ELEVENTH EDITION

Guiding Children's Learning of Mathematics

Leonard M. Kennedy
Professor Emeritus
California State University, Sacramento

Steve Tipps
University of South Carolina Upstate

Art Johnson
Boston University

THOMSON

WADSWORTH

AUSTRALIA BRAZIL CANADA MEXICO SINGAPORE SPAIN UNITED KINGDOM UNITED STATES

THOMSON

WADSWORTH

Guiding Children's Learning of Mathematics, **Eleventh Edition**
Leonard M. Kennedy, Steve Tipps, Art Johnson

Education Editor: Dan Alpert
Development Editor: Tangelique Williams
Assistant Editor: Ann Lee Richards
Editorial Assistant: Stephanie Rue
Marketing Manager: Karin Sandberg
Marketing Assistant: Teresa Jessen
Marketing Communications Manager: Shemika Britt
Project Manager, Editorial Production: Trudy Brown
Creative Director: Rob Hugel

Art Director: Maria Epes
Print Buyer: Karen Hunt
Permissions Editor: Bob Kauser
Production Service: Newgen–Austin
Text and Cover Designer: Lisa Buckley
Copy Editor: Mimi Braverman
Cover Image: Dorling Kindersley/Getty Images
Compositor: Newgen–Austin
Text and Cover Printer: Courier Corporation, Kendallville

Library of Congress Control Number: 2006939472
ISBN-13: 978-0-495-09191-2
ISBN-10: 0-495-09191-X

Thomson Higher Education
10 Davis Drive
Belmont, CA 94002-3098
USA

For more information about our products, contact us at:
Thomson Learning Academic Resource Center
1-800-423-0563

For permission to use material from this text or product, submit a
request online at **http://www.thomsonrights.com**.
Any additional questions about permissions can be submitted by
e-mail to **thomsonrights@thomson.com**.

To Rebecca Poplin for her inspiration
and constant support.
—S. T.

For my uncle Anthony Sideris.
His integrity and adherence
to the highest moral principles
continue to influence me.
—A. J.

Brief Contents

Contents

List of Activities

Preface

When contemplating the 11th edition of *Guiding Children's Learning of Mathematics*, the authors started by thinking about what has been happening in mathematics education in the last five years. The No Child Left Behind Act of 2002 (NCLB) has focused public attention on student performance and highlighted the demand for more and better mathematics instruction. The act requires that teachers be "highly qualified" and places an increased emphasis on their demonstrating their knowledge and skill in teaching. Certification requirements have been influenced by NCLB, with more states dividing early-childhood from elementary licensure and creating middle-grade certificates. Many teacher certification programs have also increased their requirements for mathematics background. The range of technology resources for teaching mathematics has likewise increased—especially those related to the Internet. Finally, providing appropriate instruction for all students has become more challenging, as teachers work with students from diverse cultural, economic, and language backgrounds and with varying degrees of ability. Each of these factors influences the life space of teachers and, for that reason, the way in which we have organized this edition and what we have revised and changed.

While acknowledging and incorporating changes in mathematics teaching are important in the 11th edition, however, the goal of *Guiding Children's Learning of Mathematics* is the same as that of the first edition, which was published in 1970—to provide a readable and user-friendly textbook that enables preservice and experienced teachers to develop their own understanding of mathematics and to offer them a wide array of experiential activities as examples of active learning and creative teaching. Through the years the book has changed as chapters have been revised to reflect current issues and emphases; but the philosophy of the book has remained constant:

- Mathematics enriches lives and expands worlds.
- Mathematics is challenging, fun, and rewarding.
- Mathematics is a mission and a treasure shared by teachers and learners.

We believe that teachers are the critical element in creating exciting and successful mathematical adventures for learners, through

- Active engagement of students in worthwhile mathematical tasks
- Problem solving and thinking as central goals in mathematics
- Relating mathematical concepts and skills to life experiences
- Communicating mathematical ideas in many forms

Over the years, all of the chapters have been extensively rewritten, incorporating the feedback of reviewers, editors, coauthors, and hundreds of in-service and preservice teachers who have used the text. In addition, the authors have drawn from their own experiences in order to continually improve the book. Teaching with a textbook that you yourself have written is an ongoing and humbling learning experience. As a student once asked, "Do you really agree with the textbook about . . . ?"

Organization

In the reorganization and revision for the 11th edition, we endeavor to clarify and illustrate mathematical and pedagogical issues without oversimplifying them. An obvious change is the restructuring of the text content into smaller and more focused chapters. In Part 1 of the book, the NCTM principles and standards provide the foundation for discussion of what is important and how it can be taught effectively. Each of the six principles is treated in a separate chapter.

- Part 1: Guiding Elementary Mathematics with Standards
  - Chapter 1: Elementary Mathematics for the 21st Century
  - Chapter 2: Defining a Comprehensive Mathematics Curriculum
  - Chapter 3: Mathematics for Every Child (**NEW**)
  - Chapter 4: Learning Mathematics
  - Chapter 5: Organizing Effective Instruction
  - Chapter 6: The Role of Technology in the Mathematics Classroom (**NEW**)
  - Chapter 7: Integrating Assessment

The complexities of teaching and assessment are presented as choices and decisions that teachers make. Rather than suggesting that one way is the right way for teaching everything, we suggest that many approaches may be successful if they adhere to basic principles of effective teaching, learning, and assessment. The NCTM principles are introduced and the content and process standards are described in Chapters 1 and 2 with classroom vignettes. The new curriculum focal points (2006) from NCTM are introduced in Chapter 2. These help teachers identify and focus on critical elements of the content at each grade level. Chapter 3 considers the equity issues of teaching mathematics to a diverse student population: students with gifts and talents, students who are culturally and linguistically diverse, and students with special needs. In Chapter 4, the topic of teaching and learning is explored by way of learning theory, research, and professional guidelines for establishing an effective classroom. Chapter 5 outlines the many decisions that teachers make every day with regard to planning and organizing the elements of instruction, including materials, grouping, time, and space. Chapter 6 presents new and emerging technologies that impact mathematics teaching and learning today. Chapter 7 describes the rationale for classroom assessment, using a variety of techniques that teachers employ to enhance and adjust instruction.

Having a separate chapter for each principle provides modules that may be used in a variety of ways by instructors and students. For example, the principles could be used to introduce the course, or they could be used at different times in connection with the chapters in Part 2.

In Part 2, important mathematical concepts are defined and illustrated with problems and teaching examples that now extend to grade 6. Part 2 balances the development of mathematical knowledge with methods of teaching the content and skills. In each chapter, examples and activities illustrate ways in which teachers might engage children in active mathematical thinking and problem solving. Activities in each chapter show how students can model concepts with physical objects, and then record and communicate their actions informally as well as with conventional symbolism. As they construct meaning, students are encouraged to move toward mental operations that require estimation, reasonableness, and application of mathematical concepts to numerical and geometric situations.

Content standards have been presented in paired chapters of "developing" and "extending" concepts and skills over the K–6 continuum. The "developing" chapters emphasize content typically found in early childhood and primary grades. The "extending" chapters focus on concepts and skills typical of intermediate and upper elementary grades, through grade 6, which many elementary schools include in their building and curriculum. This organization allows students and teachers to address the content appropriate to their needs and certification levels.

- Part 2: Mathematical Concepts, Skills, and Problem Solving
  - Chapter 8: Developing Problem-Solving Strategies
  - Chapter 9: Developing Concepts of Number
  - Chapter 10: Extending Number Concepts and Number Systems (**NEW**)
  - Chapter 11: Developing Number Operations with Whole Numbers
  - Chapter 12: Extending Computational Fluency with Larger Numbers (**NEW**)
  - Chapter 13: Developing Understanding of Common and Decimal Fractions
  - Chapter 14: Extending Understanding of Common and Decimal Fractions (**NEW**)
  - Chapter 15: Developing Aspects of Proportional Reasoning: Ratio, Proportion and Percent (**NEW**)
  - Chapter 16: Thinking Algebraically (**NEW**)
  - Chapter 17: Developing Geometric Concepts and Systems
  - Chapter 18: Developing and Extending Measurement Concepts
  - Chapter 19: Understanding and Representing Concepts of Data
  - Chapter 20: Investigating Probability

Chapters 10 and 12 extend the discussions of number concepts and number operations, respectively. Similarly, Chapter 14 extends the topics of common and decimal fractions. We now present two topical chapters—Chapter 15, dealing with ratio and proportion, and Chapter 16, thinking algebraically.

New Chapter Features

In Part 2, the reader will also find increased emphasis on diversity, technology, and assessment. Introduced in Part 1, these topics are integrated throughout the chapters in Part 2 via classroom vignettes and activities. In addition, each chapter in Part 2 contains new and exciting features related to assessment, technology in mathematics, and diversity in the classroom. *Misconceptions* highlight students' typical misunderstandings, thus alerting teachers to those concepts and skills that may need particular

attention. *Multicultural Connections* are suggestions for expanding subject matter to include topics and content that will appeal to the diversity in classrooms. Each chapter also contains representative end-of-chapter problems from three highly-esteemed tests: The National Assessment of Educational Progress (NAEP), Trends in International Mathematics and Science Study (TIMSS), and Professional Assessment for Beginning Teachers (Praxis).

Understanding mathematical concepts and building skills is within the capabilities of all future teachers, even if they have previously not enjoyed or felt confident with mathematics. Using this textbook invites preservice teachers to learn its content and methods through active engagement with the text, the exercises, the activities, and their peers. The experience of learning via this textbook models appropriate techniques that preservice teachers can use with their students. Many new activities are presented in Chapters 8–20, and many others have been revised. All of the activities and assessments can be implemented in field settings.

In light of new and emerging Internet resources, each chapter features an Internet lesson plan, a description of an Internet game that focuses on improving mathematics skills, and references to Internet sites with interactive activities through which students can explore chapter-related mathematics concepts. Each chapter also includes activities that are explicitly linked to each of the process standards highlighted by the National Council of Teachers of Mathematics: communication, connections, reasoning and proof, and representation.

Technology itself is also used to provide many new resources. The *Guiding Children's Learning of Mathematics* companion website (**www.thomsonedu.com/education/kennedy**) for students and instructors offers several features, including:

- Downloadable black-line masters for classroom use
- Essential web links for math education
- Activities Bank with a number of useful activities not found in the textbook
- PowerPoint® presentation with a talking-point outline for each chapter
- NCTM Standards Spotlight, a correlation of activities in the textbook with NCTM standards

Acknowledgments

We thank the Wadsworth editorial and production staff: Education Editor, Dan Alpert; Development Editor, Tangelique Williams; Editorial Production Project Manager, Trudy Brown; Assistant Editor, Ann Lee Richards; Editorial Assistant, Stephanie Rue; Marketing Manager, Karin Sandberg; and Advertising Project Manager, Shemika Britt. We also thank the reviewers who provided invaluable feedback and guidance:

Helen Gerretson, University of South Florida

Barbara B. Leapard, Eastern Michigan University

Blidi S. Stemn, Hofstra University

Ed Dickey, University of South Carolina

Edna F. Bazik, National-Louis University

Eileen Simons, Hofstra University

Fenqjen Luo, University of West Georgia

Karla Karstens, University of Vermont

Kyungsoon Jeon, Eastern Illinois University

Lisa B. Owen, Rhode Island College

Marina Krause, California State University, Long Beach

Marshall Lassak, Eastern Illinois University

Mary Goral, Bellarmine University

Nancy Schoolcraft, Ball State University

Priscilla S. Nelson, Gordon College

Zhijun Wu, University of Maine at Presque Isle

Rick Austin, University of South Florida

PART 1

Guiding Elementary Mathematics with Standards

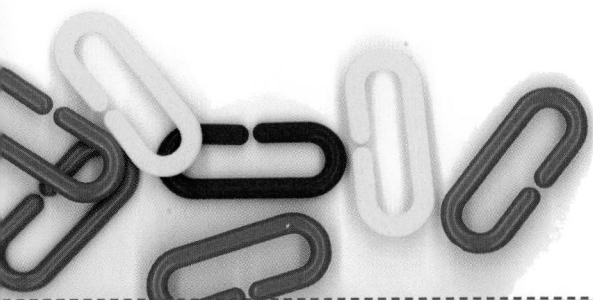

CHAPTER 1

Elementary Mathematics for the 21st Century

Elementary mathematics has been the subject of much discussion, debate, and controversy in recent years. At the center of this debate is whether children should focus on basic computation skills or develop a wider range of knowledge and skill in mathematics. The curriculum recommended by the National Council of Teachers of Mathematics (2000) and adopted by many states emphasizes thinking and problem solving related to all mathematical topics: numbers and operations, statistics, measurement, probability, geometry, and algebra. The content is connected to living, working, and solving problems in a technological and information-based society. Computational skills are still important, but students must know when and how to use numbers to solve problems.

The need for a well-balanced and coherent mathematics curriculum prekindergarten (PK) through grade 12 was also emphasized with the passage of the No Child Left Behind Act of 2001. This law mandated each state to adopt standards for academic performance and develop a testing program to demonstrate student achievement.

Just as the focus of mathematics has changed, the strategies that teachers use reflect new understanding of how students learn, based on research on cognition—the process of learning. Teachers and parents are challenged to consider mathematics differently from their school mathematics experience, which was dominated by calculations and procedures, drill and repetition, and solitary work. An ideal classroom today finds students working together on challenging problems related to their lives, explaining their thinking to each other and their teacher, and using a variety of materials to show what they understand and can do.

In this chapter you will read about:

1 Problem solving as the central idea in school mathematics

2 How the *Principles and Standards for School Mathematics* (National Council of Teachers of Mathematics, 2000) serves as a model for what mathematics should be taught and how it should be taught

3 Six principles that provide a foundation for school mathematics from preschool through grade 12: mathematics curriculum, equity, teaching, learning, assessment, and technology

Solving Problems Is Basic

Too many adults believe that they are not competent in mathematics. They may even have mathematics anxiety just thinking about mathematics. At the same time, these people use mathematics in their daily lives when they shop, cook, manage their money, work on home improvement projects, or plan for travel. Every citizen needs mathematical concepts and skills for budgeting and saving, financing a house or car, calculating a tip at a restaurant, or estimating distances and gas mileage. Often the numerical answer is only one factor considered in a decision. Other issues may be more important than the computed answer. Is a regular box of cereal for $3.75 a better buy than the smaller box for $2.75 or the giant box for $4.75 (Figure 1.1)? Does having a "50 cents off" coupon change the answer? What other factors influence the choice of cereal?

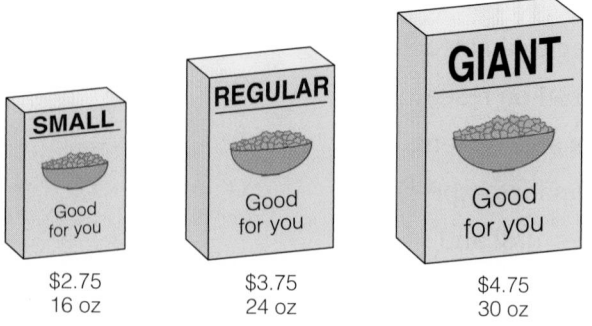

Figure 1.1 Which cereal would you buy?

EXERCISE

Using the information in Figure 1.1, work in groups of two or three to solve the cereal problem. Which box of cereal would you buy based on cost? Does a coupon change your decision? If the store doubles the coupon, does that change the decision? What else would you consider when deciding which cereal to buy? ●●●

Calculations are only part of solving problems in mathematics. Reasoning is used to decide how much cost, taste, and nutrition are considered in the final decision. Even after complex calculations, such as the cost of remodeling or the various incentives offered for buying a car, the numerical answer is only one of many other factors involved.

Adults, even those who believe they were not good in school mathematics, often develop mathematical skills in their jobs. Carpenters and contractors measure accurately and estimate job costs and materials. Accountants, graphic designers, and hospital workers use calculators and computers routinely to record and analyze information and designs. When mathematics is applied to realistic life and work situations, many adults find that they *are* capable in mathematics, despite their negative attitudes toward mathematics in school. The need to connect mathematics to realistic situations has been one motivation for reform of the mathematics curriculum and teaching.

The vision of mathematics has changed. Mathematics used to be a solitary activity done primarily on worksheets. Now teachers ask students to work together to solve interesting problems, puzzles, games, and investigations. When solving these problems, students develop the concepts, skills, and attitudes needed for life and work. Numbers and calculation are still essential, but mathematical thinking and reasoning equip all children to solve a wide variety of problems.

Elementary mathematics teachers are on the front line of the effort to develop mathematical concepts and problem-solving skills. Classroom events provide mathematical learning experiences.

- If juice boxes are packaged in groups of three, how many packs are needed for 20 children?

- How much money is needed to buy lunch, a snack, and a pencil at the school store?

- Is January a good month to take a field trip to the zoo? Why or why not?

- Will this 12×15 inch piece of paper be large enough to cover a cube for my art project?

- How many children prefer hamburgers to pizza? Hamburgers to hot dogs? Pizza to hot dogs?

Students figure out what information they need and how to use it to solve problems.

Problem-focused teachers ask, "Is there only one answer? Can anyone see another way to solve this problem?" As students discover problems with multiple answers and multiple solution paths, they become more flexible in their thinking. When problems serve as the context of teaching, children ask, "Does this answer make sense?" Information from print and electronic sources is represented in many forms: text, pictures, tables, and graphs. Students learn as they write, draw, act, read about, and model their thinking. They engage in dialogue, demonstration, and debate about mathematical ideas. When children are actively engaged in doing mathematical tasks, they are thinking about how mathematics works. This new vision of mathematics includes a balanced mathematics program for students of all ages that focuses on concepts, processes, and applications, with problem solving at its core.

Public and political concern about student achievement is another factor that influences the development of new mathematics curriculum and teaching. As a result, national and state policymakers demand more accountability of schools and teachers for student learning. The No Child Left Behind Act of 2001 requires that states adopt standards-based curricula. The standards provide common expectations for student performance, and statewide testing has been developed to measure student progress. Results are used to rate and rank schools based on student achievement. If schools do not meet performance standards, sanctions may be imposed under the act. Teachers also must demonstrate knowledge of content and teaching practices to meet "highly qualified" requirements under No Child Left Behind. The provisions of the act are controversial, and debate continues on the local, state, and national levels.

A Comprehensive Vision of Mathematics

The effort to improve mathematics education was based on several factors. School mathematics has been seen by many learners as irrelevant and boring when mathematics is actually useful and exciting when learned conceptually and practically. Research has accelerated the information available about how mathematics is learned and effectively taught. Political demands for a standard curriculum and increased assessment required a response from the mathematics education community.

The opportunity and challenge to formulate this new vision of mathematics was met by the National Council of Teachers of Mathematics (NCTM). For nearly a century, NCTM has sought to answer two central questions for teachers, parents, and policymakers:

- What mathematical concepts and skills are fundamental for students to know?

- What are the best ways to teach and learn these essential concepts and skills?

NCTM, an international professional organization of more than 100,000 professionals in mathematics education, provides resources and guidance to teachers, schools, school districts, and state and national policymakers through policy recommendations and publications. In 2000, the NCTM Board of Directors and members adopted *Principles and*

Standards for School Mathematics. This comprehensive and balanced statement describes principles to guide mathematics programs and outlines the content and processes central to teaching and learning mathematics (the report is available at **http://www .nctm.org**).

The new standards consolidated curriculum, teaching, and assessment issues into one document. Core beliefs, called *principles*, are addressed directly in the new standards. Standards are organized into four grade bands (PK–2, 3–5, 6–8, and 9–12) that address unique characteristics of mathematics content and learning needs of children throughout their school years. Five content standards and five process standards are common across all grade levels, showing the unity of mathematics knowledge and process.

Principles of School Mathematics

The principles surround all aspects of planning and teaching. Table 1.1 lists each NCTM principle and issues related to it. Teachers can ask themselves whether they are following the principles as they reflect on their teaching.

TABLE 1.1 • Six Principles for School Mathematics

Equity Principle

Excellence in mathematics education requires equity—high expectations and strong support for all students.
- Equity requires high expectations and worthwhile opportunities for all.
- Equity requires accommodating differences to help everyone learn mathematics.
- Equity requires resources and support for all classrooms and students.

Mathematics Curriculum Principle

A curriculum is more than a collection of activities:
- A mathematics curriculum should be coherent.
- A mathematics curriculum should focus on important mathematics.
- A mathematics curriculum should be well articulated across the grades.

Teaching Principle

Effective mathematics teaching requires understanding what students know and need to learn and then challenging and supporting students to learn it well.
- Effective teaching requires knowing and understanding mathematics, students as learners, and pedagogical strategies.
- Effective teaching requires a challenging and supportive classroom-learning environment.
- Effective teaching requires continually seeking improvement.

Learning Principle

Students must learn mathematics with understanding, actively building new knowledge from experience and prior knowledge.
- Learning mathematics with understanding is essential.
- Students can learn mathematics with understanding.

Assessment Principle

Assessment should support the learning of important mathematics and furnish useful information to both teachers and students.
- Assessment should enhance students' learning.
- Assessment is a valuable tool for making instructional decisions.

Technology Principle

Technology is essential in teaching and learning mathematics; it influences the mathematics that is taught and enhances students' learning.
- Technology enhances mathematics learning.
- Technology supports effective mathematics teaching.
- Technology influences what mathematics is taught.

- Curriculum: Do all children receive a well-rounded and balanced program in mathematics?

- Equity: Do all children have access and opportunities to be successful in mathematics?

- Learning: Are the methods I use based on what is known about how children learn?

- Teaching: Do the methods I use enhance learning by engaging children in mathematical thinking, developing concepts and skills, and applying their knowledge to engaging problems?

- Assessment: Do I use assessment to determine children's strengths and needs on a continuous basis and adjust my instruction accordingly?

- Technology: Do I use technology to help children explore and learn mathematical concepts?

These six principles should be integrated into every mathematics lesson (Figure 1.2).

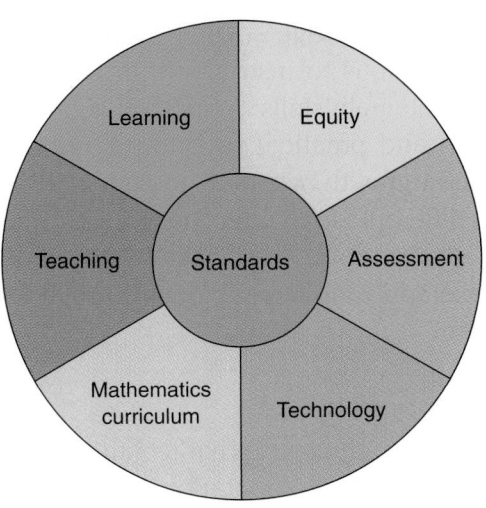

Figure 1.2 Six principles for school mathematics

ⒺXERCISE

In a classroom you are observing, give examples of how you see the six principles at work or not in evidence. ●●●

The Mathematics Curriculum Principle

The mathematics curriculum principle describes essential mathematics concepts and skills that NCTM believes are important for children to learn from preschool through grade 12. This comprehensive and

TABLE 1.2	**Content and Process Standards for School Mathematics**

Content Standards

- Numbers and operations
- Algebra
- Geometry
- Measurement
- Data analysis and probability

Process Standards

- Problem solving
- Reasoning and proof
- Communication
- Connection
- Representation

well-balanced mathematics curriculum includes five content standards and five process standards taught across all grades, PK–12.

Common standards emphasize the unity and interrelatedness of mathematics knowledge and process (Table 1.2). The content standards are organized in four grade bands (PK–2, 3–5, 6–8, and 9–12) that address unique characteristics of content and cognitive development of learners. The complete curriculum with grade band expectations is found in Appendix A. In this text, we emphasize the first two grade bands, PK–2 and grades 3–5, with additional attention to grade 6 because it is often included in elementary certification and school organization. In Chapter 2 we present each of the content and process standards with descriptions of how they are integrated into daily teaching. Standards and expectations are also discussed in the appropriate chapters in Part 2 of the text as content and activities are introduced for each topic.

The Equity Principle

Equity means that the full mathematics curriculum, balanced with content and process, is available to *all* students. Students in schools possess many characteristics. They may be male or female; represent many different cultures, ethnic groups, and languages; and possess a variety of background experiences, mathematical interests, and abilities. Despite the differences among students, they all need mathematics to carry out daily tasks, to work, and to be informed citizens in a technological world. Rather than being a gate or filter that allows only a few students to move forward, equity emphasizes that the mathematics door is open to all students from the first day of their education and throughout their lives. All students need opportunities to develop technical, vocational, and practical mathematics and to develop reasoning skills.

Equity does not mean that every student receives exactly the same program. It means that no child is deprived of the opportunity to learn; no arbitrary limits are set on individuals. Because students have different goals, abilities, and interests, mathematics must address individual needs as well. Gifted students need opportunities to explore beyond the basic curriculum. Students who experience difficulties in mathematics need extra assistance to attain the knowledge and skills outlined in the standards. When instruction is flexible enough to allow children the time and resources to explore topics of special interest to them, it serves all students. In Chapter 3 we discuss how to provide a challenging and comprehensive mathematical program for all students.

The Learning Principle

Understanding how children learn is the foundation of teaching; teachers must understand learning theories to design appropriate instructional activities. Current research supports effective teaching practices such as discussion and writing in mathematics, active engagement with significant mathematical tasks, higher order thinking about mathematical problems, and use of models, materials, and multiple representations of mathematical concepts. In Chapter 4 we present knowledge from learning theories and research about effective teaching and learning in classrooms as a coherent guide for organizing instruction.

The Teaching Principle

Teaching is directly related to learning. Knowing how students learn leads to teaching techniques that help students to develop an understanding of mathematical concepts, think strategically about problems, and develop strong process skills. Teachers consider many things as they make many decisions about instruction: grade-level standards, goals and progress for each child, strategies and activities, materials, time and space, and grouping of children. Their decisions and choices determine the climate of the classroom and the nature of the mathematical conversation they encourage. Some choices limit the conversation, interaction, and collaboration; other choices encourage dialogue, demonstration, and engagement. In Chapter 5 we make suggestions for developing a mathematics classroom that encourages student involvement. In the chapters in Part 2, we present lessons, activities, and ideas for teaching content and process.

The Assessment Principle

Instead of giving tests at the end of each reporting period, the assessment principle envisions continuous interaction between learner and teacher before, during, and after instruction. Assessment occurs daily through asking questions and observing student work, by reviewing written work done in class or at home, by monitoring activities and exercises, by reading and responding to journals, and by reviewing portfolios and projects. Some assessments are snapshots of knowledge so that teachers can make daily adaptations to instruction. Projects allow students to integrate skills and knowledge in a more integrated and practical situation. Portfolios and journals show growth over time. In Chapter 7 we present many different techniques that can be used to collect information about student knowledge and skill, and we exemplify these techniques throughout Part 2 of the text.

The Technology Principle

Many parents and teachers fear that technology inhibits children's skill with computation. Technology is not a substitute for knowing numbers and operations or for building fundamental concepts; instead, technology is a tool for learning and applying mathematical concepts. Computers and calculators can help children learn mathematics in powerful and meaningful ways.

> In a first-grade classroom, students discovered that when they keyed in 5 + and repeatedly touched =, the calculator displayed 10, 15, 20, 25, 30. . . . The students started skip counting by 5's as the display guided their chant. Irma noticed that all the numbers ended in 0 or 5 and were in two horizontal lines on the hundreds chart.

Some children experimented with 25 + or 100 + as the starting number. Racing for the biggest number, they found that larger starting numbers grew in length very fast. One child got an error message; then they all wanted to get "ERROR" and to learn what that meant.

The children were deeply engaged with numbers: how to count in different ways, when is a number too big for the calculator, and multiplication. The calculator became a tool for exploration of mathematics concepts instead of being limited to checking answers. The challenge is finding ways to integrate technology into a learning event.

Technology also changes what is taught and the time spent on topics. How many problems of multiplication and division are required after students demonstrate understanding of the meaning and process? Do children really need to learn the algorithm for square root? When a calculator has a built-in graphing program, how many hand-drawn graphs are required? Teachers must reconsider both what content is taught and the time needed for practice and reallocate time to teaching concepts and problem solving. In Chapter 6 we extend the discussion of technology use for learning mathematics.

Implementing the Principles and Standards

The principles and standards provide the vision of what mathematics can and should be for elementary students. Since adoption of the standards in 2000, teachers have worked to implement the vision through their instruction. The purpose of this textbook is to provide content background and examples of teaching for beginning and experienced teachers. In Chapters 2 through 7 we develop the six principles through discussion and examples of their classroom implementation. In Chapters 8 through 20 we focus on mathematics curriculum by describing activities and processes that give life to the principles and standards each day for elementary students.

Study Questions and Activities

1. Consider your own mathematics experiences in schools. Were your experiences consistent with the NCTM principles?
   - Did you have a well-balanced curriculum?
   - Were all students provided opportunity and support to be successful?
   - Did teachers use a variety of teaching techniques that motivated and challenged each student's learning?
   - Was technology used to enhance your learning mathematics?
   - Did teachers assess your learning frequently with a variety of techniques?
2. Recall your experiences in mathematics. Does your background illustrate positive or negative examples of the principles?
3. Do a web search about the No Child Left Behind Act, and locate sources that support the act and those that express reservations. What are the major requirements of No Child Left Behind? What are the specific areas of disagreement and concern? Are there any points of agreement?

Teacher's Resources

Ben-Hur, Meir. (2006). *Concept-rich mathematics instruction: Building a strong foundation for reasoning and problem solving.* Alexandria, VA: Association for Supervision and Curriculum Development.

Checkley, Kathy. (2006). *Priorities in practice: The essentials of mathematics, K–6—effective curriculum, instruction, and assessment.* Alexandria, VA: Association for Supervision and Curriculum Development.

National Council of Teachers of Mathematics. (2000). *Principles and standards for school mathematics.* Reston, VA: Author.

CHAPTER 2

Defining a Comprehensive Mathematics Curriculum

The vision of mathematics presented in the *Principles and Standards for School Mathematics* (National Council of Teachers of Mathematics, 2000) emphasizes thinking and problem solving within a well-balanced curriculum of content knowledge and process skills for PK–12 students. Students are actively engaged in interesting and meaningful activities to develop mathematics concepts and build critical skills while solving problems. In this chapter we describe the National Council of Teachers of Mathematics (NCTM) content and process standards through classroom vignettes and examples that demonstrate how content and process standards are developed in student-centered classrooms.

In this chapter you will read about:

1 Five content standards and classroom or real-life situations for each standard

2 Five process standards and classroom or real-life examples for each standard

3 How process and content standards are integrated into teaching

Connecting Concepts, Skills, and Application

The NCTM curriculum standards present a comprehensive overview of what students should know and be able to do in mathematics as they progress in school from PK through grade 12. Instead of memorizing procedures and definitions out of context, students learn concepts and mathematical procedures through problems that require mathematical reasoning.

The NCTM standards provide a model for many state-adopted mathematics standards-based curricula. When first looking at state standards, teachers may feel overwhelmed if they believe that each standard is an isolated topic or skill. However, the standards actually encourage teachers to build connections and relationships among concepts, skills, and applications in mathematics and other subject areas. In one lesson or activity, several related concepts or skills can be introduced, developed, or reviewed. Classroom vignettes and examples in this chapter illustrate how teachers connect mathematics concepts with each other, with other subjects, and with children's interests and experiences.

What Elementary Children Need to Know in Mathematics

The five content standards and five process standards in the NCTM standards identify the content knowledge and the mathematical processes developed over the PK–12 curriculum. In this chapter we explain the importance and meaning of both

---

TABLE 2.1 • Mathematics Curriculum Principle: Content Standards

Numbers and Operations

Instructional programs from PK through grade 12 should enable all students to
- Understand numbers, ways of representing numbers, relationships among numbers, and number systems
- Understand meaning of operations and how they relate to one another
- Compute fluently and make reasonable estimates

Algebra

Instructional programs from PK through grade 12 should enable all students to
- Understand patterns, relations, and functions
- Represent and analyze mathematical situations and structure using algebraic symbols
- Use mathematical models to represent and understand quantitative relationships
- Analyze change in various contexts

Geometry

Instructional programs from PK through grade 12 should enable all students to
- Analyze characteristics and properties of two- and three-dimensional geometric shapes and develop mathematical arguments about geometric relationships
- Specify locations and describe spatial relationships using coordinate geometry and other representational systems
- Apply transformations and use symmetry to analyze mathematical structures
- Use visualization, spatial reasoning, and geometric modeling to solve problems

Measurement

Instructional programs from PK through grade 12 should enable all students to
- Understand measurable attributes of objectives and the units, systems, and processes of measurement
- Apply appropriate techniques, tools, and formulas to determine measurement

Data Analysis and Probability

Instructional programs from PK through grade 12 should enable all students to
- Formulate questions that can be addressed with data and collect, organize, and display relevant data to answer them
- Select and use appropriate statistical methods to analyze data
- Develop and evaluate inferences and predictions that are based on data
- Understand and apply basic concepts of probability

SOURCE: Reprinted with permission from *Principles and Standards for School Mathematics* (2000) by the National Council of Teachers of Mathematics. All rights reserved.

TABLE 2.2 **Mathematics Curriculum Principle: Process Standards**

Problem Solving

Instructional programs from PK through grade 12 should enable all students to
- Build new mathematical knowledge through problem solving
- Solve problems that arise in mathematics and other contexts
- Apply and adapt a variety of appropriate strategies to solve problems
- Monitor and reflect on the process of mathematical problem solving

Reasoning and Proof

Instructional programs from PK through grade 12 should enable all students to
- Recognize reasoning and proof as fundamental aspects of mathematics
- Make and investigate mathematical conjectures
- Develop and evaluate mathematical arguments
- Select and use various types of reasoning and methods of proof

Communication

Instructional programs from PK through grade 12 should enable all students to
- Organize and consolidate their mathematical thinking through communication
- Communicate their mathematical thinking coherently and clearly to peers, teachers, and others
- Analyze and evaluate the mathematical thinking and strategies of others
- Use the language of mathematics to express mathematical ideas precisely

Connections

Instructional programs from PK through grade 12 should enable all students to
- Recognize and use connections among mathematical ideas
- Understand how mathematical ideas interconnect and build on one another to produce a coherent whole
- Recognize and apply mathematics in context outside of mathematics

Representation

Instructional programs from PK through grade 12 should enable all students to
- Create and use representations to organize, record, and communicate mathematical ideas
- Select, apply, and translate among mathematical representations to solve problems
- Use representations to model and interpret physical, social, and mathematical phenomena

content and process standards. Tables 2.1 and 2.2 provide an overview of the content standards and the process standards, respectively. In Appendix A the content standards for students' mathematical growth and proficiency across four grade bands include expectations that provide benchmarks for teachers. In Part 2 of the textbook we provide activities, lessons, and examples that show how content is taught within the framework provided by the process standards. Rather than being separate topics, the process standards are integrated into lessons and activities presented to children.

Numbers and Number Operations

Learning about numbers and number operations has been and still is a central element of elementary school mathematics. Although computational pro-ficiency is essential, understanding how numbers work and reasoning about numbers, called number sense and computational fluency, respectively, are emphasized. Rather than memorizing isolated facts and procedures, students construct understandings about numbers and number systems as the foundation for learning operations, facts, and procedures.

For children, understanding numbers progresses from counting objects and matching sets with numerals, to using objects, pictures, and symbols that represent place values for tens, hundreds, even millions and billions. Concepts of addition, subtraction, multiplication, and division begin with stories about everyday events using simple numbers. The stories provide the problems that are solved through action, pictures, and number sentences. Stories with larger numbers or fractions draw on understanding of operations and allow students to solve problems. Computational fluency is the ultimate goal for students, because they can solve problems using paper-and-pencil techniques, technology, or estimation or mental computation. They should know which computational technique is most appropriate and how precise they need to be to get a reasonable answer. Throughout the development of number sense, thinking about numbers is emphasized so that students can solve more complex problems, justify their strategy, and explain whether the answer is reasonable.

While students learn about numbers, they can also be learning about other standards. In this primary-grade vignette, a teacher bridges from number facts to an algebraic number pattern.

Ms. Munoz shows two beads on a string (Figure 2.1), then adds three more beads. She asks students what number sentence to write, and students suggest $2 + 3 = 5$. With

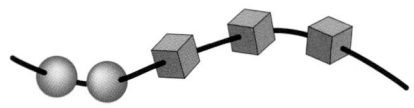

Figure 2.1 Beads showing $2 + 3$

blocks at their desks, children create more examples of adding 3, draw pictures of their blocks, and write other number sentences. After recording several sentences on the board, she asks: "What is 5 plus 3? What is 8 plus 3? What is 12 plus 3?" Using a hundreds chart, students mark a starting number with a green chip and put a red chip on "plus 3." After several examples, Ms. Munoz asks if they see a pattern for "plus 3," and they respond that plus 3 is like counting 3 more. Finally, she says, "I am thinking of a mystery number. Now I add 3 and have 26. What was the mystery number?" Children put the red chip on 26 and count down 3 to find 23. They continue finding mystery numbers with partners. The teacher asks children to generalize a rule for adding 3 that encourages them to think about how numbers work. Asking about a mystery number, Ms. Munoz engages children in algebraic thinking $x + 3 = 26$. The teacher not only develops under-

standing of number operations and algebra but also integrates processes of problem solving, representation, reasoning, and communication into the lesson.

EXERCISE

Why would the teacher ask students to generate rules for number operations? How is making a rule different from learning the addition and subtraction facts? ●●●

Geometry

Geometry and spatial sense are central mathematical ideas in our three-dimensional world. Many activities—playing sports, driving, gardening, keyboarding—require spatial sense. People use spatial awareness when they arrange furniture, pack baggage, and wrap presents. Artists, architects, and engineers create sophisticated and aesthetic products that use an understanding of geometry.

Many mathematical concepts are represented with geometry. The number line is a one-dimensional model for addition and subtraction. A map is a two-dimensional grid representation showing relative locations of buildings, streets, and cities. The same two-dimensional coordinate grid is used for graphing algebraic equations and showing area.

In elementary mathematics, children learn about geometry and develop spatial sense in their environment. They find relationships among shapes and angles as they explore their world. Geometry activities activate creativity, problem solving, and reasoning in students' pictures and designs, such as quilt patterns.

Kai watches his grandmother use the "diamond in a square" pattern to make a quilt (Figure 2.2). He finds graph paper and starts drawing the quilt designs with squares and triangles. He finds that the triangles are really larger squares rotated 45 degrees around the center square. He has to figure out how long the side of each new square is and notices that the sides get longer, but the angles stay the same.

When Kai takes his quilt to school, his third-grade teacher, Ms. Scott, recognizes that quilts are a good way to integrate geometry, art, and measure-

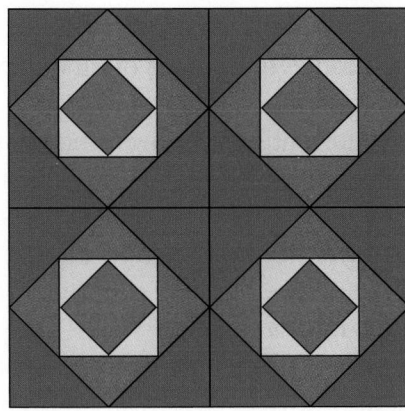

Figure 2.2 Quilt pattern: diamond in square

ment into a social studies unit on pioneers and the westward movement.

ⒺXERCISE

Find three or four quilt patterns that show geometric concepts. Share them with classmates. ●●●

In the sixth grade, Ms. Ledford finds quilt patterns with 3-4-5 triangles to introduce similar triangles and the Pythagorean theorem. To extend her students' understanding, she takes the class outside, where she has placed a 2-meter upright bar in the ground that is casting a 1.5-meter shadow (Figure 2.3). She asks the students how they could use this information to estimate the height of the oak tree in the school yard. This lesson involves students in problem solving, calculations, algebraic reasoning, and connecting geometric principles to the real world.

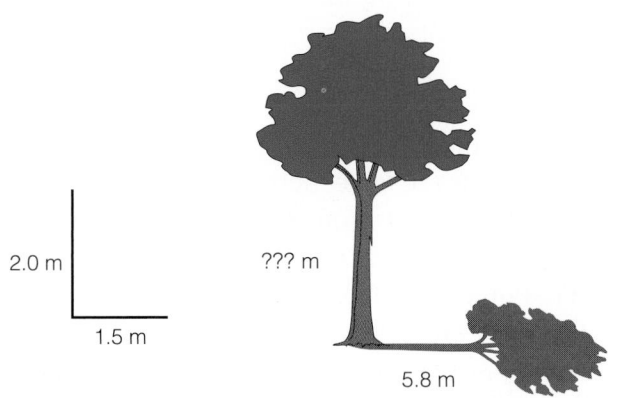

Figure 2.3 Measuring a tree with similar triangles

ⒺXERCISE

What is the approximate height of the tree shown in Figure 2.3? How does this activity connect geometry with measurement? ●●●

Measurement

People measure length, area, volume and capacity, mass, angle, time, temperature, and money nearly every day. Likewise, elementary school children learn measurement concepts and skills through their daily activities. They weigh fruit and vegetables on a variety of scales. They measure the length of the hall, the room, and their bodies. They use television or bus schedules to plan activities. They measure angles and areas when creating art projects. Measurement is a natural activity for students, and the concepts and skills of measurement, such as iteration, benchmarks for common units, approximation, and precision, develop through these experiences.

Measuring the area of rectangles (Figure 2.4) may begin as a counting exercise, but students soon realize that multiplication is a faster way to determine the area. When area is represented as a multiplication fact—$4 \times 6 = 24$—they have the first step of an algebraic formula (length $\times$ width = area) to represent any rectangular area.

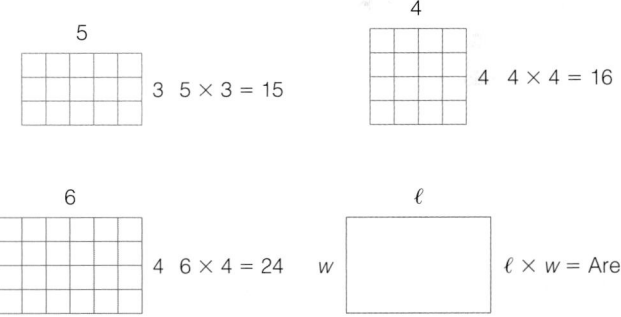

Figure 2.4 Area of rectangles

ⒺXERCISE

Measure the area of a book cover, desktop, or table top using sticky notes or square pieces of paper. Use two or three different sizes of paper. Does this activity help you understand length $\times$ width = area? ●●●

Classroom activities highlight the real-life connection to measurement. A classroom savings account shows compounding interest. Telling time is a basic skill for organizing life activities, and thermometers are essential tools for weather and personal health. Comparison shopping is done with flyers from newspapers, catalogs, and advertisements. Sy Ning uses her knowledge of measurement to decide which pizza is the best deal for the Liu family.

Sy Ning compares the price of small, medium, and large pizzas (Figure 2.5). She estimates the area of each pizza using πr^2, approximating $\pi = 3$. She concludes that the area of the 12-inch pizza is more than twice that of the 8-inch pizza, but the price is less than double. Because one large pizza costs almost $5.00 less than two small ones, the family buys a large pizza with one-half cheese and pepperoni and one-half vegetarian toppings.

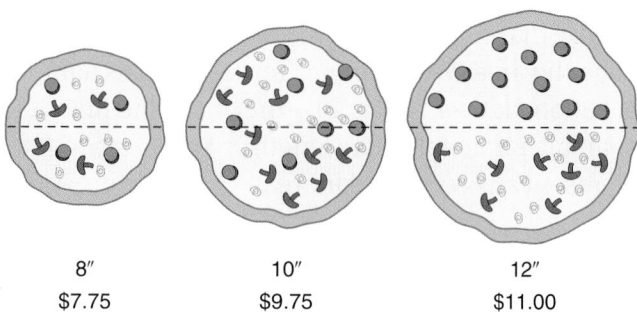

| 8″ | 10″ | 12″ |
| $7.75 | $9.75 | $11.00 |

Figure 2.5 Comparing pizzas

Solving the problem involved more than calculations; favorite toppings and personal choices were also considered in the solution. Classroom activities highlight real-life connections to measurement. Making a schedule with routine and special events uses the clock and calendar as tools. Charting heights, temperature, and rainfall makes measurement meaningful and provides important data for analysis.

ⒺXERCISE

What are typical high and low temperatures in your area in the winter? in the summer? What is the average annual rainfall? Where do you find this information? ●●●

Data Analysis and Probability

In an information age, data are often organized and presented in the form of tables and graphs. Newspapers display information in charts, and content reading in social studies and science depends on interpretation of graphical information. Graphs showing average temperature and average rainfall help students understand the climatic differences between a desert and a rainforest.

By organizing, displaying, and analyzing information that they have collected, students learn how to interpret data and draw conclusions. Children collect information about birthdays, favorite pizza, letters in names, hair color, and height of plants grown from seeds. They turn these data into tables, charts, and graphs. When students have collected information from their classmates and the students in the next class, they can compare and contrast the information gathered.

ⒺXERCISE

Find a table, chart, or graph in a newspaper. Write three to five questions about the information displayed, including both factual and inferential questions. Trade with classmates to answer the questions they have written. What did you learn from the activity? ●●●

Probability is the study of chance—how likely an event will occur. Forecasting weather involves probability based on atmospheric conditions. Health and auto insurance premiums are calculated for different people on the likelihood of their having illnesses or being involved in an accident. Understanding chance is an important mathematical concept for understanding many aspects of life. Probability experiments also provide opportunities for data collection.

After the experiment of rolling one die 60 times (Figure 2.6), students see that the expected and the observed results are not exactly the same, but when they add all the results from all the groups, they find that the expectation of equal probability for each number is quite accurate. Before students roll two dice 60 times and record their results in a chart, Mr. King asks them to predict how many of each sum they will roll. Based on their previous experiment, they predict 5 of each number 1 through 12.

By displaying the results in a table, chart, or graph, students saw their results and interpreted them with more confidence. They discovered that their predictions were not very accurate.

Roll 1 die 60 times	Number of 1s	Number of 2s	Number of 3s	Number of 4s	Number of 5s	Number of 6s
Expected	10	10	10	10	10	10
Observed	8	11	12	7	9	13

Figure 2.6 Expected and observed values of 60 rolls of a die

Ⓔ X E R C I S E

Conduct the experiments with one die and two dice with two or three partners. How do your results for rolling one die compare to those of the students? What happens when you combine all the results in the class? Based on your experiment with two dice, what problems did the students find with their predictions? ●●●

The newspaper reported that the state lottery was worth $157 million, and fifth-grade students wanted to know how people could win. Mrs. Imari asked students what they knew about the lottery. When she found they had little understanding, she decided to introduce probability experiments and simulations.

Figure 2.7 Sampling exercises

The next day, Mrs. Imari introduced a bag with 99 yellow chips and 1 red chip (Figure 2.7). Each child removed a chip, recorded the color, and put it back in the bag. Only 2 students out of 117 students in the fifth grade had drawn a red chip. The ratio of 2 to 117 meant that the chance of getting a red chip was about 1 in 60 compared to the actual ratio of 1 red to 99 yellow. Next, in a learning center, students experimented by drawing one chip from a bag holding 999 yellow chips and 1 red chip; no student

picked a red chip. After other sampling exercises with objects and computer simulations, students concluded that as the number of chips increases, the chance of winning is reduced. When they talked about the lottery, they saw that the chance of picking six winning numbers out of all the possible combinations meant that any one person would have a very low probability of winning. The lottery ticket states that the chance of winning is 1 in 16,000,000, or 0.00000000625—close to zero probability.

Activities and lessons with data and probability are engaging for students. Students enjoy taking surveys and comparing results. They enjoy rolling dice, spinning spinners, and drawing chips from a bag. These activities are also easy to integrate into other subject lessons.

Ⓔ X E R C I S E

What is the probability of drawing any specific number from a bag of tiles numbered 1 to 50? What is the probability of drawing any specific number after the first number has been removed? How would you calculate the probability of drawing those two numbers in sequence? ●●●

Algebra

Algebra has been the traditional topic for high school mathematics, but the 2000 NCTM standards included algebra as a priority for all grades. Although algebraic concepts and thinking have been embedded in elementary mathematics, they were not recognized or well developed. Concepts of patterns, relationships, change, variability, and equality are fundamental to the study of numbers, operations, geometry, measurement, and data. Algebra is just one more step when a teacher asks students to use their observations to create a general rule, predict, estimate, and reason about missing information. A kindergarten class performs algebra when they analyze a pattern and represent it in many forms.

Ms. McDowell's children in kindergarten can find, read, label, and extend patterns of pictures and shapes. She wants them to represent patterns in other ways. She asks them how to act out the shape pattern—circle-

Figure 2.8 Representations of A-B-C pattern

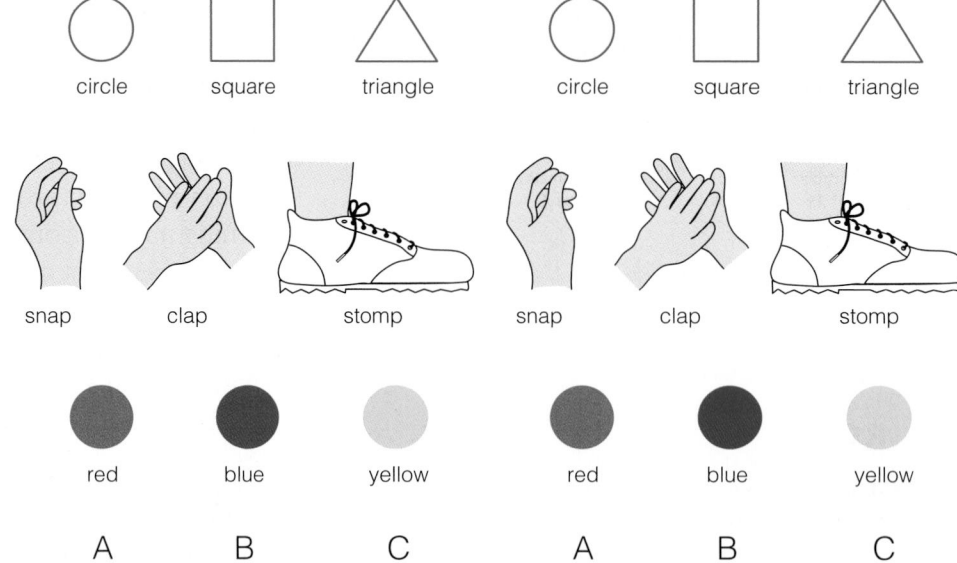

| A | B | C | A | B | C |

square-triangle, circle-square-triangle—using actions and sounds. They respond with snap-clap-stomp and animal sounds: "woof-meow-oink." She asks how many different sounds or actions are in each sequence, they reply "three." Finally, she asks if they could write the sequence using letters. They decide they would need three different letters (Figure 2.8).

Patterns are the beginning of algebraic thinking. Collecting observations about concrete models in a table makes number patterns and sequences more apparent.

EXERCISE

Work with a partner to represent a pattern of your own in five different ways: shape, picture, sound, action, symbols. ●●●

(a) Stacked blocks

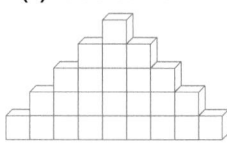

Students in the fourth grade at Viejo Elementary School build a triangle-shaped tower with cubes (Figure 2.9a). They count the number of blocks on each level: 3, 5, 7, 9, . . . , and the total number. They note that each row increases by 2 and predict that the next row will have 11 blocks in it. They predict the total will be 35 because 24 + 11 = 35; then they build the next level and confirm their reasoning. Mrs. Simmons challenges them to answer the question "How

many total blocks would be in a tower having 10 rows?" without building all 10 rows. The students organize their results in a table (Figure 2.9b) to find a pattern. The exploration was not over because a student was puzzled.

(c) Stacked blocks

The next day, Yolanda asked why the top row was missing. Mrs. Simmons asked if that would change their results. When they put one cube on the top (Figure 2.9c), they found a different pattern (Figure 2.9d). Sebastian said that the totals of the blocks 1, 4, 9, 16, 25, . . . were squared numbers because they were the result of multiplying a number by itself: $1 \times 1, 2 \times 2, 3 \times 3, 4 \times 4, ...$ Kaylee explained that when you got to the 10th row, the total number of

(b) Table of number patterns

Row	No. of blocks	Total
1	3	3
2	5	8
3	7	15
4	9	24
5	11	35
. . .	. . .	. . .
. . .	. . .	. . .
10	. . .	. . .
. . .	. . .	. . .
50	. . .	. . .
. . .	. . .	. . .
100	. . .	. . .

(d) Table of number patterns

Row	No. of blocks	Total
1	1	1
2	3	4
3	5	9
4	7	16
5	9	25
. . .	. . .	. . .
. . .	. . .	. . .
10	. . .	. . .
. . .	. . .	. . .
50	. . .	. . .
. . .	. . .	. . .
100	. . .	. . .

Figure 2.9 Finding a number pattern with blocks

blocks would be 100 because $10 \times 10 = 100$. Mrs. Simmons asked how many blocks it would take to build a triangle shape with 20, 50, and 100 rows. Then she asked her students to compare their tables to see if they could find a formula for the total number of blocks in the first tower.

ⒺXERCISE

What would be the total number of blocks needed to complete the tower with 12 rows—without the top block and with the top block? ●●●

Through exploration with a concrete model, students found several patterns and ways to represent the towers. Algebraic teaching and algebraic thinking occurs every time students ask questions about combinations and possibilities.

- What comes next?
- What is missing?
- What would happen if . . . ?
- If this changed, what would happen?

Opportunities for finding and extending patterns, using variables, observing change, and using symbolic notation are found in almost every lesson.

Learning Mathematical Processes

The five process standards (see Table 2.2) emphasize how children learn and think about mathematics. The process standards are threaded through the content standards emphasizing the context for learning mathematics. The five process standards introduced in this chapter are integrated into Part Two of this book with content activities and lessons.

Problem Solving

Many people recall learning mathematics by memorizing facts followed with a few word problems at the end of the unit or chapter. In a modern mathematics program, problems are not an afterthought. Instead, children begin with stories and situations that require them to develop concepts and skills to solve problems. In "learning through problem solving" (Schroeder & Lester, 1989), real-life and simulated problem situations provide context and reason for learning mathematics. Problem solving is the central goal of mathematics instruction.

Students need a variety of engaging experiences to develop proficiency in problem solving. Newer elementary textbooks and supplemental materials implement the standards with many stories and situational problems for students and teachers to solve. Puzzles and games also develop problem-solving strategies. Interesting problems are also found in newspapers or on the Internet. An article about the world's largest dormitory (Hoppe, 1999) included statistics about the largest dormitory in the United States at the University of Texas. A listing of the gallons of water used, pounds of cereal and dozens of eggs eaten, and tons of garbage hauled away generated questions about consumption and waste at school and at home. These topics became mathematical investigations connected to science and social studies.

Many good problems are encountered in classrooms throughout the school year. Teachers and students identify problems and investigate alternative solutions.

- A class needs sashes for a school program. Each sash has three stripes of different-colored material, and each stripe is 4 inches wide and 48 inches long. How many sashes are needed? How many yards of each color of material are needed? What is the cost of 1 yard of material? What will be the cost of all the sashes?

- Two computers are in the classroom. How can everybody get a turn? What is the best way to schedule the computers with the least interruption of other activities?

- A class is investigating climatic changes in its region of the country. What is the average monthly rainfall for the past 5 years? How do these averages compare with the same averages for the past 100 years? Has the average for any given month changed? How has temperature changed over the past 100 years?

- A class is studying nutrition as part of a health unit. What number of calories is recommended for girls in the class? for boys? What ratio of calories from fats to total calories is recommended? What is the average daily intake of calories of each child in the class? How are the calories for each child distributed among the food types? How much does each child's calorie intake vary from what is recommended?

Realistic and open-ended problems invite realistic and open-ended problem solving. Nonroutine problems involve important mathematics concepts and skills. Classroom investigations are called **problem-based learning**. Thorp and Sage (1999) describe problem-based learning as "focused, experiential learning (minds-on, hands-on) organized around the investigation and resolution of messy, real-world problems." By creating a "learning adventure," teachers work with students to solve problems with meaning. All the sources of problems contribute to the development of problem solving and provide a variety of problems for student engagement. In Chapter 8 we introduce some problem-solving strategies that are used by children and adults when they encounter problems.

Reasoning and Proof

Elementary students demonstrate reasoning and proof when they explain their thinking. In the context of mathematics-rich activities and problems, students tell, show, write, draw, and act out what they are doing and explain why. By providing experiences for students to construct their own solutions and understandings, teachers encourage children's thinking.

The teacher may initiate problems that are rich with mathematical concepts or follow up on a student interest. The lottery vignette describes a real-life problem of interest to students. Students experienced simple samples, then more complex samples, and drew conclusions based on the data and evidence they generated. Throughout the investigations, they predicted, hypothesized, conjectured, and reasoned using data.

During learning, children often have partial understanding or misconceptions. Young children are preoperational, meaning that their thinking is strongly influenced by visual impressions.

Mariel, age 5, has learned to identify squares, rectangles, circles, and triangles. The triangle shape used in her classroom is

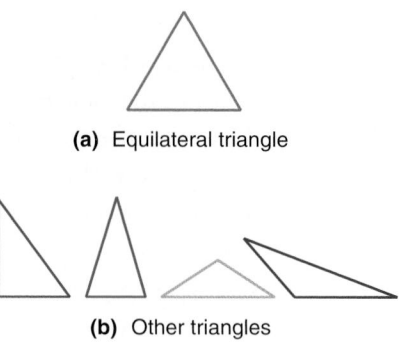

(a) Equilateral triangle

(b) Other triangles

Figure 2.10 Triangles

an equilateral triangle (Figure 2.10a). When introduced to another triangle, she refuses to name it a triangle. The name is limited by her understanding of "triangles."

As students develop cognitively, they reason more flexibly. Classification based on the relationship between shapes is a powerful reasoning process. After working with a set of triangles, third graders recognize that some attributes are common to all triangles and that some characteristics identify specific triangles. One writes a journal entry explaining what the cooperative group decided about triangles.

All triangles have three sides and three angles. Equilateral triangles are special because they have three congruent sides and three congruent angles of 60 degrees. Right triangles are special because they all have one right angle. If right triangles have two sides the same length, they are isosceles right triangles. Scalene triangles have no congruent sides. Scalene triangles might also be right triangles.

Teachers encourage mathematical discourse by asking open-ended questions based on mathematical tasks that engage students' interest and thinking. Teachers must resist the temptation to provide quick and easy answers. Instead, they should ask students to explain their reasoning whether the answer is correct or not. Errors are opportunities for students to develop reasoning and sound mathematical concepts. Disagreements and arguments are important in a classroom that encourages thinking.

Communication

The NCTM principles and standards challenge teachers to organize classrooms so that they promote communication and collaboration. Mathematics is often remembered as a solitary exercise of writing answers in workbooks or worksheets. Today, talking, reading, writing, acting, building, and drawing are valued ways of learning mathematics.

Communication is as fundamental to learning mathematics as it is to reading and language arts. In every lesson, children share their thinking and improve their reasoning through oral discussions, written descriptions, journals, tables, charts, and graphs. In the vignette about block towers, students constructed models and counted blocks. Data placed in tables led to conclusions, predictions, and new questions. Students who snap, clap, and stomp various patterns are communicating understanding of sequence and repetition that they then symbolize with pictures and symbols. As children listen to explanations and solutions, they hear alternative ways of thinking and may clarify their ideas.

In the real world, people often work together on common goals or problems. The elementary classroom models cooperative efforts of information sharing and task focus. A new play area calls on children to collaborate and negotiate the design. Each grade level could work on the task and make recommendations using diagrams and written explanations.

POINT OF VIEW

Students need opportunities not just to listen, but to speak mathematics themselves—to discuss what they have observed, why procedures appear to work, or why they think their solution is correct. Students read hundreds of mathematical exercises in their textbooks; they also need opportunities to read about mathematics and to write about the mathematical ideas they have. (Silver et al., 1990, pp. 7–8)

- A new surface is being put on the school's playground, and markings for old activities will be covered. What game and activity spaces should be laid out on the new surface? What is the best way to lay out the spaces for the least possible interference among players of different games?

Talking, sharing, discussing, and even arguing contrasts with traditional classrooms where students work in isolation on getting the one right answer. Promoting mathematics as a collaborative and communicative enterprise challenges teachers to rethink their ground rules for teaching mathematics.

Connection

Connecting mathematics asks students and teachers to find mathematics in the real world, especially things related to students' lives and interests, associations among mathematical concepts, and ways that mathematics are related to other school subjects and topics. "When am I ever going to use this?" is answered through activities and problems that connect mathematics to real problems that make sense to children.

School mathematics can be taught in connected ways or in disconnected ways. Disconnected mathematics is sometimes directed by textbooks and other materials. Connected mathematics is still focused on the development of concepts and skills but is open to many opportunities to build these skills through problem solving. The problems can be real, invented, based on classroom situations, drawn from other subjects, or generated by student interest. The lottery problem connected the interest of students to mathematical concepts of probability, data analysis, and number operations and to processes of problem solving, reasoning, and communication. Many classroom situations illustrate connections to children's experiences.

- A third-grade class sells pizzas at a Parents' Night program. How much should the pizzas cost? How many pizzas will be needed? How many slices can be cut from one pizza? What is a fair price to charge for one slice? What is a reasonable profit?

- A science unit on plant growth includes experiments comparing growth under different light conditions. What measurements need to be made and how often? What units and measuring instruments are required? What is the best way to record observations? How should the results of the project be reported?

- Ms. Wolfgang asks the students to use the newspaper advertisements from the home improvement store to determine how much it would cost to carpet a platform being built for a stage and reading area (Figure 2.11). The platform is 8 feet 6 inches by 11 feet 9 inches, but the cost of carpet is given in dollars per square yard. One group of students decides to calculate the dimensions in

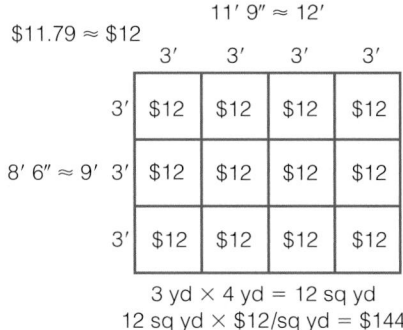

Figure 2.11 Estimated area and cost of carpet

feet and then in square feet, or approximately 9 feet × 12 feet = 108 square feet, and then converts to square yards (108 ÷ 9 = 12 square yards). Another group converts feet to yards and approximates with 3 yards × 4 yards = 12 square yards. If carpet is priced at $11.79 per square yard, they determine the cost as about $144, and then remembered the sales tax of 7.5% that must be added. They decided $150 was a good estimate of the total cost.

Solving the carpet problem requires measurement, addition, division, multiplication, estimation, and percent. The diagram allows students to see how multiplication is used to solve area (3 × 4 = 12 square yards) and find the total cost (12 yards × $12 per yard = $144). Students may also want to look at different flooring materials related to economics topics in social studies.

Interdisciplinary teaching with integrated themes and activities (Table 2.3) builds children's sense of how concepts in one subject link to concepts in mathematics.

ⒺXERCISE

Find an example of an integrated, interdisciplinary unit on the Internet. How well are mathematics concepts and skills developed in the unit? ●●●

Mathematical Representation

When adults recall their experiences with mathematics in school, they often only remember filling out worksheets with numbers or writing on the board. Mathematical ideas can be expressed in many ways: physical models, pictures, diagrams, tables, graphs, charts, and a variety of symbols. The

block tower problem was represented concretely with blocks, graphically in a table, and symbolically with formulas. The lottery problem was acted out through sampling, recorded in tables, and could be simulated with computer programs. "Half" is shown in pictures of areas and sets and symbolically as a common fraction, a decimal fraction, or a percent. Although "mean" and "median" are computed in specific ways, students are sometimes confused by the differences. When means and medians for various data sets are displayed graphically, the differences may be more apparent. Using different representations contributes to the meaning and complexity of a concept.

Place value representation is a complex notion that children develop over several years. Children start with a naïve notion of one numeral or name for each amount. Two is one more than 1, 6 is one more than 5, 11 is one more than 10. The idea that numbers are just a never-ending sequence of words related by "plus 1" must change before students compute with larger numbers. They need to see and know that the number system is based on groups of 10 and that number values can be represented in many ways. The number 16 can be shown by 16 blocks arranged in many ways, pictures of 16 objects, 1 rod and 6 cubes with place value blocks, a 4 × 4 grid,

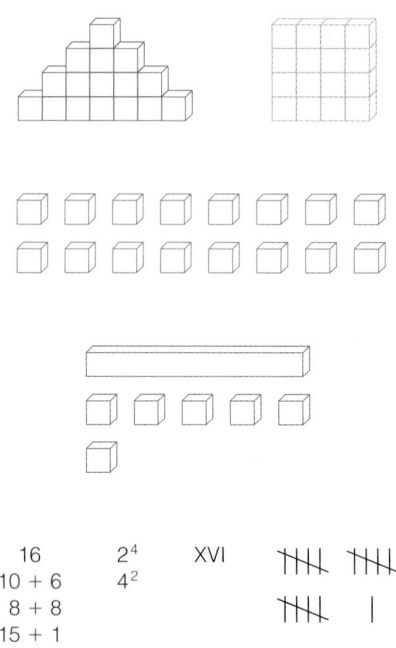

Figure 2.12 Representations of 16

TABLE 2.3	**Interdisciplinary Connections for Mathematics**

Mathematics and Science

- Taking and recording temperature, wind speed, and air pressure in a weather unit
- Investigating the conditions for putting an object in orbit around Earth
- Using a scale of hardness to classify various kinds of rocks and minerals

Mathematics and Social Studies

- Investigating various devices for telling time, such as sundials, sand timers, and water clocks
- Investigating the mathematics used by ancient Egyptians during construction of the pyramids
- Studying Southwest Native American rugs, bowls, and baskets to understand the iconography and how symmetry and tessellation create meaningful designs
- Comparing (1) the highest and the lowest places on land and (2) the highest place on land with the deepest place underwater

Mathematics and Art

- Making a scale drawing of a backdrop for a class play and measuring and preparing the paper for the backdrop
- Planning and making an Escher-like tessellation (see Chapter 9)
- Creating Japanese origami

Mathematics and Health

- Keeping a height chart for a year
- Determining calories in school meals and home meals
- Measuring heart rate before and after exertion

Mathematics and Reading/Language Arts

- Looking for patterns in words, classifying words as rhyming and nonrhyming, and looking for palindromic words and phrases
- Researching and writing about famous mathematicians
- Analyzing text to determine the frequency of letters (students can connect this to the television game show *Wheel of Fortune*)

Mathematics and Physical Education

- Counting the number of hops while jumping rope
- Using movement activities to investigate geometric transformations: slides, flips, and turns
- Organizing games on a play area
- Timing races

and numerals and expressions such as 16, 4^2, 2^4, 15 + 1, 10 + 6, 20 − 4, and XVI. Instead of being limited to one idea about 16 (Figure 2.12), children must understand that multiple representations are essential to developing a true understanding of number.

Integrating Process and Content Standards

Mathematics content and processes develop through many experiences with mathematics-rich activities and situations coupled with opportunities to communicate and connect those experiences. Effective teachers integrate content and process standards into every lesson and unit. In each of the vignettes and examples in this chapter, concepts and pro-

cesses have been highlighted. A unit on statistics has students measure and record their heights in inches (Figure 2.13a) and centimeters (Figure 2.13b). Then they organize the measurements for the class in a table (Figure 2.13c) and a graph (Figure 2.13d). Information from the table and the graph describes the heights of children in the room and allows for conclusions about heights of the group.

- "All the students are shorter than 70 inches (180 centimeters) tall, and everybody is taller than 45 inches (110 centimeters)."

- "Most students are about 55 inches (140 centimeters) tall."

- "Most children are between 53 inches (130 centimeters) and 58 inches (145 centimeters) tall."

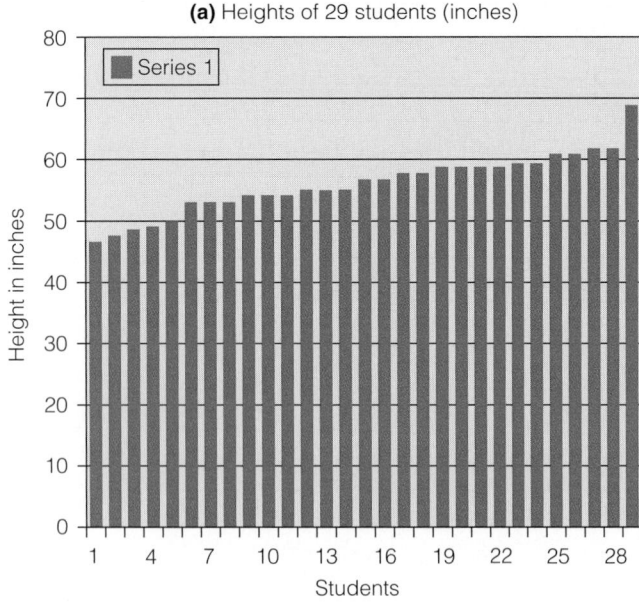

(a) Heights of 29 students (inches)

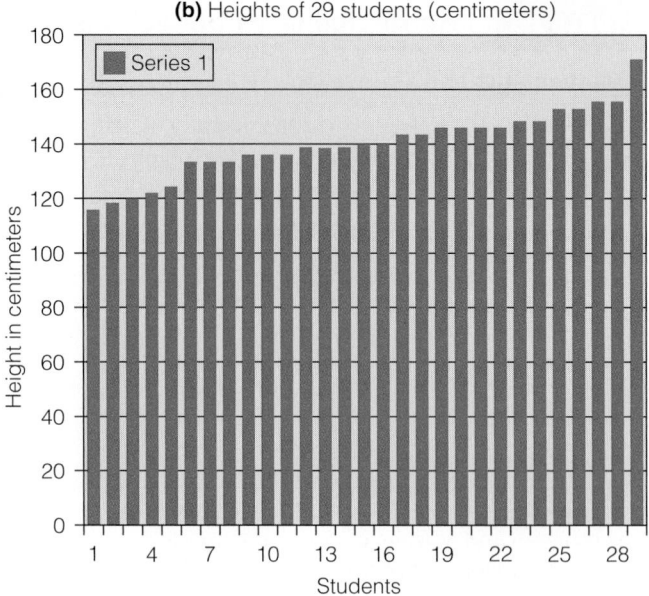

(b) Heights of 29 students (centimeters)

(c) Table of heights (inches)

Height in inches	Number of students
44	0
45	0
46	1
47	1
48	1
49	1
50	1
51	0
52	0
53	3
54	3
55	3
56	2
57	2
58	4
59	2
60	0
61	2
62	2
63	0
64	0
65	0
66	0
67	0
68	1

(d) Graph of heights (inches)

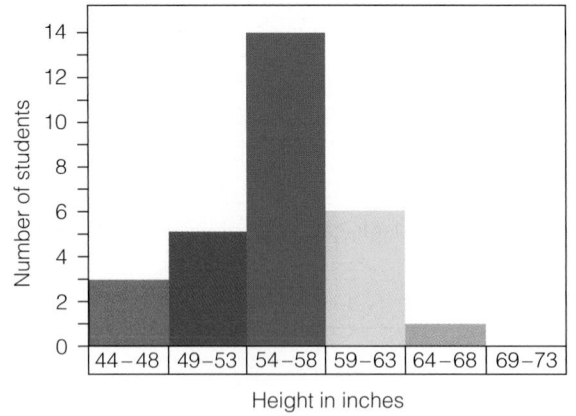

Figure 2.13 Data analysis and display of children's heights

median, and mean to data on rainfall and temperature. Some teachers fear that the greater emphasis on testing will limit their efforts to do exciting projects and stimulating teaching. In reality, instruction based on the NCTM principles and standards develops essential concepts and skills in the curriculum and the demands for accountability. When children learn important mathematics in meaningful ways, they learn the mathematics they need for their lives.

Many resources are available for teachers. NCTM provides publications and materials that support teachers' efforts in implementing standards-based instruction. Membership in NCTM includes a subscription to one of three journals. For elementary and early childhood teachers, *Teaching Children Mathematics* is recommended. *Mathematics Teaching in the Middle School* is written for middle-grade teachers. The NCTM website **http://www.nctm.org** provides many helpful links for teachers, such as sample e-lessons, technology integration, and activities in the Illuminations website. NCTM also sponsors local, state, regional, and national conferences each year with presentations and exhibits for teachers. Many other publishers and suppliers of mathematics teaching materials have coordinated their materials and publications with the standards.

Students note extremes or limits, variation in heights, and a tendency of heights to cluster. These observations introduce statistical concepts of range, mean, median, and mode. The focus for this lesson is statistical concept, skills, and language, but students also use knowledge of numbers and number operations, measurement, and algebraic thinking. Later in the year, an integrated unit in social studies and science on climate provides another chance to apply range,

Working with teachers in your school or on your team helps you to focus on the needs of the children in your room or grade level. Sharing ideas, articles, and materials with colleagues helps you to grow professionally. Many school districts employ a mathematics consultant or coordinator who knows about available resources. An experienced mentor also can help a new teacher find resources and learn how to use them.

Finding Focus

Teachers sometimes feel overwhelmed by national and state standards. In response to the concern that the curriculum was "a mile wide and an inch deep," the National Council of Teachers of Mathematics in September 2006 published *Curriculum Focal Points for Prekindergarten through Grade 8 Mathematics* that highlights three core ideas, called focal points,

---

TABLE 2.4 • **Curriculum Focal Points**

Kindergarten Focal Points

Number and Operations: Developing an understanding of whole numbers, including concepts of correspondence, counting, cardinality, and comparison
Geometry: Identifying shapes and describing spatial relationships
Measurement: Identifying measurable attributes and comparing objects by using these attributes

Grade 1 Focal Points

Number and Operations and Algebra: Developing understandings of addition and subtraction and strategies for basic addition facts and related subtraction facts
Number and Operations: Developing an understanding of whole number relationships, including grouping in tens and ones
Geometry: Composing and decomposing geometric shapes

Grade 2 Focal Points

Number and Operations: Developing an understanding of the base-10 numeration system and place-value concepts
Number and Operations and Algebra: Developing quick recall of addition facts and related subtraction facts and fluency with multidigit addition and subtraction
Measurement: Developing an understanding of linear measurement and facility in measuring lengths

Grade 3 Focal Points

Number and Operations and Algebra: Developing understandings of multiplication and division and strategies for basic multiplication facts and related division facts
Number and Operations: Developing an understanding of fractions and fraction equivalence
Geometry: Describing and analyzing properties of two-dimensional shapes

Grade 4 Focal Points

Number and Operations and Algebra: Developing quick recall of multiplication facts and related division facts and fluency with whole number multiplication
Number and Operations: Developing an understanding of decimals, including the connections between fractions and decimals
Measurement: Developing an understanding of area and determining the areas of two-dimensional shapes

Grade 5 Focal Points

Number and Operations and Algebra: Developing an understanding of and fluency with division of whole numbers
Number and Operations: Developing an understanding of and fluency with addition and subtraction of fractions and decimals
Geometry and Measurement and Algebra: Describing three-dimensional shapes and analyzing their properties, including volume and surface area

Grade 6 Focal Points

Number and Operations: Developing an understanding of and fluency with multiplication and division of fractions and decimals
Number and Operations: Connecting ratio and rate to multiplication and division
Algebra: Writing, interpreting, and using mathematical expressions and equations

SOURCE: From *Curriculum Focal Points for Prekindergarten through Grade 8 Mathematics* (2006) by the National Council of Teachers of Mathematics.

at each grade level. The principles and standards are still the framework for mathematics curriculum and instruction with problem solving as the central theme. The focal points listed in Table 2.4 identify three critical knowledge and skills at each grade level. The purpose was not to narrow the curriculum to three concepts, but to help teachers organize instruction with attention to some essential developmental knowledge.

The publication as well as the website **www.nctm .org** describe ways teachers can utilize the focal points in planning and teaching. For example in grade 4, knowledge and skill with multidigit multiplication, area of two-dimensional shapes, and decimal fractions are emphasized. Students might cover boxes with centimeter grid paper and find connections among multiplication, area, and decimal fractions.

Summary

The worlds of 1910 and 2010 are different, and the mathematics that students need to live and thrive in the 21st century is different. A balanced program of number, geometry, algebra, measurement, and data analysis concepts and skills replaces a mathematics program focused primarily on computation. Development of thinking skills and application of mathematics to solving problems breaks away from a focus on memorization. Understanding what problems to solve and when and how to solve them is the center of the modern mathematics program.

NCTM recognizes the changing need of content and context for school mathematics in *The Principles and Standards for School Mathematics* (National Council of Teachers of Mathematics, 2000). Five content standards and five process standards provide a coherent vision of mathematics to help students become productive and thinking citizens. Five major content topics are developed across all grade levels: numbers and operations, algebra, geometry, measurement, and data analysis and probability. Learning content occurs when students are communicating about mathematics, reasoning and solving problems, connecting mathematics to their world, and demonstrating their understanding in a variety of ways. The standards serve as a framework for state curricula in mathematics. They challenge teachers to focus on important mathematical content and skills that enable students to become proficient problem solvers.

Study Questions and Activities

1. Find the curriculum standards for your school or state on the Internet. Compare the NCTM content and process standards to your state or local mathematics curriculum. If you do not know the URL for your state's department of education website, search for "mathematics standards state." What similarities or differences do you find between the NCTM standards and your school or state's standards?

2. Observe in a mathematics classroom, and decide whether you see principles and standards in practice.

3. Describe an ideal classroom that would exemplify the principles and standards. What would you expect to see and hear in the classroom?

4. Look through a catalog of mathematics materials. Identify materials related to each of the content and process standards.

5. Go to http://www.nctm.org and read about the principles and standards. Look at the resources available to teachers on this website.

6. Not all educators and parents agree with the NCTM standards. Conduct an Internet search for sites that raise objections to the standards. Do you agree or disagree with their arguments?

Teacher's Resources

National Council of Teachers of Mathematics. (2000). *Principles and standards for school mathematics.* Reston, VA: Author.

CHAPTER 3

Mathematics for Every Child

Mathematics knowledge and skill provide a key for entry into a rapidly changing technological world. In the middle of the last century the idea that only a few students, primarily white male students, could be successful in mathematics was widely accepted in American society. This perception denied female and minority students, students with special needs, and students with linguistic differences access to advanced mathematics programs. As a result, females and minorities had fewer opportunities to learn and faced limited opportunities in college and vocational choices.

In 1998–1999, the NCTM Board of Directors renewed the challenge to schools and educators to provide equal opportunities (National Council of Teachers of Mathematics, 2000, p. 13):

> The Board of Directors sees the comprehensive mathematics education of every child as its most compelling goal. By "every child" we mean every child—no exceptions. We are particularly concerned about students who have been denied access in any way to educational opportunities for any reason, such as language, ethnicity, physical impairment, gender, socioeconomic status, and so on. We emphasize that "every child" includes
>
> • learners of English as a second language and speakers of English as a first language;
>
> • members of underrepresented ethnic groups and members of well-represented groups;
>
> • students who are physically challenged and those who are not;
>
> • females and males;

- students who live in poverty and those who do not;

- students who have not been successful and those who have been successful in school and in mathematics.

The Board of Directors commits the organization and every group effort within the organization to this goal.

In a recent position statement (2005) NCTM restates and extends this commitment and challenge (**http://www.nctm.org**):

> Every student should have equitable and optimal opportunities to learn mathematics free from bias—intentional or unintentional—based on race, gender, socioeconomic status, or language. In order to close the achievement gap, all students need the opportunity to learn challenging mathematics from a well-qualified teacher who will make connections to the background, needs, and cultures of all learners.

In this chapter you will read about:

1 Ways to include diverse cultural aspects in mathematics teaching

2 The role of ethnomathematics in teaching mathematics

3 Strategies for teaching mathematics to English-language learners

4 Teaching strategies for students with learning disabilities

5 Characteristics of students who are gifted and talented in mathematics

6 Multiple intelligences and learning styles

Equity in Mathematics Learning

Whether teachers work in a self-contained setting or as specialists in mathematics, they have a professional responsibility to provide a mathematics-rich environment for all—boys and girls, students with limited English proficiency, members of all cultural and ethnic groups, students who are physically and learning challenged, students who are gifted and talented, and learners of every style and orientation. Meeting the needs of every student is not easy, but every teacher must work toward that goal. When students fail to develop their full potential in mathematics in elementary school, they have difficulty with mathematics in later grades. Those in high school who lack the prerequisite understanding and skills for college and university study are unprepared to enter many occupations. The social and economic implications for individuals and society as a whole are great when students are not nurtured in mathematics.

POINT OF VIEW
A recognition of individual differences must be basic to an educator's philosophy. (Guild & Garger, 1998)

In this chapter we consider equity in mathematics learning from several viewpoints: gender, ethnicity, limited English proficiency, technological equity, special needs, giftedness, and learning styles. Each of these groups presents its own challenges for the classroom teacher, challenges that must be met to ensure that every child in each of these groups is able to learn interesting and valuable mathematics.

Gender

Only a few decades ago one of the truisms in education was "Math is for boys, English is for girls." Not that girls didn't achieve in mathematics—some did. But the expectation was that boys *should* do well in mathematics. Test scores in high school and college enrollment figures supported the truism. In the minds of many, mathematics was the domain of men, not women.

In recent years evidence put this "truism" to rest forever. Girls can do mathematics as well as boys, and recent test scores support that stand. The most recent test results of the National Assessment of Educational Progress (2005) show only a slight difference in mathematics scores between boys and girls (girls' score, 278; boys' score, 280). The difference between the genders has remained about the same over the past decade, and scores for both have continued to rise. Thus, as a percent of the mean test score for boys and girls, the difference between the genders continues to shrink, to the point that any differences are now statistically insignificant. A meta-analysis of recent mathematics scores on the SAT shows no difference in girls' and boys' scores (Barnette & Rivers, 2004). Girl's enrollment in mathematics courses in high school and college continues to rise but still trails boys' enrollment figures.

Although the facts show no gender differences in mathematics achievement, there are still reports of girls being treated differently from boys in mathematics classes in subtle ways. In the past teachers at all levels devoted more classroom time to helping boys. Boys were encouraged more than girls to think through a problem, as opposed to being given direct cues or directions for solving it. Teachers tended to call on boys more than girls during class discussions, and boys were praised more frequently than girls (Huber & Scanlon, 1995; Sadker & Sadker, 1994; Tapasak, 1990). Although today's classrooms show less of this gender distinction, there is still work to be done. Even parents' attitudes reflect this distinction in mathematics. Parents tend to attribute their girls' mathematics achievement to hard work, but the boys' achievement is attributed to natural talent (Gershaw, 2006; McCookLast, 2005).

Children learn that being a boy or a girl makes a difference in what they are expected to be, do, think, and feel. This learning process is called gender socialization. Differences in treatment and expectations . . . influence the kinds of skills each sex develops, how confident children feel as learners, and even what intellectual risks they are willing to take. . . . Girls learn to approach math and science with greater uncertainty and ambivalence than boys, with inadequate practice and uncertainty in particular skill areas (like spatial skills) and, more generally, with conflicts about competence and independence. (Davenport, 1994, pp. 1–2)

Even when teachers treat students equally, derogatory remarks from male students about female students' capabilities and interests in mathematics have negative effects on females. Female students may downplay their interest and skills when they reach middle school because of beliefs that females are not or should not be as good in mathematics as males. Gallagher and Kaufman and Campbell provide a fuller discussion of causes and effects of gender differences in mathematics (see Gallagher & Kaufman, 2004; Campbell, 1995).

Even though these societal attitudes fly in the face of facts and educational policies, they do have an effect on young women. Fewer girls enroll in upper-level mathematics courses in high school or become mathematics majors in college. One study found that 9% of girls in grade 4 expressed a dislike for mathematics. By grade 12 the percentage had risen to 50% (Chacon & Soto-Johnson, 2003). A long-term study followed students from middle school through high school for a period of 17 years. The findings showed that although girls had higher grades, they had a lower interest in math than boys at every grade level and their interest in math declined every year from grade 7 through high school (Steeh, 2002). Clearly much more must be done to ensure that our young women remain confident in their mathematics ability and that they develop and maintain a desire to pursue more advanced mathematics.

There are always going to be differences between the genders in classrooms. Training little boys to be more like girls in their decorum or little girls to imitate boys in their energy level is counterproductive. Both genders benefit the classroom. It is important

POINT OF VIEW

Addressing gender equity in the mathematics classroom is a complex process. Since the forces shaping mathematics education are in a constant state of change, teachers will continually be facing new gender-equity dilemmas. (Ambrose et al., 2002, p. 447)

to recognize those benefits and to help all students gain from them.

One stereotypical difference between boys and girls that can benefit boys in mathematics is boys' risk-taking tendency. A stereotypical elementary school classroom can find boys out of their seats, noisily interacting with others, and taking and issuing dares to each other. Most of the girls are composed, on task, and following the teacher's directions. When these behaviors are extended to mathematics, they can work to the boys' benefit. Consider the approach to nonroutine problems that each type of student will take. Students who have practiced only the routine algorithms (a set of instructions used to solve a problem, such as the procedure for long division) and solution strategies presented by the teacher in class may find that such routine approaches are not helpful with nonroutine problems. Risk-takers who have tried alternative approaches, used guessing, and created their own solution strategies are in a position to try something different and so are not intimidated by a problem that is unfamiliar and cannot be solved by the routine algorithms learned in class. A teacher who is alert to such stereotypical tendencies will help girls confront and solve nonroutine problems. At the same time the teacher will assist the boys to master classroom procedures and strategies when they are explored.

Research suggests that gender affects spatial sense. The ability to view objects, mentally manipulate them, and move between two and three dimensions is related to gender. Among children, only 17% of girls achieved the average score that boys did on tests of spatial sense (Linn & Petersen, 1986). Further research has supported this gender factor in spatial sense (Greenes & Tsankova, 2004; Levine et al., 1999). If no intervention is done, then the gap in spatial sense becomes larger as children move from grade to grade, until the difference begins to affect other areas of mathematics learning. The solution is simply to teach spatial sense in the elementary classroom along with other mathematics topics. When students (regardless of gender) who

have a poorly developed spatial sense are given the opportunity to improve and extend that ability, they quickly erase any deficit within a few grades. Thus the single-gender difference in mathematics may be overcome with a focused effort in the primary and elementary classrooms. See Chapter 17 for activities that develop spatial sense.

In closing, gender is no barrier to achievement in mathematics. Girls and boys bring various talents and abilities to their mathematics, which serve to enrich a mathematics classroom. At one time mathematics may have been only for boys, but not anymore. More than ever, mathematics belongs to everyone, and the role of the classroom teacher is to ensure that both girls and boys believe and achieve in mathematics.

Ethnic and Cultural Differences

Students from ethnic or cultural groups different from the dominant culture may encounter inequitable treatment. According to Secada (1991), a mathematics curriculum that fails to reflect the lives of children from culturally different groups may stereotype mathematics as belonging to a few privileged groups. In addition, in the United States expectations for achievement in mathematics are sometimes not as high for these students as for Asians and white students. Gloria Ladson-Billings (1995, p. 38) illustrates this difference:

White, middle-class students are treated as if they already have knowledge, and experience instruction as *apprenticeship*. However, African American students often are treated as if they have no knowledge and experience instruction as *teaching*.

When students are apprenticed, they are afforded the opportunity to perform tasks that they have not fully learned. . . . In the classroom, this apprenticing is played out by teachers treating white, middle-class students as if they are competent in areas they are not. They are treated as if they come with knowledge (which they do).

However, African American youngsters often are treated as if they have no knowledge.

Thus, as "empty vessels" they must be filled.

Ladson-Billings noted that African American students received more teacher-directed lessons in specific knowledge and skills and fewer opportunities to engage in problem-solving situations that required independent thought and action.

No evidence supports any claim that African American, Latino American, Native American, Asian American, or any other group of students lacks the ability to learn mathematics. What is lacking in many instances is a common *background* for learning mathematics. Many students live in socioeconomic environments that offer different background-building experiences. Ladson-Billings (1995) cites a specific example of how socioeconomic circumstances influence students' thinking: A problem asks, "Which is a more economical way to commute to work, a bus pass that costs $65 a month or a one-way fare for $1.50?" The answer depends on experience. One student might consider one-way fares better because a parent's transportation cost would be $60 when commuting to a single job for 20 workdays each month. Other students could view the pass as less costly than individual fares, if a monthly pass would allow for unlimited trips between home, employment, shopping, and other important sites. Socioeconomic conditions and a narrow range of experiences may impede early learning, but they are not reasons for believing that students are less able to learn mathematics and should aim for less lofty goals than other students. In keeping with the key point for teaching diverse students, it is important to provide all children with a fair and equitable opportunity to learn mathematics.

Multiculturalism

When students are from different cultural or ethnic backgrounds, introducing multicultural aspects into the mathematics classroom can be constructive. Multiculturalism in mathematics suggests using materials from many cultures to explain mathematics concepts, to apply mathematical ideas, and to provide a context for mathematics problems. Thus there is more to multiculturalism than hanging posters on the wall or focusing on a few special holidays.

Grounding mathematics in meaningful contexts for children is crucial; otherwise mathematics becomes a dance of symbols and abstract numerical relationships.

Putting mathematics in meaningful settings involves more than changing the names of people in word problems to reflect different ethnic backgrounds. It involves problems in real-life settings that children from different ethnic backgrounds will find compelling. Children can be a source of multicultural mathematics material. A teacher who knows the children in the classroom and their backgrounds can place mathematics in meaningful contexts for them. When mathematics is couched in significant situations for children, they begin to understand that mathematics is a valuable subject, one that has real worth in their personal lives, as reflected in their ethnic background. Generic settings that can appeal to children from various ethnic backgrounds include native cooking and recipes, crafts involving measurement and geometry, designing and building a house, shopping for native foods and goods. Reading multicultural stories with mathematics themes is an effective way to fold multiculturalism into mathematics class. Table 3.1 is a list of some multicultural storybooks with mathematics themes to them.

Storytelling can also feature multicultural themes. An effective storyteller can be more engaging than a story in a book. These stories or folktales can come from a variety of sources, including the students themselves (see Goral & Gnadinger, 2006). An advantage of storytelling is that the teacher can adjust the story to emphasize a particular point or mathematics concept. In addition to stories, songs that feature mathematical concepts or numbers may also be part of mathematics class. The list in Table 3.2 is adapted from Galda and Cullinan (2006). It contains songs and folktales that feature a specific number.

Ethnomathematics

In 1985, Uribitan D'Ambrosio introduced the term *ethnomathematics*. He used it to refer to mathemat-

TABLE 3.1 ○ **Multicultural Books with a Mathematics Theme**	
Anansi the Spider: A Tale from the Ashanti, Gerald McDermott, 1987	African
The Black Snowman, Phil Mendez, 1989	African American
Count on Your Fingers African Style, Claudia Zaslavsky, 2000	African
Count Your Way Through Africa, Jim Haskins, 1989	African
Fun with Numbers, Jan Masslin, 1994	Mayan and African
The Girl Who Loved Wild Horses, Paul Gobel, 1978	Native American
Grandfather Tang's Story, Ann Tompert, 1990	Chinese
The Hundred Penny Box, Sharon Bell Mathis, 1975	African American
Legend of the Indian Paintbrush, T. de Paola, 1988	Native American
A Million Fish . . . More or Less, Patricia McKissack, 1992	Native American
The Patchwork Quilt, Valerie Flournoy, 1985	African American
Popcorn Book, T. dePaola, 1978	Native American
The Rajah's Rice, Dave Barry, 1994	Indian
Sadako and the Thousand Paper Cranes, Eleanor Coerr, 1993	Japanese
The Story of Money, Carolyn Kain, 1994	Multicultural
Story Quilts of Harriet Powers, Mary Lyons, 1997	African American
Thirteen Moons on the Turtle's Back, Joseph Bruchac, 1992	Native American
Two Ways to Count to Ten: A Liberian Folktale, Ruby Dee, 1988	African
The Village of Round and Square Houses, Ann Grifalconi, 1986	African

ics as seen through a cultural filter. Ethnomathematics is the "study of the interaction between mathematics and human culture" (Johnson, 2006). All mathematics developed from a cultural need, regardless of the historical setting. Geometry concepts grew out of a need to measure land, build dwellings, and find one's way between villages and cities. The rise of commerce set in motion the development of accounting and the algorithms we use today. Consequently, ethnomathematics reflects situations that led to the development of mathematics in various cultures. Ethnomathematics informs teachers and students about how mathematics was developed in response to societal needs, and it is shaped by cultural settings and issues today. Thus ethnomathematics delves more deeply into the interplay between mathematics and culture than does multiculturalism.

Every culture developed mathematics to fit a particular need. Children illuminate these developments by asking their parents how they used mathematics in their native land, under what situations they learned to use mathematics, and how they use mathematics in their everyday lives. Rather than sanitize mathematics from all cultural influences, mathematics becomes the shaper and tool of all civilizations. Minority students are encouraged by and involved in mathematics that is intimately connected to their cultural background. Table 3.3 presents 10 ways of including culturally relevant activities in the classroom. These topics and related projects can motivate students from diverse ethnic backgrounds to learn mathematics.

Multicultural themes should be integrated into the mathematics curriculum. They could be the settings that introduce mathematics concepts, illuminate those concepts, or summarize the study of a particular concept. Multiculturalism is not an

TABLE 3.2 ○ **Folk Songs and Folktales That Feature Numbers**	
Number	**Folk Songs and Folktales**
One	*Puss in Boots*
Two	*Jorinda and Jorongel* *Perez and Martina*
Three	*Three Wishes* *Three Little Pigs* *Three Billy Goats Gruff* *Three Little Kittens* *Goldilocks and the Three Bears*
Four	*Bremen Town Musicians* *Four Gallant Sisters*
Six	*Six Foolish Fishermen*
Seven	*Seven Blind Mice* *Her Seven Brothers* *Seven with One Blow* *Snow White and the Seven Dwarfs*
Twelve	*Twelve Dancing Princesses* *Twelve Days of Christmas*

TABLE 3.3 ● **Activities That Draw on the Cultural and Ethnic Background of Children**

1. History of Mathematics

Biographies and anecdotes about Chinese, Hindu, and Persian mathematicians can be sources of interesting, humanizing stories for children. Teachers can relate these stories to students at appropriate times during mathematics class. Children could also act out the stories, playing the roles of mathematician and others in these minidramas (see Johnson, 1991, 1999).

2. Number Systems

Studying the numerical systems of the Egyptians, Native Americans, or the Maya is broadening for all children. Children can make posters describing the other systems. They can also change the prices on price tags or in circulars to show prices in other numerical systems.

3. Counting Language

Learning to count in the language of another student can be a means of introducing multiculturalism into the classroom. Many languages have a counting system that is much more logical than ours. In many languages, 11 is expressed as "ten-one," 12 is "ten-two," up to 19, "ten-nine"; 21 is "two-ten-one," 22 is "two-ten-two," 31 is "three-ten-one," and so forth. Children can teach the class to count in their native language. They could also show their counting words in a visual exhibit such as a poster or table display.

4. Algorithms

The algorithms we use for computation may be different in another culture. Ask children to share their algorithms. Russian peasant multiplication or lattice multiplication are interesting and effective alternatives to algorithms commonly used in the United States. Students can explain the algorithms that they or their parents use that are alternative algorithms to the ones studied in class. A homework assignment might be to compute using an alternative algorithm.

5. Problem Contexts

Teachers might provide contexts for story problems that are drawn from settings and activities familiar to other cultures. Students can write out meaningful contexts or problems to use in class.

6. Multicultural Literature

Folktales or foreign literature may be used to teach mathematics in context. Children can ask parents and relatives to relate these tales to them. The children can then bring the tales to class.

7. Art

Symmetry patterns or artworks from different cultures may be used to promote geometric understandings. Navajo basket designs, African mandalas, or Asian needlepoint designs are full of symmetry and geometric figures. Some students may have native artwork at home that they can bring to class. Children can produce artwork that resembles the native art. Children can also cut out examples of native art in magazines and assemble collages to represent the native artwork.

8. Recreational Mathematics

Games such as Pente, GO!, Sudoku, or Mancala involve strategies that promote logical thinking. One station of an activity center can be stocked with these different games.

9. Calendars

Calendars from different cultures include different names for months, days of the week, and frequently different ways of recording the date. Foreign names might be included in the daily calendar reading. Several foreign language calendars could be displayed around the classroom, and different students assigned to read the date each day.

10. Notation

It can be beneficial to have children show and explain their different notations for familiar representations. For example, some Latin American children will correctly write $\overset{\angle}{ABC}$ for $\angle ABC$ or $\overset{\triangle}{QRS}$ for $\triangle QRS$. Children can share the notation they learned in their native land at appropriate times during mathematics class. Groups of students could design posters to show the notations that other cultures use.

add-on to supplement the study of mathematics. It is the vehicle for the very study of mathematics.

Every mathematics classroom has its own culture, either one that recognizes and prizes the various ethnic backgrounds of its students or one that ignores all cultural backgrounds and sets mathematics in a culturally neutral context. To best encourage ethnically diverse students, the teacher must acknowledge their cultural and ethnic backgrounds and use those backgrounds to enliven and enhance their study of mathematics.

POINT OF VIEW
Honor and respect the children's home and ancestral culture(s). (Delpit, 1999)

Mathematics may be the first subject area that culturally diverse students begin to learn, but teachers cannot assume that students with computational proficiency understand number and operational concepts. Certainly, many children from all cultural backgrounds have learned pencil-and-paper computations. However, focusing exclusively on computations deprives the student of language and concept development needed for problem solving and reasoning. Problem solving, best done in the context of real-world story problems, should be based on children's experiences. Zanger (1998) reports a classroom project of collecting and publishing math problems written by students and parents. At first the parents were wary, but when the book was published, it became an immediate hit with students, who now had problems related to their experiences. Students unable to express themselves fully in English might write out problems in their first language accompanied by graphic depictions. These problems can then be translated by another student or faculty member. When the teacher writes real-world problems, the problems should be concise, clear, and free of slang or unfamiliar idioms.

Many school districts provide professional development for teachers who work with cultural, ethnic, and language diversity. A new teacher should take advantage of these professional opportunities. Understanding the principles of good mathematics is a foundation, but additional preparation provides the background to become more sensitive to the specific cultural and ethnic groups in the local district and to become familiar with programs for language learners offered in and beyond the classroom.

Students Who Have Limited English Proficiency

The United States has a well-deserved reputation as a melting pot of races, cultures, and nationalities. In the nation's classrooms nearly 6 million students have limited English proficiency (LEP). By some estimates, within 20 years most students in American schools will not speak English as a first language. As the number of such students has grown, educational policies for these students have changed. More and more states are eliminating bilingual or foreign language classrooms in favor of schooling LEP students in regular English-speaking classrooms. The result is that more and more teachers will have LEP students in class.

POINT OF VIEW
Teachers need help to understand the strengths and needs of students who come from diverse linguistic backgrounds. . . . To accommodate differences among students effectively and extensively, teachers also need to understand and confront their own beliefs and biases. (National Council of Teachers of Mathematics, 2000, p. 12)

The first language of LEP students is intimately tied to their cultural or ethnic background. It is the language spoken at home and in their social community, and it is the means by which LEP students communicate with family, peers, and neighbors about their neighborhood and community, all of which are immersed in their native culture. Many LEP students might speak English only at school.

LEP students learn English over several years. Table 3.4, adapted from the Virginia State Board of Education, gives some sense of how long it can take for LEP students to communicate effectively in English.

The timeline in Table 3.4 assumes continuous living in the United States. Many LEP children return to their native lands every year, sometimes for weeks at a time. During their visit they will rarely speak or hear English, and so such visits may delay the development suggested in the table. With Table 3.4 as a guide, teachers can begin to understand why a child who can carry on a perfectly good English conversation in the playground can rightly claim he cannot understand the English discussions in the classroom. By some estimates, instructional class-

TABLE 3.4	Time Needed for Language Acquisition
State of Language Acquisition	**General Behavior of Students Who Have Limited English Proficiency**
Silent/Receptive Stage • 6 months to 1 year • 500 receptive words	• Point to objects, act, nod, or use gestures • Speak hesitantly
Early Productive Stage • 6 months to 1 year • 1,000 receptive/active words	• Produce one- or two-word phrases • Use short repetitive language • Focus on key words and context clues
Speech Emergence Stage • 1–2 years • 3,000 active words	• Engage in basic dialogue • Respond using simple sentences
Intermediate Fluency Stage • 2–3 years • 6,000 active words	• Use complex statements • State opinions and original thoughts • Ask questions
Advanced Fluency Stage • 5–7 years • Content area vocabulary	• Converse fluently • Understand grade-level classroom activities • Read grade-level textbooks • Write organized and fluent essays

SOURCE: Virginia Department of Education (2004).

room English lags behind conversational English by up to 5 years. An added factor is that mathematics has its own language, which is quite different from conversational English. Words and terms that children hear only in a mathematics class include *denominator, numerator, quotient, isosceles, greatest common factor,* and *composite,* to name a few. As a consequence, mathematics English is even more challenging than general classroom English.

A number of teaching strategies can help LEP students in the classroom. For example, speaking slowly and clearly and carefully pronouncing each word is helpful to LEP students. In spoken and written speech teachers should avoid slang, colloquialisms, and other unusual linguistic expressions, including contractions. It can be beneficial to LEP students to use familiar phrases and vocabulary, especially when introducing new concepts. That way they are able to focus on the mathematics involved and not have to wrestle with the English content. Sometimes a simple alteration in speech patterns can be advantageous. Instead of using pronouns, teachers can use full referents. Not "What is *its* area?" but "What is *the circle's* area?" Do not expect LEP students to copy material from the board or overhead screen. Instead, prepare a handout for them (actually for the whole class) so they can focus on discussions and explanations and not on the task of accurate copying. In a similar light, when writing on the board, print rather than use cursive.

Extralinguistic clues are particularly helpful to LEP students. Appropriate gestures, facial expressions, examples and nonexamples, and models or manipulatives can illuminate a discussion that might otherwise be unintelligible to LEP students. When introducing new terms or vocabulary, teachers can write these on the board beforehand and point to the specific word as it is being discussed, along with some model or action to clarify its meaning, such as pointing to a picture of a rectangle when that term is used.

A well-meaning teacher may use childish vocabulary and an extremely slow pace in conversations directed to LEP students. LEP students can perceive these childish speech patterns and may react negatively to them. Avoid speaking louder than normal to LEP students, as some people do when assisting a foreign tourist with directions. LEP students can sense this and may react against it. If a teacher makes any of these errors, recognizing the error and correcting it is the key.

Grouping is another way to support learning English. English learners can work in small groups to solve story problems or open-ended problems. An all-English-learning group allows children to communicate freely with one another about the problem and its potential solutions. At other times, English learners might be grouped with English speakers who can model procedures and behaviors appropriate for the mathematics classroom. English learners can also be grouped with bilingual children. Such a grouping validates their culture and supports the maintenance of their first language while learning mathematics. As language learners gain confidence, they may make an oral presentation to a small group, where they can make use of gestures, intonations, and visual aids.

Another aspect of teaching mathematics to LEP students involves the mathematics itself, the words and symbols of mathematics. There are many terms in mathematics that have entirely different meanings in conversational English. A list of these words includes:

Right	Volume	Left
Square	Face	Variable
Mode	Median	Round

Native English speakers can tell from the context which meaning of the term is suggested, but not LEP students. They need time to develop the ability to discern what meaning such words convey.

Consider mathematics homophones, such as one/won, whole/hole, cent/scent, and arc/ark. Even a native English-speaking child needs assistance to discern the correct word and meaning. LEP students require more time and experience before they can do so. Then there are soundalike words that are difficult for LEP students to distinguish: line/lion, three/tree, leave/leaf, graph/graft, four/fourth, and angle/angel. In all these cases the teacher who pays careful attention to the mathematics vocabulary seeks to clarify any confusion before it becomes problematic.

Another aspect of mathematics to consider is the symbols of its language. Many symbols are not as universally used and accepted as we might ex-

POINT OF VIEW
The most important feature of multicultural mathematics is to let students' motivation to do mathematics grow out of their natural cultural environment. (D'Ambrosio, 1997)

pect. For example, the number 3.14 is written 3,14 by some cultures, whereas the number 3,452 is written 3.453. We write $1 but read this as "one dollar," with the leading symbol ($) read last. However, we read 5¢, 3′, 4 lbs, and 6 yds from left to right, as the symbols appear. Some LEP students read right to left, so the number 86 means "sixty-eight" to them.

A simple expression such as $8 \div 2$ is read several different ways in English:

8 divided by 2

2 goes into 8

2 divided into 8

8 divided in half

Consider how confusing this simple expression and others can be to LEP students. Becoming aware of the subtle aspects of language is an important first step for teachers to help LEP and other students become successful in mathematics.

ⒺXERCISE

Give four English expressions that are equivalent to the mathematics expression 7 − 2. ●●●

Assessing LEP students in mathematics can be challenging. Is the difficulty with a mathematics concept or a homework problem due to a language issue or the mathematics involved? At times LEP children might frame an explanation in their native language. Another child or a teacher might then translate the answer. This enables the child to communicate without the burden of trying to write in a new language, and the teacher has a more accurate understanding of the child's progress.

Many LEP students learn different algorithms for the four basic operations in their native lands. It may be more advantageous to allow LEP students to continue to use the algorithms they have already learned rather than insist that they adopt the familiar algorithms we use in the United States. Allowing LEP students to use their native algorithms also validates the students' cultural background, as suggested in the section on multiculturalism. For example, students from some Latino cultures will perform two-digit subtraction as shown here.

$$
\begin{array}{ccc}
83 & 8 & 13 \\
-47 & -5 & 7 \\
\hline
 & 3 & 6
\end{array}
$$

$$83 - 47 = 36$$

This algorithm avoids regrouping. Instead, 10 units are added to the units of the larger number, and one 10 is added to the tens digit of the smaller number. Because both numbers were increased by 10, the difference between the resulting values is the same as it was for the original values.

It is important to remember that LEP students may be further advanced in their mathematics than the rest of the students in the class. They simply need to develop a command of English that will enable them to contribute to the class and progress in their mathematical knowledge. With your help they can succeed.

Technological Equity

Technological advances have changed the landscape of mathematics education. Calculators, computer software, and the Internet have had profound effects on the teaching and learning of mathematics. These new and emerging technologies will have a yet undetermined effect on mathematics teaching and learning. We advocate taking appropriate advantage of existing technologies to improve mathematics learning.

The positive effects of technology must be viewed through the lens of equity. Not all students have the same access to the technologies we discuss throughout the text. Many schools provide calculators and software programs. The question of equity arises with access to the Internet. Many students can use a computer at home to explore the Internet and to try some of the interactive lessons in later chapters. However, Internet access is not universal. According to a recent *Education Week* survey, about 1 in 5 students does not have a computer at home (*Education Week*, 2006). Not all children with a computer at home have Internet access. For some children with Internet access, one or both parents

may work from home and cannot give up valuable computer time. Teachers may interview students to assess their home computer situation. See Chapter 6 for information about how useful the computer, calculator, and the Internet are for helping children learn mathematics.

What about children who do not have any Internet access at home? What can be done to ensure that all children have appropriate opportunities to use the Internet? A teacher can arrange for students to use the classroom or school library computers during the school day or before or after school or a computer in the public library. Children once went to the library to use the encyclopedias and other reference texts. Library opportunities for children, however, must be carefully considered. To require a child to visit a public library several times a week seems unfair when others in the class can use a computer at home. Even one public library visit in a two-week period may be burdensome because of location or transportation. Teachers can get all the facts involving their students before deciding what is reasonable for out-of-school computer use. The central tenet is that all students should have equitable and appropriate opportunities to succeed in mathematics.

Students Who Have Difficulty Learning Mathematics

Difficulty learning mathematics denotes a wide range of impediments that students must deal with. One child may have a disability in reading, whereas another may have difficulty in mathematics; one child with disabilities may be hyperactive, whereas another may be quiet and withdrawn. Difficulty learning mathematics can stem from a variety of sources, including emotional, learning, and cognitive disabilities. In other words, children with learning disabilities are a heterogeneous group (Mercer, 1992, p. 25).

The Individuals with Disabilities Education Act (IDEA), a federal law, requires that children with disabilities have free public education in the "least restricted environment." Rather than being placed in isolated special education settings, more and more students with disabilities are being included in the regular classroom, sometimes with instructional support from aides or special education teachers. **Inclusion** means that teachers work with students with a variety of cognitive abilities, learning styles, social problems, and physical challenges. The challenge is to find strategies that maximize learning for all learners.

The learning expectations and nature of the instructional support for students with special needs is outlined in an individualized educational plan, commonly referred to as IEP. Based on individualized goals, the teacher may modify instructional techniques and assignments as described in the plan. Growing evidence shows that active engagement of students is as beneficial for students with learning disabilities as for those without diagnosed disabilities. Table 3.5 outlines types of problems associated with students who have learning disabilities.

For many children with special needs, especially those with learning and cognitive disabilities, their difficulty comes from the fact that their processing time is slower than that of regular children. They may require more time to understand a mathematics concept, apply it, and make it theirs. One approach to help children access new mathematics might be termed *overlearning*. Overlearning involves learning, practicing, and drilling the same math fact, procedure, or algorithm many times to achieve the ability to use it without prompting. For example, all children practice the algorithm for multiplication with whole numbers, so they learn it and can develop the habit of using it automatically, without having to think through each step of the algorithm every time they use it. Alternative algorithms, discussed in Chapter 12, may be less confusing for many students who struggle with traditional algorithms. Students with special needs will require more time with such an algorithm, careful and repeated modeling of the algorithm by their teacher, and many repeated practice sessions to achieve a measure of mastery. However, it is not necessary to insist on mastery of math facts or a particular algorithm before children with leaning disabilities can move forward with their mathematics learning.

Students with disabilities can also benefit from math cards. Students write their own math facts on an index card, or they write information to help them with a mathematical concept or process. For example, the math card shown on page 39 was used by a child with special needs to help him recall the steps in the long division algorithm. He had previously engaged in developmental activities to build his understanding of division but needed help to complete the steps in the division algorithm.

TABLE 3.5 ● **General Learning Disabilities: Area of Disability**		
Academic	**Social-Emotional**	**Cognitive**
Poor reading skills	Lack of motivation	Short attention span
Inadequate reading comprehension	Easily distractible	Perceptual difficulties
Problems with math calculation	Inadequate social skills	Lack of motor coordination
Math reasoning difficulties	Learned helplessness	Memory deficits
Deficient written expression	Poor self-concept	Problem-solving hurdles
Listening comprehension problems	Hyperactivity	Difficulty evaluating one's own learning processes

SOURCE: Adapted from Mercer (1992, p. 53).

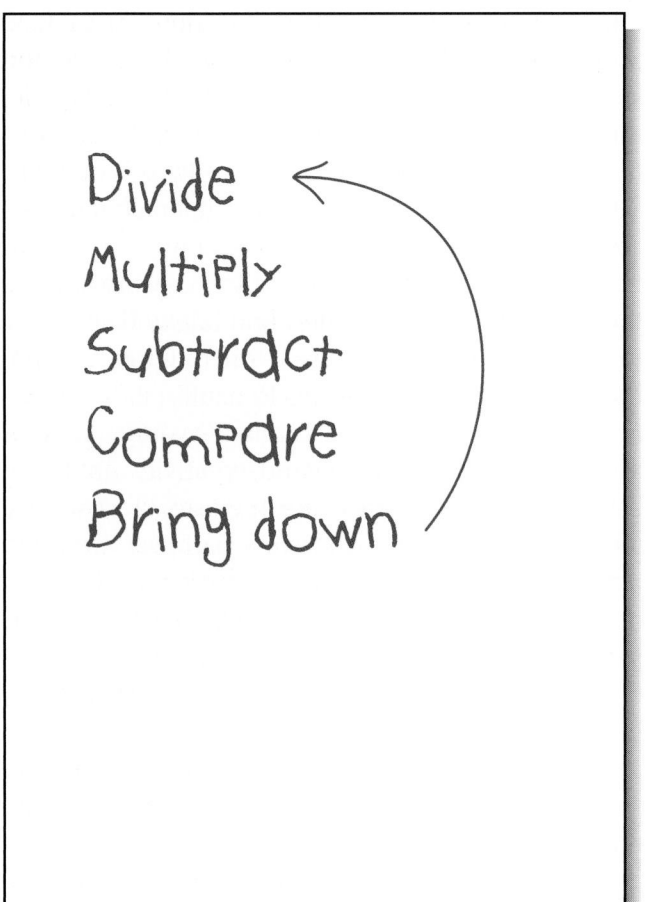

Divide ←
Multiply
Subtract
Compare
Bring down

Read

Draw a picture of what is happening.

What is the question?

Do I need the exact answer?

What operation do I need?

Do I use a calculator, pencil, or mental math?

Figure out

Check my answer

Another math card (adapted from Bley & Thornton, 2001) helped a student relate mathematical processes, symbols, and English expressions.

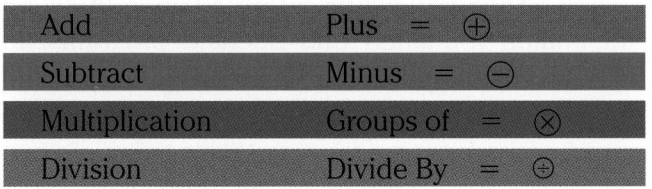

Add	Plus	=	⊕
Subtract	Minus	=	⊖
Multiplication	Groups of	=	⊗
Division	Divide By	=	⊕

Note that the colors help the child relate each operation and symbol to the appropriate English representation.

Another math card helped one student to solve word problems. She listed each important step for solving every word problem she confronted.

These math cards and similar learning aids should be available to students whenever they need them. Sometimes children outgrow them and do not require the prompts the cards provide. In other cases the cards continue to serve as a security blanket, a quick reminder to students of what they have already mastered. Still other children will require the math cards for all their academic lives and may use similar cards for life outside the classroom.

Many students with special needs have difficulty with their visual perception. The page of a standard mathematics textbook might be an overwhelming swirl of colors, pictures, and symbols. Students might cover up the nonessential part of a page when solving a problem from their book. They might use a piece of cardboard with a rectangular opening cut in it. The opening could be shifted around the page to reveal a problem, diagram, or example. Children with visual difficulties or trouble with fine motor skills will find some of the algorithms difficult because of the requirement of precise placement of digits as they use the algorithm. The algorithm for multiplication with whole numbers requires

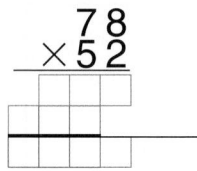

children to line up columns of numbers, which can prove challenging. One possible solution to children's difficulty is to provide a grid for them to use, as shown here.

There are many Internet resources for special-needs children. These sites contain lesson plans or links to other sites with lesson plans that might be used with students with special needs:

http://mathforum.org/t2t/faq/faq.disability.html

http://www.teachingld.org/teaching_how-tos/math/default.htm

http://www.ricksmath.com

http://www.col-ed.org

http://www.learnnc.org/lessons/

http://www.mathforum.com

http://www.kidsdomain.com

http://www.mathsolutions.com

http://www.teachersfirst.com

http://www.arches.uga.edu

http://www.crayola.com/educators/lessons

http://www.teachers.net/lessons/

http://www.yale.edu/ynhti/curriculum/units

http://www.remc11.k12.mi.us/bcisd/curriculum.html

http://www.successlink.org

Physical Disabilities

http://www.sedl.org/about/termsofuse.html#access

http://www.rit.edu/~comets/bibliopage1.htm

Gifted and Talented Students

Why are students who are gifted and talented included in a chapter on equity in mathematics? After all, if these students are gifted, do they really need any assistance to achieve? The point here is not to help gifted and talented students meet a specific achievement level that is established for all students. Rather, the point is to meet their specific needs. All children, including gifted and talented children, deserve a challenging mathematics curriculum, one that will advance their knowledge of mathematics at a pace that will continue to motivate them. In ad-

dition, many gifted and talented students are at risk. Surprisingly, the dropout rate for gifted and talented students (about 20%) nearly matched the dropout rate of the general student population (about 25%) in several studies (Ruf, 2006; Renzulli & Park, 2002; Schneider, 1998). Thus gifted and talented students deserve a place in a chapter on equity.

At one time, intelligence test scores were used as the sole determiner of gifted and talented students; today, identification is based on multiple criteria. Laurence Ridge and Joseph Renzulli (1981) identified three clusters of traits: above-average general ability, task commitment, and creativity. Table 3.6 lists the characteristics of each cluster. Test scores, teacher observations, and work samples are often used to evaluate these characteristics. In the past, qualified gifted students were eligible for various services, ranging from special programs and activities during the school day to enrichment classes and extracurricular programs.

The federal No Child Left Behind Act has had some unexpected consequences for gifted and talented education. The act focuses attention on underachieving groups, seeking to raise their mathematics performance, but it ignores gifted and talented students. As of 2004, 22 states did not contribute any funds to gifted and talented programs, and 5 others earmarked only $250,000 to support gifted and talented education. At present, only 2 cents of every $100 in federal funds for education is dedicated to gifted and talented learning (Bilger, 2004). An example of how gifted and talented funding is drying up can be found in Illinois. In 2002, Illinois provided $19 million for gifted and talented programs. In 2004, all gifted and talented funding was eliminated (Shermo, 2004).

Gifted students are far more likely to be in a regular classroom for the entire school day. Although gifted students will be able to achieve basic mathematics without any special attention, these students who are gifted in mathematics deserve as much attention to their needs as any other group of students to meet their full potential in mathematics.

In addition to the characteristics listed in Table 3.6, classroom teachers should also recognize other pertinent characteristics of gifted students in mathematics. Gifted students may immerse themselves in one or two mathematics topics intensely for a period of time. They often have original ways of thinking

TABLE 3.6 **Characteristics or Traits of Gifted and Talented Students**

Above-Average General Ability	Task Commitment	Creativity
Accelerated pace of learning; learns earlier and faster	Highly motivated	Curious
Sees relationships, readily grasps big ideas	Self-directed and perceptive	Imaginative
Higher levels of thinking; applications and analysis easily accomplished	Accepts challenges, may be highly competitive	Questions standard procedures
Verbal fluency; large vocabulary, expresses self well orally and in writing	Extended attention to one area of interest	Uses original approaches and solutions
Extraordinary amount of information	Reads avidly in area of interest	Flexible
Intuition; easily leaps from problem to solution	Relates every topic to own area of interest	Risk taker, independent
Tolerates ambiguity	Industrious and persevering	
Achievement and potential have close fit	High energy and enthusiasm	Masters advanced concepts in field of interest

SOURCE: Ridge & Renzulli (1981).

and a willingness to try different approaches and inventive problem solutions. Despite the stereotype of gifted children as ideal students, they are individuals with the full range of behaviors, including being stubborn, messy, forgetful, or rebellious. Traits of gifted students—such as questioning authority, extreme imagination, and absolute focus on one topic—often dismay teachers but may be signs of boredom and a need for additional responsibility and challenge.

Gifted students do not learn concepts and skills automatically; they need to participate in a planned, systematic mathematics program in which they learn basic mathematical concepts, develop reasonable proficiency with basic facts and algorithms and other skills, and apply their knowledge to solving problems. However, gifted students may learn at a rapid pace and need additional opportunities beyond the basic curriculum.

To challenge and provide quality mathematics to gifted and talented students, teachers need to identify gifted and talented students in the class. Test scores and grades might assist in identifying these students, but they are not the only identifying characteristics. Additional characteristics, listed in Table 3.7, were developed by Russian educator Igor Krutetskii, who found that gifted and talented students in mathematics exhibited a number of these characteristics to a high degree.

After identifying potential gifted and talented students in mathematics, what helps them reach their full potential? In a word, challenge. If gifted children are not challenged by the curriculum early in their school years, they will equate smart with easy. As a result, challenges and hard work will feel threatening to their self-esteem. Many gifted children sit through lessons that they fully understand and could easily teach to the rest of the class.

TABLE 3.7 **Krutetskii's Characteristics of Mathematics Giftedness**

Resourcefulness	Flexibility
Economy of thought	Use of visual thinking
Ability to reason	Ability to generalize
Mathematical memory	Ability to abstract
Enjoyment of mathematics	Mathematical persistence

SOURCE: Krutetskii (1976).

Challenges for gifted students can take many forms. A well-meaning teacher might provide extra problems to keep a gifted student on task, but this serves only to punish students who complete an assignment quickly. In this case gifted and talented children quickly learn that their hard work results only in more work to do. Instead of assigning more of the same types of problem, challenge problems such as brainteasers might be used to spark attention and motivate gifted students to move beyond the typical problems at hand. In many cases gifted students could prepare a presentation to the class of their findings or solution strategies. At a minimum they could explain their results to the teacher in written and/or oral form.

When assigning homework to a class, some teachers allow students to try the most difficult problems first. If students can solve the most difficult problems, then they do not need to solve all the problems on the assignment. In this instance all students should have the opportunity to try solving only the difficult problems. It may be surprising to see who tries to do so. At times students who successfully solve the most difficult problems are not the ones the teacher might have identified as gifted and talented.

Another approach used by some teachers provides the opportunity for gifted students to test out of a unit of study. For example, a gifted student might try the unit test at the start of the unit. If the child scores high enough, then she might spend mathematics time on a project or exploration in lieu of the unit topic. This will prevent gifted students from spending time in what they do not need, review of a topic that the rest of the class must practice. As suggested earlier, the results of their explorations might be reported to the class and certainly to the teacher.

A common strategy that many teachers use is to have gifted and talented children tutor or assist students who are having difficulty with a particular topic. It is true that both can benefit from such an arrangement; the struggling students receive individualized help, and the gifted students explicitly explain the mathematics at hand, perhaps formalizing their innate understanding of a topic. However, gifted and talented students are in school to advance their own mathematics, not to teach others, which is the teacher's responsibility. We recommend that gifted and talented students be used sparingly as tutors or teachers.

All the preceding discussion applies to large-group instruction or individualized assignments. When forming small groups with gifted and talented students, teachers should place one gifted student in a group with regular students or form a group composed of all gifted and talented students. When a gifted student is in a small group with regular students, both benefit. Regular students benefit from observing the effort and time on task that many gifted students exhibit. They also benefit from the insights gifted children have and the conclusions that they make. The gifted children benefit by developing interpersonal skills and by framing their mathematics concepts into formal expressions that they can communicate to others. By doing so, they solidify the foundations for building even more advanced mathematical understandings.

When only gifted students work together in a small group, they have the opportunity to work with peers who are able to assimilate and organize information quickly and completely. They can work with group members who are able to conceptualize relationships and make conclusions as quickly as they can. As a group, much should be expected of them. They should produce excellent results, far beyond those expected of other groups. In addition, they should make a class presentation of their findings so that the entire class can benefit from their concerted efforts.

In closing, having gifted students in the classroom requires a teacher to ensure that their educational needs are met, just as the needs of all other children are met. At times, gifted students can be frustrating, charming, and inspiring, all in the same day. That is simply who they are, and it is the challenge for a classroom teacher to help these children achieve and meet their potential in mathematics.

Individual Learning Styles

Mathematics teachers work not only with students of many ethnic and cultural backgrounds, language differences, and learning capabilities but also with students with individual learning styles. Recent research and theories about learning point out differences in children's learning styles and strengths.

Multiple Intelligences

The **theory of multiple intelligences** was first proposed by Howard Gardner in 1983. In *Frames of the Mind: The Theory of Multiple Intelligences,* Gardner asserts that people are capable, or even gifted, in different ways. Gardner, Kagan and Kagan, and other advocates of multiple intelligences believe that no single description of intelligence exists. Intelligence tests focus on only one type of learning, typically verbal knowledge, but individuals are "smart in different ways" (Kagan & Kagan, 1998, p. xix). Gardner initially identified seven intelligences: linguistic, logical/mathematical, spatial, body/kinesthetic, musical, interpersonal, and intrapersonal. He has since added an eighth intelligence: naturalist. Figure 3.1 gives a short description of each of the eight intelligences.

In each intelligence area, individual differences also occur. Individuals may feel more comfortable with some of the intelligences and less comfortable with others. Differences may occur within an intelligence; a person might be comfortable writing prose but not at all comfortable writing poetry or speaking before an audience. A person with the naturalist intelligence may be comfortable around plants but have little interest in animals. Linguistic (verbal) intelligence has been the mainstay of traditional schooling. Even logical/mathematical intelligence, strongly related to problem solving, reasoning, and mathematical thinking, receives little attention in classrooms where teacher-directed lessons are the primary means of instruction.

In real-world activities the intelligences are integrated, and several may be needed to complete complex tasks. Carpeting a house requires a number of intelligences: drawing a picture of each room (spatial), measuring each room (bodily/kinesthetic), calculating square yards and cost (logical/mathematical), and discussing choices and making selections (linguistic and interpersonal). By offering all children a rich curriculum with a variety of hands-on problem-solving activities, teachers provide the variety needed to appeal to and develop all the intelligences.

⒠XERCISE

Take a Multiple Intelligences Test at http://www .bgfl.org/bgfl/7.cfm?s=7&m=136&p=111,resource_ list_11. Were the results what you expected? ●●●

Learning Styles

Learning styles is another way of describing how people receive, process, and respond to their world. **Learning modalities** is one way of describing learning. Do learners prefer to process information visually, auditorily, kinesthetically, or in some combination? Do learners prefer to learn individually or in groups, with quiet or background noise, in structured or open-ended assignments (Carbo et al., 1986)? Other style descriptions focus on specific aspects of learning and personality on a continuum. Table 3.8 lists eight different learning styles with the related adjectives at the extreme points of the continuum.

Based on present research and understanding of individual differences, teachers cannot design lessons specific to the styles and intelligences of each child. Instead, effective teaching must allow for learning needs of a wide variety of learners. Variety in teaching approaches, use of materials, focus on

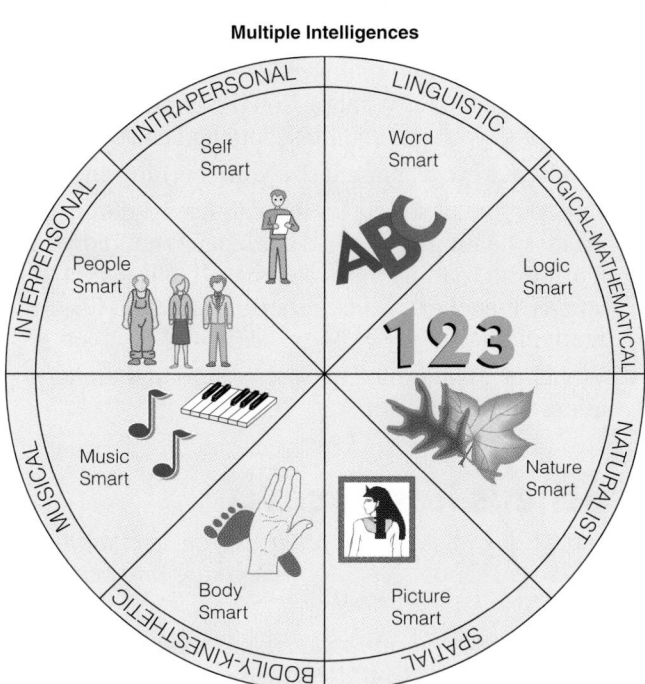

Figure 3.1 Gardner's eight multiple intelligences

TABLE 3.8 · **Learning Styles and Descriptors**		
Orientation	Dependent	Independent
Control	Internal	External locus
Stimulation	High need	Low need
Processing	Random	Sequential
Thinking	Concrete	Abstract
Personality	Introvert	Extrovert
Response	Emotional	Rational
Time	Impulsive	Reflective

meaning, and relating to individual needs and interests are key ideas in teaching the many students in any classroom. The characteristics of good teaching are congruent with constructivist principles, research on effective teaching, and strategies for a diverse classroom. A balanced approach encourages student thinking and creativity, autonomy of thought and action, and meaningful learning in many contexts. Design of worthwhile and challenging mathematics activities is the core of teaching.

❷XERCISES

What kind of learner are you? Discuss your strengths and weaknesses as a learner with a classmate. ●●●

Do you believe students should be able to concentrate on their strong areas and avoid their weak areas, or should students develop their skills in all the intelligences? ●●●

Summary

Students have special learning needs in mathematics. Students with disabilities may need classroom adaptations to support their learning. Gifted and talented students need additional challenges. Students who have limited English proficiency will require accommodations to support their mathematics learning. Multiple intelligences and learning styles underscore the need for variety in teaching and learning activities in the classroom because all students have individual learning characteristics. We no longer try to teach all students the same way, reasoning that equal treatment for all students means equitable treatment. Supreme Court Justice Felix Frankfurter said, "There is no greater inequality than the equal treatment of un-equals." Treating all children the same does not ensure that they are all treated fairly. Treating children fairly requires providing all of them with opportunities to reach their full potential in mathematics regardless of what individual accommodations are needed. Only when children's needs are met can it be said that they are treated equally.

Study Questions and Activities

1. Look through a recent elementary school mathematics textbook series to see if it portrays a good mix of male/female, majority/minority, and children with/ without physical disabilities. What effect do you believe the children portrayed in textbooks have on the children who use those books?
2. At what level of schooling—early elementary, intermediate grades, junior high, senior high, or college—do you believe the best mathematics teaching occurs? Why?
3. Do a ministudy of yourself. Which of the eight intelligences discussed in this chapter do you think best characterize you? What personal characteristics prompted you to name these intelligences?
4. How would you characterize your learning style?
5. Print out the abstracts for three to five research articles dealing with gifted students. What did you learn from reading these abstracts that is useful to you as a teacher? Which articles would you like to read in full?
6. What is the difference between ethnomathematics and multiculturalism?

Teacher's Resources

Alcoze, Thom, et al. (1993). *Multiculturalism in mathematics, science, and technology: Readings and activities.* Reading, MA: Addison-Wesley.

Ashlock, R. (2006). *Error patterns in computation* (9th ed.). Upper Saddle River, NJ: Pearson.

Bennet, Christine. (2003). *Comprehensive multicultural education: Theory and practice* (5th ed.). Boston: Allyn & Bacon.

Bley, N., and Thornton, C. (2001). *Teaching mathematics to students with learning disabilities* (3rd ed.). Austin, TX: Pro Ed.

Copley, J. (Ed.). (1999). *Mathematics in the early years.* Reston, VA: National Council of Teachers of Mathematics.

Echevarria, Jena, & Graves, Anne. (1998). *Sheltered content instruction: Teaching English-language learners with diverse abilities.* Boston: Allyn & Bacon.

Irons, Calvin, & Burnett, James. (1993). *Mathematics from many cultures.* Denver: Mimosa.

Kagan, Spencer, & Kagan, Miguel. (1998). *Multiple intelligences: The complete MI book.* San Clemente, CA: Kagan Cooperative Learning.

Kottler, E., & Kottler, J. (2002). *Children with limited English: Teaching strategies for the regular classroom.* Thousand Oaks, CA: Corwin Press.

Lumpkin, Beatrice. (1997). *Algebra activities from many cultures.* Portland, ME: J. Weston Walsh.

Malloy, Carol E. (Ed.). (1998). *Challenges in the mathematics education of African-American children.* Reston, VA: National Council of Teachers of Mathematics.

National Council of Teachers of Mathematics. (1999). *Developing mathematically promising students.* Reston, VA: National Council of Teachers of Mathematics.

Reis, S., Burns, D., & Renzulli, J. (1992). *Curriculum compacting.* Mansfield Center, CT: Creative Learning Press.

Secada, W. G. (Ed.). (2000). *Changing the faces of mathematics: Perspectives on multiculturalism and gender equity.* Reston, VA: National Council of Teachers of Mathematics.

Secada, W. G., & Edwards, C. (Eds.). (1999). *Changing the faces of mathematics: Perspectives on Asian Americans and Pacific Islanders.* Reston, VA: National Council of Teachers of Mathematics..

Secada, W. G., Hanks, J., & Fast, G. (Eds.). (2002). *Changing the faces of mathematics: Perspectives on indigenous peoples of North America.* Reston: VA: National Council of Teachers of Mathematics.

Secada, W. G., Ortiz-Franco, Luis, Hernandez, Norma G., & De La Cruz, Uolanda (Eds.). (1999a). *Changing the faces of mathematics: Perspectives on African Americans.* Reston, VA: National Council of Teachers of Mathematics.

Secada, W. G., Ortiz-Franco, L., Hernandez, N., & De La Cruz, U. (Eds.). (1999b). *Changing the faces of mathematics: Perspectives on Latinos.* Reston, VA: National Council of Teachers of Mathematics.

Schiro, Michael. (2004). *Oral story telling and teaching mathematics: Pedagogical and multicultural perspectives.* Thousand Oaks, CA: Sage.

Thornton, Carol, & Bley, N. (Eds.). (1994). *Windows of opportunity: Mathematics for students with special needs.* Reston, VA: National Council of Teachers of Mathematics.

Tiedt, Pamela, & Tiedt, Iris. (2002). *Multicultural teaching: A handbook of activities, information, and resources* (6th ed.). Boston: Allyn & Bacon.

Trentacosta, Janet (Ed.). (1997). *1997 yearbook: Multicultural and gender equity in the mathematics classroom—the gift of diversity.* Reston, VA: National Council of Teachers of Mathematics.

Tucker, B., Singleton, A., & Weaver, A. (2002). *Teaching mathematics to all children: Designing and adapting instruction to meet the needs of diverse learners.* Upper Saddle River, NJ: Prentice Hall.

Zaslavsky, Claudia. (1993). *Multicultural mathematics: Interdisciplinary cooperative learning activities.* Portland, ME: J. Weston Walsh.

For Further Reading

Battista, Michael T., & Larson, Carol Novillis. (1994). The role of JRME in advancing learning and teaching elementary school mathematics. *Teaching Mathematics to Children* 1(3), 78–82.

The focus of research reported in the *Journal for Research in Mathematics Education* (JRME) has shifted from a behaviorist perspective, focusing on what children do, to a constructivist approach, focusing on how they think. Battista and Larson give practical suggestions for using research to improve instruction.

Carroll, William M., & Porter, Denis. (1997). Invented algorithms can develop meaningful mathematical procedures. *Teaching Children Mathematics* 3(7), 370–374.

Carroll and Porter interviewed and observed children in second-, third-, and fourth-grade classrooms who learned computation with whole numbers by using invented algorithms, which allows students to make sense of the mathematics they are doing.

Curcio, Frances R., & Schwartz, Sydney L. (1998). There are no algorithms for teaching algorithms. *Teaching Children Mathematics* 5(1), 26–30.

Curcio and Schwartz believe that students are active inventors of rules of relationships, that teachers continue to struggle with determining how and when to formalize an algorithm, and that the most effective resource for making instructional decisions is students themselves.

Kerssaint, Gladis, & Chappell, Michaele. (2001). Capturing students' interests: A quest to discover mathematics potential. *Teaching Children Mathematics* 7(9), 512–517.

Mathematics problems centered on what is relevant to students' cultural and experiential background may benefit students.

Krause, Marina C. (2000). *Multicultural mathematics materials* (2nd ed.). Reston, VA: National Council of Teachers of Mathematics.

These games and activities come from around the world to bring ethnic and cultural diversity to the mathematics curriculum in grades 1–8. The book, which introduces children to the ethnic heritage of others and encourages an appreciation of cultural diversity, contains convenient, reproducible activity pages for classroom distribution.

Midobuche, Eva. (2001). Building cultural bridges between home and the mathematics classroom. *Teaching Children Mathematics* 7(9), 500–502.

Students benefit from the cultural backgrounds of diverse students.

Moldavan, Carla. (2001). Culture in the curriculum: Enriching numeration and number operations. *Teaching Children Mathematics* 8(4), 238–243.

Numeration systems and alternative algorithms from different cultures can enrich the study of math for elementary school students.

Neel, K. (2005). Addressing diversity in the mathematics classroom with cultural artifacts. *Teaching Mathematics in the Middle School* 11(2), 54–58.

Neel describes how multiculturalism is enhanced when students bring in cultural artifacts that become part of classroom explorations.

Perkins, Isabel. (2002). Mathematical notations and procedures of recent immigrant students. *Mathematics Teaching in the Middle Grades* 7(6), 346–352.

Perkins discusses awareness of the differences in standard notation and algorithms of students in the class when planning lessons and activities.

Willis, Jody, & Johnson, Aostre. (2001). Multiply with MI: Using multiple intelligences to master multiplication. *Teaching Children Mathematics* 7(5), 260–269.

One theory of learners claims eight different intelligence strengths for children. Knowledge about these different intelligences can be used to enhance children's learning of multiplication.

Zaslavsky, Claudia. (2001). Developing number sense: What can other cultures tell us? *Teaching Children Mathematics* 7(6), 312–319.

Mathematics from other cultures can be used to great advantage in the classroom to illuminate various mathematical concepts.

CHAPTER 4

Learning Mathematics

When states and local school districts develop curricula using the NCTM principles and standards, they answer the question, What mathematics should students know? According to the standards in *Principles and Standards for School Mathematics* (National Council of Teachers of Mathematics, 2000), students need conceptual knowledge and skills in numerical operations, geometry, measurement, data analysis, probability, and algebra with an emphasis on problem solving and application in meaningful contexts.

The next question for teachers is, How should I teach mathematics? The NCTM principle of teaching and the principle of learning address this question. Knowledge about learning and effective teaching are based on learning theory and research and are verified in classroom practice. Teachers who understand how children grasp concepts in mathematics provide instructional experiences that support the needs of the learner and the demands of the content. The learning needs of a diverse student population reinforce the need for teachers to understand how students learn mathematics. In this chapter we review theories of learning and research on learning mathematics.

In this chapter you will read about:

1 Learning theories and their implications for elementary mathematics instruction

2 Research on teaching mathematics and recommended instructional practices

Learning is a complex cognitive process. For more than 100 years psychologists have observed people as they mastered skills; from their observations they formed new concepts and developed learning theories to explain this complex process. No single theory explains all the nuances and complexities involved in learning. However, understanding various learning theories provides a foundation for the choices that teachers make in their teaching. A brief synopsis of learning theories as they relate to teaching mathematics reinforces information from child development or educational psychology in the context of mathematics instruction.

Theories of Learning

Behaviorism

Behaviorism is a theory of learning that focuses on observable behaviors and on ways to increase behaviors deemed positive and decrease behaviors deemed undesirable. In the late 19th century the "mental discipline" theory of learning influenced the way mathematics was taught. According to this theory, the mind is like a muscle and benefits from exercise, just as muscles do. Early in the 20th century stimulus-response theory explained that learning occurs when a bond, or connection, is established between a stimulus and a response. Thorndike, Pavlov, Skinner, and others demonstrated the effects of different conditioning plans on a variety of animals. Positive reinforcement, such as rewards of food or water, led animals to perform a task again and again. Animals could be trained to respond to a certain stimulus by prior rewards.

Behaviorism has a long history in teaching, as many teachers subscribe to the **stimulus-response theory** by "exercising" the brain. Drill and practice of facts and mathematical procedures is based on a belief that repetition establishes strong bonds. Since the 1930s researchers and theoreticians have challenged the stimulus-response theory as too simplistic to explain all learning. If learning occurs only as a response to a stimulus, how can people create new words, new art, new music, new inventions, or even new theories? Cognitive and information theories explore how learning is influenced by language and culture, individual and social experiences, intention and motivation, and neurophysiological processes.

❷XERCISE

Can you think of something you have learned through repetition? What happened when you continued to practice the skill or knowledge? What happened when you stopped practicing? ●●●

Cognitive Theories

Cognitive theories share a common belief that mental processes occur between the stimulus and response. Mental processes, or cognitions, although not directly observable, result in highly individualized responses or learning; therefore human beings learn by creating their own unique understandings from their experiences. The major differences between behaviorist and cognitive theories are summarized in Table 4.1.

Different cognitive theories explain learning by emphasizing different aspects. Some cognitive theories focus on how complex learning proceeds from one level or stage to the next. **Cognitive-developmental theories**, such as those of Jean Piaget, Richard Skemp, and Jerome Bruner, propose levels of successively more complex intellectual understanding or conceptualization. Other theories explain learning through the functions or mechanisms that are involved. Information-processing models compare learning to computer functions, and brain-based theories explain learning in terms of how the brain receives, stores, and retrieves information. **Constructivism** is another term associated with cognitive theories. Regardless of the particular model used, cognitive theories center around the idea of constructing meaning from experience.

Key Concepts in Learning Mathematics

Focus on Meaning

In the 1930s the **meaning theory** of William Brownell challenged the mental exercise and training focus of the stimulus-response theory. Brownell's meaning theory suggested that children must understand what they are learning if learning is to be permanent. When children generate their own solutions to problems while investigating the meanings of mathematical concepts with manipulative materials and other learning aids, they are demonstrating

TABLE 4.1 ● **Comparison of Behaviorism and Cognitivism**

	Behaviorism	Cognitivism
Principal concepts	Stimuli, responses, reinforcement	Higher mental processes (thinking, imagining, problem solving)
Main metaphors	Machinelike qualities of human functioning	Information-processing and computer-based metaphors
Most common research subjects	Animals; some human research subjects	Humans; some nonhuman research subjects
Main goals	To discover predictable relationships between stimuli and responses	To make useful inferences about mental processes that intervene to influence and determine behavior
Scope of theories	Often intended to explain all significant aspects of behavior	Generally more limited in scope; intended to explain more specific behaviors and processes
Representative theorists	Watson, Pavlov, Guthrie, Skinner, Hull	Gestalt psychologists, Bruner, Piaget, connectionist theorists

SOURCE: Lefrancois (2000, p. 194).

the meaning theory (Brownell, 1986). Marilyn Burns, a leading mathematics educator, also emphasizes the importance of meaning in learning mathematics. She suggests that teachers must do "what makes sense" rather than teaching by rote (Burns, 1993).

❷XERCISE

Can you think of something you "learned" even if you did not understand it? How did that experience make you feel? How do you feel when you learn something you really understand? ●●●

Developmental Stages

Piaget described learning in four stages: sensorimotor, preoperational, concrete operational, and formal operational. The **sensorimotor stage** occurs between birth and age 2–3 years. Foundations for later mental growth and mathematical understanding are developed at this stage. For instance, children learn to recognize people and things and to hold mental images when the people or things can no longer be seen. This ability, called **object permanence**, is essential for recalling past experiences to connect with new experiences. Rather than "out of sight, out of mind," children need to be able to remember events, objects, and ideas even when they are no longer present.

During the **preoperational stage** (age 2–3 to age 6–7), children gradually change from being egocentric and dominated by their idiosyncratic perceptions of the world to beginning to become aware of feelings and points of view of others in their world. Children develop symbol systems, including objects, pictures, actions, and language, to represent their experience. Blocks can be buildings or trucks, cups or plates, people or numbers. Representing ideas and actions with objects is an important step toward understanding pictures and, later, symbols. Children's concepts of number and space start with concrete objects and interactions with peers and adults.

During the **concrete operational stage** (ages 7–12), children master the underlying structure of number, geometry, and measurement. Work with concrete objects is the foundation for developing mathematical concepts represented with pictures, symbols, and mental images. Children learn about classification systems based on attributes of objects, events, and people and how they are alike and different. They gradually consider multiple attributes simultaneously: The cube is red, rough, thick, and big; the triangle is yellow, thin, smooth, and small (Figure 4.1). Children recognize actions that are reversible or inverses, such as opening and closing doors or joining and separating sets. Addition and subtrac-

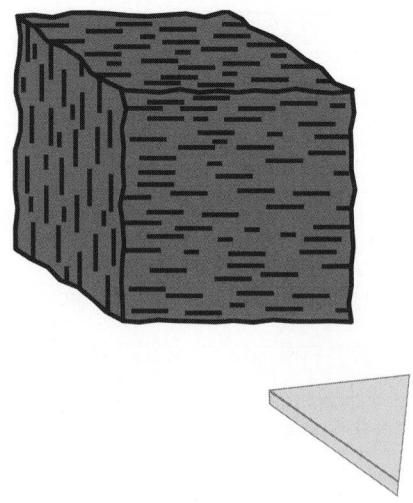

Figure 4.1 Attributes of geometry blocks

tion are reversible because one reverses, or undoes, the other. Children learn to think about parts and wholes needed in fractions and division. Manipulations of objects and pictures develop into mental images and operations as children internalize those actions.

Starting at ages 11–13, more sophisticated ways of thinking about mathematics, including proportional reasoning, propositional reasoning, and correlational reasoning, begin and continue to develop during the teenage years and into adulthood. **Formal operational** thinking enables children and adults to form hypotheses, analyze situations to consider all factors that bear on them, draw conclusions, and test them against reality.

Through the stages of learning and interaction with objects, events, and people in their world, children construct meaning for new experiences in relation to old ideas and experiences. Complex mental structures, or *schema*, represent the unique understanding of how the world works. As new experiences are assimilated, or taken into the mental framework, they are compared to existing schema. If they do not correspond, they create a state of *disequilibrium*. Disequilibrium ends when learners reconcile new experiences through accommodation or by modifying their understanding. Piaget saw learning as a continual process of assimilation and accommodation. Confusion and making mistakes in the process of assimilation and accommodation are natural and necessary parts of constructing new schema.

Social Interactions

Lev Vygotsky believed that interactions between the learner and the physical world are strongly influenced by social interactions; his theory is called **social constructivism**. According to Vygotsky (1962), learning is enhanced as adults and peers provide language and feedback while learners process experiences. The *zone of proximal development* is just beyond the learner's current capabilities but can be reached with assistance from adults or peers. *Scaffolding* occurs when adults or peers support learners while they construct meaning from their experience.

Concrete Experiences

Richard Skemp describes learning at two levels: experience and abstraction. Interaction with physical objects during the early stages of concept learning provides a foundation for later internalization of ideas. Later, physical experiences are processed again at the abstract level. An underlying structure, or *schema*, allows prior learning to serve as a basis for future learning. Time for reflection and opportunity to use knowledge are essential for organizing thoughts.

Similar ideas about using physical models for conceptual learning were proposed by Dienes (1969). His work with manipulatives, such as base-10 blocks (Dienes blocks), convinced him that learning improved when concepts were shown in "multiple embodiments" rather than a single representation; place value can be demonstrated with base-10 blocks in addition to bundles of stirring sticks, bean sticks, and Unifix cubes.

Levels of Representation

Jerome Bruner (1960) was interested in how children recognize and represent concepts. Like Dienes, Bruner advocated discovery learning and learning through hands-on activities. Bruner's first stage of representation is *enactive*, suggesting the role of physical objects in learning. The second level is *ikonic*, referring to pictorial and graphic representations. Finally, the *symbolic* level involves using words, numerals, and other symbols to represent ideas, objects, and actions. Bruner's levels of representation are related to both Piaget's stages and Skemp and Dienes's ideas about the need for physical experiences in the development of meaning.

Procedural Learning

Learning a procedure, how to do something, is another important aspect in mathematics. James Hiebert and Patricia Lefevre (1986) define procedural knowledge as recognizing symbols and learning rules. Recognizing symbols is illustrated when a child identifies "+" as a plus or addition sign but does not know what addition means. Learning the rules and steps of an algorithm is procedural learning. If students learn procedures without their meanings, they often use the procedures at inappropriate times. "Invert and multiply" is a procedure that is often misapplied because students do not understand when or why the procedure makes sense.

Conceptual knowledge provides meaning for procedures. Conceptual knowledge is a schema built on many rich relationships. A student who knows when joining sets is needed and follows the symbols and procedures in solving a problem demonstrates both conceptual understanding and procedural knowledge of addition. Estimation skills draw on understanding the concepts behind procedures. If asked to find the square root of 950, a student might say, "I don't remember the steps, but the answer is a little more than 30 because 30×30 is 900." A student who has only memorized the procedure for calculating square roots will say, "I don't remember the rule, so I don't know the square root of 950."

Short-Term to Long-Term Memory

Although cognitive scientists agree that cognitive processes occur between stimulus and response, exactly how learning occurs is still a subject of lively debate. One cognitive theory—**information processing**—uses a computer as a metaphor for learning. Instinctual behavior is similar to read-only memory (ROM) in a computer; it is preprogrammed. Random access memory (RAM) is short-term memory that the computer receives and stores temporarily but does not retain when turned off. Learning becomes permanent when new ideas and experiences are transferred from short-term memory to long-term memory, where it is stored for later retrieval and use. Information is stored in the computer's permanent memory based on the needs and choices of the computer user.

Lefrancois (2000) describes the similarities and differences between learning by humans and learning by computers with models and metaphors. The neural network, or connectionist, model has appeal because it mirrors the structure of the human brain and accounts for the dynamic nature of learning. Neural networks are similar to the constructivist idea of schema. Which memories are stored and how they are retrieved in the brain are apparently controlled by the learner's emotions, motivations, and intentions. Deciding what is important to remember and making meaning from experience increase retention and retrieval. Strong emotions also appear to aid memory. The brain mechanisms behind human emotions, motivations, and intentions are not fully understood, although many cognitive scientists continue to investigate brain anatomy and functioning.

Pattern Making

In the past 30 years new technologies designed for medical diagnosis have enabled researchers to "see" which parts of the brain are active during learning activities. According to Leslie Hart, learning occurs because the brain is built to find patterns and to make connections between experiences. "Learning [is] the extraction from confusion of meaningful patterns" (Hart 1983, p. 67). Hart suggests six premises about how the brain is built to learn:

1. The brain is by nature a magnificent pattern-detecting apparatus, even in the early years.

2. Pattern detection and identification involves both features and relationships and is greatly speeded up by the use of clues and categorizing . . . procedure[s].

3. Negative clues play an essential role.

4. The brain uses clues in a probabilistic fashion, not by . . . adding up.

5. Pattern recognition depends heavily on what experience one brings to a situation.

6. Children and youngsters must often revise the patterns they have extracted, to fit new experiences.

Instead of being a passive receiver of stimuli, the brain is an active processor of information. How the brain turns experience into knowledge is still being explored, but the formation of synaptic and dendritic connections between brain cells appears to be the biological mechanism of learning. Regardless, the conclusion is that the brain makes sense of experiences by finding relations and connections between old and new information (Jensen, 1998, pp. 90–98). Children process experiences into knowledge and skills because they have human brains.

Thinking to Learn

In reviewing the implications of brain research for teaching, Eric Jensen (1998) found two elements important: "First, the learning is challenging, with new information and experiences. . . . Second, there must be some way to learn from the experiences through interactive feedback" (pp. 32–33). If learners are engaged in novel, complex, and varied experiences, they become critical thinkers and problem solvers. Interactive feedback includes both internal and external information: what children tell themselves and information received from adults, peers, and interactions with the physical world. Physical and social interactions provide new information for the construction of linguistic, social, scientific, and mathematical knowledge.

The metaphors for learning from computer and brain models connect with constructivist theories of learning:

- People create meaning by finding relationships and patterns in their experiences.

- What people learn and how they learn and how long they remember depend on unique motivations, intentions, and emotions of individual learners.

Human beings undoubtedly learn some things in behaviorist ways. The hot stove is a stimulus that evokes a strong, immediate, and long-lasting response in the unwary toddler or adult. Repeating a telephone number keeps it active in short-term memory. But humans use more sophisticated learning strategies than instinct and repetition; they perform unexpected and complex cognitive tasks when they learn concepts, act creatively, and solve problems. Cognitive theories conjecture that people transcend their immediate physical sensations and think. Cognitive theories are generalizations about learning because individuals learn in idiosyncratic ways based on their experiences, intentions, social interaction, and maturity. The theories are complex because human learning is complex.

Research in Learning and Teaching Mathematics

Theories about learning are developed and tested through research studies on how children learn and how teachers teach mathematics. Through educational research, educators and psychologists ask and answer questions about how children learn and how teachers can improve their effectiveness in teaching. Research describes, explains, and provides information about learning and teaching.

By reading research and research summaries, teachers learn more about how children learn and what techniques can be used to improve their learning. With electronic databases and search engines, teachers can find research studies on almost any topic in teaching or learning mathematics. The ERIC Clearinghouse for Science, Mathematics, and Environmental Education is the major source of research information about mathematics with the AskERIC database (available at **http://ericir.syr.edu**). For example, by entering the key words *fractions, elementary mathematics*, and *research*, a complete bibliography of research studies and other articles provide research about teaching and learning fractions. Figure 4.2 shows the abstract of a study from the ERIC database that describes misconceptions about fractions. A search on "research" into "problem solving" strategies yields an abstract (Figure 4.3) that explains kindergartners' problem-solving processes. After reading the abstract, teachers can decide whether they want to read the entire study.

In educational journals and full-text online services, teachers can find complete studies that include questions they are trying to answer, the subjects who participated in the study, how data were collected and analyzed, and conclusions or answers drawn from the data. InfoTrac College Edition and EBSCO are other database services that allow searches and offer many full-text articles.

ⒺXERCISE

Read the research abstracts in Figures 4.2 and 4.3. What questions were the researchers trying to answer? What did they find out, and how could that be useful to you as a teacher? ●●●

Title: Hispanic and Anglo Students' Misconceptions in Mathematics

ERIC Digest

Author(s): *Mestre, Jose*

Publication Date: March 1, 1989

Descriptors: *Concept Teaching; *Error Patterns; *Hispanic Americans; *Mathematical Concepts; *Mathematics Instruction; *Misconceptions; Anglo Americans; Concept Formation; Elementary Secondary Education; Student Attitudes

Identifiers: *ERIC Digests*

Abstract: Students come to the classroom with theories that they have actively constructed from their everyday experiences. However, some of these theories are incomplete half-truths. Although such misconceptions interfere with new learning, students are often emotionally and intellectually attached to them. Some common mathematical misconceptions involve: (1) confusion between variables and labels, with failure to understand that variables stand for numerical expressions; (2) mistakes about the way that an original price and a sale price reflect one another; (3) misconceptions about the independent nature of chance events; and (4) reluctance to multiply fractions. Hispanic students display some unique mathematical error patterns resulting from differences in language or culture. In addition, linguistic difficulties increase the frequency with which Hispanic students commit the same errors as Anglo students. Since students will not easily give up their misconceptions, lecturing them on a particular topic has little effect. Instead, teachers must help students to dismantle their own misconceptions.

One effective technique induces conflict by drawing out the contradictions in students' misconceptions. In the three steps of this technique, the teacher probes for qualitative, quantitative, and conceptual understanding, asking questions rather than telling students the right answer.

In the process of resolving the conflicts that arise, students actively reconstruct the concept in question and truly overcome their misconceptions.

This digest contains 10 references. (SV)

Figure 4.2 Research abstract on misconceptions about fractions

---

Title: Models of Problem Solving:
A Study of Kindergarten Children's Problem-Solving Processes

Author(s): *Carpenter, Thomas P., and Others*

Source: *Journal for Research in Mathematics Education v24 n5 p428-41 Nov 1993*

Publication Date: November 1, 1993

ISSN: 00218251

Descriptors: *Cognitive Processes; *Cognitive Style; *Heuristics; *Problem Solving; *Word Problems (Mathematics); Addition; Division; Interviews; Kindergarten; Learning Strategies; Mathematical Models; Mathematics Education; Mathematics Instruction; Models; Multiplication; Primary Education; Schemata (Cognition); Subtraction

Identifiers: *Representations (Mathematics); Mathematics Education Research*

Abstract: After a year of instruction, 70 kindergarten children were individually interviewed as they solved basic, multistep, and nonroutine word problems.

Thirty-two used a valid strategy for all 9 problems, and 44 correctly answered 7 or more problems. Modeling provided a unifying framework for thinking about problem solving. (Author/MDH)

Figure 4.3 Research abstract on kindergarteners' problem-solving processes

Reviews of Research

Single research studies provide clues about learning and teaching, but they do not allow researchers to draw strong conclusions by comparing and contrasting similar studies. Professional organizations make research summaries and syntheses available for professional educators in their journals: *Teaching Children Mathematics, Journal of Educational Research, Journal of Research in Mathematics Education,* and *Elementary School Journal.* The *Handbook of Research on Mathematics Teaching and Learning* (Grouws, 1992) and the *Handbook of International*

TABLE 4.2	Recommendations Based on Research for Improving Student Achievement in Mathematics

1. The extent of the students' opportunity to learn mathematics content bears directly and decisively on student mathematics achievement.

2. Focusing instruction on the meaningful development of important mathematical ideas increases the level of student learning.
   - Emphasize the mathematical meanings of ideas, including how the idea, concept, or skill is connected in multiple ways to other mathematical ideas in a logically consistent and sensible manner.
   - Create a classroom learning context in which students can construct meaning.
   - Make explicit the connections between mathematics and other subjects.
   - Attend to student meanings and student understandings.

3. Students can learn both concepts and skills by solving problems.
   Research suggests that it is not necessary for teachers to focus first on skill development and then move on to problem solving. Both can be done together. Skills can be developed on an as-needed basis, or their development can be supplemented through the use of technology. In fact, there is evidence that if students are initially drilled too much on isolated skills, they have a harder time making sense of them later.

4. Giving students both an opportunity to discover and invent new knowledge and an opportunity to practice what they have learned improves student achievement.
   Balance is needed between the time students spend practicing routine procedures and the time they devote to inventing and discovering new ideas. To increase opportunities for invention, teachers should frequently use nonroutine problems, periodically introduce a lesson involving a new skill by posing it as a problem to be solved, and regularly allow students to build new knowledge based on their intuitive knowledge and informal procedures.

5. Teaching that incorporates students' intuitive solution methods can increase student learning, especially when combined with opportunities for student interaction and discussion.
   Research results suggest that teachers should concentrate on providing opportunities for students to interact in problem-rich situations. Besides providing appropriate problem-rich situations, teachers must encourage students to find their own solution methods and give them opportunities to share and compare their solution methods and answers. One way to organize such instruction is to have students work in small groups initially and then share ideas and solutions in a whole-class discussion.

6. Using small groups of students to work on activities, problems, and assignments can increase student mathematics achievement.
   When using small groups for mathematics instruction, teachers should:
   - Choose tasks that deal with important mathematical concepts and ideas
   - Select tasks that are appropriate for group work

Research in Mathematics Education (English, 2003) collect current reviews of research on important topics for teaching and learning. ERIC digests provide short summaries of research and research-based best practices.

Based on a review of research, Grouws and Cebulla (2002) made 10 recommendations (available at **http://www.ericse.org/digests/dse00-10.html**) with direct application for teachers of mathematics. Current research is also available through the website of the National Center for Improving Student Learning and Achievement in Mathematics and Science (available at **http://www.wcer.wisc.edu /ncisla/**).

Recommendations given in Table 4.2 support cognitive theories about learning. Constructivist teaching depends on teachers knowing how children learn and connecting important content to the needs and interests of the learner. Galileo wrote, "You cannot teach a man anything; you can only help him find it within himself." Constructivist teaching has roots in the theories of Piaget, Bruner, Skemp, and Vygotsky and is consistent with current research on teaching and learning. Research is the foundation for the recommendations about learning and teaching found in the *Principles and Standards for School Mathematics* (National Council of Teachers of Mathematics, 2000). NCTM continually updates research through its publications such as *Lessons Learned from Research* (Sowder & Schappelle, 2002). Gerald A. Goldin (1990, p. 31) cites six themes on which teaching mathematics in a constructivist manner is based:

TABLE 4.2 • Continued

- Consider having students initially work individually on a task and then follow with group work where students share and build on their individual ideas and work
- Give clear instructions to the groups and set clear expectations
- Emphasize both group goals and individual accountability
- Choose tasks that students find interesting
- Ensure that there is closure to the group work, where key ideas and methods are brought to the surface either by the teacher or the students, or both

7. **Whole-class discussion following individual and group work improves student achievement.**

   It is important that whole-class discussion follows student work on problem-solving activities. The discussion should be a summary of individual work in which key ideas are brought to the surface. This can be accomplished through students presenting and discussing their individual solution methods, or through other methods of achieving closure that are led by the teacher, the students, or both.

8. **Teaching mathematics with a focus on number sense encourages students to become problem solvers in a wide variety of situations and to view mathematics as a discipline in which thinking is important.**

   Competence in the many aspects of number sense is an important mathematical outcome for students. Over 90% of the computation done outside the classroom is done without pencil and paper, using mental computation, estimation, or a calculator. However, in many classrooms, efforts to instill number sense are given insufficient attention.

9. **Long-term use of concrete materials is positively related to increases in student mathematics achievement and improved attitudes toward mathematics.**

   Research suggests that teachers use manipulative materials regularly in order to give students hands-on experience that helps them construct useful meanings for the mathematical ideas they are learning. Use of the same materials to teach multiple ideas over the course of schooling shortens the amount of time it takes to introduce the material and helps students see connections between ideas.

10. **Using calculators in the learning of mathematics can result in increased achievement and improved student attitudes.**

    One valuable use for calculators is as a tool for exploration and discovery in problem-solving situations and when introducing new mathematical content. By reducing computation time and providing immediate feedback, calculators help students focus on understanding their work and justifying their methods and results. The graphing calculator is particularly useful in helping to illustrate and develop graphical concepts and in making connections between algebraic and geometric ideas.

SOURCE: Grouws & Cebulla (2002).

1. Mathematics is viewed as *invented* or *constructed* by human beings; it is not an independent body of "truths" or an abstract and necessary set of rules.

2. Mathematical meaning is *constructed by the learner* rather than imparted by the teacher.

3. Mathematical learning occurs most effectively through *guided discovery, meaningful application,* and *problem solving* rather than imitation and reliance on the rote use of algorithms for manipulating symbols.

4. Study and assessment of learners must occur through individual interviews and small-group observations that go beyond paper-and-pencil tests.

5. Effective teaching occurs through the creation of classroom *learning environments* that encourage the development of diverse and creative problem-solving processes in students.

6. Teachers must consider the origins of mathematical knowledge to understand that such knowledge is constructed and that mathematical learning is a constructive process.

A constructivist teacher develops opportunities for children to activate prior knowledge and to acquire, understand, apply, and reflect on knowledge (Zahorik, 1995). Teachers who understand both the structure of mathematics and the processes of learning create classrooms that lead to success for the learners.

Teachers and Action Research

Many teachers do not realize that by asking and answering questions about student learning and effective teaching, they conduct research in their classrooms. Teachers describe, explain, and try methods to improve their students' learning. They assess student learning by collecting data, drawing conclusions, and changing their techniques to increase learning. This process, called **classroom action research**, is central to improving teaching and learning. Many articles in the journal *Teaching Children Mathematics* are based on practices that teachers deem successful. For example, Ambrose and Falkner (2001) report on students' thinking, understanding of concepts, and use of geometry vocabulary as a result of building polyhedra. In some issues of *Teaching Children Mathematics* a problem for students is presented, and several months later a follow-up article shows different student solutions with a discussion of various strategies. This feature gives teachers insight into student thinking and models classroom research.

Summary

Learning theories and research provide understanding of learning and teaching processes for teachers. Although behaviorist theories and practices of drill and practice have often dominated mathematics instruction, new research supports a more cognitive approach to teaching. The cognitive approach recognizes the importance of individual differences in motivation, emotion, experience, language, and culture and how these differences can influence how and what students learn. Key ideas for teaching based on cognitive theories include focus on meaning, developmental stages in learning, social interaction, concrete experiences with multiple representations, learning meaningful procedures, building long-term strategic memory, and finding patterns. As indicated by cognitive research and theories, teachers need to provide instruction that engages students actively in constructing mathematical concepts and building skills in a meaningful context.

Through journals and technology teachers have access to the latest research about learning and teaching. Specific studies or reviews of research that summarize and synthesize current research are found in journals and online. Teachers also ask and answer questions in their own classrooms as they assess student learning and determine which techniques are most effective for learners.

Study Questions and Activities

1. Bransford and colleagues (1999, p. 108) said, "The alliance of factual knowledge, procedural proficiency, and conceptual understanding makes all three components usable in powerful ways. Students who memorize facts or procedures without understanding often are not sure when or how to use what they know, and such learning is often quite fragile." Is this approach more behaviorist or cognitive in nature? Explain your answer.

2. Compare the recommendations for teachers from research by Grouws and Cebulla (2002) with the "key ideas" from cognitive theories. Which points match between them and which do not?

Teacher's Resources

Benson, B. (2003). *How to meet standards, motivate students, and still enjoy teaching.* Thousand Oaks, CA: Corwin Press.

Clements, D. (2003). *Learning and teaching measurement.* Reston, VA: National Council of Teachers of Mathematics.

Kirkpatrick, J., Martin, W. G., & Schifter, D. (2003). *A research comparison to principles and standards for school mathematics.* Reston, VA: National Council of Teachers of Mathematics.

Posamentier, A., Hartman, H., & Kaiser, C. (1998). *Tips for the mathematics teacher.* Thousand Oaks, CA: Corwin Press.

Ronis, D. (1997). *Brain-compatible mathematics.* Thousand Oaks, CA: Corwin Press.

Sowder, J., & Schappelle, B. (2002). *Lessons learned from research.* Reston, VA: National Council of Teachers of Mathematics.

Tate, M. (2005). *Worksheets don't grow dendrites.* Thousand Oaks, CA: Corwin Press.

Tomlinson, C., & McTighe, J. (2006). *Integrating differentiated instruction and understanding by design: Connecting content and kids.* Alexandria, VA: Association for Supervision and Curriculum Development.

Wolfe, P. (2001). *Brain matters: Translating research into the classroom practice.* Alexandria, VA: Association for Supervision and Curriculum Development.

CHAPTER 5

Organizing Effective Instruction

Effective teaching strategies in mathematics emerge when learning theories, research on teaching and learning, and successful teaching practices are taken into consideration and drawn upon. Constructivism is the theory that best explains the complexities of learning mathematical concepts and procedures in a developmental process. By exploring materials and discussing interesting mathematics-rich problems, students construct mathematical concepts and develop skills. In a challenging and supportive classroom, teachers organize mathematical tasks and encourage student engagement and communication by the way they manage space, time, and materials. In this chapter we describe how teachers make plans and implement instruction and how the decisions they make foster conceptual and procedural knowledge.

In this chapter you will read about:

1. Characteristics of successful teachers
2. Long-range and short-range planning based on curriculum objectives
3. Teaching approaches and strategies that support learning
4. Cooperative learning to encourage student achievement and communication
5. Organization of time, space, and materials that support learning and student interaction

What Is Effective Mathematics Teaching?

New and experienced teachers ask two questions about their mathematics teaching:

1. What concepts, skills, and applications should children learn?

2. What are the most effective ways to develop these concepts, skills, and applications?

The first question, about the expected content and processes of mathematics, can be answered by referring to the state and district learning objectives, which are often based on the NCTM standards presented in Chapters 1 and 2. The answer to the second question, about teaching content and process skills, is further developed in Part 2 of this text.

Effective teaching depends on the knowledge and skills that teachers bring to instruction decisions and the choices teachers make in implementing this pedagogical knowledge. Teachers must make many decisions about the way they teach. Teachers plan worthwhile mathematics experiences, interact with children while they are learning, and monitor student's progress. Successful teachers understand how children learn and vary their teaching based on group and individual needs. Because no single instructional approach works for every child and every concept, effective teachers build a repertoire of instructional skills and techniques with characteristics suggested by theory, research, and practice, such as those cited in Chapter 4.

- Teachers engage children actively in learning.

- Teachers encourage students to reflect on their experiences and construct meaning.

- Teachers invite children to think at higher cognitive levels.

- Teachers help children connect mathematics to their lives.

- Teachers encourage children to communicate their ideas in many forms and settings.

- Teachers constantly monitor and assess students' understanding and skill.

- Teachers adjust their instruction to fit the needs, levels, and interests of children.

- Teachers create a positive learning environment that supports critical and creative thinking.

Using Objectives to Guide Mathematics Instruction

Three classroom vignettes illustrate how teachers at different grade levels adapt lessons to match the content with the level of students. The general objective for each lesson is for students to collect data and represent information on a bar graph with a title and key and to draw conclusions based on the data.

First-Grade Graphing

Mr. Gable plans a lesson on classification and representation for first-graders using the objective "Students will sort 20 wooden blocks into groups by color and display the information on a bar graph." Students gather in a circle on the floor. Mr. Gable places a red flower on red construction paper, a blue glove on blue paper, and a yellow fire engine on yellow paper. Students notice the objects match the color of the paper. He asks students where new objects belong, and children place them on the corresponding color. Students talk about which color has the most or least objects, how many more red has than yellow, and so forth (see Figure 5.1a).

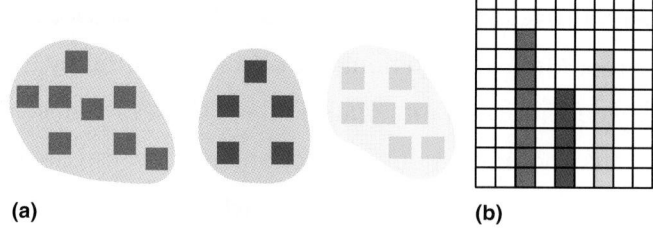

(a)   **(b)**

Figure 5.1 (a) Object graph and (b) bar graph

Then Mr. Gable gives each pair of students 20 blocks of three colors and matching construction paper. He asks them to sort the blocks by color and to count them. After placing the blocks in groups, students move the blocks on 1-inch graph paper and color in the squares on the paper (see Figure 5.1b).

After putting graphs on a bulletin board, Mr. Gable asks questions: "How many graphs show seven or more red cubes? Are there any graphs with fewer than three of a color? Which graph has the most red cubes?" Activities and lessons over several weeks focus on classifying and graphing.

Third-Grade Data Collection

Mrs. Alfaro plans a lesson with this objective: "Given centimeter-squared paper, students will collect data on a topic of their choice and construct a bar graph, including a title and key, showing the results." She asks students to write their favorite sandwich on 2-inch sticky notes with their initials. Students put their sticky notes on a white board with others of the same type: peanut butter, peanut butter with jelly, grilled cheese, bologna, bacon and tomato, and "other." After grouping, they line the sticky notes up, starting at the base.

An overhead transparency of graph paper shows labeled columns with the six types of sandwiches. Initials of each child are transferred to a corresponding square on the transparency. Finally, Mrs. Alfaro asks students to supply a title; the group decides on "Yum-Yum: Our Favorite Sandwiches." She writes, "1 square = 1 sandwich" beneath the title and labels it the "key" for the graph (see Figure 5.2).

The next day, students work in groups of three to poll each other about other favorites: pizza, ice cream, sports teams, pets, singing groups, colors, and dream cars. Over two or three days, the stu-dents collect data, organize them, and display them on graphs with titles and a key. The activity is concluded when groups show their graphs and report conclusions drawn from them.

Students poll students in other classes to compare their class results with those for other groups.

Sixth-Grade Rainfall Graph

Ms. Clary's students have had experiences with bar graphs and know how to determine the mean average for a set of numbers, so she wants them to work independently on graphing for an interdisciplinary social studies and science unit on weather. The performance task is, "Given a chart of the monthly rainfall for the last 10 years, students will use a computer spreadsheet to compute the mean average rainfall for each month, create a bar graph showing the mean average monthly rainfall, and write a short paragraph in which they describe weather trends over the 10 years using mean averages and extremes." She allows the students to pick any city in the United States using data from almanacs and the Internet. After entering the data on the computer, students use the average function on the spreadsheet and create bar and line graphs. Students take turns working as computer consultants if problems occur.

After a week, each student has a table and bar graph of mean rainfall (see Figure 5.3) and an essay

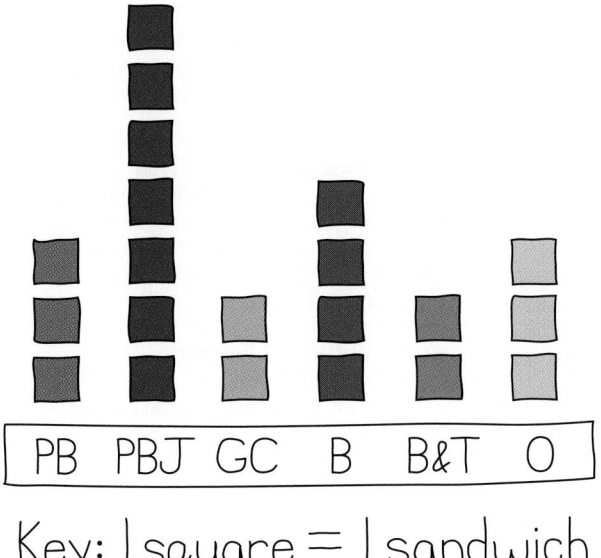

Figure 5.2 Yum-Yum: Our Favorite Sandwiches graph

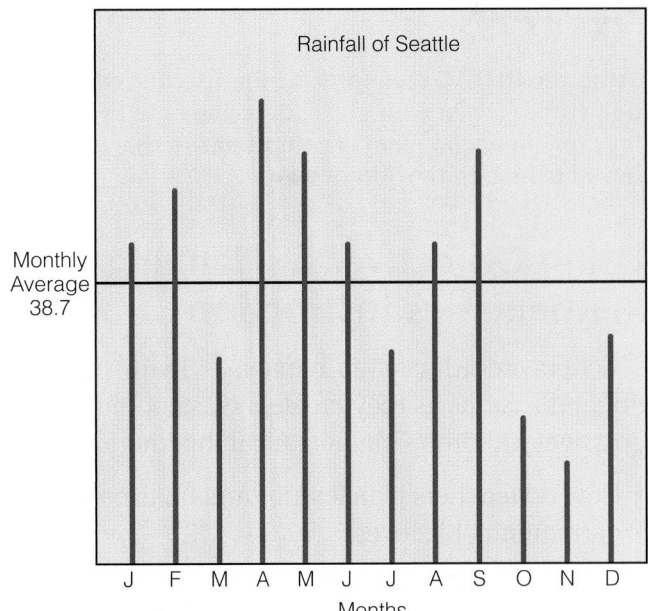

Figure 5.3 Rainfall graph

about the weather pattern in the city. As they look for similarities and differences in rainfall patterns across the United States, they identify weather patterns such as droughts, events such as El Niño and La Niña, and hurricanes.

Using standards and objectives as beginning points, these three teachers demonstrate characteristics for successful teachers through their flexibility and adaptation. The content objectives and skill levels are met with different tasks and materials, but all challenge students and encourage thinking.

Becoming an Effective Teacher

The three teachers from the vignettes exhibit excellent teaching techniques. However, acquiring all the qualities of effective teaching does not occur overnight; teaching is a continuous improvement process. Ten principles for preparing new teachers were adopted by the Interstate New Teacher Assessment and Support Consortium (INTASC). The INTASC standards, listed in Table 5.1, outline what beginning teachers should know and be able to do. These statements provide a framework for new teachers entering the profession and are adapted by many states for new teachers. In practice, the 10 standards are not 10 separate practices. Combined they represent what good teachers know and do on a daily basis.

ⒺXERCISE

Using the INTASC standards or the teacher education standards in your state, describe how the teachers in each vignette exhibited the characteristics of effective teaching. ●●●

Using Objectives in Planning Mathematics Instruction

Teachers coordinate and manage many instructional decisions as they create a classroom that encourages children's mathematical thinking.

- How do teachers plan lessons and units based on curriculum objectives?
- What teaching approaches and strategies engage students in worthwhile learning activities?

Many states and school districts adopt or adapt the NCTM standards when writing their curriculum goals

TABLE 5.1 ● **INTASC Beginning Teacher Standards**

1. Content Pedagogy
The teacher understands the central concepts, tools of inquiry, and structures of the discipline he or she teaches and can create learning experiences that make these aspects of subject matter meaningful for students.

2. Student Development
The teacher understands how children learn and develop and can provide learning opportunities that support a child's intellectual, social, and personal development.

3. Diverse Learners
The teacher understands how students differ in their approaches to learning and creates instructional opportunities that are adapted to diverse learners.

4. Multiple Instructional Strategies
The teacher understands and uses a variety of instructional strategies to encourage student development of critical thinking, problem solving, and performance skills.

5. Motivation and Management
The teacher uses an understanding of individual and group motivation and behavior to create a learning environment that encourages positive social interaction, active engagement in learning, and self-motivation.

6. Communication and Technology
The teacher uses knowledge of effective verbal, nonverbal, and media communication techniques to foster active inquiry, collaboration, and supportive interaction in the classroom.

7. Planning
The teacher plans instruction based on knowledge of subject matter, students, the community, and curriculum goals.

8. Assessment
The teacher understands and uses formal and informal assessment strategies to evaluate and ensure the continuous intellectual, social, and physical development of the learner.

9. Reflective Practice: Professional Growth
The teacher is a reflective practitioner who continually evaluates the effects of his or her choices and actions on others (students, parents, and other professionals in the learning community) and who actively seeks out opportunities to grow professionally.

10. School and Community Involvement
The teacher fosters relationships with colleagues, parents, and agencies in the larger community to support students' learning and well-being.

and **performance objectives**. Wording of objectives varies, but the scope and sequence are often similar. Performance objectives, also called instructional objectives and learning targets or benchmarks, describe what students should know and be able to do as a result of instruction. By knowing the expectations for the grade level they teach, as well as objectives for earlier and later grades, teachers see how content and skills develop over time. By aligning the curriculum, teams of teachers on the same grade level and across grade levels in a school coordinate their objectives, instructional practices, and assessments so that all children have a positive learning experience.

Long-Range Planning

In a long-range plan teachers outline how instructional topics and objectives for the year are developed and sequenced. Planning across the year allows time for development, review, and extension of topics and balances instructional time so that all standards receive attention and build on one another. With increasing emphasis on accountability, teachers also consider when state assessments are scheduled and make sure that content is developed and reviewed before the test. A fourth-grade teacher's preliminary plan for the year is shown in Table 5.2. A long-range plan is subject to change to take advantage of learning opportunities and learner needs.

Unit Planning

Teachers create two- or three-week instructional units based on the long-range plan that included varied lessons and activities. A three-week instructional unit on addition and subtraction of two- and three-digit numbers in third grade might include eight directed teaching/thinking lessons, six learning center and computer-based activities, three games, and two investigations or student-centered projects. Multiple learning experiences provide for varied learning styles, interests, and abilities within the topic. Unit planning also considers various student groupings from whole class to small group to individual learning.

Learning activities are sequenced so that new concepts and skills are introduced and developed in a logical way. A real-life or imagined problem captures children's interest. Good instructional problems motivate learning and have mathematical concepts and skills embedded in them. A teacher starts a lesson or unit with problems based on a children's book, newspaper article, children's lives, or manipulatives. *How Many Snails: A Counting Book* (by Paul

TABLE 5.2	Long-Range Plan (Grade 4): Mathematics

September
Review geometry concepts and terminology—symmetry, 2-D and 3-D figures.
Introduce area and volume measurement.

October
Review concepts and basic facts for four operations.
Develop algorithms for two- and three-digit numbers for four operations.
Introduce estimation and calculator strategies for larger numbers.

November
Continue estimation and algorithms.
Review and extend common fractions—concepts, equivalence, comparisons.
Introduce addition and subtraction with fractional numbers concretely.

December
Review and extend linear, area, and volume measure.
Review addition and subtraction models of fractions.
Review and extend data gathering and graph making.

January
Introduce probability using common and decimal fractions.
Continue estimation and algorithms for four operations, including fractions.
Introduce transformational geometry and coordinate geometry.

February
Introduce statistics and interpretation of graphs.
Review and extend estimation and algorithms with whole and fractional numbers.
Review and extend measure of volume and weight (with science).

March
Continue decimal fraction concepts (money), statistics, and probability.
Review place value and extend to decimal fractions.
Introduce measurement of angles.

April
Review and extend four operations with decimal fractions.
Review and extend probability concepts.
State assessments.

May
Review and extend data collection and analysis.
Review and extend transformational geometry.
Review and extend estimation and algorithms for four operations.

Giganti) introduces counting, classification, subtraction, and fractions by asking students to count sets of objects with different attributes. A newspaper article states that the state is running out of telephone numbers and brings up questions about how many

Figure 5.4 Area of a triangle

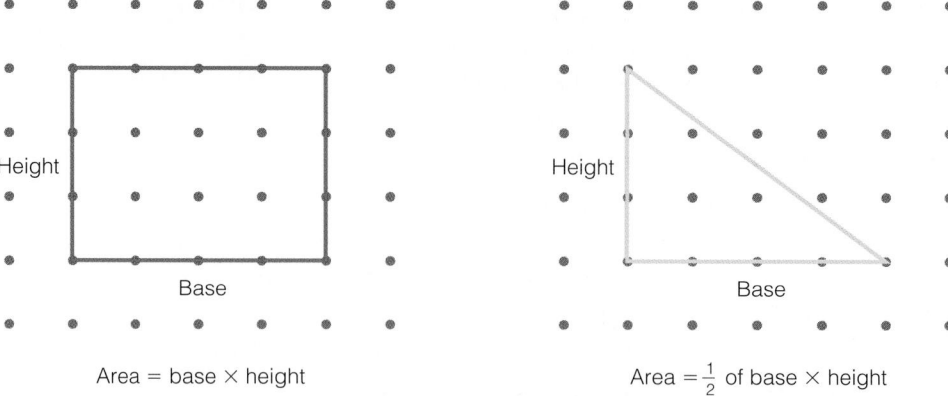

Area = base × height   Area = $\frac{1}{2}$ of base × height

telephone numbers are possible in any area code. This discussion includes large numbers, multiplication, and combinations.

Teachers also consider the sequence of activities in a unit. Teachers introduce new concepts with simple examples and move to more sophisticated concepts as children become successful. Patterning might be explored with A-B repetition first, then A-A-B, then A-B-C and A-B-C-B. Measurement of length is modeled with paper clips and a chain of paper clips before the ruler is introduced. Students compare and classify the size of angles on triangles. Little, big, and corner angles are later renamed "acute, obtuse, and right" angles and are compared to angles found in different figures. As students gain skill and confidence, situations and vocabulary become more complex.

Effective teachers incorporate different levels of representation in lessons moving from concrete objects to pictures to symbols and eventually to mental images and operations. Mathematical concepts are developed using stories, models, pictures, tables and graphs, and number sentences or formulas. This sequence of introducing material to students builds understanding of essential attributes of mathematical concepts. Realistic contexts give way to symbolic representations. Mental computation, number sense, reasonableness of answer, estimation, and spatial sense are indicators of students' ability to reason abstractly.

Students also develop from specific to general solutions. Learning the blue-blue-red pattern with blocks is specific, but patterning is a fundamental thinking skill that extends beyond learning one pattern. Identifying and labeling many patterns in many situations and many forms (A-B-C, A-B-C-B, A-A-B-C) creates a generalized skill. Finding the area

of a rectangle or a triangle by counting square units is a solution strategy for that shape. However, noting that the area of rectangles is determined by multiplying the length by the height is a generalized rule. Finding that the area of a triangle is half the area of its related rectangle extends the first rule (Figure 5.4). As children take specific solutions and generate a formula for the area of all triangles, they are thinking algebraically. Figure 5.5 summarizes some important sequences that teachers consider in planning their units to maximize student learning.

PROBLEM SOLVING

Problem → Concept → Skill → Solution → New problem

COMPLEXITY

Simple → Complex

SITUATION

Specific → General

REPRESENTATION

Concrete → Pictorial → Symbolic → Mental

Figure 5.5 Developmental sequence for activities

Daily Lesson Planning

The daily lesson plan focuses on the activities presented in a single day in the context of the unit plan as well as the long-range plan. Instructional decisions on a daily lesson plan are specific, because teaching optimizes student learning. Teachers ask, "What types of activities should I plan for today?" to guide children toward mastery of the objectives for the unit. Each day contributes to attainment of the unit, and teachers have several approaches available.

Varying Teaching Approaches

Some teachers believe that standards or curriculum objectives limit their creativity and flexibility in teaching mathematics. Although standards guide instructional goals, effective teachers choose the techniques and activities that address student learning styles, preferences, intelligences, and needs. Meeting all students' needs requires varied instructional approaches, including informal or exploratory activities, directed teaching/thinking lessons, and problem-based projects or investigations.

Informal or Exploratory Activities

When planning daily lessons, some lessons should provide time for students to informally explore concepts. Work with manipulatives, playing games, and setting up learning centers are informal approaches that have many benefits for student learning. Informal activities with manipulatives prepare children for directed teaching episodes and investigations with materials. Children are fascinated by new materials, so experienced teachers provide students exploratory time with materials before using them in directed activities. When students have worked with materials before a directed lesson, they concentrate on the content of the lesson rather than on the novelty of the materials. Manipulatives have mathematics concepts and skills embedded in them. When children spontaneously build a stair-step pattern with Cuisenaire rods (Figure 5.6), they are modeling the plus-1 rule for learning basic facts: $1 + 1 = 2, 2 + 1 = 3, 3 + 1 = 4$, and so on. Arranging pattern blocks is an exploration of proportionality and fractional parts (Figure 5.7). Informal experiences give students a head start on understanding because they have already experienced a concept through their hands-on exploration. Finally, informal explorations invite cre-

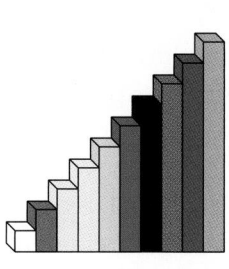

Figure 5.6 Cuisenaire rod stairs demonstrate +1.

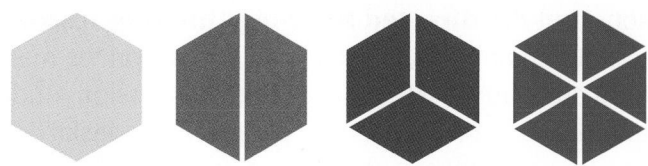

Figure 5.7 Pattern blocks show fractional parts.

ativity and critical thinking through open-ended tasks. Students create new uses and new rules with games and objects. Informal activities allow students to individualize their learning. The teacher serves as a guide and facilitator while students work informally.

- Individual student's needs and interests can be addressed by offering choice as part of informal activities. Different children learn at different levels of understanding with the same materials. Informal activities encourage independent thought and autonomous action, and they provide variety in the instructional approaches in the classroom.

- By selecting the materials and the tasks carefully, teachers extend engaged learning time for students. While teachers work with individuals or small groups, students in the classroom explore materials and activities related to the objectives using directions from printed materials or task cards. Task cards coordinated with manipulatives challenge students to complete an activity. For example, a task card on patterning with colored shapes may leave several blank spaces for students to complete the pattern with pattern blocks.

Informal activities provide valuable learning for all students when teachers select appropriate materials and tasks, monitor and assess student work, discuss the concepts being encountered, and introduce vocabulary related to the activities. If students establish a purpose for exploratory activities, they are more likely to see them as important. Children in all elementary grades, as well as middle and secondary levels, need exploratory experiences as new concepts and materials are introduced. Informal activities, learning centers, and games extend skills and topics from a previous grade or earlier in the year.

Directed Teaching/Thinking Lessons

A different approach to daily planning is a directed teaching/thinking lesson. Some people see direct teaching as teacher-controlled or even scripted lessons, but the **directed teaching/thinking lesson** in mathematics is interactive and incorporates manipulative materials, visual aids, discussion and argument, and interesting performance tasks to encourage thinking. A directed teaching/thinking lesson can be taught to small groups or the whole class. Small groups are often more effective because the teacher closely observes children's work with materials, watches their eyes, and listens to their comments.

During a unit, the teacher uses the directed teaching/thinking format to introduce, reinforce, and extend key concepts and skills several times while working toward student mastery. A lesson plan serves as a road map for a well-thought-out lesson with a destination (the instructional objective) and a route (procedures needed to master the objective). Robert Gagne (1985) describes a well-planned lesson in nine events that can be grouped into three phases: preparation, presentation, and practice.

Preparation (Motivation and Preparation: Setting the Stage)

- Gain the learner's attention.
- Inform the learner of the learning objective or task.
- Recall prior experiences, information, and prerequisite skills.

Presentation (Instructional Input and Modeling)

- Present new content or skills by demonstrating and describing critical attributes.
- Provide guided practice with additional examples.
- Elicit performance on a learning task.
- Check for understanding.

Practice (Independent Practice)

- Provide feedback and assess performance.
- Apply content or skill in new situation.

In the first phase the teacher creates the mind set for learning. A stimulating introduction helps students focus their attention on the concept being explored. Teachers have many ways of creating an expectancy or anticipation for learning: a children's literature book on a concept, a manipulative for modeling, or a problem situation related to the concept being de-

veloped. A mystery box might contain something related to the lesson, and students guess the contents; for example, an orange in the mystery box might introduce spheres. A recent newspaper headline or personal experience might pique student interest in a new topic. A number puzzle gets students thinking about mathematics. These activities motivate students to shift their attention from a previous activity, such as recess or reading, to mathematics and activates prior knowledge for the concept or skill being addressed.

In the second phase of a directed teaching/thinking activity, students develop understanding of new content. According to Gagne's plan, the teacher explains and models the new content or skill and the student models what the teacher has done. However, a more constructivist approach, described in Chapter 4, places the teacher as a facilitator of student learning. In this role the teacher prepares a problem or situation that engages students' thinking about an important mathematical concept or skill. Rather than tell the students what to do and think, the teacher asks questions and elicits student ideas. The performance task requires the student to think mathematically. When children rearrange blocks to show regrouping for two-digit addition or roll two number cubes and record the results on a graph, the activity itself carries the content. Students learn by doing mathematics. In this way the critical attributes of the concept are developed by the learner. As the activity progresses, the teacher labels the actions with more formal vocabulary and introduces symbols as they are needed.

As teachers check for understanding, they discover that some students need more explanation and examples, whereas others are ready for guided practice. During guided practice, students work in pairs or independently on problems that extend their thinking and skill. The teacher monitors student work and gives corrective feedback or guiding questions as needed. As students progress, the teacher asks students to generate their own problems. Students who show understanding of the concept or skill are ready for the third phase; others need more time and examples.

In the third phase of the directed teaching/thinking lesson the teacher still monitors student work but the student works more independently. Independent practice is appropriate when students understand

Figure 5.8 Seven-step lesson cycle

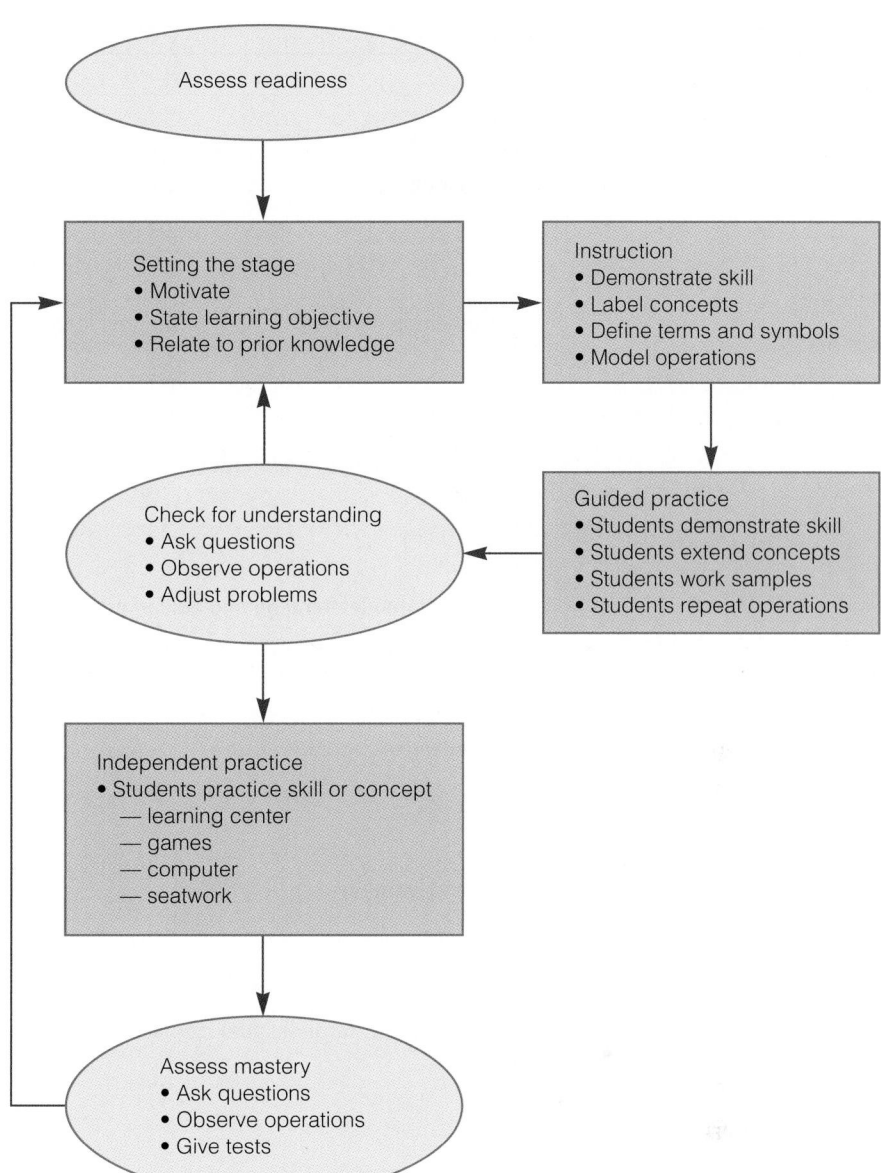

the skill or content (Figure 5.8). Students may also practice and extend their new concepts and skills through problems, projects, and investigations.

ⒺXERCISE

The lesson cycle in Figure 5.8 is often called the Hunter lesson model, named for educator Madeline Hunter, who popularized it. Discuss the lesson cycle with a classmate, and compare it to Gagne's events of instruction. ●●●

Writing Plans for Directed Teaching/Thinking Lessons. When writing lesson plans, teachers realize that all activities support the core concept of the unit. Whether called the focus, the big idea, or

the essential question, teachers and students connect each day with the unit goals. Without focus on the central concept, individual lessons become disjointed. The NCTM standards and expectations help teachers find the central ideas for planning.

Lesson plans can be written in many formats, but they typically include four or five common elements: instructional objectives; step-by-step procedures for introducing, guiding, and generalizing the concept or skill; materials needed; evaluation techniques; and modifications for special learners. The blank lesson plan format in Figure 5.9 is based on the lesson cycle; a sample lesson plan is shown in Figure 5.10. In Chapters 8 through 16 lesson plans and activities for each content standard are presented.

Figure 5.9
Blank lesson plan form

Teacher _Lorenz_   Date _10/24/2007_

Instructional Objective: _____

Materials: _____

Motivation and preparation: setting the stage

Instructional input and modeling

Check for understanding and guided practice

Independent practice

Extend learning

Modifications for individual learners

EXERCISE

Many activities and lesson plans can be found on the Internet or in teacher manuals that accompany elementary mathematics textbooks. Find three lesson plans on the Internet and determine how well they match the lesson plan format in Figure 5.9. What is similar and what is different? ●●●

Problem-Based Projects and Investigations

Another instructional approach is **problem-based projects or investigations**. While investigating a problem, students explore and apply concepts and skills, expand ideas, and draw conclusions. Investigations can be initiated by the teacher or by students

with the teacher providing technical assistance and support. Sometimes, students may require specific instruction on a mathematics concept related to their problem.

Investigation or projects reflect classroom or real-world situations. In Ms. Hale's fifth-grade class passing trains were visible from the classroom window. One student kept a log of the trains and their schedules on the north and south routes. With encouragement the student researched the trains and discovered coal was the cargo, where the coal was coming from and where it was going, the speed of the train, and how scheduling prevented train wrecks. A retired train engineer served as a resource person for the project. The culmination of the investigation was a paper, posters, and a presentation to classmates. A

Figure 5.10
Sample lesson plan for subtraction

Teacher _Lorenz_   Date _10/24/2007_

Instructional Objective: Students will solve story problems using subtraction of 3-digit numerals by modeling decomposition with manipulatives and recording the regrouping.

Materials: Have students prepare 3 × 5 cards in learning center in packs of 100s, 10s, and 1s with rubber bands. Distribute 1000 3 × 5 cards for each group of 4, so that each group has some of each amount.

Procedure: Motivation and preparation: Setting the stage
- Review place value with dice game, placing numerals to make the largest 4-digit number.
- Model several subtraction stories with two digit numbers.
- Tell stories to match the numbers in the problems. Students may use the 100s chart to find the answers

$$\begin{array}{ccc} 37 & 83 & 95 \\ -22 & -48 & -73 \end{array}$$

- Introduce the regrouping and renaming subtraction model with packs of cards and have students follow. "You had 37 cents and spent 22 cents on a pencil."
- Put 3 packs of 10 and 7 single cards on the board tray. Remove 22 of them. Ask how many are still on the tray.
- Model several other problems.
- Compare the answers to answers using the 100s chart.
- When students demonstrate understanding of regrouping, tell a story with larger numbers: "In January, Mrs. Cardwell ordered 1000 Valentine cards for her card shop. On Monday, February 1, she still had 862 cards for sale. By Friday, February 5, she only had 374 cards on the shelf. How many had she sold during the week?"

Instructional input and modeling
- Ask students to show how many cards she had at the start with the card sets.
- Ask students to remove enough cards to show what she had on Monday using regrouping.
- Then ask them to show how many cards she sold during the week.

$$\begin{array}{cc} 1000 & 862 \\ -862 & -374 \\ \hline 138 & 488 \end{array}$$

- After a few minutes, ask groups to share their solutions and process.
- If students used subtraction processes other than decomposition, such as equal addition or compensation, accept these solutions and have students discuss different approaches.

Check for understanding and guided practice
- Provide several more problems.
- Ask students to tell a story for each subtraction example and model it with cards. They also may use one of the other processes to see if they get the same answer.

$$\begin{array}{cccc} 125 & 284 & 284 & 731 \\ -73 & -143 & -198 & -374 \end{array}$$

- Monitor work with cards and written work.
- Ask students who are modeling accurately to make up several more problems together.
- For students who are showing difficulty, plan a small-group reteach. Students who are catching on can pick three problems from page 93 to work. Go back and review simple subtraction.

Extend learning with a journal problem
How many cards do you think Mrs. Cardwell should have on hand for the rest of the Valentine season? Justify your answer.

Modifications for individual learners
Decide if students are ready to work three problems from page 93 or to wait another day until process is stronger.
For Mable: Pair with Sy Ning.
For Sean and Tran: Introduce virtual blocks on computer and have them teach others.
For Jeffri: Be alert to frustration. Simplify problems as needed.

teacher who is aware of student interests can make time for such projects. Other students might be interested in horses, dinosaurs, or astronauts, which could generate investigations that lead to mathematical questions and concepts as well as interdisciplinary ideas.

- How fast can different horses run?
- How big were dinosaurs? How much did they eat?
- How fast does the shuttle fly when taking off and while in orbit?

Classroom projects provide investigation opportunities. Ms. Shivey asked first-graders to design board games for practicing addition and subtraction facts. They played commercial board games to become familiar with game structure. Using poster board, dice, index cards, and colored pens, they designed and constructed games, played their game with peers, and revised the game. A two-week creative project resulted in many weeks of fact practice as well as problem solving, communicating, and reasoning. Although penalties were favorite design features, the first-graders learned quickly that nobody wanted to play games that were impossible to win.

Newspapers are sources of problem-based projects. When the newspaper reported that a new area code was needed, students wanted to know why. They discovered that telephone companies reserved thousands of telephone numbers for future use by new subscribers and for new technologies, such as cell phones and fax machines. This investigation led to population statistics and work with large numbers. Another article showed how far different animals could jump compared to their body length: fleas, rabbits, kangaroos, and the best human jumpers. Interest in jumping animals led to interest in world records and then led to activities in linear measurement.

Because investigations are open-ended, student success is based on whether they complete their task and demonstrate the target knowledge and skill. Assessment reflects the learning goal, the choice of suitable sources of information, the completeness and accuracy of information, and the manner in which it is summarized and reported. Many teachers use a K-W-H-L chart for organizing investigations. Students list what they *k*now, what they *w*ant to know, and *h*ow they are going to conduct the investigation (including resources they will use) and finally report on what was *l*earned. Investigations provide curriculum differentiation for gifted and talented students; however, all students benefit from an investigation approach. Some students complete several investigations in a year; others may work on only one or two. Investigations on different topics can go on simultaneously. Although curriculum goals are established by standards, problem-based investigations provide a way that students can push the curriculum. Providing time and support for project-based learning stimulates students to be independent learners.

Integrating Multiple Approaches

Because children learn mathematics in many ways, as discussed in Chapters 3 and 4, teachers must teach using various approaches. When teachers vary their instruction with informal activities, directed teaching/thinking lessons, and investigations, they provide for students who have different learning strengths and needs. Within a unit, teachers want to balance exploratory, teacher-guided, and project-type activities.

Each instructional approach invites children to construct mathematical knowledge and to develop skills. Informal experiences build background and provide practice and maintenance of skills. Directed teaching/thinking lessons provide engagement and interaction as teachers and students develop concepts, skills, and vocabulary. Investigations allow students to pursue mathematical and interdisciplinary projects beyond the predetermined curriculum. Individual students may need specific modifications based on their individual plans, but many times accommodations that work for one student can also help other students.

Delivering Mathematics Instruction

The success of each instructional approach is influenced by other decisions that teachers make about mathematics instruction and its delivery. New and experienced teachers ask questions about the amount and types of practice and homework they should assign. They also make decisions about how to organize students for instruction. In addition, they encourage mathematical conversations by the type of questions they ask. Decisions on these topics influence how they teach and the learning environment they create.

Practice

Practice is often equated with intense, isolated drills of number facts. In a constructive classroom, practice has a broader meaning. Practice in a constructivist sense means having many rich and stimulating experiences with a concept or skill rather than repetition of the same experience. The concept of area is developed when students measure various surfaces using tiles, cards, or sticky notes of different sizes. Understanding of area measurement is not expected to be a one-time event but an accumulation of related experiences. Informal games and learning center activities provide multiple experiences in learning. The trading game described in Chapters 9 and 10 helps students at different levels come to new understandings of how numbers work.

Guided and independent practice built into directed teaching/thinking lessons allows the teacher to observe and question students during learning. By assessing students, teachers decide whether some need additional developmental work and which ones are ready for independent practice or projects. Only after students have demonstrated understanding of concepts and proficiency is independent practice appropriate. Unless students are 70–80% proficient, practice may reinforce incorrect thinking. If sufficient time is spent on conceptual development with a variety of activities and teaching approaches, students build strong understanding, which reduces time and energy spent with practice.

When students understand number operations and develop strategies for learning facts, most are successful with fact practice. Without understanding or strategies, however, most find fact practice frustrating and defeating. Timed drills are cited as a major source of mathematics anxiety. By following some simple guidelines, teachers can avoid harmful aspects of drill:

- Develop concepts and skills before independent practice is started.

- Emphasize understanding and accuracy as the most important outcome. Speed is a secondary goal and varies from student to student.

- Keep practice sessions short, perhaps 5 minutes.

- Use a variety of practice activities, including games, flash cards, and computer programs.

- Avoid comparison of students. The time required to master the facts differs from student to student.

- Allow children to monitor their own progress and record their improvement.

Homework

Homework seems like a rather simple issue, but homework practices are often complicated by issues such as the age of the child, the demands of the content, and the support and expectations of parents. Schools may adopt formal policies about the nature and amount of homework at different grade levels to provide some consistency in practice, but many homework policies are unwritten. New teachers should ask about the homework policies in a school.

Homework activities are usually of two types: exploratory or conceptual activities and independent practice of skills. At-home exploratory or conceptual activities connect school mathematics to home and back. Kindergartners might bring an object or picture that is "round" or "square" from home. Third-graders can find how far they travel from home to school on the bus, in the car, or by walking. Sixth-graders could look at the calories on food packages and create menus using a balanced food plan. Teachers also develop take-home backpacks with mathematics games, puzzles, or books to stimulate exploratory or practice activities.

Independent practice or drill activities often come from worksheets or textbook pages. Students should understand what they are to do so that they can complete the sheet with little assistance. Parents complain when students do not know what to do and when the homework takes too long to complete. More is not better. If students understand and are successful, 10 to 20 examples are sufficient. If students cannot complete 10 or 20 examples, assigning 50 or 100 creates frustration for students and parents. Some teachers set a time limit on homework, such as "work as many examples as you can in 10 minutes."

Responding to homework is another issue with many different opinions. Some teachers insist on grading homework, while others check for accuracy and understanding. By removing the emphasis on grading, teachers and students look at homework differently. Students who check their own homework can see what they got right and wrong. Self-assessment allows them to find out what they understand. With a quick check of homework, teachers identify strengths and weaknesses of the class or individuals. A mistake on homework or seat work provides an opportunity to correct a misunderstanding.

Grouping

Flexible grouping means that the teacher uses different instructional groups appropriate to the task or situation. Students can work independently, in small groups, or in the whole-class setting. Groups are not fixed but are reorganized periodically so children can work with a variety of peers on different tasks. Each grouping format has advantages and disadvantages. Students working alone gain independence but miss the opportunity to discuss, explain, and justify their work with peers. Whole-class instruction seems efficient because all the students appear to be learning the same thing, but individuals may not be engaged with the group task at all. When whole-group instruction is the only instructional format, some students are unchallenged and bored while other students are lost. Small groups of three to six students have many instructional advantages. Students of similar abilities or interests can work together for a unit or project.

POINT OF VIEW
Students' learning is supported when they have opportunities to describe their own ideas, hear others explain their thoughts, and explore various approaches. . . . Not only do students have more opportunities to speak more often [in small groups], but they may be more comfortable taking the risk of trying out their thinking during problem solving situations in the setting of a small group. (Burns, 1990, p. 25)

Flexible grouping avoids the dangers of **tracking**, or grouping students by ability and keeping students together for long periods. Tracking frequently works to the detriment of lower-ability students, with instruction that deemphasizes concepts and overemphasizes isolated skills. Tracking also isolates the lower-ability students from the modeling and support of more proficient students. The lower-track students often have the least qualified and least experienced teachers and the least opportunity to experience a full and balanced curriculum.

The equity principle advocates a balanced, stimulating curriculum for all students. When children have the opportunity to work together to learn and solve problems, all are advantaged. Using multiple instructional approaches increases interest in learning with lessons that draw on students' background experiences. Informal activities and projects increase enrichment of the curriculum, greater personalization of instruction, and student interaction and discussion.

Cooperative Group Learning

Cooperative learning is a grouping strategy that is designed to increase student participation by capitalizing on the social aspects of learning. In mathematics, students cooperate while working together on a geometry puzzle, measuring the playground, or reviewing for a test. Spencer Kagan (1994) identified basic principles for implementing cooperative learning successfully: positive interdependence, individual accountability, equal participation, and simultaneous interaction. **Positive interdependence** means that team success is achieved through the successes and contributions of each member. **Individual accountability** requires that team members be held accountable for contributions and results of the team effort. Every student on the team is responsible for learning the content and skill, and the team is accountable for all the team members' being successful. **Equal participation** means that team members have equal opportunity to participate; an activity is not dominated by one member, nor can members choose not to participate. In traditional instruction, interchanges are often between the teacher and one student at a time. Cooperative learning involves several students at the same time—**simultaneous interaction**.

In cooperative learning students are organized in groups, or teams, that are heterogeneous so that students with different skill levels, ethnic and cultural backgrounds, socioeconomic status, and other characteristics work together. English-language learners work with bilingual students or English speakers. Teachers balance teams with higher-, middle-, and lower-skill students. Simpler, shorter mathematics tasks, such as covering the desk with tiles or playing a game on addition facts, may be done in pairs.

Cooperative-learning activities may be done with two to six students, but many teachers prefer teams of four because they are small enough for active participation by everyone and large enough for diversity of members and roles. Larger teams result in students' withdrawing from tasks and observing rather than participating. Many teachers assign specific roles within the teams, such as recorder, reporter, materials manager, teacher contact, and convener. Students rotate roles so they all gain social and organizational skills.

Team building and cooperative skills are also essential to cooperative learning. Team members bond by sharing who they are, where they have been, and what they aspire to become. Choosing a team name, designing an insignia, or creating a motto encourages team pride and identity. Students learn about each other and appreciate the skills and experience each one brings to the task. Interpersonal skills are developed through cooperation with teammates. Students learn to participate actively and equally, to share and rotate responsibilities, and to report results of group activities. An effective teacher promotes cooperative skills by modeling them, selecting students to role-play for practice, and holding discussions and evaluations of cooperative efforts.

Kagan (at **http://www.cooperativelearning.com**) describes 20 cooperative learning structures for different purposes from complex to simple tasks. Students unfamiliar with cooperative learning begin with simple activities and structures for a specific task for a short time. In Pairs/Check two students solve problems, check each other, and correct each other if needed. For Think/Pair/Share individuals work individually on a problem or task, then discuss their results with a partner, and finally share with all members of the team to see if all team members understand the content or process.

A cooperative structure of intermediate complexity is Numbered Heads Together. When a learning task and objective is presented, each team is responsible for all members' mastering the content or skill. The teacher calls on team members by number. If the team member answers a question or demonstrates a skill, the team earns points. In Jigsaw students leave their home team to become part of an expert group. Each team member becomes an "expert" on one aspect of the content or skill and teaches the home team (Figure 5.11). If the topic is

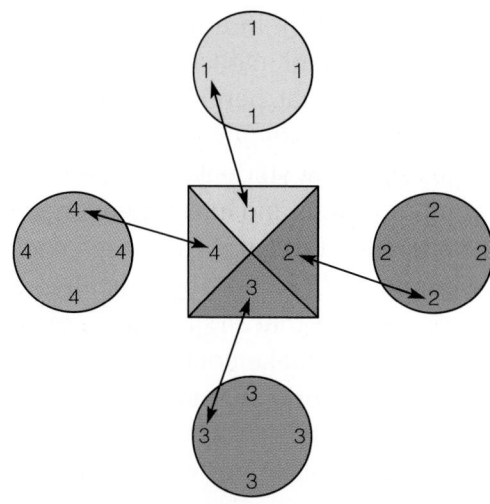

Figure 5.11 In Jigsaw members of the home team join an expert team to learn something new, then return to teach their teammates what they learned.

angles, students become experts on acute angles, right angles, obtuse angles, and measuring angles. When all parts of the content come together, students gain a complete understanding of angles. Jigsaw places responsibility on each team member to contribute to the overall completion of a divided task, story, or chapter.

Students learning English benefit from cooperative learning because they use and hear English in a less threatening context than whole-class discussions. Cooperative groups accommodate students with learning disabilities as well as gifted and talented students. Students with learning disabilities benefit from interaction with other students. Students proficient in mathematics extend their understanding when they teach others and exchange ideas with team partners. For students with limited mathematics proficiency, group cooperation supports their learning.

Cooperative learning also benefits students from different cultural and ethnic backgrounds. Lee Little Soldier (1989) says that cooperative learning supports the Native American value of learning based on cooperation rather than competition. She notes that "traditional Indian families encourage children to develop independence, to make wise decisions, and to abide by them. Thus the locus of control of Indian children is internal, rather than external, and they are not accustomed to viewing adults as authorities who impose their will on others" (pp. 162–163).

Carol Malloy (1997), in a discussion of African American students and mathematics, observes, "Instructional models that permit students to participate in cooperative rather than competitive learning activities will allow students to take advantage of their community focus and interdependence as well as their preference for learning through social and affective emphases" (p. 29). The structure of cooperative groups means that all students have opportunities to participate, make contributions, and share the results of their work. Instead of every person for him- or herself, cooperative learning is based on the Three Musketeers philosophy of one for all, and all for one. The group succeeds only when all the partners succeed.

Cooperative learning has been the subject of research for more than 30 years. Research and reviews of the literature about cooperative learning by Slavin (1987, 1989) attest to its benefits for student achievement. Of 68 studies on cooperative learning that were judged to be adequately controlled, 72% showed higher achievement for cooperative-learning groups. Cooperative approaches are effective over a range of achievement measures and different students; the more complex the outcomes (higher-order processing of information, problem solving), the greater the effects. Marzano and colleagues (2003), in an extensive review of research on instructional strategies, found that cooperative learning was highly effective in raising student achievement an average of 30 percentile (Marzano, 2003).

Encouraging Mathematical Conversations

Teachers encourage or discourage talk and thinking with the questions they ask children. While watching informal activities, checking for understanding in a lesson, or guiding an investigation, teachers need to ask more open-ended questions. **Open-ended questions** ask students to explain their reasoning. **Closed questions** call for short, specific answers.

Closed Questions	Open-Ended Questions
What is the area of the rectangle?	How do you determine the area of the rectangle?
Does Cereal x cost more or less than Cereal y?	Would you buy Cereal x or Cereal y? Why?
What is the formula for the area of this triangle?	Given this triangle, how could you determine its area? Is there more than one way to show it?

Asking good questions is an important teaching skill to develop. Without preparation, teachers tend to ask questions that have short, factual answers. Good questions challenge students to think at a deeper level. The teacher can write several open-ended questions in a lesson to elicit student understanding and misconceptions. After asking higher level questions, teachers should also allow enough time, called wait time, so that one or more students can respond and engage in discussion.

Managing the Instructional Environment

Managing the instructional environment also influences instruction. Teacher decisions about the time, space, materials, textbooks, and other resources for teaching can encourage or discourage student interaction and increase or decrease independence and responsibility of children managing their own learning.

Time

Teachers seldom say that they have too much time for teaching. Careful planning helps teachers maximize engaged learning time for active learning. Long-range planning helps teachers balance topics throughout the year. Standards have a scope and sequence of content and process, but teachers allocate time for introduction, development, and maintenance of concepts and skills throughout the year. Teachers also balance time for mathematics with other subjects. If mathematics is scheduled for 1 hour daily, the teacher has about 180 hours to develop knowledge and skills. Every minute is precious.

Teachers maximize time by integrating mathematics with different subjects. Measuring temperature or mass addresses science and mathematics standards. A graphing lesson that compares state or country populations includes mathematics skills and social studies content. Interdisciplinary planning means instructional time does double duty

If mathematics lasts 50 minutes or an hour, an effective teacher maximizes student engaged time with a variety of activities by using a parallel schedule (Figure 5.12). Some students participate in directed lessons while others work in learning centers, on projects, on the computer, or on seat work. The teacher teaches a whole-group lesson, reteaches with a small group, assesses individuals, and moni-

Figure 5.12
Parallel-activities schedule

	15–20 minutes		30–45 minutes		
What the Teacher Does	Whole-Class Lesson	Monitor	Small-Group Reteaching	Assessment	Closure
What the Students Do	Whole-Class Lesson	Exploration and Investigation *Learning Centers *Games *Small Group		*Seatwork *Computer *Individual Assessment	Closure

tors student work during the period. The teacher provides closure to the math period by reviewing major points and discussing issues and questions raised by students. Offering a variety of different learning activities is important whether teachers plan a fixed mathematics period, an integrated day, or a parallel-activity schedule.

Space

How teachers organize space in the classroom also influences the classroom climate. A classroom with desks lined up in rows with the teacher's desk in front implies a teacher-centered approach. If desks are arranged in groups of four or tables with centers and materials displayed around the room, the room invites more student interaction (Figure 5.13). Even

if student desks are in rows, teachers may allow students to move their desks together for activities or to work together on the floor or at a table. Changing the room arrangement is natural as children progress and new topics are introduced. Displaying student work on bulletin boards also reinforces the topics being studied. Students can post samples of work or alternative answers to problems. Then the bulletin board contributes to discussion of mathematics concepts and ideas.

Learning Centers

Learning centers are areas in the classroom set up with materials that students can use in their learning. With learning centers students engage in informal or exploratory work, review and maintain

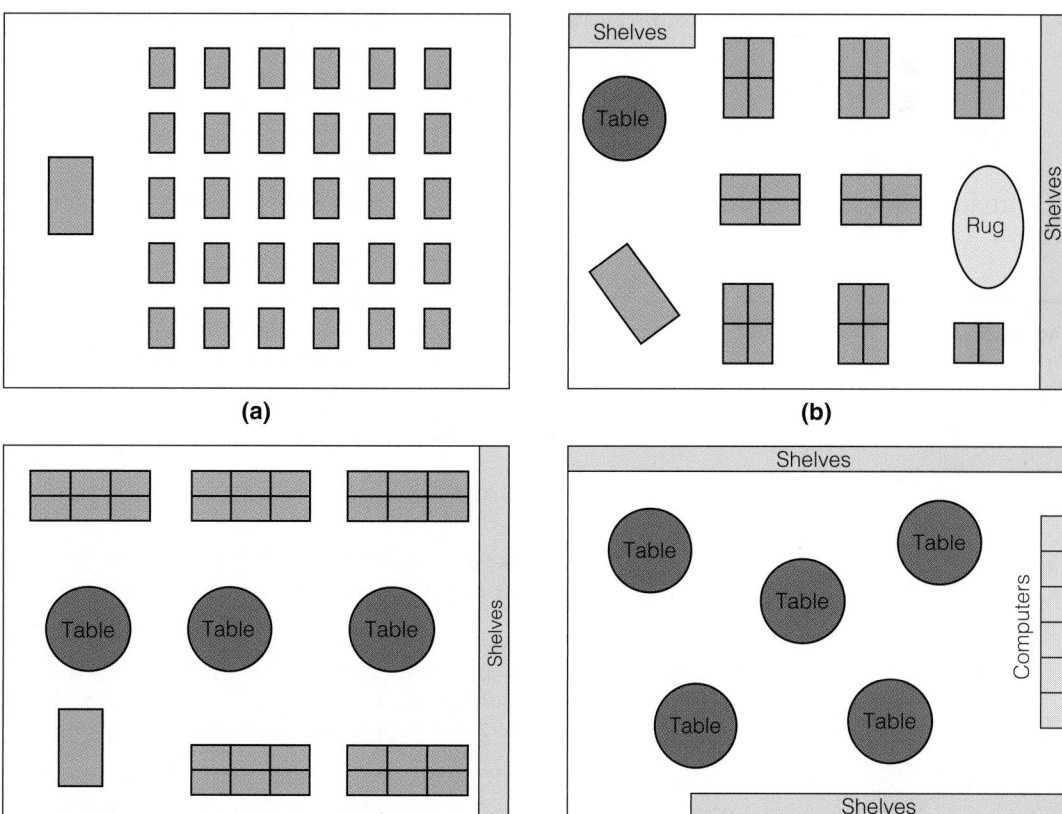

Figure 5.13 Classroom arrangements: (a) traditional classroom; (b) classroom with table and rug for group work, games, or manipulatives; (c) classroom with tables for projects and learning centers; (d) mathematics laboratory

prior skills, and conduct problem-based investigations. Students can work independently and/or have specific tasks that are required. Some learning centers contain a variety of manipulatives that can be used every day in mathematics instruction: calculators; games, puzzles, and books; paper, crayons, and marking pens. Other centers support specific instructional objectives. For studying geometry, the center might include geometry puzzles, geoboards, tangrams, and pattern blocks.

- A data center may contain spinners, number cubes, a clipboard for data collection, and a computer for entering data, analyzing, and displaying graphs.

- A sand or water tub with plastic containers of various sizes and units provides exploration of volume and capacity.

- A game center includes games and puzzles for developing strategy, practicing number facts, or learning geometry terms.

- Computers are set up with software selected to support the instructional goal or maintain skills from earlier units.

- A classroom store may be adapted to different instructional purposes. Play money and empty product boxes are all that primary-grade children need to play store while they learn about the exchange of money for goods. Third- and fourth-graders pay and make change, practicing subtraction skills. Fifth- or sixth-graders can set up a real store in which students buy school pencils or

notebooks and keep records of the profit and loss in the store.

Task cards or other assignment options in the learning center encourage independent work. For probability the assignment shown in Figure 5.14 might be posted. The task card for measurement illustrated in Figure 5.15 guides students' measurement activities with a centimeter ruler. Advance planning and selection of materials is essential for implementation of learning centers, but because they do not require constant supervision by the teacher, the teacher can be engaged in other instructional or assessment tasks. However, rotating and updating materials in the center is important because new options increase students' interest.

Manipulatives

Manipulatives, sometimes called objects to think with, include a variety of objects—for example, blocks, scales, coins, rulers, puzzles, and containers. Stones or sticks were probably the first manipulatives used; today the choice of materials seems endless, with educational catalogs full of materials that support mathematical thinking (see Appendix B). Manipulatives can be as simple as folding paper to demonstrate fractional parts or as elaborate as a classroom kit of place-value blocks. The value of a manipulative is in its use. Skilled teachers help students discover mathematics embedded in the materials. Matching the manipulatives to the concept or operation being taught is the key for using them to scaffold students' understanding.

Figure 5.14
Probability assignment for learning center

Exploring Probability

Each group is to select one probablility device: spinner, die, or coin. Follow the directions and record the number of times for each result.

- If you choose a spinner, spin it 50 times and count how many times the pointer stops at each color.

- If you select a die, roll it 50 times and count how many times each number lands on top.

- If you have a coin, toss it 50 times and record the number of heads and tails.

When you have completed the task, discuss the results, make a table or graph showing the results, and write a statement that tells what you have observed. Was this the result you expected, or did it surprise you?

This activity should take about 15 minutes. You may repeat this assignment three times with different probability devices. Place the results of your experiment, with conclusions, in your folder.

Figure 5.15
Task card for measurement

Using Centimeters

Use the centimeter ruler to measure the items and answer the questions. Use a complete sentence to answer each question. Compare your answers with those of another student. If there are any discrepancies, measure the objects again to resolve them.

1. How many centimeters long is the plastic pen?

2. How many centimeters long is the yellow spoon?

3. How many centimeters long is the film box? How wide is it? Is the end of the film box shaped like a square?

4. How many centimeters long is the strip of blue paper?

5. What are three things in the room that are less than 20-centimeters long? How long is each thing?

Manipulatives can be packaged for easy distribution and compact storage. Plastic shoeboxes and zip bags are often used for these reasons. Because schools cannot buy every manipulative for every teacher; sharing resources is essential. With a central mathematics storage area for the school or grade level, teachers can check out materials as they teach a topic.

Some people believe that manipulatives are just for younger children or for slow learners. However, manipulatives support learning of concepts by creating physical models that become mental models for concepts and processes. Many manipulatives can be used for several mathematics concepts. Teachers need to know what concepts are being developed by the manipulative so they can encourage students to develop the concept or skill. Table 5.3 shows the connection between mathematical concepts with appropriate manipulatives.

Textbooks and Other Printed Materials

Although recent textbook series claim to address the NCTM and state standards, research shows that they are only partially successful. Written to appeal to the widest audience, textbooks include a little of everything. Used in a conceptual teaching plan, textbooks provide units and lessons with activities, games, extension activities, and evaluation strategies. Teachers exercise professional judgment by determining how well any materials connect to standards and learning expectations of the state and district. Effective teachers start with the standards, not the textbook chapters, to balance topic coverage of them. Relying on a textbook for a long-range plan may put too much emphasis on a topic of limited value and reduce treatment of other topics. Checking the developmental sequence of skills is important. One teacher found that measurement to the quarter inch was presented before students had studied fractional parts. She introduced fractions before starting the measurement lesson.

Textbooks and other materials are effective only if they serve the learning needs of the students. Even when a textbook includes informal and exploratory activities to open a lesson, some teachers start with sample problems. Whether teachers use the developmental lesson from the textbook or create their own, concept development is essential. Eliminating exploratory developmental activities undermines children's understanding of the core concept.

NCTM and many commercial publishers provide supplementary materials that support the standards. The number of lessons, games, and activities available on the Internet is almost limitless; however, many materials posted on the Internet have not undergone editing or a selection process. Reviewing activities is required to match the content and learning needs of the children. Vendors can also provide

TABLE 5.3 **Mathematical Concepts and Their Appropriate Manipulatives**

Angles
Protractors, compasses, geoboards, Miras, rulers, tangrams, pattern blocks

Area
Geoboards, color tiles, base-10 blocks, decimal squares, cubes, tangrams, pattern blocks, rulers, fraction models

Classification and Sorting
Attribute blocks, cubes, pattern blocks, tangrams, two-color counters, Cuisenaire rods, dominoes, geometric solids, money, numeral cards, base-10 materials, polyhedra models, geoboards, decimal squares, fraction models

Common Fractions
Fraction models, pattern blocks, base-10 materials, geoboards, clocks, color tiles, cubes, Cuisenaire rods, money, tangrams, calculators, number cubes, spinners, two-color counters, decimal squares, numeral cards

Constructions
Compasses, protractors, rulers, Miras

Coordinate Geometry
Geoboards

Counting
Cubes, two-color counters, color tiles, Cuisenaire rods, dominoes, numeral cards, spinners, 10-frames, number cubes, money, calculators

Decimals
Decimal squares, base-10 blocks, money, calculators, number cubes, numeral cards, spinners

Equations/Inequalities;
Equality/Inequality; Equivalence
Algebra tiles, math balance, calculators, 10-frames, balance scale, color tiles, dominoes, money, numeral cards, two-color counters, cubes, Cuisenaire rods, decimal squares, fraction models

Estimates
Color tiles, geoboards, balance scale, capacity containers, rulers, Cuisenaire rods, calculators

Factoring
Algebra tiles

Fact Strategies
10-frames, two-color counters, dominoes, cubes, numeral cards, spinners, number cubes, money, math balance, calculators

Integers
Two-color counters, algebra tiles, thermometers, color tiles

Logical Reasoning
Attribute blocks, Cuisenaire rods, dominoes, pattern blocks, tangrams, number cubes, spinners, geoboards

Measurement
Balance scale, math balance, rulers, capacity containers, thermometers, clocks, geometric solids, base-10 materials, color tiles

Mental Math
10-frames, dominoes, number cubes, spinners

Money
Money

Number Concepts
Cubes, two-color counters, spinners, number cubes, calculators, dominoes, numeral cards, base-10 materials,

Cuisenaire rods, fraction models, decimal squares, color tiles, 10-frames, money

Odd, Even, Prime, and Composite Numbers
Color tiles, cubes, Cuisenaire rods, numeral cards, two-color counters

Patterns
Pattern blocks, attribute blocks, tangrams, calculators, cubes, color tiles, Cuisenaire rods, dominoes, numeral cards, 10-frames

Percent
Base-10 materials, decimal squares, color tiles, cubes, geoboards, fraction models

Perimeter and Circumference
Geoboards, color tiles, tangrams, pattern blocks, rules, base-10 materials, cubes, fraction circles, decimal squares

Place Value
Base-10 materials, decimal squares, 10-frames, Cuisenaire rods, math balance, cubes, two-color counters

Polynomials
Algebra tiles, base-10 materials

Probability
Spinners, number cubes, fraction models, money, color tiles, cubes, two-color counters

Pythagorean Theorem
Geoboards

Ratio and Proportion
Color tiles, cubes, Cuisenaire rods, tangrams, pattern blocks, two-color counters

Similarity and Congruence
Geoboards, attribute blocks, pattern blocks, tangrams, Miras

Size, Shape, and Color
Attribute blocks, cubes, color tiles, geoboards, geometric solids, pattern blocks, tangrams, polyhedra models

Spatial Visualization
Tangrams, pattern blocks, geoboards, geometric solids, polyhedra models, cubes, color tiles, Geofix Shapes

Square and Cubic Numbers
Color tiles, cubes, base-10 materials, geoboards

Surface Area
Color tiles, cubes

Symmetry
Geoboards, pattern blocks, tangrams, Miras, cubes, attribute blocks

Tessellations
Pattern blocks, attribute blocks

Transformational Geometry: Translations, Rotations, and Reflections
Geoboards, cubes, Miras, pattern blocks, tangrams

Volume
Capacity containers, cubes, geometric solids, rulers

Whole Numbers
Base-10 materials, balance scale, number cubes, spinners, color tiles, cubes, math balance, money, numeral cards, dominoes, rules, calculators, 10-frames, Cuisenaire rods, clocks, two-color counters

Concepts matched with manipulatives developed by National Supervisors of Mathematics (1994).

many written and computer-based instructional resources that can be used in planning and implementing exciting instruction.

Children's Literature

Only 20 years ago few children's books that focused on mathematics were available beyond simple number books. Now concept books on every mathematical topic are a great addition to the materials teachers can use for teaching and learning. Books introduce concepts in realistic or imaginary settings that stimulate children's interest and thinking. In Chapters 8–20 children's books on each content topic are listed. Bibliographies of children's books organized by concept are available on several Internet sites, with activities to extend the concept.

ⒺXERCISE

Find a bibliography of mathematics concept books with an Internet search. Compare the topics to the NCTM content and process standards. ●●●

Summary

Effective teachers actively engage students in meaningful mathematics tasks using a variety of instructional approaches, including informal and exploratory activities, directed teaching/thinking lessons, and projects and investigations. Exploratory activities involve students in independent work with manipulatives and games and allow them to develop an intuitive understanding of concepts through their experiences. In directed teaching/thinking lessons teachers guide students through a series of interactive experiences. Lessons are not lectures and are not passive in nature; they require students to engage in a problem or situation that requires development of mathematics skills and concepts. Projects and investigations are good extensions of learning that allow students to refine their understanding and apply skills. Using a variety of instructional approaches allows students with different skills, interests, and needs to be challenged. Unit planning, weekly planning, and daily planning provide a structure to build concepts in a logical sequence of lessons and activities that move from simple to complex, concrete to symbolic, and specific to generalized.

Teachers confront many issues and make many organizational and management decisions that influence the learning environment. Decisions are based on understanding state and local curriculum standards and providing a safe and stimulating environment for learning. The role and amount of practice and homework are practical issues. Homework can consist of conceptual or practice activities. Practice should be assigned only if students have developed a skill, or else they will be frustrated and will practice the skill incorrectly.

Teachers decide whether to teach large groups, small groups, or individuals, depending on the needs of students on a specific lesson. Cooperative-learning groups require students to work together to complete tasks and master content. Cooperative learning benefits students with learning disabilities, gifted and talented students, ethnic and cross-cultural groups, and English-language learners because all students are supported in a positive social climate focused on learning.

Decisions regarding grouping and teaching strategies connect to classroom decisions about time allocation, space arrangements, and choice of materials. Because teachers have limited time, careful scheduling is required to provide time for different instructional approaches, activities, and groupings. Flexible seating arrangements encourage group cooperation and sharing. Learning centers contain learning materials and assignments for investigations, projects, and independent tasks. Manipulatives are an essential part of teaching mathematics because they help students develop physical models to represent mathematics operations. All students need the benefits of manipulatives in learning mathematics. Textbooks can be valuable resources when teachers use them to support developmental learning. They contain lessons using manipulatives and provide many suggestions for games and enrichment. Teachers must review textbooks and other resource materials carefully to make sure they support the scope and sequence of their curriculum. Children's literature that addresses mathematical concepts is available for all topics. Children's literature helps students relate mathematics to real or imagined situations. Lists of books and lesson plans are available on the Internet.

Study Questions and Activities

1. Select one performance objective from your state or district objectives. Find a lesson plan on the Internet that might be used to teach the objective. Does the lesson plan include all the parts of the model lesson plan?

2. Observe a mathematics lesson. Did the teacher's lesson fit the lesson cycle or the model lesson plan?

3. Interview a teacher who uses cooperative learning. Ask how activities are organized. Are any structures that are described in this textbook used in the class? If you cannot find a teacher who uses cooperative learning, ask if they have ever used cooperative learning and what they found were the strengths and weaknesses of cooperative learning.

4. Observe two classrooms and note how each teacher organizes the classroom. Consider student grouping, classroom arrangement, use of time, and availability of resources for student learning. How do the classrooms compare to the suggestions in this textbook?

5. Examine the teacher's manual from a recent elementary mathematics series. Is the book aligned with your state or district objectives? Do the lessons specify the performance objectives for each lesson? Are concepts adequately developed with activities and manipulatives before guided and independent activities are introduced? Are supplemental games and activities suggested? Is this a textbook you would like to use in your teaching? Why or why not? If you know a teacher who uses the textbook, ask for a response to the textbook.

Teacher's Resources

Andrini, B. (1998). *Cooperative learning and mathematics*. San Clemente, CA: Kagan Cooperative Learning.

Andrini, B. (1990). *Just a sample video*. San Clemente, CA: Kagan.

Brooks, J., & Brooks, M. (1999). *In search of understanding: The case for constructivist classrooms*. Alexandria, VA: Association for Supervision and Curriculum Development.

Burns, M. (1997). *What are you teaching my child?* Videotape. Sausalito, CA: Math Solutions Inc.

Checkley, K. (2006). *Priorities in practice: The essentials of mathematics K–6*. Alexandria, VA: Association for Supervision and Curriculum Development.

Debolt, V. (1998). *Write! Mathematics: Multiple intelligences and cooperative learning writing activities*. San Clemente, CA: Kagan Publishing.

Kagan, S. (1997). *Cooperative learning*. San Clemente, CA: Kagan Cooperative Learning.

Kagan, S., Kagan, L., & Kagan, M. *Reaching the mathematics standards through cooperative learning: Video and teacher guide (Grades K–8)*. San Clemente, CA: Kagan Publishing.

Kenney, J., Hancewicz, E., Heuer, L., Metsisto, D., & Tuttle, C. L. (2005). *Literacy strategies for improving mathematics instruction*. Alexandria, VA: Association for Supervision and Curriculum Development.

Silbey, R. (n.d.). *Mathematics higher-level thinking questions: Elementary (Grades 3–6)*. San Clemente, CA: Kagan Publishing.

Torp, L., & Sage, S. (2002). *Problems as possibilities: Problem-based learning for K–16 education* (2nd ed.). Alexandria, VA: Association for Supervision and Curriculum Development.

Wirth, D. (2004). *35 Independent math learning centers: K–2*. New York: Scholastic Inc.

CHAPTER 6

The Role of Technology in the Mathematics Classroom

The boundaries of mathematics education are moving, never to return to their former positions. New and emerging technologies are expanding how children learn mathematics and how teachers teach mathematics. Technological advances in mathematics are nothing new. Past technological advances, including the abacus (500 B.C.E.–1000 C.E.), the slide rule (c. 1600), and the pencil (c. 1800), had lasting effects on how mathematics was discovered, taught, and learned. The influence of these inventions pales in comparison to the technological advances of the 20th century. The inventions of the calculator, the computer, and the Internet promise to change mathematics learning to a far greater degree than the earlier inventions and will continue to do so, perhaps in ways we can not imagine.

POINT OF VIEW
Technology is an essential tool for teaching and learning mathematics effectively; it extends the mathematics that can be taught and enhances students' learning. (*NCTM News Bulletin,* January/February 2004, p. 2)

NCTM included a technology principle in *The Principles and Standards for School Mathematics* (National Council of Teachers of Mathematics, 2000). The technology principle states (p. 24):

Technology is essential in teaching and learning mathematics; it influences the mathematics that is taught and enhances students' learning.

As the technology principle suggests, the calculator, computer, and the Internet are no longer extravagant frills or add-ons. They are now essential for teaching and learning mathematics in the 21st century.

In this chapter you will read about:

1 Appropriate uses of handheld calculators in the classroom

2 Research that supports using calculators to learn mathematics

3 Criteria for selecting effective mathematics software programs

4 The Internet as a tool for teaching mathematics

5 Research that validates using virtual manipulatives to learn mathematics

Calculators

Calculator use in the mathematics classroom has sparked more controversy than any other technological development. Opponents of calculators in the classroom fear the erosion of students' skills, their diminished memory of basic facts, and their inability to perform mental math or make everyday estimations. Such concerns are not unreasonable, and many parents share these concerns. Teachers can help parents allay these concerns and develop a more positive attitude toward calculators in the classroom (see Hillman & Malotka, 2004). To be sure, calculators in the hands of students without any guidance is not necessarily a good thing. However, appropriate use of calculators can enhance students' ability to perform mathematics.

NCTM has taken the following position (National Council of Teachers of Mathematics, 2005):

> School mathematics programs should provide students with a range of knowledge, skills, and tools. Students need an understanding of number and operations, including the use of computational procedures, estimation, mental mathematics, and the appropriate use of the calculator. A balanced mathematics program develops students' confidence and understanding of when and how to use these skills and tools. Students need to develop their basic mathematical understandings to solve problems both in and out of school.

Calculator Use

Calculators are neither the cure-all for learning mathematics nor the end of learning basic facts and algorithms. The calculator is a tool that, if properly used in the classroom, augments understanding of numbers and operations. But it is not a substitute for understanding an algorithm process or knowing basic number facts. A fifth-grade student who reaches for a calculator to determine 7×6 is not making suitable use of this tool, neither is a fourth grader who needs a calculator to decide if $5.00 is sufficient to purchase two items that cost $1.99 each. In contrast, a suitable use of a calculator might be to determine average daily high and low temperatures for a given time period.

These examples highlight the balance a classroom teacher must provide when calculators are used in the classroom. Sometimes mental mathematics should be used, whether recalling a number fact or solving 82×5 by mentally reforming the problem to $(80 \times 5) + (2 \times 5)$. In many cases mathematics problems and settings require estimation skills, as with the problem of purchases with $5 suggested earlier. Of course, there are times when a problem involves complex numbers and repetitious computations or when an exact answer is required. In these cases the calculator is the right tool.

Depending on the problem, however, computing an exact answer by mental math or paper and pencil can be faster than using a calculator. The following problems demonstrate how number sense can be more efficient than competent calculator use.

$$3\tfrac{3}{4} + 3\tfrac{3}{4} + 3\tfrac{3}{4} + 3\tfrac{3}{4} + \tfrac{1}{4} + \tfrac{1}{4} + \tfrac{1}{4} + \tfrac{1}{4} = ?$$

$$23 \times 10,000 = ?$$

$$86 + 74 = ?$$

When students have many experiences with problems that use mental math, estimation, pencil-and-paper computations, and calculations with a calculator, they develop the ability to discern the judicious use of a calculator while developing estimation and mental math skills. Teachers need to help students develop a sense about these types of mathematics solution strategies so students do not unnecessarily rely on a calculator to solve every mathematics problem.

Appropriate calculator use must be considered even with complex problems that require a specific answer. The objective of the problem itself can help determine if using a calculator is called for. If the objective of a problem is **process oriented**, then children can benefit from pencil-and-paper computation, using algorithms they have learned. A process-oriented problem concentrates students' efforts on getting the answer by using familiar algorithms. The method, or the process, is the focus. Such problems enable students to apply their algorithms in real-life situations and to appreciate how empowering such algorithms are, in contrast to sterile rote computations performed from a set of skill problems on a worksheet. Students might use their knowledge of multiplication to determine the area of their classroom in square feet and in square inches. If the objective of the problem is **product oriented**, then the focus is on the product students obtain to solve a problem. The calculator frees students from computational boredom and allows them to concentrate on the product or the answer. They can think about the problem itself and not on the computations that the problem requires. For example, a calculator would be a proper tool to use when finding the mean age in years and days of a classroom of students. Naturally many problems have elements of both process and product orientations, but usually one of them dominates the problem, as suggested by the problems here.

Benefits of Using a Calculator

Calculators can be used to enhance children's understanding of mathematics. Consider the following problem:

- Use each of the digits 4–9 only once to form two three-digit numbers with the largest product possible.

This problem is tedious to explore using pencil and paper to perform the computations. In fact, such a problem might not even be appropriate for pencil and paper. The problem requires too much time and effort to solve using a pencil. Using a calculator frees students from the time-consuming drudgery of computation and allows them to discover patterns and relationships about the multiplication algorithm that they use to produce the largest possible product.

> **POINT OF VIEW**
> For some the thinking is to allow calculator use for only those students who have mastered a concept. We provide crutches to the kids who don't need them. (Usiskin, 1988)

The calculator can also help students explore mathematics concepts for the first time. Imagine a child entering 21.34679 into a calculator and then multiplying by 10 repeatedly. The child then observes how the decimal point changes positions as each multiplication by 10 is entered. The calculator becomes a tool for understanding multiplication with powers of 10. Similarly, the child could enter a decimal fraction and then repeatedly divide by 10. Young children can enter a digit (say, 5), then press +, then =. The result will be 10. Press = again and the result is 15, and so forth. Children can produce the multiples of any number this way and thus can learn to skip count using the calculator.

Newer calculators allow students to enter and display common fractions and mixed numbers. A student who enters $\tfrac{1}{5} + \tfrac{1}{5}$ may be surprised to see the answer $\tfrac{2}{5}$ displayed rather than $\tfrac{2}{10}$ (computed incorrectly by adding the numerators and the denominators). Repeating the process with several more pairs of fractions will help the student anticipate a different

TI-15 Calculator

process for adding fractions than merely summing numerators and denominators.

ⒺXERCISE

Use a calculator to find the following products: 11 × 11, 111 × 111, and 1,111 × 1,111. Predict the product 11,111 × 11,111. Explain the pattern you discern. How did using a calculator help you? ●●●

TI-10 Calculator

As a practical condition when using calculators in the classroom, each student or each pair of students needs a calculator. In primary grades children may bring a calculator from home. Although all calculators follow the same logic in their computational operations, different manufacturers use different color keys and displays. Different models of calculators include a variety of operation keys beyond the digits and the four major operations (+, −, ×, ÷). These extra keys may confuse younger students. When possible, a school set of calculators appropriate for the grade level is the best choice so that all students are using the same calculator in class and from year to year.

Research on Calculators in the Classroom

Research has long supported appropriate calculator use in mathematics classrooms. For example, in an early meta-analysis of nongraphing calculator studies, the researchers concluded that "the use of hand-held calculators improved student learning" (Humbree & Dassart, 1994). In addition, students' attitudes toward mathematics also improved.

Subsequent studies have continued to show the benefits of using calculators in the classroom (Dunham & Dick, 1994; Groves, 1994). A recent synthesis of 54 research studies on the use of calculators in the classroom resulted in several important findings. A statistical meta-analysis of the studies showed that using calculators in the classroom had a positive effect on children's computational and conceptual mathematics development. Using calculators in the classroom was also linked with students' positive attitude toward mathematics. Perhaps surprisingly, students who used calculators did better on mental computation problems than did nonusers (Ellington, 2003).

The meta-analysis compared mathematics achievement on standard tests among classes that used calculators in different ways. One finding was that children who used the calculator in the classroom but not on the test performed up to expectations. These children maintained their pencil-and-paper skills despite using a calculator in class. Another finding was that for calculator use to benefit students, the students had to use calculators in their classroom for at least 9 weeks. Using calculators for shorter periods did not benefit students, and a few studies showed that such short-term use of calculators actually lowered students' achievement.

The conclusion of this meta-analysis was that "calculators should be carefully integrated into K–2 classrooms to strengthen the operational goals of these grades, as well as foster students' problem-solving abilities" (Ellington, 2003, p. 461). Subsequent studies have also continued to support the benefit of calculators to students' mathematics learning (Grouws & Cebula, 2004). For more about calculator use in the classroom, see **http://www.nctm.org/dialogues/1999-05.pdf**.

The subject of calculators in the classroom can be particularly worrisome for parents. Some parents still fear that their children's mathematics skills will waste away if they regularly use a calculator in mathematics. As part of informing parents about their children's education, a letter to parents describing how the calculator will be used in class can alleviate many parental concerns.

Dear Parent,

We are using calculators in your child's third-grade class this year. The calculator is another learning tool that will help your child discover mathematical relationships and learn mathematics concepts. We will use the calculator to explore whole number patterns and decimal patterns. We will also use the calculator to solve problems that would require long and tedious computation by hand. We will not use the calculator to replace learning mathematics facts or appropriate mathematics operations.

If you have questions about how we are using calculators at any time during the school year, ask your child to explain how we used calculators that week. If you have other questions please feel free to contact me.

Sincerely,

Ms. Nother

Middle school students can use the graphing capabilities of advanced calculator models for exploring statistical and algebraic concepts, for example, using graphing calculators to plot and identify coordinates of points. Students in upper middle school grades can use graphing calculators to investigate lines on a coordinate plane and the equations that produce these lines. These same graphing calculators can also perform geometry explorations using an adapted dynamic geometry software program (see Johnson et al., 2004).

Computers

The impact of computer technology on public education continues to expand. Almost one-fourth of school districts now provide laptop computers for their students (Borja, 2006). Some states are considering a graduation requirement that requires all students to pass an online course (Canavale, 2005).

Research About Computers in the Classroom

Some concerned educators and commentators fear that all the money and efforts being devoted to educational technology may be misplaced. Critics who fear a rush to computer technology frequently cite Ted Oppenheimer's "Computer Delusion" (1997). In this article Oppenheimer suggests that "computers are lollipops that rot your teeth," and he terms computers "just a glamorous tool" (pp. 46 and 47).

Learning in the Real World is a group of editors and parents who are also concerned about the growing trend to use computers in education. The concerns of this group are that computer funds might be better spent in other areas, that the isolation of students who work alone on a computer is not beneficial, and that the contrast between a virtual world and the real thing is lost. In their publications Learning in the Real World cites journals and newspapers around the country to support its position. For example, the group quotes the executive director of the National Association of Elementary School Principals, "If computers make a difference, it has yet to show up in achievement" (Learning in the Real World, 2000). Such concerns are well meaning and should be examined.

Certainly the computer is not a cure-all for every problem in education, especially mathematics. It is not enough to place a few computers in a classroom and expect improvement. Improvement will not come even if every child has her or his own computer. Along with the technology must come appropriate use of the computer, effective programs that take advantage of the computers, and proper training and knowledge by teachers who will use the computers in the classroom. When these criteria are met, then computer technology can benefit students. The research is clear: "Students can learn more mathematics, more deeply with the appropriate use of technology" (National Council of Teachers of Mathematics, 2000, p. 25).

POINT OF VIEW

Technology can be used in the elementary grades to enhance a concrete experimental approach to mathematical topics, enabling students to have greater success with a more symbolic, abstract approach later in school. (Flores, 2002, p. 96)

School districts that provided laptops to their students have seen grade point averages rise without any other changes in the education program (Borja, 2006). A study in Missouri found that providing one Internet-connected computer for every two students also improved students' test scores (Beglau, 2005). Other research findings support improved learning and student achievement when students use computers. When computer use is combined with effective software programs, engaging lessons, or the Internet, student achievement becomes clear (Anderson, 2000; Clements & Sarama, 2002; Cordes & Miller, 2000; Dirr, 2004; Marshall, 2002; North Central Regional Education Laboratory, 2005; Schacter, 1999; Wenglinsky, 1998).

Computer Software

In most cases classroom computers are linked to software programs or to the Internet. (We discuss the Internet later in this chapter.) In the early days of computers in the classroom, computer programs were essentially programmed learning tools. At the end of the session, the student's score was tabulated and this score determined the starting point for the next session. From this simple, pedantic start, educational software has evolved into a wide variety of learning tools.

Today the computer allows interactive exploration, discovery, practice, review, and much more. Mathematics software products available to teachers and parents run the gamut from simple entertaining games to a complete K–12 mathematics course. Research confirms that these programs can be effective teaching tools. Similar research supports other programs, for example, two dynamic geometry software programs, Geometer's Sketchpad and Cabri Geometry (Battista, 2002). Dynamic geometry software programs allow students to draw, distort, and measure shapes and explore a wide range of geometry concepts. These software programs help children "develop personally meaningful ways of reasoning that enable them to carefully analyze spatial problems and situations" (Battista, 2001, p. 74). Other software programs from various commercial vendors are frequently supported by research as well.

Fewer school districts are purchasing stand-alone software programs, preferring to use software that is bundled in an entire curriculum program (see **http://www.Riverdeep.com**) or associated with a mathematics textbook adoption. In addition, many teachers have found activities on the Internet that duplicate the activities of software programs. Nevertheless, the number of software programs continues to expand, focusing more on home use and less on school use. It can be beneficial to help parents determine what software programs they might purchase for their children. All programs are not created equal. It is important to select an effective mathematics software program for the classroom or the home. The following criteria may be helpful in selecting software programs for mathematics.

- Is the mathematics content correct?
- Is the mathematics at the appropriate level?
- Is the mathematics meaningful?
- Is the program user-friendly? (Not too dull, but not too many bells and whistles)
- Is the program at an appropriate level?
- Is the program highly interactive?

- Is the program engaging for students?
- Does the program develop mathematics thinking or simply drill mathematics facts/procedures?
- Does the program do what it claims?
- Does the program require higher-order thinking?
- Are there printed support materials such as blackline masters and student sheets?
- Is there an Internet site for further materials, teacher assistance, and updates?

The software programs in Table 6.1 meet these criteria and have been well received by young children and preservice elementary school teachers. Additional software programs are referenced in Chapters 8–19.

Before purchasing any software program, it is advisable to preview the program. Many vendors will supply interested teachers or parents with a CD containing a sample of their programs. Vendors also use the Internet to provide a preview of their software program.

EXERCISE

Interview a classroom teacher to determine what mathematics software is available for his or her students. ●●●

Some commercial publishers have begun to include a CD with their textbooks. The CDs contain a variety of materials, including games, lesson plans, problems, black-line masters, and interactive mathematics explorations. For example, each book in the Navigation series by NCTM contains a CD that provides additional reading for teachers, interactive explorations for students, and further materials on the Navigation topic. (The Navigation series is published by the National Council of Teachers of Mathematics. The series contains a book for each content strand at each grade band.) These CDs can be an effective ancillary for any textbook and should be carefully considered when purchasing a book or adopting a text for the classroom. See **http://www.ct4me.net/software_index.htm**, the home page of Computing Technology for Math Excellence, for an extensive list of mathematics software materials.

A growing trend is for publishers to put substantial parts of their textbook or the entire textbook

TABLE 6.1	Mathematics Software Programs
Grade	**Program**
4–6	Building Perspectives Deluxe (Pleasantville, NY: Sunburst Technology)
3–6	The Cruncher 2.0 (Torrance, CA: Knowledge Adventure)
4–8	Data Exploration Software (Emeryville, CA: Key Curriculum Press)
4–6	Data Explorer (Pleasantville, NY: Sunburst Technology)
4–7	Factory Deluxe (Pleasantville, NY: Sunburst Technology)
2–8	FASTT Math (http://www.tomsnyder.com)
4–8	Fathom Dynamic Statistics (Emeryville, CA: Key Curriculum Press)
4–7	The Geometer's Sketchpad (Emeryville, CA: Key Curriculum Press)
K–6	Glory Math Learning System (http://www.gloryschool.com)
2–6	The Graph Club 2.0 Deluxe (Watertown, MA: Tom Snyder Productions)
K–4	Graphers (Pleasantville, NY: Sunburst Technology)
4–6	Green Globs and Graphing Equations (Pleasantville, NY: Sunburst Technology)
1–8	MathAmigo (http://www.valiant-technology.com)
4–6	Math Arena (Pleasantville, NY: Sunburst Technology)
4–7	Math Munchers Deluxe (Novato, CA: Riverdeep/The Learning Co.)
K–10	Riverdeep Math Programs (many) (http://www.riverdeep.net)
4–8	Tabletop (Cambridge, MA: TERC/Broderbund)
4–8	Tinkerplots (http://www.keypress.com)
4–6	Zoombinis Island Odyssey (Novato, CA: Riverdeep/The Learning Co.)
4–6	Zoombinis Logical Journey (Novato, CA: Riverdeep/The Learning Co.)
4–7	Zoombinis Mountain Rescue (Novato, CA: Riverdeep/The Learning Co.)

on a CD. It is not clear how this new trend will play out. CD versions of nearly every major school-level mathematics text are available, although the issues of implementation are not clear. Some school districts are eliminating all books for middle and high school students and going electronic. There may be a desk copy of a mathematics book for students to use in school, but they have no personal book to take home. Instead, they access the book by using a CD on their laptop or the Internet. It is too early to assess the effects that such an electronic approach will have on student learning, but no doubt research studies will soon reveal their findings. Suffice it to say that the potential for a totally electronic mathematics class is here.

The Internet

More than calculators or any software program on a computer, the Internet has the potential to completely change mathematics learning and teaching. Hundreds of Internet sites provide lesson plans, test items, word problems, and interactive mathematics activities. The list of sites grows larger every month, with no signs of slowing down.

In Chapter 3 we addressed the question of equity that should be considered when using the Internet with students. Equity issues are important, but they may be mitigated by the numbers of students who are actively online. According to a 2006 survey by the Pew Internet and American Life Project, 87% of 12–17-year-olds are online (Cassidy, 2006). The reasonable expectation is that younger siblings also have Internet access. Such a high percent will likely increase, perhaps eliminating any concerns about equity.

Many Internet sites are designed to assist the teacher in almost every aspect of planning for teaching mathematics. Table 6.2 lists a few sites that are sources for assistance, but there are many more. These resources are only a few of the sites that are available to teachers (and students) at the click of a mouse.

The value of any website can be weighed in much the same manner as we suggested to evaluate software. In the case of lesson plans, determine if a site is juried. That is, are all the lesson plans submitted to a jury of professionals who determine if the plan meets demanding criteria before it is included on the site? Some websites will accept any lesson plans that are submitted, regardless of how poorly conceived. Similarly, other websites should be reviewed for their effectiveness before fully adopting them for any classroom use.

ⒺXERCISE

Go to http://www.LessonPlanz.com and find four mathematics lesson plans. Describe the features of the best and worst of the plans from the four plans you selected. ●●●

Another use of the Internet is for research and data gathering. In Chapter 19 we discuss the many ways data can be represented. The Internet has a

TABLE 6.2	Useful Mathematics Internet Sites

General Sites
- National Council of Teachers of Mathematics (http://www.nctm.org)

This is the website of the national mathematics teacher's organization. It contains many useful sites and links to many more.

- Math Forum (http://mathforum.org)

This website is full of interesting activities, virtual manipulatives, and engaging problems.

- PBS Mathline (http://www.pbs.org/teachersource/math.html)

This website contains detailed, well-written lesson plans on a wide variety of topics.

Lesson Plans
- http://www.thegateway.org
- http://www.LessonPlanz.com
- http://www.nytimes.com/learning/teachers/lessons/mathematics.html
- http://mathforum.com/alejandre/

Mathematics Dictionary
- http://www.wolfram.com
- http://www.didax.com/mathdictionary
- http://Pantheon.org/mythica.html
- http://www.teachers.ash.org.au/jeather/maths/dictionary.html
- http://www.amathsdictionaryforkids.com

Mathematics History
- http://www.hpm-americas.org
- http://www-groups.dcs.st-and.ac.uk:80/~history/
- http://www.agnesscott.edu/Lriddle/women/women.html

Word Problems
- http://www.mathstories.com
- http://www.mathsurf.com/teacher
- http://www.aaamath.com/

Graphing Software
- http://www.pair.com/ksoft/
- http://nces.ed.gov/nceskids/graphing
- http://www.cradlefields.com
- http://www.coolmath.com/graphit/index.html

limitless supply of engaging data that students can use to create various visual displays, from simple bar graphs to box-and-whisker plots. Table 6.3 is a list of websites that contain data about many different topics.

Virtual Manipulatives

The most exciting development on the Internet is the emergence of interactive or *virtual manipulatives*. A virtual manipulative is "an interactive, Web-based visual representation of a dynamic object that presents the opportunity for constructing mathematical knowledge" (Moyer et al., 2002, p. 372). Interactive activities (sometimes called *applets,* for "small applications") present children with an ever-expand-

ing number of interactive explorations that encompass all aspects of elementary mathematics, from simple counting and spatial visualization activities to graphing statistical data and explorations involving the Pythagorean theorem.

Virtual manipulatives can be especially beneficial to students who have special needs or speak English as a second language (Figures 6.1 and 6.2). Some applets allow children to perform explorations that would be difficult if not impossible in a classroom with real materials. In addition, older students who might consider some manipulative activities as too childish will engage in similar activities using virtual manipulatives.

TABLE 6.3	Internet Data Resources

Data Sets
- The Data Library: http://www.mathforum.org/workshop/sum96/data_collections/datalibrary
- InfoNation: http://www.cyberschoolbus.un.org
- Quantitative Environmental Learning Project: http://www.seattlecntral.org/qelp
- Exploring Data: www.exploringdata.cqu.edu.au
- StatLib: http://lib.stat.cmu.edu/datasets
- Statistical reference data sets: http://www.itl.nist.gov/div898/strd
- U.S. Census data: http://factfinder.census.gov/home/saff/main.html?_lang=en

Real-Time Data
- Air quality index from the EPA: http://www.epa.gov/airnow
- Earthquake activity from the USGS: http://www.earthquake.usgs.gov
- Weather information: http://iwin.nws.noaa.gov
- Satellite images: http://www.noaa.gov/satellites.html
- Marine data: http://www.oceanweather.com/data

NCTM-Sponsored Sites

NCTM sponsors several websites that are excellent resources for mathematics teachers:
- Illuminations: http://illuminations.nctm.org/Weblinks.aspx

This website links to hundreds of virtual manipulative websites. The sites can be searched by grade band (preK–2, 3–5, 6–8) and by topic.
- On Math: http://my.nctm.org/eresources/journal_home.asp?journal_id=6

On Math contains a number of interactive tasks imbedded in full lesson plans.
- Electronic journals: http://www.nctm.org

Electronic versions of *Teaching Children Mathematics* and *Mathematics in the Middle School* are available at this website.
- Figure this: http://www.figurethis.org/

This website contains more than 100 engaging problems that are colorfully presented. They are designed for students to solve with parents in a family math setting.

Table 6.4 provides a brief list of websites that contain many different applets for various grade levels and across many topics, as well as links to virtual manipulatives at other sites. This list is only a glimpse of the resources that the Internet provides. Use these websites as the starting point for your own explorations of sites that will enhance your teaching and provide exciting experiences for your students. We have included an Internet lesson plan in each of the content chapters in Part 2 to exemplify how to use the Internet in classroom teaching. In these chapters we have also described Internet math games that can help students learn mathematics and listed specific websites that relate directly to the mathematics content of the chapters.

EXERCISE

Visit three of the websites listed in Table 6.4, and engage in one of the activities at each site. Record your impressions after using each activity. Was the mathematics clear? What mathematics would children learn from this activity? ●●●

Many of the applets at the Internet sites listed in Table 6.4 contain activities that resemble activities of the software programs we listed earlier in this chapter. There may be some advantages to using the Internet for interactive explorations. There is no charge for using the Internet activities and no need to update any older applets. The Internet offers students constant access, regardless of their location or the time of day, allowing teachers to use out-of-class time for such explorations. Many activities can be downloaded, eliminating the need for Internet access. Internet sites allow students in many cases to

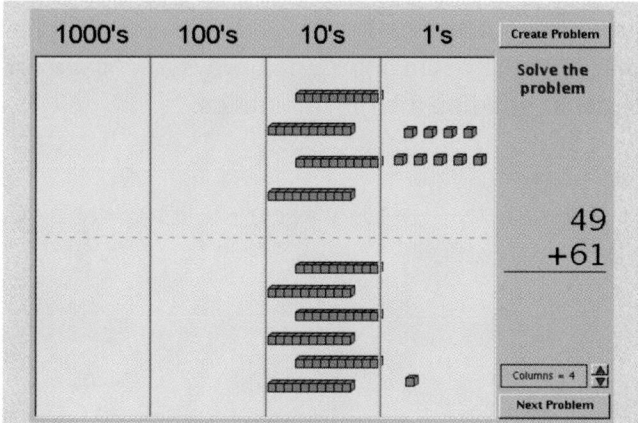

Figure 6.1 Screen capture of a virtual manipulative from the National Library of Virtual Manipulatives

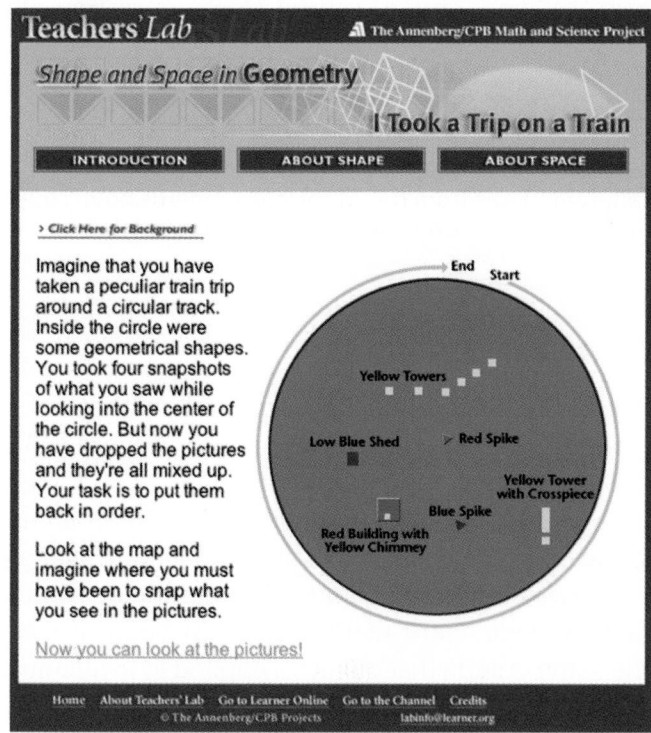

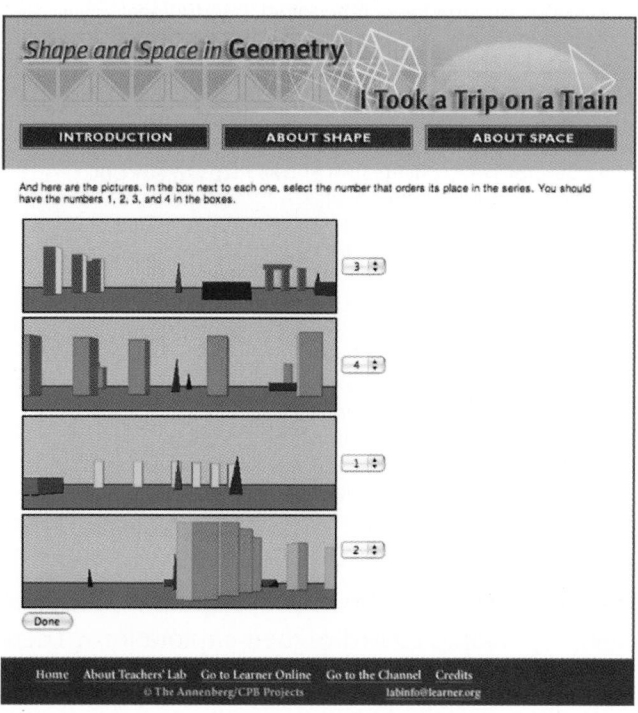

Figure 6.2 Screen capture of a virtual manipulative from the Annenberg/CPB Math and Science Project

TABLE 6.4 • **Interactive Internet Sites**

- Computer Technology for MathExcellence: http://www.ct4me.net//math_manipulatives.htm

This website provides links to the best applets of other websites and includes several of its own activities dealing with interactive calculators.

- National Library of Virtual Manipulatives: http://nlvm .usu.edu/en/nav/vlibrary.html

This website contains interactive activities from many other sites, categorized in grade bands (preK–2, 3–5, 6–8, and 9–12). Within each grade band the applets are further categorized by the five content strands that NCTM uses: number, algebra, geometry, measurement, and data/probability.

- Annenberg/CPB Math and Science Project: http:// www.learner.org/teacherslab/index.html

The Annenberg website contains several engaging applets in geometry that focus on spatial visualization and several applets that involve patterning.

- NCTM Illuminations: http://illuminations.nctm.org/ tools/index.aspx

This NCTM site contains literally dozens of engaging activities at all grade levels, categorized by grade bands (preK–2, 3–5, 6–8, 9–12) and content strands (number, algebra, geometry, measurement, and data/probability).

- Educational Java programs: http://www.arcytech.org/ java/

The mathematics activities include topics such as money, time, fraction bars, base 10 blocks, and pattern blocks.

- Shodor Education Foundation: http://www.shodor .org/interactivate/activities/index.html

This website contains more than 100 interactive explorations in the five content areas that NCTM uses: number, algebra, geometry, measurement, and data/probability.

- Math Education and Technology International Software: http://www.ies.co.jp/math/indexeng.html

This website contains 91 applets for middle school and 188 applets for higher mathematics. The middle school applets are mostly visual explorations of geometry relationships.

- The BBC Mathsfile Game Show: http://www.bbc .co.uk/education/mathsfile/

This website contains exceptional interactive games that challenge the user at several levels and in many different areas of mathematics.

- Kids Kount: http://www.fi.uu.nl/rekenweb/en

The Freudenthal Institute in the Netherlands sponsors this website. It contains extraordinary activities for developing spatial sense.

- Visual Fractions: http://www.visualfractions.com/

As the name suggests, this website presents visual displays of fraction relationships. This site contains many activities for developing fraction sense.

alter a website, add their own sketches or data, and keep a personal record of their explorations. There is an endless supply of virtual manipulatives, and cleanup is easy and instantaneous.

The full effectiveness of virtual manipulatives is still to be determined by research, but so far the findings are encouraging (Alejandre & Moore, 2003; Clements & McMillan, 1996; Keller & Hart, 2002). For children who have grown up playing video games and using computers, virtual manipulatives are not much different from using real manipulatives. Children in many cases are as comfortable manipulating tangram pieces on the computer screen as they are moving tangram pieces on a desktop (Figure 6.3). They benefit from both activities. Using the virtual or real manipulatives is not an either/or situation. Virtual manipulatives can enhance the mathematics of actual manipulatives, and vice versa. A comprehensive mathematics class will use both types of manipulatives in appropriate ways to engage students in building their mathematics.

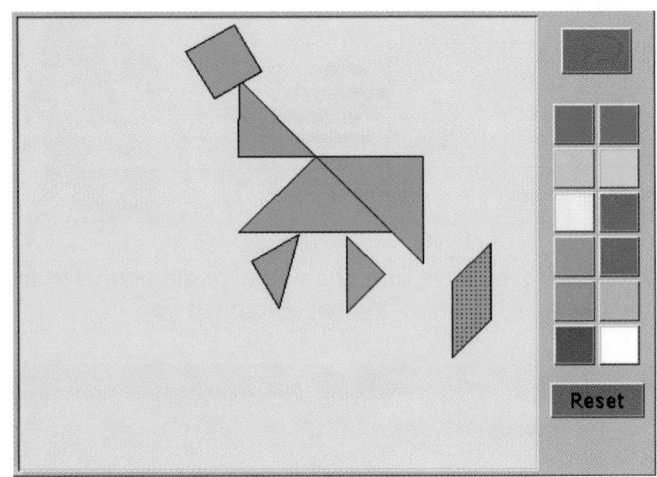

Figure 6.3 Screen capture of virtual manipulative tangram pieces from NCTM (http://standards.nctm .org/document/eexamples/chap4/4.4/#applet)

Computer Games

Another aspect of technology and mathematics learning involves electronic games (Figure 6.4). Advances in computer software and technology and the Internet have produced many entertaining games, ranging from captivating adventure games to puzzles and logic games. Can computer games help students learn mathematics? In point of fact, the same criteria that might be applied to evaluating a board game such as *Clue, Battleship,* or *Mancala* should be applied to computer games. Some factors to consider are the following:

1. What is the purpose of the game?

2. What content and/or skills will be addressed?

3. Does the game match the ability and maturity level of the students?

4. Can special-needs students play the game effectively?

5. How many students can play the game at one time?

6. How will students receive feedback?

7. What competition between students does the game encourage?

8. How can the teacher monitor and assess student learning?

Research suggests that mathematical games can be effective teaching tools. Computer games, termed digital game-based learning, can help students with a wide range of mathematical skills and content, ranging from number facts and shape identification to spatial sense and proportional reasoning (Prensky, 2000).

Computer games can help students recall number facts, practice number operations, and expand their mathematics vocabulary. In earlier times students resisted the drill and practice needed to develop their skills and recall. In the context of games, which students can play with classmates, the drudgery is essentially dissipated. Also, feedback is immediate and often comes from a colorful game character.

Engaging games can also serve as explorations or introductory experiences for students.

There are two sources of computer games: commercial software and the Internet. Examples of software games include the following:

POINT OF VIEW
When carefully selected, games can highlight specific mathematics concepts, activate strategic thinking, and create an opportunity to develop logical reasoning skills. (Martine, 2005, p. 94)

Everyday Mathematics:

- **http://www.emgames.com/demosite/index.html**
- **http://www.Techervision.com**
- Green Globs
- The Race to Spectacle City Arcade
- Math Arena
- The Amazing Arcade Adventure
- Pooling Around
- Extreme Yoiks!

Some Internet games are the following:

- **http://www.thefutureschannel.com**
- **http://my.nctm.org/standards/document/eexamples/index.htm**. See 4.2 and 6.2
- **http://www.funbrain.com**
- **http://www.mathfactcafe.com**
- **http://www.pbskids.org/cyberchase**
- **http://www.Aplusmath.com**
- **http://www.bbc.co.uk/schools/numbertime/index.shtml**
- **http://www.mathplayground.com/index.html**
- **http://www.mazeworks.com/home.htm**
- **http://www.mathcats.com**
- **http://www.bbc.co.uk/education/mathsfile/gameswheel.html**
- **http://www.mathsnet.net/puzzles.html**

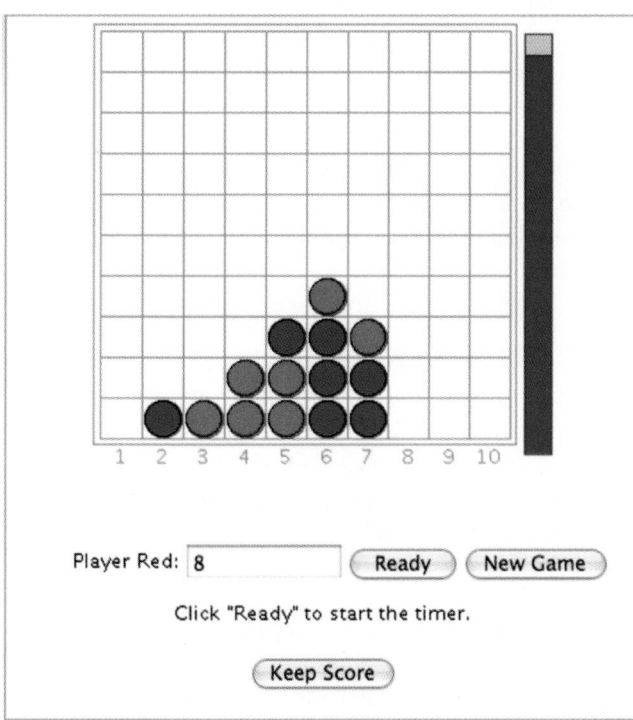

Figure 6.4 Screen capture of a BBC game

- http://www.learner.org/teacherslab
- http://www.visualfractions.com
- http://www.fi.uu.nl/rekenweb/en/
- http://www.firstinmath.com

POINT OF VIEW
Games can be utilized as a bridge to the mathematics curriculum and as a way to deepen and reinforce key concepts. (Hoyt et al., 1995, p. 3)

Research suggests that electronic games and activities using the computer and applets (interactive, dynamic activities) found on the Internet can also strengthen spatial visualization skills. Children engaged in these activities use virtual manipulatives to improve their spatial visualization skills (Keller & Hart, 2002).

Video Technology

Video technology is another recent development in educational technology. Video programming can be used to present professionals in the field using mathematics, to portray scenes from which data are derived and developed, and to present events (in real time or tape delay) that can be analyzed with mathematics, such as sporting events. Video programs can also show teachers presenting model lessons, classes of students engaged in mathematics explorations, and interviews with professionals, mathematicians, teachers, and students. Teachers can access video programming by means of DVDs, closed-circuit television, open airways, the Internet, or web casts. Two commercial sources of video programming are Futures Channel (**http://www.thefutureschannel.com**) and Annenberg Media (**htttp://www.learner.org**).

Summary

Technology has added three tools to help students learn mathematics: the calculator, the computer, and the Internet. Each has great potential for helping students build their mathematics knowledge. Nevertheless, none of them is a solution to the challenge of learning mathematics. They are not cure-alls. Inappropriate use of calculators or the computer can slow students' advancement in mathematics. A disorganized curriculum of virtual manipulatives can turn the study of mathematics into one giant video game. However, research clearly supports these technologies as effective tools for learning mathematics. We highly recommend using them in mathematics classrooms at any level.

Study Questions and Activities

1. How have you used calculators, computers, or the Internet in your mathematics learning? Did you use a calculator or the computer in your elementary classes or middle grades?
2. Visit lesson plan sites on the Internet, and read three lesson plans. Critique the lesson plans. Are they engaging? Will students learn mathematics?
3. Visit the Internet site http://www.fi.uu.nl/rekenweb/en, and play one of the games. How might this game help children learn mathematics?
4. Interview an elementary school teacher at a local school. Ask how often children use a calculator and/or a computer in class, and what mathematics lessons require their use.
5. Contact any of the software vendors listed in this chapter, and request a sample of their program (on a CD or on the Internet). Try a lesson or activity from the program, and record your impressions. Evaluate the lesson using the criteria on page 84.
6. Use each of the digits 4–9 only once to form two three-digit numbers with the smallest product possible.

Teacher's Resources

CAMP-LA. (1991). *Activities enhanced by calculator use. Book 1, Grades K–2; Book 2, Grades 3–4; Book 3, Grades 5–6.* Orange, CA: Cal State Fullerton Press.

Fey, J. (Ed.). (1992). *Calculators in mathematics education, 1992 yearbook of the National Council of Teachers of Mathematics.* Reston, VA: National Council of Teachers of Mathematics.

Kerrigan, John. (2004). *Using mathematics software to enhance elementary students' learning.* Reston, VA: National Council of Teachers of Mathematics.

Masalski, W., & Elliott, P. (Eds.). (2005). *Technology-supported mathematics learning environments: Sixty-*

seventh yearbook. Reston, VA: National Council of Teachers of Mathematics.

Olson, Judy, Olson, M., & Schielack, J. (2002). *Explorations: Integrating handheld technology into the elementary mathematics classroom.* Dallas: Texas Instruments Inc.

For Further Reading

Clements, D., & Sarama, J. (2002). The role of technology in early childhood learning. *Teaching Children Mathematics* 8(6), 340–343.

In this journal article Clements and Sarama outline the beneficial role that various facets of technology can have with early learners.

Duebel, P. (2006). Game on! How educators can translate their students' love of video games into the use of a valuable, multifaceted learning tool. *THE Journal* 33(6), 12–17.

This article relates video games to digital games that use virtual manipulatives to teach mathematics concepts. Duebel describes how classroom teachers can bridge the gap between video games and computer games that teach mathematics.

Ellington, Aimee. (2003). A meta-analysis of the effects of calculators in students' achievement and attitude levels in precollege mathematics classes. *Journal for Research in Mathematics Education* 5(34), 433–463.

Ellington summarizes the findings of 54 studies that explored the effects on student learning of using calculators in mathematics classrooms.

Hillman, S., & Malotka, C. (2004). Changing views: Fearless families conquering technology together. *Mathematics Teaching in the Middle School* 4(10), 169–179.

This article describes a workshop for parents and middle-school students that clarifies an appropriate role for using hand-held technology in learning mathematics.

Kerrigan, John. (2004). *Using mathematics software to enhance elementary students' learning.* Reston, VA: National Council of Teachers of Mathematics.

Kerrigan describes his program for encouraging students and their families to become comfortable and competent with calculators in the mathematics classroom.

Masalski, W., & Elliott, P. (Eds.). (2005). *Technology-supported mathematics learning environments: Sixty-seventh yearbook.* Reston, VA: National Council of Teachers of Mathematics.

This yearbook is a collection of articles about the practice of using technology in the mathematics classroom. Topics range from activities submitted by classroom teachers to findings by educational researchers.

Moyer, P., Bolyard, J., & Spikell, M. (2002). What are virtual manipulatives? *Teaching Children Mathematics* 8(6), 372.

Moyer and colleagues describe the benefits and limitations of using virtual manipulatives in elementary school mathematics.

Thompson, A., & Sproule, S. (2000). Deciding when to use calculators. *Mathematics Teaching in the Middle School* 4(6), 126–129.

As the title suggests, the article presents situations that are appropriate for calculator use and also presents situations when using a calculator may not benefit students.

CHAPTER 7

Integrating Assessment

Assessment is an essential skill for teachers. Without assessing what students know about mathematics and their level of skills, teachers cannot adjust instruction for students in the classroom. Accountability is another reason that assessment is essential. Statewide tests required by the No Child Left Behind Act of 2002 provide information about student achievement as it relates to state standards. They also identify general strengths and problems in the curriculum and instruction. Some tests include diagnostic information about individual student mastery of skills. But standardized tests rarely measure student readiness for learning, attitudes toward mathematics, or students' abilities to reason, solve problems, or communicate ideas about mathematics. Using a variety of assessment strategies, teachers learn about each child's strengths and needs and adjust their instruction to meet them.

In this chapter you will read about:

1 Integrating assessment with curriculum and instruction
2 Planning and organizing assessment strategies, including observations and interviews, written work, performance tasks, journals and portfolios, and paper-and-pencil tests
3 Recording student progress and determining levels of performance
4 Analyzing student work and making instructional decisions
5 Implementing assessment to determine readiness, check student understanding, diagnose problems, encourage student self-evaluation, and document mastery of curriculum objectives
6 Interpreting and using standardized tests for assessment

Connecting Curriculum, Instruction, and Assessment

Assessment is the process of finding out what students know and what they can do. As a result of assessment, teachers plan instruction to meet curriculum goals from the federal, state, and local standards. Curriculum, instruction, and assessment are three aspects of teaching that must be coordinated. Curriculum describes what concepts and skills are to be taught, instruction includes the methods and activities for learning, and assessment measures student progress toward the goals and objectives. Although instruction focuses on students' experiences to develop skills and concepts, "the fundamental role of assessment . . . is to provide authentic and meaningful feedback for improving student learning, instructional practice, and educational options" (Herman et al., 1992, p. vi). A comprehensive assessment program allows teachers to explore student performance in several ways:

- Determining prior knowledge and skills
- Understanding children's thinking
- Identifying strengths, problems, and misunderstandings
- Tracking academic progress over time
- Encouraging student self-assessment and responsibility in learning
- Evaluating mastery of a topic or skill

Standardized tests are one part of an assessment program, but teachers need classroom assessments that are more flexible for use in daily teaching and learning. They need assessments that:

- Address concepts, skills, and application of mathematics in meaningful contexts
- Coordinate with instruction and occur before, during, and following instruction
- Collect information about students through observations, interviews, written work, projects, presentations, performance tasks, and quizzes
- Use a variety of documentation techniques, including anecdotal records, checklists, rating scales, and scoring rubrics
- Allow analysis of information in planning instruction to meet needs of individuals and groups

The **scope** and **sequence** of curriculum goals and objectives provide structure for teaching and assessment. Scope describes the range of topics, concepts, and skills to be taught, whereas the sequence organizes knowledge and skills across grade levels, such as the sequence found in the NCTM grade band expectations in Appendix A. State and local schools often provide specific grade-level learning targets, or **benchmarks**.

Planning for Assessment

When teachers plan for assessment, they consider several questions about their purpose and methods of data collection, analysis, and interpretation:

- What student learning objectives or performance indicators are being assessed?
- How can students demonstrate the concept, skill, or application being assessed, or what task or assignment would be appropriate for demonstrating this objective?
- How can student work be recorded and documented?
- What levels of performance demonstrate student achievement—individually and collectively?
- What instructional actions can be taken based on assessment?

Answers to these questions are interrelated; the answer to one question influences decisions about other questions. The matrix of design questions in Figure 7.1 helps teachers consider many issues in an assessment program.

Performance Objectives and Tasks

Planning for assessment begins with clear learning objectives that guide instruction and assessment. A **performance objective** in a unit or lesson describes the expected student learning so that teachers and students understand what they are working toward. Performance objectives guide what the teacher teaches, what students are to learn, and what is going to be assessed during and after instruction. For example:

- The student counts objects in sets (less than 50) in groups of 2, 3, 4, and 5.
- The student describes and demonstrates the +0, +1, and +2 strategies for addition.

Figure 7.1
Assessment questions

Planning the assessment	Gathering evidence	Interpreting evidence	Using the results
What purpose does the assessment serve?	How are activities and tasks created or selected?	How is the quality of the evidence determined?	How will the results be reported?
What framework is used to give focus and balance to the activities?	How are procedures selected for engaging students in the activities?	How is an understanding of the performances to be inferred from the evidence?	How should inferences from the results be made?
What methods are used for gathering and interpreting evidence?	How are methods for creating and preserving evidence of the performances to be judged?	What specific criteria are applied to judge the performances?	What action will be taken based on the inferences?
What criteria are used for judging performances on activities?		Have the criteria been applied appropriately?	How can it be ensured that these results will be incorporated in subsequent instruction and assessment?
What formats are used for summarizing and reporting results?		How will the judgments be summarized as results?	

SOURCE: National Council of Teachers of Mathematics. (1995). *Assessment standards for school mathematics*. Reston, VA: Author, pp. 4–5.

- The student measures and records length in centimeters and inches.
- The student collects data and displays the data on a bar graph that is labeled and titled appropriately.

Performance indicators specify how the student demonstrates the performance objective. The objective in instruction becomes the performance indicator in assessment. The performance indicator describes what the teacher expects to see the student do, say, write, or demonstrate. It might include the situation and criterion for success. For example:

- Count sets up to 50 in groups of 2, 3, 4, and 5 accurately.
- Model +0, +1, and +2 strategies, identify examples, and generalize a rule.

- Measure and record the length of four objects using a meterstick (to the nearest centimeter) and a yardstick (to the nearest inch).
- Collect data from classmates on a favorite topic, and display the data on a bar graph that is labeled and titled appropriately. Write conclusions and/or questions about the information from the bar graph.
- Model addition problems through $9 + 9$ using manipulatives.
- Recall multiplication facts up to 10×10 with 90% or better accuracy.
- Measure mass of objects less than 1 kilogram accurately using a balance scale.
- Record results of rolling two dice in a table, and draw conclusions about the result.

- Identify critical information, and draw conclusions from tables and graphs.

Mathematical attitudes and study skills are also described with performance indicators. For example:

- Student stays with task, is persistent.
- Student contributes to discussion.
- Student cooperates with partners.
- Student presents findings using a spreadsheet or graphing program.

Creating Assessment Tasks

Lessons organized for assessment include a performance indicator—the task or assignment for students to demonstrate learning. A lesson on measuring length asks students to measure 10 objects in traditional and metric systems and record their measurements. The teacher might also make

sure that each student uses the correct technique. Assessment using two or more assessment strategies increases teacher confidence about student understanding.

Teachers can assess an objective through a variety of tasks or assignments. To identify the performance level of the learner, teachers could use concrete, pictorial, or symbolic representations in the instructional and assessment tasks. For example, in Figure 7.2 addition strategies at four different levels allow the teacher to determine levels of student understanding.

Collecting and Recording Assessment Information

When choosing assessment tasks, teachers also think about ways to collect and record student performance information. Teachers learn about student

Figure 7.2
Four levels of assessment tasks

Performance indicator:
The student generalizes the +0, +1, and +2 rules for numbers greater than 99.
The student can explain how the rules apply to numbers greater than 99.
MENTAL LEVEL (larger numbers):
Students describe their thinking about addition problems involving +0, +1, and +2 rules with numbers larger than 99, such as 457 + 1, 999 + 1, 357 + 2, 898 + 2, 588 + 0, 777 + 2.

Performance indicator:
The student uses Unifix cubes to model the +0, +1, and +2 rules.
The student can generate a rule for the result of +0, +1, and +2 addition facts.
CONCRETE TASK (model):
Given two colors of Unifix blocks, model 5 + 1, 6 + 1, 7 + 1 and 5 + 2, 6 + 2, 7 + 2.
Ask the student to give the sums. Ask the student to make more examples.
Ask if the student knows a rule for adding 1 to any number, for adding 2 to any number.
"Can you make another sum that shows +1 with the Unifix cubes? That shows +2?"
Ask the student if there is a rule for +0 and to show +0 with the Unifix cubes.

Performance indicator:
The student identifies examples of the +0, +1, and +2 rules and explains them.
PICTORIAL TASK:
Given pictures of sets illustrating +0, +1, and +2, students sort the cards by rule and explain the rules.

Performance indicator:
The student identifies examples of the +0, +1, and +2 rules and explains them.
SYMBOLIC TASK (basic facts):
Given a page of basic addition facts, ask students to circle all the ones that show the +1 rule in red, then the +2 rule in blue, then the +0 in green.
Ask students what they know about the answers to all the problems that follow the +1 rule, the +2 rule, and the +0 rule.

performance through informal interactions with students as they observe and ask questions during work in learning centers. More formally, teachers may review seat work or homework or ask students to write in their journals or create projects and portfolios related to the objectives being taught. Tests and quizzes are other means of collecting assessment information. As teachers watch students work, they mentally note their strengths and weaknesses. Keeping track of student progress mentally has limitations of memory and inconsistency. Recording student learning from the students' performance is essential for analysis and interpretation of data. Without recording and analyzing student work, teachers may reduce the diagnostic power of assessment.

Recording information ranges from informal anecdotal notes to more organized checklists, rating scales, and rubrics. When students explore mathematical concepts in a learning center, assessment procedures may be informal observations and questioning. Observation is possibly the most flexible data collection process, but it can be unfocused. To overcome this problem, teachers refer to perfor-

mance objectives and indicators to focus on the intended learning. An **anecdotal record** is a written note about what a student did and said. Teachers develop shortcuts for anecdotal notes, as illustrated in the teacher's record of Hector's thinking while he measured perimeter with Unifix cubes (Figure 7.3). The teacher noted in parentheses which questions were asked. Anecdotal records may be kept on index cards or in a notebook.

A checklist connects each student to performance objectives for the lesson or unit. In Figure 7.4 several patterning skills are recorded for an individual student on one form. The checklist can be marked in a variety of ways: check marks, stars, question marks, ratings of 1, 2, 3, or short comments. The form could be used several times for multiple observations, interview questions, or drawn patterns. Three simple patterns are included in the figure, but teachers note additional patterns created by children.

In Figure 7.5 a group of students is assessed while the students collect and organize data for display on a bar graph. Using a rating scale or scoring symbols,

Figure 7.3
Anecdotal record
for measuring perimeter

Hector   3/5/2002

Performance indicator: Measure perimeter

Assessment task: Measure perimeter of desk with Unifix cubes

Unifix Cubes Top, 30. Side, 24. Wrote 30 + 24.

30 UCs to bottom, 24 → R

30 + 24 + 30 + 24 =

(> or < 80) "More." (Why?) "4 × 20 = 80"

Estimate 100 — no 108 because 2 × 50 = 100 + 8 = 108

Figure 7.4
Assessment for one student
on patterning skill

Name: _____ Date: _____

Patterns	Model pattern with cubes	Extend pattern with cubes	Read pattern with cubes	Act out pattern with snap-clap	Symbol pattern with letters
AB AB AB					
AAB AAB AAB					
ABC ABC ABC					
Create _____					
Create _____					

Figure 7.5
Recording form
for assessment of graphing

Date: _____	Hector	Isabel	Jamie	Kristin	Lamisha
Collects data					
Constructs bar graph					
Draws conclusions					
Interprets others' graphs					
Works cooperatively					

Figure 7.6
Rating scale for assessing
an oral report

Name: _____ Date: _____

Subject/Topic: _____

Content

Accurate/appropriate	1	2	3	4
Organized main points and details	1	2	3	4
Complete	1	2	3	4

Presentation

Well organized	1	2	3	4
Spoke clearly	1	2	3	4
Used visual aids to illustrate	1	2	3	4
Answered questions	1	2	3	4

Comments:

_____

_____

_____

_____

the teacher indicates the strengths and weaknesses of individual students and is able to draw conclusions about the performance of the class as a whole.

A rating scale is a number line that indicates the level of performance from low to high. The scale in Figure 7.6 rates student performance from 1 to 4 on each aspect of an oral report. Ratings scales, sometimes called **Likert-type scales**, are quick to score but have a problem. Interpretation of the scores is often difficult because teachers may have different meanings for the same number. For one teacher a 3 on a five-point scale may mean very good work, whereas another may think that a 3 is marginal work. When teachers fail to clearly articulate what each rating means, students may not know what the expectations are. Numbers by themselves do not describe performance levels very well. Labels such as *excellent, proficient, average, satisfactory,* or *needs improvement* are judgments but do not describe what the teacher expects and what the student is expected to demonstrate.

To clarify rating scales, teachers add descriptions to each number to create a **scoring rubric**. Rubrics are an effort to create a uniform understanding for levels of performance. Rubrics can be **holistic** or **analytic**. The holistic rubric is a judgment of overall quality for an assignment or task. If a teacher were assessing student understanding of three-dimensional figures, a single performance indicator that incorporates many aspects of the assignment would be:

Understands 3-D Figures

Names and analyzes features for six 3-D figures	Names and identifies features, does not analyze	Names, does not identify or analyze features	Does not name or identify features
4	3	2	1

The analytical rubric is more detailed than the holistic rubric; it breaks down the holistic rubric into several performance indicators with rubrics for each. The general objective "Understands 3-D figures" is broken down into five more specific tasks:

- Labels cube, pyramid, cylinder, cone, triangular prism, and rectangular prism
- Identifies shape and number of faces for each figure
- Identifies number of vertices and edges for each figure
- Finds examples of 3-D figures used in everyday life
- Constructs 3-D figures using paper or manipulatives

For each task, a scoring rubric would describe the levels of performance:

- Identifies shape and number of faces for each figure

Identifies/ analyzes 3-D figures by faces	Identifies 3-D figures by faces	Identifies faces for 3 or fewer	Does not identify figures by faces
4	3	2	1

Levels of performance are shown in Figure 7.7 as a progression from rating scale to a holistic rubric to an analytic rubric that details three dimensions of multiplication—concepts, accuracy, and speed.

Teachers often adapt scoring rubrics and procedures from other sources. Before using any rubric, teachers must carefully review it to determine whether it is suitable for their content and level. The Rubistar website (**http://rubistar.4teachers.org**) provides templates for rubrics that teachers can customize for their assignments. A rubric for problem solving can be found at **http://www.nwrel.org/msec/mpm/scoregrid .html**. If teachers want to develop their own problem-solving rubrics, a generic rubric with four objectives and three levels of performance is shown in Figure 7.8. Another rubric in Figure 7.9 includes four performance dimensions with four levels of performance.

Analyzing Student Performance and Making Instructional Decisions

Analysis of student performance is the first step in drawing conclusions about student achievement. The next step is to draw conclusions about the class collectively needing more work on specific topics. Some students have weak performance in all topics, and others need enrichment and extension activities. Screening or evaluating student performance using a teacher-made preassessment or scores on the standardized test from last year is the first step; additional diagnostic assessment can be done as each topic is introduced. Computer-managed programs supplied with textbooks or in software packages include teacher reports about student progress. Teachers then ask whether student problems are conceptual or procedural in nature. A short interview to pinpoint problems can be useful in making this decision. When teachers use assessment information for instructional decisions, the time and energy spent in assessment has a great payoff.

Although teachers must analyze and interpret each unique set of data, the assessment questions are the same:

- What are the strengths and weaknesses of the group overall and of individuals?
- Are there patterns of performance that help identify needs?
- Are there unusual occurrences (anomalies) in the data that require more information?

Figure 7.7
Assessment on multiplication using rating scales and rubrics

Rating scale using Likert-type scale:

Multiplication facts to 10 × 10

1................2................3................4................5

Rating scale using Likert-type scale with general labels:

Multiplication facts to 10 × 10

1................2................3................4................5

Low   Satisfactory   Excellent

Holistic scoring rubric using general descriptions:

Multiplication facts to 10 × 10

1................2................3................4................5

Knows   Knows   Knows all
few facts   most facts   facts with speed

Analytic scoring rubric using detailed descriptions:

Multiplication facts to 10 × 10

1................2................3................4................5

| Concept | No concept | Skip count Make groups | Draw pictures Model blocks | Tell stories | Draw, tell, write number sentence |

1................2................3................4................5

| Facts | <10 | 10–30 | 30–50 | >50 | >80 |

1................2................3................4................5

| Speed | Slow response | Answers but uses counting or other strategy | on 50%+ | Rapid response on 75%+ | on 90%+ |

Figure 7.8
General guide for rubric development

	Needs work	Competent	Superior
Understands problem			
Strategies and planning			
Solution and reflection			
Presentation and communication			

With answers to these questions, teachers make instructional decisions for the group and for individuals. Analysis and interpretation of data is equally important for state or national testing results. For example, fifth-grade and fourth-grade teachers find strengths, weaknesses, and patterns from last year's scores that identify which objectives and content were academic strengths and which require more emphasis for the coming year.

EXERCISE

Find three examples of rubrics from the Internet or other sources. What do you like or dislike about them? ●●●

Figure 7.9
Criteria and performance levels for problem solving

	1 Unskilled	2 Incomplete	3 Proficient	4 Superior
Understanding of the task	Misunderstood	Partially understood	Understood	Generalized, applied, and extended
Quality of approaches/ procedures/ strategies	Inappropriate or unworkable approach	Some use of appropriate approach or procedure	Appropriate workable procedure	Efficient or sophisticated approach/ procedure
Why the student made choices along the way	No evidence of reasoning	Little justification	Reasoned decisions and adjustments	Reasoning clear, adjustments shown and described
Decisions, findings, conclusions, observations, connections, generalizations	No solution or inappropriate conclusions	Solution incomplete or partial	Solution with connections	Solution with synthesis or generalization

SOURCE: Vermont Department of Education. (1992). *Looking beyond the answer: Vermont's mathematics portfolio program*. Montpelier, VT: Author, pp. 5–7.

Implementing Assessment with Instruction

Assessment occurs before instruction starts, during instruction, and toward the end of instruction. Each stage of instruction helps the teacher know how to plan for student learning. In this section we describe how different teachers might organize assessments and use assessment information in teaching.

Preassessment

Before instruction, teachers determine if students have sufficient background and experience for the new learning objectives. Vygotsky (1962) describes the **zone of proximal development** as the gap between current knowledge or skill and the desired knowledge or skill. Students are able to learn within their zone of proximal development. If students do not have the requisite background for learning, the teacher provides experiences that develop the foundation for successful learning. For instance, if children have never handled money, then making change and calculating it will be more difficult. Students who have never cut a pizza into four, six, or eight slices do not have the same understanding of fractions as students who have varied experience with wholes and parts. Playing games such as Candyland or Yahtzee enables students to develop intuitive understandings about probability that are further developed with probability experiences.

When teachers preassess or learn about the background knowledge of their students, they plan instruction more effectively and **scaffold** student learning by supporting new skills and concepts based on student experiences. A short pretest or interview and observation may be sufficient to determine what children know. For example, a kindergarten or first-grade teacher assesses counting using a checklist that identifies several counting skills (Figure 7.10). Level of understanding is marked with an X for skilled or a slash for partially skilled or is left blank if the skill is missing. After a brief interview with each child for one or two minutes, the teacher obtains student profiles of counting skills and knows to plan appropriate counting activities for each of them.

Ⓔxercise

What conclusions would you draw from Figure 7.10 about the counting skills of the children? What experiences would you provide for different children based on your conclusions? ●●●

With a short paper-and-pencil exercise or interview, teachers can do a quick check on what students already know on a topic being introduced or reviewed. Three examples of three-digit subtraction show how well students compute and understand the regrouping process with base-10 blocks (Figure 7.11). By asking students to work each exam-

Figure 7.10
Counting assessment

	Rote count	Set count	Rote count	Set count	Rote count	Set count
	1 to 10	1 to 10	1 to 20	1 to 20	1 to 50	Blocks to 50
Arnie	X	X	X	/	X	/
Bialy	X	X	X	X	/	/
Catasha	X		X		X	
Demi	X	X	/	/	/	/
Eduardo	X	/	X	/	/	/
Finis	X	X	X	X	X	X
Gabriel	X	X	X	X	/	X

Figure 7.11
Quick preassessment for
three-digit subtraction

Name: _____   Date: _____

Computation   **Demonstration with blocks**

1. 876
   −245

2. 536
   −298

3. 876
   −417

ple and show their thinking with blocks, the teacher can see if the children understand the process both conceptually and procedurally. Afterward, students in the class who need particular attention and students who may need differentiated instruction on topics they already have accomplished can then be determined. Preassessment allows teachers to attend to the differences in achievement found in their classroom.

During Instruction

Assessment during instruction shows how students are progressing toward mastery of the lesson or unit objectives. Grading is deemphasized during instruction because students are in the process of learning. The focus on assessment is whether the students understand the concepts and skills being developed through lessons and activities. Another name for assessment during learning is *formative assessment* because it gives feedback while the concepts are still being learned.

Teachers gain insight into student understanding by watching students as they work with manipulatives, asking questions about what students are do-

ing or thinking, and reviewing class work or homework. A checklist on patterning skills summarizes student progress over a three-week unit (Figure 7.12). The teacher records student progress with bowling symbols (X for complete, / for partial, and blank or 0 for little skill). The numbers 3, 2, 1 or symbols such as check marks, plus and minus signs, or stars are other quick marking systems.

Looking at the student profiles on patterning, the teacher determines the levels of performance and the next instructional steps (see Figure 7.12):

Beatrice, Cari, and Damon have strong patterning skills; they are ready for more complex symbols and number patterns.

Amelio and Elena have made a lot of progress, but have not mastered patterning. Work in the pattern learning center would be a good way for them to develop their skill.

Frank can create patterns for himself but has not applied skills to existing patterns. He needs some small group and individual work building on his patterns. He could work with stringing beads and pattern cards.

Figure 7.12 Assessment record for patterning skills

	Find	Read	Extend	Analyze	Make
Amelio	O / X	/ / X	O / /	O O O	/ X X
Beatrice	/ X X	X X X	/ X X	O / X	X X X
Cari	/ / X	/ X X	O / X	/ / X	/ X X
Damon	X X X	X X X	/ X X	/ X X	/ X X
Elena	/ / X	/ / /	/ / /	O O /	/ O /
Frank	O O /	O O /	O O O	O O O	/ X X

Figure 7.13
Individual checklist for multiple assessments

Name: _____

Objective: The student understands common fractions demonstrated by modeling, drawing, labeling, and telling stories involving halves through tenths.

Performance indicators   Assessment events

Area models	1	2	3	4	5	6
1. Identify common fraction						
2. Model/draw common fraction						
3. Label common fraction						
4. Tell a story about common fraction						

Set models	1	2	3	4	5	6
1. Identify common fraction						
2. Model/draw common fraction						
3. Label common fraction						
4. Tell a story about common fraction						

On _____, the student has demonstrated

No understanding   Partial understanding   Full understanding

Comments:

_____

_____

_____

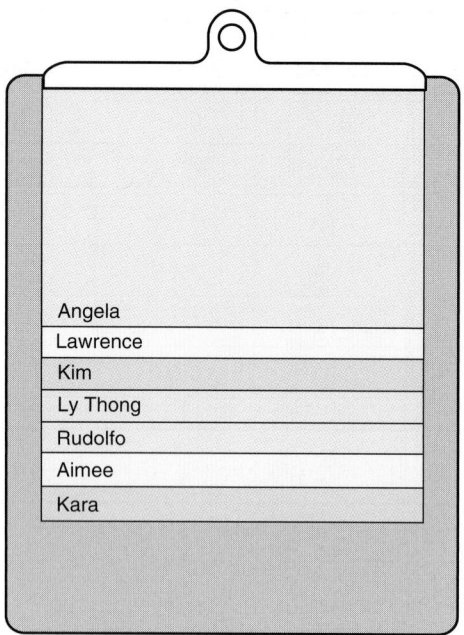

Figure 7.14 Running record on clipboard

An individual student recording sheet tracks student understanding over several assignments during a fraction unit (Figure 7.13). A **running record** of student progress is made by taping index cards on a clipboard (Figure 7.14) and is a handy way to keep up with anecdotal notes or individual checklists.

Self-Assessment During Instruction

Teachers encourage student responsibility for learning when they provide opportunities for self-assessment. Students are aware of what they understand and what they do not. Teachers can ask students to indicate whether they are understanding with a simple hand signal: thumbs up for "I understand," thumbs sideways for "I am not so sure," and thumbs down for "I am lost." Students write on personal white boards to show their answers when the teacher asks for a whole-class response. A quick scan of the responses gives immediate feedback. Green or red cups on the desk can indicate who needs help during class. A red cup asks the teacher to come by for a question while the students work on another problem.

Self-checking activities in learning centers encourage students to take responsibility for learning. Many teachers have students check their own homework and class work papers. When students find errors, they should focus on what they understand rather than on the right or wrong answers. Wrong answers are just a clue to a problem that needs to be fixed. When the emphasis is on learning rather than getting a good grade, students' self-monitoring is a powerful motivator.

Writing as Assessment

Writing is another valuable instructional and assessment technique in mathematics. Just as a ship's captain or astronauts keep a log about what happens, students write about their progress in mathematics in journals or other assignments.

> During the first ten minutes of our fifth-grade mathematics class, students are busily writing in their journals. We use journal writing to focus students on a review or to assess their ideas about a topic before its introduction. We have also used this activity to assess how well students understand a topic in progress. We find that journal writing often brings to light thoughts and understandings that typical classroom interactions or tests do not elucidate. (Norwood & Carter, 1994, p. 146)

Journals serve as a record of students' thinking and a place to raise questions or problems. Examples of questions that teachers can ask students to answer and record in their journals include:

- Draw and name five geometric shapes; describe the characteristics of each one. How are they alike, and how are they different from one another?

- What are some similarities among triangles, squares, quadrilaterals, rectangles, pentagons, and hexagons? How are they alike and different?

- The newspaper article on the bulletin board says that the average weekly allowance of 9-year-olds is $10. How would you find out if that is true for you and your friends?

- Is a square a rectangle? Is a rectangle a square? Explain your thinking.

Entries may be free-form or guided through leading questions, problems, and prompts, such as a weekly puzzler for journals:

- If you had a penny for every minute you have lived, how much money would you have?

- How many times does the numeral 1 occur in the counting numbers 1 through 100? Does 2 occur the same number of times as 1?

Journals also can be used to understand attitudes about mathematics:

- What do you think you do best in mathematics?
- What is your favorite part of mathematics? Why?
- When I think of multiplication and division, I . . .
- Today in math, I had trouble with . . .

Through writing, students reveal their understanding of the topics and progress toward objectives by working problems, explaining their thinking, and asking questions about something they do not understand. As formative assessments, journals provide information that can be used for daily instruction.

Assessment at the End of Instruction

At the culmination of instruction, teachers hope and expect that all students have mastered the concepts and skills and can apply them in problem-solving situations. Assessments following instruction, also called **summative assessment** or **mastery assessment**, give information about mastery of learning targets. Summative assessment provides accountability for students and for teachers. Traditionally quizzes were used for summative evaluation, such as the short subtraction quiz in Figure 7.15, which shows whether students have developed computational skills in subtraction.

However, a paper-and-pencil quiz may not adequately assess conceptual understanding, problem-solving, reasoning, or application objectives. A better mastery assessment might be a performance task, project, presentation, or portfolio showing student work and progress. To check conceptual understanding of multiplication, students could write a story, draw a picture, and write a number sentence for three multiplication situations. Understanding of "greater than" and "less than" is observed when students play "battle" with number cards. The number cards could be single-digit or larger, and the game could be varied to ask students to find numbers to the hundreds place.

A performance task, such as that given in Figure 7.16 on volume, asks students to go beyond computation and solve a problem in which they must show understanding of volume. Figure 7.17 is a performance task that requires understanding of area and solving a problem. In both cases the performance criteria are stated so that students understand the expectation for demonstrating mastery.

At the end of instruction students have had time and opportunity to develop understanding and skills. Teacher conclusions about student accomplishment is often reported with grades, but grades are poor indicators of mastery. Instead, a checklist that shows mastery of a topic would be a better summative report. On a subtraction quiz the teacher decides that mastery level is three out of four questions correct (or four out of five correct) and determines who has mastered the content. A mastery checklist shows which students need reteaching. Follow-up diagnosis identifies the source of the problem and helps the teacher decide what instructional action to take; using interviews may locate the misunderstanding.

Figure 7.15 Subtraction quiz: Problems with and without regrouping

Subtraction with Whole Numbers Name: _____ Date: _____

A	36 − 7	B	43 − 21	C	40 − 8	D	36 − 19
E	43 − 9	F	50 − 27	G	70 − 2	H	45 − 22
I	60 − 25	J	38 − 19	K	80 − 29	L	78 − 42
M	90 − 3	N	86 − 18	O	31 − 4		

Figure 7.16 Performance task on volume and capacity

Performance objective. Students calculate the volume of rectangular solids accurately with cubic units.

You have packed a box for shipping, containing 20 packages. It was _____ tall, _____ wide, and _____ deep. Its volume was

_____.

In your journal, record information about three different boxes you have packed. They should have different dimensions and measurement units (English and metric). The first two boxes may be designed with a friend. The last box should be individually designed. For each of the three boxes, be sure that you include the following elements:

- Sketch and label the dimensions of your box, and calculate its volume. It may be a scaled-down sketch. Be sure to include units.

- What common object or objects might fit in this box?

- Would UPS accept your box for shipment? Why or why not? Would FedEx accept this box? Would the USPS accept this box for shipment?

Figure 7.17 Problem-solving task and criteria

| Your new collie puppy will need a kennel to live in. The open space in your backyard is 15 feet by 60 feet. There are 48 feet of wire fence for the dog's kennel. If you use whole numbers only, what different sizes and shapes of rectangular kennels can you make? Which shape will give your dog the most space inside the kennel? Which kennel would you make for your dog? Explain why you selected your kennel. | I will look for these things as I evaluate your work:

1. Evidence that you understand the problem
2. The quality of your approaches and strategies
3. The decisions, conclusions, generalizations, or connections you make
4. How well you use mathematical sentences, drawings, or other means to represent your work
5. How well you express the reason you give for selecting a particular kennel |

Checklists or rubrics that give specific information about student achievement and progress can also be used in grading. A grading plan showing how different types of assessment are balanced between quizzes, projects, and daily work is illustrated in Figure 7.18.

A rubric or rating scale has a quality dimension instead of indicating simply right or wrong. When using a rubric in a grading plan, the teacher can create a grade associated with total points on a rubric. On a five-point rubric a 3 could indicate satisfactory demonstration for each of the five dimensions. In this case 20–25 points would be an A, and 15–19 points would be a B. Fewer than 15 points could mean that the student needs to revise and resubmit the project or portfolio.

Portfolios allow students to demonstrate learning over time. In a unit on measurement students could collect measurement assignments and tasks for a linear measurement, an area measurement, and a volume measurement. A rubric with the portfolio describes the expectations for the unit, such as problem-solving tasks and routine activities from the students' text or workbook. The portfolio would also include summary statements for each type of measurement in which students explain what they have learned. A portfolio is a good summative assessment strategy that combines daily instructional activities, problem solving, and self-assessment.

ⒺXERCISE

If you are in a school, ask the teacher if you can grade a set of mathematics quizzes. Look at the test items to see if you can detect strengths and weaknesses shown on the test. If you find weaknesses, what would you do to help students learn the missing concept or skill? ●●●

Figure 7.18 Incorporating alternative assessment in grading

Grading Plan for Fractions Unit		
Completion of daily work	30 points	Checklist of daily work completed
Quiz 1	10 points	Day 8
Fraction project	30 points	Project assignment and rubric Day 12
Quiz 2	30 points	Day 15

Interpreting and Using Standardized Tests in Classroom Assessment

Standardized testing is not new in classrooms; however, greater emphasis has been placed on student test scores because of the No Child Left Behind Act of 2002. As a result, teachers need new knowledge and skill with standardized tests. Teachers who provide a full and meaningful curriculum for all students through active and relevant instruction, as recommended in the NCTM principles and standards (National Council of Teachers of Mathematics, 2000), approach standardized testing in a positive way. They understand how the test is constructed, what objectives it covers, what the test scores mean, and how they are used. They are often expected to explain what tests mean to parents about their children's performance in mathematics. Standardized tests can provide the classroom teacher with useful information about student learning.

Standardized tests are classified as norm referenced or criterion referenced, although some tests include both types of scoring information. **Norm-referenced tests** compare the scores of individual students to the scores of a large group of students who have taken the test. The bell curve, also called the **normal distribution** (Figure 7.19), is a graphic display of the number of students at each percentile rank. Half the students' scores are above the 50th percentile and half are below the 50th percentile. A student who performs in the lowest third compared to others who took the test would have a percentile rank between the 1st and 34th percentile. A student who performs in the average range would have a rank between the 35th and 65th percentiles. A student who performs above average would have a rank between the 66th and 99th percentiles. Students scoring in the lowest third are in need of extra support and enriched instruction because they have not mastered the content on the test. Students in the upper third may need more challenging opportunities to expand their understanding.

Percentile scores allow comparison of student performance to national and state scores; however, they do not provide much diagnostic information

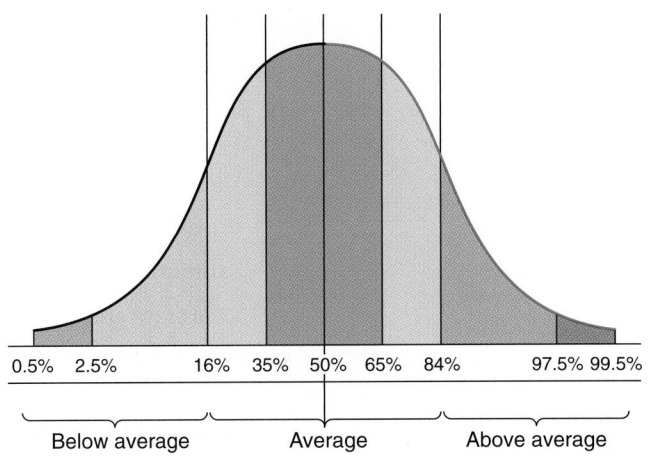

Figure 7.19 Bell curve (normal curve) used for interpreting normative tests

about the skills and content that each student has mastered. Subtest scores, such as computation, concepts, or problem solving, give the teacher some clues about strengths and weaknesses, but classroom assessment is needed to identify specific problems.

Criterion-referenced tests usually provide more diagnostic information for teachers because they show which concepts and skills each student has mastered instead of comparing students to each other. Mastery is determined by the number of items answered correctly for each performance objective and the number of objectives mastered. A criterion-referenced test for the fourth grade might have 10 performance objectives with four or five questions on each objective. By answering correctly three of four questions related to an objective, a student indicates mastery of that objective. If mastery of the entire test is 80%, the student would be required to master eight of the ten objectives. If fewer than eight objectives were mastered, the student would not meet the criterion. A student's profile from a criterion-referenced test in Figure 7.20 shows that the student mastered five of ten objectives but did not master five other objectives. Even if the student answered some question on the other objective correctly, not enough items were correct to show mastery. Diagnostic follow-up with an interview or observation can help the teacher find exactly which skills or concepts were weak, and the teacher can plan for reteaching. When teachers review student profiles for a class or grade level, they find objectives that were mastered or not mastered by most of the students in the class and identify individual students who need special help. Even when standardized testing is used, classroom assessment is necessary to identify specific student strengths and weaknesses.

Standardized tests and their use have raised many concerns. Many parents and teachers believe that such tests have narrowed the curriculum and have created too much "teaching to the test." They also dislike the pressure that standardized tests place on children. Another concern is whether standardized tests adequately measure the range of skills and abilities in mathematics. Standardized tests may measure what is easy to test rather than what is important. Deciding what the test items should be and how difficult they are is a major concern in test development. Furthermore, several states have ex-

Figure 7.20
Student profile from criterion-referenced test

Student
Grade 4

	Items on test	Number of correct items for mastery	Correct	Mastered
Whole number concepts	5	4	3	X
Addition/subtraction	4	3	3	M
Multiplication/division	4	3	3	M
Fractions	4	3	3	M
Geometry	5	4	3	X
Measurement	4	3	3	M
Data analysis	4	3	3	M
Problem solving	6	4	2	X
Estimation	4	3	2	X
Representations	5	4	2	X
Required for mastery	45	34		7 of 10 objectives
Summary for student			27	5 of 10 objectives

perienced problems with accurate scoring of standardized tests.

Test bias is another point of concern. Test bias means that items on the test provide an advantage or disadvantage as a result of content or wording that is more familiar to one group than another. Minority students and those learning English may experience test bias, although students who speak English also interpret questions differently depending on geographic, cultural, and linguistic backgrounds. Effort has been made to improve standardized tests; however, many questions still remain about their validity and use.

EXERCISE

Find the website that describes your state testing program. The content of the test may be described as well as scores for the state and school districts. Is the state test a criterion-based or normative test? ●●●

Summary

Assessment is the process of collecting, organizing, analyzing, and using information about student achievement and progress to improve instruction. Assessment and instruction are based on curriculum goals and objectives. Before instruction, teachers discover students' background knowledge and plan with this information. During instruction, feedback on student progress guides daily planning. At the conclusion of instruction, assessment shows whether students have learned the content and identifies the strengths and weaknesses for the group and for individual learners.

Performance objectives and indicators describe how students demonstrate their knowledge and skill. Assessment planning allows teachers to gather information, analyze, and interpret information about learning. Written work, interviews, observations, projects, performance tasks, portfolios, and quizzes are sources of assessment information. Anecdotal notes, checklists, rating scales, and rubrics may be used to record and summarize student achievement. After analysis, teachers determine instructional strategies and activities for students who have mastered the objectives and for students who need additional experiences.

The emphasis on standardized testing brought about by the No Child Left Behind Act has distressed many teachers and parents because of the time spent on testing and preparing for the test, the narrow focus of instruction, and problems with the validity of the testing program. Good teachers provide rich mathematical experiences based on the curriculum. They combine standardized testing information with classroom assessment to gain a more complete understanding of student performance and needs and to improve their teaching.

Study Questions and Activities

1. Do you remember having checklists, ratings scales, and rubrics as part of the assessment process in elementary school? high school? college? If so, what did you like or dislike about them?

2. Interview two or three elementary school teachers. Ask how they assess student learning. Do they use alternative, or informal, assessment strategies such as performance tasks, projects, or portfolios? If students keep portfolios or journals, ask if you may look at them. What features of portfolios or journals described in this chapter do you see in the students' products?

3. Select one or two students to observe over several mathematics class periods. Ask the students to show you their work and explain what they are doing. Take anecdotal records, and draw some conclusions about their skill and knowledge.

4. Ask two teachers for their perspective on state or district testing programs. What do you think about your state testing program?

5. Many schools are required by their state department of education to post their test results on the Internet. Find a school report card, and look at the test results for a school near you. How well are the students in the school doing in mathematics? Are the students' scores reported by percentile, mastery level, or both?

6. One teacher says that he is "teaching to the test," and another says that she is "teaching the test." Which approach is more defensible for teachers?

7. A parent has come to you with a newspaper headline that states that 50% of fourth-graders are at or below grade level in mathematics. How would you explain this to the parent?

8. Two major critics of standardized testing and interpretation are Alfie Kohn and Gerald Bracey. Search on the Internet for articles by them, and summarize their major concerns about the use of standardized tests.

Teacher's Resources

Bracey, G. (2004). *Setting the record straight: Misconceptions about public education in the U.S.* Portsmouth, NH: Heinemann.

Bush, W. (Ed.). (2001). *Mathematics assessment: Cases and discussion questions for grades K–5.* Reston, VA: National Council of Teachers of Mathematics.

Depka, E. (2001). *Developing rubrics for mathematics.* Thousand Oaks, CA: Corwin Press.

Kallick, B., & Brewer, R. (2000). *How to assess problem-solving skills in math.* New York: Scholastic.

Pokay, P., & Tayeh, C. (2000). *256 assessment tips for mathematics teachers.* Parsippany, NJ: Dale Seymour.

Sherman, H., Richardson, L., & Yard, G. (2004). *Teaching children who struggle with mathematics: A systematic approach to analysis and correction.* Alexandria, VA: Association for Supervision and Curriculum Development.

Stenmark, J., & Bush, W. (Eds.). (2001). *Mathematics assessment: A practical handbook for grades 3–5.* Reston, VA: National Council of Teachers of Mathematics.

For Further Reading

Atkins, S. L. (1999). Listening to students: The power of mathematical conversations. *Teaching Children Mathematics* 5(5), 289–295.

When teachers listen to what children say, they learn much about their understanding and misunderstandings in mathematics.

Beto, Rachel. (2004). Assessment and accountability strategies for inquiry-style discussions. *Teaching Children Mathematics* 10(9), 450–455.

Beto discusses assessment strategies that increase child interactions and focus on problem solving and inquiry.

Buschman, Larry. (2001). Using student interviews to guide classroom instruction. *Teaching Children Mathematics* 8(4), 222–227.

Buschman presents guidelines for developing student interviews that relate to classroom teaching.

Corwin, Rebecca. (2002). Assessing children's understanding: Doing mathematics to assess mathematics. *Teaching Children Mathematics* 9(4), 229–235.

Teachers are educational researchers as they gather information about student performance.

Crespo, Sandra, Kyriakides, Andreas, and McGee, Shelly. (2005). Nothing "basic" about basic facts: Exploring addition facts with fourth graders. *Teaching Children Mathematics* 12(2), 60–65.

Assessment uncovers problems that fourth-graders are having with learning basic addition facts and leads to instruction to improve student understanding and fluency.

Leatham, Keith R., Lawrence, Kathy, and Mewborn, Denise S. (2005). Getting started with open-ended assessment. *Teaching Children Mathematics* 11(8), 413–417.

Open-ended assessment items with fourth-graders give the teacher better information about student understanding. Suggestions for using open-ended assessment items are included.

Rowan, Thomas E., & Robles, Josepha. (1998). Using questions to help children build mathematical power. *Teaching Children Mathematics* 4(9), 504–509.

Open-ended questions and prompts are used in problem solving and assessing student thinking.

Silver, Edward, & Cai, Jinfa. (2005). Assessing students' mathematical problem posing. 12(3), 129–134.

Silver and Cai discuss what assessments reveal about student understanding when the students are creating mathematical problems.

Warfield, Janet, & Kloosterman, Peter. (2006). Fourth-grade results from national assessment: Encouraging news. *Teaching Children Mathematics* 12(9), 445–454.

Warfield and Kloosterman analyze the fourth-grade results on the National Assessment of Educational Progress test from 1990 to 2003 and find encouraging results and some concerns.

Wilson, Linda D. (2004). On tests, small changes make a big difference. *Teaching Children Mathematics* 11(3), 134–138.

How tests are worded and presented can result in differences in student performance and can raise questions of test validity.

PART 2

Mathematical Concepts, Skills, and Problem Solving

CHAPTER 8

Developing Problem-Solving Strategies

Problem solving is central to teaching and learning mathematics. This long-standing NCTM position regarding problem solving was reiterated in the 2000 *Principles and Standards for School Mathematics*:

> By learning problem solving in mathematics, students should acquire the ways of thinking, habits of persistence and curiosity, and confidence in unfamiliar situations that will serve them well outside the mathematics classroom. In everyday life and in the workplace, being a good problem solver can lead to great advantages. (National Council of Teachers of Mathematics, 2000, p. 52)

As the first process skill, problem solving is critical for developing other process skills and content knowledge. Students who learn from a problem-solving perspective construct their own understanding of mathematics instead of memorizing rules that they do not comprehend.

In this chapter you will read about:

1 The central place of problem solving in learning concepts and skills in mathematics

2 Problem-solving strategies and activities to develop strategies

3 Implementing problem solving through a variety of classroom activities

At one time, problem solving in mathematics instruction was equated with a few word problems at the end of a chapter; students would pick numbers from the problem and apply the most recently learned computation. Without development of problem-solving skills, word problems became a source of much frustration and little success for many students. Students were often perplexed when they encountered realistic problems and had to decide which operations to use, what numbers to include, and whether their answers made sense.

Today, problem solving is a central focus of mathematics teaching and learning. A balanced approach found in the NCTM standards (National Council of Teachers of Mathematics, 2000) recognizes the importance of computation and the vitality that problem solving gives to learning mathematics. Problem solving is the first process skill in the NCTM standards and is fundamental to the comprehensive mathematics curriculum described in Chapter 2.

Effective elementary teachers encourage creative and critical thinking in all subjects. Teachers find realistic problems in children's experiences that help teach mathematical skills and concepts. Realistic situations, imagined events, puzzles, games, and manipulatives create problems that students can confront and engage in. Students discover concepts and procedures and apply them in interesting and novel situations; they become mathematicians as they solve a variety of problems.

When business, government, and other leaders look at essential job skills for employees, they emphasize the abilities to think critically and creatively, to solve problems, to communicate effectively in written and spoken form, and to work cooperatively on a team. The connection between a problem-solving approach and real-life skills is obvious.

> . . . to function in our complex and changing society, people need to be able to solve a wide variety of problems. The elementary math curriculum must prepare children to become effective problem solvers. (Burns, 2000, p. 4)

With a repertoire of problem-solving strategies, students can understand a problem, develop a plan, and carry out their plan. Then they can consider whether their answer is reasonable and whether there are alternative answers or approaches, and finally they can communicate their answer and their reasoning. The ability to compute accurately is essential in problem solving, but thinking is at the core of mathematics teaching and learning.

Every lesson can teach problem-solving skills, as Ms. Eckelkamp found when she asked her third-grade class to consider transportation for a field trip.

Ms. Eckelkamp: Since we are studying animals and habitats, we are going to the zoo. We have 27 children in our class. Let's talk about how we are going to go to the zoo.

Evan: We could walk to the zoo.

Tara: It's too far; we should ride in cars.

Ms. Eckelkamp: How many cars would we need?

Kayleigh: Our car has two seatbelts in the front and three in the back, so four children can ride in each car. Six cars carry four children: Six cars with four children is 24 children.

Kim: But we have 27 children. We would need seven cars for everybody unless three people were sick.

Joaquina: Some cars have two seatbelts in the back. Three children could ride in some cars. Twenty-seven divided by three is nine cars. Some cars hold four children and others three; I think we need eight cars.

Ali: Our van has seven seats—everybody could ride in four vans.

Jorge: One van is the same as one large car and one small car.

Terrell: One school bus would hold everybody with room for Ms. Eckelkamp and parents.

Real-life problems require more than computing $27 \div 4 = 6$, remainder 3. For problems similar to the one illustrated, the National Assessment of Education Progress found that many students in elementary and middle grades gave the computed answer of 6, remainder 3, rather than the realistic answer of 7. In addition to calculating, it is essential that students explain whether the answer makes sense, how conditions might affect the answer, and how the answer was derived. Problems can have different answers depending on the factors considered.

ⒺXERCISE

Give three situations from your experience when you used mathematics to solve a problem. ●●●

Approaches to Teaching Problem Solving

Teaching About, Teaching for, and Teaching via Problem Solving

Schroeder and Lester (1989) describe three approaches to problem-solving instruction:

- Teaching *about* problem solving.
- Teaching *for* problem solving.
- Teaching *via* problem solving.

Teaching *about* problem solving focuses on teaching steps and strategies. Problems are exercises to practice the strategies. When teaching *for* problem solving, teachers introduce strategies with exercises based on real-world situations. In the third approach, teaching *via* problem solving, problem solving becomes the carrier for both content and process. Solving a problem requires comprehension of the problem and understanding a variety of strategies that might be applied; as a result of solving the problem, students develop both the answer or answers and the content and skills needed for the problem. Addition is learned from problems in which children combine sets to find the answer.

POINT OF VIEW

Problems are valued not only as a purpose for learning mathematics but also as a primary means of doing so. The teaching of a mathematical topic begins with a problem situation that embodies key aspects of the topic, and mathematical techniques are developed as reasonable responses to reasonable problems. A goal of mathematics is to transform certain nonroutine problems into routine ones. The learning of mathematics in this way can be viewed as a movement from the concrete (a real-world problem that serves as an instance of the mathematical concept or technique) to the abstract (a symbolic representation of a class of problems and techniques for operating with these symbols). (Schroeder & Lester, 1989, p. 33)

Division is learned when children divide a set into equal groups according to the situation. Measurement skills and concepts develop from activities such as measuring heights, scheduling events in class and at home, and determining the cost of a new classroom printer and how to get the funds. By confronting a variety of problems with different challenges, students develop concepts, procedures, flexibility in thinking, and confidence in attacking new situations.

The Four-Step Problem-Solving Process

Students need many realistic, open-ended problems because realistic problems offer the opportunity to uncover important mathematics content. A problem is a situation that has no immediate solution or known solution strategy. If the answer is already known, there is no problem. If the procedure is known, the solution involves substitution of information into the known process. If neither the answer nor the procedure is known, students need techniques for solving the problem. George Polya, in his pioneering book *How to Solve It* (1957), suggests a four-step problem-solving process. This general strategy or organizer, called a **heuristic**, applies to all problem solving and parallels the scientific method.

Scientific Method	**Polya's Problem-Solving Steps**
1. Understand the problem.	1. Identify the problem or question.
2. Devise a plan.	2. Propose a solution.
3. Organize an experiment or observation.	3. Carry out the plan.
4. Gather data and analyze them.	4. Look back or evaluate.
5. Draw conclusions.	
6. Interpret and evaluate the solution.	

Polya's problem-solving steps are commonly included in elementary mathematics textbooks as a problem-solving guide for students, using terms such as *understand, plan, do,* and *check back*. In real-life problems the learner considers various strategies, makes decisions about the effectiveness and reasonableness of processes and solutions, and draws conclusions and generalizations about the results.

Eleven Problem-Solving Strategies: Tools for Elementary School Students

Problem-solving strategies are tools that students use to solve problems. They help students understand the problem, develop and implement their plan, and evaluate the reasonableness of their solution. Reasoning, communicating, representing, and connecting are involved when students solve problems:

> Many of the process skills needed in mathematics are similar to reading skills, and when taught together would reinforce each other. (Sutton and Krueger, 2002, p. 17)

Students develop and refine strategies as they solve different problems, including nonroutine, open-ended, and divergent situations. Having a repertoire of strategies allows them to use strategies in flexible ways to approach new situations. Eleven problem-solving strategies, or tools, are important for elementary students:

1. *Find and use a pattern:* Students identify a pattern and extend the pattern to solve the problem.

2. *Act it out:* By acting out a problem situation, students understand the problem and devise a solution plan.

3. *Build a model:* Students use objects to represent the situation.

4. *Draw a picture or diagram:* Students show what is happening in the problem with a picture or a diagram.

5. *Make a table and/or a graph:* Students organize and record their data in a table, chart, or graph. Students are more likely to find a pattern or see a relationship when it is shown visually.

6. *Write a mathematical sentence:* If the problem involves numbers and number operations, strategies often lead to a mathematical sentence or expression of a relationship with numbers or symbols.

7. *Guess and check, or trial and error:* By exploring a variety of possible solutions, students discover what works and what doesn't. Even if a potential solution does not work, it may give clues to other possibilities or help the student to understand the problem.

8. *Account for all possibilities:* Students systematically generate many solutions and find the ones that meet the requirements of the problem situation.

9. *Solve a simpler problem, or break the problem into parts:* If a problem is too large or complicated to attack, students can reduce the size of the problem or break it into parts to make it more manageable.

10. *Work backward:* Considering the goal first can make some problems easier. Starting with the end in mind helps students develop a strategy that leads to the solution by backing through the process.

11. *Break set, or change point of view:* When a strategy is not working, students need flexibility in their thinking. They may need to discard what they are doing and try something else or think about the problem in a different way.

These 11 strategies are tools for understanding, organizing, implementing, and communicating problems, solutions, and mathematical concepts. One strategy may lead to a solution, but often a combination of strategies is required. Many mathematics textbooks and trade books include excellent exercises for developing the strategies. However, strategy instruction is a means rather than the end of problem solving.

Find and Use a Pattern. Humans live in a world full of patterns: in art, architecture, music, nature (Figure 8.1), design, and human behavior. Patterns are generally defined as repeated sequences of objects, actions, sounds, or symbols. Patterns may also include variations or anomalies because they are not perfect. Patterns are related to expectations and predictions. If something has happened before, humans expect that it will happen again. Novelty occurs when something unexpected happens. Patterns can be simple or complex, real or abstract, visual or aural. Recognizing and using patterns is a critical human thinking ability.

> The ability that even infants have to gradually sort out an extremely complex, changing world must be considered astounding, as well as evidence that this is the natural way

Figure 8.1 Example of a pattern as seen in nature: a sunflower

learning advances. But more surprising still is the clear fact that the learner manages to learn from input presented in a completely random, fortuitous fashion—unplanned, accidental, unordered, uncontrolled. (Hart, 1983, p. 65)

Without the ability to find and use patterns to organize their world, humans would live in a world of chaos.

Young children create patterns based on color with common manipulatives: pattern blocks, color tiles, links, and multilink cubes. Commercial or teacher-made templates guide children's pattern work (Figure 8.2) from simple two-element patterns to more complex patterns with three or four elements. Students match patterns, read color patterns, and extend pattern:

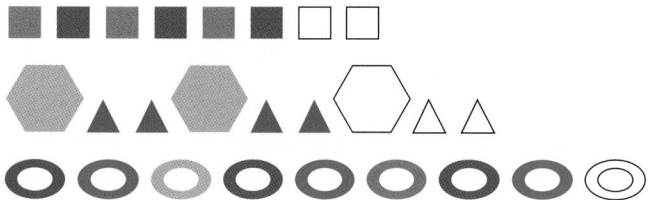

Figure 8.2 Pattern templates

Red, blue, red, blue, red, blue, . . .

Yellow, green, green, yellow, green, green, . . .

Blue, green, yellow, blue, green, red, blue, green, yellow, . . .

Other patterns can be found and made using the children themselves. They can arrange themselves by type of shoe, color of eyes, or positions:

Sandal, sneaker, sandal, sneaker, . . .

Brown, blue, green, brown, blue, green, . . .

Sit, stand, sit, stand, sit, stand, . . .

Rather than limiting instruction to one or two examples, teachers should present many patterns of different types and ask students to find and extend them. Activity 8.1 shows how people patterns develop into symbolic notation for patterns. As students gain understanding of patterns, they begin to create their own patterns that demonstrate their understanding. In Chapter 7 an assessment strategy for patterns shows how teachers can document students' developing skills.

Patterns are a foundation skill for algebra and algebraic thinking (Figure 8.3). Even numbers are those numbers that can be broken down into pairs, giving a numerical sequence of 2, 4, 6, 8, ... Prime numbers are those that have only one set of factors: $17 = 1 \times 17$. Intermediate-grade students work with patterns and sequences that increase, decrease, and overlap in more complex ways than the patterns used with younger students. More complex patterns can be found in the relationships between numbers.

Increasing sequence: 1, 1, 2, 4, 3, 9, 4, 16, . . .

Decreasing sequence: 100, 90, 81, 73, 66, 60, . . .

× × ○ × × △ × × □ × × ○ . . .   1, 1, 2, 3, 5, 8, 13, . . .

‖₁‖₁‖₁‖ . . .   1, 8, 27, 64, . . .

☆ ○ ☆ ☆ ○ ☆ ○ ○ ☆ ○ ☆ ○ . . .   1, 4, 2, 7, 3, 10, 4, . . .

Figure 8.3 Patterns

In Chapter 16, the role of patterns in algebraic thinking demonstrates how patterns are represented physically, in pictures, numerically, and, finally, in symbolic notation. Algebra often is a generalized expression of a pattern: n^2 is an expression for all

ACTIVITY 8.1   Making People Patterns

Level: Grades PreK–2
Setting: Small groups or whole group
Objective: Students make people patterns.
Materials: Cards for pattern labels

- Call on children to stand in a pattern created according to their characteristics and their clothing:

  Boy-girl, boy-girl, boy-girl, . . .

  Athletic shoes, leather, athletic shoes, leather, . . .

  Black hair, blond hair, brown hair, black hair, blond hair, brown hair, . . .

- Lead the children in "reading" the pattern ("black hair, blond hair, brown hair, . . ."). Ask what goes next, and have children join the pattern. Allow children to suggest other patterns.

- Have students join in as soon as they understand the pattern. Nodding the head for the "pause" is a good way to maintain the rhythm.

- Have children hold label cards for the characteristics and read the pattern again.

  Boy   Girl   Boy   Girl   Boy   Girl   Boy   Girl

- Substitute letters for the labels

  B   G   B   G   B   G   B   G

- Have children make patterns with Unifix cubes, buttons, or other manipulatives. Provide index cards to use as labels for these patterns.

---

square numbers, $2n$ is an expression for all even numbers, $b \times h/2 = A$ is a formula for the area of a triangle.

Activity 8.2 demonstrates how counting the number of squares in a geometric design turns into a pattern activity with algebraic implications. Primary children count and look for a pattern; older children use the pattern to generate a rule or mathematical expression. Beginning with simple patterns and progressing to more complex forms, students learn that patterns are powerful thinking skills for problem solving.

Learning about patterning is not limited to mathematics but is connected to other school subjects. When children learn to play patterns with musical instruments, they develop skills used in reading sentences and words. Rhyming words, short and long vowel sounds, and prefixes and suffixes are other important patterns in reading. Science is often described as the study of patterns in the natural world. Students discover patterns in plant leaves, by observing the change of tadpoles to frogs, and from the chemical reactions between vinegar and different rocks.

ⒺXERCISE

Look in a textbook or resource book for examples of patterns and sequences. Share those examples with classmates. Do you find opportunities for students to find patterns, extend patterns, and create patterns of their own? ●●●

Act It Out. In the act-it-out strategy children dramatize or simulate a problem situation to help them understand the problem and create a plan of action. When the situation is acted out with readily available props, the solution is often obvious. A new mathematical operation, such as takeaway subtraction, is presented through stories, as seen here:

- Ignacio has seven bananas. He gives three bananas to Marta.

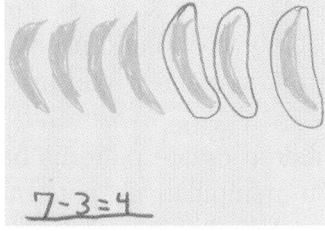

- Mary Lou collected 16 basketball cards. She sold four of her cards to Roby.

Children take turns acting out the story and then talk about the result of the action. After several stories have been acted out, children can make up

ACTIVITY 8.2   How Many Rectangles? (Reasoning, Representation)

Level: Grades 3–6
Setting: Small groups
Objective: Students count the rectangles in a row of dominoes.
Materials: Dominoes

- Have students place one domino on their desk. Ask how many rectangles they see. For this exercise a domino is counted as one rectangle. Other rectangles are combinations of whole dominoes.

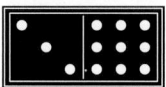

- Have students place two dominoes in a row. Ask how many rectangles they see now. (Answer: Three, from two single dominoes and one made of two dominoes.)

- Next, have them look at three dominoes and determine how many rectangles are shown. (Answer: Six, from three single dominoes, two double dominoes, and one triple domino rectangle.)

- Make a table to show the results.

Dominoes	Number of Rectangles
1	1
2	3
3	6
4	?
5	?
.	
.	
.	
10	?

- Look at the table, and ask if they see a pattern in the number of rectangles. (Answer: Students will likely see the pattern of adding 2, 3, 4, and so on to the number of rectangles. They may also see that the additional number of rectangles is equal to the number of dominoes.)

- Ask students how many rectangles they believe they might find if they lined up 4, 5, 6, . . . , 10 dominoes.

- Introduce the idea of triangular numbers being numbers that can be drawn in a triangle shape. Older students may also find that the expression $\frac{n(n+1)}{2}$ gives the triangular numbers.

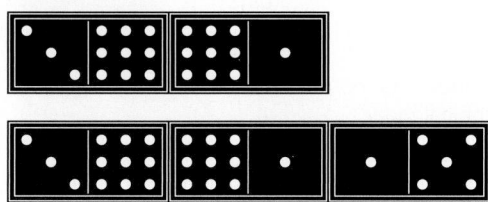

their own stories and act them out. The action of takeaway subtraction is developed in a problem setting, and the solution is represented with objects, through actions, in pictures, and finally with number sentences. Many informal activities invite students to act out mathematical situations. Children can make purchases at a classroom store stocked with food and household product containers.

Role playing serves as a motivator for investigations and projects:

- Plan a menu for the week. Make a grocery list, and use the newspaper ads to get prices for your shopping list. How much do you estimate it will take to buy your groceries for the week?

- Create a household budget. Creating a household budget requires a record of earnings and payments. A game simulation would have each student draw a weekly Earn card and four Bill cards. The class bank cashes the Earn card. Bills are paid in the class stores.

- Design a room. Measure, make a scale model, and show your selections of furniture, carpet, paint, and accessories. Several programs on television model the design process.

Board games, from Junior Monopoly to Clue, include role playing that develops thinking skills and strategies. *To Market, To Market* (Santa Cruz, CA: Learning in Motion; available at **http://www.learn .motion.com**) is a computer simulation of shopping that presents children with many problem-solving situations.

Children's literature that focuses on mathematical concepts, such as *The Doorbell Rang* (Hutchins, 1986), offers opportunities for acting out stories and exploring mathematical ideas. In *The Doorbell Rang* the concept of division is explored when the number of cookies per person is reduced as more people ring the doorbell and come in. On *Who Wants to Be a Millionaire?* contestants answer questions for prizes that double repeatedly in value from

ACTIVITY 8.3   **Payday (Reasoning, Representation)**

Level: Grades 3–6

Setting: Cooperative groups or pairs

Objective: Students represent a pattern by acting out a situation.

Materials: Blank calendars and play money purchased or created by teams of children. Students will need large and small denominations. Ask them to find out which denominations of money are printed.

- Pose the following situation: You are offered a job, and you can choose how to get paid: either $50,000 for a month or $1 on day 1, $2 on day 2, $4 on day 3, $8 on day 4, and doubling for each workday in the month. Which job would you take? Why?

- Ask students to predict which would be more: $50,000 or doubling their pay for 20 days of work.

- Have students count out $50,000 with play money. Then have them act out getting paid $1 on day 1, $2 on day 2, and so on. Print a calendar of the current month for students to record the amount of money earned each weekday, and keep a running total.

	September					

- Ask if it would make any difference if they worked 22 days in the month or 25 days?

Extensions

- Have students represent the amounts in exponents of 2 on the calendar.

- Have students look at average salaries for different occupations and the educational requirements for them. Ask if they see a relationship between education and salaries.

$100 to $1,000,000. In Activity 8.3 students act out two scenarios about getting paid with play money. They also explore the geometric progression of doubling. Compounding with interest is another interesting progression that can be estimated with the expression 72 divided by the rate of interest, which gives the number of years an investment doubles. For example, 72 divided by 8 percent interest gives 9 years to double an investment. Ask students how many years it would take to become a millionaire starting with $1,000.

Acting out situations and representing the results in writing and symbols enhances algebraic thinking because students can see patterns emerging from their actions.

Build a Model. Working with manipulatives (pencils, teddy bears, plastic beads) can create interest in new topics and helps students construct their understanding of concepts. With younger children more realistic materials are better. Plastic dinosaurs are more obvious models in a story about dinosaurs. After having many problem-solving experiences, students realize that dinosaurs and other real objects can be represented with cubes, tiles, or sticks. Manipulatives can be easily rearranged to show actions in a story problem. They show the beginning

and ending situation through their arrangement. Models invite students to try various solutions free from a sense of failure.

In Activity 8.4 modeling with pattern block triangles shows a relationship between the number of triangles in a row and the perimeter of the figure. In Activity 8.5 modeling with wheels is used to answer the question of how many unicycles, bicycles, and tricycles were rented.

EXERCISE

Consider the Research for the Classroom feature on page 122. What conditions in schools and outside schools might account for the changes in girls' spatial ability over the past 20 or 25 years? ●●●

Draw a Picture or Diagram. Pictures and diagrams have many of the same benefits as models in visualizing problems and clarifying thinking. However, teachers should not allow students to get lost in drawings that are too elaborate or detailed. The purpose of the drawing is to illustrate the situation of the problem. Children should become comfortable with simple "math art" rather than try to make everything look realistic. Tally marks, stick figures, circles,

ACTIVITY 8.4   Triangles Up and Down (Reasoning, Representation)

Level: Grades 1–4

Setting: Small groups

Objective: Students find a rule for the relationship of the number of triangles in a row.

Materials: Pattern block triangles

- Have students line up triangles in a straight line with triangles alternately pointing up and pointing down. Start with one triangle, then two, then three, and so on.

- Ask students to predict whether the tenth triangle will point up or down and to explain their thinking.

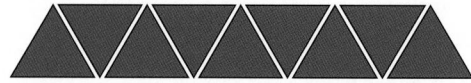

- Ask students to count the perimeter of the line of triangles as they add triangles to it. The perimeter units are the sides of each triangle. Have students make a table

that shows the number of triangles and the resulting perimeter. Using the pattern found, can they predict the perimeter of a line of 10 triangles?

Triangles	Perimeter
1	3
2	4
3	5
4	6
5	?
.	
.	
.	
10	?

ACTIVITY 8.5   Renting Cycles (Reasoning, Representation)

Level: Grades 2–6

Setting: Cooperative groups

Objective: Students make a model, account for all possibilities, and guess and check to solve the problem.

Materials: Plastic disks, poker chips, or counters to serve as models of wheels

- Seven people rent cycles for a ride at the beach. They have their choice of unicycles, bicycles, and tricycles. For seven riders, what is the largest and smallest number of wheels possible? (Answer: 21 for the largest number of wheels and 7 for the smallest.)

- Ask students to model different combinations of wheels and to report their solutions. What combinations of cycles could the cyclists have rented?

- Record their answers in a table to show the three types of cycles and the total. Students should be encouraged to look for many possible combinations.

Unicycles	Bicycles	Tricycles	Total
1 wheel	2 wheels	3 wheels	
7 × 1	0 × 2	0 × 3	7 wheels
3 × 1	2 × 2	2 × 3	13 wheels
2 × 1	1 × 2	3 × 3	13 wheels
?	?	?	16 wheels
1 × 1	1 × 2	5 × 3	18 wheels

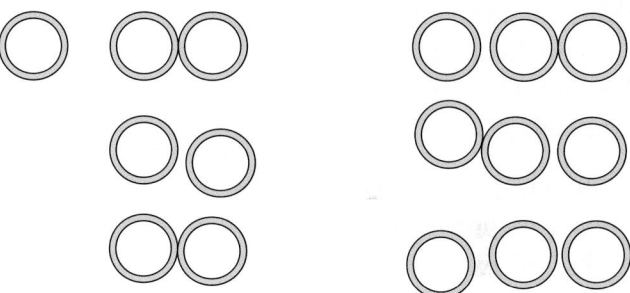

- After everyone has rented a cycle, the riders count and find that there are 16 cycle wheels. Which combination or combinations give a total of 16 wheels?

Extension

- Ask students to model different combinations if they know only the number of wheels such as seven, but not the number of riders. As students become more systematic in their approach, the number of wheels can increase. Students should see quickly that the possible solutions become large.

- When students are ready for more symbolic representation, the table can be written in algebraic form.

  2 Unicycles + 2 Bicycles + 3 Tricycles = 15 wheels

  $2U + 2B + 3T = 15$ wheels

- Use coins and ask students to find combinations of coins that total 56 cents. Which combinations result in the largest and smallest number of coins? Which solutions are possible if they know that one of the coins is a quarter? Which solutions are possible if at least one of the coins is a quarter?

Research for the Classroom

In the 1980s girls generally were found to have lower spatial scores on tests. In 1982 Joan Skolnick and her associates cited research concluding that young girls are less likely than boys to engage in play activities that involve objects (models) such as blocks, balls, toy trains, and airplanes (Skolnick et al., 1982). They thought that different play activities might contribute to the differences in spatial visualization. As a result, girls' spatial visualization skills may not be as fully developed as boys'. In a 1997 study in Sweden, Swensson and colleagues reported changes in spatial reasoning ability. They tested different groups of boys and girls over 25 years and found increases for both sexes, but the girls' scores had increased more rapidly and almost equaled the boys' scores by 1995 (Swensson et al., 1997). Bruer (1999) concluded that spatial skills of boys and girls based on tests differ in only minimal ways.

triangles, and doodles can represent situations simply and quickly. Rubber stamps of animals, shapes, flowers, and other designs can also illustrate problems and reduce the time needed for drawing. As children mature in their understanding, numerical and other symbolic expressions can replace models, pictures, and diagrams. A sketch of distances in Activity 8.6 shows what is known about a problem and what is unknown. Labeling the diagram makes the number sentence and solution easier.

Venn diagrams help students visualize situations in which classification and belonging to part of a group are important.

- John and Joe own a total of 12 dogs. They own four dogs together, and John owns three by himself. How many dogs does Joe own by himself?

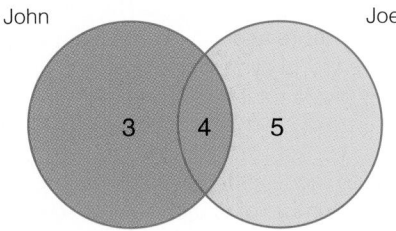

John   Joe

3   4   5

Knowing that the boys own a total of 12 dogs and that John owns 3 and shares ownership of 4 enables the problem solver to draw a Venn diagram and write a number sentence: $12 - 7 = 5$. As relationships become more complex, Venn diagrams are more important in understanding a problem and finding an answer, as shown by a question from the fifth-grade level of the Texas Assessment of Academic Skills in the spring of 2002 (Figure 8.4). More than 90 percent of the students were successful on the item.

EXERCISE

Look at the item from the Texas Assessment of Academic Skills test (see Figure 8.4). Which was the correct answer? How did you determine the answer? How could you change the numbers in the table so that a different answer on the test would be correct? ●●●

Make a Table and/or a Graph. Learning to make a table or a graph is simultaneously a problem-solving strategy and mathematical content. Concepts and skills related to data collection, analysis, and display enable students to organize and interpret information from problems. Recording data gives a visual display so that students can see what information they have collected; then they can look for patterns and relationships.

- Lena has 17 cents. What combinations of pennies, nickels, and dimes could she have? What is the largest number of coins she could have? What is the smallest number of coins she could have?

A third-grader made the table shown here to show the possible combinations of coins.

Pennies	Nickels	Dimes
17	0	0
12	1	0
7	2	0
2	3	0
7	0	1
2	1	1

Figure 8.4 Release item from the Texas Assessment of Academic Skills Test, spring 2002, grade 5

Electronic Devices Used While Traveling

Electronic Device	Number of People
Cellular phone only	5
Cellular phone and CD player only	12
Cellular phone and computer only	2
Cellular phone, CD player, and computer	6
CD player only	7
CD player and computer only	3
Computer only	1

Which diagram below was drawn from the information in the chart?

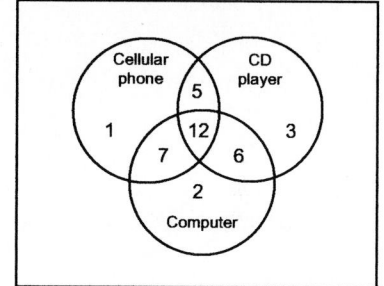

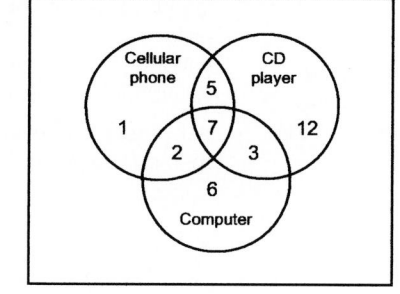

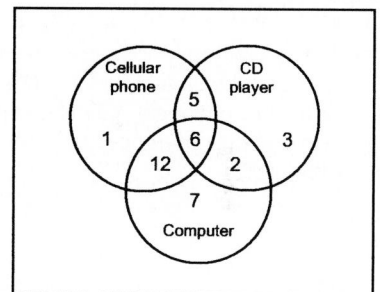

Children can refer to the table to answer additional questions.

- If Lena had one nickel, what other coin combinations could she have?

- If Lena had seven pennies, what other coin combinations could she have?

- If Lena had one dime, what other coin combinations could she have?

As students gain skill and confidence, they can change the parameters in the problem:

- If Lena had 76 cents, how many coin combinations could she have?

As the problem becomes more complex, a collaborative table might be placed on the bulletin board so that children can post different answers as they find them. When many solutions are posted, children pose questions based on the variety of solutions.

A rate table is often used to show the relationship between two sets of numbers.

- At the back-to-school sale, Clothesmart offered a dollar off for a purchase of more than one shirt,

ACTIVITY 8.6   How Far? (Reasoning, Communication)

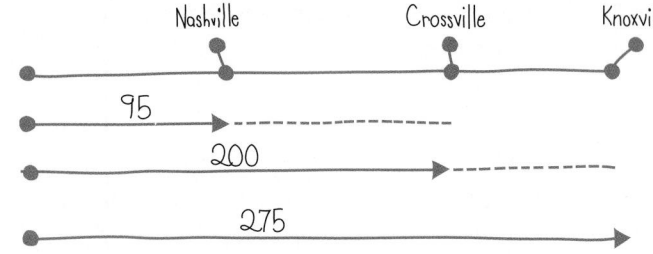

Level: Grades 3–6

Setting: Small groups

Objective: Students draw a diagram to show what is known in a problem and what is unknown.

Materials: Handmade road sign for distances in your area, a road map

- Present this story to students: Starting from their home in western Tennessee, John's family drove to visit his grandmother in Knoxville. When they left home, they saw a road sign.

- Show the road sign, and discuss the information it gives you.

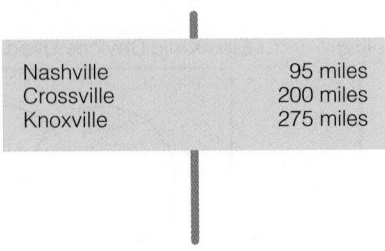

Nashville	95 miles
Crossville	200 miles
Knoxville	275 miles

- When they got to Nashville, John wanted to know how many miles were left until they reached Crossville and Knoxville.

- Ask students to draw a diagram and label the known distances. The unknown distances can be shown with a dotted line.

- The diagram may allow students to label the distance between the cities by inspection. They can see that the difference between 275 miles and 200 miles is 75 miles. Likewise the difference between 200 miles and 95 miles is 105 miles.

- Students can also express the mileages in different number sentences and equations.

200 − 95 = distance from Nashville to Crossville
200 − 95 = 105 miles

200 − distance from Nashville to Crossville = 95
200 − 105 = 95 miles

95 + distance from Nashville to Crossville = 200
95 + 105 = 200 miles

Extensions

- Connect to social studies with a map of Tennessee. Identify some possible locations for John's home and starting point. This will allow students to find the location of the sign on the map.

- For the trip, find places on the route for rest stops and sightseeing.

- Estimate the time between the towns and rest stops using 60 miles per hour and 70 miles per hour. How many gallons of gasoline are needed if the car gets 20 miles per gallon? 25 miles per gallon? 30 miles per gallon? What would the trip cost using current gas prices?

- Ask students to create similar problems using the map of their state to make road signs.

blouse, pants, or shorts. One piece of clothing was $8, two were $7 each, and three cost only $6 each. If more were bought, they were also $6 each. Students can use a spreadsheet to create a rate table and a graph of the cost of 1 through 10 pieces of clothing, as done here. What do you notice about the cost of clothing as the number of pieces of clothing increase?

Pieces of clothing	1	2	3	4	5	6	7	8	9	10
Regular price	$8	$16	$24	$32	$40	$48	$56	$64	$72	
Sale price	$8	$14	$18	$20	$20	$18	$14	$8	0	

(a)

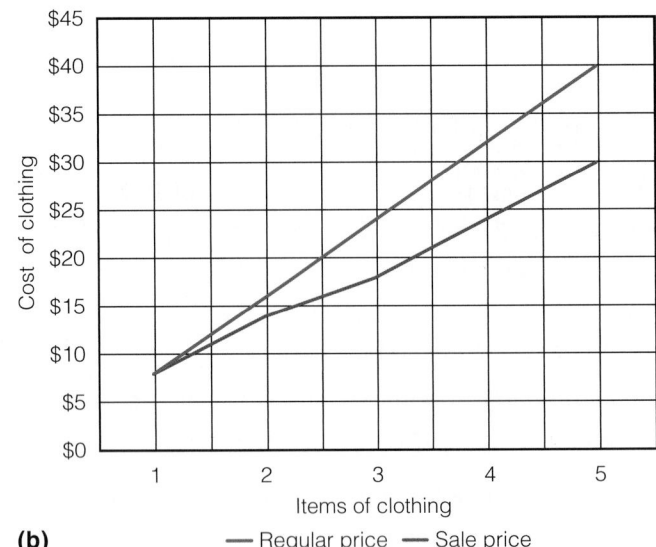

(b)

Many examples from other problem-solving strategies include creation of a table to record the results of the strategy of modeling or seeking a pattern. Tables and graphs make relationships, changes, and trends more apparent so that students can find and interpret patterns.

Write a Mathematical Sentence. While solving problems, students communicate and represent their thinking through modeling, acting, drawing, and writing. A word sentence describes the problem situation, as does a number sentence.

• Natasha has four apples and five oranges. She has a total of nine pieces of fruit.

$$4 \text{ apples} + 5 \text{ oranges} = 9 \text{ pieces of fruit}$$
$$4 + 5 = 9$$

As seen in many examples in this chapter, a number sentence developed from models, drawings, and acted-out problems summarizes the problem situation. Even when the computation is routine or the answer is evident, the skill of writing a number sentence is critical. The state assessment of academic skill in Texas asks students to write or choose a number sentence that describes the problem. Two items from the released test for fifth-grade are shown in Figure 8.5; 89% of the students answered item 22 correctly, and 83% were correct on item 27.

ⒺXERCISE

What are the answers to the two questions in Figure 8.5? How did you solve the problems? Were the answers obvious, or did you use a strategy? ●●●

Writing a number sentence is important when students learn about the basic operations of addition, subtraction, multiplication, and division. When learning about multiplication, for example, a story with an addition sentence provides the foundation for understanding multiplication and its representation in a number sentence.

• Jonas has 5 quarters. How much money does he have?

$$25 + 25 + 25 + 25 + 25 = 125$$
$$5 \times 25 = 125$$

Writing a number sentence is also important in showing division as repeated subtraction. Students can model repeated subtraction with coins and see how division is related to subtraction.

• Veena had $2.00. She spent $0.30 for each eraser. How many erasers did she buy?

$$\$2.00 - 0.30 - 0.30 - 0.30 - 0.30 - 0.30 - 0.30$$
$$= 0.20$$
$$\$2.00 \text{ divided by } 0.30 = 6 \text{ erasers}$$
$$\text{with } 0.20 \text{ left over}$$

Students usually write their own number sentences to solve problems rather than eliminate equations, as done in the test examples. Calculators allow students to concentrate on the problem rather than on computations as they compare several possible answers.

• Amber shopped at the grocery store for supper. She wanted to buy bread for $3.00, milk for $3.00, spaghetti sauce for $4.00, hamburger for $5.00,

---

Figure 8.5 Items from the Texas Assessment of Academic Skills Test, spring 2002, grade 5

22 The Givens family had a party at a skating rink. The rink charged admission of $5.95 for each adult and $3 for each child. There were 8 adults and 14 children at the party. Which number sentence can be used to find C, the total admission charge for the party?

F $\quad C = (8 \times 5.95) + (14 \times 3)$
G $\quad C = (8 \times 3) + (14 \times 5.95)$
H $\quad C = (8 + 14) \times (5.95 + 3)$
J $\quad C = (8 + 14) + (5.95 + 3)$
K $\quad C = (8 - 5.95) \times (14 - 3)$

27 Janelle makes wind chimes to sell in her mother's booth at a craft fair. She sells each wind chime for $2.25. At the last fair she sold 16 chimes and used the money to buy a $30 vest. Which number sentence can be used to find the amount of money Janelle had left?

A $\quad (30 - 16) \times 2.25 = \square$
B $\quad 30 - (16 + 2.25) = \square$
C $\quad (16 \times 2.25) - 30 = \square$
D $\quad 16 \times (30 - 2.25) = \square$
E $\quad (30 - 2.25) \times 16 = \square$

butter for $3.00, spaghetti noodles for $4.00, ice cream for $4.00, and cookies for $3.00. She had $20. What do you think she should buy to stay within her budget?

• A new car was advertised in the newspaper for $16,999. How much would Kane pay each month if he made payments for 36 months with no money down and no interest? How much would he pay each month for 36 months if he paid a down payment of $2,000 and an interest rate of 6%?

• Determine distances for trips from Miami, Florida, to Seattle, Washington, using three different routes on interstate highways.

Guess and Check, or Trial and Error. *Guess and check*, also called *trial and error*, is an all-purpose problem-solving technique in which several possible solutions are attempted to solve a problem. Instead of going for the right answer immediately, students see what works and what doesn't. Even if the attempts do not yield the answer, they often give clues to the solution. On the second or third try students may find a pattern that leads to the desired result. Using a calculator, students in Ms. McCuen's class examine several results to a number puzzle.

• Two numbers multiplied together have a product of 144. When the larger number is divided by the smaller number, the quotient is 4.

Kara: I know 12 × 12 is 144.

Keesha: But 12 divided by 12 is 1, so the two numbers can't be 12 and 12.

Josue: I multiplied 4 and 36 and got 144.

Lollie: But 36 divided by 4 is 9, not 4.

Jonice: Let's make a table so we can see the numbers we have tried.

Guess	Number 1	Number 2	Product	Quotient
#1	12	12	144	1
#2	4	36	144	9
#3	6	24	144	4

Joaquin: What number is between 12 and 4? I think it will have to be even to get an even product. Let's try 6 and 8.

Kara: If you divide 144 by 6, you get 24.

Keesha: That's it! Twenty-four divided by six is four. Does 8 work too?

Joaquin: I made up another puzzle. Two numbers multiplied together are 180, and the difference between them is 3.

In this case students recognized that a table would help them organize guess-and-check solutions. When teachers refrain from demanding immediate solutions, they encourage thinking. In problem solving, "See what works" is a good strategy.

Guess-and-check does not mean making wild guesses but making reasonable choices. If a large jar of gumballs is presented, students may guess anything from 100 to 1,000,000. If teachers provide a benchmark, or referent, they guide students to reasonable guesses. A large jar filled with gumballs is displayed along with a smaller jar containing only

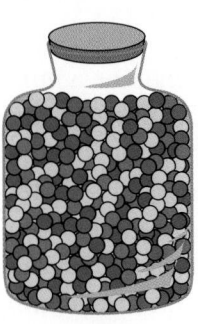

50 gumballs. Students compare the number in the smaller jar to the size of the large jar, then write their estimates on a chart or in their journal: "My estimate for the number of gumballs in the large jar is ____ because ____ ." Another approach is to exhibit the smaller referent jar after students have made initial estimates. Students count the number in the referent and adjust their estimates. Original estimates might range from 100 to 5,000, but after counting the referent jar of 133, estimates become more consistent and accurate, such as 800 to 1,330. Reasonableness is the goal in estimation, so teachers should avoid giving prizes for the best estimate. Instead, they should help students identify a range of good estimates, such as 1,000–1,200.

Number puzzles (Figure 8.6) also invite guess-and-check thinking. In Figure 8.6a the numerals 0 to 8 are arranged so that all the sums down and across are 12. In Figure 8.6b the numerals 1 to 8 are placed so that the sums on each side of the square are all 11. To solve the puzzles, students try several arrangements of numbers. If numerals are written on small pieces of paper, they can be easily moved, making number puzzles faster and less frustrating. The wrong combination can give clues for the correct answer. After solving the first set of puzzles, students see if they can find solutions for other sums, such as 10 or 13.

(a) Place the numbers 0 through 8 in the circles so that the sum of each row and column is 12.

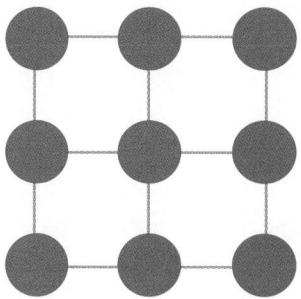

(b) Place the numbers 1 through 8 in the circles so that the sum of each row and column is 11.

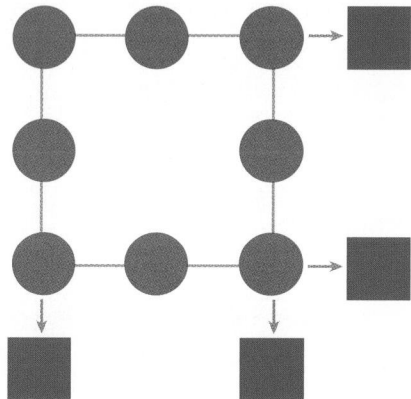

Figure 8.6 Number puzzles

ⒺXERCISE

With a friend or classmate, work the puzzles in Figure 8.6. Did you use trial and error in your problem solving? Did you find combinations that helped you find the solution? ●●●

Account for All Possibilities. Accounting for all possibilities is a strategy that is often used with other strategies. Using the guess-and-check strategy may naturally lead to an organized approach of what works and what does not. Creating a table of possible answers often is used to identify a pattern or relationship, such as riders and wheels or combinations of coins. In primary grades children model all the possible sums for 7 with Unifix cubes (Figure 8.7). When they list all their answers (0 + 7, 1 + 6, 2 + 5, 3 + 4, 4 + 3, 5 + 2, 6 + 1, 7 + 0), they see a pattern of the first number increasing as the second one decreases.

When students list coin combinations for 56 cents, the solutions that meet a requirement, such as one quarter, simplify the task by limiting the possibilities. A trip to the ice cream store is another situation for finding all the possibilities.

- If the store sells four flavors of ice cream and three toppings, can every child on the soccer team of 19 players have a different ice cream sundae?

This problem can be solved with a model, a drawing, or a diagram, as shown in Figure 8.8. In Figure 8.8a, for example, brown paper squares represent chocolate topping on four circles, each representing a different ice cream. Ice cream and topping combinations can also be used to illustrate multiplication in a Cartesian cross-product (Figure 8.8d).

Activity 8.7 is a target game with Velcro balls. As children play the game, they see that each ball has a score depending on where it sticks. After playing the game, children predict all the possible scores with

Figure 8.7 Unifix towers showing possible combinations of 7

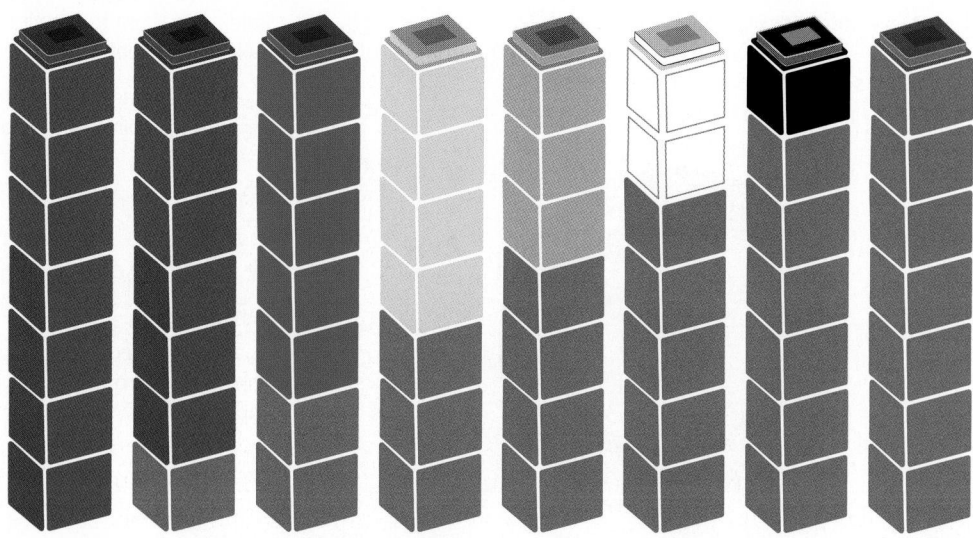

Figure 8.8 Ice cream sundae combinations

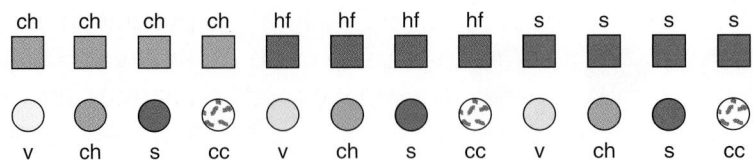

a. Model with colored paper

| ch | ch | ch | ch | hf | hf | hf | hf | s | s | s | s |

v   ch   s   cc   v   ch   s   cc   v   ch   s   cc

b. Sketch of sundaes with toppings

ch →   hf →   s →

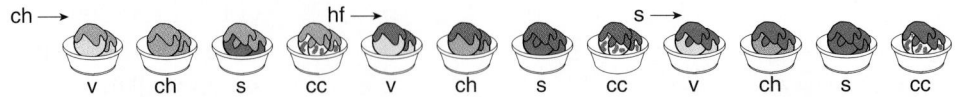

v   ch   s   cc   v   ch   s   cc   v   ch   s   cc

c. Diagram of sundaes

$$\frac{ch}{v} \quad \frac{ch}{ch} \quad \frac{ch}{s} \quad \frac{ch}{cc} \quad \frac{hf}{v} \quad \frac{hf}{ch} \quad \frac{hf}{s} \quad \frac{hf}{cc} \quad \frac{s}{v} \quad \frac{s}{ch} \quad \frac{s}{s} \quad \frac{s}{cc}$$

d. Cross diagram of possible sundaes

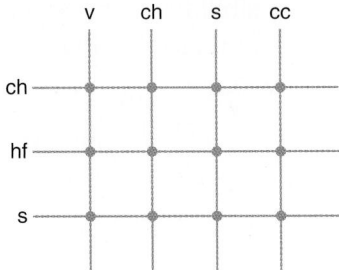

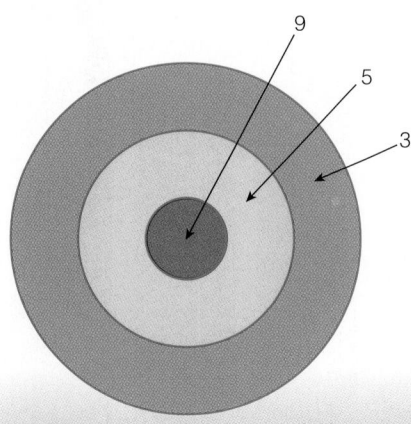

ACTIVITY 8.7 **Targets (Reasoning, Communication)**

Level: Grades 2–4

Setting: Learning center

Objective: Students determine the possible scores from throwing three dart balls at a target.

Materials: A Velcro target with Velcro balls. Label the target with point values, such as 9 for the center, 5 for the middle ring, and 3 for the outside ring.

- Have students play the target game and keep score on a score sheet with three columns showing the number of points for each round of three balls.

- After the students have played several games, ask them what the highest possible score is and what the lowest possible score is.

- Ask whether the score could be 4, 9, 14, 15, 18, or 20 if all three balls stuck on the target. Ask for their thinking behind their answers. Is there a pattern that helps them determine which scores are possible and which are impossible? Ask them to list all the possible combinations using their score sheet.

Game	Center, 9 points	Middle, 5 points	Outer, 3 points	Total
#1	1	1	1	17
#2	1	0	2	15
#3	0	1	2	11
#4	0	3	0	15

Extension

- Change the values of the targets and the number of balls. Ask students to think about the high, low, possible, and impossible answers.

three balls. Identifying the high and low scores gives boundaries to the possibilities, and a table helps to organize the information and show patterns. Pascal's triangle has many applications in mathematics and is a good subject for an investigation. In Activity 8.8 it is used to find several patterns.

Solve a Simpler Problem, or Break the Problem into Parts. Some problems are overwhelming because they appear complex or contain numbers that are large. Breaking a complex problem into smaller and simpler parts is an important problem-solving strategy. Sometimes, substituting smaller numbers in a problem helps students understand what is going on in the problem. Solving a simpler problem gives students a place to start.

Many realistic problems are solved in parts. When measuring the area of an irregularly shaped room for carpet, students can measure the room in parts and add the parts together (Figure 8.9a). The surface area of a cereal box (rectangular prism) is found by adding the areas of each face (Figure 8.9b).

Many mental computation strategies are based on making a more difficult combination into an easier computation. For example, a teacher wants students to work on mental computation strategies for adding 9's. If $4{,}567 + 999$ is too hard as a first example, the teacher could start with $47 + 9$. Students can find that answer by using a number line and counting forward to 56. They can also see that adding $47 + 10$ is easier to compute mentally, but the sum has to be corrected by subtracting 1 to get 56.

Starting with $47 + 10$, $323 + 100$, or $4{,}567 + 1{,}000$, the pattern of adding an easy number is established before working on $47 + 9$, $323 + 99$, or $4{,}567 + 999$. Learning the principle of *compensation* by adding and then subtracting with simple numbers encourages mental computation strategies for addition and subtraction in many situations.

Work Backward. Working backward is helpful when students know the solution or answer and are finding its components. Some teachers introduce working backward in "known-wanted" problems. Students begin with the solution and think about the information that would give that result.

- Edmundo has seven pets that are dogs and cats. Five are dogs. How many cats does he have?

Children can model or draw seven pets, identify five as dogs, and find that the missing part is two cats. The number sentence is a subtraction problem that can be written either in addition or subtraction form.

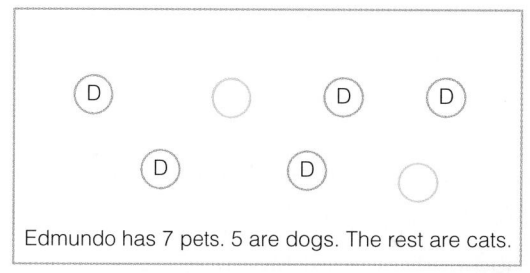

Edmundo has 7 pets. 5 are dogs. The rest are cats.

$$7 \text{ pets} = 5 \text{ dogs} + \underline{\quad} \text{ cats}$$
$$5 \text{ dogs} + \underline{\quad} \text{ cats} = 7 \text{ pets}$$
$$7 \text{ pets} - 5 \text{ dogs} = \underline{\quad} \text{ cats}$$

(a)

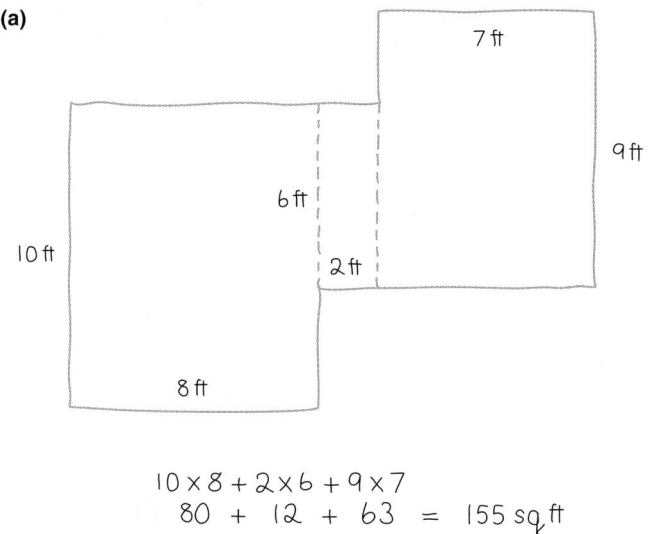

$$10 \times 8 + 2 \times 6 + 9 \times 7$$
$$80 + 12 + 63 = 155 \text{ sq ft}$$

(b)

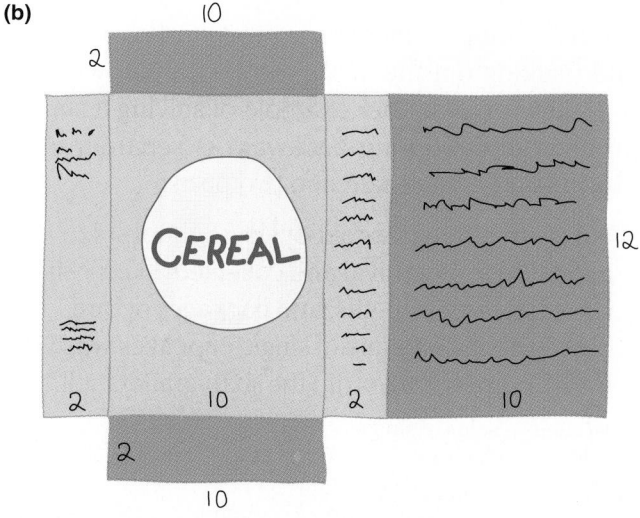

Figure 8.9 Breaking area into smaller parts: (a) area of a room to be carpeted, (b) surface area of a cereal box

ACTIVITY 8.8   Pascal's Triangle (Reasoning, Communication)

Level: Grades 4–6
Setting: Whole group
Objective: Students explore the patterns in Pascal's triangle.
Materials: Copies of Pascal's triangle

- Tell students that they are going to work with Pascal's triangle. (Pascal was a French mathematician who invented the first computer, but it could only add and subtract numbers.)

- Display the first few rows of Pascal's triangle, one row at a time. After three or four rows, ask the students what pattern they see.

```
              1
            1   1
          1   2   1
        1   3   3   1
      1   4   6   4   1
    1   5  10  10   5   1
  1   6  15  20  15   6   1
1   7  21  35  35  21   7   1
```

- Ask students to conjecture what numbers are in the next row and to explain their thinking.

- Reveal the next row, and have students compare the numbers to the conjecture.

- Ask students what they notice about the order of each row. (Answer: The numbers in each row are palindromic—they are the same front to back and back to front.)

- Ask students about the number of numerals in each row. (Answer: Some are odd, others are even.)

- Ask students if they see a pattern in the sums of each row. (Answer: The sum of each row is double the sum of the previous row. The sum of each row is 2 raised to a power: $2^0 = 1$; $2^1 = 2$; $2^2 = 4$; and so on.)

A similar process of working backward from the known is used in a more complex problem.

- Chen had $20.00 when he went to the grocery store. After buying a chicken for $2.09, celery for $0.79, milk for $1.39, and a loaf of bread, he received $13.96 in change. Estimate how much the bread cost.

Knowing that the total has to be $20, students can find several ways to express their thinking.

$$\$14 = \$20 - \$2 - \$1 - \$1 - \text{bread}$$
$$\$2 + \$1 + \$1 + \text{bread} + \$14 = \$20$$
$$\$20 - \$14 = \$2 + \$1 + \$1 + \text{bread}$$

All the number sentences involve starting with $20 and backing out the amounts that are known until only $2 is left. Another example of solving a similar problem and working backward is separating the proceeds of a bake sale into two parts.

- The sixth-grade class at Bayview School sold cupcakes at a carnival and collected $50.00. Single cupcakes cost 25 cents, and packages of three cost 50 cents. The sale of single cupcakes was $30. How many cupcakes did the sixth-graders sell?

Total sales = sales of singles + sales of packages:	$50 = $30 + $20
Each dollar for single cupcakes buys four cupcakes:	30 × 4 = 120 cupcakes
Each dollar for packages of three buys six cupcakes:	20 × 6 = 120 cupcakes

Single cupcakes + packaged cupcakes = total:	120 + 120 = 240 cupcakes

In these examples students work backward to find the elements that are part of a known total or answer. Rush Hour is a challenging spatial puzzle that begins with toy cars and trucks in a gridlock. Students rearrange toy cars and trucks to undo the gridlock and free the red car stuck in traffic. The difficulty of the puzzles increases with more vehicles in the traffic jam.

A number puzzle also illustrates working forward and backward.

- Pick a number, triple it, add 3, double the result, subtract 6, divide by 3. If Sue's answer was 12, what was her beginning number?

Try several numbers, and see if you find a pattern. Start with 12 and go backward, reversing each step.

Undo step 5	Multiply by 3	12 × 3 is 36
Undo step 4	Add 6	36 + 6 is 42
Undo step 3	Divide by 2	42 divided by 2 is 21
Undo step 2	Subtract 3	21 − 3 is 18
Undo step 1	Divide by 3	18 divided by 3 is 6 Sue started with 6.

This number puzzle can be made simpler with fewer steps or more complex with larger numbers. Students can create their own puzzles: "How would you make 7 into 99?" or "Make 99 into 7." Many teachers maintain a file of number puzzles for warm-ups, learning centers, and sponge activities for the odd minutes in the school day.

ⒺXERCISE

Sudoku is a number puzzle that has become popular. The rule for solving the puzzle is simple: Fill each row, column, and nine-square section with the numbers 1 through 9. However, the combinations are not simple. Look for an easy Sudoku puzzle in the newspaper, a book, or on the Internet to work with a friend or classmate. Which strategies did you use? ●●●

POINT OF VIEW

Whenever possible, give your students the opportunity to work on a problem independently. If they have trouble getting started, do not tell them which strategy to use; try only to ask questions that will lead them to choose an appropriate strategy. Help your students to realize that they may need to test several strategies before an appropriate one is found. (Lechner, 1983, p. 17)

Break Set, or Change Point of View. Creative thinking is highly prized in today's changing world. Persistence is an important attribute of good problem solvers. Problem solvers also need to understand when they have met a dead end. At a dead end they have to change their strategy, or how they are thinking about the problem.

Being able to break old perceptions and see new possibilities has led to many technological and practical inventions. The inventor of Post-it Notes was working on formulating a new glue and found an adhesive that did not work very well. Instead of throwing his failure out, he thought how it might be useful for temporary cohesion.

Put nine dots on your paper in a 3 × 3 grid. Connect all nine dots with four straight lines without lifting your pencil from the paper. After several attempts, you may agree with others that the problem cannot be solved. However, when lines extend beyond the visual box created by the nine dots, the solution is not difficult. Having permission to try something "outside the box" opens up new possibilities. Past experience can be helpful or limiting.

Being flexible is less a strategy and more a mindset of seeing alternative possibilities. In the number puzzles in Figure 8.6, students rearrange the numbers several times to get the sums and the order of numbers to work. When one answer is correct, students resist changing it even when it is necessary to solve the entire puzzle.

Children may be less set in their ways of thinking and therefore may have less difficulty changing their point of view compared with adults, who can become fixed in their thinking. Both children and adults need to learn to ask themselves, "Is there another way?" In Figure 8.10 squares are drawn on a grid. The first square has an area of 1 unit. The second square has an area of 4 units. The challenge is to draw other squares with areas of 2 square units, 3 square units, 4 square units, 5 square units, 6 square units, 7 square units, 8 square units, and 9 square units. To be successful in this task, students must change their point of view and recognize that squares can be drawn at different orientations and that some squares may not have solutions.

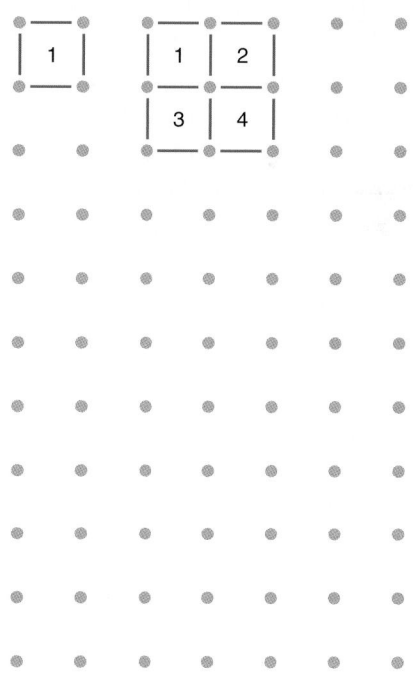

Figure 8.10 Grid for area puzzle

ⒺXERCISE

How did you have to change your point of view to draw the squares in Figure 8.10? How many were possible? ●●●

Implementing a Problem-Solving Curriculum

Flexibility of thinking is essential in problem solving. In the past teachers might present only one way to approach a problem or one way to think about it. Students who had alternative ideas were frustrated and discouraged. Most problems can be solved in a variety of ways; learning to use problem-solving strategies encourages students to try several approaches. Even when teachers introduce strategies by themselves, students soon learn that the strategies are more powerful when they are used together. As children mature, complex problem situations involve a broader range of mathematics topics and concepts. Solving a variety of problems in different ways develops many skills and attitudes that support algebraic thinking.

Many teaching/thinking lessons and informal activities that link problem solving to algebra are found in the Navigations Through Algebra series (Cuevas & Yeatts, 2001; Greenes et al., 2001), in *Teaching Children Mathematics*, on the NCTM website (**http://www.nctm.org**), and in supplemental materials from educational publishers. Good problems are found in many resources, including textbooks and supplemental materials. Puzzles and games provide many opportunities for problem solving. Classroom situations over the school year also offer many problems that students can work together to solve, as discussed in Chapter 2.

Teachers who promote thinking and problem solving for their students find support in national and state standards. Because a problem-based classroom may look messier or seem noisier than a traditional classroom, teachers should be proactive with principals and parents by explaining the importance of problem solving. Parent information sessions organized by teachers at the first of the year can alleviate tension about problem-based mathematics curriculum. Parents often want to know that their children will learn basic computational skills, and teachers can reassure them that computation is an important goal. Students need reasons for learning the facts and applying them in interesting problems. Because the process and answer are both important, assessment of problem solving focuses on whether students understand a problem, can devise a strategy, and can come to a reasonable solution that they can explain. Assessment suggestions for problem solving are found in Chapter 7.

Newsletters to parents suggest games and activities for learning facts and for developing mathematical thinking. At workshops or parents' mathematics nights, students can teach their parents how they are solving problems with strategies. Parents experience problem-solving activities that model how students learn mathematics in new ways. Marilyn Burns (1994) produced a video for teachers and parents titled *What Are You Teaching My Child?* which describes why problem solving is essential for all students and how it is used in real life (the video is available at **http://www.mathsolutions.com/mb/content/publications**). The videotape also shows the modern elementary classroom and why it looks different from the classroom that many parents remember.

Take-Home Activities

Dear Parents,

We have been working with pattern blocks and solving number problems with them. Your student has a zipper bag with 20 pattern blocks in it. The small green triangles are worth 1 point, the blue parallelograms are worth 2 points, the red trapezoids are worth 3 points, and the yellow hexagons are worth 6 points. Using the pattern blocks, you and your child can solve the following problems:

- Make a turtle with the pattern blocks. Write a number sentence showing the total value of the blocks you used.
- Make a model of something using pattern blocks that has a value of 26 points. Trace around the picture and write the number sentence you used.
- Make a pattern with the pattern blocks using red and blue blocks. Read the pattern.
- Show four combinations of blocks with a total value of 18 points.

After solving these problems, see if you can make up other problems using the pattern blocks.

Sincerely,

Take-Home Activities

Dear Parents,

How do students spend their time? We are investigating this question and asking students to keep a log of their activities one day this week. Using a daily schedule, students mark which activity is most important in each half hour. One copy of the schedule is for midnight to noon, and another is for activities from noon until midnight. After collecting this information, we will make circle graphs and compare the amount of time students spend on different activities.

Name:

Activity	School/Study	Play	Sleep	Eat/Bath	Other
12:00					
12:30					
1:00					
1:30					
2:00					
2:30					
3:00					
3:30					
4:00					
4:30					
5:00					
5:30					
6:00					
6:30					
7:00					
7:30					
8:00					
8:30					
9:00					
9:30					
10:00					
10:30					
11:00					
11:30					

Thank you for your help.

Summary

Problem solving has been the focus of instruction in elementary education for several decades. Students act as mathematicians as they discover and refine concepts and procedures needed to solve a variety of problems. Problem solving also involves process skills of reasoning, connecting, communicating, and representing mathematical ideas. Creative and critical thinking skills are important attributes for working in the technologically demanding world of the twenty-first century.

Learning processes and strategies for solving problems begins in elementary school and continues through secondary education. The problem-solving process suggested by George Polya leads elementary students through four steps: understand, plan, carry out the plan, and check to see if the solution is appropriate and sensible. Development of problem-solving strategies, such as finding and using patterns, guessing and checking, breaking a problem into smaller parts, or making a table or graph, provides students with tools that apply to different problems, often in conjunction with each other.

Teachers have several responsibilities for building an environment that encourages flexibility of thinking. They need to choose worthwhile and interesting mathematical tasks that interest children. Many classroom and interdisciplinary situations are good problem-solving tasks. Games, puzzles, and informal activities also develop problem-solving skills and attitudes. When teachers recognize how algebra is embedded in many problem-solving situations, they can help students grow in their understanding and skill in algebra.

Study Questions and Activities

1. Which of the 11 problem-solving strategies have you used? Which strategies do you think are most important? Why?

2. What is your understanding of teaching *via* problem solving? What do you need to do to become more skilled at this approach?

3. Find five problems for students at a grade level of your interest in resource books, in teacher's manuals, and on the Internet. Solve them and analyze your thinking. Which strategies did you use in solving the problems? Share your problems with fellow students to build a file of classroom problems.

4. How do you interpret the following statement: "A good problem solver knows what to do when he or she doesn't know what to do."

Teacher's Resources

Algebraic thinking math project. (1999). Alexandria, VA: PBS Mathline Videotape Series.

Andrews, A. G., and Trafton, P. (2002). *Little kids—powerful problem solvers*. Westport, CT: Heinemann.

Burns, M. (1994). *What are you teaching my child?* Sausalito, CA: Math Solutions Inc. (video). Available at http://www.mathsolutions.com/mb/content/publications

Egan, L. (1999). *101 brain-boosting math problems*. Jefferson City, MO: Scholastic Teaching Resources.

Findell, C. (Ed.). (2000). *Teaching with student math notes* (v. 3). Reston, VA: National Council of Teachers of Mathematics.

Greenes, C., & Findell, C. (1999). *Groundworks: Algebraic thinking series (grades 1–7)*. Chicago: Creative Publications.

Kopp, J., with Davila, D. (2000). *Math on the menu: Real-life problem solving for grades 3–5*. Berkeley, CA: UC Berkeley Lawrence Hall of Science.

NCTM. (2001). *Navigations through algebra*. Reston, VA: National Council of Teachers of Mathematics.

O'Connell, S. (2000). *Introduction to problem solving: Strategies for the elementary math classroom*. Westport, CT: Heinemann.

O'Connell, S. (2005). *Now I get it: Strategies for building confident and competent mathematicians*. Westport, CT: Heinemann.

Shiotsu, V. (2000). *Math games*. Lincolnwood, IL: Lowell House. Available from ntcpub@tribune.com

Trafton, P., and Thiessen, D. (1999). *Learning through problems: Number sense and computational strategies*. Westport, CT: Heinemann.

Children's Bookshelf

Anno, M. (1995). *Anno's magic seeds*. New York: Philomel. (Grades 3–5)

Bayerf, J. (1984). *My name is Alice*. New York: Dial Books. (Grades 1–3)

Burns, M. (1999). *How many legs, how many tails?* Jefferson City, MO: Scholastic. (Grades 1–3)

Ernst, L. (1983). *Sam Johnson and the blue ribbon quilt*. New York: Lothrop, Lee & Shepard. (Grades 1–3)

Hutchins, P. (1986). *The doorbell rang*. New York: Greenwillow Books. (Grades 3–5)

Pinczes, E. (1993). *One hundred hungry ants*. Boston: Houghton Mifflin. (Grades 2–4)

Scieszka, J., & Smith, L. (1995). *The math curse*. New York: Viking. (Grades 3–6)

Singer, M. (1985). *A clue in code*. New York: Clarion. (Grades 4–6)

Weiss, M. (1977). *Solomon Grundy, born on Monday*. New York: Thomas Y. Crowell. (Grades 4–6)

For Further Reading

Civil, M., & Khan, L. (2001). Mathematics instruction developed from a garden theme. *Teaching Children Mathematics* 7(7), 400–405.

Making a garden motivates students to confront many mathematics and interdisciplinary problems and issues.

Contreras, Jose (Ed.). (2006). *Posing and solving problems*. Focus issue of *Teaching Children Mathematics*, 12(3).

This focus issue contains five feature articles about ways to engage students with problems and to develop their thinking.

Evered, L., & Gningue, S. (2001). Developing mathematical thinking using codes and ciphers. *Teaching Children Mathematics* 8(1), 8–15.

Codes and ciphers demand reasoning and perseverance for problem solving.

Methany, D. (2001). Consumer investigations: What is the "best" chip? *Teaching Children Mathematics* 7(7), 418–420.

Nutritional data and taste preferences are considered in a classroom research project to find the best chip.

O'Donnell, B. (2006). On becoming a better problem-solving teacher. *Teaching Children Mathematics* 12(7), 346–351.

O'Donnell presents a classroom example of how teachers can expand their implementation of problem solving.

Outhred, L., & Sardelich, S. (2005). A problem is something you don't want to have. *Teaching Children Mathematics* 12(3), 146–154.

Outhred and Sardelich conduct classroom action research of primary students engaged in a problem-solving activity and show how the students improved their skills.

Rowan, T. E., & Robles, J. (1998). Using questions to help children build mathematical power. *Teaching Children Mathematics* 4(9), 504–509.

Teacher questions have a major impact on classroom discourse and reasoning. Examples of questions are given as models, with three vignettes of classroom questioning practice.

Schneider, S., & Thompson, C. (2000). Incredible equations: Develop incredible number sense. *Teaching Children Mathematics* 7(3), 146–147.

Children create extended equations and develop number sense as they solve them.

Silbey, R. (1999). What is in the daily news? *Teaching Children Mathematics* 5(7), 190–194.

A newspaper report about the blooming of cherry trees in Washington, D.C., stimulates student inquiries and problem solving.

Silver, E., & Cai, J. (2005). Assessing students' mathematical problem solving. *Teaching Children Mathematics* 12(3), 129–135.

Problem posing is presented as an important aspect of learning to solve problems. Students understand the process better when they are actively engaged in finding problems.

Yarema, C., Adams, R., & Cagle, R. (2000). A teacher's "try"angles. *Teaching Children Mathematics* 6(5), 299–303.

Problems and patterns provide background for number sentences and equations.

Young, E., & Marroquin, C. (2006). Posing problems from children's literature. *Teaching Children Mathematics* 12(7), 362–366.

Young and Marroquin make suggestions and provide resources for teachers to develop children's books as the source of interesting mathematical problems.

CHAPTER 9

Developing Concepts of Number

Learning about numbers, numerals, and number systems is a major focus of elementary mathematics. Children's number sense and knowledge of number begin through matching, comparing, sorting, ordering, and counting sets of objects. Rote and rational counting are important milestones in the development of number. Number is represented in stories, songs, and rhymes and with concrete objects and numerals. As students count beyond 9, they encounter the base-10 numeration system used for larger numbers. They also explore number patterns in the base-10 number system through 100 using a variety of experiences and activities in the classroom.

In this chapter you will read about:

1. Basic thinking-learning skills for concept development in mathematics

2. Characteristics of the base-10 numeration system

3. Different types of numbers and their uses

4. Activities for developing number concepts through manipulatives, books, songs, and discussion

5. Rote and rational counting skills and problems some children have with counting numbers

6. Assessment of children's number conservation, or number constancy

Numbers and counting probably emerged from practical needs to record and remember information about commerce and livestock. Today, numbers are used in many ways, but the basic utilitarian nature is the same. Accountants and bankers track and manage millions of dollars around the globe; social and natural scientists research population trends and topics in medicine, physics, or chemistry using computers; computer programmers and analysts manipulate numbers and symbols to develop new languages and applications. In daily life families track income and expenses. Counting and number development start early in life. Children use numbers naturally as they play games, sing songs, read picture books, and solve problems. The NCTM standards for algebra include basic thinking skills of classifying, sequencing, and patterning. Such skills are also fundamental for the development of number concepts.

NCTM Standards for Number and Operations

Instructional programs from prekindergarten through grade 2 should enable all students to:
Understand numbers, ways of representing numbers, relationships among numbers, and number systems
Understand meanings of operations and how they relate to one another
Compute fluently and make reasonable estimates
Pre-K–2 Expectations:
In prekindergarten through grade 2 all students should:
- count with understanding and recognize "how many" in sets of objects;
- use multiple models to develop initial understandings of place value and the base-ten number system;
- develop understanding of the relative position and magnitude of whole numbers and of ordinal and cardinal numbers and their connections;
- develop a sense of whole numbers and represent and use them in flexible ways, including relating, composing, and decomposing numbers;
- connect number words and numerals to the quantities they represent, using various physical models and representations.

NCTM Standard for Algebra

Instructional programs from prekindergarten through grade 2 should enable all students to:
Understand patterns, relations, and functions
Represent and analyze mathematical situations and structures using algebraic symbols
Use mathematical models to represent and understand quantitative relationships
Analyze change in various contexts

Pre-K–2 Expectations:
In prekindergarten through grade 2 all students should:
- sort, classify, and order objects by size, number, and other properties;
- recognize, describe, and extend patterns such as sequences of sounds and shapes or simple numeric patterns and translate from one representation to another.

Primary Thinking-Learning Skills

Thinking-learning skills appear to be innate in humans. Brain research shows that infants actively make sense of their world. Thinking-learning skills provide a foundation for all cognitive learning, including development of numbers and number operations. Three skills are discussed in this chapter, and patterning is developed more fully in Chapter 16:

- Matching and discriminating, comparing and contrasting
- Classifying, sorting, and grouping
- Ordering, sequence, and seriation

Matching and Discriminating, Comparing and Contrasting

When children match and compare, they find similar attributes. Discriminating and contrasting involve identifying dissimilar attributes. Infants respond differently to familiar or unfamiliar faces, sounds, and smells. They gaze at pictures resembling faces and avoid pictures showing scrambled face parts. Recognizing similarities and differences can often occur simultaneously, such as when children match the mare with the colt, the cow with the calf, and the bear with the cub; children see the relationship between the adult and young animals at the same time they recognize the differences. Matching begins with the relationship between two objects. Relationships can be physical (large red triangle to large red triangle), show related purpose (pencil with ballpoint pen, key with lock, or shoe with sock), or connect by meaning (a cow with the word *cow*).

Learning activities based on similarities and differences extend from early childhood through high school and were found by Marzano (2003) to be the most effective teaching strategy for increasing student achievement. In the primary grades many games are based on finding similarities and differences. Lotto games have many variations; children

Figure 9.1 Feeling box

might match a red apple with a green apple; a calf with a cow; three oranges with three apples; or three oranges with the numeral 3. A teacher can place several objects in the feeling box (Figure 9.1) and suggest matching and discriminating tasks for students. Later, children can bring objects for the feeling box and create similar tasks for classmates.

Children develop matching and discriminating skills and comparing and contrasting skills through a variety of experiences and activities.

Matching Tasks	**Discriminating Tasks**
Find two keys.	Find two keys—one heavy and one light.
Match two balls of the same size.	Find two balls—one large and one small.
Find two pencils with the same length.	Find two pencils—one long and one short.

A teacher can adapt an activity from *Sesame Street* with four objects so that "one of these things is not like the others" (Figure 9.2). Drawings of five clowns

Figure 9.2 One of these things is not like the others.

Figure 9.3 What is different about each clown?

are almost identical in Figure 9.3, but each one has a distinguishing characteristic for children to find. Other search puzzles may show hidden objects or ask which picture is different.

Card games, such as Go Fish and Crazy Eights and Uno, match and discriminate by number, color, or suit. In the game Set, each card has four attributes: number, color, shape, and shading. Students make "sets" of three cards (Figure 9.4) that match on each attribute or differ on the attributes. Children match objects to shape outlines in Activity 9.1. In Activity 9.2, children explore bolts, nuts, and washers and find which ones match.

Matching and discriminating tasks are found in other subject areas. In language and literature, metaphors and similes express comparisons and contrasts.

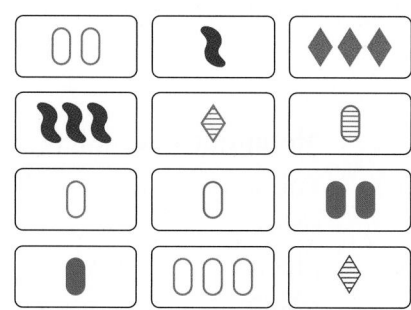

Figure 9.4 Set game cards

ACTIVITY 9.1 Matching Objects to Pictures (Reasoning)

Level: Grades: K–1
Setting: Learning center
Objective: Students match objects to pictures or outlines.
Materials: Various

- Sketch pictures or outlines of common objects on a large sheet of heavy tagboard. The pictures may vary from detailed to outline-type illustrations.
- From a collection of common objects in a box, students match the real objects with their pictures and outlines.

Variations

- Students recognize many things by shape or logo: stop sign, McDonald's golden arches, Toyota icon, and many others. Make a collection of shapes and icons on cards or in a book to which students can add new examples.
- Make a mask from a file folder with a small hole cut in it. Put a picture inside the file folder so that only part of the picture can be seen. Ask students to identify the pictured object from the part they can see.

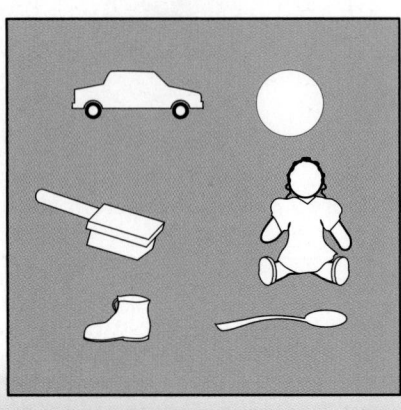

ACTIVITY 9.2 Nuts and Bolts (Reasoning)

Level: Grades K–2
Setting: Learning center
Objective: Students match, classify, and seriate objects.
Materials: Nuts, bolts, and washers of various sizes

- Collect an assortment of nuts, bolts, and washers of various sizes. Put different numbers and sizes of nuts, bolts, or washers in different boxes so that each box has combinations that match or do not match.
- Ask students to match, classify, and line up the objects in the box.

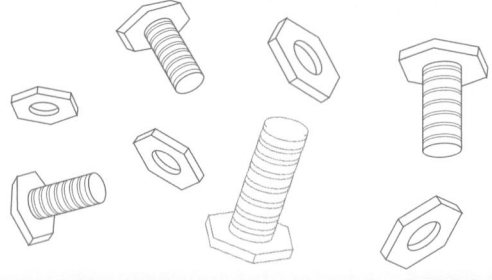

Simile Examples	**Metaphor Examples**
The sky was like an ocean of stars.	The sky was an ocean of stars.
The road was like a silver ribbon.	The road was a silver ribbon.

Compare and contrast tasks encourage student reasoning at all grades and subjects:

- Compare and contrast Lewis and Clark's explorations of the Pacific Ocean to the first explorations of space.
- What is alike and different about the stories *The Little Red Hen* and *The Grasshopper and the Ant*?
- What is alike and different about *Charlotte's Web* as a book and as a movie?

- Compare and contrast the monthly rainfall in Portland, Maine, and Portland, Oregon.

- Compare and contrast the expected and observed outcomes of rolling two dice.

- Describe the relationship between dog years and people years.

- Describe how measuring the length of the football field in centimeter cubes and with a trundle wheel would be similar and different.

- Show one-half in six different ways with objects, pictures, and symbols.

Classifying

Classification, also called sorting or grouping or categorizing, extends matching two objects that are similar to matching groups of objects that share common characteristics, or attributes. Classification is an important skill in all subject areas. In science children sort objects that sink or float and objects that are living or nonliving. Groupings of tree leaves and animals are based on similarities and differences. In reading children find words that rhyme, have the same initial consonants, or have long vowel versus short vowel sounds. They use classes of letters called consonants and vowels that have different uses and sounds and find that classification systems can have exceptions. Identifying needs and characteristics of people around the world is a core concept in social studies. People living in different places have unique languages, art, and music, but they all exhibit these cultural characteristics in some way. All peoples have a staple food that is cooked, mashed, and eaten with other foods, whether that staple is rice, wheat, corn, or taro root. The commonalities help children understand the similarities and differences among cultures.

MULTICULTURALCONNECTION

Different cultures have a food staple made of a grain (e.g., wheat, rice, quinoa, or corn) or a root vegetable (e.g., potato or taro). Ask parents of students from different cultures to demonstrate how they cook the staple into a bread or porridge. Students can develop a Venn diagram of how the different foods are alike and different.

As students become more sophisticated in classifications, simple classes give way to complex classifications. Calling "kitty" demonstrates that the child has attached a label to a group of furry, four-legged animals. When an adult replies, "Spot is a dog. He barks," or "Spot is bigger than cats," the child begins to form two classes of animals that are small, furry, and four-legged. A broader classification system is developed as children learn about a variety of other animals with different attributes. Elephants have four legs but are large and have a trunk. Gradually children develop a *schema*, or understanding, of the attributes that define specific animals and describe complex relationships between different animals. They are able to group animals in many ways: size, type of skin covering, what they eat, where they live, sounds they make, and many other ways to organize animals by their characteristics. This ability to create flexible and complex classification systems is critical for conceptual learning.

Consistent classification develops over time and with experience. When the child lines up a red shoe, a green shoe, a green car, a police car, a police officer, and a firefighter, the thinking behind the sorting may not be obvious (Figure 9.5). By listening, a teacher may hear the child "chain" the objects rather than classify: "Red shoe goes with a green shoe, a green shoe goes with a green car, a green car goes with a police car." Attribute blocks emphasize simple classifications by color, shape, size, thickness, or texture or two-way classification. Real-life objects are typically more complex in the ways they can be organized because they have many attributes.

Figure 9.5 Chaining objects

Children may sort buttons by size (big, medium, small), texture (rough, smooth), color, number of holes, and material, as well as not-button. They also see that buttons have more than one attribute. The big red button is big and red and belongs to two classes at the same time. The double-classification board in Figure 9.6 challenges students to find two characteristics at the same time. Sorting boxes contain collections of objects, such as plastic fishing worms, washers of various sizes, assorted keys, small plastic toys, buttons, plastic jar lids, and other common items. These collections provide many

Figure 9.6 Double classification board

experiences for sorting objects by different attributes: color, shape, material, letters on them, and so on. Activity 9.3 demonstrates students' classification skills with collections of objects.

ⒺXERCISE

How would you describe a chair? Which attributes are essential for a chair? Why is a sofa or stool not a chair? What attributes keep them from being a chair? Make a chart or diagram showing the relationships between different types of seating. ●●●

Ordering, Sequence, and Seriation

Another basic thinking-learning skill involves finding and using the orderly arrangements of objects, events, and ideas. **Order** has a beginning, a middle, and an end, but placement within the order can be arbitrary. When threading beads on string, children may put a red bead first, a yellow bead second, and a green bead last, but they could easily rearrange the beads. Juan could be at the first, middle, or end of the lunch line. In **sequence**, order has meaning. Days of the weeks have fixed sequence, but the classroom schedule may vary from day to day depending on special events. Calendars mark the passage of days, months, and years, and time lines show the

---

ACTIVITY 9.3   **Sorting Boxes (Problem Solving and Reasoning)**

Level: Grades Pre-K–2

Setting: Learning center

Objective: Students classify objects based on common characteristics.

Materials: Collections of objects, such as toy cars, toy animals, bolts, pencils and pens, coins, canceled stamps, socks, shells, beans, rocks

- A math box is a collection of objects that children can manipulate and organize in various ways. Watch as students work with these collections.

- Ask questions or make statements to model language and extend thinking. "Are there enough shirts for all the

pants?" "Are there enough washers for all the bolts?" "Do you have enough garages for all the trucks?" "Which shells do you like best? Why?" "I see three big dinosaurs." "I see two blue cars and three green trucks."

Variation

With older children the same skills can be developed with other materials or examples: names of the 25 largest cities in the United States, rainfall in the 25 largest cities in the United States, rivers and their lengths, cards with zoo animals, examples of different kinds of rocks.

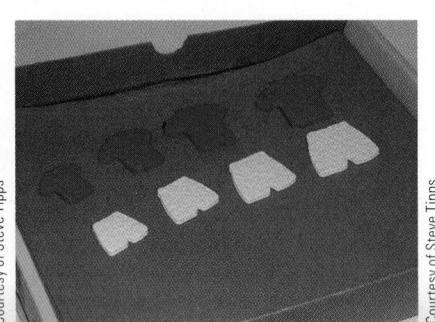

sequence of historical events, geological periods, or presidents. The sequence of events in a story provides structure for the plot. Drawings of plant growth show the sequence in development. **Seriation** is an arrangement based on gradual changes of an attribute and is often used in measurement. For example:

- Children line up from shortest to tallest.
- Red paint tiles are arranged from lightest to darkest.
- Bolts, nuts, and washers go from the largest to the smallest in diameter.
- Each stack of blocks has one more block in it than the last one.

Comparative vocabulary develops with seriation: good, better, best; big, medium, small; lightest, light, heavy, heaviest; lightest, light, dark, darkest. Activity 9.4 describes comparison of length with drinking straws.

Games follow a sequence of turns and rules; most board games are based on roll, move, and take the consequences, as in Activity 9.5.

Beginning Number Concepts

Experiences with matching, discriminating, classifying, sequencing, and seriating are important skills needed for development of number concepts. Objects can be classified by size, color, or shape, but they can also be sorted by the number of objects: five apples, five cars, five pencils. "Five" or the idea of "fiveness" is the common characteristic. Number is an abstract concept rather than a physical characteristic; it cannot be touched, but it can be represented by the objects.

Order, sequence, and seriation also play a role in number concept. **Counting** is a sequence of words related to increasing number: 1, 2, 3, 4, 5. . . . Children learning to count may say numbers out of order or have limited connection between a number word and its value. An adult asks, "How old are you?" The toddler responds with three fingers and says "two." With more counting experience, children recognize number in many forms: objects in a set, spoken words, and written symbols.

Beginning number concepts are a major focus in early childhood because they are the foundation for

---

ACTIVITY 9.4   Drawing Straws (Reasoning)

Level: Grades K–3
Setting: Learning center
Objective: Students compare and seriate objects by length.
Materials: Five or six straws or dowels cut into different lengths

- Make a format board by tracing the straws or dowels in a row from the shortest to the longest on poster board.
- Put the straws or dowels into a box. Have students draw straws or dowel pieces and place them on the board.

Variations

- Have students arrange straws from smallest to largest without the board.
- Make a board with only a few lengths of straws drawn on it. Children take turns picking out straws. They can choose straws that match the lengths, or they can place shorter straws or longer lengths in the correct positions between those drawn.
- Make a board on which the lengths are marked at random.

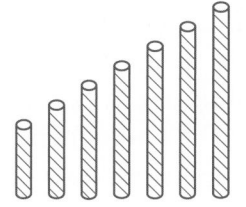
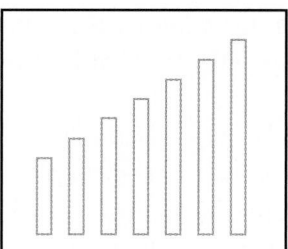
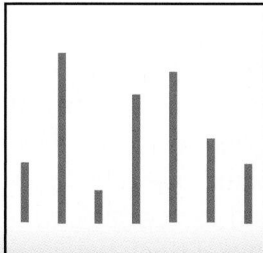
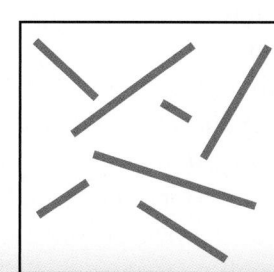

ACTIVITY 9.5   Follow the Rules (Problem Solving)

Level: Grades 1–3

Setting: Small groups

Objective: Students develop a sequence of attribute blocks that follow a change rule.

Materials: Attribute materials or a set of objects with at least three attributes, transparency attribute blocks

- Make a game board such as the one shown.

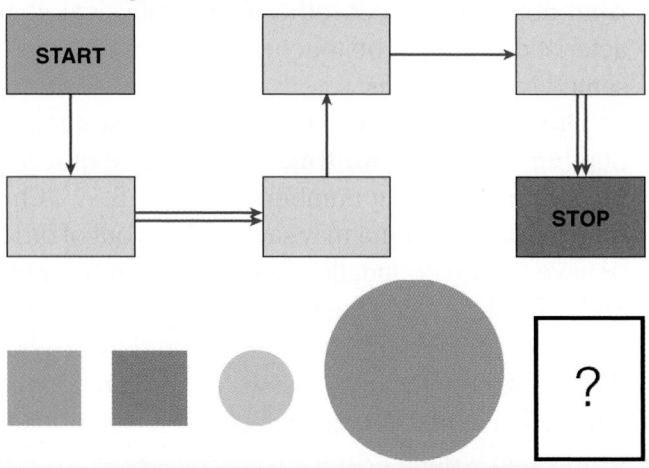

- The arrows represent rules for changing the shapes in the rectangles:
  - → Change one attribute (a big red rough square to a small red rough square)
  - ⇒ Change two attributes (a big red rough square to a small red rough circle)

- Display a pattern on the overhead using transparency attribute blocks. Each block differs in one attribute from the previous attribute block.

- Ask students which blocks they can find to continue the sequence.

- Distribute a set of attribute blocks to each group. Most sets of 32 attribute blocks have four shapes in four colors of two sizes.

- Have children put a shape in the Start box and follow the rules to the Stop box.

- Ask them to start with a different block and show the same sequence rule—one attribute changes.

Variation

Older students can make a sequence that has a "two attributes change" rule.

---

understanding the Hindu-Arabic numeration system and number operations. Although numbers up to 10, 20, or even 100 may seem simple to adults, number concepts and number sense are important cognitive goals for young children. Teachers and other adults encourage numerical thinking through the activities and conversations about number.

The **Hindu-Arabic numeration system** is a base-10 system that developed in Asia and the Middle East. As early as A.D. 600, a Hindu numeration system in India was based on place value. The forerunners of numeric symbols used today appeared about A.D. 700. Persian scholars translated science and mathematics ideas from Greece, India, and elsewhere into their language. The Arabic association with the system came from translation and transmission to other parts of the world. *The Book of al-Khowarazmi on Hindu Number* explained the use of Hindu numerals. The word *algorithm* comes from the author's name, al-Khowarazmi; algorithms are the step-by-step procedures used to compute with numbers (Johnson, 1999). Increased trade between Asia and Europe and the Moorish conquest of Spain further spread the Hindu-Arabic numeration system

across the Mediterranean into Europe. The Hindu-Arabic system gradually replaced Roman numerals and the abacus for trade and commerce in Europe. For a brief time the two systems coexisted, but eventually the algorists, who computed with the new system, won out over the abacists. By the 16th century the Hindu-Arabic system was predominant, as people recognized its advantages for computation.

Five characteristics of the Hindu-Arabic system make possible compact notation and efficient computational processes:

1. Ten is the base number. During early counting, people undoubtedly used fingers to keep track of the count. After all fingers were used, they needed a supplemental means for keeping track. A grouping based on 10, the number of fingers available, was natural.

2. Ten symbols—0, 1, 2, 3, 4, 5, 6, 7, 8, 9—are the **numerals** in the system.

3. The number value of a numeral is determined by the counting value and the position: The numeral 2 has different values in different positions of 2, 20, and 200. Place value is based on pow-

ers of 10 and is called a **decimal system**. The starting position is called the units or ones place. Positions to the left of the ones place increase by powers of 10.

10^5	10^4	10^3	10^2	10^1	10^0
100,000	10,000	1,000	100	10	1

Place value to the right of the ones place decreases by powers of 10, so that negative powers of 10 represent fractional values:

10^0	10^{-1}	10^{-2}	10^{-3}	10^{-4}	10^{-5}
1.0	0.1	0.01	0.001	0.0001	0.00001

A decimal point signifies that the numbers to the left are whole numbers and that the numbers to the right are decimal fractions. From any place in the system, the next position to the left is 10 times greater and the next position to the right is one-tenth as large. This characteristic makes it possible to represent whole numbers of any size as well as decimal fractions with the system. The metric system for measurement and the U.S. monetary system are also decimal systems.

4. Having zero distinguishes the Hindu-Arabic system from many other numeration systems and allows compact representation of large numbers. A zero symbol in early Mayan writings also has been documented. The term *zero* is derived from the Hindu word for "empty." Zero is the number associated to a set with no objects, called the empty set. Zero is also a placeholder in the place-value system. In the numeral 302, 0 holds the place between 3 and 2 and indicates no tens. Finally, 0 represents multiplication by the base number 10 so that 300 is $3 \times 10 \times 10$.

5. Computation with the Hindu-Arabic system is relatively simple as a result of algorithms developed for addition, subtraction, multiplication, and division. **Algorithms** are step-by-step calculation procedures that are easy to record. Although most people learn a single algorithm for each operation, several algorithms are discussed in Chapter 12.

Children begin learning about the Hindu-Arabic system by counting objects and recording numerals. Throughout the elementary years they learn about the place-value system and computational strategies that the system makes possible.

Number Types and Their Uses

Numbers have three main uses: to name or designate; to identify where objects and events are in sequence; and to enumerate, or count, sets (Figure 9.7). Identification numbers or numbers on football jerseys and hotel rooms are **nominal** because they are used to identify or name, although they may code other information. Single digits on football uniforms may indicate players in the backfield. A room number of 1523 may be the 23rd room on the 15th floor or the 23rd room on the 5th floor of the first tower. Automobile license tags are identifying numbers that may also code information such as county of residence.

Ordinal numbers designate location in a sequence:

- Evan is *first* in line; Kelly is *last.*
- Tuesday is the *seventh* day of school.
- Toni ate the *first* and *fourth* pieces of cheese in the package.

Cardinal numbers are counting numbers because they tell how many objects are in a set. Number

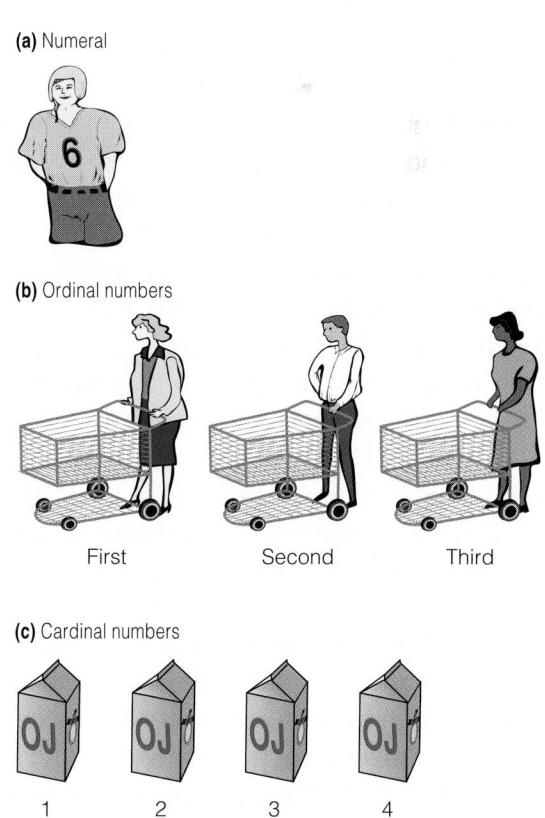

(a) Numeral

(b) Ordinal numbers

First   Second   Third

(c) Cardinal numbers

1   2   3   4

Figure 9.7 Three uses of numbers

describes an abstract property of every set from 1 to millions.

- Ishmael has 1 dog. Tandra has 2 cats. Nguyen has 3 goldfish.

- We counted 23 cars, 8 pickup trucks, and 12 vans and sport utility vehicles in the parking lot.

- The distance to the moon ranges between 356,000 kilometers and 406,000 kilometers.

- The movie *Pirates of the Caribbean* earned more than $600 million at the box office.

Written symbols for numbers are *numerals*; 19 is the numeral for a counted set of 19 objects.

Children use nominal, ordinal, and cardinal numbers from an early age. They learn addresses and telephone numbers that are identified with particular people. They know what *first* and *second* mean when they run races from one end of the playground to the other. By singing counting songs and reading counting books and through many other experiences, children construct a comprehensive understanding of numbers, their many uses, and the words and symbols that represent them.

Counting and Early Number Concepts

The growth of children's understanding of number is so subtle that it may escape notice. Children younger than 2 years of age have acquired some idea of "more," usually in connection with food—more cookies or a bigger glass of juice. Counting words are heard in the talk of 2- and 3-year-old children. When young children hold up three fingers to show age, they are performing a taught behavior rather than understanding what "three" means. They repeat a verbal chain of 1, 2, 3, 4, 5 that receives approval and attention from adults. Some children count up to 10, 20, or 100 using memorized verbal chains, although the meaning behind the words may not have developed.

Early number work involves oral language. Number rhymes, songs, and finger-play activities stimulate children's enjoyment of number language and support the connection of number words with number ideas. Through rhythm, rhyme, and action children associate counting words with their meanings. Books of finger plays and poems for young children

include many counting and number ideas. "Five Little Monkeys" is a counting-down favorite that appears in song and story versions. Each verse has one fewer monkey jumping on the bed, illustrating counting down or backwards.

Many counting and number books invite counting aloud. Some involve puzzles and problems for students to solve through counting. Eve Merriam's text and Bernie Karlin's illustrations in *12 Ways to Get to 11* build a subtle message about number constancy. On each two-page spread the number 11 is represented in different situations and different arrangements. As a follow-up, children could make boxes for the numbers 11 through 19 and fill them with different objects each day for several weeks. Activity 9.6 describes an activity using *Anno's Counting Book*.

Children's literature promotes understanding of mathematical concepts in situations and stories that relate to children. Number books, counting books, and number concept books have many advantages for teachers and children (National Council of Teachers of Mathematics, 1994, p. 171):

- Children's literature furnishes a meaningful context for mathematics.

- Children's literature celebrates mathematics as a language.

- Children's literature integrates mathematics into current themes of study.

- Children's literature supports the art of problem posing.

Counting and number concept books are listed at the end of this chapter in the Children's Bookshelf section. Bibliographies found on the Internet, such as **http://www.geocities.com/heartland/estates/4967/math.html**, contain a wide variety of mathematical books on counting, number, and other mathematical concepts.

Rote counting is a memorized list of number words. The verbal chain of 1, 2, 3, 4, . . . provides prior knowledge for number concepts. **Rational counting**, or meaningful counting, begins when children connect number words to objects, such as apples, blocks, toy cars, or fingers. *Three* becomes a meaningful label for the number of red trucks or bears or mice or candles on the cake. Counting is a complex cognitive task requiring five counting prin-

ACTIVITY 9.6   Counting with Anno

Level: Grades K–2
Setting: Whole group
Objective: Students relate number to counting.
Materials: *Anno's Counting Book*, by Mitsumasa Anno (New York: HarperCollins Children's Books, 1977), Unifix cubes

Anno's Counting Book engages children in counting from 0 to 12 in a series of pages that depict the development of a community over seasonal changes. This wordless book invites children to develop understanding of the numbers 0 through 12. An almost blank page shows a winter snow scene that introduces zero. Each page displays more objects to count. As the spring thaw sets in, children see two trees, two rabbits, two children, two trucks, two men, two logs, two chimneys.

Each page shows progressively more complex illustrations that require a more intense search for numbers. On each page a set of blocks illustrates the number featured in the illustration.

- Show the book through the first time without interruption. Have the students look at each picture.
- The second time through, ask students what they notice about each page. Model counting, and have students count with you or by themselves.
- Place the book and Unifix cubes at a reading station. Ask students to match a number of cubes with the pictures.
- Assign different numbers to groups of two or three, and let students make posters using stickers.
- Have individuals or small groups write stories about the posters or list what they find on a page.

Extension

- Use the book to introduce multiples and skip counting.

---

ciples, which were identified by Rachel Gelman and C. R. Gallistel (1978, pp. 131–135):

1. The *abstraction principle* states that any collection of real or imagined objects can be counted.

2. The *stable-order principle* means that counting numbers are arranged in a sequence that does not change.

3. The *one-to-one principle* requires ticking off the items in a set so that one and only one number is used for each item counted.

4. The *order-irrelevance principle* states that the order in which items are counted is irrelevant. The number stays the same regardless of the order.

5. The *cardinal principle* gives special significance to the last number counted because it is not only associated with the last item but also represents the total number of items in the set. The cardinal number tells how many are in the set.

Through counting objects and interactions with adults and peers, children begin to understand the pattern of numbers and their names: 1-more-than-1 is two, 1-more-than-2 or 2-more-than-1 is three, and so on. Numbers are developed progressively with concrete materials: 1 through 5, followed by 1 through 10, then 1 through 20. Stress the last or *cardinal number* of a set as objects are counted: "One, two, three,

four, *five*," then ask questions such as "What is the last number you counted?" or "How many cars did you count?" A commercial number chart, or one made by the children, demonstrates the "one more" idea between counting numbers, as shown in Figure 9.8. Counting sets aloud connects the sequence

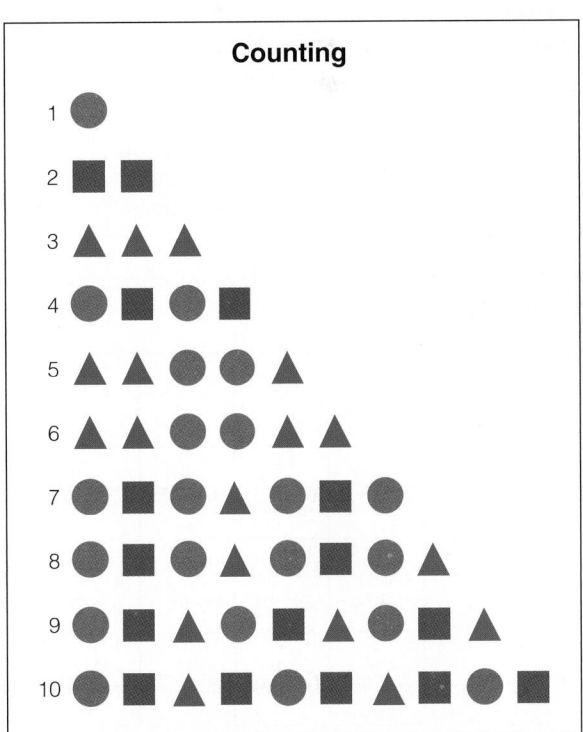

Figure 9.8 Counting chart

of numbers and the objects, as shown in Activity 9.7. Activities with manipulative materials demonstrate numbers created in different ways so that children become flexible in their ideas about number (see Activities 9.8 and 9.9).

Listening to children count shows whether students have learned the sequence of numbers. By counting objects, children coordinate number words with objects one to one. Conservation of number, or constancy of number, indicates an understanding that the number property of a set remains constant even when objects are rearranged, spread out, separated into subsets, or crowded together. Without number constancy children may count two sets of six objects but believe that one set is larger because it looks longer or more dense or more spread out.

Zero requires special attention because children may not have encountered it as a number word. How-ever, children have had experiences with "all gone" and "no more" that can be used to introduce zero. In Activity 9.10 sorting objects into color groups and story situations illustrates zero, or the empty set.

Number Constancy

By using Piaget's conservation of number task, teachers can assess a child's level of number understanding and skill as preconserver, transitional, or conserver (Piaget, 1952). Adults who are not familiar with this task are usually surprised at children's answers to what appears to be a simple task. However, the development of number constancy, or conservation, is a critical cognitive milestone. Without number constancy or number permanence, work with larger numbers, place value, operations, symbols, and number sense is difficult or impossible. Most students develop number understanding at about 5 or 6 years of age because they have sufficient

---

ACTIVITY 9.7   **Counting Cars (Representation)**

Level: Grades K–2

Setting: Learning center

Objective: Students sort and graph objects.

Materials: Plastic cars or other small objects in assorted colors, paper grid with car-size squares

- Place plastic cars (or animals or colored cubes) on the table so that each color of cars is a different number, 1–9, depending on the numbers being emphasized.

- Ask students to sort the cars by color.

- Have a piece of paper marked with squares large enough to hold the cars.

- Ask students to line up the cars so that only one car is in one square. Start with the largest number of cars on the bottom line, and place the smallest number on the top line. Fill in the middle lines so that the sets of cars are arranged from largest to smallest.

- Ask students to count the number of cars in each line. Add the numeral to the chart.

- Read *Counting Jennie*, by Helena Clare Pittman (Minneapolis, MN: Carolrhoda Books, 1994). Have students take a counting walk and record what they count.

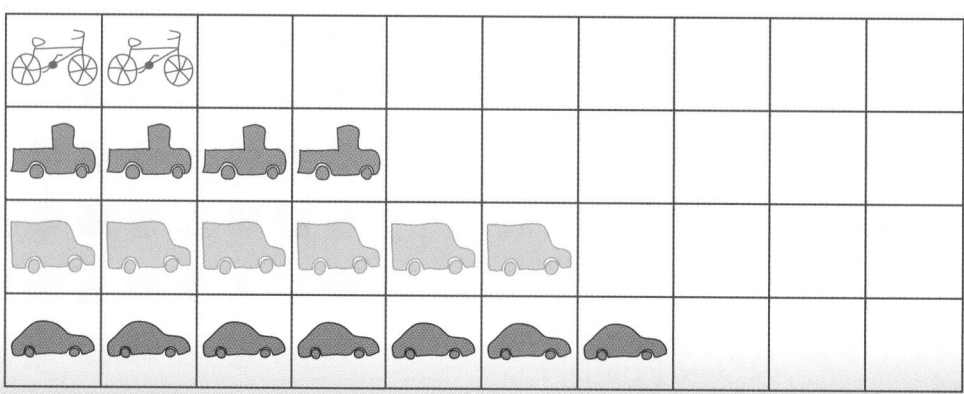

ACTIVITY 9.8   Unifix Cube Combinations (Representation)

Level: Grades K–2

Setting: Learning center or small group

Objective: Students demonstrate that the same number can be made in different ways.

Materials: Unifix cubes

- Create a Unifix tower of seven cubes of the same color.
- Ask students to make other towers the same height using two colors of cubes. They will make tower combinations of two colors for 1 + 6, 2 + 5, 3 + 4, 4 + 3, 5 + 2, and 6 + 1. Some students will notice that 1 + 6 and 6 + 1 are similar but reversed.
- Ask them to make towers of 5 or 7 with three colors. Have students discuss all combinations to see if they have found them all without duplication. Ask if any of the towers have the same numbers made with the colors in different orders.
- Ask how many cubes are in your tower and how many are in each of their towers. Ask them to tell what they learned

about the number 7. Repeat the lesson with other numbers and objects until students understand that a number can be made with many combinations.

ACTIVITY 9.9   Eight (Representation)

Level: Grades K–1

Setting: Small groups

Objective: Students discover cardinal property of number for sets.

Materials: Objects for sorting and counting, paper plates

- Arrange two or three sets of eight objects, each set on a separate paper plate.
- Ask: "How are these sets different?" Discuss the differences the children see, such as size, color, or type of objects.

- Ask: "How are these sets the same?" (Answer: Each one has eight in it.)
- Ask: "How can we make each of the sets have seven? nine?"
- Ask: "What was done to keep all the sets equal in number?"
- Read *Ten Black Dots*, by Donald Crews (New York: Greenwillow, 1986), and have students make pages for a number book using black dots.

ACTIVITY 9.10   No More Flowers (Representation)

Level: Grades 1–2

Setting: Small groups

Objective: Students recognize the word zero and the numeral 0 as symbols for the empty set.

Materials: Felt objects and flannel board, or magnetic objects on a magnetic board

- Put three felt objects on a flannel board.
- Tell a story about the objects, such as: "These flowers were growing in the garden. How many do I have?"
- Remove one of the objects and ask: "When I went to my garden on Saturday, I picked one of the flowers. How many were left?"

- Repeat the story two more times and remove two flowers. Ask how many are left in the garden. Students respond with "none," "not any," "they are all gone," and so on.
- Show several empty containers (boxes, bags, jars). Ask students to describe their contents. Some will say they are empty. They may or may not know zero. If they do not, introduce the word *zero* and the numeral 0 for a set that contains no objects.

mental maturity and have had appropriate experiences with objects and language. Teachers and parents of young children may be tempted to "teach" children the right answer to the conservation task. The ability to conserve is not learned directly but is constructed through interactions with objects and people as well as through mental maturation. Within a short time a student may move from preconserver to transitional to conserver through his or her own reasoning and understanding process.

Piaget developed assessment interviews on many concepts in mathematics: number, length, area, time, mass, and liquid volume. Although materials change for each concept, the steps of the interview are the same for each concept (Copeland, 1984; Piaget, 1952; Wadsworth, 1984):

Step 1. Establish that the two sets or quantities are equivalent.

Step 2. Transform one of the sets or objects.

Step 3. Ask whether the two sets or quantities are still equivalent.

Step 4. Probe for the child's reasoning.

Step 5. Determine the level of reasoning on the task.

Activity 9.11 describes how to conduct an assessment on number constancy, or conservation. Whether the child thinks the sets of checkers are

---

ACTIVITY 9.11 Number Conservation (Assessment Activity and Reasoning)

Level: Grades K–2 (can also be used diagnostically with older children experiencing problems with number concepts)

Setting: Individual

Objective: Students demonstrate number conservation.

Materials: Red and black checkers, 5–10 of each color

An interview for conservation, or constancy, of number determines whether a child can hold the abstract concept of number even when objects are rearranged. This protocol is for individual assessment. The interviewer should refrain from teaching at this time. The purpose is developmental assessment.

Step 1. Establish that the two sets or quantities are equivalent. Put seven red checkers and seven black checkers in parallel rows so that the one-to-one correspondence between the rows is obvious. Say: "I have some red checkers and some black checkers. Do I have the same number of red checkers and black checkers?"

If the child does not recognize that the number of checkers is the same in both rows, the interview is over. The child does not conserve number yet or does not understand the task. If the child responds that the number of red and black checkers is the same, the interview continues.

Step 2. Transform one of the sets or objects. The teacher changes the arrangement of one of the rows by pushing the checkers closer together, spreading them out, or clustering them as a group. The rearrangement is done in full view of the child.

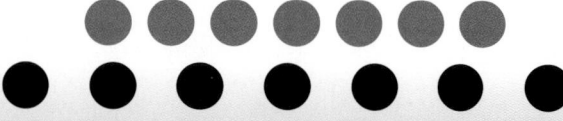

Step 3. Ask whether the two sets or quantities are still equivalent. "Look at the checkers now. Are there more checkers here (pointing to the top row), more checkers here (pointing to the bottom row), or is the number of checkers the same?" The student may respond "more red," "more black," or "the same." Sometimes the student is confused or does not answer.

Step 4. Probe for the child's reasoning. This is the most important part of the interview because it reveals how the child is thinking. "How did you know that the number of black checkers was more (or that the number of red checkers was more or that the number of red and black checkers was the same)?"

Step 5. Determine the level of reasoning on the task. Based on the child's answer, determine the level of conservation.

Preconserver: Child does not yet recognize equivalence of the sets. Some may not even understand what the question is or may not have the vocabulary to understand the situation.

Transitional: Child recognizes equivalence in parallel lines but is confused when the sets are rearranged. These children look intently at the checkers and think out loud: "I thought they were the same, but now they look different." "They aren't the same anymore, but they used to be." "They look different, but they are the same." Wavering between different and same is typical of the transitional learner.

Conserver: Child recognizes, often immediately, that the two sets were equivalent and are still equivalent regardless of the arrangement. When asked to explain why the two are the same, their reasoning may vary, but students who conserve number are absolutely sure about their answer.

the same number or different, the teacher asks for their reasoning. Some children recount the sets of checkers or rearrange them. Others reply that "none were added, none were taken away"; their reasoning is more abstract. Transitional students are puzzled by the task because they are not sure whether the number is the same or different. Some children offer no reason for their answer.

Children move through the concrete operational stage during the elementary years as they develop constancy of length, area, volume, elapsed time, mass, and other concepts. Piaget's structured interview is a good model for assessment of any mathematics content: student engagement with a specific assessment task, followed by questions to discover the child's thinking.

Teachers who focus on student thinking design concrete experiences and avoid abstractions and symbolizations too early. Throughout elementary school, children need objects as aids in their thinking because abstract thinking begins only around ages 11 to 13 and develops slowly into adulthood. Manipulatives in mathematics are objects to think about. Also, adults often use concrete materials and models to help children learn about new ideas and solve problems.

Linking Number and Numeral

Many experiences with manipulative and real objects, games, computer software, books, songs, and conversation develop number concepts and skills. Children who enter preschool and kindergarten with meager informal number and counting experiences or limited English language proficiency need extended time and varied experiences. Unfortunately, children who need additional oral language and concrete experiences are sometimes rushed into symbolic experiences without sufficient background.

As children gain proficiency with verbal and physical representations of number, they also encounter the written symbols 0, 1, 2, 3, 4, 5, 6, 7, 8, 9 matched with sets. Unifix number boats and number indicators, shown in Figure 9.9, structure connecting number to numeral because the number of blocks inside the boat matches the numeral. Unifix number indicators fit on any tower of cubes, so children must determine which indicator goes with which tower. Peg number puzzles, another

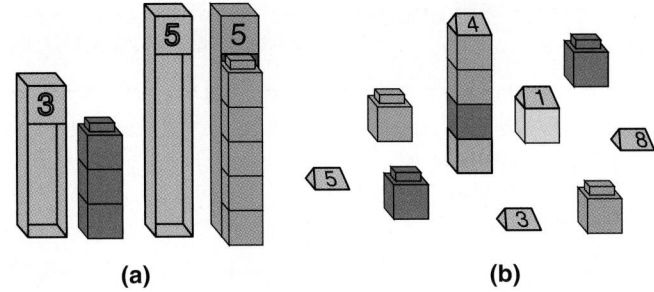

Figure 9.9 (a) Unifix cubes and number boats; (b) Unifix cubes and number indicators.

structured material, show the numeral with the correct number of peg holes. Students fill up the puzzle for each number and then put the numbers together in correct numerical order, as shown in Figure 9.10.

Children also develop mental images of numbers. After working with dice, dominoes, and cards, children develop a strong visual image for number that they recognize without counting the dots or pips. This ability is called *subitizing* and shows a growing sophistication with number. Students soon call out the numbers while playing board games and connect the number with the action. A number line is a spatial, or graphic, arrangement of counting numbers (Figure 9.11). The number line introduces

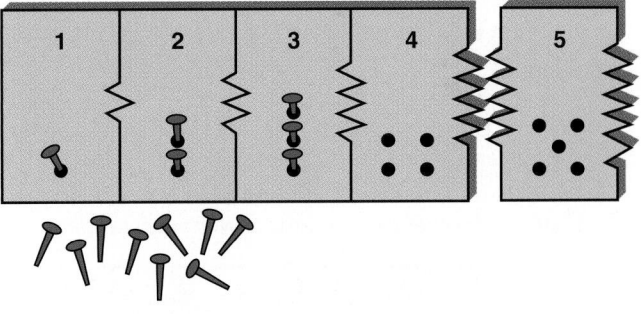

Figure 9.10 Interlocking number puzzles with pegs

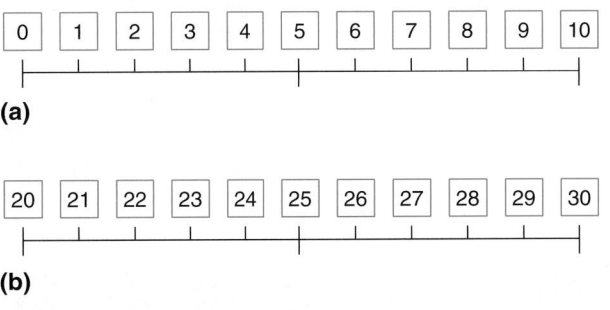

Figure 9.11 Number lines

ACTIVITY 9.12   Plate Puzzles and Cup Puzzles (Representation)

Level: Grades K–2

Setting: Learning center

Objective: Students connect sets with numerals.

Materials: Paper plates, scissors, paper cups

- Make puzzles out of paper plates. Cut each paper plate so that it has a distinct configuration.
- On one piece of the plate, write a numeral; on the other piece, draw a picture or put stickers corresponding to the numeral.

- Write a numeral on an inverted paper cup. Use golf tees to punch the corresponding number of holes in the bottom of the cup. Children fit the correct number of tees into the holes in the cup.
- Have children make their own cup and plate puzzles.

ACTIVITY 9.13   Matching Numeral and Set Cards

Level: Grades K–2

Setting: Learning center

Objective: Students match sets with numerals.

Materials: Pocket chart and sets of cards for matching

A pocket chart can be used in many ways. If made with library pockets on a poster board strip, it makes a learning center that can sit on the chalk tray. At first, the matches made are simple, but the variations suggest many ways of extending the use of the pocket chart.

- Put cards that have pictures of sets on them in the pockets for 0–9 or 1–10. Pictures or stickers can be used. Children can also be given the task of making additional sets of cards.
- Put a set of picture cards in the pockets. Ask students to match with other picture cards or with numeral cards.

- If students need more clues, the cards can match by color as well as by number. Additional sets should not have the color cues.

Variations

- Reverse the order of the sets, or mix up the order of the sets.
- Add a set of number words to match to the sets and the numerals.
- Add a set of addition cards (5 + 1) and subtraction cards (4 − 3) to match the numbers.
- The pocket chart can be used later as a place-value chart for large numbers.

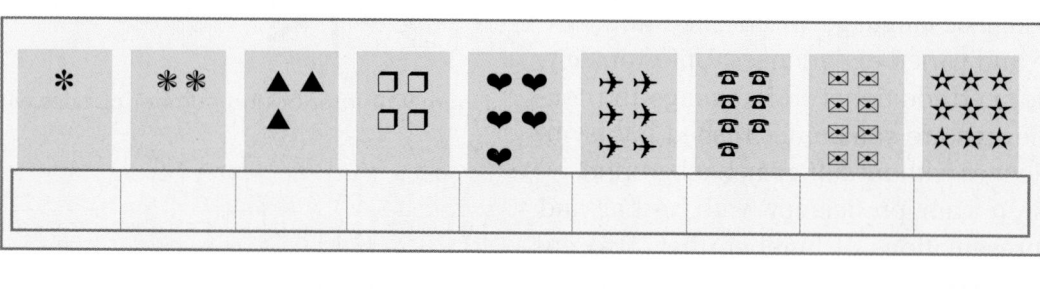

the idea of counting up by walking forward on the number line. Students can also count down by walking backward or turning around. Counting up with objects or on the number line connects counting to addition and subtraction.

Games and puzzles are informal activities that are introduced and placed in learning centers as exploratory and independent activities. Activity 9.12 shows simple puzzles to match sets with numerals. In Activity 9.13 picture cards are matched with appropriate numeral cards. Activity 9.14 is a concentration game for matching numerals and sets.

ⒺXERCISE

Play a board game, card game, or number puzzle game with primary students and observe them. Which mathematics concepts and skills are they learning and practicing? Are all the students equally proficient with the skill? What could you do to help the student be more successful with the game and skill? ●●●

Writing Numerals

Writing names and numerals is a major achievement that gives children more independence in recording their mathematical ideas. Number work does not have to be delayed until children can write. Numeral cards allow children to label sets and sequence numbers. Children usually have developed many number concepts and can recognize many numerals before they can write them. They may also type or use a computer mouse to select numerals without controlling a pencil.

When handwriting instruction begins, correct form is modeled by the teacher and in the materials used. Students trace over dotted or lightly drawn numerals to build their proficiency. Children who write numerals correctly and neatly during writing practice sessions may be less careful at other times. A chart showing the formation of numerals can be posted on the wall, or a writing strip of letters and numerals can be placed at the top of each desk. Different schools adopt different handwriting systems,

---

ACTIVITY 9.14 **Card Games for Numbers and Numerals**

Level: Grades K–4

Setting: Learning center

Objective: Students match numerals and sets.

Materials: Sets of playing cards or index cards with stickers on them

Concentration

- Make a set of 10 index cards with 1 to 10 stickers on them and another 10 cards with the numerals 1 to 10 on them. Arrange the cards face down in a 4 × 5 array.
- A child turns over two cards at a time.
- When a match is made between number and numeral, the child keeps the two cards. If there is not a match, the cards are returned to their places face down, and the next child turns over a pair.

Variations

- Match two sets of numeral cards.
- Pick a target number, and turn over combinations of cards with that sum.
- Play battle with the cards. Each child has half a deck, and they turn over the cards simultaneously. High count wins

both cards. An alternative is to turn over two cards and the highest sum takes all the cards. Ask students to suggest what should be done if the two cards have the same sum.

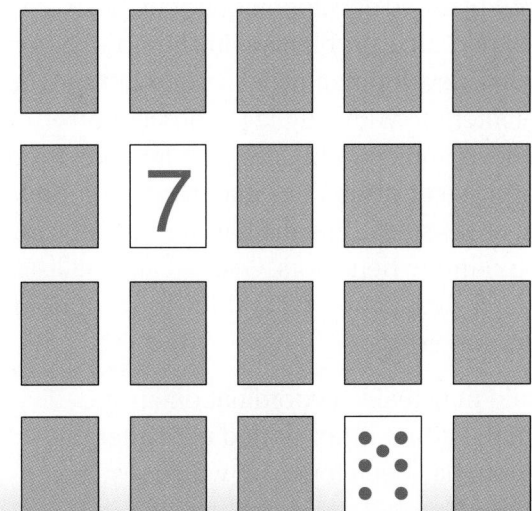

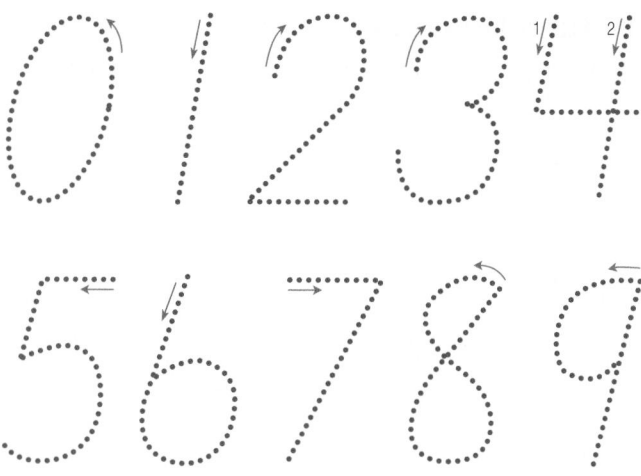

Figure 9.12 D'Nealian numeral forms

such as the D'Nealian number forms shown in Figure 9.12. You will probably need to practice the adopted handwriting systems so that you are a good model for children.

Writing opens up many new opportunities for children to make their own books and displays. On a page, "one" and "1" are written, and the child draws or pastes examples of one object. On the "two" page, two objects are drawn or pasted. Posting children's work or making books for the class library extends interest as children go back to these products again. Booklets are also good home projects, from simple counting projects to special number topics such as odd and even numbers, multiples, and number patterns.

Misconceptions and Problems with Counting and Numbers

Despite well-planned developmental activities, some children experience problems with number. Some children have developmental delays or other special needs that interfere with language, motor control, or cognitive development. Children with limited vision or certain physical disabilities may need larger materials that are easier to see and handle. In analyzing children's counting behaviors, Gelman and Gallistel (1978, pp. 106–108) observed and identified a number of common errors:

- A child may make a coordination error when the count is not started until after the first item has been touched, which results in an undercount, or when the count continues after the final item has been touched, which results in an overcount.

- A child may make omission errors when one or more items are skipped.

- A child may make a double-count error by counting one or more items more than once.

- A child may use idiosyncratic counting sequences such as "1, 2, 4, 6, 10."

If children have difficulty with counting and make coordination, omission, or double-counting errors, they can count objects on a paper or a magnetic board with a line marked down the center. As children count each object, they move it from the left half to the right half. This action reduces the opportunity to begin or end the count improperly, to skip one or more objects, or to double-count some. After counting proficiency is achieved, a child may not need to move the objects.

Reversal errors in writing numerals, as with 6 and 9 or 5 and 2, are common among children. Eye-hand and fine muscle coordination are needed before children can write with accuracy and comfort. If children count accurately, written reversals should not cause concern. If the problem persists into the second or third grade, the teacher may refer the student for visual or motor coordination problems. Adapting material for students with visual or motor impairments might include providing larger materials or using materials with rough surfaces.

Introducing Ordinal Numbers

Ordinal numbers describe relative position in a sequence or line. Ordinal numbers occur in many situations that students and teachers can discuss and label. Children can stand at the first, sixth, or tenth place from zero on the number line. When children line up for recess or dismissal, they notice who is first, last, second, fifth, or middle. The bases in baseball are also first, second, third, and home (or last) base. Discussing sequence in stories, in days of the week or month, or in each day's events uses ordinal numbers. Asking questions calls attention to ordinal concepts:

- Who was the third animal that Chicken Little talked to?

- Who is second in line today?

- What happens during the second week of this month?

When children see the ordinal usage occur in common classroom situations and hear adults use the various terms correctly, most have little trouble with this use of numbers.

Other Number Skills

From their first encounters with numbers and counting, students learn some important number skills that extend their understanding of how numbers work. Skip counting and concepts of odd and even are introduced in primary grades.

Skip Counting

First experiences in counting are based on one-to-one correspondence between objects and the natural numbers 1, 2, 3. Skip counting is performed with objects that occur in groups of 2, 3, 4, 5, or others. Skip counting encourages faster and flexible counting and is connected to multiplication and division.

- How many eyes are in our room? Count by two.

- How many chair legs are in the room? How can we count them quickly?

- We have 15 dimes and 7 nickels. What is a quick way to count our money?

A hundreds board or chart is a visual way for children to investigate skip counting (see Activity 9.15).

One-to-One and Other Correspondences

Children use one-to-one correspondence as the basis for relating one object to one counting number. They also need experience with other correspondences and relations: one-to-many, many-to-one, and many-to-many. One-to-many correspondences and many-to-one correspondences are used every day in many reversible situations; some examples are shown in Table 9.1.

A good problem-solving strategy for many-to-many correspondences is a rate table. If three pencils cost 25 cents, how many pencils will 75 cents buy? The ratio between pencils and cents is 3:25 which is extended as far as it is needed to answer the question.

Pencils	3	6	9	12	15	18	21	24	27
Cost		25¢	50¢	75¢	?	?			

ⒺXERCISE

Look at a state map. Using the scale on the map, estimate the distance between two places in your state. ●●●

ACTIVITY 9.15 **Patterns on the Hundreds Chart**

Level: Grades 2–5

Setting: Small groups

Objective: Students find patterns on the hundreds chart.

Materials: Hundreds chart on paper or transparency (see Black-Line Master 9.1)

- Ask students to color numbers as they skip-count by twos on the chart. Ask students to describe the design made by multiples of 2.

- Have students in each group color the hundreds chart for multiples of 3, 4, 5, and so on, and watch for designs made by the patterns. After students have completed individual number pages, make a book in which they describe the patterns found.

- Pose questions such as, "What skip-counting pattern begins at the top left and moves downward toward the bottom right corner?" "Name a skip-counting pattern that begins at the top right and moves diagonally downward to the left."

1	2	3	4	5	6	7	8	9	10
11	12	13	14	15	16	17	18	19	20
21	22	23	24	25	26	27	28	29	30
31	32	33	34	35	36	37	38	39	40
41	42	43	44	45	46	47	48	49	50
51	52	53	54	55	56	57	58	59	60
61	62	63	64	65	66	67	68	69	70
71	72	73	74	75	76	77	78	79	80
81	82	83	84	85	86	87	88	89	90
91	92	93	94	95	96	97	98	99	100

TABLE 9.1   Some Common One-to-Many, Many-to-One, and Many-to-Many Correspondences

	One-to-Many	Many-to-One	Many-to-Many
Place value	1 ten = 10 ones	10 ones = 1 ten	
Value	1 nickel = 5 pennies	5 pennies = 1 nickel	
Linear measure	1 foot = 12 inches	12 inches = 1 foot	
	1 meter = 100 centimeters	100 centimeters = 1 meter	
Time/distance	1 hour for 55 miles	55 miles in 1 hour	
Shopping	1 dozen has 12 bagels	12 bagels in 1 dozen	
Time	1 day has 24 hours	24 hours in 1 day	
Maps	1 inch stands for 25 miles		
Fuel economy			15 gallons goes 350 miles
Food			3 cans for $1.45
Tires			4 tires cost $125.00

Odd and Even Numbers

Counting by twos prompts children's thinking about odd and even numbers. Counting eyes, or ears, or feet, or twins helps students recognize naturally occurring situations of even numbers. **Even numbers** are a set of numbers divisible by 2 with no remainder. **Odd numbers** are the set of numbers not divisible by 2 evenly and they cannot be organized into pairs. Skip counting by 2 is a way to identify even numbers. In Activity 9.16 children use plastic disks to determine which numbers are even and which are odd. Objects that can be arranged in pairs represent even numbers. Knowledge of even and odd numbers establishes a pattern that is also used for finding other patterns and relationships.

The number line and hundreds chart are used for further investigations with even and odd numbers. Children make a variety of observations about the number chart:

- Beginning at 2, every other number is an even number; beginning at 1, every other number is odd.

- The column on the left side of the chart contains all odd numbers ending in 1. Each alternate column ends in 3, 5, 7, and 9.

- The second column from the left contains all even numbers that end in 2.

- Each alternate column across the chart contains even numbers ending in 4, 6, 8, and 0.

- Even numbers are all multiples of 2.

Similar conclusions can be made about 3, 4, 5, and other numbers as students explore patterns. Intermediate-grade students can study even and odd numbers at a more abstract level. They should develop and justify these generalizations during their investigations.

ACTIVITY 9.16   Even and Odd (Reasoning)

Level: Grades 1 and 2

Setting: Student pairs

Objective: Students recognize odd and even numbers by pairing objects.

Materials: Counting disks or other objects

- Ask students to arrange eight disks in two rows. Ask if they can put the same number in each row.

(a)
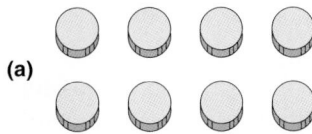

- Ask students to find other numbers of disks to make two equal rows. Put their numbers on a chart, or mark them on a hundreds chart.

- Ask students to arrange seven disks in two rows. Ask if the two rows are equal.

(b)
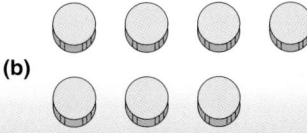

- Ask students to find other numbers that do not make two equal rows. Put these numbers on the board, or mark them with a different color on the hundreds chart.

- Say: "Numbers that make two equal rows have a special name." If students do not volunteer "even," supply it.

- Say: "Numbers that cannot make two equal rows also have a name." If students do not know "odd," supply it.

- After every even number is an odd number, which can be expressed as $2n + 1$.

Students may be asked whether zero is an even number and to explain their thinking.

Research for the Classroom

Various research findings have determined that young children learn to count and use numbers in purposeful ways at an early age. Caulfield (2000) suggests that the human brain is "born to count" as a natural way of organizing the physical world. Suggate and colleagues (1997) studied mathematical knowledge and strategies of 4- and 5-year-olds over a year. Most students had a high level of numerical proficiency at the beginning of the year and improved over the year. However, a few students showed little improvement over the year. Wright (1994) also studied the growth of forty-one 5- and 6-year-olds for a year. However, his findings emphasize the mismatch between the children's numerical competence and the demands of the curriculum.

Jones and colleagues (1992) reported that first-grade students engaged in a tutoring program became more flexible in their numerical strategies and were successful at tasks that were more complex than usually expected of them. The tutoring program involved working in pairs with a teacher on inquiry and exploratory mathematical tasks. The mentor-teachers also changed their practices and beliefs about what students could learn as a result of participation in the program.

In summary, young children have many numerical skills and can learn new strategies if teaching is interactive, relevant, and encourages thinking about number rather than memorizing processes without understanding.

Summary

Children use numbers in many ways: to label, to order, to count, and to solve problems in their lives. Young children classify and sequence objects based on physical qualities. Through a variety of manipulative and language experiences, children learn about number as an abstract property of sets that can be represented with objects, in pictures, and with symbols, called numerals. Interactions with numbers in books, songs, poems, puzzles, games, and objects contribute to the development of number and numerals. Rote counting, rational counting, and number conservation are important achievements in learning about numbers. In rote counting children can recite number words, whereas rational counting demonstrates the relationship between number words and objects. Understanding that number is constant regardless of the arrangement of objects is called number conservation or constancy and is a developmental milestone about age 6 for children.

When children encounter numbers in meaningful settings and situations, they begin to think about numbers in terms of number patterns, reasonableness, and estimation. Questions such as what number is after 99, what number is between 43 and 45, or which numbers are odd and even serve as the foundation for number sense with larger numbers, computation, and algebraic thinking. Recognizing patterns in numbers up to 100 sets the stage for understanding the Hindu-Arabic, or base-10, numeration system. Hindu-Arabic numeration is a place-value system based on the number 10 that allows numbers of any size to be represented in an economical way. Developed over centuries, the Hindu-Arabic system provides efficient algorithms for computation.

Study Questions and Activities

1. Number sense is a major goal of instruction in numbers. How aware of numbers are you in everyday life? Do you notice how much groceries cost? how much you tip a server? how long you wait on line? how much you save on an item on sale?

2. Ask several young children, ages 4, 5, or 6, to count aloud for you to 20. Then ask them to count a set of 12 pennies or other small objects. Record what each child does. Did you find any differences in their rote and rational counting abilities? Did any of them demonstrate the common counting errors listed by Gelman and Gallistel? What procedures would you recommend for helping a child overcome counting errors?

3. Read a counting book with a group of young children. Observe their reactions to the pictures, numerals, and story. What did you learn about children's understanding of numbers and number concepts?

Praxis

The Praxis II test includes items on early mathematics. Try the following three items to check your understanding of the concepts and teaching methods in items similar to those found on the Praxis test.

4. When Mrs. Rodriquez greets children by counting them first, second, third, fourth, . . . , which use of number is she demonstrating?
   a. Cardinal
   b. Nominal
   c. Counting
   d. Ordinal

5. Mr. Kinski asks students to classify classroom objects into three groups. What mathematical concepts and skills are used?
   a. Recognizing similarities and differences
   b. Counting
   c. Relating numbers to numerals
   d. Recognizing two-dimensional and three-dimensional shapes

6. Miss Shalabi asks students to extend the pattern made with the following attribute blocks. Benito places a square then a triangle at the end of the pattern. What response would be the best way to help Benito?

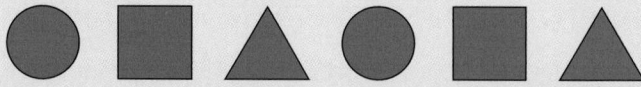

   a. No, that is wrong. Put a circle then the square and triangle.
   b. Read the pattern with me. What pattern do you hear?
   c. How many shapes are in the pattern?
   d. Let me show you how to finish the pattern.
   Answers: 4d, 5a, 6b.

Teacher's Resources

Kamii, C., & Housman, L. (2000). *Young children reinvent arithmetic: Implications of Piaget's theory* (2nd ed.). Williamston, VT: Teachers College Press.

Shaw, J. (2005). *Mathematics for Young Children*. Little Rock, AR: Southern Early Childhood Association.

Wheatley, G., & Reynolds, A. (1999). *Coming to know number: A mathematics activity resource for elementary school teachers*. Tallahassee, FL: Mathematics Learning.

Whitin, D., & Wilde, S. (1995). *It's the story that counts: More children's books for mathematical learning, K–6.* Portsmouth, NH: Heinemann.

Wright, R., Martland, J., and Stafford, A. (2000). *Early numeracy*. Thousand Oaks, CA: Corwin Press.

Children's Bookshelf

Anno, Mitsumasa. (1977). *Anno's counting book*. New York: Harper-Collins. (Grades PS–3)

Bang, Mary. (1983). *Ten, nine, eight*. New York: Greenwillow. (Grades PS–1)

Blumenthal, Nancy. (1989). *Count-asaurus*. New York: Macmillan. (Grades PS–3)

Coats, Lucy. (2000). *Nell's numberless world*. London: Dorling Kindersley. (Grades 2–4)

Crews, Donald. (1986). *Ten black dots* (rev. ed.). New York: Greenwillow. (Grades PS–3)

Dee, Ruby. (1988). *Two ways to count to ten*. New York: Henry Holt. (Grades K–3)

Ernst, Lisa Campbell. (1986). *Up to ten and down again*. New York: Mulberry. (Grades K–2)

Feelings, Muriel. (1971). *Moja means one: A Swahili counting book*. New York: Dial. (Grades PS–3)

Freeman, Don. (1987). *Count your way through Russia*. Minneapolis: Carolrhoda. (Grades 1–3)

Hoban, Tana. (1985). *1, 2, 3*. New York: Greenwillow. (Grade PS)

Hoban, T. (1998). *More, fewer, less*. New York: Greenwillow. (Grades K–2)

Johnson, S. (1998). *City by numbers*. New York: Viking. (Grades 2–6)

Merriam, Eve. (1992). *12 ways to make 11*. New York: Simon & Schuster. (Grades 1–3)

Morozumi, Atsuko. (1990). *One gorilla*. New York: Farrar Straus & Giroux. (Grades K–2)

Pittman, Helena Clare. (1994). *Counting Jennie*. Minneapolis: Carolrhoda Books. (Grades K–2)

Schmandt-Besserat, D. (1999). *The history of counting*. New York: William Morrow. (Grades 4–6)

Zaslavsky, Claudia. (1989). *Zero: Is it something? Is it nothing?* New York: Franklin Watts. (Grades 1–4)

For Further Reading

Fuson, K., Grandau, L., & Sugiyama, P. (2001). Achievable numerical understanding for all young children. *Teaching Children Mathematics* 7(9), 522–526.

Fuson and colleagues describe young children's developmental understanding of number and methods to enhance understanding.

Huinker, D. (2002). Calculators as learning tools for young children's explorations of number. *Teaching Children Mathematics* 8(6), 316–322.

Young children with calculators make dynamic discoveries about numbers, counting, and number relationships.

Kline, Kate. (1998). Kindergarten is more than counting. *Teaching Children Mathematics* 5(2), 84–87.

The ten-frame is a visual image for representing numbers and counting ideas.

Pepper, K., & Hunting, R. (1998). Preschoolers' counting and sharing. *Journal of Research in Mathematics Education* 29(2), 164–183.

Research report on early counting strategies used in sharing situations.

Reed, K. (2000). How many spots does a cheetah have? *Teaching Children Mathematics* 6(6), 346–349.

Children explore the number of spots on a cheetah and invent counting and estimation strategies.

CHAPTER 10

Extending Number Concepts and Number Systems

As children master basic number concepts and can count and write numbers through 20, understanding larger numbers using the base-10 place-value system becomes the focus of instruction. Representing larger numbers with the Hindu-Arabic numeration system is a foundation for computation and number sense. Reasonableness and estimation are essential for development of number sense—the ability to think with and about numbers. In this chapter activities develop understanding of place value and emphasize numbers sense.

In this chapter you will read about:

1 The essential role of number sense and number awareness in elementary mathematics

2 Representing numbers in many forms

3 Using the base-10 numeration system to represent larger numbers

4 Activities and materials for teaching exchanging and regrouping in base 10

5 Activities and materials for learning about larger numbers

6 Activities and materials for number sense, rounding, and estimation

7 Extending understanding of number through patterns, operation rules for odd and even numbers, prime and composite numbers, and integers

NCTM Standards and Expectations

Understand numbers, ways of representing numbers, relationships among numbers, and number systems.

In prekindergarten through grade 2 all students should:
- Count with understanding and recognize "how many" in sets of objects;
- Use multiple models to develop initial understandings of place value and the base-10 number system;
- Develop understanding of the relative position and magnitude of whole numbers and of ordinal and cardinal numbers and their connections;
- Develop a sense of whole numbers and represent and use them in flexible ways, including relating, composing, and decomposing numbers;
- Connect number words and numerals to the quantities they represent, using various physical models and representations.

In grades 3–5 all students should:
- Understand the place-value structure of the base-10 number system and be able to represent and compare whole numbers and decimals;
- Recognize equivalent representations for the same number and generate them by decomposing and composing numbers;
- Explore numbers less than 0 by extending the number line and through familiar applications.

Number Sense Every Day

Number sense should be an everyday event in classrooms. Teachers stimulate children's thinking with and about numbers by posing questions based on daily occurrences.

- Last week, the estimation jar held 300 cotton balls. This week it is full of golf balls. Do you think the jar holds more than 300 golf balls or fewer than 300 golf balls? Why do you think so?

- Our class has 22 students, and 20 are eating in the cafeteria. If lunch costs 85 cents, will 20 lunches cost more or less than $20?

- Sada put 200 color tiles in the bag. When groups each picked out five samples of 20, they reported these results:

	Red	Blue	Yellow	Green
Group 1	43%	24%	17%	16%
Group 2	35%	28%	20%	17%
Group 3	39%	25%	21%	15%

What is your best estimate of the number of tiles of each color in the bag?

- If everybody in our classroom had one pet, how many pets would we have? What if everybody had two pets? three pets? How could we find out how many pets we really have in our classroom?

- The newspaper reports that the population of our state is growing by 30,000 each year. If 1 out of 3 individuals is of school age, how many new schools do we need to build each year?

Children with number sense see how numbers are represented and operated on in various ways, allowing them to use number flexibly in computation and problem solving.

- Half a gallon of ice cream is $\frac{1}{2}$, 0.5, or 50% of a gallon or 2 quarts or 4 pints or 8 cups.

- If an $80 coat is reduced by 25% on sale, one-fourth of $80 is $20. The coat costs $60 plus tax.

- One meter is slightly longer than 1 yard; running a 100-meter race should take slightly longer than running a 100-yard race.

- The product of 3.8 and 9.1 is approximately $4 \times 9 = 36$.

At the core of number sense is flexible understanding of numbers and how they can be represented in various ways. Rather than memorizing rules, students are asked to develop numbers as they solve problems, estimate, and draw reasonable conclusions from numerical information.

Teachers who engage children in mathematical conversation encourage children to think about numbers and their meaning. Ms. Chen wants to know whether her second-grade students recognize different representations for 27 using a hundreds chart and base-10 materials.

Amani: Twenty-seven comes after 26 and before 28.

Guillermo: Twenty-seven is three more than 24 and three smaller than 30.

Lisette: Twenty-seven is two groups of ten and seven ones.

Yolanda: Twenty-seven is 10 more than 17 and 10 less than 37 on the hundreds chart.

Ian: I can count to 27 by threes: 3, 6, 9, 12, 15, 18, 21, 24, 27, but counting by fours is 28.

Jermaine: Twenty-seven is an odd number because you skip it when you count by twos.

When making 27 with base-10 materials, some display 27 with two orange rods and seven white cubes;

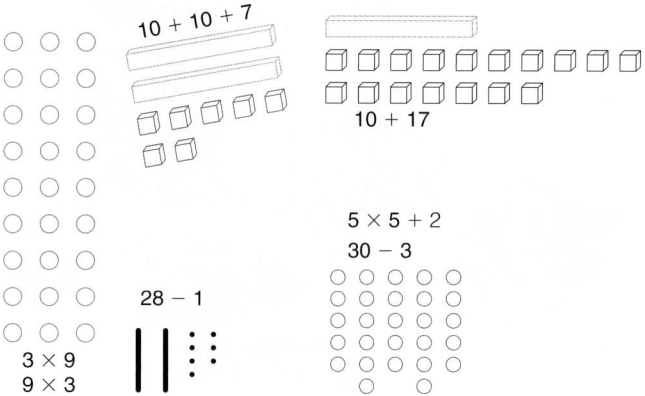

Figure 10.1 Several ways of representing 27

others line up 27 loose cubes, 2 bean sticks and 7 beans, or 9 groups of 3 (Figure 10.1).

By observing and listening to children, the teacher learns whether they understand many numeral expressions for 27. From student comments and demonstrations, Ms. Chen believes that students have developed a flexible understanding of number and its many representations, so she is ready to introduce the place-value system in a more comprehensive way. Extending their understanding of number and place value to hundreds and thousands is critical for understanding number operations with larger numbers.

Understanding the Base-10 Numeration System

When students are learning to count, they often think of each number as having its own unique name. Numbers 0–9 do have unique names, but learning a different name for all the numbers from 10 to 999,999 would be impractical and impossible to remember. Instead the place-value system allows the same 10 symbols to have different values depending on the position in a numeral: 6 could have a value of 6 in the ones position, 60 in the tens position, or 600 in the hundreds position. The hundreds chart (Figure 10.2) illustrates for children the pattern of tens and ones that structures the base-10 numeration system.

Counting by tens and the hundreds chart introduce the pattern of tens in the number system. Base-10 materials represent numbers concretely. Commercial and teacher-made materials (bean sticks, bundles of stir sticks, graph paper, or strings of

MISCONCEPTION
English counting words above *ten* (*eleven, twelve, thirteen* through *nineteen*) hide the place-value meaning. *Eleven* means 10 + 1, *twelve* is 10 + 2, and *thirteen* is 10 + 3. Connecting the values from 11 to 19 to their place-value meaning is important. Some teachers have the students use "count ten, ten plus one, ten plus two," and so on as an alternative counting language up to 19. Above 20 the place-value system and counting language correspond: 21 means 2 tens plus 1.

beads) are useful for representing values to 1,000 (see Photo 10.1).

Place-value materials can be either proportional or nonproportional. **Proportional materials** show value with the size of the materials. When the manipulative piece representing one unit is determined, the tens piece is 10 times larger, and the hundreds piece is 10 times the tens place. Some materials allow students to create their own base-10 materials. A tower of 10 Unifix cubes represents 10. If one tongue depressor or popsicle stick is the unit, a bundle of 10 represents tens, and 10 bundles are 100. A paper clip is 1, a chain of 10 paper clips would be the tens, and ten chains hooked together show 100. Base-10 blocks, Cuisenaire rods, and bean sticks are proportional materials with the tens unit already joined together.

Nonproportional materials can also represent place values, although the one-to-ten relationship is not shown in the size of materials. Money is the most familiar nonproportional material. Dimes are not 10 times as large as pennies, and dollar coins or bills are not 10 times as large as dimes. Nonproportionality makes money exchange confusing for younger

1	2	3	4	5	6	7	8	9	10
11	12	13	14	15	16	17	18	19	20
21	22	23	24	25	26	27	28	29	30
31	32	33	34	35	36	37	38	39	40
41	42	43	44	45	46	47	48	49	50
51	52	53	54	55	56	57	58	59	60
61	62	63	64	65	66	67	68	69	70
71	72	73	74	75	76	77	78	79	80
81	82	83	84	85	86	87	88	89	90
91	92	93	94	95	96	97	98	99	100

Figure 10.2 Hundreds chart (see Black-Line Master 10.1)

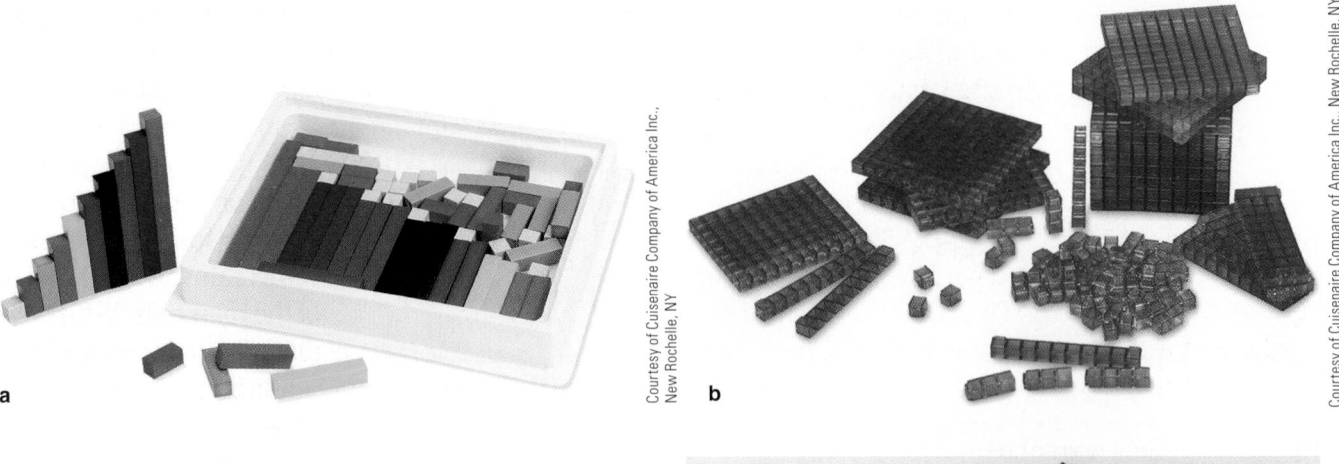

Courtesy of Cuisenaire Company of America Inc., New Rochelle, NY

Courtesy of Cuisenaire Company of America Inc., New Rochelle, NY

Courtesy of Didax Educational Resources, Peabody, MA

Courtesy of Scott Resources, San Francisco

Photo 10.1 Base-10 materials: (a) Cuisenaire rods; (b) base-10 blocks; (c) Unifix cubes; (d) chip trading materials

children. They have to remember the relationship rather than seeing the relationship. Chip trading materials and an abacus are also nonproportional materials. Value of a number is indicated by color and position rather than by size. The Hindu-Arabic numeration system is also nonproportional because numerals are evaluated by their position.

Both proportional materials and nonproportional materials are useful, but proportional materials emphasize the relative value of the places and

---

ACTIVITY 10.1 Trains and Cars (Representation)

Level: Grades K–2

Setting: Pairs

Objective: Students recognize 10 as an organizer for counting numbers larger than 10.

Materials: Unifix cubes

- Give pairs of children a bowl of Unifix cubes. Have each student count 10 single cubes and put them together to make a train.

- Ask them how many trains they can make with the cubes in their bowl. Ask how many trains and how many extra cars.

- Let the students tell what they have in their bowl. Have each pair compare the number of cubes in their trains with those in other trains.

- Ask two groups to combine their trains and extra cars to see how many trains they have together.

- Count trains by tens, and ask students if any group has 10 trains. Emphasize that 10 trains is 1 hundred.

are recommended for initial instruction in the base-10 system. Children enjoy making a set of base-10 materials by bundling stirring sticks to show groups of 10, then bundling 10 groups of 10 into a big bundle of 100. Working with a variety of materials shows children that place value is a characteristic of the number system rather than a particular manipulative. Activity 10.1 introduces place value with Unifix cubes and trains of 10. Activity 10.2 introduces a train-car work mat with a tens column and a ones column. Additional task cards guide children during independent learning activities.

Place-value materials and activities continue through grade 6 as students represent larger numbers and model problems in addition, subtraction, multiplication, and division. Children show their understanding of place value with materials, actions, simple diagrams (e.g., Figure 10.3), and numerals. Exchanging 10 ones for 1 ten and 10 tens for 1 hundred establishes the place-value pattern for thousands, millions, and billions. Children notice that the 9 is a precursor for the next larger place. The calculator is a learning tool for place value as students repeatedly add 1 and note changes each time 9 is reached, such as $99 + 1$ becomes 100. Introduction of the exchange from 99 to 100 is often celebrated on the hundredth day of school to call attention to the importance of 100. Students bring displays of 100 beans, 100 cotton balls, and 100 peanuts.

Figure 10.3 Example of a simple diagram of base-10 blocks showing 237

Exchanging, Trading, or Regrouping

When working with place-value materials, children trade, or exchange, ones for tens and tens for hundreds, or the reverse. Exchanges between place values is most accurately called **regrouping and renaming**, but *trading up* and *trading down* are common terms. Both are more accurate terminology than "carrying" or "borrowing" because they accurately describe the physical actions. Many games

and activities illustrate exchanges with any place-value manipulatives. Activity 10.3 is an important informal introduction to creating numbers up to 100 or 1,000 by accumulating and trading up with proportional materials of beans and sticks. Trading down begins with the 10 tens sticks, and children remove beans and sticks as they roll the die. This activity also serves as an informal assessment of children's understanding of place value. Nonproportional materials, such as poker chips or color tiles, can be used to play the same game. Beans spray-painted yellow, blue, green, and red are inexpensive substitutes for commercial materials. Game mats can be made of file folders or tagboard.

Through teacher questioning with physical modeling of place value, students begin to understand how place value works and should become comfortable with physical representations of larger values. As they progress, students discuss how many hundreds, tens, and ones are in each number they create. Symbolic representation also begins. Activity 10.4 uses children's names as the source for counting ones, tens, and hundreds. In Activity 10.5 players have seven turns to accumulate 100 points without going over. The game can be played with place-value materials on a game mat or with symbols as students are learning addition with regrouping.

Assessing Place-Value Understanding

Some students experience difficulty in understanding place value. By working at the concrete level and not rushing the transition to symbolic representation, most students construct place-value meaning by the third grade. However, some students have continuing difficulty with the meaning of tens and ones. Kamii (1986) developed a structured interview for place value. The interview can be done with any number using the steps shown in Activity 10.6.

MULTICULTURAL CONNECTION

English counting language may also contribute to children's confusion about tens and ones. In Asian and Latin-based languages, counting language emphasizes the place-value structure (Table 10.1). In Spanish, for example, 16 is *diez y seis*, or "10 and 6." Students from various cultures might be invited to teach counting words in their language. With a chart such as Table 10.1, students notice the patterns based on tens in languages such as Chinese.

ACTIVITY 10.2 Train-Car Mats

Level: Grades 1–2

Setting: Pairs

Objective: Students use a two-column mat as a structure for place value.

Materials: Unifix cubes, two-column mat

- Give pairs of students sets of 12–30 Unifix cubes and a two-column mat.

- As children assemble trains with 10 cubes, have them put them in the left column on the mat. Have them put extra cars in the right column. Ask students to report how many items they have as "___ trains and ___ cars."

- As students understand the format, work up to sets between 30 and 100.

- Provide index cards with numerals on them so that students can label the columns: 2 tens or 20 with index cards in one color, and 11, 12, 13 in another color.

Variation

- Use counting chips, tongue depressors, or stirrers with a place-value mat.

- Have the children stack the chips or bundle the tongue depressors or stirrers with a rubber band.

- Ask children where the bundle of 10 should go on the place-value mat.

- Discuss 11 as "10 and 1," 12 as "10 and 2," and so on.

- Provide task cards for students to continue work independently.

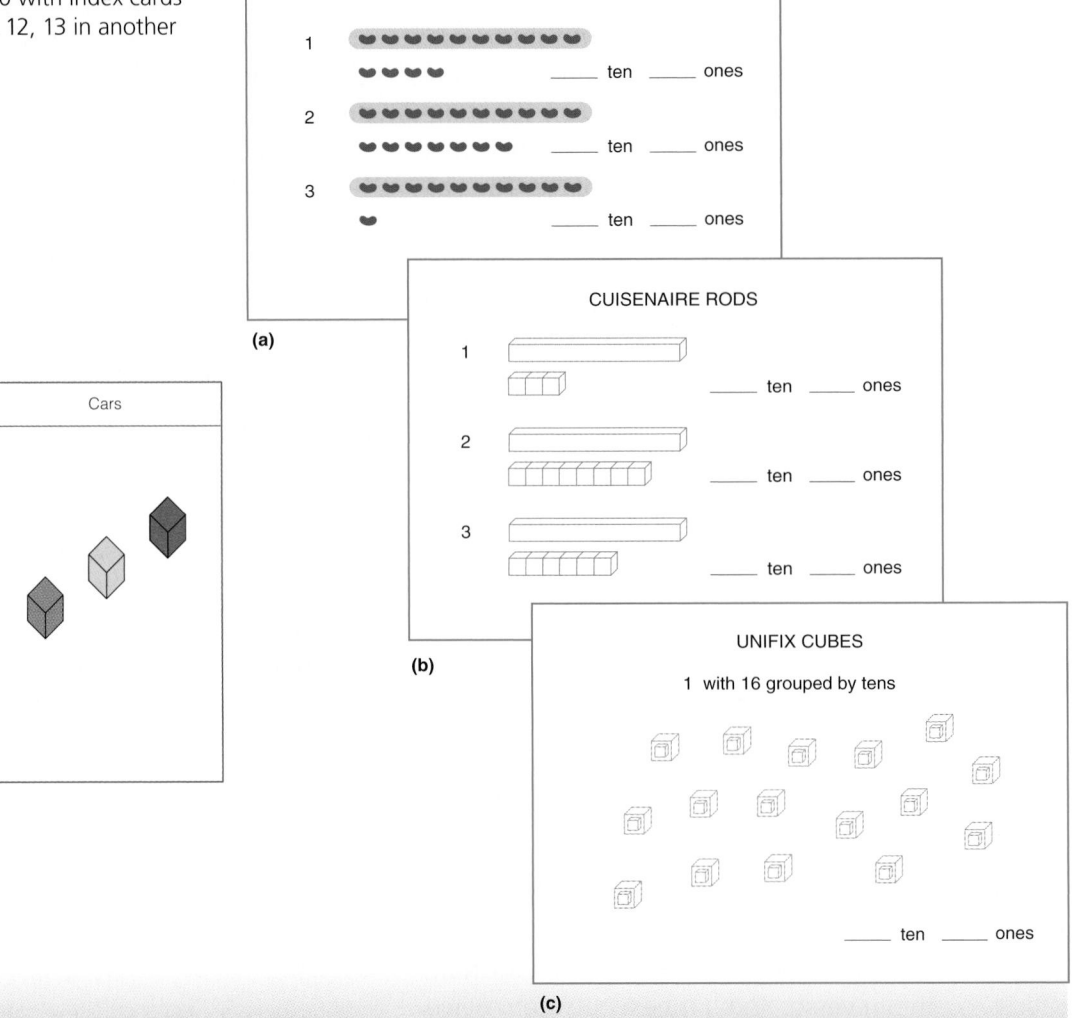

ACTIVITY 10.3 Beans and Sticks (Representation)

Level: Grades 2–5

Setting: Small groups of 3 or 4 students

Objective: Students represent numbers in the place-value system.

Materials: Beans, bean sticks of 10, and bean flats of 100 (or other base-10 materials); two-, three-, or four-column mat; number spinner or number cubes

- Play a game with beans, sticks, the place-value mat, and a spinner or number cubes. Each player spins or rolls, counts that many beans, and puts them in the ones column. Players should take turns spinning or rolling.

- As each player accumulates 10 loose beans, he or she trades 10 beans for a bean stick and puts it on the mat in the tens place. Play continues until all players have ten bean sticks and can trade for a bean flat.

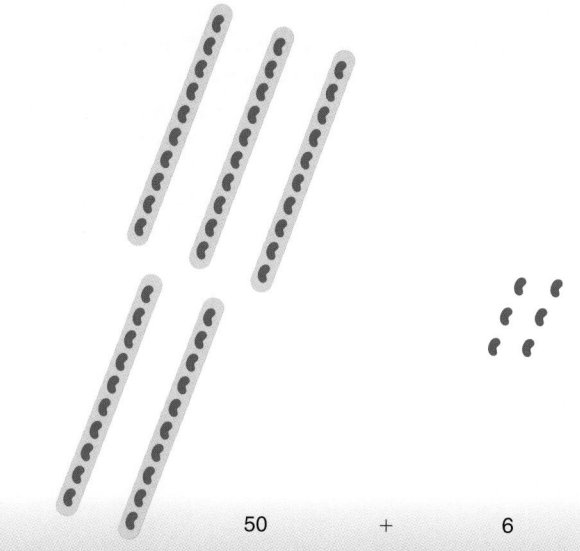

50   +   6

- The game continues into hundreds using a three-column mat, or to thousands with a four-column mat.

- Give each group two spinners or two dice, and ask them to decide how to use two numbers on each turn.

- Assess student knowledge and skill with a checklist identifying skills: count to 10; exchange accurately, call the correct number; write the numeral; explain tens and ones in number.

Variation

Play the same game with nonproportional materials, such as yellow, blue, green, and red chips or poker chips. Label the game mat with colors, starting with yellow at the right, then blue, green, and red on the left. Each group needs 5 red chips and 40 each of green, blue, and yellow chips, one game mat for each player, and one die.

- After students have had ample time to play the game, ask them what they noticed about playing the game. Emphasize the trading rule and the number of chips that can be in each color space.

- Students can experiment with other trading rules, such as "trade 4" or "trade 9." Younger children can also play the game with a trading rule such as "trade 4" to practice counting to 4.

- Players start with a red chip and trade down until one player has cleared her or his mat.

Working with Larger Numbers

Large numbers are encountered as children think about stars in the sky, pennies in a piggy bank, or a large bag of popcorn kernels. Interest in big numbers and their names helps students explore the meaning and representation of numbers larger than 1,000. Numbers greater than 1,000 are seldom counted physically in real life. Although people could count to 10,000 or 1,000,000, they seldom actually physically count that many objects. Instead they represent large number values symbolically. Even if counting a large number is necessary, people usually create many smaller amounts and aggregate the total. A bank teller creates rolls of pennies, nickels, dimes, and quarters and bundles of bills before

coming up with a total. Population of a city, for example, is done by counting how many people live in specific blocks or areas and adding for a grand total. Computer-based inventory systems keep track of large inventories in supermarkets and retail stores after inventories are taken by counting the number of items on the shelves of each store.

Manipulative work with numbers 1 through 1,000 sets the stage for understanding how the base-10 number system works. Thousands, millions, or billions follow the place-value pattern established with ones, tens, and hundreds and extends students' understanding that number is abstract and infinite and that the place-value system represents infinitely large numbers in a compact form. Two books by

ACTIVITY 10.4 E-vowel-uation (Representation)

Level: Grades 2–5

Setting: Small groups or whole group

Objective: Students recognize that the position of the numeral determines its value.

Materials: Index cards

- Ask students to write their first name (or first and last names) in block letters on one side of an index card. Announce that vowels are worth 1 cent each and that consonants are worth 10 cents each. Have them count or add up the value of their names.

KARA THOMPSON   KRTHMPSN = 80 cents   AAOO = 4 cents = 84 cents

JUAN RODRIGUEZ   JNRDRGZ =   70 cents   UAOIUE = 6 cents = 76 cents

- Ask students to line up from the lowest total to the highest total. Look at names that have low totals and high totals. Ask students to suggest reasons for the low and high totals.

- Change the rule. Consonants are worth 1 cent each, and vowels are worth 10 cents each. Ask students if they think the total of their name will be larger or smaller. Let them calculate the new totals.

- Ask what they notice about the values of their names with a new rule. Some children will have the same value under both rules. Some will notice that their name value switched from 35 cents to 53 cents. Ask why their names had the same or a different value.

- Line up again using the new evaluation to see if the lineup is the same or different.

Variations

- Put the cards on a bulletin board or in a card box, and order them from high to low or from low to high.

- Using the two rules, look for names or words worth $1.00.

- Using the two rules, look for names with large totals and small totals.

- Have capital letters worth a bonus of $1 each. Most students will have a $2 bonus, but some may have $3 or $4.

- Use a different system for evaluating letters, such as place in the alphabet (A = 1, B = 2, etc.) or Scrabble scoring for letters.

ACTIVITY 10.5 Seven Chances for 100 (Reasoning)

Level: Grades 2–5

Setting: Small groups or pairs

Objective: Students apply place value in a game and develop a strategy.

Materials: Die, base-10 blocks, two- or three-column place-value mat

- Organize groups of two to four children. Players take turns rolling the die. On each roll, students can decide whether the number will go with the tens or the ones: a 5 on the die can be worth either 50 (5 rods) or 5 (5 cubes). Each player will have *exactly* seven turns to get as close to 100 points without going over. During play, students trade 10 units for a tens rod. Remind students that they have to take all seven turns.

- After playing for several days, ask students if they have developed a strategy for getting close to 100 without going over.

- After playing the game with the base-10 materials, some students can write the scores on a tens and ones chart and keep a running total.

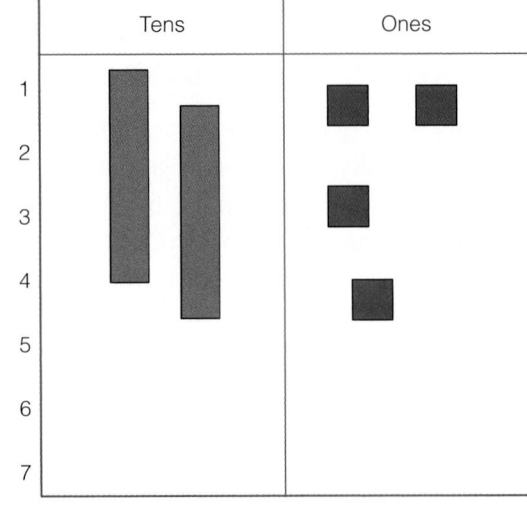

ACTIVITY 10.6   Place-Value Assessment

Level: Grades 1–4
Setting: Individuals
Objective: Students demonstrate an understanding of place value.
Materials: Cubes, paper and pencil

Based on the interview by Kamii (1986), ask students to identify the value of a two-digit numeral as well as the value of each numeral. The interview proceeds in five steps:

1. Give a student 12 to 19 cubes, and then ask the student to count out 16 cubes and draw a picture of them on paper.

2. Ask the student to write the numeral (e.g., 16) for the number of cubes.

3. Ask the student to circle the number of drawn cubes shown by the numeral 16.

4. Point to the 6 in the numeral 16, and ask the student to circle the number of cubes that goes with that numeral.

5. Point to the 1 in the numeral 16, and ask the student to circle the number of cubes that goes with that numeral.

Evaluate the students' understanding of the number.

The figure illustrates responses to the interview. Many students circle the 16 cubes for "16" and 6 cubes for the "6" correctly, but for the "1" they circle only one block instead of ten. Based on her interviews, Kamii concluded that misconceptions about place value persist into third or fourth grade. Whether this problem is due to maturation or inappropriate instruction is not clear, but teachers should be sensitive to students and provide more

developmental activities as needed. Concrete models for trading are essential to illustrate the dynamic nature of place value.

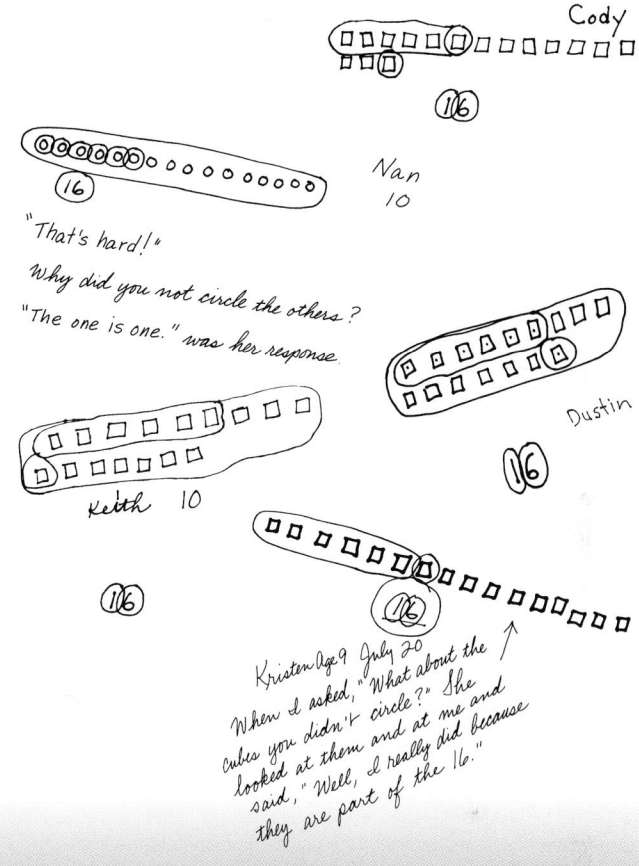

TABLE 10.1   Counting Language: English Versus Chinese

English	Chinese	English	Chinese	English	Chinese
one	yi	eleven	shi-yi	twenty-one	er-shi-yi
two	er	twelve	shi-er	twenty-two	er-shi-er
three	san	thirteen	shi-san		
four	si	fourteen	shi-si		
five	wu	fifteen	shi-wu	thirty	san-shi
six	liu	sixteen	shi-liu		
seven	qi	seventeen	shi-qi		
eight	ba	eighteen	shi-ba	forty	si-shi
nine	jiu	nineteen	shi-jiu		
ten	shi	twenty	er-shi	fifty	wu-shi

ACTIVITY 10.7 Think of a Million (Reasoning and Representation)

Level: Grades 3–6

Setting: Whole group

Objective: Students visualize the magnitude of large numbers.

Materials: *How Much Is a Million?* by David Schwartz, illustrated by Steven Kellogg (New York: Lothrop, Lee & Shepard, 1985); package of popcorn kernels or dried beans

- Show students a package of popcorn kernels or dried beans. Ask if they think there could be a million kernels in the package. Have students count the number in one package.

- Based on the number, ask students how many packages they would need to get to a million. Use multiplication by 10 and 100 as a quick way to determine the number of packages. A rate table is useful for this.

Packages	1	10	100	200	300	400
Number	2,317	23,000	230,000	460,000	690,000	920,000

- Introduce Schwartz's book, and read through it, stopping to discuss the illustrations and questions posed in the text.

- Ask students to suggest other things that could be a million. Cooperative groups select a topic and determine how to make a million. Students may wish to refer to Schwartz's calculations in the back of the book.

Extension

Another book by David Schwartz, also illustrated by Steven Kellogg, is *If You Made a Million* (New York: Lothrop, Lee & Shepard, 1989). This book engages children in thinking about money and the responsibilities that come with large amounts of it.

ACTIVITY 10.8 Spin to Win (Representation and Reasoning)

Level: Grades 3–6

Setting: Whole group

Objective: Students demonstrate place-value knowledge and develop a strategy.

Materials: Spinner, numeral cards (0–9), standard die or a die with numerals 0–10 for each group

- On the overhead projector, show a transparency with four boxes labeled thousands, hundreds, tens, and ones. Have students make a similar board on their paper.

Thousands	Hundreds	Tens	Ones

- Announce the goal of the game, such as making the largest four-digit number.

- Using a spinner, number cards, or a die to randomly generate numbers, call out one number at a time. After each number is called, write it in one of the four place-value boxes on the overhead. Once a number is placed, it cannot be moved.

- Spin, roll, or draw cards, and have students fill in their forms. After four numbers have been picked, ask students to tell the largest number anyone made. Ask for the largest number possible.

- In cooperative groups, have students take turns at the spinner while other students fill in the place-value chart.

- Vary the game goals: Make the smallest numeral with the four numbers called out. Make a number that is closest to 7,000. Make a number between 4,000 and 6,000.

- The number of places can be reduced to three for younger students and increased for older students.

Variation

After students are proficient with the game, the game goal and board can be changed to include addition, subtraction, multiplication, and division. Create a game board with three blanks on the top line and two on the bottom line. Place numbers in the blanks to make the largest sum, the smallest sum, the largest difference, the smallest difference, the largest product, the smallest product, or the smallest dividend. Students can create their own boards and game goals.

ACTIVITY 10.9   Big City (Reasoning and Connections)

Level: Grades 3–5

Setting: Whole group

Objective: Students find data with large numbers to use for identifying place value, comparing numbers, ordering, rounding, and estimating.

Materials: Table of data on populations

- Ask students to list large cities in North America. They may want to think of professional sports teams.

- Explain that large cities are often part of a metropolitan area that includes a central city or cities plus the suburbs and surrounding smaller towns.

- Display a table showing the populations of the 15 largest metropolitan areas, and have students organize the data. These data may be found in an almanac or on the Internet.

- In cooperative groups, have students create three to five questions to be answered with the data display.

- Which cities have populations of more than 5 million?
- Which cities have more population than Dallas and Houston put together?
- Which cities are 4,000,000 larger than another city?
- Round the populations of all the cities to the nearest million.
- Which cities have half the population of Chicago?

Extensions

- Find population data for the 10 largest cities and towns in your state. Put the cities and their populations on index cards for grouping and ordering.

- Locate the 15 largest U.S. metropolitan areas on a map of the United States. Are there any patterns to where the cities are located?

- Compare populations in 2000 to populations in 1950. What cities have been added, and which have lost rankings? What factors might contribute to the changes?

Rank	Metropolitan Area Name	State	2000 Population
1	New York–Northern New Jersey–Long Island	NY, NJ, CT, PA	21,199,865
2	Los Angeles–Riverside–Orange County	CA	16,373,645
3	Chicago-Gary-Kenosha	IL, IN, WI	9,157,540
4	Washington-Baltimore	DC, MD, VA, WV	7,608,070
5	San Francisco–Oakland–San Jose	CA	7,039,362
6	Philadelphia–Wilmington–Atlantic City	PA, DE, NJ	6,188,463
7	Boston-Worchester-Lawrence	MA, NH, ME, CT	5,819,100
8	Detroit–Ann Arbor–Flint	MI	5,456,428
9	Dallas–Fort Worth	TX	5,221,801
10	Houston-Galveston-Brazoria	TX	4,669,571
11	Atlanta	GA	4,112,198
12	Miami–Ft. Lauderdale	FL	3,876,380
13	Seattle-Tacoma-Bremerton	WA	3,554,760
14	Phoenix-Mesa	AZ	3,251,876
15	Minneapolis–St. Paul	MN, WI	2,968,806

SOURCE: http://geography.about.com/library/weekly/aa010102a.htm

David Schwartz, *How Much Is a Million?* (1985) and *If You Made a Million* (1989), invite children to imagine the magnitude of large numbers. In Activity 10.7, *How Much Is a Million?* stimulates investigation into ways of representing large numbers.

In Activity 10.8 children create the largest or smallest possible numeral with four rolls of a die or spinner. As they play, students develop strategies to maximize the number and develop an understanding of chance. Populations of cities provide meaning for large numbers in Activity 10.9. Students compare, order, and combine the populations of cities and also discuss meanings related to the location and other characteristics of large cities.

Real-world settings provide context for large numbers. When children understand how the place-value system represents large numbers, they begin to comprehend such things as the size of the population of the United States relative to that of other countries (Table 10.2).

Newspapers and almanacs are also resources for a "big number" search. When students find big numbers, they write them on index cards with what they represent and put them on a classroom

TABLE 10.2	Populations of Selected Countries (2006)
China	1 313 973 700
India	1 095 352 000
United States	300 176 000
Brazil	188 078 000
Japan	127 463 600
Mexico	107 449 500
France	60 876 100
Italy	58 133 500

SOURCE: http://geography.about.com/cs/worldpopulation/a/most

chart (Figure 10.4). The cards can be classified, compared, and sequenced. Big numbers with meaning motivate children to learn names for large numbers: millions, billions, trillions, and so forth.

Big numbers

10,000,000 and larger	1,000,000 to 9,999,999 Millions	100,000 to 999,999 Hundred thousands	10,000 to 99,999 Ten thousands	1000 to 9,999 Thousands	0 to 999 Hundreds

Figure 10.4 Classification chart for big numbers

A place-value chart to millions or billions highlights the structure, pattern, and nomenclature of the numeration system. Each grouping of three numbers is called a period; the three numbers in the period are hundreds, tens, and ones. Students should be familiar with the smallest period and how to read numbers having three numerals, for example, 379 as three hundred seventy-nine. If the number were 379,379, the second period would be called three hundred seventy-nine thousand. The convention for writing large numbers in the United States is to separate each period of three numerals with commas. Internationally, spaces are often used instead of commas to separate the period groupings, as shown here:

United States	489,321,693,235
United States	489,321,693,235
International	489 321 693 235

ⒺXERCISE

Do you prefer using spaces or commas for separating the periods in large numbers? What are the advantages and disadvantages of each notation system? ●●●

After establishing the meaning of numbers with base-10 materials, students are ready to record numbers in various ways, including compact and expanded numeral forms. The compact form for numerals such as 53,489 is most common, but it can be represented in several ways:

With words: Fifty-three thousand four hundred eighty-nine

With numerals and words: 5 ten thousands, 3 thousands, 4 hundreds, 8 tens, 9 ones; or 53 thousands, 4 hundreds, 8 tens, 9 ones

With numerals: 50,000 + 3,000 + 400 + 80 + 9

With expanded notation: $(5 \times 10,000) + (3 \times 1,000) + (4 \times 100) + (8 \times 10) + 9$

With exponents: $5 \times 10^4 + 3 \times 10^3 + 4 \times 10^2 + 8 \times 10^1 + 9 \times 10^0$

Exponential notation for large and small numbers is written with powers of 10 or exponents: 20,000 becomes $2 \times 10,000$ or 2×10^4. Intermediate- and middle-grade students learn scientific or exponential notation for larger numbers, such as distances in space.

Thinking with Numbers

While learning about the Hindu-Arabic numeration system, students also become aware of how important numbers are in daily living. Numbers also provide useful information for the classroom. Becoming aware of the role of numbers is a first step in number sense.

- How much does a gallon of milk cost?

- How far is the grocery store, and how long does it take to walk? to drive? to take the subway?

- How long will it take to do my homework? Do I have time before supper to finish?

- If I need 12 pages of paper for my booklet, how many pages does everyone in the class need for their projects?

The answers to many questions are estimations and approximations.

- Milk is about $3 a gallon.

- The grocery store is about 5 miles away. It takes 10 minutes by car, 75 minutes walking, and 20 minutes by subway.

- I can finish this homework in 25 minutes and still have 15 minutes to play basketball before dinner.

- We are going to need about 250 pages of paper for 20 projects.

People learn from experience to make educated guesses. Working with large numbers is a good time to emphasize number sense, the ability to think about numbers in meaningful and reasonable ways. Exact answers are not always required. If the airport reported 1,212,678 outgoing passengers this year, is that number absolutely accurate? Is it possible that somebody did not get counted? Does 1 person or even 10 or 1,000 people make that much difference in a number the size of 1 million?

Rounding and estimating are important numerical thinking skills. **Rounding** expresses vital information about a number without being unnecessarily detailed. The number of passengers in the airport could be expressed as "more than 1 million," "1.2 million," or "nearly one and a quarter million." Rounding emphasizes the important information without the less important details. Different people might need more or less precision in a number. The airport manager and board may need the detailed information, but the citizens only need to know "a little more than 1 million."

Estimation is a reasonable guess, hypothesis, or conjecture based on numerical information. It is more than rounding, although rounding is often

used in estimation. If somebody wanted to know the average number of passengers that traveled each day of the year, they could divide 1,212,678 by 365 days and get a computed answer that 3,322.4054 people traveled each day. However, the computed answer is not a meaningful answer for several reasons, especially the 0.4054 person. Reasonably rounded numbers allow ease of computation or even mental computation.

- Think: 1,200,000 divided by 300 is 4,000.

- Think: 1,200,000 divided by 400 is 3,000.

A reasonable estimate would be between 3,000 and 4,000—maybe 3,500 passengers on average. An estimate communicates numerical information with meaning. Students might also note that the number of passengers is larger than average on the busiest travel days of the year and less than average on other days.

ⒺXERCISE

What times of the year do most airports have the largest and smallest passenger counts? Which days might be busiest for airports in Orlando? Puerto Rico? Denver? ●●●

Students learn to think about rounding and estimation in the context of working with larger numbers. Teachers report that students resist estimation. Students who have been taught about numbers with an emphasis on accuracy and getting the right answer may not be comfortable with "close enough" as an answer. Children may also resist textbook exercises in rounding and estimation because the numbers are small enough that they can be calculated and understood without rounding or estimation. Should students estimate the sum of 34 + 47 when they can easily calculate it? Rounding down to 30 and up to 50 for an estimated answer of 80 is more trouble and work than adding the two numbers and getting the accurate answer 81. Numbers less than 1,000 may be used to introduce the processes, but rounding and estimation should move quickly to examples that illustrate their utility with larger numbers and their meaning.

Rounding

Thoughts about rounding begin when children compare numbers and see them on a number line or hundreds chart. Using a number line, students visualize the order and relative position of numbers and discuss how numbers relate to each other.

* What number comes after 38? 49? 87?

* What numbers are found between 38 and 52? Is 43 closer to 38 or to 52? Is 49 closer to 38 or to 52?

* What is the hundred after 365? What is the hundred before 365?

* What is a number between 300 and 400? Is it closer to 300 or 400?

* Is 385 closer to 300 or to 400? Is 307 closer to 300 or to 400?

Rounding is introduced with numbers between 0 and 100. When looking at 67 on a number line (Figure 10.5a), children can see that 67 is between 60 and 70 but only three steps from 70. They recognize that 67 is nearer to 70 than to 60. On the other hand, 62 is closer to 60 than to 70 (Figure 10.5b). Because 65 is five steps from 60 and five steps from 70, they learn that midway numbers are usually rounded upward, so 65 is rounded to 70 and 650 is rounded to 700. Some teachers have students draw the number line between 60 and 70 as a hump with 65 at the top (Figure 10.5c). This visual clue shows that numbers below 5 slide back and numbers above the midway point slide forward.

When rounding to the hundreds, students find the numeral in the hundreds place, think next largest hundred, and determine whether the tens and ones are more or less than 50. They can draw a number line segment, such as Figure 10.5d, to see whether 383 is closer to 300 or to 400. Likewise, 834 is rounded to 800 because it is closer to 800 than to 900 (Figure 10.5e). Because 650 is midway between

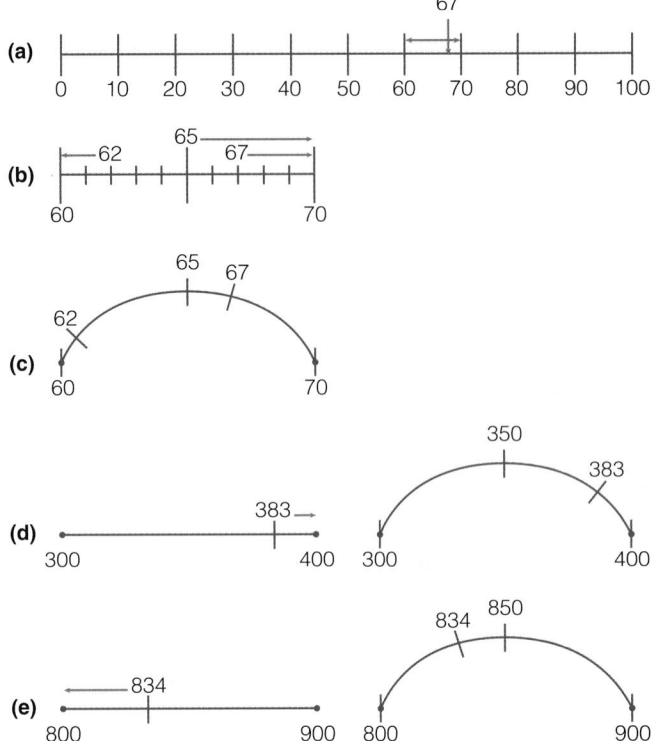

Figure 10.5 Number lines for rounding

600 and 700, the convention is to round it upward to 700. After learning the process of rounding to the nearest ten and hundred, students can use the same process to round to any place value depending on the precision wanted. When rounding is taught as a thinking process rather than as a mechanical one, students ask themselves whether 74,587 is closer to 74,000 or to 75,000.

* The population of our county is 74,587. Round to the nearest thousand and to the nearest ten thousand.

* Round the population of the United States in 2006 to the nearest million.

Some students may talk through the process or circle numbers as a reminder. Having verbal and visual cues helps students think about the number and process of rounding as they become more skilled. Once children understand rounding numbers, problem-solving activities provide practice and application of the process. The task card shown in Figure 10.6 provides practice with rounding numbers from real situations.

Figure 10.6
Problem card used to practice rounding numbers

> Round each number to the nearest hundred, then to the nearest thousand:
>
> - The baseball game was attended by 3291 fans.
>
> - The trip from London, England, to Sydney, Australia, stopped in New York. The total distance was 14,648 miles.
>
> - The telethon collected $113,689 for multiple sclerosis.
>
> Think about each situation. Does it make more sense to round to the hundreds or to the thousands?

ⒺXERCISE

What are your answers to the task card in Figure 10.6? What process did you use to round the numbers? Was your process more a step-by-step process that you learned or more thinking about the situation? ●●●

Estimation

When people do not have specific information or need a precise answer, they often make an educated guess.

- How much time should I plan for commuting this morning?

- How much money do I need for a vacation at the beach?

- Would a couch or two loveseats fit best in the room?

- How much have I spent on groceries today?

An estimate is an educated or reasonable guess based on information, prior knowledge, and judgment. Even when information is known, the situation may call for estimation. The carpenter measures the room for flooring as 10 feet by $12\frac{1}{2}$ feet, calculates the area, then increases the estimate by 10% to account for waste, matching pattern, or irregularities in product. A chef decides how much meat, pasta, vegetable, and bread must be stocked by estimating the number of customers who are likely to order different meals.

Estimation of quantity improves when a **benchmark**, or referent, is used. A benchmark gives students a comparison unit or amount to use for an es-

timate. Without a benchmark, students have a hard time making a reasonable estimate and refining it. Students then resort to wild guessing instead of thoughtful estimation. Activities with an estimation jar help students develop their idea of number. As students fill jars with different objects, they can use benchmarks to explain their estimates.

- "If the baby food jar holds 943 popcorn kernels, the jelly jar should hold about 3,000 because it is about three times as big."

- "The mayonnaise jar holds 4,000 popcorn kernels. It might hold 100 cotton balls because the cotton balls are much bigger than popcorn. But cotton balls will squeeze up so it might hold more than 100."

- "The jar holds 126 jelly beans, but I think the number of marshmallows will be fewer than 126 because they are bigger; maybe 50 marshmallows?"

- "The little jar is less than half as big as the liter jar; maybe it holds 400 milliliters to 500 milliliters."

The goal is to find an acceptable range of estimates and to recognize whether an estimate is out of that reasonable range. Through activities such as Activity 10.10 with an estimation jar, students learn the difference between wild guesses and reasonable estimates. The difficulty of the estimate depends on the size of the jar and the size of the objects. It can be adapted for kindergarten so that the number of objects is 20 to 30 or into hundreds for older children. Teachers should take care not to give prizes for the closest estimate but recognize all students as they make reasonable estimates.

ACTIVITY 10.10 How Many Beans? (Reasoning)

Level: Grades 3–5

Setting: Whole group

Objective: Students estimate the number of beans in a glass jar.

Materials: Jar filled with jelly beans (lima beans, etc.), smaller jar or cup, extra beans, ruler

- Display the jar filled with beans. Ask for first estimates, which can be written on a chart. Tell students to use any strategy they wish—short of removing the beans from the estimation jar and counting them. When students estimate for the first time, they will be guessing.

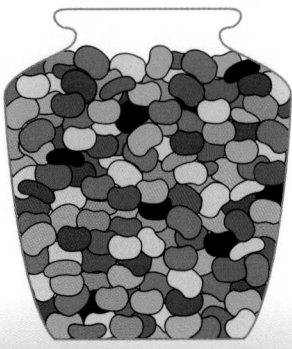

- Discuss the first estimates: high, low, middle, cluster of estimates, range (high to low). Students can also talk about how they determined their estimates.

- Provide a benchmark for their estimate either in a smaller jar or the same size jar with a set number of jelly beans, such as 50.

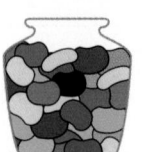

  - Ask if students want to revise their estimates based on the new information.

  - Post the revised estimates, and compare them.

  - Have students count the jelly beans in groups of 10 or 20. Post a final number. Compare second estimates to the posted number. Avoid a "winner," but ask students to decide which estimates were reasonably close to the actual number. The goal of an estimation jar is to find all the estimates that were reasonable.

- Display estimate jars of different sizes with different sizes of beans and different objects, such as marbles, rice, or packing peanuts.

MISCONCEPTION

Many students feel estimation results in the "wrong" answer, especially if mathematics emphasized getting the right answer rather than number sense. Students need comfort and skill for thinking about "close enough." Problems and projects that require approximate rather than exact answers help students develop skill and confidence.

Problems related to other content and real life also involve estimation. Estimating packages of popcorn for a class party is based on past experiences of popping corn and how much popcorn each child will eat. Children's prior knowledge and number awareness are essential to estimation and reasonableness. Students can also predict future events based on information.

- A population graph for the United States shows an increase from 250,000,000 to 275,000,000 between 1990 and 2000. What do you estimate it to be by the year 2008 if the growth rate stays the same? What if the growth rate increases; what population would you estimate in 2010?

- If the water in a jar evaporates 1 centimeter per day at a room temperature of 75 degrees and 5 centimeters per day at 85 degrees, how much do you think will evaporate at a temperature of 95 degrees?

- If the car travels 408 miles on a tank of gas, how many tanks are needed for a 1,000-mile trip?

In addition to numerical situations, estimation applies to problems and situations in geometry, measurement, statistics, probability, and fractions. Activity 10.11 suggests how to develop estimations using information from previous events.

POINT OF VIEW

Estimation serves as an important companion to computation. It provides a tool for judging the reasonableness of computations. (National Council of Teachers of Mathematics, 2000, p. 155)

Addition, subtraction, multiplication, and division calculations with larger numbers are often estimated because exact answers are not needed. The following problems can be answered by computation, by calculator, or by estimation. Rounding is useful in finding numbers that are easier to estimate.

- If the largest city in the state has a population of 2,218,899, and the second largest city has a

ACTIVITY 10.11   Snack Stand Supply Problem (Reasoning)

Level: Grades 3–6
Setting: Small groups
Objective: Students estimate, using data from a classroom project.
Materials: Table with data from an earlier fundraising effort.

Each year the fifth-grade class of Hopewell School raises money for field trips by selling food at the spring parents' meeting. Over the past six years, they have sold cookies, popcorn balls, and fruit punch.

Year	2001	2002	2003	2004	2005	2006
Cookies	98	108	117	130	126	142
Popcorn balls	72	87	99	91	101	113
Fruit punch	123	143	158	160	165	172

- Organize cooperative groups and describe their task.
  1. Have students use the information from prior years to estimate how much food they should have for the 2007 sale.
  2. Have students explain how they came up with each of their estimates.
  3. Ask the students to write down any question or issues that came up in their estimations that they believe would improve their estimate.
  4. Have each group compare its projections with those of other groups. Have the groups tell whether their estimates are similar to or different from other groups' estimates.
- Use newspapers or almanacs to find other data that show changes over time, such as population or crops. Develop some questions for another cooperative group to answer using the data and estimation.

population of 1,446,219, approximately how many people live in these two cities?

- The state budget is $5,251,793,723. Of that amount, $2,463,723,192 is spent for education. What percent of the budget is spent on all other expenses?

- The chocolate factory produces an average of 57,123 chocolate bars each week. How many chocolate bars are likely to be produced in a year?

- The chocolate bars are packaged in boxes of 48. How many boxes are needed each week?

Questions such as these can be placed on index cards for an estimation center. Additional exercises involving number sense and estimation are found in Chapter 12.

EXERCISE

Answer the previous four questions using estimation. How accurate do you think your estimate needs to be? How did you think about your estimate? What other factors might be considered in explaining your estimate? ●●●

Research for the Classroom

Recent research studies have investigated the computational strategies used by children as well as their understanding of the strategies they have been taught. The conclusion is that students can develop computational strategies, although not all students develop the same level of skill with strategies or from the same instruction.

Murphy (2004) interviewed three children to determine whether they were using compensation in two-digit addition problems. She found that one used primarily counting on and two employed both counting on and the associative law to raise one number to a multiple of 10, then added the remainder. She instructed the three students on compensation (adding 19 by adding 20 and subtracting 1) and interviewed them a week later and found each modified the taught strategy. The researcher interpreted the results as supportive of the constructivist approach because all three had the same instructional experience, but each had developed a slightly different understanding.

Montague and van Garderen (2003) compared the estimation strategies used by learning-disabled, average, and gifted students in the fourth, sixth, and eighth grades. They found that all three groups scored poorly on estimation. However, the LD students used fewer strategies and were less successful overall than the average or gifted students.

Ainsworth, Bibby, and Wood (2002) worked with forty-eight 9- and 10-year-old students on their estimation skills using a computer program that provided feedback about the accuracy of their estimation. The program guided students' estimation process using front-end and truncation strategies. Students in the control group showed no improvement, but students with pictorial and numerical feedback reduced the number of errors in their estimation. Differences were found in student understanding of the pictorial and numerical representations.

Other Number Concepts

Patterns

Looking for patterns and relationships among numbers is fundamental to number sense and algebraic reasoning. Even before efficient algorithms, people studied number lore and the relationships among numbers. Many computational puzzles and games are based on relationships between numbers.

Intermediate-grade students can explore a wider variety of patterns, including increasing and decreasing patterns. They encounter these in many situations as they explore geometry and fractions. The ancient Greeks thought of numbers as geometric in nature. Square numbers are those numbers that form squares, and cubic numbers form cubes. For example, 4 tiles form a 2×2 square and 9 tiles make a 3×3 square; 8 cubes form a $2 \times 2 \times 2$ cube and 27 cubes form a $3 \times 3 \times 3$ cube.

Square numbers:	1	4	9	16	25	36	49
Cubic numbers:	1	8	27	64	125	216	343

Another sequence, called the Fibonacci sequence, describes the growth of plants and other natural phenomena: 1, 1, 2, 3, 5, 8, 13, . . .

In the primary grades students recognize odd and even numbers. In the intermediate grades children discover odd and even rules for number operations. In the following vignette Mr. Greene provides examples and asks questions so students can find a rule that will help them think about number combinations.

Mr. Greene: I am going to put some addition examples on the board. I want you to look at the numbers and the answers to see if you can find a pattern or rule for each group.

Group 1

$$
\begin{array}{ccccc}
4 & 2 & 8 & 12 & 26 \\
+4 & +8 & +14 & +6 & +18 \\
\hline
8 & 10 & 22 & 18 & 44
\end{array}
$$

Dahntey: I see a lot of 8's and 4's because $4 + 4$ is 8 and $8 + 14$ is 22.

Josh: 4 and 8 are even numbers.

Catasha: I think all the numbers are even numbers.

Emily: She is right. All the numbers are even, the addends and the answers.

Mr. Greene: What rule could we write about adding even numbers?

Catasha: When you add two even numbers, the answer is even?

Josh: What about adding three even numbers?

Dahntey: I tried three even numbers, and the answer is even.

Mr. Greene: Can you find any examples when our rule for adding even numbers does not work?

Other rules can be derived in a similar manner by giving examples.

- The quotient of two even numbers is always even.
- The difference between an odd number and an even number is an odd number.
- The product of two odd numbers is an odd number.
- The sum of one odd number and one even number is odd.

EXERCISE

Give three examples that illustrate rules about subtraction of odd numbers from even numbers and multiplication of two odd numbers. What rule could you write about the multiplication of even numbers? ●●●

Prime and Composite Numbers

Work with prime and composite numbers extends understanding of factors, divisors, and multiples encountered in the study of multiplication and division. Some numbers have several factors and are called **composite numbers**. Other numbers that have only one set of factors—the number 1 and itself—are called **prime numbers**. Activity 10.12 allows students to investigate array patterns and factors with cubes and disks. A large classroom chart shows numbers from 1 to 30 and identifies numbers with only one set of factors and numbers with multiple sets of factors.

A composite number is factored completely when all the factors are prime numbers. When 18 is factored, it is expressed as $2 \times 3 \times 3$; 36 is factored as $2 \times 2 \times 3 \times 3$. Finding factors by examination is easy when the product is one of the basic multiplica-

ACTIVITY 10.12   Prime and Composite Numbers (Reasoning and Representation)

Level: Grades 3–6
Setting: Small groups
Objective: Students use arrays to find factors of numbers.
Materials: Tiles or other counting materials

- Have students put six tiles in all possible rectangular row and column arrangements that they can find. Label the arrays with the factors of 6.

- When students understand the task, have them arrange sets from 1 through 20 tiles in arrays.

- Put the results of the student exploration in a table listing the factors for each number 1 through 20.

- Ask students to examine the table. "Some whole numbers—2, 3, 5, 7, 11, 13, 17—have only two arrays, such as 5: $1 \times 5, 5 \times 1$." "5×1 and 1×5 are really the same." "The arrays are just one line." "Other numbers have several arrays." "They can be arranged in one or more rectangular patterns as well as in straight lines."

- Introduce the terms *prime numbers* for numbers that have only one set of factors (1×5 and 5×1) and *composite numbers* for numbers with more than one set of factors (2×3, 3×2 and 1×6 and 6×1).

- Ask students what they notice about all the factors of prime numbers.

Extension

Ask students whether the number 1 is prime or composite and why. Research the answer on the Internet.

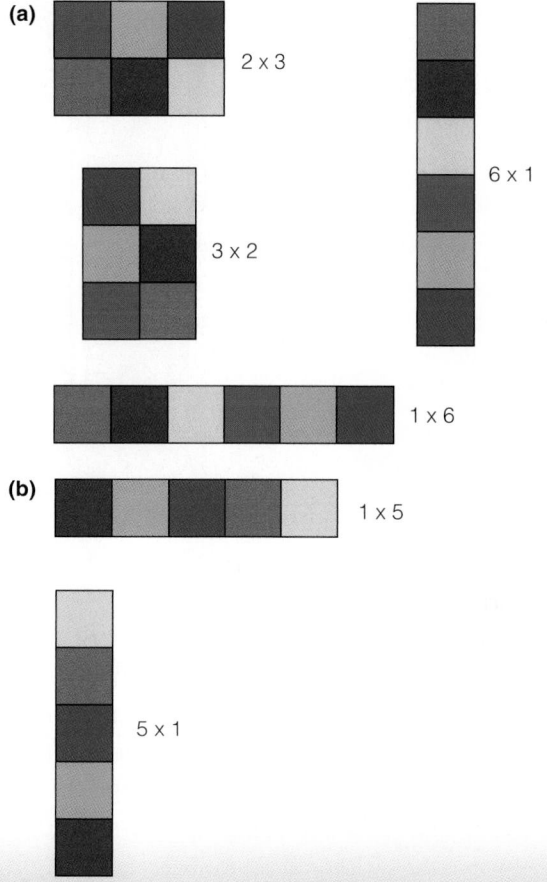

tion facts and has only two factors, such as 4, 6, 15, and 63. However when factoring 12, children might name either 2×6 or 3×4, but they are not finished; because one of the factors is not prime, further factoring is needed to find that the prime factorization for 12 is $2 \times 2 \times 3$.

Factor trees are suitable for larger numbers. Factor trees are created by expressing a composite number in terms of successively smaller factors until all factors are prime numbers. The process is described in Activity 10.13, where different factor trees for 24 are developed.

Activity 10.14 shows how to find prime and composite numbers not already known by students using the *sieve of Eratosthenes*. Eratosthenes, a Greek astronomer and geographer who lived in the third century B.C., devised a scheme for separating any set of consecutive whole numbers larger than 1 into prime and composite numbers. Interested students can extend the sieve process for larger numbers. Some students might search for twin primes, such as 3 and 5, 5 and 7, 11 and 13, which have only one composite number between them. Challenge students to find other twin primes between 100 and 300. Work with the sieve is a good place to incorporate the calculator to reduce the drudgery of calculation and emphasize the mathematical pattern.

Integers

Numbers used for counting discrete quantities are called **whole numbers**. In other situations numbers are needed that express values less than 0 as well. The temperature may be below 0 degrees (Figure 10.7a); Death Valley is lower than sea level, which is considered 0 (Figure 10.7b); and a check written on insufficient funds can put the checking account below 0, commonly called in the red (Figure 10.7c). A football team may lose yardage on a

Figure 10.7 Negative integers

(a)

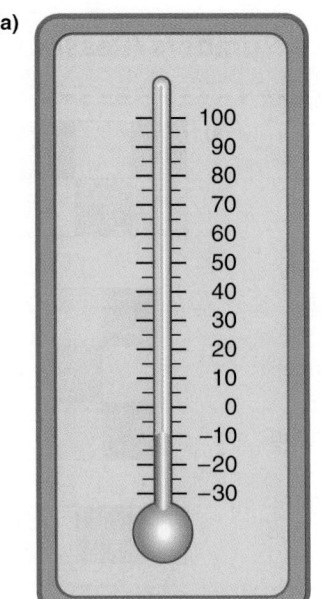

(b)

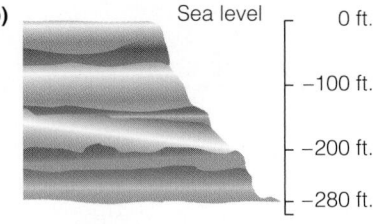

(c) $50 - $60 = - $10

(d)

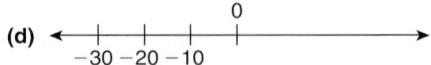

play or penalty, and contestants go "in the hole" on some television quiz programs.

Positive and negative numbers are part of the **integer** number system. Number lines can be extended to the left past 0. The same rules of number sequence, magnitude, and more than and less than apply to negative integers. When comparing whole numbers, children see that numbers increase as you move to the right and decrease to the left. When you move past 0 to the left, the numbers become negative and their negative value increases. Negative temperatures get colder and colder as the temperature moves away from zero: −20 degrees is colder than −10 degrees. Similarly, negative bank balances get worse as the balance moves down from zero: −$200 is worse than −$10.

ACTIVITY 10.13 Factor Trees (Representation)

Level: Grades 3–5
Setting: Small groups
Objective: Students use a factor tree to find prime factors.
Materials: Chalkboard and chalk

- Write 24 on the chalkboard. Ask: "What are two numbers that when multiplied have a product of 24?" Accept 1 × 24, and write it to the side. Ask for another set of factors.
- Write factors beneath their product.
- Ask if either of the factors can be factored again.
- Complete one factor tree for 24.
- Write 24 again, and ask if 24 has two other factors not used in the first example. Complete the second factor tree.
- Write 24 a third time, and ask for factors. Complete the third factor tree.
- Ask what students notice about all the factor trees. (Answer: They all have the same factors even if they are written in different orders. Every composite number has only one set of prime factors, a rule called the **fundamental theorem of arithmetic**.)

- Ask why you did not use 24 × 1 as a starting place.
- Ask students to make factor trees with other numbers from 10 to 100, and post them on the board. Write prime numbers that they find on one side of a poster or bulletin board and composite numbers on the other side.

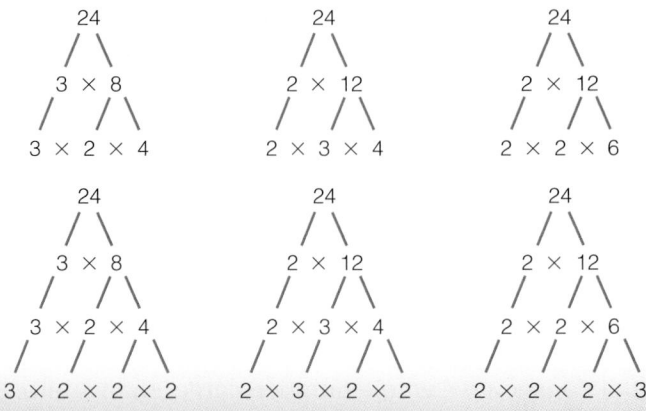

ACTIVITY 10.14   Sieve of Eratosthenes (Reasoning)

Level: Grades 3–5
Setting: Small groups
Objective: Students identify composite and prime numbers.
Materials: Hundreds chart (see Black-Line Master 10.1)

• Ask students to put a square around 1 on the chart because 1 is a factor of all numbers including itself. It is neither prime nor composite.

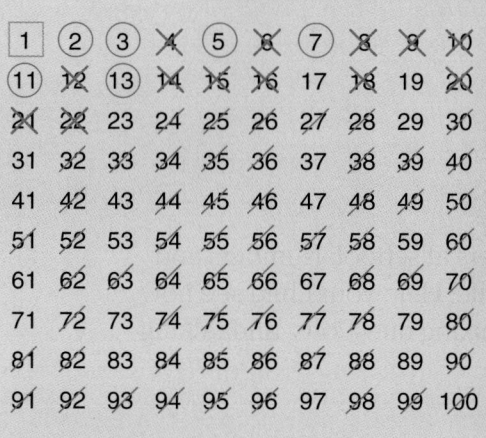

• Go to 2 on the chart, circle it, and cross out all the multiples of 2 up to 100.

• Go to 3, circle it, and cross out multiples of 3 on the chart.

• Go to 4, and ask why all the multiples of 4 are already crossed out. (Answer: They are all multiples of 2.)

• Go to 5. Ask students whether 5 is prime or composite, and how they know. Circle 5, and cross out the multiples of 5 that remain.

• Let students continue circling prime numbers and crossing out multiples. Have them post their hundreds charts with prime numbers circled and other numbers marked out. Have them compare their charts to see if they agree or disagree. After discussion, have students prepare a list of all prime numbers under 100.

Variations

• Find prime numbers between 100 and 200, or larger.

• In 2003 the largest prime number was found to contain 2,090,960 digits. Search the Internet for the largest prime number known.

• Look on the Internet for uses of prime numbers.

In elementary school teachers can introduce the idea of negative number situations with money, football, temperature, and the number line. Activities provide background for understanding positive and negative integers and their symbols, such as +4 and −4. The use of these signs may lead to confusion with addition and subtraction signs. For this and other reasons, formal work with integers is now recommended for middle school rather than elementary school students. Some simple activities based on pairing positive and negative numbers introduce operations. Red chips are positive numbers and blue chips are negative integers. The format for positive and negative numbers should show superscript plus and minus signs for positive and negative to distinguish the signs from regular plus and minus signs for addition and subtraction. Adding three red and three blue chips creates a sum of zero because each positive chip and negative chip pair has a sum of zero. Students may call the chips matter and antimatter to show that they cancel each other out.

3 red + 3 blue = 0
$^{+}3 + {}^{-}3 = 0$

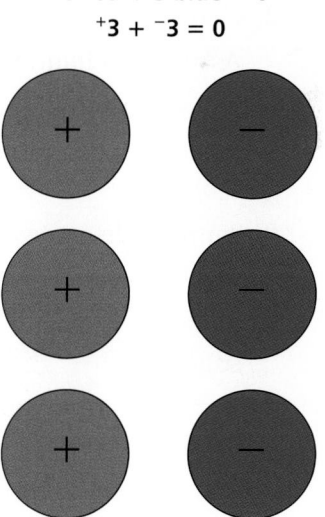

Take-Home Activities

Take-home letters invite parents to extend and support student learning. Both of these letters ask parents to engage children with numbers at home. Because connections is one of the process standards in *Principles and Standards for School Mathematics* (National Council of Teachers of Mathematics, 2000), students need to see how numbers are used in real life. The first letter suggests ways that parents can talk with students about numbers in the grocery store, on television, and in games. The second letter asks parents to work with students to complete an extension of a classroom project.

Numbers All Around

Dear Parents,

Your child is learning about counting and numbers at school. Numbers and counting are also important in the child's home life. Help your child see how numbers are used every day by playing games, asking questions, and talking about numbers. Here are some suggestions.

1. Numbers in the grocery store:

   Ask which brand of bread is more expensive.

   Find items that are on sale. Ask how much you can save.

   Estimate how much you have bought, and compare it to the register total.

2. Numbers on television:

   Ask which channels broadcast special shows.

   Ask when certain programs begin and end.

   Ask how much money people are winning on *Wheel of Fortune* or *Jeopardy.*

3. Numbers in games:

   Play card games, such as Battle, that compare number values.

   Play card games, such as Gin, that match numbers or put numbers in sequence.

   Play dominoes. You can begin by matching dots and later introduce scoring.

   Play Yahtzee or Junior Yahtzee.

These simple activities can be fun for you and your child. Next month, we will be having a math game night to introduce more games that you and your child can play.

Take-Home Activities

Big Number Hunt

Dear Parents,

For the past three weeks, the fourth- and fifth-graders have been studying numbers larger than 10,000. Children have learned about millions, billions, and trillions. Here are some examples we have found:

· Man wins $31,000,000 in lottery.
· The tanker spilled more than 4,000,000 gallons of crude oil; 16,000,000 gallons are still on board.
· The airplane flies at 45,000 feet.

This week everyone is hunting for five large numbers in newspapers, on the Internet, or from any other source to add to our big number collection. We will use them for comparing and classifying, for making big number books, and in rounding and estimating. You can work together with your child to find big numbers. On Thursday we are planning a big number circus.

Summary

Number sense is an awareness of numbers in daily life and an understanding of how they work. Children with many experiences develop an understanding of numbers and of the Hindu-Arabic, or base-10, numeration system; they are able to think about numbers as well as compute with them. The Hindu-Arabic numeration system is a place-value system based on multiples of 10 that can represent large numbers efficiently. The system, which was developed over centuries, also allows the use of efficient algorithms in computation.

After developing basic number concepts up to 20 with objects, pictures, and numerals, children are ready to extend their knowledge to larger numbers in the hundreds or thousands. Through modeling with Unifix cubes, bundled tongue depressors, base-10 and Cuisenaire materials, and bean sticks, students can see the relative size of numbers and recognize the structure and rules of the Hindu-Arabic numeration system. The base-10 system accommodates numbers of all sizes; millions and billions adhere to the same rules as smaller numbers. They can represent large numbers in both compact and expanded forms.

At the same time children learn the number system, they develop number awareness and number sense. They become aware of the many uses of numbers in their world and develop flexible thinking about using numbers. Answers do not always need to be exact. Students learn that some answers can be "close enough" to keep their meaning. Rounding and estimation are two skills that allow students to draw reasonable conclusions about the precision needed for numbers. Other relationships about numbers and the number system are also explored: number patterns, prime and composite numbers, and positive and negative integers.

Study Questions and Activities

1. Number awareness and number sense are major goals of instruction in numbers. How aware of numbers are you in everyday life? Do you notice how much groceries cost? how much you tip a server? how long you wait on line? how much you save on a sale?

2. Use one of the base-10 materials to represent the following numbers:

   a. 128

   b. 478

   c. 397

   d. 1,153

   If you do not have access to a set of commercial materials, such as Cuisenaire rods or Unifix cubes, draw a diagram to show the numbers.

3. List two examples of when you round numbers and estimate. How comfortable and skilled are you with rounding and estimating?

Using the Technology Center

The activities described here (courtesy of Texas Instruments, Dallas, Texas) are examples of how both primary- and intermediate-grade students can use calculators to enhance their understanding of numbers.

Calculator Counting

Students work with a calculator singly or in pairs. Tell students that they are to figure out how to make the calculator count by ones. When they have done this, have them count by twos, fives, tens, or any other number. Give challenges: "Can you count by fives to 500 in a minute?" Have one child time the other with the second hand on a classroom clock or another timepiece. "Tell me how many numbers are in each of these sequences: 8, 15, 22, . . . , 113; 10, 19, 28, . . . , 118." Young children can see numbers "grow" by entering a number—say, 453—then pressing +, then 1, entering 100, pressing +, then 1, and so on. Older children can do the same activity with a number such as 43,482 and repeatedly adding 1,000. Stop the activity periodically to discuss what happens. Ask: "How many times do you press the equals key to go from 436 to 536 when you repeatedly add 10? How many hundreds are 10 tens?" "How much larger is 23,481 after you add 100 ten times? Ten hundreds are equal to how many thousands?"

TI-10 calculator

Courtesy of Texas Instruments

Wipeout

This activity can be used with place value in larger numbers. Children work singly or in pairs. The object of the activity is to wipe out a number in a particular place-value position. For example, when given a calculator showing the number 547, the student is to wipe out the 4 tens with one subtraction. To do this, the student must understand that the "4" represents 4 tens, or 40: 40 is subtracted from 547, leaving 507. Numbers in any place-value position other than the extreme left or right can be wiped out. The size of numbers should increase as children mature; older students can use numbers in the millions.

Teacher's Resources

Burns, Marilyn. (1994). *Math by all means: Place value, grades 1–2*. Sausalito, CA: Math Solutions (distributed by Cuisenaire Company of America).

Fraser, Don. (1998). *Taking the numb out of numbers*. Burlington, Canada: Brendan Kelly.

Verschaffel, L., Greer, B., & de Corte, E. (2000). *Making sense of word problems*. Lisse, Netherlands: Swets and Zeitlinger.

Wheatley, G., & Reynolds, A. (1999). *Coming to know number: A mathematics activity resource for elementary school teachers*. Tallahassee, FL: Mathematics Learning.

Children's Bookshelf

Clements, Mike. (2006). *A million dots*. New York: Simon and Schuster Children's Publishing. (Grades 1–4)

Cuyler, M. (2000). *100th day worries*. Riverside, NJ: Simon & Schuster. (Grades 1–3)

Schmandt-Besserat, D. (1999). *The history of counting*. New York: William Morrow. (Grades 4–6)

Schroeder, Peter, & Schroeder-Hildebrand, Dagmar. (2004). *Six million paper clips: The making of a children's Holocaust memorial*. Minneapolis: Kar-ben. (Grades 2–5)

Schwartz, David. (1985). *How much is a million?* New York: Lothrop, Lee & Shepard. (Grades 2–6)

Schwartz, David. (2001). *On beyond a million: An amazing math journey*. New York Dragonfly Books. (Grades 4–6)

Technology Resources

Videotapes

Both sides of zero: Playing with positive and negative numbers. PBS Video.

Factor 'em in: Exploring factors and multiples. PBS Video.

Number sense. Reston, VA: National Council of Teachers of Mathematics.

Soaring sequences: Thinking about large numbers. PBS Video.

For Further Reading

Fuson, K., Grandau, L., & Sugiyama, P. (2001). Achievable numerical understanding for all young children. *Teaching Children Mathematics* 7(9), 522–526.

Fuson and colleagues describe young children's developmental understanding of number and outline methods to enhance understanding.

Lang, F. (2001). What is a "good guess" anyway? *Teaching Children Mathematics* 7(8), 462–466.

Lang presents procedures and activities that support estimation and reasonableness.

Ross, S. (2002). Place value: Problem solving and written assessment. *Teaching Children Mathematics* 8(7), 419–423.

Ross describes strategy for assessing place value through problem solving.

Sakshaug, Lynae. (1998). Counting squares. *Teaching Children Mathematics* 4(9), 526–529.

The task of counting squares in pyramid shape leads to discoveries about number patterns.

Taylor-Cox, J. (2001). How many marbles in the jar? *Teaching Children Mathematics* 8(4), 208–214.

Estimation activities demonstrate different types of estimation.

Thomas, C. (2000). 100 activities for the 100th day. *Teaching Children Mathematics* 6(5), 276–280.

Thomas presents many activities to celebrate the 100th day of school.

Zaslavsky, C. (2001). Developing number sense: What can other cultures tell us? *Teaching Children Mathematics* 7(6), 312–319.

Cultural differences in numerical representations and language help students understand the numbers we use.

CHAPTER 11

Developing Number Operations with Whole Numbers

As elementary students work with objects, they encounter problems that require combining and separating them. They add the value of coins to pay for a snack; they remove animals from the farm diorama; they skip-count the number of shoes in the class by 2's; and they share a bag of cookies equally among their friends. Realistic situations such as these introduce number operations of addition, subtraction, multiplication, and division. With a strong conceptual base through stories, models with manipulatives, pictures, and symbolic representations, students build an understanding of how each operation works and learn the strategies that lead to computational skill with basic facts. Building conceptual and strategic understanding makes mastery of the facts a successful first step in computational fluency. Chapter 12 extends the number operations to larger numbers, computational algorithms, and estimation strategies.

In this chapter you will read about:

1 Curriculum standards for number operations with whole numbers

2 The importance of problem solving in learning number operations

3 The situations and actions associated with addition and subtraction and activities to model and develop the concepts

4 Properties of addition and subtraction and their application

5 Strategies and activities for learning addition and subtraction facts

6 Situations and actions for multiplication and division and ways and activities to model and develop the concepts

7 Properties of multiplication and division and their uses

8 Interpretation of remainders in division in different situations

9 Strategies for learning multiplication and division facts

10 Guidelines for developing accuracy and speed with number combinations

Building Number Operations

Addition and subtraction situations are part of everyday life for children. Examples of the ways that children use addition and subtraction every day include:

- Adding to determine the number of boys and girls in the class.

- Determining the number of blue and red blocks in a tower.

- Paying for food at the market with bills and getting change.

- Comparing one's own allowance to a friend's allowance.

Multiplication and division events are also common in children's lives. For instance, in kindergarten each child gets a juice box and three crackers during snack time and the total number of crackers must be computed; at the grocery store with a parent, children see that each orange costs 50 cents and six oranges are purchased; or at home a pizza is delivered and it is cut into eight pieces.

Experiences with combining, removing, and sharing provide realistic contexts for number operations. As children tell stories, draw pictures, and write number sentences, they explore number patterns and relationships leading to properties and strategies for number combinations. Then students extend their skill to computational procedures for larger numbers and continue work on number sense with rounding, estimation, and reasonableness. In the elementary grades the goal for children is computational fluency.

The approach to teaching number operations and number sense has changed in contemporary mathematics programs. In the past, number opera-

POINT OF VIEW

Knowing basic number combinations—the single-digit addition and multiplication pairs and their counterparts for subtraction and division—is essential. Equally essential is computational fluency—having and using efficient and accurate methods of computing. . . . Regardless of the particular [computation] method used, students should be able to explain their method, understand that many methods exist, and see the usefulness of methods that are efficient, accurate, and general. Students also need to be able to estimate and judge the reasonableness of results. (National Council of Teachers of Mathematics, 2000, p. 32)

tions were often taught only as memorized facts for each operation. Then a few dreaded story problems were placed at the end of the chapter. Today, problems are posed in realistic settings that require students to consider the relationships among numbers. As they solve problems, children learn the four number operations and the basic facts that are critical for all computational procedures. When children understand how numbers work together, they have a foundation for large number operations using computational strategies such as estimation and reasonableness, whether they are working on paper or with calculators.

What Students Need to Learn About Number Operations

The NCTM standards for number and operations identify three broad expectations for students in prekindergarten through grade 5 (National Council of Teachers of Mathematics, 2000):

1. To understand numbers, ways of representing numbers, relationships among numbers, and number systems.

2. To understand meanings of operations and how they relate to one another.

3. To compute fluently and make reasonable estimates.

The complete standards are the following:

NCTM Standards for Number and Operations

Pre-K–2 Expectations
In prekindergarten through grade 2 all students should:
- develop a sense of whole numbers and represent and use them in flexible ways, including relating, composing, and decomposing numbers;
- understand various meanings of addition and subtraction of whole numbers and the relationship between the two operations;
- understand the effects of adding and subtracting whole numbers;
- understand situations that entail multiplication and division, such as equal groupings of objects and sharing equally;
- develop and use strategies for whole-number computations, with a focus on addition and subtraction;
- develop fluency with basic number combinations for addition and subtraction;
- use a variety of methods and tools to compute, including objects, mental computation, estimation, paper and pencil, and calculators.

Grades 3–5 Expectations
In grades 3–5 all students should:
- understand various meanings of multiplication and division;
- understand the effects of multiplying and dividing whole numbers;
- identify and use relationships between operations, such as division as the inverse of multiplication, to solve problems;
- understand and use properties of operations, such as the distributivity of multiplication over addition;
- develop fluency with basic number combinations for multiplication and division and use these combinations to mentally compute related problems, such as 30×50;
- develop fluency in adding, subtracting, multiplying, and dividing whole numbers.

Developing proficiency with number operations proceeds through four interrelated phases:

1. Exploring concepts and number combinations through realistic stories, with materials, and through representations of situations using pictures and number sentences.

2. Learning strategies and properties of each operation for number combinations.

3. Developing accuracy and speed with basic facts.

4. Extending concepts and skills for each operation with large numbers to gain computational fluency.

The first three steps to proficiency with number operations occur chiefly in the primary grades but continue throughout the elementary grades. Table 11.1 illustrates how the concepts and skills build over the elementary grades. Basic facts are important for computational fluency, but knowing when and where the operations are used to solve problems is equally important. In the upper grades of elementary school place-value concepts join with understanding of addition and subtraction so that children extend their understanding of whole-number operations to larger numbers, including estimation, algorithms, calculators, and number sense. Extending whole-number operations to larger numbers is found in Chapter 12.

When students understand operations, they are empowered to solve a wide variety of problems and gain confidence as they attempt more complex problems in later grades. Fluency and flexibility with numbers extend students' understanding of numbers to algebraic situations.

Standards and grade-level expectations are *guidelines* for teachers. Individual children, however, learn number operations at different rates and in different manners. In a third-grade classroom one child might count objects for addition, whereas another might estimate sums in the millions. Teachers face the constant issue of balancing the expectations of the curriculum and the needs of individual children.

❷XERCISE

Compare the elementary mathematics standards in your state curriculum with another state's curriculum standards. Describe how your state standards are similar to or different from the NCTM standards. Do you find a sequence of skill development similar to the phases described in this chapter? ●●●

TABLE 11.1 · Sequence of Concepts and Skills for Addition and Subtraction		
Concepts	**Skills**	**Connections**
Number concepts 1–100	Rote counting Rational counting with objects in sets Representing numbers with pictures and numerals	Addition and subtraction
Numbers 1–1,000	Representing numbers with base-10 materials Exchange rules and games Regrouping and renaming	Algorithms Estimation

Numbers larger than 1,000	Representing numbers with numerals
	   in the base-10 system
	Learning names of large numbers and realistic
	   situations for their use
	Visualizing larger numbers
		Algorithms

Operation of addition	Stories and actions for joining sets Representing addition with materials, pictures, and number sentences	Problem solving, multiplication

Operation of subtraction	Stories and actions for separating sets
	Stories and actions for whole-part situations
	Stories and actions for comparison
	   situations
	Stories and actions for completion
	   situations
	Representing subtraction with materials,
	   pictures, and number sentences
		Problem solving, division
		Problem solving, fractions
		Problem solving,
		   measurement
		Problem solving,
		   open sentences

Basic facts for addition
and subtraction
	Finding and using strategies
	   for basic facts
	Recognizing arithmetic rules and laws
	Achieving accuracy and speed with basic facts
		Estimation and
		   reasonableness
		Algebraic rules and relations
		Mental computation

Addition and subtraction
operations with larger
numbers
	Story situations and actions with larger numbers
	Developing algorithms with and without regrouping
	   with materials (to 1,000) and symbols
	Estimation
	Using technology: calculators and computer
		Problem solving
		Computational fluency,
		   mental computation
		Reasonableness
		Problem solving,
		   reasonableness

What Teachers Need to Know About Addition and Subtraction

As teachers begin their work with addition and subtraction, they introduce students to stories that illustrate the situations, meanings, and actions associated with the operations.

Addition is the action of joining two or more sets.

- Juan has four red pencils and three blue pencils.

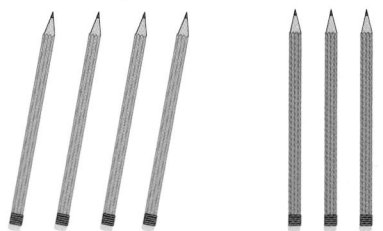

- Heather has 37 books in her library. She receives five books as presents for her birthday.

- The school collection for earthquake victims was $149 on Friday and $126 on Saturday.

The natural question is how many or how much is in the joined set. In each situation the total, or **sum**, is found by combining the number of pencils, the number of books, or the amount of money collected on Friday and Saturday. The numbers related to each set being joined are **addends**.

In contrast to addition with one action, subtraction is used to solve four problem situations.

1. *Takeaway*: Removing part of a set.

2. *Whole-part-part*: Separating a set into subsets.

3. *Comparison*: Showing the difference between two sets.

4. *Completion*: Finding the missing part needed to finish a set.

Takeaway subtraction is used when part of an original set is moved, lost, eaten, or spent.

- Jeff collects wheelie cars. He had 16, but traded 3 of them for a new track.

- Janyce had $94 saved from birthday money. She spent $33 on new shoes, $14 for a new top, and $27 for a new skirt.

- Jamal had 36 cookies. He gave two cookies each to 12 friends.

In takeaway situations the question or problem asks how much is left or how many are left after part of the set is removed. The answer is called the **remainder**.

Whole-part-part subtraction identifies the size of a subgroup within a larger group. The whole group has a common characteristic, but parts or subgroups have distinct characteristics.

- The class has 25 children. Fourteen are girls.

- Deidre has 17 stuffed animals. Fourteen are bears.

- Sally has 48 snapdragons. Thirty of them are white. The rest are yellow.

- Darius counted 114 people at the family reunion. Forty-nine had his same last name.

Whole-part-part subtraction identifies membership in two subgroups that are included in the whole group. The number in one part of the whole is known, and the question posed is how many belong in the other part. In whole-part-part stories no items are removed or lost, as in takeaway situations.

Comparison subtraction, not surprisingly, compares the size of two sets or the measure of two objects. The quantity of both sets or measurement of both objects is known.

- In the NBA game the shortest player is 5 feet, 3 inches, and the tallest player is 7 feet, 6 inches.

- On Friday, $149 was collected for flood victims; on Saturday, $126 was collected.

- The circus put on two performances. The matinee was attended by 8,958 people, and the evening performance attracted 9,348 people.

The comparison question in subtraction asks how much larger or how much smaller one set is than the other. "What is the **difference**?" is another way of expressing comparison between the two sets.

Completion is similar to comparison in that two sets are being compared. However, in completion situations the comparison is between an existing set and a desired set or between an incomplete set and a completed set.

- Saundra has saved $9. The CD she wants costs $16.

- Shaeffer is collecting state quarters. He already has 23.

- Mr. Lopez is making lemonade for the party. The recipe calls for 3 cups of water for each can of concentrate. He used 6 cans of concentrate and has put in 10 cups of water so far.

The question for completion stories is how many more are needed or how much more is needed. Completion is subtraction because the total and one addend are known, and the other addend represents the part of the set that is needed or missing. Completion problems can be written in subtraction form, for example, $9 - 5 = ?$, but are sometimes written as addition sentences, $5 + ? = 9$, called the missing-addend form.

Developing Concepts of Addition and Subtraction

Understanding of addition and subtraction concepts and procedures develops through children's informal experiences with numbers. During play, children share cookies, count blocks, compare heights and distances, complete sets, and classify objects by attributes. Without rich mathematical experiences children have a weak foundation for mathematical concepts and skills. Early childhood teachers provide many informal experiences that help build children's experiential background for numbers and operations. Children's intuitive understanding of addition and subtraction builds on counting skills to 10 and beyond.

- Throw six beanbags in the basket. Now throw two more. Count how many beanbags are in the basket now.

- You have nine leaves in your box. When you take three out, how many are left in the box?

- One Unifix tower has nine red blocks, and another tower has six green blocks. Which one is taller? How much taller is it?

- We have 12 napkins and 15 children. How many more napkins do we need?

Many children's books engage students with numbers in active ways as they hear the stories, count pictures, and search for pictures that complement the text. A walk-on number line models addition and subtraction kinesthetically. Addition is a forward movement on the number line, and subtraction reverses the action.

Introducing Addition

Addition is a process of combining sets of objects and is introduced through story situations that pose a problem to be solved. After hearing the number problem, children act out the story with physical objects and find the results.

- I had two apples in a bowl. Then I put in three oranges.

After actions with physical models are developed, the same stories can be represented with simple pictures or diagrams. Then the situation is recorded symbolically with numerals and mathematical signs.

- Two apples and three oranges are five pieces of fruit: $2 + 3 = 5$.

This process is repeated with different stories. Students gain understanding and confidence with ad-

ACTIVITY 11.1 Solving Problems with Addition (Representation)

Level: Grades K–2

Setting: Small group or whole class

Objective: Students demonstrate addition by joining objects contained in two or more groups.

Materials: Stuffed animals (or other suitable objects), books, math box materials

- Begin with a story about some stuffed toys: "I like to collect stuffed animals. I recently went looking for them at garage sales. I found these two at one house (show two animals) and these three at another house (show three more animals). How many stuffed animals did I find?"

- Ask students to tell how they determined the answer. They might say, "I counted," "I counted two more, beginning at 3," "I just looked and knew."

- Repeat with other familiar objects, such as books and pencils.

- Have children work in pairs with math box materials to share "joining" stories. Take turns making up stories.

- Introduce the combining board for addition. Students put the objects in the two rectangles and pull them down into the larger rectangle.

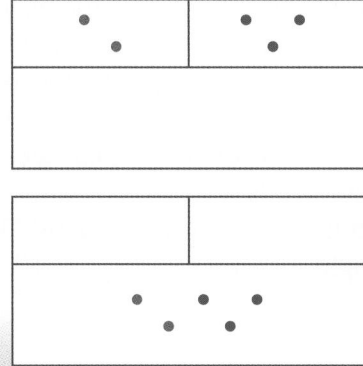

ACTIVITY 11.2 More Cats (Representation and Communication)

Level: Grades K–2

Setting: Whole group

Objective: Students model addition.

Materials: So Many Cats! by Beatrice Schenk de Regniers, illustrated by Ellen Weiss (New York: Clarion Books 1985); pictures of cats; magnetic numbers and symbols

So Many Cats! describes how a family collected cats. They started with one, but more cats arrived, and none could be resisted. After each new arrival, the cats are counted again. The book ends with yet another cat at the window.

- Read through the book once. On the second reading have children count each time new cats appear. Pictures of cats can be placed on the board rail to show the number of cats.

- Talk about the progressive accumulation of cats. "They had three, and three more came." "They had six, and two more came."

- As students are ready, write addition sentences as each new cat or cats arrive (e.g., $6 + 2 = 8$).

- Have children tell a progressive story, real or imaginary, about pets (e.g., "I had one frog, then two alligators followed me home."). Each child can add new animals to the story. Children may model stories using pictures or counters and write addition sentences.

Extension

- Invent new stories about cats that come or leave. Ask the children to model how many cats there are as you tell the story. Begin with one or two cats arriving or leaving at a time, and progress to larger numbers. Discuss how many cat eyes or cat paws are in the house with the addition or subtraction of cats as a foundation for multiplication.

dition represented in physical, pictorial, oral, and written forms that will lead to images of addition and mental operations.

Activity 11.1 presents addition situations with familiar objects. Story problems introduce concepts by having students act out the situation described. Activity 11.2, based on *So Many Cats!* by Beatrice

Schenk de Regniers, illustrates addition as more and more cats arrive at a house.

Concrete materials and realistic situations for addition and subtraction allow the teacher to draw on the environment and experience of students from varying backgrounds. Stories can be personalized with familiar names and situations. Some students advance quickly to more symbolic representations; others remain at the concrete level longer. Children need not be hurried to represent addition and subtraction with symbols because they can use number combinations cards, such as 2 + 3, to label the joined sets.

After modeling addition stories and actions with concrete materials, introduce the addition sentence 2 + 3 = 5, read "two plus three equals five." When written below the word sentence, the plus sign takes the place of "and" and the equal sign substitutes for "are" or "equals." Working with objects, pictures, and number cards prepares students to write addition sentences alone or with a partner. One child might separate beads strung on a card or wire into two sets, and the other would respond "Three plus five equals eight" or write "3 + 5 = 8" (Figure 11.1).

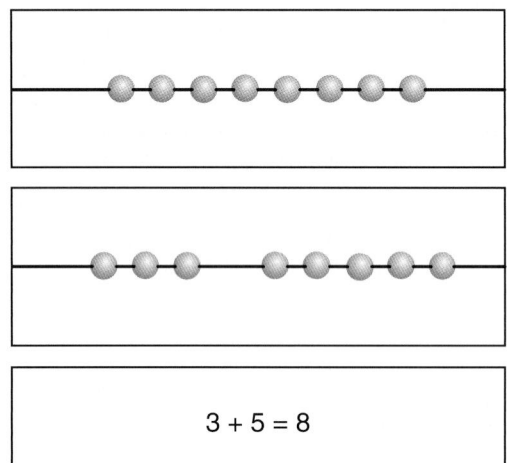

Figure 11.1 Bead cards for representing addition combinations

Magnetic objects and a pan balance are suggested in Activity 11.3 for modeling addition and introducing the addition sentence with the equal sign. This activity also develops the algebraic concept of equality. Although adults understand that the equal sign means balanced or equal, many children do not understand that the equal sign means that the number combinations on each side of the equal sign are the same. Their understanding is more "do it now" rather than "is the same as." In Activity 11.4 the teacher demonstrates writing addition sentences with the equal sign.

Many other activities demonstrate addition. Beans painted different colors are good for exploring number combinations (Figure 11.2a). One child puts seven beans painted red and blue in a cup and dumps them out on a paper saucer. The second child finds and reads the number sentence card for the combination shown by the red and blue beans: 4 + 3 = 7. Dominoes also represent addition combinations up to 6 + 6 (Figure 11.2b). Double dominoes represent addition facts up to 12 + 12. With Cuisenaire rods a child can select one length rod and build all the two-rod combinations of the same length. Combinations for the dark green rod are shown in Figure 11.2c. Sentences based on color (yellow + white = dark green) or number sentences (5 + 1 = 6) describe the combinations. As children are exploring the concept of addition and recording their findings, the teacher can introduce the terms *addend* and *sum*.

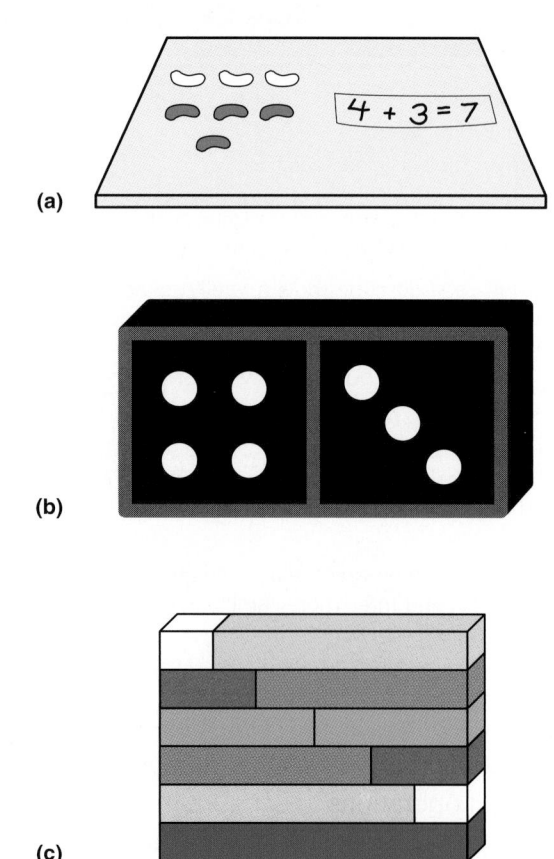

Figure 11.2 Addition demonstrations

ACTIVITY 11.3   Introducing the Equal Sign (Problem Solving and Representation)

Level: Grades K–2

Setting: Small groups or whole class

Objective: Students represent joining objects in two or more sets with the addition sentence.

Materials: Counting objects such as bears; pan balance; magnetic board objects, such as animal outlines or flowers; large magnetized numerals and equal sign for the magnetic board

- Place several uniformed-weighted objects, such as small counting bears, on one side of a pan balance. Ask children what is needed to make the two sides level. They will answer, "Put some bears on the other side."

- Put bears on the other side of the pan balance one at a time so that gradually the balance is level.

- Count the bears on each side to establish equality of number.

- Introduce the equal sign to children, and explain that the equal sign indicates that the same amount is on both sides of the equal sign in the equation.

- Ask children to make up and share other addition stories with objects or with the pan balance. They can select

number sentence cards or write number sentences for their discoveries.

- Place the pan balance in a learning center for students to experiment with different combinations.

- An inexpensive number scale can also be purchased that has weighted numerals.

Children can explore balance by hanging 3 and 4 on one side of the scale and balancing it with 6 and 1. Make number sentence cards or a whiteboard available for recording.

Extension

- Add the medium-size and large bears from sets of counting bears to encourage exploration of equivalence by weight. This introduces the element of variability into the process because the bears have different weights. One large bear is equal to or weighs the same as three small bears.

ACTIVITY 11.4   Addition Sentence (Representation)

Level: Grades K–2

Setting: Whole class and pairs

Objective: Students represent joining objects in two or more sets with the addition sentence using an equal sign.

Materials: Various counters, such as interlocking cubes or two-color counters; combining board from Activity 11.1; number sentence cards or whiteboards with markers.

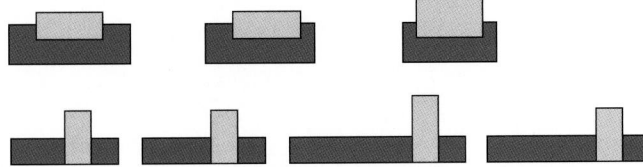

- Place three cars and four trucks on the magnetic board and tell a story about them. "Three red cars and four trucks were on the highway." Tell the students that a number sentence represents the same story. Have one student put a 3 beneath the cars and a 4 beneath the trucks.

- Place a plus sign between the 3 and the 4, and read "Three cars and four trucks." Ask what the plus sign means.

- Ask how many vehicles were on the highway. Place an equal sign and a 7 to complete the addition sentence, and read "Three cars and four trucks are equal to seven vehicles." Ask students what the equal sign means. (Answer: 3 plus 4 is the same as 7.) Reply, "Seven is another name for three plus four."

- Reduce the number sentence to $3 + 4 = 7$, and read "Three plus four equals seven."

- Ask students to work together to create more number stories and sentences. They may use the combining board from Activity 11.1. Ask them to find cards that match the addition stories they are telling or to write number sentences on their whiteboards.

Place-value material activities (discussed in Chapter 10) can continue when operations are introduced. Number combinations with sums greater than 10 should not present any great difficulty as children count to 20, 30, and more. Children see that the numbers 11–19 are combinations of ten and ones represented with Cuisenaire rods, bundles of stir sticks, and bean materials. With Cuisenaire rods a dark green (dg) rod and a black (bk) rod make a train equal in length to a train made with an orange (o) rod and three white (w) rods (Figure 11.3).

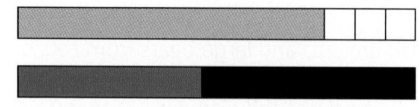

Figure 11.3 Cuisenaire train for 13

$$\text{dark green} + \text{black} = \text{orange} + \text{white} + \text{white} + \text{white}$$
$$dg + bk = o + 3w$$
$$6 + 7 = 10 + 3$$

When six loose beans and eight loose beans are joined, ten beans are exchanged for one bean stick and four loose beans remain.

Teachers assess whether students understand the concept of addition by observing and questioning children as they work with materials, draw pictures, tell stories, and write number sentences. A class checklist or rating scale in Figure 11.4 keeps a weekly record of student progress over time.

ⒺXERCISE

Based on Figure 11.4, what conclusions can you draw about each child's conceptual understanding of addition? What does this information suggest for instruction? ●●●

Introducing Subtraction

Subtraction, like addition, is introduced with realistic stories and is modeled with real objects and materials such as chips, blocks, and Unifix cubes. Takeaway stories are often the first of four subtraction actions presented.

• I have six books. If I give two to Nia, how many books will I keep?

As children act out this story, ask how many books each has. Use of varied stories, objects, and numbers allows students to describe their actions and the results in many contexts.

• Eight elephants were on the shore; three waded into the lake for a drink. How many were left on the shore?

Children can also illustrate stories with simple pictures and record the results with a number sentence $(8 - 3 = 5)$. As children make up new stories for subtraction, they see the relation between action and notation.

Subtraction is the **inverse operation** for addition; takeaway subtraction "undoes" addition. Other inverse operations can be modeled by opening and closing a door or by turning the lights on and off. Activities for subtraction typically follow introduction of addition, but the connection between operations is easily modeled as sets are joined and separated. The inverse relationship between addition and subtraction can be modeled with stories, objects, and pictures.

• Six adult elephants and two baby elephants were at the watering hole. The baby elephants got full and left the watering hole. How many were still drinking?

1—not yet Student Name	Tell Addition Story	2—developing Model Addition	Draw Pictures	3—proficient Write Number Sentence
Lilith	1 2 2 2	2 2 2 2	1 2 2 3	1 1 1 2
Anthony	1 2 2 2	1 1 1 2	1 1 2 2	1 1 1 1
Veronica	1 2 2 3	1 2 2 3	1 2 2 3	1 2 2 3
Josephina	1 2 2 3	1 2 3 3	1 2 3 3	1 2 3 3
Sandy	1 2 3 3	1 3 3 3	1 3 3 3	1 2 3 3

Figure 11.4 Class assessment checklist on addition and number sentences

A large domino drawn on a file folder demonstrates the inverse relationship and resulting number sentences by folding back one side of the folder at a time.

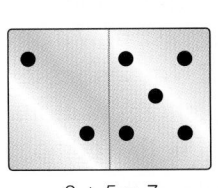   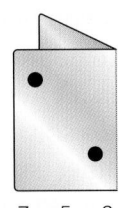   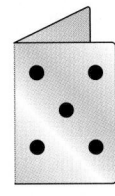

  2 + 5 = 7   7 − 5 = 2   7 − 2 = 5

Children become familiar with mathematics symbols and develop an understanding of inverse operations as they connect the actions and their meanings. The plus sign indicates joining and is read "plus"; the minus sign indicates separation in the takeaway story and is read as "minus."

Takeaway is one of four subtraction situations and should not be used as the name for the minus sign. The other subtraction situations are whole-part-part, comparison, and completion. Just as with addition and takeaway, children's experiences provide context for stories that are told, acted out, modeled, and recorded. When all types of subtraction stories are developed, students gain a broader understanding of subtraction. Students who have only been introduced to takeaway stories are frustrated when confronted by other subtraction types in a textbook or on tests.

Whole-part-part subtraction involves a whole set that is divided into subsets by some attribute.

- Bill saw eight airplanes fly overhead. Five of the planes were painted red. How many of the planes were not red?

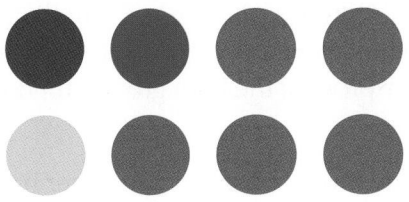

Plastic airplanes or counters or triangles can be used to represent the eight airplanes with five of them red. Children talk through the problem by describing what they see. "I see eight airplanes and five are red; three are not red." Sorting activities are also a good time to highlight whole-part-part subtraction.

- You have 15 buttons and 8 are gold. How many are not gold?

- There are 22 boys and girls here today. Let's count the boys. How many girls are here?

After several examples, children determine that they can write a subtraction number sentence for the stories. The sum is the whole and the addends are the two parts. Activity 11.5 describes how to

ACTIVITY 11.5 How Many? (Representation)

Level: Grades K–2

Setting: Small groups or whole group

Objective: Students model whole-part-part subtraction.

Materials: How Many Snails? by Paul Giganti, illustrated by Donald Crew (New York: Greenwillow, 1988)

How Many Snails?—a picture counting book with patterned text—has two-page pictures of dogs, or snails, or clouds with different characteristics. Children are asked to count the number of dogs, the number of spotted dogs, and the number of spotted dogs with their tongues out. The idea of whole-part-part is introduced.

- The first encounter with the text will probably be as a counting book. The picture and text invite student participation; read one display at a time with students counting the clouds (the whole group) and big, fluffy clouds (subgroup).

- Following the initial presentation, read the book again and ask an additional question: "How many clouds are not big and fluffy?"

- Ask students to tell the total number of clouds (8), the number of big, fluffy clouds (3), and the number of clouds that are not big and fluffy (5).

- Write the number sentence 8 − 3 = 5. Ask what each number represents.

- After reading several more pages, ask students to make their own picture for a page for a classroom book. Depending on their level, children may draw a picture or include the repetitive text on their own page. Share picture pages with the group, post them on the bulletin board, and make a classroom book.

introduce whole-part-part subtraction using the book *How Many Snails?* by Paul Giganti.

Children have daily experiences comparing ages, amounts, and lengths. Their language already includes comparison words such as older, younger, bigger, smaller, taller, shorter, more, and less. Preschool children are often asked whether one set is bigger or smaller. Such comparison experiences and vocabulary provide the background for comparison subtraction.

• Antoinette has 12 baseball cards; her brother has 9. How many more cards does Antoinette have than her brother?

Show two sets of cards, and ask which set has more cards in it (the set with 12 cards) and which has fewer (the set with 9 cards). Matching the cards one to one shows three unmatched cards in the larger set. Count each set and ask, "How many more cards does Antoinette have? How can we write a subtraction sentence to show how many more cards Antoinette has." Write two statements:

Antoinette's cards − brother's cards = difference
$$12 - 9 = 3$$

The fourth subtraction situation, completion, is similar to comparison, but children often find it more difficult to understand. In comparison children see two existing sets, but completion compares an existing set with a desired set. The existing set is incomplete and the problem or aim for the student is to complete the set.

• Miguel has saved $6 for a CD. The CD costs $9.

• Ari can get a free kite by saving nine lids from her favorite yogurt. She already has six lids.

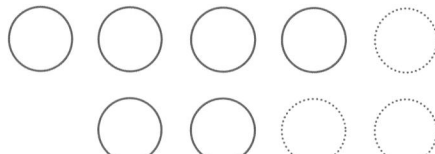

Counting-on is a successful approach for completion problems. After telling the story of Miguel, put

six play dollar bills or counters on a magnetic board. Ask, "How many dollars does Miguel need for the CD?" (Answer: 6.) Ask, "How many dollars does Miguel have?" (Answer: 9.) Let students count-on, "1, 2, 3" or "7, 8, 9," as you place the three more dollars or counters on the board. Finally, ask how many were added. (Answer: 3.) Activity 11.6 describes the counting-on strategy to solve completion situations.

Balancing is another strategy for the completion type of subtraction. Put nine disks on one side of a pan balance and six on the other side (Figure 11.5). Ask student to estimate how many more disks balance the scale, and count as you add disks. The number sentence can be written either as subtraction, $9 - 6 = 3$, or as addition, $6 + 3 = 9$. The missing addend is an algebraic equation form that shows that something is missing and needs to be balanced: $6 + ? = 9$.

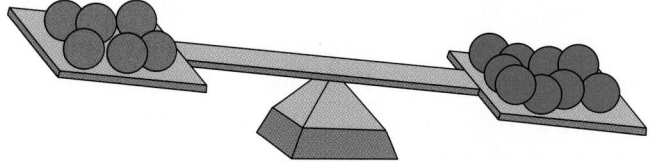

Figure 11.5 Completion subtraction with a balance scale

As important as modeling addition and subtraction with manipulatives is, activities alone do not guarantee meaningful learning. Like any tool, manipulatives are the means rather the ends of an activity. Discourse between students, and with a teacher, is essential for scaffolding mathematical ideas. Mathematical conversations encourage students to transfer learning from short-term to long-term memory. Drawing the subtraction stories is an important problem-solving strategy that helps students understand how subtraction works. Each story situation demands a slightly different picture. Students may need help to draw the story rather than the number sentence. In takeaway or whole-part-part subtraction the student draws the total number and identifies a part that is removed or a part that belongs to a subgroup of the total. For comparison and completion problems children model or draw two sets and show how they compare or measure with each other. Students may want to draw both the sum and the addend. Help students depict the story first; then write the number sentence as a summary of the story situation.

ACTIVITY 11.6 Counting On (Problem Solving and Reasoning)

Level: Grades 1–3

Setting: Small groups

Objective: Students use counting-on strategies to learn subtraction facts.

Materials: Counting-on cards, counters, or painted lima beans

- The counting-on strategy is one way to have children conceptualize how many more of something are needed. It is best used when the difference between two numbers is relatively small, such as in $9 - 2 = 7$.

- Tell a story: "Janell has $5, but the CD she wants costs $8. How much more money does she need?" Show a counting-on card with eight circles, five filled in and three

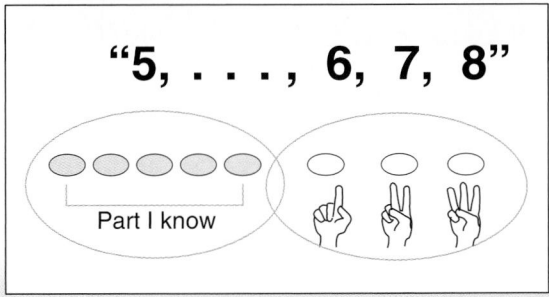

"5, . . . , 6, 7, 8"

Part I know

blank. Ask what the five stands for, and the three. (Answer: She has five; she needs three more.) Use the card to illustrate how to count on from 5: "6, 7, 8."

- Have students model the situation with counters or beans. Each child counts five showing one color and three of another color.

- Follow the action by having children say the appropriate sentence for the combination: "She wants eight, she has five, she needs three more; eight minus five equals three."

- Repeat with similar stories, counting-on cards, and manipulatives.

Source: Adapted from Fennell (1992, p. 25).

Extension

- With beans (or other objects) and small cups, label each cup with numerals 1 through 18. Put the corresponding number of beans in each cup. Remove a few beans from the cup, and put them on the table. Ask how many more counters are in the cup to complete the number in the set.

- Six children were at the party. Two went home.

If the children start by writing $6 - 2$, the picture they draw may not accurately show the story. Pictures are a problem-solving strategy that students use to understand the problem and develop a plan. Starting with addition and subtraction situations, children learn that accurate representation of the story is important (Figure 11.6).

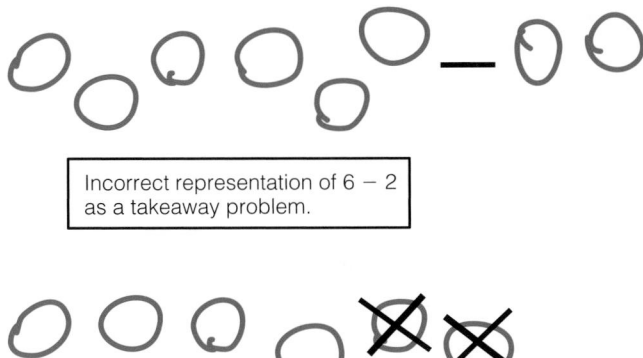

Incorrect representation of $6 - 2$ as a takeaway problem.

Correct representation of $6 - 2$ as a takeaway problem.

Figure 11.6 Children's drawings of subtraction

Vertical Notation

Early in learning number operations, mathematical sentences are recorded horizontally, like a word sentence. The horizontal form has two benefits:

1. The order of numerals in a sentence is the same as the verbal description and reinforces the meaning of a problem story. Joining three apples and four apples is described as "I had three apples and got four more. I now have seven apples." The mathematical sentence is $3 + 4 = 7$.

2. Horizontal notation is later used for formulas and algebraic expressions.

Making the transition is not difficult when attention is paid to the meaning and order of the stories being recorded. Compare two addition situations.

- Four parents were watching soccer practice. Then six more joined them. $4 + 6 = ?$

- Six parents were sitting in the stands watching soccer. Four more joined them. $6 + 4 = ?$

When the horizontal number sentence and its meaning are established, students are introduced to the vertical, or stacked, notation form. The number sentences $4 + 6 = 10$ and $6 + 4 = 10$, respectively, are written in stacked form:

$$\begin{array}{r} 4 \\ +6 \\ \hline 10 \end{array} \qquad \begin{array}{r} 6 \\ +4 \\ \hline 10 \end{array}$$

Preserving the order of the numbers from horizontal sentences to stacked forms reinforces the logic of the story. A magnetic board with moveable numbers allows for easy translation of the numbers from horizontal to vertical notation, as seen in Activity 11.7.

Order in subtraction sentences is more critical because subtraction is not **commutative**.

- Four parents were watching soccer practice. Two had to leave early. $4 - 2 = 2$.

$$\begin{array}{r} 4 \\ -2 \\ \hline 2 \end{array}$$

Although $2 - 4$ is a valid sentence with negative integers, it does not describe this story.

Simple addition and subtraction problems can be presented in either form; however, as students work with larger numbers, alignment of place values shows the advantage of vertical notation.

What Teachers Need to Know About Properties of Addition and Subtraction

As students work with addition and subtraction, the properties of the operations should be emphasized because they are so important in learning the basic facts. The **commutative property of addition** states that the order of the addends does not affect the sum.

Commutative law: $2 + 3 = 3 + 2$

$$n_1 + n_2 = n_2 + n_1$$

Subtraction is not commutative: $7 - 6$ is not equal to $6 - 7$.

The **associative property of addition** applies to three or more addends. Addition is a binary operation involving two addends. When working with three or more addends, two are added, then another addend is added, and another, until the sum is determined. If the problem shows the associative property, the order in which pairs of addends are added does not change the sum. Subtraction is not associative.

Associative law: $8 + (2 + 3) = (8 + 2) + 3$

$$a + (b + c) = (a + b) + c$$

ACTIVITY 11.7 **Vertical Form (Representation)**

Level: Grades 1 and 2

Setting: Small groups or whole class

Objective: Students use horizontal and vertical notation for addition.

Materials: Magnetic board shapes; numerals; +, −, and = signs

- Tell the following story: "Two children were playing kick ball and four more joined the game." Arrange two sets of shapes in a horizontal row on a magnetic board. Ask children to use magnetic numerals and symbols to write the number sentence for the objects. Read the sentence: "Two plus four equals six."

- Rearrange the shapes to form a vertical column. Put two shapes at the top and the other four beneath. Ask whether the number of shapes has changed.

(Answer: No.) Ask what has changed. (Answer: The arrangement.)

- Transform the number sentence from horizontal to vertical also. Put the numerals alongside the shapes with the plus sign to the left of the bottom numeral. Read the sentence: "Two plus four equals six."

- Tell other stories and have students represent them with magnetic shapes and numbers in both horizontal to vertical form.

Assessment

- Ask children to draw pictures for an addition and a subtraction story, and record the numbers for the problem in horizontal and vertical form.

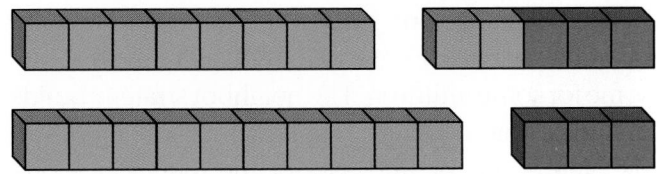

When adding five addends, such as $4 + 5 + 3 + 6 + 7$, the commutative and associative laws work together to make addition easier by finding combinations of 10: $4 + 6$ is 10; $7 + 3$ is 10; $10 + 10 + 5$ is 25. Looking for easy combinations of 10, 100, or 1,000 is a mental computation strategy called **compatible numbers**.

Zero is the **identity element** for both addition and subtraction because adding or subtracting zero does not change the sum. When working with concrete materials, students model stories with zero and find that zero does not change the sum regardless of the size of the number.

Identity element: $5 + 0 = 5$ $72 - 0 = 72$

  $n + 0 = n$ $n - 0 = n$

Learning Strategies for Addition and Subtraction Facts

As children gain understanding and confidence with addition and subtraction, the emphasis of instruction moves toward learning number combinations. Children who learn addition and subtraction conceptually with realistic stories and materials have already encountered most or all combinations. Learning strategically is more efficient than memorization alone and has longer term benefits for number sense. Instead of learning 100 addition and 100 subtraction combinations as isolated facts, children learn a strategy, generalization, or rule that yields many facts. Learning properties and rules emphasizes how numbers work and fosters number sense and mental computation.

The 100 basic addition facts are all the combinations of single-digit addends from $0 + 0 = 0$ to $9 + 9 = 18$, although some teachers or state standards extend number combinations up to $12 + 12 = 24$. The subtraction facts are the inverse of the 100 addition facts. The basic facts are shown on the addition-subtraction table in Figure 11.8. As students learn a new rule or generalization, they can fill in the 10×10 addition and subtraction fact table (Figure 11.7, Black-Line Master 11.1). The fact table becomes a record

of the strategies students are learning. Some facts are learned with several strategies so that students choose the best strategy for their own learning.

The *commutative law for addition* means that the order of the addends does not change the sum: $3 + 6$ and $6 + 3$ have the same sum. Because each fact is paired with its reverse, students who understand the commutative law can use knowledge of one fact to learn its partner. The strategy is illustrated by rotating a Unifix cube train or a domino. "Turn-around facts" or "flip-flop facts" are other names for the commutative facts in addition. Figure 11.8 shows the symmetrical relation of commutative facts. Students should also understand that the commutative law does not apply to subtraction because $9 - 6$ does not equal $6 - 9$.

The identity element of zero for addition is demonstrated by putting three cubes in one hand and leaving the other hand empty. Putting the hands together shows that adding "three plus *no more*" is three. After several examples, ask students to develop a rule for adding zero. They will say "adding zero doesn't change the answer" or similar phrasing. The "plus 0" rule accounts for 19 facts on the addition table (Figure 11.9).

Counting-on is a particularly effective strategy for adding one or two, and some students may even use counting-on for adding

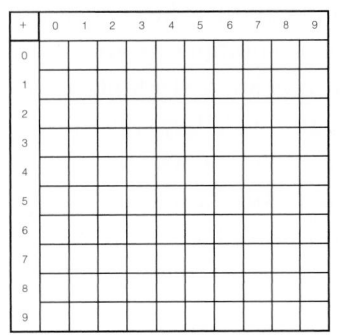

Figure 11.7 Blank addition table

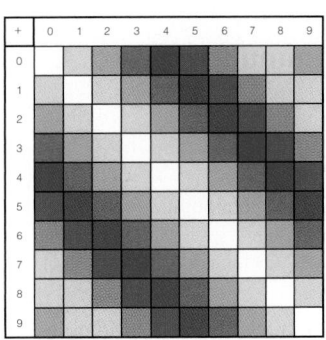

Figure 11.8 Addition table with commutative facts

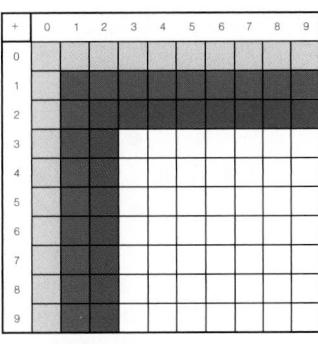

Figure 11.9 Strategy of plus 0, plus 1, and plus 2

three. Model the "plus 1" rule with four cubes in one hand and one cube the other. After seeing further examples, such as 5 + 1, 8 + 1, and 2 + 1, students will generalize that "adding 1 is just counting to the next number." The "plus 2" and "plus 3" rules are extensions. The "plus 1" strategy yields 17 basic facts, and the "plus 2" rule gives 15 more facts (Figure 11.9). With only three strategies of "plus 0," "plus 1," and "plus 2," students have strategies for almost half the addition facts.

The *associative law* is an important strategy because it encourages students to think flexibly about combinations and to use combinations that they already know as building blocks. If students know 4 + 2 but have problems with 4 + 3, they split the fact and recombine it as 4 + 2 + 1. Activity 11.8 is a lesson on the commutative and associative properties.

Most children learn the *double* facts, such as 1 + 1 = 2 and 4 + 4 = 8, with ease. Perhaps repetition is a musical cue because many children almost sing the double combinations. The 10 double facts occupy a diagonal in the addition table (Figure 11.10).

Near doubles or neighbor facts include combinations such as 8 + 9 and 7 + 6 that may be troublesome for some children. The neighbor strategy builds on the doubles strategy. Display six red counters and six blue counters, and ask for the total. Place one more red counter, and ask how many there are now. After similar examples using a double fact plus one, many children will notice, "It's just one more than the double fact." Ask children to show how neighbor facts line up beside the doubles on the addition chart (Figure 11.10). Some children do not make the connection immediately and need additional time and experience with the near doubles. Activity 11.9 introduces near doubles.

"**Make 10**" emphasizes combinations with a sum of 10 that fill the

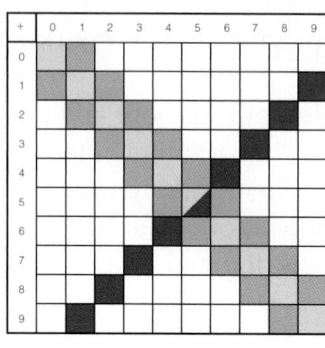

Figure 11.10 Doubles, near doubles, and combinations of 10

ACTIVITY 11.8 Commutative and Associative Properties (Representation)

Level: Grades 1–3

Setting: Small groups or whole class

Objective: Students demonstrate the commutative and associative properties of addition.

Materials: Beans and paper plates, Cuisenaire rods, a sheet of number lines for each child

- Give each student a paper plate with a line dividing it in half. Also give each student 20 beans. Ask students to put five beans in one half of the plate, and three in the other half. Then have them combine the beans on one side.

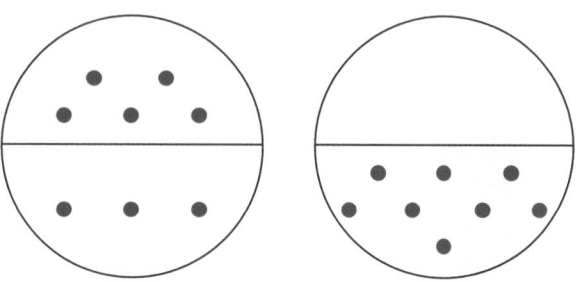

- Ask for the total number of beans. (Answer: 8.) Ask which of the students put three beans with five and which put five beans with three. Ask if the answer was the same.
- Say: "Tell me about the two number sentences."

- Have students repeat with other numbers of beans.
- Ask students to generalize what they found out. (Answer: The sum is the same, no matter which number is first.) You may decide to tell them they have discovered the commutative property of addition.
- Ask how they could show the commutative property with Cuisenaire-rod trains and with the number line.

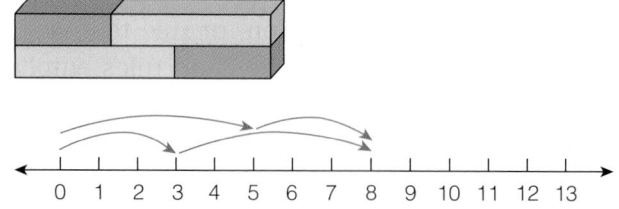

Extension

- The same materials and procedures can be changed slightly to demonstrate and develop the associative property. Children place three sets of beans on a plate showing thirds. Move the plates around in various sequences, and write the number sentences such as 3 + 4 + 2 and 2 + 4 + 3. Students can combine any two sets first and then add the third addend. Ask which combinations are easiest for them to recall.

ACTIVITY 11.9 Near Doubles (Reasoning)

Level: Grades 1–3

Setting: Small groups

Objective: Students use double number combinations to find a near-double strategy.

Materials: Double cards for each child, set of near-double cards (double dominoes can be used), worksheet for each child

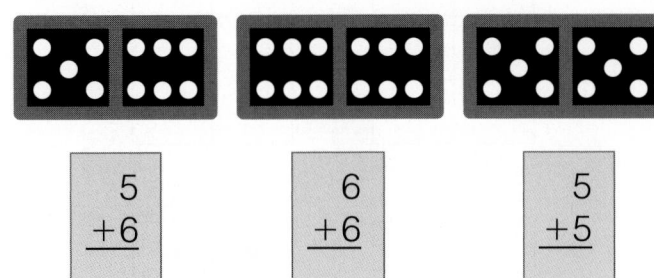

- Ask students which addition facts are doubles. When they answer 1 + 1, 2 + 2, 3 + 3, and so forth, ask why they are called doubles. (Answer: Because both addends are the same number.)

- Have each child make a set of double facts cards on 4 × 6 index cards.

- Hold up a near-double card, such as 5 + 6. Say: "Look at your double cards and find one that is almost the same. Show me that card." Some children will hold up 5 + 5; others might hold up 6 + 6.

- Ask students how their card is similar to 5 + 6. (Answer: 5 + 5 is 10, so 5 + 6 will be one more, or 11; or 6 + 6 is 12, so 5 + 6 is one less.)

- Ask what strategies were used for changing the double fact to a new fact. (Answer: The first suggests a "double plus 1" combination. The second card suggests a "double minus 1" combination.) Either strategy is useful, and students should be encouraged to consider them both.

- Ask students to find another double-fact card and near-double facts that are related to it.

Assessment

- On a fact worksheet, ask students to circle double facts in blue and near doubles in orange.

---

opposite diagonal in Figure 11.10. Students have had many experiences with tens in place-value activities. The Exchange game from Chapter 10 requires students to count 10 as they trade up and down. Work with pennies and dimes provides many experiences for sums of ten. The tens frame in Figure 11.11 is also good for developing the make 10 strategy.

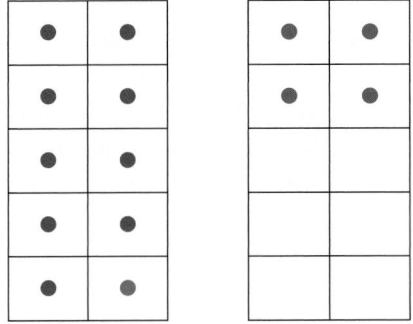

Figure 11.11 Tens frames

"Ten plus" is based on the associative property and combines "make 10" with counting-on. For 8 + 5 the child thinks how to make 10 starting with 8 and renames 5 as 2 + 3. The problem becomes 8 + 2 + 3, or 10 with 3 extra.

$$8 + 5 = \underline{\quad} \qquad 8 + (2 + 3) = 10 + 3 = 13.$$

When students begin working with more than two addends, the make-ten and ten-plus strategies are particularly useful because they look for compatible numbers totaling 10.

$$7 + 6 + 3 = 7 + 3 + 6 = 10 + 6 = 16$$

Rearranging the numbers to make a more difficult problem into an easier one continues the theme of thinking about how numbers relate.

Activity 11.10 uses the tens frame (Black-Line Master 11.2) to demonstrate a visual strategy for ten-plus combinations.

"Ten minus 1" is used for fact combinations with 9 as an addend. With the tens frames shown in Figure 11.11, ask, "What is the sum of 10 plus 4?" When students respond 14, remove one counter from the 10: "What is the sum of 9 plus 4?" After several examples, give students examples starting with 9 + 7 and ask them to explain their thinking. The tens frame is also useful to show the 10 minus 1 strategy.

Understanding addition and subtraction begins conceptually through activities with concrete materials and examples and continues with the development of properties, strategies, and rules for the number combinations. Knowing the properties and rules

ACTIVITY 11.10   Making Ten with the Tens Frame

Level: Grades 1–3

Setting: Small groups or student pairs

Objective: Students use the add-to-ten strategy for finding sums greater than 10.

Materials: Tens frames on overhead or board, magnetic shapes, math boxes

- Tell a story that has a sum greater than 10, such as "Juan had seven dimes and then got six more dimes. How many dimes did he have?" Model the problem $7 + 6 = ?$ on the tens frame. Use one color of counter on one frame and a different color on the other.

- Ask: "Does anyone see a way to rearrange the counters to make the answer easy to see?" Ask a student to explain while moving three counters from one tens frame to another tens frame. Ask if they could have moved the counters the opposite way.

- Ask: "How much is 10 and 3 more?" Ask whether this is an easier way to think about adding the two numbers.

- Tell several other stories for pairs of students to model with the tens frame.

- Ask students to generalize a rule for the sums they have been working with. (Answer: First, make ten. Then see how many are still in the other tens frame and add that to the ten.)

- Have children work in pairs with counters and tens frames to model several other problems.

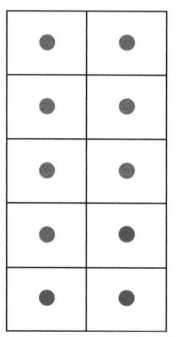
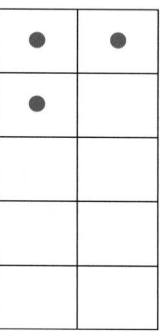

supports students' thinking while they are learning the facts. If they cannot remember a fact, they can reconstruct the fact. Strategies develop mental computation and number sense and are a critical step in learning the facts.

Strategies for Subtraction

Many subtraction strategies are counterparts of addition strategies. Counting-down strategies for subtraction are shown by walking backward on the number line or removing items from a set. Students will say, "It is just the number before." This leads to strategies of "minus 1" and "minus 2." Students can also recognize situations in which the difference between the sum and the known addend is one or two.

- Juan's dog had 10 puppies. He found new homes for nine of the puppies: $10 - 9 = 1$.

- We want to buy a book that costs $7.00, but we have only $5.00: $7 - 5 = 2$.

These stories make good "think-aloud" examples for students.

When students understand that subtraction is the inverse operation for addition through many activities, they find that each pair of addition facts also yields a pair of subtraction facts. A "fact family" involves the commutative law of addition and the inverse relationship between addition and subtraction to produce four related facts. A triangle flashcard (Figure 11.12) shows how three numbers form four number sentences.

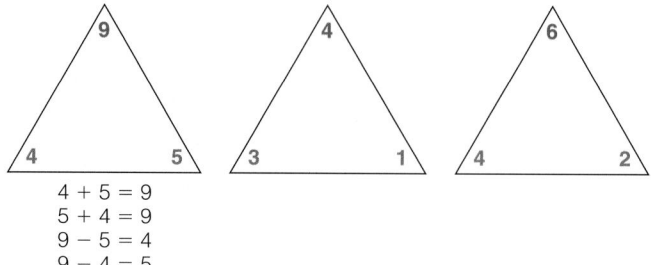

Figure 11.12 Triangle flash cards

A child covers one number on the flash card and asks the partner for the number sentence that completes the relationship of addition or subtraction.

Students describe the identity property of the "minus 0" strategy as not taking anything away, so that they still have what they had at the beginning.

- I have six oranges and gave none of them away: $6 - 0 = 6$.

Children sometimes generalize incorrectly. For example, when the problem involves subtracting a number from itself, the zero rule sometimes causes difficulties.

- I have six oranges and gave six away: $6 - 6 = 0$.

If a child confuses subtraction facts involving zero, act out several stories to show different situations. Ask children to generate a rule for a number subtracted from itself as "you don't have any left." This conclusion has an algebraic generalization of $n - n = 0$. Activity 11.11 describes an activity in which students imagine the missing number in a subtraction situation.

Developing Accuracy and Speed with Basic Facts

If students do not develop useful fact strategies, they revert to less efficient methods, such as finger counting, marking a number line, knocking on the desk, or drawing pictures. Although these behaviors are useful in developing the concept, continued reliance on them inhibits quick, confident responses with number facts. Many children move from concrete to abstract symbolic representations quickly and give up concrete materials; others need them for longer periods of time. However, teachers should avoid letting students become dependent on physical strategies. Thinking strategies for number operations are an important link between understanding concrete meaning and achieving accuracy and ready recall of number facts.

Activities that focus on accuracy and speed with basic facts occur after children understand concepts and symbols for operations and have developed strategies for many facts. The goal of practice activities is *ready recall*—knowing the sum or difference with accuracy and appropriate speed. Without ready recall of basic facts, various algorithms, estimations, and mental computation with numbers larger than 100 become laborious and frustrating.

ACTIVITY 11.11   **Subtracting with Hide-and-Seek Cards (Reasoning)**

Level: Grades 1–3

Setting: Student pairs or small groups

Objective: Students use the hide-and-seek strategy for learning subtraction facts.

Materials: Teacher-made hide-and-seek cards for several subtraction combinations (picture different objects on cards), math boxes

- Have students work in pairs with math box materials. Ask students to place a set of objects on a plate (e.g., 11 objects). Have one student cover part of the set with paper or a paper plate cut in half.

- Ask: "How many do you see?" and "How many are hiding?" The students identify both numbers and say, for example, "Eleven minus five equals six."

- Students repeat with other combinations of objects, taking turns covering objects on the plate.

- Show students a hide-and-seek card with numerals on flaps folded back. Have students identify the "whole" (e.g., 12).

- Cover both portions by folding flaps over them. Have students identify the total number (12). Uncover one part of the picture. Have students identify the amount seen (e.g., 6) and the number still "hiding" (6). Ask students to say and write the number sentence.

- Have children work with several different cards.

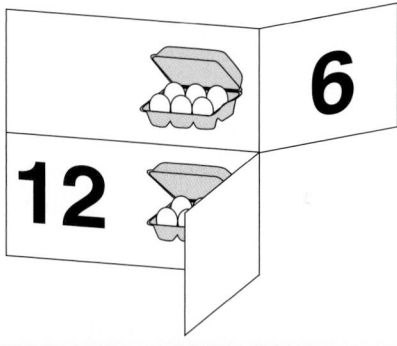

Source: Adapted from Thompson (1991, pp. 10–13).

How much emphasis to place on basic facts is a continuing issue in mathematics education. Many adults remember speed demands and "timed tests" as a negative emotional experience that tainted their attitude toward mathematics for the rest of their lives. Some children enjoy the challenge of taking timed tests and seeing their progress on public display, whereas others shut down emotionally and cognitively. Competition between students and public displays that show which students have learned their facts may seem benign, but many adults recall them as a discouraging advertisement of their failures.

Knowing the negative impact of timed tests and other drill situations, effective teachers should carefully consider methods for encouraging accuracy and speed with basic facts. The following guidelines suggest how practice might be handled in a more positive manner.

- Develop accuracy with facts before speed. Speed is the secondary goal.

- Expectations for speed will be different for each child. The time required to master the facts differs from student to student. Students should not be compared to each other, but they can be encouraged to monitor their own progress and improvement.

- Help children develop strategies that make sense to them. Begin with the easy strategies and facts such as the "plus 1" and "minus 1" rules and then move to more complex strategies and facts, such as fact families or combinations for 10.

- Review already learned facts, and gradually add new ones. Have students record their mastery of the strategies and facts in a personal log or table.

- Keep practice sessions short, perhaps five minutes.

- Use a variety of practice materials, including games, flash cards, and computer software. Flash cards encourage mental computation, whereas written practice pages may slow down thinking due to focus on writing.

- Avoid the pressure of group timed tests. Instead allow children to test themselves individually

with a kitchen timer and keep their own record of facts learned rather than facts missed. When children set their own reasonable time limits, they are more motivated to see learning the facts as a personal accomplishment.

The goal is for all children to have ready recall of facts so that they can move forward in their computational fluency. Many computer programs offer individual practice routines set for individual speed and different challenges as well as report scores and progress over sessions for the student and teacher. Card games such as bingo, memory, and matching provide variety in practice.

0	6	18	9	15
4	3	11	8	7
5	7	Free	17	16
6	15	13	2	4
10	1	12	14	6

When students make flash cards for the facts as they learn them, they can practice alone or with a partner.

- If you can say the answer before you flip the flash card over, put the card in your fast stack. If there is a delay, put that card in a second stack to work on later.

This activity is also used as an assessment technique in Activity 11.12. Children identify the facts they know and the ones they are working on. The personal set of flash cards can be taken home to practice with siblings or adults.

Self-assessment puts students in charge of their learning. They may keep personal improvement charts that show how many facts they answered correctly in 5 minutes, then 4 minutes, and 3 minutes. They can mark the combinations they know on an addition table or write entries in their journals: "I am very fast with the 9s. I know $9 + 6$ is 15 because it is 1 less than $10 + 6$."

Effective teachers also watch for signs of frustration or confusion. If students know only a few facts, they are frustrated by practice and avoid it. If students revert to finger counting, tally marks, or con-

ACTIVITY 11.12 Assessing with Flash Cards

Level: Grades 2–5

Setting: Individuals

Objective: Student accuracy and speed with subtraction facts is assessed, and self-assessment is encouraged.

Materials: Commercial flash cards or child-made flash cards made with index cards. Put the number combination on the front with the answer on the back so that when the flash card is flipped, the answer is right side up.

- As students learn a strategy, have them make their own set of flash cards or choose the flash cards for that strategy.

- Let students work through the flash cards with partners.

- After practice, do a quick assessment with the flash cards that the students have. Have students place the cards in three stacks: I know the answer fast; I know the answer but have to think about it; I don't know the answer yet.

- Have the students mark cards green for the first stack, yellow for the second, and red for the third.

- Note on a checklist or addition table which addition facts are in each stack.

- Add new cards as new strategies are learned, and check for progress.

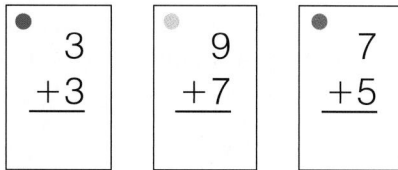

This assessment encourages students to take responsibility for learning the facts and also demonstrates progress as the green stack gets bigger. The assessment takes only a couple of minutes and clearly identifies problems and difficulties.

ACTIVITY 11.13 Practice Addition and Subtraction Number Facts with Calculators

Level: Grades 1–4

Setting: Pairs

Objective: Students build accuracy with number facts, and they compare the speed of a calculator with thinking.

Materials: Set of student- or teacher-made fact cards, calculator

Use this activity with children who are reasonably proficient with basic facts for addition and subtraction.

- Students work in pairs with two identical sets of 15 fact cards. One student is the Brain, and the other is the Button. The Brain recalls the answers for the fact combinations and writes them on a piece of paper.

- The Button must key each combination into a calculator, then write the answers. As the activity begins, ask: "Who will complete the work first, the Brain or the Button?"

- Start each pair of students simultaneously. An easy way to time the activity is to record elapsed time in seconds on the chalkboard or overhead projector: 8, 10, 12, 14, ... Each student notes the time it took her or him to finish the task. Discuss the results to help students see how knowing the facts speeds their work.

Variations

- Use subtraction, multiplication, and division facts.
- Use three or four single-digit addends.

crete strategies, they may be indicating weakness in understanding or strategies. In both cases students need work with concepts and strategies before working on accuracy and speed. Even when students have become proficient with facts, they need to refresh their knowledge of strategies and recall of facts. At the beginning of the school year a teacher might ask students to assess their understanding of strategies and recall of facts. Activities for review and maintenance should be based on student strengths and needs. Activity 11.13 uses a calculator to provide practice with basic facts. A benefit of this activity is that it points out the advantage of knowing the facts: the brain usually wins over the button.

Research for the Classroom

Arthur Baroody and his colleagues Meng-Lung Lai and Kelly Mix have compiled a review of the literature on the development of young children's number and operations sense (Baroody et al., 2005). Based on this research, Baroody (2006) advocates a number sense approach for students who are learning number combinations. He proposes helping students to find patterns that connect number combinations by starting with the idea that the same number can be represented in many forms; 8 can be renamed 1 + 7, 2 + 6, 5 + 3, and 4 + 4. Flexible thinking about numbers allows students to compose and decompose them in ways that make learning facts easier: 8 + 5 = 8 + 2 + 3 = 10 + 3. Baroody also suggests that common instructional techniques emphasize counting strategies that may inhibit learning of facts beyond sums of 10. Overemphasis on counting may limit investigation of other more useful and generative patterns. Students—in particular, students with learning disabilities—are trapped by inefficient strategies that limit their understanding of relationships between numbers and their combinations. Students should build a variety of strategies that create groups of related facts such as fact families. Although practice has a role in learning number combinations, it should be based on reasoning strategies that become automatic rather than on drill of isolated facts.

What Students Need to Learn About Multiplication and Division

As with addition and subtraction, the goal of instruction in multiplication and division of whole numbers is **computational fluency**—knowing when and how to compute accurately when solving problems. Experiences that children have with modeling, drawing, and representing addition and subtraction problems in everyday situations provide a model for work with multiplication and division. Understanding multiplication and division begins in kindergarten and the primary grades when children skip-count, share cookies at snack times, or make patterns with linking cubes. Such activities set the stage in second and third grade for directed teaching/thinking lessons about multiplication and division situations, actions, and strategies for learning number combinations.

The NCTM curriculum standards referring to whole-number operations emphasize that they should be taught in meaningful ways. Table 11.2 outlines an instructional sequence for multiplication and division that addresses number concepts, connections between operations, and computational fluency with larger numbers. Children who understand how numbers and operations work make connections between whole numbers and fractions, see relationships among the four basic operations, and grasp topics in number theory such as divisibility.

⒠XERCISE

Compare your state mathematics curriculum with the NCTM standards for learning multiplication and division. Does the state curriculum emphasize learning the operations by using realistic situations and materials and by solving problems? Does your state curriculum address how technology is used in learning multiplication and division? ●●●

What Teachers Need to Know About Multiplication and Division

Adults who use multiplication and division in a variety of settings in their everyday life may not realize the varied situations and meanings for the operations.

Multiplication Situations, Meanings, and Actions

Multiplication has three distinct meanings in real-world situations:

1. *Repeated addition*: The *total in any number of equal-size sets*.
2. *Geometric interpretation*: The number represented by a rectangular array or area.
3. *Cartesian product*: The number of one-to-one combinations of objects in two or more sets.

TABLE 11.2 **Development of Concepts and Skills for Multiplication and Division**

Concepts	Skills	Connections
Number concepts 1–100	Skip counting Recognizing groups of objects Thinking in multiples	Multiplication and division
Numbers 1–1,000	Representing numbers with base-10 materials Exchange rules and games Regrouping and renaming	Algorithms Estimation Mental computation
Numbers larger than 1,000	Expanded notation Learning names for larger numbers and realistic situations for their use Visualizing larger numbers	Alternative algorithms
Operation of multiplication	Stories and actions for joining equal-sized sets: repeated addition Stories and actions for arrays and area: geometric interpretation Stories and actions for Cartesian combinations Representing multiplication with materials, pictures, and number sentences	Multiples, factors Area measurement Probability and combinatorics Problem solving
Operation of division	Stories and actions for repeated subtraction division Stories and actions for partitioning Representing division with materials, pictures, and number sentences	Fractions Divisibility rules Problem solving
Basic facts for multiplication and division	Developing strategies for basic facts Recognizing arithmetic properties Achieving accuracy and speed with basic facts Achieving accuracy and speed with multiples of 10 and 100	Estimation and reasonableness Algebraic patterns and relations Mental computation Estimation, mental computation
Multiplication and division with larger numbers	Story situations and actions with larger numbers Developing algorithms with and without regrouping using materials (to 1,000) and symbols Estimation Using technology: calculators and computer	Problem solving Computational fluency, mental computation Reasonableness Problem solving, reasonableness

Repeated addition, the most common multiplication situation, involves finding a total number belonging to multiple groups of the same number.

4 packages of 3 juice boxes

- Johnny had four packages of juice boxes. Each package had three juice boxes.

$$3 + 3 + 3 + 3 = 12 \text{ juice boxes}$$
$$4 \times 3 = 12 \text{ juice boxes}$$

- Diego had five quarters in his pocket.

$$25 \text{ cents} + 25 \text{ cents} + 25 \text{ cents} + 25 \text{ cents} + 25 \text{ cents} = 125 \text{ cents}$$
$$5 \times 25 \text{ cents} = 125 \text{ cents}$$

5 quarters

The **geometric interpretation** is represented as a row-and-column arrangement and is also called a rectangular array. Area is one example of the geometric meaning of multiplication.

- Paolo arranged the chairs in four rows with five chairs in each row: $4 \times 5 = 20$ chairs.

4 rows of 5 chairs

- Gina measured the room. It was 9 feet by 10 feet.

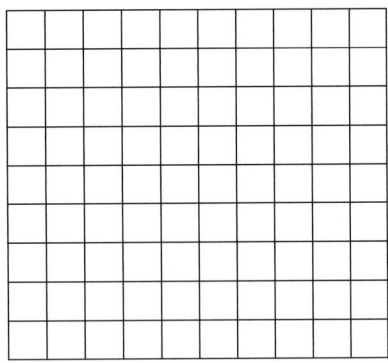

9 feet x 10 feet

The third type of multiplication, **Cartesian cross-product** or **combinations**, shows the total number of possibilities made by choosing one option from each group of choices.

- Emma hung up five blouses and three pants to see all the outfits she could make. Five blouses paired with three pants makes 15 possible outfits: $5 \times 3 = 15$.

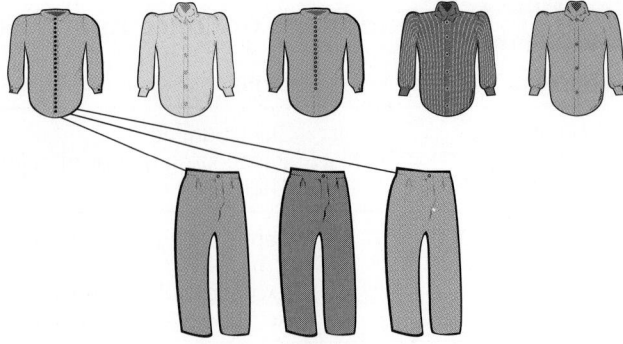

Combinations of blouses and pants

- Kara had two kinds of cake (yellow and chocolate) and three flavors of ice cream (vanilla, strawberry, and chocolate mint). Two kinds of cake paired with three flavors of ice cream gives six possible dessert choices: $2 \times 3 = 6$.

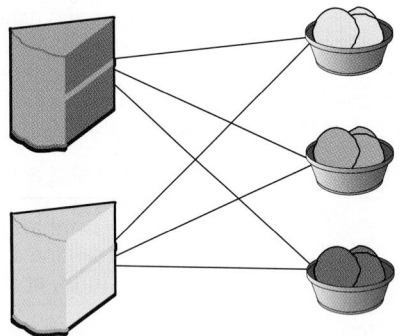

Combinations of cake and ice cream

If Kara offered four types of toppings (chocolate, hot fudge, butterscotch, berry), the number of possible dessert combinations would be $2 \times 3 \times 4 = 24$. The important limitation on this is that only one choice can be made in each category.

Numbers multiplied together are called **factors**. The result of multiplication is the **product**.

Division Situations, Meanings, and Actions

Division is the *inverse operation* of multiplication. In multiplication two factors are known and the product is unknown. In division the total or product is known, but only one factor is known. The total or product is called the **dividend**, and the known factor is the **divisor**. The unknown factor is called the **quotient**. There are two types of division situations:

1. *Repeated subtraction, or repeated measurement*: How many groups of the same size can be subtracted from a total?

2. *Sharing, or partitioning*: The total is equally distributed among a known number of recipients.

Because division is the inverse operation of multiplication, a multiplication situation can illustrate the difference between the two types of division.

Multiplication

- Three boys had four pencils each. How many pencils did they have?

$$3 \text{ groups of } 4 = 12$$

When the known factor is the number of pencils for each boy, the question is, How many boys can get pencils? The pencils are being measured out in groups of 4.

Repeated Subtraction

- John had 12 pencils. He wants to give four pencils to each of his friends. How many friends can John give pencils to?

$$12 - 4 - 4 - 4 = 0 \quad \text{Subtract 4 three times.}$$
$$12 \div 4 = 3$$

When the known factor is the number of boys, the question is how many pencils each will get.

Sharing

- John has 12 pencils and 3 friends. How many pencils can John give to each of his friends?

The pencils are shared one at a time among the friends. John gives each friend one pencil, a second, a third, and then a fourth pencil before exhausting the pencils.

$$12 \div 3 = 4$$

When the known factor is the number belonging to each group, the unknown factor is the number of groups. This division situation is called **repeated subtraction**, or **repeated measurement**. Measurement division asks how many groups of a known size can be made. Measurement division is called repeated subtraction because the number in each group is repeatedly subtracted from the total.

- Marisa baked 24 cookies and wants to serve 5 cookies to each person at her party. How many people can attend, including herself?

24 cookies, serving size 5

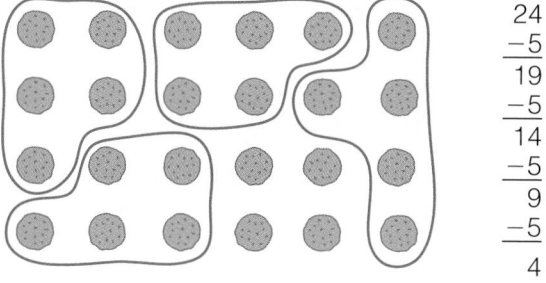

$$
\begin{array}{r}
24 \\
-5 \\
\hline
19 \\
-5 \\
\hline
14 \\
-5 \\
\hline
9 \\
-5 \\
\hline
4
\end{array}
$$

$$24 \div 5 = 4 \text{ remainder } 4$$

Figure 11.13 Repeated subtraction, or measurement division

Figure 11.13 shows how Marisa measured the cookies into groups of five. Marisa can serve four people and has four extra cookies.

24 cookies divided by 5 cookies
= 4 people at the party plus 4 extra cookies
$$24 \div 5 = 4, \text{ remainder } 4$$

In an earlier example Paolo arranged 20 chairs with 5 chairs in each row. How many rows?

20 chairs in rows of 5 chairs = 4 rows

When the number of groups is known but the size of each group is not known, the division situation is called **partitive**, or **sharing**. The action involves distributing, or sharing, the number as evenly as possible into the given number of groups. Partitive division asks how many are in each group.

- Kathleen dipped 19 strawberries in chocolate. If she is filling three gift boxes, how many strawberries go in each box?

Kathleen distributes the 19 strawberries one at a time into three boxes.

19 strawberries separated into 3 boxes =
6 strawberries in each box with 1 extra strawberry.
$$19 \div 3 = 6, \text{ remainder } 1$$

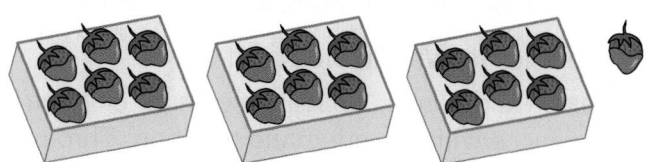

If division is done with numbers that can be evenly divided, the result is two whole-number factors. But division does not always work out evenly in real life. The groups or objects that are not evenly divided are called *remainders*. Depending on the situation, remainders can change the interpretation of the answer by rounding up or down, making fractions, or ignoring the remainder altogether.

- If 4 children can go in each car, how many cars are needed for 21 children?
- If you have 26 cookies for seven children, how many cookies does each child receive?
- A farmer has 33 tomatoes and is packing them 4 to a box. How many packages are needed?

In each of these cases, the remainder has a specific meaning or multiple possibilities. Helping students consider the meaning of remainders is an important aspect of teaching division.

EXERCISE

What is the calculated answer for each of the remainder stories? What is a realistic way to interpret the remainder in each case? Is there more than one way to consider the remainder? ●●●

Developing Multiplication and Division Concepts

Many experiences with counting, joining, and separating objects and groups of objects in preschool and first grade should prepare students for multiplication and division. During the second and third grade children's earlier informal experiences enable them to invent and understand multiplication and division from realistic problems. Just as for addition and subtraction, multiplication and division follow an instructional sequence that moves from concrete to picture to symbol to mental representations and from simple to complex problems that stimulate children's thinking. As children learn how multiplication and division work, they uncover basic number combinations, properties, and strategies.

Introducing Multiplication

Repeated-addition multiplication extends children's experiences with counting and addition. Through skip-counting by 2's, 3's, 5's, and 10's and working with groups of buttons, small plastic objects, or similar materials, children have established a fundamental idea for multiplication—adding equal-size groups. Addends for addition can be any value, but in multiplication all the addends must have the same value. Teachers help students find and chart common objects found in equal-size groups.

- Groups of 2: Eyes, ears, hands, legs, bicycle wheels, headlights.
- Groups of 3: Triplets, tripod legs, tricycle wheels, juice boxes.
- Groups of 4: Chair legs, car tires, quadruplets.
- Groups of 5: Fingers, nickels, pentagon sides.
- Groups of 6: Soft drinks, raisin boxes, hexagon sides, insect legs,
- Groups of 7: Days of the weeks, septagon sides, spokes on wheels.
- Groups of 8: Octopus legs, octagon sides, spider legs.
- Groups of 9: Baseball teams, cats' lives.
- Groups of 10: Fingers, toes, dimes.
- Groups of 12: Eggs, cookies, soft drinks, dodecagon faces.
- Groups of 100: Dollars, metersticks, centuries, football-field lengths.

Children represent the equal groups with objects, pictures (Figure 11.14), and numbers.

Patterns are another way that students represent multiplication. Linking-cube trains are arranged in patterns of two, three, four, or other numbers of cubes. Children counting a three-cube pattern and emphasizing the last object in each sequence learn to skip-count.

One, two, *three*, four, five, *six*, seven, eight, *nine*, . . .
Three, six, nine, . . .

Children often skip-count by 2's, 5's, and 10's, and the multiplication facts for these numbers are among the easiest for children to learn. Skip counting by 3, 4, 6, 7, and other numbers helps students learn those facts as well. Skip counting with the calculator is easy. Many calculators allow students to key in 6, press the + key, and press the = key repeatedly. The display will show 6, 12, 18, 24, and so forth. The MathMaster calculator keeps track of the number of groups of 6's on the left side of the display and the total number of cubes on the right side (Figure 11.15).

(a) 4 sets of 2 eyes   **(b)** 3 chairs have 12 legs   **(c)** 6 ladybugs have 36 legs

Figure 11.14 Multiples

Focusing on groups instead of individual items helps children move to multiplicative thinking. Instead of counting each insect leg, students can think of six legs for each insect, and four insects have "6, 12, 18, 24 legs." Thinking in multiples is quicker for determining the total in equal-size groups than counting each item. Activity 11.14 illustrates one way to encourage thinking in multiples.

1	6
2	12
3	18
4	24
5	30

Figure 11.15 Numbers and group display on MathMaster calculator

Students write stories, draw pictures, and write number sentences to record multiplication situations. For example, in Figure 11.16 children write the addition sentence $7 + 7 + 7 = 21$ to represent the story. Students notice that both the picture and

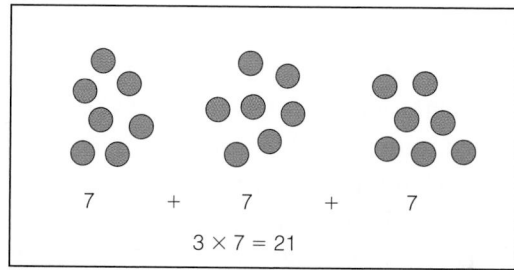

7   +   7   +   7

$3 \times 7 = 21$

Figure 11.16 Markers used to illustrate the multiplication sentence $3 \times 7 = 21$

ACTIVITY 11.14 **Repeated Addition (Representation)**

Level: Grades 2–4

Setting: Groups of four

Objective: Students describe the relationship between multiplication and repeated addition.

Materials: Counting cubes

- Each team of four students is given four different multiplication word problems.
  - Sadie buys gum in packages that have seven sticks each. When she buys four packages, how many sticks does she get?
  - Conrad has five packages of trading cards. How many cards does he have if each package holds five cards?
  - Jawan has three packages of frozen waffles. How many waffles does he have if each package has eight waffles in it?

- Jaime has eight boxes of motor oil. Each box contains four cans of oil. How many cans of oil does Jaime have?

- Each team member models one story with objects and shares the results with team members.

- Ask children to explain their solution using different techniques: repeated addition, skip counting, and multiplicative thinking. Write addition sentences and multiplication sentences for the problems on the board.

- Have teams make up problems to send to other teams to solve.

the addition sentence show three 7's. The 3 is the number of sets, and 7 is the number in each set. The answer, 21, tells the total number of objects in 3 sets of 7.

$$7 + 7 + 7 = 21$$
$$3 \text{ groups of } 7 = 21$$
$$3 \times 7 = 21$$

This situation can be used to introduce the symbols for multiplication. The multiplication sentence for "three groups of seven" is written $3 \times 7 = 21$ beneath the addition sentence. Reading the number sentence as "three groups of seven equals twenty-one" emphasizes the *multiplier* meaning of the 3. The first factor is called the *multiplication operator* or **multiplier** because it acts on the second factor, the **multiplicand**, which names the number of objects in each set. Activity 11.14 shows how cooperative groups explore and share story problems that model repeated addition and multiplication.

Because children are already familiar with stacked notation for addition, both the multiplication sentence in horizontal and stacked notation can be introduced, with one difference. In the horizontal notation the first number is the multiplier; in the vertical notation the multiplier is the bottom number. Both forms are read "three groups of seven." The order of factors has meaning when related directly to a multiplication story and when algorithms are introduced.

The *geometric interpretation* of multiplication shows the graphic arrangement of objects in rows and columns called rectangular **arrays**. Arrays are seen in the desk arrangement in some classrooms, ceiling and floor tiles, cans at the grocery store, window panes, shoes boxes on shelves, and rows of a marching band. As students identify arrays in their world, they can draw pictures for the bulletin board and write journal entries to share with classmates.

Students also show understanding by arranging disks or tiles into arrays. When exploring rectangular arrays, students discover that some numbers can be arranged in only one array; these numbers are *prime numbers*. Other numbers (composite numbers) can be arranged in several ways to show whole-number factors, such as 16 tiles: 1 row of 16, 2 rows of 8, or 4 rows of 4 (Figure 11.17).

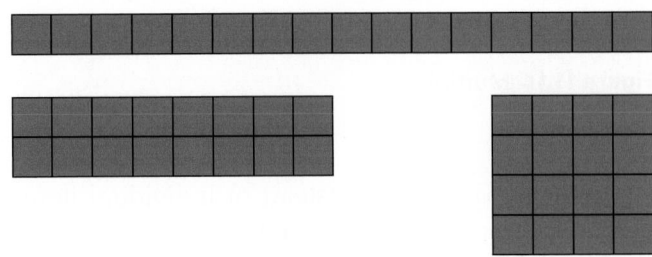

Figure 11.17 Arrays of 16 tiles

Arrays also illustrate the commutative property of multiplication, as in Figure 11.18. Library book pockets and index cards in Figure 11.19 show arrays

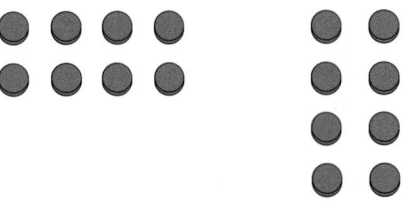

Figure 11.18 Commutative property of multiplication: 2×4 array, 4×2 array

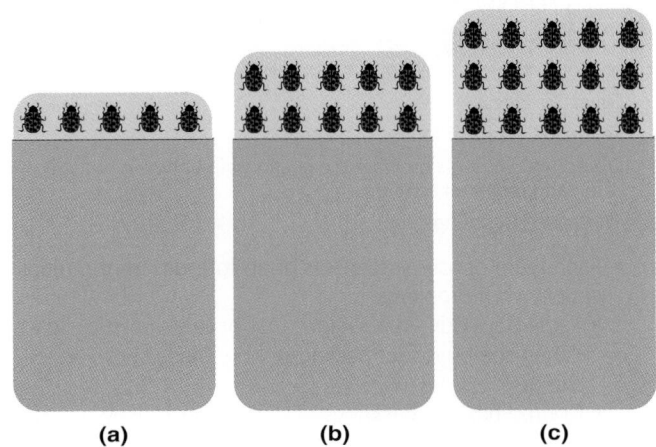

(a) (b) (c)

Figure 11.19 Library book pocket and index cards can be used to show arrays.

of bugs with 5 as a factor: One row of 5 bugs (a); 2 rows of 5 bugs is 10 (b); 3 rows of 5 bugs is 15 (c). As each row is revealed, students skip-count. Students can make index cards for other multiplication combinations.

Area measurement of rectangles is related to multiplication arrays. In an informal measurement activity, children cover their desktop or book with equal-size squares of paper, sticky notes, or tiles. They soon discover that they only need to cover each edge of the rectangle to compute the total number needed to cover the top by multiplying. Coloring rectangles on a piece of centimeter grid paper also shows arrays. Two number cubes generate the length of the sides. The length of each side and the total number of squares create a multiplication sentence (Figure 11.20). Area measurement is discussed further in Chapter 18.

(a) Cutouts

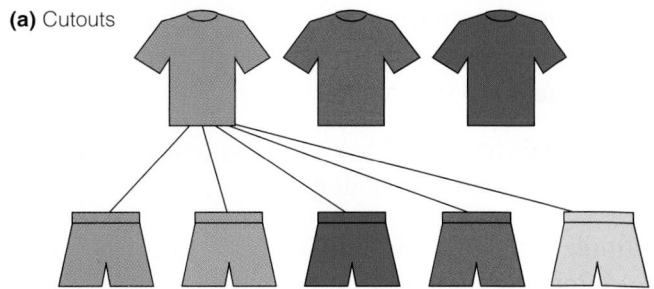

(b) Cubes

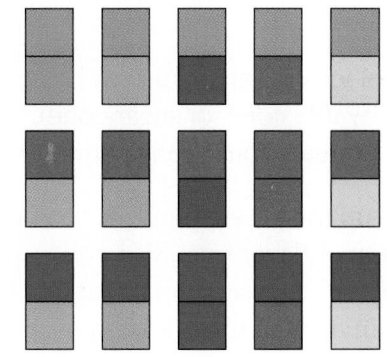

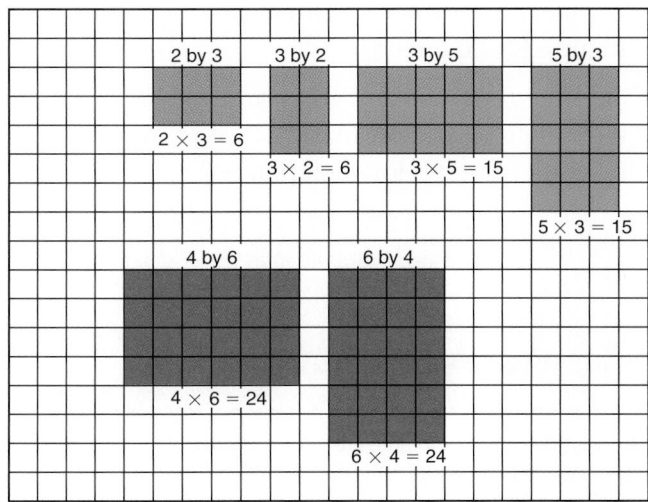

Figure 11.20 Geometric interpretation of multiplication: area measurement

(c) Letter code

B–B	B–T	B–G	B–R	B–Y
R–B	R–T	R–G	R–R	R–Y
G–B	G–T	G–G	G–R	G–Y

(d) Lattice

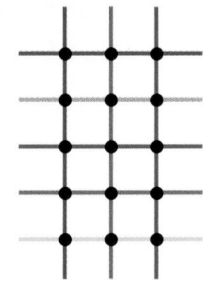

Figure 11.21 Four representations of Cartesian combination

The third multiplication interpretation is *combinations*, or the *Cartesian cross-product*, which gives the number of combinations possible when one option in a group is matched with one option from other groups.

• Tracy has three shirts (red, blue, white) and five pairs of pants (blue, black, green, khaki, brown). How many outfits are possible?

Combinations of three shirts and five pairs of pants are represented in four different ways in Figure 11.21. Cutouts of shirts and pants are the most literal representations, while the same combinations are shown by color cubes. More symbolic representations of combinations of shirts and pants are letter-coded combinations and a lattice diagram showing 15 points of intersection.

Additional stories provide exploration of other combinations with objects, drawings, diagrams, or symbols.

- In an ice cream shop, Ari chooses from vanilla, chocolate, or strawberry ice cream and either cone or cup for container.

Six choices are possible so long as only one choice is possible from each category.

Vanilla Cup, Vanilla Cone, Chocolate Cup, Chocolate Cone, Strawberry Cup, Strawberry Cone

3 kinds of ice creams × 2 types of containers = 6 options

$3 \times 2 = 6$

- With four flavors of ice cream and three choices of container (cup, waffle cone, or sugar cone), how many different treats could Tonya buy?

Children can make up their own menus for choices in the ice cream shop (1 flavor from 31, 1 cone from 4, 1 topping from 6) or other situations that involve making choices from a set of options such as pizza (crust, toppings) or automobiles (color, engine, interior). A cooperative learning activity in Activity 11.15 involves creating color combinations for custom-ordered bicycles.

ⒺXERCISE

Create stories for the multiplication sentence 3 × 5 = 15 that illustrate repeated addition, geometric arrays or area, and Cartesian products. Draw a picture for each story. Can you extend your stories for 3 × 4 × 5? How would you show three factors with an array or combinations? ●●●

Introducing Division

Division is the inverse operation for multiplication. Multiplication is used for situations when the factors are known to calculate a product. For division the product, or total, is known but only one factor is known. Children need experience with two division situations—measurement and partitive—illustrated by realistic stories and modeled with manipulatives.

- *Multiplication*: I am making breakfast for four people. If I cook each of them two eggs, how many eggs do I need?

- *Measurement, or repeated subtraction, division*: I have eight eggs. How many people can be served if I cook two eggs for each person?

ACTIVITY 11.15 **Color Combinations for Bicycles (Representation)**

Level: Grades 2–4
Setting: Groups of four
Objective: Students model concepts of multiplication.
Materials: Pieces of red, silver, gold, and black paper; six different colors of yarn; clear tape

- Present this situation: Each team of four is a work crew in a bicycle manufacturing plant. The company's designer has decided that the plant will produce bicycle frames in four colors: red, silver, gold, and black. Each bicycle will have one color of trim painted on it, chosen from six possibilities. The task will be to create color samples for the bicycles before making them. How many different bicycles can be made from four frame colors and six trim paints?

- Assign a role to each team member. One student is the manager; the manager reads the directions and keeps the team on track. The second student is the layout worker; the layout worker organizes the bicycles (colored papers) by color. The third student is the trim worker; the

trim worker distributes the trim colors (yarn). The fourth member of each team is the trim painter; the trim painter applies the trim (tapes the yarn to the paper).

- Each team has 15 minutes to complete the samples. Before teams begin work, team members plan how to organize different combinations of colors.

- After 15 minutes, ask the teams to report and show their color samples and the number of combinations. Ask students whether all the combinations are likely to be equally popular.

- Ask the teams to determine the number of combinations for five frame colors and three trim paints and for four frame colors and five trim paints. During discussion of the new situations, ask students if there is a way to know the number of different combinations without making the samples. What is the advantage of making all the samples?

In measurement division the total (8 eggs) and the size of each group (2 eggs) are known. The number of groups (people) is unknown. Children act out the problem by placing two plastic eggs each on one plate, two plates, three plates, and four plates until all the eggs are gone. Repeated subtraction, another name for measurement, is modeled by students removing two eggs, then two more, then another two, and finally two more.

- *Partitive, or sharing, division*: I have eight eggs to divide equally among four people. How many eggs can I cook for each person?

In a partitive division story the total number of eggs (8) and the number of people (4) are known, but the number of eggs for each person is unknown. Children share eggs by putting one egg on each person's plate, then another for each person, until all the eggs are gone (Figure 11.22). Sharing is another name for partitive division.

Measurement division: 8 eggs are distributed 2 each to 4 plates.

Partitive division: 8 eggs are distributed one at a time to 4 plates.

Measurement stories are preferred by many teachers because subtraction is a well-known model

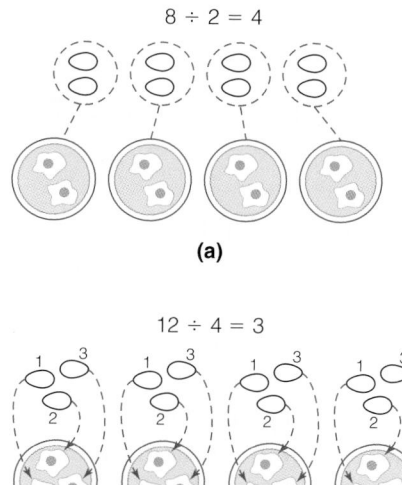

(a)

(b)

Figure 11.22 (a) Measurement division; (b) partitive division

for children. As soon as students see how division is working, teachers can introduce situations with remainders.

- Natasha bought a package of 14 pencils. If she gave four pencils to each friend, how many friends would get four pencils? Four pencils are put into three cups with two extra pencils.

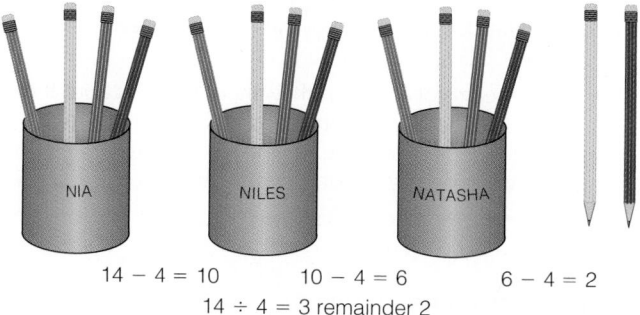

$$14 - 4 = 10 \qquad 10 - 4 = 6 \qquad 6 - 4 = 2$$
$$14 \div 4 = 3 \text{ remainder } 2$$

From their actions students see that 14 is the original group of pencils, 4 indicates the size of each group of pencils being subtracted, and 3 represents the number of groups. Two pencils are not in a cup because they are not a complete group of 4. The teacher asks students what they might do with the two extra pencils.

Division stories of both types are acted out with materials and represented with pictures; the teacher introduces the division sentence and symbols. As children see repeated subtraction, they write three subtraction sentences. After 4 is subtracted three times, 2 pencils are left undivided. The horizontal division sentence is introduced to show the same information. The division sentence is read "Fourteen divided by three equals four with a remainder of two."

Students act out familiar situations of sharing items such as cookies to illustrate partitive division. If they begin with 17 cookies, they can share the cookies with three people, four people, five people, or six people. After students have acted out several sharing situations and represented the actions in pictures or diagrams, record their work with a division sentence:

$$17 \div 5 = 3, \text{ remainder } 2.$$

The Doorbell Rang, by Pat Hutchins (New York: Harper Collins, 1986), is a picture book that models sharing (Activity 11.16). Each time the doorbell rings,

---

ACTIVITY 11.16   Sharing Cookies (Problem Solving, Connection, and Representation)

Level: Grades 2–4

Setting: Groups of four

Objective: Students model and describe the meaning of partitive division situations.

Materials: "Cookies" cut from construction paper, other manipulative materials selected by teams

- Read *The Doorbell Rang*, by Pat Hutchins (New York: Harper Collins, 1986) through once.

- Tell the teams of four that they are going to act out the story. Give the students the construction paper cookies. Read the book again, and have each team model the situations described as the story progresses.

- Have students discuss what happens as the number of people increases.

- Tell each team to create a story about sharing things and prepare to act it out (allow approximately 5 minutes).

- Each team acts out its story while other teams observe. After each story, discuss what was demonstrated by the actors.

- End the lesson by giving each group a small bag of cookies or other treats, which they must share equally among themselves.

---

more guests come to the party, and the cookies are shared to accommodate all the guests.

When division is introduced with materials, most children recognize that division and multiplication are *inverse* operations. Multiplication joins sets, just as addition does; division separates, just as subtraction does. Children also learn mathematical vocabulary associated with division. The number being divided is the *dividend*, the number by which it is divided is the known factor or *divisor*, and the answer is the unknown factor or *quotient*.

The meaning of the dividend never changes; it always tells the size of the original group. But the roles of divisor (the known factor) and quotient (the unknown factor) are interchanged, depending on the situation. In measurement the divisor tells the size of each group, and the quotient tells the number of groups. In a partitive situation the divisor tells the number of groups, and the quotient tells the size of each group. Children also recognize that a dividend in division is related to a product in multiplication. As children develop number sense about division, they think about the meaning of the remainder in context rather than by rule.

ⒺXERCISE

Write a measurement story and draw a picture for the sentence 34 ÷ 5 = 6, remainder 4. Write a partitive story and draw a picture for the same sentence. ●●●

Working with Remainders

Introducing remainders early through division stories allows students to see remainders as a natural event. They find that some situations involve numbers that divide without a remainder and that some do not. When remainders are included in examples, children discuss the meaning of remainders in different situations and develop options for working with them.

- The basket had 25 apples in it. If 25 apples are shared equally by three children, how many apples will each have?

25 ÷ 3 = 8 remainder 1

Children may suggest, "Eat 1 apple yourself and don't tell," "Cut it up so that everybody gets some," "Put it back in the box," "Give it to grandmother," and so forth. Sometimes the remainder can be divided into equal parts; other times the remainder is ignored or might call for an adjustment of the final answer up to the next whole number. Talking about remainders helps students understand that the remainder needs to be considered in the calculated answer and its meaning.

Various examples illustrate the different meanings for the remainder.

- We have 32 children in our class. If we play a game that requires three equal-size teams, how many players will be on each team?

The computed answer is 10 children on each team with 2 children left over. A calculator answer is 10.67 or $10\frac{2}{3}$. However, cutting children into parts is not reasonable. Students may decide that the practical solution requires two teams of 11 and one team of 10. They might decide that three equal teams of 10 is better and assign two students tasks such as keeping score, managing equipment, or refereeing. Students can recognize the difference between a computed answer and a practical answer.

- Sixty-eight apples are to be put into boxes. If each box holds eight apples, how many boxes are needed?

> **MISCONCEPTION**
>
> Many tests, such as the National Assessment of Educational Progress (NAEP), report that proper interpretation of remainders in division problems causes errors by many students even through middle and high school. Even if students can compute an answer correctly, they do not consider how the remainder is used in a problem context. Introducing remainders in stories and asking students to consider how remainders should be treated establishes a foundation for reasoning about their meanings.

The paper-and-pencil answer is 8, remainder 4, and a calculator answer will be 8.5. The physical answer to the question is eight full boxes and another half-box. The practical answer could be eight if the remainder is disregarded or nine if all the apples need to be placed in boxes even if they are not full. The remainder might be ignored if only the number of full boxes is considered, or students may suggest that they need nine boxes, even though one box is not completely full.

- Three cans of cat food cost $0.98. How much will one can cost?

When $0.98 is divided by 3, the answer is $0.3266667. However, students should understand that the price will be rounded up to $0.33 when only one can is bought.

- Our grade has 52 children who will ride to camp in minivans. If each van can carry six children and their gear, how many vans will be needed?

The computed answer for $52 \div 6$ is 8, remainder 4, or 8.6667. Acting out or modeling this situation shows that four children are without transportation after eight vans have been filled. One more van will be needed for the four remaining children. A total of nine vans is needed, so the number is raised to the next whole number. More discussion about the fractional treatment of remainders is included in Chapter 14.

What Teachers Need to Know About Properties of Multiplication and Division

An *identity element* is a number that does not change the value of another number during an arithmetic operation. Multiplying by 1 does not change the value of a number, so 1 is the identity element for multiplication. For example, consider $12 \times 1 = 12$. The identity element for division is also 1. Consider $12 \div 1 = 12$.

The **commutative property of multiplication**, similar to the commutative property of addition, is illustrated when the order of factors is switched but the product is the same.

- A fruit stand has gift boxes of four apples. How many apples are in six boxes?

(a) 6 boxes of 4 apples

- A fruit stand has gift boxes of six apples. How many apples are in four boxes?

(b) 4 boxes of 6 apples

Division is not commutative, as students should recognize when they consider $35 \div 5$ and $5 \div 35$.

The **associative property for multiplication** is similar to the associative property for addition. When three or more factors are multiplied, the order in which they are paired for computation does not affect the product.

- Robin was taking inventory at the grocery store. The cans of green beans were stacked three cans across, two cans high, and six cans back.

The associative property allows factors $3 \times 2 \times 6$ to be grouped for multiplication in several ways:

$$(3 \times 2) \times 6 = 6 \times 6$$
$$2 \times (3 \times 6) = 2 \times 18$$
$$3 \times (2 \times 6) = 3 \times 12$$
$$(6 \times 2) \times 3 = 12 \times 3$$
$$(n_1 \times n_2) \times n_3 = n_1 \times (n_2 \times n_3)$$

The associative property, like the commutative property, applies to multiplication but not to division.

The **distributive property of multiplication and division over addition** allows a number to be separated into addends and multiplication or division to be applied or distributed to each addend.

- The stools cost $27 each. Ms. Turner wanted to buy four of them.

In the case of $4 \times \$27$, the multiplier 4 can be applied to $20 + 7$, to $25 + 2$, or to $15 + 12$:

$$4 \times (20 + 7) = (4 \times 20) + (4 \times 7) = 80 + 28 = 108$$
$$4 \times (25 + 2) = (4 \times 25) + (4 \times 2) = 100 + 8 = 108$$
$$4 \times (15 + 12) = (4 \times 15) + (4 \times 12) = 60 + 48 = 108$$

The distributive property of division over addition also means that the dividend can be broken into parts that are easier to calculate. For example, when 39 is divided by 3, 39 can be thought of as $30 + 9$ or as $24 + 15$ and division can be performed on each addend:

$$39 \div 3 = (30 + 9) \div 3, \text{ or } (30 \div 3) + (9 \div 3) = 10 + 3 = 13$$
$$39 \div 3 = (24 + 15) \div 3, \text{ or } (24 \div 3) + (15 \div 3) = 8 + 5 = 13$$

Learning Multiplication and Division Facts with Strategies

As students work with equal-size groups, arrays, area models, and Cartesian product situations, they become familiar with the multiplication of number combinations. Learning $2 \times 5 = 10$ is not difficult for children who understand two groups of five and have experience skip counting 5, 10, 15, ... Un-

derstanding the inverse relationship between multiplication and division connects the multiplication facts to division facts. In fact, when students are acting out division problems, they often discover this connection.

Learning number facts through strategies means that students are going beyond memorization; they understand the fundamental rules and properties for multiplication and division that support mental calculations and number sense. Some multiplication and division strategies are similar to strategies for addition and subtraction facts, so children should be familiar with them. Because many facts can be learned with a variety of strategies, children can adopt the strategy that works best for them. The multiplication chart is a good way to organize facts as students learn strategies.

Skip counting is the first valuable strategy because the "verbal chain" of multiples (2, 4, 6, 8, . . . and 5, 10, 15, 20, . . .) is a familiar sequence. Most children learn the facts for 2, 5, and 10 easily. Learning skip counting for other facts by counting multiples on the hundreds chart supports the meaning of multiplication. On the multiplication chart (Black-Line Master 11.3) students can fill in the multiplication facts for 2's and 5's.

The *commutative law for multiplication* states that the order of the factors does not change the products so that each multiplication fact has a mirror fact: $6 \times 4 = 4 \times 6$. Activities with arrays illustrate the commutative law graphically. When children recognize that the commutative law gives them pairs of equivalent facts, they can use this strategy for learning facts.

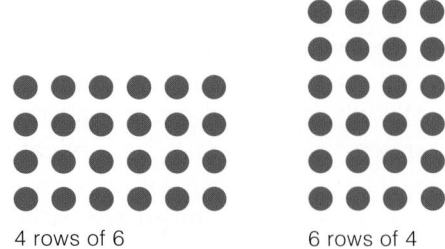

4 rows of 6   6 rows of 4

Multiplying with 0 is modeled with no cubes in one cup, no cubes in two cups, up to no cubes in nine cups. "How many are in one group of zero? two groups of zero? nine groups of zero? a million groups of zero?" The question can also be asked, "How many are in zero groups of five? no groups of

17? zero groups of a thousand?" Students develop the rule that "multiplying with zero gives you zero" or similar phrasing.

Multiplication with 1 introduces the identity element for multiplication. It is also easy to model with language similar to that used for multiplication by zero. Put one cube in several cups. "How many is two groups of one? six groups of one? ninety-nine groups of one?" The commutative situation is also presented. "How many are in one group of six? one group of 50? one group of a million?" Reasoning from the model leads most children to the realization that "multiplying by 1 doesn't change the number."

Multiplication by 2 connects skip counting 2's and relates to double facts in addition. Because 3 + 3 is 6, two groups of three are six. This pattern is easy to illustrate with linking cubes, and children recognize that "a number multiplied by 2 is the same as adding a number twice."

The **squared facts** are those facts found when a number is multiplied by itself, such as 4 × 4 or 7 × 7. The geometric interpretation makes a strong visual impression that the square facts are also square arrays. The **near squares**, or **square neighbors**, occupy the spaces on either side of the square facts and can be thought of as one multiple more or one multiple less than the square fact. If 8 × 8 is 64, then 7 × 8 is 64 − 8 = 56 and 9 × 8 is 64 + 8 = 72. Skip counting by 8's provides good background for this mental computation.

Multiplying with 9 as a factor can be developed with several strategies. One strategy involves multiplying by 10's—which students have already learned using skip counting. If 10 × 9 is 90, then 9 × 9 is 90 minus 9. If 10 × 5 is known to be 50, then 9 × 5 is 50 minus 5. Other interesting patterns are explored in Activity 11.17.

The distributive law of multiplication provides another strategy for learning multiplication facts by breaking an unknown product into two known products. If the answer to 7 × 6 is unknown, the problem can be distributed as (7 × 3) + (7 × 3) or 21 + 21 (Figure 11.23). This strategy will become important as children work with algorithms in intermediate grades.

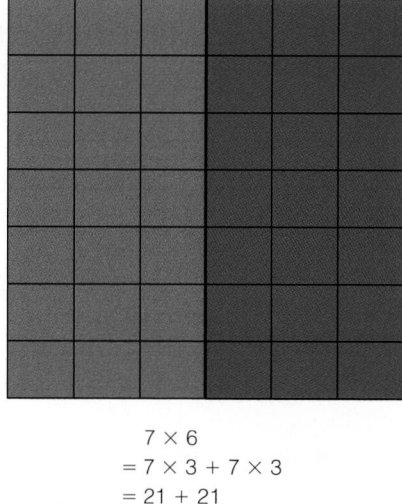

7 × 6
= 7 × 3 + 7 × 3
= 21 + 21

Figure 11.23 Using the distributive property to learn multiplication facts

Division Facts Strategies

When students understand that division and multiplication are *inverse operations*, students use the multiplication facts to learn division facts through activities that focus on a product and its factors. A factor tree introduces students to a missing factor. By drawing a factor tree, they can see that the factors for 24 could be 6 × 4, 8 × 3, 12 × 2, or 24 × 1. While looking at the various trees, the teacher can ask, "If 24 is a product and 4 is a factor, what is the missing factor?"

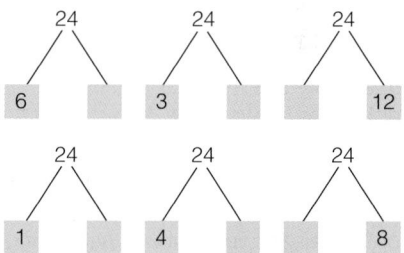

Other properties and rules are also useful in learning division facts.

Zero in division can be used in two ways. When the total being divided is zero, the quotient is also zero. Children enjoy the absurd notion of dividing zero objects into groups.

- I had no oranges in my basket. I divided them among seven friends. How many oranges did each get? Each friend gets 0 oranges.

However, zero is never used as a divisor. Stories illustrate the logical absurdity of dividing by zero.

ACTIVITY 11.17 **Putting on the Nines (Reasoning)**

Level: Grades 2–5

Setting: Small groups or whole class

Objective: Students explore the multiplication facts with 9 to find patterns in the products.

Materials: Linking cubes

- Ask students to use linking cubes to make rods of 10 and write the number facts for 10 in a chart.
- Ask students to make rods of 9 with the linking cubes and write the number facts for 9 next to the 10's facts in a chart.

Rods	10's	9's
1	10	9
2	20	18
3	30	27
4	40	36
5	50	45
6	60	54
7	70	63
8	80	72
9	90	81
10	100	90

- Ask students to look for patterns and relationships between the two lists of facts. They may suggest several different patterns in the facts:
  - The digits in each of the 9 facts all add up to 9.
  - A product can be matched with another product that has the same numbers but reversed, such as 81 and 18.
  - You can count to get the facts for 9. Write 9, 8, 7, and so forth in the ones place; then start at the bottom and write 9, 8, 7, and so forth in the tens place.
  - The 9 facts are less than the 10 facts.
  - The difference between the 10 facts and the 9 facts is the number of rods. Some students may express the difference with a number sentence: $n \times 9 = (n \times 10) - n$.
- Ask students which patterns help them remember the facts for 9. Their answers will vary depending on the pattern that they notice and use.

Extension

The facts for 9 can also be shown with ten fingers. Tell students that you will show them how to multiply by 9 using their finger calculator. Ask them to hold both hands up so that they can see their palms. Model this action.

For the math fact 4×9, ask students to bend down the fourth finger. Tell them the three fingers to the left of the bent finger are worth ten each and the six fingers to the right of the bent finger are worth one each. Ask students the math fact for 36. When you bend the fourth finger down say, "4×9 is 36." Ask students to see if the finger calculator works for all the 9 facts starting with the first finger. After students are able to multiply with their finger calculator, ask them why the finger calculator works for 9's but not for other facts.

4×9
Bend down 4th finger from the left (represents the "4" in the equation)
Three fingers before bent finger represent 3 tens
Six fingers after the bent finger represent 6 ones
$4 \times 9 = 36$

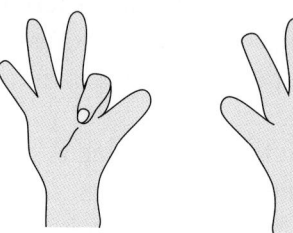

8×9
Bend down 8th finger (represents the "8" in the equation)
Seven fingers before bent finger represent 7 tens
Two fingers after the bent finger represent 2 ones
$8 \times 9 = 72$

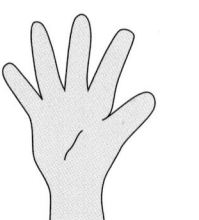

Although the basic multiplication facts go through 9×9, including the facts through 10×10 is common because the 10's are easy and important for later computation. Many teachers also encourage students to learn number combinations for multiples of 11 and 12. The combinations for 11 are easy using the 11's pattern and skip counting: 11, 22, 33, 44, 55, 66, and so on. When students learn the multiplication facts for 12, they should notice the relationship between the 12 facts and facts already learned for 6.

- I had seven oranges and divided them between two friends. How many oranges did each friend get?

- If I divided seven oranges between one friend, how many would the friend get?

- If I divided seven oranges between no friends, how many would the friends get?

Dividing any amount into zero groups is implausible and impossible; in mathematics, division by zero is undefined.

In Activity 11.18 children fill in the multiplication table to show 19 facts with 0 as a factor, 17 identity facts (1 as a factor), and 15 double facts (2 as a factor). These three strategies supply 51 quick and easy multiplication facts. When the facts for 5 are also placed on the table, only 36 facts remain. Various strategies might be used to simplify these 36 facts, such as pairing facts using the commutative law (e.g., 7×9 and 9×7). The associative law is also useful for facts involving 6, 7, and 8 when students know easier facts. The squared facts, such as 3×3

ACTIVITY 11.18   Find the Facts (Reasoning)

Level: Grades 3–5

Setting: Small groups

Objective: Students identify the easy facts and the difficult multiplication facts.

Materials: Multiplication table through 9×9

- Put a blank multiplication table on an overhead transparency (see Black-Line Master 11.3).

×	0	1	2	3	4	5	6	7	8	9
0										
1										
2										
3										
4										
5										
6										
7										
8										
9										

- Point out the factors across the top and down the left side; products will be at the intersection of two factors.

- Begin with 0 on the left side as a factor: "If we multiply each number in the top row by 0, what are the products?" (Answer: They are all 0.) Fill in the cells after each question: "Where else will there be products that are 0?" (Answer: Down the first column of cells.) "How many multiplication facts have 0 as a factor?" (Answer: 19.)

- Use 1 as a factor and ask: "What is the product when we multiply each number in the top row by 1?" (Answer: Each product is the same as the number in the top row.) "Where else do we find factors that work this way?" (Answer: When numbers in the left-hand column are multiplied by 1 in the top row.) Ask how many facts are

found with the identity element of 1. (Answer: 17 more facts—those that have 1 as a factor, excluding those that have 0.) Add 19 and 17 to show that by knowing the role of 0 and 1 in multiplication, students know more than one-third of the basic facts.

- The third row and third column of cells have 2 as a factor. Ask students about skip counting by 2's, or doubles. Write the 15 products for these combinations in the table. Point out that the easy combinations with 0, 1, and 2 contain more than half the basic facts.

- Combinations with 5 as one factor offer little difficulty to most children because of skip counting by 5's. Add these to the table. They contribute another 13 facts.

- Most students probably already know the remaining combinations for cells in the upper left-hand part of the table: 3×3, 3×4, 4×3, and 4×4.

- Ask how many facts are not yet written in. Ask which of those facts the students already know. Different children may already know some of these facts. This process highlights the 20 or so facts that usually take extra work, and students can concentrate on them in their practice.

×	0	1	2	3	4	5	6	7	8	9
0	0	0	0	0	0	0	0	0	0	0
1	0	1	2	3	4	5	6	7	8	9
2	0	2	4	6	8	10	12	14	16	18
3	0	3	6	9	12	15				
4	0	4	8	12	16	20				
5	0	5	10	15	20	25	30	35	40	45
6	0	6	12			30				
7	0	7	14			35				
8	0	8	16			40				
9	0	9	18			45				

and 7×7, are on a diagonal on the multiplication chart. Ten square facts and 18 neighbor facts mean that almost a quarter of the facts can be learned with this strategy.

A table also demonstrates the relationship between multiplication and division facts. Factors are on the left side and top row, with products in the center of the table; for every product the two factors can be identified by tracing up and to the left. For $48 \div 8$, find 48 in the table and trace left to the 8 and up to the 6 or left to 6 and up to 8.

Building Accuracy and Speed with Multiplication and Division Facts

Knowledge of multiplication and division facts is expected of elementary school students. When students understand the operations and have strategies for learning and remembering the number combinations, they are ready to work on ready recall.

Accuracy is the first priority in developing ready recall and speed, which varies among children. Practice activities for multiplication and division follow the same guidelines presented for addition and subtraction facts; practice should be short, frequent, and varied in method, with an emphasis on personal improvement. Classroom procedures used for practicing number combinations can support confidence and motivation, or undermine them.

Many practice activities can be used, including computer software, flash cards, and partner games. Consider triangle flash cards (Figure 11.24a). When children pair up to play, one child covers the product 63, the other child multiplies the factors to find the product: $7 \times 9 = 63$. For division one child covers one factor such as 9, and the partner says, "$63 \div 7 =$

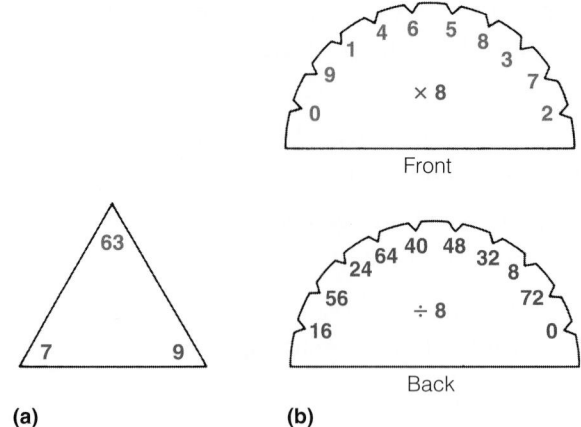

Figure 11.24 Two types of flash cards for practicing multiplication and division facts

9." The partner card in Figure 11.24b shows all multiplication facts with 8 as a factor on the front and all related division facts with 8 as a divisor on the back. Students take turns putting a pencil or fingertip in a notch next to a number, such as 9. One partner says "$9 \times 8 = 72$" or "$8 \times 9 = 72$" and is checked by the partner on the opposite side of the card. For division the partner on the division side might say "$72 \div 8 = 9$" and be checked.

Many drill games and activities for improving accuracy and speed are available on the Internet and in commercial packages. Student improvement has been reported as a result of using these materials.

ⓔXERCISE

What role, if any, do you think timed tests should play in developing accuracy and speed with the facts? ●●●

Take-Home Activities

Take-home activities show parents that the curriculum includes more than practicing computation with algorithms. The two accompanying activities require reasoning to determine correct solutions. The challenge of each activity will intrigue many parents as well as students. They are good cooperative-learning activities for adults and students at home.

Addition with Number Squares

Work this puzzle with other people in your home.

- Cut out nine 1-inch squares of paper.
- Put the numeral 1 on one square of paper, the numeral 2 on the next, and so forth until each square is numbered (1 to 9).
- Arrange the squares so that you have a large square with 3 three-place numbers and so that the sum of the numbers made by the squares in the top and middle rows equals the number made by the squares in the bottom row.

Can you arrange the squares in more ways than one and get a correct answer each time? Can you find a pattern that will help you make arrangements that work? Write your solutions in your journal as you work so that you can share them with classmates and your teacher tomorrow.

Number Puzzles

Below are some algorithms in which letters have been substituted for numbers:

ABA	XYZ	BOX	YOU
−ACD	−MNO	−OUT	−FOR
EAB	OZR	ORB	USA

A letter stands for the same number each time it appears in the algorithm.

See how many of these puzzles you can solve. It is possible to have more than one solution to a given puzzle.

Make one addition and one subtraction puzzle and bring them to school tomorrow for a friend to solve.

Summary

Curriculum standards emphasize student understanding of four arithmetic operations, when and how to use the operations to solve problems, and accurate recall of basic number facts. Development of number operations begins while children are counting, classifying, and comparing sets of concrete objects. During the conceptual development phase of number operations, children tell stories, model problems, draw pictures, and write number sentences as they construct meanings and actions for addition, four subtraction situations (takeaway, whole-part-part, comparison, completion), three multiplication interpretations (repeated addition, geometric interpretation, Cartesian product), and two division types (measurement, or repeated subtraction, division; partitive, or sharing, division). During this time, students explore all the number combinations and properties of the operations.

As students understand each operation, they find strategies and properties to organize the number combinations. Strategies based on arithmetic properties and rules about how numbers work make learning facts more meaningful and easier. Instead of memorizing, students learn how numbers work as a foundation for number sense and estimation. Finally, students need time to develop ready recall of number combinations. Practice with number combinations might include flash cards, partner games, computer games, and worksheets. Because individual children differ in their progress with number facts, personal improvement and success are crucial elements to a successful practice program. Overemphasis on speed, such as timed tests, is cited as a major cause of mathematics anxiety.

When students understand each of the operations, have learned meaningful strategies for learning number combinations, and have developed ready recall of facts, they have foundational skills for computational fluency. They will extend these skills as they add, subtract, multiply, and divide larger numbers with a variety of algorithms, through technology, and with number sense such as estimation and checking for reasonableness.

Study Questions and Activities

1. Tell stories that illustrate addition and each of the four types of subtraction. Model each story with counters, draw a picture of the story, and write a number sentence for it. Which of the stories were easiest for you? Were any more difficult?

2. Using counters or interlocking cubes, model the commutative property, the associative property, and the identity element for addition. Can you think of real-life situations that illustrate ideas similar to commutativity, associativity, or identity?

3. Write a subtraction question and draw a simple picture or diagram for each of the following situations. Label each situation with the type of subtraction it illustrates.
   a. Mr. Ramirez had 16 boys in a class of 25 children.
   b. Joan weighed 34 kilograms, and Yusef weighed 41 kilograms.
   c. Mrs. Bennett bought two dozen oranges and served 14 of them to girls after soccer practice.
   d. Mr. Hoang had 18 mathematics books for 27 students.
   e. Diego had 34 cents. The whistle costs 93 cents.

4. Write stories to illustrate the three multiplication interpretations. Draw pictures and diagrams for each. Are there any similarities in your diagrams for the three interpretations?

5. Identify each of the following situations as measurement or partitive. Write the question that goes with the situation, and draw a picture for one problem of each type of division. Then write a number sentence for the picture. What would you do with the remainder, if any, in each of these cases?
   a. Geraldo shared 38 stickers with six friends so that each got the same number of stickers.
   b. Juan had 25 chairs. He put six of them in each row.
   c. Mr. Hui imported 453 ornaments. He packaged 24 ornaments in each box to ship to retailers.
   d. Ms. Krohn divided $900 evenly among her four children.

6. Do you remember learning about remainders? Do you agree or disagree with the idea to introduce remainders early in learning about division? Why?

7. Look at an elementary school textbook, and see how addition and subtraction are introduced. Do the teaching/learning activities in the teacher's manual use stories, pictures, and manipulatives to model the operations? Does the textbook emphasize the development of strategies for learning number facts?

8. Obtain a practice page of 100 addition or subtraction facts, and take a 3-minute timed test. How many did you complete? How many of the completed answers were correct? How did you feel at the end of the test? Discuss with fellow students their memories of timed tests. What are the possible harmful aspects of this practice? What ways can you think of to overcome the pressure and anxiety many students feel from such tests?

Teacher's Resources

Baroody, A., and Coslick, R. (1998). *Fostering children's mathematical power: An investigative approach to K–8 mathematics instruction*. Mahwah, NJ: Lawrence Erlbaum Associates.

Fosnot, C., & Dolk, M. (2001). *Young mathematicians at work: Constructing number sense, addition, and subtraction*. Westport, CT: Heinemann.

Kamii, C., & Housman, L. (2000). *Young children reinvent arithmetic: Implications of Piaget's theory* (2nd ed.). Williamston, VT: Teachers College Press.

Kirkpatrick, J., Swafford, J., and Findell, B. (Eds.). (2001). *Adding it up: Helping children learn mathematics*. Washington, DC: National Academy Press.

Children's Bookshelf

Butler, M. Christina. (1988). *Too many eggs*. Boston: David R. Godine. (Grades PS–2)

Calmenson, Stephanie. (1984). *Ten furry monsters*. New York: Parents Magazine Press. (Grades PS–3)

Chorao, Kay. (1995). *Number one number fun*. New York: Philomel Books. (Grades K–2)

Chwast, Seymour. (1993). *The twelve circus rings*. San Diego: Gulliver Books, Harcourt Brace Jovanovich. (Grades K–4)

de Regniers, Beatrice Schenk. (1985). *So many cats*! New York: Clarion Books. (Grades PS–3)

Edens, Cooper. (1994). *How many bears*? New York: Atheneum. (Grades K–3)

Matthews, Louise. (1980). *The great take-away*. New York: Dodd, Mead. (Grades K–2)

McMillan, Bruce. (1986). *Counting wildflowers*. New York: Lothrop, Lee & Shephard. (Grades PS–2)

Moerbeck, Kees, & Dijs, Carla. (1988). *Six brave explorers*. Los Angeles: Price/Stern/Sloan. (Grades PS–3)

Viorst, Judith. (1978). *Alexander who used to be rich last Sunday*. New York: Aladdin/Macmillan. (Grades 1–3)

Technology Resources

Commercial Software

There are many commercial software programs designed to help students with their number sense, recall of number facts, and applications of number operations. We list several of them here.

How the West Was One + Three × Four (Sunburst)
Math Arena (Sunburst)
Math Munchers Deluxe (M.E.E.C.)
Oregon Trail (Broderbund)
The Cruncher 2.0 (Knowledge Adventure)

Also, programs published by Tabletop Press and the Nectar Foundation are helpful.

Internet Game

At **http://www.fi.uu.nl/rekenweb/en** there are a number of interesting games. *Make Five* allows students to play alone or with a partner. The object of the game is to capture five squares in row on a 10×10 grid. Children capture a square by solving the problem in the square. Students can select addition facts, subtraction facts, or multiplication facts for their grid problems.

Find more games at

http://www.bbc.co.uk/education/mathsfile/
http://www.bbc.co.uk/schools//numbertime/games//index.shtml
http://www.subtangent.com/index.php

Internet Activity

This activity is for children in grades K–1. Students play a game of electronic concentration where the cards contain a digit, the numeral word, or a number of dots. Students can turn over any two cards to try to find a matching pair. The object here is to find all the matching pairs in the fewest number of turns.

Students will find Concentration at **http://illuminations .nctm.org/Activities.aspx?grade=1&grade=4**. Demonstrate how to play the game and then allow pairs of students the opportunity to play a game. They should keep track of how many turns they used, and keep a list of the matching pairs of cards.

Internet Sites

For virtual manipulatives to practice number facts, go to

http://nlvm.usu.edu/en/nav/vlibrary.html (see Base Blocks, Base Blocks—Addition, Base Blocks—Subtraction, Number Line Arithmetic, Number Line Bounce, Number Line Bars, Abacus, and Chip Abacus)

http://Illuminations.nctm.org (see Five Frame, Ten Frame, Electronic Abacus, and Concentration)

http://www.arcytech.org/java/ (see BaseTen Blocks and Integer Bars)

For sites to practice math facts, go to:

Math Flash Cards: **http://www.aplusmath.com/Flashcards**

Interactive factor trees: **http://matti.usu.edu/nlvm/nav/category_g_3_t_1.html**

Interactive Flash Cards: **http://home.indy.rr.com/lrobinson/mathfacts/mathfacts.html**

Mathflyer (a space ship game that employs multiplication facts): **http://www.gdbdp.com/multiflyer/**

Math Facts Drill: **http://www.honorpoint.com/**

Mathfact Cafe: **http://www.mathfactcafe.com**

228

For Further Reading

Baroody, A. (2006). Why children have difficulties mastering the basic number combinations and how to help them. *Teaching Children Mathematics* 13(1), 22–31.

Baroody compares a number sense view of learning number combinations with what he calls conventional wisdom. He suggests that problems with learning combinations are based on poor instructional procedures that concentrate on memorization rather than on building understanding of number operations and relationships.

Behrend, J. (2001). Are rules interfering with children's mathematical understanding? *Teaching Children Mathematics* 8(1), 36–40.

Behrend uses a case study to explore misinterpretation of rules for addition and the problems children experience as a result of learning rules without understanding.

Computational fluency (special issue). (2003, February). *Teaching Children Mathematics* 9(6).

This focus issue on computational fluency contains nine featured articles on the topic.

Russell, S. (2001). Developing computational fluency with whole numbers. *Teaching Children Mathematics* 7(3), 154–158.

Russell provides strategies, rather than rote procedures, that build number understanding and computation fluency.

Whitenack, J., Knipping, N., Novinger, S., & Underwood, G. (2001). Second graders circumvent addition and subtraction difficulties. *Teaching Children Mathematics* 8(1), 228–233.

Second graders confront and solve addition and subtraction difficulties.

CHAPTER 12

Extending Computational Fluency with Larger Numbers

I n the primary grades students begin work with number and number operations encountered in the context of realistic situations and problems. They learn to count objects and sets; they represent numerical situations with materials, pictures, and numerals; and they establish basic understandings of place value and properties of number operations. These concepts and skills are the foundation for computational fluency, and their use continues through intermediate and middle grades. Computational fluency refers to the use of numbers with confidence and ease in problem-solving situations. Students with computational fluency know when and how to calculate to solve problems with the four basic operations. Fluency is more than memorizing computational rules or learning key words; it includes estimation, number sense, and incorporating higher-order thinking skills, such as judgments about the reasonableness of computed answers. In this chapter activities and examples extend basic concepts and skills with number operations by introducing written algorithms, including alternative approaches for all four operations, estimation, mental computation, and use of technology.

In this chapter you will read about:

1 Computational fluency with larger numbers and development of four approaches to computation: paper-and-pencil algorithms, estimation, calculators, and mental computation

② Activities for addition and subtraction of whole numbers to 100 using base-10 blocks and the hundreds chart

③ Representing addition and subtraction of larger numbers with base-10 models and with traditional and alternative algorithms

④ Estimation strategies for addition and subtraction of larger numbers

⑤ Activities and models for multiplication and division of larger numbers

⑥ Traditional and alternative algorithms for multiplication and division of larger numbers

⑦ Estimation strategies and mental computation for multiplication and division

Number Operations with Larger Numbers

In primary grades students begin their work with numbers up to 100 or 200 that allow them to explore addition, subtraction, multiplication, and division in problem situations. They learn properties of number operations and strategies for number facts to develop accuracy and speed. In intermediate and middle grades students extend their understanding of operations, strategies, and facts when working with two-digit and three-digit numbers. Operations with smaller numbers can be modeled with base-10 blocks and represented in pictures, and these models are useful for understanding that the same properties of operations also apply to larger numbers. Solving problems through concrete, pictorial, and symbolic representations builds the foundation for computational fluency with larger numbers, which are more difficult to represent physically.

The NCTM standards on extending number and number operations are the following (National Council of Teachers of Mathematics, 2000):

NCTM Standards on Extending Number and Operations

Instructional programs from prekindergarten through grade 12 should enable all students to:
- Understand numbers, ways of representing numbers, relationships among numbers, and number systems;
- Understand meanings of operations and how they relate to one another;
- Compute fluently and make reasonable estimates.

In prekindergarten through grade 2 all students should:
- Develop a sense of whole numbers and represent and use them in flexible ways, including relating, composing, and decomposing numbers;
- Connect number words and numerals to the quantities they represent, using various physical models and representations;
- Understand various meanings of addition and subtraction of whole numbers and the relationship between the two operations;
- Understand the effects of adding and subtracting whole numbers;
- Understand situations that entail multiplication and division, such as equal groupings of objects and sharing equally;
- Develop and use strategies for whole-number computations, with a focus on addition and subtraction;
- Develop fluency with basic number combinations for addition and subtraction;
- Use a variety of methods and tools to compute, including objects, mental computation, estimation, paper and pencil, and calculators.

In grades 3–5 all students should:
- Understand the place-value structure of the base-10 number system and be able to represent and compare whole numbers and decimals;
- Recognize equivalent representations for the same number and generate them by decomposing and composing numbers;
- Explore numbers less than 0 by extending the number line and through familiar applications;
- Describe classes of numbers according to characteristics such as the nature of their factors;
- Understand various meanings of multiplication and division;
- Understand the effects of multiplying and dividing whole numbers;
- Identify and use relationships between operations, such as division as the inverse of multiplication, to solve problems;

- Understand and use properties of operations, such as the distributivity of multiplication over addition;
- Develop fluency with basic number combinations for multiplication and division and use these combinations to mentally compute related problems, such as 30 × 50;
- Develop fluency in adding, subtracting, multiplying, and dividing whole numbers;
- Develop and use strategies to estimate the results of whole-number computations and to judge the reasonableness of such results;
- Select appropriate methods and tools for computing with whole numbers from among mental computation, estimation, calculators, and paper and pencil according to the context and nature of the computation and use the selected method or tools.

In grades 6–8 all students should:

- Develop an understanding of large numbers and recognize and appropriately use exponential, scientific, and calculator notation;
- Use factors, multiples, prime factorization, and relatively prime numbers to solve problems;
- Develop meaning for integers and represent and compare quantities with them;
- Use the associative and commutative properties of addition and multiplication and the distributive property of multiplication over addition to simplify computations with integers, fractions, and decimals;
- Understand and use the inverse relationships of addition and subtraction, multiplication and division, and squaring and finding square roots to simplify computations and solve problems;
- Develop and use strategies to estimate the results of rational-number computations and judge the reasonableness of the results.

Addition and Subtraction Strategies for Larger Numbers

Introducing children to addition strategies with larger numbers follows the same instructional sequence used for introducing and teaching children basic addition. Problem situations are represented with materials and pictures and finally recorded with numerals and symbols. For example:

- Yesterday Jorje had 40 baseball cards. Today he bought 30 more. How many cards does he have (see Figure 12.1a)?
- Angela had 72 cents in dimes and pennies. She spent 45 cents on a pencil. How much money does she have now (see Figure 12.1b)?

Students model problems such as these with baseball cards or coins. They can represent the operations with index cards, plastic coins, or base-10 blocks showing tens and ones. They can also draw pictures and write number sentences.

Modeling operations with materials shows students how adding (combining) or subtracting (separating) larger numbers follows the same rules as basic facts. While working with materials and explaining their actions, students may "invent" the traditional algorithm or alternative strategies (Activity 12.1). Each operation has several valid algorithms, and some are the dominant ones in other cultures and countries.

Algorithms for Addition. The traditional, or conventional, algorithm for addition is commonly referred to as carrying, but it is more accurately called **regrouping and renaming** or trading up. Students who have played the exchange game in

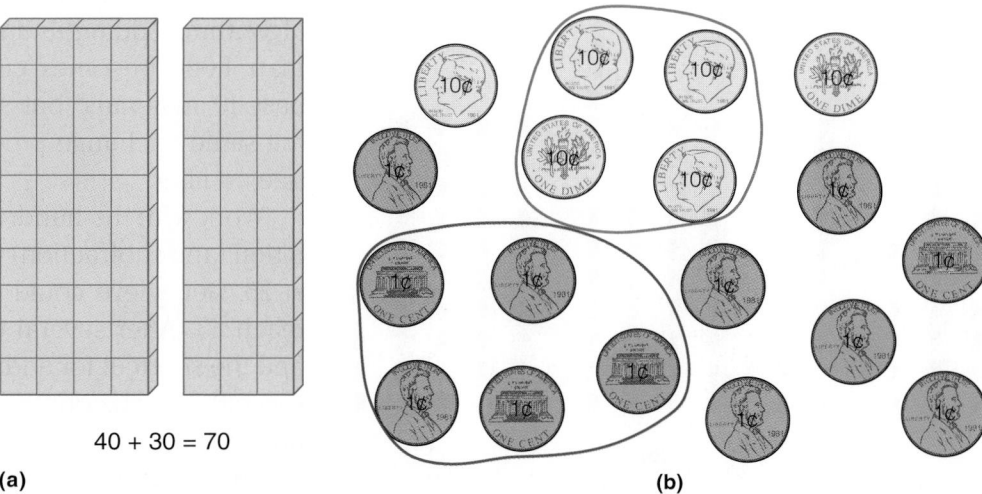

Figure 12.1 (a) Base-10 rods illustrating 40 + 30 = 70. (b) Six dimes and 12 pennies (with 4 dimes and 5 pennies circled)

40 + 30 = 70

(a)   (b)

ACTIVITY 12.1   **Thinking Strategies for Two-Digit Addition (Problem Solving, Reasoning, and Mathematical Representation)**

Level: Grades 1–3
Setting: Whole class
Objective: Students add two numbers between 9 and 100.
Materials: Counters, base-10 materials

- Tell a story based on a classroom situation. For example, "There are 28 children in Ms. Quay's class and 29 in our class. If everybody can go on the field trip to the zoo, how many children are going?"

- Ask students to model the situation with objects, place-value materials, or pictures. Some count a set of 28 and a

set of 29 objects, and others use place-value materials to show 20 + 8 + 20 + 9 = 57. Some might draw a picture, or use a different sequence such as 30 + 30 = 60 and then subtract 3.

- Ask students to discuss their thinking. Compare the answers to see if the strategies work.

- Record the thinking that students present in number sentences and/or vertical notation.

Chapter 10 understand the rules for trading 10 ones for 1 ten and 10 tens for 1 hundred. For example:

- Genevieve had 26 colored markers in her art kit. Her uncle gave her 17 markers. How many did she have?

Bean sticks show the regrouping for Genevieve's markers in Figure 12.2. After putting the three bean sticks together, combine the loose beans (6 + 7), and then trade 10 beans for a bean stick, leaving 3 loose beans. The new bean stick combines with the existing 3 for a total of 4 bean sticks, or 4 tens.

Using manipulatives as a model for operations allows students to record what they see, to talk through the process they have completed, and then to write the steps:

Ronnie: We put the sticks together. That gives us 3 sticks, or 30.

Enrique: We'll add the beans 6 + 7 for 13 beans.

Liane: Then, we regroup 10 beans and exchange them for a stick.

Johanna: Write down 3 for the number of beans, and put the tens stick with the other tens.

Teacher: How can we record that we have an extra ten?

Justin: Write it in the tens column because it is 1 ten.

Huang: Now we have 1 ten + 2 tens + 1 ten, or 4 tens. Write the 4 in the tens column below the line.

$$
\begin{array}{r}
1 \\
26 \\
+17 \\
\hline
43
\end{array}
$$

Manipulative materials are a physical model to demonstrate the operation, but they have served their purpose when students understand the actions with numbers up to 1,000. Some students need concrete models longer than other students and continue to use them until they feel confident with the algorithm. Adding and subtracting numbers larger than 1,000 becomes cumbersome to model with base-10 materials, but students have learned that the same exchange processes take place with any size number.

Work with the hundreds chart also illustrates addition (and subtraction) with tens and ones. Starting at 26, Genevieve could count forward 17 places to reach 43. After several examples, children usually find the shortcut for adding 10 by moving down one row rather than counting forward 10. They may also notice that they can go down two rows to 46 and left 3 numbers to 43. Adding 20 and subtracting 3 has the same result as adding 17 (Figure 12.3).

(a)   (b)   (c)

Figure 12.2 Bean sticks showing 26 + 17 = 43

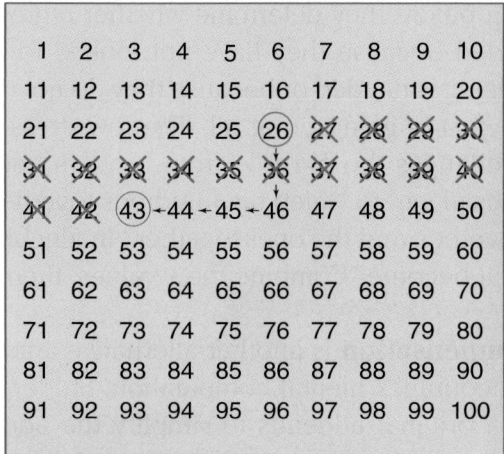

Figure 12.3 Addition on the hundreds chart

While students are learning about regrouping, they are also learning that regrouping is not always necessary. If they survey the problem, they can decide whether the sums in any column are greater than 10. By presenting regrouping and nonregrouping problems, teachers encourage students to think about each problem before starting. Different problems can be solved in different ways.

Most people learned the traditional addition algorithm with regrouping, but regrouping is not the only, or even the best, algorithm in all situations. All the operations have alternative algorithms with steps that differ from the traditional algorithm, but the results are equally valid mathematical processes. **Alternative algorithms**, also referred to as *low-stress, transitional,* or *teaching algorithms,* have advantages for many students. They often preserve the meaning of the number and place value better, are easy to model with materials, connect to estimation and mental computation processes, and require less memorization of steps than the traditional algorithms. Alternative algorithms also require students to think about the procedure and recognize that several solution strategies are possible. Instead of learning only one right way, they begin to think, "Which procedure makes more sense to me?" and "Which procedure is most efficient and effective in this situation?"

In addition, a common alternative algorithm involves adding numbers in the largest place value (left digits) first and recording that partial sum. In turn, each place value to the right is then added, and partial sums are recorded. For example, the model and discussion for adding 26 pencils and 17

pencils leads to an expanded alternative algorithm and a low-stress alternative algorithm. Note that the low-stress algorithm is a form of expanded notation addition.

Traditional	Expanded	Low Stress	
1			
26	$20 + 6$	26	
$+17$	$10 + 7$	$+17$	Think:
43	$30 + 13 = 43$	30	$20 + 10$
		13	$6 + 7$
		43	$30 + 13$

The usefulness of the low-stress algorithm is more apparent as the numbers grow in size:

- Mr. Gilbert ordered bags of birdseed. He had 358 in the storeroom and received a new shipment of 267. How many bags of birdseed did he have?

Figure 12.4 shows a student model for adding the ones, tens, and hundreds with materials. These models can be recorded in either expanded notation or the low-stress form. These models provide a bridge to the traditional algorithm as students see that regrouping is represented in three different formats.

Because both the expanded notation and the low-stress algorithm move students toward understanding the traditional algorithm, many teachers introduce them first, thus the names transitional or teaching algorithms. Base-10 blocks can also be used to model the steps for the expanded notation or low-stress algorithm by putting the hundreds together and writing that sum, then the tens, then the ones:

Mr. Gilbert's birdseed

Low Stress		Traditional	
		11	Think:
358		358	$8 + 7 = 15$
$+267$	Think:	$+267$	Write 5 in ones place and
500	$300 + 200$	625	regroup 1 ten
110	$50 + 60$		$10 + 50 + 60 = 120$
15	$8 + 7$		Write 2 in tens place and
625	$500 + 110 + 15$		regroup 1 hundred
			$100 + 300 + 200 = 600$
			Write 6 in hundreds place

The side-by-side comparison illustrates the simplicity of the expanded and low-stress algorithms. Both algorithms develop estimation and mental computation skills. Front-end estimation uses the left-most digit because its place value gives it the greatest value.

Many students have problems with the traditional algorithm. They do not know why they put "flying 1's" above the addends. Many also have alignment problems writing the regrouped numbers above the problem. Some even begin by putting 1's over every

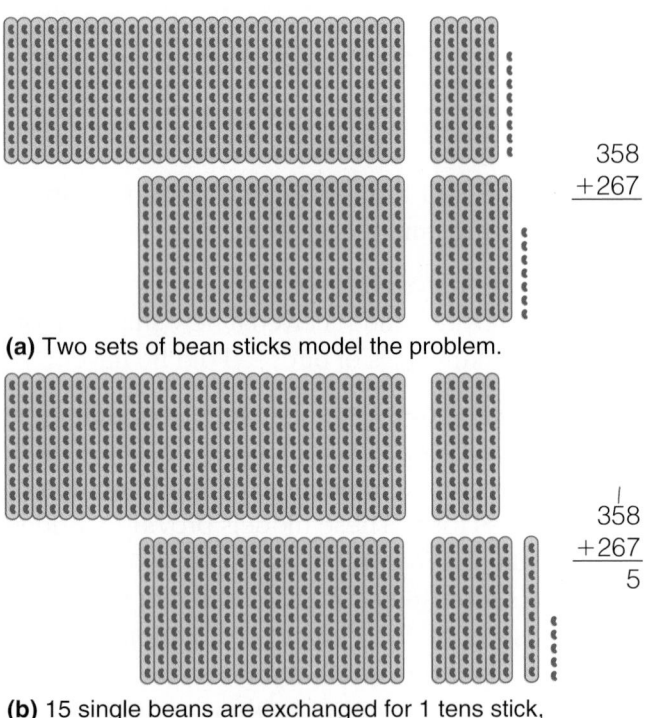

(a) Two sets of bean sticks model the problem.

$$\begin{array}{r} \overset{\scriptstyle|}{358} \\ +267 \\ \hline 5 \end{array}$$

(b) 15 single beans are exchanged for 1 tens stick, with 5 loose beans remaining.

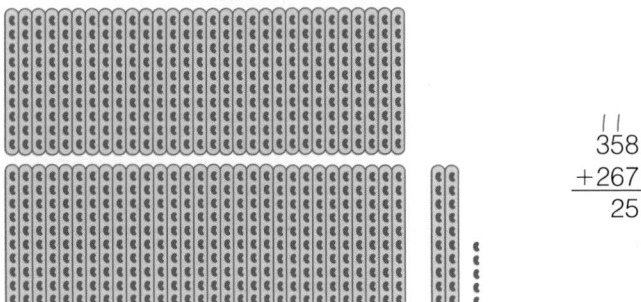

$$\begin{array}{r} \overset{\scriptstyle||}{358} \\ +267 \\ \hline 25 \end{array}$$

(c) 10 tens sticks are exchanged for a hundreds raft, with 2 sticks remaining.

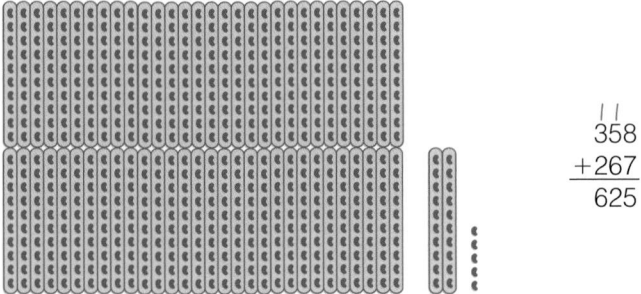

$$\begin{array}{r} \overset{\scriptstyle||}{358} \\ +267 \\ \hline 625 \end{array}$$

(d) The hundreds rafts are combined.

Figure 12.4 Traditional algorithm with bean sticks illustrating 358 + 267 = 625

column before they determine whether regrouping is needed because they have not looked to see if regrouping is needed or because they do not understand what is going on at all. The low-stress algorithm changes the old rule from "Always begin in the ones place" to "Keep the hundreds together, the tens together, and the ones together." In algebra this rule will become "Combine the x values, then the y values."

Compensation is another alternative approach that encourages mental computation. Students adjust the original addends to simplify the addition. Then they correct, or compensate, in the final answer. Students who have played the exchange game from Chapter 10 are familiar with compensation. If they have 7 ones on the trading board and roll 5 on the dice, instead of counting out five more cubes, students learn to pick up a rod for 10 and put 5 cubes back in the bank. The result is still 12 on the board, but students have arrived at the result through compensating—adding 10 and subtracting 5. Here is another example:

Teacher: Ms. Gideon started driving to Salt Lake City at 8:00 in the morning. At 1:00 in the afternoon, her trip odometer read 287 miles, and she saw a sign "Salt Lake City 100 miles." How many miles will she drive on her trip? Work the problem on your place-value mat, and tell me what you did.

Keisha: We put 2 hundreds, 8 tens, and 7 ones on our mat. Then we added 100 on the mat. The trip was 387 miles long (Figure 12.5a).

Teacher: What is the distance if the sign reads 99 miles to Salt Lake City?

Lindo: It would be 386 miles because it was 1 mile shorter.

Teacher: Start with 287 on your board. How could you show addition of 99? Is there more than one way?

Huang: We put 9 tens and 9 ones on the mat and regrouped to get 386.

Walter: We put 100 on the mat and took off 1 because it is the same as adding 99 (Figure 12.5b).

When students are comfortable with the process of adding 100 and subtracting 1, they find ways to use compensation to adjust a cumbersome regrouping problem into an easier problem for mental computation and eliminate regrouping in many problems.

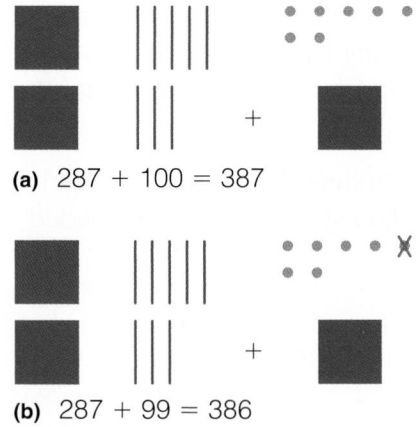

(a) 287 + 100 = 387

(b) 287 + 99 = 386

Figure 12.5 Compensation algorithm for addition

Traditional

  11   Think:
 499   9 + 9 = 18
+789 Write 8 in ones place and regroup 1 ten
1,288 10 + 90 + 80 = 180
         Write 8 in tens place and regroup 1 hundred
         100 + 400 + 700 = 1,200
         Write 1 in thousands place and 2 in
           hundreds place

Compensation

          Think:
 500 − 1   499 = 500 − 1
+789
1,289 − 1 = 1,288
         Decrease the answer by 1

ⒺXERCISE

Assess understanding of addition by interviewing three to five students. Present each of the following problems, and ask them to "think aloud" as they work. Do they use the traditional algorithm? Does their thinking reflect knowledge of regrouping? Do any of them use the low-stress algorithm or compensation?

    123 + 100 =   123 + 99 =
    345 + 300 =   345 + 289 =
  1,297 + 500 =   1,297 + 511 = ●●●

Algorithms for Subtraction. Procedures for subtraction with larger numbers are related to addition processes. Subtraction between 20 and 100 can be modeled with manipulatives and simple pictures or on the hundreds chart. Subtraction of tens is easily understood when children have been count-

ing down by tens and using the hundreds chart to model subtraction:

- A length of rope 70 feet long has 40 feet cut from it. How many feet remain?

In Figure 12.6, 70 feet of rope is represented by 7 ten rods; 4 rods (40 feet of rope) are removed and 3 rods (30 feet of rope) remain.

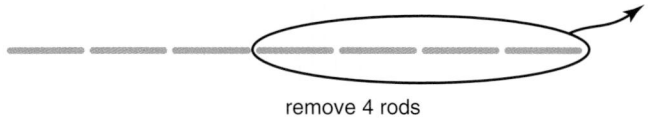

remove 4 rods

Figure 12.6 Rods representing 70 feet − 40 feet

Decomposition, the traditional subtraction algorithm, is modeled in the exchange game from Chapter 10 when students start with 100 or 1,000 and remove chips on each turn. Although commonly called borrowing, decomposition is another example of regrouping and renaming, or trading down. Decomposition involves the same steps as addition but involves trading down rather than trading up:

- Bandar saved $50 and spent $30 for clothes. How much does he have?
- The sneakers cost $47. I have $29 now. How much more do I need?
- Ani's family was shopping for a digital camera. The list price was $573. The same camera was for sale on the Internet for $385. How much can they save?

The stories can be acted out using play money, then with base-10 blocks. Students regroup and rename hundreds to tens and tens to ones with materials in each situation, or they draw simple diagrams. Students can represent $573 with base-10 materials, as shown in Figure 12.7a. In Figure 12.7b a ten rod has been exchanged for 13 one rods. Figure 12.7c shows that 100 is exchanged to make a total of 16 tens. After regrouping, 5 ones, 8 tens, and 3 hundreds are removed (Figure 12.7d). As in addition, decomposition is related to expanded notation:

Expanded

  500 + 70 + 3   400 + 160 + 13   Regroup
 −300 − 80 − 5 −300 − 80 −5   Subtract
               100 + 80 + 8 = 188

Decomposition

    5 7 3   4   16 13   Regroup
   −3 8 5   −3   8   5   Subtract
                1   8   8

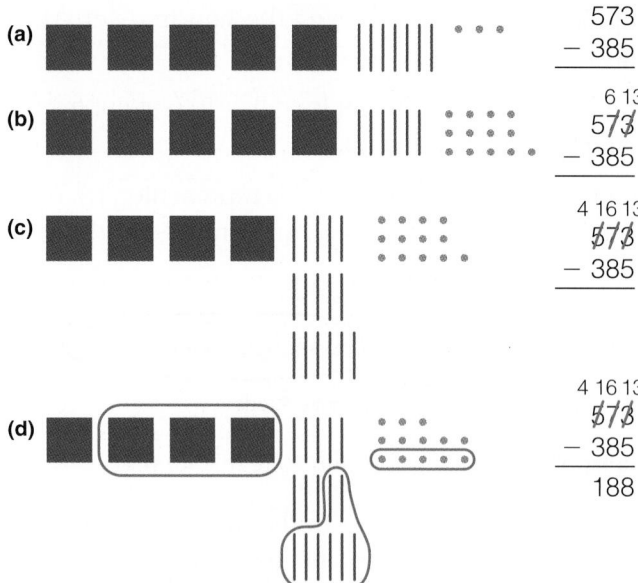

Figure 12.7 Base-10 blocks show subtraction with regrouping: (a) 5 flats, 7 rods, 3 units; (b) regroup 1 rod; (c) regroup 1 flat; (d) subtract by removing 385.

A cooperative activity in Activity 12.2 illustrates students exploring decomposition.

Decomposition is difficult for many children if they memorize steps because each problem has a unique regrouping situation. Instead, they can look at each place value and decide if regrouping is needed.

Experience with physically trading from hundreds to tens to ones is important. Frances Thompson (1991) found that students who actually manipulated materials showing the decomposition

process understood and retained skill in subtracting two-digit numbers better than those who watched demonstrations but did not actually exchange the materials. For example:

- If 306 plants were purchased for the garden and 148 were already planted, how many still needed to be planted?

Expanded

Think:
$$306 = 30 \text{ tens} + 6 \text{ or}$$

306	29 tens + 16	200 + 90 + 16
−148	−14 tens − 8	−100 − 40 − 8
	15 tens + 8 = 158	100 + 50 + 8 = 158

Decomposition

29 16
3̶0̶6̶　　Regroup 30 tens to 29 tens and 10 ones
−1 4 8　　Subtract 29 tens − 14 tens, 16 ones − 8 ones
1 5 8

Students who are comfortable with various representations of 306 know that it can be called 30 tens and 6 ones. By regrouping 1 ten as 10 ones, they have 29 tens and 16 ones, or 2 hundreds, 9 tens, and 16 ones. Subtraction is completed by subtracting 8 from 16, 4 tens from 9 tens, and 1 hundred from 2 hundreds, or 29 tens − 14 tens and 16 ones − 8 ones.

Alternative Algorithms for Subtraction. Several alternative algorithms are possible for subtraction of larger numbers. The **equal-addition algorithm** for subtraction is well known in Europe and other parts of the world but has been used infrequently in the United States. The mathematical concept behind the algorithm is simple—many subtraction combinations have the same answer. For example, many subtraction problems have a difference of 28:

57	58	59	60	61	62	164	168	781	780
−29	−30	−31	−32	−33	−34	−136	−140	−763	−762
28	28	28	28	28	28	28	28	28	28

Some number combinations are easy to calculate $(58 - 30)$, whereas others (e.g., $164 - 136$) are perceived as more difficult.

Let each student list their current age and the age of another person who is older. Ask what the difference in age is now. Then ask what the differ-

ACTIVITY 12.2 Decomposition Algorithm (Reasoning and Representation)

Level: Grades 3–5
Setting: Cooperative learning
Objective: Students develop the decomposition algorithm for subtracting two-digit numbers.
Materials: Base-10 materials

- With the team/pair/solo structure, four team members solve the first problem, pairs solve the second problem, and individuals solve the final problem.

- Present a problem situation: "Ms. Hons packed 82 boxes of apples to sell at a fruit stand. At the end of the day, 53 boxes remained. How many boxes were sold during the day?"

- Tell each team to solve the problem, using any way they choose. Ask each team to write the mathematical sentence for the situation with their answer: $82 - 53 = ?$.

- Present a second, similar problem. Team members work in pairs to solve this problem. When pairs are finished, they compare their work and clear any discrepancies.

- Present a third problem, which each member of a team solves. Again, team members compare their answers.

- Call on one team member to explain the solutions to each of the problems. Different strategies may be presented for each solution. Probe for decomposition as an effective strategy.

---

ence will be when both of them are 3 years older, 5 years older, and 10 years older. Students will recognize that the number of years between the two ages remains constant. Ask them to suggest a rule for what they see, for example, "If the same number is added to both ages, the difference is still the same." Students who understand how this rule works are ready to use equal addition as a written algorithm or mental computation strategy:

- Hawthorn School had 678 students. When a new school was built, 199 Hawthorn students were transferred to it. How many students are enrolled at Hawthorn now?

Subtracting 199 from 678 is seen as a hard problem by many children, but subtracting 200 from 679 seems simple. Increasing both 678 and 199 by 1 makes a hard computation into an easier one.

Traditional	**Expanded**	**Equal Additions**
5 16 18 6̶ 7̶ 8̶	$500 + 160 + 18$	Think: $678 + 1 = 679$ Add 1
		$-(199 + 1) = -200$ Add 1
-199	$100 - 90 - 9$	479 Subtract
4 7 9	$400 + 70 + 9 = 479$	

Students who understand the logic of equal additions find it a quick mental computation strategy for some problems.

- The Olympic torch was carried across the United States on a journey of 7,592 miles. At Columbus, Ohio, the runners had already covered 2,305 miles. How many miles were left?

In this case students look for a convenient number to add or subtract from both numbers in the problem. The 5 in 2,305 appears to be an easy number to subtract, but adding 5 to each number also simplifies the computation.

Think: Add 5 to both numbers
$$7,592 \quad \text{Add 5: } 7,592 + 5 = \quad 7,597$$
$$\underline{-2,305} \quad \text{Add 5: } 2,305 + 5 = \underline{-2,310}$$
$$5,287$$

Or subtract 5 from both numbers
$$\text{Subtract 5:} \quad 7,592 - 5 = \quad 7,587$$
$$\text{Subtract 5:} \quad 2,305 - 5 = \underline{-2,300}$$
$$5,287$$

Equal-addition reasoning also leads to a more sophisticated type of equal-addition problem. If students put 497 on the place-value mat and add 10 to it, they could add 10 ones or 1 ten. Adding 100 to any number could be done by adding 10 tens or by adding 1 hundred. In the Olympic torch problem both the total miles and the current mileage are adjusted by 10. The total miles has 10 ones added to the ones place; the addend has 1 ten added to the tens place:

	Think:	Th H T O
7592	Add 10 ones	7 5 9 12
-2305	Add 1 ten	-2 3 1 5
	Subtract	5 2 8 7

After the numbers are adjusted by adding 10 to each of them, subtraction proceeds left to right or right to left, because the regrouping is already completed.

Students skilled with equal additions perform subtraction rapidly. Students who went to school in another country might demonstrate the process for the class.

See "Subtracting with Equal Additions," one of many activities on the companion website, for an example of how to introduce the equal-addition algorithm.

Compensation with subtraction is similar to compensation with addition. In the Hawthorn School problem of losing 199 students to a new school, students might notice that 199 is close to 200, allowing them to subtract 200 and then add 1 back:

$$\begin{array}{r} 678 \\ -199 \\ \hline \end{array} \qquad \begin{array}{r} 678 \\ -200 \\ \hline \end{array} \quad \text{Think: Subtract 200 and add 1}$$
$$478 + 1 = 479$$

After inventing or learning about alternative algorithms, students are able to consider whether decomposition, expanded notation, equal additions, or compensation is the efficient way to approach the problem. Making decisions about the faster and easier computational approach is part of computational fluency.

The low-stress algorithm for subtraction is similar to the low-stress algorithm for addition with an additional element of negative integers. After working with positive and negative numbers on a number line or thermometer, intermediate-grade students should be comfortable with the idea of "below zero." Beginning at the left, subtraction is done for each place value, including those resulting in a negative value:

- The school carnival collected \$5,162. They paid \$3,578 for supplies and concessions.

$$\begin{array}{rl} 5,162 & \\ -3,578 & \text{Think:} \\ 2,000 & 5,000 - 3,000 \\ -400 & 100 - 500 \\ -10 & 60 - 70 \\ -6 & 2 - 8 \\ \hline 1,584 & 2,000 - 400 \text{ is } 1,600; 1,600 - 10 \text{ is } 1,590; \\ & 1,590 - 6 \text{ is } 1,584 \end{array}$$

Many students find that a low-stress procedure is easier than decomposition because each place value is calculated by itself before combining them for the final answer. Low-stress algorithms also prepare students for front-end estimation and can be a mental computation strategy.

EXERCISE

Solve the following problems using the traditional, compensation, equal-addition, and low-stress algorithms. Write your thinking steps, and compare with a partner. Which strategy works best for you in each problem?

$$\begin{array}{r} 342 \\ -168 \\ \hline \end{array} \qquad \begin{array}{r} 633 \\ -287 \\ \hline \end{array} \qquad \begin{array}{r} 517 \\ -393 \\ \hline \end{array} \quad \bullet\bullet\bullet$$

Mental Computation. Mental computation is used with estimation and rounding and instead of algorithms to get exact answers. People look for number combinations and multiples of 10, 100, or 1,000 that make calculations easy. Numbers that add to combinations and multiples of 10 are called **compatible numbers**. For example:

- The votes for Geraldo for class president were 72, 15, 36, 43, and 93.

Rearranging numbers in the tens column gives 70 + 30 and 10 + 90 plus 40 = 240. In the ones column, 2 + 3 + 5 = 10 and 6 + 3 = 9, totaling 19. The mental sum is 240 + 19 = 259.

Mental calculations for subtraction use techniques from estimation and alternative algorithms. Several different approaches to mental calculations are possible.

- Yusef needed \$75 to buy a DVD player. He had saved \$48. How much more did he need?

Round to nearest \$5 and compensate:
$$\$75 - \$50 = \$25 \qquad \$25 + \$2 = \$27$$

Add 2 to both numbers and subtract:
$$\$77 - \$50 = \$27$$

Expand and subtract:
$$\$70 - \$40 = \$30$$
$$\$5 - \$8 = -\$3 \qquad \$30 - \$3 = \$27$$

Think-aloud practice with mental computation and estimation at the beginning of a class period can be done by writing four addition or subtraction examples. Have students work in pairs and compare their answers.

EXERCISE

Work the following examples using compatible numbers. Explain your thinking to another student.

$$16 + 23 + 7 + 4 = \underline{\quad}$$
$$20 + 392 + 680 = \underline{\quad}$$
$$246 + 397 + 3 = \underline{\quad}$$
$$476 + 385 + 24 = \underline{\quad} \quad \bullet\bullet\bullet$$

Multiplying and Dividing Larger Numbers

Exploring Multiplication Algorithms. Multiplication and division of two- and three-digit numbers are a logical extension of earlier work with the operations. Following development of place value, understanding of operations, and basic facts, students apply commutative, associative, and distributive properties with base-10 materials to explore traditional and alternative algorithms:

• Johnny bought 3 dozen bagels for the meeting. Instead of getting 12 in a dozen, he got a baker's dozen of 13 bagels. How many bagels did he buy?

Modeling the story with materials, as in Figure 12.8a, students see that 3 groups of 13 is the same as 3 groups of 10 and 3 groups of 3:

$$3 \times 13 = 3 \times (10 + 3)$$
$$(3 \times 10) + (3 \times 3) = 30 + 9$$

Expanded notation using the distributive property reflects the place-value model and sets the stage for the traditional algorithm (Figure 12.8b). A lesson using books is described in Activity 12.3.

Traditional and alternative algorithms use the distributive property; however, the steps can be recorded in different ways

• If Johnny bought 7 bags of oranges with 13 oranges in each bag, how many oranges would he have?

Expanded	Alternative	Traditional
		2 Think:
$7 \times 13 = 7 \times (10 + 3)$ 13		13 $7 \times 3 = 21$
$= 70 + 21$ $\times 7$ Think:		$\times 7$ Write 1 in ones place
$= 91$ 21 7×3		91 Regroup 2 tens
70 7×10		$7 \times 10 = 70$
91 $21 + 90$		$7 + 20 = 90$
		Write 9 in tens place

Think: $7 \times 10 = 7$ tens

Think: $70 + 20 = 9$ tens

As multiplication numbers grow in size, the simplicity of the alternative algorithm becomes even more obvious:

• The scouts sold 15 dozen cookies in an hour. How many cookies were sold?

Figure 12.9 shows each part of the multiplication process with base-10 blocks:

$$15 \times 12 = (10 + 5) \times (10 + 2)$$
$$= (10 \times 10) + (10 \times 2) + (5 \times 10) + (5 \times 2)$$

Students can model 15×12 using blocks to show the partial products from the alternative algorithm (Figure 12.9).

Figure 12.8 Modeling (a) 3 baker's dozens and (b) 7 baker's dozens

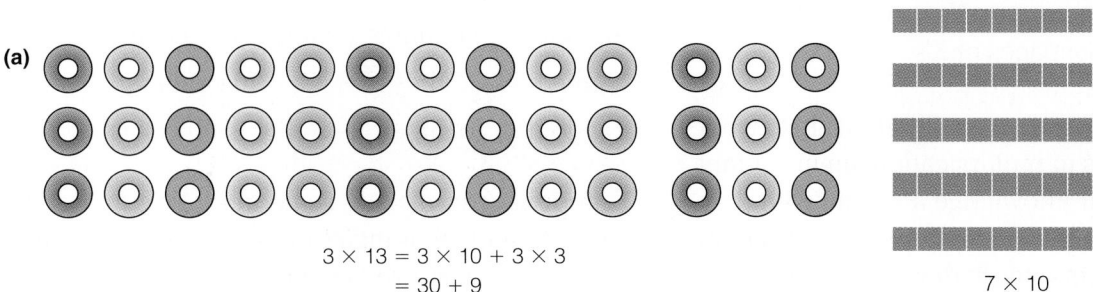

$3 \times 13 = 3 \times 10 + 3 \times 3$
$= 30 + 9$
$= 39$

7×10 7×3

$70 + 21$

Alternative		**Transitional**		**Traditional**	
12		12		₁	Think:
×15	Think:	×15	Think:	12	5 × 2 = 10
100	10 × 10	10	5 × 2	×15	Regroup 1 ten
20	10 × 2	50	5 × 10	60	5 × 10 = 50 and add 10
50	5 × 10	20	10 × 2	+120	Write 60
+10	5 × 2	100	10 × 10	180	Think: 10 × 12 = 120
180		180			Write 120
					Add 60 + 120

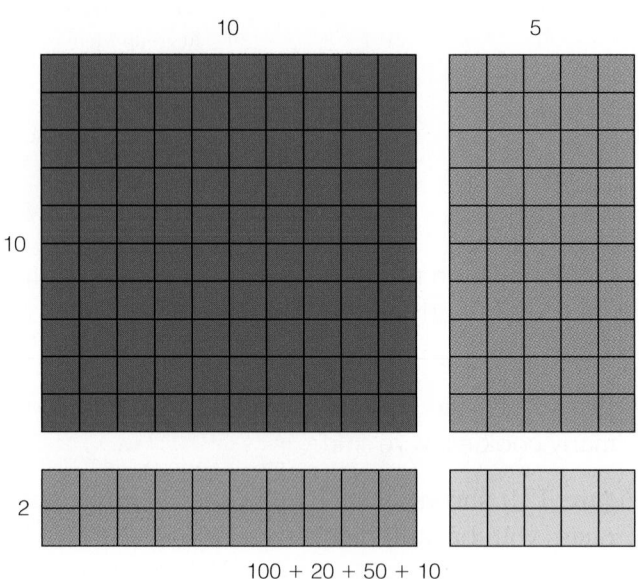

Figure 12.9 Array for 12 × 15 showing distributive property

The traditional algorithm requires short-term memory while performing other operations as students switch back and forth between multiplication and addition. The alternative algorithm records each step with partial products. All the multiplication operations are completed before addition is performed. Writing the entire number for each partial product also keeps the place values lined up without use of blank spaces or X's.

Decade Multiplication. As children begin to work with larger numbers in multiplication, an important step is building their knowledge and skill with multiples of 10 and 100. Because products greater than 1,000 become cumbersome to draw or to model with

> **MISCONCEPTION**
>
> Notation for the traditional algorithm creates problems for many students. Teachers may suggest leaving spaces or putting X's as placeholders during multiplication, but these tend to weaken mathematical understanding of multiplication by 10, 100, or larger multiples. The partial sums found in the alternative and transitional algorithms preserve the value of numbers. If the traditional algorithm needs regrouping twice or in both the ones and the tens place, many children have difficulty keeping numbers organized and separated. Others cannot remember whether to multiply and then add or to add and then multiply the renamed tens and hundreds. These procedural problems relate to poor understanding of place value.

materials, children should develop confidence with mental calculations for problems such as 20 × 30 and 40 × 800. These products are needed for alternative and traditional algorithms. Because these problems involve multiples of 10, they are called *decade multiplication*. Decade multiplication is critical for success with multiplication, division, mental computation, and estimation of larger numbers, but it is sometimes taught as a rule without developing the reason behind it.

Teachers should introduce multiplication with 10 and 100 in realistic situations and as an extension of learning number facts so that students see patterns of multiplication by 10 and 100:

- A dime is 10 pennies; 2 dimes is 20 cents.
- Jaime had 7 dimes: 7 × 10 = 70 cents.
- Diego had 20 dimes: 20 × 10 = 200 cents.

Students can make a scale model of the school grounds using an orange Cuisenaire rod = 100 feet. The front fence is 7 rods long: 7 × 100 = 700 feet.

ACTIVITY 12.3   Distribution (Representation and Reasoning)

Level: Grades 3–5

Setting: Small groups or whole class

Objective: Students multiply a two-digit number by a one-digit number without regrouping.

Materials: 36 books (preferably identical, such as a set of reading texts), linking cubes for each child

- Arrange the 36 books into sets of 12. Display the three sets and tell the children, "I have 3 sets of 12 books. How many books are there all together?"

- Have students consider the problem and discuss ways to determine the answer. For example: Count the books; add $12 + 12 + 12$; skip count by 12's; or multiply 3×12.

- Write the multiplication sentence $3 \times 12 = 36$ and then the vertical notation:

$$\begin{array}{r} 12 \\ \underline{\times 3} \\ 36 \end{array}$$

- Separate the books so that each set shows 10 books and 2 books. Hold up the 3 groups of 2 books. Ask: "How many books are in these 3 sets of 2 books?" Show the multiplication of 3×2 in the algorithm.

- Point to the 3 groups of 10 books. Ask: "How many books are in 3 sets of 10 books?" Show the multiplication of 3 times 10 in the algorithm, and add the partial products:

$$\begin{array}{r} 12 \\ \underline{\times 3} \\ 6 \\ \underline{30} \\ 36 \end{array}$$

- Children can also use Unifix cubes to illustrate combinations that demonstrate partial products and their sums: 6×11, 3×13, 4×12.

- Cloris read that a bridge is 3,000 feet long: 30 rods $\times$ 100 feet = 3,000 feet.

Other illustrations use different multiples of 10 or 100:

- Thirty classes at Upward Elementary each raised $50 for hurricane relief: $30 \times \$50 = \$1,500$.

- The school sweatshirts cost $20, and 150 students ordered one: $150 \times \$20 = \$3,000$.

- On the 100th day of school, students determined how many minutes they had been in school: 300 minutes per day $\times$ 100 days = 30,000 minutes.

The calculator is an excellent learning tool for students to explore a variety of decade products. Have students work the following examples using a calculator:

$$2 \times 40 = 80$$
$$2 \times 400 = 800$$
$$20 \times 40 = 800$$
$$20 \times 400 = 8,000$$
$$200 \times 40 = 8,000$$
$$200 \times 400 = 80,000$$
$$5 \times 60 = 300$$
$$5 \times 600 = 3,000$$

$$50 \times 60 = 3,000$$
$$50 \times 600 = 30,000$$
$$500 \times 60 = 30,000$$
$$500 \times 600 = 300,000$$

From a study of situations like these, ask students to propose a decade multiplication rule. After some discussion they will state something like "Multiply the numbers at the front and put zeros on the end." This is a good start, but it needs more work. They clearly see the pattern related to the number of zeros. The more important idea is that the number of zeros is the number of tens being multiplied shown in expanded notation using the associative and distributive laws. Students also need to be aware of situations when the multiplication of the leading numbers results in a factor of 10. Students who have an understanding of the number of tens being multiplied are also setting a foundation for exponential notation:

$$30 \times 100 = (3 \times 10) \times (1 \times 10 \times 10) = (3 \times 1) \times (10 \times 10 \times 10) = 3 \times 1,000 = 3,000$$
$$50 \times 400 = (5 \times 10) \times (4 \times 10 \times 10) = (5 \times 4) \times (10 \times 10 \times 10) = 20 \times 1,000 = 20,000$$

Division problems with multiples of 10 and 100 also use expanded notation. What is sometimes referred to as "canceling zeros" is actually dividing by multiples of 10 or 100:

$$300 \div 100 = (3 \times 100) \div (100) \text{ or}$$
$$(3) \times (100 \div 100) = 3 \times 1 = 3$$

Students can make generalizations about multiplying and dividing by 10's and 100's:

$2 \times 10 = 20$	$20 \div 10 = 2$
$2 \times 100 = 200$	$200 \div 100 = 2$
$9 \times 30 = 270$	$270 \div 30 = 9$
$70 \times 10 = 700$	$700 \div 10 = 70$

Extending Algorithms for Larger Numbers. By learning decade multiplication and division, children develop mental computation strategies, establish skills for front-end estimation, and take an important step toward multiplication and division with larger numbers before they begin working with algorithms. Consider the following problem:

• Each box contains 24 apples. Jamie has 47 boxes to sell. How many apples are being sold?

The distributive property of multiplication over addition is the foundation for algorithms. A major difference between the traditional algorithm and an alternative algorithm is notation. The alternative algorithm records a partial product for each multiplication, starting at the left with the largest place value. A transitional algorithm also records all the partial products but starts with multiplication in the ones place. The traditional algorithm has all the same steps but requires that students regroup and remember whether they are multiplying or adding during each step.

Activity 12.4 illustrates multiplication with regrouping in a cooperative group lesson. This format encourages students to explore multiplication and to create alternative algorithms.

Students should not devote extensive time to multiplying three-digit and larger numbers. All children should learn one or more algorithms that they can use efficiently and accurately for these problems. Students who are efficient with alternative or transitional algorithms may never need to learn a traditional algorithm. Other students prefer the compact and efficient nature of the traditional algorithm and seem to have no problems with the notation. Some students switch from one algorithm to another depending on the numbers. Learning different algorithms gives all students power and flexibility with multiplication of larger numbers, although in real life they are more likely to use a calculator or to use estimation. Several other multiplication algorithms are interesting for students to explore. The historical algorithms in Activity 12.5 show that mathematics has evolved over many centuries and that many cultures have contributed.

Introducing Division Algorithms. Division with larger numbers builds on ideas and skills developed for division with smaller numbers and place value. To use division algorithms successfully, students should understand both partitive and measurement division situations, know the multiplication and division facts, including decade multiplication, and be able to add and subtract accurately. When working with early division situations, students recognize that division is related to multiplication facts.

Alternative		**Transitional**		**Traditional**
47		47		1$\overset{2}{2}$
×24	Think:	×24	Think:	47
800	20×40	28	4×7	×24
140	20×7	160	4×40	188
160	4×40	140	20×7	+94
+28	4×7	+800	20×40	1128
1128		1128		

ACTIVITY 12.4 **Multiplication with Regrouping (Representation)**

Level: Grades 3–5

Setting: Cooperative groups

Objective: Students multiply two-digit numbers by one-digit numbers with regrouping.

Materials: Place-value materials of students' choice

- Write a sentence and algorithm on the chalkboard:
  7 × 14 = ?.

$$\begin{array}{r} 14 \\ \underline{\times 7} \end{array}$$

- Allow time for each team to discuss how to determine the product. When agreement is reached, each member solves the problem using the procedures. Have team members consult a second time to check their work.

- Have each team explain what it did. Teams should demonstrate how materials were used. For example, one team might use squared paper. Call on a student to explain. For example, a student may say, "First, we colored squares to show 7 times 14. Next, we cut the paper to show 7 times 4 and 7 times 10. We know that 7 times 4 is 28 and 7

times 10 is 70, so 28 and 70 make 98." Teams that used algorithms might have representations such as these:

$$\begin{array}{r} 14 \\ \underline{\times 7} \\ 70 \\ 28 \\ \underline{} \\ 98 \end{array}$$

$$7 \times 14 = 7 \times (10 + 4)$$
$$7 \times 10 = 70$$
$$7 \times 4 = 28$$
$$= 98$$

- During discussion of models and algorithms, help students to see that the number of ones is greater than 10. If the standard algorithm is introduced, tens from the ones place are regrouped and added to the tens place in the product:

$$\begin{array}{r} 2 \\ 14 \\ \underline{\times 7} \\ 98 \end{array}$$

- Repeat with examples such as 3 × 26, 6 × 12, and 4 × 24.

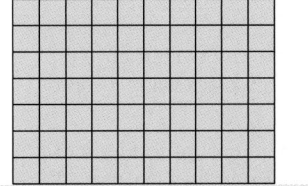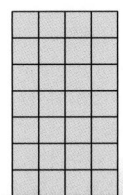

- Twenty-eight marbles are shared equally by six children. How many marbles will each child have?

When students divide 28 objects into 6 groups, they place 4 objects in each group with 4 extra (Figure 12.10). They also record the word and number sentences to represent this story.

- Twenty-eight marbles divided by 6 people = 4 marbles each with a remainder of 4:

$$28 \div 6 = 4, \text{remainder } 4$$

Each child has four marbles, but there are not enough for each child to have five. This situation is partitive or sharing; however, the reasoning is similar in measurement, or repeated subtraction, division situations.

- Twenty-eight marbles are put in gift bags with six marbles in each bag. How many bags of marbles can be made?

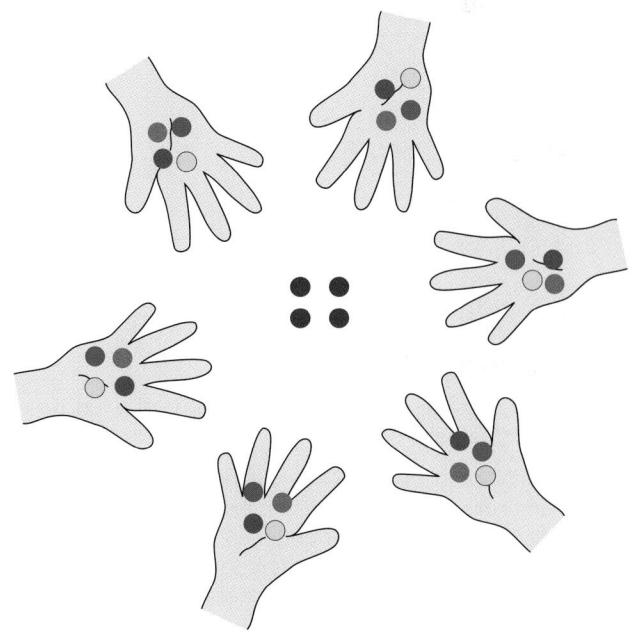

Figure 12.10 Marbles used to model 28 ÷ 6

ACTIVITY 12.5 **History and Multiplication Algorithms**

Level: Grades 3–5

Setting: Individual or group investigation

Objective: Students explore historical multiplication algorithms to see how they work.

Materials: None

Lattice, or Gelosia, Multiplication

Multiplication using the lattice method is done in a lattice, or gelosia. The lattice method is easy to use because no addition is done until all multiplication is completed. The method is demonstrated with the multiplication of 23 and 68:

- Make a lattice, and write one factor across the top and the other down the right side.
- Ask students to multiply 3×8, 3×6, 2×8, and 2×6 and to write the product for each pair of numbers in the appropriate cell of the lattice.
- Add the numbers in each diagonal, beginning at the lower right. The excess of tens in the diagonal that contains 6, 2, and 8 is regrouped and added in the next diagonal. The product is represented by the numbers outside the lattice, beginning at the top left.
- Ask students to compare the lattice to the alternative or traditional algorithms and to tell how place value is represented on the lattice.
- Have students work individually or in groups to figure out how this method works with larger numbers, such as 236 × 498.

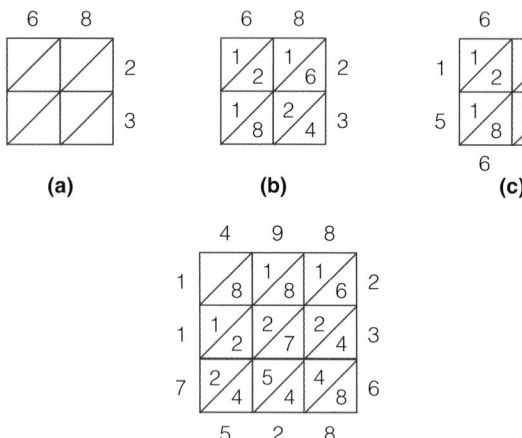

(a)   **(b)**   **(c)**

Egyptian Multiplication

The Egyptian process of multiplication is one of doubling and adding partial products:

- Model the problem 7×21 by writing two columns. In the first column place 1, and in the second column 21. In the next row, double the 1 and the 21; in the third row, double both numbers again. Stop doubling when any combination of numbers in the left column adds to 7 or higher.

1	21
2	42
4	84
7	147

- Ask students to explain how the Egyptian method works. What property is demonstrated in this method? (Answer: Distributive property of multiplication over addition.)
- Ask students to figure out how to multiply 13×26 using the Egyptian method:

*1	26
2	52
*4	104
*8	208
13	338

Russian Peasant Multiplication

The Russian peasant process, similar to the Egyptian process, is based on doubling. However, a different method determines which partial products are kept.

- Demonstrate the Russian peasant process for 48×28. Write 48 in the first column and 28 in the second column. In the next row the 48 is divided by 2 and 28 is doubled. The division-by-2 and doubling process continues until 1 is at the bottom of the left column. Then add the doubled numbers in the second column that appear next to odd numbers in the first row. Doubled numbers adjacent to even numbers are discarded.

48 ×	28
24	56
12	112
6	224
3	448
1	896
	1,344

- If an odd number is divided by 2, the remainder of 1 is dropped, as in the following example, 37×57. Again, only the doubled numbers adjacent to odd numbers are added to determine the product. Those next to even numbers are discarded.

37 ×	57
18	114
9	228
4	456
2	912
1	1,824
	2,109

- The rationale for this process is more difficult to determine than for Egyptian multiplication. Challenge students to see if they can figure out how it works. Can you?

Extension

Napier's rods, another multiplication process, was invented by John Napier in 1617. Students should be able to find several websites that describe Napier's rods and how to construct them. Challenge students to find an explanation of Napier's rods, or Napier's bones, and to make a set to demonstrate this early computational device.

The divisor is subtracted from the dividend as many times as possible.

• How many times did we distribute the six marbles? (Answer: Four times.)

• How many marbles were unshared? (Answer: Four marbles.)

The repeated subtractions are shown in number sentences and in the division bracket:

$$
\begin{array}{ll}
28 - 6 = 22 & 28 \div 6 = 4, \text{ remainder } 4 \\
22 - 6 = 16 & \quad\ 4, \text{ remainder } 4 \\
16 - 6 = 10 & 6\overline{)28} \\
10 - 6 = \ \ 4 & \ \underline{-24} \\
& \quad\ \ 4
\end{array}
$$

Many division problems can be solved by inspection because they draw on knowledge of multiplication facts. Using multiplication facts to solve division problems with dividends up to 100 is developed with "think-back" flash cards. A child is shown the front of the card with the division algorithm and thinks of the closest fact associated with that division.

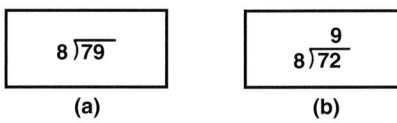

(a)   **(b)**

Figure 12.11 Example of a think-back flash card: (a) Front shows division algorithm; (b) back shows the associated basic fact.

The back of the card shows the nearest fact. If a student is shown the card in Figure 12.11, the student thinks of the related division fact "72 divided by 8 equals 9."

When a student cannot think back to the correct basic fact, show the fact on the back of the card. Frequent group and individual work with these cards helps children develop skill in naming quotients.

As the numbers increase in size, students have difficulty predicting appropriate trial quotients through inspection. An alternative algorithm, called the ladder method, allows students to see each subtraction and gives them great flexibility in choosing their trial quotients. Division is a more efficient way to record the process than many subtractions.

Activity 12.6 shows how children use base-10 blocks to model division and relate the materials to recording the algorithm. Because the parts of the algorithm can be directly related to actions with bean sticks or other manipulative materials, stu-

dents see meaning in the steps as the algorithm is completed.

Real-world situations help students understand division involving larger numbers just as they did with basic facts. Children who use the traditional algorithm of guessing, multiplying, subtracting, and bringing down often have difficulty predicting reasonable numbers for starting the division. They also have difficulty lining up numbers and knowing how many numbers to bring down. The alternative algorithm allows students to build the final answer by multiplying any two numbers that the child finds easy instead of having to get the best or closest trial quotient. In either case children should have skill and confidence in mental calculations, including decade multiplication. Without ready recall of addition, subtraction, and multiplication facts, they cannot focus on the meaning of division with larger numbers. For example:

• A farmer has 288 oranges to bag for market. If she puts the oranges into 24 bags, how many oranges will be in each bag?

How many times can I subtract 24 from 288?

$$
\begin{array}{r|l}
24\overline{)288} & \\
\underline{-240} & 10 \\
48 & \\
\underline{-48} & 2 \\
0 & \\
\end{array}
\qquad
\begin{array}{l}
\text{Think:} \\
10 \times 24 = 240 \\
288 - 240 = 48 \\
2 \times 24 = 48 \\
48 - 48 = 0
\end{array}
$$

24 can be subtracted from 288 12 times.

Relate each numeral in the algorithm to the problem situation so that students understand each one's meaning. When talking through the problem, model the actions by putting 10 oranges in each bag in the algorithm, then place 2 more in each bag. The ladder algorithm uses the same thinking questions as the teacher and student record their work.

Students usually need several more examples with guided practice or working with a partner before they gain confidence in the ladder method. The alternative method gives students flexibility when they cannot identify a trial quotient. They use any reasonable quotient that is easy to multiply and subtract. Different students may find quotients by using facts that they consider easier. The ladder algorithm can be simplified once the process is understood.

Alternative		**Traditional**	
$\begin{array}{r} 2 \\ \times 10 \\ \hline 24\overline{)288} \\ -240 \\ \hline 48 \\ -48 \\ \hline 0 \end{array}$	Think: $10 \times 24 = 240$ $288 - 240 = 48$ $2 \times 24 = 48$ $48 - 48 = 0$	$\begin{array}{r} 12 \\ 24\overline{)288} \\ -24 \\ \hline 48 \\ -48 \\ \hline 0 \end{array}$	Think: $1 \times 24 = 24$ $28 - 24 = 4$ Bring down 8 $2 \times 24 = 48$ $48 - 48 = 0$

Only the multiplier needs to be written down, either on the side or above the bracket:

• Sam drove 3,174 miles on 123 gallons of gas. What was his mileage (miles per gallon)?

Despite using different number combinations, both students calculated the answer correctly. The remainder 99 is interpreted as $\frac{99}{123}$ (or about 0.8 of a gallon). The fuel efficiency of the car was almost 26 miles per gallon.

Enough work is needed so that students understand the meaning and the thinking behind the algorithm. However, extensive exercises with division of larger numbers are no longer seen as useful. Instead, more time should be spent on problem-solving situations with multiplication and division in

---

ACTIVITY 12.6 **Division with Regrouping (Representation, Problem Solving, and Reasoning)**

Level: Grades 3–5

Setting: Pairs or small groups

Objective: Students use place-value materials to demonstrate division with regrouping.

Materials: Place-value materials, such as bean sticks, Cuisenaire rods, or base-10 materials, or bundled and loose tongue depressors

• Present a situation: "Gloria put 45 apples into three bags—the same number in each bag. How many apples did she put in each bag?"

• Have students work with place-value materials to solve the problem. Bean sticks illustrate the process here.

• Ask: "Could you separate the 4 tens into 3 equal-size groups?" Allow time for students to determine that they cannot do this.

• Ask: "What can you divide into 3 groups?" (Answer: Divide 3 tens into 3 groups.)

• Ask: "What did you do next?" (Answer: Exchanged 1 ten for 10 ones and divided 15 into 3 groups.)

• Ask: "How many apples are in each bag?" (Answer: 15.)

• Have pairs of students repeat with examples such as 56 ÷ 4, 52 ÷ 2, and 78 ÷ 6. Observe and assist as needed.

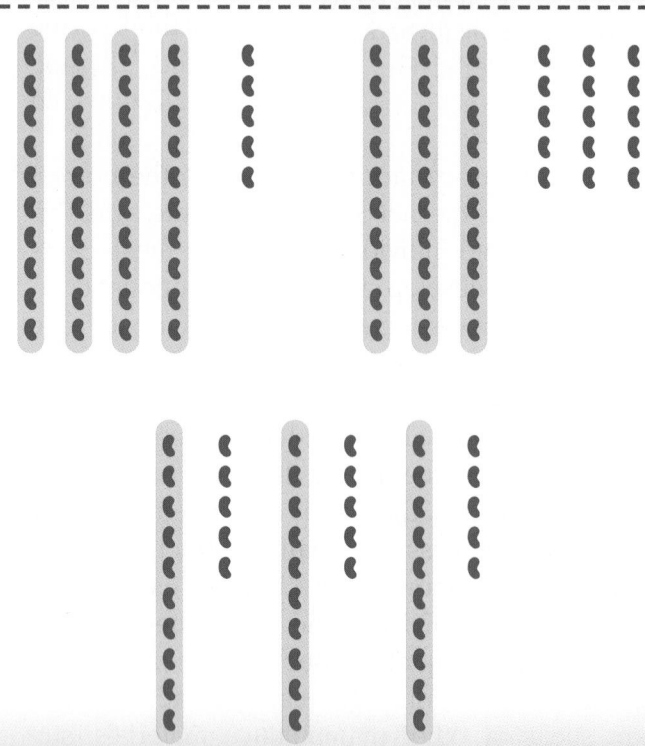

Student 1			Student 2	
5			2	
10			3	
10			20	
123)3174			123)3174	
−1230	10		−2460	20
1944			714	
−1230	10		−369	3
714			345	
−615	5		−246	2
99			99	

which students use estimation, mental calculation, and/or calculators. Mental computation with multiplication and division is less frequent than with addition or subtraction. Estimation and calculator use with larger multiplication and division problems are better strategies.

ⒺXERCISE

How many long-division problems do you think students need to complete to show their understanding of the algorithm? Look at a fifth- or sixth-grade textbook to see how much practice is given. Is it adequate? too little? too much? ●●●

Number Sense, Estimation, and Reasonableness

While students learn computational algorithms, they are also developing number sense skills, such as estimation, rounding, and reasonableness. These skills are particularly important with larger numbers. For example:

• If one bank has deposits of $45,173, 893, and the other bank holds $37,093,103, how much will be deposited if they merge?

• The population of the largest city is 10,987,463, and the population of the second largest city is 6,423,932? How many more people live in the larger city?

• The hybrid car gets 37 miles per gallon. If the gas tank holds 16 gallons of gas, how many miles can it go on a full tank?

• The seven-day cruise costs $539. What is the cost per day for the vacation?

In some instances exact calculations are needed, but often estimation, mental calculations, and calculators can be used instead of paper-and-pencil procedures. Students who possess computational fluency recognize which computational approach is best in different situations, depending on the accuracy needed.

Problems with two- and three-digit numbers demonstrate the need for estimation to attain a fast approximation. Estimation is most valuable for numbers in the thousands and larger or when several addends are considered. Procedures for *front-end estimation* and *rounding estimation* are similar to alternative algorithms that start in the largest place value for the first approximation. If more precision is needed, students can adjust the answer to improve the estimate by including the next place value. For example:

• Students were tracking the energy usage of their school. Over four months the electrical usage was 2,345 kWh, 6,526 kWh, 3,445 kWh, and 3,152 kWh.

Intermediate-grade students make a front-end estimate by adding the thousands and adjust the estimate by adding the sum of the hundreds:

	Front-End	**Adjusted**	**Rounded**
	Add thousands	Add hundreds	Round to hundreds
2,345	2,000	300	2,300
6,526	6,000	500	6,500
3,445	3,000	400	3,400
+3,152	+3,000	+100	3,200
	14,000	+1,300 = 15,300	15,400

The front-end estimate is 14,000, and the adjusted estimate is 15,300. Values in the tens and ones places are ignored because they add little to the sum. If students round the addends to the hundreds place, the estimate is 15,400. Any of these estimates serve as reasonable comparisons for an answer using a calculator. If the calculator answer is close to 19,000 or 1,500, the estimates would be clues that something is wrong, When rounding, students determine how much accuracy is needed and round each number to that place. Addends for the previous example could be rounded to the nearest 1,000, 500, or 100.

When teaching estimation strategies, teachers model the process by thinking aloud. Students then think aloud in pairs or small groups to verbalize estimation and mental computation processes. Comparing front-end estimation to adjusted and rounded estimation helps students determine whether one method is better than the other for the purpose of the problem. Estimation in subtraction also uses front-end estimation and rounding techniques:

- Lando wants to buy a car that costs $7,358. He has a down payment of $2,679. How much money will he borrow to complete the purchase?

Front-End	Adjusted	Rounded	
		Round to nearest 1,000 or 500	
7,000	7,000 + 300	7,000	7,500
−2,000	−2,000 − 600	−3,000	−2,500
5,000	5,000 − 300	4,000	5,000

The loan officer at the bank calculates the exact amount being borrowed and adds taxes and registration fees using his computer. An estimate gives a sense of what is involved before starting paperwork.

Both front-end estimation and rounding are efficient ways to estimate products. Students can use either process, depending on the size of the number and the precision. Front-end estimation might adjust the answer by using the first two largest places. Decade multiplication is critical in making estimation quick and easy. For example:

- Mr. Johnson planted 125 pecan trees. After they grow, he expects each tree to produce about 85 pounds of pecans.

Front-End	Adjusted	Rounded		
				Up and
		Up	Down	down
100	120	130	120	130
×80	×80	×90	×90	×80
8,000	8,000	9,000	9,000	8,000
	+1,600	+2,700	+1,800	+2,400
	10,600	11,700	10,800	10,400

Flexible thinking is needed as students compare and decide which result is best for different estimation procedures—front-end, adjusted, and rounding. Continuing the pecan tree example, a student might note that the front-end estimate of 8,000 is low and that rounding both factors up gives 11,700, which will be high. The other three estimates are in between, so the student thinks that the best estimate is probably about 10,500.

A sample problem on estimation from the Texas Assessment is shown in Figure 12.12. Children choose the best estimate based on reasonable low and high estimates.

26. Mr. Benjamin jogs for 33 minutes to 38 minutes every day. Which could be the total number of minutes that Mr. Benjamin jogs in 4 days?

   a. Less than 120 min

   b. Between 120 min and 180 min

   c. Between 180 min and 240 min

   d. Between 240 min and 300 min

   e. More than 300 min

Figure 12.12 Sample problem on estimation from the Texas Assessment for fifth grade

Another multiplication concept, called factorials, is shown in Activity 12.7, which is based on *Anno's Magical Multiplication Jar*. Children should see the magnitude of repeated multiplications.

➋XERCISE

Estimate each of the following products with front-end and rounding techniques. Which of these products can you calculate mentally?

27	42	94	87	348
×8	×7	×16	×23	×75 ●●●

Estimating quotients with larger numbers uses the logic learned with the alternative division algorithm or by using multiplication. Decade multiplication is an essential skill in estimation of division. For example:

- The school PTA raised $7,348 at its carnival. They decided to buy new printers for classrooms. If each printer costs $324, how many printers can they buy?

ACTIVITY 12.7   Factorials (Reasoning)

Level: Grades 3–5

Setting: Small groups or whole class

Objective: Students model factorials, a sequence of multiplications $1 \times 2 \times 3 \times 4 \times 5 \dots$

Materials: A copy of the book *Anno's Mysterious Multiplying Jar,* by Masaichiro Anno and Mitsumasa Anno (New York: Philomel Books, 1983).

Anno's Mysterious Multiplying Jar "is about one jar and what was inside it." With this simple statement, Mitsumasa Anno and son Masaichiro Anno, a writer-artist team, begin their tale about a fascinating jar and its contents, introducing the topic of factorials to intermediate- and middle-grade students. Inside the jar was a sea of rippling water on which a ship appeared. The ship sailed to a single island. The island had two countries, each of which had three mountains with four walled kingdoms on each mountain, and each kingdom had five villages. Eventually students are asked to answer the question, "How many jars were in the boxes in the houses in the villages in the kingdoms, on the mountains, in the countries?"

- Read the story, pausing to allow time for students to talk about how many countries, mountains, and kingdoms there are. Continue reading to the point where there are 10 jars in each box, and ask, "How many jars were in all the boxes together?"

- Give each student a large sheet of paper and crayons. Reread the story, allowing time for sketches to be drawn of the evolving scene.

- Have students study their sketches to see if they can determine the pattern that is developing. Have them discuss their ideas about the pattern. Ask them if they can write a multiplication sentence to show the situations in the pictures.

- Tell students that the authors have represented the island's growing number of objects. Turn to the page where the display of dots begins. Ask: "Why didn't the authors show dots for the boxes and for the jars in the boxes? Students may use calculators to determine the products of larger numbers.

- Introduce the term and numerical representation of *factorial.* Children should come away from the activity with an understanding that the factorial symbol—10!—is equal to $10 \times 9 \times 8 \times 7 \times 6 \times 5 \times 4 \times 3 \times 2 \times 1$, or 3,628,800, a very short way to write a very large number!

- Students can create their own factorial stories and illustrate them. Their stories, pictures, and computations can be displayed on a factorial bulletin board.

The teacher asks students whether the PTA could buy 10, 20, 30, 50, or 100 printers. The students reason that 10 printers would cost about $3,200; that 20 printers would cost twice as much, or about $6,400; and that 30 printers would cost about $9,600. They decide that the PTA could buy between 20 and 30 printers. Another estimation adjusts the numbers by rounding the dividend and divisor to numbers that are easy to divide. Different students find different number combinations for estimation:

Ian: 7,500 divided by 500 is 15, and 7,500 divided by 250 is 30; the answer is halfway between 15 and 30 or about 22.

Heather: 7,000 divided by 350 is 20, so we should be able to buy a few more than 20 printers.

Sara: 7,200 divided by 600 is 12 and divided by 300 is 24. I think the answer is close to 25.

Students compare their answers and thinking to see whether their estimates were reasonable. Both front-end estimation and rounding processes allow students to find a similar but simpler division problem.

EXERCISE

What estimated quotients would be reasonable for each of the following divisions? Tell a story that might go with the numbers in the following problems. Try both front-end estimation and rounding methods or a combination to find numbers that are easier to compute mentally. Compare the numbers you used with someone else's estimation process.

368 ÷ 42 is about?   1,268 ÷ 87 is about?
5,383 ÷ 677 is about?   15,383 ÷ 913 is about? ●●●

Take-Home Activities

Repeated Subtraction with a Calculator

Most calculators allow you to subtract repeatedly by setting up a problem such as this one:

$$597 \; \boxed{-} \; 19 \; \boxed{=} \; \boxed{=} \; \boxed{=} \; \boxed{=}$$

How many times do you think that you will have to touch the equal key to get the remainder to less than 19? How long do you think it will take you to reach that number?

Estimate the number of times you will subtract the divisor for the following problems:

		Estimate	Actual Number
238 divided by 41	$238 \; \boxed{-} \; 41 \; \boxed{=} \; \boxed{=}$	_____	_____
571 divided by 16	$571 \; \boxed{-} \; 16 \; \boxed{=} \; \boxed{=}$	_____	_____
1,200 divided by 63	$1{,}200 \; \boxed{-} \; 63 \; \boxed{=} \; \boxed{=}$	_____	_____
4,594 divided by 425	$4{,}594 \; \boxed{-} \; 425 \; \boxed{=} \; \boxed{=}$	_____	_____
9,007 divided by 113	$9{,}007 \; \boxed{-} \; 113 \; \boxed{=} \; \boxed{=}$	_____	_____
15,073 divided by 743	$15{,}073 \; \boxed{-} \; 743 \; \boxed{=} \; \boxed{=}$	_____	_____

Create problems for yourself and a friend to estimate and repeatedly subtract.

_____ divided by _____	_____ $\boxed{-}$ _____ $\boxed{=} \; \boxed{=}$	_____	_____
_____ divided by _____	_____ $\boxed{-}$ _____ $\boxed{=} \; \boxed{=}$	_____	_____
_____ divided by _____	_____ $\boxed{-}$ _____ $\boxed{=} \; \boxed{=}$	_____	_____

Tiling with Coins

Tiling your desk with quarters? You might use some of the existing artwork showing quarters covering a surface.

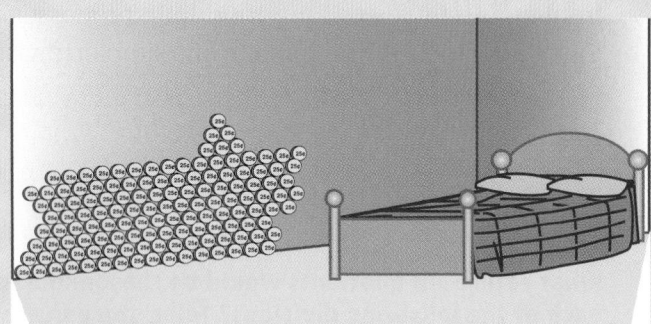

How many quarters would it take to cover the top of a table or large book at your house? How many quarters would you need to estimate the number to cover the table? What could you use instead of real quarters?

What would be the value of the quarters needed to cover the table?

How many dimes would it take to cover the table? What would all the dimes be worth? How many nickels would be needed to cover the table? What would the nickels be worth?

Object being covered?   _____

Number of quarters?   _____

Value of quarters?   _____

Number of dimes?   _____

Value of dimes?   _____

Number of nickels?   _____

Value of nickels?   _____

If you could keep the coins needed to cover the floor of a room, would you rather cover it with quarters, dimes, or nickels? Explain your reasons.

Summary

Traditional algorithms can be taught; however, many students have difficulty with the traditional algorithms. The algorithms are often confusing because of placement of answers and because they involve switching from one operation to another several times. The larger the numbers become, the more complex the algorithm becomes and the more it places a memory burden on many students who are trying to remember the steps.

Each of the operations has one or more alternative algorithms that help students to develop their skill in computing with larger numbers. Many algorithms are based on expanded notation, which emphasizes place value of numbers. Some algorithms allow students to adjust the numbers in a given problem to make the computation easier. Many alternative algorithms simplify computation by allowing students to write down partial answers as they work. In general, the alternative algorithms for each of the operations build on understanding of the operations, preserve the meaning of numbers as students work, are easy to model with base-10 materials, and require less memory of steps while students are working. Many students are successful in computing with alternative forms; others use the traditional algorithm readily.

As students model problems and record answers, they build skills with estimation, rounding, and mental computation. Several alternative algorithms parallel front-end estimation strategies because they are based on the numbers in the largest place value. Students can compare the results of different estimation strategies to decide what are reasonable answers to problems with large numbers. This skill is also valuable when using calculators and computers. Students should check calculator answers against estimated answers to determine whether their estimates were reasonable. Computational fluency and flexibility means that teachers spend less time practicing paper-and-pencil algorithms and more time solving problems with larger numbers using a variety of computational approaches.

Study Activities and Questions

1. Recall your own learning of algorithms for larger numbers. Were they hard or easy for you to remember and perform? Did you learn or develop for yourself any of the alternative algorithms?

2. Look at a current elementary textbook or teacher's guide. Do they include alternative algorithms for students? If so, how do the materials present the algorithms for children?

3. Think of five or six ways that you computed answers in the last week. Did you use the calculator? Did you use estimation? Did you use a paper-and-pencil algorithm to get the answer? What led you to use different approaches?

4. Use place-value devices such as base-10 materials to demonstrate the following examples. Write a story to go with each of them. Work each example using both the traditional algorithm and one of the alternative algorithms.

   a. 24
   + 48

   b. 64
   − 26

   c. 23
   ×18

   d. 536 ÷ 24

5. Estimate the answers to the following examples. What process did you use for estimation? Was your strategy rounding or front-end estimation? Compare your strategy with other students.

   a. 269
   924
   472
   +826

   b. 3,879
   −2,091

   c. 711
   ×138

   d. 1,826 ÷ 35

6. Ask several fifth- or sixth-graders to estimate the answers in Question 5 and to think aloud as they work. Can you draw any conclusions about their skill with estimation strategies?

   Use a calculator or a computer spreadsheet to find the answers to the following problems.

7. What is the total population of the 10 largest cities in the country (or your state, province)?

8. Ms. Powell has donated a total of $348 to a library during the past 4 years. She has donated the same amount of money each year. How much money has Ms. Powell donated to the library in each of the past 4 years? (Taken from the Fourth Grade Texas Assessment of Knowledge and Skills Release Test, 2006.)

   a. $82
   b. $87
   c. $352
   d. $344

9. Ted collected 22 pounds of aluminum cans. How many ounces of aluminum cans did he collect? (Taken from the Sixth Grade Texas Assessment of Knowledge and Skills Release Test, 2006.)

   a. 6 oz.
   b. 38 oz.
   c. 352 oz.
   d. 220 oz.

Praxis (http://www.ets.org/praxis/) The average number of passengers who use a certain airport each year is 350,000. A newspaper reported the number as 350 million. The number reported in the newspaper was how many times the actual number?

   a. 10
   b. 100
   c. 1,000
   d. 10,000

NAEP (http://nces.ed.gov/nationsreportcard/) Amber and Charlotte each ran a mile. It took Amber 11.79 minutes. It took Charlotte 9.08 minutes. Which number sentence can Charlotte use to best estimate the difference in their times?

a. $11 - 9 =$ c. $12 - 9 =$

b. $11 - 10 =$ d. $12 - 10 =$

TIMSS (http://nces.ed.gov/timss/) A runner ran 3000 meters in exactly 8 minutes. What was his average speed in meters per second?

a. 3.75   d. 37.5

b. 6.25   e. 62.5

c. 16.0

Technology Resources

There are many commercial software programs designed to help students with their number sense, recall of number facts, and applications of number operations. We list several of them here:

How the West Was One + Three × Four (Sunburst)

Math Arena (Sunburst)

Math Munchers Deluxe (MEEC)

Oregon Trail (Broderbund)

The Cruncher 2.0 (Knowledge Adventure)

Internet Game

At **http://www.fi.uu.nl/rekenweb/en**, students may play a variety of challenging mathematics games ranging from number fact recall to spatial sense. In Broken Calculator students try to reach a given number by using the available keys on a calculator. In this game not all the keys are available. For example, in one game the + and × keys are missing, as are the 5, 7, and 9 keys. The task is to reach 80 beginning with a value of 150.

Find more games at **http://www.bbc.co.uk/education/maths file/**, **http://www.bbc.co.uk/schools//numbertime/games// index.shtml**, and **http://www.subtangent.com/index.php**.

Internet Activity

This activity is for students in grades 3–6. Students work in small groups to solve number puzzles on the Internet. The only material they need is a computer with Internet access. Have students go to **http://nlvm.usu.edu/en/nav/ vlibrary.html** and follow the links to the activity Circle 21. This activity asks students to arrange numbers in each of the regions formed by overlapping circles so that each entire circle has a sum of 21. Have students solve three of the puzzles and turn in the completed puzzles. Once they have solved three puzzles, challenge each group to create three original puzzles to use with the class.

Internet Sites

For Internet sites that allow students to explore and work with integers, go to the following websites:

http://nlvm.usu.edu/en/nav/vlibrary.html (see Circle 21, Circle 3, Circle 99, Color Chips, and Rectangular Multiplication of Integers)

http://lluminations.nctm.org (see Voltage Meter)

For explorations with modular systems go to the following website:

http://www.shodor.org/interactivate/activities/index.html (see Clock Arithmetic)

For websites to practice math facts, go to:

Math Flash Cards: **http://www.aplusmath.com/Flashcards**

Interactive factor trees: **http://matti.usu.edu/nlvm/nav/ category_g_3_t_1.html**

Interactive Flash Cards: **http://home.indy.rr.com/lrobinson/ mathfacts/mathfacts.html**

Mathflyer (a space ship game that uses multiplication facts): **http://www.gdbdp.com/multiflyer/**

Math Facts Drill: **http://www.honorpoint.com/**

Mathfact Cafe: **http://www.mathfactcafe.com**

For Further Reading

Baek, J. (2006). Children's mathematical understanding and invented strategies for multidigit multiplication. *Teaching Children Mathematics* 12(5), 242–247.

Classroom research shows teachers how children think about multidigit multiplication, revealing misconceptions as well as understanding.

Bass, H. (2003). Computational fluency, algorithms, and mathematical proficiency: One mathematician's perspective. *Teaching Children Mathematics* 9(6), 322–327.

The purpose and value of alternative algorithms is advocated for development of understanding how numbers work.

Computational Literary Theme Issue. (February 2003). *Teaching Children Mathematics* 9(6).

This themed issue of *Teaching Children Mathematics* contains several articles that describe computational fluency and gives examples of strategies to build operational fluency for students across the elementary grades.

Ebdon, S., Coakley, M., & Legrand, D. (2003). Mathematical mind journeys: Awakening minds to computational fluency. *Teaching Children Mathematics* 9(8), 486–493.

Teachers encourage flexible thinking about numbers and operations, and students consider alternative ways to represent solutions on mind journeys. Thinking aloud is used in the classroom discussion.

Fuson, K. (2003). Toward computational fluency in multidigit multiplication and division. *Teaching Children Mathematics* 9 (6), 300–306.

Computational algorithms serve two purposes: computation skill and understanding how operations work.

Whitenack, J., Knipping, N., Novinger, S., & Underwood, G. (2001). Second graders circumvent addition and subtraction difficulties. *Teaching Children Mathematics* 7(5), 228–233.

Second-graders develop meaning for tens and ones in subtraction situations through stories, models, and pictures.

CHAPTER 13

Developing Understanding of Common and Decimal Fractions

Children's study of fractional numbers begins as early as kindergarten and continues through middle school. Fractional numbers and concepts related to them—in the form of common fractions, decimal fractions, and percentages—are encountered in everyday settings by children and adults. Common fractions are used to express parts of wholes and sets, to express ratios, and to indicate division. "One-half of a pie" refers to part of a whole; "one-half of 12 apples" refers to part of a set. If one apple is served for every two children, a ratio of 1:2 exists between the number of apples and the number of children; this ratio is also expressed as $\frac{1}{2}$. Division, such as "2 divided by 4," can be written as the common fraction $\frac{2}{4}$. Common fractions are an integral part of the English, or common, system of measure, as indicated by quarter-inches, half-pounds, and thirds of cups. Decimal fractions are used to express parts of wholes and sets divided into tenths, hundredths, thousandths, and other fractional parts of tenths. They are used to express money in our monetary system ($1.23 and $0.07) and represent various measurements in the metric system (0.1 decimeter or 0.01 meter).

As with other numbers, children's work with fractional numbers begins with real-world examples, and representations of fractional numbers are modeled with real materials and manipulatives. In all grades concrete representations help children develop a clear understanding of these numbers, their uses, and the mathematical operations associated with them. In this chapter we focus on activities for developing foundational concepts of fractional numbers expressed as common and decimal fractions and related concepts. Activities featured in this chapter focus on concepts and skills involving operations with fractional numbers. Although percent is commonly linked with the study of fractions, we have chosen to consider percent in a different chapter. Chapter 15 includes a full discussion of percent and ratio and proportion.

The NCTM standards for number and operations suggest the following standard for fractions at this level.

NCTMConnection

Understand numbers, ways of representing numbers, relationships among numbers, and number systems

Pre-K–2 Expectations

In prekindergarten through grade 2 all students should
- understand and represent commonly used fractions, such as $\frac{1}{4}$, $\frac{1}{3}$, and $\frac{1}{2}$.

In this chapter you will read about:

1. Uses of common and decimal fractions from everyday life commonly studied in grades K–3

2. Real and classroom learning aids for representing parts of wholes and sets to help children develop their understanding of common and decimal fractions

3. Activities emphasizing equivalent common fractions and comparison of unlike fractions

4. Materials and procedures for helping children learn how to round decimal fractions

5. Ways to extend the concept of place value to include decimal fractions

6. A take-home activity dealing with common fractions

POINT OF VIEW

No area of elementary school mathematics is as mathematically rich, cognitively complicated, and difficult to teach as fractions, ratios, and proportionality. (Smith, 2002, p. 18)

Teaching children about common and decimal fractions extends their understanding of number concepts beyond knowledge about whole numbers. Knowledge of fractional numbers allows children to represent many aspects of their environment that would be unexplainable with only whole numbers, and it allows them to deal with problems involving measurement, probability, and statistics. Helping children build knowledge of fractions also broadens their awareness of the power of numbers and extends their knowledge of number systems. The concepts of common and decimal fractions developed in elementary school lay the foundations on which more advanced understandings and applications are built in later grades.

What Teachers Need to Know About Teaching Common Fractions and Decimal Fractions

The role of manipulatives in learning about both common fractions and decimal fractions is extremely important. At times, teachers are tempted to hurry students beyond manipulatives and concrete models of fractional numbers into abstract computations. When students are moved along too quickly from concrete models to abstract computations, they never fully develop basic understandings of the fractional concepts and relationships. Consequently, they advance their understanding of fractional numbers by rote memorization and not from any conceptual understanding. Knowledge about fractional numbers gained in this way is fragile. Teachers need to allow children sufficient time to engage with various models that represent fractions before they move on to symbolic aspects of fractional numbers. When students develop concepts about, and processes with, fractional numbers slowly and carefully through activities with concrete materials and realistic settings, they avoid misconceptions that must be corrected later. Children also construct meaning of fractional numbers by interacting with peers and adults. During this process, their understanding of fractions may not be identical to their teacher's. Overemphasis of the teacher's way of viewing these new numbers may inhibit students' progress in understanding them. It is important, especially during early work with fractional numbers, to allow students time to explore the meaning of these numbers and to build their conceptual understanding.

Table 13.1 suggests when various topics for common and decimal fractions might be beneficially introduced to children. Notice that introductory activities may stretch across several years in order to build a foundational understanding. Introductory activities are then followed by activities that maintain and/or extend understanding.

For example, the fact that common fractions $(\frac{1}{2})$ and decimal fractions (0.5) represent the same number is not understood by many students. One reason the connection between the two types of numerals may seem obscure is that instruction of common and decimal fractions is often completely separated. When students work with common fractions at one time and decimal fractions at a different time, connections are often unclear or not made at all. Another reason is that most people use the term *fraction* when they refer to common fractions and the term *decimal* when they refer to decimal fractions. Using the terms *common fraction* and *decimal fraction* helps students understand that both types of numerals are used to represent fractional numbers. Both numerals refer to parts of units or sets; the difference is that a common fraction represents units or sets separated into any number of parts (3 out of 5 or $\frac{3}{5}$), whereas a decimal fraction represents units or sets separated into 10 parts or parts that are powers of 10 (0.6 or $\frac{6}{10}$; 0.03 or $\frac{3}{100}$). When percent is used, the unit or set is separated into 100 parts. When the terms *common fraction* and *decimal*

> The modern English term *fraction* was first used by Geoffrey Chaucer (1300–1342), author of *The Canterbury Tales*. It has the meaning "broken number" in Middle English.

TABLE 13.1 Sequence for Fraction Topics in School							
Topic	K	1	2	3	4	5	6
Basic understanding	I	I	M	M	M	M	M
Equivalent fractions			I	I	I	M	M
Improper fractions			I	I	I	M	M
Mixed numbers				I	I	M	M
Ordering fractional numbers				I	I	I	M

I, topic introduced. M, topic maintained.

fraction are used throughout the school years, children learn that both are representations of fractional numbers.

Mathematically, fractional numbers are part of the set of rational numbers that can be expressed in the form $\frac{a}{b}$, where a is any whole number and b is any nonzero whole number. Symbolically, fractional numbers are expressed as common fractions ($\frac{1}{2}$ and $\frac{2}{3}$), as decimal fractions (0.5 and 0.6666. . .), and as percents (50% and $66\frac{2}{3}$%).

Five situations that give rise to common fractions are discussed in the following sections.

Five Situations Represented by Common Fractions

Unit Partitioned into Equal-Size Parts

Objects such as cakes, pies, and pizzas are frequently cut into equal-size parts. When a cake is cut into four equal-size parts, each part is one-fourth of the entire cake; the common fraction $\frac{1}{4}$ represents the size of each piece. Many measurements with the English system of measurement require common fractions. When you need a more precise measurement than is possible with a basic unit of measure, such as an inch, the object is subdivided into equal-size parts. When an inch is subdivided into eight equal-size parts, each part is one of eight equal-size parts made from the whole, or $\frac{1}{8}$ of an inch.

The digits in a common fraction show this part-whole relationship. In the numeral $\frac{1}{2}$, the 2 indicates the number of equal-size parts into which the whole, or unit, has been subdivided and is called the **denominator**. The 1 indicates the number of parts being considered at a particular time and is called the **numerator** (Figure 13.1a). For the common fraction $\frac{3}{8}$, the whole has 8 equal-size parts, and 3 of the 8 parts are indicated (Figure 13.1b). Division of a unit into its parts is also referred to as an area or geometric model.

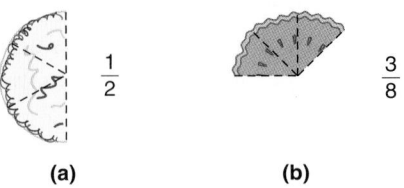

Figure 13.1 Fractions represent parts of a whole: (a) one-half of a cake is represented by the common fraction $\frac{1}{2}$; (b) three-eighths of a pizza is represented by $\frac{3}{8}$.

Set Partitioned into Equal-Size Groups

When a collection of objects is partitioned into groups of equal size, the setting is clearly one that involves division. When 12 objects are divided into two equal-size groups, the mathematical sentence $12 \div 2 = 6$ describes the setting. The child thinks, "How many cookies will each person get when a set of 12 is divided equally between two people?" The whole number 6 represents the amount of one of the two parts. A different interpretation of the same setting is to find $\frac{1}{2}$ of a set of 12 objects, or $\frac{1}{2}$ of $12 = 6$. The child thinks, "What is $\frac{1}{2}$ of a set of 12?" Now the whole number 6 refers to $\frac{1}{2}$ of the set (Figure 13.2a).

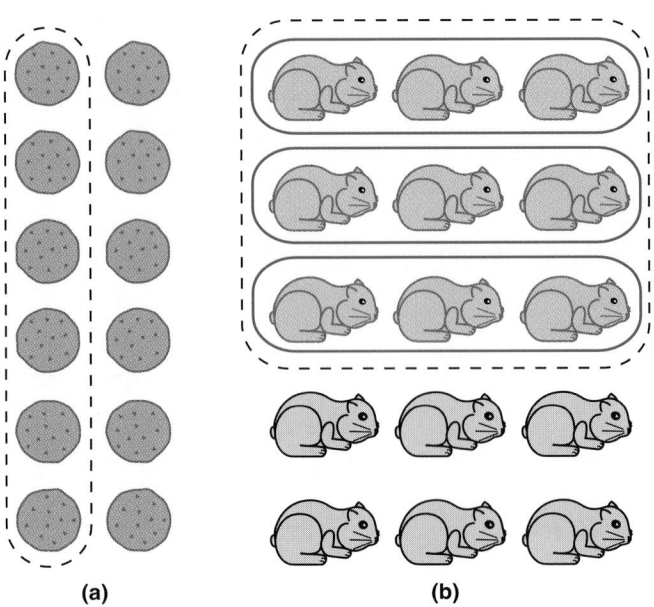

Figure 13.2 Fractions represent parts of a set: (a) 6 is $\frac{1}{2}$ of 12; (b) 9 is $\frac{3}{5}$ of 15.

If $\frac{3}{5}$ of 15 hamsters are brown, children must think of first separating the 15 hamsters into five groups of equal size. Each group of 3 hamsters relates to the size of the original set of 15 hamsters so that each group is $\frac{3}{15}$, or $\frac{1}{5}$, of the entire set. The denominator in $\frac{3}{5}$ indicates the number of equal-size parts into which the set is subdivided (5), and the numerator indicates the number of groups being considered (3). If $\frac{3}{5}$ of the 15 hamsters are brown, then there are 9 brown hamsters (Figure 13.2b).

Comparison Model

Fractional relationships can also be represented as a comparison between two sets. Figure 13.3 shows $\frac{2}{3}$ using the comparison method. The number of red buttons compared to the number of green buttons is $\frac{2}{3}$ (Figure 13.3a), as is the number of red cans compared to the number of green cans (Figure 13.3b). For 2 red buttons there are 3 green buttons, and for 2 red cans there are 3 green cans. In both cases the numerator and the denominator are distinct.

In contrast to the part-whole model for fractions, the fractional part is not embedded in the whole. Counting out or removing the numerator (2 red buttons) for examination will not affect the denominator (3 green buttons), because each part exists independently. This method of representing common fractions parallels the meaning of fraction as a ratio.

Expressions of Ratios

The relationship or comparison between two numbers is often expressed as a ratio. Although a full discussion of ratio and proportion is presented in Chapter 15, it is appropriate to briefly consider the concept of ratio here, in contrast to fraction concepts. The following are examples of common situations that exhibit ratios.

- *The relationship between things in two groups.* In a classroom in which each child has six textbooks, the ratio of each child to books is 1 to 6. This can be represented by the expression 1 to 6, 1:6, or by the common fraction numeral $\frac{1}{6}$ (Figure 13.4a).

- *The relationship between a subset of things and the set of which it is a part.* When there are 3 blue-covered books in a set of 10 books, the ratio of blue-covered books to all books is 3 to 10, 3:10, or $\frac{3}{10}$ (Figure 13.4b).

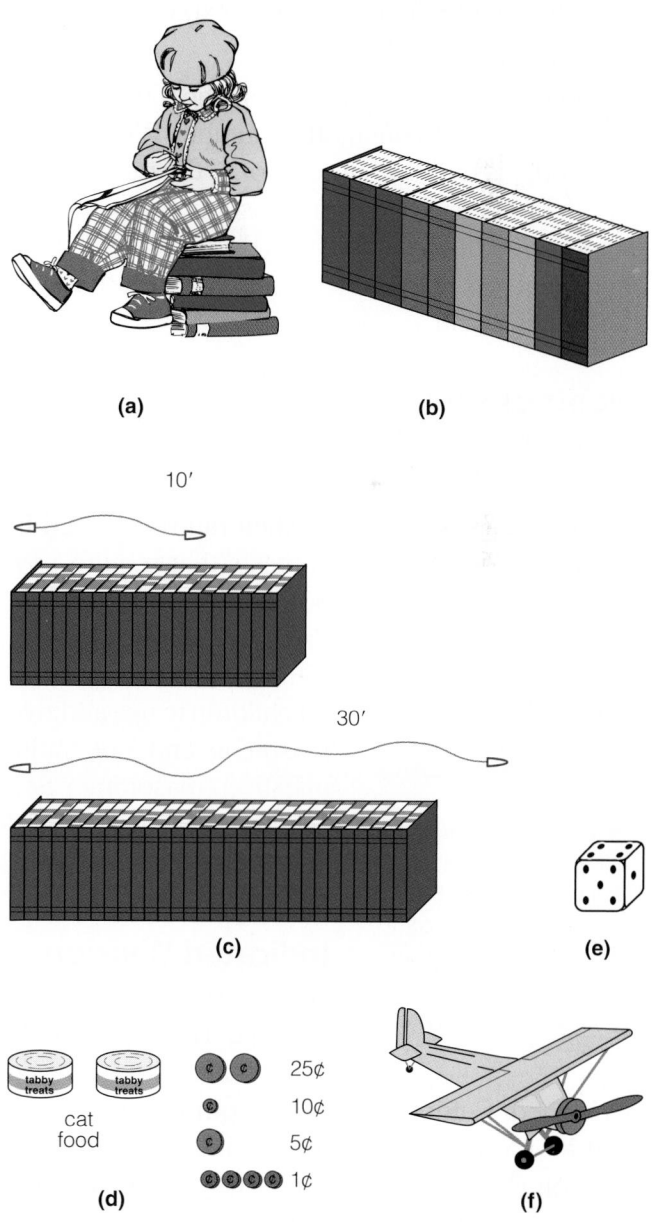

(a)   **(b)**

10′

30′

(c)   **(e)**

(d)   **(f)**

Figure 13.4 Fractions representing ratios: six examples

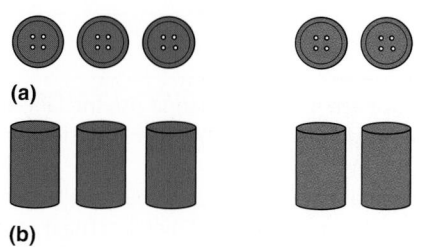

(a)

(b)

Figure 13.3 Fractions represent comparisons: (a) $\frac{2}{3}$ as many red buttons as green buttons; (b) $\frac{2}{3}$ as many red cans as green cans

- *The relationship between the sizes of two things or two sets.* When a 10-foot jump rope is compared with a 30-foot jump rope, the ratio between the two ropes is 10 to 30, 10:30, $\frac{10}{30}$, or $\frac{1}{3}$. When a set of 20 books is compared with a set of 30 books, the expressions 20 to 30, 20:30, $\frac{20}{30}$, and $\frac{2}{3}$ are used (Figure 13.4c).

- *The relationship between objects and their cost.* If the price of two cans of cat food is 69 cents, the ratio between the cans of cat food and their cost is 2 for 69, 2:69, or $\frac{2}{69}$ (Figure 13.4d).

- *The relationship between the chance of one event occurring out of all possible events.* When a regular die (*die* is singular for the plural *dice*) is rolled, the chance of rolling a 4 can be expressed as 1 in 6, 1:6, or $\frac{1}{6}$ (Figure 13.4e).

- *Ratio as an operator.* In this case the ratio is a number that acts on another number. When a toy or model is built with a scale of $\frac{1}{50}$, the ratio acts as an operator between a measurement of the model and the actual object (Figure 13.4f). If the actual object is 150 feet long, then the model is 3 feet long ($150 \times \frac{1}{50} = 3$).

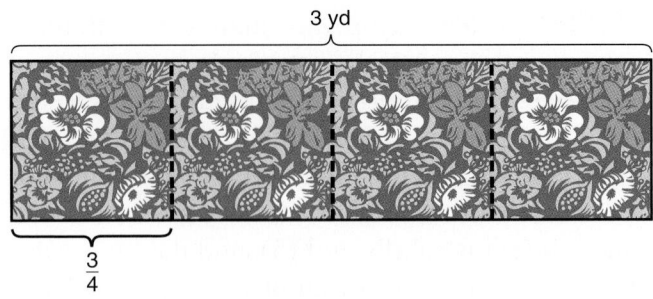

Figure 13.5 Fractions representing division: 3 yards of cloth is cut into 4 equal-sized parts; each part is $\frac{3}{4}$ yard long.

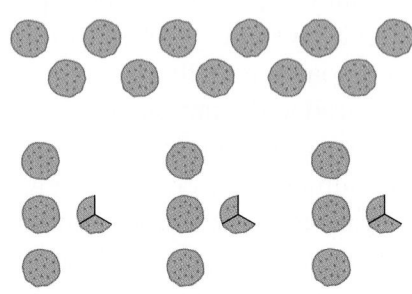

Figure 13.6 Fractions representing division: 11 cookies divided equally among 3 children; each child gets $\frac{11}{3}$, or $3\frac{2}{3}$ cookies.

When children simply form a ratio between two numbers, they will generally have little difficulty. It is when ratios are used in contexts that require proportional reasoning that difficulty can arise. In such settings, the tendency is for children to use additive reasoning and not multiplicative reasoning. See Chapter 15 where ratio and proportional reasoning is discussed more fully.

Indicated Division

Sentences such as $3 \div 4 = ?$ and $11 \div 3 = ?$ indicate that division is to be performed. Cutting a piece of cloth that is 3 yards long into four equal-size pieces illustrates the first situation (Figure 13.5). Another way to indicate this division is by using the common fraction numeral $\frac{3}{4}$. A setting that illustrates the second sentence is the equal sharing of 11 cookies by three children (Figure 13.6). Division for the second sentence can be expressed as $\frac{11}{3}$. When the division is completed, the answer (3 with a remainder of 2) can be represented as the mixed numeral $3\frac{2}{3}$, or each child's fair share of the 11 cookies.

The term *numerator* is derived from the Latin term *numeros*, meaning "number," and *denominator* is from the Latin term *denominaire*, meaning "namer." Thus the denominator names the fraction (according to how many parts make up the whole), and the numerator indicates the number of individual parts. (Bright & Hoffner, 1993)

The first European mathematician to use the familiar fraction bar was Leonardo of Pisa (c. 1175–1250), better known as Fibonacci.

The horizontal fraction bar symbol ($\frac{3}{4}$) is called an *obelus*, from the Greek word meaning "obelisk." The diagonal fraction bar symbol (3/4) is called a *solidus*. The term is derived from the Latin term meaning "monetary unit."

Research for the Classroom

An interesting research finding involves the difference between representing a common fraction with a set of discrete objects and representing it with a continuous object. Hunting (1999) found that young children can represent a common fraction of a set of marbles by setting aside some of the marbles, as for example, setting aside two out of a set of six marbles to represent $\frac{1}{3}$ of the set. The same children had great difficulty marking $\frac{1}{3}$ of a rectangle or separating $\frac{1}{3}$ of a licorice stick. Many children could not represent any common fractions at all with continuous objects. Thus, although children may appear to have a good understanding of fraction representation when using discrete objects, they may require more experience with common fractions before they can represent common fractions with continuous objects such as a number line.

Introducing Common Fractions to Children

Primary-grade children typically encounter common fractions through work with real objects and models while learning about simple common fractions such as halves, thirds, and fourths. Small sets of objects can also be separated into equal-size groups. Early on, common fraction numerals such as $\frac{1}{2}$ or $\frac{1}{4}$ are introduced as names for common fractions, but foundational understanding of fractions continues throughout the primary grades. Children label parts of wholes or sets as *one-half* and *two-thirds* or refer to *one part out of two parts* or *two parts out of three parts*. When students do begin to write common fraction numerals, they should write their fractions with a horizontal bar, not a diagonal one. A horizontal fraction bar will make future operations with fractions, especially multiplication and division, much easier (see Chapter 14). As understanding of the concepts of common fractions for parts of units and parts of groups becomes established, children will be able to work with other common fractions (fifths, sixths, eighths, and tenths) and will learn to recognize and name the parts of numerals such as $\frac{3}{5}$, $\frac{2}{6}$, and $\frac{3}{8}$. When children use realistic settings, stories, and models of common fractions, they recognize that a given common fraction, such as $\frac{1}{2}$, has many equivalent common fractions, such as $\frac{2}{4}$, $\frac{3}{6}$, and $\frac{4}{8}$. The following photo shows typical commercial models for elementary school children. Many teachers have children use paper circles, squares, rectangles, and triangles and drawings when commercial materials are not available.

Fraction kit

Image courtesy of ETA/Cuisenaire

MULTICULTURALCONNECTION

Antonio y Oliveres, a Spanish mathematician writing in Mexico in the mid 1800s, first began the use of the solidus (/) to represent fractions. The solidus is a popular alternative to the common fraction bar because it allows printers to set type for fractions on a single line.

Partitioning Single Things

Most children have experiences in which they share parts of whole objects or collections of objects by using fractional parts long before the concept of common fractions is introduced in school. They help parents and others cut and share pizzas, cookies, sandwiches, and myriad other items. These and similar common experiences can be illustrated on a bulletin board to form a basis for discussing the process of cutting things into parts and sharing pieces (Figure 13.7).

Squares, rectangles, circles, and other shapes cut from paper can extend real-life experiences during introductory activities. Activity 13.1 shows one

We share many kinds of food.

Figure 13.7 A bulletin board can be used to show how food is shared.

way to help young children use the share concept to learn about one-half. Children can also fold paper shapes to show fourths and eighths and to show thirds and sixths, as shown in Figures 13.8 and 13.9.

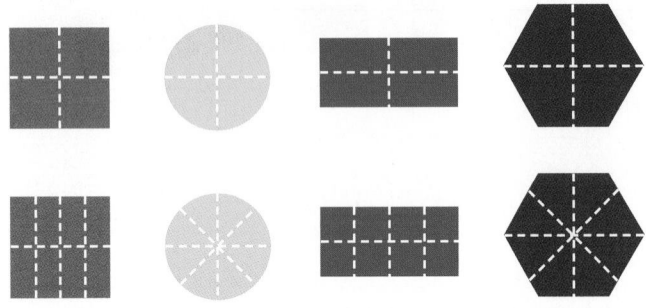

Figure 13.8 Geometric regions to show fourths and eighths

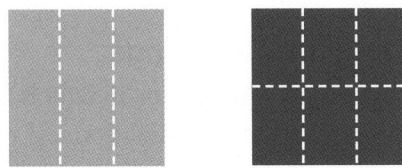

Figure 13.9 Squares marked to show where to fold to make thirds and sixths

Folding a shape to show three equivalent parts is difficult, so fold lines should be marked to show how to fold the shape during early experiences. When the idea of fair shares is well understood and the idea of cutting regions into equivalent pieces is clear, numerals for common fractions can be introduced. You might begin with a shape cut into four equivalent pieces: "Into how many parts has this

shape been cut?" (Answer: 4.) "How many parts is my finger touching?" (Answer: 1.) Write $\frac{1}{4}$ on the chalkboard. Repeat a similar dialogue with $\frac{1}{3}$, $\frac{1}{2}$, and other familiar fractions. Help children recognize that the bottom numeral indicates the *number* of parts into which the unit has been cut and that the top numeral indicates *one* of the parts. Children typically refer to the numerator as the "top number" and the denominator as the "bottom number."

Accept Their Language in Early Work. Insisting that primary school children use the terms *numerator* and *denominator* may serve only to complicate their understanding of fractions. As children mature and meanings become established, introduce the terms *denominator* and *numerator* to identify the two parts of a common fraction.

As work advances, children need activities that extend beyond unit fractions. A **unit fraction** is one in which the numerator is 1. Activities similar to Activity 13.1 should be used to develop understanding of fractions with numerators other than 1, such as $\frac{2}{3}$, $\frac{2}{4}$, and $\frac{3}{4}$. (See Black-Line Masters 13.1, 13.2, and 13.3 for fraction circle and fraction strips templates.) See "Quarters, Quarts, and More Quarters: A Fraction Unit" on the companion website for an example of a fraction unit that introduces simple common and decimal fractions.

ⒺXERCISE

Use fraction manipulatives to solve the following problem: If 9 hamsters are $\frac{3}{5}$ of the total number of hamsters in a pet store, how many hamsters are there? ●●●

Assessing Knowledge of Common Fractions

A quick way to assess children's understanding that common fractions represent fair-share, or equivalent, parts of a whole is by using shapes that show both examples and nonexamples of the fractions. Prepare some shapes that have shading showing halves, thirds, or fourths and other shapes showing nonexamples of halves, thirds, or fourths (Figure 13.10). You can gain a good idea of a child's understanding by placing the shapes in an array and directing the child, "Point to each shape that shows $\frac{1}{4}$, $\frac{1}{2}$, $\frac{1}{3}$." When a child correctly identifies all the halves,

ACTIVITY 13.1 Introducing Halves (Representation)

Level: Kindergarten and Grade 1

Setting: Whole class

Objective: Students develop the concept of one-half.

Materials: Large circles, squares, and rectangles cut from newsprint or colored construction paper

- If space permits, have children sit on the floor in a semi-circle, with you at the opening (they can work at their tables or desks, if necessary).

- Nearly all young children have experiences with "fair share" settings. Asking children to tell of their experiences will elicit comments that reveal the extent of their knowledge of the concept of sharing things.

- Give each child one of the shapes cut from newsprint or colored construction paper. Ask them to name a type of food each shape might represent (e.g., circle: pizza, tortilla, cake, pie, cookie; square: brownie, waffle; rectangle: cake, lasagna, candy bar). Tell them that they are to fold each shape so that there are two fair-share parts. Challenge them to see if a shape can be folded in more than one way to form two fair shares.

- Use the folded shapes to develop new knowledge. Have children discuss and show their fair shares. Be sure that

children with unique folds have opportunities to show and explain their work. It is easy to see that two parts are the same size when a rectangle is folded along a center line so the opposite edges come together. It is more difficult to see that pieces are the same size when a fold is made along a diagonal or in some other way. It may be necessary to cut along a fold line so that one piece can be flipped or rotated to make it fit atop the second piece. Help children see that even though a circle can be folded many times to show halves, the fold is always made in the same way.

- Develop understanding of the children's knowledge by saying, "Raise your left thumb if you can tell me what we call each part when we make two fair-share parts" (Answer: one-half.) Discuss the meaning of one-half.

- Reflect on their knowledge by asking children to name times when they have used one-half. They might discuss such things as $\frac{1}{2}$ of an hour, an apple, a candy bar, or a soft drink.

---

thirds, and fourths, verify the understanding by asking, "Are there any other fourths (halves, thirds) shown on the shapes?" A child who is certain will say no. Table 13.2 provides a scoring rubric for this assessment. In Activity 13.2 children fold an equilateral triangle into smaller shapes and compare the area of each resulting part to the whole area of the original triangle. In Activity 13.3 children use Cuisenaire rods to explore part-whole relationships of common fractions.

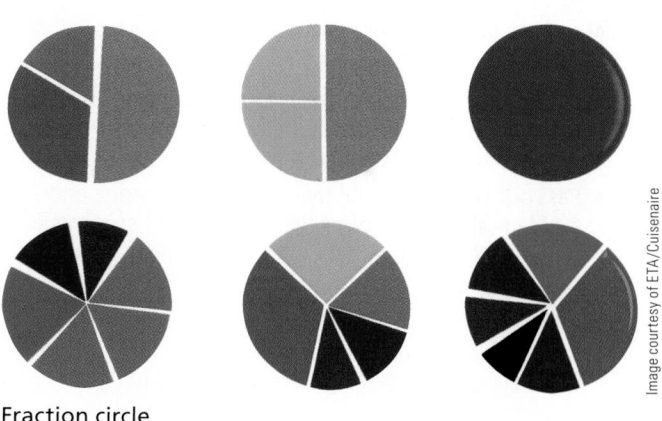

Fraction circle

Image courtesy of ETA/Cuisenaire

Figure 13.10 Shape cards for testing understanding of examples and nonexamples of $\frac{1}{2}, \frac{1}{3}$, and $\frac{1}{4}$

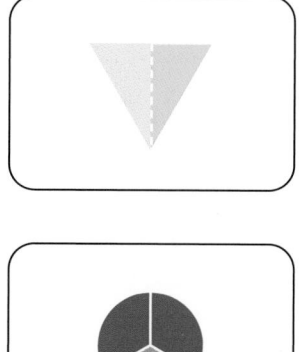
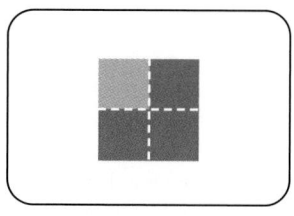
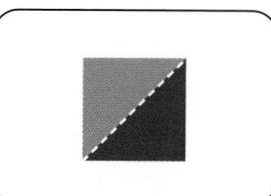
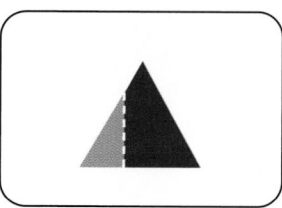
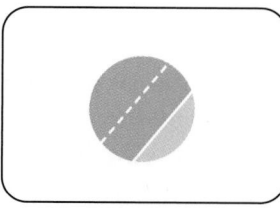

TABLE 13.2 ● Scoring Rubric for Assessing Understanding of Unit Fractions

Inadequate Product or Solution	Acceptable Product or Solution	Superior Product or Solution
Doesn't understand the concept	Develops the concept	Understands/applies the concept
Identifies few or no examples or nonexamples of $\frac{1}{2}$, $\frac{1}{3}$, or $\frac{1}{4}$	Identifies most but not all examples of $\frac{1}{2}$, $\frac{1}{3}$, or $\frac{1}{4}$; is uncertain of some nonexamples	Identifies all shapes correctly
Unable to explain why a display is or is not a representation of $\frac{1}{2}$, $\frac{1}{3}$, or $\frac{1}{4}$	Able to explain each shape as an example of $\frac{1}{2}$, $\frac{1}{3}$, or $\frac{1}{4}$; unsure about some nonexamples	Gives clear explanation of why shapes are examples or nonexamples

ACTIVITY 13.2   Fractions on a Triangle (Connection)

Level: Grades 2 and 3

Setting: Student pairs

Objective: Students identify various fractional parts of an equilateral triangle.

Materials: Two equilateral triangles (see Black-Line Master 13.4), scissors

- Pair students by their order in your class roster. Pair the first student and the last student, the second student and the next-to-last student, and so forth.

- Pass out two equilateral triangle sheets, scissors, and a data table to each pair of students. Direct students to work through the folding steps given here. Be sure that students fill in the data table following each question.

  1. Cut out both equilateral triangles.

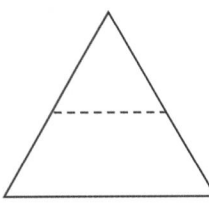

  2. Fold on the dotted line shown here so that the top angle of the triangle touches the middle of the bottom side.

  3. What shape is this new figure? If the original triangle has an area of 1, what fraction area is this new figure?

  4. Fold on the new dotted line shown here to get another shape.

  5. What shape is this new figure? If the original triangle has an area of 1, what fraction area is new figure?

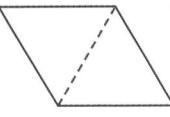

  6. Fold again, this time along the new dotted line shown here.

  7. What shape is this new figure? If the original triangle has an area of 1, what fraction area is this new figure?

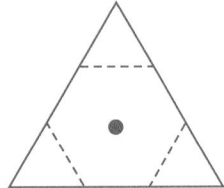

  8. Take the other equilateral triangle and fold on the dotted lines shown here so that each vertex folds onto the center point.

  9. What shape is this new figure? If the original triangle has an area of 1, what fraction area is this new figure?

Triangle Fractions Data Table

Draw your folded shape.	Name the shape.	What fraction is the shape compared to the original equilateral triangle?
1.		
2.		
3.		
4.		

ACTIVITY 13.3 Cuisenaire Fractions

Level: Grades 1–3

Setting: Student pairs

Objective: Students look to identify different Cuisenaire rods as fractional parts of longer rods.

Materials: Full set of Cuisenaire rods (10 white rods, 5 of each other color) for each pair of students; overhead set of Cuisenaire rods

- Display teal, green, red, and white rods on the overhead.

- Ask students to speculate about which color rod is exactly half the length of the teal rod.

- Once students have a chance to give their thoughts, discuss how to be sure which rod is actually half. Probe for using two same-color rods to line up with the teal rod for an exact fit. Because two green rods are the same length as a single teal rod, each green rod represents half the teal rod ($\frac{1}{2}t = g$, where t represents the length of the teal rod and g represents the length of the green rod).

- Speculate aloud about whether there are other combinations of same-color rods that are the same length as the teal rod. Have students explore this possibility with their partners, using their Cuisenaire rods. Children should find that six white or three red rods are the same length as the teal rod.

- Suggest to students that there are rods that have equal-length same-color combinations. Their task is to search for them and record their findings by making sketches of their rods and writing out the fractions shown by the shorter rods.

- Post the results on the board. Once all students' findings are posted, ask if students notice anything missing. The red, black, green, and yellow rods have no same-color combinations except white that match their lengths. As it turns out, these are prime numbers. Although you may not be ready to introduce such a concept or the vocabulary, simply noting the fact that some lengths or numbers cannot be divided up evenly into part-whole pieces (except for unit pieces) will lay the foundation for later work with prime and composite numbers.

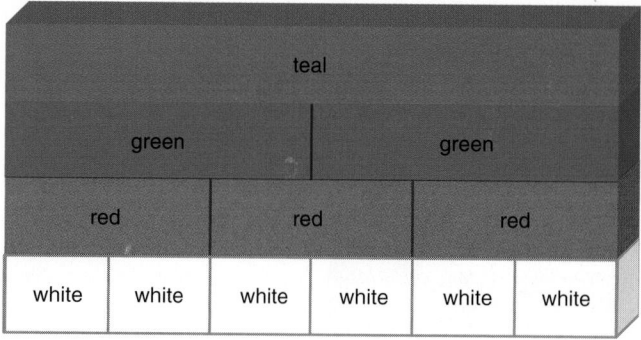

(b) Green is $\frac{1}{2}$ of teal

Red is $\frac{1}{3}$ of teal

White is $\frac{1}{6}$ of teal

(a) Green is $\frac{1}{2}$ of teal

ⒺXERCISE

Describe several common objects or settings to use during an introductory partitioning-a-whole activity and a partitioning-a-set activity, other than the ones used in the text. Draw a simple picture to illustrate a partitioning-a-whole setting and a partitioning-a-set setting. ●●●

Another example of a representation of a part-whole relationship might be a number line. In the number line shown in Figure 13.11, $\frac{1}{3}$ is shaded. As in the Unifix cubes example on page 265, some students may compare the shaded portion of a number line to the unshaded portion, rather than to the entire line segment. Thus they may see the part-part relationship, or $\frac{1}{2}$, instead of the part-whole relationship of $\frac{1}{3}$. Although it can be beneficial to represent any mathematics concepts with different models, it might be best to use the number line representation after basic concepts are introduced and understood. One research study (Ball, 1993) indicates that the only students who beneficially used a number line in their study of fractions were those who

Figure 13.11 Number line representing $\frac{1}{3}$

ACTIVITY 13.4   The Fraction Wheel

Level: Grades 1–3

Setting: Whole class

Objective: Students develop their ability to identify common fractions in an area model.

Materials: An angle wheel (see Black-Line Masters 13.5 and 13.6)

- Draw a circle on the board with $\frac{1}{4}$ shaded. Ask a student volunteer to explain how much of the circle is shaded.

- Draw a second circle on the board, this time with $\frac{2}{3}$ shaded. Again ask a student volunteer to explain how much of the circle is shaded.

- Show the angle wheel with $\frac{1}{4}$ shaded. Ask a volunteer to explain how much of the shaded part is showing. Be sure that all the children understand that the shaded part of the angle wheel shows part-whole fractions, then have a second student explain why the correct answer matches the shaded part showing on the fraction wheel. Use only unit fractions at first so that all the shaded portions are less than half of the circle.

- Quickly show a different angle, and call on a student to give the part-whole fraction that the shading represents.

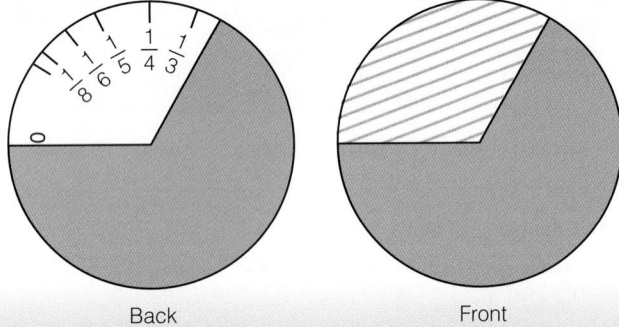

Back   Front

If the answer is incorrect, quickly move to another student for another answer.

- Continue until a student gives the correct answer, and then have another student explain why the correct answer matches the shaded part showing on the fraction wheel.

- Show several unit fractions to the class ($\frac{1}{2}$, $\frac{1}{3}$, $\frac{1}{4}$, $\frac{1}{5}$, $\frac{1}{6}$, and $\frac{1}{8}$), and repeat the unit fractions as needed, so that each child has an opportunity to give an answer and/or explain an answer.

- Once all the children have had an opportunity to give or explain at least one answer, show a common fraction between $\frac{1}{2}$ and 1, such as $\frac{2}{3}$. When you display $\frac{2}{3}$, ask the children how this new fraction is different from all the preceding fractions. Probe for the concept that this fraction is greater than $\frac{1}{2}$. That means that no unit fractions can be represented by shading that is greater than $\frac{1}{2}$ the circle. Show several fractions greater than $\frac{1}{2}$ ($\frac{3}{4}$, $\frac{2}{3}$, $\frac{5}{6}$, $\frac{7}{8}$, . . .) following the same procedure with the wheel as before.

- As students explain answers, probe for the half-circle as a *benchmark* to help determine the value of the common fraction.

- Now display any of the preceding fractions on the angle wheel, mixing all the common fractions used to this point. The goal of the activity is to move quickly from one student to another as they give estimates of the part-whole fraction you display on the angle wheel. Although it is not critical that students be able to discriminate $\frac{1}{6}$ from $\frac{1}{8}$, the first few times you work with the angle wheel, all the children should be able to use $\frac{1}{2}$ (and possibly $\frac{1}{4}$ and $\frac{3}{4}$) as a benchmark to help them make a reasonable estimate of the part-whole fraction that the angle wheel displays.

had already developed their foundational conceptions of fractions and part-whole relationships. A manipulative called the fraction wheel is the focus in Activity 13.4. When students use two pieces to model common fractions, they can manipulate and even remove the part without affecting the whole. The companion website activity "Mystery Fraction Pieces" uses a circle to build children's foundational understanding of part-whole relationships. Fraction stencils shown in the photo allow children to make their own fraction representations. The companion website activity "Tangram Fractions" explores fractions in an area representation using tangram pieces. "A Handful of Fractions" is another activity on the companion website that stresses the set model of

Fraction stencils

MISCONCEPTION

When children use manipulatives to model part-whole relationship of fractions, they may use an area model (see Activity 13.4) or a linear model to represent fractions. However, when children are beginning to formulate fractions from either model, they may form several different fractions from the same setting. Note the Unifix cube train in Figure 13.12. A student trying to write what fraction of the train is blue may write $\frac{2}{3}$ and not $\frac{2}{5}$. Do you see why?

The child is comparing the part of the train that is blue (2) to the remaining part of the train that is green (3) instead of to the entire length of the train (5). The child sees a part-part relationship and not a part-whole relationship. One reason this happens is that young children remove the blue cubes from the train and then try to make sense of what remains. With the area and linear models for part-whole relationships, once the numerator pieces are removed, there is no longer any whole to use as a reference. The whole no longer exists as a model.

Students can make a similar error with the array shown in Figure 13.13. The fraction that represents the part-whole relationship for green squares is $\frac{3}{8}$, but children who are just beginning to express fractions might render it as a part-part relationship, or $\frac{3}{5}$. It is important to help children in these early stages to be sure they do not develop such misunderstandings, which can become difficult to break, and thus hold back their advancement in laying a foundation for fraction concepts.

Figure 13.12 Unifix cube train

Figure 13.13 Unifix array representing $\frac{3}{8}$

---

fractions. A vignette on the website illustrates how California teacher Dee Uyeda had her third-graders work in cooperative groups to further their understanding of fractions.

Partitioning Sets of Objects

The concept of a fractional part of a set should be introduced only after children demonstrate that they can conserve numbers, have a good grasp of whole numbers, and are skillful in counting objects in sets. Activity 13.5 provides a real-world setting for dealing with fractional parts of groups. Later, children should be able to partition sets into equal-size groups without using fractional regions or markers as cues. As they work, children notice that not every set can be separated into equal parts with a whole-number answer for each part. This realization sets the stage for understanding mixed numerals and common fractions greater than 1.

Fractional Numbers Greater than 1

Many students seem to believe that all fractions are between 0 and 1. This is why students need opportunities to deal with common fractions greater than 1,

such as $\frac{6}{3}$, $\frac{3}{2}$, and $\frac{9}{4}$. Pictures cut from magazines can be used to present real-world settings for introducing these numerals. Later, paper shapes and number lines can be used as representations of common fractions. The pizza problem discussed earlier provides a real-world setting for looking at common fractions with numerators greater than denominators. Children see that if the family of three gets one pizza, the family of six must have two pizzas to have the same amount of pizza per person. When one pizza is cut into three equal-size parts, the common fraction is $\frac{3}{3}$. When two pizzas are each cut into three equal-size pieces, the common fraction is $\frac{6}{3}$. When two pies are each cut into six equal-size pieces, the common fraction is $\frac{12}{6}$. When two and one-half cakes are cut into six equal-size parts, the common fraction is $\frac{15}{6}$. Figure 13.14 illustrates each of these common fractions modeled with pictures of popular food items. Common fractions with numerators greater than the denominator have traditionally been called *improper* fractions. But it is more meaningful to children to call them common fractions that are greater, or larger, than 1. Fractional numbers greater than 1 are sometimes converted to whole numbers

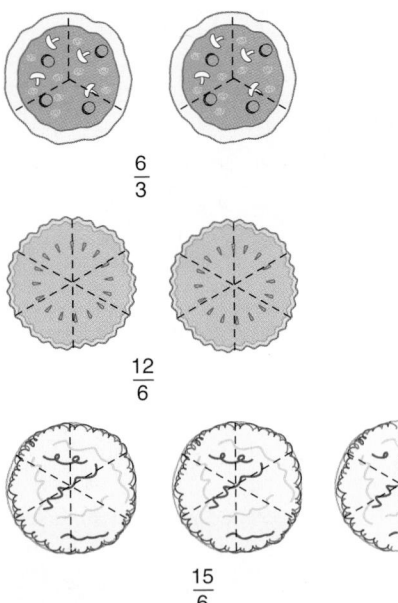

$$\frac{6}{3}$$

$$\frac{12}{6}$$

$$\frac{15}{6}$$

Figure 13.14 Fractional numbers greater than 1 represented by common items of food

or to a combination of a whole number and a common fraction. The term *mixed numeral* refers to a combination of a whole number and a fractional number. When 13 cookies are divided fairly among four people, the common fraction $\frac{13}{4}$ can be used to represent the result. This is an indicated division interpretation of a common fraction. Twelve cookies are divided into four groups of three cookies each, and the remaining cookie is cut into four equal-size parts. Each person gets three whole cookies and $\frac{1}{4}$ of another, or $3\frac{1}{4}$ cookies. The number $3\frac{1}{4}$ is read "three *and* one-fourth." This is because a mixed number is composed of a whole number (3) and a common fraction ($\frac{1}{4}$). When students read mixed numbers, call their attention to the word *and* in the number name. Have children explain why the word *and* is critical in understanding the mixed number they are reading. One last aspect of common fraction value is worth mentioning here, in the form of a question:

ACTIVITY 13.5   The Fruit Dealer and His Apples (Communication)

Level: Grades 3–5

Setting: Cooperative learning

Objective: Students demonstrate strategies for finding nonunit parts of a collection of objects.

Materials: Green or yellow plastic beads or disks; small pieces of paper to represent bags

- Organize children for a pairs/check cooperative-learning experience.
- The activity develops as children use beads or disks to represent apples. Present this story: "A fruit dealer has 36 Granny Smith apples. He wants to put his apples in bags with an equal number of apples in each bag. How many different ways can he bag the apples so that each bag contains the same number of apples?"
- One student in each pair groups the apples without consulting the partner. When the student is finished, the part-

ner accepts or rejects the way the apples were grouped. A written record of the grouping is made. The students alternate making groupings until they agree that all possible groupings have been made and they have recorded all the groupings. Pair by pair, ask children to report on one way they separated the apples. Some pairs may have only two or three groupings; others may have all possible groupings. As each pair reports, ask, "What part of 36 apples is each of your two groups? three groups? four groups?" and so on. List groupings and fractional parts on the chalkboard: 2 apples are $\frac{1}{18}$ of 36, 3 apples are $\frac{1}{12}$ of 36, and so on.

- Have children use the information on the chalkboard to deal with nonunit common fractions: "If you buy two bags that each contain 6 apples, what part of the 36 apples do you have?" Continue with other fractional parts of 36, such as $\frac{3}{4}$, $\frac{2}{3}$, and $\frac{5}{6}$. (Children's level of understanding of and ability to solve earlier problems will determine how many problems you present.)
- Discussion following each question enables children to reflect on their learning by confirming the accuracy of their work.

Is $\frac{1}{2} > \frac{1}{3}$? Are you sure? Consider this conversation between two fourth-graders, who are comparing the two fraction pieces shown in Figure 13.15.

Denyse: I still say one-half has to be bigger than one-third. Remember that the more pieces you need to make a whole, the smaller each piece is.

Alexa: I know, but look at this piece. It's $\frac{1}{3}$, but it's a lot bigger than this piece $(\frac{1}{2})$.

Denyse: You're right. It is bigger. Hmm. Maybe it's if the bottom number is bigger, then the fraction is bigger.

Alexa: But that's not what we did yesterday.

Denyse: I know, but look at the two pieces. One-third is bigger than one-half.

Alexa: I know. That's what I said.

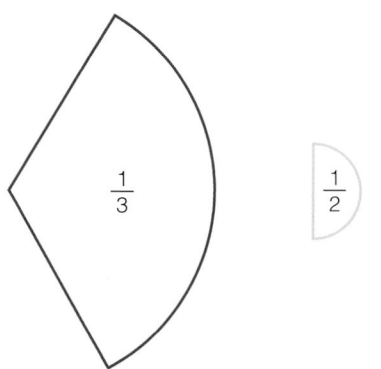

Figure 13.15 Is $\frac{1}{2}$ greater than $\frac{1}{3}$?

As you can see in Figure 13.15, the $\frac{1}{3}$ piece is certainly larger than the $\frac{1}{2}$ piece. What is confusing these students? They are comparing fractional pieces from two different-size wholes. The $\frac{1}{3}$ piece is from a larger circle than is the $\frac{1}{2}$ piece. The $\frac{1}{3}$ piece is larger than the $\frac{1}{2}$ piece in the same sense that $\frac{1}{3}$ of 300 (100) is larger than $\frac{1}{2}$ of 100 (50). Many students have this misconception because common fraction comparisons are done with abstract number representations, devoid of context. Although using numerical expressions out of context is not inappropriate and is, in fact, useful for practicing many mathematical operations, it is still important to stress that all common fractions must be based on the same whole set in order to be compared.

Activity 13.6 is an Internet activity that uses virtual manipulatives as area models of fractions to explore fractional numbers greater than 1.

Introducing Decimal Fractions

Decimal fractions are used to find parts of units and of collections of objects, just as common fractions are. The difference between the two fractional numbers is that the denominator of a common fraction can be any whole number except 0, whereas decimal fractions are confined to tenths, hundredths, and other powers of 10.

Teaching children about decimal fractions along with the study of common fractions is an integral part of the mathematics curriculum in the primary grades. The goal in the early grades is to lay a foundation that enables older students to avoid misconceptions and procedural difficulties. Children who investigate the meaning of decimal fractions and learn about them through activities with models will have the understanding needed for more advanced concepts and uses in later grades. An understanding of decimal fractions and their relationship with common fractions develops gradually, so work with physical materials, diagrams, and real-world settings is extended over a period of years.

Children's understanding of whole numbers and common fractions forms the basis for their understanding of decimal fractions. Real-world examples of things separated into tenths and hundredths are

---

ACTIVITY 13.6 Exploring Fractions (Internet Lesson)

Level: Grades 3–5

Setting: Pairs of students

Objective: Students use an Internet applet to explore improper fractions.

Materials: Internet access

- Go to http://illuminations.nctm.org/Activities.aspx?grade=2. Click on Fraction Models II.

- Have students use the circle representation of fractions.

- Have students enter larger values into the numerator than the denominator and observe the resulting circle representation. Repeat for these four fractions: $\frac{8}{11}, \frac{5}{2}, \frac{7}{4}, \frac{10}{3}$.

- Repeat with the rectangle representation.

- Ask students to explain how to represent $\frac{7}{3}$ using circles and using rectangles. Students can then use the applet to check their answers.

less common than are examples of common fractions. Metric units of measure, such as a meter stick, can represent decimal fractions, as does our monetary system. White and orange Cuisenaire rods also display a decimal relationship. Commercial or student-made materials are needed for individual and group activities. Any commercial base-10 product can serve as a model to represent decimal fractions. When base-10 materials are used, a large flat becomes a unit, a rod a one-tenth piece, and a small cube a one-hundredth piece.

Base-10 blocks

When commercial materials are unavailable, colored construction paper with half-inch or centimeter squares can be laminated and cut to make an activities kit. Each child might make a kit consisting of 10 square mats that are 10 units along each side, 20 strips that are 1 unit wide and 10 units long, and 150 one-unit squares.

Introducing Tenths

Activities involving different materials help children acquire a well-developed understanding of tenths and decimal notation for tenths. When children learn to write whole numbers, a decimal point is not part of the number. It is not needed because the whole number represents one or more whole units. Decimal numbers indicate that parts of units are involved. The decimal point separates the whole-number part of a numeral from the fractional part of a numeral. When only a decimal part of a numeral is written, it is common practice to write a zero in the ones place of the numeral, as in 0.3. The zero helps make it clear that the numeral indicates a decimal fraction. When no zero is written, it is possible to overlook the decimal point and misread the numeral.

A zero after the decimal point, as in 1.0, also has meaning. In 1.0 it indicates that a unit has been separated into 10 parts and that all 10 parts are being considered; it is equivalent to the common fraction $\frac{10}{10}$, and the zero should not be omitted. The decimal point also indicates precision of measurement, indicating that 3.0 meters, for example, is accurate to the nearest tenth, in contrast to 3 meters, which may have been rounded to the nearest meter.

> **MULTICULTURALCONNECTION**
> Any activities that use money can use currency and coins from the native countries of minority students.

Activity 13.7 illustrates an introductory lesson using Cuisenaire rods. Construction paper can replace the rods in this lesson. In Activity 13.8 a strip of paper with units separated into 10 equal-size parts is used to extend decimal fractions beyond 1. In Activity 13.9 a decimal fraction number line is used.

> Flemish mathematician Simon Stevin (1542–1620) first used decimal fractions in his book *La Thiende*. When he wrote common decimals, Stevin used a small circle instead of a decimal point. The word *dime* is derived from the title of the French translation of his book, *La Disme*.

Introducing Hundredths

Children's understanding of the decimal fraction representation of hundredths is developed through extension of activities with tenths. The hundredth pieces are included in kits for the new activities. An introductory lesson is shown in Activity 13.10. An activity built around Cuisenaire rods and a meter stick is useful for helping students to understand tenths and hundredths and to show how decimal fractions are used to indicate parts of a meter. Let children work in groups of three or four. Each group has a meter stick, 10 orange rods, and 100 small cubes. First, the children align the 10 rods end to end alongside the meter stick (Figure 13.16).

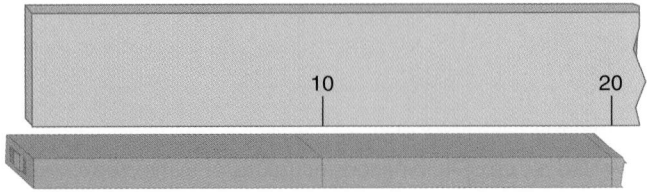

Figure 13.16 A meter stick and Cuisenaire rods used to show tenths

ACTIVITY 13.7 Introducing Tenths

Level: Grades 2–4

Setting: Whole class

Objective: Students are able to explain the meaning of decimal tenths.

Materials: Cuisenaire flats, orange rods (construction paper may be used instead)

- When they are used with whole numbers, a large flat in a Cuisenaire set is considered to be 100, an orange rod 10, and a white cube 1. Tell the children that for this lesson, each flat represents one unit, or 1.

- Tell each child to cover a flat with orange rods.

- Ask, "How many rods does it take to cover the unit piece?" Verify with the children that there are 10. Ask, "What part of the unit piece is covered by one rod?" Verify that it is 1 of 10, or $\frac{1}{10}$. Write $\frac{1}{10}$ on the chalkboard.

- Ask volunteers to give names for two rods or strips (2 of 10, or $\frac{2}{10}$), three rods or strips (3 of 10, or $\frac{3}{10}$), and so on,

until $\frac{9}{10}$ is reached and all common fractions have been written on the chalkboard.

- Introduce the decimal notation 0.1, and write it next to the $\frac{1}{10}$. Tell the children that both numerals are read as "one-tenth." Select students to write decimal fractions for each of the other common fractions.

- Tell the students that 1.0 is the numeral to use when all 10 parts are being considered. The decimal point and zero indicate that the unit has been cut into 10 parts and that all 10 parts are being considered.

- Use money to help children understand how a dime shows one-tenth of a dollar. Display a dollar bill and ask, "What coin is one-tenth of a dollar?" (Answer: dime.) "What two ways can we write the value of a dime?" (Answer: 10 cents or $0.10.) Ask, "Three dimes are what part of a dollar?" (Answer: $\frac{3}{10}$.) "What two ways can you write 30 cents?" Repeat with other numbers of dimes. (Note: Do not use either a nickel or a quarter during these early decimal fraction activities. Neither coin supports the base-10 aspect of common decimals.)

- Summarize the lesson by pointing out that the common fractions and the decimal fractions are both ways to designate the same quantity.

ACTIVITY 13.8 Fraction-Strip Tenths

Level: Grades 2–4

Setting: Cooperative learning

Objective: Students are introduced to mixed decimals and money as an application of decimal fractions.

Materials: One 3-unit-long fraction strip for each pair of children; a die for each pair; plastic dimes or dime-stamped squares of paper

- Organize the children as partner pairs. Give each pair a fraction strip, a die, and replica dimes.

1									
0.1	0.1	0.1	0.1	0.1	0.1	0.1	0.1	0.1	0.1

- Present these instructions: You will take turns to roll your die four times. After each roll, the partner not rolling the die covers the strip, one square at a time, with enough dimes to equal the number showing on the die for that roll. When you have finished the four rolls, write numbers with a dollar sign to show the total value of the dimes on your strip.

- When all have completed their rolls, call for attention, then write the words "low," "middle," and "high" on the chalkboard. In their pairs, students decide whether they have a low, middle, or high amount of money and then

tell in which column to place their money. Write the dollar values beneath the words.

- Have students remove the dimes and mark an X in place of each one, then write the decimal numeral that indicates the number of tenths covered by X's. Write the decimal numerals alongside the corresponding dollar amounts, and compare the two numerals. (The difference will be the dollar sign and a zero in the hundredths place in each money numeral.)

- This lesson presents a good opportunity to discuss ideas related to the probability of events occurring (see Chapter 20). For example, you can discuss the smallest number of squares (4) and the highest number of squares (24) that could be covered. "What would have to occur if only four squares were covered?" (Answer: Four 1's would be rolled.) "If 24 squares were covered?" (Answer: Four 6's would be rolled.) "Did this happen with any of you?" "Why are there more numbers in the middle column than in the low or the high column?" (Answer: The likelihood of getting four 1's or four 6's is much less than that of getting a mixture of numbers. A mixture of numbers will be closer to the middle.)

ACTIVITY 13.9 Number-Line Decimals

Level: Grades 2–4

Setting: Cooperative learning

Objective: Students are introduced to a decimal fraction number line and lay a foundation for adding and subtracting decimal fractions.

Materials: Duplicated copies of decimal numbers lines with tenths to 3.0, pencils, paper

- Organize children in pairs for a send-a-problem activity. Each pair has a duplicated copy of the number line, two pieces of paper, and a pencil. Each pair is to write four questions of the following type: Where do you stop when you start at 0 and go seven steps along the line? Where

do you stop when you start at 0.4 and move eight steps to the right? Where do you stop if you start at 1.7 and move three steps to the left? Pairs write their questions on one paper and their answers on the second paper.

- Each pair exchanges papers with the other pair on its team and answers the questions. When all questions are completed, students meet in groups of four to check their answers.

- Students take turns reading the decimal numerals for their answers. Each group is to resolve any situations in which there are discrepant answers.

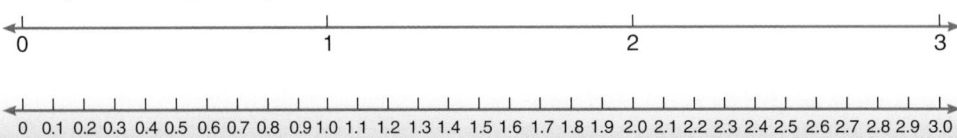

ACTIVITY 13.10 Introducing Hundredths

Level: Grades 3 and 4

Setting: Whole class

Objective: Students demonstrate understanding of the concept of decimal hundredths.

Materials: Cuisenaire flats, orange rods, and white cubes (construction paper can be used); cards containing numbers between 0 and 1, such as 0.01, 0.23, 0.40, 0.57, 0.99 (a different number on each card, one for each child)

- Review prior knowledge by having each student display a flat; then cover it with orange rods. Review the notation for decimal tenths.

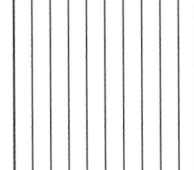 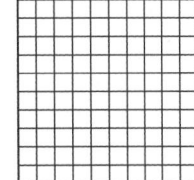

- Instruct the children to remove one tenths piece from the flat and cover it with white cubes. Ask, "How many white cubes cover one tenths piece?" (Answer: 10.) "What part of a tenth is one white cube?" (Answer: $\frac{1}{10}$.) Ask, "If it takes 10 white cubes to cover one orange rod, how many will it take to cover all 10 rods?" (Answer: 100.)

- Discuss the fact that 100 white cubes will cover the flat.

- Ask, "What part of a flat is one white cube?" (Answer: $\frac{1}{100}$.) Introduce the decimal notation 0.01. Ask, "How does this notation differ from the notation 0.1?" Help children understand that the two numerals to the right of the decimal point represent hundredths; in this case, it is one-hundredth.

- Present other decimal fractions for children to represent with the Cuisenaire materials: 0.15, 0.36, 0.86, 0.40.

- Use money as a way to extend understanding of hundredths. Ask, "What part of a dollar is one penny?" (Answer: $\frac{1}{100}$.) "What are two ways we can use money notation to show one cent?" (Answer: 1 cent and $0.01.) Have the children write notations to show money amounts such as 24 cents, 50 cents, 97 cents, 8 cents.

Variation

- Use a line-up cooperative-learning activity to extend children's thinking about decimal hundredths.

- Give each student a card containing a decimal number with hundredths.

- At a signal, the children form a line that puts the numbers in order from smallest to largest.

- When the order is correct, each student turns to the one on either side and says, "My number is _____. It is larger/smaller than your number."

Discuss that there are 10 rods and that their ends are at points along the meter stick that indicate decimeters. Next, the children align the 100 small cubes side by side along the orange rods. Build on knowledge of the relationship of the cubes to rods to enable children to see that there are 100 small cubes and that each one represents one-hundredth (0.01) of the meter, or 1 centimeter. An orange rod is one-tenth (0.1) of the meter, or 1 decimeter. Activity 13.10 expands children's knowledge of tenths and hundredths. Activity 13.11 uses a calculator to help children explore the base-10 aspects of decimal fractions.

Introducing Smaller Decimal Fractions

When children learn about decimal fractions smaller than hundredths, a large unit region marked into 1,000 parts can illustrate thousandths, but it is impractical to make models to show 10,000 and 100,000 parts. Older children who work with numbers smaller than thousandths can visualize that each thousandth has been cut into 10 equal-size parts to make ten-thousandths and then that each

ten-thousandth has been cut into 10 parts to make hundred-thousandths.

Some children may have initial difficulties reading decimal fractions because the name for the decimal fraction seems to be off by one. Consider 0.34. This decimal fraction is read as "thirty-four *hundredths*," although *hundreds* in whole numbers indicates three digits. Similarly, the decimal fraction 3.456 is read "three and four hundred fifty-six *thousandths*." In this case, a three-digit decimal fraction has the label *thousandths*, which, for children,

---

MISCONCEPTION

Some students think that the decimal point marks a symmetrical location in a decimal fraction. Actually, the units position in a decimal fraction is the point of symmetry. Can you see why?

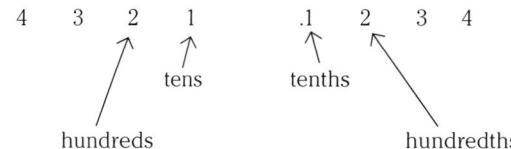

![ACTIVITY 13.11] **Decimal Fractions on a Calculator (Reasoning and Proof)**

Level: Grades 2 and 3

Setting: Pairs of students

Objective: Students use a calculator to develop an understanding of magnitude with decimal fractions.

Materials: Student calculators

The calculator provides the opportunity for students to explore decimal fractions before they are able to use any common algorithms for operations using decimal fractions.

- Pass out a calculator to each student pair.
- Ask students to enter 0.1 into the calculator. Allow time for students to locate the decimal point button.
- Most calculators will display 0.1 even if students enter ".1". Explain that the 0 is used to emphasize that the decimal fraction is less than 1. Remind students to enter all subsequent decimal fractions less than 1 with the leading 0.
- Once all students have successfully entered 0.1 into their calculators, have them clear the entry and this time enter 0.1 + 0.1 =. All should have 0.2 on their display.
- Now ask students to press the + key again. This should add 0.1 to the display of 0.2 for a new display of 0.3.

- Have students continue to press the + key until the display reads 0.9, then ask student pairs to predict the display when they press + the next time. Discuss students' conjectures as a class.
- Allow students to press the + key to obtain 1.0. Ask student volunteers to explain the result. Have students continue to press the + key until they reach 1.9. Again ask students to predict the display when they press + again, and discuss as before.
- Have students repeat using 0.2, 0.3, and 0.4 in place of 0.1 in their initial number sentence. Ask them to predict how the display will read as they press the + key, and then verify their prediction by using the calculator.

TI-10 Calculator

evokes a four-digit whole number. In the case of hundredths the number of hundredths will not exceed 99; we never reach 100. If there are more than 99 hundredths, then the result is a mixed number. It is good to acknowledge this apparent mismatch between the number of digits and the decimal fraction name as children are learning to read decimal fractions and to help them understand why it is proper.

MULTICULTURALCONNECTION

Newspapers and magazines are good sources for demonstrations of decimal fractions. Sports magazines, such as *Sports Illustrated* and *Sports Illustrated for Kids*, and newspaper sports sections contain many team and individual statistics from other countries and from the Olympics and World Cup soccer competitions. Monetary exchange rates are also represented as decimal fractions. Students can find examples and display them on a bulletin board or in a class book. Children can also record in their journals examples of decimal fractions observed at home and other places outside the classroom.

Introducing Mixed Numerals with Decimal Fractions

Whole numbers and decimal fractions form mixed numerals in the same ways that whole numbers and common fractions do. Measurements made with meter sticks often result in whole meters plus decimeters or centimeters. The measure of the length of a room might be recorded as 4.3 meters. This means that the room is 4 meters plus 3 decimeters long. When children record measurements made with a meter stick, explain that people read mixed numerals that contain decimal fractions in two ways. Although a measurement of 4.3 meters is commonly read as "four point three meters" rather than "four and three-tenths meters," the first reading hides the meaning of the number. As children begin to read decimal fractions, avoid the common reading "four *point* three." When children read decimals by simply reading numerals and inserting "point" where the decimal appears, they mask the mathematical value of the decimal fraction. The decimal fraction 2.4 is properly read as "two and four-tenths," and 5.35 is read "five and thirty-five hundredths." Reading mixed numerals with a decimal fraction in this manner helps children build an understanding of the decimal fraction included with the whole number.

Comparing Fractional Numbers

Children compare whole numbers in many ways. They match objects in one set with objects in a second set and conclude that the one with excess objects has a larger number than the other set. They learn that larger numbers are to the right of smaller ones on a number line, in numerical sequence, and that the difference between any two consecutive whole numbers is 1. They need to have similar experiences to learn that fractional numbers can also be ordered by size. When children order and compare whole numbers, they learn that there is a *finite* number of whole numbers between any pair of numbers. When they order and compare fractional numbers, they learn that there is an *infinite* number of fractional numbers between any pair of numbers.

Initial experiences comparing common and decimal fractions come through investigations with models of various kinds. We discuss activities with three different models that are appropriate for second-, third-, and fourth-graders, followed by more abstract procedures suitable for older children.

Comparing Common Fractions

Commercial kits and construction paper can be used to model settings in which children compare fractions whose numerators are 1. Models show that $\frac{1}{2}$ is more than $\frac{1}{3}$, $\frac{1}{4}$, or any other unit fraction for an object with a given size and shape. The patterns that become apparent when models are arranged in sequence from smaller to larger or larger to smaller help children order these common fractions.

Fraction strips cut from colored construction paper are used in Activity 13.12 to compare common fractions. The strips consist of a unit piece and half, fourth, third, sixth, eighth, and twelfth pieces. Children manipulate the pieces at their desks as they complete the activity.

Comparing Common and Decimal Fractions with Number Lines

Number lines marked with common fractions provide a more abstract way to compare fractional numbers than do regions or strips. Children extend their understanding by connecting their knowledge of those models to the more abstract number lines. Activity 13.13 provides a setting in which children use communication and reasoning skills as they compare common fractions on number lines.

ACTIVITY 13.12 Fraction Strips (Representation)

Level: Grades 3–5

Setting: Cooperative learning

Objective: Students demonstrate a strategy for comparing common fractions.

Materials: Multiple sets of fraction strips cut from colored construction paper, four different colored marking pens, large sheets of butcher paper, masking tape, paper containing eight questions similar to the following:

1. How many $\frac{1}{2}$ strips are as long as the 1 strip? How many $\frac{1}{3}$ strips are as long as the 1 strip? Which is longer, a $\frac{1}{2}$ strip or a $\frac{1}{3}$ strip?

2. What is the shortest fraction strip in this set? Name the strips that are longer than this strip. Use the fraction strips to put these common fractions in order, beginning with the largest and ending with the smallest: $\frac{1}{8}, \frac{1}{2}, \frac{1}{3}, \frac{1}{6}, \frac{1}{4}$.

3. Which is longer, two $\frac{1}{2}$ strips or two $\frac{1}{3}$ strips?

4. Which is longer, two $\frac{1}{6}$ strips or one $\frac{1}{4}$ strip?

5. Which is shorter, two $\frac{1}{3}$ strips or two $\frac{1}{8}$ strips?

6. Use the strips to put these common fractions in order, beginning with the smallest and ending with the largest: $\frac{2}{3}, \frac{3}{6}, \frac{3}{8}, \frac{3}{4}$.

7. Name three common fractions that are equivalent to $\frac{1}{2}$.

8. Name two common fractions that are equivalent to $\frac{4}{12}$.

- Put a set of strips, four marking pens, and a question sheet together in a food storage bag for each team. Roll a sheet of butcher paper for each team and secure with a rubber band.

- Organize the children into team-project cooperative-learning groups consisting of four children. Distribute one bag of materials and a sheet of butcher paper to each team.

- Team members rotate responsibilities as they answer the eight questions. Each member is to use the strip material, if necessary, to complete two questions while the other three serve as consultants. Answers are written on the butcher paper, with each student using a different colored pen.

- Tape the answer sheets side by side on the chalkboard or a wall. Students check from their desks to see if there are any discrepancies in answers. Discuss any discrepancies.

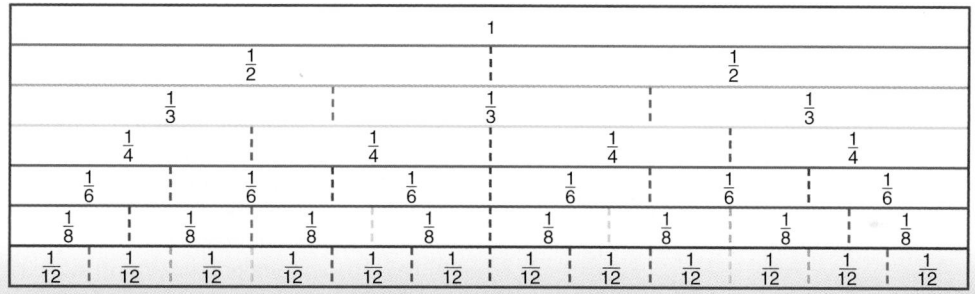

Children can also use a set of number lines to compare decimal fractions. Display three number lines on a large sheet of paper or overhead transparency—one showing a unit, one showing tenths, and one showing hundredths—placed one above the other so that the starting points are in a vertical line (Figure 13.17). You can provide leads similar to those in Activity 13.14 to focus attention on comparisons:

- Which is more, 3 tenths or 27 hundredths?

- Name a number of tenths that is more than 80 hundredths.

- What is the number of tenths that is equal to 70 hundredths?

- Which is more, 89 hundredths or 9 tenths?

An important concept about numbers—that there is no smallest fractional number—can be developed intuitively by using number lines like the ones in Activity 13.16 and Figure 13.17. In the following vignette a fourth-grade teacher uses both common fraction

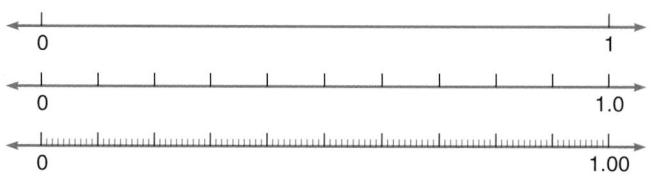

Figure 13.17 Number lines for comparing decimal fractions

ACTIVITY 13.13 **Common Fractions on a Number Line (Communication)**

Level: Grades 2–4

Setting: Whole class

Objective: Students order and compare common fractions.

Materials: Large sheet of paper showing number lines with only whole-number locations marked, black marking pen, paper and pencil for each student. The lines and marks must be visible to all students; the set of lines can be displayed on an overhead projector.

- Direct students' attention to the top line, and point out the unit segment.

- Go to the second line, and mark the point midway between 0 and 1. Darken and label the marks that show the $\frac{1}{2}$ and $\frac{2}{2}$ points on the line.

- Say, "Raise your right hand if you can tell me the denominator for common fractions on the third line." Darken and label points for $\frac{1}{4}$, $\frac{2}{4}$, $\frac{3}{4}$, $\frac{4}{4}$, and $\frac{5}{4}$.

- Continue to the bottom line, where thirty-seconds will be marked and labeled.

- Raise and discuss questions such as these:

  1. How many of the $\frac{1}{2}$ segments match the length of the unit segment?
  2. What is the shortest segment on the chart?
  3. How many of the $\frac{1}{16}$ segments are equivalent to a $\frac{1}{8}$ segment?
  4. Which is longer, a $\frac{1}{16}$ segment or a $\frac{1}{4}$ segment?
  5. Which are shorter, two $\frac{1}{8}$ segments or two $\frac{1}{4}$ segments?
  6. What number of $\frac{1}{8}$ segments are equivalent to a $\frac{1}{2}$ segment? to a $\frac{1}{4}$ segment? to a whole segment?
  7. What is the order of these segments, from longest to shortest: $\frac{1}{4}$, $\frac{3}{8}$, $1\frac{9}{32}$, $\frac{1}{2}$, $\frac{3}{4}$, $\frac{30}{32}$, $\frac{3}{16}$?
  8. Which fraction is nearer to 0: $\frac{1}{8}$ or $\frac{1}{16}$? $\frac{1}{4}$ or $\frac{1}{32}$?
  9. Which fraction is nearer to 1: $\frac{5}{8}$ or $\frac{15}{16}$? $\frac{7}{8}$ or $\frac{5}{16}$?
  10. Which fraction is closer to $\frac{1}{2}$: $\frac{1}{16}$ or $\frac{15}{32}$? $\frac{3}{8}$ or $\frac{7}{8}$?

- Use questions like these to help children develop generalizations about common fractions: "What do you see about common fractions that are close to 1 on the number line?" (Answer: Their top numbers [numerators] are almost as large as their bottom numbers [denominators].) "What can you tell me about common fractions that are close to $\frac{1}{2}$ on the number line?" (Answer: Their top numbers [numerators] are about half as big as their bottom numbers [denominators].) "Common fractions that are close to 0 can be recognized in what way?" (Answer: They have a small top number [numerator] and a large bottom number [denominator].)

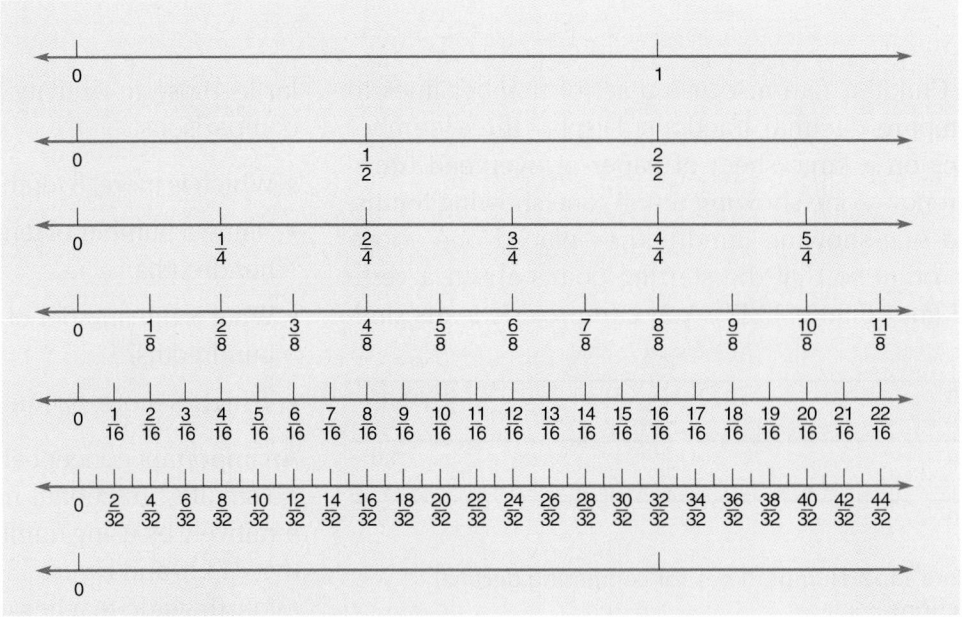

ACTIVITY 13.14 Using Benchmarks to Order Fractions

Level: Grades 4–6
Setting: Small groups
Objective: Students develop their ability to order common fractions.
Materials: Ruler, paper, pencils

- Draw a number line on the board like the one shown here.
- Ask for a few common fractions from a student volunteer.

$$\longleftarrow \overset{|}{0} \qquad\qquad \overset{|}{1} \longrightarrow$$

- Discuss where these fractions might be placed. Probe for using $\frac{1}{2}$ and 1 (and possibly $\frac{1}{4}$ and $\frac{3}{4}$) as benchmarks.
- Write these common fractions on the board, and direct each group to place them on a number line like the one drawn on the board: $\frac{7}{8}, \frac{1}{2}, \frac{3}{2}, \frac{2}{3}, \frac{3}{8}, \frac{1}{4}, \frac{7}{8}, \frac{1}{2}, \frac{10}{29}, \frac{4}{3}, \frac{1}{3}, \frac{1}{6}$.
- Ask for group volunteers to place one common fraction on the number line you have posted on the board.
- As each group posts a common fraction, ask group members to explain how they located it on the number line. Again, probe for students' use of benchmarks.

and decimal fraction number lines to conduct a discovery lesson designed to elicit children's thoughts about numbers and infinity.

Teacher: I started at $\frac{1}{2}$, which is midway between 0 and 1. Then I marked the midpoint between 0 and $\frac{1}{2}$. What point is that?

Marcella: It's $\frac{1}{4}$.

Teacher: What is the midpoint between 0 and $\frac{1}{4}$?

Ben: It's $\frac{1}{8}$.

Teacher: Yes, it is $\frac{1}{8}$. Put your thumbs up if you think you know the next point I'll mark. [Teacher looks around to see who is predicting and calls on a student.]

Juanita: I think it will be $\frac{1}{16}$.

Teacher: Why do you think it will be $\frac{1}{16}$?

Juanita: Because $\frac{1}{16}$ is a half of $\frac{1}{8}$. If you had $\frac{2}{16}$ you would have the same as $\frac{1}{8}$.

The teacher marks $\frac{1}{16}$ and then $\frac{1}{32}$ on the last numbered line and then asks, "What will be the name of the midpoint on the blank number line beneath the one that shows thirty-seconds?"

Alf: It will be $\frac{1}{64}$.

Teacher: I've run out of space for more points on these lines. Does that mean there are no fractional numbers between $\frac{1}{64}$ and 0?

Salena: No.

Teacher: How do you know?

Morgan: There has to be a smaller one. It wouldn't make sense for them to just stop.

Lorrie: When I look at the points we've marked so far, I see a pattern.

Teacher: Explain the pattern you see, Lorrie.

Lorrie: First, we marked $\frac{1}{2}$, then $\frac{1}{4}, \frac{1}{8}, \frac{1}{16}, \frac{1}{32}, \frac{1}{64}$.

Roberto: I get it, the bottom number doubles each time.

Liu: The next one will be $\frac{1}{128}$.

Teacher: What will the next one be?

Lorrie: It will be $\frac{1}{256}$.

Lin: Gee, the fractions are getting mighty small.

Teacher: Let's leave the common fraction lines and look at the decimal fraction lines. The spaces between hundredths are too small to separate into 10 parts. Imagine that we can separate the space between zero and one one-hundredth on the number line into 10 equal-size parts. What would be the size of each part?

Carlos: One one-thousandth.

Teacher: Good. So far, we see a pattern of tenths, hundredths, thousandths. What is the next decimal fraction for this pattern?

Steve: Ten-thousandths.

Teacher: Does this pattern ever end?

Al: No.

Teacher: Can you explain why?

Al: We divided the second number line into 10 equal-size parts, and the third line into hundredths. If the line was bigger, one part of a hundredth line could be cut into 10 parts to show thousandths. Even though the parts get too small to see and to show on the number lines, there is always a smaller decimal fraction than the last one we considered.

Teacher: Good explanation. Now, who will summarize what we have discovered about common and decimal fractions?

Lakeesha: There is no "smallest" common fraction and no "smallest" decimal fraction. They go on forever.

Teacher: Can anyone tell me what we call a sequence of numbers that never stops?

Kareem: It's called infinity.

Teacher: That's about right. A sequence of numbers that never stops is an infinite set. There is no way to count the numbers. We say that the numbers can go on forever, or to infinity. Now, let's look at one other idea about common and decimal fractions. Do you believe we can count the common fractions between 0 and 1?

Josh: I don't think so, but I'm not sure.

Teacher: Josh is right. Raise your hand if you can explain to the class why we can't count the common fractions between 0 and 1.

Carlos: We saw that when you marked fractions from 1 toward 0 they kept getting smaller but never stopped. So, I think that you can never stop stuffing fractions between 0 and 1. If they don't stop, there will be no way to count them.

Teacher: That's correct. We say that there is an infinite number of common fractions between any pair of numbers. Do you think that is true of decimal fractions?

Class: Yes!

Teacher: You are thinking about some powerful ideas here. You are learning something about what infinity means.

Different modes of representing numbers are not always evident to every child. One important goal is to help children connect the different representations of numbers and make sense of them. A skillful teacher helps children develop the higher-order thinking skills needed to participate in discussions that expand their thinking beyond the obvious. A teacher's skillful use of models, questions, responses, and acceptance will encourage children to expand their thinking, as did the children in the vignette.

Discussions of number concepts often lead children to continue their investigations beyond $\frac{1}{512}$, $\frac{1}{1024}$, and so on. They may also investigate patterns for $\frac{1}{3}$, $\frac{1}{5}$, or some other unit fraction. Some children may be interested in naming and writing the decimal fractions for very small fractional numbers. Such children should be encouraged to write their numerals and stories about them in their journals or learning logs.

Equivalent Fractions

Materials used to help students understand common fractions will also help them understand the meaning of equivalent common fractions. Students can use identical-size shapes such as fraction circles to see that $\frac{1}{2}$ is equivalent to $\frac{2}{4}$, $\frac{3}{6}$, and $\frac{4}{8}$, as they stack pieces for fourths, sixths, and eighths on one-half of the shape. Fraction strips (see Activity 13.12) and number lines (see Activity 13.13) provide the means for additional study of equivalent common fractions. Students can work individually or in small groups to determine the equivalency of common fractions illustrated by each device. Encourage children to find the pattern that develops for an equivalent class of fractions. An *equivalent class* contains common fractions that are names for a given part of a whole. The equivalent class for $\frac{1}{2}$ is $\frac{1}{2}$, $\frac{2}{4}$, $\frac{3}{6}$, $\frac{4}{8}$, $\frac{5}{10}$ . . . . When children examine the common fractions in this set, they see that the numerator of each successive numeral is one greater than the preceding numerator and that each denominator is two greater than the denominator of the preceding numeral.

EXERCISE

Write a successive sequence of equivalent common fractions for $\frac{1}{3}$, $\frac{1}{5}$, and $\frac{1}{7}$. What pattern do you see for each of your sets of equivalent fractions? ●●●

Ordering Fractions

When children have a good foundational understanding of the role of the numerator and denominator in a common fraction, they are able to order fractions by magnitude without resorting to models or a number line to compare them. One way they can order fractions, as suggested in Activity 13.14, is to use *benchmarks*. Children can easily tell if a fraction is greater than 1, so they can use 1 as a benchmark to order the fractions $\frac{7}{8}$ and $\frac{15}{11}$. Because the numerator in $\frac{15}{11}$ is larger than the denominator, $\frac{15}{11}$ is larger than 1 ($\frac{15}{11} = \frac{11}{11} + \frac{4}{11}$). Common fractions can also be ordered by comparison to $\frac{1}{2}$. Consider $\frac{2}{5}$ and $\frac{5}{9}$. Children can tell that $\frac{5}{9}$ is greater than $\frac{1}{2}$ by doubling the numerator of each fraction and then comparing the result to its respective denominator. In the case of $\frac{2}{5}$, when the numerator is doubled ($2 \times 2 = 4$) the result is less than the denominator of 5, so $\frac{2}{5}$ is less than $\frac{1}{2}$. In the case of $\frac{5}{9}$, when the numerator is doubled ($2 \times 5 = 10$) the result is greater than the denominator 9, so $\frac{5}{9}$ is larger than $\frac{1}{2}$.

When two common fractions have the same denominator, they are easy to compare. For example, given the common fractions $\frac{3}{7}$ and $\frac{5}{7}$, it is easy for children to determine that $\frac{5}{7}$ is the larger common fraction. The reasoning is that $\frac{3}{7}$ represents only 3 parts out of 7, whereas $\frac{5}{7}$ represents 5 parts out of 7 (Figure 13.18a).

Similarly, when the numerators are the same, children can quickly determine the order of fractions. To compare $\frac{3}{5}$ and $\frac{3}{8}$, children can reason that each common fraction involves 3 parts out of the whole. In the case of $\frac{3}{5}$, there are 5 pieces to a whole, but for $\frac{3}{8}$ there are 8 pieces to the whole. The size of the pieces is larger for $\frac{3}{5}$ than for $\frac{3}{8}$; therefore $\frac{3}{5} > \frac{3}{8}$ (Figure 13.18b). This line of reasoning can also be used to compare two fractions, such as $\frac{8}{11}$ and $\frac{11}{14}$. In this case both fractions are 3 parts short of a whole—$\frac{3}{11}$ and $\frac{3}{14}$, respectively.

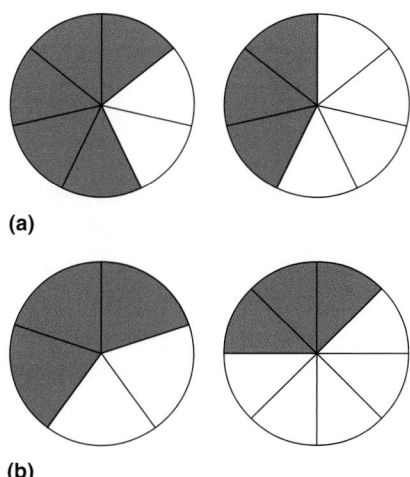

(a)

(b)

Figure 13.18 Comparing fractions with (a) the same denominator and (b) the same numerator

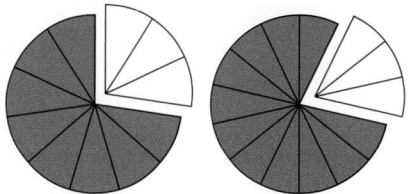

Figure 13.19 Comparing fractions when numerator and denominator differ by the same amount

Notice that $\frac{3}{11}$ and $\frac{3}{14}$ have the same numerator. Using the method just discussed, we can conclude that $\frac{3}{11} > \frac{3}{14}$ (Figure 13.19). That means that $\frac{8}{11}$ needs a larger part to be equal to a whole, so $\frac{8}{11}$ is the smaller of the two fractions.

ⒺXERCISE

Put these fractions in descending order: $\frac{1}{4}$, $\frac{3}{5}$, $\frac{11}{27}$, $\frac{7}{9}$, $\frac{10}{100}$, $\frac{7}{12}$. ●●●

Rounding Decimal Fractions

A major goal of mathematics is for children to reason as they work with numbers. One aspect of reasoning is the ability to judge whether answers make sense. The ability to round decimal fractions empowers children to make estimates to determine whether their answers are reasonable.

Number lines help children learn to round whole numbers; they can also be used to learn how to round decimal fractions. The number lines pictured in Figure 13.17 can be extended to give children a model that shows a decimal number line that extends beyond the number 1. Paper adding machine tape is a handy source of paper on which to make an extended number line. In Activity 13.15 children use a cooperative-learning strategy to learn to round decimal tenths to whole numbers. A number line that is divided into hundredths can be used in a similar way to show how to round hundredths to tenths or to whole numbers.

To round a decimal hundredth to tenths, children apply a rule similar to the one they used for rounding tenths to whole numbers. For example, the number 0.67 is rounded to 0.70 because it is closer to 0.70 than 0.60 on the line. The number 0.23 is

ACTIVITY 13.15 Rounding Decimals to Whole Numbers

Level: Grades 4–6

Setting: Cooperative learning

Objective: Students demonstrate a strategy for rounding decimal tenths to whole numbers.

Materials: A number line, made from adding machine tape, marked to show tenths to 4.0, with "Dump the Trash" written at 1.0, 2.0, 3.0, and 4.0, two for each team. (A line about 3 feet long is suitable; a few trees and shrubs along the line adds realism.)

- Tell the children to imagine that they are participating in a clean-up day along a 4-mile hiking trail. Each mile is marked in tenths, and there is a Dump-the-Trash station at each milepost. Each team of four is to determine which mileposts are the ones to go to to push their cart of trash the shortest distance each time it is unloaded. Write these decimals on the chalkboard: 2.3, 3.6, 0.7, 2.5. These numbers tell where a team is each time they have a full load of trash.

- There are four students in each group, organized into two two-member teams. Both teams solve the same problems. The first member of a team determines where to go with trash from 2.3 miles on the trail. The other member can coach, if necessary. When each pair has finished the first problem and the coach determines that it is correct, they switch roles. When two problems have been solved, the

teams stop working and check with each other. If all four agree on the answers, they proceed to the next two. If they disagree, they review each other's thinking to reach agreement before moving on.

- When all groups are finished, ask each team to tell whether they agreed throughout the lesson or whether there were disagreements. How were the disagreements resolved? Is everyone on the team satisfied with the agreements?

- Discuss the rules for rounding decimal fractions: When the tenths part of the number is less than 5, the number is rounded to the next lower whole number. When the tenths part of the number is greater than 5, the number is rounded to the next larger whole number. When the decimal is 0.5, the number is rounded to the next larger whole number. (This is the way it is most commonly done. A second method considers the whole number when determining which way to round. When the whole number is even, the number is rounded up. When the whole number is odd, the number is rounded down.)

- Tell the children that a decimal less than 1 is rounded to 1 if the number in the tenths place is 5 or more. Decimals less than 0.5 are not rounded to whole numbers.

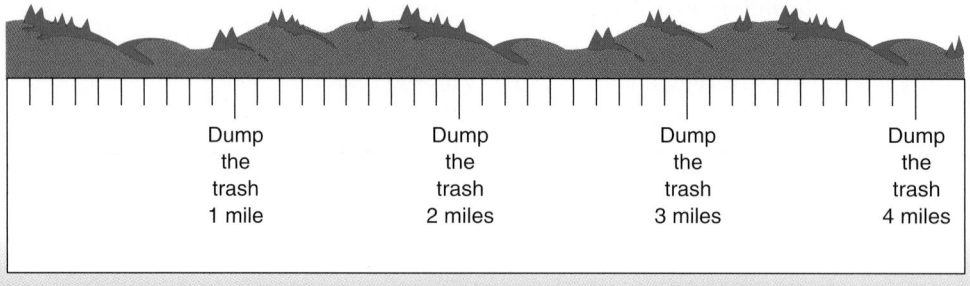

Dump	Dump	Dump	Dump
the	the	the	the
trash	trash	trash	trash
1 mile	2 miles	3 miles	4 miles

rounded to 0.20 because it is closer to 0.20 than 0.30. The number 0.25 is rounded to 0.30. The extended number line shows that when a decimal hundredth is rounded to a whole number, the point midway between two whole numbers determines whether a number is rounded down or up. The decimal fraction 1.23 is rounded down to 1.00 because its decimal part is less than 0.50, whereas the number 1.65 is rounded up to 2.00 because its decimal part is more than 0.50.

The values 2.5 and 3.4 are both properly rounded to 3 when rounded to the nearest whole number. The expression 3.0 represents a decimal fraction that measures 3 to the nearest tenth. Activity 13.16 provides an opportunity for children to explore the effects of rounding to whole numbers. This activity helps children understand the effect of rounding decimal fractions and the importance of representing decimals accurately. Activity 13.17 is an assessment activity for writing fractions.

ACTIVITY 13.16 **Rounding Decimal Circles**

Level: Grades 4–6

Setting: Pairs of students

Objective: Students use several sets of decimal circles to establish the effects of rounding on decimal fractions.

Materials: Decimal circles (see Black-Line Master 13.7), ruler, scissors

- Pair students by using your alphabetized class roster to match the first and last children, second and next to last, and so forth.

- Pass out to each student pair a sheet of circles, a scissors, and a ruler.

- Direct students to cut out the entire rectangles containing each set of circles.

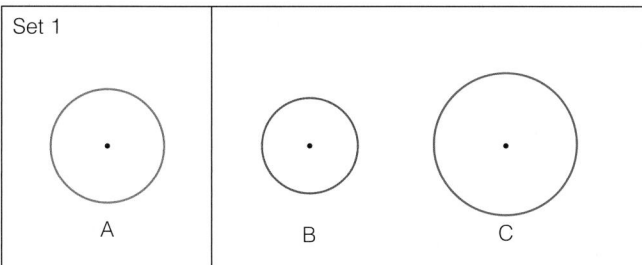

Set 1

A   B   C

- Have students measure the diameter of each circle in Set 1 and record their measurements in a chart, as shown here.

	Actual measure to 0.1 cm	**Rounded measure to nearest whole cm**	**Fit in the hole? Yes or No**
Circle A			
Circle B			
Circle C			

- For Set 1, have children cut out the entire rectangle containing Circle A, and then cut out Circle A without cutting into the remaining part of the rectangle. Be sure children save the resulting rectangle with the hole in it. Now they

should cut out Circles B and C, and discard any remaining parts of the rectangle that contained these two circles. Students should now have one rectangle with a hole and two circles.

- Ask children to try to fit each circle into the hole. Suggest that since the hole and the two circles all have the same rounded value, they should be a good fit.

- Ask children to record on their chart what happened when they tried to fit the circles into the hole.

- Repeat with Set 2 and Set 3.

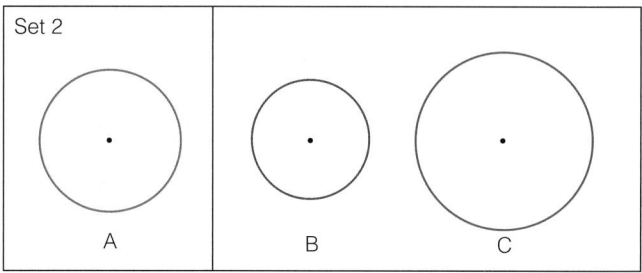

Set 2

A   B   C

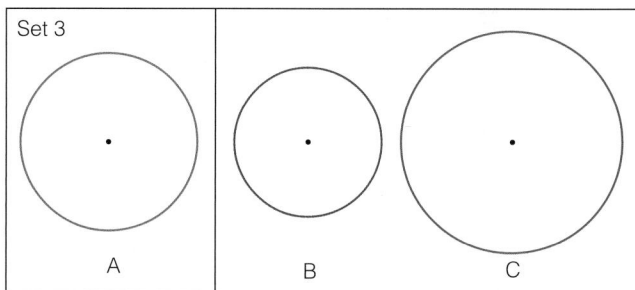

Set 3

A   B   C

- Once each pair has completed recording their measurements, ask what is true about their rounded decimal fractions for each circle. (Answer: They are the same.)

- As a culminating activity, ask each pair of students to explain how it can be that all three circles seemingly have the same diameter once rounded, but two of the circles do not fit into the third circle.

ACTIVITY 13.17   **An Assessment Activity**

Level: Grades 4–6

For each picture or shape, write the fraction shown by the shaded or circled part.

1.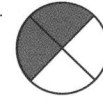

2.

3.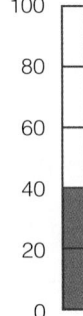

4.

5.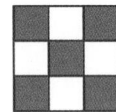

6.

7.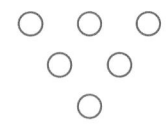

8.

9.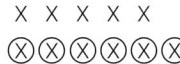

10.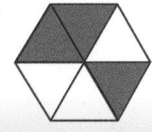

11.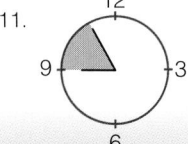

12.

Take-Home Activities

This take-home activity provides opportunities for parents and children to interact as they deal with common fractions. Playing pieces for the activity can be cut from colored construction paper on which shapes have been duplicated. A die can be made with a wooden block and round adhesive labels on which the fractions have been written. Zippered plastic bags can be used to hold the materials needed for one game. (Parents who do volunteer work in classrooms can prepare materials for both in-class and take-home activities.)

Frontier School
1234 Pioneer Place
Goldtown, CA 95643
(421) 439-2938

Dear Parent:

Accompanying this letter are directions and materials for two games that will help your child understand the meaning of common fractions and learn about common fractions that are equivalent to each other. The plastic bag contains whole circles; pieces that show halves, thirds, fourths, sixths, and eighths; and a die marked $\frac{1}{2}, \frac{1}{3}, \frac{1}{4}, \frac{1}{6}, \frac{1}{8}$, and $\frac{2}{8}$. Here are directions for the games.

Cover the Circle: This game can be played by as many as four players. Each player begins with a whole circle. In turn, players roll the die and cover their circles with parts of circles. For example, when a player rolls $\frac{1}{4}$, a part showing one-fourth of a circle or two parts showing one-eighth of a circle can be put on the whole circle. When a person cannot cover the remaining space on a circle with the piece or pieces indicated by a roll of the die, he or she must wait for another turn. The first person to cover a circle is the winner.

Uncover Your Circle: This game can be played by up to four players. Players begin by covering their circles with two of the half pieces. In turn, players roll the die and uncover their circles by removing the fractional amount indicated by the die. Exchanges of pieces will be needed as the game is played. If $\frac{1}{4}$ comes up on the first roll, a one-half piece can be exchanged for two one-fourth pieces, then one one-fourth piece can be removed. If a player does not have a piece to remove or cannot make an exchange after a roll of the die, he or she must wait for another turn. The first player to uncover a circle is the winner.

Summary

Activities that give children an understanding of common and decimal fractions are an essential part of the elementary school curriculum. The work done in the early years serves as a foundation for more abstract concepts in higher grades. The intent in elementary school is to provide children with basic ideas about these numerals.

Common fractions have several meanings, depending on the context in which they are used. Children learn that common fractions are used to express parts of a unit or set of objects that has been partitioned into equal-size parts or groups, to express ratios, and to indicate division. Decimal fractions are used to represent parts of wholes or collections of objects but have denominators that are 10 or a power of 10. The denominator is not written but is indicated by the number of numerals there are to the right of the ones place in a decimal numeral. Students need experiences with concrete and semiconcrete models that represent both types of numerals and their uses. Geometric regions, fraction strips, markers, number lines, and various manipulatives are used during initial activities. These same materials help students to learn about equivalent fractions and to compare common fractions. Basic concepts of ratio can be developed with investigations of settings involving purchases of common items, such as gum or pencils.

Materials such as Cuisenaire sets, construction paper kits, fraction strips, and number lines are aids that students can use to learn the meaning of decimal fractions. Once the meaning of decimal fractions is understood and students can write decimal numerals accurately, they are ready to learn to round decimals to the nearest whole unit or to another decimal place.

Study Questions and Activities

1. Think back to your own experiences with common and decimal fractions in elementary school. Do you believe that the instruction you received helped you develop a good understanding of these numbers? Envision a classroom in which the teacher invokes teaching procedures based on the philosophy of this chapter. How does the classroom you envision compare with classrooms of your experience?

2. Which representation of fractions is more appealing to you, fraction strips or fraction circles? Explain your answer.

3. How can having a good visual conception of fraction benchmarks benefit children?

4. Create a scenario for a pairs/check cooperative-learning exercise that can be used to help children learn to round decimal hundredths to tenths and/or to whole numbers (see Activity 13.16).

   Praxis (http://www.ets.org/praxis/) Which of the following is equal to a quarter of a million?

a. 40,000

b. 250,000

c. 2,500,000

d. 1/4,000,000

e. 4/1,000,000

NAEP (http://nces.ed.gov/nationsreportcard/) Shade $\frac{1}{3}$ of the rectangle below.

TIMSS (http://nces.ed.gov/timss) A cake was cut into eight pieces of equal size. John ate three pieces of the cake. What fraction of the cake did John eat?

a. $\frac{1}{8}$

b. $\frac{3}{8}$

c. $\frac{3}{5}$

d. $\frac{8}{3}$

Using Children's Literature

(Grades 3–4) The plot in *Alexander, Who Used to Be Rich Last Sunday* (Judith Viorst, New York: Aladdin Paperbacks, 1978) involves Alexander, a boy who gets $1.00 on Sunday from his grandparents. In the course of the week Alexander fritters the whole dollar away. Children can write the numerical representation for each part of the story. For example, one of Alexander's brothers has two dollars, three quarters, one dime, seven nickels, and eighteen pennies. Children can also write the numerical equations that keep track of Alexander's money. At various times during the week Alexander spends 11 cents, then 15 cents, and then 12 cents. The amount of money that remains after each day can be linked to stages in the story.

Teacher's Resources

AIMS. (2000). *Proportional reasoning: AIMS activities*. Fresno, CA: Activities in Mathematics and Science Educational Foundation.

Barnette, Carne, Goldenstein, Donna, & Jackson, Babette (Eds.). (1994). *Fractions, decimals, ratios, and percents: Hard to teach and hard to learn?* Portsmouth, NH: Heinemann Press.

Curcio, Frances R., & Bezuk, Nadine S. (1994). *Understanding rational numbers and proportions*. Reston, VA: National Council of Teachers of Mathematics.

Currah, Joanne, & Felling, Jane. (1997). *Piece it together with fractions*. Edmonton, Canada: Box Cars and One-Eyed Jacks.

Litwiller, Bonnie (Ed.). (2002). *Making sense of fractions, ratios, and proportions*. Reston: VA: National Council of Teachers of Mathematics.

Long, Lynette. (2001). *Fabulous fractions: Games and activities that make math easy and fun*. New York: Wiley.

Reys, Barbara J. (1992). *Developing number sense in the middle grades*. Reston, VA: National Council of Teachers of Mathematics.

Wiebe, Arthur. (1998). *Actions with fractions*. Fresno, CA: AIMS Educational Foundation.

Children's Bookshelf

Dennis, Richard. (1971). *Fractions are parts of things*. New York: Thomas Y. Cromwell. (Grades K–3)

Hoban, Lillian. (1981). *Arthur's funny money*. New York: Harper & Row. (Grades K–3)

Hutchings, Pat. (1986). *The doorbell rang*. New York: Greenwillow Books. (Grades 2–4)

Leedy, Loreen. (1994). *Fraction action*. New York: Holiday House. (Grades 1–4)

Maestro, Betsy, & Maestro, Guilio. (1988). *Dollars and cents for Harriet*. New York: Crown. (Grades K–3)

Matthews, Louise. (1979). *Gator pie*. New York: Dodd, Mead. (Grades K–3)

McMillan, Bruce. (1991). *Eating fractions*. New York: Scholastic. (Grades PS–2)

Most, Bernard. (1994). *How big were the dinosaurs?* San Diego: Voyager Books. (Grades 2–5)

Pomerantz, Charlotte. (1984). *The half-birthday party*. New York: Clarion Books. (Grades K–3)

Thaler, Mike, & Smath, Jerry. (1991). *Seven little hippos*. New York: Simon & Schuster. (Grades 1–3)

Technology Resources

Applets

One of the most exciting developments in educational technology is the growing number of mathematics applets available on the Internet. An applet is an interactive dynamic program that allows the user to manipulate images on the screen to discover and demonstrate mathematics relationships. The applet discussed here was produced by the National Council of Teachers of Mathematics (NCTM). The applet—or mathlet, as NCTM designates these interactive activities—is called Fraction Pie (available at **http://illuminations.nctm.org**). It is one of many mathlets maintained by NCTM for all mathematics levels, from Pre-K–2 to 9–12.

Students can use this particular mathlet to explore in a dynamic setting what happens to the value of a common fraction when the numerator and/or denominator is changed. The screen captures of the applet shown here demonstrate how $\frac{1}{6}$ and $\frac{1}{10}$ are displayed at the site. Students can change the size of the denominator by dragging the appropriate slider. As they do so, all the data on the page change, as does the diagram. Students can experiment freely to build their understanding of how an increase in the denominator shrinks the size of a common fraction. In this case students see $\frac{1}{6}$ change to $\frac{1}{7}$, then $\frac{1}{8}$, then $\frac{1}{9}$, and finally $\frac{1}{10}$. This website has the ability to display fractions with numerators and denominators up to 100.

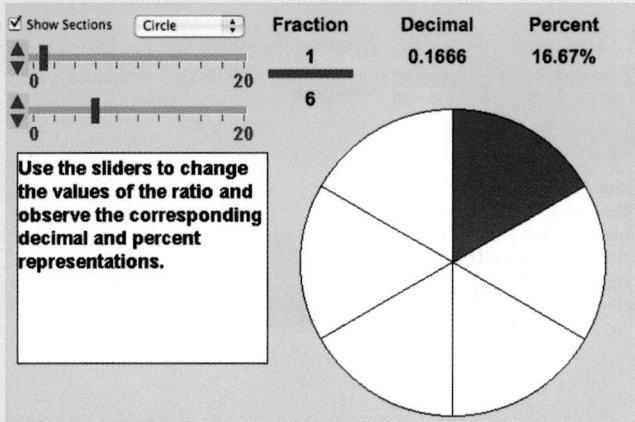

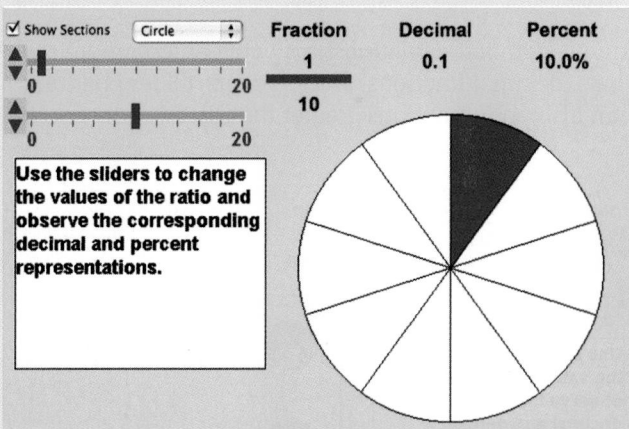

Similarly, children can change the value of the numerator in a fraction and determine that as the number increases in a numerator, so does the value of the resulting common fraction. The screen captures show this function using a rectangle for the whole. Here children can see $\frac{1}{6}$ change to $\frac{2}{6}, \frac{3}{6}, \frac{4}{6}$, and finally $\frac{5}{6}$.

The mathlet also represents common fractions as parts of sets, so children can experiment with these fractions in three different representations: circles, rectangles, and sets. Older children can take advantage of the display of equivalent decimal fractions and percents for every common fraction they enter to build their

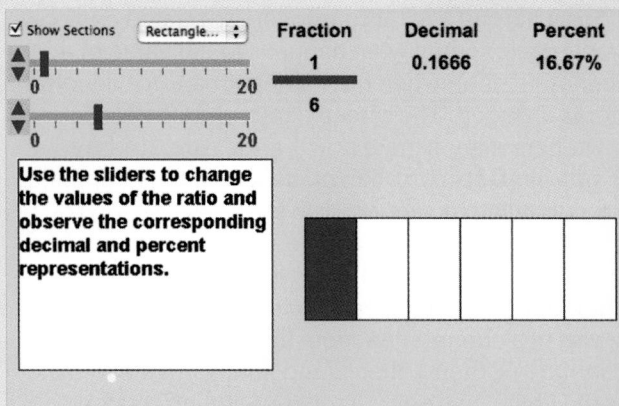

Use the sliders to change the values of the ratio and observe the corresponding decimal and percent representations.

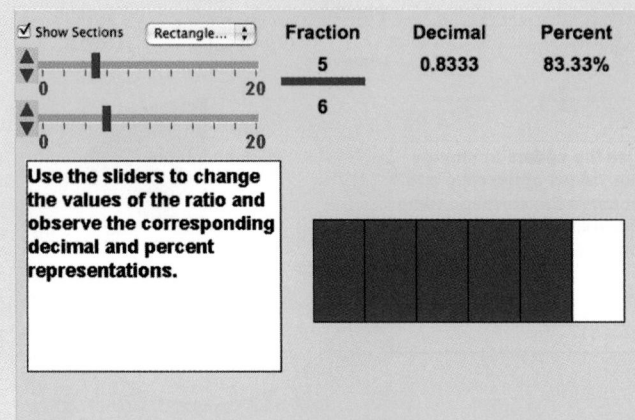

Use the sliders to change the values of the ratio and observe the corresponding decimal and percent representations.

knowledge of the relationships between common fractions, decimal fractions, and percents. Older children can also enter fractions greater than 1.

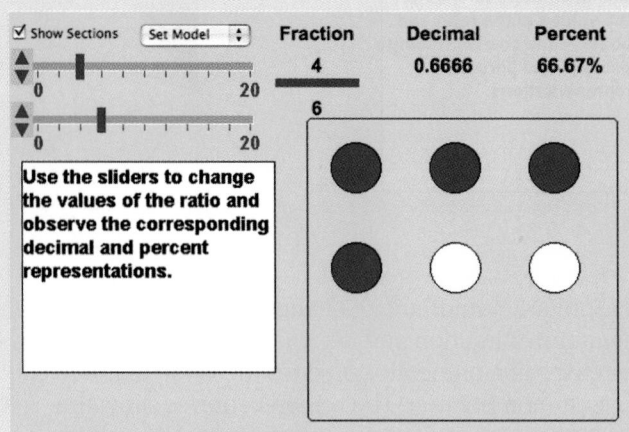

Use the sliders to change the values of the ratio and observe the corresponding decimal and percent representations.

The Fraction Pie mathlet can be found at **http://illuminations.nctm.org**. Once at the site, click on Fraction Pie: Version 2.

Internet Websites

General fraction websites:

http://www.visualfractions.com

http://www.k111.k12.il.us/king/math.htm#

To display models of basic fractions, see the following website:

http://illuminations.nctm.org

To explore equivalent fractions, try these websites:

Equivalent fractions: http://illuminations.nctm.org and http://nlvm .usu.edu/en/nav/vlibrary.html

Equivalent fractions pointer: http://www.shodor.org/interactivate/ activities/index.html

For fraction decimal representations, try the following websites:

Converter: http://www.shodor.org/interactivate/activities/index .html

For ordering fractions, see

Fraction Sorter: http://www.shodor.org/interactivate/activities/ index.html

For fraction comparing with fraction strips, see

http://www2.whidbey.net/ohmsmath/webwork/javascript/

Comparing Fractions: http://www.visualfractions.com/compare .htm

Internet Game

The game Builder Ted, available at **http://www.bbc .co.uk/education/mathsfile/index.shtml**, shows players a set of decimal fractions. The challenge is to order the decimals one at a time for Builder Ted. There are three levels to the game, with the highest level including decimal fractions less than 0. There are sound effects that are amusing but could be distracting. The sound effects can be turned off.

For Further Reading

Anderson, C., Anderson, K., & Wenzel, E. (2000). Oil and water don't mix, but they do teach fractions. *Teaching Children Mathematics* 7(3), 174–176.

This article describes an oil-water activity that provides a concrete model for fraction relationships.

Empson, Susan. (2002). Equal sharing and the roots of fraction equivalence. *Teaching Children Mathematics* 7(7), 421–423.

Empson presents several student-invented strategies for finding equivalent fractions. These lead to students eventually developing efficient methods for finding equivalent fractions.

Ploger, D., & Rooney, M. (2005). Teaching fractions: Rules and reason. *Teaching Children Mathematics* 12(1), 12–17.

The authors present a conceptual model for balancing foundational understanding of fractions with the need to recall rules that describe fractional relationships.

Siebert, D., & Gaskin, N. (2006). Creating, naming, and justifying fractions. *Teaching Children Mathematics* 12(8), 394–397.

In this article the authors suggest additional ways, besides whole number combinations, that children can think about fractions.

Watanabe, T. (2006). The teaching and learning of fractions: A Japanese perspective. *Teaching Children Mathematics* 12(7), 368–372.

This article presents the basic approaches used in Japanese schools for teaching fraction concepts and relationships.

Watanabe, T. (2002). Representations in teaching and learning fractions. *Teaching Children Mathematics* 8(8), 457–464.

Part-whole, set, and comparison models for representing fractions are discussed, along with the inherent weaknesses of each model for young children's learning about fractions.

CHAPTER 14

Extending Understanding of Common and Decimal Fractions

Instruction about common and decimal fractions in the lower grades is directed not so much toward making children skillful in performing operations but toward building a foundation that can be expanded in the higher grades. The focus in lower grades is on conceptual understanding of the meaning of fractions, both common and decimal. According to *Professional Standards for School Mathematics* (National Council of Teachers of Mathematics, 2000, p. 152), middle-grade students "develop their understanding of and ability to employ the algorithms for the basic operations with common and decimal fractions. They should be able to develop strategies for computing with familiar fractions and decimals." Younger students might engage in some activities that introduce the concepts of the four operations with fractions, but the formal study of the respective algorithms and fluency in them is a focus of the middle-grades mathematics curriculum.

In the early grades children construct their understanding of common and decimal fractions and learn about addition and subtraction with rational numbers. Work with common and decimal fractions continues in upper elementary school as children deal with these fractions on a more symbolic level, advance their understanding of addition and subtraction, and learn the meaning of multiplication and division. In the middle grades the familiar algorithms for all four operations with common and decimal fractions are emphasized, as is development of proportional reasoning and problem solving with percents. In this chapter we discuss the mathematical procedures for computing (algorithms) with common and decimal fractions, but these algorithms are the final result of many activities and experiences that build students' conceptual understanding of them. Students should use these algorithms because the specific procedure makes sense in the context of a problem and not because they have memorized a set of computational steps. Thus we focus on those concept-building activities first and then discuss the algorithms that develop from them.

In this chapter you will read about:

1 Ways to extend the concept of place value to include decimal fractions

2 Ways to model addition and subtraction with common and decimal fractions and to develop understanding of these operations and their respective algorithms

3 Realistic situations and concrete materials and pictures for modeling multiplication and division and for introducing algorithms with common and decimal fractions

4 Activities dealing with renaming common fractions

5 Activities dealing with common and decimal fraction relationships

6 Ways to use the calculator to explore common and decimal fraction relationships

7 Activities that use the Internet to explore fractional numbers

8 A take-home activity dealing with common fractions

Standards and Fractional Numbers

State mathematics standards agree that when teaching children about common and decimal fractions, the emphasis should be on connecting the two ways of representing fractional numbers. Students should see mathematics as unified rather than as a series of separate ideas. When children understand that common and decimal fractions and percents are different representations of the same numbers, they are empowered to deal confidently and accurately with problems that involve these numbers using concrete, pictorial, and symbolic representations as well as technology. Although we have chosen to consider percent in Chapter 15 as part of proportional reasoning, we maintain that percent concepts and skills should be developed at the same time as common and decimal concepts and skills. Activities with common and decimal fractions provide students with connections between the numerals and processes—and with the real-world situations from which they arise. Once settings and algorithms are understood, children can decide whether to use a paper-and-pencil algorithm estimation, mental computation, or a calculator or computer to solve problems.

Teaching Children About Fractional Numbers in Elementary and Middle School

POINT OF VIEW

A significant amount of instruction time should be devoted to rational numbers in grades 3–5. The focus should be on developing students' conceptual understanding of fractions and decimals—what they are, how they are represented, and how they are related to whole numbers—rather than on developing computational fluency with rational numbers. Fluency in rational-numbers computation will be a major focus of grades 6–8. (National Council of Teachers of Mathematics, 2000, p. 158)

The topics in this chapter—common fraction operations and decimal fraction operations—are generally emphasized in the middle school curriculum (grades 6–8). In *Principles and Standards for School Mathematics* the National Council of Teachers of Mathematics (2000, p. 215) states, "In the middle grades (6–8) students should become facile in working with fractions, percents, and decimals." Elementary grades provide the foundation for work with fractions, decimals, and percents. Only on a firm foundation of conceptual understanding can children later become facile with operations and applications of fractions, decimals, and percents.

The topics in this chapter include some topics that are developed more fully in the middle grades, for several reasons. First, elementary school teachers need a sense of the mathematics and related applications and activities to come in the middle grades in order to prepare their students for middle-grade mathematics topics. Second, elementary school teachers provide activities that introduce these middle school topics for their elementary school students. Finally, all children in the United States in grades 3–8 are required by the No Child Left Behind Act to take tests in reading and mathematics. The specific content of these tests varies from state to state, according to the mathematics framework of each state. Where

POINT OF VIEW

By studying fractions, decimals, and percents simultaneously, students can learn to move among equivalent forms, choosing and using an appropriate and convenient form to solve problems and express quantities. (National Council of Teachers of Mathematics, 2000, p. 150)

you teach will determine what aspects, if any, of the topics considered in this chapter are part of the grade 4, 5, or 6 tests for your students.

NCTM Number and Operations Standard

Grades 3–5 Expectations:

In grades 3–5 all students should:

Understand numbers, ways of representing numbers, relationships among numbers, and number systems

- understand the place-value structure of the base-ten number system and be able to represent and compare whole numbers and decimals;
- recognize equivalent representations for the same number and generate them by decomposing and composing numbers;
- develop understanding of fractions as parts of unit wholes, as parts of a collection, as locations on number lines, and as divisions of whole numbers;
- use models, benchmarks, and equivalent forms to judge the size of fractions;
- recognize and generate equivalent forms of commonly used fractions, decimals, and percents;
- explore numbers less than 0 by extending the number line and through familiar applications;
- describe classes of numbers according to characteristics such as the nature of their factors.

Understand meanings of operations and how they relate to one another

- understand various meanings of multiplication and division;
- understand the effects of multiplying and dividing whole numbers;
- identify and use relationships between operations, such as division as the inverse of multiplication, to solve problems;
- understand and use properties of operations, such as the distributivity of multiplication over addition.

Compute fluently and make reasonable estimates

- develop fluency with basic number combinations for multiplication and division and use these combinations to mentally compute related problems, such as 30×50;
- develop fluency in adding, subtracting, multiplying, and dividing whole numbers;
- develop and use strategies to estimate the results of whole-number computations and to judge the reasonableness of such results;
- develop and use strategies to estimate computations involving fractions and decimals in situations relevant to students' experience;
- use visual models, benchmarks, and equivalent forms to add and subtract commonly used fractions and decimals;
- select appropriate methods and tools for computing with whole numbers from among mental computation, estimation, calculators, and paper and pencil according to the context and nature of the computation and use the selected method or tools.

Grades 6–8 Expectations:

In grades 6–8 all students should:

Understand numbers, ways of representing numbers, relationships among numbers, and number systems

- work flexibly with fractions, decimals, and percents to solve problems;
- compare and order fractions, decimals, and percents efficiently and find their approximate locations on a number line;
- develop meaning for percents greater than 100 and less than 1;
- understand and use ratios and proportions to represent quantitative relationships;
- develop an understanding of large numbers and recognize and appropriately use exponential, scientific, and calculator notation;
- use factors, multiples, prime factorization, and relatively prime numbers to solve problems;
- develop meaning for integers and represent and compare quantities with them.

Understand meanings of operations and how they relate to one another

- understand the meaning and effects of arithmetic operations with fractions, decimals, and integers;
- use the associative and commutative properties of addition and multiplication and the distributive property of multiplication over addition to simplify computations with integers, fractions, and decimals;
- understand and use the inverse relationships of addition and subtraction, multiplication and division, and squaring and finding square roots to simplify computations and solve problems.

Compute fluently and make reasonable estimates

- select appropriate methods and tools for computing with fractions and decimals from among mental computation, estimation, calculators or computers, and paper and pencil, depending on the situation, and apply the selected methods;
- develop and analyze algorithms for computing with fractions, decimals, and integers and develop fluency in their use;
- develop and use strategies to estimate the results of rational-number computations and judge the reasonableness of the results;
- develop, analyze, and explain methods for solving problems involving proportions, such as scaling and finding equivalent ratios.

Extending Understanding of Decimal Fractions

By the time children enter the upper elementary grades, they have learned that decimal fractions are one way to represent and work with fractional numbers. Children in grades 5 and 6 are ready to deal with more complex concepts involving these numerals. We now discuss ways to help students extend their understanding of the place-value scheme for whole numbers to include decimal fractions.

Children use a variety of materials and procedures to learn that 0.3, 0.13, and 1.3 are equivalent to the common fractions $\frac{3}{10}$, $\frac{13}{100}$, and $\frac{13}{10}$. Lessons such as the ones that follow help children see that deci-

mal fractions extend the Hindu-Arabic numeration system to represent fractional parts as well as whole units. Activity 14.1 uses a place-value pocket chart to help students recognize that decimal fractions are an extension of whole numbers in the Hindu-Arabic numeration system. In Activity 14.2 a classroom version of an abacus is used. This abacus can be made with wooden beads on pieces of coat-hanger wire stuck in a 2-foot piece of 2×4 wood. When an abacus represents decimals, a rod other than the one on the far right indicates the ones place. Activity 14.3 helps older students complete the connection between place value for whole numbers and place value for decimal fractions. As they do this activity, children learn that the ones place, not the decimal point, is the point of symmetry for place value in the Hindu-Arabic numeration system. Moving in both directions from the ones place, students find tens and tenths, then hundreds and hundredths, then thousands and thousandths, and so forth.

Decimal Fractions and Number Density

Once children understand how to name decimal fractions, teachers can use decimal fractions to help children understand the density of numbers. The **density property of numbers** stipulates that there is always another number between any two numbers. This is difficult to show with common fractions— for example, $\frac{1}{5}$ and $\frac{1}{6}$. It is easier to demonstrate density with decimal fractions. For example, what is a number between 1 and 2? Children who are beginning a study of decimal fractions could locate these two numbers on a number line and divide the interval between 1 and 2 into 10 parts (Figure 14.1a). Any decimal fraction represented by the interval markings is a number between 1 and 2. In Figure 14.1a the number 1.3 is represented. Students can then be asked to locate one of the numbers between 1 and 2 on the number line (1.3 as shown here). Teachers can locate other values between 1 and 2 and then

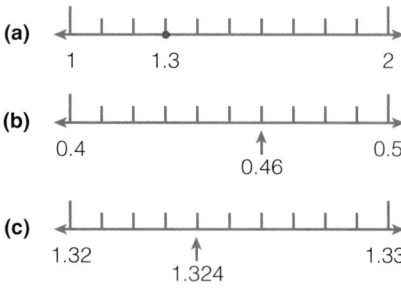

Figure 14.1 Number lines

ACTIVITY 14.1 Place-Value Pocket Chart

Level: Grades 3–5

Setting: Whole class

Objective: Students extend their concept of place value to include decimal fractions.

Materials: A place-value pocket chart. This is a device about 24 inches wide and 18 inches high with three or four parallel slots that hold 3 × 5 cards. It is used to represent place value. For this lesson a chart will represent ones and tenths. Also needed is a kit of decimal fraction learning aids for each child. Use Cuisenaire rods or any other materials with which the children are familiar.

- Have children recall previous knowledge with a quick review of place value for whole numbers.

- Write the decimal fraction 3.4 on the chalkboard, and instruct each child to represent it with a chart from their kit materials, as shown here.

- Show a pocket chart that contains three bundles of tenths pieces and four single tenth pieces. Explain that each card stands for one-tenth. Ask: "How are three bundles of tenths cards like the three unit pieces in your kits." (Answer: They represent three units.) "How are the four tenths in the chart like the tenth pieces in the kits?" (Answer: They represent four-tenths.)

- Repeat with other decimal fractions, including some with no tenths and some with no units. The display in the first chart shown below has no units; the correct numeral for this display is 0.5. In the second chart there are no tenths; the numeral is 4.0.

- Ask: "How do the numerals 10 and 1.0 differ? What does the "1" in 10 stand for?" (Answer: 1 ten.) "What does the "0" stand for?" (Answer: no ones, or 0 ones.) "What does the "1" in 1.0 stand for?" (Answer: 1 one.) "What does the "0" stand for?" (Answer: no tenths, or 0 tenths.) Point out that tens are to the left and tenths are to the right of the ones place.

Ones	Tenths
	‖‖‖‖‖

Ones	Tenths
‖‖‖	‖‖‖‖

Ones	Tenths
‖‖‖‖	

ACTIVITY 14.2 Decimals on an Abacus

Level: Grades 3–5

Setting: Cooperative learning

Objective: Students demonstrate how to place decimal points correctly to represent mixed decimal fractions and to read the numbers.

Materials: A classroom abacus, $8\frac{1}{2}$ × 11 paper containing 534123 written six times in large numerals, marking pen for each student

- Organize the class into groups of four for a think-share cooperative-learning activity. Display the abacus with a decimal point located between the first and second rods at the right to represent the number 53,412.3. Tell each team to place the decimal point in the number repre-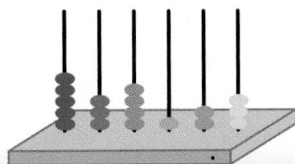sented on the abacus in the numeral at the top of the paper. Teams meet to check agreement of responses. When all teams agree, move on.

- In think-share cooperative learning, students respond independently to a problem from the teacher or a fellow student. The setting for this activity is: "There are five numerals on your papers. Each of you is to move the decimal point to the left, one position at a time, as you go down the paper. When all members of your team are finished, meet and take turns reading the numbers. Each member must read one of the numbers." Give students time to think and talk.

- The final group assignment is to collaborate on a statement that explains the value of each of the numerals 5, 3, 4, 1, 2, and 3 in one of the numbers. Each team selects its own number. For example, if a group selects 5,341.23, then students would evaluate each numeral in the number (e.g., the numeral 5 represents five thousand).

- Groups share their statements. If any numbers were not selected, the class discusses the place value of numerals in them.

ACTIVITY 14.3 Place-Value Chart

Level: Grades 3 and 4

Setting: Whole class

Objective: Students demonstrate the concept of symmetry around the ones place in the decimal place-value scheme.

Materials: A chart like the one given here, displayed on a large piece of butcher paper or an overhead projector transparency:

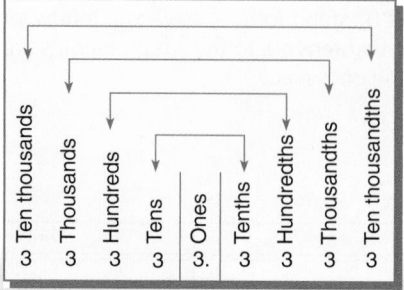

- Display the chart. Point out that the ones place is in the center of the chart.

- Ask: "What is the value of the 3 to the left of the ones place?" (Answer: 3 tens.) "What is the value of the 3 to the right of the ones place?" (Answer: 3 tenths.)

- Repeat with the 3's in the hundreds and hundredths places and the 3's in the thousands and thousandths places.

- Discuss that the ones place is the point of symmetry, or balance, and that the tens place is to its immediate left and the tenths place is to its immediate right, the hundreds place is two places to the left and the hundredths place is two places to the right, and so on.

- Point out that each place-value position has a value that is 10 times greater than the position to its immediate right and that a value is one-tenth as much as that of the position to its immediate left, regardless of where it is in relation to the ones place.

repeat the activity with other numbers, such as 4 and 5, 15 and 16, and 98 and 99.

The same process can be used for decimal fractions that appear to be adjacent, such as 0.4 and 0.5. These two decimal fractions might also be located on a number line and the interval between them divided into 10 equal parts (Figure 14.1b). The decimal fraction that names any of the intervals is a number between 0.4 and 0.5, in this case 0.46. Similarly, the same technique will work for other decimal fractions, such as 1.32 and 1.33. The two decimal fractions can be displayed on a number line, and the interval between them divided into 10 parts (Figure 14.1c). As shown here, one of the numbers between 1.32 and 1.33 is 1.324.

Expanded Notation for Decimal Fractions

By the end of grade 6 some children will be ready to learn an abstract way to think about and represent decimal fractions. These forms are extensions of earlier expanded notation forms introduced with whole numbers. In expanded notation, 54,326 is represented as

$$54{,}326 = (5 \times 10^4) + (4 \times 10^3) + (3 \times 10^2)$$
$$+ (2 \times 10^1) + (6 \times 10^0)$$

These expanded decimal notations are appropriate only for children who have a mature understanding of numbers and for whom the notations will have

meaning. Children with a good understanding of negative numbers can learn the full exponential notation of decimal fractions in the form

$$343.68 = (3 \times 10^2) + (4 \times 10^1) + (3 \times 10^0)$$
$$+ (6 \times 10^{-1}) + (8 \times 10^{-2})$$

Extending Concepts of Common and Decimal Fraction Operations

Addition and Subtraction with Common and Decimal Fractions

Children have a solid understanding of and skill in performing addition and subtraction operations with whole numbers by the time they encounter addition and subtraction with common and decimal fractions. A strong conceptual understanding of addition and subtraction serves as the foundation for study of the same operations with fractional numbers. Just as children used physical models as they learned about whole number operations, they should learn how operations with fractions work in the same manner. Addition of fractional numbers is a joining operation, just as addition of whole numbers is. Subtraction with fractional numbers arises from the same four situations as those with whole numbers: takeaway, comparison, completion, and whole-part-part (Figure 14.2).

ⒺXERCISE

Create different examples that illustrate each of the four subtraction settings in Figure 14.2. ●●●

Addition and Subtraction with Common Fractions

Addition and subtraction with common fractions involves computation when there are like denominators (e.g., $\frac{2}{5}$ and $\frac{4}{5}$), unlike denominators (e.g., $\frac{2}{3}$ and $\frac{3}{4}$), and mixed numerals (e.g., $2\frac{3}{8}$ and $6\frac{1}{6}$). Work

with these operations is spread over several years, to accommodate the different levels of difficulty and children's increasing maturity, and moves progressively from common fractions with like denominators to common fractions with unlike denominators and finally to mixed numerals. An integral aspect of a smooth progression through these different types of common fractions is a basic understanding of the parts of a fraction and their effect on the value of a fraction, as stressed in the early part of this chapter. For example, a student who understands the difference between $\frac{2}{3}$ and $\frac{2}{5}$ also understands that they

Figure 14.2 Four situations involving subtraction with common fractions

TAKEAWAY

"Carmen has $3\frac{3}{4}$ pounds of ground beef. If she uses $1\frac{1}{2}$ pounds for a meat loaf, how much ground beef will she have left?"

(a) There were $3\frac{3}{4}$ pounds of ground beef, (b) $1\frac{1}{2}$ pounds were removed, and (c) $2\frac{1}{4}$ pounds were left.

COMPARISON

"John walks $\frac{3}{4}$ of a mile to school, and Jason walks $\frac{7}{8}$ of a mile. How much less does John walk than Jason?"

John's walk is shown on the top line, and Jason's is shown on the bottom line. The difference is $\frac{1}{8}$ of a mile.

COMPLETION

"Sarah has $\frac{7}{8}$ of a cup of flour. How much more does she need for a recipe that requires $1\frac{1}{2}$ cups of flour?"

The cup contains $\frac{7}{8}$ of a cup of flour. Another $\frac{5}{8}$ cup is needed to make $1\frac{1}{2}$ cups.

WHOLE-PART-PART

"The dry ingredients for a cake recipe total $2\frac{1}{4}$ cups. If there are $1\frac{3}{4}$ cups of flour, how much sugar and other dry ingredients are there?"

The bottom portion of the container shows that $1\frac{3}{4}$ cups of the ingredients is flour. The upper portion shows that $\frac{2}{4}$ cup, or $\frac{1}{2}$ cup, is sugar and other dry ingredients.

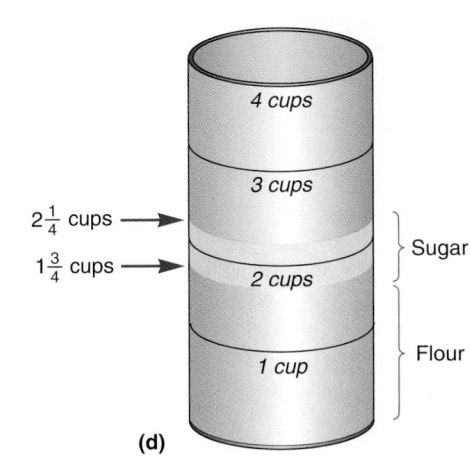

Research for the Classroom

In a recent study (Aksu, 1997), sixth-grade students were given a series of problems involving all four operations with common fractions (addition, subtraction, multiplication, and division). The study was done in two settings: computational and contextual. In the computational setting the examples were devoid of any context and were simply presented to the students in a form such as $2\frac{2}{3} \times 4\frac{1}{5} = ?$. In the contextual setting the fraction operations were embedded in word problems.

One finding of Aksu's study was that there was no difference in success (problems solved correctly) with any of the operations in the computational setting. The students were able to complete examples using all four operations equally well. Their success was far higher with the com-

putational problems than with the contextual problems. In every operation, students did significantly better when they could solve the problem without any context. Among the contextual problems themselves, addition problems were the simplest and multiplication operations were the most difficult.

There are several implications for the classroom. Students need ample experience solving fraction problems in context, not just in isolated computational settings. Many realistic stories should form the problem-solving context for fraction work. Furthermore, the difficulty students had with multiplication problems in context points to the need to provide students with many experiences with such problems (Aksu, 1997).

cannot be added directly because they name different fractional parts of a whole. A common fractional part for these two fractions (common denominator) is needed in order to add them.

Adding and Subtracting with Like Denominators

The setting within which children work should be stocked with familiar learning aids: geometric regions left whole and cut into fractional parts, fraction-strip sets, and number-line charts. Activity 14.4 illustrates a problem that can be used for children's first work with addition of common fractions. As you read the activity, note that the addition does not begin with the simplest combinations, such as $\frac{1}{4} + \frac{1}{4}$ or $\frac{1}{2} + \frac{1}{2}$. Children who have many experiences with fraction manipulatives develop a good understanding of common fractions. They "just know" easy combinations such as $\frac{1}{4} + \frac{1}{4} = \frac{1}{2}$ and that $\frac{1}{2} + \frac{1}{2} = \frac{2}{2}$, or one whole, through early experiences with various fraction manipulatives. In Activity 14.4 children use the processes that make sense to them at the moment. The teacher makes no suggestions about how to proceed. Rather, children determine the answer to the problem in many ways, through manipulation of concrete materials and with mental and symbolic processes.

Student presentations and discussions of the different processes help children refine their thinking as they discover simpler and faster ways to work. Many children will abandon learning aids in favor of mental and symbolic processes as they move along in Activity 14.5 and subsequent activities. Thus, although the goal is to have children develop confidence and facility with symbolic processes, children use manipulatives whenever they need to. At first, the symbols record what the student can see and do with the manipulative objects. Children who have sufficient experiences with manipulatives can eventually work efficiently with symbols. Activity 14.5 uses a calculator to introduce addition with common fractions.

Using Algorithms to Compute with Fractional Numbers

Mathematics educators disagree about whether elementary school children should be taught standard algorithms for computing with common fractions. Advocates for allowing students to continue using invented algorithms, such as the one used by Jawawn in Activity 14.4, delay introducing standard algorithms. Others contend that introducing algorithms in the elementary grades lays the foundation for using symbols and algorithms in algebra. As students expand their understanding of operations through problem-solving activities, such as those of Activities 14.4 and 14.5, they develop the standard algorithms. When children move from invented algorithms to standard algorithms in this manner, they have a strong understanding and recall of the

EXERCISE

Use fraction circles to model $\frac{3}{4} + \frac{3}{4} = 1\frac{1}{2}$. ●●●

In this discussion we use mathematical sentences as the format for algorithms for adding and subtracting common fractions:

$$\frac{1}{2} + \frac{1}{4} = \frac{2}{4} + \frac{1}{4} = \frac{3}{4}$$

It is not necessary that a vertical notation, as shown here, be used. The vertical notation of the algorithm can create unnecessary confusion.

$$\frac{2}{3}$$
$$+\frac{2}{3}$$
$$\overline{\frac{4}{3}}$$

However, a decision about whether to show children this vertical form should be determined by local and state mathematics standards as well as by the tests mandated by local, state, and federal policy.

Adding and Subtracting When Denominators Are Different

When addition and subtraction are performed with common fractions that have unlike denominators, the situation is more complex than when denominators are the same. Begin with problems that use reasonable denominators (10 or smaller), and allow children time to determine solutions. Activity 14.6 illustrates a way to introduce addition with unlike denominators. In the activity children use pairs/check cooperative learning with models of their choice to solve problems involving addition of unlike fractions. The problems in Activity 14.6 are successively more difficult. In the first problem one of the two denominators is a multiple of the other. The second problem has denominators that are multiples, but there are four addends. Neither denominator is a multiple of the other in the third problem; this type is most difficult for children.

A situation in which one denominator is a multiple of the other is illustrated in this takeaway example:

- When Billy checked, he found $\frac{5}{6}$ of a pizza in the refrigerator. When he ate a piece that was $\frac{1}{3}$ of the original pizza, how much pizza was left?

ACTIVITY 14.6 Adding with Unlike Denominators

Level: Grades 3–5

Setting: Small groups

Objective: Students discover strategies for adding common fractions with unlike denominators.

Materials: Fraction kit materials, commercial or teacher-made; common fraction number line; paper and pencils

- Begin with a review of different ways that common fractions can be named. For example, $\frac{1}{2}$ can be $\frac{2}{4}, \frac{3}{6}, \frac{4}{8}$, and so on. Have the children give other names for $\frac{1}{4}, \frac{1}{3}, \frac{1}{5}$, and $\frac{1}{6}$.

- Tell the children to use the pairs/check format. Present a problem: "While making clothes for her doll, Mae used $\frac{1}{2}$ yard of material for a skirt and $\frac{1}{4}$ yard for a blouse. What part of a yard did she use for the outfit?"

- Have pairs work and check their answers. They can use any materials and procedures they choose. Share results in groups of four.

- Examples of the responses are:
  - Kelly used a one-half and a one-fourth fraction strip and got three-fourths.
  - Abdul used one-half of a circle and one-fourth of circle. When he put them together, he had three-fourths of a circle. The answer is three-fourths of a yard.

- Lamont thought: One-half is the same as two-fourths, add two-fourths to one-fourth and you have three-fourths.

$$\frac{1}{2} + \frac{1}{4} = \frac{2}{4} + \frac{1}{4} = \frac{3}{4}$$

- Give additional problems to solve and share responses:
  - Andrea sewed a border on a head scarf. Two sides were $\frac{7}{8}$ yard long, and the other two sides were $\frac{1}{2}$ yard wide. How many yards of border did she use?
  - Chun Lei used $\frac{3}{4}$ of a cup of onion and $\frac{5}{6}$ of a cup of bok choy in a stir fry dish. How many cups of vegetables did she use?

- When discussion of the three problems is complete, have one child write the sentence for the first problem on the chalkboard and explain the algorithm.

- Have student volunteers write sentences and explain processes for the other two problems.

By the time children deal with situations like these, they should have had experiences with a variety of models, and many of them will "just know" that $\frac{1}{3}$ equals $\frac{2}{6}$, and if they take $\frac{2}{6}$ from $\frac{5}{6}$, the answer is $\frac{3}{6}$, or $\frac{1}{2}$. These children have little difficulty adding and subtracting with simple common fractions. Those who demonstrate that they can compute answers mentally should not be required to use models or paper-and-pencil processes. The teacher's role is to encourage children to use mental computation when possible and to help them recognize situations when it should or should not be used. Mental math is most effective with denominators such as the ones given here. A problem that uses, for example, 2, 4, or

8 for denominators or 2, 3, or 6 might be solved using mental math rather than a process that involves having to record every step of the algorithm.

If children have not had sufficient experiences with equivalent fractions by grade 3, the teacher should provide time and use the activities suggested earlier in this chapter and in Chapter 13. Some children will require activities and explorations that focus on the need for a common denominator when adding or subtracting common fractions with unlike denominators. Activity 14.7 models a fraction circle to help these children understand the need for a common denominator in such cases. Fraction circles and fraction stencils are available commercially.

ACTIVITY 14.7   Using Fraction Circles to Explore Adding Fractions with Unlike Denominators (Representation)

Level: Grades 4–6

Setting: Small groups

Objective: Students develop an understanding of the need for a common denominator when combining common fractions with unlike denominators.

Materials: Fraction circles, including an overhead projector set

- Give several sets of fraction circles to each small group. Ask students to form the following sum using the $\frac{1}{2}$ piece and a $\frac{1}{3}$ piece.

- Once all student groups have placed their pieces as shown in the figure, ask for the sum of the two pieces. Propose that the sum of the two pieces is a multiple of $\frac{1}{2}$ or $\frac{1}{3}$ (it is not), and ask students to examine if either case is possible. Children will find that one $\frac{1}{2}$ piece will not cover both pieces and that two $\frac{1}{2}$ pieces will overlap both pieces. Similarly, two $\frac{1}{3}$ pieces will not cover both pieces, and three $\frac{1}{3}$ pieces will overlap both pieces.

- Suggest that students try other fraction pieces to find the sum of $\frac{1}{2}$ and $\frac{1}{3}$. When students try to cover both pieces with $\frac{1}{6}$ pieces, they will find that five of the $\frac{1}{6}$ pieces will exactly cover both pieces. Thus $\frac{1}{2} + \frac{1}{3} = \frac{5}{6}$.

- Have a student volunteer demonstrate the number sentence on the overhead using transparent fraction pieces.

- Ask if there is any other way to determine the sum of $\frac{1}{2}$ and $\frac{1}{3}$. Probe for completing the sum to make a whole. As shown here, when a single $\frac{1}{6}$ piece is combined with the original $\frac{1}{2}$ and $\frac{1}{3}$ pieces, the result is one whole. Help students reason that because the $\frac{1}{2}$ and $\frac{1}{3}$ pieces equal 1 (or $\frac{6}{6}$) when a $\frac{1}{6}$ piece is added to them, then their total without the $\frac{1}{6}$ piece must be $\frac{5}{6}$.

- Have student groups use their fraction pieces to represent the following sums and write the number sentence that results:

$$\frac{1}{2} + \frac{1}{4}$$

$$\frac{1}{3} + \frac{1}{4}$$

$$\frac{2}{3} + \frac{1}{6}$$

$$\frac{1}{3} + \frac{2}{4}$$

$$\frac{2}{6} + \frac{1}{2}$$

$$\frac{1}{3} + \frac{1}{2}$$

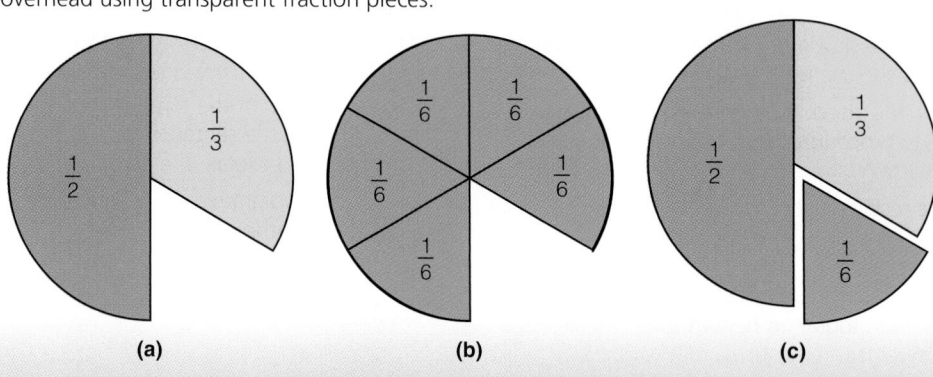

(a)   (b)   (c)

Even after many experiences representing addition and subtraction with various models, some students benefit from viewing a model algorithm. The model algorithm may be one they are helped to develop, it may be one from a group member, or it may be provided by the teacher. Such a model algorithm should be easy to follow.

$$\frac{2}{3} \text{ (Find common)} \qquad \frac{?}{12} \qquad \frac{8}{12}$$
$$+\frac{1}{4} \text{ denominator)} \qquad +\frac{?}{12} \qquad +\frac{3}{12}$$
$$\qquad\qquad\qquad\qquad\qquad\qquad \frac{11}{12}$$

Given time to think about and discuss processes, children use prior knowledge to solve the more difficult problems, but later they develop more symbolic and more mental ways to compute. Initially they may rely on learning aids to visualize and solve problems, but later they develop understandings that enable them to use more symbolic ways to compute. It is critical that children do not rush to an algorithm before they develop these symbolic understandings. A child who moves to a memorized algorithm without understanding it needs constant review to remember the algorithm. Once children have built a foundation about common fractions, they should have sufficient time to develop and practice algorithms for common fractions and mixed numerals.

Adding and Subtracting with Mixed Numerals

Adding and subtracting with mixed numerals is an extension of prior work with common fractions and their operations. The complexity increases when operations involve mixed numerals, because now there are both whole and fractional numbers. Situations that involve adding and subtracting mixed numerals are numerous. They arise frequently in delicatessens, bakeries, pizza parlors, and other food establishments where pies, cakes, pizzas, and other foods are cut into fractional parts of a whole to make serving-size portions. They arise during handicraft

activities, where materials are measured and cut for woodworking, clothing, basketry, and other projects. Activity 14.8 uses a deli as a setting to introduce addition of mixed numerals.

One type of subtraction with mixed numerals is bothersome for many children. It arises from a situation such as this:

- Reuben started with $6\frac{1}{3}$ yards of a crepe paper streamer when he made a banner for a track meet. He returned $1\frac{2}{3}$ yards to the craft table. How much of the streamer did he use?

One way to illustrate this is with a length of crepe paper streamer or adding machine tape. Cut a strip $6\frac{1}{3}$ yards long (Figure 14.3). A class discussion might proceed like this:

Teacher: Here is the piece of the streamer that Reuben began with. How long is it? (Two students extend the streamer across the front of the room.)

Jane: Six and one-third yards long.

Teacher: How much of the streamer did Reuben return to the table?

Maribel: One and two-thirds yards.

Teacher: Antonio and Felicia, use this yardstick to measure the part that Reuben returned to the table. (The piece is measured and cut.)

Teacher: How can we determine the amount of streamer Reuben used?

Antonio: Measure the piece we are holding. (The piece is measured and the answer, $4\frac{2}{3}$ yards, is noted.)

Teacher: Let's write down what we did:

$$6\frac{1}{3} - 1\frac{2}{3} = 4\frac{2}{3}$$

Teacher: What do you notice about the common fractions in this problem?

Ming: $\frac{1}{3}$ is less than $\frac{2}{3}$.

Teacher: We need to do something with the common fractions before we subtract them. What do you think we can do?

Figure 14.3 A length of butcher paper illustrates the subtraction $6\frac{1}{3} - 1\frac{2}{3} = 4\frac{2}{3}$: (a) the original piece of paper; (b) $1\frac{2}{3}$ marked for removal; (c) the remaining piece of paper.

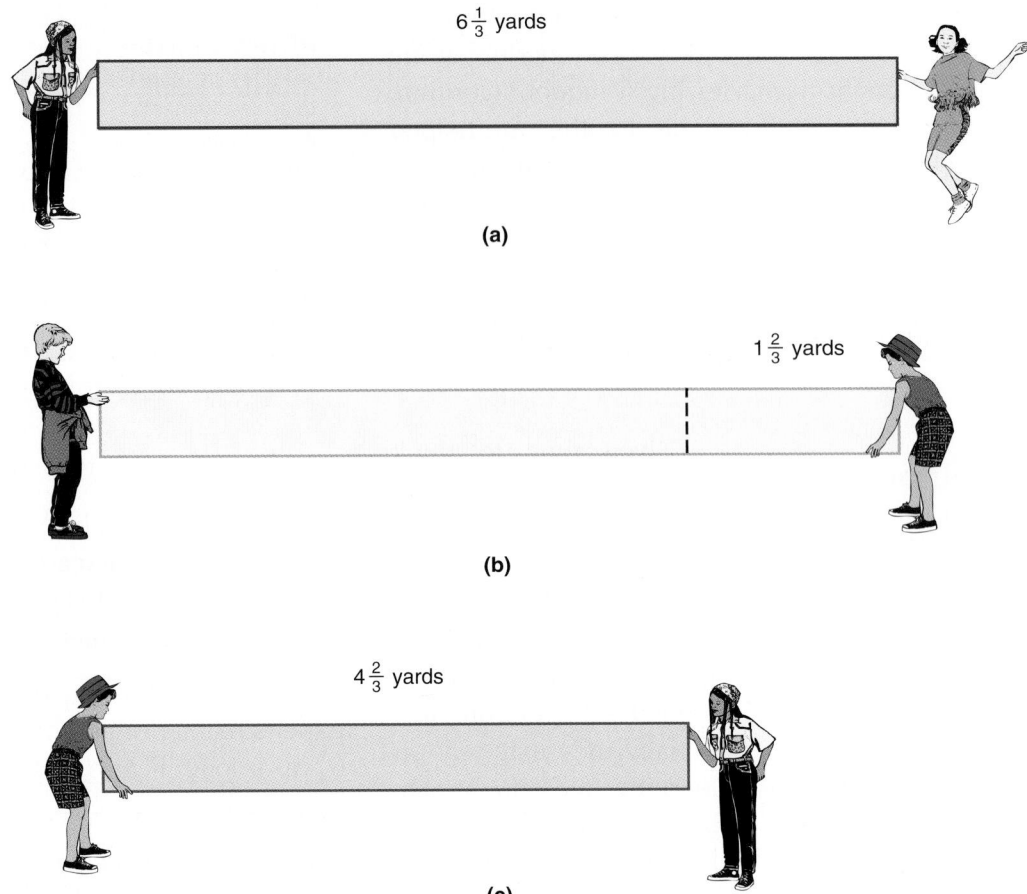

Le: Can we change one of the wholes into thirds?

Brandon: If we change one 1 into thirds and add it to the one-third, we will have four-thirds. Then we can subtract two-thirds from four-thirds. That leaves two-thirds ($\frac{4}{3} - \frac{2}{3} = \frac{2}{3}$).

Althea: And then we can subtract 1 from 5. That leaves 4.

Jason: Four and two-thirds is the answer we got when we cut and measured the paper.

Teacher: Is there another way to think about the problems? We can rename $6\frac{1}{3}$ as $5\frac{4}{3}$. Then $5 - 1 = 4$ and $\frac{4}{3} - \frac{2}{3} = \frac{2}{3}$, so $6\frac{1}{3} - 1\frac{2}{3} = 4\frac{2}{3}$.

This scenario suggests one algorithm for subtracting mixed numerals with regrouping. As with other processes in mathematics, some students will invent their own algorithms, such as representing $6\frac{1}{3}$ and $1\frac{2}{3}$ as thirds ($\frac{19}{3}$ and $\frac{5}{3}$). As suggested earlier in this text, you can acknowledge such invented algorithms and allow students to use them as initial methods for solving problems. It may be that the invented algorithm will enable the student to solve problems as well as

the standard algorithm. Consider Krystal's method for subtracting mixed numerals with regrouping:

$$
\begin{array}{r}
7\frac{1}{6} \\
-3\frac{1}{3}
\end{array}
\qquad
\begin{array}{r}
7\frac{1}{6} \\
-3\frac{2}{6} \\
\hline
4 - \frac{1}{6} = 3\frac{5}{6}
\end{array}
$$

Can you follow Krystal's solution method? Notice that she subtracts the whole numbers and the fractions separately. In the case of the common fractions, because the top common fraction is smaller than the bottom, when she subtracted, she ended up with a negative fraction ($-\frac{1}{6}$). This is easily combined with the whole number 4 to result in the correct answer of $3\frac{5}{6}$. When Krystal's teacher asked her to demonstrate her method to her class, several of her classmates readily adopted Krystal's method as their own (Johnson, 1999).

Note that Krystal's algorithm is as efficient as the standard algorithm with regrouping in the final steps. The logic is easy to follow. Students in Krystal's class who adopt this method may never need the standard algorithm. Students' invented algorithms serve

ACTIVITY 14.8 Cakes at the Deli (Connections)

Level: Grades 3–5

Setting: Groups of four

Objective: Students develop strategies and algorithms for adding mixed numerals and introduce a standard algorithm.

Materials: Fraction kit materials, commercial or teacher-made; common fraction number lines; paper and pencils

- Tell the children that they are going to work in cooperative groups to show one way to model the following problem and one way to compute an answer using pencil and paper: "There are $1\frac{1}{2}$ white cakes and $1\frac{1}{4}$ chocolate cakes at a deli counter at 8 o'clock one evening. On an average night between 8 and 9, the deli sells enough slices to equal three cakes. Is there enough cake on hand for average sales on this evening?" This activity could use real cakes or brownies as a culminating activity of fraction study.

- Each pair from a group is to use concrete materials or a drawing to solve the problem. Then they are to use symbols that show a solution based on the concrete materials or drawing. When finished, each pair compares its solutions with the group's other pair.

- One pair might use rectangular regions to represent the problem:

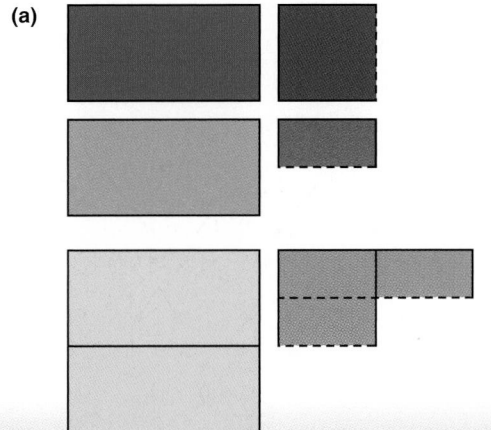

(a)

Their written solution is

(b)
$$1 + \frac{1}{4} + 1 + \frac{1}{2} = 2 + \frac{3}{4} = 2\frac{3}{4}$$

They explain that they added 1 and 1 to get 2 and $\frac{1}{2}$ and $\frac{1}{4}$ to get $\frac{3}{4}$, so there were 2 and $\frac{3}{4}$ cakes. The deli did not have enough cake for an average night.

- Have other pairs explain the ways that they solved the problem.

- Following discussion of models and diagrams, show an algorithm for the problem. Have children explain how their models and diagrams are represented by numerals in the algorithm.

(c)
$$
\begin{array}{r}
1\frac{1}{2} \longrightarrow 1\frac{2}{4} \\
+\ 1\frac{1}{4} \longrightarrow 1\frac{1}{4} \\
\hline
2\frac{3}{4}
\end{array}
$$

- Point out that when this algorithm is used, the common fractions are renamed with a common denominator. The $\frac{1}{2}$ is renamed as $\frac{2}{4}$, and the addition is completed.

- Give additional problems to solve, and share responses:
  - "A customer purchased $2\frac{1}{8}$ pounds of salami and $1\frac{3}{4}$ pounds of ham sliced for sandwiches. How much sandwich meat did the customer purchase?"
  - "A recipe lists $8\frac{1}{2}$ pounds of cake flour, $2\frac{3}{4}$ pounds of sugar, and $\frac{1}{8}$ pound of baking powder for a large cake. How many pounds of dry ingredients are in the cake?"
  - "There were $2\frac{1}{3}$ apple pies and $3\frac{5}{6}$ peach pies in the dessert case. How much pie was there?"

them well and may be the algorithms they will always use. If Krystal's approach were less efficient or more time-consuming, students would want to compare the two approaches critically and determine which was best for them. Children in Europe and South America learn to compute with different algorithms and do well in mathematics. Allowing students to explore, explain, and evaluate various algorithms helps them to understand that mathematics has many paths for solving problems.

As time passes, children need to maintain their skill with algorithms. Practice that emphasizes thinking rather than memorized procedures is important.

For example, students may write stories and draw pictures that illustrate addition and subtraction sentences. Sentences such as the following can be used to review addition and subtraction with common fractions:

$$\frac{6}{8} + \frac{7}{8} = \frac{13}{8} \quad \text{or} \quad 1\frac{5}{8}$$

$$\frac{11}{12} - \frac{5}{12} = \frac{6}{12} \quad \text{or} \quad \frac{1}{2}$$

$$3\frac{5}{8} + 6\frac{2}{8} = 9\frac{7}{8}$$

$$7\frac{1}{6} - 4\frac{1}{3} = 2\frac{5}{6}$$

Children who can create reasonable word or story problems for each of these sentences demonstrate that they understand the meanings of addition and subtraction with common fractions.

ⓔXERCISE

Create a problem situation for each of the number sentences in the previous paragraph. If this exercise is difficult for you, why do you think this is so? How does the creation of a word problem for a mathematical sentence provide evidence that a student understands a given operation? ●●●

Least Common Multiples and Greatest Common Factors

When students add and subtract common fractions with unlike denominators, they need to find common denominators. Many times the denominators are multiples, for example,

$$\frac{1}{3} + \frac{5}{6} = ?$$

where the common denominator is 6. Renaming $\frac{1}{3}$ as $\frac{2}{6}$ is easy for students who have worked with fraction materials. In other cases the common denominator is found by simply determining the product of the two denominators, for example,

$$\frac{3}{4} - \frac{1}{3} = ?$$

where the common denominator is 12 (3 × 4). This process of multiplying the denominators always results in a common denominator, but the resulting denominator may be much larger than needed, requiring much more computation than necessary. Consider the following example:

$$\frac{7}{24} + \frac{5}{36} = ?$$

POINT OF VIEW
It is more difficult for students to acquire conceptual understanding once they have learned rote procedures. Thus, it is essential to focus initial instruction on building conceptual understanding. (Owens & Super, 1993)

The common denominator that results from finding the product of 24 and 36 (864) is far larger than necessary. If 864 were used as the common denominator in this problem, the solution would require a great deal of unnecessary computation. There are many other common denominators that are smaller than 864. Finding the **lowest common denominator** (the common denominator with the smallest value) makes sense for addition and subtraction problems because the lowest common denominator, also known as the **least common multiple** (LCM; the common multiple with the smallest value), will greatly decrease the amount of computation needed to solve the given problem.

One way to find the LCM is to complete a prime factor tree for each denominator. The factor trees for 24 and 36 are shown in Figure 14.4a. Each number is broken into a pair of factors. These factors are, in turn, broken down into pairs of factors until only prime factors remain. The prime factors of 24 are 2, 2, 2, and 3 (2 × 2 × 2 × 3 = 24). The prime factors of 36 are 2, 2, 3, and 3 (2 × 2 × 3 × 3 = 36). Once the two denominators are represented as prime factors, the LCM can be determined. The common factors of 24 and 36 are 2, 2, and 3, as shown in Figure 14.4b. The LCM is found by taking the product of the common factors (2, 2, and 3) and the remaining factors of the two factor trees: 2 remains from the factors of 24, and 3 remains from the factors of 36. Thus the LCM is 2 × 2 × 2 × 3 × 3, or 72.

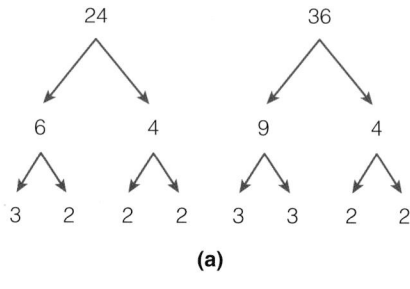

(a)

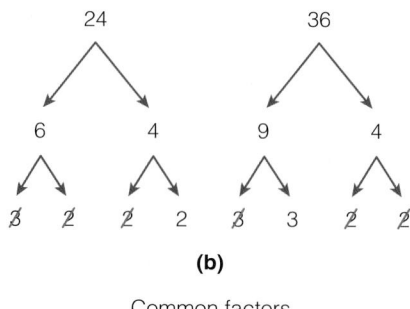

(b)

Common factors
2, 2, 3

Figure 14.4 Using factor trees to find the LCM of 24 and 36

Another method for finding the LCM is one that students may invent for themselves using equivalent fractions. For x + y they can write equivalent fractions for each addend and look for a common denominator. This requires that students understand that equivalent fractions are found by multiplying a fraction by 1 expressed as $\frac{2}{2}$ or $\frac{3}{3}$ and so on.

$$\frac{5}{36} = \frac{10}{72}$$
$$\frac{7}{24} = \frac{21}{72}$$

Because 72 is the smallest multiple of 36 and 24, 72 is the LCM. This same process can be used for the problem $\frac{3}{16} + \frac{5}{12}$:

$$\frac{3}{16} = \frac{6}{32} = \frac{9}{48} \quad \text{or} \quad \frac{3}{16} \times \frac{3}{3} = \frac{9}{48}$$
$$\frac{5}{12} = \frac{10}{24} = \frac{15}{36} = \frac{20}{48} \quad \text{or} \quad \frac{5}{12} \times \frac{4}{4} = \frac{20}{48}$$

The denominator 48 is the smallest multiple of both 16 and 12, so 48 is the LCM. In each case, multiplying both the numerator and the denominator of these fractions by the same number has the same effect as multiplying by 1 ($\frac{3}{3} = \frac{4}{4} = 1$).

Rods, tiles, or graph paper can be used to model this thinking. Figure 14.5 shows how rods can be used to find the LCM of 5 and 6. Notice that the 5 rods are lined up alongside the 6 rods until the two trains of rods have exactly the same length. In this case the length of each of the rod trains is 30. The LCM for 6 and 5 is 30.

Figure 14.5 Using rods to model the LCM of 5 and 6

Another approach to finding the LCM uses Venn diagrams, as shown in Figure 14.6. The circles contain the prime factors of 24 and 36. The factors that 24 and 36 have in common (2, 2, and 3) are

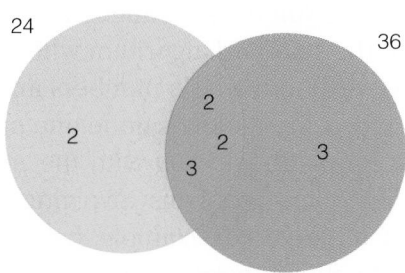

Figure 14.6 Using a Venn diagram to model the LCM of 24 and 36

displayed in the area that the circles have in common, where they overlap. The LCM is the product of all factors shown ($2 \times 2 \times 2 \times 3 \times 3 = 72$). This approach visually clarifies the factors that are common to each number and thus the factors that are part of any common denominator.

There is another benefit to representing the prime factors in a Venn diagram. Notice the common factors where the circles intersect. These factors (2, 2, 3) are the factors of the **greatest common factor** (GCF; the common factor with the largest value). The GCF is useful when students are renaming fractions in their lowest terms. For $\frac{24}{36}$ the diagram shows that the GCF is $2 \times 2 \times 3$, or 12. When 24 and 36 are each divided by 12, the resulting common fraction, $\frac{2}{3}$, is in its simplest form:

$$\frac{(24 \div 12)}{(36 \div 12)} = \frac{2}{3}$$

When both the numerator and the denominator of any fraction are divided by the same number—in this case 12—it is the same as dividing by 1 ($\frac{12}{12} = 1$).

Some children will find appealing the "outside-in" method for determining common factors of two numbers. To find the GCF for two numbers using the outside-in method, the first step is to find the smallest factor (2) of one number (24) and write it with its matching factor (12):

$$24$$
$$2 \qquad\qquad\qquad 12$$

Next, find the next largest factor (3) and its matching factor (8):

$$24$$
$$2 \qquad 3 \qquad\qquad 8 \qquad 12$$

The process continues until there are no factors between the last factor pair:

$$24$$
$$2 \qquad 3 \qquad 4 \qquad 6 \qquad 8 \qquad ⑫$$

This is the factor list for 36:

$$36$$
$$2 \qquad 3 \qquad 4 \qquad 6 \qquad 9 \qquad ⑫ \qquad 18$$

The two factor lists show that the GCF of 24 and 36 is 12.

$$24 \div 12 = 2 \text{ and } 36 \div 12 = 3$$

John Venn (1834–1923) was an English mathematician who used the circles known as Venn diagrams. Venn was not the first to use circles to represent mathematics concepts. Leonhard Euler (1707–1783) used the same circle arrangements more than a century earlier, but they were not used extensively until Venn's application to modern algebra concepts of British mathematicians. Venn was in the right place at the right time.

Using a Calculator to Add Common Fractions

Modern calculators permit students to perform many operations easily and quickly. Students should leave elementary school knowing how to use a calculator to perform operations with whole numbers and common and decimal fractions, to simplify common fractions, to determine greatest common factors, and to determine averages (means). Children must have opportunities to learn to use calculators accurately and in appropriate ways and at appropriate times. You can integrate calculators into the curriculum so that children view them as a tool for computing and solving problems. For ex-

I-15 Explorer

Casio FX-55 calculator

ample, when students learn to add and subtract common fractions using paper-and-pencil algorithms, they should learn to use a calculator to perform the same operations. Once children can use a calculator to perform operations, they need opportunities to practice and maintain their skills.

Interesting and entertaining learning and practice materials have been developed for this purpose. Producers of calculators and book publishers are sources of worthwhile activities. Some publications contain activities for a particular calculator; other publications apply to all calculators that have common functions. *A World of Mathematics: Activities for Grades 4, 5, and 6 Using the TI-15* (Christ, 2000) is an example of a text designed to be used with a specific calculator. However, the activities are easily adjusted to any fraction-capable calculator. Many books provide activities suitable for any four-function calculator, such as *Explorations: Integrating Hand-Held Technology into the Elementary Mathematics Classroom* (Olson et al., 2002).

An activity from *Activities for Casio FX-55 Fraction Calculator* (Casio, 1994) is an example of material from a book designed to help children learn to use a calculator. The activity is a game for two or three in which children use a calculator to add common fractions and mixed numerals. The game provides practice in adding while encouraging children to estimate sums before computing. To be successful at the game, a player must have reasonable mathematical sense about common fractions.

Addition and Subtraction with Decimal Fractions

Students who have a good understanding of fractional numbers and their decimal fraction representations generally experience little difficulty learning to compute with decimal fractions because the algorithms for decimals resemble the algorithms for whole numbers. Numerals are aligned by place-value positions in the standard algorithm when adding or subtracting with both whole numbers and decimal numbers, and computation is done one place-value position at a time, beginning with the position on the right. Everyday problems involving money or metric measurement, for example, help students to recognize situations that involve decimal fractions and to grasp the importance of understanding each

Name _____ Date _____

And the Winner Is...

Adding Fractions and Mixed Numbers

Choose a partner and play a game using a calculator with the fraction boxes shown below. Take turns with your partner and circle two boxes of your choice. Then find the sum of the fractions or mixed numbers in the boxes you chose. Record the answer as a score. Continue playing the game until all of the boxes have been chosen. The player with the highest total score wins!

$\frac{2}{3}$	$2\frac{1}{4}$	$\frac{3}{8}$	$\frac{3}{20}$	$\frac{9}{10}$	$6\frac{1}{12}$
$\frac{7}{9}$	$4\frac{7}{8}$	$1\frac{3}{5}$	$\frac{1}{20}$	$\frac{5}{6}$	$3\frac{3}{4}$
$8\frac{4}{7}$	$\frac{8}{11}$	$\frac{6}{11}$	$9\frac{5}{8}$	$3\frac{4}{5}$	$\frac{9}{11}$
$7\frac{3}{10}$	$\frac{9}{20}$	$5\frac{10}{11}$	$1\frac{1}{5}$	$\frac{9}{16}$	$10\frac{1}{5}$
$\frac{5}{7}$	$7\frac{2}{9}$	$\frac{4}{11}$	$4\frac{7}{12}$	$\frac{1}{9}$	$8\frac{3}{7}$
$4\frac{3}{5}$	$\frac{9}{11}$	$7\frac{3}{7}$	$9\frac{1}{3}$	$\frac{5}{8}$	$3\frac{7}{10}$

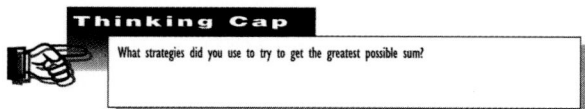

Thinking Cap

What strategies did you use to try to get the greatest possible sum?

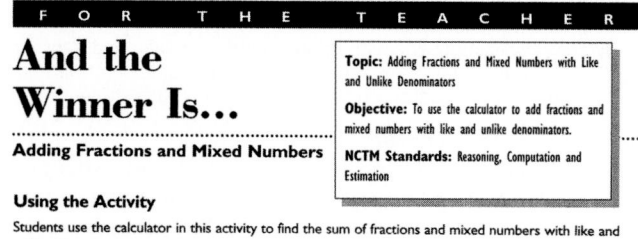

F O R   T H E   T E A C H E R

And the Winner Is...

Adding Fractions and Mixed Numbers

Topic: Adding Fractions and Mixed Numbers with Like and Unlike Denominators

Objective: To use the calculator to add fractions and mixed numbers with like and unlike denominators.

NCTM Standards: Reasoning, Computation and Estimation

Using the Activity

Students use the calculator in this activity to find the sum of fractions and mixed numbers with like and unlike denominators.

- The `b/c` key can be used to enter fractions.
- The `a` and `b/c` keys can be used to enter mixed numbers.

Example Suppose the first player circles $8\frac{4}{7}$ and $\frac{8}{11}$. The calculator should be used to find the sum: 8 `a` 3 `b/c` 7 `+` 9 `b/c` 10 `=` $9\frac{4}{5}$. The player should record this sum and all other sums of the numbers in the two boxes chosen at each turn. Once all of the boxes have been chosen, each player should use the calculator to add all of his or her recorded sums.

Assessment Encourage students to check their sums by estimating the sums before finding them on the calculator.

Answers

Answers will vary depending upon the boxes chosen by each player.

Thinking Cap

As an extension, students describe any strategies they used while playing the game. Encourage students to think of other possible strategies they might use if they played the game again.

Answers

Possible answer: I tried to choose the two greatest possible numbers from the ones that were left.

operation. Activity 14.9 illustrates addition settings with tenths and hundredths. A number line is used to model the first setting, and base-10 blocks are used for the second. Similarly, base-10 blocks can be used to represent subtraction in a fashion similar to what was done with whole numbers. Although subtraction with decimal fractions is done in the same way as subtraction with whole numbers, students still need to work with realistic situations that lead to subtraction. Activity 14.10 uses a calculator for early explorations of decimal addition with tenths.

Perhaps you learned the rule "When adding or subtracting decimals, line up the decimal points." Students who follow this rule can set up any addition or subtraction problem involving decimals correctly, but they may not understand why the rule works. If students have worked with decimal materials, blocks, or coins, they should understand that lining up the decimals really is aligning the place values. As the following problem shows, when decimal fractions are aligned so that the decimal points line up, the rule ensures that, as with whole numbers, digits that are added together have the same place value. Thus tenths in each of the decimal frac-

tions are combined with each other and not with units or hundredths.

$$
\begin{array}{r}
2.\mathbf{3}4 \\
4.\mathbf{1} \\
0.\mathbf{9}85 \\
+\ 25.\mathbf{7} \\
\hline
\end{array}
$$

Lining up the place values also helps with the estimation of the answer by adding the whole numbers (2 + 4 + 25) or by rounding (2 + 4 + 1 + 26).

Multiplication with Common Fractions

The commonly used algorithm for multiplication of common fractions is deceptively easy for teachers to teach and children to use. Here is a set of rules presented in a book for teachers (Muschla & Muschla, 1995, p. 25):

Multiplication of Fractions

1. Multiply the numerators.

2. Multiply the denominators.

3. Simplify if possible.

ACTIVITY 14.9 Adding with Decimal Fractions

Level: Grades 3–5

Setting: Whole class

Objective: Students develop strategies and algorithms for adding with decimal fractions.

Materials: Number line with decimal tenths on overhead transparency; base-10 flats, tens and ones pieces; erasable pen; overhead projector; individual chalkboard and chalk for each student

- Begin with a problem: "Danielle earns pocket money by using her bicycle to do errands. She measures distances in kilometers with a metric odometer. For one errand she recorded the distances 0.7, 0.3, and 0.8 kilometers. How many kilometers did she ride for that errand?"

- Discuss the meaning of the three numbers in the story and what is to be found. "What will you do to determine the answer?" (Answer: add the three numbers.)

- Have students write a mathematical sentence for the situation on their individual chalkboards:

  $$0.7 + 0.3 + 0.8 = ?$$

- Display the number line marked with tenths, and have a student mark the three stages of Danielle's errand. Have the student tell how far she rode.

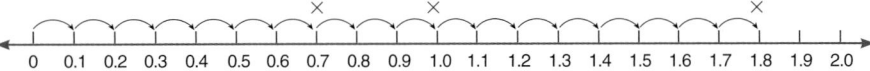

- Write a vertical algorithm:

  $$\begin{array}{r} 0.7 \\ 0.3 \\ +0.8 \\ \hline \end{array}$$

- Add the numbers in the algorithm:

  $$\begin{array}{r} 0.7 \\ 0.3 \\ +0.8 \\ \hline 1.8 \end{array}$$

- Present a second story: "Sara went to the store to buy 2 pounds of cheddar cheese. None of the packages showed a weight of 2 pounds, but Sara found a package with 0.87 of a pound and another with 0.95 of a pound. She knew that this was nearly 2 pounds. How much was it?"

- Discuss the problem and have students write an algorithm for the situation:

  $$\begin{array}{r} 0.87 \\ +0.95 \\ \hline 1.82 \end{array}$$

- Model the situation on the overhead with base-10 pieces:

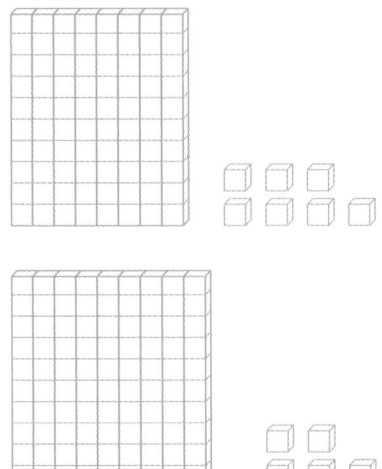

- Discuss actions with the blocks as the hundredths pieces are composed first, followed by the tenths pieces. Repeat discussion with an algorithm.

- Present other problems, or have each child create one for tenths or hundredths to share with a classmate.

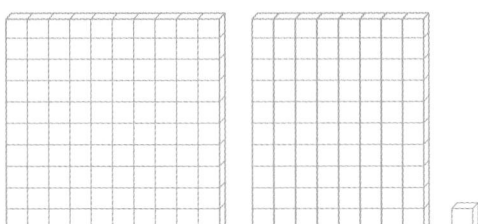

- A similar procedure can be followed to represent subtraction with decimal fractions, following the same concepts involving composing and decomposing numbers as was used with whole-number subtraction.

Children who are taught rules for performing computation with this algorithm can multiply pairs of fractional numbers with ease. However, if they compute by rules alone, they will understand little of the meaning behind the computation and have difficulty recalling the steps in the algorithm. Students need to explore the meaning of common fraction multiplication and division. Learning effective algorithms for multiplication and division should come from exploration of realistic situations modeled with learning materials. The final thing children should learn about multiplying and dividing fractional numbers is an effective algorithm. Teachers who adopt the philosophy of this book will use realistic situations and learning aids, not simply rules, as they explore with students the meanings of multiplying and di-

ACTIVITY 14.10 **Adding Common Decimals with a Calculator**

Level: Grades 3–5

Setting: Pairs

Objective: Students develop regrouping when adding common decimal fractions.

Materials: Calculator, paper and pencils

- Remind students how to perform repeated addition on a calculator by putting the following number sentence on the board: 2 + 2 = ?.

- Ask students to enter the sentence into the calculator, and be that sure all have the same result (4).

- Now have students press the + key again. The reading should now be 6. Pressing the + key added 2 to the previous sum. Repeatedly striking the + key will add 2 to any previous sum.

- Have students practice finding 8 × 7 by performing repeated addition on 7 (7 + 7 + 7 + ⋯ = 56).

- Now ask students to enter 0.2 + 0.2 = into their calculators. The result should be 0.4. Have students make repeated additions until they reach 0.8. Now ask students to speculate about the next reading when the + key is pressed. Have students press = and discuss the result. Many students will expect 0.10, not 1.0, as the result. Discuss why the result is 1.0.

TI-10 Explorer

Image courtesy of Texas Instruments

- Use 0.1, 0.3, 0.4, and 0.5, and follow the same procedure. Do not stop with the first number to equal or exceed 1.0; continue beyond 5.0 for each example.

- Ask students to write out the readings for the following sentence: 0.6 + 0.6 = ?, assuming that the + key is pressed seven times. Students then check their work by using the calculator.

viding with common fractions. Research has shown that "procedural knowledge should be developed on a foundation of conceptual understanding. . . . Once students understand a computational procedure, practice will help them become confident and competent in using it. But when students mimic a procedure without understanding it, it is difficult for them to go back later and build understanding" (Sutton & Krueger, 2002, p. 81).

MISCONCEPTION

As children learn to do multiplication with whole numbers, they see that the product is larger than either factor (except when 0 or 1 is a factor). Thus the rule "Multiplication makes bigger, division makes smaller" seems to be reasonable. Of course, such a rule is patently untrue when common fractions are involved. For instance, when children multiply with common fractions between 0 and 1, they see that the product is smaller than either factor, except when 1 is a factor. This difference points to the need for careful development of understanding of multiplication with common fractions through the use of realistic situations, learning aids, and connections between this multiplication and multiplication with whole numbers.

Multiplication with fractional numbers involves three situations: multiplying a common fraction by a whole number, multiplying a whole number by a common fraction, and multiplying a common fraction by a common fraction. Figure 14.7 illustrates these three types of multiplication in situations suitable for use in elementary school. These and the problems in Activities 14.11 through 14.14 are examples to use with children.

Multiplying a Fractional Number by a Whole Number

One way to interpret multiplication is as repeated addition. With whole numbers the thinking is that there are a number of groups of a certain size—say, five groups of four apples; the answer, 20, is determined by adding 4 five times:

$$4 + 4 + 4 + 4 + 4 = 20 \text{ or } 5 \times 4 = 20$$

Repeated addition with common fractions uses the same thinking, except that the second factor is a common fraction. In the example in Figure 14.7a,

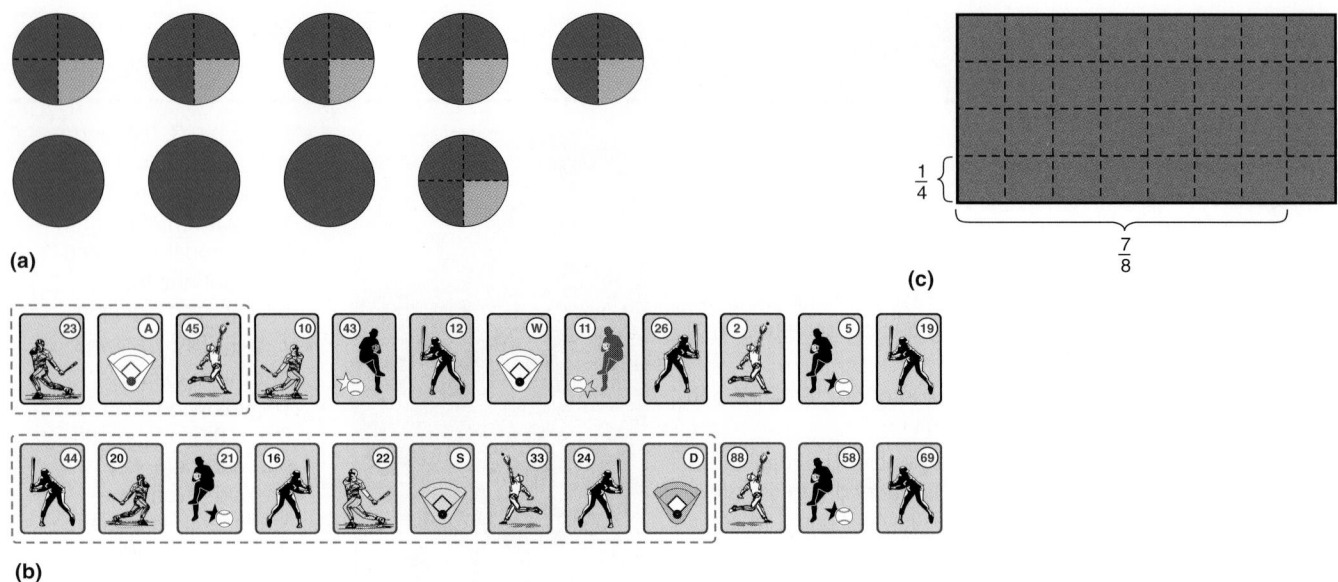

Figure 14.7 Multiplication situations involving common fractions

there are 5 three-quarter hours. The answer can be determined by adding $\frac{3}{4}$ five times:

$$\frac{3}{4} + \frac{3}{4} + \frac{3}{4} + \frac{3}{4} + \frac{3}{4} = \frac{15}{4} = 3\frac{3}{4}$$

or

$$5 \times \frac{3}{4} = \frac{15}{4} = 3\frac{3}{4}$$

The connection between repeated addition with whole numbers and repeated addition with fractional numbers can be made by engaging children in a lesson like the one in Activity 14.11:

1. Oletha practices goal tending for her soccer team for $\frac{3}{4}$ of an hour five nights a week. How many hours does she practice each week? (Answer: There are 5 three-quarter circles, each representing $\frac{3}{4}$ of an hour. The combined circles represent $3\frac{3}{4}$ total hours: $5 \times \frac{3}{4} = \frac{15}{4}$, or $3\frac{3}{4}$.)

2. Harold had 12 baseball trading cards. He traded $\frac{3}{4}$ of them for one Hank Aaron card. How many cards did he trade for the one card? (Answer: There are 12 cards. One-fourth of 12 is 3, so three-fourths of 12 is 9: $\frac{3}{4} \times 12 = 9$.)

3. Ben had $\frac{7}{8}$ of a sheet of poster board. He used $\frac{1}{4}$ of the sheet for an art project. What part of the entire sheet did he use for the project? (Answer: Seven of the eight parts are bracketed to show $\frac{7}{8}$. The seven eighths are cut into fourths, and one of the fourths is bracketed. One-fourth of seven-eighths is $\frac{7}{32}$ of the piece of board: $\frac{1}{4} \times \frac{7}{8} = \frac{7}{32}$.)

Multiplying a Whole Number by a Fractional Number

Many practical situations give rise to the need for multiplying a whole number by a fractional number. In Figure 14.7b the baseball card setting is this type. Figure 14.8 illustrates other common examples: one-quarter of a block of butter weighs one-fourth of a pound, so the weight is $\frac{1}{4}$ of 16 ounces, or 4 ounces. One-third of a foot is the same as $\frac{1}{3}$ of 12 inches, or 4 inches; one-half of a dollar is $\frac{1}{2}$ of 100 pennies, or 50 cents. Frequent encounters with these and similar applications enhance children's understanding of the practical uses of this multiplication. Activity 14.12 presents a whole-class lesson dealing with this type of multiplication. Eventually, students learn that multiplication of a whole number by a common fraction—for example, $\frac{2}{3} \times 18$—can be completed by either of the following algorithm procedures:

$$2 \times \frac{18}{3} = \frac{36}{3} = 12$$

$$\frac{18}{3} \times 2 = 6 \times 2 = 12$$

Multiplying a Fractional Number by a Fractional Number

Multiplying a fractional number by a fractional number is the most difficult for students to visualize and understand. Care must be taken to ensure that meanings are clear. The poster board problem in Figure 14.7c is this type. The following are addi-

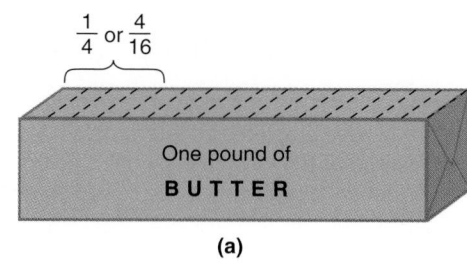

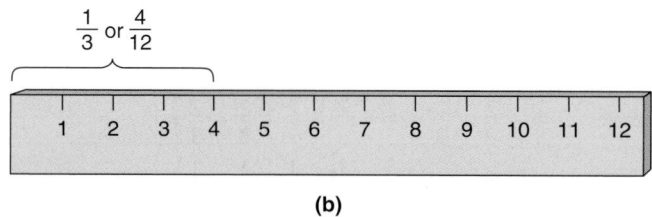

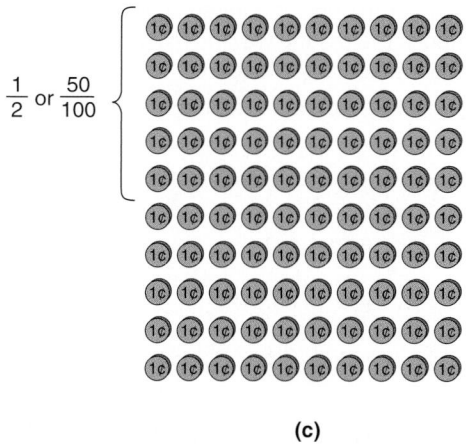

Figure 14.8 (a) One-fourth of a pound of butter (16 ounces) is $\frac{4}{16}$; (b) one-third of a foot (12 inches) is $\frac{4}{12}$; (c) one-half of a dollar (100 pennies) is $\frac{50}{100}$.

tional situations that provide a connection between the real world and multiplying one common fraction by another:

- A popcorn-ball recipe uses $\frac{3}{4}$ of a cup of sugar. If only $\frac{1}{2}$ of a recipe is prepared, how much sugar is used?

- Rosie had $\frac{3}{4}$ of a pound of ground beef. When she used $\frac{1}{3}$ of it for a burger, how much ground beef was in her burger?

- Mas spends $1\frac{1}{2}$ hours doing homework each evening, He does $\frac{1}{2}$ of his homework before dinner and $\frac{1}{2}$ after dinner. How much time does he work before dinner? after dinner?

These problems can all be solved quickly using a memorized algorithm such as the one in the teacher's book referred to earlier. The algorithm for the first problem ($\frac{3}{4} \times \frac{1}{2}$) suggests the following solution:

Multiply the numerators: $3 \times 1 = 3$
Multiply the denominators: $4 \times 2 = 8$
$$\frac{3}{4} \times \frac{1}{2} = \frac{3}{8}$$

When students memorize a rote procedure such as this, no matter how simple, they lose a conceptual understanding of the process involved and retain little number sense about whether the solution they obtain is reasonable. We strongly recommend that students need experiences such as Activity 14.12 and 14.13 before they begin to apply any formal algorithms.

Understanding the meaning of multiplication of two fractional numbers can be developed with a presentation using real objects and an overhead projector. Figure 14.9 illustrates a plan for a lesson to develop the concept. Note that this lesson does not introduce the algorithm. (The same scheme could be used with small groups of students if enough ingredients and other materials are on hand, so children could measure and work out answers for themselves.)

Once the children show that they can visualize situations involving multiplication of two common fractions and understand their meanings, an algorithm can be introduced. Raise questions that cause children to think about the new multiplication and its relationship to concepts they already know. For example:

- What is different about this multiplication compared to multiplication with common fractions that we've already done? (Answer: Here we are multiplying two common fractions. Before we had one common fraction and a whole number.)

- Do you think we can use the same algorithm as before for this type of multiplication? Let's see. (Write algorithms for the recipe changes with answers.)

$$\frac{1}{2} \times \frac{1}{4} = \frac{1}{8}$$
$$\frac{1}{2} \times \frac{1}{2} = \frac{1}{4}$$
$$\frac{1}{2} \times \frac{1}{3} = \frac{1}{6}$$
$$\frac{1}{2} \times \frac{3}{4} = \frac{3}{8}$$

ACTIVITY 14.11 Multiplying a Fraction by a Whole Number (Reasoning and Proof)

Level: Grades 4–6

Setting: Groups of four

Objective: Students develop strategies and an algorithm for multiplying a common fraction by a whole number.

Materials: Common fraction manipulatives, common fraction number lines, paper and pencils

- Give each team a printed copy of the following problem: "Sarah practices ballet for three-quarters of an hour each day. How many hours does she practice in a week?"

- Teams share work in a modified roundtable format. In this format the first team member reads the problem and conducts a discussion about its meaning. The second member chooses a concrete learning aid appropriate for solving the problem. The third uses the learning aid to represent the problem, and the fourth member solves the problem with the learning aid.

- One child might select circular pieces from a common fraction kit. The child who represents the problem sets up 7 three-quarter circles. The child who solves the problem combines the circles to show that Sarah practices for $5\frac{1}{4}$ hours in a week.

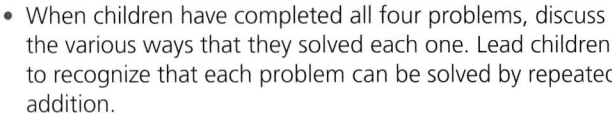

- Another child might select a number line. The child who represents the problem marks off 7 three-quarter jumps and the child who determines the answer converts $\frac{21}{4}$ to $5\frac{1}{4}$ hours.

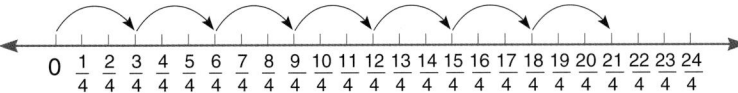

- Present the following three additional problems for groups to solve. Members rotate functions until each one has performed each function.
  - "Flora has 6 pieces of candy. Each weighs $\frac{5}{6}$ of an ounce. What is the total weight of the candy?"
  - "Jam will use $\frac{2}{3}$ foot of framing material for each side of a square picture. How much framing material will he need for two pictures?"
  - "The oval track at Wilson School is $\frac{1}{4}$ mile around. Hark ran five laps around the track. How far did she run?"

- When children have completed all four problems, discuss the various ways that they solved each one. Lead children to recognize that each problem can be solved by repeated addition.

- Write an addition sentence for each problem:

$$\frac{3}{4} + \frac{3}{4} + \frac{3}{4} + \frac{3}{4} + \frac{3}{4} + \frac{3}{4} + \frac{3}{4} = ?$$

$$\frac{5}{6} + \frac{5}{6} + \frac{5}{6} + \frac{5}{6} + \frac{5}{6} + \frac{5}{6} = ?$$

$$\frac{2}{3} + \frac{2}{3} + \frac{2}{3} + \frac{2}{3} + \frac{2}{3} + \frac{2}{3} + \frac{2}{3} + \frac{2}{3} = ?$$

$$\frac{1}{4} + \frac{1}{4} + \frac{1}{4} + \frac{1}{4} + \frac{1}{4} = ?$$

- Add the numerators in the addition sentences. Compare answers with the answers that children arrived at using learning aids. Connect this addition to repeated addition with whole numbers. Discuss the way in which repeated addition and multiplication are related.

- Have children name a multiplication sentence for each problem:

$$7 \times \frac{3}{4} = ?$$

$$6 \times \frac{5}{6} = ?$$

$$8 \times \frac{2}{3} = ?$$

$$5 \times \frac{1}{4} = ?$$

- Guide children to note that multiplying the whole number by the numerator and writing the product over the denominator yields the answer. The answer can be converted to a whole number or whole number and fraction.

Figure 14.9 Lesson plan for discovery lesson with mixed numerals

TEACHER
Joshua Jones   DATE 12/14/06
TOPIC
Multiplying common fraction by common fraction

MATERIALS NEEDED
2 glass measuring cups, popped popcorn, sugar, jar of corn syrup, salt, water, vanilla, fraction kit materials, overhead transparency with recipe, projector

SET THE STAGE AND STATE THE OBJECTIVE
"I made some small popcorn balls for holiday decorations last night. Here is the recipe I used." Show recipe on overhead.

| 3 quarts popcorn | $\frac{3}{4}$ cup sugar | $\frac{1}{3}$ cup corn syrup |
| $\frac{3}{4}$ cup water | $\frac{1}{4}$ tsp. salt | $\frac{1}{2}$ tsp. vanilla |

"I made a half recipe. How much of each ingredient did I use?"

PROVIDE INSTRUCTIONAL INPUT AND MODELING
Show 3 qts. of popcorn. Discuss what $\frac{1}{2}$ is. Pour $\frac{3}{4}$ cup sugar into measuring cup. Talk about what $\frac{1}{2}$ would be. Use measuring cups and ingredients to discuss other portions.

CHECK FOR UNDERSTANDING AND GIVE GUIDED PRACTICE
Use Louie's hamburger and Mas's homework problems (see main text) for students to solve with kit materials, drawings, or mentally. Discuss.

GIVE INDEPENDENT PRACTICE
None

ACTIVITY 14.12 Multiplying a Whole Number by a Fractional Number

Level: Grades 4–6

Setting: Whole class

Objective: Students develop strategies and an algorithm for multiplying a whole number by a common fraction.

Materials: Sets of 24 individual objects (disks, plastic animals, etc.) for each child; 2-foot loops of colored string or yarn, several per child

- Say: "I want each of you to use your disks to make a 3 × 6 array." Monitor to check for accuracy. Have the students recall a multiplication sentence for this array: 3 × 6 = 18.

- Say: "I want each of you to put a loop of yarn around one-third of your array." Monitor for accuracy.

- Discuss the fact that to determine one-third of the set, it is necessary to think in terms of three equal-size subgroups. Each subgroup is one-third of the entire set of disks, so $\frac{1}{3}$ of 18

is 6. Write the multiplication sentence $\frac{1}{3} \times 18 = 6$ on the chalkboard.

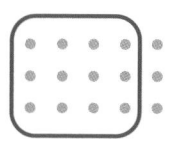

- "Now I want you to move your loop to show how many disks are in two-thirds of the array." Monitor for accuracy.

- Write a sentence for this situation: $\frac{2}{3} \times 18 = 12$.

- Repeat with another set that can be separated into equal-size sets without remainders, such as $\frac{3}{4}$ of 16, $\frac{2}{5}$ of 20, and $\frac{5}{6}$ of 12.

- Provide guided practice by having students work in pairs/check format to complete these examples. Alternatively, one child uses markers and string to solve a problem while the other checks the work.

ACTIVITY 14.13   Using Paper Folding to Multiply Common Fractions

Level: Grades 3–5

Setting: Small groups

Objective: Students will use the results of paper folding to develop an algorithm for multiplying common fractions.

Materials: Several sheets of paper per student

- Hold up a single piece of paper. Tell children that you are holding the world's cheapest calculator.
- Relate that this is a special calculator that will do multiplication with fractions.
- Write $\frac{1}{2} \times \frac{1}{2} = ?$ on the board and ask students to get their calculator (piece of paper) so that they can use it to solve the problem.
- Slowly fold the paper in half and then in half again. Ask students to explain why the folding represents $\frac{1}{2} \times \frac{1}{2}$. (Folding the paper in half is the same as taking $\frac{1}{2}$ of the paper, or multiplying by $\frac{1}{2}$. The resulting rectangle is the answer to the problem $\frac{1}{2} \times \frac{1}{2} = ?$)

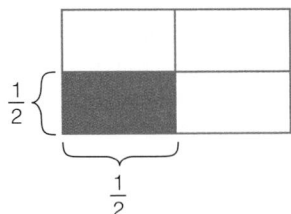

- Unfold the paper and ask what part of the whole paper is represented by the rectangle (Answer: $\frac{1}{4}$.).
- Write the completed problem on the board: $\frac{1}{2} \times \frac{1}{2} = \frac{1}{4}$.
- Ask children to fold paper to represent the following problems, then record the number sentence and answer:

$$\frac{1}{2} \times \frac{1}{3} = ?$$
$$\frac{1}{3} \times \frac{1}{4} = ?$$
$$\frac{1}{2} \times \frac{1}{2} \times \frac{1}{2} = ?$$

- Ask for student volunteers to write the number sentences on the board.
- Challenge students to find the pattern to solving these sentences and use that pattern to solve the following problems:

$$\frac{1}{2} \times \frac{1}{4} = ?$$
$$\frac{1}{3} \times \frac{1}{8} = ?$$
$$\frac{1}{2} \times \frac{2}{3} = ?$$
$$\frac{3}{4} \times \frac{2}{3} = ?$$

- Have students in each group explain their solution strategies.

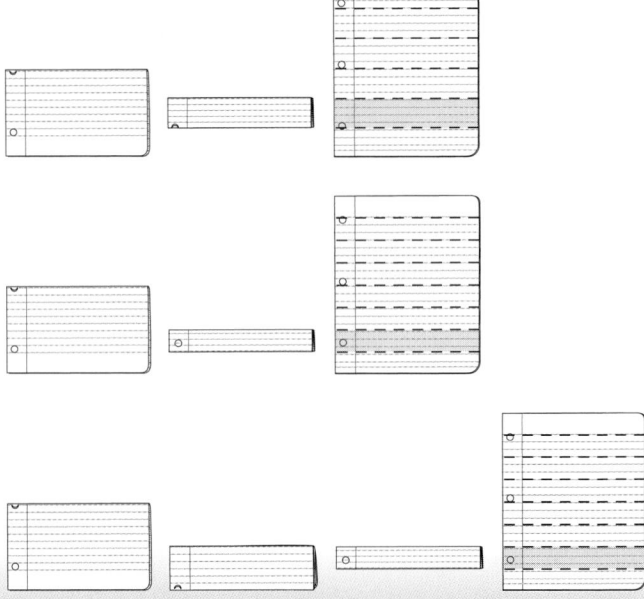

- How is the multiplication completed with the algorithm? (Answer: The numerator of one fraction is multiplied by the numerator of the other fraction, the denominator of one fraction is multiplied by the denominator of the other, and the two products form another common fraction.)

Activity 14.13 uses paper folding to help children develop the algorithm for multiplying two common fractions.

ⒺXERCISE

Make up an additional word problem for each of the four multiplication sentences in the preceding example. Sketch a sequence of steps for each sentence with models that illustrate each one. ●●●

Multiplying Mixed Numerals

Situations that involve multiplication with mixed numerals occur in a variety of settings. We used a reduction of ingredients in a recipe to illustrate one

ACTIVITY 14.14 Multiplying with Mixed Numerals

Level: Grades 4–6

Setting: Groups of four

Objective: Students develop strategies for multiplying pairs of mixed numerals.

Materials: Jigsaw cards (explained in activity), lemon soufflé recipe, paper and pencils

- Give each team of four students a copy of the lemon soufflé recipe:

  16 eggs

  $2\frac{1}{3}$ cup sugar

  $\frac{3}{4}$ teaspoon salt

  9 tablespoons lemon juice

  grated rind of $\frac{1}{2}$ lemon

  $\frac{3}{4}$ tablespoon vanilla

  This recipe serves 18 people.

- Explain the jigsaw problem-solving cooperative-learning format. Four clues for solving a problem are distributed to a team, one to each child. The problem for this activity is: "One soufflé made from the recipe serves 18 people. How much of each ingredient will you need to make enough soufflé to serve 45 people?"

  Clue 1: If you want to make enough soufflé for 36 people, how do you determine the quantity of each ingredient?

  Clue 2: Determine the quantity of each ingredient when you double the recipe.

  Clue 3: By how much will you increase the ingredients to make enough soufflé to serve 9 more people, for a total of 45 people?

  Clue 4: What is the total amount of each ingredient?

- Children discuss and solve the clues in order, making certain that each one understands their meaning.

- Call on team members to explain their work.

  Hot Rods: "We used markers to represent eggs. We counted out 16 eggs for one recipe and 16 more for a second recipe. That's enough for 36 people. We needed enough eggs for 9 more people. Eight is $\frac{1}{2}$ of 16, so we counted 8 more markers; that made 40 eggs in all."

16 eggs for 18 people   16 eggs for 18 people   8 eggs for 9 people

40 eggs for 45 people

Go Getters: "We used a measuring cup and sand to determine the amount of sugar. First, we filled a measuring cup to show 2 cups and poured that into a bowl. Then we measured $\frac{1}{3}$ and put that in the bowl. That was enough sugar for soufflé that serves 18 people. We did that a second time, and had enough sugar for 36 people. Then we measured 1 cup, that's half of 2, and then measured $\frac{1}{2}$ of $\frac{1}{3}$. That gave us $\frac{1}{6}$ cup or enough for 9 more servings. When we added everything together, we had $2\frac{1}{3}$ plus $2\frac{1}{3}$ plus $1\frac{1}{6}$. That's $5\frac{5}{6}$ cups of sugar."

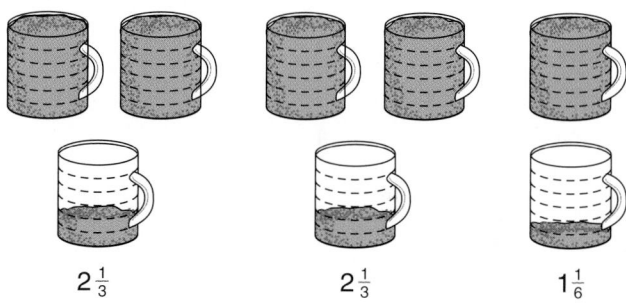

$2\frac{1}{3}$ $2\frac{1}{3}$ $1\frac{1}{6}$

- Each of the other groups explains another part of the problem.

- A culminating activity might be to actually prepare a soufflé.

setting for multiplying a pair of common fractions. When the ingredients in a recipe are increased, multiplication with mixed numerals can occur. If a recipe that includes $1\frac{1}{2}$ cups of sugar is doubled to make a larger cake, then 3 cups of sugar is needed. When that same recipe is increased $2\frac{1}{2}$ times, the amount of sugar must be increased $2\frac{1}{2}$ times. Activity 14.14 shows one way to introduce multiplication with mixed numerals. The first and second steps in this activity provide a base from which to solve the third and fourth steps.

Once the recipe is doubled (from 18 to 36 servings), the amount needed for 45 servings can be determined by finding $\frac{1}{2}$ the recipe amount of each ingredient and adding it to the doubled amount. Children who recognize this can complete much of the work mentally.

Before introducing an algorithm for multiplying with mixed numerals, spend some time reviewing the process of changing mixed numerals to common fractions. Ask questions such as "How many halves in $2\frac{1}{2}$?" (Answer: 5.) "How many fourths in

$3\frac{1}{4}$?" (Answer: 13.) "How many sixths in $2\frac{5}{6}$?" (Answer: 17.) You might have students demonstrate that $2\frac{1}{2} = \frac{5}{2}$ by using fraction pieces or models, as illustrated in Figure 14.10.

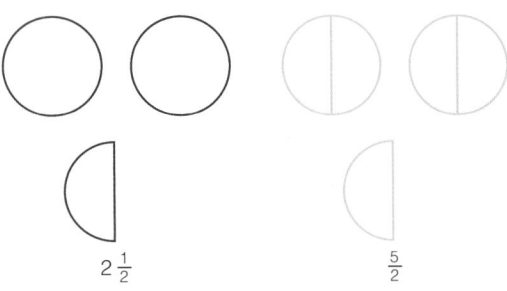

$2\frac{1}{2}$ $\frac{5}{2}$

Figure 14.10 Changing mixed numerals to common fractions using fraction pieces

This review sets the stage for doing the same thing in the algorithms. Following discussion of the soufflé problem in Activity 14.14, introduce a mathematical sentence for each part:

$$2\frac{1}{2} \times 16 = ?$$

$$2\frac{1}{2} \times 9 = ?$$

$$2\frac{1}{2} \times \frac{3}{4} = ?$$

$$2\frac{1}{2} \times 2\frac{1}{3} = ?$$

$$2\frac{1}{2} \times 1\frac{1}{2} = ?$$

Discuss each sentence in terms of the students' models, drawings, or mental solutions. The sentence $2\frac{1}{2} \times 16 = ?$ can be thought of as $2 \times 16 = 32$ and $\frac{1}{2} \times 16 = 8$, or 40, which is represented by the Hot Rods markers: 2 groups of 16 and $\frac{1}{2}$ of a group of 16. The sentence $2\frac{1}{2} \times 2\frac{1}{3} = ?$ can be thought of as $2 \times 2 = 4, \frac{1}{2} \times 2 = 1, 2 \times \frac{1}{3} = \frac{2}{3}$, and $\frac{1}{2} \times \frac{1}{3} = \frac{1}{6}$, which is rep-

resented by the Go Getters' modeling with measuring cups and sand: 4 cups + 1 cup + $\frac{2}{3}$ cup + $\frac{1}{6}$ cup. Note that the distributive property for multiplication is applied to mixed numerals in each of these situations. Associate each of the other sentences with the models children used to solve a part of the problem.

The next step leads to a standard algorithm for multiplying mixed numerals. Point to the first sentence and ask: "How many halves in $2\frac{1}{2}$?" (Answer: 5.) Change the sentence from $2\frac{1}{2}$ to $\frac{5}{2}$. Point out that this is now a whole number multiplied by a common fraction, so $5 \times 16 = 80$; divide 80 by 2; the answer is 40. The other algorithms should be completed in the same way.

$$2\frac{1}{2} \times 1\frac{1}{2} = ?$$

$$\frac{5}{2} \times \frac{3}{2} = ?$$

$$\frac{5}{2} \times \frac{3}{2} = \frac{15}{4} = 3\frac{3}{4}$$

In addition to using models and real-life applications, it is also beneficial to use an expanded notation, as suggested in the discussion of Activity 14.14. When children read the problem $2\frac{1}{2} \times 3\frac{1}{4} = ?$, they will read "two *and* one-half, three *and* one-fourth." This correct reading of the mixed numerals clearly indicates that there are two numbers represented in each mixed numeral, a whole number *and* a fractional number. Thus the expanded notation for this problem is simply a recognition of this already known fact. The original problem can be written in expanded notation as follows:

$$2\frac{1}{2} \times 3\frac{1}{4} = ?$$

$$\left(2 + \frac{1}{2}\right) \times \left(3 + \frac{1}{4}\right) = ?$$

MISCONCEPTION

When working with multiplication of mixed numerals with children, it is helpful to know that some children typically want to multiply mixed numerals as follows:

$$2\tfrac{1}{2} \times 3\tfrac{1}{4} = 6\tfrac{1}{8}$$

Can you tell what the error is? The student multiplied the whole numbers ($2 \times 3 = 6$) and then multiplied the fractional numbers

($\frac{1}{2} \times \frac{1}{4} = \frac{1}{8}$). Why might children use such a strategy? Many factors could explain why this incorrect method is used, but one reason is that children carry over the rules for addition and subtraction with mixed numerals to work multiplication. While learning addition and subtraction, children first add (or subtract) the fractional numbers and the whole numbers separately. Children bring the same reasoning to multiplication of mixed numerals.

The resulting expanded notation algorithm can be solved using the distributive law [8(3 + 4) = 8(3) + 8(4) = 24 + 32 = 56], resulting in these four partial products: $(2 \times 3) + (2 \times \frac{1}{4}) + (\frac{1}{2} \times 3) + (\frac{1}{2} \times \frac{1}{4})$. The final product is the sum of these four partial products. Every mixed numeral multiplication problem can be solved this way.

> Students may have used a similar expanded notation with multiplication of whole numbers:
>
> $16 \times 32 = (10 \times 30) + (10 \times 2) + (6 \times 30) + (6 \times 2) = 300 + 20 + 180 + 12 = 512.$

In comparison to the expanded notation method, the familiar algorithm for multiplying mixed numerals is efficient. Both mixed numerals are renamed as a *single* fractional number; then the two fractional numbers are multiplied to complete the algorithm. Thus the original problem can be solved as follows, using the familiar algorithm shown here:

$$2\frac{1}{2} \times 3\frac{1}{4} = \frac{5}{2} \times \frac{13}{4}$$
$$= \frac{(5 \times 13)}{(2 \times 4)}$$
$$= \frac{65}{8} = 8\frac{1}{8}$$

MULTICULTURALCONNECTION

Students can draw on their cultural background when developing word problems and contexts for fractional problems. For example, when recipes are the context, students can use recipes for ethnic dishes.

Division with Common Fractions

Division with fractional numbers arises from the same two settings as division with whole numbers—namely, repeated subtraction (measurement) and sharing (partitive) settings. The examples in Figure 14.11 illustrate measurement and partitive settings for division involving common fractions that are suitable for elementary students. Students can model these and other problems using fraction manipulatives or drawings.

Students' early experiences should include problem-solving work for which they devise solutions. The purpose of early activities is not to teach an algorithm ("invert and multiply") but to help students

understand division situations. These activities help children develop an intuitive base on which to build understanding of division algorithms. Activity 14.15 illustrates how measurement division involving common fractions can be introduced. Activity 14.16 is an introductory lesson dealing with partitive division with common fractions.

ⓔXERCISE

Create a story problem for a measurement situation and one for a partitive situation that could be used with children. Illustrate each problem with materials children might use to represent it as they solve the problem. ●●●

Developing Understanding of Division Algorithms

As mentioned earlier, in the elementary grades work with division involving common fractions helps children develop an intuitive understanding of algorithms involving these numbers. Two algorithms are used for dividing with common fractions. One is the common denominator algorithm, and the other is the invert-and-multiply algorithm. Both can be developed intuitively by following discovery lessons such as those in Activities 14.15 and 14.16.

Examples illustrate the measurement situations in Figure 14.11 to suggest a way to introduce the common fraction algorithm:

6 sheets of paper, how many $\frac{1}{2}$ pieces? $6 \div \frac{1}{2} = ?$
$\frac{2}{3}$ of pizza, how many $\frac{1}{6}$ pieces? $\frac{2}{3} \div \frac{1}{6} = ?$
$2\frac{1}{2}$ quarts ice cream,
    how many $\frac{1}{4}$ servings? $2\frac{1}{2} \div \frac{1}{4} = ?$

Discuss each situation: "If we change 6 to halves, how many halves are there?" (Answer: 12.) Rename 6 as $\frac{12}{2}$. "If we rename $\frac{2}{3}$ as sixths, how many are there?" (Answer: 4.) Rename $\frac{2}{3}$ as $\frac{4}{6}$. "If we rename $2\frac{1}{2}$ as a common fraction, what is the fraction?" (Answer: $\frac{5}{2}$.) "If we rename $\frac{5}{2}$ as fourths, how many fourths are there?" (Answer: 10.) Rename $\frac{5}{2}$ as $\frac{10}{4}$. Rewrite each division sentence:

$$\frac{12}{2} \div \frac{1}{2} = ?$$
$$\frac{4}{6} \div \frac{1}{6} = ?$$
$$\frac{10}{4} \div \frac{1}{4} = ?$$

Figure 14.11 Measurement

MEASUREMENT

- Six pieces of paper are cut in half. How many pieces are there? (Answer: $6 \div \frac{1}{2} = 12$.)

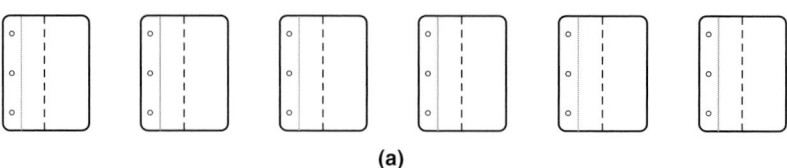

(a)

- Two-thirds of a pound of plant food is separated into two smaller packets. How much does each packet weigh? (Answer: $\frac{2}{3} \div 2 = \frac{1}{3}$.)

(b)

- Two and one-half quarts of ice cream are separated into one-fourth quart portions. How many portions are there? (Answer: $2\frac{1}{2} \div \frac{1}{4} = 10$.)

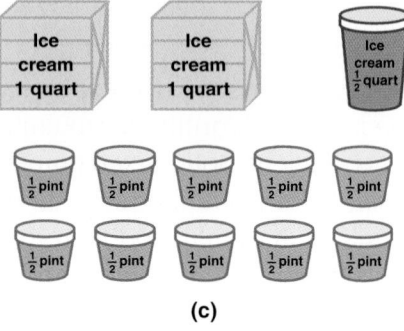

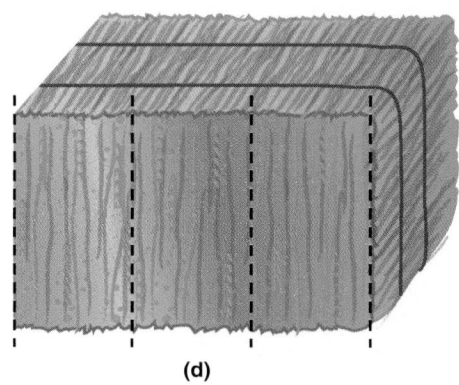

(c)

These measurement problems illustrate repeated subtraction situations. Each can be solved by subtracting the number that is the divisor until zero or an amount less than the divisor is reached, then counting the number of times it was subtracted.

PARTITIVE

- Three-fourths of a bale of hay is in a barn. It is divided into three equal-size packs. What part of a whole bale is each pack? (Answer: $\frac{3}{4} \div 3 = \frac{1}{4}$.)

(d)

- A half gallon of milk is poured into eight equal-sized containers. What part of a gallon is in each container? (Answer: $\frac{1}{2} \div 8 = \frac{1}{16}$.)

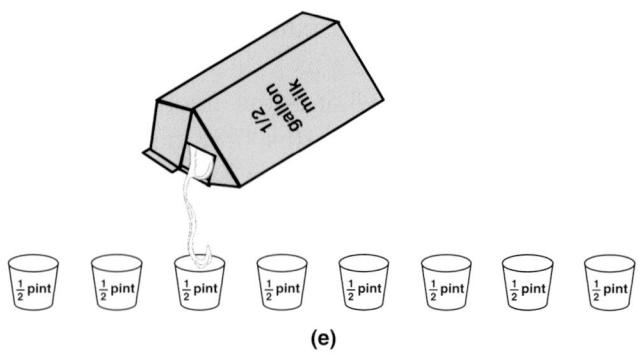

(e)

- Two and one-half apples are cut so that there are five equal-size pieces. What is the size of each piece? (Answer: $2\frac{1}{2} \div 5 = \frac{5}{10}$, or $\frac{1}{2}$.)

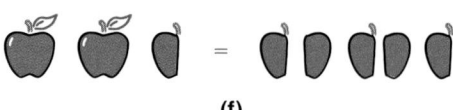

(f)

These partitive problems are "What is the size of each part?" situations. Each can be solved by dividing the quantities or objects into a number of equal-size parts and naming the size of each part.

ACTIVITY 14.15 Dividing by a Common Fraction

Level: Grades 4–6

Setting: Whole class

Objective: Students develop an understanding of measurement division with common fractions.

Materials: Demonstration markers and magnetic board, 3-foot length of craft paper, rectangles cut into fourths and eighths

- Put 15 markers on a magnetic board. Ask: "If we put these markers into groups that each have three markers, how many groups will there be?" (Answer: 5.) Review the idea that this measurement situation can be solved by repeated subtraction. Demonstrate by removing groups of three markers and counting the groups. Repeat with other groups, if necessary, to help students recall the meaning of repeated subtraction (measurement) division.

- Show a 3-foot length of craft paper, and present this situation: "I have a 3-foot piece of craft paper. If I cut it into pieces that are each $\frac{1}{2}$ foot long for student projects, how many pieces will there be?"

- Help students see that this situation is similar to the whole number situation. They know the size of the original object, 3 feet; they know the size of each part, $\frac{1}{2}$ foot; they are to determine the number of pieces. Once the paper has been cut, the $\frac{1}{2}$-foot pieces can be removed one at a time, just as sets containing three markers were removed.

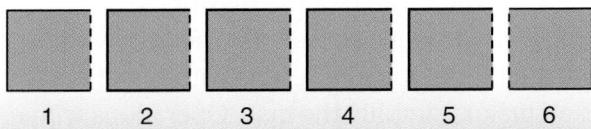

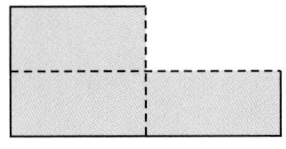

- Show a model of a sheet cake, and present this situation: "I have $\frac{3}{4}$ of a cake. When I cut it into pieces that are each $\frac{1}{4}$ of the cake, how many pieces will there be?"

- When the cake is cut into $\frac{1}{4}$-size pieces, there are three pieces.

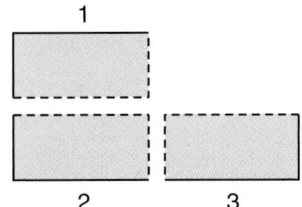

- "If I cut a cake into slices that are $\frac{1}{8}$ of the cake, how many will there be in $\frac{3}{4}$ of a cake?" By now, some students will see that if they rename $\frac{3}{4}$ as $\frac{6}{8}$, the answer will be 6, the numerator of the renamed common fraction.

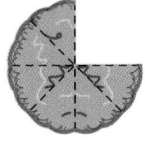 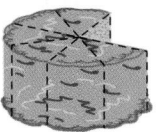

- Summarize the problems:

  15 markers in groups of 3 (5 groups)

  3 feet of paper cut into $\frac{1}{2}$-foot pieces (6 pieces)

  $\frac{3}{4}$ cake cut into $\frac{1}{4}$ slices (3 slices)

  $\frac{3}{4}$ cake cut into $\frac{1}{8}$ slices (6 slices)

- Have each child solve the measurement examples in Figure 14.11. Models or thought processes can be used to solve the problems. Have children share their models and/or thought processes.

"Look at the denominators in each example. What do you notice about them?" (Answer: They are the same number in each pair.) "Look what happens when I divide the numerators, then the denominators, in the first sentence: $\frac{12}{2} \div \frac{1}{2} = \frac{12}{1}$. What happened when I divided the denominators?" (Answer: The quotient is 1.) "What is another way to write $\frac{12}{1}$?" (Answer: 12.). "So, when we divide the numerators and the denominators, we get a new fraction that has a denominator of 1. Let's look at the other two sentences."

$$\frac{4}{6} \div \frac{1}{6} = \frac{4}{1} = 4$$

$$\frac{10}{4} \div \frac{1}{4} = \frac{10}{1} = 10$$

Summarize the process: Rename the dividend and divisor as common fractions having the same denominator, if necessary. Divide the first numerator by the second numerator, then divide the first denominator by the second denominator. Rename the quotient as a whole number or mixed numeral.

The invert-and-multiply algorithm is based on the idea that dividing one number by another is the same as multiplying the number by the reciprocal of the divisor. We use examples from Activity 14.15 to illustrate a way to develop an intuitive understanding of this algorithm. Recall with children the paper-folding work they did to determine answers to such questions as "When a half piece of paper is folded in half, what is the size of each of the two pieces?" Display the record made during that activity:

$\frac{1}{2}$ cut into 2 pieces, each piece $\frac{1}{4}$ of whole

$\frac{1}{2}$ cut into 4 pieces, each piece $\frac{1}{8}$ of whole

$\frac{1}{3}$ cut into 2 pieces, each piece $\frac{1}{6}$ of whole

$\frac{1}{6}$ cut into 6 pieces, each piece $\frac{1}{36}$ of whole

ACTIVITY 14.16 Dividing a Common Fraction by a Whole Number

Level: Grades 4–6

Setting: Whole class

Objective: Students develop an understanding of the meaning of partitive division with common fractions.

Materials: $8\frac{1}{2} \times 11$ paper (can be scrap), several pieces for each child; scissors and marking pen for each child

- List these words on the chalkboard or overhead: halves, thirds, fourths, sixths. Tell the children that they are to fold one piece of paper into halves, another into thirds, and so on, until the pieces are folded to show each of the common fractions.

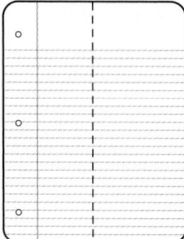 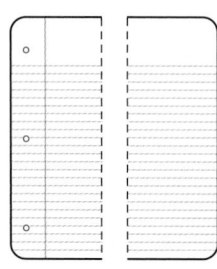 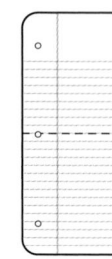

- Give these instructions: "Cut along the fold of the piece folded in half to make two parts. When you have done that, fold one of the halves so that there are two equal-size parts." When the folding is finished, tell the children to write the common fraction that tells what part of the whole sheet of paper the newly folded portion is. Have children fold the other half to make and identify four equal-size parts.

- Give instructions for folds with other pieces: Fold thirds into 2, 3, and 4 pieces; name the size of each piece.

- Fold fourths into 2, 3, and 4 pieces; name the size of each piece.

- Fold sixths into 2, 3, and 4 pieces (there will be two unfolded pieces); name the size of each piece.

- Discuss and list results of cutting and folding:

  $\frac{1}{2}$ folded in half: each piece $\frac{1}{4}$ of whole

  $\frac{1}{2}$ folded in fourths: each piece $\frac{1}{8}$ of whole

  $\frac{1}{3}$ folded in halves: each piece $\frac{1}{6}$ of whole

  $\frac{1}{3}$ folded in fourths: each piece $\frac{1}{12}$ of whole

- Emphasize the concept that when a common fraction is divided by a whole number, the quotient identifies the size of each part in relation to the entire sheet of paper.

Write division sentences along with their corresponding multiplication sentence:

$$\frac{1}{2} \div 2 = \frac{1}{4} \qquad \frac{1}{2} \times \frac{1}{2} = \frac{1}{4}$$

$$\frac{1}{2} \div 4 = \frac{1}{8} \qquad \frac{1}{2} \times \frac{1}{4} = \frac{1}{8}$$

$$\frac{1}{3} \div 2 = \frac{1}{6} \qquad \frac{1}{3} \times \frac{1}{2} = \frac{1}{6}$$

$$\frac{1}{6} \div 6 = \frac{1}{36} \qquad \frac{1}{6} \times \frac{1}{6} = \frac{1}{36}$$

Relate each pair of sentences to the corresponding description in the first listing.

EXERCISE

Write a real-life problem for the number sentence $\frac{2}{3} \div \frac{1}{2}$. ●●●

As children discuss the examples, help them see that, just as the answer to 6 divided by 3 is the same as finding $\frac{1}{3}$ of 6, $\frac{1}{2}$ divided by 2 is the same as finding $\frac{1}{2}$ of $\frac{1}{2}$. Summarize the process: To divide a common fraction by a common fraction, multiply the dividend by the inverse of the divisor.

There are few occasions when individuals compute either of the algorithms with paper and pencil. Calculators simplify the task. Operations with calculators and common fractions are presented later in this chapter. Whether you go beyond an intuitive development of either or both algorithms to have children develop paper-and-pencil skills with them will depend on goals for the setting in which you teach. If your local mathematics standards require children to learn and apply the standard algorithms, do not neglect the necessary foundational work described earlier as activities that lead to the algorithms. Procedures learned by rote tend to be brittle.

Developing Number Sense About Operations with Common Fractions

Students who have a good understanding of common fractions gained through work with regions, number lines, and other models develop a feel for fractions.

As children's sense for numbers grows, so does their skill in estimating and judging the reasonableness of answers. Teachers play a role in helping children develop a sense about numbers. During study with fraction strips and number lines, ask questions about fractions that are near 0, near $\frac{1}{2}$, and near 1. Build on this knowledge to help children think about operations with common fractions and judge the reasonableness of their own answers. Use questions such as these as children learn the four operations:

- When you add $\frac{1}{3}$ and $\frac{1}{4}$, will the sum be less than, equal to, or more than 1? Why?

- When you add $\frac{1}{2}$ and $\frac{3}{4}$, will the sum be less than, equal to, or more than 1? Why?

- When you add $\frac{2}{3}$ and $\frac{1}{4}$, the sum will be about what number? Why?

- The sum for a pair of fractions is between $\frac{1}{2}$ and 1. Is the pair $\frac{1}{3}$ and $\frac{1}{4}$, $\frac{1}{8}$ and $\frac{1}{6}$, or $\frac{2}{3}$ and 1? Why?

- When you subtract a pair of common fractions, will the answer be less than or more than 1? Why?

- When you determine $\frac{1}{2}$ of 12, will the answer be more than or less than 12? Why?

- When you divide 12 by $\frac{1}{2}$, will the quotient be more than or less than 12? Why?

- When you divide $\frac{1}{4}$ by 2, will the quotient be more than or less than $\frac{1}{4}$? Why?

- When you divide $\frac{1}{2}$ by $\frac{1}{4}$, will the quotient be more than or less than 1? Why?

- When you divide $\frac{1}{2}$ by $\frac{3}{4}$, will the quotient be less than or more than 1? Why?

Another aspect of number sense with common fractions is the ability to compute mentally. You should encourage children to become comfortable with doing much of their computation without paper and pencil. When children add or subtract simple combinations, such as $\frac{1}{2} + \frac{1}{4}$ or $\frac{1}{3} - \frac{1}{6}$, do not require that they show all their computations with paper and pencil. Those who can think "$\frac{1}{2}$ plus $\frac{1}{4}$ is $\frac{2}{4}$ plus $\frac{1}{4}$, or $\frac{3}{4}$" and "$\frac{1}{3}$ minus $\frac{1}{6}$ is $\frac{2}{6}$ minus $\frac{1}{6}$, or $\frac{1}{6}$" should be allowed to record the sum or difference without written computation. The same holds true for multiplication and division. However, asking children to show computations on occasion serves as an assessment of their understanding of algorithms. Standardized tests that students are required to take at the end of certain grade levels in some states include algorithmic computation, so children should maintain skill with each algorithm they learn.

"Thinking aloud" about procedures for multiplication and division of fractional numbers helps students develop mental computation skills:

- There are 240 students in a school. Three-fourths of them arrive by bus each day. How many are bused to school? Help students to think, "One-fourth of 240 is 60, so three-fourths will be 3 times 60, or 180. That means 180 are bused to school."

- There are 40 pounds of cheese in a round. How many $\frac{1}{4}$-pound pieces can be cut from the round? Help students to think, "There are 4 quarter-pound pieces in 1 pound, so there will be 40 times 4 pieces, or 160, in the round."

ⒺXERCISE

Discuss the validity of the rule "Division makes smaller." ●●●

Renaming Fractions in Simpler Terms

A common practice in the past was to have students rename every fraction answer in its simplest form. Answers were often considered wrong if they could be but had not been "reduced to lowest terms," even when all other aspects of the work were correct. A simple example where this rule violates good practice is in check writing. When a check is written for a purchase costing $78.95, the cent part is written as $\frac{95}{100}$, not $\frac{19}{20}$. In keeping with the philosophy that students should understand what they are doing, it is better that they consider the nature of each problem before they make a decision about renaming an answer. Consider these two examples:

- Pedro's father uses fine gold wire to make jewelry. The jewelry wire costs $5.00 per quarter inch. One day he purchased one piece of wire that was $3\frac{1}{4}$ inches long and another that was $4\frac{1}{4}$ inches long. What is the total length of the two pieces? What was the cost of the wire?

In this problem precision of measurement is important because the price is based on quarter-inch segments. It is necessary to know how many quarter-inches are purchased in order to determine the cost. Retaining $7\frac{2}{4}$ inches as the answer reflects the nature of the situation; renaming it as $7\frac{1}{2}$ inches does not. To solve the problem, the sum can be renamed as $\frac{30}{4}$; 30 times 5 shows that the cost of the wire is $150.00.

- There were $29\frac{1}{4}$ yards of cloth on a bolt. How much is left after a customer purchases $2\frac{3}{4}$ yards of the cloth?

In this case the answer $26\frac{2}{4}$ can be renamed as $26\frac{1}{2}$ because cloth is sold by the yard and precision is not significant. Discussions that help students make decisions about how to treat common fractions in answers should replace the practice of having them rename every answer in simplest terms.

During early work with fraction models and number lines, children learn that there are equivalent classes of fractions, such as $\frac{1}{2}, \frac{2}{4}, \frac{3}{6}$, and $\frac{4}{8}$. As their understanding matures, they easily rename $\frac{1}{2}$ as $\frac{2}{4}$, $\frac{1}{3}$ as $\frac{2}{6}$, and $\frac{4}{8}$ as $\frac{2}{4}$ or $\frac{1}{2}$. It is when common fractions become larger that children see that renaming is not so easily done.

Discussion of the process can begin with simple examples:

$$\frac{1}{2} = \frac{2}{4} \qquad \frac{2}{3} = \frac{4}{6} \qquad \frac{4}{8} = \frac{12}{24} \qquad \frac{4}{10} = \frac{16}{40}$$

Point out that the numerator and the denominator in $\frac{2}{4}$ are two times as large as in $\frac{1}{2}$. Ask: "How much larger are the numerator and denominator in $\frac{4}{6}$ than in $\frac{2}{3}$?" (Answer: two times as large.) "How much larger are they in the third example?" (Answer: three times as large.) "In the fourth example?" (Answer: four times as large.) "Can you name a rule for changing a common fraction so that it is in higher terms?" (Answer: Multiply the numerator and denominator by the same number.) Point out that this is the same as multiplying by 1:

$$\frac{1}{2} \times 1 = \frac{1}{2} \times \frac{2}{2} = \frac{2}{4}$$
$$\frac{2}{3} \times 1 = \frac{2}{3} \times \frac{2}{2} = \frac{4}{6}$$
$$\frac{4}{8} \times 1 = \frac{4}{8} \times \frac{3}{3} = \frac{12}{24}$$
$$\frac{4}{10} \times 1 = \frac{4}{10} \times \frac{4}{4} = \frac{16}{40}$$

Changing to lower terms (simplifying) is the inverse of changing to higher terms, so you can reverse the process to rename the common fractions in simpler terms:

$$\frac{2}{4} \div 1 = \frac{2}{4} \div \frac{2}{2} = \frac{1}{2}$$
$$\frac{4}{6} \div 1 = \frac{4}{6} \div \frac{2}{2} = \frac{2}{3}$$
$$\frac{12}{24} \div 1 = \frac{12}{24} \div \frac{3}{3} = \frac{4}{8}$$
$$\frac{16}{40} \div 1 = \frac{16}{40} \div \frac{4}{4} = \frac{4}{10}$$

Discuss the rule: To rename a common fraction in simpler terms, divide both the numerator and the denominator by the same number.

Multiplying and Dividing with Decimal Fractions

Multiplying with Decimal Fractions

Work with decimal fractions in the early years is confined to developing understanding of the numerals. Later, children learn about addition and subtraction with them. In higher grades they learn processes for multiplying and dividing with decimal fractions. Because fractional numbers expressed as decimal fractions can be multiplied using the same algorithm as when whole numbers are multiplied, teachers must guard against having the process become mechanical for students. Unless conceptual knowledge is developed along with procedural knowledge, children's understanding is shallow. A number of practical applications of multiplication with decimal fractions are relevant for elementary school children. The examples in Activities 14.17 and 14.18 can be used to foster children's thinking about multiplication with decimal fractions.

Multiplication of decimal fractions involves multiplying a decimal fraction by a whole number, a whole number by a decimal fraction, or a decimal fraction by a decimal fraction. Activity 14.17 shows a way to introduce multiplication of a decimal fraction by a whole number. Whole-class lessons present situations involving multiplication of a whole number by a decimal fraction (see the companion website activity "Multiplying a Whole Number by a Decimal Fraction") and a decimal fraction by a decimal fraction (see Activity 14.18). Estimation is also an important part of helping children make sense of multiplication with decimal fractions.

After students understand the meaning of the three multiplication settings, they will be ready to learn an algorithm. The commonly used algorithm

ACTIVITY 14.17 Multiplying a Decimal by a Whole Number

Level: Grades 4–6

Setting: Groups of four

Objective: Students develop strategies and an algorithm for multiplying a decimal fraction by a whole number.

Materials: No specific materials; students may select from materials center, use diagrams, or do all work mentally or with paper and pencil.

- Present the following four numbered problems, one for each team member.
  1. Josie is repairing her railroad track layout. She needs six pieces of wire, each 0.6 of a meter long. How much wire does she need for her layout?
  2. Onterrio paid $0.49 each for eight cans of corn. What was the total cost of the corn?
  3. Marty has four bags of dog food, each weighing 0.75 of a kilogram. What is the total weight of the dog food?
  4. A restaurant recipe uses 1.5 liters of milk for each bowl of pancake batter. How much milk is used to make 15 bowls of batter?

- Distribute a copy of each problem to each team. Team members decide which member will solve which problem. Each team member chooses a method by which to work and solves the problem. Members who finish first may coach other members.

- Teams discuss their solutions.

- On a signal, the children who worked problem 1, those who worked problem 2, those who worked problem 3, and those who worked problem 4 assemble in groups to share their work.

- Students return to desks for a discussion of the problems. Points to bring out during the discussion should include the following :
  - Each of these problems can be solved by repeated addition. For example:

    $0.6 + 0.6 + 0.6 + 0.6 + 0.6 + 0.6 = ?$

    or $6 \times 0.6 = ?$

  - Estimation helps determine the reasonableness of some answers. When $0.49 is rounded to $0.50, 8 times 50 indicates that the answer will be around $4.00. An answer of $39.60 or $0.3960 is not a reasonable answer.

  - Multiplication with decimal fractions is done the same way as multiplication with whole numbers.

  - Numbers can be renamed from decimal fractions to common fractions to solve some problems mentally. Thus 0.75 can be renamed $\frac{3}{4}$. Four $\frac{3}{4}$'s are $\frac{12}{4}$, or 3. Or, two $\frac{3}{4}$'s are $1\frac{1}{2}$; two $1\frac{1}{2}$'s are 3.

ACTIVITY 14.18 Multiplying a Decimal Fraction by a Decimal Fraction

Level: Grades 4–6

Setting: Whole class

Objective: Students develop strategies for multiplying a decimal fraction by a decimal fraction.

Materials: Two transparencies, each with a square marked to show tenths; light-colored marking pens; wiping cloth

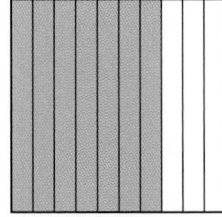

- Explain this situation: "Art foil comes in sheets that are 10 centimeters square." Place one of the transparent squares on the projector, with the lines vertical. "I am going to color 0.7 of this square, which represents a sheet of foil." Color 7 tenths.

- "If I cut off 0.3 of the 7 tenths for an art project, how much of the original sheet will I cut off?" Place the second transparency on top of the first with lines crosswise. Shade 3 tenths of it.

- Point out that the answer is represented by the 21 parts that are shaded twice. Each of the 21 parts represents one of the 100 parts into which the entire unit was separated, so the product is 0.21.

- Write and complete the multiplication sentence $0.3 \times 0.7 = 0.21$.

- Relate this multiplication to working with percent by altering the problem: "A store advertised a 30% reduction in the cost of 70 cent ballpoint pens. What was the amount of the reduction for each pen?" Discuss how this problem is like the original problem. (Answer: 30% is the same as 0.3, $0.70 is the same as 0.7.) Help children see that multiplying 0.7 by 0.3 is one way to determine the amount of reduction for the sale.

is the same for this multiplication as for multiplying whole numbers. Once children recognize this, they need meaningful ways to determine where to place the decimal point in each product. One way to determine where to place the decimal point is to round decimal fractions to whole numbers, then estimate products. For example, when 0.9 and 2.1 are multiplied, the product is 181 without the decimal point. By rounding 0.9 to 1 and 2.1 to 2, an estimated product is 2. When considering where to place the decimal point, 1.81 is the only reasonable response; 18.1 is far too large and 0.181 is much too small.

The product of 23.2 times 1.95 is 45240 without the decimal point. By rounding 23.2 to 20 and 1.95 to 2 and multiplying 2 times 20, an estimated answer of 40 is obtained. Where should the decimal point be placed in 45240 to reflect the estimated answer of 40?

It is not always possible to round decimal fractions smaller than 1 to make estimates. A different strategy is needed for estimating answers to examples of multiplication such as 0.46 times 0.23. This strategy uses knowledge that decimal fractions can be renamed as common fractions, and vice versa. To estimate a product for 0.46 times 0.23, use the thought process shown in Figure 14.12. An alternative way to think about this problem is shown in Figure 14.13. Exercises containing examples such as those in Figure 14.14 can be given to students for practice in making decisions about where to place decimal points in products.

Dividing with Decimal Fractions

Students' understanding of division with decimal fractions is enhanced by connecting the new work to division with whole numbers. Students need to see that the same two situations prevail for division with decimal fractions as for division with whole numbers: determining the size of each group when a set is divided into a given number of groups (partitive division) or finding the number of groups when a set is divided into groups of a given size (measurement division). The same algorithm can be used for division with decimal fractions as for whole numbers. The new element for students is placement of a decimal point in the quotient. As with other new topics, this division should be introduced in relevant settings and with meaningful materials. Activity 14.19 suggests procedures that can be used.

Introduce the division algorithm for each problem following an activity like the one in Activity 14.19. Relate numerals in each algorithm to action with models. In part a of the equations, segments of a 0.3-meter cord were cut; there were eight segments, with a 0.1-meter piece of cord left over. In part b, each of the eight parts into which the cord was cut is approximately 0.3 meter long. For this activity it is not necessary to carry division beyond the tenths place. Later, you may want to extend the division beyond tenths (part c) as a way to indicate a more precise measurement.

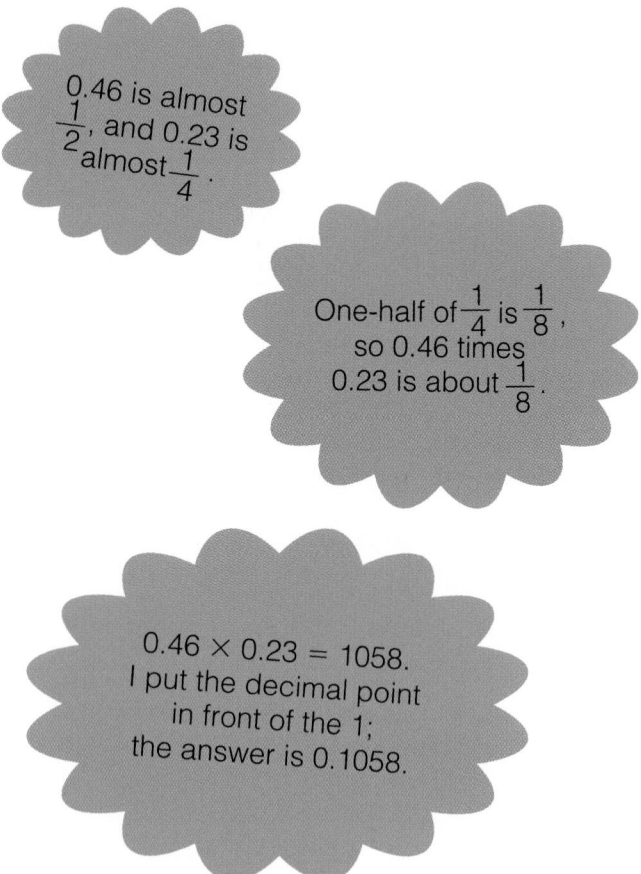

(a)

$$0.3\overline{)2.5}$$ with quotient 8

$$\begin{array}{r} 8 \\ 0.3\overline{)2.5} \\ \underline{24} \\ 1 \end{array}$$

(b)

$$\begin{array}{r} 0.3 \\ 8\overline{)2.5} \\ \underline{24} \\ 1 \end{array}$$

(c)

$$\begin{array}{r} .3125 \\ 8\overline{)2.5000} \\ \underline{24} \\ 10 \\ \underline{8} \\ 20 \\ \underline{16} \\ 40 \\ \underline{40} \end{array}$$

Figure 14.12 Estimating decimal products in terms of common fractions

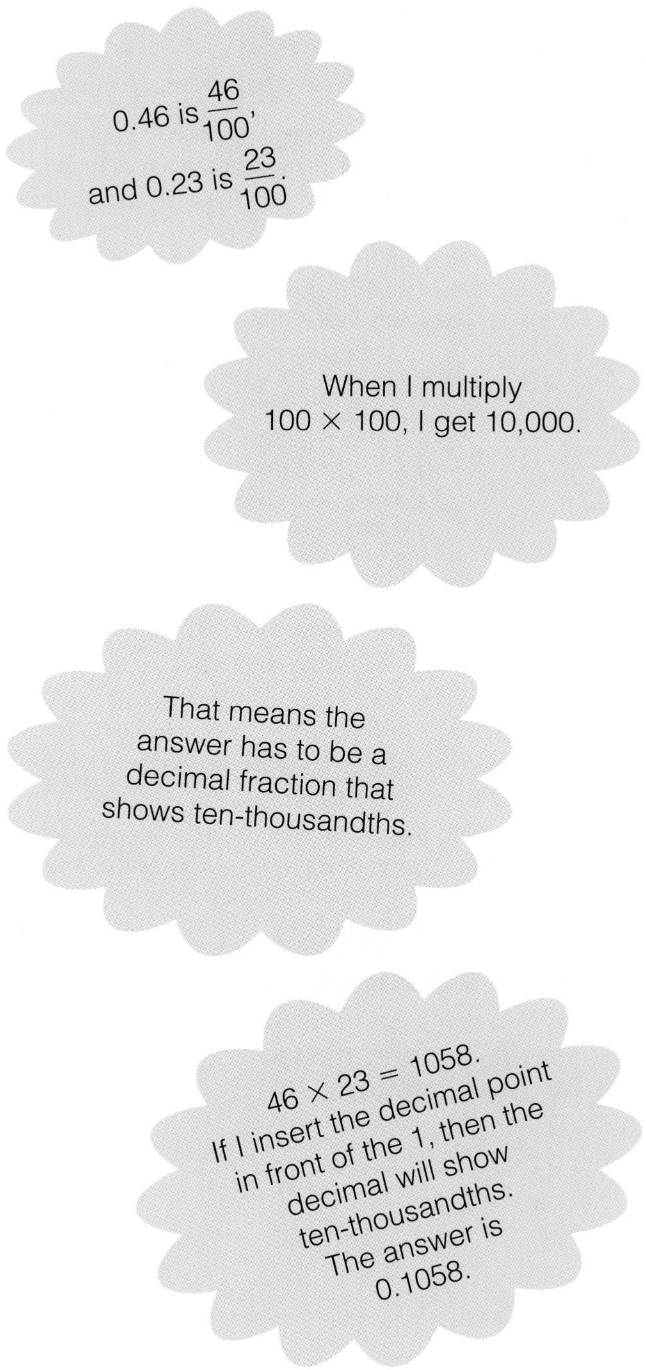

0.46 is $\frac{46}{100}$, and 0.23 is $\frac{23}{100}$.

When I multiply 100 × 100, I get 10,000.

That means the answer has to be a decimal fraction that shows ten-thousandths.

46 × 23 = 1058. If I insert the decimal point in front of the 1, then the decimal will show ten-thousandths. The answer is 0.1058.

Figure 14.13 Estimating decimal products (alternative method)

Estimation is one way to determine where to place the decimal point in many quotients. To estimate the quotient for a pair of numbers, as in the sentence 29.52 ÷ 6 = ?, students should think, "29.52 can be rounded to 30; 30 divided by 6 equals 5, so 29.52 divided by 6 will be about 5." When the quotient is determined, students should place the decimal point to make the answer 4.92. Discuss examples such as the following to help students make estimates for putting a decimal point in the correct place:

$$69 \times 0.3 = 230$$
$$811.8 \times 22 = 369$$
$$20.74 \times 3.4 = 61$$

Students who estimate their answers before using their algorithm can readily recognize any errors they might make when placing the decimal point in the quotient. Activity 14.20 assesses students' ability to perform operations with common and decimal fractions.

Relating Common Fractions to Decimal Fractions

One last topic to be considered is the relationship between common and decimal fractions. Certainly students should view both representations as naming fractional numbers. Converting decimal fractions to common fractions is fairly straightforward, especially if children are accustomed to reading decimal fractions as we suggest. For example, 0.45 should be read as *forty-five hundredths*. When children read decimal fractions this way, it is a simple task to convert the decimal fraction to its common fraction $\left(\frac{45}{100}\right)$.

Converting common fractions to decimal fractions can be a bit more challenging. Certainly some common fractions are easily represented as decimal fractions. Many common fractions can be written as

Figure 14.14 Exercise for estimating and placing decimal points in products

Name: _____   Date: _____

Directions: Underline the correct product for each of these multiplications.

2.4 × 6.8 =	16.32	1.632	163.2	1632
10.6 × 3.68 =	3.900.8	390.08	39.008	3.9008
9 × 2.98 =	2.682	268.2	2.682	26.82
0.78 × 4.13 =	32214	3.2214	32.214	322.14
0.33 × 0.74 =	2.442	244.2	0.2442	24.42

ACTIVITY 14.19 Measurement and Partitive Division

Level: Grades 4–6

Setting: Groups of four

Objective: Students develop a strategy for dividing with decimal fractions.

Materials: 2.5-meter lengths of cotton cord, two pieces for each pair of children; meterstick, marking pen, and scissors for each pair of children; printed copies of the two problems

- Give each pair of students a copy of the following two problems, along with the other materials. Instruct them to read the problems and proceed to solve them.
  1. Juanita has a cord that is 2.5 meters long. She will cut pieces that are 0.3 meter long to make ties for a volleyball net. How many ties will she have?
  2. Leong has a cord that is 2.5 meters long. He will cut eight equal-size pieces for ties on a volleyball net. How long will each tie be?

- Tell the children that they will work in a pairs/check format. Each pair on a team will use materials from the bag and a meterstick to solve each of the problems. (The scissors are for cutting the cord.) When both pairs on a team are finished, the pairs compare their work and clear up any discrepancies.

- When all pairs are finished, collect the printed problems with answers from each pair. Discuss the problems and their solutions. If you find answers that are not in agreement, call on team members to explain their work. (Disregard minor differences caused by irregularities in measuring or rounding numbers.)

- Discussion should reveal that the first problem is a measurement type problem (How many pieces of a given size are there?) and that the second is a partitive type problem (What is the size of each piece?).

- Point out that as they cut the cord for the first problem, they removed, or *subtracted*, 0.3 meter with each cut until only a too-small piece remained. Show this with repeated subtraction:

$$2.5 - 0.3 = 2.2$$
$$2.2 - 0.3 = 1.9$$
$$1.9 - 0.3 = 1.6$$
$$1.6 - 0.3 = 1.3$$
$$1.3 - 0.3 = 1.0$$
$$1.0 - 0.3 = 0.7$$
$$0.7 - 0.3 = 0.4$$
$$0.4 - 0.3 = 0.1$$

- There are eight subtractions. Write the division sentence:

$$2.5 \div 0.3 = 8 \text{ and a remainder}$$

- When the students cut the second cord, they marked and cut eight equal-size pieces. Write the division sentence for this problem:

$$2.5 \div 8 = 0.3 \text{ (approximately)}$$

- Discuss reasons why the answer is recorded no more precisely than tenths. (Answer: It was not possible to fold and cut the cord precisely. A meterstick is not precise enough to determine a measurement beyond tenths.)

ACTIVITY 14.20 Operations with Common and Decimal Fractions (Assessment Activity)

Level: Grades 4–6

- Solve each of these problems, and write a real-life setting for each one.
  1. $2\frac{1}{2} + 3\frac{2}{3} = ?$
  2. $5\frac{3}{4} - \frac{21}{3} = ?$
  3. $5.3 + 6.23 = ?$
  4. $7.3 - 4.5 = ?$
  5. $4 \times 4\frac{1}{4} = ?$
  6. $6\frac{2}{3} \div \frac{2}{3} = ?$
  7. $6.12 \times 7 = ?$
  8. $8 \div 0.25 = ?$

equivalent fractions with a denominator of 10, 100, or 1,000.

$$\frac{1}{2} = \frac{5}{10} = 0.5$$

$$\frac{1}{4} = \frac{25}{100} = 0.25$$

$$\frac{3}{4} = \frac{75}{100} = 0.75$$

$$\frac{1}{8} = \frac{125}{1,000} = 0.125$$

$$\frac{3}{8} = \frac{375}{1,000} = 0.375$$

Decimal representations of these and other common fractions are **terminating decimals**. When such a fraction is converted to a decimal with the division algorithm, the quotient eventually terminates. Many fractions do not have terminating decimal representations. Their decimal representations are repeating decimals that extend infinitely. Activity 14.21 presents students with the opportunity to use calculators to explore the nature of terminating ($\frac{1}{2} = 0.5$) and repeating decimal representations of common fractions (e.g., $\frac{1}{3} = 0.33333\ldots$).

ACTIVITY 14.21 Exploring Terminating and Repeating Decimals

Level: Grades 5–6

Setting: Student pairs

Objective: Students will distinguish between terminating and repeating decimals.

Materials: Calculator

- Post the fraction $\frac{1}{8}$ on the board. Demonstrate how to use the calculator to convert $\frac{1}{8}$ to a decimal fraction.
- Repeat for $\frac{1}{3}$.
- Ask students to compare their two results. Probe for students to recognize the difference between repeating and terminating decimals.

- Ask students to use their calculators to represent the following fractions as decimals and then to categorize the results as either terminating or repeating: $\frac{1}{2}, \frac{1}{3}, \frac{1}{4}, \frac{1}{5}, \frac{1}{6}, \frac{1}{7}, \frac{1}{8}, \frac{1}{9}, \frac{1}{10}, \frac{1}{11}, \frac{1}{12}, \frac{1}{13}, \frac{1}{14}, \frac{1}{15}, \frac{1}{16}, \frac{1}{17}, \frac{1}{18}, \frac{1}{19}, \frac{1}{20}, \frac{1}{25}, \frac{1}{30}, \frac{1}{35}, \frac{1}{40}, \frac{1}{45}, \frac{1}{50}$.
- Ask student pairs to determine what common fractions produce terminating decimals.
- After a short time suggest that students write the denominator of the fraction as prime factors. Students will then observe that if the denominator of a fraction is composed of only 2 and 5 as primes, then it will terminate.

Using a Calculator to Develop Understanding of Decimal Fractions

One of the first calculator activities is learning how to enter whole numbers. Students learn that to enter the number 243, for example, they have to enter the numerals 2, 4, and 3 in that order. Students should be able to enter decimal fractions in a similar fashion. The first calculator activity that follows provides an interesting way to practice this skill. The second activity is the game of Wipeout played with decimal fractions. The third and fourth activities deal with estimating products and quotients while computing with decimal fractions.

- Write each of the following decimal number words and decimal numerals on the chalkboard, or duplicate them for distribution to students:

two and five-tenths	sixty-one and forty-hundredths
four and three-tenths	seventy-five and sixty-seven-hundredths
six and nine-tenths	four and twenty-one-hundredths
five and seven-tenths	ninety-six and nine-hundredths
19.4	237.37

Instruct each student to enter the decimal numbers for the words in the first list into a calculator, pushing the + key after each entry. The numbers will have been read and entered correctly if the sum equals the decimal fraction at the bottom of the list. Repeat with the second list.

- The game of Wipeout was introduced earlier when it was played with whole numbers. Now it is played with decimal fractions. The object is to wipe out a number in a particular place-value position in one move. For example, when shown the number 23.42, students are to wipe out the 4 in the tenths position in one subtraction. To do this, students must know that the "4" represents 4 tenths and that it can be wiped out by subtracting 0.4 from 23.42. The tenths are wiped out, leaving 23.02.

Write numbers such as the following on the chalkboard, or have them on cards for each pair of students:

Wipe Out Tenths	Wipe Out Hundredths	Wipe Out Thousandths
62.6	23.45	61.304
21.934	23.59	22.498
43.186	52.092	324.987

Variation: Have students use a 0–9 spinner to generate numbers to wipe out. Each player gets four spins to get as close to 0 as possible in each place-value position.

- In this activity students first use estimation to determine the placement of the decimal point in each answer. Then have students compute the answers with a calculator to check their estimations.

21.3	0.78	0.789	3.621
× 4.8	× 4.3	× 26.3	× 0.4
10224	3354	207507	14484

$$263 \qquad 654 \qquad 0051 \qquad 632$$
$$3)\overline{7.89} \quad 3.8)\overline{248.52} \quad 0.9)\overline{0.459} \quad 2.7)\overline{170.64}$$

- Provide a list of 22 multiplication combinations:

0.4×9	3.6×1	3×1.2	60×0.6
0.12×30	1.8×2	2×1.8	0.05×720
1.0×36	0.04×0.9	4×0.9	18×0.2
9×0.04	0.3×12	0.6×0.6	36×0.1
120×0.03	6×0.6	72×0.5	360×0.01
18×0.02	40×0.09		

Students are to put a check mark next to each combination that they believe has a product of 3.6. When they have finished, students use calculators to compute the answers and check their work.

Using Calculators with Common Fractions

Three calculators with capabilities to perform operations with common fractions are the Sharp EL-500L, the Texas Instruments TI-15, and the Casio FX-55. With each of these calculators a student can enter and simplify common fractions, convert from common fractions to decimal fractions and vice versa, and perform addition, subtraction, multiplication, and division.

Simplifying Common Fractions. Children use regions, fraction strips, and number lines to deal with groups of related common fractions, such as $\frac{1}{2}, \frac{2}{4}, \frac{3}{6}$, and so on, which are all names for one-half. This and every other equivalence class have a common fraction that is in simplest form.

Once students understand the idea that each given part of a region or point on a line has many

names, they can use calculators to identify the simplest form for any common fraction. For example, given the common fraction $\frac{2}{4}$, what is the simplest form? This is one that students will know to be $\frac{1}{2}$. What about $\frac{48}{96}$? The fact that its simplest form is also $\frac{1}{2}$ may not be readily apparent.

Converting from Common to Decimal Fractions and Vice Versa. Each calculator is capable of converting a common fraction to a decimal fraction, and vice versa. On the Casio and the TI-15, the key marked F-D renames a fractional number from one form to the other. The common fraction $\frac{7}{8}$ is renamed 0.875 when F-D is pressed; the same key renames 0.875 as $\frac{7}{8}$. The Sharp calculator operates differently. It uses the 2nd Deg key to change from one form to another. When the common fraction mode is being used, a number appears as $\frac{7}{8}$. The numeral is renamed 0.875 by changing to the decimal fraction mode.

Computing with Common Fractions. Children who understand the meaning of problem situations that require one or another of the operations and who can compute with paper-and-pencil algorithms are ready to use calculators to compute with common fractions. A calculator is faster and more accurate than paper-and-pencil computation.

The three calculators mentioned (EL-500L, TI-15, and FX-55) do not perform the four operations in identical ways, but each begins an operation in the same way: Enter the first common fraction, press the operation key, enter the second common fraction, and press the + key. The differences lie in the display that unfolds as an operation is performed.

- On the TI-15 the first common fraction appears as it is entered, the + sign appears when it is pushed, and the second common fraction appears when it is entered. When the = key is pressed, the answer is given in simplified form.

- The display on the Casio FX-55 is similar to that on the TI-15 except that the first fraction does not remain on the display when the operation sign appears with the second common fraction. To divide $\frac{3}{4}$ by $\frac{1}{4}$ with this calculator, enter $\frac{3}{4}$, $\div$, and $\frac{1}{4}$. The $\frac{3}{4}$ appears first; then the $\div$ sign and $\frac{1}{4}$ appear simultaneously. When = is pressed, the quotient 3 is displayed.

Sharp EL-500L calculator

- The Sharp EL-500L displays the entire algorithm as an operation is performed. When you multiply $\frac{1}{2}$ and $\frac{2}{8}$, you see "$\frac{1}{2} \times \frac{2}{8}$" build on the display as entries are made. When = is pressed, the screen shows the product in simplest form without the algorithm.

Whatever calculator students use, they should have opportunities to learn to perform operations with common fractions using that calculator. Activity 14.22 is an assessment activity involving operations with common and decimal fractions.

ACTIVITY 14.22   Operations with Common and Decimal Fractions (Assessment Activity)

Level: Grades 4–6

Have students solve each of the following problems, and write a real-life setting for each one.

1. $2\frac{1}{2} + 3\frac{2}{3}$
2. $5\frac{3}{4} - 2\frac{1}{3}$
3. $5.3 + 6.23$
4. $7.3 - 4.5$
5. $4 \times 4\frac{1}{4}$
6. $6\frac{2}{3} \div \frac{2}{3}$
7. 6.12×7
8. $8 \div 0.25$

Take-Home Activity

This take-home project involves advertising circulars to determine the prices of grocery items. Students compute the cost of a typical weekly grocery list using the circular.

Westlands School
150 Dalton Rd.
Chelmsford, MA

Dear Parent,

Your daughter/son will be using a weekly grocery store circular to complete this project. They will try to compile a weekly grocery list with a total cost that comes as close as possible to, but not exceeding, $75.00. Please help your child to develop a reasonable shopping list for items that are contained in the circular.

If I can answer any questions, I can be contacted at school.

1. Have your child select one grocery store circular to use for the project.
2. Go through the circular, pointing out all items that you would usually purchase for the week, along with other items you might purchase less frequently.
3. Check your child's final list and cost to be sure that the list contains items you usually purchase.

Summary

Activities that give children an understanding of common and decimal fractions are an essential part of the elementary school curriculum. The work done in primary grades serves as a foundation for more abstract concepts in higher grades. The intent in elementary school is to provide children with basic ideas about common and decimal fractions.

Common fractions have several meanings, depending on the context in which they are used. Children learn that common fractions are used to express parts of a unit or set of objects that has been partitioned into equal-size parts or groups, to express ratios, and to indicate division. Decimal fractions are used to represent parts of whole objects or collections of objects but have denominators that are 10 or a power of 10. The denominator is not written but is indicated by the number of numerals there are to the right of the ones place in a decimal numeral. Students need experiences with concrete and semiconcrete models that represent both common and decimal fractions and their uses. Geometric regions, fraction strips, markers, number lines, and various manipulatives are used during initial activities. These same materials help students to learn about equivalent fractions and to compare common fractions. Materials such as Cuisenaire sets, kits made from construction paper, fraction strips, and number lines are aids that students can use to learn the meaning of decimal fractions.

Operations with fractional numbers expressed as common and decimal fractions require the same careful development as operations with whole numbers. Even though children are older when operations with fractional numbers are developed, the processes are developed through carefully sequenced activities with appropriate learning aids rather than by rules alone.

Real-world problems illustrate situations that give rise to addition and subtraction with common and decimal fractions. Geometric regions, fraction strips, number lines, and decimal fraction models should accompany real-world problems to give meaning to the operations. References to similarities between operations with whole numbers and those with fractional numbers should be stressed whenever appropriate. Addition and subtraction with mixed numerals are a challenge to many children. Children need to learn the meaning of multiplication and division with common fractions through activities that develop the processes intuitively. They do this by dealing with real-world situations that involve multiplication and division.

Activities involving estimation when multiplying and dividing with decimal fractions help children learn to place decimal points properly in products and quotients. As children mature, they learn how to name common fractions in their simplest forms. At the same time they learn that the need to simplify fractions is determined by the situation in which they are used. Each of the four operations can be done with both common and decimal fractions on a calculator that has the capability of handling common fractions, such as the Texas Instruments TI-15, the Casio FX-55, or the Sharp EL-500L.

Study Questions and Activities

1. A number of the operations discussed in this chapter, especially multiplication and division with common fractions, are not well understood by students. Consider your own understanding of this chapter's operations. Which do you believe you understand well? Which ones do you not understand well? Think not only about your ability to perform each operation but also your understanding of situations that give rise to each one. Are there any operations that you understand better now than you did before you read the chapter? To what do you attribute your good or poor understanding of any of the operations?

2. Word problems are used frequently in this chapter to present situations leading to multiplication and division with common and decimal fractions. Develop your own skill in creating word problems for real-life situations by writing a problem for each of the following sentences. Also sketch the objects or use real objects to model each sentence. Which sentences can be interpreted as repeated addition? Which of the division sentences represent partitive situations? measurement situations?

   a. $3 \times \frac{4}{5} = 2\frac{2}{5}$

   b. $\frac{2}{3} \times 18 = 12$

   c. $\frac{1}{2} \times 1\frac{1}{2} = \frac{3}{4}$

   d. $12 \div \frac{1}{4} = 48$

   e. $\frac{1}{2} \div 3 = \frac{1}{6}$

   f. $4 \times 2.2 = 8.8$

   g. $0.5 \times 12 = 6$

   h. $12 \div 0.2 = 60$

3. Estimation is recommended as a way to help students learn how to place a decimal point in a product or quotient when they compute with decimal fractions. Explain the thought process that a child might use to estimate a product or quotient for each of these examples:

   a. $4.8 \times 2.3 = 1104$

   b. $36.2 \times 1.08 = 39096$

   c. $48.36 \times 51 = 246636$

   d. $21.8240 \div 3.2 = 682$

   e. $9.966 \div 33 = 302$

4. Explained in this chapter are ways that calculators can simplify common fractions, rename improper fractions as mixed numerals, and perform operations with fractional numbers. Practice each process

and operation with a suitable calculator until you can do them easily. Write a statement in which you explain your position on student use of a calculator for work with common fractions. How do you envision calculators changing the way common fractions are taught and learned in the elementary school of the future? If you believe they will not—or should not—lead to any changes, state your reasons.

5. Research the standardized tests administered in your state. Do any of the tests allow for calculators? What effect does this have on teaching common and decimal actions?

Praxis (http://www.ets.org/praxis/) Jerry is 50 inches tall and is growing at the rate of $\frac{1}{24}$ inch per month. Adam is 47 inches tall and is growing at the rate of $\frac{1}{8}$ inch per month. If they continue to grow at these rates for the next four years, in how many months will they be the same height?

a. 24

b. 30

c. 36

d. 42

NAEP (http://nces.ed.gov/nationsreportcard/) On the number line given here, what number would be located at point P?

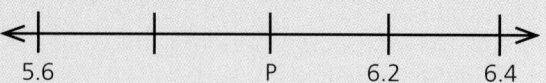

TIMSS (http://nces.ed.gov/timss/) In which of these pairs of numbers is 2.25 larger than the first number but smaller than the second number?

a. 1 and 2

b. 2 and $\frac{5}{2}$

c. $\frac{5}{4}$ and $\frac{11}{4}$

d. $\frac{11}{4}$ and 3

Using Children's Literature

Watson, Clyde. (1972). *Tom Fox and the apple pie*. New York: Thomas Y. Cromwell. (Grades 4–6)

In *Tom Fox and the Apple Pie*, Tom Fox buys an apple pie at the county fair and carries it home. On the way home he envisions sharing the pie with the rest of his family—all 15 of them! Because cutting a pie into 16 pieces would make very small pieces, Tom schemes to wait until his brothers and sisters are out of the house before cutting up the pie; that way, there would be only eight pieces, and each piece would be larger. But not large enough for Tom. He then plans to serve this pie to only four people, then two, and finally concludes the pie is just right for only him.

Here are some assessment activities and questions for this book:

· Write a fraction to describe one piece of pie as Tom imagines 16 pieces, 8 pieces, 4 pieces, and 2 pieces.

· Compare these fractions, and tell how the denominator changes. How many pieces would a pie have if one piece were $\frac{1}{25}$ of the pie?

· As the denominator increases in these fractions, what happens to the size of one piece of pie?

· Have students cut paper dinner plates into the same number of pieces that Tom imagines for his pie: 2, 4, 8, and 16. Have them write the fraction that describes one piece of each pie, and then compare the pieces. (How many sixteenths are in one-eighth? in one-fourth? in one-half? How many fourths are in one-half? and so forth.)

· Have students reassemble a single pie by using different-size pieces to make their composite pie. Have student volunteers show their different composite pies and describe who in the story would be able to share the pie.

Teacher's Resources

Barnette, Carne, Goldenstein, Donna, & Jackson, Babette (Eds.). (1994). *Fractions, decimals, ratios, and percents: Hard to teach and hard to learn?* Portsmouth, NH: Heinemann Press.

Curcio, Frances R., & Bezuk, Nadine S. (1994). *Understanding rational numbers and proportions*. Reston, VA: National Council of Teachers of Mathematics.

Currah, Joanne, & Felling, Jane. (1997). *Piece it together with fractions*. Edmonton, Canada: Box Cars and One-Eyed Jacks.

Litwiller, Bonnie (Ed.). (2002). *Making sense of fractions, ratios, and proportions*. Reston, VA: National Council of Teachers of Mathematics.

Long, Lynette. (2001). *Fabulous fractions: Games and activities that make math easy and fun*. New York: Wiley.

Reys, Barbara J. (1992). *Developing number sense in the middle grades*. Reston, VA: National Council of Teachers of Mathematics.

Wiebe, Arthur. (1998). *Actions with fractions*. Fresno, CA: AIMS Educational Foundation.

Children's Bookshelf

Adams, Laurie, & Coudert, Allison. (1983). *Alice and the boa constrictor*. Boston: Houghton Mifflin. (Grades 4–6)

Ash, Russell. (1996). *Incredible comparisons*. London: Dorling Kindersley. (Grades 3–6)

Beneduce, Ann. (1996). *Gulliver's adventures in Lilliput*. New York: Putnam & Grosset. (Grades 4–7)

Carle, Eric. (1970). *Eric and the beanstalk*. New York: Putnam & Grosset. (Grades 3–6)

Clement, Rod. (1991). *Counting on Frank*. Milwaukee: Garth Stevens. (Grades 3–6)

Cole, Joanna. (1986). *The magic school bus at the waterworks*. New York: Scholastic. (Grades 3–5)

Conford, Ellen. (1989). *What's cooking, Jenny Archer?* Boston: Little, Brown. (Grades 4–6)

Klevin, Jill. (1974). *The Turtle Street Trading Company*. New York: Harcourt Brace Jovanovich. (Grades 4–6)

Levetin, Sonia. (1974). *Jason and the money tree*. New York: Harcourt Brace Jovanovich. (Grades 4–6)

Schwartz, David. (1989). *If you made a million*. New York: Lothrop, Lee & Shepard. (Grades 3–5)

Smoothey, Marion. (1995). *Ratio and proportion*. New York: Marshall Cavendish. (Grades 4–8)

Stienecker, David L. (1996). *Fractions*. New York: Benchmark Books. (Grades 3–5)

Thompson, Lauren. (2001). *One riddle, one answer*. New York: Scholastic. (Grades 4–6)

Wells, Robert E. (1993). *Is a blue whale the biggest thing there is?* Morton Grove, IL: Albert Whitman. (Grades 3–6)

Wells, Robert E. (1997). *What's faster than a speeding cheetah?* Morton Grove, IL: Albert Whitman. (Grades 3–6)

Wells, Robert E. (1995). *What's smaller than a pigmy shrew?* Morton Grove, IL: Albert Whitman. (Grades 3–6)

Technology Resources

Computer Programs

Math Tools. (1997). Englewood Cliffs, NJ: Prentice Hall.

The Fraction Bar section with a calculating tool provides opportunities for adding, subtracting, multiplying, and dividing with common fractions. There are no visual clues to assist in understanding an operation's meaning.

Mighty Math: Number Heroes. (1996). San Francisco: Edmark Corporation.

The Fraction Fireworks section includes a fraction calculator and activities for adding, subtracting, and multiplying with common fractions.

Internet Sites

General fraction sites:

http://www.visualfractions.com

http://www.k111.k12.il.us/king/math.htm#

To display models of basic fractions:

Fraction Models I, II, and III:

http://illuminations.nctm.org

To explore equivalent fractions:

Equivalent Fractions and Fraction Game:

http://illuminations.nctm.org

Fraction Four and Equivalent Fractions Pointer:

http://www.shodor.org/interactivate/activities/index.html

Fractions–Equivalent: **http://nlvm.usu.edu/en/nav/vlibrary .html**

Decimal fraction representations:

Converter: **http://www.shodor.org/interactivate/activities/index .html**

Denominator to Repeating Decimal Checker and Common Fraction to Decimal Fraction:

http://www2.whidbey.net/ohmsmath/webwork/javascript/

Ordering common fractions:

Fraction Pointer: **http://www.shodor.org/interactivate/ activities/index.html**

Fraction-Comparing with Fraction Strips:

http://www2.whidbey.net/ohmsmath/webwork/javascript/

Comparing Common Fractions:

http://www.visualfractions.com/compare.htm

Operations:

Subtraction with Common Fractions: **http://www.jason .org/eprise/main/jason_public/web_pages/mathemagica/ math_tools/number_sense.htm**

Common Fractions—Adding:

http://www.visualfractions.com/add.htm

Common Fractions—Rectangle Multiplication:

http://nlvm.usu.edu/en/nav/vlibrary.html

Internet Game

The game Saloon Snap, available at **http://www.bbc .co.uk/education/mathsfile/gameswheel**, shows players a common fraction and a decimal fraction. The challenge is to recognize equivalent representations before a character in the games does. There are three levels to the game, with the highest level including percent representations. There are sound effects that are amusing but could be distracting. The sound effects can be turned off.

Internet Activity: Multiplying Mixed Numerals

This Internet activity is for children in grades 5 and 6. Students should work in pairs. The objective is for students to explore multiplying with mixed numerals.

Have student pairs go to **http://www.visualfractions. com/MultEasy.htmld**. Demonstrate for students how the applet at this site works, and then challenge student pairs to use the applet to solve five problems. The student pairs should print the final screen image that supports their answers to each of the problems. Select student pairs to show one of their solutions to the class and explain their thinking. Ask for other solution strategies for the problem.

For Further Reading

Anderson, Cindy, Anderson, Kevin, & Wenzel, Edward. (2000). Oil and water, but they do teach fractions. *Teaching Children Mathematics* 7(3), 174–178.

Oil and water do not mix but are perfect for demonstrating how to add common fractions with unlike denominators. In this activity fractions of a cup of water and a cup of oil are combined in a larger container, and the total amount of liquid serves as the setting for adding fractions.

Bay-Williams, Jennifer, & Martinie, Sherri L. (2003). Thinking rationally about number and operations in the middle grades. *Teaching Children Mathematics* 8(6), 282–287.

Bay-Williams and Martinie describe the use of engaging contexts to reveal the foundations of rational numbers. These problem contexts help students understand the results of division and multiplication by numbers less than 1.

Brinker, Laura. (1998). Using recipes and ratio tables. *Teaching Children Mathematics* 5(4), 218–224.

Brinker describes how increasing and decreasing recipe ingredients can enhance children's understanding of and work with ratios and proportions. Examples of the teacher's and students' involvement in the activities are cited.

Mack, Nancy K. (1998). Building a foundation for understanding the multiplication of fractions. *Teaching Children Mathematics* 5(1), 34–38.

Children's work with multiplication involving common fractions was built on their informal knowledge, which was determined by having them react to equal-sharing situations. Real-world situations were presented, and children used drawings and verbal descriptions to explain the meaning of multiplication with common fractions. The practice laid a foundation for later work with mathematical sentences.

Moss, Joan. (2003). Introducing percents in linear measurement to foster an understanding of rational-number operations. *Teaching Children Mathematics* 9(6), 335–339.

Moss makes a compelling case for introducing percents even before fractions as a means of dividing up a number line into smaller segments. Once students can use percents to do so, they are then introduced to equivalent fractions and decimals.

Perlwitz, Marcella. (2005). Dividing fractions: Reconciling self-generated solutions with algorithmic answers. *Teaching Children Mathematics* 10(6), 278–283.

Perlwitz relates how one teacher used student-generated methods to fortify students' understanding of traditional algorithms.

Telese, James, & Abete, Jesse, Jr. (2002). Diet, ratios, proportions: A healthy mix. *Mathematics Teaching in the Middle School* 8(1), 8–13.

The project described in this article uses data from various foods to produce ratios and proportions that are then graphed, used to compare various diets, and ultimately used to examine the school lunch menu. Students' work for all parts of the project is displayed, along with evaluation comments.

Warrington, Mary Ann, & Kamii, Constance. (1998). Multiplication with fractions: A constructivist approach. *Mathematics Teaching in the Middle School* 3(5), 339–343.

Kamii was an assistant to Piaget, and her approach to teaching the fraction operations of multiplication and division reflects her background. This article presents activities that can be used to help children understand multiplication and division with fractions before learning any algorithms or set of rules.

CHAPTER 15

Developing Aspects of Proportional Reasoning: Ratio, Proportion, and Percent

Proportional reasoning involves understanding how quantities vary in relation to each other. It is the relationship between two quantities that may vary but remain in the same relationship or ratio. Proportional reasoning is an overarching principle of all mathematics and is central to all subdisciplines of mathematics. For example, proportional reasoning is used in geometry with similar figures and dilations (see Chapter 17); in algebra with slopes of lines, work problems, and rate problems; in probability to determine chances of events happening; and in calculus with related rates problems. Anyone who computes miles per gallon, changes a recipe for a larger number of servings, or purchases fruit at a grocery store uses proportional reasoning.

In middle school, students reason proportionally when they compute percentages, and when, with decimal and common fractions, they work with rates, determine probabilities, and explore similar figures. Outside school, children reason

POINT OF VIEW
Ratio and proportion are difficult concepts for children to learn. They constitute one of the stumbling blocks of the middle-school curriculum, and there is a good possibility that many people never come to understand them. (National Council of Teachers of Mathematics, 2000, p. 211)

proportionally when they make purchases based on rates, reading maps, or doubling a recipe. NCTM identifies proportionality as a key mathematical concept for all grades and proportional reasoning as a major method of thinking in mathematics, deeming the study of proportional reasoning "of such great importance that it merits whatever time and effort must be expended to assure its careful development" (National Council of Teachers of Mathematics, 1989, P. 82).

In this chapter you will read about:

1 Proportional reasoning as a multiplicative relationship

2 The difference between ratios and fractions

3 Ways to introduce proportional reasoning to children

4 Different ways to solve proportion problems

5 A proportional approach to teaching percent

Proportional Reasoning

Despite the emphasis on proportional reasoning in school mathematics, middle school and high school students have difficulty with situations that require them to reason about proportional relationships. Data from the Third International Mathematics and Science Study (TIMSS) show that proportionality is the most difficult problem area for students in the middle grades (Beaton et al., 1996). Even preservice teachers can have difficulty reasoning proportionally (Cramer et al., 1989). Thus it is critical to introduce appropriate real-world settings that will lay the foundation for proportional reasoning in the elementary and middle grades.

What Teachers Should Know About Teaching Proportional Reasoning

Proportional reasoning can be a difficult concept for children, even in the middle grades. Teachers should give careful attention to the development of proportional reasoning in students. The tendency is for students to solve problems using an additive approach. Teachers should counteract this by building students' understanding of multiplicative relationships.

Solving proportion problems should be approached from the vantage point of multiplicative

relationships. Algorithms, such as the cross-product algorithm, should not be introduced until students have fully developed and refined their understanding that proportional relationships involve multiplicative relationships.

Students' understanding of all the facets of percent is closely linked to their understanding of proportional relationships. Students should use proportional relationships to solve percent problems, rather than rely on an algorithm applied by rote or a memorized rule to solve a problem.

Few NCTM standards explicitly cite proportional reasoning (see later discussion). However, for earlier grade levels the standards for number and operation that involve fractions, decimals, and even multiplication relationships could be considered part of proportionality. We have not included those standards here, only those that specifically mention ratio, proportion, or percent.

NCTM Standards and Expectations

Grades 6–8 Expectations:

In grades 6–8 all students should:

- work flexibly with fractions, decimals, and percents to solve problems;
- compare and order fractions, decimals, and percents efficiently, and find their approximate locations on a number line;

- develop meaning for percents greater than 100 and less than 1;
- understand and use ratios and proportions to represent quantitative relationships.

(b)

Ratios as a Foundation of Proportional Reasoning

To begin to work with proportions and proportional reasoning, students must have a foundational understanding of ratios. (A proportion is an equality between two or more ratios, such as $\frac{2}{3} = \frac{4}{6} = \frac{6}{9}$.) A ratio can be expressed in several forms: as a fraction ($\frac{2}{3}$), in colon notation (2:3), or in common English expressions (two to three or two out of three). The two different symbolic notations are not troubling to students, who can easily move between $\frac{2}{3}$ and 2:3. However, there is much more to ratio and proportional reasoning than notation. As suggested in Chapter 12, a ratio can be considered a fraction in the part-whole sense that fractions represent. However, a ratio can represent other mathematical relationships.

> The most famous number in mathematics, π, is a ratio between the circumference C and the diameter d of a circle (C/d).

Meanings of Ratio

Part-Whole Sense

In this representation the ratio describes a subset and the entire set, for example, the ratio of the number of red marbles (6) compared to all the marbles (10) in the bag is 6:10 or $\frac{6}{10}$ (Figure 15.1a).

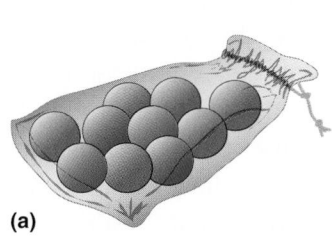

(a)

Figure 15.1

Part-Part Sense

The ratio in this setting describes the relationship between two subsets of the same set, for example the ratio of the number of blue yo-yos to the number of green yo-yos is $\frac{4}{7}$ (Figure 15.1b).

Relationship Between Two Independent Sets

In this case the two sets may be unrelated, such as the number of milk cartons (4) and the number of cookies (9). This ratio of cartons to cookies is 4:9. This relationship can also be described as the number of cookies to cartons, 9:4. The two sets can also be units of measurement, such as the ratio of the length of a yardstick to the length of a 12-inch ruler, 36:12 (Figure 15.1c).

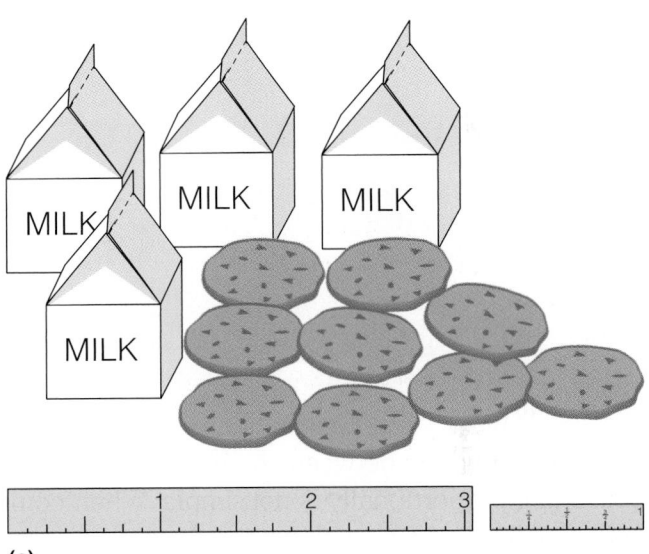

(c)

Ratio as a Rate

A ratio can describe pricing information, such as 2 pounds of bananas for 69 cents (2:69), or a rate, such as 55 miles per hour (55:1) (Figure 15.1d).

(d)

Probability Relationships

The chance of rolling an even number with a single number cube is 3:6 (Figure 15.1e).

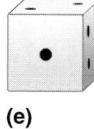

(e)

Ratio as an Operator

In this case the ratio is not an expression to describe a relationship between two sets but a rate or number that acts on another number. For example, a stuffed toy bear is designed to look like the real thing but is smaller in size. Such a toy is perhaps $\frac{1}{12}$ the height of a real bear. The scale factor is 1:12, and if a real bear is 6 feet tall, then the stuffed toy bear is $6 \times \frac{1}{12} = \frac{1}{2}$ foot or 6 inches tall (Figure 15.1f).

(f)

The connection between common fractions and reasoning proportionally is not simple. When common fraction representations are used to indicate ratios, they should be interpreted differently from when they represent part-whole relationships. Common fractions do not require labels for each of their numerical parts because they are both drawn from the same set. For example, the number of green marbles (9) in a bag of 22 marbles is represented as $\frac{9}{22}$. In a ratio, each numerical term should be labeled to convey the correct representation that the ratio portrays. The fraction $\frac{9}{22}$ can be considered a ratio. The ratio $\frac{9}{22}$ might convey the relationship of the number of automobiles to the number of cell phones among a group of high school seniors. In this case the numerator of the ratio expression tells the number of objects in one set (number of automobiles) and the denominator tells the number of objects in an entirely different set (cell phones). Furthermore, a ratio may have 0 in the denominator—for example, the

ratio of days in a week compared to the number of pigs with wings $(\frac{7}{0})$.

Another difference between ratios and fractions can be exhibited by considering a classroom with 12 boys and 14 girls. The ratio describing the relationship between the number of girls and boys can be represented as either $\frac{12}{14}$ (boys to girls) or $\frac{14}{12}$ (girls to boys). The fraction $\frac{12}{14}$, which describes 12 marbles out of 14 marbles can never be represented as $\frac{14}{12}$. Suppose that two boys and three girls join the class. The ratio of the newcomers is $\frac{2}{3}$. The new ratio of boys to girls is $\frac{14}{17}$, found by adding the two numerators and two denominators [(12 + 2)/(14 + 3)]. Common fractions cannot be added in this manner.

Ratios are not independent numerical expressions. They must be understood in the context of the relationships they represent. Consequently, care must be used when fraction notation is introduced as a way of indicating ratios to be sure that children understand the difference between common fractions and ratios from the very start.

Teaching Proportional Reasoning

Fluency and full applications with ratio and proportional reasoning are a focus of the middle school curriculum. However, younger children can engage in a number of activities and explorations that will help them begin to develop their proportional reasoning skills.

The common difficulty that children (and many adults) have with proportional reasoning is that they do not understand that proportions represent multiplication or multiplicative reasoning. Instead, they believe that many proportional situations show addition or additive relationships. Consider the following problem:

> **MISCONCEPTION**
>
> Because ratios can be represented in the familiar common fraction form, some children believe that they can be used in fraction computations. Given a common fraction, there are many equivalent fractions, $\frac{2}{5} = \frac{4}{10} = \frac{6}{15} = \frac{8}{20}$. However this is not true with ratios. Consider a setting in which there are two children who must share five cookies. This ratio of $\frac{2}{5}$ is not equivalent to a ratio of $\frac{4}{10}$ because there are neither 4 children nor 10 cookies.

- For every four laps around the track that Janelle ran, Keith ran three laps. Janelle ran eight laps. How many laps did Keith run?

In this proportional setting, solving the problem correctly requires multiplicative reasoning. The ratio of laps Janelle ran to the number of laps Keith ran is 4:3 or $\frac{4}{3}$. The correct answer is that since Janelle *doubled* the number of laps she ran (2 × 4), Keith would *double* the number of laps he ran. The answer is that Keith ran 6 (3 × 2) laps. The ratio of the final number of laps is $\frac{8}{6}$, which is equivalent to the original ratio of $\frac{4}{3}$. Children who are reasoning from an additive perspective will instead reason that since

Janelle ran 4 *more* laps, Keith will run 4 *more* laps, or 7 (3 + 4) laps. Children require many activities before they can comfortably reason about proportions using multiplicative reasoning. It might be said that students who cannot reason multiplicatively are thinking at a concrete level. In order to reason multiplicatively (proportionally), they must reason at a more abstract, or operational level. Moreover, additive approaches to such a problem can be likened to a default strategy. That is, students who are unsure of how to proceed tend to fall back on additive procedures.

Activity 15.1 presents children with a qualitative problem—that is, one without direct computation. Such qualitative problems eliminate the need for involved computations and a specific numerical solution. Instead, in this activity students compare lemonade recipes and decide if new recipes will taste sweeter, sourer, or the same as the original, but they do not quantify their answers by determining how

ACTIVITY 15.1 Qualitative Proportions (Reasoning and Proof)

Level: Grades 4 and 5
Setting: Small groups
Objective: Students solve qualitative problems that develop proportional thinking.
Materials: Several large plastic containers, measuring cup

- Ask children how to make lemonade. Probe for a recipe that includes lemon juice, sugar, and water. Discuss how the lemon juice and the sugar each affect the taste of the lemonade.

- Put a recipe for lemonade on the board: 1 cup juice, 1 cup sugar, 3 cups water.

- Mimic making this recipe by adding a pretend cup of sugar from one container and a pretend cup of lemon juice from another container into the pretend water container and mixing thoroughly.

- Now ask what happens if you make lemonade with a new recipe. Ask children for volunteers to act out adding 1 cup of juice and 2 cups of sugar to the water. Ask students to compare the new lemonade to the original recipe. Is the new flavor the same, sweeter, or sourer? As students talk in their groups, be sure they have an explanation for their decision.

- Discuss various groups' reasons as a class. Students may correctly reason that because there is now more sugar than lemon juice, then the recipe will make a sweeter lemonade.

- Repeat with a different recipe: 2 cups of juice and 1 cup of sugar with 2 cups of water.

- Have children consider the flavors offered by these recipes as their groups compare each one to the original recipe:

Cups of Juice	Cups of Sugar	Outcome
2	2	Same
2	3	Sweeter
3	3	Same
3	2	Sourer
4	2	Sourer

- As children talk about the flavors, move about the groups to listen to their discussions. Look for opportunities to ask groups to explain their reasoning when they have correct answers. Probe for multiplicative reasoning in the discussions by asking why one of the recipes (3 cups sugar and 3 cups juice) tastes the same as the original recipe. Ask for new recipes that would taste the same as the original.

- Similar qualitative problems can involve a fruit salad recipe, chocolate flavoring and milk, and ingredients for fruit punch.

much sweeter or sourer. Thus students can focus on the multiplicative aspects of the problem without the concern for manipulation of the numbers.

Developing Proportional Reasoning Using Rate Pairs and Tables

By the time the concepts of ratio and proportion are introduced in upper elementary and middle school, children have had many experiences that provide familiar situations through which to introduce ratios and their notation. When children assemble a bag of marbles with two red and four green marbles, they express the ratio between the two colors as 2:4 or 1:2. They then add more marbles of each color to the bag, making sure that the resulting ratio of red to green marbles is still 1:2. To do so, they might build a table of marble colors that shows the ratio of 1:2 for each pair of entries. A table such as the fol-

lowing, which shows the same rate between the two objects, is called a *rate table*:

Red	1	2	3	4	5	6
Green	2	4	6	8	10	12

Children's experiences with money and the cost of objects provide another setting because there is a ratio between the object and the money. If one package of candy costs 27 cents, there is a ratio of 1 package for every 27 cents. This ratio can be expressed as 1 to 27, 1:27, or $\frac{1}{27}$. There is a ratio between time and distance traveled. A driver whose speed averages 55 miles per hour has the ratio 55 miles traveled for every 1 hour. The ratio of miles to hours can be expressed as 55 to 1, 55:1, or $\frac{55}{1}$. Ratios such as these are rate pairs. A rate is usually a ratio representing two different sets or measures so that one of the terms of the ratio is 1, such as miles per hour (1 hour), heartbeats per minute (1 minute), or $6.75 per pound (1 pound). Activity 15.2 shows

---

ACTIVITY 15.2   Rate Pairs (Connections)

Level: Grades 4–6

Setting: Cooperative learning

Objective: Students develop the concept of ratio and proportion using rate pairs.

Materials: Real or representative miniboxes of raisins, sports trading cards, apples, and similar items that children might buy; representative coins—pennies, nickels, dimes, quarters; direction card denoting cost of various items; copies of blank ratio tables; and a different colored pencil for each student. Package the items in separate bags—a dozen of one item and $3.00 worth of coins in each bag. Make one set for each team of four children.

- Tell the children that they are to use the Round Robin cooperative-learning format. Each team will have a bag containing several items and some coins. Their task is to complete the table by indicating the cost of various groupings of items. For example, a direction card says, "There are three trading cards in each package. Three cards cost 49 cents." (Use a different ratio on each direction card.)

The team is to fill in the rate table to show the cost of 6, 9, 12, . . . cards.

Number of items	3	6	9	12	15	18	21
Cost	$.49	$.98					

- One member of the team lays out one pack of cards and 49 cents in coins, and a second fills in the first cells in the table. The third child lays out another pack and another 49 cents, and the fourth fills in the next column of cells. Action rotates as each new set of materials and coins is laid out and cells are filled. Each child uses a different colored pencil to fill in cells.

- Each team completes the same routine with its set of materials.

- When all teams are finished, each one explains its work to classmates. Discussion should emphasize the concepts of ratios, proportions, and rate tables. In this situation, *ratio* refers to the number of items and their cost. The ratio for three cards and their cost is 3 to 49 cents, expressed as 3:49 or $\frac{3}{49}$; the ratio for six cards is 6:98 or $\frac{6}{98}$.

Extension

- Have students gather average gas mileage figures for sport utility vehicles, and make rate tables showing gasoline consumed and distance traveled. Information is available in brochures from auto dealers and, for some makes of automobiles, on the Internet. For example, connect with the General Motors Company website for information about GM vehicles.

ACTIVITY 15.3 Ratios at Work

Level: Grades 4–6

Setting: Whole class

Objective: Students develop a strategy for using ratios and proportions to solve problems.

Materials: Overhead transparency with blank rate-pair table, marking pen, projector, problem cards, printed copies of blank rate-pair tables

- Begin with this story: "Carla and Carmen share responsibility for managing a gift shop. Carla is at the shop four days a week, and Carmen is there three days. When Carla has been at the shop for 20 days, how many days has Carmen been there?"

- Project the blank rate-pair table. Discuss the ratio formed by comparing the two work schedules. Write different representations beneath the table: 4 to 3, $\frac{4}{3}$, 4:3.

- Have children give the first entry, and write it in. Fill in the table until 20 and 15 are entered.

- Discuss the meanings of the entries. Point out that the rate table shows that when Carla has worked 20 days, Carmen has worked 15 days. Write the ratio: $\frac{20}{15}$ or 20:15.

- Ask: "What numbers from the table are given in the problem?" (Answer: 4, 3, and 20). "How can I express those numbers as a proportion?" (Answer: $\frac{4}{3} = \frac{20}{n}$). Help children see the connection between this situation and equivalent common fractions. "If we rename $\frac{4}{3}$ as an equivalent fraction with a numerator of 20, by what number is 4 multiplied?" (Answer: 5). "How will we determine the denominator for the new fraction?" (Answer: multiply 3 by 5). "What is the denominator?" (Answer: 15). Verify the answer with the table.

Carla	4	8	12	16	20
Carmen	3	6	9	12	15
	4 to 3	$\frac{4}{3}$	4:3		

how a shopping situation can be used to introduce the concept of rate pairs and to help children understand and record ratios. See Activity 15.3 for an activity that has students identify and interpret rate pairs from a rate table.

Many rates are familiar to adults but not to children. For instance, when a car travels 300 miles using 25 gallons of gas, we think in terms of miles per gallon: $\frac{300}{25} = 12$ miles per gallon. Although miles per gallon is the conventional expression, these data could just as well be used to determine gallons per mile: $\frac{25}{300} = 0.08$ gallon per mile. To children who are inexperienced with real-life applications, either rate is perfectly reasonable. As you design problems for children to explore, help them to become familiar with the generally accepted rates commonly used in real-life applications. Activity 15.4 presents common situations for students to represent in two different ratios, as before, and then asks students to select the ratio that they think represents the common ratio for each problem.

EXERCISE

Name three additional examples of rate-pair situations. Money was involved in Activity 15.2. Include money in only one of your situations. Give three other examples of proportion situations. ●●●

When children first begin to work with ratios and rate pairs (Activities 15.2 and 15.3), they may not use

any multiplicative understandings. In the following rate table, for example, some children will complete the second row by simply adding $0.39 to the previous total.

Packs of mints	1	2	3	4	5	6
Total price	$0.39	$0.78	$1.17	?	?	?

Packs of mints	1	2	3	4	5	6
Price of mints	$.39	$.78	$1.17	?	?	?

They can complete the table correctly, but they do not understand the multiplicative underpinnings of ratios, rates, and proportions. Children require many activities that help them make the leap in rate situations from applying addition to applying multiplication instead. Problems involving rate pairs can be a good place to introduce algebraic concepts, including using a variable to reference a missing value (see Chapter 16).

Working with Proportions

Using Equivalent Fractions

Proportion is the equality between two or more ratios. There is a proportional relationship between 1:39 and 2:78 and any other rate pair in the rate table given in the previous section ($\frac{1}{39} = \frac{2}{78} = \frac{3}{117}$, . . .). As shown in this section, proportions are a key part of solving problems that involve proportional reasoning.

ACTIVITY 15.4 **Finding the Right Rate (Communication)**

Level: Grades 5 and 6
Setting: Groups of three students
Objective: Students explore the meanings of common rates.
Materials: Paper and pencils

- Post the rate 55 mph on the board. Ask students if they know what mph stands for. Then ask students in their groups to explain what 55 mph means to someone who is driving a car. Probe that the traveled distance is 55 miles in *1* hour.

- Now post 0.018 hpm (hours per mile) on the board. Describe this as "eighteen-thousandths of an hour per mile." Ask students in their groups to explain if this rate could describe the speed of a car. Probe that although the decimal fraction is quite small, the speed of a car could be described by what part of an hour was needed to travel 1 mile, in this case 0.018 hour or about 1 minute. Such a rate is difficult to understand, especially with a rate less than 1. Most students will readily dismiss this rate as a way of representing speed.

- Ask students to explain why 55 mph is easier to understand than 0.018 hpm.

- Suggest that there are other rates that are common but that may be written in this *inverse style*. Ask students to represent two different rates for the following common situations, and then select the rate they think is most meaningful. (Note: Many times students have not had the out-of-school experiences that adult consumers have, so it can be quite challenging for them to select the better rate representation. In some cases, such as 4 or 6, either rate is acceptable.)

1. Six apples cost $2.00.
2. A human heart beats 540 times in 8 minutes.
3. Dean rode his bike 18 miles in 3 hours.
4. Five dollars ($5.00) is worth £3 (British pounds).
5. There are 30 CDs in 6 cases.
6. The willow tree grew 18 feet in 3 years.
7. Jose earned $54 in 9 hours.

Teachers help children connect the concepts of ratios and proportions to the concept of equivalent fractions as another means of solving proportions. For example, a dessert recipe for three people calls for 2 cups of flour. At this same rate, how many cups of flour does the same recipe require for 12 people? The proportion for this problem consists of the two ratios specified in the problem. The two ratios are equal, because the ratio of cups of flour to the number of people must remain the same for any number of people for the recipe to be correct. The proportion may be represented as

$$\frac{3}{2} = \frac{12}{?}$$

Students can use equivalent fractions to solve for the missing term, 8 cups of flour. (Note that applying the cross-product algorithm could solve the problem. We discuss the algorithm later in this chapter and suggest delaying its use in elementary school.)

Any problem solved using a rate table can be solved using a proportion. Solving a problem using proportions is more efficient than using a rate table. To avoid rote use of proportions by students, teachers should be sure that students are confident using rate tables before setting up and solving proportions.

Proportional relationships involving ratios are frequently used in problem solving. Consider the situation in Activity 15.1. This activity will give most children a good foundation for understanding ratios and proportions. Because proportional thinking is developmental, according to Piaget, students grow in their ability to reason competently about proportional relationships through middle school and even high school. Nevertheless younger children benefit from introductory activities such as Activities 15.1 and 15.2.

Solving Proportions Using a Multiples Table

Once students are comfortable using rate tables to solve proportion problems (see Activities 15.2–15.4), they are then ready to use a multiples table. Students can use a multiples table (Table 15.1) to solve many different proportion problems.

Consider the following problem.

- Two pounds of chocolates costs $5.00. How much will 12 pounds of chocolates cost?

TABLE 15.1 ○ Multiples Table

1	②	3	4	⑤	6	7	8	9	10
2	4	6	8	10	12	14	16	18	20
3	6	9	12	15	18	21	24	27	30
4	8	12	16	20	24	28	32	36	40
5	10	15	20	25	30	35	40	45	50
6	⑫	18	24	[30]	36	42	48	54	60
7	14	21	28	35	42	49	56	63	70
8	16	24	32	40	48	56	64	72	80
9	18	27	36	45	54	63	72	81	90
10	20	30	40	50	60	70	80	90	100

In Table 15.1 the known values of the problem are circled: 2, 5, and 12. Notice that because 2 and 5 both refer to the same data fact, they are located in the same row. They could be represented as the ratio $\frac{2}{5}$, for pounds of chocolate to cost in dollars. The other known value is 12, which refers to a different number of pounds of chocolate. What number in the rate table would form an equivalent ratio with 12? That number must appear in the same column as 5 in order to produce an equivalent ratio. Each of the pairs of numbers in the 2 column and the 5 column produce equivalent ratios. The answer to the problem is the number in the square, 30. A multiples table such as the one in Table 15.1 can be used to solve a variety of proportion problems.

The problem might also be solved using only part of the multiples table, much like using a rate table.

②	3	4	⑤
⑫	18	24	㉚

Older children may solve the problem in a variety of ways: writing it as $\frac{2}{5} = \frac{12}{x}$ and using equivalent fractions, using a cross-product algorithm, or mentally without using any particular process. Activity 15.5 assesses students' ability to set up and solve proportions using a multiples table.

Notice that in Activity 15.5 the tables result in whole-number relationships; that is, each rate pair is related to the original rate pair by some factor that is a whole number—$2, 5 pounds, 12 pounds,

---

ACTIVITY 15.5   Using a Multiples Table with Proportions (Assessment Activity)

Level: Grades 5 and 6

Setting: Pairs of students

Objective: Represent and solve proportion problems on a multiples table.

Materials: Multiples table

Use the multiples table to set up and solve the following problems. Be sure to write the proportion first, and then the answer to the problem.

1. Potatoes cost $3 for 5 pounds. How many pounds of potatoes will $18.00 buy?

2. A basketball team wins two out of every three games that they play. At this rate, how many games will they need to play to win 12 games?

3. Two days out of every seven days are weekend days. How many weekend days are there in 56 days?

4. Lee ran five laps for every three laps that Susan ran. If Lee ran 15 laps, how many laps did Susan run?

5. Peaches cost $2 for five peaches. How much will 10 peaches cost?

$30. Children might be given the option to solve these proportion problems by using what they have learned about equivalent fractions (see Chapters 13 and 14). Students who opt to use equivalent fractions instead of a rate table might be asked to explain their reasoning to the class.

What solution strategies can children use in addition to equivalent strategies?

Two other methods that students can use to solve proportion problems are *unitizing* and using the *unit rate*. Unitizing can be used to solve a problem such as "Apples cost $1.50 for 2 pounds. How much will 9 pounds cost?" In this case, the amount of apples, 2 pounds, is taken as a unit or chunk. How many of these chunks are needed to be equivalent to 9 pounds? Four chunks is 8 pounds (4 × 2), and 5 chunks is 10 pounds (5 × 2). So $4\frac{1}{2}$ chunks will make the 9 pounds. The $4\frac{1}{2}$ chunks will also apply to the cost. If 1 chunk of cost is $1.50, then $4\frac{1}{2}$ chunks will be the total cost of the apples. Four chunks is $6.00 (4 × $1.50), and half a chunk is $0.75 ($\frac{1}{2}$ × $1.50). So the total cost is $6.75 ($6.00 + $0.75). A rate table could help children solve this type of problem even though it does not represent whole number relationships.

2	4	6	8	9	10
$1.50	$3.00	$4.50	$6.00	?	$7.50

Unitizing can be used with many problems, but in some cases the numbers in the problem do not lend themselves to unitizing, such as when pears cost $1.59 for 5 pounds and a person wishes to purchase 9 pounds. In that case, a method that students might use is *unit rates*. This problem-solving strategy involves finding the unit rate, in this case, the price of *one* pound of apples (1 pound is the unit). Grocery stores frequently post the unit rate or unit price of their products. Unit rates can be used to solve the following problem: "Apples cost $1.98 for 3 pounds. How much do 10 pounds cost?" In this case, the price for a single pound of apples (the unit) is $1.98 ÷ 3 = $0.66. The cost for 10 pounds is 10 × $0.66, or $6.60.

Unit rates can be combined with estimation to comparison shop. For example, consider the following situation:

• A 12-ounce bottle of herbal vinegar costs $4.49, and a 10-ounce bottle costs $3.95. Which is the better buy?

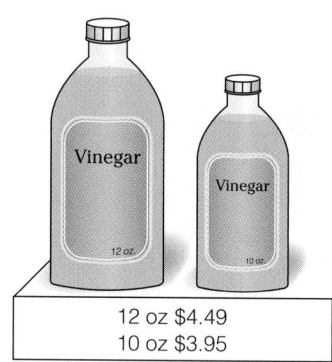

12 oz $4.49
10 oz $3.95

In this case, unit rates combined with estimation can determine the better buy. The cost per ounce for the 10-ounce bottle is approximately $0.40 ($3.95 ÷ 10). At that rate, the 12-ounce bottle would cost approximately $4.80, which is more than $4.49 (12 × $0.40 = $4.80), so the 12-ounce bottle of vinegar is the better buy.

Proportional reasoning is required in many geometry settings. Consider the two similar rectangles shown here.

The rectangles are similar, so their sides are in proportion. The side lengths of the larger rectangle are three times the side lengths of the smaller rectangle (2 × 3 = 6). Thus the length of the missing side is 15 (5 × 3). Some students will incorrectly reason that because

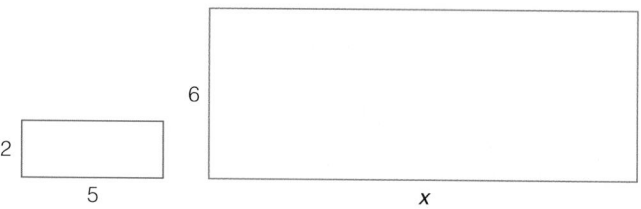

the corresponding side of the larger rectangle is 4 units longer than the matching side in the smaller rectangle, then the missing side is also 4 units longer and so must have a length of 9 (5 + 4).

When children have had many opportunities to use both methods, they are able to use unitizing in those problems where it is most appropriate, allowing them to find the answer quickly. They are also able to use unit rates for problems that do not lend themselves to unitizing. Activity 15.6 uses the Internet as a means to allow students to change distance and rates to determine the race winner. Students can plan their solutions using both unitizing and unit rates.

EXERCISE

A store is selling used CDs at five for $12. At the same rate, how much will nine CDs cost? Solve this problem using unitizing and unit rates. Which method do you prefer? ●●●

Solving for Proportion Using the Cross-Product Algorithm

What about using the cross-product algorithm to solve proportion problems? There is no question that the

$$\frac{4}{5} = \frac{7}{x}$$
$$4x = 35$$
$$x = \frac{35}{4}$$

cross-product algorithm (as illustrated) is effective and efficient. It can be used to solve any proportion problem, whether it includes all whole number values or not.

> **MISCONCEPTION**
> Students who have a shallow understanding of proportional relationships will frequently confuse the cross-product algorithm with the algorithm for multiplying fractions. They fail to discern the difference between these two mathematical operations (see later discussion) and will apply the incorrect algorithm, using the cross-product algorithm, for example, when multiplying common fractions.

Consider the following proportion, formed from two pairs of sides of similar rectangles in Figure 15.2. This problem is difficult to solve using rate tables or unitizing. It could be solved using unit rates, but the computations would be challenging and tedious to some students. The cross-product algorithm can be used here to quickly solve the problem.

$$\frac{3}{7} = \frac{x}{5}$$
$$7x = 15$$
$$x = \frac{15}{7}$$

ACTIVITY 15.6 Racing for Fame (Internet Activity)

Level: Grades 5 and 6

Setting: Groups of three students

Objective: Students explore rates and speed in an interactive setting.

Materials: Internet access

- Go to http://my.nctm.org/standards/document/eexamples/index.htm (see Activity 5.2).
- Demonstrate how to change starting positions and length of strides for each character.
- Ask students to decide who will win the race using various starting positions and stride lengths you select; then run the applet to show the results.
- Allow students the opportunity to experiment with changing starting positions and stride lengths.
- After students have had sufficient time to experiment with the applet, have them produce starting positions and stride lengths to match the following stories:

1. The boy and girl start from the same place. The boy gets to the tree ahead of the girl.

2. The girl starts behind the boy. The girl gets to the tree before the boy.

3. The boy starts at the tree and the girl starts at the house. The girl gets to the tree before the boy gets to the house.

4. The girl starts halfway to the house and the boy starts at the tree. They both get to the house at the same time.

5. The boy has a stride that is four times as long as the girl's stride. If the boy starts at the tree, where must the girl start to get to the house at the same time as the boy? Be sure to have students explain their answers to this one.

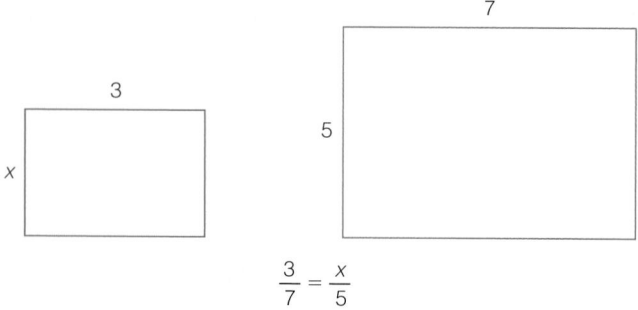

$$\frac{3}{7} = \frac{x}{5}$$

Figure 15.2 Similar rectangles

The cross-product algorithm should be the last proportion-solving strategy that students learn in middle school grades. Only after students have used the other processes presented in this chapter should they apply the cross-product algorithm. Students who learn the cross-product algorithm early in their development of proportional reasoning may never understand the multiplicative aspect of proportions. In addition, without the foundational understandings developed by the processes described earlier, students will apply the algorithm without any thought to the proportional relationships involved. Teachers should delay teaching students the cross-product algorithm until the students have experienced many proportional situations using a variety of strategies.

Developing and Extending Concepts of Percent

A complete understanding of percent requires the same multiplicative reasoning used with proportions. The pervasive nature of percent makes it important that students acquire a good understanding of its meaning and uses. In practice, percent is used in a variety of ways, and its applications are numerous in business, government, science, and industry, as well as in many aspects of daily life. In one day, one of us encountered these uses:

- The Federal Reserve Board lowered the short-term interest rate by 0.25%.

- You can get 2.9% interest on a new car loan through the month of October.

Research for the Classroom

Several research studies indicate that children must develop a variety of approaches to solve problems that require proportional reasoning. One such study focused on what seem to be straightforward missing-term proportion problems such as the following: Five shirts require 10 yards of cloth. How many yards of cloth will 15 shirts require?

This problem can be solved using a proportion linking shirts and cloth or by using proportions linking shirts to shirts and cloth to cloth. Both of these proportions are shown here.

shirts/cloth = shirts/cloth   shirts/shirts = yards of cloth/
                                                  yards of cloth

$$\frac{5}{10} = \frac{15}{?}$$ $$\frac{5}{15} = \frac{10}{?}$$

It may appear that the proportions are essentially the same. Mathematically they are equivalent, and both will result in the correct solution to the problem. However, they are conceptually different. The first proportion relates values within the understood comparison between shirts and cloth. The second proportion relates values across the given comparison of shirts and cloth, relating independent quantities of shirts to each other and independent quantities of cloth to each other. The research findings were that children who had ample opportunities to use both forms of the proportion used the form that best fit a problem in their view. In other words, the children did not use the same form of the proportion for all problems but used the form that appealed to their personal conceptualization of the problem.

The implication for classroom teachers is that the teachers' way of viewing a proportion problem may not be the way their students view it. Rather than following a preconceived relationship that does not reflect students' understanding of the problem, teachers need to provide the tools to construct proportional relationships that make sense to their students in the context of a particular problem (Lamon, 1999, 1994; Vergnaud, 1983). Thus teachers should provide experiences where students form proportions that represent both within and between relationships.

- The registrar of voters predicts a turnout of 32% of registered voters for the November general election.

- Sacramento County's sales tax was raised to 7.75% with approval of an additional 0.50% for transportation improvements.

- A computer sales company advertised promotional prices of up to 70% off on selected merchandise.

Meaning of Percent

Percent expresses a relationship between a number and 100. The symbol % indicates a denominator of 100; the word *percent* names the symbol and means "per hundred" or "out of 100." For example, 15% is an expression of the ratio between the numbers 15 and 100; it means 15 parts per 100 or 15 out of 100.

State and local governments use a sales tax as a means of raising revenue. A tax of 6 percent means that for every 100 cents ($1.00) of the purchase price of an article, a tax of 6 cents (0.06 of $1.00) will be collected by the merchant and remitted to the state. This setting provides a basis for discussing terms used in connection with percent. When an item is sold for $10, the cost is the **base** to which the tax is applied, 6% is the **rate** of tax, and 60 cents is the amount of tax, or **percentage**.

Table 15.2 illustrates some common ways that percent is used. The table helps clarify confusion about the terms *percent* and *percentage*. Because confusion is likely, a teacher must make it clear that *percent* indicates the rate (of sales tax, discount, increase, or whatever), whereas *percentage* indicates the amount, or quantity (of tax, discount, increase, or whatever). Base and percentage always represent numbers that refer to the same units (dollars, cups of water, bottles of soda), and percent is the rate by which the percentage compares with the base.

Another point of confusion arises when a given percent is applied to different bases. Consider a price increase as an example: The price of a $5.00 hat is increased 20% to $6.00. If, at a later time, the price is reduced back to $5.00, is the percent of decrease the same as the percent of increase? In both cases, the amount is the same; the price went up a dollar, and it came down a dollar.

The number lines in Figure 15.3 show that the rates in this increase-decrease setting are different. In Figure 15.3a, the first pair of segments represents the original price (blue segment), which was $5.00; and the price after it was increased to $6.00 (red segment). The increase is $\frac{1}{5}$ of the original line (red segment compared to blue segment). One out of 5 is 20% of the whole, so the *rate* of increase was 20%. In Figure 15.3b, the blue segment represents the new base: $6.00. The decrease of $1.00 represented by the red segment is $\frac{1}{6}$ of the top line's length (red segment compared to the blue segment). One out of 6 is $0.16\frac{2}{3}$, so the rate of decrease is $16\frac{2}{3}\%$, not 20%.

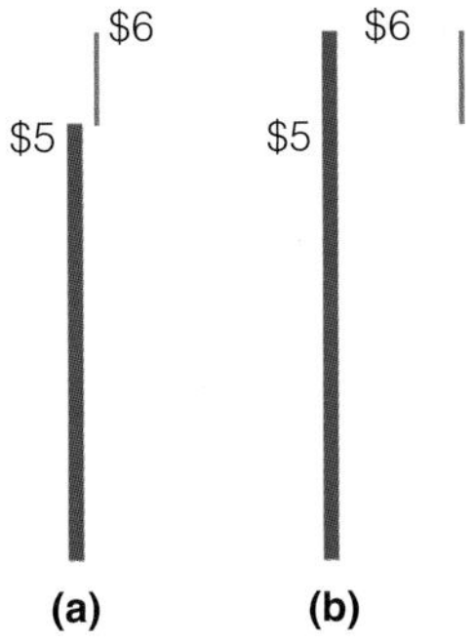

Figure 15.3 Linear representation of changes in percent

ⒺXERCISE

If the price of the $6.00 hat is reduced by 20%, what will it cost? ●●●

TABLE 15.2	Common Uses of Percent		
	Rate	**Base**	**Percentage**
Sales tax	6% sales tax	$12.00 sale	$0.72 added to sale price
Percent off sale	20% off retail	$60.00 retail	$12.00 reduction in price of coat
Increase in tax	4% raise in property tax	Property tax of $1,000.00	$40.00 increase in taxes
Ratio	Quarterback completed 50% of passes	Quarterback threw 30 passes	Quarterback completed 15 passes

Teaching and Learning About Percent

The content readiness that children need before they are introduced to percent is an understanding of both common and decimal fractions. The pedagogical readiness required is an understanding of the learning aids they will use. During introductory and developmental activities, each whole unit or set should be one that is easily subdivided into 100 parts. It is easier for children to understand the meaning of percent when they deal with portions of the 100 parts of a unit or collection of objects than when they deal with units or sets that cannot be partitioned into 100 parts. As children mature, they need experiences that relate percents to groups other than 100.

Although children need an understanding of common and decimal fractions before percent is introduced, mastery of fractions is not required. We recommend that early uses of percent can quickly follow initial experiences with common fractions and decimals. A percent is simply another way to represent common or decimal fractions. Some children find initial experiences with percent quite easy to understand because all percents are based on 100, in contrast to different denominators with common fractions and different powers of 10 with decimal fractions.

One introductory lesson (Activity 15.7) uses the same Cuisenaire materials used to introduce decimal fractions. An assessment activity (Activity 15.8) provides an early assessment that links common fractions, decimal fractions, and percent to familiar area models. Activity 15.9 helps students develop common fraction, decimal fraction, and percent equivalents. In Activity 15.10 students estimate linear percentages and verify them with an elastic percent ruler. In Activity 15.11 students consider percent in yet another context, money.

Children in grades 5 and 6 who have had experiences that connect the three ways to represent fractional numbers—common and decimal fractions and percent—will easily shift their thinking from one form to another. An exercise (see Figure 15.4) in which children convert forms can serve as a quick way to assess their ability to relate one representation to another.

Working with Percent

Students who successfully complete the percent concept-building activities in Figure 15.4 are ready to use percent to solve problems. Being able to find a percent of a number is based on knowledge of and skill in using common and decimal fractions to find parts of wholes and groups. For example, when a $50 item is on sale with a 40% discount, the amount of the discount is determined by finding 40% of 50 using either 0.4 of 50 or $\frac{4}{10}$ of 50. In either case the answer is determined by applying a known skill—multiplication with a decimal or common fraction—in a new situation. Here are examples of

---

ACTIVITY 15.7 Cuisenaire Rod Percents (Representation)

Level: Grades 4–6

Setting: Whole class

Objective: Students demonstrate understanding of the basic concept of percent.

Materials: One Cuisenaire flat, 9 orange rods, and 100 small white rods for every two students (construction-paper kit materials may be used)

- Activate prior knowledge by having children recall that each white rod is $\frac{1}{100}$, or 0.01, of the flat. Write the numerals $\frac{1}{100}$ and 0.01 on the chalkboard.

- Have pairs of children put 50 white rods on the flat, and then write the common fraction and decimal fraction numerals: $\frac{1}{2}$ and 0.50. Ask: "What is the common fraction if we change the denominator to 100?" (Answer: $\frac{50}{100}$). Have them repeat with other numbers of white rods: 10,

44, and 72. (Children may substitute 1 orange rod for every 10 white rods as they work.)

- Write the numerals in a table like the one below.

Common Fraction		Decimal Fraction	Percent
$\frac{1}{2}$	$\frac{50}{100}$	0.50	50%
$\frac{1}{10}$	$\frac{10}{100}$	0.10	10%
$\frac{44}{100}$		0.44	44%
$\frac{72}{100}$		0.72	72%

- Use a discussion of the chart to extend the children's understanding of fractional numbers to include percent. They should learn that common fractions, decimal fractions, and percent are all notations for parts of wholes and sets.

ACTIVITY 15.8 **Assessment Activity**

Level: Grades 2–4
Setting: Individual students

For each figure, show the ratio of the shaded portion to the unshaded portion.

1.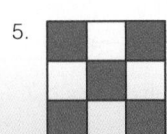

2.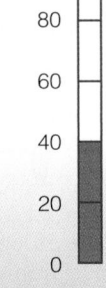

3. 100

6.

7.

4.

5.

8.

9.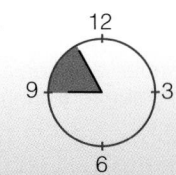

ACTIVITY 15.9 **Hundred Day Chart**

Level: Grades 2–4
Setting: Individual students
Objective: Students write out equivalent common fractions, decimal fractions, and percents.
Materials: A large chart with 100 squares on it

In primary grades, one way that teachers help young children with their counting is to focus on Hundred Day. This activity uses Dollar Bill Day instead, focusing on the four equivalent representations for each day: common fractions, decimal fractions, money, and percents.

• As early as possible in the school year, post a chart with 100 squares. Explain that this is a Dollar Bill Day Chart. The class will use the chart to record each school day.

• For each day of school, have a different student write the numeral of the date into the next empty square of the Dollar Bill Chart.

• As each day is written into the chart, each student should record the day and its various equivalents in their own chart as shown here.

Day	Dollar Equivalent	Common Fraction	Decimal Fraction	Percent
1	$0.01	$\frac{1}{100}$	0.01	1%
2	$0.02	$\frac{2}{100}$ or $\frac{1}{50}$	0.02	2%

• Older students could also write the simplified common fraction for the specific day.

• Students might keep their charts in a notebook or folder in the class, or collect their chart at the start of class to record their new Dollar Bill Day data and then return the chart to its place.

• Periodically check the charts to be sure that students are recording information correctly, especially if you expect students to simplify the common fractions.

• On Dollar Bill Day, commemorate the event by completing the class Dollar Bill Chart, and then have children complete their own chart.

ACTIVITY 15.10 Elastic Percent Ruler

Level: Grades 4–6

Setting: Pairs of students

Objective: Students use the elastic percent ruler to help them estimate linear percentages.

Materials: 1.1-meter lengths of $\frac{1}{2}$-inch elastic, permanent markers, meter sticks, sticky notes, paper adding-machine tape

In this activity, children will make their own elastic percent ruler by marking an elastic with percent markings.

- Distribute a length of elastic to each pair of students. Direct students to mark one end of the elastic 0 and then mark every 10 centimeters until they reach 100 centimeters, close to the other end of the elastic. The elastic should lie flat on a table or desk when students make their marks. It should be fully extended, but not be stretched.

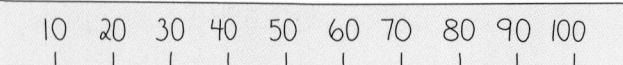

- Once students have finished, have them check to be sure that their unstretched elastic percent ruler is the length of a meter stick.

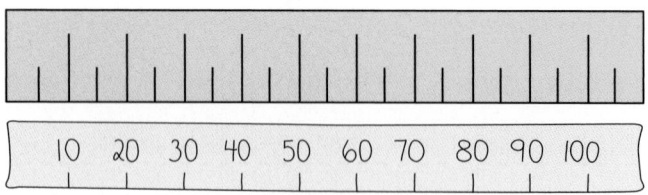

- Assign students various objects around the room to measure; the objects should be longer than a meter but not longer than the stretched elastic. Your desk, a panel of

chalkboard, and the width/length of a window are some possibilities.

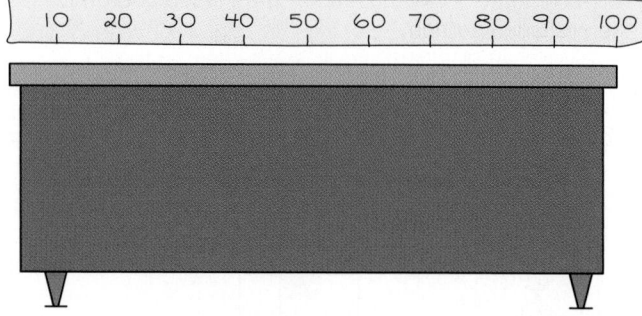

- Students are to estimate specific linear percentage lengths from one end of the object to the other, either marking them with chalk or pencil or placing a sticky note at the point they select. Some linear percentage lengths to ask students to mark are 30%, 50%, 75%, 90%, 10%, and 40%.

- After estimating, children should use their elastic percent ruler to find the actual linear percentage. They should continue with each percent, first estimating and then verifying with their elastic percent ruler.

- As students are engaged in the activity, circulate to see how their estimation accuracy improves as they measure more objects with their elastic ruler.

- As a culminating activity, give each group a random length of paper adding-machine tape (between 1.3 and 2 meters in length). The group's task is to mark and label with a pen several linear percentages that you assign. They then exchange paper tape with another group and use their elastic rulers to verify each other's estimations.

---

situations that can be used to help children make this connection:

- A basketball team sank 65% of 40 free throws in a game. How many free throws did the team make?

- A gardener planted 20 tulips in a group. Seventy-five percent were red. How many red tulips were there?

- On average, 2.5% of the days in a year have a snowfall of at least 1 inch. What is the average number of days per year that have an inch or more of snow?

- An auto shop sold 55% of 180 tires in July. How many tires did the auto shop sell?

By providing a mixture of situations, teachers can help children distinguish between situations that can be easily solved with mental computation—the tulip problem, in which students think "What is $\frac{3}{4}$ of 20?" and compute the answer in their heads—and situations for which pencil and paper or a calculator is needed.

Some students might compute the free-throw situation mentally, thinking that 10% of 65 is 6.5, so 40% of 65 is 4 × 6.5, or 26. Other students may reason that 40 times 65 is 260 to determine that 26 is the answer. Do not pressure students who do not readily understand explanations of classmates' mental processes to adopt them for themselves. Over time,

ACTIVITY 15.11 Another Look at Percent

Level: Grades 4–6

Setting: Cooperative learning

Objective: Students develop a strategy for understanding percent.

Materials: Students select suitable manipulative materials. Every group needs paper and pencils plus two tables on butcher paper (overhead projector tables can be used).

- This lesson uses a partners cooperative-learning format with four-member teams.

- Tell this story: "A sixth-grade class had a cupcake sale to raise money for a trip. Ten students each baked four chocolate and six white cakes for the sale. What percent of Gleneece's cakes were chocolate?"

- Each pair of team members prepares a presentation, using manipulative materials or drawings, to illustrate and explain how they determined their answers. Team pairs share their presentations.

- Add to the story: "Don baked four chocolate and six white cakes. How many cakes did he and Gleneece bake? What percent of the 20 cakes were chocolate cakes?"

- Again, pairs illustrate and explain the situation to team partners.

- Show a table that displays two entries that show what has been done so far.

Chocolate	4	8
Number	10	20

- Point out that the table shows the relationships between chocolate cakes and all cakes when there are 10 and 20 cakes. "Raise your hand to tell me what goes in the next column." Have different students contribute as you complete the table.

Chocolate	4	8	12	16	20	24	28	32	36	40
Number	10	20	30	40	50	60	70	80	90	100

- Have children study the table and describe what they see. Possible responses: "The numbers in the top row increase by 4." "The bottom numbers increase by 10." "If you make common fractions of the top and bottom numbers you have a set of equivalent fractions." "Each common fraction is equal to 40%." "Each baker made 40% chocolate cakes."

- Make a table for the white cakes; solicit comments about it. Probe for all ratio pairs representing the same percent.

Chocolate	6	12	18	24	30	36	42	48	54	60
Number	10	20	30	40	50	60	70	80	90	100

- Children who know about ratios might recognize that they are dealing with a ratio setting. When they determine what percent each type of cake is of the total, they determine the ratio between a given type of cake and the total number of cakes. Another way of thinking about 40% is to think of it as the part that 40 is of 100. The number of chocolate cakes baked compared with all cakes baked by each student can be represented as 4:10, and the percent as 40%.

- Give each team a different, similar setting: "The town council ruled that 2 acres of every 10 acres of land in new developments was to be set aside as parkland. If there are 50 acres of new development, how many acres of parkland are there?" "Students at Bonheim School averaged a $3.00 profit on every $10.00 of sales in their school-supply store. If they had $120.00 worth of sales, how much was their profit?" Teams solve and share with classmates.

Name _____   Date _____

1. Rename each decimal fraction as a percent:
   a. 0.65 = _____   b. 0.21 = _____   c. 0.95 = _____
   d. 0.08 = _____   e. 0.86 = _____   f. 0.30 = _____

2. Rename each common fraction as a decimal fraction:
   a. $\frac{1}{4}$ = _____   b. $\frac{1}{2}$ = _____   c. $\frac{3}{4}$ = _____
   d. $\frac{2}{10}$ = _____   e. $\frac{6}{10}$ = _____   f. $\frac{1}{10}$ = _____

3. Rename each common fraction as a percent:
   a. $\frac{1}{4}$ = _____   b. $\frac{1}{2}$ = _____   c. $\frac{3}{4}$ = _____
   d. $\frac{2}{10}$ = _____   e. $\frac{6}{10}$ = _____   f. $\frac{1}{10}$ = _____

4. Rename each percent as a decimal fraction:
   a. 13% = _____   b. 47% = _____   c. 99% = _____
   d. 5% = _____   e. 60% = _____   f. 21% = _____

5. Rename each percent as a common fraction:
   a. 20% = _____   b. 50% = _____   c. 19% = _____
   d. 75% = _____   e. 90% = _____   f. 5% = _____

Figure 15.4 Worksheet for practice with converting forms of fractional numbers

students will construct their own understanding of those mental processes that make sense to them. A calculator is useful for computing increasingly complex problems involving percent, and children should learn to use them for this purpose.

In each of the preceding situations, the base and rate were known and multiplication by a common or decimal fraction determined the percentage. In other situations, the base and percentage are known and the percent is to be determined or the percent and percentage are known and the base is to be determined.

Consider the following three problems:

1. A shirt is on sale at 25% off. The regular price of the shirt is $25.00. Find the discount.

2. The number of students in an elementary school increased by 120. The school originally had 600 students. By what percent did the number of students increase?

3. Jim got 12 questions correct on his mathematics test. That was 80% of the number of items on the test. How many questions were on Jim's test?

Each of these questions presents a different aspect of percent problems. In Question 1, the task is to determine the percentage, given the rate and the base. In Question 2, the task is to determine the rate, given the base and the percentage. In Question 3, the task is to determine the base, given the rate and the percentage.

In times past, these questions were designated Case I, Case II, and Case III, respectively. First, children identified the type of problem they were solving; then, they applied a memorized division or multiplication procedure to solve each type of problem. The focus was on memorizing rules rather than understanding the relationships in the problem. We suggest a different approach that builds on children's knowledge of ratio and proportion and is developed in an intuitive way.

Recall the three terms associated with percent: base, rate, and percentage. Remember, too, that *percent* means *per 100*. These terms are all part of the following problem:

• A farmer plants 25% of his 200-acre farm with corn. How many acres are planted with corn?

A diagram of the farm (Figure 15.5) helps clarify the situation. Students who have a good understanding

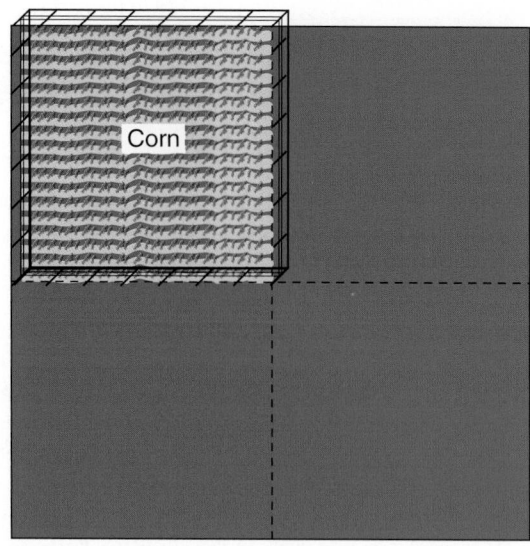

Figure 15.5 A simple drawing can illustrate a percent situation

of fractional numbers, including percent, should readily recognize that if 25% of the 200-acre farm is planted with corn, that is the same as $\frac{1}{4}$ planted in corn, or $\frac{1}{4} \times 200 = 50$ acres planted in corn.

Pose another situation:

• Look at the picture this way. It shows that part of the 200 acres is planted in corn. How many acres of corn does the picture show? (Answer: 50). What part of the 200 acres is the 50 acres? (Answer: $\frac{1}{4}$). One-quarter is the same as what percent? (Answer: 25).

Then present the situation differently:

• If 50 acres of corn is 25% of the entire farm, how many acres are there on the farm? Fifty acres is what part of the farm? (Answer: 25%, or $\frac{1}{4}$). If 50 acres is $\frac{1}{4}$ of the farm, how large is the farm? (Answer: 4×50, or 200 acres).

Following discussion, show a proportion for the first situation:

$$\frac{25}{100} = \frac{?}{200}$$

• What does the $\frac{25}{100}$ represent? (Answer: the percent of the farm in corn).

• What does the 200 represent? (Answer: the size of the farm).

• What does the question mark represent? (Answer: the acres planted in corn).

TABLE 15.3 • Three Types of Percent Problems		
Total Acreage (Base)	**Percent Corn (Rate)**	**Acres in Corn (Percentage)**
200	25%	?
200	?	50
?	25%	50

- What number replaces the question mark to make this a proportion? (Answer: 50).

Repeat this discussion with each of the other situations:

$$\frac{?}{100} = \frac{50}{200}$$

$$\frac{25}{100} = \frac{50}{?}$$

All three problems are represented in Table 15.3.

Another way to represent the problem is with a detailed diagram. If the diagram is drawn as shown in Figure 15.6, it can be used to easily answer any of the preceding questions. Notice that the farm is divided into 25% *chunks* that are labeled with the number of acres represented by each chunk.

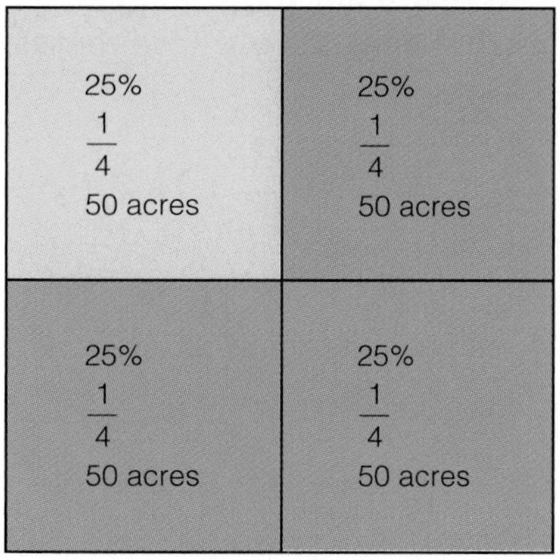

25% $\frac{1}{4}$ 50 acres	25% $\frac{1}{4}$ 50 acres
25% $\frac{1}{4}$ 50 acres	25% $\frac{1}{4}$ 50 acres

Figure 15.6 Diagram representing a percent situation

A number line is another way to visualize these same problems (Figure 15.7). Draw a line with 0 at the left end and 100 at the right end. Divide it into 10 equivalent parts, and put percent numbers along the bottom. The base for this situation—200—goes above the 100. Half the base is 100; write that above 50 on the line. Have children tell where 50 and 150 acres would go on the line. Use the line as you

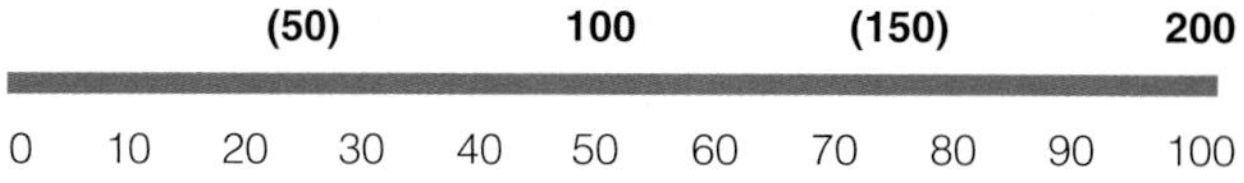

Figure 15.7 Number line used to represent a percent situation

discuss the proportion situations involving acres of corn.

Proportional Reasoning and Percent

As children begin to apply proportional reasoning in their mathematics, they can do so with percents. The proportional relationship that can be used to solve all percent problems can be represented as follows:

$$\frac{\text{part}}{\text{whole}} = \frac{\%}{100}$$

The first problems children solve using proportions should involve numbers that enable children to use chunking or equivalent fractions to find the solution. Only after much experience with proportionality situations will children be able to understand and use the cross-product algorithm. Only then should you use numbers that require the cross-product algorithm in their computations.

Percent problems can be the setting for introducing algebraic processes and variables. In each of the proportions, a variable can be used to represent the missing term, and the resulting proportions can be solved using the cross-product algorithm.

ⒺXERCISE

Briefly describe a situation other than the cornfield that can be used to practice the proportion method of dealing with problems involving percent. How can you illustrate the situation? ●●●

Use what you know about percents to solve this problem: Flormart is selling a coat that normally costs $120 at 25% off. A competitor, Bullseye, sells the same coat for $150 but is offering it at 40% off. Which store has the better sale price for the coat?

Working with Percents Greater Than 100

There is one aspect of percent that proves confusing for students, even at the high school level: percents greater than 100. Because teachers stress that percent means what part of 100, students imagine that all percents are between 0 and 100. "After all," they might reason, "how can you have more than 100% of anything?" When working with percent is restricted to physical models that represent a whole, and all percents are part of the whole, such a misconception can become entrenched. Students need experiences working in situations where percents are greater than 100. For example, if the price of a movie ticket increases from $4.00 to $9.00, the amount of the increase is $5.00. What is the percent of increase compared to the original price of a ticket?

$$\frac{5}{4} = \frac{x}{100}$$

$$x = 125\%$$

Notice that the part/whole = %/100 format must be adjusted for this problem because the solution depends on values that change over time. A related format might be

$$\frac{change}{starting\ value} = \frac{\%}{100}$$

Percents greater than 100 can also be shown with area models. Figure 15.8 shows 50% and 150% of the same-sized circle. When teachers provide many early experiences that portray percents greater

than 100 along with common and decimal fractions greater than 1, students will not find such percents challenging once they become part of their regular study in upper middle school.

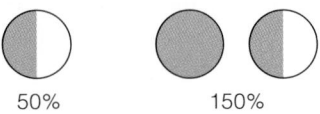

50%   150%

Figure 15.8 Representing percents greater than 100

A chart that shows the relationship between common and decimal fractions, percents, and money can also be helpful. Note that the following chart includes percents larger than 100.

25¢	=	25%	=	$0.25	=	$\frac{25}{100}$	=	$\frac{1}{4}$
50¢	=	50%	=	$0.50	=	$\frac{50}{100}$	=	$\frac{1}{2}$
125¢	=	125%	=	$1.25	=	$\frac{125}{100}$	=	$\frac{5}{4}$
175¢	=	175%	=	$1.75	=	$\frac{175}{100}$	=	$\frac{7}{4}$

Activity 15.7 can be adapted to use Cuisenaire Rods to represent percents greater than 100. For example, if the red rod is 100%, what percent does the teal rod represent? the green rod? the black rod?

ⒺXERCISE

In a set of Cuisenaire Rods, the magenta rod represents 100%. What does the blue rod represent? ●●●

Take-Home Activities

These take-home activities invite students and parents to work together to enhance the children's understanding of uses of percent and ratio. In the first activity parents and students find uses of per-cent in newspapers and magazines. In the second activity children should be encouraged to complete the body-ratio activity for each family member.

Arrowhead School
12345 Lake View Road
Wizard Mountain, Idaho

Dear Parents:

Children in your child's class have been studying about percent and its uses. One way for students to connect with what they are doing in the classroom is to locate examples of the mathematics they are learning in real-world situations. You and your child can investigate uses of percent in newspapers and magazines and on television. We will discuss the results of students' investigations in class next week.

This chart will help your child to record information to bring to class for the discussion. In the first column, name the magazine, newspaper, or television show. In the second column, briefly describe the situation—sale, population statistics, budget information, and so on. In the third column, write examples of information, such as a pie chart showing percents, percent off in a sale, and so on.

Source	Situation	Example

Please have your child bring the information to class on Tuesday the 14th.

Thank you.

A Sierra School Mathematics Take-Home: Body Ratios

Here are directions for doing some body measurements. Please ask a parent, other adult, or older brother or sister to assist you as you work.

Cut a length of string equal to your height. Use this string to gather some information about body ratios. How many times do you think your string will wrap around your neck? Predict first, then find out. What have you discovered? It takes the circumference of _____ necks to equal 1 body height, or the circumference of 1 head equals _____ of my height. Write this information in ratio form. Repeat for your height and the circumference of your head.

Use your string to find three or four other body ratios. For example, how many of one of your feet equals your height, or how many of one wrist circumference equals your waist? (Remember to predict first.) Do you think the same ratios would be true of babies? of adults? How could you find out? Use the information you have gathered about your body ratios to make a scale drawing of yourself. By what percent (or what fraction) will you have to reduce each of your measurements to fit on a page of your journal?

Write the results of your investigation in your journal. Be sure to tell which body parts fit each of the ratios you put in your journal.

Summary

Proportional reasoning is a key concept in mathematics, and children's understanding of the multiplicative aspect of proportionality is apt to be slow in developing. Be sure to take the time that is needed for students to gain an understanding of proportions. The cross-product algorithm is the most efficient method for solving proportion problems, but it can cloud students' understanding of proportional situations. It should be the last method introduced to students for solving proportions, well along into the middle grades.

The use of common fractions to express ratios and solve problems involving proportions should be introduced through simple examples of patterns and tables. Working with percent is closely related to working with ratios and proportions and should be approached through situations involving proportions. Students' solution strategies for percent problems should develop from their understanding of percent and multiplicative relationships.

Two take-home activities presented in this chapter give children opportunities to explore uses of percent in newspapers and magazines and to extend their understanding of ratios by examining relationships among various parts of their bodies.

Study Questions and Activities

1. Compose two problems dealing with money, one that uses additive relationships and one that uses multiplicative relationships.

2. Why delay demonstrating to students the cross-product algorithm for solving proportions?

3. What is the benefit to children to study introductory aspects of common fractions, decimal fractions, and percents at the same time?

4. Give two real-life examples of percents greater than 100.

5. Draw a diagram and a number line to fit the following situations. Write a proportion for each situation.

   a. A mixture of coffee beans weighs 50 kilograms. If 48% of the beans are grown in Hawaii, how many kilograms of coffee are from Hawaii?

   b. A mixture of coffee beans contains 24 kilograms of coffee grown in Hawaii. If this is 48% of the entire mixture, what is the total weight of the mixture?

   c. A mixture of coffee that weighs 50 kilograms has 24 kilograms of coffee grown in Hawaii. What percent of the mixture is coffee from Hawaii?

   Would you use this situation or the cornfield situation for children's first experience with solving these types of problems? Why do you prefer your choice?

6. In what ways are percents similar to common and decimal fractions? How are they different?

Praxis (http://www.ets.org/praxis/) Jerry is 50 inches tall and is growing at the rate of $\frac{1}{24}$ inch per month. Adam is 47 inches tall and is growing at the rate of $\frac{1}{8}$ inch per month. If they each continue to grow at these rates for the next four years, in how many months will they be the same height?

a. 24

b. 30

c. 36

d. 42

NAEP (http://nces.ed.gov/nationsreportcard/)

Bay City		Exton		Yardville

On the road shown above, the distance from Bay City to Exton is 60 miles. What is the distance from Bay City to Yardville?

a. 45 miles

b. 75 miles

c. 90 miles

d. 105 miles

TIMSS (http://nces.ed.gov/timss/) If the ratio of 7 to 13 is the same as the ratio of x to 52, what is the value of x?

a. 7

b. 13

c. 28

d. 364

e. 91

Using Children's Literature

Strauss, Stephen. (1995). *Sizeauarus: From hectares to decibels to calories—a witty compendium of measurements.* New York: Kodansha International. (Grades 4–6)

This book provides a number of interesting data tables that students in grades 4–6 can use to make comparisons between the attributes of various physical objects. Children could be asked to find several ratios that interest them. The ratios might be rounded to single-digit common fractions. The following are examples of possible ratios children might compute (Strauss, 1995):

· The area of the Atlantic Ocean to the area of the Pacific Ocean (p. 126)

· The area of a pool table to the area of a baseball diamond (p. 127)

· The density of rubber to that of gold or platinum, or of tooth enamel (p. 130)

· The kilowatt-hours used by a clock to the kilowatt-hours used by a television, a fan, an air conditioner, or a hair dryer (p. 145)

- The weight of a dime to that of a quarter, or of a raccoon to that of a moose (p. 171)

Teacher's Resources

AIMS. (2000). *Proportional reasoning: AIMS activities.* Fresno, CA: AIMS Educational Foundation.

Barnett, Carne, Goldstein, Donna, & Jackson, Babette (Eds.). (1994). *Fractions, ratios, and percents: Hard to teach and hard to learn?* Portsmouth, NH: Heinemann.

Carpenter, T., Fennema, E., & Romberg, T. (Eds.). (1993). *Rational numbers: An integration of research.* Hillsdale, NJ: Lawrence Erlbaum Associates.

Curcio, Frances R., & Bezuk, Nadine S. (1994). *Understanding rational numbers and proportions.* Reston, VA: National Council of Teachers of Mathematics.

Currah, Joanne, & Felling, Jane. (1997). *Piece it together with fractions.* Edmonton, Canada: Box Cars and One-Eyed Jacks.

Harel, G., & Confrey, J. (Eds.). (1989). *The development of multiplicative reasoning in the learning of mathematics.* Albany: State University of New York Press.

National Council of Teachers of Mathematics. (2002). *Making sense of fractions, ratios, and proportions.* Reston: VA: Author.

Children's Bookshelf

Adams, Laurie, & Coudert, Allison. (1983). *Alice and the boa constrictor.* Boston: Houghton Mifflin. (Grades 4–6)

Ash, Russell. (1996). *Incredible comparisons.* London: Dorling Kindersley. (Grades 3–6)

Banks, Lynne. (1980). *The Indian in the cupboard.* New York: Avon Books. (Grades 3–6)

Beneduce, Ann. (1996). *Gulliver's adventures in Lilliput.* New York: Putnam & Grosset. (Grades 4–7)

Clement, Ron. (1991). *Counting on Frank.* Milwaukee: Garth Stevens Children's Books. (Grades 5–7)

Dodds, Dayle Ann, & Manders, John. (2004). *Minnie's diner.* London: Candlewick Press. (Grades 2–5)

Most, Bernard. (1994). *How big were the dinosaurs?* San Diego: Voyager Books. (Grades 2–5)

Schwartz, David. (1989). *If you made a million.* New York City: Lothrop, Lee, and Shephard Books. (Grades 4–6)

Waverly, B. (1990). *How big? How fast? How hungry?* Milwaukee: Raintree. (Grades 3–6)

Wells, Robert E. (1993). *Is a blue whale the biggest thing there is?* Morton Grove, IL: Albert Whitman. (Grades 3–6)

Wells, Robert E. (1995). *What's smaller than a pigmy shrew?* Morton Grove, IL: Albert Whitman. (Grades 4–6)

Wells, Robert E. (1997). *What's faster than a speeding cheetah?* Morton Grove, IL: Albert Whitman. (Grades 4–6)

Technology Resources
Computer Software

Mighty Math: Number Heroes. (1996). San Francisco: Edmark Corporation.

This software includes several sections dealing with percents and conversions between percents and common fractions and decimals.

SimCalc. (1998). Free from http://www.analyzemath.com/distancespeed/distancespeed.html

The focus of this software is the relationship between distance and rate and time. This software allows children to experiment by changing any or all of these variables and then assessing the results.

Internet Sites

For activities relating common fractions, decimal fractions, and percent, go to the following websites:

http://nlvm.usu.edu/en/nav/vlibrary.html (see Percentages)

http://illuminations.nctm.org (see Fraction Pie Overview)

For an interesting applet that simulates viewing an object through a tube so that proportions are maintained as the location of the person or the length of the tube is changed, go to the following website:

http://illuminations.nctm.org (see Tube Viewer simulation)

Internet Game

One of the many games at a site maintained by the British Broadcasting Corporation is *Saloon Snap. Saloon Snap* is located at **http://www.bbc.co.uk/education/mathsfile/**. The game challenges students to decide which of two mathematics expressions is larger. The setting is a saloon, and students compete against a saloonkeeper to make the correct choice. The game has three levels of difficulty, and the reaction time can be adjusted in each level from slow to fast.

In the game the numerical representations can be percents, decimals, or fractions. The game is accompanied by sound effects (in this case a "raspberry" follows an incorrect choice) that can be turned off. A game consists of 10 items, and the score is shown on the screen at the end of every round of 10 challenges.

For Further Reading

Abrahamson, D., & Cigan, C. (2003). A design for ratio and proportion instruction. *Mathematics Teaching in the Middle School* 8(9), 493–501.

Abrahamson and Cigan describe how to use number charts and rate tables to formulate proportion quartets for solving proportion problems.

Billings, E. (2001). Problems that encourage proportion sense. *Mathematics Teaching in the Middle School* 7(1), 10–14.

Billings describes using nonnumeric problems to develop proportion senses and the cross-product algorithm in children.

Boston, M., Smith, M., & Hillen, A. (2003). Building on students' intuitive strategies to make sense of cross multiplication. *Mathematics Teaching in the Middle School* 9(3), 150–155.

Boston and colleagues detail various activities and strategies that build students' understanding of proportions before using cross-product algorithms.

Bright, G., Joyner, J., & Wallis, C. (2003). Assessing proportional thinking. *Mathematics Teaching in the Middle School* 9(3), 166–171.

Bright and colleagues present several assessment activities and children's responses to them. They analyze the responses and discuss the implications. They suggest that deep understanding of proportionality may be lacking even in children who can correctly answer typical ratio and proportion problems.

Brinker, Laura. (1998). Using recipes and ratio tables. *Teaching Children Mathematics* 5(4), 218–224.

Brinker describes how increasing and decreasing recipe ingredients can enhance children's understanding of and work with ratios and proportions. Examples of the teacher's and students' involvement in the activities are cited.

Doyle, Shelley. (2000). Promoting percent as a proportion in eighth-grade. *School Science and Mathematics* 7(100), 380–392.

Doyle describes the findings of a research study that supports solving percent word problems as proportions rather than by using different word problem strategies.

Langrall, C., & Swafford, J. (2000). Three balloons for two dollars: Developing proportional reasoning. *Mathematics Teaching in the Middle School* 6(4), 154–261.

Langrall and Swafford set out essentials for foundational understanding of proportions, even for those students who have had formal instructions in proportions. Informal reasoning strategies of children are described and analyzed.

Moss, Joan. (2003). Introducing percents in linear measurement to foster an understanding of rational-number operations. *Teaching Children Mathematics* 9 (5), 335–340.

Moss makes a compelling case for introducing percents even before fractions as a means of dividing up a number line into smaller segments. Once students can use percents to do so, they are then introduced to equivalent common and decimal fractions.

Telese, James, & Abete, Jesse, Jr. (2002). Diet, ratios, proportions: A healthy mix. *Mathematics Teaching in the Middle School* 8(1), 8–13.

The project described in this article uses data from various foods to produce ratios and proportions that are then graphed, used to compare various diets, and ultimately used to examine the school lunch menu. Student work for all parts of the project is displayed, along with evaluation comments.

CHAPTER 16

Thinking Algebraically

A chapter on algebra in a book that focuses on mathematics at the K–6 level may surprise new teachers. After all, most people remember algebra as a dance of symbols with a goal of solving for x. Algebra was a high school course where they studied equations and graphing. But algebra is more than solving for x; it is a study of patterns, functions, and relationships. Algebra allows students to generalize from arithmetic to discern relationships, to make predictions from observed patterns, and to use a powerful problem-solving tool to solve problems. In short, algebra is a way for students to "recognize order and organize their world" (National Council of Teachers of Mathematics, 2000, p. 91).

In this chapter you will read about:

1. The value of patterns and patterning activities for younger children

2. Activities to introduce the concept of variable to children

3. The importance of equality in equations

4. Common misconceptions students hold about algebraic relationships

5. The concept of functions in developing algebraic reasoning

6. What research says about young children using letters as variables

In this chapter we focus on three aspects of algebraic reasoning: patterns, equations and variables, and functions. The study of each of these begins in the primary grades and extends through the entire mathematics curriculum, to high school grades and beyond. In truth, the foundation for the development of algebraic thinking begins at the lowest grades and continues through the entire elementary school mathematics program. NCTM has designated algebra as one of the five content standards for school mathematics. The algebra standards for younger children are:

POINT OF VIEW
While in the past, algebra instruction was reserved for older students and focused primarily on the manipulation of symbols and the solutions to equations, today's algebra instruction should begin with the youngest students and focus more on the "big ideas" of algebra and on reasoning algebraically. (Greenes, 2004, p. 8)

NCTM Algebra Standard

Algebra instructional programs from prekindergarten through grade 12 should enable all students to:
    Understand patterns, relations, and functions

Pre-K–2 Expectations:
In prekindergarten through grade 2 all students should:
- sort, classify, and order objects by size, number, and other properties;
- recognize, describe, and extend patterns such as sequences of sounds and shapes or simple numeric patterns and translate from one representation to another;
- analyze how both repeating and growing patterns are generated.
    Represent and analyze mathematical situations and structures using algebraic symbols

Pre-K–2 Expectations:
In prekindergarten through grade 2 all students should:
- illustrate general principles and properties of operations, such as commutativity, using specific numbers;
- use concrete, pictorial, and verbal representations to develop an understanding of invented and conventional symbolic notations.
    Use mathematical models to represent and understand quantitative relationships

Pre-K–2 Expectations:
In prekindergarten through grade 2 all students should:
- model situations that involve the addition and subtraction of whole numbers, using objects, pictures, and symbols.
    Analyze change in various contexts

Pre-K–2 Expectations:
In prekindergarten through grade 2 all students should:
- describe qualitative change, such as a student's growing taller;
- describe quantitative change, such as a student's growing two inches in one year.

The NCTM standards move algebra beyond simply solving for x or graphing lines. The focus of algebraic thinking in the lower grades is to analyze change by observing and extending patterns. Algebraic thinking provides tools to children to represent relationships that they observe through patterns and then generalize these relationships to represent the changes they can observe in various contexts.

What Teachers Should Know About Teaching Algebra

Algebra is the study of patterns and numerical relationships. Children who are able to form patterns build a foundation for the algebraic concept of functions. Patterning is the concept of functions that is central to algebra. Students use functions to generalize a relationship from patterns they have formed. The ability to generalize a relationship from specific data is a hallmark of algebraic reasoning. For example, the following table shows the temperature and the number of cricket chirps recorded in 15 seconds:

Chirps in 15 seconds	10	15	20	25
Temperature	49	54	59	64

From these data a generalization is that to find the temperature, add 39 to the number of cricket chirps. Teachers can help students develop algebraic thinking by providing many experiences with generating data and formulating functional relationships; by working through these activities, students will learn to avoid simply manipulating numbers and symbols in equations. Another key concept in algebra is the balance aspect of equations. Students need to understand that the equal sign in an equation indicates a balance or equality between the numerical expressions on both sides of the equation.

POINT OF VIEW
Mathematics is a science of pattern and order. (National Research Council, 1989, p. 60)

Patterning as Algebraic Thinking

Humans use patterns to make sense of a chaotic and seemingly random world of experiences. By finding and using patterns, humans develop concepts and skills for living. Patterns occur in natural and human-designed settings. Trees and plants are recognized

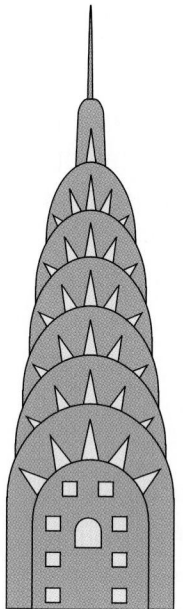

Figure 16.1 Example of a pattern seen in architecture: New York's Chrysler Building

by the patterns of their leaves, shape, and bark. By recognizing which trees and plants had curative value, people in many cultures developed medicines and avoided plants that were poisonous. In art, architecture, and design, patterns create unity and harmony through repetitions of colors and shapes (Figure 16.1). Repetition of melodies and rhythm bring unity to music from Bach and Mozart to Prince and Eminem.

Science is based on identifying regular and predictable occurrences in the physical world. What weather factors predict the occurrence of tornadoes and hurricanes? What influence does El Niño or La Niña have on weather patterns? New elements were predicted even before they were discovered because physicists and chemists recognized patterns in the periodic table of elements. Good readers and writers use word and letter patterns when they decode or spell similar words (*enough, tough, rough*), although English has many irregularities that confuse children and adults (*bough, gruff*).

Many patterns are also found in mathematics because mathematics is a way of describing the events in the world. Prime and composite numbers, odd and even numbers, and square numbers are patterned sequences of numbers. For example,

1	4	9	16	25	36
1^2	2^2	3^2	4^2	5^2	6^2

Whole numbers in the Hindu-Arabic number system are based on a pattern of increasing powers of 10, called **place value**:

1	10	100	1,000	10,000	100,000
10^0	10^1	10^2	10^3	10^4	10^5

Negative numbers extend place value with a pattern of negative powers of 10:

0.0001	0.001	0.01	0.1	1	10	100	1,000	10,000	100,000
10^{-4}	10^{-3}	10^{-2}	10^{-1}	10^0	10^1	10^2	10^3	10^4	10^5

Finding and using patterns is an essential strategy for living, in mathematical thinking, and in problem solving.

ⒺXERCISE

Describe a pattern that you use to organize your life and activities. ●●●

Patterns in Mathematics Learning and Teaching

Patterning is a central element in algebraic thinking. Patterns are generally defined as a repeated sequence of objects, actions, sounds, or symbols. Starting with simple patterns, children recognize, represent, extend, and create patterns with different arrangements of elements. A simple pattern with two elements repeated can take many forms.

People: boy-girl, boy-girl, . . .

Blocks: red-white, red-white, . . .

Actions: snap-clap, snap-clap, . . .

Sounds: quack-moo, quack-moo, . . .

Symbols: A-B, A-B, . . .

The specific objects, events, or actions change, but the pattern is the same. Patterns may have three elements repeated, as in A-A-B/A-A-B, or four elements repeated, as in A-B-C-B/A-B-C-B. Patterns may progress or change, such as A-B-C/B-C-D/C-D-E or A-A-B/A-A-C/A-A-D. Numerical patterns may increase or decrease in value or demonstrate other relationships and rules.

Children learn about patterns with simple activities, but the goal in patterning exercises is to recognize patterns in many situations. When children recognize a pattern, as with the cricket chirp data, they are beginning to think algebraically. Kindergarten and

POINT OF VIEW
The ability that even infants have to gradually sort out an extremely complex, changing world must be considered astounding, as well as evidence that this is the natural way learning advances. But more surprising still is the clear fact that the learner manages to learn from input presented in a completely random, fortuitous fashion—unplanned, accidental, unordered, uncontrolled. (Hart, 1983, p. 65)

primary-grade children learn visual, word, and sound patterns. When children learn to play patterns with musical instruments, they develop skills used in reading sentences and words. Rhyming words, short and long vowel sounds, and prefixes and suffixes are other important patterns in reading. While teaching patterns to primary children, teachers should emphasize general skills of finding, extending, and making different patterns rather than limit instruction to one or two examples.

Patterns can be explored in a classroom pattern center supplied with rubber stamps and paper, colored beads and cord, pegboards and golf tees, pattern blocks, small colored tiles, and colored disks. Task cards can guide children in their pattern work

(Figure 16.2). In the art center shapes cut from construction paper are glued to paper to show patterns. Patterned beats of a drum or rhythmic handclaps help young children recognize auditory patterns. As children mature, they represent visual or rhythmic patterns in other forms. Activities 16.1 and 16.2 suggest other ways teachers might introduce patterns and help students represent patterns in several different ways.

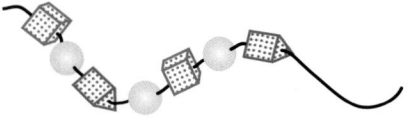

Make this pattern with beads and lace.

Make this pegboard pattern.

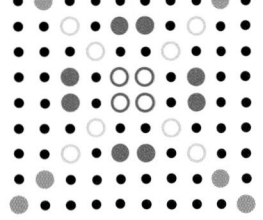

Figure 16.2 Task card for directing pattern activities

Patterning is a broader skill than learning the A-B pattern. Intermediate-grade students (grades 3–5) work with patterns that increase, decrease, and

overlap in more complex ways than A-B-C. A jumping game using number lines or a hundreds chart illustrates number patterns that begin with simple rules but progress in complexity. Students follow the directions and record the sequence of numbers that results from moving forward and back (adapted from Greenes et al., 2001, pp. 22–23):

Rule: Start at 2, jump 3 spaces forward 4 times. Where do you land?

Rule: Start at 0, jump 3 spaces forward and 1 space back. Repeat 3 times. Keep track of all the numbers you landed on.

Rule: Start at 1. Jump forward 1. Where did you land? Jump that number forward. Repeat 3 times.

Rule: Start at 1. Jump forward 1. Where did you land? Double the number and jump forward. Repeat 3 times.

When students follow the rules, they create a number pattern. Then they invent a rule to challenge classmates. This pattern activity models addition and subtraction on the number line and helps them see how the number system works. For children in grades 2–4 the teacher can begin with simple number or letter sequences and ask students to find the next term in the sequence and then explain the rule they used:

2, 6, 14, 26, 42, 62, . . .

5, 10, 15, 20, . . .

a, c, e, g, . . .

3, 7, 5, 9, 7, 11, 9, 13, 11, 15, 13, 17, . . .

8, 6, 4, 2, 0, . . .

w, v, u, t, . . .

100, 90, 81, 73, 66, 60, 55, 51, . . .

7, 21, 35, 49, . . .

a, z, b, y, . . .

MISCONCEPTION

Some students examine only the first two terms of a series and then try to determine all subsequent terms in the series, regardless of what other terms follow. This approach works if all terms show the same increase or decrease. However, consider this pattern: 1, 3, 6, 10, 15, ... The difference between the first two terms (+2) is not the difference for subsequent terms. A student who used the +2 rule from the first two terms would mistakenly conjecture that the next term in this series is 17 (15 + 2).

ACTIVITY 16.1   Making Rhythm Patterns

Level: Grades Pre-K–2

Setting: Small groups or whole group

Objective: Students make auditory patterns with percussion instruments.

Materials: Drum, cymbals, rhythm sticks, tambourine, and tone block

- Children sit in a circle. Begin beating the drum with a steady beat: thump, thump, thump. Children clap with the rhythm.

- After the students can keep the steady rhythm, ask them to listen to a new pattern. Instead of beating regularly, introduce pauses in the pattern: Thump-thump-pause, thump-thump-pause, . . . Thump-pause, thump-pause, thump-pause, . . .

- Have students join as soon as they understand the pattern. Nodding the head for the pause is a good way to maintain the rhythm.

- Ask volunteers to model a pattern of beats using another rhythm instrument, and have others join in with their instruments or by clapping.

- Ask two or three students to demonstrate patterns with combinations of instruments. Students can stand in a row and repeat the sequence.
  - triangle, drum, cymbals   triangle, drum, cymbals
    sticks, sticks, bell   sticks, sticks, bell

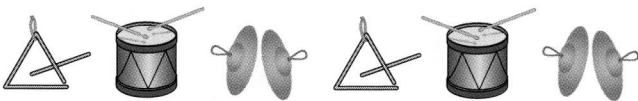

- Introduce pictures of the instruments on cards, and rearrange the cards to show different combinations of instruments and different sequences. Have students with different instruments play their instruments in the pattern shown.

- Ask questions about which instruments are in each sequence, if any instruments play more than once, and how many sounds are in each sequence.

ACTIVITY 16.2   One Pattern with Five Representations

Level: Grades K–2

Setting: Small groups

Objective: Students demonstrate five different representations of a pattern.

Materials: Sentence strips with drawn and symbol patterns

- Begin with a display of geometric shapes cut from one color of poster board. Read the pattern with the children in unison—for example, square-circle-triangle, square-circle-triangle, ...

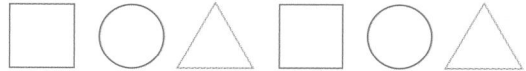

- Ask children to name the shapes in the pattern. Have them tell how many shapes are in one sequence, and where the sequence begins and ends.

- Ask: "What action could we make every time we see the square, the circle, the triangle?" Take the suggestions and perform the actions—for example, stomp-clap-snap, stomp-clap-snap, ...

- Ask: "What sound could we make every time we see the square, the circle, the triangle?" Take the suggestions and make the sounds, such as oink-moo-meow.

- Ask: "Could we use alphabet letters to show this sequence?" Students may suggest different letter combinations, such as S-C-T. Tell them that they can choose any three letters to represent the pattern. Many times the letters A, B, C, D, and so forth are used to represent the elements in a pattern.

- Show other patterns on sentence strips or tagboard, and have students act out, make sounds, or use symbols to represent the same pattern. Let students continue the pattern.

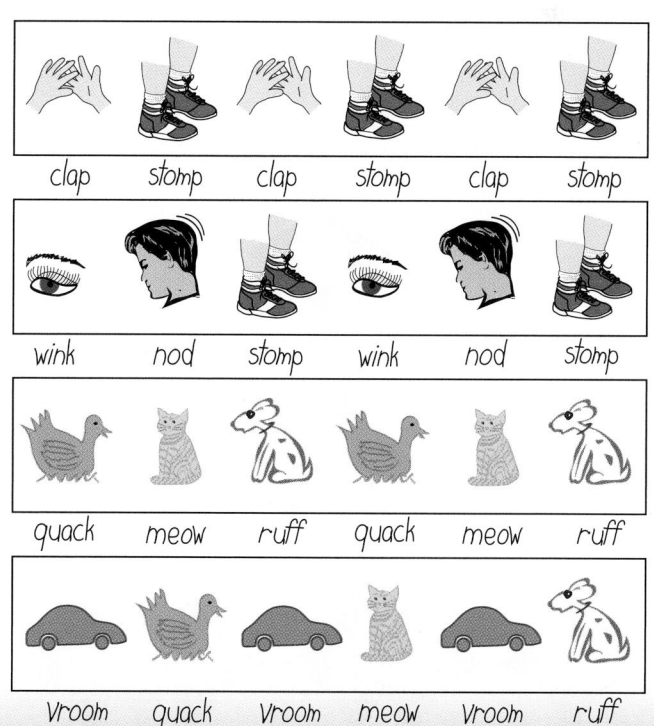

For many people the word pattern calls to mind a geometric design or template for creating a piece of clothing, such as a dress pattern. Children can use geometric shapes to explore patterns. Activity 16.3 uses pattern blocks to extend children's knowledge about patterns.

1	2	3	4	5	6	7	8	9	10
J	U	N	I	J	U	N	I	J	U

The pattern for the letter N is 3, 7, 11, 15, ... Children can conjecture about the next two squares that contain N. Similarly, they can observe patterns with other letters in their name. In this activity and in many other pattern explorations, children could use a calculator. For example, the letter J appears in every four squares. Thus, starting at Box 1, students could press +4 repeatedly to find the subsequent terms or boxes that will contain J in the JUNI pattern.

MULTICULTURALCONNECTION

Many of the early advancements in algebra were due to Arabic and Persian mathematicians in the Middle Ages. The word *algebra* is from the title of a book written by Persian scholar Al-Khwarizmi in A.D.825. The title was *Hisab al-jabr w'al-muqabalah*, which loosely translated means "the science of reunion and reduction."

Activity 16.4 uses patterns of children's names. When a child's name is the pattern train, the children can observe patterns to when specific letters appear in the pattern. For example, note the pattern train shown for the name Juni, J-U-N-I. This four-letter train then repeats to form the pattern:

POINT OF VIEW
Patterns weave mathematical topics together. Through the study of patterns, children learn to see relationships and make connections, generalizations, and predictions about the world around them. Working with patterns nurtures the kind of mathematical thinking that empowers children to solve problems confidently and relate new situations to previous experiences. (Leiva, 1991, p. 1)

Many patterns are also observable on a hundreds chart. Multiples of 2 end

---

ACTIVITY 16.3 Exploring Patterns with Pattern Blocks

Level: Grades K–2

Setting: Small groups

Objective: Students discern and extend patterns using pattern blocks.

Materials: Pattern blocks

- Draw the following design on the board, and ask students to make it using their pattern blocks:

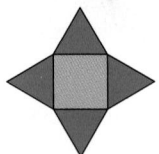

- Have students extend the pattern, as shown here:

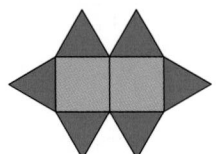

- Ask students to extend the pattern to the next stage.

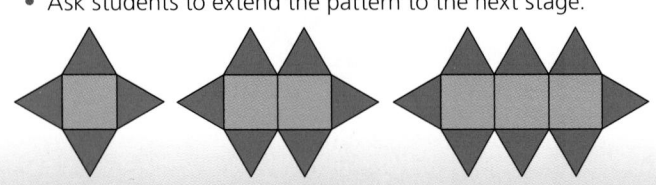

- Once children have completed Stage 3 of the pattern, ask them to explain how they would make Stage 4 of the pattern. Discuss how many new shapes are needed for this stage and the next two stages.

- Have students record their data for the first three stages in a table.

Stage	1	2	3
Squares	1	2	3
Triangles	4	6	8

- Have students extend the data table for Stage 4 and Stage 5, and then build each stage to check their data. Have students discuss how they knew what shapes to use before they built each stage.

- Ask older students to use the pattern to answer the following questions:
  - If there are 6 squares, how many triangles are there?
  - If there are 8 squares, how many triangles are there?
  - If there are 10 squares, how many triangles are there?
  - If there are 20 squares, how many triangles are there?

ACTIVITY 16.4 **Exploring Letter Patterns in a Name**

- -

Level: Grades 2–4
Setting: Individual
Objective: Students discern and extend letter patterns.
Materials: Graph paper

- Write out three pattern trains of a child's name, such as Logan.

- Ask students to predict the next two terms of the pattern. Ask students to explain their answer.

- Ask students when the letter A will next appear in the pattern. (Answer: term 14.)

- Discuss students' conjectures, and continue the pattern to verify the answer.

L	1	6	11	16
O	2	7	12	17
G	3	8	11	18
A	4	9	14	19
N	5	10	15	20

- Have students write out three pattern trains for their name on graph paper. Be sure that students number each square.

- Challenge students to use their pattern to answer the following questions:

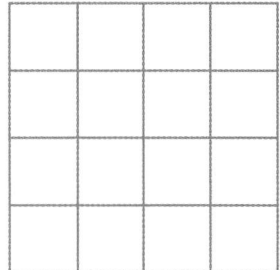

- When will three of the letters in their name next appear?
- What letter will be in term 20? in term 30? in term 50?
- How many times will the first letter in their name appear in the first 30 terms? in the first 50 terms? in the first 100 terms?

- Children could also write their name to fill in a 4 × 4 array of squares. The task would be to predict what letter falls in the last square. The task could be repeated with a 5 × 5 or 6 × 6 array.

in 2, 4, 6, 8, or 0. Multiples of 5 form two columns of numbers that end in 0 or 5. Children can examine these and other patterns to describe the visual pattern that the multiples form and the characteristics of the numbers in the visual pattern. Figure 16.3 shows the multiples of 9 on a hundreds chart. The multiples form a diagonal. The numbers in the multiples pattern for 9 all have digits that sum to 9.

1	2	3	4	5	6	7	8	9	10
11	12	13	14	15	16	17	18	19	20
21	22	23	24	25	26	27	28	29	30
31	32	33	34	35	36	37	38	39	40
41	42	43	44	45	46	47	48	49	50
51	52	53	54	55	56	57	58	59	60
61	62	63	64	65	66	67	68	69	70
71	72	73	74	75	76	77	78	79	80
81	82	83	84	85	86	87	88	89	90
91	92	93	94	95	96	97	98	99	100

Figure 16.3 Hundreds chart with multiples of 9 highlighted

Young children can use patterns in many settings beyond mathematics. At the end of this chapter we describe how children can use patterns when they read the storybook *And Meatballs for All*, by Marilyn Burns, and *The Rajah's Rice*, by David Barry. In both stories children can use patterns to extend the story line and add to the information in the books.

Variables and Equations in Mathematics and Algebraic Thinking

Using variables, or symbols, to represent numbers is a fairly new development in mathematics. Variables became part of formal mathematics only about 400 years ago. For thousands of years before the 17th century, mathematicians had struggled with mathematical expressions, in some cases using entire words to refer to the unknown quantity in an equation. The point here is that the concept of using variables to replace unknown numbers is not as obvious as it may appear. If it took mathematicians thousands of years to develop the concept of variables, it is understandable that the topic may be challenging for students today.

Variables are commonly used in mathematics in several ways:

1. $2x = 10$
2. $5y < 30$
3. $\square + \triangle = 12$
4. $A = bh$
5. $F = \frac{9}{5}C + 32$

The first statement, an open sentence, is true or false depending on the value that x represents. If x represents 5, then the sentence or equation is true. If x represents another value, then the sentence is false. Open sentences are typical of the types of equations that younger children work with in mathematics. The goal is to determine the value for x that makes the sentence or equation true.

Statement 2 is an inequality. The variable y represents an infinite number of values, any value less than 6. Children have difficulty with the ambiguity of inequalities. There are an infinite number of values that will make the inequality true. Thus y can repre-

> **MISCONCEPTION**
>
> Once students begin to use variables, they focus on the value that the variable represents. One consequence is that for many students each variable in an equation must have its own value and no two variables can have the same value. For instance, many children would consider $x + 4 = 4 + y$ to be false, because they mistakenly reason that x and y cannot have the same value. Similarly, many students would say $q = r$ must be false, without knowing anything about either value that these variables represent. Again they mistakenly assume that two different variables must represent different quantities.

sent an infinite number of values. This contradicts most of what mathematics has been for students, a study of problems and challenges that have a single answer, not a multitude of possible solutions.

The equation in Statement 3 has shapes to hold a number. Younger children are familiar with number sentences with a missing value, usually represented by a box, a blank, or a question mark. Equation (1) could have been easily represented as $2\square = 10$. The value for either $\square$ or $\triangle$ cannot be determined independently. Once a value is selected for $\square$, say 7, then the value of $\triangle$ can be determined (5). This relationship is called a function and is developed more fully later in this chapter. Note that there are an infinite number of value pairs that $\square$ and $\triangle$ could represent.

Statement 4 represents the formula for the area of a rectangle, where b is the length of the base, h is the height, and A is the area. These letters represent real-world relationships, much as variables do in other formulas.

Finally, Statement 5 is an equation that represents the relationship between Fahrenheit and Celsius temperatures. The variables refer to a specific temperature measurement system.

With so many different uses of variables in mathematics it is important that teachers provide students with foundational experiences using variables in equations so that students clearly understand the role of variables in representing numbers. The challenge is compounded by the use of letters as names

Research for the Classroom

In the recent past mathematics educators advised against using variables in primary grades. Rather than asking children to solve an equation with an unknown, such as

$$X + 5 = 7$$

teachers were advised to use a blank, an empty box, or a similar construct to represent the missing value:

$$\_\_ + 5 = 7$$
$$? + 5 = 7$$
$$\square + 5 = 7$$

The concept of variable was regarded as a difficult concept to understand. With number sentences such as those shown here, children could still engage in algebraic think-

ing without the concept of variable to further confuse them.

Recent research findings indicate that even young children can use variables to represent unknowns and then solve for the numbers that the variables represent. Researchers concluded that children as young as first-graders can confidently use variables in number sentences and equations. Proper experiences are required to introduce the concept of variable, and supporting activities must support their understandings. With proper classroom experiences such as the activities that follow, the evidence suggests that even the youngest children can work with variables (Carraher et al., 2006; Tsankova, 2003; Dobrynina, 2001).

or designations in nonmathematical settings, such as Exit 44A, grades of A or B, outline subheadings, and newspaper comics on page 4E. In none of these cases does the designation of a letter indicate any numerical representation. Rather, the letters are used as a designation or name for the item. It is understandable how children can have difficulty understanding the proper role and use of variables in mathematics.

Whether a teacher chooses to use a letter, an empty box, a question mark, or a dash to represent a missing number in a sentence, children need many experiences with open sentences. Activities 16.5 and 16.6 provide different experiences with open sentences. In Activity 16.5 students hide one term of the sentence and challenge others to determine the hidden number and then write the complete sentence. In Activity 16.6 a file card is used to hide

---

ACTIVITY 16.5   What Number Is Hiding?

Level: Grades 1–3

Setting: Small groups

Objective: Students solve for the missing value in a number sentence.

Material: Poster board or oak tagboard

- Write the number sentence 3 + 4 = 7 on the poster board.
- Hold up the poster board but cover the 4 with your hand. Ask students to discuss the missing number in the group.

$$3 + \text{✋} = 7$$

- Have one group present their findings and the reason for their answer.

- Hold up the poster board again, but remove your hand to reveal the number.
- Repeat with several more challenges.
- Ask each group to write out 10 number sentences.
- Groups challenge each other to find the missing number in the number sentences they have created. When a group shows a number sentence to another group, one person holds a finger over one number for the other group to find and someone from the group being challenged writes out the completed number sentence.

ACTIVITY 16.6   "How Many Are Hiding?" (Reasoning and Proof)

Level: Grades 1–3

Setting: Groups of four students

Objective: Students determine how many chips are "hiding" beneath the index card.

Materials: Counters, file cards

- Arrange some chips on a desk, and hide some beneath a file card, as shown here:

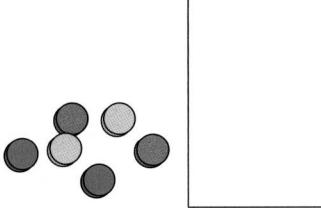

- Tell students that there are eight chips altogether but that some are hiding behind the card. Ask students how many chips are hiding under the card.
- Allow groups to work out their answer, and then ask for an explanation from a group.

- Pairs work in the groups to design four challenge problems like this one.
- Each pair presents their problems to the other pair in their group by arranging the proper number of counters and writing the total number of chips (hidden and exposed) on the file card, as shown here:

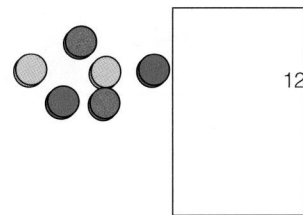

- If the pairs do not agree about a problem solution, the class can observe, question, and decide on the correct solution.
- Each pair selects their best problem to present to the class.

some chips. Students are challenged to determine how many chips are hiding.

In each of these and similar activities, teachers should ask for the value that makes the equation true, rather than simply "What's the number?" Although the difference may seem subtle, asking for the value that makes the equation true implies that the variable may take many possible values but that only one value will balance or make true the given equation or number sentence. When students build such a conceptual understanding of variable and equation from the beginning, they are better able to maintain these concepts when they are performing more complex operations within equations.

Students continue to expand their experiences with variables with activities such as Activities 16.7 and 16.8. In Activity 16.7 students represent equations using playing cards. In Activity 16.8 students are challenged to solve open sentences with many different representations of a missing value, including letters as variables. When students have many experiences with variables, they are less likely to think of algebra as a process of symbol manipulation to solve for an unknown.

One final aspect about variables for younger children is when there is no single value that the variable represents. Students, even through high school, are so accustomed to finding the answer to any mathematics problem that an equation with more than one value for a variable is difficult to understand. The ambiguity of multiple answers is the challenge for teachers as they encourage students to think about all the possible answers that could be true.

One way to have younger children begin to work with multiple solutions to a problem story is to use a table. For example, "Juanita has 10 pencils. Some are blue and some are red. How many blue pencils and how many red pencils does she have?"

$$Blue + Red = 10$$

Blue	Red
1	9
2	8
3	7
...	...

Older children would work with a different form of the equation to represent this situation: $a + b = 10$. There are 10 pairs of solution values for this problem. Activity 16.9 uses such a problem to develop children's sense of a variable.

ACTIVITY 16.7 **What Does the Card Say?**

Level: Grades 1–3
Setting: Small groups
Objective: Students determine the value of a playing card.
Material: Playing cards with no picture cards

- Hold up two cards for all the class to see, one facing the class, one facing you.
- Ask students to guess the value of the card they cannot see. Probe that there is no way to be sure of its value.

- Form a number sentence with the two cards, either addition or subtraction. Now ask for the value of the unknown card. Have students explain their strategies to solve for the unknown card.
  - $8 - ? = 3$
- Repeat with other pairs of cards.

ACTIVITY 16.8 Replacing the Number

Level: Grades 1–3

Setting: Pairs

Objective: Students solve for the missing number in number sentences.

- Write the number sentence $3 + 5 = 8$ on the board.
- Erase one of the numbers and replace it with a question mark. Ask students for the missing number.
- Repeat with many different symbols, replacing each of the three numbers in random order. Each time ask for the number that is "hiding" behind the symbol. Be sure to write the answer in the form of, for example, $x = 11$ for each problem.
- Pass out these problems (see Black-Line Master 16.1) for each pair of students to solve.

1. $q + 4 = 9$
2. $x - 3 = 8$
3. $\square - 8 = 3$
4. $6 + r = 13$
5. $8 - t = 2$
6. $\heartsuit + 7 = 16$
7. $\square - 4 = 5$
8. $9 - 3 = \diamondsuit$
9. $\triangle + 7 = 10$
10. $\bigcirc - 2 = 1$
11. $? - 3 = 10$
12. $5 + \_\_ = 6$

ACTIVITY 16.9 Multiple Value Variables

Level: Grades 1–3

Setting: Whole class

Objective: Students find all possible values for variables in an equation.

Materials: None

- Post this equation on the board: $\square + \bigcirc = 6$
- Ask students to volunteer possible answers. Post answers on the board.
- Ask for an explanation for each pair given. Look for students selecting a value of one variable and computing the other.
- Challenge students to find all the possible value pairs for $\square + \bigcirc = 10$.

Extension

- Students in upper elementary grades might examine the pairs of addends by graphing them. They could represent the data in a t-chart first, then graph the data to observe the relationship between the two addends in a graphical representation.

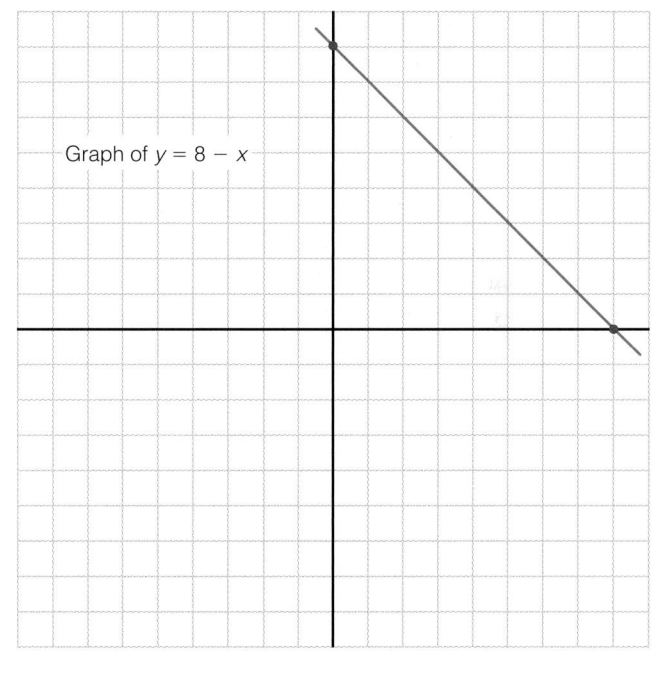

Graph of $y = 8 - x$

x	y
0	8
1	7
2	6
3	5
4	4
5	3
6	2
7	1
8	0

Equations in Algebraic Thinking

Equations are a powerful means of expressing mathematical relationships, from area formulas and temperature conversions to representations of word problems. Centuries of mathematical thought have refined both how to write and how to solve equations, resulting in an efficient universal process for solving many different types of mathematics problems. The central feature of an equation is that it shows the equality of two quantities in a relationship as simple as $2 + 2 = 4$ or as complex as $x^2 + 5x = 6$. In all equations the equal sign indicates equality between the two quantities.

One way to think of an equation is as a balance, with each side of the equation representing a quantity on a scale or pan balance. If the quantities are equal or the same, then they balance. In any equation this balance aspect must be maintained or the equal sign is no longer valid. Consider the number sentence $8 + @ = 11$. The equation will balance if and only if @ is 3. If any other value replaces @ (e.g., 5), then the equation will not balance, and the equation with 5 replacing @ will not be true ($8 + 5 \neq 11$).

This balance aspect of an equation may seem straightforward, but it is fairly challenging for students to internalize. Many students can routinely manipulate symbols about an equation in an algebra class but lack this fundamental understanding of an equation. As a result, these students run into difficulty if an equation or a problem diverges in any respect from the practice problems they have been solving. Their memorized rote procedures have overwhelmed any real understanding of the fundamental balance aspect of equations.

Some activities stress the balance aspect of an equation and make explicit use of an actual balance. The balance pictured here enables students to place blocks at marked positions on each balance arm to represent numerical value. For example, students could use such a scale to represent and then solve $3x = 18$. First students would put a block in the 8 position and a block in the 10 position on one balance arm. The task is then to put three blocks in the same position on the other arm to balance $8 + 10$. If three blocks are put on the 6 position, then the two quantities balance and in the equation $3x = 18$, $x = 6$. Some students understand an expression such as $3x$ to represent a number in the 30s, because they see a 3 in what they understand to be the tens place, leaving only the ones place to be determined.

The Balance Principle

The Zero Principle

3 Steps of Solving Equations

Step 1: Model
Step 2: Simplify & Solve
Step 3: Check

Balance scale

Younger children should have some experiences using balance scales from their work with measurement activities (see Chapter 18). Activity 16.10 uses a balance scale to develop the understanding of equality in number sentences and equations.

After some experiences children can move from real pan balances to drawings of pan balances. The balance scales (Figure 16.4) help children begin to

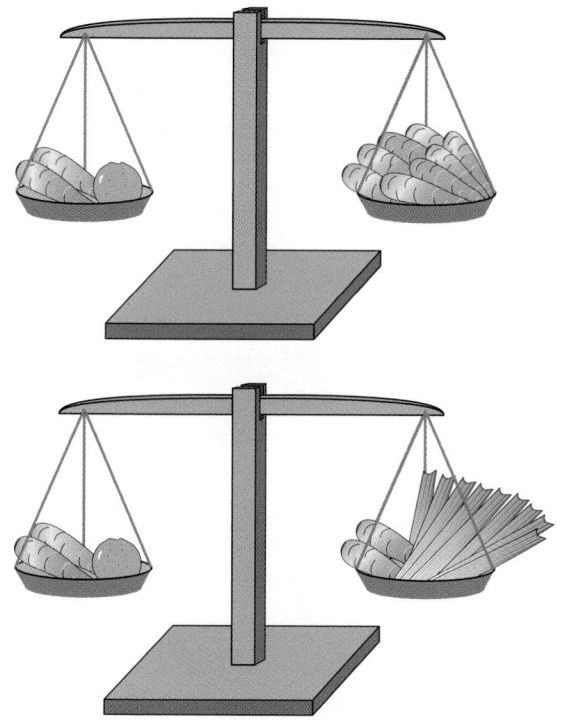

Figure 16.4 Balance scales used to determine unknown values

use the balance concept as a means to determine the value of an unknown. With the first scale students could draw the scale and then mimic removing two carrot sticks from each pan, resulting in one tangerine balancing six carrot sticks. With the second balance scale students can remove two carrot sticks from each pan to determine that one tangerine balances nine celery sticks.

Several more experiences balancing real objects will help students become comfortable with the balance concept, which we discuss further with drawings of blocks. Note that in each example the blocks have different relationships.

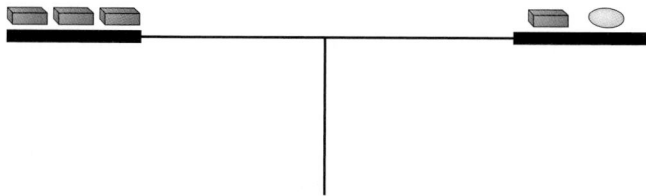

• How much does a sphere weigh?

In this problem a student could reason that by taking off one cube from each balance pan, the scale would still balance. That would leave one sphere on

one balance pan and two cubes on the other pan. So one sphere balances two cubes.

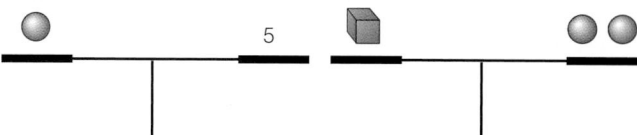

• How much does a cube weigh?

In this problem a sphere weighs 5 kilograms. The student can use this information with the second balance to determine how many kilograms a cube weighs. A cube weighs as much as two spheres, or 10 kilograms.

Activities 16.11 and 16.12 focus on each of these uses of a balance to represent an equation.

Functions in Algebraic Thinking

The idea of functions is a central concept to algebraic reasoning. A function is the pairing of members of two sets so that given the value of a member of one set, the related member of the second set can be predicted or determined. The cricket chirp data are an example of a function. Reasoning with functions is common in everyday life. When determining the cost of 3 pounds of bananas, where 1 pound costs $0.59 per pound, we use a function ($3 \times$ price per pound, or $3 \times \$0.59$) to compute the price of 3 pounds ($1.77). Determining sales tax for an item involves functions. Estimating how far we can drive on a full tank of gas also uses a function. If a car travels 25 miles on 1 gallon of gas, it will travel 250 miles on 10 gallons and 500 miles on 20 gallons.

Functions are really a generalization of specific relationships. The power of algebraic reasoning is generalization from specific cases to general relationships. The role of a function is to reveal the general relationship or to produce a result based on the general relationship. Thus a cook can use the general function of 1 hour of cooking for every 3 pounds of turkey (cooking hours = pounds ÷ 3) to determine that a 15-pound bird must be cooked for 5 hours:

Pounds	3	6	9	12	15
Hours	1	2	3	4	X

Students use functions when exploring patterns. In the pattern 2, 4, 6, 8, . . . , the rule for finding

ACTIVITY 16.10   Balancing Bears (Representation)

Level: Grades K–3

Setting: Learning center

Objective: Students explore the concept of equality using weighted bears.

Materials: Pan balance, weighted bears, number scale, double arm scale

- Place a pan balance in the mathematics center with an assortment of weighted bears. Students put bears of different sizes on each side of the scale.

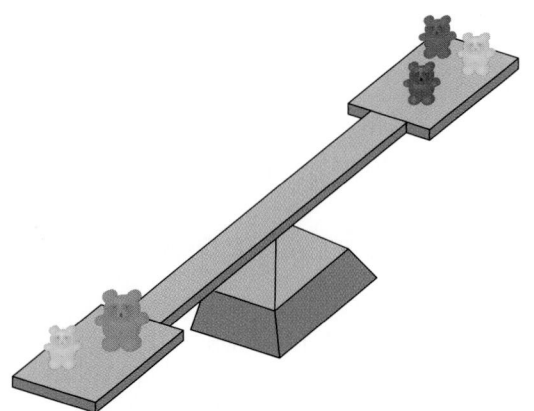

- Ask the students if they see a pattern or relationship between the weight of the small, medium-size, and big bears. For example, how many small bears balance a large bear?

- Put other small objects in the center for students to weigh with bears. Have students draw or write their observations about how many bears balance each object. For example:
  - A pencil weighs more than a small bear but less than a big bear.
  - A book is too heavy to use. There are not enough bears to balance it.
  - Three middle bears weigh the same as the staple remover.
  - One small, two middle, and three large bears weigh the same as a tennis ball.

- Place a number scale with weighted numbers (shown here) or a balance scale in the center for further exploration. You may tape an equal sign at the pivot point of the balance. Students place numbers on either side to make equations that balance: $2 + 3 = 1 + 4$, $5 + 5 = 2 + 1 + 7$, and the like.

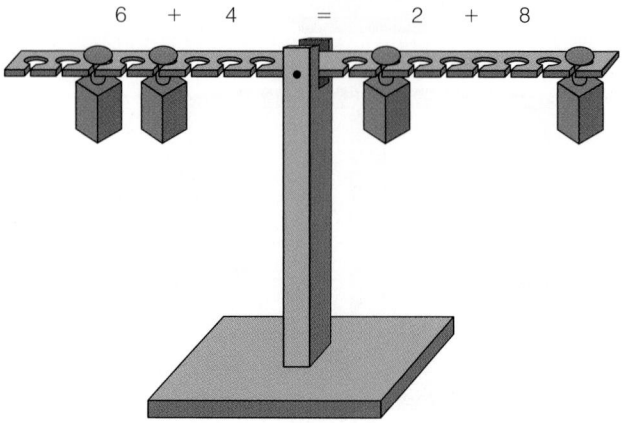

$$6 \quad + \quad 4 \quad = \quad 2 \quad + \quad 8$$

- On task cards labeled "What Number Is Missing?" ask students to find the number needed to make the equation balance.

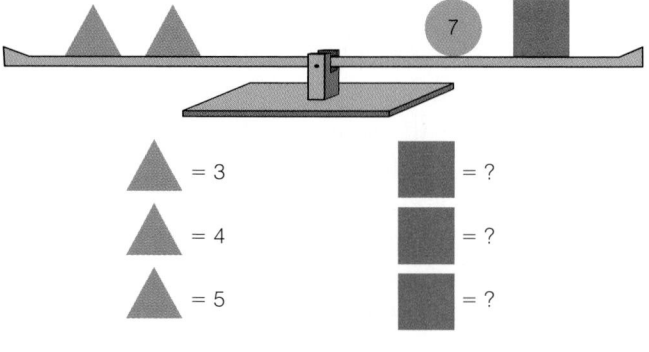

- Ask the students if they see a pattern or relationship between the weight of the small, medium-size, and big

subsequent terms is to add 2. To determine the tenth term in this pattern, a child would have to determine the first nine terms (2, 4, 6, 8, 10, 12, 14, 16, 18) and then add 2 to the ninth term to find the tenth term (20). When a student can state a function that describes a pattern, she does not have to list all the preceding terms to find the tenth (or any) term. The rule, or function, for determining any term in the above pattern is $2n$, where n is the term position in the pattern. Thus the tenth term is $2(10)$, or 20, and the hundredth term is $2(100)$, or 200. Every term has a specific value. An important feature of a function is that every term or value in the first set has one,

and only one, resulting value in the second set. The graphic display in Figure 16.5 can help to illustrate the characteristics of a function. Notice the three sets in Figure 16.5. The relationship between the sets

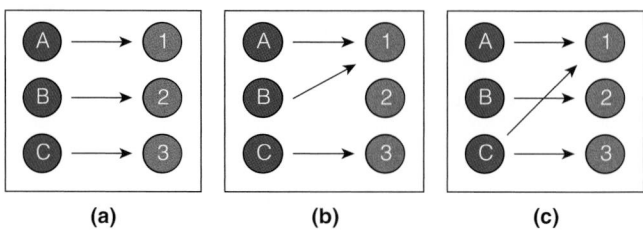

Figure 16.5

ACTIVITY 16.11 Weighing Blocks

Level: Grades 2–4

Setting: Student pairs

Objective: Students determine the weight of various blocks on a pan balance.

Materials: Black-Line Master 16.2

- Pass out Black-Line Master 16.2, which portrays several balance problems.

- Draw this balance on the board, and ask children for suggestions about how to solve the problem.

- Probe for undoing or taking the same block off each pan. Be sure to stress the need to maintain the balance of the scale.

- Students then work to solve the problems on the black-line master.

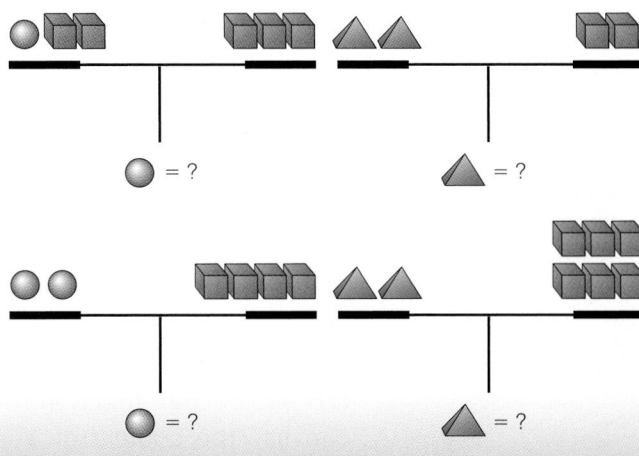

ACTIVITY 16.12 What Does It Weigh?

Level: Grades 2–5

Setting: Small groups

Objective: Students determine the weight of blocks on balance scales.

Materials: Black-Line Master 16.3

- Pass out Black-Line Master 16.3.

- Draw both balances on the board, and ask children for suggestions about how to solve for how much a cube weighs.

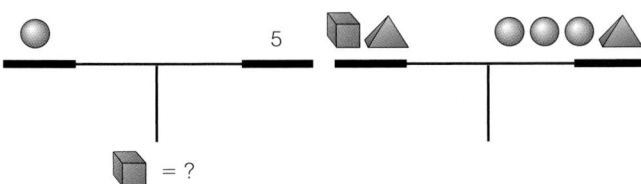

- Probe for "undoing" or taking the same block off each pan. Be sure to stress the need to maintain the balance of the scales.

- Students then work to solve the problems on the black-line master.

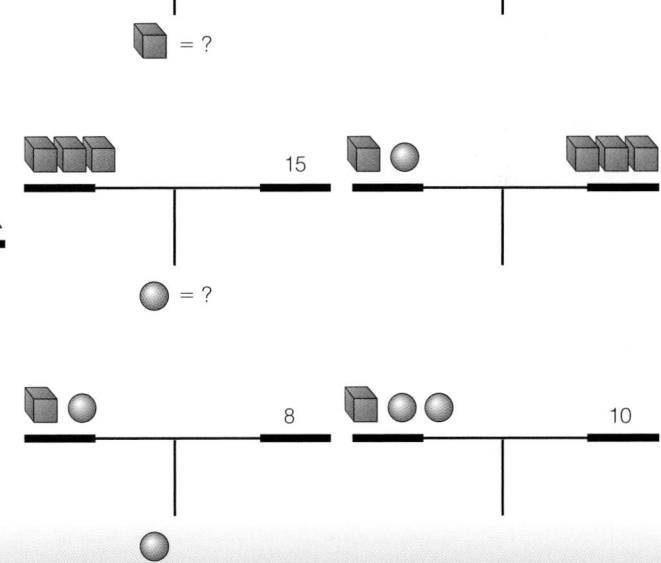

may or may not represent the definition of a function, depending on how the members of set Q {A, B, C} are paired with the members of set R {1, 2, 3}.

In Figure 16.5a each member of set {A, B, C} is paired with only one member of set {1, 2, 3}, so the relationship between the two sets represents a function. Figure 16.5b also shows a function. Even though two members of {A, B, C} are paired with 1 in {1, 2, 3}, the figure still represents a function, because every member of {A, B, C} is paired with only one member of {1, 2, 3}. Figure 16.5c does not display a function. In this case one member of {A, B, C} is paired with two different members of {1, 2, 3}. This violates the definition of a function, where there is a one-to-one pairing between the given set and the resulting set.

Formal definitions of functions are not very beneficial to elementary students. Students in elementary and middle school can best learn about functions by exploring function relationships, solving function problems, and applying functions to real-life situations as described here.

POINT OF VIEW

Change is an important idea that can be studied using the tools of algebra. (National Council of Teachers of Mathematics, 2000, p. 163)

Younger children can begin to work with functions using straightforward relationships between the input and output values (called *domain* and *range*). Activities involving functions can use the context of a function machine to help children understand functions. For example, younger children can be asked about horses on a farm. If there is one horse (input), how many eyes does it have (output)? What if there are two horses? three? four? Suppose that there are 10 horses. Children reason that there are twice as many eyes as horses. It may not be beneficial to introduce notation to represent the number of eyes in the primary grades, but by grade 4 the notation

$2 \times h$ can be appropriate. For younger children a t-chart such as that used in Activity 16.9 is helpful.

A classroom function machine can be made from a large cardboard box (one large enough to hold an adult) with two slots cut into it, one marked "input" and one marked "output" (Figure 16.6). Instead of using numbers for input values, drawings can help children understand the basics of a function machine. For example, when a child puts a piece of paper with a single triangle into the input slot, the adult in the box slides a piece of paper with two triangles out of the output slot. When a child inputs a piece of paper with two triangles, the adult in the box slides a piece with three triangles out of the output slot, and so forth. If an adult aide is not available to "operate" the machine, perhaps an older child from an upper grade can provide the output results. Children will quickly catch on to the rules that the "machine" is using.

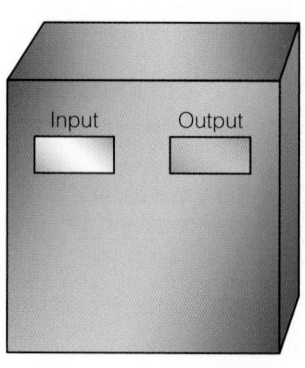

Figure 16.6 Function box with input and output slots

ACTIVITY 16.13   Magic Math Box

Level: Grades 2–5

Setting: Whole group

Objective: Students generate a rule to explain the relation between two numbers.

Materials: Index cards

- Draw a magic math box on an overhead or on the board.
- Tell the students that the box changes any numbers that are written inside it.

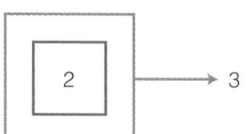

- Demonstrate by writing 2 inside the box (input) and 3 outside the box (output).
- Ask children about a rule for these numbers. They might guess + 1, × 2, − 1, and other possible rules. Have them suggest new input numbers; write the output number for each input number until they agree on a rule that works for all the examples.
- Write another number inside the box, and ask students to guess the result using the new rule. If the rule is + 1 and the inside number is 5, the outside number is 5 + 1 = 6.

- Have students explain the rule and then take turns making up new rules, such as $n + 2$, $n - 1$, $3n + 1$, and so forth.

Extension

- Have students make their own set of magic math cards. Fold 3 × 5 note cards in half. Write the input number on the outside of the card, and the output number on the inside. Make several more cards using the same rule. Fold back the cards with a rubber band and put them in a learning center. Children unfold the cards one at a time and guess the rule. Each new card can confirm or reject the rule.

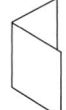

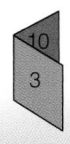  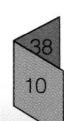 

Then pairs of children can replace the adult aide and produce output data from inside the box.

Activity 16.13 uses a drawing of a function machine to explore functions with children.

When younger students have a proper introduction to unknown quantities through regular explorations with number sentences and then equations, they develop a solid understanding of the role of a variable and its value in problem solving. Equally important is the balance aspect of equations. Children who understand that the equal sign indicates that two parts of an equation are equal, or balanced, will not fall into the common trap of rote symbol manipulation to solve equations with no recognition of the balance aspect of equations.

Extending Algebraic Thinking

Older children move beyond intuitive activities in algebraic reasoning to more abstract experiences. They begin to explore algebraic relationships using equations and functions that they represent on paper. The NCTM algebra standards for older children follow.

NCTM Algebra Standard

Algebra instructional programs from prekindergarten through grade 12 should enable all students to:
> Understand patterns, relations, and functions

Grades 3–5 Expectations:
In grades 3–5 all students should:
- describe, extend, and make generalizations about geometric and numeric patterns;
- represent and analyze patterns and functions, using words, tables, and graphs.

Grades 6–8 Expectations:
In grades 6–8 all students should:
- represent, analyze, and generalize a variety of patterns with tables, graphs, words, and, when possible, symbolic rules;
- relate and compare different forms of representation for a relationship;
- identify functions as linear or nonlinear and contrast their properties from tables, graphs, or equations.
> Represent and analyze mathematical situations and structures using algebraic symbols

Grades 3–5 Expectations:
In grades 3–5 all students should:
- identify such properties as commutativity, associativity, and distributivity and use them to compute with whole numbers;
- represent the idea of a variable as an unknown quantity using a letter or a symbol;
- express mathematical relationships using equations.

Grades 6–8 Expectations:
In grades 6–8 all students should:

- develop an initial conceptual understanding of different uses of variables;
- explore relationships between symbolic expressions and graphs of lines, paying particular attention to the meaning of intercept and slope;
- use symbolic algebra to represent situations and to solve problems, especially those that involve linear relationships;
- recognize and generate equivalent forms for simple algebraic expressions and solve linear equations.
> Use mathematical models to represent and understand quantitative relationships

Grades 3–5 Expectations:
In grades 3–5 all students should:
- model problem situations with objects and use representations such as graphs, tables, and equations to draw conclusions.

Grades 6–8 Expectations:
In grades 6–8 all students should:
- model and solve contextualized problems using various representations, such as graphs, tables, and equations.
> Analyze change in various contexts

Grades 3–5 Expectations:
In grades 3–5 all students should:
- investigate how a change in one variable relates to a change in a second variable;
- identify and describe situations with constant or varying rates of change and compare them.

Grades 6–8 Expectations:
In grades 6–8 all students should:
- use graphs to analyze the nature of changes in quantities in linear relationships.

Extending Understanding of Patterning

As older children develop their algebraic thinking, their study and analysis of patterns becomes more sophisticated, with more challenging patterns to analyze. They move from simply determining the next term in a pattern or from identifying a pattern (such as A-B, A-B, A-B, . . .) to using patterns to solve problems, much like the cricket chirp pattern. The pattern may be generalized to produce solutions to problems that would be difficult to solve otherwise. Activity 16.14 shows a problem that could be studied at two levels. Notice that at one level the challenge is to find a pattern and use it to determine the number of squares in the next figure, a 5 × 5 grid. Students then verify their answer by counting all the squares on the grid. As an extension, students move beyond discerning the pattern and predicting the next term in the pattern. They generalize from the pattern to determine the number of squares in a 10 × 10 grid without having to determine the number of squares in all the smaller grids. Activity 16.15 examines a growing pattern. In this pattern each subsequent stage is a larger increase than the previous stage. In

Activity 16.16 older students find a growing pattern and then use it to develop a generalized relationship between the number of sides in a polygon and the number of diagonals in the polygon.

ⒺXERCISE

Find the next term for each of the patterns in Figure 16.7. ●●●

× × ○ × × △ × × □ × × ○ ...   1, 1, 2, 3, 5, 8, 13, ...

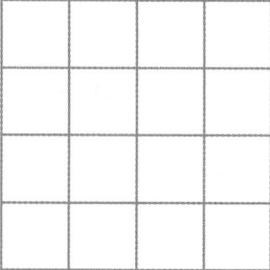   1, 8, 27, 64, ...

☆ ○ ☆ ☆ ○ ☆ ○ ○ ☆ ○ ☆ ☆ ○ ...   1, 4, 2, 7, 3, 10, 4, ...

Figure 16.7 Find and extend patterns

Older students can also discern patterns in more complex series of numbers. The following series of numbers have a pattern that will allow students to predict the next term and perhaps determine an expression for determining the number in any term of the pattern:

2, 4, 6, 8, 10, . . .

0, −3, −6, −9, −12, . . .

1, 4, 9, 16, 25, . . .

1, 2, 2, 3, 5, 8, . . .

1, 3, 6, 10, 15, . . .

a, b, d, g, k, . . .

For example, in the pattern 5, 10, 15, 20, 25, the pattern shows the factors of 5. Each term is a factor of

---

ACTIVITY 16.14 How Many Squares? (Communication)

Level: Grades 5 and 6

Setting: Small groups

Objective: Students count the squares in a diagram and record their counting to find a pattern and generalize a process.

Materials: None

- Have students look at a 4 × 4 diagram and count all the squares they can find. Remind them that squares can come in different sizes.

- As students complete their work, record their answers on the board, such as 16, 17, 21, 28, 29, and 30.

- Ask: "Which squares did you find first? Which were harder to find? How many squares did you find of each size?"

- As individuals report their process and talk about the different-size squares, draw a t-chart showing the size of squares and the number (see t-chart). For each size, ask students to confirm the count until everyone is satisfied. When these counts are totaled, students should agree on 30. Ask students if they see any patterns.

Size	Number
4 × 4	1
3 × 3	4
2 × 2	9
1 × 1	16

- Ask: "What do you think the next number in the sequence will be?" Have students use the 5 × 5 diagram to check their conjecture.

Extension

- Extend the thinking about patterns and representations of patterns by presenting a 10 × 10 square diagram. Ask: "How many squares total are there in a 10 × 10 square?"

- Begin by reviewing the data for 5 × 5.

Size		Number	Square
5 × 5	or 25	1	1^2
4 × 4	or 16	4	2^2
3 × 3	or 9	9	3^2
2 × 2	or 4	16	4^2
1 × 1	or 1	25	5^2

- Again, encourage discussion of patterns. At some point, students should realize that, rather than counting all the squares, they can simply add the square numbers 1 + 4 + 9 + 16 + ··· + 100.

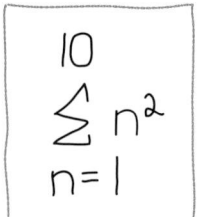

- Finally, say: "Let me show you a symbol for summing numbers." Introduce Σ as a summation symbol that can be used any time the sum of a series of numbers is to be determined.

- Discuss the idea of a general solution and a concise symbolization result from extending the lesson to a situation in which physical counting is too difficult and cumbersome.

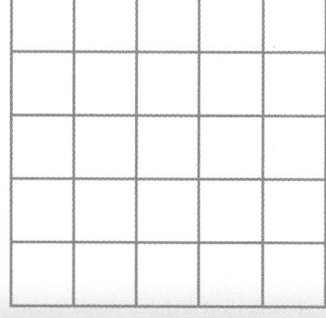

5 and the term in position 6 is 5 × 6. The term in position 9 is 5 × 9, and the term in the *n*th position is 5*n*. When students are able to represent a pattern in this way, they are beginning to use one of the most powerful tools of algebra, generalizing a relationship from data taken from their observations.

Some students enjoy patterns that involve a series of items that are neither numbers nor alphabet letters. In the patterns shown here the letters in the series are the first letters of terms in the series. For example, the third series could be represented as W, A, J, M, . . . :

S, M, T, W, T, . . . (days of the week)

J, F, M, A, M, . . . (months of the year)

Washington, Adams, Jefferson, Madison, . . .

Lincoln, Jefferson, Roosevelt, Washington, . . .

ACTIVITY 16.15 Building Houses

Level: Grade 3–6

Setting: Small groups

Objective: Students model a row of houses and find a rule for the relationship.

Materials: Pattern blocks

- Ask students to make a house using a square and a triangle. Then have them make a row of houses. The houses are attached to one another, as shown.

 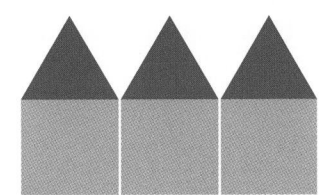

- Ask students how many outside edges, including the roof, one house has. (Answer: 5.) Have them count the number of outside edges for two houses, three houses, and four houses.

- Have students make a table or t-chart to record the number of houses and the number of outside edges. Ask if they see a pattern. (Answer: The number of edges increases by 3 for each house.)

Number of Houses	Number of Edges
1	5
2	8
3	11
4	14
5	?

- Ask students to predict the number of edges for 5, 6, 7, 8, 9, and 10 houses.

- Ask if they can think of a rule for the number of houses and the number of edges. (Answer: The number of edges is the number of houses times 3, plus 2.)

- Ask the students to explain how the rule applies to the first house (Answer: three sides on the house and two edges on the roof) and to the added houses (Answer: add two sides and adjoin one side, add two edges for the roof).

- Extensions: Depending on the experience and understanding of the students, the relationship can be graphed and written as a formula: edges = 3 × houses + 2, or later, $y = 3x + 2$.

ACTIVITY 16.16 How Many Diagonals? (Connections)

Level: Grades 5 and 6

Setting: Small groups

Objective: Students use patterns to determine the number of diagonals in dodecagons by observing a pattern.

- Draw a pentagon on the board. Ask students to describe a diagonal and then ask for a volunteer to draw a diagonal in the pentagon.

- Using the same vertex, ask for volunteers to draw another diagonal from that vertex.

- Have students draw their own pentagon and then draw and count all possible diagonals.

- Once students can correctly draw and count the diagonals in a pentagon (there are five), challenge them to predict the number of diagonals in a dodecagon by looking for a pattern to the number of diagonals in polygons.

- Students should explore the number of diagonals in various polygons by drawing each polygon and all possible diagonals.

- Students should record their data for polygons up to eight sides in a table, as shown here.

Number of sides	3	4	5	6	7	8
		+2	+3	+4	+5	+6
Number of diagonals	(0	2	5	9	14	20)

- The pattern here shows that the change in the number of diagonals is not constant. The change in the number of diagonals increases by 1 for each successive polygon. By continuing his pattern, students can determine that a dodecagon has 54 diagonals.

Calendar pages are another source of patterns, some of which we describe here. Students can verify that any block of four dates will have the same sum along both diagonals. Every date is 7 less than the date directly below it. Activity 16.17 uses the calendar as the focus for patterns.

Activity 16.18 is an assessment activity where students determine the next two terms of patterns. Activity 16.19 builds on Activity 16.18 by asking students to examine two series and graph them.

Students can also use graphing to find the solution to a problem that is revealed by a pattern of data. In the following problem students can find the answer by graphing the data on a coordinate grid:

- An intake system fills a silo with grain. The time needed to fill the silo to various depths is given in the data table. How long will it take to fill the silo to a depth of 31 feet?

Minutes	1	2	3	4	5	6	⋯	?
Depth in feet	1	4	7	10	13	16	⋯	31

This problem could be solved by filling in all the missing data in the table to find the number of minutes for 31 feet. Students could also develop an expression for the relationship between the number of hours (h) and the depth of grain (d): $d = 3h - 2$. For this problem it may be easier to graph the data. Certainly it would be easier to graph using a graphing calculator, but we will assume that students will do their graphing using graph paper. Figure 16.8 shows the graph of this problem. The data are plotted on the coordinate grid, and the line joining the data points

---

ACTIVITY 16.17 **Calendar Patterns**

- -

Level: Grades 3–6

Setting: Whole group

Objective: Students derive a general rule for adding three consecutive numbers.

Materials: Calendar

- Have students look at the calendar. Ask them to add any three dates that appear next to each other (consecutively) and look for a pattern.

October						
			1	2	3	4
5	6	7	8	9	10	11
12	13	14	15	16	17	18
19	20	21	22	23	24	25
26	27	28	29	30	31	

- Ask students to write their number sentences for three consecutive dates on index cards, and post them on the bulletin board.

- After students have posted several examples, ask if anyone has found a pattern. Students should see that the sum of three consecutive numbers is the same as the middle number added three times.

  $9 + 10 + 11 = 10 - 1 + 10 + 10 + 1 = 10 + 10 + 10$

- Ask why the equation is true. (Answer: The first number is 1 less than the middle, and the last number is 1 more, so they add to 0.)

  $$\text{middle} - 1 + \text{middle} + \text{middle} + 1$$
  $$= \text{middle} + \text{middle} + \text{middle}$$

- They may express this as sum

  $$= m + m + m, \text{ or sum} = 3 \times m$$

Variation

- Ask students to look at the Fridays in the month and to note the dates of the Fridays (e.g., 3, 10, 17, 24, 31).

- Ask if they see a pattern, and why they think this pattern works. What is the number rule to express this pattern?

- Have students answer questions such as the following: If Friday is March 6, what is the date two Fridays later? If Sunday is April 13, what date is the following Sunday? the following Monday? the following Saturday?

ACTIVITY 16.18 What's Next? (Assessment Activity)

Level: Grades 5 and 6

Setting: Student pairs

Objective: Students demonstrate an understanding of patterns.

Materials: None

• Post the following series on the board:

  1, 2, 4, 8, 16, 32, . . .   4, 8, 12, 16, 20, . . .

  1, 3, 6, 10, 15, 21, . . .   2, 1, 4, 3, 6, 5, . . .

  M, T, W, T, F, . . .   a, c, e, g, i, k, . . .

  20, 15, 10, 5, 0, . . .   4, 16, 64, 256, . . .

• Instruct students to work in pairs to find the next two terms of the patterns.

• Students should also explain how they determined the next two terms.

• Students should produce two patterns of their own that will be given to the class to solve at a later time.

The numerical patterns given here show either the same additive difference between terms (e.g., 4, 8, 12, 16, which has a difference of 4 between terms) or a varying difference between terms (e.g., 1, 3, 6, 10, 15, 21). When these two series are graphed, the difference between them becomes apparent. The data for each series can be recorded in t-charts and then graphed.

Term	Value	Term	Value
1	4	1	1
2	8	2	3
3	12	3	6
4	16	4	10
5	20	5	15
6	24	6	21

The data of the first series form a line. They are in a *linear* relationship that can be represented as $N + 4$ or $y = x + 4$. The second series does not generate points in a straight line. This series forms a curve. Activity 16.19 asks students to examine these two series and to graph them.

ACTIVITY 16.19 Graphing Numerical Patterns

Level: Grades 5 and 6

Setting: Student pairs

Objective: Students relate a graphical representation to numerical series.

Materials: None

• Tell students that "not all patterns are created equal." Allow students to agree or disagree and to explain their stand.

• Put both of the following numerical series on the board:

  4, 8, 12, 16, 20, . . .   1, 3, 6, 10, 15, 21, . . .

• Ask students to find the next two terms in each series, to explain how to find the next term in the series, and to graph the data for each numerical pattern.

• Have several student pairs report their findings to the class.

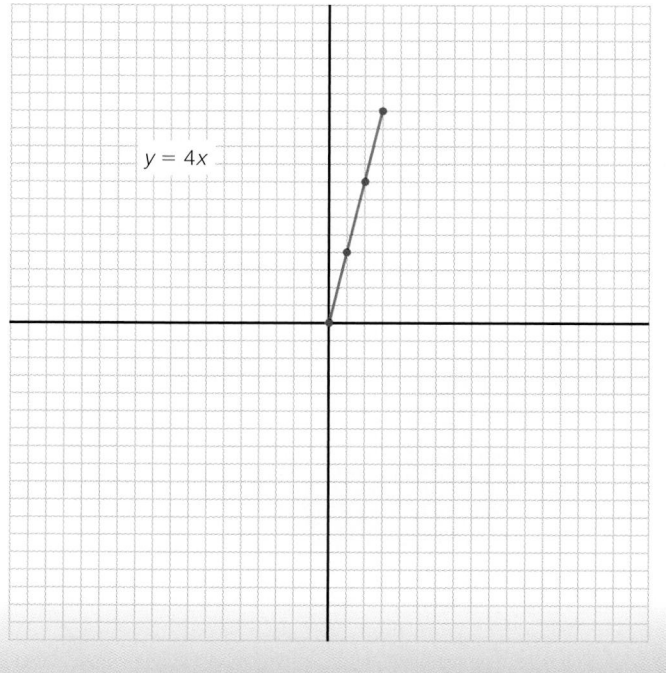

$y = 4x$

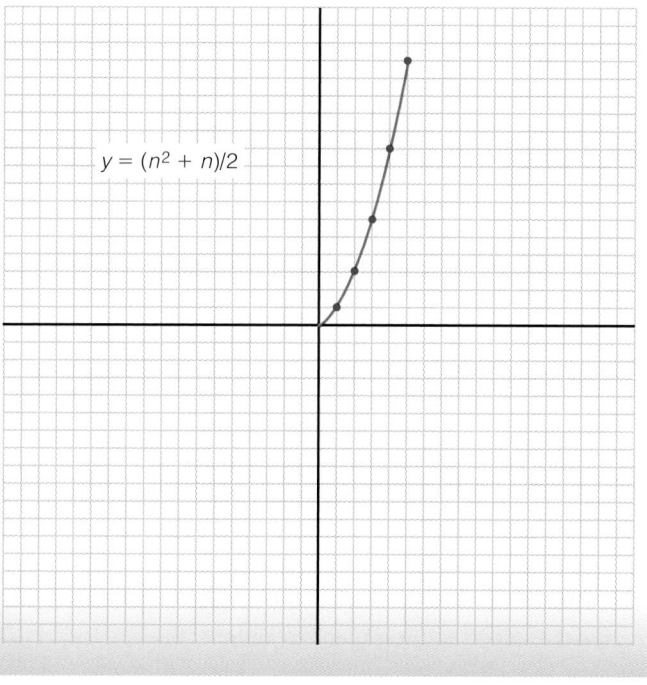

$y = (n^2 + n)/2$

is extended. The line will eventually pass through the point where the depth is 20. That point has a value of 58. Thus, filling a silo to a depth of 20 feet requires 58 minutes. Activity 16.20 asks students to use a graph to solve a problem involving the depth of a swimming pool.

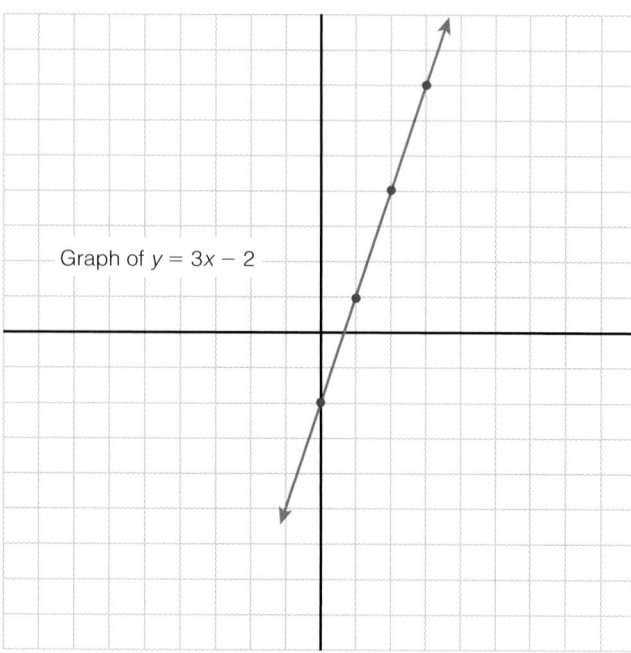

Figure 16.8 Graph of $y = 3x - 2$

Extending Understanding of Equations

Students in upper elementary school and middle school continue to develop their understanding of equations by representing relationships in problems with equations and then solving those problems. The balance aspect of equations for students is still important so that they do not lose this underlying idea in solving equations. Some students focus so much on manipulating equations to solve for x that they disregard the idea of equality in equations. Activities 16.21 and 16.22 extend this balance aspect of equations.

Experiences with the balance aspect of equations help students to observe equations as consisting of two equal parts on each side of the equal sign. They understand the need to perform identical operations to both sides of an equation to maintain the balance. One approach to solving equations makes use of the idea of undoing an equation by performing the same procedure to both sides. Consider the following equation:

$$3x + 4 = 19$$

The student covers the first part of the equation that needs undoing.

$$3x + \text{✋} = 19$$

ACTIVITY 16.20 How Long Will It Take?

Level: Grades 5 and 6

Setting: Pairs

Objective: Students use a graph to solve a problem.

Materials: Graph paper

- Ask students if any of them have a swimming pool. Discuss how long it takes to fill or empty a pool using a typical garden hose.

- Display the following data table to students, and explain that it represents the time needed to empty a pool. The challenge for them is to determine how long it will take to empty the pool.

Hours	0	1	2	3	4
Depth	10	9.5	9	8.5	8

- Ask students to use a graph to find the answer.

- After all pairs are finished, have several pairs display their graphs on the overhead projector and explain how they determined the answer using their graphs.

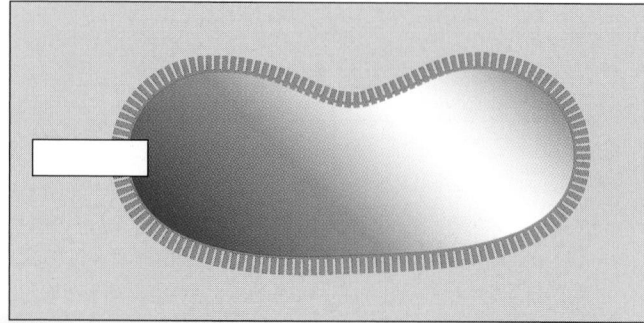

ACTIVITY 16.21   Does It Balance?

Level: Grades 5 and 6

Setting: Student pairs

Objective: Students use the balance concept to tell if an equation balances.

Materials: None

- Show this balance to students.

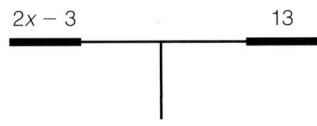

- Ask whether the pans balance if $x = 5$. What about if $x = 6$? 8? 10? Discuss the results for each value.

- In the discussion help students understand that depending on the value given for x, the balance tilts to the left (if $x = 5$ or 6), balances (if $x = 8$), or tilts to the right (if $x = 10$). There is only one value that solves the equation ($x = 8$), the same value that balances the scale.

- Have students solve the following balances, deciding whether the scale tilts left or right or balances.

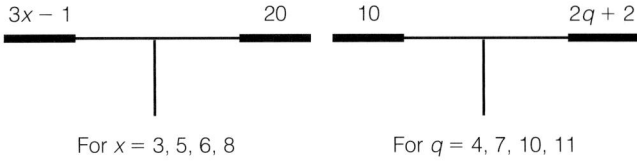

For $x = 3, 5, 6, 8$ For $q = 4, 7, 10, 11$

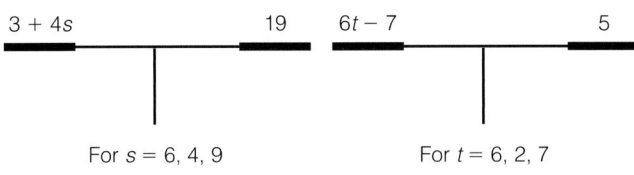

For $s = 6, 4, 9$ For $t = 6, 2, 7$

To undo the $+4$, 4 must be subtracted from both sides of the equation, resulting in

$$3x = 15$$

$$x = 15$$

To undo the 3, both sides must be multiplied by $\frac{1}{3}$, and this results in the correct answer:

$$x = 5$$

Algebra tiles are a common manipulative with many uses in the algebra curriculum. The square represents x^2, the long piece represents x, and the square piece represents 1. Students can represent equations using the tiles. For example, the equation $2x + 4 = 8$ is shown here with algebra tiles.

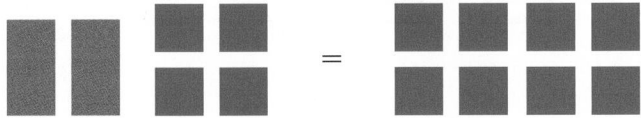

Students can move the tiles to replicate solving the problem, similar to how they can represent and solve equations using a balance scale. Algebra tiles are also used in higher grade levels to represent multiplying binomials and factoring quadratic equations.

Algebra tiles

Extending the Meaning of Functions

The role of function with older students grows in importance, because students at this level begin to use functions to make sense of many relationships both in and out of school. The basic concept of function that these students learned in earlier grades has not changed. What is different is the complexity of functions and the application of functions to an expanding variety of situations.

As stated earlier in this chapter, the relationship between two sets of numbers is a function; each item in one set matches, or maps onto, an item in the other set. A rate table is often used to show the relationship between two sets of numbers.

- Ms. Sund wants to increase the sale of CDs in her music store. She decides to offer an incentive by

reducing the price of CDs by $1 for each additional CD purchased. What advice would you give her about this plan?

The cost of CDs at the regular price is shown in one rate table (Figure 16.9a), and the cost of CDs on sale is shown in a different rate table (Figure 16.9b). By graphing the data (Figure 16.9c), students can compare the cost of CDs at the regular price and at the sale price and then predict, calculate, and graph the cost of buying 6, 7, and 8 CDs. Extending the pattern

---

ACTIVITY 16.22 What Does the Scale Tell You?

Level: Grades 5 and 6

Setting: Student pairs

Objective: Students demonstrate an understanding of balancing equations.

Materials: None

- Post the following balance on the board, and ask students for any conclusions.

- Have students explain their reasoning for any conclusions. Probe for the balance showing equality between two blocks and a single sphere.

- Have student pairs work through balance problems on Black-Line Master 16.4. When all pairs are finished, have volunteer pairs explain their answers to the problems.

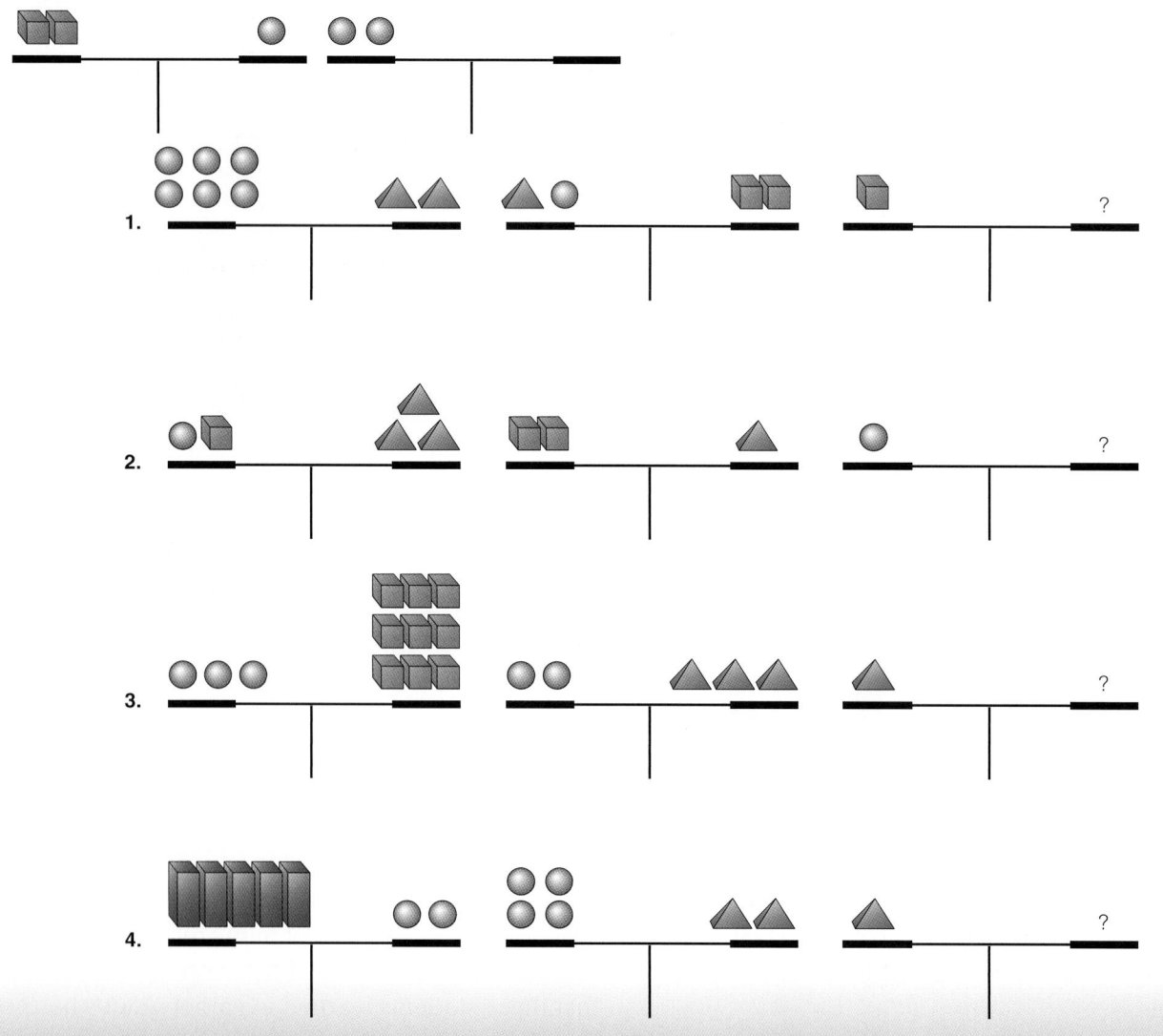

may yield some surprising results and advice for the record shop owner about her sale plans. (As a customer purchases more CDs, the total price begins to decrease!) The price of CDs is a function of the number of CDs. The relationship between the number of CDs and the price of regularly priced CDs shows a constantly increasing function. The rate table for the sale CDs shows a changing relation between number and price. Tables and graphs make relationships, changes, and trends more apparent so that students can find and interpret patterns.

(a)

Number of CDs	1	2	3	4	5
Regular price	$12	$24	$36		

(b)

Number of CDs	1	2	3	4	5
Sale price	$12	$22	$30		

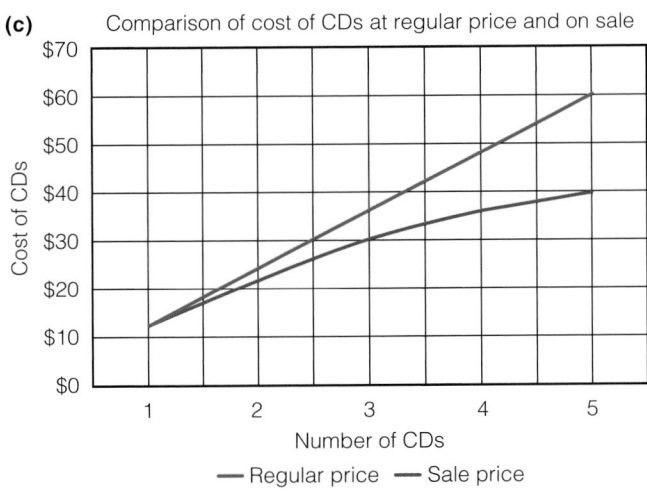

(c)

Figure 16.9 Rate table and graph for the price of CDs: regular and sale

• The sink has a depth of 40 centimeters. Water fills the sink at a rate of 5 centimeters per 10 seconds. How full will the sink be in 1 minute? When will the sink overflow?

The relation between time and depth of the water is shown in the rate table in Figure 16.10a, but the graph brings more meaning to the information (Figure 16.10b). By extrapolating (extending the data pattern), students can predict the depth after 1 minute

and when the sink will overflow. The graph in Figure 16.10c also shows the depth of water in the sink over time. In this graph the relation is not linear. Students can interpret the graph and hypothesize what may have caused the changes in depth.

(a) Table

Time (s)	10	20	30	40	50	60
Depth (cm)	5	10	15	20		

(b) Graph

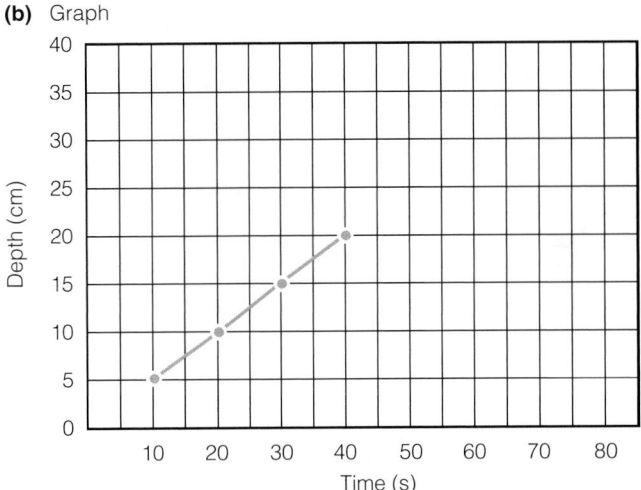

(c) What happened?

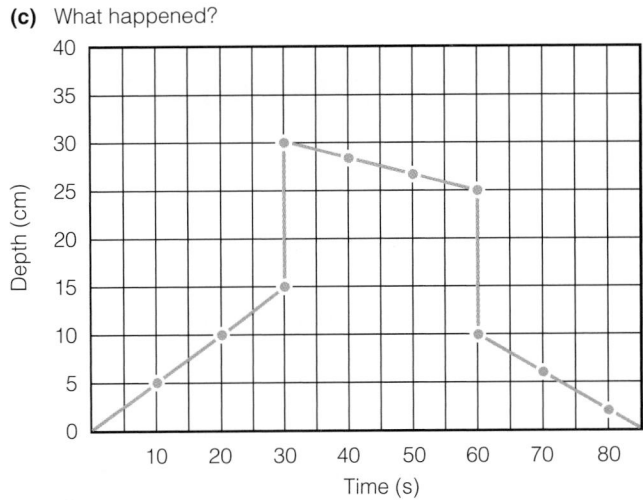

Figure 16.10 Filling a sink with water

ⒺXERCISE

Read the graph in Figure 16.10c. How would you explain changes in the depth of water shown in the graph? ●●●

ACTIVITY 16.23 Find the Mystery Function I

Level: Grades 4–6

Setting: Student pairs

Objective: Students try to determine the rules of function machines.

Materials: None

- Draw a function machine on the board. Explain to students that this function machine has two steps for the function.

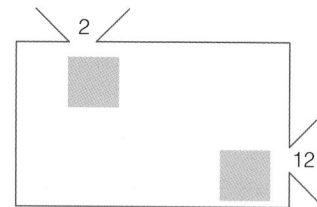

- Ask for a volunteer to offer a number for input.
- Write the resulting number or output on the function machine and in a t-chart.
- Ask for another input number and then record the output.

Input	Output
1	10
2	12
3	14
4	16
n	$2(n + 4)$

- Continue for three more outputs, and then ask student pairs to determine the function. Ask pairs to express the function as an algebraic rule.
- Discuss the various rules that student pairs present to the class. The rule for the function machine data shown here can be expressed as $2(n + 4)$ or $2n + 8$. The function machine can be completed as shown in Figure 16.6.

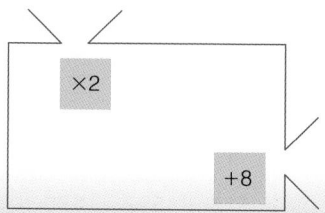

ACTIVITY 16.24 Mod(ular) Math Functions

Level: Grades 5 and 6

Setting: Small groups

Objective: Students produce functions based on clock arithmetic.

Materials: None

- Write the number sentence $8 + 5 = 1$ on the board. Ask for students in their groups to conjecture when this statement is true.
- Write $6 + 8 = 2$, $4 + 10 = 2$, and $11 + 8 = 7$ on the board. Ask groups to prepare t-charts to determine the function used in these number sentences.

- Ask groups to volunteer to present their functions.
- Discuss how their functions can be represented on a 12-hour clock.
- Ask groups to use a different clock or modular system for a series of equations that they will present to the class.

Another way to explore functions is to focus on the functions themselves. Activity 16.23 uses a two-step function machine, Activity 16.24 applies a clock as the starting point for examining modular arithmetic functions, and Activity 16.25 draws on a function machine found on the Internet. In modular or clock arithmetic the base of the number system is the number of digits on the clock. Our number system is a base-10 number system and can be represented on a clock with 10 digits. Consider a base-12 system, represented on a clock with 12 digits. The problem $8 + 6 = ?$ can be represented by first moving the clock hand to 8. Then advancing the hand of the clock 6 more hours. The hand would make a complete revolution and then begin another turn around the dial. In this case the hand ends up pointing to 2. Thus on our 12-hour clock $8 + 6 = 2$

A simple clock is a four-hour clock with 0, 1, 2, and 3 for digits. What is the sum of $3 + 2$ on this clock? First the hand moves to 3, and then advances two more hours. It would end up moving to 1. Thus on this clock $3 + 2 = 1$. Subtraction and multiplication might also be explored with this clock.

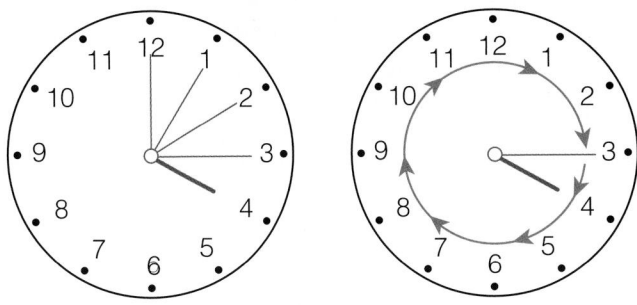

In addition to using a clock to explore this function, students might compile a data table to show addition facts on a 4-hour clock:

+	0	1	2	3
0	0	1	2	3
1	1	2	3	0
2	2	3	0	1
3	3	0	1	2

For more information about clock arithmetic and clock arithmetic activities, see Brown and Jones (2005).

ACTIVITY 16.25 Find the Mystery Function II (Internet Lesson Plan)

Level: Grades 4–6

Setting: Student pairs

Objective: Students try to determine the functions of mystery challenges.

Materials: Internet access to http://www.learner.org/teacherslab; follow the links to Mystery Operations in Number Patterns.

• Demonstrate how to use the website to identify a mystery function. Show students how to ask for more than one

example of a function acting on a number before venturing to identify the function.

• Challenge students to identify four mystery functions at this website.

• Have students record the information given to them for each mystery function, and the functions they identified.

Take-Home Activities

Many teachers have prepared manipulative kits for children to take home. Informal activities such as games and puzzles allow parents and children to work together in a different way than paper-and-pencil homework. Here are two letters and directions for a primary kit and an intermediate kit that highlight patterning.

Primary Kit

Dear Parent,

We have been studying patterns. In the plastic bag, you will find blocks that join together. The blocks can be used to show many patterns. Here is one example. Your child should be able to make this pattern, read "red-blue, red-blue," and add blocks that continue the pattern.

With the blocks, you can make other patterns for your child to work with. Make a record of the patterns you create together.

Your child may also find other examples of patterns around the house. Patterns occur in music when sequences of notes are repeated and in art when colors or designs are repeated. Your child will find patterns in clothing with stripes or plaid designs. He or she will also find patterns in many daily routines, such as getting ready for bed, cleaning up after a meal, or shopping for groceries. It is also important for your child to notice when a pattern is changed, disrupted, or incomplete.

Looking for patterns helps children recognize how important and useful patterns are to us in everyday life.

Thank you for your help.

Take-Home Activities

Intermediate Kit

Dear Parents,

We have been learning about patterns this year. Patterns are important thinking skills in mathematics. This pattern puzzle can be completed with tiles or blocks or by coloring.

It begins with one tile on the grid paper. The next size square has 4 tiles in it and needs 3 more tiles. The next square has 9 tiles and takes 5 more tiles to complete. We have worked this far in class. When each new square is made, the number of tiles needed follows a pattern based on the length of the side of the squares.

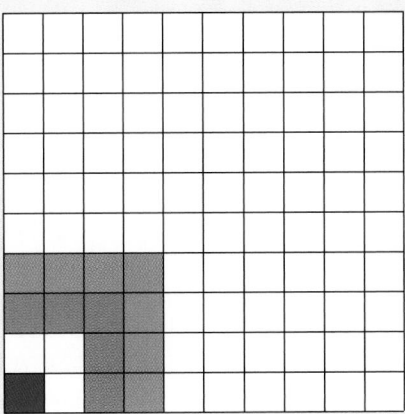

Square	Number of Tiles	Tiles to Add	Number Sentence
1	1 × 1	3	1 + 2
4	2 × 2	5	2 + 3
9	3 × 3	7	3 + 4
16	4 × 4	9	4 + 5
25	_____	___	_____
36	_____	___	_____
49	_____	___	_____
64	_____	___	_____
81	_____	___	_____
100	_____	___	_____

Add tiles to finish the squares on the grid. Your student can extend the pattern to 10 × 10 and record results in the table. What patterns were found?

Thank you for your assistance.

Summary

When NCTM included algebra as one of the content standards for grades K–12, they made a major realignment in the curriculum for elementary school. They called for elementary school students to begin work in algebra. But algebra in elementary school was not to be an abstract manipulation of x and y. Instead, algebra was a natural extension of problem solving with numbers, geometry, measurement, and data collection. In these activities students encounter the algebraic thinking and themes related to pattern, variables, equality, relations and function, representation, and change.

Patterns are a central theme of algebraic understanding, and children should see many different types of patterns, ranging from patterns with numbers and letters to patterns using sounds, objects, and real-world data. One goal of exploring patterns is to use them to solve real-life problems. It is important that children have many opportunities to engage in algebraic reasoning with manipulatives, such as pan balances, so that they have concrete experiences that provide a solid understanding of the balance aspect of equations. Finally, students should have many opportunities to work with functions, using real data and then generalizing to algebraic expressions to describe the functions.

Study Questions and Activities

1. What do you remember of your algebra experiences in high school and college? What are your feelings and thoughts about those memories?

2. What was your first reaction to teaching algebra in elementary school? What is your impression after reading this chapter?

3. What are the themes of algebra? Find one activity to highlight each of the themes.

4. How would you explain algebraic reasoning to the parent of a second-grader?

5. Read an article on the Internet about algebra in elementary school. Are you comfortable with the level of mathematics it describes for elementary school? Why or why not?

Praxis (http://www.ets.org/praxis/) If $4x - 3(x + 1) = 5$, what is the value of x?

a. 2
b. 4
c. 6
d. 8

NAEP (http://nces.ed.gov/nationsreportcard/) The terms in this sequence are the squares of consecutive odd numbers:

$$1, 9, 25, 49, 81, \ldots$$

The same rule is applied to each number in the given pattern. What is the sixth number in the pattern?

a. 40
b. 100
c. 121
d. 144
e. 169

TIMSS (http://nces.ed.gov/timss/) n is a number. When n is multiplied by 7 and then 6 is added, the result is 41. Which of these equations represents this relation?

a. $7n + 6 = 41$
b. $7n \pm 6 = 41$
c. $7n \times 6 = 41$
d. $7(n + 6) = 41$

Using Children's Literature

Burns, Marilyn. (1997). *Spaghetti and meatballs for all.* New York: Scholastic. (Grades K–3)

In the story *Spaghetti and Meatballs for All*, Mrs. Comfort invites 32 people to a family reunion at her house. She decides to seat them at adjoining tables. How many tables does she need? Students could make a table to keep track of the data in the story and find the pattern to the number of tables and number of people who can sit at them. Students could also use sticky notes for tables and rearrange them as the story requires.

Tables:	1	2	3	4
People:	4	6	8	10

Students can complete the table, and then answer how many tables Mrs. Comfort would need for a reunion of 40 or 48 people.

Barry, David. (1994). *The Rajah's rice: A mathematical folktale from India.* San Francisco: W. H. Freeman. (Grades 4–6)

The Rajah's Rice presents the tale of Chandra, who cures the Rajah's elephants. He is willing to reward her with gold and jewels, but she asks only for some grains of rice on a chessboard. Her request of one grain on the first square, 2 on the second, 4 on the third, and so forth results in quite a surprise for the Rajah. Students can make a table to compute the number of grains on the first 10 squares.

1	2	3	4	5	6	7	8	9	10
1	2	4	8	16	32	64	128	256	512

After students discern the pattern for the number of grains of rice, ask them to make an estimate of the total number of grains on square 25, on square 50, and on square 64. After each estimate, allow students to use a calculator to compute the number of grains of rice. Conclude by asking students to explain why the Rajah could not fulfill Chandra's request.

Teacher's Resources

Algebraic thinking math project. (1999). Alexandria, VA: PBS Mathline Videotape Series.

Burns, M. (1994). *What are you teaching my child?* Sausalito, CA: Math Solutions Inc. (video). Available at http://www.mathsolutions.com/mb/content/publications

Cuevas, G., & Yeatts, K. (2001). *Navigating through algebra, 3–5.* Reston, VA: National Council of Teachers of Mathematics.

Egan, L. (1999). *101 brain-boosting math problems.* Jefferson City, MO: Scholastic Teaching Resources.

Findell, C. (Ed.). (2000). *Teaching with student math notes,* v. 3. Reston, VA: National Council of Teachers of Mathematics.

Friel, S., Rachlin, S., & Doyle, D. (Eds.). (2001). *Navigating through algebra, 6–8.* Reston, VA: National Council of Teachers of Mathematics.

Greenes, C., Cavanaugh, M., Dacey, L., Findell, C., & Small, M. (2001). *Navigating through algebra, PK–2.* Reston, VA: National Council of Teachers of Mathematics.

Greenes, C., & Findell, C. (1998). *Algebra puzzles and problems series (Grades 4–6).* Chicago: Creative Publications.

Greenes, C., & Findell, C. (1999). *Groundworks: Algebraic thinking series (Grades 1–7).* Chicago: Creative Publications.

Greenes, C., & Findell, C. (Eds.). (2004). *Developing students' algebraic reasoning abilities.* Lakewood. CO: National Council of Supervisors of Mathematics.

Greenes, C., Findell, C., & Caufield, T. (2003). *The abc's of algebra.* Chicago: Creative Publications.

Kopp, J., with Davila, D. (2000). *Math on the menu: Real-life problem solving for grades 3–5.* Berkeley, CA: UC Berkeley Lawrence Hall of Science.

O'Connell, S. (2000). *Introduction to problem solving: Strategies for the elementary math classroom.* Westport, CT: Heinemann.

Shiotsu, V. (2000). *Math games.* Lincolnwood, IL: Lowell House.

von Rotz, L., & Burns, M. (2002). *Lessons for algebraic thinking: K–2.* Sausalito, CA: Math Solutions Publications.

Wickett, M., Kharas, K., & Burns, M. (2002). *Lessons for algebraic thinking: 3–5.* Sausalito, CA: Math Solutions Publications.

Children's Bookshelf

Anno, M. (1995). *Anno's magic seeds.* New York: Philomel. (Grades 3–5)

Bayer, J. (1984). *My name is Alice.* New York: Dial Books. (Grades 1–3)

Barry, D. (1997). *The Rajah's rice: A mathematical folktale from India.* San Francisco: W. H. Freeman. (Grades 4–6)

Burns, M. (1997). *Spaghetti and meatballs for all.* New York: Scholastic Press. (Grades 2–4)

Burns, M. (1999). *How many legs, how many tails.* Jefferson City, MO: Scholastic. (Grades 1–3)

Ernst, L. (1983). *Sam Johnson and the blue ribbon quilt.* New York: Lothrop, Lee & Shepard. (Grades 1–3)

Glass, J. (2000). *Counting sheep.* New York: Random House. (Grades 1–3)

Holzman, K. (1995). *A quarter from the tooth fairy.* New York: Scholastic. (Grades 2–4)

Hutchins, P. (1986). *The doorbell rang.* New York: Greenwillow Books. (Grades 3–5)

Pinczes, E. (1993). *One hundred hungry ants.* Boston: Houghton Mifflin. (Grades 2–4)

Pitman, H. (1986). *A grain of rice.* New York: Scholastic. (Grades 4–6)

Scieszka, J., & Smith, L. (1995). *The math curse.* New York: Viking. (Grades 3–6)

Singer, M. (1985). *A clue in code.* New York: Clarion. (Grades 4–6)

Stevens, J. (1995). *Tops and bottoms.* San Diego: Harcourt Brace. (Grades 1–3)

Taback, S. (1997). *There was an old lady who swallowed a fly.* New York: Viking. (Grades 1–3)

Weiss, M. (1977). *Solomon Grundy, born on Monday.* New York: Thomas Y. Crowell. (Grades 4–6)

Williams, A. (1989). *A chair for my mother.* New York: Hooper Trophy. (Grades 1–3)

Wood, A. (1984). *The napping house.* Orlando: Harcourt. (Grades 2–4)

Zimleman, N. (1992). *How the second grade got $8,205.50 to visit the Statue of Liberty.* Pacific Grove, CA: Albert Witman. (Grades 1–3)

Technology Resources

Computer Programs

There are many software programs that effectively develop children's algebraic reasoning. Any of the programs on this list will advance students' mathematics understanding.

Alge-Blaster (Torrance, CA: Davidson)

Graph Links Grades 1–6 (Orlando, FL: Harcourt Brace)

Green Globs and Graphing Equations (Pleasantville, NY: Sunburst Communications)

Mighty Math Astro Algebra (Orlando, FL: Edmark)

Tabletop (Novato, CA: Broderbund)

Internet Sites

For pan balance activities, go to the following websites:

http://illuminations.nctm.org/ (see Pan Balance [3 applets])

http://nlvm.usu.edu/en/nav/vlibrary.html (see Algebra: Balance Scales)

http://mathforum.org/te/exchange/hosted/palu (see Solving Equations with Balance Strategy)

For patterning activities, go to the following websites:

http://nlvm.usu.edu/en/nav/vlibrary.html (see Algebra: Pattern Blocks, Space Blocks)

For function box activities, go to the following websites:

http://nlvm.usu.edu/en/nav/vlibrary.html (see Algebra: Function Machine)

http://www.shodor.org//interactivate/activities/index.html (see Algebra: Function Machine)

For activities that involve evaluating expressions, go to the following websites:

http://www.bbc.co.uk/education/mathsfile/ (see Algebra: Late Delivery Game, Dice Substitution, and Equation Match Game)

http://mathforum.org/te/exchange/hosted/palu (see True-Makers)

Internet Game

At **http://www.bbc.co.uk/education/mathsfile/** there is an algebra matching game. In the game file Equation Match, students match equation solutions in a grid of squares. When a correct pair is matched, the grid reveals two squares of a picture. The goal is to reveal the entire picture. Students can try to solve the equations mentally or use pencil and paper. There are three levels of difficulty to the equations, ranging from simple one-step equations to two-step equations to equations that require using the distributive law to solve. The amusing sound effects can be turned off for those students who find them distracting.

For Further Reading

Bay-Williams, J. (2001). What is algebra in elementary school? *Teaching Children Mathematics* 8(4), 196–200.

Rationale and activities for algebra in the elementary classroom.

Brown, E., & Jones, E. (2005). Using clock arithmetic to teach algebra concepts. *Mathematics Teaching in the Middle School* 2(11), 104–110.

Brown and Jones show how a simple clock can be the tool for exploring modular arithmetic and signed number operations and for solving equations.

Civil, M., & Khan, L. (2001). Mathematics instruction developed from a garden theme. *Teaching Children Mathematics* 7(7), 400–405.

Making a garden motivates students to use algebraic reasoning to confront many mathematics and interdisciplinary problems and issues.

Elliot, P. (2005). Algebra in the K–2 curriculum? Billy goats and bears give us the answer. *Teaching Children Mathematics* 12(2), 100–104.

Elliot relates algebraic concepts to many familiar storybooks for young children. The stories are used to help young children develop algebra thinking in the context of the stories.

Mann, R. (2004). Balancing act: The truth behind the equals sign. *Teaching Children Mathematics* 11(2), 65–69.

Mann discusses activities using a real balance scale to develop the concept of equality of the equal sign in an equation.

Reeves, C. (2006). Putting fun into functions. *Teaching Children Mathematics* 12(5), 250–259.

In this article Reeves describes how his students built their own function machines using boxes and containers as a way to introduce functions into his classes.

Rivera, F. (2006). Changing the face of arithmetic: Teaching algebra to children. *Teaching Children Mathematics* 12(6), 306–311.

Rivera describes recent research in algebra learning at the elementary level, focusing on implications for classroom teaching.

Schneider, S., & Thompson, C. (2000). Incredible equations: Develop incredible number sense. *Teaching Children Mathematics* 7(3), 146–147.

Children create extended equations and develop number sense as they solve them.

Soares, J., Blanton, M., & Kaput, J. (2006). Thinking algebraically across the elementary school curriculum. *Teaching Children Mathematics* 12(5), 228–235.

Soares and colleagues describe algebraic concepts and activities developed from reading books in various subjects, thus incorporating algebra into the curriculum.

Vennebush, G., Marquez, E., & Larsen, J. (2005). Embedding algebraic thinking throughout the mathematics curriculum. *Mathematics Teaching in the Middle School* 2(11), 86–93.

Vennebush and colleagues explain how to develop algebraic thinking by modifying tasks that involve geometry, data, and number sense.

Yarema, C., Adams, R., & Cagle, R. (2000). A teacher's "try" angles. *Teaching Children Mathematics* 6(5), 299–303.

Problems and patterns provide background for number sentences and equations.

Ziemba, E., & Hoffman, J. (2006). Sorting and patterning in kindergarten: From activities to assessment. *Teaching Children Mathematics* 12(5), 236–241.

In this article Ziemba and Hoffman describe how assessments in patterning and sorting can be successfully done by very young schoolchildren.

CHAPTER 17

Developing Geometric Concepts and Systems

For many years geometry instruction was limited to naming shapes and measuring angles. Today, geometry plays a central role in elementary school mathematics. Geometric systems and spatial sense are partnered with number systems and numerical thinking as foundations for elementary and higher mathematics. Geometry also has many practical applications. Many everyday activities require spatial sense to provide an orientation with surroundings, whether finding a missing set of keys, making a trip to the grocery store, or walking from one room to another.

People use their spatial sense to arrange furniture, pack luggage, and park cars. They also use geometric relationships to measure distances and estimate length and area. Geometric and visual thinking are essential in art, architecture, design, graphics, animation, and dozens of other vocational and recreational settings.

Rich experiences in geometry develop problem-solving and reasoning skills and connect with many other topics in mathematics and with the real world.

In this chapter you will read about:

1 The essential role geometry plays in the world of the child and in the elementary and intermediate school curriculum

2 The importance of spatial sense in mathematics and seven skills that define spatial sense

3 Developmental stages in children's understanding of geometry

4 Four geometry systems that are taught in elementary and intermediate school: topological, Euclidean, transformational, and coordinate

5 Activities and materials that develop concepts of topological geometry and spatial sense

6 Plane shapes and solid figures and activities that teach children about them

7 Activities for learning about points, lines, rays, and line segments

8 Activities for learning and extending concepts about symmetry, similarity, and congruency

9 Transformational geometry and activities such as tessellations for learning about slides, turns, and flips

10 The Pythagorean theorem and its extensions and applications

11 Coordinate geometry, with activities and materials used in developing related skills

Geometry provides strong connections to our world. Both practical and aesthetic aspects of geometry are found in art and architecture, space exploration, home planning, and clothing and automobile design. Such topics interest students and can be used to develop children's geometry knowledge and skills, spatial sense, and problem-solving abilities. Materials and activities in geometry require that children describe geometric forms, search for patterns, organize data, build and interpret models, make conjectures, and draw conclusions.

NCTM identified geometry as one of the five content strands in mathematics education. The specific recommendations for geometry at the Pre-K–2 level are shown here.

NCTM Geometry Standard

Instructional programs from prekindergarten through grade 8 should enable all students to:

Analyze characteristics and properties of two- and three-dimensional geometric shapes and develop mathematical arguments about geometric relationships

Pre-K–2 Expectations:
In prekindergarten through grade 2 all students should:
- recognize, name, build, draw, compare, and sort two- and three-dimensional shapes;
- describe attributes and parts of two- and three-dimensional shapes;
- investigate and predict the results of putting together and taking apart two- and three-dimensional shapes.

Specify locations and describe spatial relationships using coordinate geometry and other representational systems

Pre-K–2 Expectations:
In prekindergarten through grade 2 all students should:
- describe, name, and interpret relative positions in space and apply ideas about relative position;
- describe, name, and interpret direction and distance in navigating space and apply ideas about direction and distance;
- find and name locations with simple relationships such as "near to" and in coordinate systems such as maps.

Apply transformations and use symmetry to analyze mathematical situations

Pre-K–2 Expectations:
In prekindergarten through grade 2 all students should:
- recognize and apply slides, flips, and turns;
- recognize and create shapes that have symmetry.

Use visualization, spatial reasoning, and geometric modeling to solve problems

Pre-K–2 Expectations:
In prekindergarten through grade 2 all students should:
- create mental images of geometric shapes using spatial memory and spatial visualization;
- recognize and represent shapes from different perspectives;
- relate ideas in geometry to ideas in number and measurement;
- recognize geometric shapes and structures in the environment and specify their location.

Children's Development of Spatial Sense

Many topics and skills in elementary school build on children's spatial sense. Fractions, measurement, estimation, positive and negative integers on a number line, map reading, and concepts in science and social studies have a spatial quality. Algebra, trigonometry, calculus, and topics in higher mathematics also require spatial thinking.

Spatial sense, also called *spatial perception* or *spatial visualization*, helps students understand the relationship between objects and their location in a three-dimensional world. It also helps them to orient themselves in their three-dimensional world. Spatial sense is the ability to perceive objects in relation to one another and to oneself, the ability to mentally change the orientation of an object in relation to other objects or to oneself.

Spatial sense is an intuitive feel for one's surroundings and the objects in them. To develop spatial sense, children must have many experiences that focus on geometric relationships; the direction, orientation, and perspectives of objects in space; the relative shapes and sizes of figures and objects; and how a change in shape relates to a change in size (National Council of Teachers of Mathematics, 1989, p. 49).

POINT OF VIEW
Geometry helps us represent and describe in an orderly manner the world in which we live. Children are naturally interested in geometry and find it intriguing and motivating; their spatial capabilities frequently exceed their numerical skills, and tapping these strengths can foster an interest in mathematics and improve number understandings and skills. (National Council of Teachers of Mathematics, 1989, p. 48)

One of the eight multiple intelligences proposed by Howard Gardner (1982) is the spatial ability that all people have and that can be developed through experience. In fact, many great scientists, mathematicians, and inventors—including Einstein—report that they saw how things worked before they were able to explain or demonstrate their discoveries.

Del Grande and Morrow (1989, pp. 1–3) identified seven skills that contribute to spatial sense:

1. *Eye-motor coordination* is the ability to coordinate the eye with other parts of the body in various activities.

2. *Figure-ground perception* is the visual act of identifying a figure against a complex background.

3. *Perceptual constancy* is the ability to recognize figures or objects in space, regardless of size, position, or orientation.

4. *Position-in-space perception* is the ability to relate an object in space to oneself.

5. *Perception of spatial relationships* is the ability to see two or more objects in relation to oneself or in relation to each other.

6. *Visual discrimination* is the ability to distinguish the similarities and differences between or among objects.

7. *Visual memory* is the ability to recall objects no longer in view.

POINT OF VIEW
Geometry offers an aspect to mathematical thinking that is different from, but connected to, the world of numbers. (National Council of Teachers of Mathematics, 2000, p. 97)

Through work with two- and three-dimensional objects, children develop their spatial sense. The activities in this section are all designed to enhance younger students' spatial visualization skills, although older students may also benefit from these experiences. Activity 17.1 focuses on the spatial perception children use to orient themselves in a three-dimensional world.

When adults read storybooks to young children, they expect children to readily interpret two-dimensional drawings as representative of three-dimensional objects. When children see a picture of a kite or a dog in a storybook, they realize that these objects in a book with length and width represent length, width, and depth. Activity 17.2 helps students focus attention on the careful translation of two-dimensional sketches to three-dimensional shapes. The activity can be made more challenging for older children by using more complex diagrams and asking students to determine the number of blocks in a block structure without actually building it. An extension of the activity might be to ask students to design and draw their own block structures using isometric dot paper (see Black-Line Master 17.1 and page 392).

For children in the early grades Activity 17.3 concentrates on a different spatial sense skill: perceiving individual and overlapping shapes in a composite figure. Activity 17.4 takes advantage of children's love of solving mazes. In this interactive electronic activity, found on the Internet, children plot a path through a maze by giving careful directions to a lost ladybug. Such an activity helps younger children

Research for the Classroom

Recent research and children's performances on national and international tests support the claim that there is no real gender advantage as far as mathematics is concerned. The myth that "math is for boys and English is for girls" is simply not sustained by any hard evidence. However, there is one mathematics area in which research shows that boys have an advantage over girls: spatial sense. Young boys outscore young girls in several areas of spatial sense, including mazes, mental rotations, block designs, and block building (Levine et al., 1999). Mental rotation is particularly difficult for young girls, with only 17% of young girls performing at the average level of the boys (Linn & Petersen, 1986). This gap in mental rotation ability is all the more important because this ability is linked to SAT scores, with a higher correlation than either mathematics self-confidence or mathematics anxiety (Casey et al., 1997).

Earlier research has demonstrated that spatial visualization skills are not established at birth but can be learned and enhanced through a variety of experiences (see Activity 17.1). In view of this gender difference in spatial vi-

sualization skills, teachers need to be sure to include many spatial sense activities in the early years. Emerging research suggests that girls can catch up to boys in the early grades when they have ample opportunities to develop and extend their early spatial sense (Casey et al., 2004). Thus, in response to these research findings, teachers will need to explicitly help students, both boys and girls, to develop their spatial sense.

All students have an innate spatial sense, but it is important to remember that students enter school with different spatial sense abilities. Early experiences, before and outside school, help awaken and begin the spatial sense of some children. Other children may not have access to comparable early exposure. Children who have played with jigsaw puzzles, constructed Lego buildings, and built sand castles may have enhanced their natural spatial sense. Classroom teachers must allow for these differences and provide activities for students that will extend and enhance their students' spatial sense, regardless of their grade level.

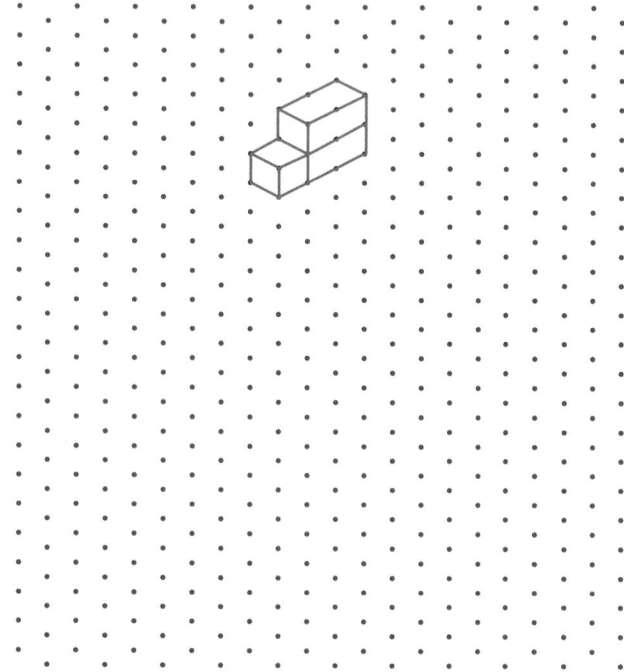

focus on directions and terminology, such as turn, left, and right.

Several of the companion website activities foster spatial sense. The activity "Matching Outlines" challenges children to match a three-dimensional

object with its outline. The activity "Mirror Partners" asks students to imitate the motions of a face-to-face partner.

What Teachers Need to Know About Teaching Geometry

Research following the van Hieles's studies, discussed later, has supported the general framework of the levels of geometry thinking. There are several implications for teachers. It is critical that activities match the van Hiele levels of students. If students are reasoning at a lower level than the level of the activities, the result will be that students will revert to rote memorization in an attempt to complete tasks.

Spatial sense is not an innate ability and must be developed. Many children will have developed their spatial sense with out-of-school activities. For those who have not, their teacher must help to develop their spatial sense by using activities that expand and enhance spatial abilities.

Geometry is part of everything humans do. To describe and understand the two- and three-dimensional world we live in, mathematicians have developed several different geometric systems. The need

ACTIVITY 17.1 Move Around the Solid City

Level: Grades K–4

Setting: Groups of four

Objective: Students identify the order of viewing positions around a mock town.

Materials: Solid figures such as View Thru Solids, simple sketches of Solid City from several viewpoints

- Organize students into groups of four. Number each group.
- Have each group member sit on one side of a table.
- Put several solids such as a cube, pyramid, cone, or other relatively simple three-dimensional shapes in the center of the table. Tell the students these are part of Solid City. (A clear plastic model is preferred because students can see through it to lines and points not facing them.) Caution the students not to move the solids once they have been put before them.

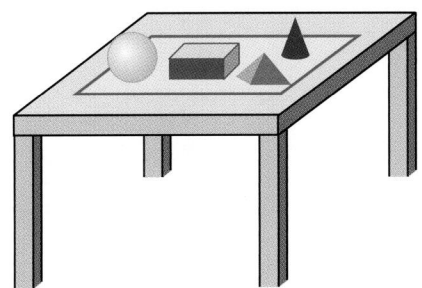

- Each group is given a set of Solid City sketches. Their task is to determine where to stand around the table to see the same view that is depicted in each sketch.
- Once students in a group have determined each viewpoint, they should put the sketches in the order of views a student would see as the student walked clockwise around the table.
- Have students explain how they decided on the order of the sketches.

Extension for Older Students

- Each student in a group stands in a different position around the table. Each student is to sketch the view of the solids from her or his perspective. Some children may sketch edges of the solids that are hidden from view. They can use solid lines for edges facing the drawer and broken lines for those that are away from the drawer.
- The four sketches are put into a pile and then exchanged with another group.
- Students who receive drawings from the other group have to put them in order according to the views a student would see if he or she walked around Solid City.
- Ask students to label their drawings by naming the shape or shapes they see from each perspective.
- Have students rearrange their town, make new sketches, and exchange them with another group.
- After several exchanges, ask students how they decided to organize the sketches.
- Add a multicultural dimension to the activity by asking students what familiar building or structure each of the shapes calls to mind.

Extension

Sunburst has developed a software program, Building Perspective, that provides experiences for children to analyze, design, and build block structures.

ACTIVITY 17.2 How Many Blocks?

Level: Grades 1–6

Setting: Small groups or individual

Objective: Students build three-dimensional structures from two-dimensional drawings.

Materials: Inch or centimeter cubes, activity sheets

- Students use cubes to build three-dimensional structures drawn on their activity sheets.
- Circulate as students are building. Ask if there are blocks in their building that they cannot see in the drawing
- Have students record in a table how many blocks are needed to build each structure.
- Question whether a given drawing can be built with a different number of blocks.

Variation

- Older children can work with more complex buildings and might be challenged to determine the number of blocks by observation, without building the structures.

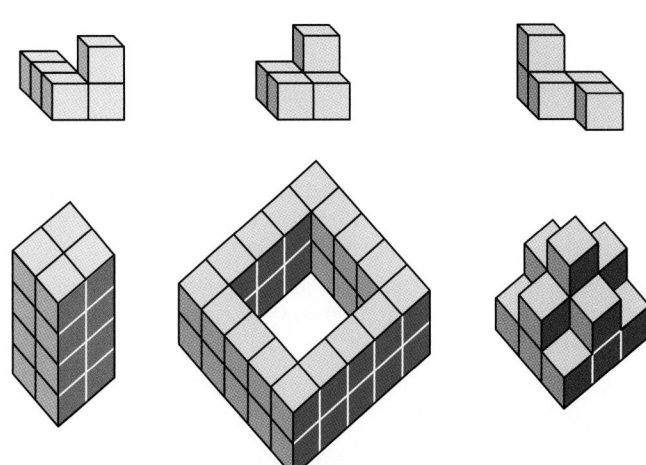

ACTIVITY 17.3   Embedded Triangles

Level: Grades 2–4

Setting: Groups of four

Objective: Students search for and record triangles in a composite figure.

Materials: Diagrams of a composite figure on a sheet of paper, crayons or colored pencils

- Display the composite figure to students.
- Ask students to describe the figure to classmates.
- If students do not suggest that the figure is composed of several triangles, probe for that insight as students relate their descriptions.
- For younger students, pass out several copies of the composite figure and ask students to color the various triangles with different colors. For example, on one sheet students could color the six triangles a, b, c, d, e, and f. On another sheet they might color triangle abc and triangle def.
- For older students, ask them to label all the triangles they can see. One method of labeling is to label each vertex of the figure and use three vertex points to designate each triangle.

- Another method is to label each area of the figure with a letter or number and then designate the triangles by using the composite areas. In the figure below, labeled by areas, the triangles are:

a, b, c, d, e, f

ab, bc, de, ef, be, cf

abc, def

abde

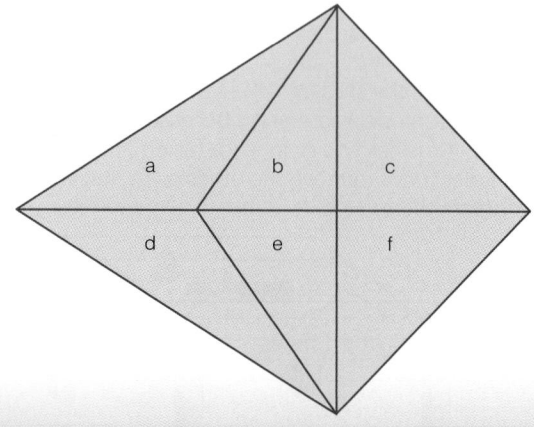

ACTIVITY 17.4   Ladybug Maze (Internet Activity)

Level: Grades K–4

Setting: Pairs of students or individual

Objective: Students plan a route for a ladybug through a maze using an activity on the Internet.

Materials: Internet access

- Go to http://my.nctm.org/standards/document/eexamples/index.htm. Follow the link to Ladybug Maze.
- Help students understand the directions for the applet. Students use the applet to plan a path and then engage the ladybug to follow the path they have designed.
- When students have compiled the directions for the path, ask them to describe how the ladybug will move when it follows a specific command in the path plan.
- When students create a path for the ladybug through the maze, have them print out the maze with and without the path.
- Have them give the unmarked maze to another pair of students and then describe their successful path to them.
- The students try to trace out the successful path following the directions they are given.

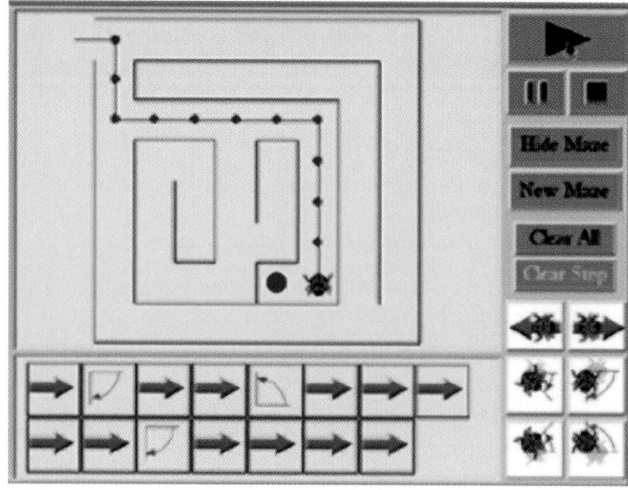

Used with permission from illuminations.nctm.org, copyright © 2000–2002 by the National Council of Teachers of Mathematics Inc. All rights reserved. The presence of the screen shot from http://standards/nctm.org/document /eexamples/chap4/4.3/index.htm does not constitute or imply an endorsement by NCTM.

to make distinctions among these systems in elementary school is not great, but children learn basic aspects of at least four different geometric systems:

- Topological geometry
- Euclidean geometry
- Coordinate geometry
- Transformational geometry

Although the geometric systems are interrelated, each system uses a slightly different set of rules and vocabulary. Topological geometry describes where objects are located in relation to each other. A child's first geometric experiences are topological, according to Piaget. A child views everything in relation to his or her own location or personal perspective. By moving around and locating things in their environment, children develop a mental understanding and an extensive vocabulary for objects in their space—far and near, above and below, before and behind, first and last.

Euclidean geometry, the geometry learned exclusively by most students in high school, is the geometry of shapes and objects in two- and three-dimensional space. In Euclidean geometry students learn the characteristics of objects: points and lines, circles and spheres, triangles and pyramids, squares and cubes, rectangles and prisms, and the many other flat shapes and solid figures. These characteristics and the relationships between them are organized into simple rule systems and formulas.

Coordinate geometry imposes a grid system on two- or three-dimensional space that has many simple and complex uses. The grid system on a city map shows that a particular building can be located in grid K-10. The grid system used by air traffic controllers allows them to locate and give information to landing and departing aircraft.

Transformation geometry is sometimes called motion geometry, or the geometry of slides, flips, and turns. As objects and shapes are moved or transformed by sliding, flipping, or turning, they can be combined in many different ways. Frank Lloyd Wright, the great American architect, envisioned all buildings as combinations and rearrangements of the simple building blocks he played with as a child. Moving a figure in transformation geometry may appear to change its appearance, but it will not change its fundamental characteristics. A kite can be seen in the sky, on the ground, from either side, sitting on its end or on its side, but it is still a kite, and none of its characteristics—length, width, shape—has changed.

Concepts and skills from each of these geometry systems are introduced informally in the elementary grades with engaging activities and materials. Because concepts from one system are related to concepts from another system, many activities overlap. Teachers do not need to differentiate among the four geometry systems for elementary students. However, you may find that different objectives in your curriculum emphasize different geometric systems. Figure 17.1 provides a graphic organizer for

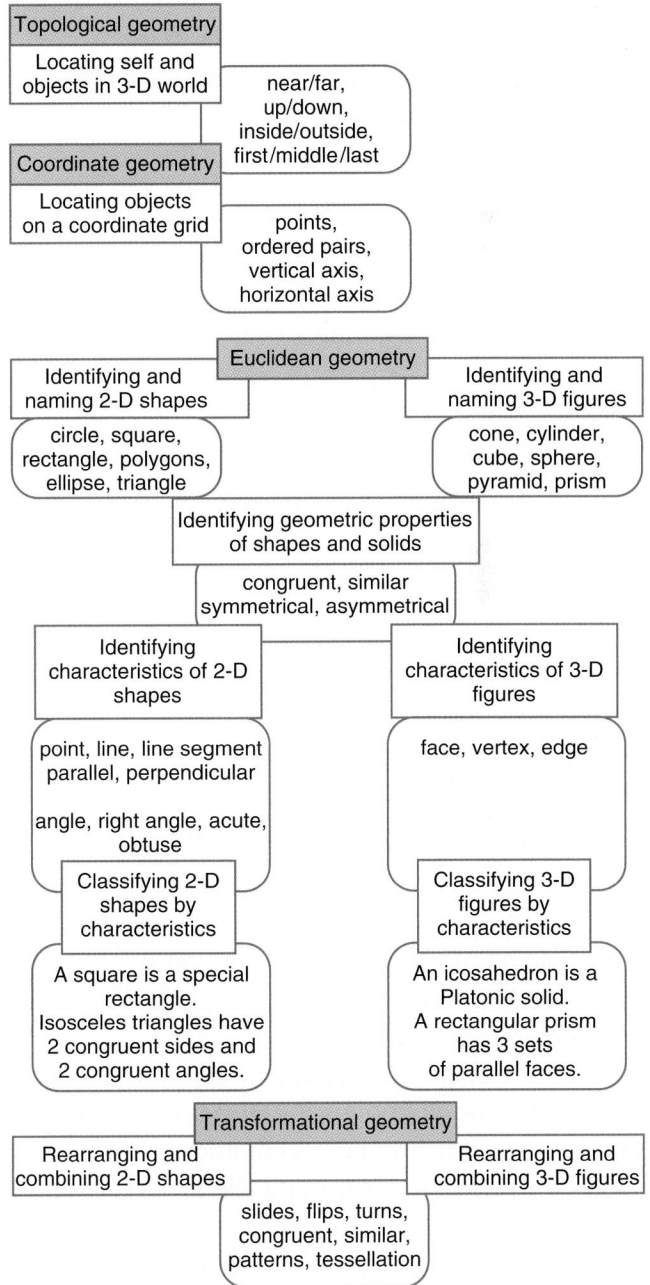

Figure 17.1 Geometric systems and concepts

major geometry topics that are often included in elementary mathematics.

> Euclidean geometry is named for Greek mathematician Euclid (ca. 300 B.C.E.). Euclid organized all the known geometry of his time into a series of assumed facts (postulates) and provable statements (theorems).

Ⓔ XERCISE

Review your state or local curriculum standards. Do you find objectives related to all four geometry systems? ●●●

Development of Geometric Concepts: Stages of Geometry Understanding

Pierre Marie van Hiele-Geldof and Dina van Hiele (a husband and wife who were Dutch middle school teachers and mathematicians) spent many years investigating and describing how children develop their understanding of Euclidean geometry (Fuys & Tischler, 1988, p. 7). They concluded that individuals pass through five stages of geometric understanding:

Stage 0: Visualization—recognizing and naming the figures

Stage 1: Analysis—describing the attributes of figures

Stage 2: Informal deduction—classifying and generalizing figures by their attributes

Stage 3: Deduction—developing proofs using postulates and definitions

Stage 4: Rigor—working in various geometric systems

The first three stages occur during the elementary school years. By understanding children's development, teachers can design appropriate geometry activities.

The first stage (visualization) starts in a child's early years and continues into the primary grades. Children recognize and label common plane figures such as circles, squares, triangles, and rectangles. They recognize simple solids such as cubes, spheres, pyramids, and cones and name them with those labels or with less formal names such as boxes and balls. At this stage children begin to develop and

expand the spatial visualization skills they acquired before entering school.

> Progress from one [van Hiele] level to the next . . . is more dependent upon instruction than on age or biological maturation, and types of instructional experiences can affect progress (or lack of it). (Taylor et al., 1991, p. 9)

During the second stage (analysis), students become more proficient in describing the attributes of two- and three-dimensional shapes. The language they use is a mixture of mathematical terminology and less precise nouns and adjectives. A triangle has three sides and three points, or corners. A sphere is a "ball" and is round all over—but a cone is round and flat on one end and "pointy" (or has a "round point") on the other. A square has "straight" corners. Teachers accept children's language but consistently use correct terminology in response:

Teacher: The ball is also called a sphere.

Teacher: All six faces of this cube are squares.

Teacher: The corners of the triangle are called angles.

Teacher: This is a 90-degree angle and is called a right angle.

Children learn to identify the unique characteristics of all plane and solid figures through work with various geometric situations and materials.

The third van Hiele stage (informal deduction) begins in the intermediate grades, as children classify and organize two- and three-dimensional figures according to their characteristics. A debate about whether a square is a rectangle or a rectangle is a square is valuable in clarifying the relationships between squares and rectangles. (A square is a special rectangle because it has all the characteristics of a rectangle plus four congruent sides.) As they mature, children learn that all four-sided figures are quadrilaterals despite different appearances. Quadrilaterals can be either regular (a square) or irregular (all other quadrilaterals). Children find that certain shapes fit side to side to make designs and that others do not. The questions and problems encountered in elementary school provide background for the later, more formal deductive study of geometry in middle and senior high school and beyond, which is done at the fourth and fifth van Hiele stages.

The fourth stage (deduction) and fifth stage (rigor) occur well after elementary school. A typical high school geometry course is designed to fully develop students' deduction abilities with the postulate-theorem-proof of Euclidean geometry. The final stage of rigor describes the geometry thinking needed for graduate-level geometry courses.

With these stages of development in mind, teachers can plan activities for children's study of geometry. The van Hieles found that every student must pass through each of the stages of geometric thinking in order. Thus a student who is operating at the visualization stage (Stage 0) will be unable to fully engage in an activity that stresses analysis (Stage 1) or informal deduction (Stage 2). Once a student is competent in visualization, then activities that stress the next van Hiele level can be offered. Because elementary students will focus on the first three stages, they are not expected to use deductive proofs as they deal with geometric concepts and forms. This does not mean that children cannot engage in activities that involve some aspect of deduction. Children learn to play games such as Clue and Battleship, which require logical thinking. They can solve mystery stories that require deductive reasoning, such as the stories involving Amelia Bedelia or Encyclopedia Brown. Many geometry activities can involve discovery and conjecture as a means to develop children's geometric thinking. By using task cards and activities designed for individual and group work, students can explore geometry concepts in an informal manner. Through manipulation of real objects and graphic representations, they name and describe geometric shapes and figures and their characteristics, relationships, position, and properties.

Teaching and Learning About Topological Geometry

Topological geometry describes how objects in space relate to each other. A topological view does not require that figures maintain a rigid or fixed shape, as in Euclidean geometry. Rather, a shape can be altered so that it assumes a new configuration, much as if it were drawn on a sheet of rubber that can be stretched in all directions. For example, a square can be stretched to the shape of a rectangle, an oval, or another simple closed figure. An open figure such as the letter C can be reshaped to look like the letter S. Certain characteristics, such as being a closed or open figure, remain unchanged, even though the shape can take different forms.

Children's perspective of the world, including their understanding of space, is **idiocentric**, or self-centered. According to Piaget, young children do not view people and objects as stable and unchanging but see them in the topological sense. To children in the sensorimotor and preoperational stages, people and objects change as the position from which they are viewed changes. Therefore Piaget suggests that children's early concepts of the spatial world are topological (Piaget et al., 1960). Investigations of four topological relations—proximity and relative position, separation, order, and enclosure—provide early spatial learning for preschool, kindergarten, and primary-grade students.

Proximity and Relative Position

Proximity refers to the relative location of objects in space—how near or far one object is from another. Naturally, young children are interested in things close to them because they can touch and manipulate them. Things far out of their reach are usually of little interest, unless the child sees something that is eye-catching, such as a shiny part of a swinging mobile. Objects that are out of sight do not exist in the mind of a child in the early sensorimotor stage.

Gradually, children recognize that out-of-sight objects do exist, and they can identify the location of objects in space. Early experiences with spatial concepts and vocabulary such as *near, far, close to, under, above, below, up, down, beside, between, next to*, and so on come from children's everyday experiences and free-play activities.

Parents and teachers help develop children's spatial understandings by using topological geometry terms tied to real experiences drawn from multicultural settings:

- Put the yellow sarong *on top of* the table.

- Juanita is standing *between* Alexa and Candace.

- The tower is going *up, up, up*. It is almost as tall as you are.

- Bring the chair that is *beside* the computer into the listening center.

- Walk *close to* the wall during the fire drill.

Working with collections of miniature toys and counting manipulatives also leads to language about location and proximity:

- Which red car is *farther from* the green car?
- Which bead is *next to* the blue bead?

Flannel-board shapes or magnetized objects can also be arranged so that teacher and students talk about their locations:

- Emily, please move the blue car *inside* the red garage.
- Which car is *closest to* the red airplane? *farthest from* it?

Spatial directions can be incorporated into simple games such as Simon Says, Mother May I, or I Spy. The teacher or students can identify objects in the room by describing their characteristics and position:

- I spy something yellow *on top of* the coat closet.
- I spy something *under* the desk nearest the wall.
- I spy someone *far from* Sean and *close to* Paloma.

Children enjoy hiding objects to find when they play I Spy.

An obstacle course is another game for highlighting relative positions. Students move through a series of obstacles in the classroom or outdoors to demonstrate "over the chair," "under the desk," and "around the monkey bars."

Children enjoy planning a path through a maze. They can describe the various turns made as they negotiate their escape path. Learning positional vocabulary does not just build topological concepts; the same words are also important in language, reading, and directions. An active approach to learning topological terms is one way to promote language development and understanding for students who are learning English as a second language.

Separation

Until children achieve an understanding of separation, they cannot clearly visualize an object as having separate parts or a collection as being made up of separate objects. Children's drawings, especially those of human figures, demonstrate their poor understanding of separation. Early drawings are often egg-shaped, with odd lines for mouth, arms, and legs. The head may be an integral part of the body, rather than separate. Gradually, children differentiate body parts and add a distinct head, torso, and limbs. Finally, they draw details such as fingers, toes, and all parts of the face and head in the proper places. This progression clearly demonstrates the idea of separation, or differentiation, of whole and parts, which takes several years to develop. A teacher finds various opportunities to illustrate whole and parts:

- The class is divided into two separate teams. Each team stands on one side of the room.
- The library separates books for the primary grades from books for upper-grade children.
- A fence separates cows from horses.
- Some of the children drink orange juice, some drink milk, and some drink water.
- Part of my allowance is for snacks, and part of my allowance is for a movie.

Classification activities also help children learn about parts and wholes. A set of toy animals can be divided into groups of dogs, cats, elephants, cows, horses, and monkeys. Recognizing sets and subsets is an important aspect of separation that leads to understanding of number concepts and common fractions. Classification is also an important aspect of organizing an understanding of various geometric shapes and their relationships.

Order

A sequence of events has two orders: beginning to end and end to beginning, or forward and backward. Developing a sense of reversibility, or opposite order, is an important thinking skill. Young students do not maintain the order of a set of events or objects. Patterning and sequence activities help establish a regular order of events and objects. The vocabulary for order is developed with the activities: *first, last, middle, next to last,* and so on.

Thinking forward is generally easier than thinking backward, so teachers need to engage students in a variety of activities that deal with reverse actions. Teacher-led activities direct attention to forward and backward sequences. Children can form a tight circle on the floor. At the teacher's direction they enlarge the circle by moving backward until told to stop. After they reverse and tighten the circle, they can talk about what happened to the circle. Students of many ages enjoy palindromic words and numbers. *Palindromes* are words and numbers that read the same forward as they do backward, such as 2002, 12321, MOM, DAD, BOB, OTTO, MADAM, and MADAM, I'M ADAM. Ask children what is special about these words, numbers, and phrases, and challenge them to find other examples. Counting from 1 to 10, then from 10 to 1, is another example of reversibility. The countdown to a rocket takeoff is "10, 9, 8, 7, 6, 5, 4, 3, 2, 1, blast off!" Students also encounter reversibility of a sort when they see that subtraction can be considered the reverse of addition, and division the reverse of multiplication.

A learning center can be established with activities for dealing with order. Make four- or five-figure patterns of rubber-stamped animals, birds, or flowers on a strip of paper. Then ask children to make the patterns in reverse. Teachers sometimes plan a "Backward Day," in which the children do things backwards, and daily activities are reversed. At lunch they eat dessert first; they wear their shirts and blouses backwards; and they think of other ways to do things in reverse. The companion website activity "Balls in a Tube" provides experiences for younger children as they build their understanding of forward and backward sequences.

Enclosure

In simplest terms enclosure identifies locations inside, outside, in, out, and between. Similar to relative position, enclosure refers to (1) the position of one point between two others on a line, (2) a point within a closed curve on a plane, or (3) a point within a closed three-dimensional figure in space (Figure 17.2).

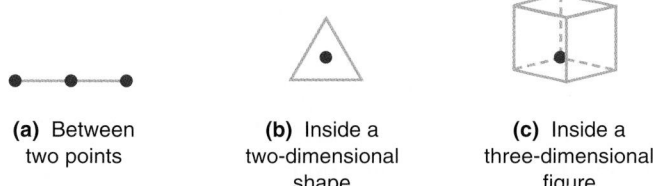

(a) Between two points   **(b)** Inside a two-dimensional shape   **(c)** Inside a three-dimensional figure

Figure 17.2 Enclosures

An understanding of enclosure on a line is important because children frequently encounter the idea of "between" in mathematics. Have five students stand in a row facing the rest of the class; ask about their positions:

- Who is *between* Kasheen and Thun?
- How many children are *between* Amy and José?
- Who is *inside* the block corner? *outside* the circle?

Have children find examples of enclosure, or being between, in the room:

- The fish is *inside* the aquarium.
- The bird is *outside* the cage.
- The flag is *between* the door and the chalkboard.
- The file cabinet is *between* a bulletin board and a corner.

A block corner where children build corrals for horses and fenced lots for cars and trucks is an excellent place for children to explore enclosure within a plane figure.

Demonstrating enclosure and separation in three dimensions can be done by placing a block inside a jar. When the lid is on, the block cannot be removed. The jar *encloses* the block. The jar separates the block from the space outside the jar. The block is *inside* the jar. Have the children find other examples of items that are enclosed in boxes or jars inside the classroom. Containers with and without lids are used for storage. Use questions and comments to stress the fact that a container does not enclose an object if there is no lid. Raise a question about things in a file cabinet or closet:

- Does the cabinet or closet enclose them?
- Does a wastebasket enclose objects that are inside it?

For an activity that explores enclosures, see the companion website activity "Fences." In the activity "Simple Closed Curves" on the companion website children explore various curves that they form using yarn, seeking to identify those yarn curves that are simple closed curves.

Topical geometry is strongly related to spatial perception. As children engage in activities that involve topological geometry, they are also building spatial sense.

EXERCISE

Think of three examples for proximity, separation, order, and enclosure that you might use in the classroom or at home. What questions might you ask, or directions might you give, to develop the topological concepts? ●●●

Topological Mazes and Puzzles

There are many activities that involve topological types of challenges. Working maze puzzles and drawing figures without lifting the pencil from the paper are topological activities that develop spatial sense and problem-solving skills. Figure 17.3 illustrates three topological puzzles that children enjoy. More examples can be found in the comics pages of newspapers or puzzle books in bookstores. Activity 17.5 provides a topological challenge for young children using alphabet letters.

Topology activities for older children can be provided by having them work with maps and mazes. For example, children might describe different routes from Los Angeles to New York on a map of the interstate highway system, using routes that never double back or cross over each other. Although the answers may vary greatly, topologically they are all continuous lines.

> ### MULTICULTURALCONNECTION
> On a map, students might trace a journey between cities in their native country and shade provinces or states in their native country.

Another common topological puzzle is to color a state map of the United States. The challenge is to do this with the fewest number of colors so that no state touches another state with the same color. The teacher might challenge whether this can be accomplished with two colors, three colors, four colors, five colors, six colors, or more. (No matter how complex a map, at most four colors are needed to color it.) Students may also wish to look at printed maps to see possible coloring solutions.

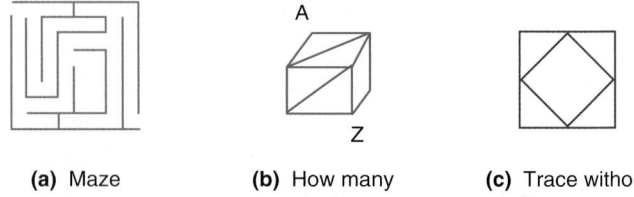

(a) Maze   **(b)** How many paths from A to Z?   **(c)** Trace without lifting pencil.

Figure 17.3 Topological mazes and puzzles

Teaching and Learning About Euclidean Geometry

Plane figures are shapes that have two dimensions, such as squares, triangles, rectangles, circles, ellipses, and other closed figures. **Space figures** have three dimensions. Examples are boxes and blocks, balls and world globes, cones, pyramids, and eggs. Young children typically learn about two-dimensional shapes before they learn about some of the building blocks of geometry, such as points, lines, segments, and angles. They also begin to explore solid shapes before learning about characteristics of two-dimensional shapes, such as congruence, similarity, and symmetry. The presentation of topics in this section follows this same order.

Geometry in Two Dimensions

Plane Figures. Plane figures are common in children's environments. Classrooms have windows, doors, and other objects with square, rectangular, circular, and triangular shapes that children can locate and identify. They can also find shapes in pictures and on clothing designs. Children at the visualization stage of the van Hiele model of geometry thinking may categorize all shapes with curved surfaces as circles. Similarly, they may consider many rectangles as squares. At higher van Hiele levels they will separate squares and rectangles and

---

ACTIVITY 17.5   Simple Letters

Level: Grades K–2

Setting: Pairs of students

Objective: Students list the block capital letters that can be made without lifting the pencil off the paper.

Materials: A full alphabet of block letters

- Demonstrate to students that the letter C is a simple letter because it can be drawn without lifting the pencil off the paper.

- Ask students if they think the letter X is a simple letter. Then demonstrate that X cannot be drawn without lifting the pencil off the paper.

- Pass out sets of letters to each pair of students, and ask them to make a list of simple letters.

- Ask children if any of their names are "simple names" when printed, such as BOB.

distinguish between circles and other shapes with curved lines.

Activity 17.6 presents an activity that can be explored at different levels, depending on the number of figures used and the geometric thinking of the children. The task is to sort various random geometric shapes (see Black-Line Masters 17.2, 17.3, 17.4, 17.5, and 17.6) into different groups.

MISCONCEPTION

Young children at the visualization level may recognize only equilateral triangles as triangles because their experience in viewing and identifying triangles has consisted exclusively of equilateral triangles. In Figure 17.4 you can see a first-grade student's attempts to draw as many different triangles as possible. Despite their appearances, all the triangles are equilateral triangles. Also note that all the triangles are oriented so that the bases are parallel to the bottom edge of the paper. Experiences with many types of triangles are needed so that children see that any shape with only three sides and three angles must be a triangle. The change from simply identifying shapes to recognizing attributes of shapes is the developmental progress suggested by the van Hieles in Stage 1 (analysis).

Many books for children are excellent for identifying plane figures and their characteristics. Books featuring geometry are noted in the Children's Bookshelf at the end of this chapter. Students can take digital photographs of different shapes seen during a "shape" walk to display on a bulletin board or in a multimedia presentation. Written material can accompany photos on a bulletin board. Oral descriptions can be developed for a multimedia presentation.

Students may also draw their shapes for a shape book. Children enjoy making shape books or posters by cutting pictures from magazines. Sponges can be cut into geometric shapes, and students can use tempera paint to make designs with them. Large shapes can be outlined on the classroom floor with masking tape or painted permanently on the playground or multipurpose room floor so that children can walk around them. A shape scavenger hunt might be developed for the classroom or the entire school.

Experiences with physical models help children think about and visualize geometric figures. Shape puzzles and shape templates are often found in early childhood classes. Templates can be bought commercially or cut from plywood, fiberboard, cardboard, or recycled polystyrene meat trays. The templates and cut-out forms are useful for tracing, for puzzles, and for art projects. Activity 17.7 suggests how templates help children understand the characteristics of common geometric figures.

Many shapes convey meanings. In fact, identifying the meaning of shapes in the environment is an important step in literacy development. An activity with traffic signs helps children connect shapes with their meaning. Common traffic signs, pictured in Figure 17.5, can be purchased or drawn and can be used in discussion and in acting-out exercises:

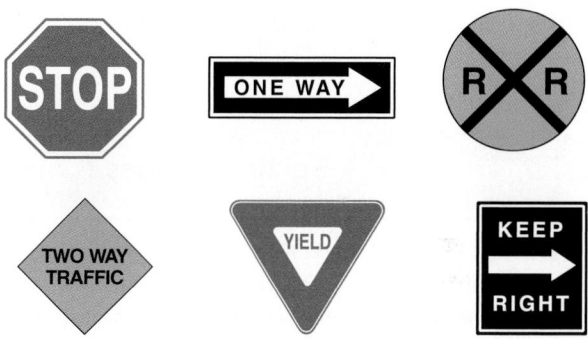

Figure 17.5 Common highway signs that children should become acquainted with by shape and color

- "Here is a round sign with a large X on it. Has anyone seen a sign like this? Where?" (Answer: At the railroad track.) "What does the X mean you should do?" (Answer: Be careful; look before you cross.) "What other signals have you seen at the railroad crossing that tells you to stop?"

- "Here are two more signs. One of them is red and has eight sides. What word is on this sign?" (Answer: Stop.) "What do the word, the color, and the sign tell you to do? How many sides does the yellow sign have?" (Answer: Three.) "It has the word *yield* on it. What does *yield* mean?" (Answer: Look to see if something is coming before moving ahead.) "What should you do if you see this sign?" (Answer: Look before you go.)

Figure 17.4 A first-grade student's triangles

A geoboard is another learning aid for shape identification. Geoboards have square grid patterns of 25, 36, or more pegs, or pegs in the shape of a circle. Rubber bands are stretched around the pegs to form shapes and designs. Larger boards allow students to construct several figures at the same time. Geoboard pattern paper should be available so that children can record their geoboard figures (see Black-Line Masters 17.7 and 17.8). Primary-grade students gain an intuitive understanding of plane figures, points, and line segments as they make and talk about the geoboard figures. Older students use geoboards to study different types of triangles, quadrilaterals, and other figures and to learn about regular and irregular figures, concave and convex figures, congruence, similarity, and symmetry.

Children commonly study polygons along with circles and ellipses in elementary school. **Polygons** are closed figures with no curved lines. They are named for the number of sides in the polygon: triangle (3), quadrilateral (4), pentagon (5), hexagon (6),

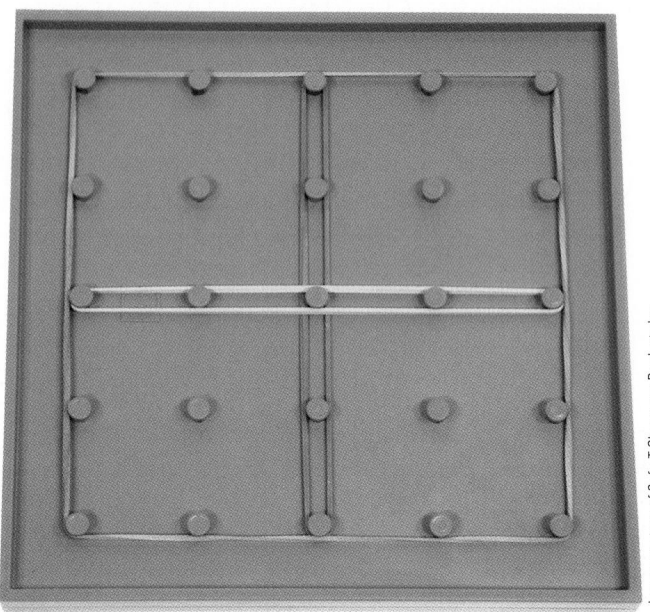

Geoboard

Image courtesy of Safe-T Classroom Products Inc.

ACTIVITY 17.6 Sorting Shapes (Communication)

Level: Grades 1–5

Setting: Pairs of students

Objective: Students sort random geometric shapes into groups, using various schemes to differentiate between the shapes.

Materials: Geometric shapes cut from Black-Line Masters 17.2–17.6

- Before cutting out the shapes from the black-line masters, it is best to laminate them to increase their durability. Lamination will also make the pieces easier for younger children to manipulate.

- For younger children, perhaps shapes 1–9 or 1–15 will be sufficient for the activity. Older children will be able to use all the shapes without becoming overwhelmed with so many figures.

- Pass out a set of shapes to each pair of students, and ask them to place the shapes into groups. They may use as many different groups as they wish, and not all shapes need to be included in the groups that students devise.

- As students form groups with their shapes, ask them to write a sentence about the group and which shapes they put into that group.

- Some students may be distracted by the numbers on the shapes or may group shapes using the numbers. To avoid any difficulties with the numbers on the shapes, you might ask students to keep the shapes number side down.

- Once students have sorted their shapes, ask for pairs of students to place their groups of shapes on the overhead projector and then challenge the rest of the class to determine their criteria for forming the group. Younger children will focus on number of sides, resemblance to familiar shapes, and the like. Older children may focus on parallel sides, angle measure, diagonals, and symmetry.

- Children of all ages will use criteria that are not straightforward geometric relationships to sort their shapes, as the two student examples here demonstrate.

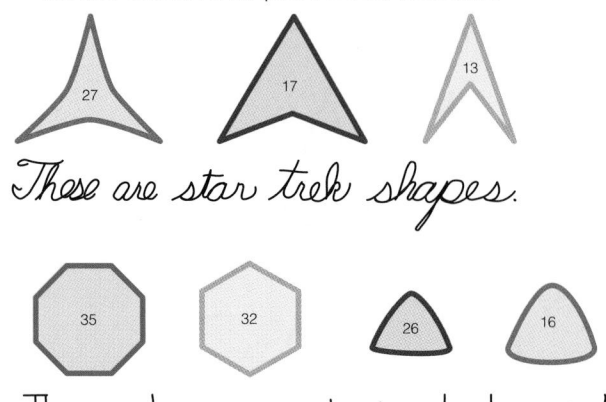

heptagon (7), octagon (8), enneagon (9), decagon (10). A **regular polygon**, such as a square, equilateral triangle, or regular hexagon, has congruent sides *and* congruent angles. Figure 17.6 illustrates

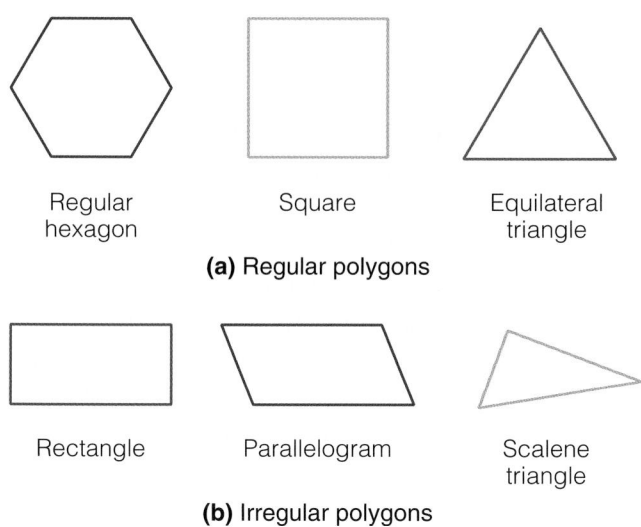

(a) Regular polygons

Regular hexagon | Square | Equilateral triangle

(b) Irregular polygons

Rectangle | Parallelogram | Scalene triangle

Figure 17.6 Polygons

several regular and irregular polygons. Activity 17.8 uses exemplars to help students clarify their conception of polygon. The activity also suggests a means to assess students' understandings.

Points, Lines, Rays, Line Segments, and Angles

As children learn about two- and three-dimensional shapes, they also encounter geometric elements such as points, lines, rays, line segments, and line intersections, which provide the foundation for Euclidean geometry. The abstract nature of geometric points and lines makes them difficult for many children to understand fully. For this reason young children learn about geometric shapes and their attributes *before* learning about points, lines, rays, and angles. A **point** is actually a location in space that has no dimension; a **line** is a set of points that extends infinitely. This description of a line allows for curved and straight lines. In general, at the elementary level all lines in geometry are assumed to be straight lines

---

ACTIVITY 17.7 Feeling and Finding Shapes

Level: Grades K–2

Setting: Small groups or individual

Objective: Students determine shapes by touch and identify by characteristics.

Materials: Geometric templates and shapes cut from them

- Give the templates and cut-out shapes to students, and have them run their fingers around the hole and along the edges of several shapes.
- Let them put their shapes into templates.
- Blindfold a child (or ask to close eyes). Have the child feel the outlines of shapes and identify the matching template. Repeat with other students.
- After the activity, ask students to tell how they knew which shape would fit. Probe for specific characteristics.

- Accept their descriptions of the shapes.
- Ask them to compare a selected shape to a circle and one shape to another. Write their observations about each shape on a chart or table.

Variations

- Have students find shapes that fit into templates in their home (e.g., door into door frame, picture into picture frame).
- Have students find pictures in magazines that show shapes, and make a picture book of shapes. Each child can make one, or the class can make a book together.

unless otherwise specified. The concepts of infinity (∞) and something that has no dimensions are difficult ideas to conceptualize until age 11 and older. However, children can learn something about these abstract ideas through real objects and picture representations. Activity 17.9 uses real materials to represent points, rays, and line segments.

A point can be represented by a dot, an infinite line by arrows on both ends of a drawn segment, a line segment as part of a line with a dot at each end, and a ray as part of a line with a dot at one end and an arrow at the other end (Figure 17.7). (Again, lines can also be curved, although the term *line* usually means a straight line in most geometry texts.)

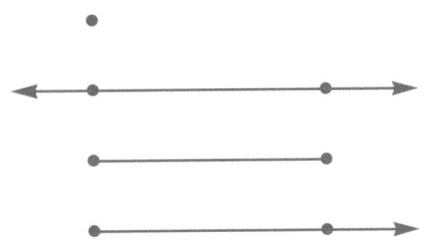

Figure 17.7 Representations of (from top to bottom) a point, a line, a segment, and a ray

Two rays with the same endpoint form an angle. Two children can form angles with their bodies by lying on the floor with their feet at the same vertex

point. If their heads are close together, their bodies form an acute angle; if their heads are far apart, their bodies form an obtuse angle. If they lie down on perpendicular lines with their feet at the same point, their bodies form a 90° angle.

Oak tag segments joined at one end with a metallic paper fastener make good models of angles. In Figure 17.8 the oak tag segments show (a) an obtuse angle (greater than 90°), (b) an acute angle (less than 90°), and (c) a right angle (90°). Flexible soda straws can also represent angles. When the end of one flexible straw is fitted into the opposite end of another flexible straw, the flexible part of the straw serves as an effective vertex for the straw angle. This technique is used in Activity 17.10. Notice that in this activity children designate one of three angle categories for the angles. They do not stipulate a degree measure. Degree measure is a topic for older children.

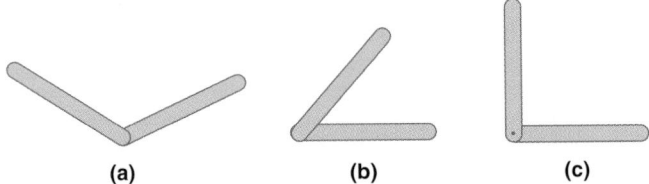

(a)   (b)   (c)

Figure 17.8 Oak tag segments joined by a fastener to represent (a) an obtuse angle, (b) an acute angle, and (c) a right angle

---

ACTIVITY 17.8 **What Is a Polygon? (Assessment Activity)**

- -

Level: Grades 1–4

Setting: Pairs of students or individual

Objective: Students develop a visual concept of polygon by examining polygons and nonpolygons.

Materials: Geometric figures sheet

- Pass out exemplars sheet to students.
- Have students use the exemplars sheet to designate the five polygons in a set of 10 geometric figures.
- Have students display their polygon selections to the class and explain their choices.

Extension

- Older students might compose a definition of polygon using the exemplar sheet. After several students have shared their definition with the class, students can discuss the various definitions and develop a class definition.

Assessment

- After the class has heard and critiqued several potential definitions, have each student write a definition of polygon in his or her notebook.

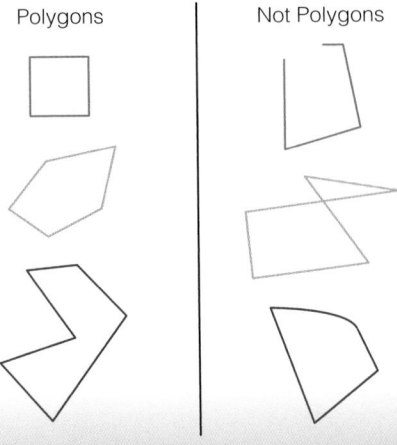

Polygons   Not Polygons

ACTIVITY 17.9   Lines, Segments, and Rays

Level: Grades 1–3
Setting: Whole group or small groups
Objective: Students model lines, line segments, and rays.
Materials: Yarn, twine

- Take the students to a playing field. Stretch a skein of yarn or ball of twine across the field as far as it will go.

- Have the students line up across the field and hold onto the string to keep it taut. Tell them that the string is part of a line that keeps going forever, even after the string comes to an end. Ask what the line would touch as it moved beyond each end of the string.

- Each student touching the string is a point on the line, and the space between each pair of them is a line segment, or part of the line.

- Name points after the children, for example, Latasha, Jamal, Sera, Jason. Name line segments by calling the names of students: line segment Latasha-Jason. The named students hold onto the string, and the students between them let go. This shows how long each line segment is. Let students take turns calling pairs of names to identify line segments.

- Ask students to remember which students are standing on either side of them. Return to the classroom, and draw a picture of a line and points on the chalkboard. Put an arrow at each end to indicate that the line keeps going in both directions. Ask students to label the points on the lines with their names.

- Ask the students to describe how the chalkboard line represents their experience outdoors. (Answer: The arrows show that the line goes on without end. The points where students' names appear show that a line segment has definite ends. Two names identify specific segments.)

- Ask students to write the names for two different segments.

- Draw a picture of a ray. Ask the students to tell what they see and what they think a ray is. (Answer: A ray includes an endpoint and all points extending in one direction from that point.)

- Relabel the chalk drawing with A, B, C, D, . . . in place of the students' names. Introduce how to write line, segment, and ray (notation).

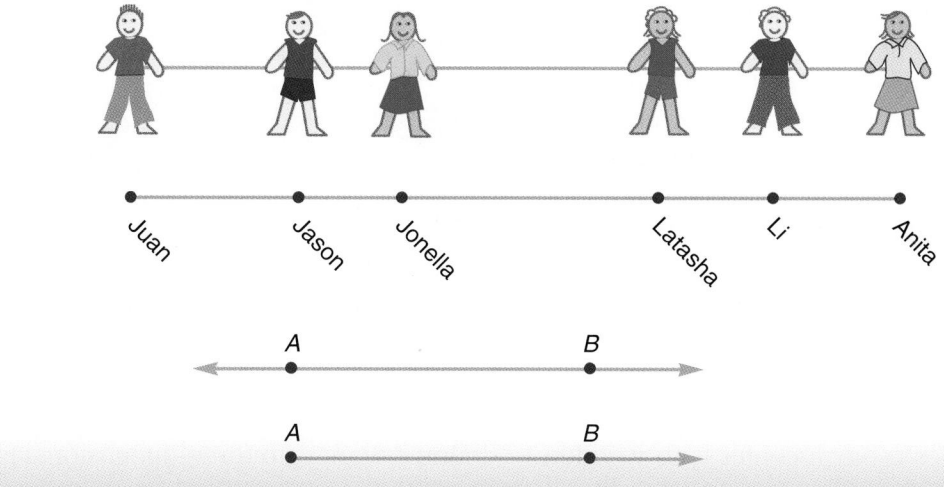

Another angle activity is done with paper plates. Provide each student with paper plates on which the center has been marked. Students cut straight lines from the outside edge to the center to make acute, right, and obtuse angles. Pose challenges to older children such as these: "Can you cut a plate so that you have one obtuse and three acute angles? Can you cut a single plate so you have a right, an acute, and an obtuse angle?" Children can also challenge each other to make different combinations of angles. Older students learn the standard way to label angles. When rays *BA* and *BC* meet at point *B*, as shown in Figure 17.9, children learn that this angle can be named either ∠*ABC* or ∠*CBA*.

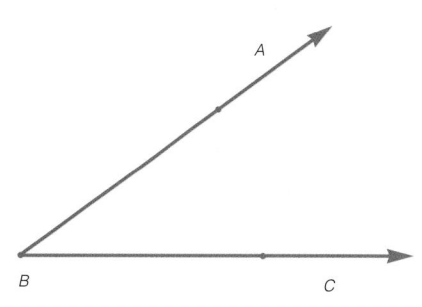

Figure 17.9 Angle *ABC* or angle *CBA*

ACTIVITY 17.10   Name My Angle

Level: Grades 2–4

Setting: Large groups

Objective: Students develop visual discrimination for acute, right, and obtuse angles.

Materials: Two flexible straws fashioned into an angle

- Draw an acute, a right, and an obtuse angle on the board.
- Ask students to name each angle.
- Write the name of each angle beneath it.
- Hold up the flexible straw angle for students to see.
- Quickly ask one student to name the angle you show.

- If a student gives the incorrect answer, give the correct one, and quickly form another angle.
- Ask another student for the correct name of the new angle formed by the straws.
- If a student answers correctly, repeat the name, and quickly form another angle.
- After a few minutes of angle identification, ask several student volunteers how they can tell the difference between acute, right, and obtuse angles.

Geometry in Three Dimensions: Space Figures

Children have daily experiences with three-dimensional objects. Classroom activities with space figures for children at van Hiele Stage 0 (visualization) build on early experiences by using common three-dimensional models in familiar settings. A classroom grocery store contains boxes with many shapes and sizes. Cans are cylinders; cereal boxes are rectangular prisms; specialty boxes are collected to provide experiences with cones and pyramids. A scavenger hunt can be a search outside school for three-dimensional figures for a classroom collection and display. Formal terms such as *cylinder* and *rectangular prism* are not necessary immediately but are introduced gradually as mathematical terminology for objects that may be described by students as "rollers" and "boxes."

In primary grades a block center with wooden or plastic blocks provides opportunities to construct three-dimensional structures. Older students also benefit from work with blocks—either standard blocks or desk sets of blocks—to construct houses, cities, furniture for dolls, or abstract arrangements. The companion website activity "Solid-Shape Search" involves children in finding real-life objects that resemble models of solids, such as a cereal box that resembles a model of a rectangular prism or a tennis ball that resembles a sphere.

Analyzing and combining three-dimensional shapes is an important spatial objective. An art project in which children build three-dimensional collages from small cereal boxes and bathroom tissue and paper towel tubes gives them an opportunity to combine and rearrange three-dimensional figures.

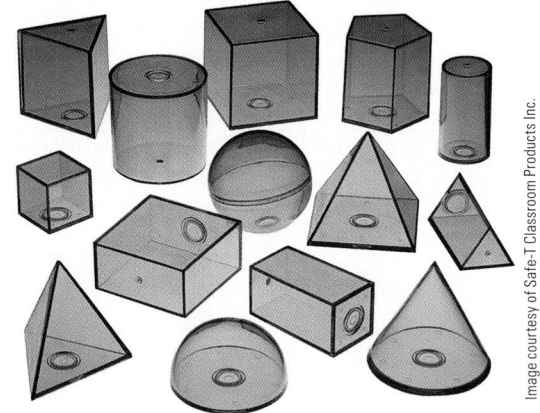

Geometry solids

Image courtesy of Safe-T Classroom Products Inc.

Glue and tempera paints are the only materials needed. Some constructions may look like trucks or boats; others may be more fanciful. Simple carpentry projects using odds and ends of lumber also let children work with three-dimensional forms.

Children can build solids using clay or plasticine. Younger children simply make and talk about their creations; older children investigate the cross-sections of the various figures (Figure 17.10). Depending on which three-dimensional solid is cut and how it is cut, the plane surfaces of the cross-sections are circles, ellipses, squares, triangles, rectangles, or

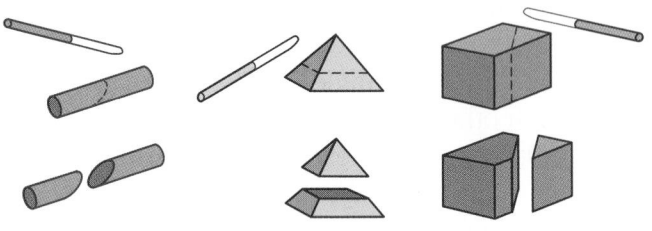

Figure 17.10 Clay shapes and cross-sections

other shapes. Older children may compile a table of the cross-section shapes that were formed by checking either yes or no next to each of the potential cross-sections.

Cross-Sections of a Cube	Yes	No
Isosceles triangle	Yes	No
Equilateral triangle	Yes	No
Scalene triangle	Yes	No
Square	Yes	No
Rectangle	Yes	No
Rhombus	Yes	No
Trapezoid	Yes	No
Pentagon	Yes	No
Hexagon	Yes	No
Octagon	Yes	No

Polyhedrons are space figures made up of plane faces. *Poly* and *hedron* are Greek terms meaning "many" and "seat" (formed by two flat surfaces), so *polyhedron* means "many flat surfaces." Commercial materials such as Geofix Shapes are available for constructing three-dimensional shapes. Students can make their own space figures with tagboard and other materials. Plastic soda straws and chenille pipe cleaners cut in 2-inch lengths can be used for an interesting investigation with solid figures. Children can build polyhedrons using gumdrops or mini-marshmallows for vertex points and coffee stirrers as edges. Display or demonstrate a figure built with such materials, and give students the opportunity to build their own polyhedrons. A pyramid formed by connecting four coffee stirrers to four gumdrops is easiest to make. Ask children to describe the solid (e.g., "It has four congruent faces that are the same size and shape; it has four vertices; it has six edges.")

Children should be encouraged to use proper terms when describing a polyhedron or its parts.

> **MISCONCEPTION**
>
> Many times children (and most adults) will use *side* when they mean a surface or face of the polyhedron. To help students use the correct term, teachers can contrast the side of a square with the face of a cube.

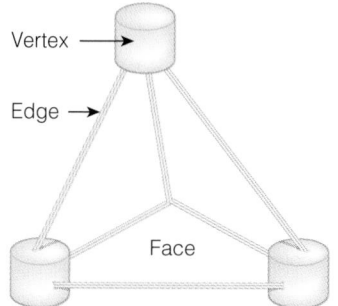

Geometric Properties: Congruence and Similarity

Two polygons are **congruent** if one fits exactly on the other. If all points on one line segment match exactly with all points on another segment, they are congruent. Any two plane or space figures are congruent when all their corresponding points match exactly. When children organize blocks by stacking the ones that fit on top of each other on the same shelf, they are demonstrating congruence. As students stack up the yellow pattern blocks in a tower, they are showing that all the yellow blocks are congruent. When students separate pattern blocks into their respective shapes, they are demonstrating congruence. Congruence is also used in linear and area measurement. The width of a desk is matched to 37 centimeter cubes lined up, and the area can be measured by covering the top with congruent squares. Students could use 37 different centimeter cubes to find another desk with the same width and use the same number of congruent squares to find a desk with the same area. Recognizing the congruence of length and area measurement units in geometry is a key to success in measurement. Uniform standard measures are based on the recognition of congruence; the meter is still a meter whether measured with 10 decimeters or 100 centimeters.

> At the entrance of his school, the Academy, Plato erected this sign: "Let No One Ignorant of Geometry Enter Here."

Two polygons are **similar** when they have the same shape. When they have the same shape, they have congruent corresponding angles and their corresponding sides are all in the same ratio. Two regular polygons with the same number of sides must be similar. Regular polygons have all sides the same length and all angles the same size. Equilateral triangles and squares are regular figures. All squares and equilateral triangles are similar, because all squares have 90° angles and all equilateral triangles have 60° angles, and each pair of corresponding sides between two squares or between two equilateral triangles will show the same ratio. Quadrilaterals, pentagons, hexagons, or other polygons can be similar but are not necessarily so, because their angles may not be congruent and their corresponding side lengths may have different ratios. The two quadrilaterals shown here are similar. Note that their corresponding angles are congruent ($\angle A \cong \angle W$,

$\angle B \cong \angle X$, $\angle C \cong \angle Y$, $\angle D \cong \angle Z$). The corresponding side lengths have the same ratio, thus

$$\frac{AB}{WX} \cong \frac{BC}{XY} \cong \frac{CD}{YZ} \cong \frac{DA}{ZW}$$

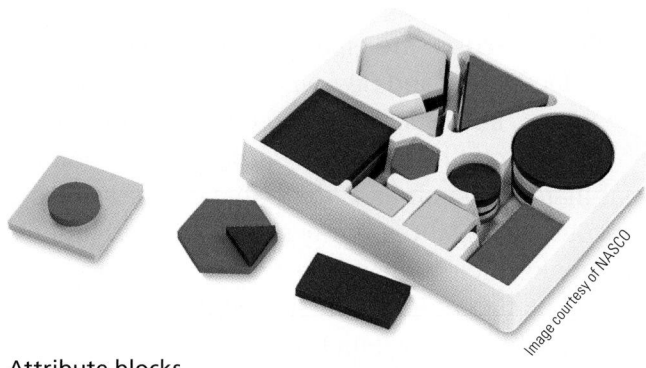

Children will find many examples of similarity as they work with the concepts of big and small. A set of counting bears contains small, medium, and large bears that have the same shape and proportions but different sizes, as do the porridge bowls in *Goldilocks and the Three Bears* or the size of the doghouses in *La Quintetta*. Congruent and similar polygons are shown in Figure 17.11.

Younger children recognize similar figures by inspection and will not give any explicit attention to congruent angles or the lengths of corresponding sides. Children's understanding of congruence and similarity grows through activities with geometry materials. A typical attribute block set of 60 blocks includes blocks of five shapes, three colors, two thicknesses, and two sizes, as shown in the photo. Each block has a unique combination of four attributes: shape, color, thickness, and size. Initially, children often sort with shape as the distinguishing attribute. They put the 60 pieces into subsets consisting of circles, squares, rectangles, triangles, and hexagons. The teacher can foster thinking about

size and shape with questions. "Why did you sort the blocks this way?" prompts children to explain that the pieces in each set have the same shape. "Are all the circles exactly the same size?" prompts them to notice and talk about the fact that some are large and some are small. Third- and fourth-graders can use the terms *congruent* and *similar* to describe their sorting. The teacher may point out that a large red square and a large blue square are congruent and that a large blue (or red) square and a small red square are similar. The teacher can then ask the children to identify other examples of congruent and similar shapes.

Image courtesy of NASCO

Attribute blocks

❷XERCISE

Sketch three sets of pentagonal or hexagonal shapes: one that demonstrates congruence, one that demonstrates similarity, and one that shows neither congruence nor similarity. Compare your drawings with those of three other students in the class. ●●●

Figure 17.11 Congruent and similar polygons

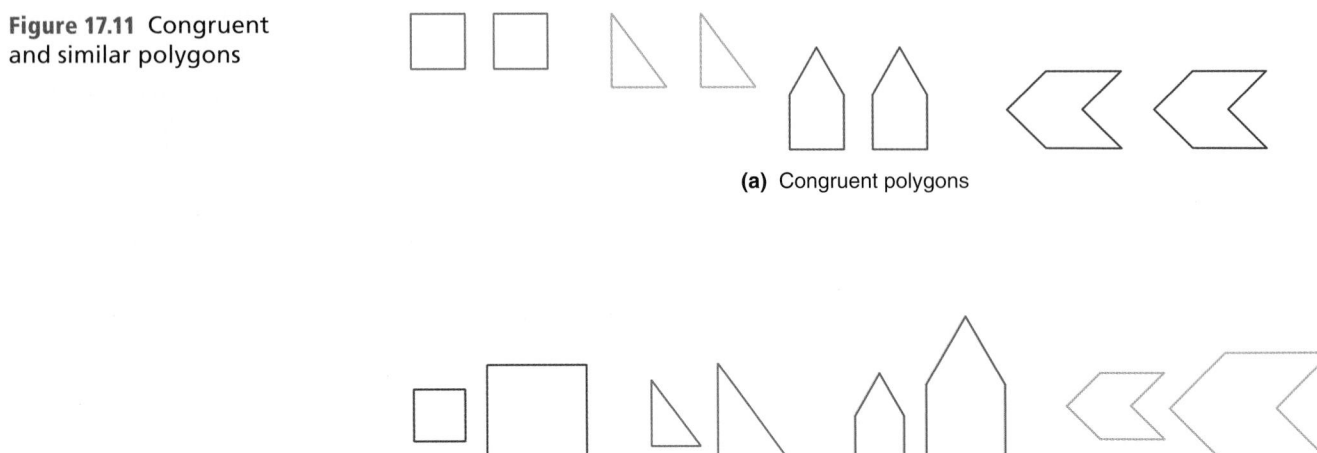

(a) Congruent polygons

(b) Similar polygons

Geometric Properties: Symmetry

As children work with pattern blocks, they often create designs by adding a shape to one side of an imaginary line and the same shape to the opposite side. Another common design is one that has four or six spokes around the center. In both cases children are demonstrating the geometric concept of **symmetry**.

Symmetry is often easier to show than to define. Children may say that something "looks the same on both sides" or "turns around the middle." Explorations and investigations help children develop an appreciation of symmetry in art and enable them to find examples in natural and human-made objects. Many commercial products use logos with line and/or rotational symmetry (see Figure 17.12). Understanding all facets of symmetry requires many experiences with

Figure 17.12 Some common logos that use symmetry

real objects and geometric manipulatives. Activities 17.11 and 17.12 take advantage of children's natural affinity for symmetry in their explorations.

Children often make patterns and structures that have balance and symmetry; this tendency may reflect the pattern-making nature of the brain to make order out of chaos. Sorting pattern block designs as symmetric or asymmetric can be done at the object level with blocks or at the pictorial level with stamped images, cutouts, or tracings. Pictures can then be placed on bulletin boards for students to classify. While children work with materials, they also talk and write about their products.

Children can find many examples of symmetry in their everyday lives. Logos of many automobile brands are symmetric, as are brand logos of other common products (see Figure 17.12). Many objects in nature, such as butterflies and flowers, have symmetry. Students can make a picture album or class book of logos, graphic and human-made objects, and natural objects and indicate whether objects have line or point symmetry or both. Many computer draw-and-paint programs have a feature called

MULTICULTURALCONNECTION

Some symmetry designs can be found in Navajo rug patterns, mandala designs, and baskets from many cultures.

Image courtesy of Safe-T Classroom Products Inc.

Pattern in a Navajo rug

ACTIVITY 17.11 Blob Art

Level: Grades K–4

Setting: Individual

Objective: Students create personal examples of symmetric designs.

Materials: 12 inch × 18 inch art paper, paints, small mirrors (optional), string

- Have the students fold their art paper in half.

- Have them put dabs of different colors of paint on one side of the paper. Fold the other half of the paper over onto the still-wet painted side and smooth it.

- Open the paper to see the design. After the papers are dry, make a bulletin board of the pictures. Some students may want to decorate the pictures by adding the same lines to both sides.

- Have an unbreakable mirror or Mira available for students to place on the fold. Discuss the fact that the mirror image is the same as the design hidden behind the mirror. Tell the students that the line along the fold is a line of symmetry. It divides the design into two identical halves.

Variation

- Dip a string in the paint. Curl the string around on one side of the paper. Fold the clean half over the string and hold it down gently while pulling the string from the folded paper.

ACTIVITY 17.12   Geoboard Symmetry

Level: Grades 2–6
Setting: Individual
Objective: Students explore symmetry with a geoboard.
Materials: Geoboard, rubber bands

- Ask students to use their rubber bands to "make something that will fly."

- Once all students have finished, have students show their designs to one another.

- Ask students what it is that most designs have in common. (Answer: They show line symmetry.)

- Ask students to explain why a few designs may not be symmetric. Students who show a top-down view of their object will have a design with line symmetry. Students with a side view will not.

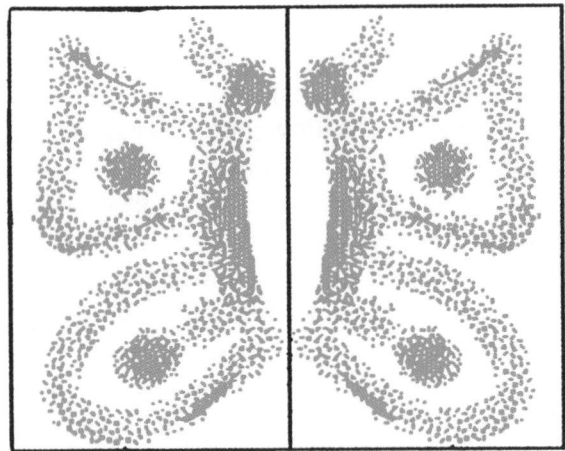

Figure 17.13 Symmetric design from a computer printout

Mirrors that allows children to create designs that contain lines of symmetry. Figure 17.13 illustrates a design created with such a program. Even the letters of the alphabet from different computer fonts and/or cultures offer an intriguing investigation of line and point symmetry and graphic design history.

Elementary students can recognize both line symmetry and rotational symmetry. **Line symmetry** can be visualized by considering a Hanukkah menorah (Figure 17.14a). If a symmetry line is drawn down the menorah's stem, each side of the symmetry line is a mirror image of the other. Every example of line symmetry produces mirror images that can be "folded" along the symmetry line onto one another.

The second symmetry type, **point** or **rotational symmetry**, can be visualized by considering a sunflower that is rotated about its center (Figure 17.14b). As it is turned, the appearance is virtually unchanged; the sunflower is symmetric around the center point.

> **MISCONCEPTION**
>
> Many students mistakenly conclude that if a figure is divided into two congruent parts by a line, then the line must be a symmetry line. To help students overcome this misconception, they should have many experiences examining figures such as a rectangle with a diagonal, in which the line divides the rectangle into two congruent parts, but the diagonal is not a symmetry line. In this case the diagonal fails the fold test.

Figure 17.14 (a) A Hanukkah menorah shows line symmetry; (b) a sunflower shows point or rotational symmetry.

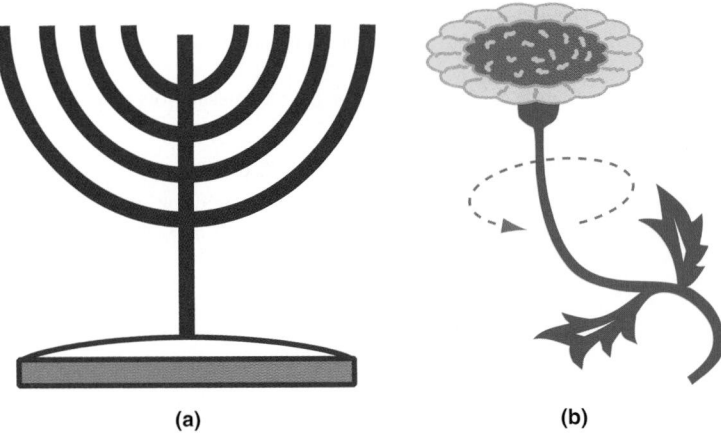

(a)   (b)

Symmetry introduces children to flips. When children make "dab" patterns, such as the one illustrated in Activity 17.11, the right half of the paper is "flipped" to create the symmetric pattern of paint on the left half. The two parts of the symmetric design are reflections of each other. In Activity 17.12 students make a free-form design on a geoboard, then check the design for line symmetry.

EXERCISE

Draw all the symmetry lines of the quadrilaterals in Figure 17.15. ●●●

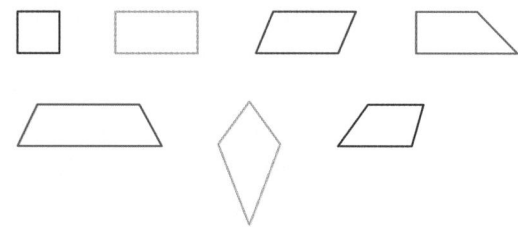

Figure 17.15 Quadrilaterals

EXERCISE

Compare the symmetry lines in an equilateral triangle, square, regular pentagon, and regular hexagon. How do you think the lines of symmetry in regular figures with an odd number of sides compare to the lines of symmetry in regular figures with an even number of sides? Children can find many examples of symmetry in their everyday lives. ●●●

MULTICULTURALCONNECTION

Ask students to explore symmetry using letters and fonts from their native language.

EXERCISE

Draw two examples of designs that have line symmetry and two examples of point or rotational symmetry. Compare your two examples with a classmate's drawings. ●●●

Teaching and Learning About Transformational Geometry

Motion, or transformational, geometry focuses on how shapes and objects appear as they are moved about in space. Although their orientation changes,

the shapes themselves remain the same. **Translations** are sliding motions, **rotations** are turning motions, and **reflections** are flipping motions. *Slide, turn,* and *flip* are terms often used in elementary school; however, the terms *translation, rotation,* and *reflection* should be introduced as well.

Flips, turns, and slides are an integral part of working with tangram pieces (see Figure 17.16). Some writers claim that an old folktale relates the origin of the first tangram. In ancient China an emperor was carrying a square tile; he dropped it and saw it break into seven pieces. In the process of recreating the tile, he found that he could assemble the pieces to form many shapes besides the original square.

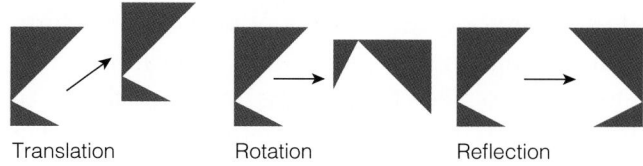

Translation   Rotation   Reflection

Figure 17.16 Translation, rotation, and reflection

EXERCISE

Using a book, pencil, or an object from you pocket or purse, demonstrate a slide, a flip, and a turn. Which of these transformations changes the orientation of the figure in the plane? ●●●

Although classroom sets of plastic tangram pieces are commercially available, children can trace them and cut the seven pieces from colored art board (see Black-Line Master 17.12). The seven tangram pieces can be used to make many recognizable shapes, such as boats and birds, as well as fanciful figures. Figure 17.17 illustrates how to assemble the pieces to form a square and three other designs. Children can be challenged to use the seven pieces to make a design or figure of their own.

Tangrams from commercial sources may have all the pieces of a design outlined on the easier task cards, with more difficult designs having only the outline of an entire figure. Children's original designs, copied on 5 × 8 index cards, may be added to the commercial designs. Young children can begin with designs requiring only two or three tangram pieces. As they gain experience, they complete five-, six-, and seven-piece designs.

Figure 17.17 Tangram figures

As children work with tangrams, geoboards, and nets, they constantly make transformational moves. The movements are a natural part of completing pictures or reproducing designs. When children form figures using tangram pieces, they slide, flip, and rotate pieces to place them in the proper position. All three motions, singly or in sequence, are involved in describing the moves. Children might describe the moves they make with one tangram piece as they are forming a tangram figure.

ⒺXERCISE

Can you assemble the purple figure in Figure 17.17 with tangram pieces? ●●●

Teaching and Learning About Coordinate Geometry

Places on a city map are often located using grid lines. The horizontal order (A, B, C, . . .) is joined, or coordinated, with the vertical order (1, 2, 3, . . .) to identify places on the map.

For instance, a school may be located on a map in the square labeled C-4. By looking across the map to C and up or down to 4, readers can find the school and its nearby streets and landmarks. This coordinate grid is a mathematical contribution of René Descartes (1596–1650) and is the basis for **coordinate geometry**, sometimes called **Cartesian geometry**.

Elementary school children can be introduced to the coordinate plane through activities that extend their use of number lines. Children use a single number line to show addition and subtraction by moving forward and backward on the line. The coordinate grid is formed by two number lines—one extending horizontally and the other vertically. The numbers or letters on each number line become the location markers for the coordinate grid. Activity 17.13 is designed to develop children's understanding of points and lines on the coordinate plane. It applies the coordinate plane to the classroom seating plan.

> One account of Descartes's life suggests that he first got the idea of coordinate geometry while lying in bed one morning, trying to describe the path of a fly crawling across his bedroom ceiling!

A square geoboard is arranged as a coordinate plane. Children who have worked with geoboards already know that its pegs form a grid, so naming the pegs with coordinate numbers is easily done. In Activity 17.14 children develop the guess-and-check problem-solving strategy by locating objects on the grid. A coordinate grid puzzle can be made by coloring various shapes on a 10 × 10 grid. Clues along each edge show how many spaces are filled in each line. Figure 17.18 shows one puzzle to be solved by

Find where the worm and two flowers are, using clues at edge of grid.

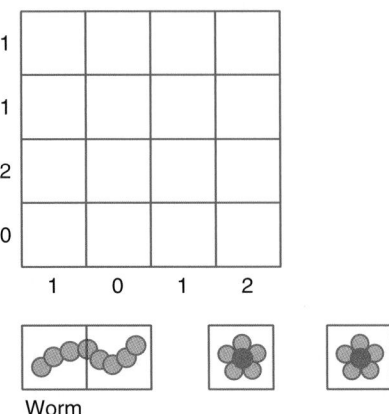

Figure 17.18 Coordinate grid puzzle

ACTIVITY 17.13 Coordinate Classroom

Level: Grades 3–6

Setting: Whole class

Objective: Students use their classroom seats to model coordinates.

Materials: Students in rows of classroom seats

- Ask students to line up their desks into vertical rows (columns) and horizontal rows.
- Establish the coordinate axes, as shown here, for the entire classroom.
- Demonstrate how to give the "address" of a student by using coordinates.
- Ask a student to stand at the origin and call out the coordinate addresses of students you name. Repeat for several more students.
- Ask students to give their coordinates from their seats.

Variation for Older Children

- Call out two pairs of coordinates, and ask those students to exchange seats or move into an empty seat.
- For older students the origin might be moved to produce negative coordinates.

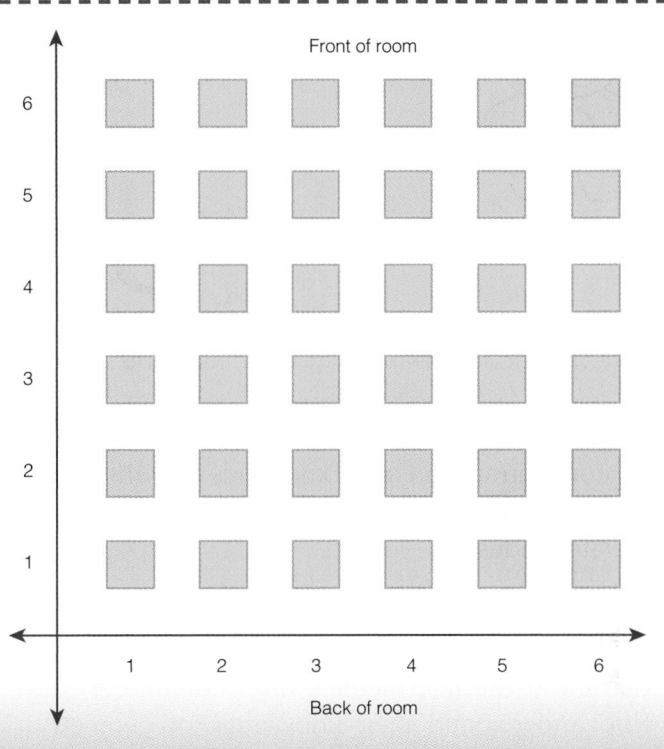

ACTIVITY 17.14 Find My Washer (Reasoning)

Level: Grades 1–4

Setting: Student pairs

Objective: Students locate objects on a coordinate grid using ordered pairs.

Materials: Geoboard for each partner, washers (painted two colors) to mark locations on the geoboard, barrier between partners

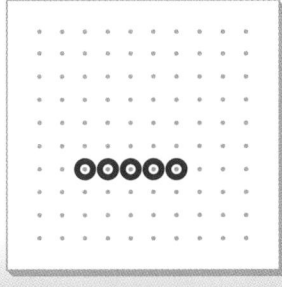

- Mark geoboards with numbers from 0 to 9 across the bottom and up the left side.
- One student secretly places five washers of one color in a row on pegs going vertically, horizontally, or diagonally.
- The second student, who cannot see the first board, makes guesses to locate the five washers. A guess consists of naming a point ("I guess point 2, 3") on the grid. The first student answers yes if there is a washer in that position. If there is not, the answer is no. Both students keep track of guesses by putting washers of the other color on "no" pegs.
- Ask students to create a scoring procedure. The game can be played competitively or noncompetitively.

coordinating the information given along each edge of the coordinate grid.

The coordinate grid can also be used to mark off a picture for a scale drawing. The picture is enlarged by drawing each piece of the grid on a large square and reassembling the result. Figure 17.19 shows a picture and portions of its enlarged version using coordinate squares. This activity can also be used

with older children when studying symmetry. The original figure and its enlargement are similar to each other.

Primary school children experience the many facets of geometry through a variety of engaging activities. They build, draw, explore, and design individual and composite geometric shapes in two and three dimensions. They enhance their spatial sense

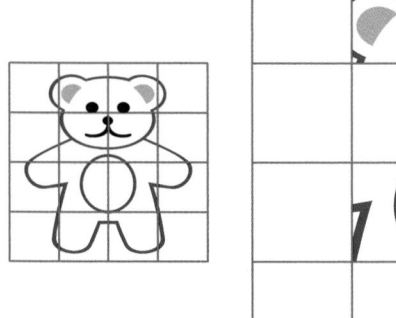
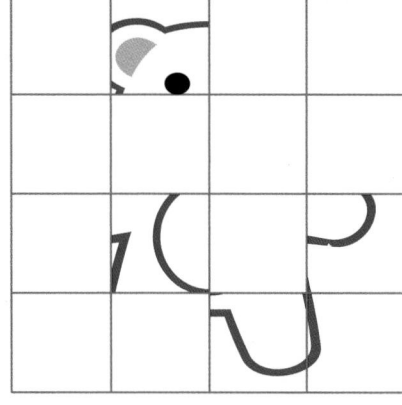

Figure 17.19 Scale drawing using coordinate grid

with activities that extend their sense of observation and concentration. Their experiences lay the foundation for extending geometry thinking in the intermediate grades.

Extending Geometry Concepts

Children at the intermediate level continue to develop and expand their knowledge of geometry. They still engage in activities to enhance their spatial sense, especially with the interplay of two- and three-dimensional representations. Topics that were introduced and considered at the visualization Van Hiele stage in earlier grades, such as similarity, symmetry, and transformations, are now studied in greater depth. New topics include dilations, the Pythagorean theorem, and formal coordinate geometry. These new topics are reflected in the NCTM geometry standards for older children.

NCTM Geometry Standard

Instructional programs from prekindergarten through grade 8 should enable all students to:

> Analyze characteristics and properties of two- and three-dimensional geometric shapes and develop mathematical arguments about geometric relationships

Grades 3–5 Expectations:

In grades 3–5 all students should:

- identify, compare, and analyze attributes of two- and three-dimensional shapes and develop vocabulary to describe the attributes;
- classify two- and three-dimensional shapes according to their properties and develop definitions of classes of shapes such as triangles and pyramids;
- investigate, describe, and reason about the results of subdividing, combining, and transforming shapes;
- explore congruence and similarity;
- make and test conjectures about geometric properties and relationships and develop logical arguments to justify conclusions.

Grades 6–8 Expectations:

In grades 6–8 all students should:

- precisely describe, classify, and understand relationships among types of two- and three-dimensional objects using their defining properties;
- understand relationships among the angles, side lengths, perimeters, areas, and volumes of similar objects;
- create and critique inductive and deductive arguments concerning geometric ideas and relationships, such as congruence, similarity, and the Pythagorean relationship.
> Specify locations and describe spatial relationships using coordinate geometry and other representational systems

Grades 3–5 Expectations:

In grades 3–5 all students should:

- describe location and movement using common language and geometric vocabulary;
- make and use coordinate systems to specify locations and to describe paths;
- find the distance between points along horizontal and vertical lines of a coordinate.

Grades 6–8 Expectations:

In grades 6–8 all students should:

- use coordinate geometry to represent and examine the properties of geometric shapes;
- use coordinate geometry to examine special geometric shapes, such as regular polygons or those with pairs of parallel or perpendicular sides.
> Apply transformations and use symmetry to analyze mathematical situations

Grades 3–5 Expectations:

In grades 3–5 all students should:

- predict and describe the results of sliding, flipping, and turning two-dimensional shapes;
- describe a motion or a series of motions that will show that two shapes are congruent;
- identify and describe line and rotational symmetry in two- and three-dimensional shapes and designs.

Grades 6–8 Expectations:

In grades 6–8 all students should:

- describe sizes, positions, and orientations of shapes under informal transformations such as flips, turns, slides, and scaling;
- examine the congruence, similarity, and line or rotational symmetry of objects using transformations.
> Use visualization, spatial reasoning, and geometric modeling to solve problems

Grades 3–5 Expectations:

In grades 3–5 all students should:

- build and draw geometric objects;
- create and describe mental images of objects, patterns, and paths;
- identify and build a three-dimensional object from two-dimensional representations of that object;
- identify and draw a two-dimensional representation of a three-dimensional object;
- use geometric models to solve problems in other areas of mathematics, such as number and measurement;
- recognize geometric ideas and relationships and apply them to other disciplines and to problems that arise in the classroom or in everyday life.

Grades 6–8 Expectations:

In grades 6–8 all students should:

- draw geometric objects with specified properties, such as side lengths or angle measures;
- use two-dimensional representations of three-dimensional objects to visualize and solve problems such as those involving surface area and volume;
- use visual tools such as networks to represent and solve problems;
- use geometric models to represent and explain numerical and algebraic relationships;
- recognize and apply geometric ideas and relationships in areas outside the mathematics classroom, such as art, science, and everyday life.

Students at these grade levels continue to improve their spatial sense through a variety of activities that use concrete manipulatives. Although children may have engaged in activities to improve their spatial sense in earlier grades, they benefit from activities that continue to extend their spatial sense. Activity 17.15 can be used with a wide range of students. The activity examines the Mobius strip, a shape with unusual properties, not the least of which is that it has only one side or surface (Figure 17.20). Students predict and then describe the resulting shapes that these activities with the Mobius strip can produce. A Mobius strip is formed by attaching the ends of a strip of paper to each other, much like a link in a paper chain. The only difference is that one end of the paper strip is twisted a half-turn (180°) before taping the ends together.

Figure 17.20 A Mobius strip

> **MISCONCEPTION**
>
> Many children expect squares to be oriented so that the top and bottom are parallel to the top and bottom of the geoboard. Thus they will not recognize a square that is oriented so that the square is in a *tilted* position. Children usually call such a shape a diamond and not a square, much as adults call a baseball playing field a diamond, when it is actually a square.

Activity 17.16 challenges students to find all the different-size squares on a geoboard. This activity helps children to recognize squares in a tilted orientation.

Children in the intermediate grades should be moving out of van Hiele Stage 0 (visualization) and into Stage 1 and Stage 2. All the activities in this section are adaptable for

ACTIVITY 17.15   The Mobius Strip

Level: Grades 2–6
Setting: Small groups
Objective: Children explore the properties of the Mobius strip.
Materials: Paper tape, transparent tape

- Have groups cut three strips of paper tape for each member of the group. The strips should be approximately 12 inches long and $1\frac{1}{2}$ inches wide.
- Demonstrate to the class how to create a Mobius strip.
- Have students create their own Mobius strips.
- Ask groups to perform the following explorations and record their findings. Before children perform each exploration, have them write out their predictions.
  1. Draw a line down the middle of the Mobius strip. Keep drawing until the line meets itself. (Predict before you draw.)
  2. Cut the Mobius strip along the whole length of the line in Step 1. (Predict before you cut.)
  3. Make another Mobius strip. This time twist one end with a full turn before taping. Draw a line down the middle of this new band and then cut along the entire line. (Predict before you draw and cut.)

- Have groups report their findings. How did their predictions compare with their results?

How closely do their recorded descriptions match their actual results?

Variation

- Older children use a new Mobius strip and draw a line $\frac{1}{3}$ of the width in from the edge of the band. Children will have to go around twice before the line meets itself. Now they can cut along the whole length of the line.
- Children tape two paper chain links together and cut along the dotted lines as shown here. Again, ask for a prediction before children perform the exploration.

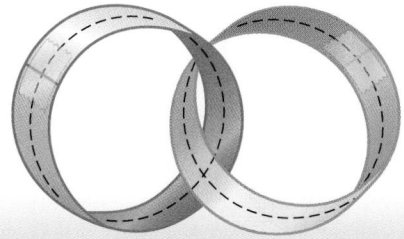

children working at van Hiele Stage 1 (identifying characteristics of each shape) and Stage 2 (looking for relationships among shapes).

Pentominoes are two-dimensional figures made by joining five equal-size squares in different ways. Twelve different pentominoes can be formed using combinations of five squares. In Activity 17.17 students try to form all the pentominoes. A common error that students make in this activity is to form reflections or rotations of previously found pentominoes. Figure 17.21 shows the same pentomino in different orientations. The second pentomino is a rotation of the first, and the third pentomino is a reflection of the first. In Activity 17.17 the focus is on finding all the pentominoes without any duplications resulting from rotations or reflections.

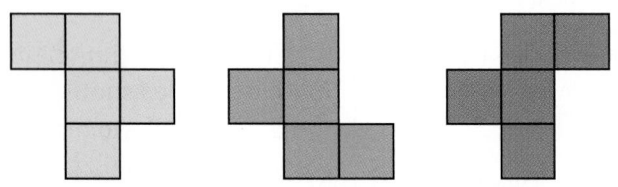

Figure 17.21 Equivalent pentominoes

EXERCISE

Which pentomino pieces do you believe can be folded into open boxes? Discuss this question with a classmate. Do you agree on your choices? How can you demonstrate which ones will fold into boxes? ●●●

Intermediate-grade children should include three-dimensional shapes in their spatial visualization activities. Moreover, the relationships between two-dimensional representations of three-dimensional figures should also be explored by means of work with isometric drawings (see Activity 17.2) and also with nets. A **net** is a two-dimensional shape that can be cut, folded, and taped to form a geometric solid. Certain pentominoes can be considered the nets of an open box. Some combinations of six squares can be folded into cubes, and others cannot. Students could use Geofix Shapes (or nets drawn and cut out from 1-inch graph paper) to

> German Renaissance artist Albrecht Dürer coined the word *net* for the two-dimensional representation of a three-dimensional figure. Dürer was among the first artists to study the geometry of perspective drawings.

ACTIVITY 17.16 Searching for Squares

Level: Grades 3–6

Setting: Pairs of students or individual

Objective: Students find all the different-size squares on a geoboard regardless of orientation.

Materials: Dot paper, geoboards, rubber bands

- Give each pair of students a geoboard, several rubber bands, and dot paper.
- Challenge students to find as many different-size squares as possible on their geoboard.
- Most students will find the four squares shown on the geoboard.
- Encourage students to look for other squares shown below the geoboard. Suggest that they change the orientation of the geoboard to help in their search.

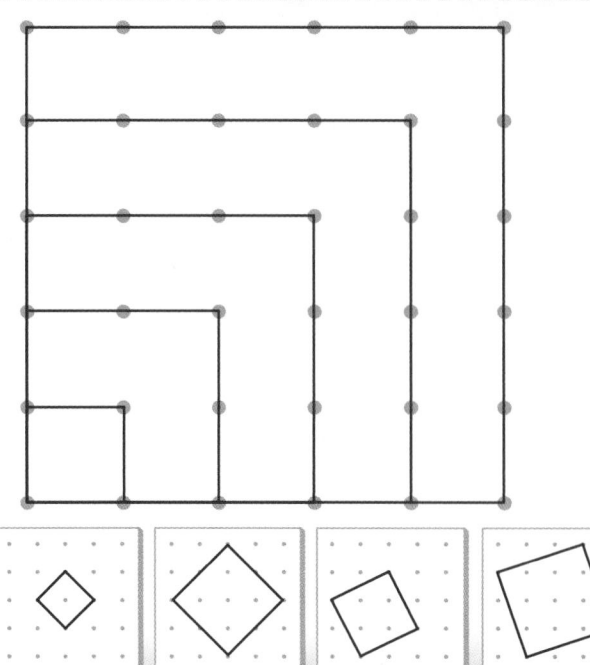

search for all the nets of a cube. See the companion website activity "Nets of a Cube."

Classifying Polygons

The earliest van Hiele stage is visualization, where children recognize some general forms of geometric shapes but make no analysis or comparisons between the shapes. Children at the intermediate-grade level begin to examine two- and three-dimensional shapes to determine their characteristics and critical attributes for identification. Squares and rectangles are familiar shapes to even young children. The activities for this section involve explorations with these and other familiar quadrilaterals. Activity 17.18 asks children to gather data about the attributes of various quadrilaterals. See the companion website activity "Exploring Diagonals of Quadrilaterals" for further explorations involving the diagonals of quadrilaterals. Activities 17.19 and 17.20 are designed for students who are entering the van Hiele analysis stage. In Activity 17.19 students create specific quadrilaterals out of a long piece of yarn and then defend their final result by referencing the attributes of the specific quadrilateral. In Activity 17.20 children try to categorize quadrilaterals in terms of their common attributes. In this activity children wrestle with deciding whether a square is always a rectangle or whether a rectangle is always a square.

Note that the template for the Venn diagrams in Activity 17.18 will accommodate trapezoids if the definition of a trapezoid is that it is a quadrilateral with *only* one pair of parallel sides. In this case a trapezoid is unlike any of the other quadrilaterals and so should be placed in one of the two separate circles in the Venn diagram. Some texts define a trapezoid as a quadrilateral *with at least* one pair of parallel sides. According to this definition a parallelogram (or rectangle, rhombus, or square) is a trapezoid (all

---

ACTIVITY 17.17 How Many Pentominoes?

Level: Grades 3–5
Setting: Small groups or individual
Objective: Students try to assemble the 12 different pentominoes.
Materials: Five square tiles, 1-inch graph paper

- Demonstrate to students how the square tiles must fit together.

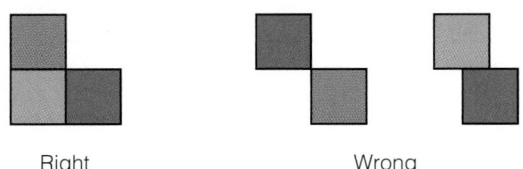

    Right   Wrong

- Challenge students to find all possible pentominoes by making an organized search.

- Students should sketch each of their combinations on graph paper.

- If a group cannot find all 12 pentominoes, they may send a representative to a group that has found them all. The visiting representative can look at the group's sketches and then return to relate which pentominoes are missing.

- Have students categorize their 12 pentominoes into several groups, using a scheme they devise. Ask a reporter to present the group's results and explain their categorization scheme. After finding all the pentominoes in this activity, students must provide an argument that there are no others. Some ineffective arguments will take the form of "We can't find any more pentominoes, so these are all there are." Probe for arguments that relate to possible combinations of pentominoes, such as "There is one pen-

tomino with five squares in a row," "There are only two pentominoes with four squares in a row," and so forth.

Extension

- Ask students to determine which 8 of the 12 pentominoes will fold up into a box with an open top. After students have categorized each pentomino as either able or not able to be folded into a box, allow groups to draw each pentomino on graph paper. They can then cut out each pentomino and verify whether it can be folded to form an open box. See the companion website activity "Nets of a Cube" for a similar activity involving the nets of a cube. Another companion website activity, "This Side Up," provides students with the opportunity to cut up boxes to form nets, which they then analyze.

ACTIVITY 17.18 Exploring Quadrilaterals

Level: Grades 4–6

Setting: Small groups

Objective: Children explore the properties of quadrilaterals.

Materials: rulers, protractors, quadrilateral shapes

- Have groups gather data from each quadrilateral.
- Groups should record their data in the table shown here with their findings.

- Discuss as a class the difference between these various quadrilaterals based on their findings.
- Post the results on the board with students reporting their findings from their group to fill in the grid.

Shape	Number of Pairs of Opposite Sides Parallel	Number of Pairs of Opposite Sides Congruent	Right Angles	Diagonals Congruent
Parallelogram				
Rectangle				
Rhombus				
Square				
Isosceles trapezoid				

ACTIVITY 17.19 Yarn Quadrilaterals

Level: Grades 3–5

Setting: Small groups

Objective: Students create large quadrilaterals out of yarn by using the appropriate attributes.

Materials: Yarn (30–40 feet for each group)

- This activity is best done in a large open area, such as the gymnasium or outside the classroom.
- Give each group of five students a length of yarn.
- Challenge students to use their entire length of yarn to form a specific quadrilateral. Select from the following list: parallelogram, rectangle, square, kite, rhombus, trapezoid.
- Suggest to students that they should justify their finished shape by referring to appropriate attributes and not simply because "it looks like it."
- Once students have formed a figure and provide a rationale for it being the correct shape, have them record in their journals the figure by name and diagram and the attributes they used to be sure the shape is correct.
- Repeat with other quadrilaterals.

ACTIVITY 17.20 **Categorizing Quadrilaterals**

Level: Grades 5–6
Setting: Small groups
Objective: Children categorize quadrilaterals.
Materials: Venn diagram sheet

- Give each student a copy of the Venn diagram shown here, and have them place in the diagram the following quadrilaterals: square, trapezoid, rectangle, rhombus, parallelogram, kite.

- Have students in each group compare their individual effort, and then design a Venn diagram for the entire group.

- When all groups are finished, have each group post their results and then discuss them with the entire class.

- Possible questions for discussion:
  - Is a rectangle always a square?
  - How is a rhombus like a square?
  - How are rectangles like squares?

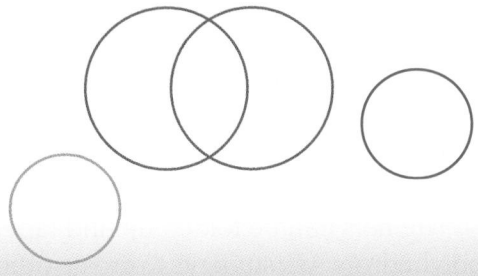

have at least one pair of parallel sides). The Venn diagram for this trapezoid definition would appear as follows. It is important for teachers to determine which of the definitions a text or state mathematics framework specifies and then select the correct diagram for this activity.

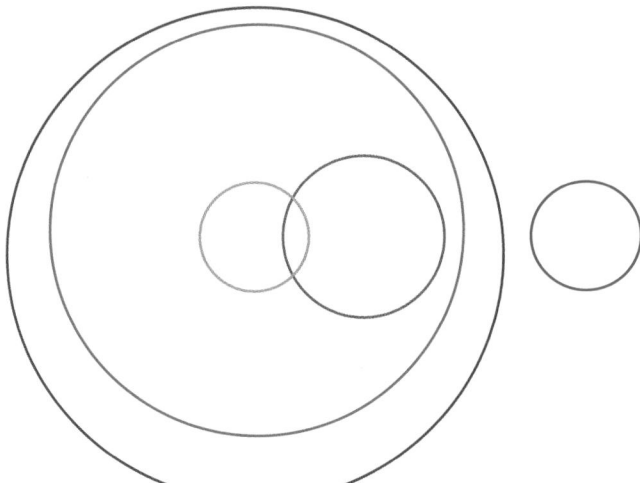

Children thinking at van Hiele Stage 0 or 1 have great difficulty categorizing a square as a rectangle. They view squares and rectangles as distinct polygons

Many geometric terms are derived from ancient Greek words that are related to the attributes of the figure. *Isosceles* is derived from Greek words meaning "equal legs"; *scalene* is taken from the Greek word for "uneven."

In the lower grades children work with various triangles and learn to recognize them by both angle and sides. Younger students use informal descriptions, but older students learn standard terms to describe triangles. The activity "Exploring Triangles" on the companion website describes a lesson on triangles for intermediate grades. Children create many different types of triangles during this activity and classify them. Triangles classified by their sides are equilateral, isosceles, or scalene. **Equilateral triangles** have three equal, or congruent, sides; **isosceles triangles** have two congruent sides; and **scalene triangles** have no congruent sides. Triangles can also be classified by their angles. **Right triangles** have a 90° angle. All angles in **acute triangles** are less than 90°; **obtuse triangles** have one angle larger than 90° (see Figure 17.22).

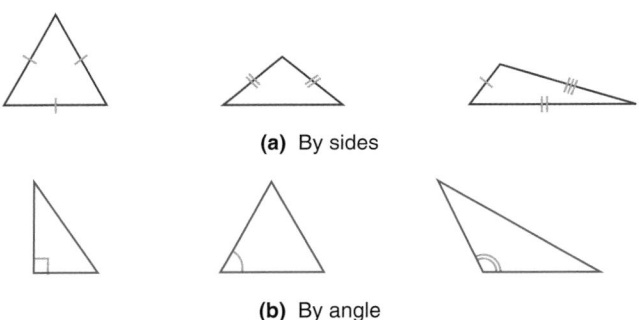

(a) By sides

(b) By angle

Figure 17.22 Classifying triangles

By the end of fifth or sixth grade, children should be able to name and describe the attributes of common polygons, see relationships between and among polygons based on attributes, and begin to categorize polygons according to their characteristics rather than their appearance.

Activity 17.21 is an assessment activity that examines children's process and results as they gather data about the number of diagonals in various polygons. They use their data to generate a conjecture about the pattern for the number of diagonals in polygons and then look for a number sentence or a formula to represent the number of diagonals in polygons.

Extending Geometry in Three Dimensions

At the upper elementary level children begin to analyze polyhedrons, find their surface areas and volumes, and explore relationships among them. A polyhedron with congruent faces, with the same number of faces meeting at each vertex, is a **regular** solid. There are five such regular solids. They are called *Platonic solids* after the Greek philosopher Plato, who lived about 428–348 B.C.E. The Platonic solids are shown in Figure 17.23: (a) a hexahedron, or cube, (b) a tetrahedron, (c) an octahedron, (d) a dodecahedron, and (e) an icosahedron. Tetrahedrons, hexahedrons, and octahedrons can reasonably be made with commonly used materials for making solid figures (see page 406). The other two Platonic solids, dodecahedrons and icosahedrons, have many faces and vertices and are tedious to assemble with any of these materials. Commercial materials such as Geofix Shapes are more suitable for building them. If such building materials are not available, students can cut out nets of the various polyhedrons (See Black-Line Masters 17.9, 17.10, and 17.11). The nets can be folded up and taped to form the polyhedron. Ask students to create other polyhedrons with their materials; then have them discuss and critique the figures.

Both commercial and teacher-made materials can help children visualize solid figures represented

---

ACTIVITY 17.21 **Diagonally Speaking (Assessment Activity)**

Level: Grades 4–6

Setting: Individuals

Objective: Students find a pattern associated with the number of sides and the number of diagonals in polygons.

Materials: Geoboard, rubber bands, unfinished table for recording answers

- Have students make the following figures on a geoboard: triangle, quadrilateral, pentagon. Use rubber bands to show the diagonals in each figure.

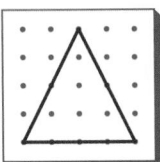 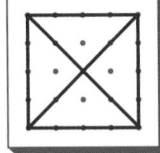 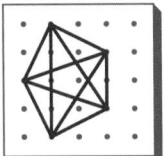

- Have students write the number of sides and diagonals for each figure in the table presented here.

Figure	Sides/Angles	Diagonals
Triangle	3	0
Quadrilateral	4	2
Pentagon	5	?
Hexagon	6	?
Heptagon	?	?
Octagon	?	?
Enneagon	?	?
Decagon	?	

- Now have the students make other figures, each one having one more side than the last. Have them write the number of sides and the number of diagonals for each of these new figures in the table.

- When at least six figures have been listed in the table, have the students study it to find a pattern. Ask the students to use the pattern to predict the number of diagonals in the remaining figures in the table.

- Ask students to explain how they found the number of diagonals in the figure with 10 sides.

- Have students develop a number sentence (formula) for finding the number of diagonals in a figure with any number of sides.

Figure 17.23 Regular solids:
(a) cube, or hexahedron;
(b) pyramid, or tetrahedron;
(c) octahedron;
(d) dodecahedron; and
(e) icosahedron

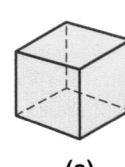 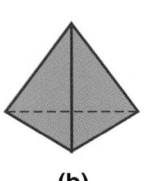 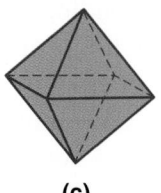 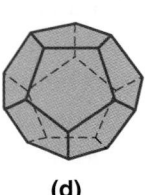 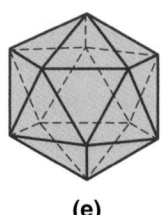

(a)   (b)   (c)   (d)   (e)

Image courtesy of Didax Educational Resources Inc.

Geofix Shapes

on a two-dimensional surface. Experiences relating real three-dimensional objects to their two-dimensional representations enhance children's spatial visualization capabilities.

ⒺXERCISE

A regular icosahedron is composed of 20 equilateral triangles. How many vertex points does an icosahedron have? ●●●

In Activity 17.22 children expand their spatial sense by examining three-dimensional figures for a pattern in the number of faces, edges, and vertices. The result is that children use their data to discover Euler's formula. Euler's formula is $V + F = E + 2$, where V represents the number of vertex points, F is the number of faces, and E is the number of edges. For a cube Euler's formula is $8 + 6 = 12 + 2$.

> Leonhard Euler (1707–1783) was a Swiss mathematician who was the most prolific author in mathematics history. His writings fill more than 800 large volumes.

Extending Congruence and Similarity

Geoboard activities with congruence and similarity are described in Activities 17.23 and 17.24. A teacher who observes children as they complete the activities gains insight into their capabilities in following directions and understanding the concept of ratio. Similarity is related to ratio, or the proportional thinking needed for reading a map or an architect's drawing. The scale for each map shows a ratio between the distance between two locations shown on the map and the same distance as it is in reality. Thus a map that shows the streets in a village will have a different scale from a map of the same size that shows the major highways of an entire state. In

---

ACTIVITY 17.22 **Euler's Formula (Reasoning and Proof)**

Level: Grades 4–6

Setting: Small groups

Objective: Students count faces, vertex points, and edges of polyhedrons.

Materials: Commercial pieces such as Geofix Shapes, or stirrers and marshmallows, or models constructed using Black-Line Masters 17.9, 17.10, and 17.11

- Have each student build two polyhedrons.
- Students count the faces, vertex points, and edges of each polyhedron.

- Direct students to record their data in a table such as the one shown here.

Figure	Number of Faces	Number Points of Vertex	Number of Edges
Cube	6	8	12

- Once students have collected their data and checked for accuracy, challenge them to find the relationship, known as Euler's formula, that exists between the number of faces, vertex points, and edges of all polyhedrons.

similar figures each pair of corresponding sides is in the same proportion. The corresponding angles are congruent. The ratio between corresponding sides is explored in Activities 17.23–17.25. Activity 17.23 helps students discern the difference between congruent and similar figures. In Activity 17.24 students build similar figures. In Activity 17.25 students use a rubber band as a tool to draw similar figures.

Extending Concepts of Symmetry

At the upper elementary level students examine symmetry lines in figures and represent line symmetry on a coordinate plane. The companion website activity "Symmetry in Letters" asks students to consider block capital letters in terms of line symmetry and then to form entire words or names with line symmetry. Activity 17.26 uses pattern blocks to develop a strong sense of line symmetry. Students can verify the line symmetry of a pattern block design by using a nonbreakable mirror or by reflecting one-half of the design onto the other half with a reflecting manipulative such as a Mira (Figure 17.24). In Activity 17.27 students draw multiple symmetry lines for various figures.

MULTICULTURALCONNECTION

A multicultural extension might be to examine the various designs from the Alhambra to determine the symmetry used by the Islamic artists. The Alhambra is a Moorish palace complex in southern Spain. It is full of many different symmetric designs on walls, ceilings and floors.

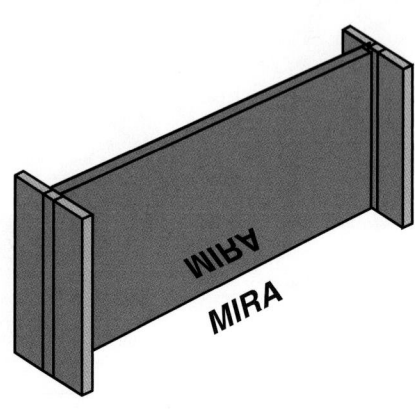

Figure 17.24 Mira

ACTIVITY 17.23 Similarity and Congruence

Level: Grades 3–5
Setting: Whole class or small groups
Objective: Students create similar and congruent figures.
Materials: Geoboards, rubber bands

- Show a right triangle on your geoboard. Have the students duplicate this triangle on their boards. Ask whether, or remind students that, the triangles are congruent.

- Have the students make two congruent triangles that are different from the one you showed them. Have students give their geoboard to a classmate to check that the triangles are congruent. Repeat several times, and monitor. Students can also make a triangle for others to match.

- Show your triangle again. This time, ask the students to make one that is like yours but with each vertical and horizontal side only half as long. Identify the two triangles as similar.

- Discuss how your triangle and theirs are alike and different.

- Make a table of the lengths of line segments for each triangle.

- Ask the students to create two new triangles—one with sides that are two times as long as the other. Monitor their work, and assess their understanding.

- Distinguish between congruent and similar. If their triangle and yours are alike in all ways, then they are congruent. If the triangles are alike in shape but are either smaller or larger, then they are similar.

Challenge

- Ask students to make similar and congruent pictures of squares, rectangles, hexagons, octagons, and their own shapes. Post their pictures on a bulletin board labeled Similar or Congruent.

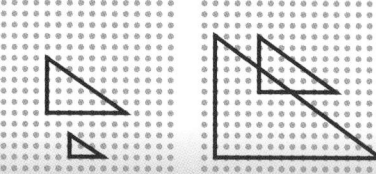

ACTIVITY 17.24 Building Similar Triangles

Level: Grades 4–6

Setting: Small groups

Objective: Students construct similar triangles and examine their attributes.

Materials: Rulers (yardsticks are best), masking tape

- Draw a triangle on the board. Ask two student volunteers to each draw a triangle on the board that is similar but not congruent to the one you drew.

- Ask students to describe similar figures based on the sketches on the board.

- Pass out the masking tape and yardsticks. Ask each group of students to make a scalene triangle on the floor using the tape. The lengths of the three sides should range between 1 foot and 2 feet.

- Students will use the yardsticks and tape to make an enlarged triangle. To do this, they measure the lengths of two sides and extend each side a distance equal to the original side length.

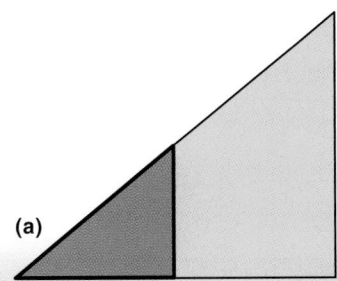

(a)

- Once the two sides are extended, students can use tape to connect the ends of the extended sides to complete the enlarged triangle.

- Have students measure the length of the original third side and the length of the enlarged third side and compare the two lengths.

- Have students compare corresponding angles in the two triangles.

- Encourage students to record their findings and report their findings to the entire class.

- Repeat the entire process, but this time mark the midpoint of the original two sides of the triangle and connect the midpoints to form the third side of a smaller triangle.

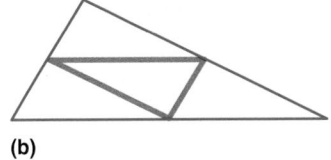

(b)

ACTIVITY 17.25 Drawing Similar Figures

Level: Grades 5–6

Setting: Pairs of students

Objective: Students will use a rubber band to draw similar figures.

Materials: Rulers, rubber band

- Demonstrate how to use a rubber band to enlarge figures.

- Have students tie a knot in the middle of their rubber band and then use it to enlarge a polygon they have drawn by tracing out the figure with the knot of their rubber band.

- Student pairs then use rulers to measure the corresponding sides to check if their enlargements have side lengths twice as long as the side lengths of their original figure.

- Have students conjecture about drawing a new figure with a rubber band that has a knot that is at $\frac{1}{3}$ the length of the rubber band. How will the side lengths of the new figure compare to the side lengths of the original figure?

- Students draw the new figure and measure side lengths to verify their conjecture.

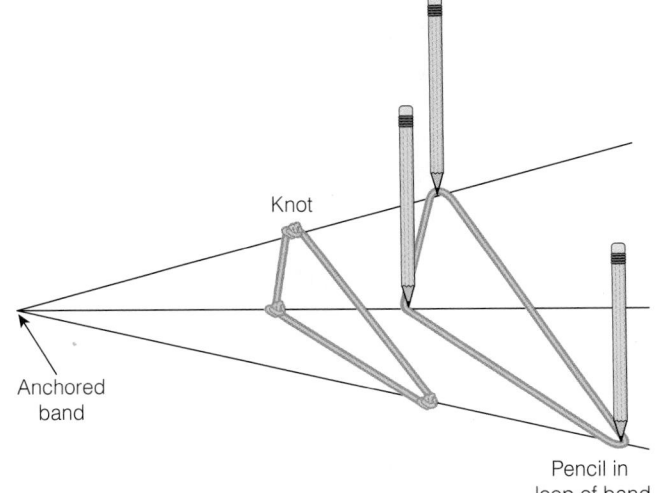

Knot

Anchored band

Pencil in loop of band

ACTIVITY 17.26 Symmetry Designs

Level: Grades 3–5

Setting: Pairs of students

Objective: Students create designs with pattern blocks to display symmetry.

Materials: Pattern blocks, Mira or mirror

- Students work in pairs to create a symmetric design by making mirror images of each other's design pieces.

- To begin, each pair of students draws a line down the middle of a piece of paper.

- One student places a pattern block so it touches the line but does not cross it.

- The partner places a pattern block on the opposite side of the line so it has line symmetry with the first pattern block.

- The same student places a second block on his or her side of the line, touching the first block. The partner must place a second block on the opposite side of the line to show line symmetry.

- Students continue alternating turns until at least 10 pattern block pieces are on the paper.

- If students cannot agree on whether a pattern block shows pattern symmetry, they can use a reflecting mirror or a Mira to determine whether it does or not.

Variation

- Students build a design with pattern blocks using at least 12 pieces. The piece must show symmetry.

- Symmetry can be verified by placing a mirror or Mira along the line of symmetry.

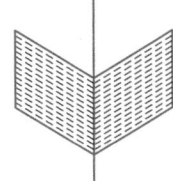

ACTIVITY 17.27 Lines of Symmetry

Level: Grades 3–5

Setting: Whole class or small groups

Objective: Students determine the number of different lines of symmetry for various polygons.

Materials: Cutouts of a square, rectangle, equilateral triangle, isosceles triangle, regular pentagon, and other regular and irregular polygons

- Challenge students to determine how many different lines of symmetry each figure has.

- Have students cut out the figures and fold them or use a Mira to verify the lines of symmetry.

- Have the students record in a table the number of lines of symmetry for each shape.

Shape	Sides	Lines of Symmetry
Square	4	4
Equilateral triangle		
Isosceles triangle		
Regular pentagon		
Regular hexagon		

- Ask students if they see a relationship between the number of sides and the number of lines of symmetry in a regular polygon. Does this relationship hold for a rectangle and an isosceles triangle? What about the other polygons? Are there any figures that have no lines of symmetry? What can be said about their shapes?

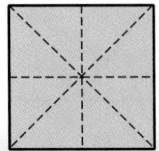 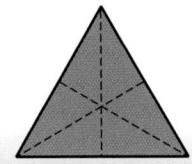 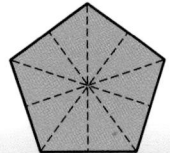

EXERCISE

Compare the number of symmetry lines in an equilateral triangle, square, regular pentagon, and regular hexagon. How do you think the lines of symmetry in regular figures with an odd number of sides compare to the lines of symmetry in regular figures with an even number of sides? ●●●

Extending Concepts of Transformational Geometry

At the upper elementary level students examine the translations more closely, moving beyond simply identifying a particular translation. They look for patterns in translations and explore translations on the coordinate plane. In addition, they begin to study a new translation, dilations. In Activity 17.28 students explore the properties of reflections in a coordinate grid. The companion website activity "Reflecting Figures in a Coordinate Grid" leads students to conclude that the commutative law holds for reflections across coordinate axes. That is, the result when a figure is reflected across the *x*-axis and then the *y*-axis is identical to the result when a figure is reflected across the *y*-axis first and then across the *x*-axis. In Activity 17.29 students describe the series of translations required to move a figure from one position to another on a coordinate grid.

Younger children become familiar with slides (translations), flips (reflections) and turns (rotations). A fourth type of transformation is a *dilation*, which is different from the other three transformations. A dilation in geometry is related to the dilation of the eye, the shrinking and enlarging of the pupil. In a dilation the resulting figure is not congruent to the original figure. Instead it is similar. A stick figure on a deflated balloon can demonstrate a dilation to children. As the balloon is inflated, the stick figure is enlarged. It changes size, but at each stage of inflation the stick figure resembles the original figure and is similar to it. Software programs such as MapQuest feature a magnifying glass on close-up, which essentially dilates, or expands, the image on the screen. Activity 17.26 used rubber bands to produce similar figures that were enlargements of a given plane figure. The resulting figures were dilations of the original figure. Activity 17.30 examines dilations in a coordinate grid.

Tessellations. Tiling patterns, or **tessellations**, are made when a surface is completely covered with one geometric figure or a combination of figures in a repeating pattern. Figure 17.25a illustrates a tessellation made with squares, Figure 17.25b a tessellation with triangles, Figure 17.25c a tessellation with regular hexagons, Figure 17.25d a tessellation with combinations of hexagons and triangles at each point, and Figure 17.25e a tessellation with octagons and squares.

Tessellations are a wonderful source of multicultural connections. Tessellations are found in architecture, in quilting, and in the artwork of various cultures. Ceramic tiles in buildings are often arranged in a repeated pattern of geometric shapes. Many quilts have an overall pattern of individual squares made from fabric shapes with a coordinated color

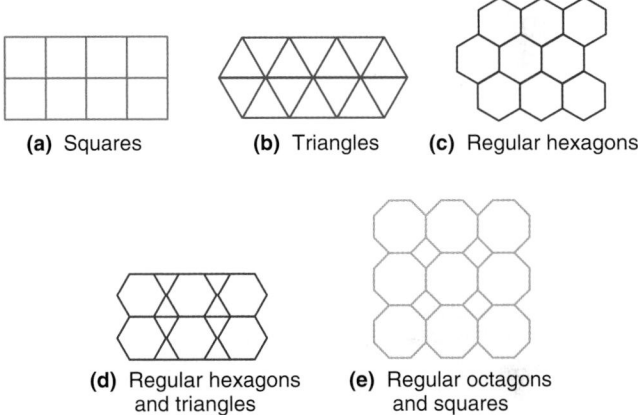

(a) Squares   **(b)** Triangles   **(c)** Regular hexagons

(d) Regular hexagons and triangles   **(e)** Regular octagons and squares

Figure 17.25 Tessellations using (a) squares, (b) triangles, (c) regular hexagons, (d) regular hexagons and triangles, and (e) regular octagons and squares

---

ACTIVITY 17.28   Reflecting Points on a Coordinate Grid

- -

Level: Grade 6

Setting: Small groups

Objective: Students will explore symmetry attributes on a coordinate grid.

Materials: Graph paper

- Review for students that when a point is reflected across a line, the resulting image point is the same distance from the symmetry line as the original point.

- Pass out graph paper, and ask students to plot the points shown here on the graph paper.

  1. (2, 4)   2. (5,7)   3. (−2, −2)   4. (−4, 3)
  5. (4, −3)   6. (3, 3)   7. (−3, −2)   8. (−3, 2)

- Ask students to reflect each of these points across the *x*-axis and to record the coordinates of both points in the table.

  Coordinates of Original Point   Coordinates of Reflected Point

- Ask groups to make a conjecture about reflecting any point across the *x*-axis. Have groups test their conjecture with point (3, −4).

- Repeat using the *y*-axis.

ACTIVITY 17.29 Geometric Transformations

Level: Grades 3–6

Setting: Student pairs

Objective: Students identify the transformation (moves) that a shape might take from one position to another.

Materials: Several congruent triangle cutouts, art paper

- Display a triangle on the overhead projector. Ask student pairs to glue one triangle on their paper and label it #1.

- Put a second triangle on the overhead. Ask: "If I move triangle #1 to where triangle #2 is, how would I have to move it?" Help the students recognize that you might have to slide it, rotate it, flip it, or perhaps make a combination of moves to put it in the second location. Repeat with other triangle placements.

- Ask students to glue several other triangles on their paper, making some upside down, backward, and on end. Label their other triangles #2, #3, #4, and so on.

- Ask: "If you move triangle #1 to where your triangle #2 is, which translations would you have to make to move it?" Remind them that they may need to slide it, rotate it, flip it, or make a combination of moves.

- Have pairs discuss what needs to be done to the first triangle to put it in the position of the other triangles. Tell the recorder for each pair to write a list of the movement(s) for triangles #2, #3, #4, and so on.

Extension

- Ask students to write directions on an index card of how to move a shape from a starting place to an ending place using slides, flips, and turns. These directions are a puzzle for others to solve. Put answers on the back of the card.

You might also introduce the notation for translations. For example, the notation $(x, y) \rightarrow (x + 4, y - 2)$ describes moving the point 4 units to the right and 2 units down.

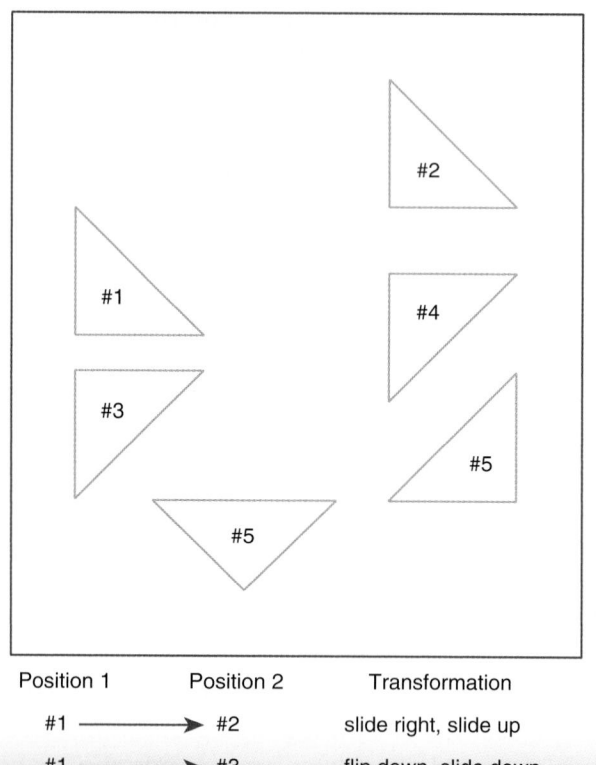

Position 1	Position 2	Transformation
#1 →	#2	slide right, slide up
#1 →	#3	flip down, slide down

scheme. The baskets, pottery, beadwork, and rugs of Native American artists often involve tessellated patterns. Lyn Taylor and her associates have written about cooperative group tessellation activities among Native Americans. They believe that because most Native American cultures are group oriented and emphasize cooperation, the noncompetitive nature of these activities can foster cross-cultural understanding among students of all ethnic groups. The creation of tessellations helps to develop spatial visualization skills. During their exploration of pattern blocks, children find which blocks fit together to cover the surface with no gaps and build an initial understanding of the tessellation concept. Older children find even more complex combinations of shapes that tessellate a surface. Squares, rectangles, equilateral triangles, and regular hexagons tessellate by themselves, and some can be combined in a recurring pattern (Figure 17.26). Regular pentagons and octagons leave gaps that must be filled

with another shape. An open-ended probe such as "What do you notice about shapes that tessellate alone?" helps children focus on the geometric properties of the shapes. Younger children will focus on equal side lengths among figures that tessellate. Older children will be able to relate the angle

Figure 17.26 Tessellation using squares, hexagons, and triangles

ACTIVITY 17.30 Exploring Dilations

Level: Grades 5–6

Setting: Pairs of students

Objective: Students explore characteristics of dilations on a coordinate grid.

Materials: Graph paper, ruler

- Direct students to draw a triangle on the coordinate grid.
- Explain to students the meaning of $(x, y) \rightarrow (2x, 2y)$ in terms of dilations.
- Ask students to plot the resulting figure from $(x, y) \rightarrow (2x, 2y)$ and to compare the side lengths of the original figure and the resulting enlargement.
- Repeat for $(3x, 3y)$
- Ask students to show how they might produce a figure with side lengths that are five times the side lengths of their original figure.
- Have groups report their findings. How did their predictions compare with their results?

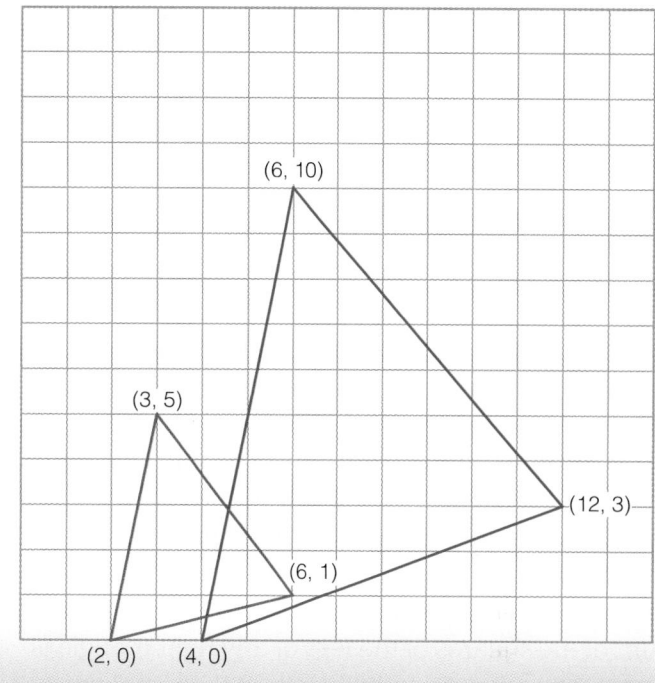

measures of the shapes to their ability to tessellate. The sum of the angles at every vertex in a tessellation must total 360°. Thus equilateral triangles will tessellate, with six triangles at each vertex ($6 \times 60° = 360°$); squares will tessellate, with four squares at each vertex ($4 \times 90° = 360°$); and regular hexagons will tessellate, with three hexagons at each vertex ($3 \times 120° = 360°$).

After students have had ample opportunity to use pattern blocks and cut-out shapes to explore tessellations, square and triangular dot paper will allow children to copy, extend, and create their own simple tessellations.

More intricate tessellation shapes are formed using a technique called the bite-and-push method. The steps for creating a tessellation using the bite-and-push method are shown in Figure 17.27. Begin with a simple tessellating shape, such as a square (Figure 17.27a). Take a "bite" out of one side by cutting a piece from one edge. Put the bite exactly across the figure on the opposite side by sliding it across (Figure 17.27b) and taping it to the opposite edge (Figure 17.27c). It will look as though the shape has been pushed from one side to the other. The student may stop here and use the new piece as a pattern for a tessellation design or may cut a second piece from the bottom of the square, slide it to the top, and tape it (Figure 17.27d). Once

POINT OF VIEW

Creating a tiling pattern is more than just drawing a design. It is the manifestation of powerful mental operations. Making a tiling pattern requires the mental rotation of a constructed image, determining the feasibility of an anticipated placement, the conceptualization and imagination of a regular pattern of tiles, and the production of the drawing. (Wheatley, 1992, p. 43)

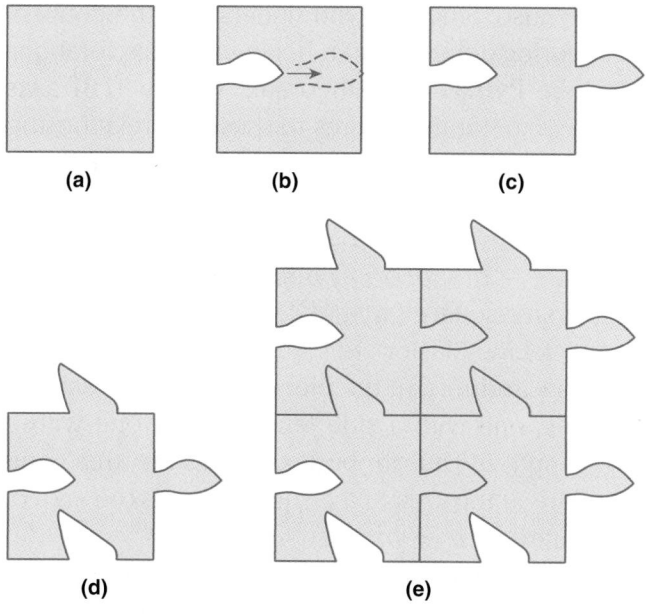

Figure 17.27 Tessellation of a unique design

satisfied with the self-created tessellation piece, the student uses it to create and color a tessellated pattern (Figure 17.27e). Other designs can be added to each piece to enhance its appearance or to further relate to a real object or animal, as do so many of the works of M. C. Escher.

The works of Dutch artist M. C. Escher (1898–1972) interest many children. Escher drew many tessellations in his body of work. Some tessellation designs show the metamorphosis of one creature into another; changing a bird into a fish is accomplished with subtle changes in the tessellating shapes. Library books and prints of Escher's art show a connection between geometry and art.

The Pythagorean Theorem. The most famous formula in all of mathematics describes the relationship between the side lengths of a right triangle. It is the Pythagorean theorem, named after Greek mathematician Pythagoras. The theorem states that the sum of the squares of the legs of any right triangle is equal to the square of the length of the hypotenuse. Using the right triangle shown here, the theorem can be represented in the familiar formula.

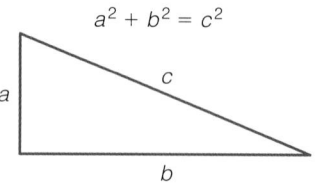

$$a^2 + b^2 = c^2$$

In the formula a and b represent either of the two leg lengths and c is the length of the longest side, the hypotenuse. Students who understand the concept of squaring a number can begin initial explorations with the Pythagorean theorem. Activity 17.31 asks students to cut up squares to show the relationship of side lengths in the Pythagorean theorem. In Black-Line Master 17.13 students cut up an a-square (area of a-square $= a \times a$, or a^2) and a b-square (area of b-square $= b \times b$, or b^2) and rearrange the pieces to form a c-square (area of c-square $= c \times c$, or c^2). In Black-Line Master 17.14 students cut up a square of side c and reform the pieces to form two smaller squares, one with a side length a and one with a side length b. Thus for both activities the area of an a-square + the area of a b-square equals the area of a c-square, or $a^2 + b^2 = c^2$.

In addition to gaining a foundational understanding of the Pythagorean theorem, students can also use the theorem to determine whether any triangles are right triangles. To do so, students need simply to substitute the three side lengths of a particular triangle into the Pythagorean theorem. If the side lengths fit the Pythagorean theorem (see Activity 17.32), then the triangle is a right triangle. When determining whether a triangle is a right triangle, students must be careful to substitute the length of the hypotenuse for c in the equation. For example, a triangle with side lengths 3, 5, and 4 is a right triangle because $3^2 + 4^2 = 5^2$, but a triangle with side lengths of 8, 9, and 10 is not a right triangle because $8^2 + 9^2 \neq 10^2$. The companion website activity "Categorizing Triangles Using the Pythagorean Theorem" extends the relationship. Students can identify acute and obtuse triangles by using a calculator to examine whether $a^2 + b^2 < c^2$ (acute) or $a^2 + b^2 > c^2$ (obtuse).

Students in upper middle school can use the Pythagorean theorem to solve various geometry problems involving right triangles. To do so, they must have learned to solve algebraic equations and to represent and work with irrational numbers. Early middle grade students might solve problems with the Pythagorean theorem, but all problems should involve Pythagorean triples. A Pythagorean triple is a combination of whole-number side lengths that fit the Pythagorean theorem. For example, 3-4-5, 6-8-10, and 5-12-13 are Pythagorean triples. Students might use an electronic spreadsheet to generate any number of Pythagorean triples. In later grades students can explore the Pythagorean theorem and its applications using noninteger side lengths.

a	b	c	a^2	b^2	c^2
3	4	5	9	16	25
6	8	10	36	64	100
9	12	15	81	144	225

MULTICULTURALCONNECTION

Students can research several multicultural aspects of the Pythagorean theorem. Chinese mathematicians knew about the relationship of the side lengths of right triangles centuries before Pythagoras. Egyptian and Babylonian architects had some knowledge of Pythagorean triples long before the time of Pythagoras.

ACTIVITY 17.31   Exploring the Pythagorean Theorem

Level: Grade 6

Setting: Small groups

Objective: Children develop the relationship of the Pythagorean theorem.

Materials: Scissors, glue sticks, Black-Line Masters 17.13 and 17.14

- Pass out copies of Black-Line Master 17.13 (Pythagorean Puzzle a) and Black-Line Master 17.14 (Pythagorean Puzzle b) to each student.

- Point out to students that the side lengths of the right triangle on each sheet are also side lengths of the different squares.

- For Black-Line Master 17.13 challenge students to cut up the pieces of both the *a*-square (side length *a*) and the *b*-square (side length *b*) to form the *c*-square (side length *c*).

- For Black-Line Master 17.14 challenge students to re-arrange the cut-out pieces of the *c*-square (side length c) to form the *a*-square (side length *a*) and the *b*-square (side length *b*).

- When students have correctly rearranged the pieces of the *c*-square to form the *a*-square and the *b*-square, they should glue the pieces in place.

- Help groups to write the formula that develops from the relationship that the *a*-square plus the *b*-square equals the *c*-square ($a^2 + b^2 = c^2$).

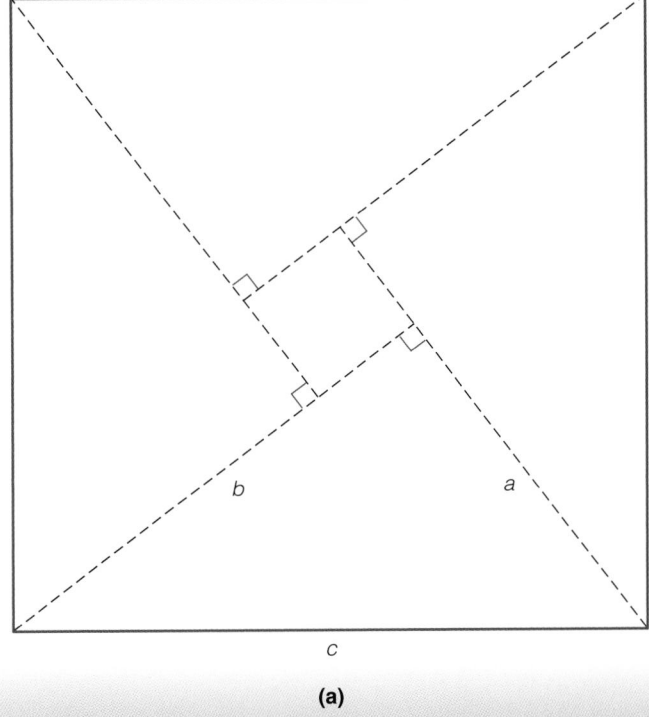

(a)

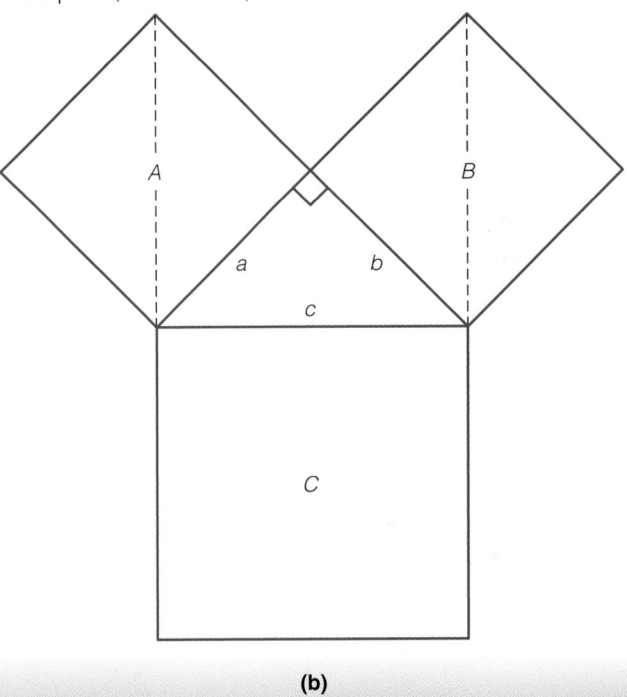

(b)

ACTIVITY 17.32   Using the Pythagorean Theorem to Find Right Triangles (Connection)

Level: Grade 6

Setting: Small groups

Objective: Students use the Pythagorean theorem to identify right triangles.

Materials: Paper, pencil, calculators

- Post this list of triangle side lengths on the board.

  a. 3, 4, 5   b. 12, 10, 16   c. 12, 13, 5

  d. 8, 8, 10   e. 10, 8, 6   f. 8, 8, 8

- Ask students whether they can tell which of them are right triangles by testing side lengths in the Pythagorean theorem. In the case of (8, 8, 8) students might recognize an equilateral triangle before applying the Pythagorean theorem to the three sides.

- When students find a right triangle, they should draw the triangle using centimeters for units. Under their drawing they should show how the side lengths of the triangle fit the Pythagorean theorem.

All these activities provide opportunities for students to communicate their knowledge of geometry and for teachers to assess them. By writing and drawing, either for display or in their journals, students demonstrate what they have learned. A short interview with students can also be used to assess their understanding. According to the objectives appropriate for each child, at each level, teachers can design appropriate assessment performance tasks. A kindergarten teacher can ask students to point to two or three examples of triangles, circles, squares, and rectangles from objects or pictures. A second- or third-grade teacher can ask students to describe shapes by the characteristics of sides and angles. A fifth- or sixth-grader can be asked to categorize quadrilaterals by various characteristics, such as parallel lines or lengths of diagonals. Short, focused interviews are good assessments because they allow students to demonstrate and explain rather than just answering on paper. During such interviews, the teacher can probe for the student's understanding of various geometric concepts and relationships.

Take-Home Activities

This chapter's take-home material is a letter to parents and involves tangram pieces for geometry activities that can be done at home. A die-cut machine can make tangram pieces to take home.

Parents are asked to help children find a family quilt, rug, or other design as a basis for a design and color activity.

Grapevine School
1954 Killian Road
Plymouth, CA 55121

Dear Parents:

For the next two weeks, students in your child's class are going to be working with geometry. Specifically, they will be looking for symmetry, congruence and similarity, and tiling patterns. These concepts have already been studied in previous grades, but we are going to extend these ideas beyond what was learned earlier. You can help your child understand these concepts better by assisting with two projects.

Your child will have a set of tangram puzzle pieces for every adult and child over age 5 in your family. Please spend some time over the next few days working as a family with the tangram pieces. For example, see if you can use the seven pieces to make two squares that are the same size, two triangles that are the same size, and a square using all seven pieces. Using the puzzle pieces, your child will find examples of congruence (the shapes fit exactly on each other) and similarity (the shapes are the same but have different sizes). Discuss these concepts when examples occur while you work. Build symmetric designs by drawing a line down the middle of a piece of paper, making a design along one side of the line, and having your child match your pieces on the opposite side of the line.

You may have a family quilt, rug, or other handcrafted item that has a repeated design. Talk about the history of the piece. Did a member of the family make it? a friend? Was it bought from the person who made it? As you sit with your child, each of you draws the design on paper and colors it in different ways. Talk about ways the pattern repeats. Are there examples of symmetry, congruence, similarity? Do geometric shapes, such as squares or triangles, cover the surface? If so, this is an example of tiling, or tessellation.

Can you find other examples of tessellation in your home? Hint: Is there ceramic tile or linoleum in the kitchen or a bathroom?

After you have done some tangram activities and have made a design, have your child write two paragraphs in her or his journal to describe the work you have done together on each activity.

Summary

Geometry is one important way we see mathematics in everyday life: clothing and building design, art and animation, suitcase packing, and map reading. Visual information constantly increases in our world. Spatial intelligence has too often been neglected by schools because it seems to be a natural ability that children bring with them to school. Research shows that spatial intelligence can be developed by activities in and out of school. Development of spatial sense, or spatial visualization, is a major benefit of geometry experiences.

Geometric understanding has been described in five stages by van Hiele-Geldof and van Hiele. The first three stages provide guidance for the elementary school teacher in designing appropriate experiences. Children learn to recognize and label shapes before they can describe the attributes of each. In the upper elementary grades students begin to use attributes to describe and generalize about shapes and to understand the relationships between plane and solid figures.

A well-rounded elementary mathematics curriculum includes activities from four different geometry systems. Children learn about topological geometry by locating and describing the space they live in, using concepts such as proximity, enclosure, order, and separation. They learn about two- and three-dimensional shapes and figures in Euclidean geometry. As they make pictures and designs with triangles, circles, and squares, they learn the names and characteristics of plane shapes and three-dimensional (space) figures and the relationships among these shapes and figures. They also become familiar with geometric properties, such as congruence, similarity, and symmetry, that are common in several geometry systems and in real-life situations. In transformational geometry they learn that rotating, flipping, and sliding shapes to new positions does not change their fundamental characteristics. As they work with coordinate geometry, they find that the location of objects can be described using two-dimensional grids and that transformations can be explored and represented on coordinate grids. Extensions of these ideas allow intermediate students to explore symmetry and similarity on coordinate grids. In grade 6 students begin their study of the Pythagorean theorem.

Learning about geometry provides a variety of activities and content in the primary and intermediate mathematics classrooms. Many of the activities use real objects and geometry manipulatives. Geoboards, pentominoes, tangrams, pattern blocks, cubes, Miras, and tiles are used to develop various concepts and terminology from the four geometric systems. Take-home activities with tangrams and tessellations connect the geometry done in school with home activities.

All the geometric systems are interrelated and essential for developing the concepts and language of geometry.

Geometry is also foundational to many other topics in mathematics, such as fractions, measurement, and probability, as well as number systems and operations. Geometry activities connect mathematics to the art of many cultures and to history.

Study Questions and Activities

1. Many activities in geometry are excellent for discovery and extension in a learning center. If task cards are available to you, look at the cards for geometry materials such as geoboards, pattern blocks, pentominoes, or tangrams. Which mathematics objectives in your state or school district curriculum are addressed in the task cards?

2. Children's spatial visualization skills can be enhanced by many out-of-school activities, such as playing with Legos or jigsaw puzzles. Make a list of such activities, and compare them to a classmate's list.

3. Make a collection of pictures that illustrate symmetric and nonsymmetric figures for a classroom bulletin board. Include examples of line and point symmetry. What can be done so that students will have an interactive experience with the pictures and concepts?

4. Using the fonts of a word processor, print out several alphabets using capital letters. Examine various letters in the different fonts to determine which ones have point symmetry, line symmetry, or both. Which letters have neither form of symmetry?

5. The van Hieles, a Dutch husband-and-wife team of researchers, identified five stages of geometric understanding, the first three of which apply to children in elementary school. List those three. Classify each numbered activity in this chapter according to the stage of understanding being developed in it.

6. Interview a kindergartner or first-grade student. Ask the student to draw a square and a triangle. Then ask the student to explain how to tell the difference between a square and a triangle.

7. Research the man Pythagoras and the Pythagorean society he founded.

8. Examine your state geometry standard and give examples of the four geometry systems that are represented.

Praxis (http://www.ets.org/praxis/) In this circle with center O and radius 2, AP has length 3 and is tangent to the circle at P. If CP is a diameter of the circle, what is the length of BC?

a. 1.25

b. 2

c. 3.2

d. 5

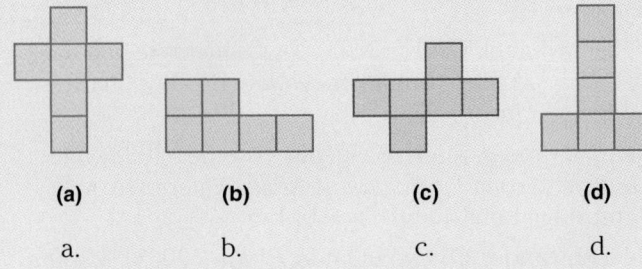

NAEP (http://nces.ed.gov/nationsreportcard/)
Which of the following can*not* be folded into a cube?

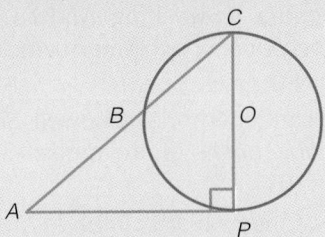

(a)   **(b)**   **(c)**   **(d)**

a.   b.   c.   d.

TIMSS (http://nces.ed.gov/timss/) Of the following, which is *not* true for all rectangles?

a. The opposite sides are parallel.
b. The opposite sides are equal.
c. All angles are right angles.
d. The diagonals are equal.
e. The diagonals are perpendicular.

Using Children's Literature

Burns, Marilyn. (1995). *The greedy triangle*. New York: Scholastic. (Grades Pre-K–3)

In *The Greedy Triangle* Marilyn Burns tells the story of a triangle who wishes to become more important by having more sides. As the triangle changes from shape to shape by adding new sides, it finds that the changes are not fully satisfying. Eventually, the moral of "being who you are" is brought home. Both the changing of the shapes and the yearning to be somebody else will strike a chord with elementary students.

· Read *The Greedy Triangle* to students.
· As you read the story, hold up large cut-out shapes to match the text.
· Have students draw or trace the various shapes into a shape book.
· In their shape book, students can record the name of each shape.
· Along with the name of the shape, students can write a story about each shape and how each shape has its own advantages and uses.

Sleator, William. (1998). *The boy who reversed himself.* New York: Dutton Publishing. (Grades 5–7)

Read the storybook aloud to young students over several class days, have older students read the story by themselves.

· Ask students what it means in the story if someone is "reversed."
· Ask how students could tell if a friend or family member was reversed.
· Ask what kinds of activities would remain unchanged if a person were reversed. What kinds of activities are impossible if a person is reversed?
· Ask students to design a new activity that would now be possible if they themselves were reversed.

Teacher's Resources

Cuevas, Gilbert (Ed.). (2002). *Navigating through geometry in grades 3–5.* Reston, VA: National Council of Teachers of Mathematics.

Del Grande, John, & Morrow, Lorna. (1993). *Curriculum and evaluation standards for school mathematics: Addenda series, grades K–6, geometry and spatial sense.* Reston, VA: National Council of Teachers of Mathematics.

Friel, S. (Ed.) 2002. *Navigating through geometry in grades 6–8.* Reston, VA: National Council of Teachers of Mathematics.

Geddes, Dorothy, Bove, Juliana, Fortunato, Irene, Ruys, David J., Morgenstern, Jessica, & Welchman-Tischler, Rosamond. (1992). *Curriculum and evaluation standards for school mathematics: Addenda series, grades 5–8, geometry in the middle grades.* Reston, VA: National Council of Teachers of Mathematics.

Greenes, Carole (Ed.). 2002. *Navigating through geometry in grades preK–2.* Reston, VA: National Council of Teachers of Mathematics.

Pohl, V. (1986). *How to enrich geometry using string designs.* Reston, VA. National Council of Teachers of Mathematics.

Restanus, Cheryl. (1994). *Math by all means: Geometry, grades 3–4.* White Plains, NY: Cuisenaire Company of America.

Seymour, D., & Britton, J. (1986). *Introduction to tessellations.* Palo Alto, CA: Dale Seymour Publications.

Children's Bookshelf

Anno, Mitsumasa. (1991). *Anno's math games III.* New York: Philomel Books. (Grades 1–4)

Brown, Marcia. (1979). *Listen to a shape.* New York: Franklin Watts. (Grades 1–4)

Bruna, Dick. (1984). *I know about shapes.* Los Angeles: Price/Stern/Sloan. (Grades PS–K)

Burns, Marilyn. (1997). *Spaghetti and meatballs for all.* New York: Scholastic Press. (Grades 3–5)

Carle, Eric. (1986). *The secret birthday message.* New York: Harper Trophy. (Grades 2–4)

Cohen, Caon Lee. (1996). *Where's the fly?* New York: Greenwillow. (Grades 1–3)

Dodds, Dayle Ann. (1994). *The shape of things.* Cambridge, MA: Candlewick Press. (Grades PS–1)

Ehlert, Lois. (1989). *Color zoo.* Philadelphia: Lippincott. (Grades PS–K)

Ellis, Julie. (2004). *What's your angle, Pythagoras?* Boston: Charlesbridge. (Grades K–2)

Ernst, Lisa Campbell. (2004) *The turn-around, upside-down book.* New York: Simon and Schuster. (Grades K–4)

Friedman, Aileen. (1994). *A cloak for a dreamer.* Jefferson City, MO: Scholastic Professional Books. (Grades 1–6)

Froman, Robert. (1972). *Rubber bands, baseballs, and doughnuts: A book about topology.* New York: Crowell. (Grades 1–4)

Froman, Robert. (1976). *Angles are easy as pie.* New York: Crowell. (Grades K–3)

Glass, Julie. (1998). *The fly on the ceiling: A math myth.* New York: Random House. (Grades 1–4)

Grifalconi, Ann. (1986). *The village of round and square houses.* Boston: Little, Brown. (Grades 1-4)

Hindley, Judy. (1994). *The wheeling and whirling-around book.* Cambridge, MA: Candlewick Press. (Grades K–4)

Hoban, Tana. (1973). *Over, under, and through, and other spatial concepts.* New York: Macmillan. (Grades PS–2)

Hoban, Tana. (1974). *Circles, triangles, and squares.* New York: Macmillan. (Grades PS–2)

Hoban, Tana. (1983). *Round and round and round.* New York: Greenwillow. (Grades K–3)

Hoban, Tana. (1986). *Shapes, shapes, shapes.* New York: Greenwillow. (Grades PS–3)

Hoban, Tana. (1992). *Spirals, curves, fan-shapes, and lines.* New York: Greenwillow. (Grades K–3)

Hoban, Tana. (2000). *Cubes, cones, cylinders, and spheres.* New York: HarperCollins Children's Books. (Grades 1–5)

Jocelyn, Marthe. (2000). *Hannah's collections.* East Rutherford, NJ: Penguin Putnam Books. (Grades 3–5)

Juster, Norton. (1971). *The phantom tollbooth.* New York: Random House. (Grades 4–6)

Juster, Norton. (1991). *The dot and the line: A romance in lower mathematics.* New York: Random House. (Grades 4–6)

Lasky, Kathryn, & Hawkes, Kevin. (1994). *The librarian who measured the earth.* Boston: Little, Brown. (Grades K–6)

MacKinnon, Debbie. (1992). *What shape?* New York: Dial. (Grades K–2)

MacKinnon, Debbie, & Sieveking, Anthea. (2000). *Eye spy shapes: A peephole book.* Watertown, MA: Charlesbridge. (Grades Pre-K–1)

Mirocha, Paul, Lauffer, Rhoda, & Lowell, Susan. (1995). *The boy with paper wings.* Minneapolis: Milkweed Editions. (Grades 4–6)

Neuschwander, Cindy. (1998). *Amanda Bean's amazing dream: A mathematical mystery.* Watertown, MA: Cambridge Publishing. (Grades 1–5)

Neuschwander, Cindy. (1999). *Sir Cumference and the dragon of PI: A math adventure.* Boston: Charlesbridge (Grades 4–6)

Neuschwander, Cindy. (2003). *Sir Cumference and the sword in the cone: A math adventure.* Boston: Charlesbridge. (Grades 4–6)

Neuschwander, Cindy, & Geehan, Wayne. (1998). *Sir Cumference and the first round table.* Watertown, MA: Cambridge Publishing. (Grades 4–6)

Neuschwander, Cindy, & Lando, Bryan. (2005). *Mummy math: An adventure in geometry.* Boston: Charlesbridge. (Grades 1–3)

Pluckrose, Henry. (1986). *Shape.* New York: Franklin Watts. (Grades 1–3)

Sharman, Lydia. (1994). *The amazing book of shapes.* New York: Dorling Kindersley. (Grades 3–5)

Silverstein, S. (1981). *Missing piece meets the big O.* New York: Harper Collins. (Grades 4–6)

Sleator, William. (1998). *The boy who reversed himself.* New York: Dutton. (Grades 5–7)

Testa, Fulvio. (1983). *If you look around you.* New York: Dial. (Grades PS–2)

Tompert, Ann. (1990). *Grandfather Tang's story.* New York: Crown. (Grades PS–2)

Walter, Marion. (1971). *Make a bigger puddle. Make a smaller worm.* New York: M. Evans. (Grades 1–3)

Yenawine, Philip. (1991). *Lines.* New York: Delacorte. (Grades K–4)

Yenawine, Philip. (1991). *Shapes.* New York: Delacorte. (Grades K–4)

Technology Resources

Internet Sites

For websites about the Pythagorean theorem, see the following:

http://www.shodor.org/interactivate/activities/index.html (see Pythagorean Explorer)

http://nlvm.usu.edu/en/nav/vlibrary.html (see Pythagorean Theorem)

http://illuminations.nctm.org (see Pythagorean Theorem Transformations)

For other practice with geometry, see the following websites:

http://nlvm.usu.edu/en/nav/vlibrary.html (see Transformations—Translations, Transformations—Rotations, Transformations—Reflections, and Transformations—Dilations)

http://www.bbc.co.uk/education/mathsfile/ (see Bath Tiles)

http://www.shodor.org/interactivate/activities/index.html (see Floor Tiles)

http://illuminations.nctm.org (see Cube Nets and Geometry Solid Tool Symmetry)

http://illuminations.nctm.org (see Mirror Tool Tessellations)

http://www.shodor.org/interactivate/activities/index.html (see Tessellate Similarity)

http://nlvm.usu.edu/en/nav/vlibrary.html (see Similar Triangles Spatial Sense)

http://www.fi.uu.nl/rekenweb/en (see Build Free, Building Houses, Houses with Height Numbers, and Island)

http://nlvm.usu.edu/en/nav/vlibrary.html (see I Took a Train and Platonic Solids)

Internet Game

At **http://www.bbc.co.uk/education/mathsfile/** there are a number of interesting games. The game Bathroom Tiles challenges students to tile a bathroom using translations, reflections, and rotations or a combination of them. There are three participant levels according to the difficulty of the tiling. Games are scored on time needed for the tiling and degree of successful tiling.

Computer Software

There are many geometry software programs for children to use. Turtle Math, developed by Douglas Clements and Julie Sarama Meredith and produced by Logo Computer Systems, is an adaptation of the computer language Logo. Turtle Math provides entertaining and challenging activities for children to explore the geometry of the turtle's world and their own. Students design the turtle's path as it travels through mazes and toward various destinations.

Other software that focuses on geometry is the Geometer's Sketchpad, a dynamic geometry program that allows students to explore geometric relationships by creating shapes and then moving and distorting them. A software similar to the Geometer's Sketchpad is Cabri Geometry, which is also available in the TI-73 calculator from Texas Instruments, a calculator designed for middle school students.

Computer Programs

Building Perspective (Sunburst Communication) (Grade 4–adult)

Cabri Geometry (Pearson Education) (Grade 4–adult)

Crystal Rain Forest (Terrapin) (Grades 4–7)

Elastic Lines: The Electronic Geoboard (Sunburst Communication) (Grades 4–8)

Factory (Sunburst Communication) (Grade 4–adult)

Geometric preSupposer (Sunburst Communication) (Grade 5–adult)

Geometry Inventor (Wings for Learning) (Grade 5–adult)

LogoWriter, school version (Logo Computer Systems Inc.) (Grades 1–12)

Math Processor (Computer Curriculum Corporation) (Grades 4–10)

Superfactory (Sunburst Communication) (Grade 6–adult)

Terrapin Logo (Terrapin) (Grades K–12)

Turtle Math (Logo Computer Systems Inc.) (Grades 2–8)

For Further Reading

Ambose, Rebecca, & Falkner, Karen. (2002). Developing spatial understanding through building polyhedrons. *Teaching Children Mathematics* 8(8), 442–447.

Children develop their spatial sense by building original polyhedrons and describing their component parts.

Barkley, Cathy, & Cruz, Sandra. (2001). Geometry through beadwork designs. *Teaching Children Mathematics* 7(6), 363–367.

This article describes a series of geometry explorations using Native American beadwork as the setting. Students design bracelets and necklaces with a focus on the geometric figures the beads represent.

Battista, Michael. (2002). Learning geometry in a dynamic computer environment. *Teaching Children Mathematics* 8(6), 333–338.

The author describes using a dynamic geometry software program with third graders to develop their understanding of two-dimensional shapes.

Britton, Barbara, & Stump, Sheryl. (2001). Unexpected riches from a geoboard quadrilateral activity. *Mathematics Teaching in the Middle School* 6(8), 490–494.

Children sort quadrilaterals by building them on a geoboard.

Curtis, Shirley. (2001). Mouse maze tournament: Connecting geometry and measurement. *Teaching Children Mathematics* 7(9), 504–507.

This article describes a project for children to design mazes for two mice. The project combines geometry and measurement relationships.

Kenehan, Garrett, & Ambrose, Rebecca. (2005). Geometry in the 3rd grade: Sorting and describing polyhedra. *ON-Math* 3(3).

The authors discuss how children develop their geometry reasoning by sorting polyhedra. The article references van Hiele levels of students as they engage in explorations with polyhedra.

Lehrer, Richard, & Curtis, Carmen. (2000). Why are some solids perfect? Conjectures and experiments by third graders. *Teaching Children Mathematics* 6, 324–329.

In this paper Lehrer and Curtis describe a series of activities that introduce Platonic solids to their children.

Lindquist, Mary, & Clements, Douglas. (2001). Geometry must be vital. *Teaching Children Mathematics* 7(7), 411–449.

Making and verifying conjectures can be at the center of geometric thinking for elementary students.

National Council of Teachers of Mathematics. (1999). Geometry and geometric thinking. *Teaching Children Mathematics* 5(6).

This focus issue on geometry and geometric thinking features eight papers, including one by Pierre van Hiele on early development.

Stein, M., & Bovalino, J. (2001). Manipulatives: One piece of the puzzle. *Mathematics Teaching in the Middle School* 6 (5), 142–145.

Stein and Bovalino consider the advantages of using manipulatives but also cite concerns for teachers who use them.

Strutchens, M., et al. (2001). Assessing geometric and measurement understanding using manipulatives. *Mathematics in the Middle School* 6(7), 402–405.

Manipulatives may be part of the assessment in mathematics classes.

Swindle, Donna M. (2001). Learning geometry and a new language. *Teaching Children Mathematics* 7(4), 246–250.

The vocabulary necessary for flexible geometric thinking is developed as students manipulate objects in space and examine them from various perspectives.

Thatcher, Debra. (2001) The tangram conundrum. *Mathematics Teaching in the Middle School* 6(7), 384–398.

The tangram serves as a manipulative for exploring linear-area relationships and for revealing irrational numbers in the lengths of some of the pieces.

CHAPTER 18

Developing and Extending Measurement Concepts

Measurement is an everyday event that children encounter in many ways: weighing and taking temperatures at the doctor's office; measuring cloth, ribbon, or wire; buying lunch or paying for a movie; pouring water into a glass to mix a fruit drink; timing the baking of a cake; or checking the television schedule. By building on measurement experiences, children and teachers develop the mathematical concepts and skills needed to be thoughtful consumers and users of measurement. Helping children understand measurement systems requires their active involvement in realistic measuring activities through which they investigate concepts and develop skills using various measuring instruments and tools.

In this chapter you will read about:

1 The meaning and characteristics of measurement and two measuring processes

2 The characteristics of the metric system and the English (customary) system and advantages of the metric system over the English system

3 A general approach to developing measurement concepts and skills, with an emphasis on children's understanding and use of estimation in measurement

4 Linear measure concepts and activities

5 Area measure and perimeter concepts and activities

6 Activities for two- and three-dimensional figures

7 Volume and capacity measure concepts and activities for figures such as cubes, rectangular prisms, pyramids, and cones

8 Mass and weight concepts and activities

9 Concepts and skills related to measuring and recording time, including beginning, ending, and duration

10 Temperature concept and skills connected with various real-life activities

11 Concept and skills with money as a medium of exchange and a measure of value

12 The meaning of angular measure and activities for helping children learn to measure angles

13 Take-home activities dealing with measurement

Measurement activities begin in preschool as children compare the length, area, capacity, and weight (mass) of familiar objects and containers. Group- and teacher-led activities continue for students throughout the grades to extend and deepen understanding of all areas of measurement. In addition to presenting examples of activities for children, in this chapter we include a discussion of the meaning of measurement, characteristics of the metric and English systems of measure, and a model for teaching all types of measurement. As with other content chapters, this chapter follows the NCTM standards. The NCTM measurement standards for Pre-K–2 are as follows:

NCTM Measurement Standard

Instructional programs from prekindergarten through grade 12 should enable all students to:
Understand measurable attributes of objects and the units, systems, and processes of measurement

Pre-K–2 Expectations:
In prekindergarten through grade 2 all students should:
- recognize the attributes of length, volume, weight, area, and time;
- compare and order objects according to these attributes;
- understand how to measure using nonstandard and standard units;
- select an appropriate unit and tool for the attribute being measured.
Apply appropriate techniques, tools, and formulas to determine measurements.

Pre-K–2 Expectations:
In prekindergarten through grade 2 all students should:
- measure with multiple copies of units of the same size, such as paper clips laid end to end;

- use repetition of a single unit to measure something larger than the unit, for instance, measuring the length of a room with a single meterstick;
- use tools to measure;
- develop common referents for measures to make comparisons and estimates.

Even before children learn to count, they exhibit a general idea about "more" and "less." At an early age children listen to stories such as *Goldilocks and the Three Bears* and compare bear sizes of Papa Bear, Mama Bear, and Baby Bear. Young children are proud to report their age in years, even though they have not yet formed a concept of time. By counting apples, oranges, plastic chips, and other **discrete**, or *countable*, objects, children learn a more precise way to compare the sizes of sets and they develop the meaning of whole numbers. Similarly, measurement concepts begin with general comparisons of a *qualitative* nature: One cookie is *bigger* than another; one building is *shorter* than another; this is a *heavier* box, a *slower* car, a *longer* room, or a *colder* day. However, these characteristics of length, volume, speed, and heat cannot be counted directly. They are **continuous** properties (continuous properties can be subdivided into progressively smaller and smaller units, such as time) that can take on an infinite number of values; in order to make *quantitative* comparisons about them (how much shorter? how much colder?), they must be measured.

Continuous properties are measured by selecting an appropriate unit and comparing that unit to the characteristic being measured. Through measurement we associate numbers with the physical qualities of length, area, capacity, volume, angles, weight (mass), and temperature. Other measured characteristics have no physical properties. A clock measures the passage of a nontangible characteristic—time. Money is a measure of value or worth or exchange. The units chosen for time are based on astronomical observation, and those for money are based on social and economic conventions.

Volume measuring kit

Direct and Indirect Measurement

Measurement uses a direct or an indirect process. Direct measurement can be used for length, area, capacity (volume), and weight by applying a unit directly to the object being measured. The length of a desk can be measured by lining up pencils, ice cream sticks, or paper clips along its edge. The capacity of a jar can be measured by counting the number of spoonfuls of salt or the number of smaller jars of water it takes to fill it. Units of measure that are applied directly possess the same attribute as the object being measured. Indirect measurement refers to processes that determine the measure of an object by nondirect means, for example, finding the height of a pole by using shadows or trigonometry.

Measuring Processes

Linear measurement tools, such as rulers, yardsticks, and metersticks, have the attribute of length and are used to measure the characteristic of length (also called height, width, depth, or distance). A yardstick can be laid end to end 100 times to verify the length of a football field. Area has two dimensions, length and width; it is measured using units also having two dimensions, such as square inches and square meters. The area of a desktop can be measured by covering the top with tiles or square-inch cards. The school play area can be painted with squares (length and width) for playing four-square games. After squeezing 100 apples in a cider press, the volume of cider can be determined by filling and emptying a cup until all the cider has been poured out; the liquid volume of cider is then expressed as the number of cups counted. On a two-arm pan balance, the weight (mass) of a book in one pan is determined by placing unit weights in the other pan. When the pans balance, the weight of the book is equal to the total of all the weights on the other side. In each situation a measurement is made with units that have the same characteristic as the object being measured.

Younger children compare the lengths of two objects by lining them up side by side. Such a direct comparison of their lengths will enable young children to determine the longer object. Of course, it is not always possible to align the two objects for such a comparison. If this is the case, younger students will use the concept of **transitivity** (transferring the measurement characteristic of an object to another object in order to make a comparison) to determine which object is the longer object. For example, if students want to compare the widths of two windows, they might cut a piece of string or paper tape to the width of the first window. They then compare the length of the string to the width of the second window. Students can then determine whether or not the second window is wider than the first window. In this case the width of the first window is transferred to the length of the string, and then the length of string is compared to the width of the second window. An example of transitivity can be found in amusement parks. Some rides have height restrictions. A pole marked at 48 inches determines who may enter the ride. The height of the shortest acceptable rider is transferred to the pole. The pole is then used to determine who may or may not enter the ride. Lobstermen use a measuring gauge to determine whether a lobster is the legal size. The gauge is applied to the body section of the lobster. If the lobster body is shorter than the gauge, the lobster is thrown back into the ocean.

In direct measurement, applying a unit of measure one or more times to an object being measured is referred to as **iteration**. The yardstick is applied, or iterated, 100 times along the length of the football field. The tiles or cards are iterated on the top of the desk, the cup is iterated in the cider, and the ounce weights are iterated to determine the weight of the book. The units can be large or small, but the process of iteration is always present in direct measure.

Even if students measure the length of an object with multiple units, such as lining up paper clips, this is still a form of iteration. With conventional measuring tools the iteration process is built into the tool. On a yardstick the iteration of 3 feet and of 36 inches is marked on the rule. The meterstick has decimeter and centimeter divisions. Weights often come in 10-gram, 50-gram, 100-gram, 250-gram, and 500-gram units that can be used in differing combinations, instead of using 1-gram units again and again.

Time and temperature cannot be measured directly; they require instruments that indirectly translate evidence of their presence into a measurable form. Indirect measurement of time is based on astronomical definitions of year, month, day, hour, and minute. Modern clocks show the passage of time in synchronicity with standard time maintained by astronomers in Greenwich, England, at the United States Naval Observatory, and at the U.S. National Institute of Standards and Technology. Temperature is also measured indirectly. Some weather thermometers have a number scale aligned with a tube that contains a liquid. Warm temperatures cause the liquid to expand and rise in the tube; cool temperatures cause it to contract and drop in the tube. The temperature is determined by looking at the scale and reading the numeral at the top of the liquid in the tube. Other thermometers have springs that expand and contract with the gain or loss of heat, moving a needle on the face of the thermometer. Body temperature is measured electronically by reading the heat in the ear canal.

Weight (mass) can be measured directly, as with a pan balance, but is more often measured indirectly. The ordinary home scale is actually a spring mechanism or electronic sensor calibrated to register pressure. The reading on the scale displays the weight that would be equivalent to a certain pressure. Electronic measuring devices are indirect measuring processes that substitute for direct measuring processes.

What Teachers Should Know About Teaching Measurement

The study of measurement begins with developing in children a foundational understanding of the various attributes that can be measured. Children develop personal benchmarks for measurement units before they convert from one unit to another. Only after children understand such concepts as perimeter, area, and volume can they begin to explore and apply formulas for computing them.

The concept of measurement involves two types of data: discrete and continuous. Counting or measuring discrete data is not challenging for children, but measuring continuous data is. Children who can iterate an inch to determine that the length of a pencil is 6 inches long may have difficulty determining the length of a pencil using a ruler, even with markings on it. In this case the data are now continuous, with no unit or iteration marks on the pencil. Similarly, area is usually a discrete data collection. Even with side lengths of a rectangle clearly marked, the notion of square units representing the area of the rectangle is really continuous data because the units are not individually represented. Time and careful development are needed for children to bridge the gap between their natural ability to count discrete measurement units and the sophistication to deal with continuous measurement data. The activities in this chapter provide examples of the types of experiences that will prepare children to work with continuous units.

Approximation, Precision, and Accuracy

Approximation. When objects in a set are counted, the number is exact: 1 or 13 or 145. When an object is measured, however, the measurement is approximate. The length of the table may be a little more or less than 13 pencils, almost 115 paper clips, or about 2 yards. The fact that measurement is always approximate stems from the nature of measurement and measurement units. At least theoretically, for any unit of measurement chosen, another smaller unit exists.

Counting the smaller units of measure yields a more precise measure for an object. For example, the height of a door measured with a meterstick might be more than 2 meters. If a decimeter is used to measure the door, the result might be a little more than 22 decimeters. Using a centimeter as the unit might show a measure of more than 222 cm but less than 223 cm. If it were practical to measure with millimeter units, the door might be a little more than 2,226 millimeters.

Each subsequent measurement is more precise, but the precision can be improved indefinitely (theoretically, if not practically) by measuring with smaller, still more precise units. Even if the measurement appears to be exact, we recognize that it is not. Saying "exactly 12 o'clock" or "A football field is exactly 100 yards long" is misleading. While you were saying 12:00, the time had already changed. A marked football field is approximately 100 yards long, rather than exactly 100 yards long. It may be 1 inch shorter or 1 inch longer than 100 yards.

Precision and Accuracy. The difference between precision and accuracy is important. *Precision* refers to units of measure. Inches are more precise than feet or yards. Milliliters are more precise than liters. *Accuracy* refers to the care with which a measurement is made. If the finish line for a 100-meter dash is only 99.8 meters from the start line, then the measurement is not accurate. An inaccuracy of this sort would negate records set on the track.

The need for precision and accuracy depends on the measurement setting. Ball bearings for the U.S. space program must be manufactured to a tolerance of 0.00001 centimeter. Cutting cloth for a shirt does not require the same accuracy, but miscutting by an inch can have serious results in fitting the shirt. An optician who measures the bifocal line inaccurately will prepare glasses unsuited for the user. Household measuring cups and spoons are precise enough for cooking but not for chemical and pharmaceutical purposes. Measuring four cups of flour rather than three, however, may ruin the cake. Human error contributes to inaccuracy in measurement—from wrongly lining up the tool, to misreading the result, to recording it incorrectly. The carpenter's adage "measure twice, cut once" is good advice for all measurement.

ⒺXERCISE

During the study of common fractions, students use number lines to develop an intuitive understanding that there is no smallest fraction. How could a teacher relate knowledge of fractions to an understanding of approximation resulting from smaller and smaller units of measure? ●●●

Selecting Appropriate Units and Tools

Choosing the unit that has the best balance of precision, accuracy, and ease of use is an important measurement skill. Measuring a football field with a yardstick would be tedious and subject to substantial error. Accurate and easy-to-use electronic and laser measuring devices have been developed to replace many mechanical devices. An electronic device will give a more accurate and precise measure of a football field than a yardstick; therefore it is more appropriate, when available. Such a device may measure the field as 3,595.72 inches, indicating that the field needs to be lengthened by approximately 4.28 inches. A football field is measured in yards, but yards are not an appropriate unit to measure the wingspan of a hummingbird, where even inches are too large for the task. A 500-gram mass eliminates the tedium of measuring apples with 500 1-gram weights; weighing a grape with a 500-gram mass would not be sensible. Measuring a door height with 2,226 separate millimeter units is not practical. A meterstick marked in millimeters is more efficient.

> Understanding that all measurements are approximations is a difficult, but important concept for students. (National Council of Teachers of Mathematics, 2000, p. 46)

Divisions on a meterstick indicating decimeters, centimeters, and millimeters allow measurement without iterating the smaller units and increasing human error. However, measuring the door may not be necessary at all. If you were covering a typical classroom door with craft paper, you would measure and cut about 2.5 meters of paper, enough to cover the surface. Selection of the unit and accuracy of measurement are subject to the demands of the task.

ⒺXERCISE

Give two examples of measurement units that are appropriate for measuring the following items. Give one inappropriate unit for each example.

- **A length of jewelry wire**
- **Contents of a cereal box**
- **Area of a hall**

What are two situations in which accuracy of measurement is important? ●●●

The English System. The English system of measurement was developed in Europe over a long period of time. Units of measure were originally derived from common usage, such as the distance from an adult's nose to the fingertip on an outstretched arm (yard), grains of barley laid end to end (inch), stones (weight), and the distance a horse could pull a plow before needing to rest (a furlong—still used in horse racing).

> The difficulty inherent in trying to use two different measurement systems was exemplified by the crash of the Martian Climate Orbiter. The loss of the $125 million spacecraft was due to miscommunication between the contractor and NASA. The contractor used English units, and NASA mistakenly assumed the units were metric.

The English, or customary, system of measurement has been used in the United States since the country's earliest years, brought from England by the original colonial settlers. Periodic efforts to convert to the metric system have been largely unsuccessful. Thomas Jefferson recommended adoption of the metric system in the early 1800s. The U.S. Congress made the system legal in 1866, and President Gerald Ford signed a voluntary Metric Conversion Act in 1975. Although the public has resisted use of the metric system, the metric system is now widely used in science, industry, and some areas of government. In recent years the U.S. government has stipulated that all suppliers to the military must produce tools, machinery, and armaments in metric units, not English units. Despite such advances, the English system is entrenched in most everyday uses in the United States. Thus children need to learn both the English and metric systems.

> The length of a yard was established by King Henry I of England (1069–1131) as the distance from the tip of his outstretched hand to the tip of the royal nose. In the following years, the length of a yard fluctuated according to the stature of the king. Eventually, Henry VII established the length of the yard as 3 feet and had a standard yard inscribed on a brass rod.

In earlier days measurements varied according to the size of a person's hand or pace, but standard units have since been established, so that inches, cups, and pounds are now the same wherever they are used. However, no common relationship exists between units for each characteristic being measured (12 inches equals 1 foot, 3 feet equals 1 yard, and 1,760 yards equals 1 mile) and from one measurement characteristic to another (between length

and capacity, for example). Tables 18.1 to 18.4 present common English units of measure for length, area, capacity (volume), and weight (mass) and show that the system lacks consistent relationship among units.

The Metric System. In contrast to the English system, the metric system was created in a systematic way during a relatively short span of time in the late 18th century. In 1790, the National Assembly of France directed the French Academy of Sciences "to deduce an invariable standard for all the mea-

TABLE 18.1 ∘ English Linear Measures

12 inches (in.)	=	1 foot (ft)
3 feet (ft)	=	1 yard (yd)
36 inches (in.)	=	1 yard (yd)
5,280 feet (ft)	=	1 mile (mi)
1,760 yards (yd)	=	1 mile (mi)

TABLE 18.2 ∘ English Area Measures

12 inches (in.)	=	1 foot (ft)
144 square inches (in.^{2})	=	1 square foot (ft^2)
9 square feet (ft^2)	=	1 square yard (yd^2)
3,097,600 square yards (yd^2)	=	1 square mile (mi^2)
4,840 square yards (yd^2)	=	1 acre (a.)
640 acres	=	1 square mile (mi^2)

TABLE 18.3 ∘ English Capacity Measures

2 tablespoons (tbsp)	=	1 fluid ounce (fl oz)
8 fluid ounces (fl oz)	=	1 cup (c)
2 cups (c)	=	1 pint (pt)
2 pints (pt)	=	1 quart (qt)
4 quarts (qt)	=	1 gallon (gal)

TABLE 18.4 ∘ English Weight Measures

16 ounces (oz)	=	1 pound (lb)
2,000 pounds (lb)	=	1 ton (T)

sures and all the weights" (Johnson & Norris, 2006). The French National Assembly wanted a new system of measurement to do away with all vestiges of the recently overthrown monarchy. All the old measurement units were tainted by association with the old regime and had to be replaced. The Academy derived its basic unit of length by calculating the distance from the equator to the North Pole and then used one ten-millionth of the distance as the length of a meter.

> The idea for a metric system of measurement was first proposed by Simon Stevin (1548–1620).

Base units for area, capacity, and weight were established at the same time as the meter (m) and were derived from the meter and its subdivisions. Area is measured in square centimeters and square meters, and volume (capacity) in cubic centimeters, cubic decimeters, and cubic meters. The base unit for land area is the *are* (pronounced "air"), measuring 100 square meters (10 m by 10 m). A hectare (ha) is 100 ares. Volume is measured in cubic centimeters (cm^3) and cubic meters (m^3). One cubic centimeter of water at 4° Celsius (the temperature at which water is most dense) is 1 gram, a basic metric unit of weight. Originally, a prototype, or standard, rod with a length of 1 meter was made from platinum and was stored in a sterile environment under constant temperature and humidity. Today, a meter is defined as 1,650,763.73 wavelengths of the orange-red line of the krypton-86 atom. Only the kilogram is still based on a physical object—a platinum-iridium solid weighing 1 kilogram kept at the International Bureau of Weights and Measures in Sevres, France. Tables 18.5 to 18.8 show commonly used units of measure in the metric system.

One significant characteristic of the metric system has already been mentioned: the measures of area, capacity, and weight are all derived from the unit for length. Another important feature is its decimal system; larger and smaller units are multiples of 10 or divisions by 10 of the base units. This connection to the Hindu-Arabic numeration system helps children develop their understanding of the metric system. Table 18.9 illustrates this attribute through the equivalence of the various units of measure for length.

The metric system has several advantages over the English system:

TABLE 18.5 Metric Linear Measures

10 millimeters (mm)	=	1 centimeter (cm)
10 centimeters (cm)	=	1 decimeter (dm)
10 decimeters (dm)	=	1 meter (m)
1,000 meters (m)	=	1 kilometer (km)

TABLE 18.6 Metric Area Measures

100 square centimeters (cm^2)	= 1 square decimeter (dm^2)
100 square decimeters (dm^2)	= 1 square meter (m^2)
100 square meters (m^2)	= 1 are
100 are	= 1 hectare (ha)

TABLE 18.7 Metric Capacity Measures

1,000 milliliters (ml)	=	1 liter (l)
1 cubic centimeter (cm^3)	=	1 milliliter (ml)
1 cubic decimeter (dm^3)	=	1 liter (l)
1,000 liters (l)	=	1 kiloliter (kl)

TABLE 18.8 Metric Weight (Mass) Measures

1,000 milligrams (mg)	=	1 gram (g)
1,000 grams (g)	=	1 kilogram (kg)
1,000 kilograms (kg)	=	1 metric ton (t)

- It is similar to the base-10 system of numeration.

- It is simple and easy to use.

- Only a few units of measure are commonly used—meter, gram, liter. Most people only need to know one or two units for each type of measurement.

- A uniform set of prefixes applies to units of measure in each area of measurement. Greek prefixes are used for units that are multiples of the basic unit (kilo = 1,000, hecto = 100, deca = 10). Latin prefixes are used for units that are divisions of the basic unit (milli = $\frac{1}{1,000}$, centi = $\frac{1}{100}$, deci = $\frac{1}{10}$).

TABLE 18.9 • Metric Equivalents		
Metric Length Equivalents	**Metric Weight Equivalents**	**Metric Capacity Equivalents**
1,000 meters = 1 kilometer (km)	1,000 liters = 1 kiloliter (kl)	1,000 grams = 1 kilogram (kg)
100 meters = 1 hectometer (hm)	100 liters = 1 hectoliter (hl)	100 grams = 1 hectogram (hg)
10 meters = 1 decameter (dkm)	10 liters = 1 decaliter (dkl)	10 grams = 1 decagram (dkg)
1 meter = 1 meter (m)	1 liter = 1 liter (l)	1 gram = 1 gram (g)
$\frac{1}{10}$ meter = 1 decimeter (dm)	$\frac{1}{10}$ liter = 1 deciliter (dl)	$\frac{1}{10}$ gram = 1 decigram (dg)
$\frac{1}{100}$ meter = 1 centimeter (cm)	$\frac{1}{100}$ liter = 1 centiliter (cl)	$\frac{1}{100}$ gram = 1 centigram (cg)
$\frac{1}{1,000}$ meter = 1 millimeter (mm)	$\frac{1}{1,000}$ liter = 1 milliliter (ml)	$\frac{1}{1,000}$ gram = 1 milligram (mg)

MISCONCEPTION

When students study the metric system, they often learn to multiply or divide by powers of 10 to convert metric measures. Some develop the mistaken rule that when converting from a smaller unit to a larger one, the correct process is to multiply. For example to change 25 centimeters to meters, some students would multiply by 100 rather than divide. (Later in this chapter we suggest other strategies to solve an example like this one.)

Once students learn and understand the metric prefixes, they can use them regardless of the measurement characteristic. Thus in Table 18.9 the measurement unit *gram* or *liter* can replace the length unit *meter*, and the result is two tables of all the metric units for weight and capacity.

The units of measure shown in Tables 18.1 through 18.8 are commonly used units and, in addition to units for time, money, temperature, and angular measure, are appropriate for study in elementary school.

ⒺXERCISE

The United States is the only industrialized nation not to use the metric system. Why do you think the United States has resisted converting completely to the metric system? ●●●

A Teaching/Learning Model for Measurement

With each type of measurement system children should have a variety of experiences that help them to understand the concept of measurement and be-

come skilled with measurement tools and appropriate units. Measurement activities in the early part of this chapter represent a teaching approach and sequence to measurement; they are intended to develop measurement concepts. As teachers work with younger children, it is useful to see how activities fit together and support the long-range instructional goals and objectives; thus a graphic organizer for measurement activities is presented in Figure 18.1. The sequence for introducing measurements concepts to children is as follows:

- Building understanding of the characteristic being measured and its use in everyday life
- Using nonstandard units with exploratory measurements
- Using standard units in both the English and metric systems, with tools focusing on determining and recording measurements
- Developing mental models for common measures
- Estimating measurements using mental models
- Engaging in projects and activities that require measurement skills
- Looking for patterns and relationships that lead to formulas for specific measures

This sequence of measurement activities connects concepts of whole numbers, fractional numbers, geometry and spatial reasoning, and patterns and relationships for algebraic thinking.

Work with measurement is spread over all the school years. Early work is largely inventive and

Figure 18.1 Teaching/ learning model for measurement

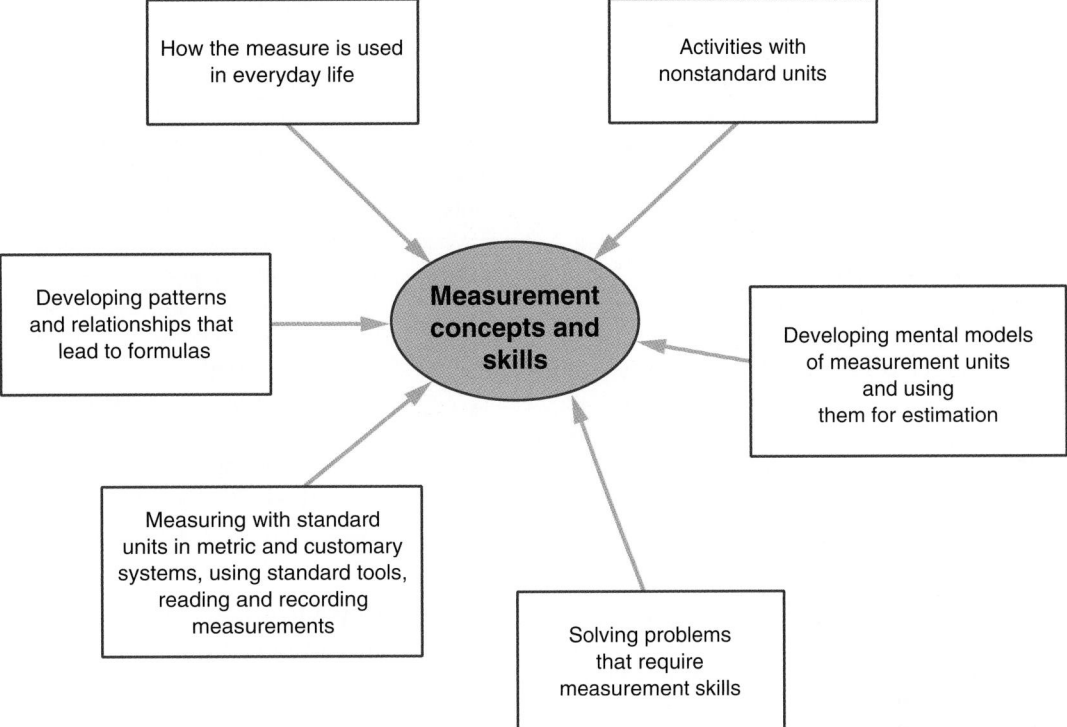

How the measure is used in everyday life

Activities with nonstandard units

Developing patterns and relationships that lead to formulas

Measurement concepts and skills

Developing mental models of measurement units and using them for estimation

Measuring with standard units in metric and customary systems, using standard tools, reading and recording measurements

Solving problems that require measurement skills

investigative by nature. Children in preschool, kindergarten, and primary grades begin with activities to establish the everyday contexts for measurement and to introduce measurement with nonstandard units. Students who conserve length, area, and volume understand that these concepts do not change, even when an object's position or appearance is altered. Students who cannot conserve length, for example, will think a yardstick is one length in a horizontal position and a different length when it is rotated to a vertical position. They do not think that the yardstick conserves or maintains the same length in all positions.

Children generally begin to conserve length and area when they are 8 or 9 years old. The ability to conserve is part of the maturation process and need not be explicitly taught. Teachers who work with nonconservers or preconservers should not be surprised at children's inconsistent use of instruments and units. However, the fact that students are not conservers should not prevent them from engaging in many activities that provide the foundation for understanding measurement. These early experiences will allow them to learn that the pencil has a fixed length whether it is horizontal or vertical or that the jar has a fixed capacity even though it can be filled by 20 small bottles or by 10 medium-size ones. Teachers can create many situations

for students to recognize ways in which they use measurement.

- A classroom height chart provides opportunities to discuss and compare heights throughout the year.
- A bucket of square ceramic or plastic tiles, or squares cut from index cards, can provide opportunities for covering desktops, books, and other surfaces.
- A sand table or plastic tub full of packing peanuts or inert packing granules with variously sized containers and measures invites comparison of volumes by filling and pouring from one container to another.
- Work with clay or plasticine allows children to feel both the volume and the mass of clay.
- A daily schedule and the calendar are discussed in terms of starting times, ending times, and time between events or time until another event.
- Checking daily temperatures helps children connect the descriptive and predictive nature of weather to reading thermometers.
- The teacher can ask students and parents to look for examples of measurement outside school.

These and many other real-life connections help students build meaning about measurement.

Research for the Classroom

Recent research has added to our knowledge of how young children master measurement concepts. Some elementary school mathematics texts suggest using iteration to begin to develop students' measurement concepts. One interesting finding from a recent study is that it is transitivity of measurement that allows students to make comparisons based on their unit iterations (Reece & Kamii, 2000b). With transitivity students "transfer" the length of an object to a second object, which is then used for comparisons to other objects. For example, the heights of two students are each "transferred" to the iterated units that students use. These two numbers of iterated units are compared to determine who is taller or shorter, and by

how much. Furthermore, the number of iterated units may in and of itself be used to represent the student's height (Reece & Kamii, 2000a).

A further finding of a related research study was that most second-grade students can use transitivity with length measurements (Reece & Kamii, 2000a). However, not until grade 3 can a large majority of students use iteration in length measurement. Iteration with volume (grade 4) and time (grade 5) develops after length iteration (Reece & Kamii, 2000a). A recommendation from these findings is to provide younger children with measurement activities that focus on both transitivity and iteration measurement concepts and not on iteration alone.

MULTICULTURALCONNECTION

Although rice, popping corn, or some other dried grains or legumes will perform well as a way to measure capacity, some students may object to what they see as a wasteful use of foodstuffs. It is important to be sensitive to such objections and to be prepared to use alternative materials, such as packaging peanuts, inert packing granules, or sand.

Activity 18.1 illustrates measurement of length, area, capacity (volume), and weight suitable for the developmental level of primary students, but the activities can be adapted for older students who need additional experiences before formal instruction in measurement. Stations 2 and 4 focus on transitivity, and Stations 1 and 3 feature iteration. Station 1 explores capacity, Station 2, weight, Station 3, length, and Station 4, time. Three of the stations involve a *qualitative comparison*, where children look for which object is heavier, longer, or slower rather than how much heavier, how much longer, or how much slower. Thus the focus is on the attribute itself rather than on any numerical representation of the attribute.

Attention to the vocabulary of measurement is important. While children are working informally with measurement materials and activities, the teacher can use different vocabulary to express similar measurement ideas. Measurement of length and distance is related to many questions: How long is it? How deep is it? How wide is it? How tall is it? How far is it from A to B? and so on.

Measurement of distance is sometimes expressed as elapsed time: It takes 30 minutes to travel from

City A to Town B. Children need to build this concept by talking about start time, stop time, and time in between start and stop. Developing a flexible measurement vocabulary is essential from these early explorations throughout the elementary grades.

Two activities on the companion website extend the measurement attributes considered in the four stations of Activity 18.1. "Drawing Straws" and "Comparing Mass in Sand Cans" provide children with the opportunity to compare lengths using straws and to compare weights (mass) using sand cans.

Activities to Develop Measurement Concepts and Skills

Nonstandard Units of Measure

Planned measurement activities frequently begin in primary grades, even though not all children are conservers. Once begun, measurement work and lessons continue throughout the elementary school years. Activities with nonstandard units bridge the gap between exploratory work and the introduction of standard units. Two goals for work with nonstandard units are to help children recognize the need for a uniform set of measures and to lay the groundwork for their understanding of the various units of standard measure.

Activities with nonstandard measurement provide experiences dealing with linear, area, capacity, and weight (mass) measures. Measuring the length of an object using dowel sticks, cardboard strips cut in uniform lengths, or other nonstandard units helps

ACTIVITY 18.1   Station Time (Reasoning)

Level: Grades K–3

Setting: Individual or student pairs

Objective: Students explore nonstandard measurement units with materials noted for each station.

Station 1: Capacity

Materials: Plastic or glass bottles marked at different levels with colored plastic tape. Put the bottles, along with several pounds of a dried grain (rice, wheat, or popcorn), a funnel, and a scoop, in a large plastic tub.

- Children use the scoop and funnel to fill the containers to the level of the tape on each bottle.

- Children may choose to count and record the scoops needed to fill each container to its mark, or you can supply a record sheet.

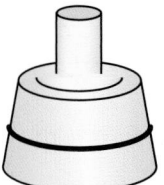 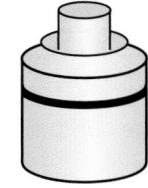 

Station 2: Heavier and Lighter

Materials: A two-pan balance or other simple balance scale; pairs of objects such as a toy car and a wooden block; a chalkboard eraser and a small bag of rice; a small rubber ball and a box of pencils

- The balance gives children opportunities to compare pairs of objects to determine heavier or lighter. In children's first work with the beam balance, they learn to make the sides balance by putting objects in both pans until the crossbar is level. They also see the crossbar go down when the object in one pan is heavier.

- Set out pairs of objects and ask students to compare their weights. Prepare a mat on which children can place objects as they work.

Station 3: Longer and Shorter

Materials: Three 10-centimeter rods from a Cuisenaire or base-10 set with sticks to be measured. Cut wooden sticks so that some are longer and some are shorter than the rods; make a large mat with the headings "Longer Than 3" and "Shorter Than 3."

- Show how to line up the rods along the sticks, beginning at one end of a stick. Children "measure" the sticks and place them on the mat, putting those that are longer than 3 rods on one side and those that are shorter than 3 rods on the other side.

- Children may also find that they need a category of "Just about 3."

Station 4: Which Is Slower?

Materials: Several cans with holes of varying sizes punched through the bottoms (avoid sharp edges); water or clean fine-grained sand in a plastic tub. Paint cans different colors, or paint a number on each.

- Have a child select a can, fill it, and hold it so the water or sand drains through the hole. (If sand is used, the child will need to gently shake the can to drain all of it.)

- Ask questions as the children observe what happens: Does the red can drain quickly or slowly? Which can drains more slowly, the red can or the blue can? What is the color of the can that drains the fastest? Can you put the cans in order from quickest to slowest? What can you tell me about the size of the hole and the speed at which the can empties?

to establish the iteration measuring process. Paper strips, each cut to the student's height, are used in Activity 18.2 to compare students' heights. New pencils are used in Activity 18.3. Students begin at one end, placing a pencil to line up with one end of the object they are measuring. They continue to line up pencils until the line of pencils is approximately equal to the length of the object. Then they count the pencils that they have laid out to determine the length of the object in pencil units. Later, they learn to use a single pencil and the iteration process.

The companion website activity "Which Unit Did You Use?" directs students to measure the length of specific items using nonstandard units, such as

ACTIVITY 18.2 How Tall Are We?

Level: Grades K–2

Setting: Small groups

Objective: Students cut paper tape to match their height and then arrange the tapes in order on a class wall or chalkboard.

Materials: Register or adding machine paper tape

- Demonstrate how to cut a length of paper tape to the height of a student. Affix a strip of paper tape to the wall next to a student. Be sure that the tape is just touching the floor.

- Mark the student's height on the tape, and then cut the tape at that mark.

- Pass out a long strip of paper tape to each student and have the groups work together to cut a strip of tape to the height of each student.

- Have students write their name on their own height tape.

- Ask each group to arrange their tapes in order of height on the chalkboard.

- Examine each group's tapes with the entire class. Whose tape is the longest? Whose tape is the shortest? Whose tape is between two others?

ACTIVITY 18.3 Pencil Measurement

Level: Grades 1–3

Setting: Student pairs

Objective: Students measure length using pencils as units.

Materials: New pencils

- Give each pair of students 8 to 10 new graphite pencils.

- Select an object such as a desktop to measure. Demonstrate how to put pencils end to end to find the length and width of the desk in pencil units. Stress the importance of not leaving gaps between pencils or having pencils overlap.

- Have students record their results, and post them for comparison. Discuss differences in measurement, and emphasize the approximate nature of measurement.

- Use problem cards such as the following to direct children's other length measurement activities.

Penciling

Use new pencils from the box to answer the following questions.

1. How long is the reading table? How wide is the reading table?
2. How wide is the door to the hallway?
3. How high is the chalk tray?
4. Can you figure out a way to decide how high the desk is without measuring it? If you can, tell how high it is.
5. Pick something else in the room, and measure its length, height, or depth.
6. Sketch what you have measured, and label your sketches with the measurements. Write about your measurements in your journal.

pencils, crayons, and stirrers. They then compare the resulting number of units they needed and explore why the numbers vary according to the unit used. As children compare the number of units they use with the length of their measurement unit, they will begin to explore the **principle of compensation**. The principle of compensation stipulates that the smaller a measurement unit is, the more of these units are required to measure an attribute. For example, if the length of a hallway is measured in meters and in inches, the number of inches that measures the hallway length is larger than the number of meters (because an inch is shorter than a meter). Similarly, your weight in ounces is a larger number than your weight in pounds, or kilograms. Walnuts, blocks, and Unifix cubes serve as nonstandard units

of weight in the companion website activity "Way to Weigh." In the companion website activity "Fill It Up" students explore capacity by comparing the capacity of varied containers. The companion website activity "Foot by Foot" focuses on using children's nonstandard personal foot lengths for measuring.

ⒺXERCISE

Problem cards are used in Activity 18.3 and in several of the companion website activities to direct children's activities with nonstandard units. Select a type of measurement—linear, weight, capacity, or area—and a nonstandard unit for it. Prepare a problem card to direct activities with your nonstandard unit and measuring processes. ●●●

In 1962, a group of students at MIT in Cambridge, Massachusetts, used a new nonstandard measure to determine the length of a bridge across the Charles River into Boston. They used the *smoot*. The smoot was the height of one of the students in the group, and they determined the length of the bridge in smoots by iterating Oliver R. Smoot Jr. across the bridge. Painted markings on the Harvard Bridge commemorate the smoot measurement unit.

Standard Units of Measure

POINT OF VIEW

Generally, if children's initial measurement explorations use a variety of units, nonstandard as well as standard, they will develop understanding about the nature of units and the need for standard units. For example, when students measure their height using a length of string and a meterstick and then compare uniformity of results, they build an awareness of the value of a standard unit. (National Council of Teachers of Mathematics, 2000, p. 46)

All the preceding activities will develop children's sense of measurement both as a concept for qualifying an attribute (length, weight, capacity) and as a process (iteration, transference). The activities also demonstrate the need for a standard unit so that any measured attribute can be easily understood and adapted to others.

To help children extend their understanding of standard units, they may find it helpful to establish personal benchmarks for some measurement units. They might use the weight of a bottle of soda as a benchmark for a pound, the span of a hand for half a foot, the width of a finger for an inch, or the distance from their chin to the floor for a meter. Personal benchmarks such as these are essential for children to develop their estimation skills with measurement and to be able to recognize reasonable measurement data. Activity 18.4 helps children establish personal benchmarks on their body for an inch and a foot and then tests their selection by measuring the length of an object using their personal unit. The companion website activity "Almost a Quarter of . . ." engages children in finding objects that are approximately $\frac{1}{4}$ yard in length. They then measure the objects and compare the actual length to their estimated length. *How Big Is a Foot?*, featured in the Using Children's Literature section at the end of this chapter, is the story of a queen's bed. It is an interesting way to emphasize the need for a standard foot measure.

As noted, children need to learn both the metric and the English systems of measurement. They learn about measurement best when they have frequent opportunities to measure objects so that they can construct their understanding of units and measuring processes. The time needed to learn both measurement systems need not be extensive. Children who understand basic measurement concepts and who understand how to use the various instruments can apply their knowledge to situations, both real and contrived, in which measuring is involved.

The study of standard units of measure also offers opportunities for children to broaden their understanding of other cultures. As indicated earlier, the United States is the only major country in the world that has not adopted the metric system of measure as its standard system. Children who began their schooling in another country may have some understanding of the metric system. They can share their knowledge of the system and some of

ACTIVITY 18.4 **When Is a Foot a Foot?**

Level: Grades 2–4

Setting: Individual

Objective: Students find lengths on their body to serve as approximations of 1 inch and 1 foot.

Materials: Rulers with inch markings

- Pass out rulers to students.
- Show students that the second knuckle of your index finger is a good approximation for an inch.

- Ask students to find two body measurements that approximate an inch and a foot.
- Have students use their two body measurements to find the width of their desk (inch unit) and the length of the chalkboard (foot unit).
- Have students record their data and then measure both lengths using the ruler to check their accuracy.

the ways they learned to use it in their homelands. At the same time, children with knowledge of the English system can share it with classmates.

Rote exercises in which children convert English to metric units and metric to English units are not meaningful ways to develop their understanding of measurement concepts or systems. According to NCTM, such activities should be avoided with younger children and are of dubious benefit for older ones; teachers should avoid extended attention to exact conversions between the two systems. However, benchmark relationships between the two systems are useful to know, and over time children need opportunities to develop them. Common relationships or benchmarks children can develop during measurement activities are these:

- One meter is slightly more than 1 yard. One yard is slightly less than 1 meter.

- Two centimeters are a little less than 1 inch. One inch is a little more than 2 centimeters.

- One kilogram is a little more than 2 pounds. One pound is a little less than one-half of a kilogram.

- One liter is slightly more than 1 quart. One quart is slightly less than 1 liter.

Learning centers are useful settings for many measurement activities. Set up a center with objects to be measured and instruments for measuring for length, area, volume (capacity), and weight (mass). Problem cards can be used as a way to direct work at the stations. Many of the activities in this chapter are designed for learning centers.

Teaching Children How to Measure Length

Building on their experiences with nonstandard measures, children are ready to begin work with a ruler. Children's first ruler should be one that has no marks along the edge; pine molding cut to lengths of 1 foot, 1 yard, or 1 meter serves nicely. Sometimes standard yardsticks or metersticks have divisions and numerals printed only on one side. These can be turned over to the blank side and used as described in what follows. Prepare problem cards to direct students' work as they measure the length and width of a desk, the distance from a classroom

> **MISCONCEPTION**
> Younger children sometimes try to fit the object to the length of a measuring unit. For example, a child who is measuring a shoe that is shorter than a foot might say, "I need more shoe."

door to the teacher's desk, or the distance between the classroom door and the principal's office. Recorded distances can be phrased such as "longer than 12 sticks and shorter than 13 sticks" or "about 13 sticks." Introducing approximate measures such as these can help children deal with measurements that are not a whole number of units.

Perimeters

Perimeter is the measure of the distance around a closed figure and is an extension of length measurement. In practical terms, perimeter is used to determine the amount of ribbon needed for the border on a place mat or bedspread and the amount of fencing needed to enclose a backyard swimming pool. Exercises dealing with realistic situations give children practical experiences that help them to determine perimeters and to distinguish perimeter from area measures.

Children can use Cuisenaire rods, trains of Unifix cubes, or centimeter rulers to find the perimeters of such things as picture and window frames, pillow covers with lace trimming, and other objects that have wooden, cloth, and paint trims (Figure 18.2). Older children can also use metric tape measures or trundle wheels to determine perimeters of class-

Figure 18.2 Unifix cubes framing the perimeter of a drawing

rooms, playground areas, and larger regions. Connections between mathematics and everyday life become evident as children engage in projects in which they, for example, determine the perimeter of a picture in order to put a border around it and investigate the cost of the chain-link fence that encloses a play area or the school grounds.

The perimeter of plane figures is determined by finding the measure of each side and adding their lengths (Figure 18.3). Students can measure the side lengths of various everyday objects such as books, posters, and placemats. See the companion website activity "Walking Around," in which students pace off the perimeter of shapes taped on the classroom floor.

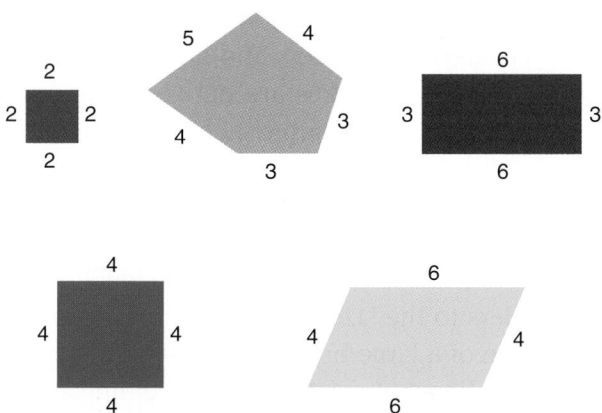

Figure 18.3 Perimeter of plane figures

Students might also measure the perimeter of figures on a geoboard or figures they have drawn on dot paper or graph paper. After similar measurement

of perimeter activities, older students better understand formulas for perimeters of common objects:

Perimeter of a square:
$$p = s + s + s + s = 4 \times s = 4s$$
Perimeter of a rectangle:
$$p = l + w + l + w = 2 \times l + 2 \times w = 2l + 2w$$
Perimeter of an equilateral triangle:
$$p = s + s + s = 3 \times s = 3s$$

ⓔXERCISE

Draw two polygons, and label each of their sides with letters. Estimate the perimeter of each shape in inches or centimeters. Write a formula for the perimeter of the two shapes. Measure each of the sides, and calculate the perimeter. How accurate were your estimates? ●●●

Teaching Children About Measuring Area

Intuitive concepts of area are developed when children cover index cards with colored squares or gummed stickers. Such an experience builds children's understanding of area as a covering, in contrast to linear measures. They also experiment with different shapes to cover a figure, such as circles or irregular figures. They discover that using shapes such as circles is not effective because of the gaps between them. Thus they gain an intuitive understanding for using square units to determine area. Activity 18.5 uses children's footprints to measure area.

ACTIVITY 18.5   Big Foot (Communication)

Level: Grades 1–4

Setting: Small groups

Objective: Students trace their foot on graph paper and approximate the area of the outline.

Materials: Graph paper

- Pass out graph paper to students in groups.

- Have students help each other trace their footprint on the graph paper.

- Have students count the number of squares that their footprint covers. They can keep track of the squares that have been counted by coloring them as they count.

- Allow student groups to decide how to deal with squares that are partially covered by a footprint.

- Have students record their data on their footprint, and post the footprints on the classroom wall.

- Have student volunteers explain how they solved the problem of the partially covered squares (counted only whole squares? counted only those at least half covered? tried to combine partially covered squares to make whole squares?).

Older children use area measures to answer the following questions:

- How many square inches of paper are needed to cover the bottom of our bird's cage?
- How much paint do we need to put a "sky" on the background prop for our play?
- How many pounds of fertilizer are needed to give a fall feeding to the school's grassy areas?
- What will it cost to have the classroom carpet cleaned if the price is 75 cents per square foot?

Many children at all grade levels in elementary school confuse area and perimeter. Activity 18.6 provides an exploration for children that compares area and perimeter using tables and chairs. In the activity children observe that any arrangement of four tables will not service the same number of chairs.

❸XERCISE

How do you remember the difference between perimeter and area? ●●●

Teaching Children About Measuring Capacity and Volume

Many real-life questions are related to capacity and volume measurement:

- How much does this jar hold?
- How much sugar do I need?
- What is the dosage of this medicine?
- How full is the cup?
- How much can I pack in this suitcase?
- Will the milk left in the carton fit into my glass?
- Which refrigerator will hold more?

Capacity and volume are two ways of thinking about and expressing the same characteristic in measurement. Capacity measures have been established for products such as liquids measured in cups, pints, quarts, and liters. Measurement of both liquid and dry ingredients with teaspoons, tablespoons, and cups is common in cooking. Capacity is measured in milliliters and liters in the metric system. Volume measures are derived from length measurements such as cubic inches and cubic feet in the English system and cubic centimeters and cubic meters in the metric system. Capacity refers to the amount that a container will hold. Volume can also refer to the amount that an object will hold, but it also refers to the size of the object, for example, the volume of a large boulder. In the metric system a direct relationship exists between volume and capacity units; a cubic centimeter is also a milliliter, and a cubic decimeter is a liter. Cups, pints, quarts, and gallons have no direct relationship to linear measures in the English system. The measure of a

---

ACTIVITY 18.6   Tables and Chairs (Communication)

Level: Grades 1–3

Setting: Small groups

Objective: Students build models of tables with their tiles.

Materials: 5 tiles (10 square), $\frac{1}{4}$-inch graph paper

- Pass out materials to students.
- Show one tile to students, and suggest that this tile is the model of a table where only one person can sit at each side.
- Have students put two tiles together as shown here, and ask how many people can sit at this long table. (Answer: 6.)
- The challenge for groups is to use four tiles to model all possible table arrangements. Each table must share at least one full side with another table.
- Students should keep track of all their tables in a chart such as this:

Drawing of Table Arrangement	Number of People Who Can Sit at the Table

- After students have collected their data, ask if the same number of tables always seats the same number of people.
- Without using the vocabulary of area and perimeter, help children to observe that although they are using four tables for each setting, the number of people who can sit at their tables varies, but the number of tables does not.
- Repeat with all five tiles.

cup is unrelated to the length of a foot, and a fluid ounce has no connection to the weight unit ounce.

Younger children enjoy filling one container with the contents of another. They might try to guess if the contents of one container will fit into another, or how many times the contents of a smaller container will fit into a larger one. The activities for younger children are similar to those outlined in Activity 18.1. Children compare capacities and rank them in order of magnitude, but all such comparisons are qualitative, with little focus on numerical presentations of volume or capacity.

Teaching Children About Measuring Weight (Mass)

As with the other attributes, younger children informally explore the attribute of weight, by holding an object in each hand. They can judge which one is lighter by using a simple pan balance. They can use nonstandard units, such as buttons or coins, to weigh objects using balance scales (see Activity 18.1, Station 2). Experiences with balance scales can help children understand the balance aspect of equations.

Children at this age (K–2) do not need to consider the difference between weight and mass. (We discuss the differences later in the chapter.) The focus for young children is on building a sensory understanding of weight and making qualitative comparisons using their bodies and simple balance scales.

Teaching Children About Measuring Angles

Measurement of angles is often considered a geometry topic, appropriate for the higher grades. However, the concept of an angle can be developed in primary grades before the introduction of degrees and protractors for measuring them. As children learn to tell time, they can form "human" clock faces with a child standing at each numeral on a circle and others acting as clock hands, moving from numeral to numeral. The angles formed by the human clock (Figure 18.4) and any demonstration clock informally introduce angles. Children can talk about

Figure 18.4 Children demonstrate angles as a human clock.

the minute hand at quarter-, half-, and three-quarter hours and whether the hour and minute hands are close together or far apart. Children can also use their index and middle fingers to form different angles.

Students explore angles by turning themselves around during physical education games or music and dance. As they make a full turn, a half-turn, and a quarter-turn, they develop their spatial sense of angles. The concept of turns and angles is embedded in geometry activities with materials such as pattern blocks, tangrams, and tessellations (see Chapter 17).

Young children also learn about squares, rectangles, and triangles, which have combinations of right, obtuse, and acute angles. While studying these figures, children demonstrate the different angles with their arms and draw them on paper. As students work with pattern blocks and tangrams, they notice the angles and which ones are the same or combine to make a larger angle. Children compare and label the angles with their own words (corner angle, little angle, big angle). The terms *right*, *acute*, and *obtuse* angles and the number of degrees in each type may not be introduced in the early grades, but gradually they are used in naming and comparing angles. In the companion website activity "Categorizing Angles" students use the corner of a file card to identify right, acute, and obtuse angles.

Teaching Children About Measuring Temperature

Children have had many experiences with temperature; *hot* is one of the first cautionary words to toddlers. Children recognize differences in activities and clothes related to outdoor and indoor temperatures and seasonal variations. Everyday experiences serve as a basis for introducing measurement of temperature. In Activity 18.7 children feel temperatures on different outdoor surfaces in sun and shade. A drawing or journal-writing activity might prompt children to recall the hottest and coldest days of their lives, and activities they enjoy most in hot and cold weather. Teachers regularly include a weather record with a graph of sun, cloud, rain, or snow pictures during calendar activities. Such activities alert children to the importance of temperature in their lives and provide a rationale for measuring and recording temperatures.

ⒺXERCISE

What ranges of temperatures do you consider hot, cold, and comfortable? Compare your temperatures to a classmate's. ●●●

Teaching Children to Measure Time

Marilyn Burns (1989) says that time appears in our lives in two different ways. One way is when we think about an interval of time—how long something takes: "Are we almost there?" "How much longer will it take?" The other way is when we are concerned with a particular time of day: "What time does school begin?" "When do I have to go to bed?"

Learning time measurement includes development of concepts of duration or elapsed time, sequences of events in time, and beginning and ending of events. These time concepts are measured with tools such as clocks and calendars. Piaget's research indicates that some children are ready to develop a full understanding of time by the age of 9; others are not ready until 10 or 11. While developing the concept of time, children may exhibit a poor sense of time duration and many misconceptions about sequences of events. For example, children can confuse which events happened before lunch and which happened after lunch. Learning to tell time is not the same as understanding elapsed time or even the concept of time itself. Many informal activities with time help children develop an understanding of elapsed time and time measurement.

Figure 18.5
Sand timer

Activities with sand or water timers, such as those described in Activity 18.1 (Station 4), help develop a sense of duration. Kitchen timers, alarm clocks, and hourglasses can also be used for timing classroom activities such as races and games (Figure 18.5). Children learn what a minute is by becoming aware of how many times they can jump, clap, or sit and stand in a minute (Activities 18.8 and 18.9).

Children also need experiences with sequences or order of events. A classroom schedule alerts them to their regular outline of activities. A televi-

---

ACTIVITY 18.7   Temperature (Connections)

Level: Grades K–2

Setting: Individual

Objective: Compare temperatures of surfaces using sense of touch.

Materials: None

- A sunny day provides a setting for an investigation and discussion about temperature. Choose an outside location where there is a sidewalk, some grass, and a patch of dry ground, and select a time when one part of each location is in sunlight and another part is in shade.

- Have the children remove their shoes and socks and walk on the sunny sidewalk. Talk about how it feels. Have them walk on the shady sidewalk, and compare its feel with that of the sunny sidewalk.

- Have the children walk on the sunny and shady portions of the other surfaces. Discuss differences in temperature, if any, between each spot and the others. Can the children order three or four locations from warmest to coolest?

ACTIVITY 18.8   How Many Can You Do?

Level: Grades 1–3
Setting: Small groups
Objective: Students estimate the number of times they can repeat a simple task in 15–30 seconds.
Materials: Clock with second hand

- Pass out a list of simple tasks such as touching one's chin, blinking one eye, snapping one's fingers, or hopping on one foot.
- Tell students that you will time them as they try to perform the task as many times as possible.
- Allow students time to estimate their task completion total.

- Have students work with a partner who will count the tasks as the partner performs them.
- Allow students the opportunity to practice their tasks before timing them.
- Time the tasks as the partner counts them, and then have the partners reverse roles and time again.
- Have students keep track of their estimated number and the number of times they performed the task in the allotted time.
- Repeat with tasks that the students suggest.

ACTIVITY 18.9   How Long Was That?

Level: Grades 1–3
Setting: Class group
Objective: Students estimate the passing of time intervals.
Materials: Clock with second hand

- Challenge students to keep track of times less than 30 seconds long.
- Explain to students that they will put their heads on their desks for a time interval of not more than 30 seconds.

At the end of the interval, ask students to estimate how many seconds have passed.

- Begin by having students put their heads on their desks. When all are ready, begin timing. After 10 seconds, have students give their estimation of elapsed time.
- Repeat with other time lengths.

sion schedule is used to find and plan television viewing. A morning schedule of getting up, eating, brushing teeth, dressing, and walking or riding to school shows daily sequences. The story sequences in children's books or films, sequences in cartoon strips, and sequences of the seasons, plant growth, and insect development provide opportunities to discuss order of events. Pictures of events and questions like these will instigate thinking about order:

- This morning we did some work with subtraction, and we made some paper bag puppets. Which did we do first? Show with thumbs up if we did subtraction first.

- We did three different things this morning. Raise your left hand if you can tell me what we did first. (Sample answer: Listened to a story.) What did we do next? (Played a math game.) What was the last thing we did? (Saw a video about animals.) What letters or icons could we use to show the order of

the three events? (Accept A-B-C or other code.) Because the game came after the story, and the video came after the game, did the video come before or after the story? (This question helps children see that if event B follows event A, and event C follows event B, then event C follows event A; it deals with transitivity, a difficult concept for children to understand.)

- What happened first in the story? Then what happened? What happened at the end of the story? What do you think happened after the book ended?

- Tell me three things you did at home before you came to school today.

- What did you do first? What did you do next? What was the last thing you did?

- When you get dressed, what do you put on first, your socks or your shoes?

Clocks and Watches

Digital and analog timepieces are part of the children's world, and they should learn to read time with both. For both digital and analog devices the underlying concept is the constant passing of seconds, minutes, and hours.

The digital clock shows the current time only. An analog clock shows current time but also does more. The 15 digits in the numbers 1–12 and moving hands enable children to note the beginning and ending times for an event and the elapsed times between. A child who says, "A half-hour has passed since we began our walk at 3 o'clock" is noting that the minute hand moved from 3:00 to halfway between 3:00 and 4:00. When a parent says, "It is 2:00; we have 45 minutes before the plane leaves at 2:45," a clock face makes it easy to see 2:00 and the distance the minute hand must move to reach 2:45. Reading times in airplane and train schedules, television guides, and other written materials also prepares students for telling time with clocks. The photo illustrates a variety of time-telling materials, including rubber stamps, student clocks, worksheets, and books.

Time measurement kits

Figure 18.6 illustrates one sequence of activities for learning to read a clock. The sequence, described in the list that follows, is not an isolated unit of instruction; the activities are spread over time and completed by the end of the primary grades (National Council of Teachers of Mathematics, 1989, p. 91). Some students are ready to read the clock in first grade; others need several years to become proficient.

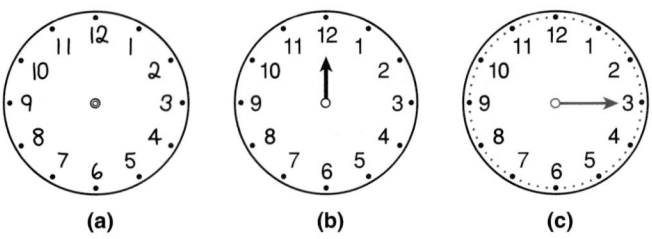

Figure 18.6 Demonstration clocks: (a) without hands; (b) with hour hand only; (c) with minute hand only

- Begin with a large demonstration clock with numerals marked prominently in black. Talk about the sequence of numbers. Children should note that 12 is at the top, 3 on the right, 6 at the bottom, and 9 on the left. Prepare a worksheet with one large clock face but no numerals. Children are to write the numerals at each hour mark (Figure 18.6a).

- Add a black hour hand to the clock. Point it at the 1. Tell children that the black hand points to a number that tells the hour. Rotate the hand from 1 to 2 to 3, and so on, as children count. Then point it at different numbers and have children tell the hour (Figure 18.6b).

- Put blue minute marks and a blue minute hand on a clock face. Tell children that while the hour hand points to the hour numerals, the minute hand points to the blue marks for minutes. They can count by fives and by ones as they move the blue hand around the clock (Figure 18.6c).

- Using both clocks, set the hour hand on an hour (say, 2) and the minute hand at 0 minutes. Read the times as the hands move forward to 2:05, 2:10, 2:15, and so on. As the minute hand goes past 30, advance the hour hand and ask why the hour hand is also moving. Ask children to predict what happens to the hour hand as the minute hand moves closer to 60 minutes.

- To help children realize the meaning of 5 minutes, have them watch the classroom clock. Remind them to watch the minute hand and the hour hand. Ask them to write in their journals what they notice.

- Use a clock with synchronized hands to show the coordinated movement of the hour hand and the minute hand. Have children watch and read the minutes as the hands turn. Ask children to compare the movement of the two hands. (Answer: While the minute hand makes one complete turn, the hour hand moves from one hour to the next.)

- Ask children to think of half a circle. Cover half of the demonstration clock, and ask children how many minutes is half of an hour. (Answer: 30.) Emphasize that when the minute hand points to 30, the hour hand is halfway between two numerals. Set the hands at different half-hour positions for children to read the time (e.g., "2 hours and 30 minutes").

- Introduce writing of time on the even hour (9 hours and 0 minutes, 9:00). As soon as that notation is set, have children read and write half-hours (2:30, 8:30) and then any hour and minute combination. Show and discuss two ways of writing time to the hour: 9:00 and 9 o'clock.

- Show the relationship between a given time and 30 minutes later by moving the minute hand as children skip count by fives to 30. Be sure that children note that the new position of the minute hand is directly across from the original position of the minute hand. The minute hand moved halfway around the clock.

Another way to help younger children gain a foundational understanding of the passing of time is to have them produce a daily event calendar, as described in Activity 18.10. Focusing on familiar events and the time during the day that each event takes place will enable younger children to gain a sense of the time durations involved between events and an

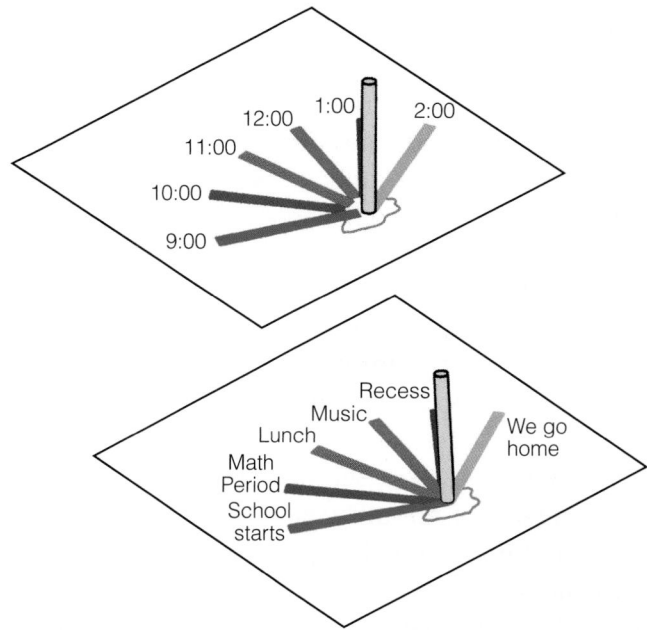

Figure 18.7 Sundials marking time and events

understanding of the routine of everyday life, with the time of day as the organizing factor.

Children in the intermediate grades continue to practice clock-reading skills. Topics can be incorporated from social studies and science units to extend children's understanding of time concepts. Interdisciplinary units might develop such topics as the establishment of uniform time zones around the world, the history of telling time, and the nature of precision instruments (e.g., electronic timers) that record time. A simple sundial set up on a sunny day gives an opportunity to see how an ancient time-telling device works (Figure 18.7). The sundial has science, social studies, and mathematical connections.

ACTIVITY 18.10 Daytimer Clock (Representation)

Level: Grades 1–3
Setting: Small groups
Objective: Students locate daily events in their lives around a clock.
Materials: Large clock face on paper

- Ask students to write down some of the activities that they do every day.

- Have students assign a time to those activities that happen about the same time every day.

- Give students the task of drawing six of their daily activities around the clock face, at the time of day when they happen.

- Have students display their completed clock faces and describe the activities they have portrayed.

Calendars

Although many primary-grade children do not possess the maturational readiness to understand fully how a calendar indicates time, they do learn about the passage of time and the sequence of events. They learn that calendars indicate days of the week, with the number, or date, for each day, the month of the year, and the year itself. Calendars such as the one in Figure 18.8 can be purchased or teacher-made and are often part of a classroom routine.

On each school day a new date is added to show the new day. Discuss with the children the month and day of the week; the number date of the day; anything special about the day, such as a classmate's birthday; and the number of days in the month that have already passed. One eventful day to note with students is Hundred Day, the 100th day of school. Older students can observe Pi Day (March 14 or 3/14) and Metric Day (October 10 or 10/10) with related activities.

Teachers can assist children's understanding of the calendar as a record of passing time by putting the days of the month in a continuous line with a balloon on each number. When the balloon is popped, the day has passed and the number of that day is revealed. The month can then be cut into strips and reorganized into the traditional month calendar. Some teachers show the entire calendar as a continuous line around the classroom. Cut a calendar with large numerals into horizontal strips showing one week each, and glue or staple the strips for the entire year end to end to a long piece of calculator tape. Labels for each child's birthday, significant school days, and holidays of ethnic and cultural groups in the class provide a reminder of past and upcoming events. Labels, pictures, or color coding for the seasons invite discussion of the seasonal cycle. Children can compare the number of days between Columbus Day and Thanksgiving to those between New Year's Day and President's Day, count the days until the next class birthday, and so on.

ᴇXERCISE

Several time expressions have diminished in common use: "quarter past five," "half past nine," and "a quarter to ten." Therefore many teachers believe children should read and write these times as "five fifteen," "nine thirty," and "nine forty-five." What is your opinion? What are the advantages and disadvantages of each expression? ●●●

In early grades calendar work should emphasize the calendar as a record of children's experience. Elementary school children are just developing a sense of historical time. Their own life is the only history they really understand, although they enjoy stories of "long ago and far away." Care must be taken in selecting which days to highlight. It is reasonable to list student's birthdays, as suggested here, but some students may be offended by any special recognition or celebration of their birthday. Likewise, religious holidays might be suitably acknowledged, but activities that revolve around such holidays may be inappropriate for children of another faith.

> **MULTICULTURALCONNECTION**
> Calendars present an opportunity to recognize special days or events for different cultures.

ᴇXERCISE

Why is a day added to February every fourth year? ●●●

Teaching Children to Use Money

Children receive and spend money at early ages. By school age many have allowances as well as lunch money. An adult may tell a child which coins to give

March						
Sun.	Mon.	Tues.	Wed.	Thur.	Fri.	Sat.
	1	2	3	4	5	

Figure 18.8 Classroom calendar with removable tabs for recording dates

to a clerk, or the child shows coins and the clerk takes the amount needed. Even with these experiences, young children have difficulty separating the value of coins from their size. For instance, a penny and a nickel are both larger than a dime, yet a dime has greater value than either of the other coins. As children grow, they learn the value of each coin and bill. Work in preschool and kindergarten begins with activities designed to acquaint children with coins in a classroom store, where they may pretend to buy things with play money. A school store with pencils, paper, and school supplies gives practical experience with real money for older children. Some schools have older students collect money in school cafeterias.

Early money activities are confined to identification of small-value coins. In the primary grades, understanding the values of coins related to 1 dollar is developed, and then bills are introduced. Real-looking plastic or pasteboard models of coins and bills are available from teacher stores and school-supply vendors.

When children work with realistic models, they may still be preoperational, and so they cannot conserve attributes of objects. One consequence is that they will not grasp the relationships between pennies and nickels, nickels and dimes, and so on. These many-to-one and many-to-many matchings are confusing because no physical relationship exists between one coin and another. A set of proportional materials helps children understand relationships among all coins and a dollar. In this model a nickel is half the size of a dime, and a quarter is five times as large as a nickel. All the other relationships between coin values are preserved in the area relationships in this model.

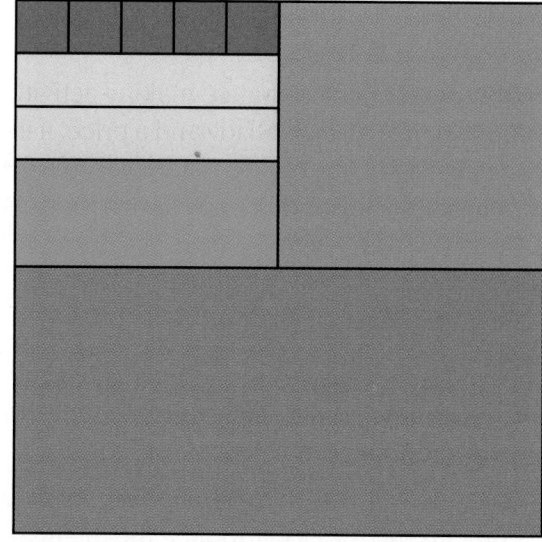

Figure 18.9 Proportional money materials

- Duplicate on tagboard a 10 × 10 grid like the one shown in Figure 18.9. Each grid piece can be about 4 centimeters square.

- The 10 × 10 grid has five small 1 × 1 squares representing pennies, two 1 × 5 rectangles representing nickels, one 2 × 5 rectangle representing a dime, a large 5 × 5 square for a quarter, and a large 5 × 10 rectangle for a half-dollar.

- Have the children make kits of money pieces by cutting out the grid and stamping or drawing pennies on one side of the tagboard and the equivalent nickel, dime, quarter, or half-dollar on the other side. They may wish to cut and mark two or three grids so that they can have more money pieces. They can leave one grid uncut as a full dollar value.

- Students can use the money pieces as puzzles to answer questions, such as
  How many pennies cover a nickel?
  How many nickels cover a dime?
  What different combinations cover a quarter?"

- As they gain confidence, they can use the pieces to show combinations:
  Show 7 cents.
  Show 32 cents.
  What are the fewest coins you can use to make 67 cents?

- Tell children that the word *cent* stands for 1 part out of 100 parts. Ask the meaning of 1 cent,

Money kits

5 cents, 10 cents, 25 cents, and 50 cents, and introduce the cent sign (¢).

- Use the coin pieces for change-making activities. Display a picture of a small toy and a price. If the toy's price is 35 cents, children start with 100 cents. They pay for the toy and see how much they have left.

- Demonstrate how to count change by first counting larger denominations and counting up: "twenty-five, thirty-five, forty-five, fifty, fifty-two."

- As students gain confidence, introduce real coins or models for the grid pieces.

- For older children learning about decimal values, the grid can be used to introduce the decimal values 0.01, 0.05, 0.10, 0.25, and 0.50.

Activities with these materials come at the point when children are beginning to grasp the concept that coins have relational values, in concert with their developmental stage when they are able to conserve. Children exemplify this understanding when they recognize that 5 pennies has the same value as 1 nickel and that 5 nickels has the value of 1 quarter. Children who are familiar with coins and small bills maintain and expand their understanding by regularly engaging in activities using money for real or vicarious situations. Working individually or in groups, they can complete simple buying activities or more advanced activities.

Older children who have an understanding of decimal fraction computation solve problems and engage in real-life activities that involve computations with money. They simulate purchases, prepare budgets for allowances, explore newspaper advertisements for a shopping cart of groceries, and engage in related activities that require decimal computation.

Michelle Craig, a primary-grade teacher in the Elk Grove, California, Unified School District, uses music and silly jingles to help children learn. One song was written to help second-graders understand the role of the decimal point in recording amounts of money. Her song "The Decimal Point Blues" has a lilting rhythm that makes it fun for children to sing and others to hear. The words to the song are on the companion website.

Extending Measurement Concepts

For older children the measurement focus is on broadening the applications of measurement to other contexts and on extending measurement concepts such as angle measure, area, and volume. The NCTM measurement standards for older children are the following.

NCTM Measurement Standard

Instructional programs from prekindergarten through grade 12 should enable all students to:

> Understand measurable attributes of objects and the units, systems, and processes of measurement

Grades 3–5 Expectations:

In grades 3–5 all students should:

- understand such attributes as length, area, weight, volume, and size of angle and select the appropriate type of unit for measuring each attribute;
- understand the need for measuring with standard units and become familiar with standard units in the customary and metric systems;
- carry out simple unit conversions, such as from centimeters to meters, within a system of measurement;
- understand that measurements are approximations and how differences in units affect precision;
- explore what happens to measurements of a two-dimensional shape such as its perimeter and area when the shape is changed in some way.

Grades 6–8 Expectations:

In grades 6–8 all students should:

- understand both metric and customary systems of measurement;
- understand relationships among units and convert from one unit to another within the same system;
- understand, select, and use units of appropriate size and type to measure angles, perimeter, area, surface area, and volume.

> Apply appropriate techniques, tools, and formulas to determine measurements

Grades 3–5 Expectations:

In grades 3–5 all students should:

- develop strategies for estimating the perimeters, areas, and volumes of irregular shapes;
- select and apply appropriate standard units and tools to measure length, area, volume, weight, time, temperature, and the size of angles;
- select and use benchmarks to estimate measurements;
- develop, understand, and use formulas to find the area of rectangles and related triangles and parallelograms;
- develop strategies to determine the surface areas and volumes of rectangular solids.

Grades 6–8 Expectations:

In grades 6–8 all students should:

- use common benchmarks to select appropriate methods for estimating measurements;
- select and apply techniques and tools to accurately find length, area, volume, and angle measures to appropriate levels of precision;

- develop and use formulas to determine the circumference of circles and the area of triangles, parallelograms, trapezoids, and circles and develop strategies to find the area of more-complex shapes;
- develop strategies to determine the surface area and volume of selected prisms, pyramids, and cylinders;
- solve problems involving scale factors, using ratio and proportion;
- solve simple problems involving rates and derived measurements for such attributes as velocity and density.

Extending Concepts About Length

In the early grades children explore the concept of length by learning how to use iteration and transference to measure lengths. They also begin to use a simple ruler to determine the lengths of specific items. Their explorations lay the groundwork for further explorations in intermediate grades. Children in the primary grades examine fairly short lengths of up to, perhaps, 10 feet.

When lengths become much greater, even a meterstick or yardstick becomes inconvenient. A trundle wheel (available from school-supply vendors) or a surveyor's wheel makes measuring easier. The wheel, which is attached to a long handle, has a circumference of 1 meter. As it is rolled across a surface, there is a "click" that indicates that one rotation of the wheel has measured 1 meter; clicks are counted to determine distances. Children can measure lengths of hallways, sidewalks, playgrounds, and other distances in and around their school with a trundle wheel (see photo).

Once children become comfortable using unmarked rulers, they are ready to use rulers with divisions on them. The first ruler of this type may show only whole-centimeter units or whole-inch units with no numerals, like the ruler in Figure 18.10. The absence of numerals means that children must count units to determine an object's length. Rulers such as these can be duplicated and cut from tagboard for Activity 18.12. Marking the starting place with green serves as a reminder to children to place the green end of the ruler at one end of the object. Numerals have been added to the ruler in Figure 18.11 so that children can determine the measure of an object with numerals rather than by counting units. The green end of the tagboard ruler becomes the "0" number on the numbered ruler.

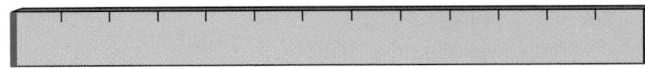

Figure 18.10 Ruler showing only centimeter unit segments and starting edge

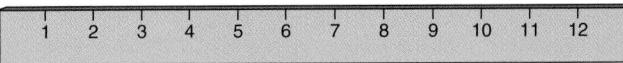

Figure 18.11 Ruler with numbered centimeter unit segments and starting edge

In Activity 18.11 students examine standard length units and select the appropriate unit for the object being measured. For example, the height of a tree should be measured in feet or meters and not in inches or millimeters. In Activity 18.12 students measure objects to the nearest centimeter.

In Activity 18.13 students measure the same object using rulers marked with increasingly detailed precision. The more detailed the precision, the more accurate the measure. As children develop their ability to measure with increasing precision, they can have difficulty interpreting the different markings on their ruler. The Master Ruler (see photo)

Trundle wheel

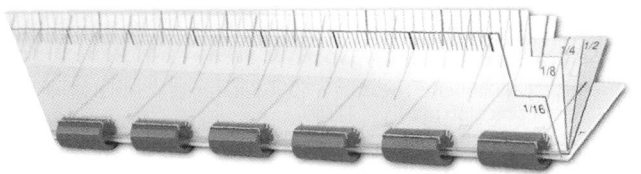

Master ruler

ACTIVITY 18.11 Name That Unit (Communication)

Level: Grades 3–5

Setting: Small groups

Objective: Students list objects that can be conveniently measured using inches, feet, yards, and miles.

Materials: Paper to record lists

• Ask students to choose between using a 1-foot ruler or a 25-foot tape measure for measuring the distance from the classroom door to the cafeteria.

• Have groups report their decision and the reasons for it to the entire class.

• Ask each group to list three lengths or distances that could be conveniently measured with inches, feet, yards, and miles.

• Have each group report their lengths and units to the entire class and discuss their decisions.

ACTIVITY 18.12 To the Nearest Centimeter (Assessment Activity)

Level: Grades 4–6

Setting: Individual or small groups

Objective: Students measure objects to the nearest centimeter.

Materials: Centimeter cubes and rods; centimeter ruler; objects to measure, 3–20 centimeters long (e.g., 35-mm film boxes, ball-point pens, books, dowels, variety of pencils)

• Lay the centimeter cubes and rods next to the object being measured. Make sure the rods are lined up with the object. Count the rods.

• Measure the same object with the centimeter ruler, stressing the importance of placing the end of the object at the end of the ruler. Emphasize careful counting.

• Compare the measures from the rods and the ruler.

• Ask students to tell which number the object is closer to, using language such as "longer than," "shorter than," or "nearly."

• Provide problem cards for further measurements.

Using Centimeters

Use centimeter cubes and rods and the tagboard ruler to measure the items and answer the following questions.

1. How many centimeters long is the plastic pen?

2. How many centimeters long is the yellow spoon?

3. How many centimeters long is the film box? How wide is the film box? Is the end of the film box shaped like a square?

4. How many centimeters long is the strip of blue paper?

5. Find three things in the room that are longer than 20 centimeters.

6. Find three things in the room that are shorter than 20 centimeters.

7. Write and draw your measurements in your journal.

Compare your answers with those of another group of students. If there are any disagreements, remeasure the objects in question to determine which is the best measurement.

ACTIVITY 18.13 The Shrinking Stirrer (Reasoning and Proof)

Level: Grades 4–6

Setting: Pairs

Objective: Students measure a coffee stirrer, using rulers with different precision marks.

Materials: Coffee stirrers cut to $3\frac{5}{8}$ inches, rulers with only 1-inch markings, rulers with $\frac{1}{2}$-inch markings, rulers with $\frac{1}{4}$-inch markings

• Pass out materials to each pair of students.

• Ask students to measure their coffee stirrer with each ruler, using first the inch ruler, then the half-inch ruler, and finally the quarter-inch ruler.

• Have students record their results for each ruler.

• Discuss with the class how it is possible for all three measurements to be correct.

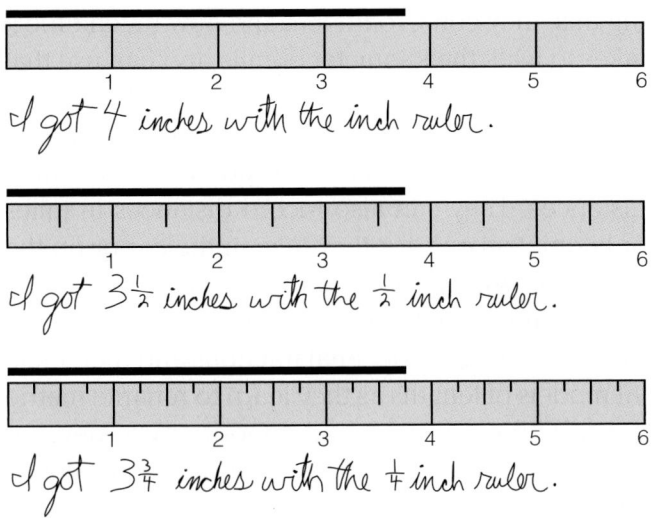

I got 4 inches with the inch ruler.

I got 3½ inches with the ½ inch ruler.

I got 3¾ inches with the ¼ inch ruler.

Figure 18.12 Student work using rulers with different precisions

enables children to measure an item with a single ruler, using different levels of precision, one after the other. The comments of Rachel, a fourth-grader who engaged in the measuring described in Activity 18.13 are shown in Figure 18.12. When asked about the different lengths for the same object, Rachel responded that it depended on the ruler. She thought it was easiest to use the inch ruler, but thought the quarter-inch ruler was best, "because it gives a closer answer." Over time, children work with metersticks, trundle wheels, and measuring tapes with subdivisions marked in decimeters, centimeters, and millimeters.

The pencil in Figure 18.13a is slightly longer than 10 centimeters, and the pencil in Figure 18.13b is slightly shorter than 10 centimeters. Children learn that, measured to the nearest whole centimeter, each one has a measure of 10 centimeters. When the endpoint of an object lies near the midpoint between two units, a judgment must be made about its measure. The first pencil might be reported as being a little more than 10 centimeters long by one

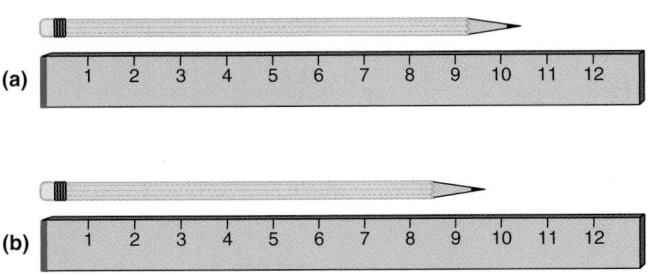

Figure 18.13 Unit rulers used to measure the length of two pencils. Each pencil has a measurement of 10 units.

child, as less than 11 centimeters by another, and as being about 10.5 centimeters by yet another. The children interpret the measure of the pencil differently, and yet each gives a correct approximate measure for it. Measurements are recorded in different ways, depending on children's maturity and understanding. For instance, children in primary grades would probably record a child's height as 138 centimeters, whereas older ones would record the same height as 1.38 meters. Unlike the English system, units are not mixed when a measurement is recorded in the metric system. The height of 1.38 meters would not be recorded as 1 meter 38 centimeters or as 1 m 38 cm, although in the English system recording a height as 5 feet 3 inches is perfectly acceptable.

> Although a conceptual foundation for measuring many different attributes should be developed during the early grades, linear measurements are the main emphasis. (Burns, 1989, pp. 23–24)

Conversion between measures in the English system can be challenging for some older students. For example, when asked to convert 180 inches to feet, students can usually recall that 12 inches equals 1 foot. However, they may be unsure whether to multiply or divide by 12 to make the conversion. They may struggle to recall, "When changing to feet, divide by 12. When changing to inches, multiply by 12." Rather than trying to have students memorize a rule about when to multiply or divide, it is more beneficial to have students first determine the magnitude of the answer. In other words, will the number of feet in the answer be larger or smaller than the number of inches given in the problem? Students can be helped to reason that since feet are a larger unit of length than inches, fewer feet are needed to equal the same length in inches (see the discussion on the principle of compensation on p. 448). Thus the number of feet in this problem must be less than the number of inches, so the number of feet is equal to 180 divided by 12. Another strategy that children might use is to draw up a table of values:

Feet	1	2	3	4	5	6	7	10	12	15
Inches	12	24	36	48	60	72	84	120	144	180

Children can use tables as an intermediate strategy before they advance to computation to solve conversion problems.

Estimation and Mental Models of Length

In many situations actual measurement is not needed. A landscaper can step off a lawn's length and width to estimate square footage and determine the amount of fertilizer needed for an adequate feeding. A bicyclist estimates distances to lay out a route for a ride of about 30 miles. As children develop mental models for different units of length, they improve their estimates. Experiences with available objects develop mental models for estimating length measures: A dime is approximately 1 millimeter thick, the nail on a child's thumb is about 1 centimeter wide, and the chalk rail in classrooms is approximately 1 meter or yard above the floor.

The best way for children to get a sense of greater distances, such as a kilometer or a mile, is to walk (or slowly drive) the distances with an adult. Establish a route on the school playground or locate landmarks that are approximately 1 kilometer or 1 mile from school—a child's house, a store, a sign. As you walk at a steady pace, have students note the time. By doing this, they come to understand how much time it takes to walk the kilometer or mile and can use that knowledge to estimate both shorter and longer distances. Activities 18.14 and 18.15 help children use paces to establish a reference point for estimating distances. They can also record distances in miles or kilometers on trips they take in the car or on the bus to the grocery store, library, or playground.

Children in the upper elementary grades can use their knowledge of decimal fractions and their mental models of lengths as they learn to rename metric units. With experience and opportunity to develop the mental models, they can find the equivalence without resorting to moving decimal points around.

- To rename 148 centimeters as meters, think: "Since 100 centimeters is 1 meter, 148 centimeters would be 1 meter and about half a meter or 0.48 meter, so 1.48 meters."
- To rename 428 meters to kilometers, think: "If 1,000 meters is 1 kilometer; 428 meters is less than half of a kilometer, so 428 meters is 0.428 kilometer."

ACTIVITY 18.14 **Step Lively! (Reasoning and Proof)**

Level: Grades 3–5
Setting: Individual
Objective: Students compare steps to 10-meter length.
Materials: None

- Measure a distance of 10 meters in the classroom or a nearby hallway.
- Have each child walk from one end to the other, counting each step, 10 times.

- Have each child determine the mean average number of steps required to walk 10 meters.
- Provide opportunities for students to use their paces to determine the approximate distance between places on the school grounds.

ACTIVITY 18.15 **How Much Is 50 Meters?**

Level: Grades 2–4
Setting: Whole group
Objective: Students estimate distance.
Materials: Chalk

- Take the children to a playground and ask them to line up along a chalk line you have marked on the hardtop (or the edge of a sidewalk).
- Instruct the children to wait for your signal to walk across the playground for the distance each thinks is 50 meters, then stop.

- Have a pair of children use a metric trundle wheel or a metric measuring tape to measure 50 meters.
- Have students note where the children who measured 50 meters are standing and evaluate their own estimates.
- Repeat the activity for 50 meters, 75 meters, 20 meters, and so on. Have children evaluate each estimate and note their own improvement.

- To rename 1.67 meters as centimeters, think: "Since 100 centimeters is a meter, 1.67 meters is 100 centimeters plus 67 more centimeters, or 167 centimeters."

> In ancient Egypt long distances were determined by professionals called rope stretchers. These men tied a specific length of rope to their ankles. They were trained to walk in a straight line for long distances, and at every stride they stretched the rope until it was taut. They measured distances by the number of strides they took. Each complete stride was eventually called a stadium.

Extending Concepts About Area

By the end of elementary school students should be able to (1) name common area units and express them in writing, (2) measure small regions directly by using square grids and cardboard pieces in both customary and metric area units, (3) estimate areas using appropriate mental models, and (4) determine area indirectly by measuring the sides of a region and developing a formula for area. The connection between multiplication arrays and area is important as students move away from determining area by counting each square and toward the use of formulas.

Measuring and Estimating Area

Measuring the areas of surfaces using nonstandard measures, such as index cards, hexagons, and pizza box lids, leads to use of standard units. Students should see that each length measure has a corresponding area unit: inch to square inch (in.^{2}), foot to square foot (ft^2), yard to square yard (yd^2), centimeter to square centimeter (cm^2), and meter to square meter (m^2). The problem card shown in Figure 18.14 involves finding areas of small regions at a learning center. The measuring device is a centimeter transparency grid that children put on top of shapes and regions to count and measure. In the regions marked B and C, areas cannot be determined by simply multiplying whole numbers as in Region A. Children must use estimation to determine their areas.

Following the problem card activities, children can explain and discuss their procedures. Depending on how they place the grids on the shapes or how they interpret the size of partial measures, children's measurements for the same region will differ and open the issue of approximation and estimation of area. A teacher-guided discussion about the area of the rectangle marked B might include these questions:

- How many square units are entirely within the region? (Answer: 32.)

- How many square units are partially within the region? (Answer: 13.)

- What is the largest possible area and the smallest possible area based on those two facts? (Answer: 32 whole squares is minimum area, and 45 squares is largest area.)

**Figure 18.14
Problem card for
area activities**

FINDING AREAS

Use plastic grids and geometric figures and free-flowing shapes to complete these activities.

1. Your first task is to determine which of the shapes have a whole number of square-centimeter units and which include parts of units along with whole units. Identify the shapes in each category by listing their letters on paper.

2. Measure each shape and write its area on your paper. Make your best estimates of the areas for shapes that do not contain just whole square-centimeter units.

3. Write explanations of how you determined the area of the different types of shapes.

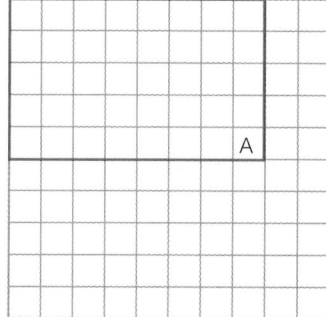
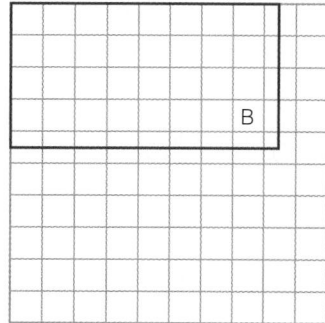
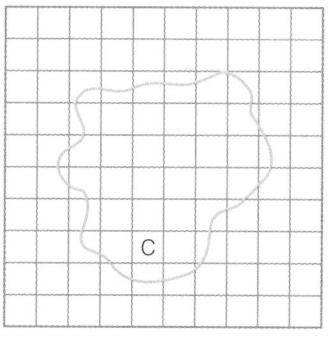

- How might you estimate the area of the 13 partial squares? (Answer: Combine the partial squares to approximate whole squares.)

- What is a good total estimate of the area? (Answer: maybe 36, 37, or 38.)

The teacher could have students work in pairs to reason about the area of the irregular shape in region C. In Activity 18.5 students used some of these area concepts as they determined the area of their footprint.

The square mile and the acre are used for most land measures in the United States. Children can learn about the acre by marking one on a playing field. To illustrate 1 acre, a teacher could place colored pylons in a square with corners approximately 70 yards apart. Students might want to find the approximate number of acres for the entire school ground or a nearby shopping center; they can use paces to estimate lengths and widths to estimate areas of larger parcels of land. Teachers could also use aerial photographs with an acre drawn on the photographs. The corresponding metric units, the *are* (10 meters by 10 meters, or 100 square meters) and the *hectare* (100 ares, or 10,000 square meters), are seldom used in the United States.

Inventing Area Formulas

As children measure rectangles and squares, they often relate them to their knowledge of the area concept of multiplication. Young children can determine that a 4 × 8 rectangular array contains 32 squares, and they can use this image to begin to learn the multiplication fact that 4 × 8 = 32. Similarly, the area of a 4-centimeter by 8-centimeter rectangular array of squares has 4 × 8 = 32 square centimeters, or more generally:

$$\text{Area of rectangle} = \text{base} \times \text{height}$$

Teacher-led activities provide the applied instruction for children to understand area formulas for parallelograms and triangles (Activities 18.16 and 18.17). When students see the area relationship between a rectangle and a parallelogram of the same height and base, they will more easily understand and remember that the formula for the area of a parallelogram is $A = bh$, as they will the area formula for a triangle, $A = \frac{1}{2}bh$. Activity 18.17 helps students focus on base length and height rather than shape or appearance when considering the area of a triangle.

The companion website activity "Geoboard Triangles" expands students understanding of triangle area by using a geoboard to form different triangles with the same base and height. No matter how different the triangles appear, they must all have the same area. The companion website activity "Half a Rectangle" uses a geoboard to relate the area of a right triangle to half the area of a rectangle.

One additional polygon that students study in the intermediate grades is the trapezoid. Children can develop the area formula for a trapezoid in much

---

ACTIVITY 18.16 Area of a Parallelogram

Level: Grades 4–6
Setting: Whole group
Objective: Students find the area of a parallelogram.
Materials: Geoboards, cutouts of rectangles and parallelograms

- Give each student a rectangle and a parallelogram with the same height and length. Ask students what the area of the rectangle is. The geoboard can be used to show that the area is length × height.

- Repeat with several other rectangles and parallelograms.

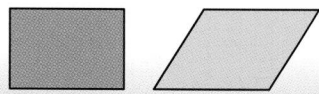

- Ask students if they can use the same formula for the area of a rectangle and the area of a parallelogram with the same height and length. (The area formula for a parallelogram is sometimes stated as $A = b \times h$, where b is the base and h is the height.)

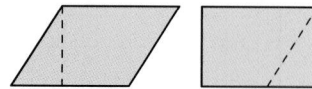

- Ask students to cut their parallelograms to make the rectangle shape. They can fold and cut off one end of the parallelograms and move it to the other end.

- Have students now compute the area of each parallelogram.

ACTIVITY 18.17   Triangles Are Half a Parallelogram (Representation)

Level: Grades 4–6

Setting: Small groups

Objective: Students develop the area formula for a triangle by linking triangles and parallelograms.

Materials: Rulers, scissors

- Pass out lined paper to students in groups.
- Have students cut out an acute triangle and then use that triangle to trace and cut out two congruent triangles.
- Challenge students to form a parallelogram out of two of the triangles.
- Ask students for the formula for the area of a parallelogram. (Answer: $A = b \times h$.)

- Have students compare the remaining triangle and the composite parallelogram.
- How do the heights compare? (Answer: They are the same.) How do the base lengths compare? (Answer: They are the same.) How do their areas compare? (Answer: The triangle area is one-half the parallelogram area.)
- Repeat with several other triangles.
- Have students answer the following questions:
  1. What is the formula for the area of a parallelogram?
  2. How does the area of a triangle compare to the area of a parallelogram with the same base and height?
  3. What is the area formula for a triangle?
  4. Use a diagram to explain why your formula in Question 3 is correct.

the same way that Activities 18.16 and 18.17 describe how to discover the area formulas for parallelograms and triangles. In the diagram here a trapezoid has two parallel bases and two nonparallel sides (legs):

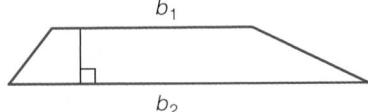

Any trapezoid can be reproduced and rotated, as shown here, to form a parallelogram. The area of the resulting parallelogram is twice the area of the original trapezoid:

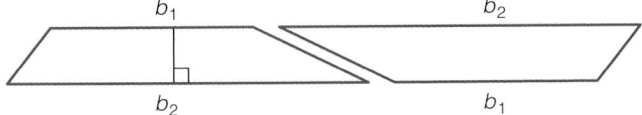

The area of the parallelogram is found with the formula: $A = bh$. In this case the height h is the same in the composite parallelogram as in the original trapezoid. The base of the parallelogram is composed of the sum of the two bases of the original trapezoid ($b_1 + b_2$). Thus the area of the parallelogram is found with the formula

$$A = bh \quad \text{or} \quad A = (b_1 + b_2)h$$

Because the original trapezoid is only half the area of the parallelogram, the formula for the area of the trapezoid is

$$A = \tfrac{1}{2}(b_1 + b_2)h$$

> **MISCONCEPTION**
>
> The area formula for a trapezoid can be challenging for some children. Some will replace the addition operation with multiplication, probably because all previous area formulas used only multiplication. Some will misapply the distributive law and apply the $\frac{1}{2}$ to only one base, rather than to the sum of the bases.

A final figure for students in the intermediate grades to study is the circle. An integral part of any study of the circle is π, a value related to both the perimeter (circumference) and area of a circle. It is commonly thought of as the circumference-diameter ratio. π is the number of times the length of the diameter of a circle will fit around the circumference. π is an irrational number. It cannot be expressed as a ratio of two integers (*a/b*). Any decimal representation of the value of π will extend to infinity with no repeating pattern in the number. As a consequence, there are two common approximations that are used for the value of π: 3.14 and $\frac{22}{7}$. These approximations are not equal but are used interchangeably according to the problem setting and the numerical values in the setting. For a problem with data in the form of decimal fractions, 3.14 would be the appropriate approximation to use.

Activity 18.18 focuses on the value of π as a ratio for the circumference to the diameter. In this activity students generate data to approximate the value of

π. Most students easily determine that the value of π is a bit more than 3, and it is common for a class result to approximate the value of π to several decimal places. However, children's first explorations using π to determine the area or circumference of a circle may be clouded when they try to use either $\frac{22}{7}$ or 3.14 as an approximation for π. When students try to use $\frac{22}{7}$ or 3.14, they become distracted with the computational aspect of the problem and lose their focus on the problem itself and the reasonableness of their answer. We recommend that students who begin to explore the circumference and area of circles use 3 for an approximation of π, with the understanding that any value used to represent π is an approximation and that 3 is a reasonable initial representation for π. Experiences with activities such as Activity 18.18 help students internalize that the value of π is a little more than 3. When students use 3 for the value of π, they are then able to concentrate on the problem and the reasonableness of their answer. In Activity 18.18 students might represent *C/d* to the nearest whole number (3) rather than to tenths or hundredths.

The area of a circle also involves the value of π. The area formula is $A = \pi r^2$. Activity 18.19 helps students discover this relationship by cutting up a circle and reassembling the pieces to form a parallelogram, much like some of the preceding activities with quadrilaterals. As shown here, the eight pieces or sectors of a circle can be reassembled to form a parallelogram. Note that the height of the parallelogram is *r*, the radius of the circle. The base of the parallelogram is $\frac{1}{2}$ the entire circumference. One way to determine *C* is by the formula $C = 2\pi r$. Thus

$\frac{1}{2}C = \pi r$. These two values can be used in the area formula for a parallelogram as follows:

$$A = bh$$
$$A = \pi r \times r = \pi r^2$$

A point of confusion for many older students is the difference between perimeter and area. These two concepts are often presented together, but they are markedly different and need to be developed carefully. Perimeter is a length measure and can be taught with length measurement activities. Children need the opportunity to engage in many activities in which they determine the area and perimeter of real objects by direct measurement. In addition, students should have ample opportunities to solve problems with real-world settings. Such activities and problems will help them distinguish between the two.

After concepts of perimeter and area measurement have been developed, investigations into relationships between the two offer opportunities for students to engage in worthwhile problem-solving activities. Questions such as the following can instigate group or individual activities and discussions:

- A plan for a flower garden requires 144 square feet for all the flowers that will be planted. The gardener wants to use the least possible amount of edging material to go around it. What shape and dimensions should the garden have?

ACTIVITY 18.18 Exploring π (Internet Activity)

Level: Grades 5–6

Setting: Small groups

Objective: Students explore the circumference-diameter ratio.

Materials: Internet connection

- Have students go to http://ejad.best.vwh.net/java/java .shtml and click *Discovering the Value of Pi*.

- Students then follow the directions in the activity to roll various circles one full revolution (circumference).

- Students record the diameter and circumference of each circle and compute *C/d* on a line.

- Ask if students have seen this value or relationship before, then link their result to π.

- Challenge students to use their findings to determine the circumference of a tower clock with a 4 foot diameter.

- As an alternative, students could use measure disks. See the companion website activity "Exploring π."

ACTIVITY 18.19 Finding the Area of a Circle (Reasoning and Proof)

Level: Grades 5 and 6
Setting: Small groups
Objective: Students explore the area of a circle.
Materials: Paper circle, scissors

- Pass out a paper circle to each student. Tell students that they already know the length of the radius, *r*.

- Direct them to fold the circle in half, fold that result in half, and fold that result in half once again.

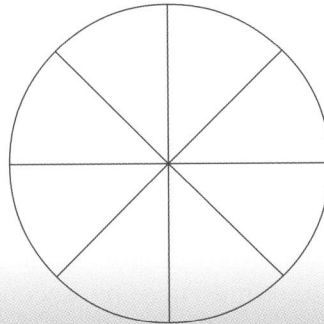

- Ask students to unfold their circle and cut out the eight pieces that the folding produced.

- Challenge students to reassemble the eight pieces to form a parallelogram, and then develop the formula for a circle from their parallelogram, as discussed in the chapter.

ACTIVITY 18.20 Tile Rectangles

Level: Grades 4–6
Setting: Small groups
Objective: Students build rectangles using all the tiles and record area and perimeter.
Materials: 36 tiles (1-inch square), $\frac{1}{4}$-inch graph paper

- Pass out materials to students.

- Ask students to use all 36 tiles to form different rectangles.

- Have students record their data in a table like this:

Diagram of Rectangle	Length	Width	Area	Perimeter

- After students have collected their data, ask them to discuss in their groups how area and perimeter are related in these rectangles. (Answer: They are not.)

- As a final discussion, ask if there is something special about the rectangle with the shortest perimeter. (It is a square.) Have students verify their conjecture by repeating this activity with 16 tiles.

- A rancher has 480 meters of fence material for her sheep pen. If each sheep requires 2 square meters of space, what are the dimensions of the rectangular pen that will hold the greatest number of sheep?

Activity 18.20 is an extension of Activity 18.6. In this activity students form different rectangles using all 36 tiles. They record the area and perimeter of each of the five possible rectangles. They can then observe in their data that there is a difference between area and perimeter for each rectangle. Furthermore, the square shape of a rectangle provides the minimum perimeter for a given area.

Extending Capacity Concepts

Younger children work with activities that will lay the foundation for understanding capacity, as suggested in Activity 18.1 (Station 1). Older children expand their understanding of capacity to identify and define capacity units, such as liter, quart, and ounce, and also engage in measurement activities using these and other capacity measurements.

In a learning center children engage in the capacity measurement activities outlined in the problem card shown in Figure 18.15. The center contains a variety of containers, some metric and some not, including at least one graduated liter measure. Several smaller metric containers are desirable but not necessary. The nonmetric containers, such as vegetable and fruit cans, plastic bottles, and wide-mouth jars, are selected to hold either more or less than a liter; labels that indicate capacity are removed. Each container is marked with a letter of the alphabet. Students compare the capacity of the jars by filling them from the graduated liter measure. Such an experience provides students with a working knowledge of the capacity of a liter. A similar center can be set up so children can learn about milliliters with specially prepared milliliter containers from school-supply companies. Small plastic medicine containers cost little or nothing. Children can use these containers to determine the capacity of smaller bottles, such as those that hold liquid food coloring, spices, or perfume.

Extending Volume Concepts

Younger children explore volume relationships in a holistic way, as suggested in Activity 18.1. Older children begin to quantify volume relationships by examining cubic measurements and using volume formulas. Volume measures such as cubic inches, cubic feet, cubic centimeters, and cubic meters are used in many practical ways to indicate the amount of space inside a three-dimensional figure. An architect who designs heating and air-conditioning systems must take into account the volume of a building and many other factors, such as building materials, windows, climate, and use by people. A manufacturer is interested in the volume of containers used to pack and ship products. A small container may not accommodate a given product; a large one may create unnecessary shipping expenses. Some manufacturers stress the large capacity of their refrigerators or SUVs in commercials.

The concept of volume builds on length and area concepts. The small metric cubes in a base-10 set have edges 1 centimeter long, faces of 1 square centimeter (cm^2), and a volume of 1 cubic centimeter (cm^3); inch cubes have length, area, and cubic measures in inches, square inches, and cubic inches. Small empty boxes and cubes can be used during an introductory lesson.

Teacher-made problem cards, such as the one in Figure 18.16, placed in the learning center direct

Figure 18.15 Problem card for capacity activity

MEASURING CAPACITY

Use the containers to complete the activities.

1. List the letters of the containers you believe hold less than a liter. List the letters of the containers you believe hold more than a liter. Do you believe any of the containers hold just one liter? If so, list their letters.

2. List the letters of the containers in the order you believe is correct from smallest to largest.

3. Use the graduated liter container and other metric containers to determine the capacity of each container. Do not fill a container higher than the bottom part of the neck. Write the letter of each container and its capacity on your paper.

4. Check your estimates against the actual measurements. List the letters of containers for which your estimate was incorrect, if any.

5. Check your ordering of the containers. If you were mistaken about the placement of any of the containers, write the correct order now.

Figure 18.16 Problem card for volume activities

MEASURING VOLUME

Use the centimeter cubes and boxes to complete these activities.

1. Fill box A with centimeter cubes. How many cubes are in one layer in the box? How many layers are there? How many cubes does the box hold? How many centimeters long is each side? The box is how many centimeters high? Write your answers on a piece of paper.

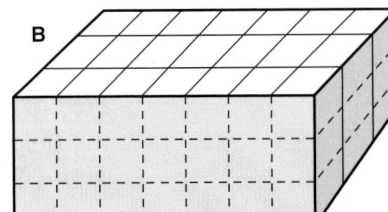

2. Fill box B. How many cubes does the box hold? How many cubes in each layer? How many layers are there? How many centimeters long is each side? The box is how many centimeters high? Record your answers.

3. Fill each of the other two boxes and answer the same questions. Record your answers.

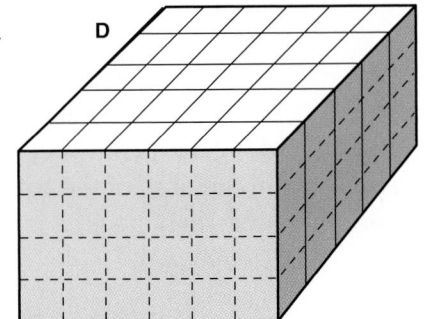

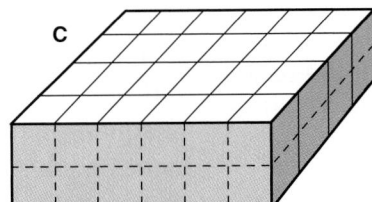

4. You have measured the volume of four boxes and have three sets of numbers for each box. One set tells the number of cubes in a box. Another set tells the number of cubes in one layer and the number of layers in a box. The third set includes the inside dimensions of each box in centimeters. Examine the numbers for box A. What connections do you see among the number of cubes in a box, the number of cubes in a layer and the number of layers, and the numbers that tell the dimensions? Write a sentence to explain these connections. See if these connections are true for each of the other three boxes.

5. Write a mathematical statement (formula) for finding the volume of any rectangular-shaped box.

group or individual measurement activities. Supply the center with centimeter cubes and several small boxes marked with a letter on each. Children work in pairs to fill each box with cubes. If they fill one that is about 7 centimeters long, 3 centimeters wide, and 3 centimeters high, as in the task card activity, students can determine that the volume is about 63 cm³ by counting the cubes in one layer (21) and then multiplying by the number of layers or height (3).

Students explore the volumes of many three-dimensional figures to develop the concept of volume and common measures. Six square-yard pieces of corrugated cardboard can be taped together to form a cube. Once students visualize what a cubic yard is, they can estimate and measure their classroom to determine its approximate volume in cubic yards (yd^3). If the ceiling is high, an adult can measure the room's height or children can estimate its height. Follow direct measurement activities with discussions to encourage students to develop an understanding of volume based on the relationship found in measuring and recording the volumes of various rectangular solids (Volume = length × width × height):

$$V = l \times w \times h$$

Another way to express the area formula is Volume = base area × height:

$$V = B \times h$$

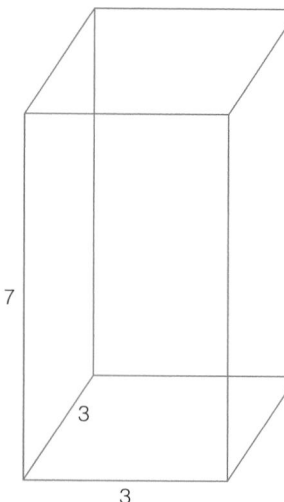

Consider a box that is 3 × 3 × 7. When a square end (3 × 3) is viewed as the base of the box, it has an area of 9 square units. The volume can be determined by multiplying the area of the base (B) times the height (h). $A = B \times h = 9 \times 7 = 63$.

Once students grasp this relationship, they have content readiness for understanding the formula for the volume of a cylinder or a triangular prism (Figure 18.17). For the triangular prism the area of the triangle at the base is determined first; then the area is multiplied by the measure of its height:

$$V = B \times h$$

In a similar fashion the volume of a cylinder equals the area of its circular base times its height. The volumes of cones and pyramids are related to the volumes of cylinders and prisms, respectively. The volume of a cone with the same base area and height as a cylinder, is found by:

$$V = \tfrac{1}{3}Bh$$

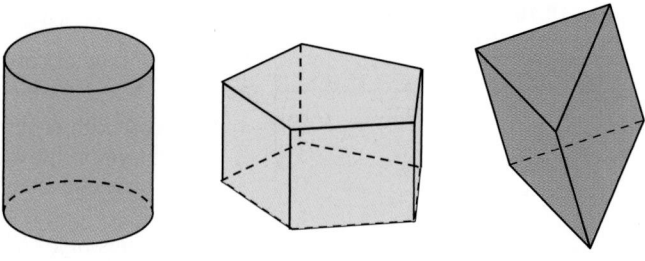

Figure 18.17 Children can find the volume of these solids by using the formula $V = B \times h$.

Similarly, when a pyramid has the same base area and height as a prism, its volume is found by the same formula ($V = \tfrac{1}{3}Bh$). Activity 18.21 engages students in volume explorations to discover this 1:3 relationship between the volumes.

One aspect of volume (and area) measures that is confusing for some students is the conversion factor between area measures and volume measures. Students mistakenly will apply the fact that 12 linear inches equals 1 linear foot to related area and volume measures, erroneously thinking that 12 square inches equals a square foot or 12 cubic inches equals a cubic foot. It is helpful to have life-size models of some area and volume units in the classroom for students to examine. When students examine a square foot of poster board and a 1-inch square tile, they can easily see that a square foot contains many more than 12 square inches (Figure 18.18a). Similarly, when students examine a 1-inch block and a cubic foot, they can easily see that a cubic foot contains far more than 12 cubic inches (Figure 18.18b).

ACTIVITY 18.21   Volume of Cones and Pyramids

Level: Grades 5 and 6

Setting: Small groups

Objective: Students compare volumes of cones to cylinders and of cubes to pyramids.

Materials: Packing materials, such as rice or inert packing materials; cone, cylinder, square pyramid, and cube from a commercial set such as View Thru Solids, or shapes constructed from templates (see Black-Line Masters 18.1 and 18.2)

- Pass out materials to students.

- Demonstrate how to pour a cone full of packing materials into the cylinder.

- Ask students to estimate how many cones will fit into the cylinder. Note for students that their bases and their heights are the same.

- Ask students to estimate how many pyramids will fit into the cube. Ask students to compare the base areas (same) and heights (same) of the two solids.

- After students make their estimates, allow them to fill and pour to verify their estimates.

- Have students write out how to find the volume of a cone if its related cylinder has a volume of 150 cubic meters.

- Have groups report their conclusions to the whole class.

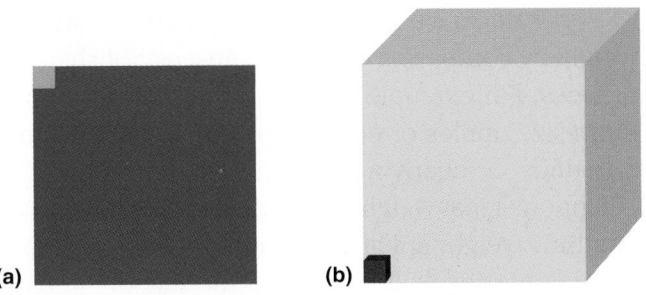

(a)   **(b)**

Figure 18.18 (a) A square inch and a square foot; (b) a cubic inch and a cubic foot

The conversion factors for area and volume units are related to the conversion factors for linear units. Students do not need to memorize all the conversion factors but can compute them, as the table for inches and feet suggests:

$$12 \text{ inches} = 1 \text{ foot}$$

144 (12×12, or 12^2, or 12 squared) square inches = 1 square foot

1,728 ($12 \times 12 \times 12$, or 12^3, or 12 cubed) cubic inches = 1 cubic foot

ⓔXERCISE

Think of a real-life setting to distinguish between square and cubic measures. ●●●

Extending Mass and Weight Concepts

Weight and mass are not the same. *Mass* is the amount of matter in an object; *weight* is the gravitational force exerted on the mass. A lunar rover has the same mass on Earth as on the moon; however, it weighs less on the moon because the moon's gravity is less. Despite the differences, *weight* is the commonly used term because we weigh objects in Earth's gravity and equate weight with an object's mass.

From comparison of different objects and a general sense about which are heavy or light (see Activity 18.1), students progress to standard measures for weight. By the time children complete elementary school, they should be able to identify English and metric weight units, use scales properly, and develop reasonable skill in estimating weights. Through measuring activities in the English system, they become familiar with their body weight in pounds and

smaller objects in ounces. A classroom display of objects weighing about a pound calls attention to an important unit for estimating weights. Weights from a barbell set may also establish what children consider heavy. Children can research and compare the weights of heavy objects (whales, elephants, or types of vehicles—compact, standard, and luxury cars, trucks, SUVs, and vans). Automobile manufacturer websites include weight information about different models. Smaller automobiles may serve as a reference object for the ton weight measure of 2,000 pounds.

The metric units of weight commonly used in science and industry are the kilogram, gram, and milligram. Just as students create a display of pound objects, they can create a display of kilogram objects and gram objects. Based on the gram objects, the weight of a milligram and its possible uses can be discussed. A unit children should know but with which they are unlikely to have direct contact is the metric ton. A metric ton (1,000 kilograms) is slightly heavier than a ton of 2,000 pounds in the English system. The similarity between the ton and the metric ton weights is more important for children than the exact equivalence.

ⓔXERCISE

Compare the weight of a shoe to the weight of this book and to the weight of another object. Which of these three objects do you think weighs closest to a pound? closest to a kilogram? ●●●

Estimating Weights and Weighing with Scales

Scales of different types are commonly used in the home, grocery store, and doctor's office. Children may have seen different scales but may not have had opportunities to explore how they work. Balance scales (see photo) can be placed in a classroom weighing center for exploration. With a two-pan scale children can directly compare the weights of objects to nonstandard weights, such as plastic bears or blocks, and to standard weights. In the classroom a scale with a set of weights, in either the English or the metric system, is needed: ounce and pound weights for English; weights of 500 grams, 250 grams, 100 grams, 50 grams, 10 grams, 5 grams, and 1 gram for metric. After direct measurement of

Image courtesy of NASCO

Balance scales

weight, children are better able to understand an indirect measurement tool such as the sliding-weight or electronic scale often used in a doctor's office.

When commercial weights are unavailable, a teacher can substitute small bags or film canisters containing clean sand for 100-, 250-, and 500-gram measures or for graduated ounce measures. Fishing weights can be used for activities requiring smaller weight units. Kitchen-type spring scales for weighing up to 5 kilograms and a platform bathroom scale should be available. Teacher-made problem cards can guide children's weighing activities (Figure 18.19) in learning centers. One requires a balance scale and food commonly sold by weight, such as apples, oranges, and hard-shelled nuts; the other requires a spring scale and a bathroom scale with plastic bags of carrots and dried beans, boxes of paper, and other heavier objects.

As students weigh objects, they learn to estimate weight by comparing objects against established references. For example, they find the number of medium-size apples or cantaloupes that weighs about 2 pounds, or nearly a kilogram, and the number of cell phones that weigh a pound. They also learn that anything weighing 1 gram or 1 ounce, such as grapes or strawberries, is light. Mental models for weights allow children to estimate the weight of unfamiliar objects. A child who envisions a gram as the weight of a paper clip can use that image to compare the weights of other objects to a gram.

Exploring Density

Younger children might begin to understand the concept of density by comparing how crowded a room can be. The more crowded the room, the greater its density. In upper elementary grade science classes, students formally confront the concept of **density**. At this level they recognize that large objects can be lightweight and small objects can be heavyweight, depending on the relationship of the mass to the volume of the object. The higher the mass to volume ratio, the greater the density of the substance or object. A snowball has a low density compared to a piece of granite or marble. A small box with a volume of 1 liter can weigh either 10 grams or 1,000 grams, depending on whether it is full of packing peanuts or sand. Experience with objects of different sizes and weights will help older elementary students understand density. The problem cards in Figure 18.20 suggest recording

Figure 18.19 Problem cards for weight

WEIGHING WITH GRAMS

Use the balance scale and weights to answer the following questions in your journal.

1. What is the weight in grams of the apple?
2. What is the weight in grams of three carrots?
3. What is the weight in grams of six walnuts?

WEIGHING WITH KILOGRAMS

Use the spring scale and the bathroom scale to answer each question in your journal.

1. How many kilograms does the bag of carrots weigh?
2. How many kilograms do ten mathematics books weigh?
3. How many kilograms does the bag of dried beans weigh?
4. How many kilograms does the box of paper weigh?

Compare your answers with those of another group of students. If there are any disagreements, reweigh the objects involved to see if one group was wrong. Could a difference be the result of the way each group interpreted the measurements, rather than an error?

Figure 18.20 Problem cards for density

DENSITY SENSITY

Weigh boxes 1 through 6 and measure the volume of each one. Record your answers in a table like the one shown.

	Cubic Feet			Liters		
	Box 1	Box 2	Box 3	Box 4	Box 5	Box 6
Weight						
Volume						
Density						

Based on your measurement, answer these questions.

1. Which box is the largest? Smallest?
2. Which box weighs the most? Weighs the least?
3. Which box is the most dense? Least dense?

HEAVY OR LIGHT?

Look at the table for 6 boxes. Based on this information, answer these questions.

	Cubic Feet			Liters		
	Box 1	Box 2	Box 3	Box 4	Box 5	Box 6
Weight	4 lb	6 lb	9 lb	2 kg	10 kg	10 kg
Volume	1 ft^3	2 ft^3	3 ft^3	2 L	2 L	5 L
Density	4 lb/ft^3	3 lb/ft^3	3 lb/ft^3	1 kg/L	5 kg/L	2kg/L

1. Which box is the largest? Smallest?
2. Which box weighs the most? Weighs the least?
3. Which box is the most dense? Least dense?

volume and weight measurements in a table. The table shows the relationship between the two measures and connects measurement to division and algebraic representation. Students can create their own density boxes to add to the collection of boxes for weighing and measuring.

Expanding Angle Concepts

The formal introduction to measuring angles will likely come in a geometry lesson when children learn that an angle is formed by two rays that have a common endpoint. One way to introduce the measuring process in intermediate grades is to have children make folds in wax paper to compare angles (Activity 18.22). Discussion during the activity leads children to realize that a new sort of unit, the degree, is needed to measure angles. One way to develop the meaning of a degree is shown in Activity 18.23.

After students understand the basis for measuring angles, teachers can introduce the standard protractor. The teacher demonstrates its use with a large protractor at the chalkboard or with a clear

MISCONCEPTION

A common error that students make is to relate the side lengths of an angle to its degree measure. Activity 18.24 helps students to dismiss this idea. As with other measurement concepts, a benchmark for angle measurement is beneficial to students. Activity 18.25 helps students to establish 90° as a benchmark for angle measure.

plastic protractor on an overhead projector. As students observe the demonstration, they discuss the meanings of the marks and numerals on the protractor. Students may notice the similarity between the clock marked off in 60 minutes and the circular protractor marked off in 360 degrees. Demonstrate measuring an acute, right, and obtuse angle so that students understand how the zero is aligned with one ray and the measurement is read where the other ray intersects the arc of the protractor.

Figure 18.21 illustrates how a protractor is positioned to measure an acute angle. This protractor has two sets of numerical scales, as do most school protractors. Students can be confused by the two

ACTIVITY 18.22 Measuring Angles

Level: Grades 4–6

Setting: Student pairs

Objective: Students represent and compare angles.

Materials: Two pieces of wax paper for each student, scissors

- Have each student fold each sheet of wax paper so that the common endpoint of two rays are at one edge of the paper. The folds form one angle on each sheet.

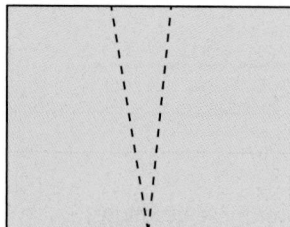 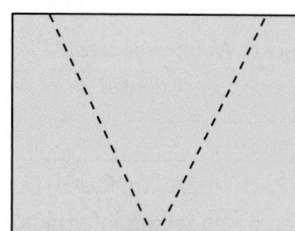

- Have students lay one sheet on top of the other so that the endpoint and one ray of the smaller angle are superimposed on the endpoint and one ray of the larger angle.

- Have students estimate the number of times the smaller angle will fit inside the larger angle. Describe the relationship as "The larger angle is less than twice as large," "The larger angle is about twice as large," or "The larger angle is more than twice as large."

- Have students cut out the smaller angle to make a unit of measure. After measuring and recording the number of times the smaller angle fits into the larger angle, have pairs of students trade their smaller angles and measure their larger angles with the new unit angle.

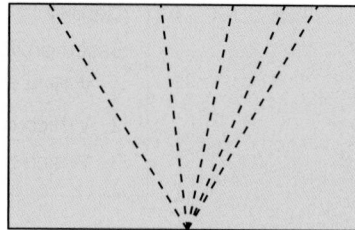

- Have students display and discuss their angle measures.
- Is the measure with the two angles the same? If not, why not?
- When you measure using a smaller angle, is the measure of the large angle a bigger or a smaller number than when you measure with a larger angle?
- Which gives a more precise measurement, a smaller angle or a larger angle?

ACTIVITY 18.23 What Is a Degree?

Level: Grades 4–6

Setting: Whole class or small group

Objective: Students define degree as a measure of angularity.

Materials: Rotating ray for overhead projector

- Show the model of a rotating ray with an overhead projector.

- Ask the children to follow the ray as it rotates around the endpoint. Imagine a ray that is rotated around its endpoint so that it makes a quarter-turn, a half-turn, and a complete rotation.

- Say: "If this ray were the minute hand of a clock, how many minutes would it pass as it made a complete rotation?" (Answer: 60 minutes.) "As the ray moves around the circle, it makes 360 stops. What part of the entire circle is the distance between each pair of stops?" (Answer: $\frac{1}{360}$.)

- Point out the angle made by the ray and the dashed line.

- Say: "The angle formed by the ray and the dashed line is 1 degree of measure. Each degree is $\frac{1}{360}$ of a full rotation of the ray."

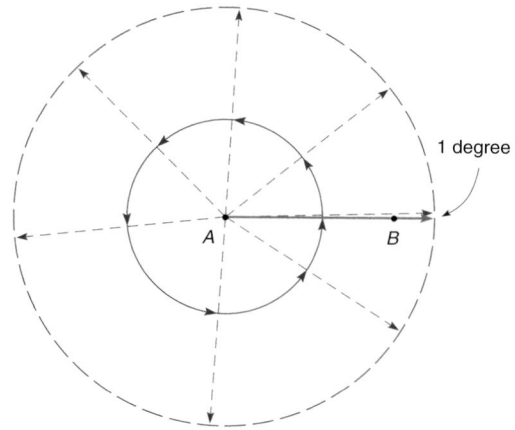

- Model a full rotation, and ask students how many degrees the ray has turned.

- Ask: "How many degrees are in one quarter turn?" (Answer: 90 degrees.) "How many degrees are in half a turn?" (Answer: 180 degrees.)

ACTIVITY 18.24 Shrinking Angles

Level: Grades 5 and 6

Setting: Small groups

Objective: Students make a pie plate angle and cut it down without changing the angle measure

Materials: Paper pie plates, rulers, scissors

- Mark the center of each pie plate, and distribute two plates per group.

- Have each student cut out an angle from a pie plate.

- Have students trace their pie plate angles.

- Ask students to cut down their angle by shortening the side lengths and compare the remaining angle to the traced angle.

- Repeat for several more cuttings.

- Have each group make a conjecture about the size of an angle and the lengths of the sides of an angle.

ACTIVITY 18.25 Angle Wheel (Representation)

Level: Grades 5 and 6

Setting: Whole class

Objective: Students estimate angle size as shown on the angle wheel.

Materials: Angle wheel made from Black-Line Master 18.3

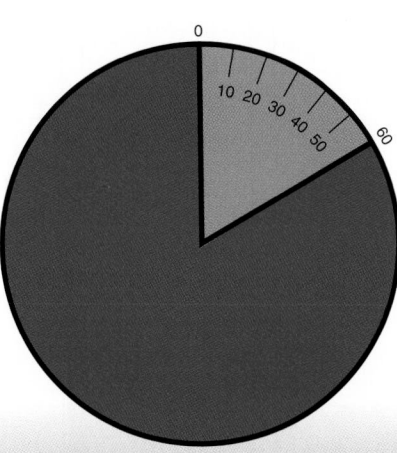

- Explain to students that you will display an angle on the angle wheel and that you want them to estimate its number of degrees. Tell students that every angle shown will be a multiple of 10°.

- Show an angle, and ask a student for its degree measure.

- Continue to ask students for the degree measure until a student is within 10°. At that point, give the correct number of degrees.

- Form another angle and repeat, but move through student estimates quickly. If a student has an incorrect measure, do not dwell on the incorrect answer. Simply repeat the given measure and quickly move on to another student until a student gives the correct answer (within 10°).

- After repeating with a number of angles, ask students how they would distinguish between a 50° angle and a 140° angle on the angle wheel. Probe for using 90° as a benchmark.

scales, unsure whether the correct reading for this angle is 60° or 120°. Instead of making a set of rules to apply to reading the protractor, students can use a benchmark of 90° (see Activity 18.25) to determine that this angle is less than 90°, so its measure is 60°, not 120°. Students can measure angles on objects, in magazine pictures, or drawn and duplicated on paper. Monitor students as they use the protractors to help those who have problems and to extend the thinking and skill of all students.

ⒺXERCISE

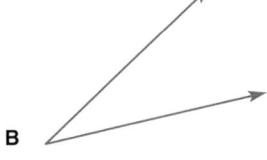

How would you help a child understand that the two angles pictured here have the same degree measure, especially since ∠A appears to be much smaller than ∠B? ●●●

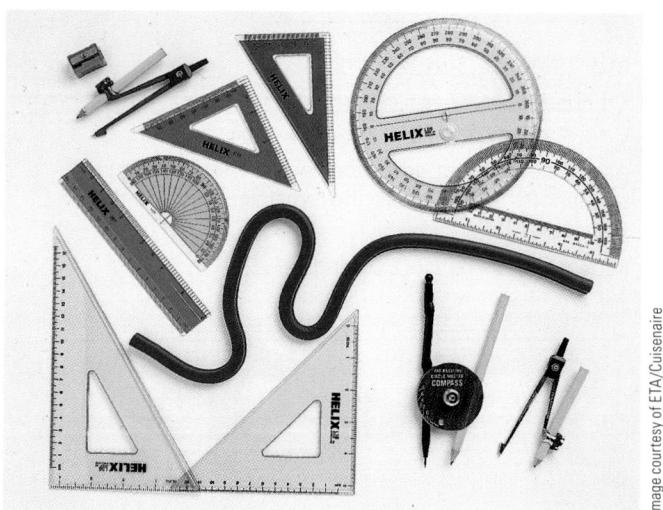

Protractors and other measuring devices

Image courtesy of ETA/Cuisenaire

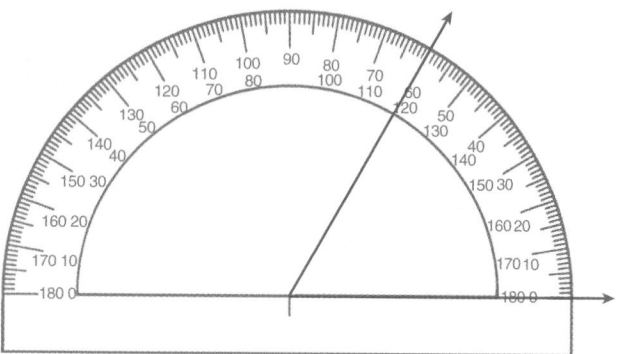

Figure 18.21 Correct alignment of a protractor to measure an angle

Older children apply their knowledge of measuring with degrees when they prepare circle (pie) graphs. Even though many computer graphing programs are available, children need opportunities to prepare simple circle graphs with protractors and compasses. Activities illustrating uses and preparation of circle graphs are discussed in Chapter 19.

Ⓔ X E R C I S E

Find examples of right, obtuse, and acute angles in the room where you are reading. Estimate the sizes of the obtuse and acute angles. If possible, measure the angles. How accurate were your estimates? ●●●

One way to assess students' understanding is with an end-of unit performance task. On the companion website two activities with scoring rubrics are presented as ways to assess students' under-

standing of volume. The box-making activity can be used to determine a student's understanding of volume. The school-volume group activity can be used as a culminating activity to assess an individual's understanding of volume measurement. Group projects can be assessed for quality of presentation and cooperation and should not be used for assigning grades. Students might do self-assessment on the group project. In Chapter 4 we discussed the development of performance tasks and rubrics to assess students' understanding.

Expanding Temperature Concepts

Older children explore applications of temperature in both Fahrenheit and centigrade (Celsius). To keep a daily temperature record, children can use large, easy-to-read thermometers and digital weather thermometers. A large demonstration thermometer, either commercially bought or made with tagboard and elastic, models how liquid in the thermometer moves up and down and is read on the Fahrenheit and Celsius scales (Figure 18.22). After reading the

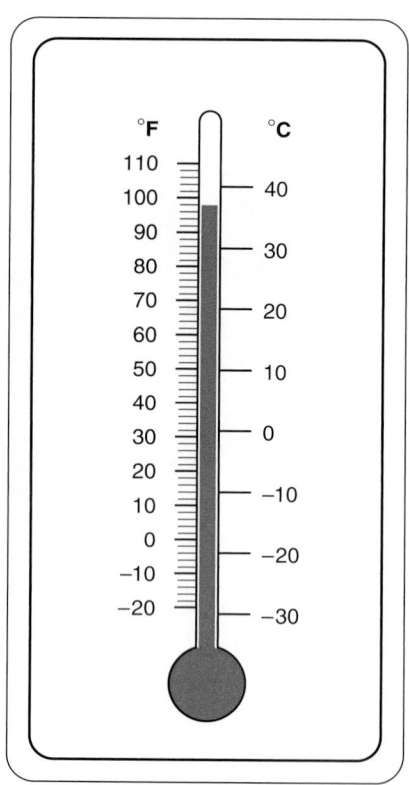

Figure 18.22 Demonstration thermometers help children learn how temperature is determined. Standard (Fahrenheit) units are shown on the left-hand side of the thermometer, and metric (Celsius) units are shown on the right-hand side.

outside temperature, the child can set the temperature on the demonstration thermometer for the entire class to read. A line graph of daily temperatures provides a record for discussion of increasing or decreasing temperatures over the month and connects mathematics and science in a realistic context.

Other science and health units also engage children in experiences with measurement of temperature. Plant experiments require that variables such as temperature, light, water, and nutrients be controlled and measured to determine their effects. Temperatures of warm- and cold-blooded animals can be considered during the study of animals. Temperature related to health is important to know and understand.

By the end of elementary school, children should know how to read both Celsius and Fahrenheit liquid and digital thermometers. Rather than spending time on conversions, students need to know that the boiling point of water is 212°F, or 100°C, and that the freezing point is 32°F, or 0°C. These two facts allow them to estimate and interpolate common temperatures such as hot, cold, and comfortable.

> A simple but reasonably accurate method for converting temperate Celsius temperatures to Fahrenheit is to double the Celsius temperature and add 30. A reading of 20°C is approximately 70°F.

Extending Concepts of Time

As older children progress in their understanding of our calendar, they begin to learn the number of days in each month. One way that children can recall the number of days in each month is to use their knuckles. If children hold up their hands as shown here, then the months can be counted off in order as either a "knuckle month" or a "space month." Knuckle months all have 31 days. Space months all have 30, with the exception of February, which has 28 days in non–leap years. Notice that with this model, there is one pair of consecutive knuckle months. These months correspond to July and August.

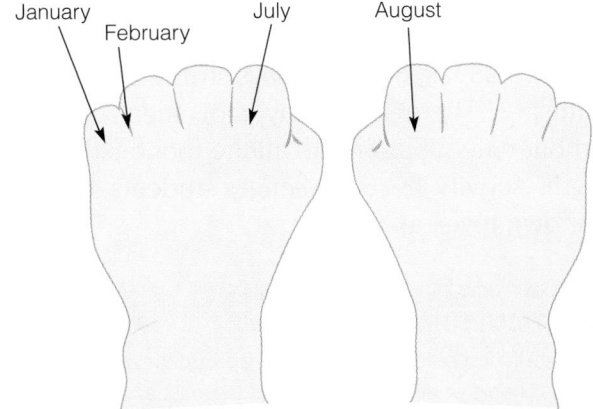

Older students can expand their understanding of time by examining time in different settings. They can explore the origins of our Gregorian calendar to determine why our calendar is named after a pope, and what events led to the present calendar after more than 1,500 years of the ancient Roman (Julian) calendar.

Older students can also explore the effect of time zones on travel. Airline schedules suggest that an airplane leaving Boston at 7 a.m. and landing in Los Angeles at 10:00 a.m. requires only 3 hours to make the transcontinental trip. Of course, the travel time is longer because there are time zones to consider, and students can grapple with this aspect of time.

Another topic for older children is the 24-hour clock. Students in your class from cultures and countries that use a 24-hour clock can explain how they were able to tell time. A final topic is suggested in Activity 18.26. Our present calendar with months

ACTIVITY 18.26 New World Calendar

Level: Grades 3–6
Setting: Small groups
Objective: Students design a new calendar
Materials: 10 grid paper

- Note for students that our calendar can be confusing. Elicit comments why this is so.
- Challenge students to design a better calendar that has all months the same length.

- Remind students that they should plan on a 365-day calendar.
- As part of their calendar design, students should clearly plan what to do with "extra days" in their year.
- Have each group report to the class about its new calendar, and post the group calendars around the room.

Standardized time zones were developed when railroad travel across the United States came about with the completion of the transcontinental railroad in 1869. In order for railroad companies to prepare and print meaningful time schedules, standardized time zones across the country were needed. Before 1869, each locale could have its own official time. The city of Chicago alone, for example, had six different time zones.

that have 28, 29, 30, or 31 days strikes some as too confusing. There are many movements to redesign our calendar to make all the months the same length. Activity 18.26 challenges students to design their own revision.

MULTICULTURALCONNECTION

An excellent multicultural activity is for students to examine the calendars of different cultures of the past and present: the Julian calendar of ancient Rome, the Mayan and Aztec calendars, and the lunar calendars of present-day and early peoples can be a fascinating study.

Measurement Problem Solving and Projects

Measurement situations abound, so it is easy to find projects and problem-solving applications that require measurement. Task cards can be used to extend measurement activities outside school. Task cards allow students to personalize and expand measurement activities that particularly intrigue them:

- Measure the length and width of one room in your house or apartment.

- Look in the newspaper for carpet ads. Measure a room, and figure out how much it would cost to cover the floor with three different qualities of carpeting.

- Find a recipe for, and bake, some oatmeal and raisin cookies.

- Weigh five different pairs of shoes. Which weighs the most? the least?

- When are the heaviest shoes worn? When are the lightest shoes worn?

- Some people say that 98.6°F is a normal temperature for a healthy person. Take the temperatures of five people who are not sick and compare them to the "normal" temperature.

- Keep a 24-hour diary of your time. How much time do you spend doing various activities?

- Take a survey of allowances in your class. What do other students spend money on each week?

- Determine how many gallons of paint are needed to paint the walls of two classrooms.

- Predict how many gallons of milk are consumed in the school cafeteria during lunch.

Take-Home Activities

Measurements are frequently made at home. One take-home activity is a measurement treasure hunt; the other has students consider questions dealing with heights of family members. Units of measure for the treasure hunt should be confined to ones that children have learned in school. A treasure list of units for older students will be more comprehensive than that for younger ones. We use English units for measurements in our example because these are the ones most commonly used at home.

Our Measurements-at-Home Hunt

Dear Parent:

Your child has been learning about measurement. We want you to help her or him find examples of measurements at home. Please take time to assist your child to complete the following work. He or she is to find things around the house whose measures match as nearly as possible the ones on the list. Here are examples: Find something that is about 7 inches long. What takes about 1 hour to complete?

If you cannot find a match for any item on the list, make a match that is as close as possible:

7 inches	4 yards	1 pound
5 pounds	5 ounces	3 minutes
1 hour	1 gallon	59 cents
90 degrees (angle)	350 degrees (temperature)	

· Have your child make a list of the measurements and the thing (or things) that matches each one.
· Have your child write a brief description of how you completed your treasure hunt. Which measurement was easiest to match? Which measurement was the most difficult to match?
· Have your child return the completed paper to school on Wednesday.

(continued)

Take-Home Activities

Our Family-Heights Activity

Dear Parents:

Your child's class has been using mathematics to collect data and analyze it in a variety of ways. One fruitful source of data is your child. This activity sheet asks questions about your child's height and the height of other family members. These data can be used with the table of average heights shown here to make predictions.

Average Heights for Children

Boys		Girls	
Age in Years	Height (cm)	Age in Years	Height (cm)
2	96.2	2	95.7
4	103.4	4	103.2
6	117.5	6	115.9
8	130.0	6	128.0
10	140.3	10	138.6
12	149.6	12	151.9
14	162.7	14	159.6
16	171.6	16	162.2
18	164.5	18	162.5

Source: Kempe et al. (1997).

NAME:_____

HOW TALL WILL I GET TO BE?

Take-Home Activities

Current Data

My height at birth: _____

I was taller/shorter than average.

My age today: _____

My height today: _____

Height Predictions

1. Based on my birth height, I predict I will be _____ cm tall when I am 16.
2. Based on my height today, I predict I will be _____ cm at age 16.
3. Which age interval on the chart showed the greatest average height growth for your sex? _____ How might that affect your height predictions?
4. If you are 140 cm tall when you are 10, will you be 280 cm tall when you are 20? Why or why not?
5. Based on your height so far, will you be taller or shorter than average when you graduate from high school?
6. Predict your height at age 18. Use the chart to help you. Explain your prediction.
7. Predict the height of a brother and sister at age 12 based on his or her birth height.
8. Make a bar graph to show the height of everyone in your family.

Summary

Children learn about measurement by measuring real objects in everyday contexts. In elementary mathematics, teachers develop the concepts and practical skills of measuring length, area, volume and capacity, weight (mass), angles, temperature, time, and money. Measurement activities build an understanding of the nature of measurement and units, present the units used to measure objects and events, and cultivate skills with measurement tools and instruments.

While engaged in many measurement activities, students discover that measurement is always approximate, not exact; measurement can always be made more precise by using smaller units. Human error creates inaccuracies in measurement. Students learn to choose appropriate measuring units and tools for different jobs; a ruler is good for measuring human height but not good for measuring a football field or a mile.

Skill with both English customary and metric units and tools is important in elementary school. The English customary system is currently entrenched in daily life in the United States, but the metric system is used virtually everywhere else in the world in everyday life and in science and commerce. The metric system is a simple scientific system in which all units are derived from the length of the meter. Units for area, volume, and mass are related to the meter and to each other based on powers of 10, like the decimal numeration system.

For each measurement characteristic, children begin with concrete experiences in realistic situations. As children learn about the units and tools in both systems of measurement, they see that the same process is used for both systems but that the units are different. Through many measuring experiences they develop mental models for common units that they can use for estimation. Older children extend their knowledge about measurement to include area, volume, and angle measure. They also learn how to compute measurements such as area and volume.

Measurement activities have many direct connections to other subject areas and home activities. Health, science, and social studies concepts relate to measurement of length, area, volume, temperature, time, and money. These measurements are also vital at home for planning and making decisions about health, cooking, decorating, purchasing, and scheduling activities. The problem-solving and realistic nature of measurement and the fact that many measurement activities can be carried out independently or in groups make measurement an excellent mathematics topic to be taught throughout the year. Teachers can prepare and introduce task cards, learning centers, and take-home activities.

Through guided discussion and debriefing of experiences, children grasp the concepts and skills of measurement.

Study Questions and Activities

1. What are your experiences with learning the metric system? Did you learn about the metric system through hands-on measurement activities?

2. Can you estimate lengths of a yard, inch, centimeter, meter, and mile? square foot, square yard, square meter? cubic foot, cubic centimeter? ounce, pound, gram, kilogram? Name common objects that would be good referents for these units.

3. In an age of digital clocks, should children learn to tell time with analog clocks? Discuss this question with two or three acquaintances. What is the consensus, and what reasons are given?

4. Search the Internet for websites on measuring instruments and processes. Report on what you find at three websites on measurement. Several manufacturers of measuring instruments have sites about their products. One manufacturer describes a distance-measuring device that is accurate to 1 foot in a mile. The National Institute for Standards and Technology maintains a site ("A Walk Through Time," available at **http://physics.nist.gov/GenInt/Time/time.html**) that chronicles the history of timekeeping and time measurement. Another website (**http://www.fraden.com**) describes the inventor of the Instant Ear Thermometer.

5. Explain how many cubic feet make a cubic yard.

6. Give a convincing argument for using the metric system rather than the English system of measurement.

7. Interview a 5- to 7-year-old child. Ask her to use a coffee stirrer to measure the length of her foot and your foot, and then compare the results.

8. Explain how the value of π is determined.

Praxis (**http://www.ets.org/praxis/**) The inside of a rectangular picture frame measures 36 inches long and 24 inches wide. The width of the frame is x inches, as shown in the figure. When hung, the frame and its contents cover 1,120 square inches of wall space. What is the length, y, of the frame in inches?

a. 44

b. 40

c. 38

d. 34

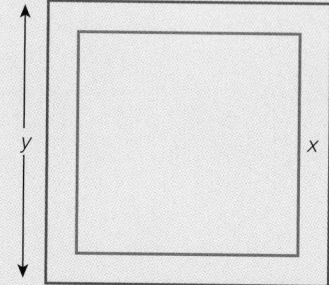

NAEP (http://nces.ed.gov/nationsreportcard/) At a picnic cider is served in cups. If 1 pint will fill 2 cups, how many cups can be filled from 8 pints of cider?

a. 4
b. 8
c. 11
d. 16

TIMSS (http://nces.ed.gov/timss/) Which of these could be the mass of an adult?

a. 1 kg
b. 6 kg
c. 60 kg
d. 600 kg

Using Children's Literature

Myllar, Rolf. (1991). *How big is a foot?* New York: Dell. (Grades K–3)

How Big Is a Foot? is the story of a carpenter and the dilemma of making a new bed for the queen. The bed was measured by the king and by the carpenter's apprentice, but because their feet were not the same size, the bed was built too small for the queen.

This story line sets the stage for measurement of lengths by students' feet.

- Students pace off the width of the room or the length of the chalkboard and write the results on a chart in Vanessa feet, Jen feet, Anwar feet, and Domingo feet.
- Have students post their data.
- Ask if anyone got an exact number of foot lengths.
- Discuss the reasons for different numbers of foot lengths.
- Ask if a giant or a mouse would need more or fewer foot lengths.

The discussion of these points brings up the need for a standard "foot" that everybody understands. Cheryl Lubinski and Diane Thiessen (1996) describe how one teacher develops these ideas over several weeks using children's literature as a basis for measurement, problem solving, and writing.

Burns, Marilyn. (1978). *This book is about time.* New York: Little, Brown. (Grades 4–6)

Want activities to stir children's interest in a unit on time? Want activities dealing with the history of time and timepieces? This book about time includes nearly all aspects of time—from evolution of the calendar to people's natural rhythms, from a history of timepieces and calendars to jet lag and "time clocks" in plants and animals. Chapter titles indicate the variety of topics: "Warm-Up Time," "It's Not the Same Time Everywhere," "Ticking Off the Day," "Portable Time," "Bits of Time," "The Calendar Story," "Nature's Amazing Clocks," "The Inside Story of People Time," "What Is Jet Lag?" and "Time in Your Life."

- Have students do their own time-check count. When do they look at their watches or clocks? Why do they look at them? (p. 10)
- Try making a list of time expressions: "Time's up." "Time flies." "Time on my hands." How many can you think of? (p. 12)
- Which civilizations made and used sundials? water clocks? sand clocks? How can children make these timepieces? (pp. 30–37)
- Have students study different types of calendars. Information in "The Calendar Story" may inspire children to do research in an encyclopedia or other sources.
- Have students identify connections between time and science that are evident in natural cycles, in the seasons, in animal migrations, and in sleep-wake cycles.

All activities are suitable for fifth- and sixth-graders who are able to read and interpret information and directions. However, many activities are suitable for younger children when adapted and presented by a teacher.

Teacher's Resources

Anderson, N., Gavin, N., Dailey, J., Stone, W., & Vuolo, J.. (2005). *Navigating through measurement in Grades 3–5.* Reston, VA: National Council of Teachers of Mathematics.

Bright, G., Jordan, P., Malloy, C., & Watanabe, T. (2005). *Navigating through measurement in grades 6–8.* Reston, VA: National Council of Teachers of Mathematics.

Clements, Douglas, & Bright, George (Eds.). (2003). *Learning and teaching measurement: 2003 yearbook.* Reston, VA: National Council of Teachers of Mathematics.

Dacey, L., Cavanaugh, N., Findell, C., Greenes, C., Sheffield, L., & Small, M. (2003). *Navigating through measurement in prekindergarten–Grade 2.* Reston, VA: National Council of Teachers of Mathematics.

Dilke, O. A. W. (1987). *Reading the past: Mathematics and measurement.* London: British Museum Press.

Geddes, Dorothy. (1994). *Measurement in the middle grades.* Reston, VA: National Council of Teachers of Mathematics.

Huong, Nguyen. (1999). *Math logic: Perimeter, area, and volume.* Bellevue, WA: Logical Connections.

Lee, Martin, & Miller, Marcia. (2000). *50 fabulous measurement activities.* New York: Scholastic.

Morrison, Philip, & Morrison, Phylis. (1982). *Powers of 10: About the relative size of things in the universe.* New York: American Scientific Library.

Strauss, Stephen. (1995). *The sizesaurus.* New York: Kondasha International.

Children's Bookshelf

Ackerman, K. (1998). *Araminta's paint box*. New York: Simon & Schuster Children's Books. (Grades 4–6)

Adams, Pam. (1989). *Ten beads tall*. Sudbury, MA: Child's Play International. (Grades PS–2)

Adler, David. (1999). *How tall, how short, how far away?* New York: Holiday House. (Grades 1–4)

Allington, Richard L., & Krull, Kathleen. (1982). *Time*. Milwaukee: Raintree. (Grades 1–2)

Anno, Mitsumasa. (1987). *Anno's sundial*. New York: Philomel. (Grades 4–8)

Ardley, Neil. (1983). *Making metric measurements*. New York: Franklin Watts. (Grades 4–6)

Carter, David A. (1988). *How many bugs in the box?* New York: Simon & Schuster. (Grades PS–2)

Clement, Rod. (1991). *Counting on Frank*. Milwaukee: Gareth Stevens Children's Books. (Grades 1–2)

Faulkner, Keith. (2000). *So big! My first measuring book*. Riverside, NJ: Simon & Schuster. (Grades PK–2)

Glass, Julie. (1998). *The fly on the ceiling*. New York: Random House. (Grades 1–3)

Gould, Deborah. (1988). *Brendan's best-timed birthday*. Scarsdale, NY: Bradbury. (Grades PS–1)

Hightower, Susan. (1997). *Twelve snails to one lizard*. New York: Simon & Schuster. (Grades 1–3)

Kain, Carolyn. (1993). *Story of money*. New York: Troll. (Grades 3–6)

Krensky, Stephen. (1989). *Big time bears*. Boston: Little, Brown. (Grades PS–K)

Laithwaite, Eric. (1988). *Size: The measure of things*. New York: Franklin Watts. (Grades 5–8)

Lasky, Kathryn. (2003). *The man who made time travel*. New York: Farrar, Strauss, and Giroux. (Grades 5–7)

Lasky, Kathryn, & Hawkes, Kevin. (1994). *The librarian who measured the earth*. Boston: Little, Brown. (Grades K–6)

Leedy, Loren. (1997). *Measuring penny*. New York: Henry Holt. (Grades 2–5)

Lionni, Leo. (1995). *Inch by inch*. New York: Morrow. (Grades K–2)

Maestro, Betsy. (1999). *The story of clocks and calendars: Making a millennium*. New York: Lothrop, Lee, & Shepard. (Grades 3–6)

Major, J. (1995). *The silk route: 7,000 miles of history*. New York: HarperCollins. (Grades 4–7)

McBratney, Sam. (1994). *Guess how much I love you*. Cambridge, MA: Candlewick. (Grades 1–4)

Miller, Margaret. (1996). *Now I'm big*. New York: Greenwillow. (Grades PS–1)

Morgan, Rowland. (1997). *In the next three seconds*. New York: Penguin. (Grades 4–8)

Murphy, Stuart, & Lum, Bernice. (2004). *Mighty Maddie*. New York: HarperCollins. (Grades PS–2)

Neasi, Barbara. (1988). *A minute is a minute*. Chicago: Children's Press. (Grades PS–3)

Neuschwander, Cindy. (1997). *Sir Cumference and the dragon of Pi: A math adventure*. Watertown, MA: Charlesbridge. (Grades 4–6)

Neuschwander, Cindy. (2001). *Sir Cumference and the Great Knight of Angleland: A math adventure*. Watertown, MA: Charlesbridge. (Grades 4–6)

Neuschwander, Cindy, & Geehan, Wayne. (1998). *Sir Cumference and the first round table*. Watertown, MA: Charlesbridge. (Grades 1–5)

Pilegard, Virginia, & Debon, Nicholas. (2004). *The warlord's kites*. New York: Pelican. (Grades 3–6)

Pluckrose, Henry. (1988). *Capacity*. New York: Franklin Watts. (Grades 1–5)

Pluckrose, Henry. (1988). *Length*. New York: Franklin Watts. (Grades 1–3)

Pluckrose, Henry. (1988). *Weight*. New York: Franklin Watts. (Grades PS–2)

Stevens, Janet, & Stevens, Susan. (1999). *Cook-a-doodle-doo!* New York: Harcourt Brace. (Grades 2–5)

Swift, J. (1991). *Gulliver's travels*. New York: Dover. (Grades 5–8)

Viorst, Judith. (1972). *Alexander and the terrible, horrible, no good, very bad day*. New York: Abrahamson. (Grades 1–3)

Wallace, Nancy Elizabeth. (2000). *Paperwhite*. Boston: Houghton Mifflin. (Grades 3–6)

Williams, Sherley Anne. (1992). *Working cotton*. San Diego: Harcourt Brace Jovanovich. (Grades 1–5)

Technology Resources

Computer Programs

Timescales (from Attainment Company Inc.) is a special program for special students. It features activities dealing with telling time that are designed for students who need special help learning to read clocks and estimating time and who benefit from multisensory feedback to strengthen cognition. It offers teachers a selection of settings to regulate the level of difficulty and to quicken or slow the pace of presentation. Students learn to read multiple clock formats in both analog and digital settings with much verbal feedback.

Internet Sites

Volume

http://nlvm.usu.edu/en/nav/vlibrary.html (see Volume and Shape [in Geometry 6–8])

http://www.shodor.org/interactivate/activities/index.html (see Surface Area and Volume [in Geometry and Measurement Concepts])

http://www.mste.uiuc.edu/carvell/3dbox/default.html
Estimation with Customary and Metric Measures

http://www.bbc.co.uk/education/mathsfile/ (see Estimation [in Shape, Space, and Measure])
Area and Perimeter

http://www.mste.uiuc.edu/carvell/rectperim/RectPerim2.html
Measurement Conversions

http://www.convert-me.com/en/
The Value of π

http://arcytech.org/java/pi/measuring.html

Internet Games

At **http://www.abc.net.au/countsin/games.htm** there are two games that enable younger children to practice their ability to judge volume and length. In game 14 (length) children select the tallest person from among a group of people. In game 15 (volume) students select the largest resulting volume of water poured into two different containers.

For Further Reading

Battista, Michael, & Clements, Douglas M. (1998). Finding the number of cubes in rectangular cube buildings. *Teaching Children Mathematics* 4(5), 258–264.

Spatial sense in two and three dimensions is emphasized in this exploration of how students understand area, volume, and visual perspective. Suggestions for assessments and action research are included.

Brahier, Daniel, & Bell, Jacqueline. (2002). Dino-mite explorations. *Teaching Children Mathematics* 8(9), 532–539.

Children reference the size of dinosaurs in this project using their own height and weight as units of measure.

Buhl, David, Oursland, Mark, & Finco, Kristin. (2003). The legend of Paul Bunyan: An exploration in measurement. *Mathematics Teaching in the Middle School* 8(8), 441–448.

Buhl and colleagues use the legend of giant Paul Bunyan to exemplify the relationships between linear, area, and volume measures of similar solids. In the article the investigators describe a class project involving building clay models of Paul, his ox Babe, and some of their personal effects to explore the measurement relationships.

Ewing, Eula. (2002). Working cotton: Toward an understanding of time. *Teaching Children Mathematics* 8(8), 475–479.

A children's reading book is the basis for expanding young children's concepts of time.

Ferrer, Bellasanta, Hunter, Bobbie, Irwin, Kathryn, Sheldon, Maureen, Thompson, Charles, & Vistro-Yu,

Catherine. (2001). By the unit or square unit? *Teaching Mathematics in the Middle School* 7(3), 132–137.

Children compare perimeter and area of various shapes to distinguish between them.

Hartletzer, Stanley. (2003). Ratios of linear, area, and volume measures of similar solids. *Mathematics Teaching in the Middle School* 8(5), 228–236.

Hartletzer delineates a classroom exploration involving paper cubes and balloons that students use to gather data for relating linear, area, and volume measures of similar solids.

Lemme, Barbara. (2000). Integrating measurement projects: Sand timers. *Teaching Children Mathematics* 7(3), 132–135.

Lemme describes a class project with students building their own sand timers and using them in a variety of activities.

Long, Betty B., & Crocker, Deborah A. (2000). Adventures with Sir Cumference: Standard shapes and nonstandard units. *Teaching Children Mathematics* 7(4), 242–245.

Activities to explore nonstandard and standard units revolve around a storybook, *Sir Cumference and the Round Table.*

Moore, Sara, & Bintz, William. (2002). Teaching geometry and measurement through literature. *Mathematics Teaching in the Middle School* 8(2), 78–84.

Moore and Bintz reference a number of literature texts as sources of explorations, discussions, and activities that develop measurement concepts in middle school students. The article includes a helpful list of references.

Preston, R., & Thompson, T. (2004). Integrating measurement across the curriculum. *Mathematics Teaching in the Middle School* 9(8), 438–441.

In this article Preston and Thompson stress the whys and hows for including measurement across the mathematics curriculum from algebra to data analysis.

Taylor, P. Mark, Simms, Ken, Kim, Ok-Kyeong, & Reys, Robert E. (2001). Do your students measure up metrically? *Teaching Children Mathematics* 7(5), 282–287.

Taylor and colleagues discuss what international test results tell us about our third- and fourth-grade students' knowledge about mathematics and the metric system in particular; they also include some recommendations for the classroom.

Young, Sharon, & O'Leary, Robbin. (2002). Creating numerical scales for measuring tools. *Teaching Children Mathematics* 8(7), 400–405.

An intermediate step for children after using nonstandard units and before using standard units is to create "standard" measuring scales with nonstandard units.

CHAPTER 19

Understanding and Representing Concepts of Data

An understanding of how information is collected, recorded, reported, and interpreted is essential for citizens in their daily lives. Numerical information can describe current events or opinions and forecast future events. Every day, newspapers, magazines, television, and Internet sites feature stories with numerical information summarized in averages and percentages and displayed in tables and graphs. Personal finance decisions about homes, jobs, savings, and purchases as well as voting on candidates and public policy depend on understanding data. An adult who cannot interpret graphical displays of data is effectively disenfranchised in matters of the national economy. Data organization and interpretation provide many experiences that develop and extend skills in problem solving, reasoning, communication, connections, and representations of mathematics.

In this chapter you will read about:

1 How students collect and organize data based on their experiences

2 Activities that help students learn how to make and analyze tables, line plots, picture graphs, bar graphs, line graphs, circle graphs, stem-and-leaf plots, and box-and-whisker plots

3 How computer graphing programs can be used to organize and analyze data

4 How data collection results in statistics that describe and summarize numerical information

5 Errors that students typically make when displaying data

6 A data-gathering take-home activity

Early work with data should be exploratory in nature and center around children's firsthand observations. The teacher first guides the collection of data and then introduces increasingly more sophisticated ways to organize and display them. Over time the teacher expands instruction to include different types of graphs. By the end of grade 6 students should be able to construct and interpret picture, bar, line, and circle graphs, stem-and-leaf-plots, and box-and-whisker plots.

NCTM Correlation

The Data Standards for Pre-K–2 are as follows:
Instructional programs from prekindergarten through grade 12 should enable all students to:
- Formulate questions that can be addressed with data and collect, organize, and display relevant data to answer them
- Select and use appropriate statistical methods to analyze data
- Develop and evaluate inferences and predictions that are based on data
- Understand and apply basic concepts of probability

Pre-K–2 Expectations
In prekindergarten through grade 2 all students should:
- pose questions and gather data about themselves and their surroundings;
- sort and classify objects according to their attributes and organize data about the objects;
- represent data using concrete objects, pictures, and graphs;
- describe parts of the data and the set of data as a whole to determine what the data show.

Data Collection

The data children collect should come from their real-life interests and activities. Many childhood activities provide data that students can organize in tables and graphs. In kindergarten and the primary grades children can gather information about birthdays; shoe sizes, types, and colors; means of getting to school; height; hair and eye colors; favorite foods; and television shows. Intermediate-grade students are interested in many of the same topics and can add, for example, favorite sports stars, clothing, video games, and performing artists.

Recording and organizing data from science and social studies topics provides rich opportunities for integrating mathematics into other areas of the curriculum. The study of weather is common in both primary and intermediate science classes. Primary-grade children can collect temperature and rainfall information and record it in tables and graphs. In later grades the study can move beyond recording the data to interpreting it. While conducting experiments in plant growth, students can record daily or weekly measurements.

MULTICULTURALCONNECTION
Data for graphs and surveys can be drawn from many different sources, including foreign countries and cultures that are important to students in the classroom. Demographic data, economic changes, results of athletic events, and the like could be used.

Children can determine the strengths of various magnets by the number of paper clips they lift. In social studies, tables and graphs of varying formats can be made to compare products, populations, or geographic sizes of states or countries. Reference books, in both print and CD-ROM formats, and Internet sites provide a variety of data sources. Whenever possible, the data collected should be related to the interests of the children so that their data-handling skills produce information that is important to them. Sometimes data will be collected and organized in a single class period. In other cases several days or weeks will be devoted to the collection, organization, and interpretation of data for a science or social studies unit. Whatever the time frame, decisions must be made before the data are collected. The following five questions frame any meaningful collection and display of data:

- What is the question that justifies the data collection?
- What information is needed to answer the question?
- How can the information be gathered?

- How can the information be organized and analyzed?
- What are the best ways to display and communicate the results or analysis?

Materials for constructing tables and graphs are readily available and inexpensive. Sheets of newsprint and centimeter- or inch-squared paper (see Black-Line Masters 19.1 and 19.2), colored cubes, picture stickers, compasses, protractors, and pens and markers are the materials children use to construct tables and graphs. Computer programs suitable for both primary- and intermediate-grade students provide ways to organize data with spreadsheets (tables) and graphs. A number of Internet sites display submitted data in a variety of representations, both graphical and tabular. By the end of grade school students should demonstrate their ability to use both student-made and computer-generated tables and graphs to organize and report data.

POINT OF VIEW
The main purpose of collecting data is to answer questions when the answers are not immediately obvious. (National Council of Teachers of Mathematics, 2000, p. 109)

What Teachers Should Know About Understanding and Representing Concepts of Data

The key reason for representing data is to make the data easily understood. It is important that children focus on representing the data meaningfully and not simply follow a procedure for producing a graph of the data. Accordingly, students should have many experiences with representing data in various forms, such as line, bar, and circle graphs, stem-and-leaf plots, and box-and-whisker plots. They should also have many opportunities to interpret these graphical representations of data so that they gain an understanding of how various representations can convey information.

Data that students represent should be engaging. Data gathered from schoolmates, family, and the community can be especially interesting to students. Additional sources of data are periodicals and the Internet.

Each measure of central tendency (mean, median, mode) has advantages and disadvantages.

In addition to computing these measures, students should understand the proper use of each measure and what information each conveys.

Teachers sometimes spend more time on collecting and displaying data than on analyzing and interpreting data. Data are useful when they are used to answer questions. Teaching children to gather and organize data is important, but from the beginning of work with tables and graphs, children should generate and answer simple questions as they gather data.

What color are your eyes?

How many pockets do you have?

How many letters are in your first name?

After collecting individual answers, students will be able to organize their data for meaningful display in tables and graphs, and analysis will be easier. Results are then categorized, and different questions can be formulated from the data collected from all the children who answered the original questions.

What color are the eyes of people in the class?

How many pockets do different people have?

What is the most frequent number of letters in first names?

Students work with topics that are important to them in life: birthdays, pets, families, foods, and so on. Data that are pertinent to students engage them in gathering data to answer important questions. Students with many experiences in analyzing data build a foundation for more sophisticated representation and interpretation of information in the intermediate grades.

Organizing Data in Tables

At the earliest levels children recognize that some ways of recording data allow them to interpret the data more quickly and accurately. A simple way to record straightforward data is with a tally system. Tally systems are among the earliest methods used by ancient peoples to record data, such as the number of animals in a herd or the number of game animals captured during a hunting season. In the tally shown here, Kimberly, a first-grade student, recorded the number of windows in her home. Note that Kimberly separated her tallies into groups of five with a cross tally at every fifth window she counted.

Kimberly can easily count up the total number of windows as she goes along or at the end by skip-counting by fives.

Even in the primary grades students encounter problems with data gathering that require them to improve their process. If they ask about favorite ice cream flavors, they may get 12 different answers from 18 children. As a result, they may decide to reframe their question: "Which one of the six kinds of ice cream is your favorite?" Whitin (2006) makes several suggestions to help students reframe their questions:

1. How were the categories chosen?
2. What will happen to data that do not fall into the chosen categories?
3. What categories were rejected?
4. What other categories could have been created?

From the earliest grades children learn that using a table to organize data is a basic problem-solving strategy. Data organized in this way allow students to handle and communicate numerical information in meaningful ways. Data for young children need to come from firsthand experiences. The shoes children wear to school can provide data for a first activity. Children can gather on the floor, remove one shoe, and place it in the center of their circle. Discussion about the different types of shoes leads to a classification scheme. Once the shoes have been sorted according to the children's classification scheme, a natural extension of the activity is to make a table to show the number of shoes in each category (Figure 19.1). Children's pets, actual or wished for, can be subjects, first for tables and then for graphs. A survey in one class of first-graders resulted in the table in Figure 19.2.

> The oldest evidence of a statistical record is a baboon leg bone estimated to be 35,000 years old. The bone has 29 individual tally marks on it.

Horse	$\|\,\|$
Cat	卌 $\|$
Fish	$\|\,\|$
Dog	卌 $\|\,\|$
Mouse	$\|\,\|$
Guinea pig	$\|$
Turtle	$\|$
No pet	$\|\,\|\,\|$

Figure 19.2 Table showing students' pets

Information from tables such as these can be represented graphically, even by young children, in a **line plot**. A line plot simply represents each item of data as an individual entry. In Figure 19.3 the data from Figure 19.1 are displayed in a line plot. Such a display is fairly simple for students to construct.

Once the columns are labeled to show the categories, students record each item in the line plot with a mark in the appropriate column. Figure 19.4 illustrates a difficulty that some students have with line plots. Autumn, a second-grader, had difficulty marking the X in each column. She could not make each X the same size, and the spaces between the Xs are not consistent. It appears that there are many more pairs of athletic shoes than leather shoes, when the difference is only one pair. In this instance students in the class were able to discern that something was wrong with the plot. They reasoned that because there are eight pairs of athletic shoes and seven pairs of leather shoes, the columns for these types of shoes should be nearly the same height. One way to help students avoid this common error is to provide graph or grid paper and be sure that students place one X in each block or square.

Figure 19.5 shows how Autumn recorded the same information with the help of a grid. Notice how the columns now more closely reflect the actual numbers of pairs of shoes. Note, too, that the line plot resembles a bar graph when it is drawn within a grid. The transition from line plots to bar graphs is a fairly easy one for children to make when they have had ample opportunities to build and interpret line plots. They make the transition to bar graph by coloring in squares of the same color to make a continuous bar. Now, instead of counting squares, they

Type of shoe	Athletic	Cloth	Leather	Sandal	Boot
Number	8	5	7	3	2

Figure 19.1 Table showing shoe types

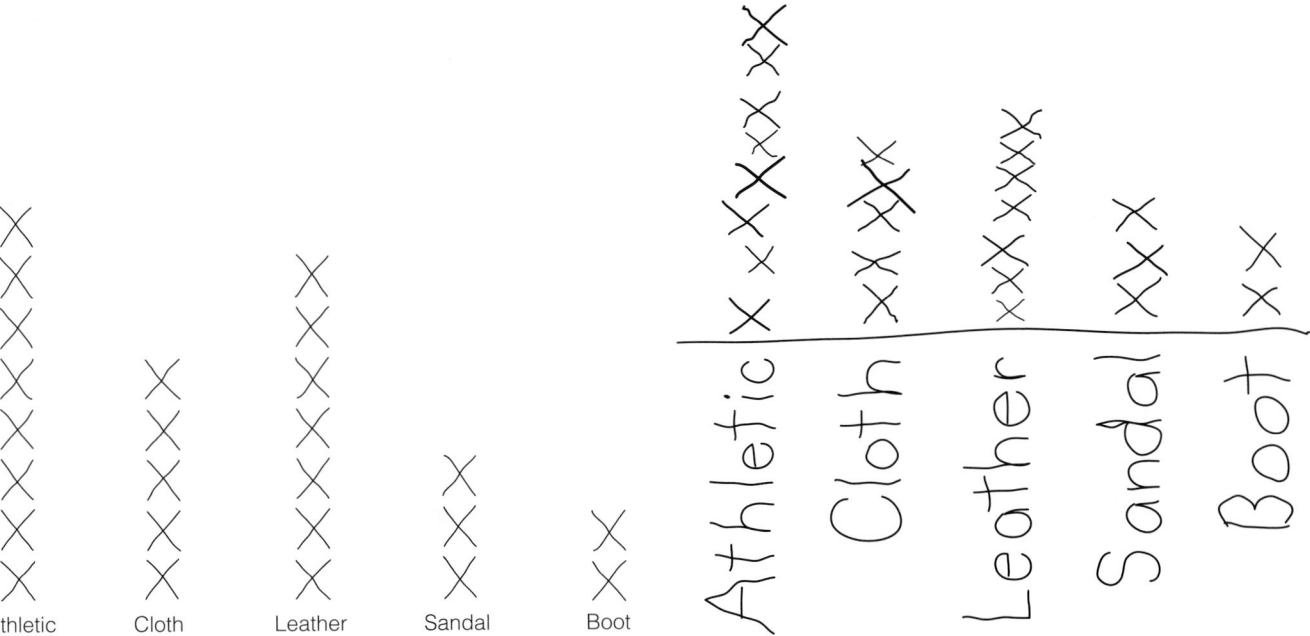

Figure 19.3 Line plot of shoe types

Figure 19.4 Student-drawn line plot without a grid

refer to the index number-line scale for the quantity that the bar graph represents.

Children use tables and graphs to identify patterns and functions. Activities leading to an intuitive understanding of function develop from situations using the relationship between two sets of numbers. During a fund-raising activity in a third-grade class, students studied the cost of toys they would use as prizes for their school carnival booth; each toy they chose cost 13 cents. When Claris suggested that they put five toys in one box as a superprize, they wondered how much five toys would cost. The teacher made a simple rate table. He began by making a blank table with the labels "Toys" and "Cost." Then he asked, "If we don't buy any toys, how much will we spend?" "If we buy one toy, how much will we spend?" As questions were asked, the teacher filled the boxes in the table (Figure 19.6). Gradually, children saw that they could get the next number by adding 13 to the preceding number. As the children studied the table, some reasoned that it was really a multiplication table for 13. They saw the relationship between the two numbers and realized that the number in each lower cell was the product of the number in the cell above it and 13.

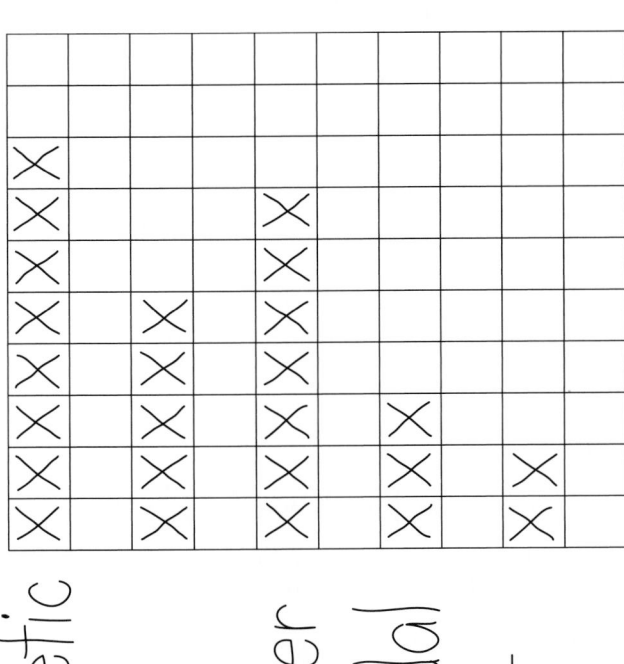

Figure 19.5 Student-drawn line plot using a grid

Toys	0	1	2	3	4	5
Cost	0¢	13¢	26¢	39¢	52¢	?

Figure 19.6 Rate table showing cost of toys

The organization of data in a table often results in the solution to a problem. Activity 19.1 suggests investigations that involve older children in determining the number of blocks in a pyramid. Organizing data in tables is one problem-solving strategy

ACTIVITY 19.1 Picture Graph (Representation)

Level: Grades K–2

Setting: Whole class

Objective: Students read and interpret an object graph and a picture graph.

Materials: Plastic animals, animal stickers portraying the same animals, two large pieces of poster board

- On each poster board, make a vertical line to serve as a baseline about 9 inches from the left edge.

- Have children sit in a circle on the floor, with a poster board in the middle. Show the table made when data on pets were collected (see Figure 19.2).

- Ask children, one by one, to name the type of pet(s) they own. Give the children plastic animals to match their pets. Children with more than one pet will get more than one animal. Have a unique "character" for children with no pet. Now, one by one, have the children put their animals on the poster board. Have the children put their animals in the appropriate places. Have them use care to align the animals at the baseline and across the poster board in rows.

- Use the object graph as a source of information for answers to questions: "Which lines are shortest?" "Are there any rows that have the same number of animals in them?" "Which pet would you say is most popular in our class?"

- Give each child a sticker to match her or his pet. Talk about how they will use the stickers to make a picture graph. Stress the importance of having a good alignment of stickers at the baseline and across the rows. Raise questions about data in this graph. Talk about the advantage of the picture graph over the object graph (e.g., it can be kept, whereas the object graph is temporary).

Our pets

for this activity. The teacher's role in these investigations is to encourage children to raise and discuss questions, to look for patterns, and to express solutions in words, with models, and with mathematical symbols.

Object and Picture Graphs

Young children's first graphs can be used to extend ongoing activities. After children have sorted and organized the shoe data in a table, the teacher can make a simple line plot to show the number of shoes in each category. Now children are ready for additional ways to organize and communicate their data. Another simple graph for the shoe data can be an **object graph**, in which actual objects, in this case the shoes, are part of the graph. An object graph can also use life-size representations of the objects instead of the actual objects themselves to display the data in a graph. (In this instance, this object graph could be considered a picture graph.) Each child gets a sheet of $8\frac{1}{2} \times 11$ colored construction paper, color coded according to type of shoes—blue for boots, red for sandals, and so on. Have students trace the appropriate shoe onto the colored paper. A length of masking tape on the classroom floor can

serve as the graph's base. Each child puts a piece of paper with the tracing of a shoe on the floor, beginning at the baseline. All children with a like color of paper place their "shoes" in the same row. The teacher helps them avoid overlapping pieces of paper or leaving large gaps between papers. Once the graph is complete, the children count the number of shoes of each kind and make comparisons among the categories (Figure 19.7).

Next, students can make a **picture graph** to give a more permanent representation of the data. A picture graph uses drawings or pictures to represent

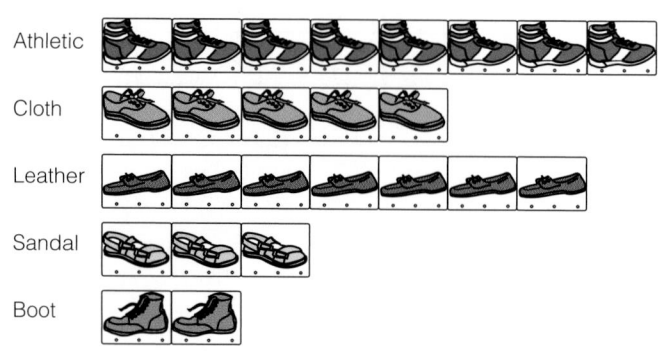

Figure 19.7 The object graph for "Shoes We Wore" investigation

the actual objects in the data set. In a picture graph each picture can represent one or more actual data objects. In this case the pictures are not life-size, as in the previous graph. Each child draws a picture of a shoe on square sticky notes. Each square is displayed with similar cards, beginning at a baseline drawn on craft paper. The teacher helps the children see that the object graph and the picture graph contain identical information in different forms. In both types of graphs, as with the tally system and the line plot, each item of data is represented by a single mark, symbol, or picture. This one-to-one relationship between the actual items and their graphical representations as symbols or pictures is critical for young children. Activity 19.1 presents other ways for children to prepare object and picture graphs. Data from the pet survey are used for these graphs.

Object and picture graphs have limitations that make them impractical for depicting some kinds of data. When real shoes and blocks are stacked to represent the shoe counting activity or the pet counting activity, the large number of objects needed makes it obvious that this is not a useful way to represent these data. Picture graphs of the same data are impractical for the same reason. Object graphs are not useful for portraying data dealing with large numbers, such as the populations of the 12 largest cities in the world (see Figure 19.8). A picture graph can be used if a single picture is used to represent a large number of people; one symbol, such as a stick

figure, might represent 10,000, 100,000, or 1 million people in a population graph. In the picture graph shown in Figure 19.8, each symbol represents 1 million people. Such picture graphs are appropriate for children in grade 3 and beyond. Older students can use picture graphs to display city and state populations of the United States in a similar fashion to how we display the populations of the 12 largest cities in the world in this chapter. Of course, they begin with simpler data representations, such as a single bicycle image to represent five bicycles.

Bar Graphs

Children who have made and interpreted object graphs, picture graphs, and line plots have little difficulty making and interpreting bar graphs. A **bar graph** is a graphical representation of numerical data that uses vertical or horizontal bars. As with the other kinds of graphs, bar graphs are used to display categorical data. Activity 19.2 explores some transitional stages between line plots or picture graphs and bar graphs. Younger children could paste squares of colored paper onto grid paper to make a simple bar graph. In a similar fashion children can

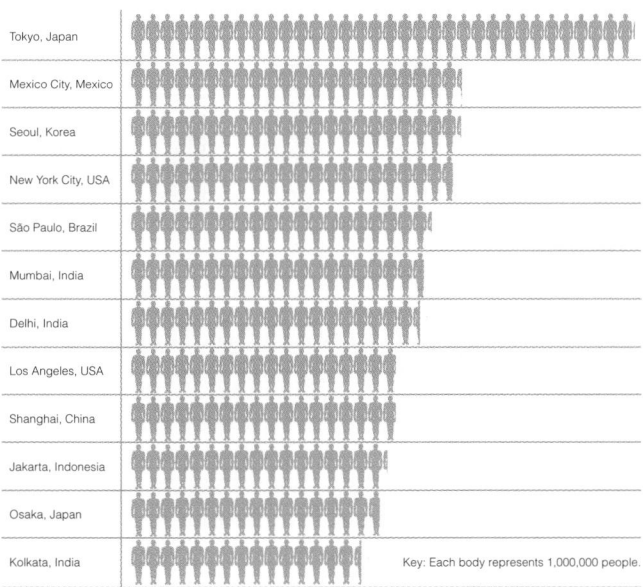

Figure 19.8 Populations of the 12 largest cities in the world

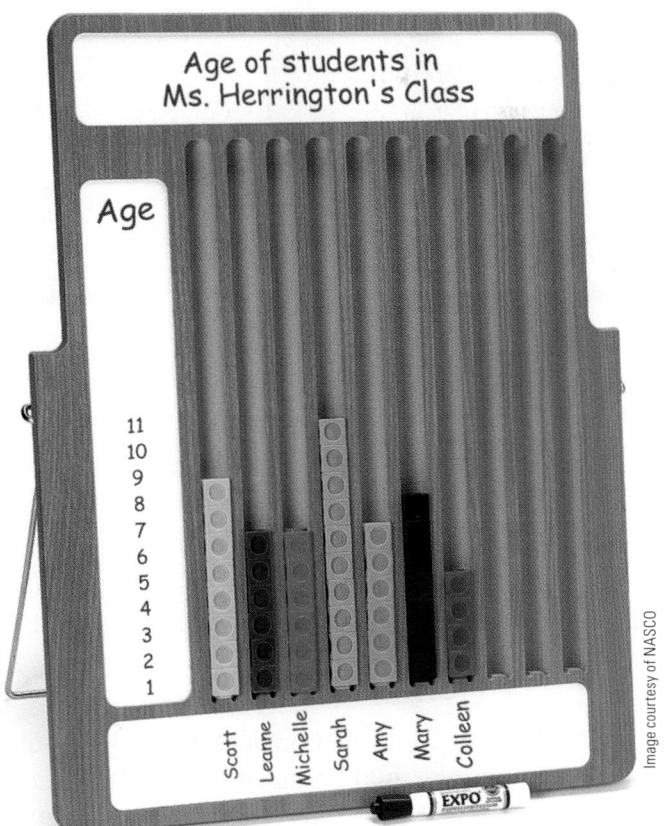

Graphing board

ACTIVITY 19.2 Bar Graphs

Level: Grades 1–3

Setting: Whole class

Objective: Students read and interpret student-made and computer-generated bar graphs.

Materials: Five colors of plastic cubes, such as Unifix cubes; four-inch squares of poster board the same colors as the cubes; large sheet of neutral-colored poster board

- Begin by displaying the table of shoe types (see Figure 19.1).

- Review the data in the table.

- Remind the children of the graph they made with squares of paper and their shoes. Show the shoe picture graph.

- Tell the children that other kinds of graphs can be used to show the same information. This time, colored cubes will be used to represent their shoes. Children with each type of shoe will have cubes of the same color. Have children with the same colors join their cubes and stand them on a table alongside the other colors. Compare the standing cubes with the table and the picture graph. Discuss the meaning of the cubes in each stack. Help children recognize that the table, the picture graph, and the colored cube "graph" all represent the shoes.

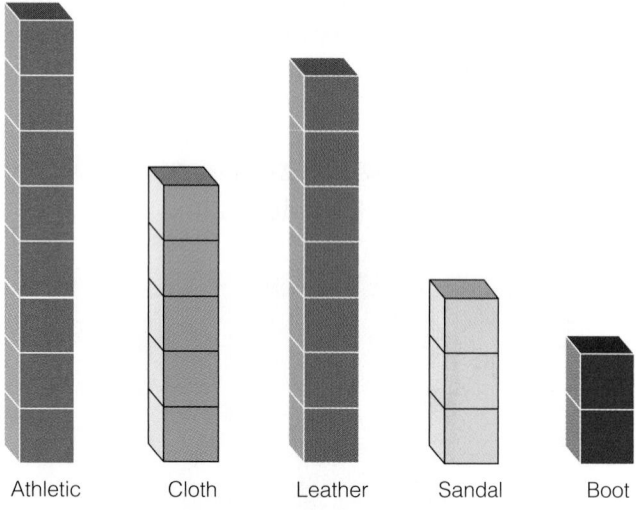

Athletic   Cloth   Leather   Sandal   Boot

- Give each child a 4-inch square of poster board with a color that matches the colored cube used earlier. Have students paste the squares onto the large sheet of poster board, which should have a baseline about 1 foot from the bottom. Name each column in the space beneath the baseline. Discuss how this graph is like the picture graph and how it is different.

- Compare the colored-squares graph with the colored-cube graph. Tell the children that the new graph is a bar graph.

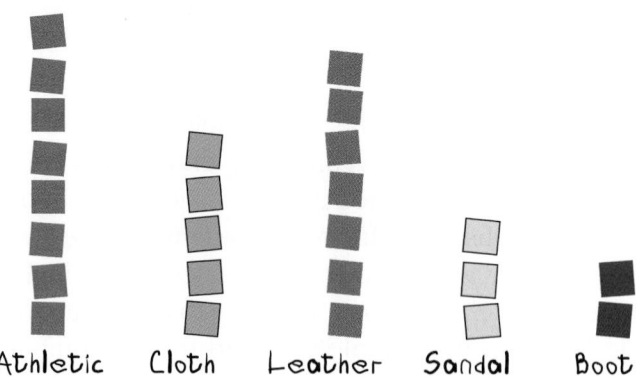

Athletic   Cloth   Leather   Sandal   Boot

- Introduce a computer graphing program. (The graphing program at http://nces.ed.gov/nceskids/Graphing/ was used for the graph shown here.) Demonstrate the program to small groups of children unless you can project a computer display to a large screen where all children can see it simultaneously. Use the program to make a table and a bar graph of the shoe data.

Number of shoes	
Type of shoes	
Athletic	8
Cloth	5
Leather	7
Sandal	3
Boot	2

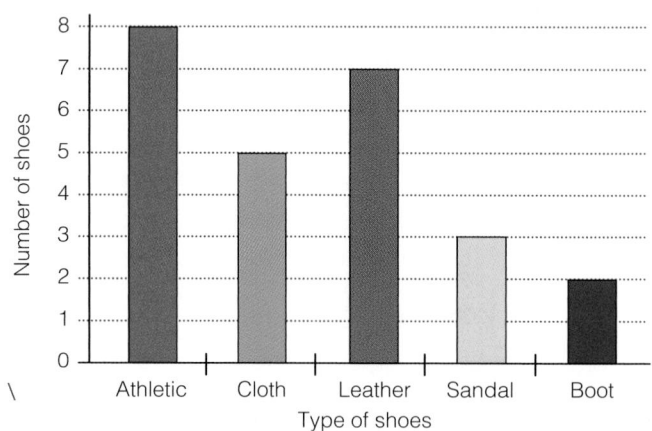

The number of shoe pairs is now determined by the scale of the graph and not by counting individual squares or cubes.

use Unifix cubes to form a similar bar graph. In both cases each individual square or cube represents an individual pair of shoes. The squares or cubes are in a one-to-one correspondence with the pairs of shoes. The final transition to a bar graph shows the same data but without individual items making up the graph. None of the bars is divided into individual squares or cubes. Activity 19.3 reverses the process. In this activity a completed bar graph is provided and children are challenged to provide

ACTIVITY 19.3 Reverse Bar Graphs (Communication)

Level: Grades 2 and 3

Setting: Individual

Objective: Students design their own data to fit a predrawn bar graph.

Materials: Predrawn bar graph, crayons, colored pencils

- Begin by displaying the predrawn bar graph to the class.
- Speculate with children about what the bar graph could represent (pets, ice cream flavors, toys, etc.).
- Tell the children that this graph could be used to represent many different data sets.
- Give each child a copy of the predrawn graph, and ask them to complete the graph by labeling the horizontal and vertical axes, coloring the bars, creating a data table, and giving the graph a title.

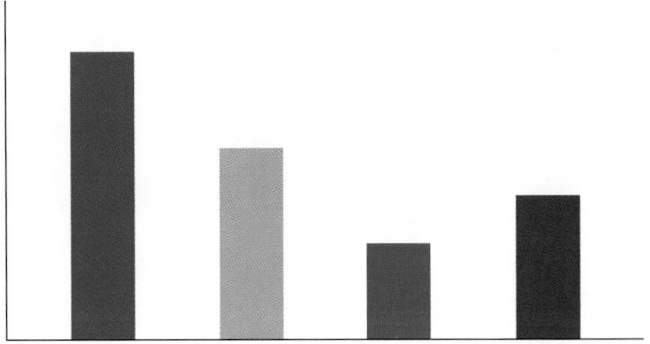

data to fit the graph. See the companion website activity "Where Is the Best Buy?" for an activity that has students use bar graphs to compare prices at different stores.

ⒺXERCISE

Identify two other types of data suitable for object or picture graphs for primary-grade children. What types of objects, real or representative, would you use for each graph? ●●●

Already prepared tables provide children with data for either handmade or computer-generated graphs. The first bar graphs students make can be put on centimeter- or inch-squared paper. A bar graph for the cost of toys table in Figure 19.6 is illustrated in Figure 19.9. Squares of colored paper

were pasted on this graph. (See Black-Line Master 19.3 for a simple template for bar graphs.) Computer programs such as the one found at **http://nces.ed.gov/nceskids/Graphing/** give students practical and easy-to-use methods for creating graphs. Computer-generated bar graphs for the pet and toy purchase situations are shown in Figure 19.10.

See the companion website activity "Our Favorite Ice Creams" for an activity that uses ice cream preferences as data that students collect, collate, and represent in tables and bar graphs.

ⒺXERCISE

The bar graph shown here displays a typical error made by students. What is the error, and why do you think such an error is common for students? ●●●

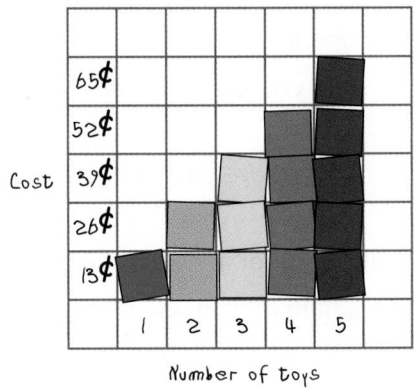

Figure 19.9 Bar graph for the toy purchase situation

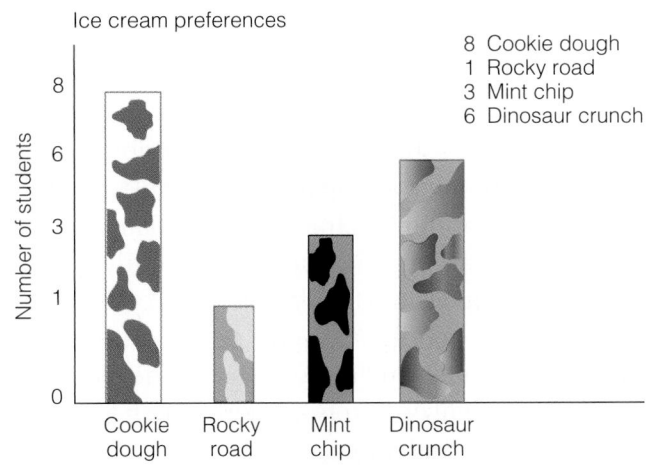

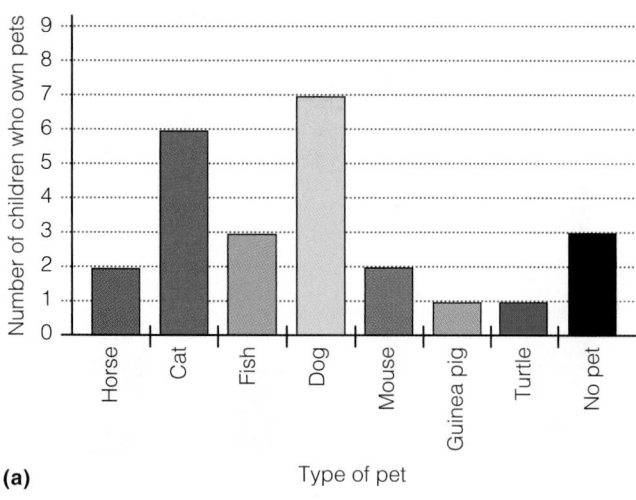

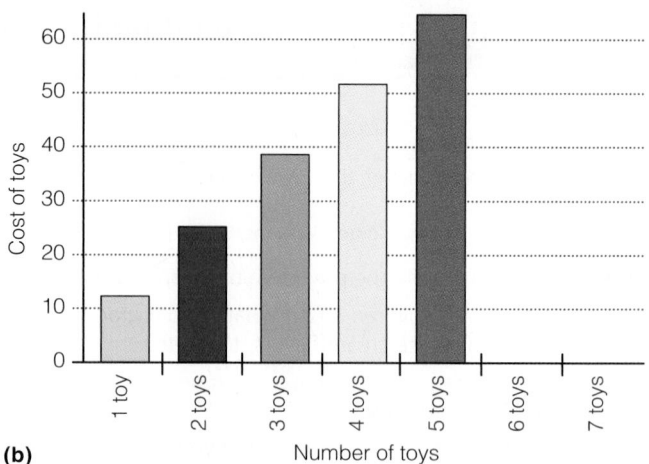

Figure 19.10 Computer-generated bar graphs for (a) pet and (b) toy situations. (These graphs were made with the program available at http://nces.ed.gov/nceskids/graphing/.)

EXERCISE

The bar graph shown here, found on the Internet, displays the population of Texas over several years. There is a misleading aspect in the display that is becoming increasingly common in the print media. This is also a common error for grade school students. What is the error, and why do you think the graph was displayed this way? ●●●

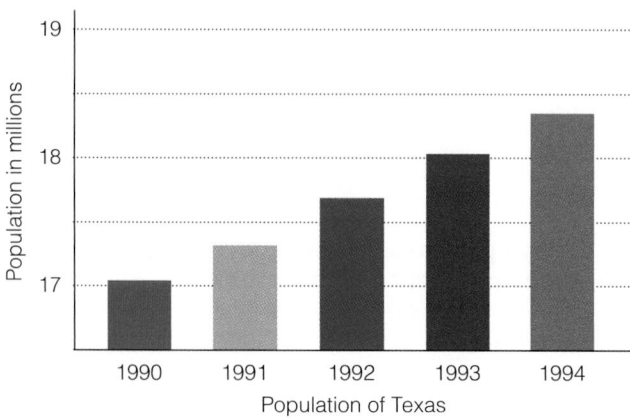

Statistics

Data are often represented in visual form in tables and graphs. Statistics are tools for describing, summarizing, and interpreting data that enable students to capture important characteristics of data numerically. Statistical language begins with early graphs when children discuss the data in terms of the most, the least, the middle, and end points of the data. Informal language and discussion provide a foundation for statistical concepts and terms such as *mode, median, mean,* and *range.*

POINT OF VIEW

In prekindergarten through grade 2, students are often most interested in individual pieces of data, especially their own, or which value is "the most" on a graph. A reasonable objective for upper elementary and middle grades is that they begin to regard a set of data as a whole that can be described as a set and compared to other data sets. (National Council of Teachers of Mathematics, 2000, p. 178)

When students conduct surveys to collect information, they ask two kinds of questions: questions with word answers that fit the different categories of the survey and questions with number answers. A first lesson in statistics should help children recognize the difference between these two kinds of questions and answers. The way information is described is based on the kind of information that was collected: categorical or numerical. Questions with word, or category, answers include:

• What is your favorite kind of pizza? (pepperoni, mushroom, or cheese)

• What pet would you like to have? (horse, cat, or fish)

• What kind of shoes are you wearing? (dress, blue, or leather)

Questions with number answers might include:

• What is the height of each student in the fifth-grade class? (45 inches, 49 inches, . . . , 64 inches)

• How many brothers and sisters do you have? (0, 1, 2, . . . , 6)

- What was your highest score in the game of Yahtzee? (193, 250, or 394)

> John Graunt (1620–1674) is credited with being the first to use statistical data. Graunt studied baptismal records and death notices to discern population trends. Based on the data he found, Graunt made reasonably close predictions about the population of London and how long it took the London population to rebound after an outbreak of the plague.

Three *measures of central tendency*—mean, median, and mode—are different ways to summarize a set of data. The mean and the median of a set of data are topics for intermediate students, and we discuss them later in this chapter. Younger children are usually interested in the **mode** because it is the most frequent value.

- Athletic shoes are worn by the largest number of students—12 out of 25.

- More students have cats than any other pet— 9 cats.

- Seven students have six letters and seven students have eight letters in their first name; six and eight letters are the most.

The term *mode* describes both categorical and numerical information and provides the answer to questions about both types of information:

- What is the most common height of students in the fifth-grade class? Look at the table, or bar graph of student heights to determine the mode.

- Which type of shoes did more children wear? How many wore that type? Eight children wore athletic shoes, five wore cloth, seven wore leather, three wore sandals, and two wore boots (see Figure 19.1). What is the mode of this set?

- Which kind of pet did most children have? Two children had a horse, six had a cat, two had a fish, seven had a dog, two had a mouse, one had a guinea pig, one had a turtle, and three had no pet (see Figure 19.2).

Some sets of data have more than one mode. The following data set lists the number of telephones in students' homes in a second-grade class: 1, 2, 3, 3, 2, 4, 2, 3, 1, 3, 4, 2, 3, 3, 4, 2, 2. Both 2 and 3 are modes for this set of data. When there are two modes for a set of data, the two values are **bimodal**. Conversely, some data sets have no mode, as the data for the world's 12 largest cities show (Figure 19.11).

Tokyo, Japan	34,100,000
Mexico City, Mexico	22,650,000
Seoul, Korea	22,250,000
New York, USA	21,850,000
São Paulo, Brazil	20,200,000
Mumbai, India	19,700,000
Delhi, India	19,500,000
Los Angeles, USA	17,950,000
Shanghai, China	17,900,000
Jakarta, Indonesia	17,150,000
Osaka, Japan	16,800,000
Kolkata, India	15,600,000

Figure 19.11 Population data for the world's 12 largest cities

Extending Data Concepts

Using Graphs to Work with Data

Older children apply more sophisticated means to represent and analyze data. They use pie charts, stem-and-leaf plots, and box-and-whisker plots. They also access real data from the Internet and other sources and draw conclusions from these real-world data. The NCTM data standards for older children follow.

NCTM Correlation

NCTM Data Standard

Instructional programs from prekindergarten through grade 12 should enable all students to:

- Formulate questions that can be addressed with data and collect, organize, and display relevant data to answer them
- Select and use appropriate statistical methods to analyze data
- Develop and evaluate inferences and predictions that are based on data

Expectations

In grades 3–5 all students should:

- design investigations to address a question and consider how data-collection methods affect the nature of the data set;
- collect data using observations, surveys, and experiments;
- represent data using tables and graphs such as line plots, bar graphs, and line graphs;
- recognize the differences in representing categorical and numerical data;

- describe the shape and important features of a set of data and compare related data sets, with an emphasis on how the data are distributed;
- use measures of center, focusing on the median, and understand what each does and does not indicate about the data set;
- compare different representations of the same data and evaluate how well each representation shows important aspects of the data;
- propose and justify conclusions and predictions that are based on data and design studies to further investigate the conclusions or predictions.

In grades 6–8 all students should:

- formulate questions, design studies, and collect data about a characteristic shared by two populations or different characteristics within one population;
- select, create, and use appropriate graphical representations of data, including histograms, box plots, and scatterplots;
- find, use, and interpret measures of center and spread, including mean and interquartile range;
- discuss and understand the correspondence between data sets and their graphical representations, especially histograms, stem and leaf plots, box plots, and scatterplots;
- use observations about differences between two or more samples to make conjectures about the populations from which the samples were taken;
- make conjectures about possible relationships between two characteristics of a sample on the basis of scatterplots of the data and approximate lines of fit;
- use conjectures to formulate new questions and plan new studies to answer them.

Intermediate-grade children continue to learn how to display data in tables in meaningful ways. Figure 19.12 shows two tables containing informa-

tion about the populations of the world's 12 largest cites; one is organized alphabetically, and the other numerically. By comparing the two tables, students should draw conclusions about which table is easier to read to answer different questions.

In which table is it easier to find the smallest city?

In which table is it easier to find the sixth and seventh largest cities?

In which table is it easier to find Mexico City?

The alphabetical listing makes it easy to locate information by name, but the numerical listing makes it easier to make numerical comparisons and judgments.

Another reason for displaying data in a table is to discern a pattern in the resulting data. In Activity 19.4 the task for students is to find the pattern for the number of building blocks in each subsequent building. In Activity 19.5 students gather data about words used in prose to identify the writer. Most writers will show a persistent use of common words, using some words more consistently than others. The pattern for word use can identify a writers' prose. For example, some historians theorize that writer Christopher Marlowe, a contemporary of Shakespeare, may have written Shakespeare's plays. A comparison of the 10 most frequently used words by both writers shows that this is highly unlikely:

Figure 19.12
Population of the world's largest cities ranked (a) alphabetically and (b) numerically

(a)	
Delhi, India	19,500,000
Jakarta, Indonesia	17,150,000
Kolkata, India	15,600,000
Los Angeles, USA	17,950,000
Mexico City, Mexico	22,650,000
Mumbai, India	19,700,000
New York, USA	21,850,000
Osaka, Japan	16,800,000
São Paulo, Brazil	20,200,000
Seoul, Korea	22,250,000
Shanghai, China	17,900,000
Tokyo, Japan	34,100,000

(b)	
Tokyo, Japan	34,100,000
Mexico City, Mexico	22,650,000
Seoul, Korea	22,250,000
New York, USA	21,850,000
São Paulo, Brazil	20,200,000
Mumbai, India	19,700,000
Delhi, India	19,500,000
Los Angeles, USA	17,950,000
Shanghai, China	17,900,000
Jakarta, Indonesia	17,150,000
Osaka, Japan	16,800,000
Kolkata, India	15,600,000

ACTIVITY 19.4 Stacking Blocks (Reasoning and Proof)

Level: Grades 3 and 4

Setting: Small groups

Objective: Students use a table to organize data.

Materials: Picture of block pattern in activity, centimeter or base-10 cubes, paper and pencils, centimeter measuring tape or meterstick for each team, overhead projector and transparency

- Present this situation: "Each team is to determine the number of blocks required to complete a pyramid that will be six layers high. You will have a top layer that is a single block resting in the center of a four-block layer beneath it. Each of these four blocks will rest on four blocks. This pattern will be used until you have completed your pyramid. Here is a picture of the top three layers. You will use blocks to build the first four layers and then will stop to decide if you can determine the total number of blocks without making the fifth and sixth layers."

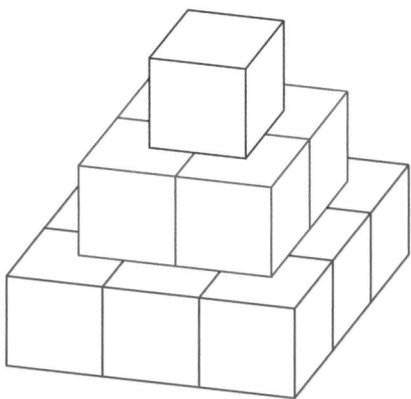

- Have students use the think-build-square cooperative group format. This format is good when manipulatives are used. Each team member has enough small cubes to construct the first four layers. First, each team member thinks about the picture and then builds a four-layer pyramid. Early finishers may coach others in their group. When the pyramids are finished, team members form a square to discuss how to solve the problem. Recommend that they use a table to organize their thinking. If a team decides it cannot solve the problem through discussion, they may add the fifth and sixth layers to one of the already made pyramids.

- Allow time for students to solve the problem; then have them discuss their solutions. Groups that made tables share them with the class. Put their tables on an overhead transparency.

Here are tables made by two groups:

Layer	1	2	3	4	5	6
Blocks	1	4	9	16	25	36

Layer	Blocks
1	1
2	4
3	9
4	16
5	25
6	36

- Have groups study the tables for a pattern. They should see that the number of blocks increases in a 1, 3, 5, 7, . . . pattern, starting at 0. They should also notice that the numbers identifying blocks in each layer are successive square numbers, beginning with 1. The number for each layer is the square of the number that indicates its position in the pyramid, top down.

- Extend the problem: "How many layers would there be if the blocks were boxes in a store display, the box at the top was at eye level for the shortest member in your group, and each box was 10 centimeters high? How many boxes would be in the display?" Have the teams solve the same problem for the tallest member in the group. Discuss the information that is needed to solve the extended problem. Allow time for students to work on the new problem.

- Discuss the groups' procedures and responses. Focus on the use of tables, patterns, or both as means of solving the problem.

Shakespeare		Marlowe	
1. the	6. a	1. and	6. my
2. and	7. you	2. the	7. that
3. I	8. my	3. of	8. in
4. to	9. that	4. to	9. a
5. of	10. in	5. I	10. with

Another way to identify a writer's work is to categorize words according to the number of letters in each word. As with common words, writers will usually use the same proportion of three-letter words, or four-letter words in their prose. See the companion website activity "Who Wrote It?" for an activity that uses lengths of words to identify a writer.

Figure 19.13 displays the data from the pyramid block activity (Figure 19.13a) and the data of world's largest cities (Figure 19.13b) in computer-generated bar graphs.

Level: Grades 5–7
Setting: Small groups
Objective: Students use a data table to organize and interpret data.
Materials: Several newspaper columns with no byline shown.

- Hold up some of the newspaper editorial columns and challenge students to identify which ones were written by the same author. Ask for possible ways to identify a common writer for any two columns.

- Suggest that writers tend to use the same words in what they write.

- Distribute columns to groups, and assign the tasks of compiling data tables showing the 10 most commonly used words in each editorial column.

- Students use their data to identify the columns written by the same person and present their findings to the class.

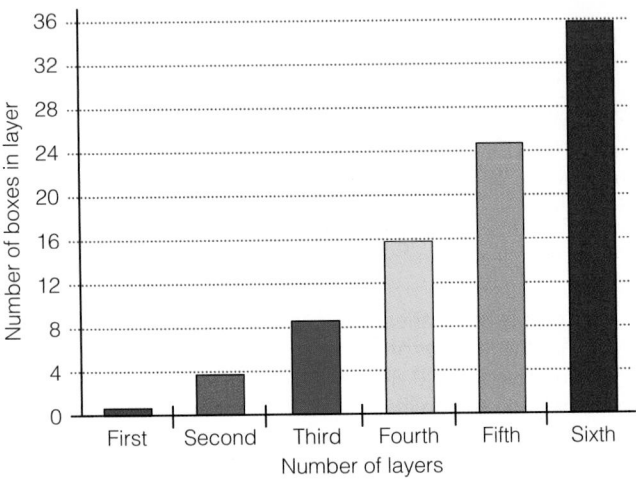

(a) This bar graph shows the number of boxes in a pyramid. We found that the number of boxes in each layer is the square of the number of boxes along one side of the layer. We added the first six square numbers to determine the number of boxes in the entire pyramid.

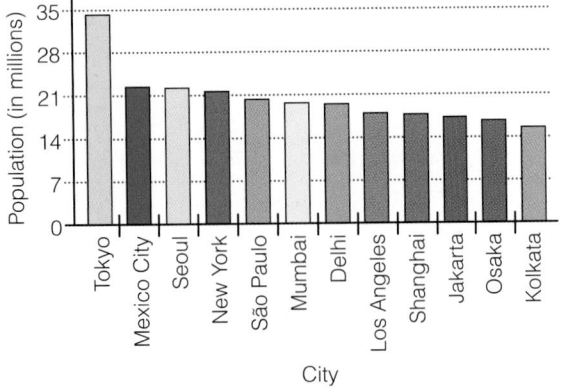

(b) This graph shows the populations of the 12 largest cities in the world, as reported at http://geography.about.com in 2006. It shows that Tokyo has about twice as many people as Jakarta.

Figure 19.13 Computer-generated bar graphs of (a) the data in the pyramid block activity and (b) the data of the world's largest cities

Histograms

Another means of representing data is a **histogram**. A histogram is a type of bar graph that represents the frequency of data that has been grouped into several intervals. Histograms are used to display numerical data rather than categorical data, as with bar graphs. The histogram shown in Figure 19.14 presents data about students in an intermediate school. Note that in the histogram the bars are adjacent (touching). The age categories are touching because they are continuous. Students move from one category (7–8) to the next (9–10). Thus a histogram is a specialized type of bar graph used to represent numerical categories that are part of a continuous group of data. In any histogram the intervals represented by the bars must be the same size; in this case each interval spans two years. All the data are represented in the histogram because the bars cover the entire range of data, from ages 7 to 12. Activity 19.6 asks students to collect data from a survey and then display the resulting data in a histogram on a poster.

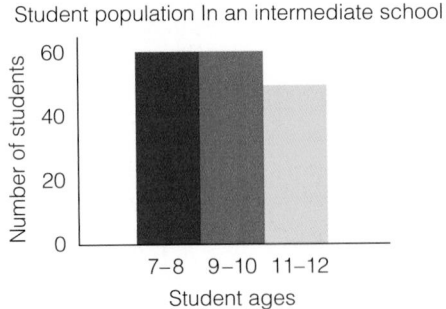

Figure 19.14 A histogram of student ages in an intermediate school

Line Graphs

Different types of graphs have been developed to display different sorts of information. Bar graphs

ACTIVITY 19.6   Histogram Survey (Representation)

Level: Grades 3–5
Setting: Small groups
Objective: Students gather and display data in a histogram.
Materials: Markers, poster board

- Present the group task to the class: Each group is to conduct a survey of their own class and of another class to gather data. The group will then display the data in a

histogram on a poster. The poster will be displayed in class for all to see.

- Groups can select their own data but suggest that the data must be continuous, such as weight, height, arm span, waist, shoe length, and pulse rate.

- Encourage groups to be sure that their intervals are the same size and that they cover the entire range of data.

---

are good for comparing information, such as shoes, pets, and populations. Bar graphs have limited value for the toy and pyramid data. A **line graph** is better for continuous data because it shows patterns, trends, and relationships more clearly. Line graphs were originally designed to represent continuous data such as height, weight, and time. Line graphs are now used mostly for showing trends over time. This ability to discern trends over time can empower students in mathematics. A line graph that shows falling CD prices or changes in global temperatures can empower children to predict trends and draw conclusions from the data.

Every line graph has a horizontal axis and a vertical axis, showing the characteristic that is expected to change with changes in the horizontal axis. If time in days is shown on the horizontal axis, then growth of a plant in inches might be recorded on the vertical axis. Figure 19.15 shows two points in time and heights measured at each time. Height at one point in time is shown at point A and height at a later point in time is recorded at point B, showing the amount of growth between the two points.

In a line graph each axis resembles a number line. Interpreting the data points according to the position of the point relative to the horizontal and vertical axes is similar to experiences children have had locating and interpreting points on a number line. Because each axis closely resembles a number line, a teacher might expect that students will quickly interpret the meaning of the line graph. However, understanding the meaning of the plotted points involves coordination of two ideas simultaneously and is difficult for many children. Young children need many experiences, such as Activity 19.7, as they are learning to internalize the relationship in the graphs. These types of graphs are qualitative, in that there are no specific numerical values in the graphs and no scale for either axis. The absence of numerical data allows students to focus on the relationship between the two axes and between the two data points without performing any computations.

POINT OF VIEW
Studies of middle school students have revealed substantial gaps in their abilities to construct graphs from given data. (Kilpatrick et al., 2001, p. 290)

Opportunities for students to make line graphs often occur during science and social studies units. Students conducting a plant growth experiment in science can measure and record the height of their plants and compare growth under various conditions. A study of the development of a state or nation might lead to preparation of a table and graph that show the growth of population over a period of years. A study of the history of transportation in the United States could include, for example, the growth of railroads in various regions. Figure 19.16 shows railroad data for the New England states in the 1850s. The Internet is a source of both descriptive and statistical information on states, nations, population, productivity, economic growth, and many other topics. An Internet site with many data sets and various graphs that display the data is **http://nces.ed.gov/nceskids**.

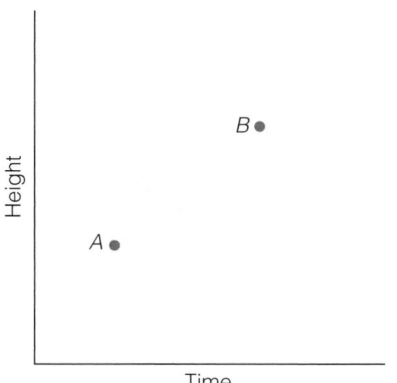

Figure 19.15 Two data points for a line graph of plant height over time

ACTIVITY 19.7   Qualitative Graphs

Level: Grades 3 and 4
Setting: Pairs
Objective: Students read and interpret qualitative graphs.
Materials: Set of qualitative graph sheets

- Pass out sheets to students. Demonstrate with student volunteers how to interpret the first graph, using the questions on the sheet.

- Ask students to answer the same questions for the other four graphs.

- Have pairs exchange papers and compare answers. If pairs disagree, then have them discuss their answers until they agree.

- For any graphs on which pairs cannot agree, post the graphs on the overhead for a class discussion.

- Have each pair make up its own qualitative graph and display it on the overhead for the class to discuss.

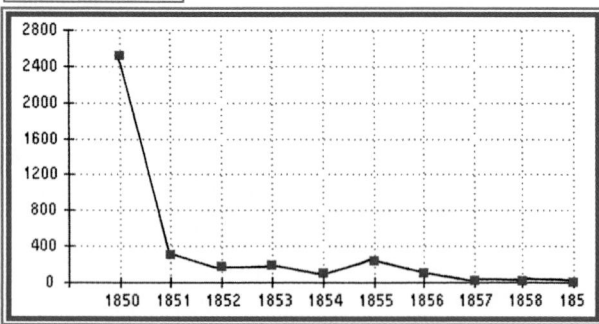

	A	B
1	1850	2507
2	1851	305
3	1852	172
4	1853	180
5	1854	97
6	1855	227
7	1856	97
8	1857	22
9	1858	17
10	1859	8

Our line graph shows the miles of railroad track built in the New England states during the 1850s. It shows that railroad companies built a lot of track in 1850 and not much each year after that. We believe that most of the cities in the states must have been connected by railroads early in the decade. We made our table and graph with Math Tools software. We found the information on the Internet.

Figure 19.16 Table, line graph, and text showing information about railroad tracks built from 1850 to 1859

Line graphs are particularly helpful for showing data from situations in which one value changes in relation to another (i.e., data involving rate pairs, or functions). Computer-generated graphs for the toy purchase and block pyramid situations show how trends are portrayed on line graphs. The line graph for toys in Figure 19.17a is a straight line, whereas the one in Figure 19.17b is a curved line whose slope increases with the addition of each new layer in the pyramid. We say that the relationship between numbers in the toy data is *linear*, whereas in the pyramid data it is *nonlinear*. Graphing programs are widely available, and once students are able to construct their own line graphs, they should use these programs to make line graphs whenever possible. Of

course, students can continue to make their own line graphs when computer programs are unavailable. In either case, students build a foundation for graphing on a coordinate system in algebra.

Ⓔ XERCISE

Look ahead to Activity 19.12. Note the double line graph, in which two sets of data are represented on a single graph. How would you compare the rainfall of the two years depicted on this graph? ●●●

Circle Graphs

Circle graphs, often called *pie charts*, use a circle to portray information so that the relationship of each part to the whole is clearly shown. Each part of the circle, or portion of the pie, displays a part-whole relationship. These graphs can be introduced as early as second or third grade. Early experiences should be with "clean" numbers—that is, numbers that are within children's present computational knowledge. The numbers in the pet situation are clean because 24 can be divided into halves, thirds, fourths, sixths, and twelfths by selecting the appropriate number of segments in the circle.

When children use data for a student-made circle graph, they first establish the total, or whole, to be considered. For the pet data (see Figure 19.2),

POINT OF VIEW
Much of students' work in grades 3–5 should involve comparing related data sets. (National Council of Teachers of Mathematics, 2000, p. 108)

24 students named a pet or no pet, so 24 is the total. Provide children with a circle marked with lines from the center to show 24 equivalent parts (see Black-Line Master 19.4). Discuss the need to sys-

EXERCISE

For each of these graphs, answer the following questions: (1) How does point B compare to point A? (Give two different answers.) (2) How does point A compare to point B? (Give two different answers.) ●●●

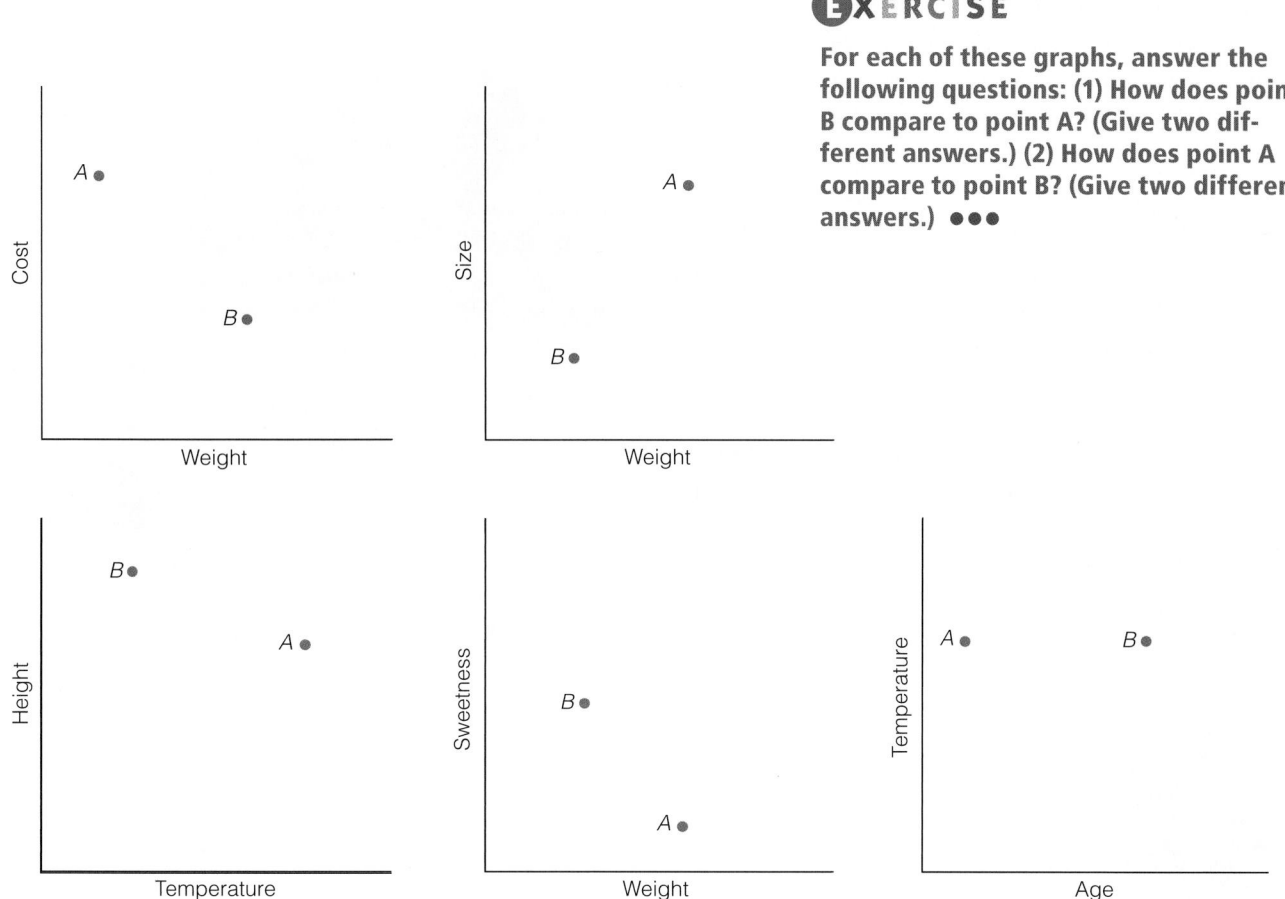

tematically count the number of parts of the circle that each type of pet will occupy and to design the graph correctly by putting all the same type of pets together. Each mark in the table (Figure 19.2) and symbol in the picture graph (see Activity 19.1) represent 1 of the 24 portions of the circle. Have children select colors to distinguish each type of pet. When children have finished coloring their graphs, show them how a key helps readers interpret the graph. Black-Line Master 19.3 is a circle graph divided into 24 equal parts. You may use it for your students' display of the pet data or with other data sets that contain 24 individual items or some factor of 24 (12 items, 8 items, and so forth).

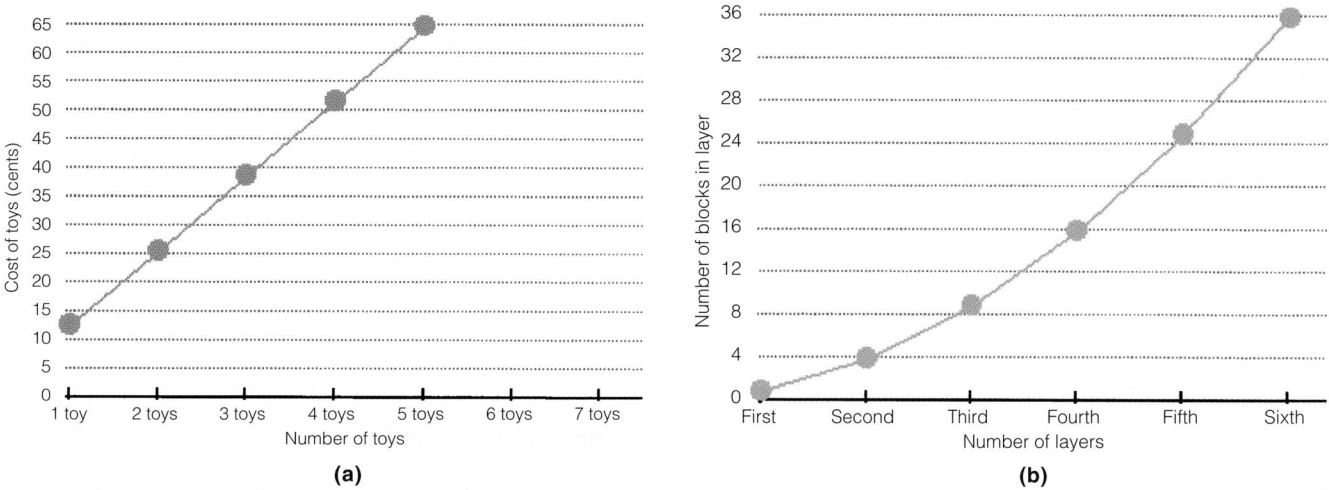

Figure 19.17 Computer-generated line graphs for the (a) toy purchase and (b) block pyramid situations. (These graphs were made with the program available at http://nces.ed.gov/nceskids/Graphing/.)

A circle graph prepared by one group of students for the pet data is shown in Figure 19.18a. The students constructed this circle graph using a template similar to Black-Line Master 19.3. Young students in grade 2 or 3 can interpret circle graphs and construct their own graphs using a template and simple data. Figure 19.18b shows a computer-generated circle graph for the pet data that displays the percents of each pet. Figure 19.19 shows a computer-generated circle graph of the population of the cities in Figure 19.8. Note how this circle graph allows for a quick comparison between the populations. These two computer-generated circle graphs would be difficult to construct by hand. To construct such circle graphs, students must have mastered a number of mathematical concepts, including angle measurement with a protractor, decimal and fraction computations, and percent. It is unlikely that students

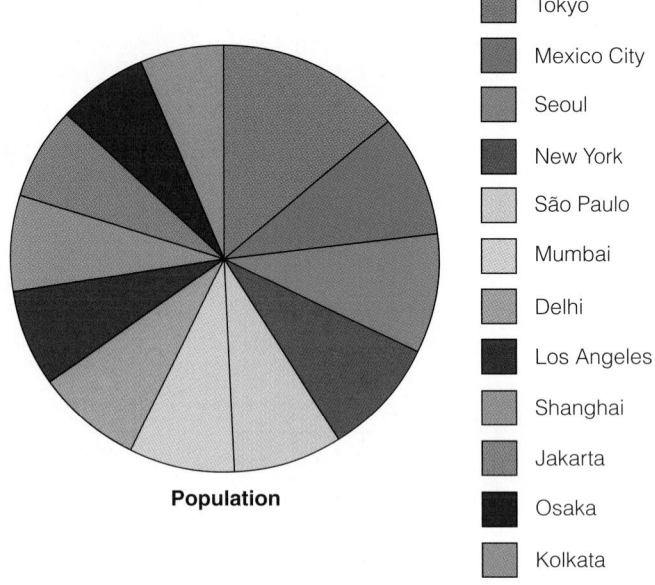

Figure 19.19 A computer-generated circle graph for populations of the 12 largest cities in the world. (This graph was made with the graphing program available at http://nces.ed.gov/nceskids/Graphing/.)

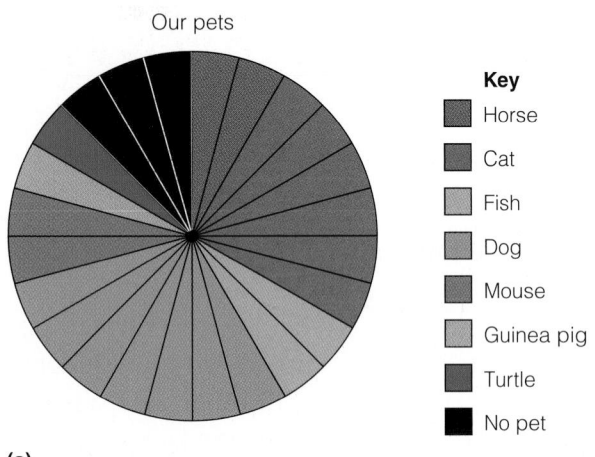

(a)

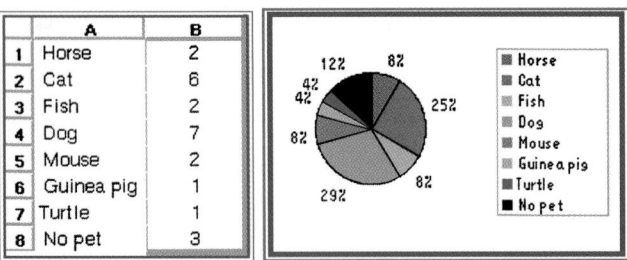

(b)

Figure 19.18 Circle graphs: (a) student-made; (b) computer-generated, with table. (These graphs were made with the program available at http://nces.ed.gov/nceskids/Graphing/.)

MISCONCEPTION

Some students confuse degree measure and percentage when making a circle graph. They will represent 25% of the data with a 25° angle instead of a 90° angle.

will be able to construct their own circle graphs with messy data that require constructing different angles until at least grade 6. In Activity 19.8 children use an Internet site to represent survey data in circle graphs.

EXERCISE

Make a table in which you list the amount of time you spent on various activities during the last 24 hours. Sketch a bar graph and a circle graph, each showing your activities for that period of time. Which graph do you believe presents the data more clearly? Why? ●●●

Florence Nightingale (1820–1910) is world renowned as the founder of modern nursing. Few people know that she designed the first circle graphs to make her case for the need for sanitary hospital facilities during the Crimean War.

Stem-and-Leaf Plots

Stem-and-leaf plots give students another way to organize and record data. A stem-and-leaf plot represents numerical data by using the left-most digit

ACTIVITY 19.8 **Circle Graph Survey (Internet Activity)**

Level: Grades 5 and 6

Setting: Small groups

Objective: Students use a pie chart to display survey information.

Materials: One computer per group

- Assign each group the task of collecting survey data from their classmates. Groups might select a topic such as favorite ice cream flavor, number of siblings, hours per day watching television, favorite cafeteria food, and so forth. Groups' questions should provide a list of three to six possible responses.

- Allow groups two or three days to survey other students in the school.

- Once student groups have collected and collated their data, they should use the pie chart generator at http://nces.ed.gov/nceskids/Graphing/ to create a pie chart to represent their survey data.

- Student groups create a poster to display their pie chart and the survey question.

of the data as a stem and the remaining digits as leaves on the graph. These plots are especially useful for comparing raw data. As an example, we use data provided by a class of fifth-grade students. The height (in inches) of each student was listed in a table, in ascending order from the top (Figure 19.20a). A stem-and-leaf plot of the children's heights was then developed from these data (Figure 19.20b). The stem-and-leaf plot is based on numbers in the table. The heights of the children ranged from 45 to 64 inches, with two students in the 40s, four in the 60s, and the rest in the 50s. The stem is made by listing each tens number—4 for 40s, 5 for 50s, and 6 for 60s—to the left of the plot under the head-

ing "Stem." Each numeral representing a ones place number is written in ascending order to the right of its stem number. In Figure 19.20b the 5 and 9 to the right of the 4 indicate heights of 45 and 49 inches, and numerals to the right of the 5 and the 6 indicate heights of other students.

The stem-and-leaf plot can be read quickly to determine that only two students are shorter than 50 inches and three are taller than 60 inches tall and that more students are 56 inches tall than any other single height. Counting the leaves tells the number of students in the class. Figure 19.20c shows a hand-drawn bar graph of the same data. A computer-generated table and stem-and-leaf plot for the same

Figure 19.20
Student-made
(a) table, (b) stem-and-leaf plot, and
(c) bar graph for heights of fifth-grade students

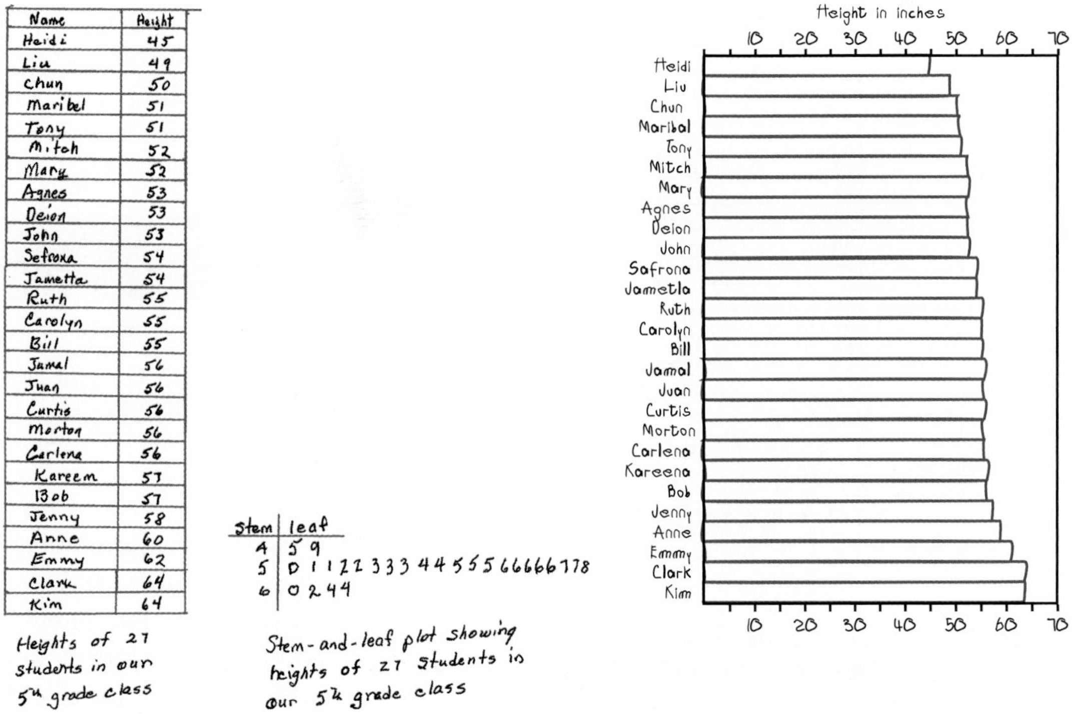

(a)

(b)

(c)

student heights are presented in Figure 19.21. Stem-and-leaf plots would not be useful for showing data from the shoe and pet activities because none of the numbers is larger than 10. A plot for the populations of the world's 12 largest cities appears in Figure 19.22.

> John Tukey (1915–2000) invented the stem-and-leaf plot while a professor at Princeton. Tukey is well known to statisticians for statistical procedures used to analyze complex data.

Information from two data sets can be compared by using a double stem-and-leaf plot. The double stem-and-leaf plot shown in Figure 19.23, representing home run leaders in the American and National Leagues, was drawn by Mark, a fifth-grade student. One set of data is entered to the left of the stem, and

Figure 19.22 A computer-generated stem-and-leaf plot for the world's largest cities. Created using the program available at http://math.about.com.

stem	leaf
15	6
16	8
17	9 2
18	0
19	8 5
20	2
21	9
22	7 3
23	
24	
25	
26	
27	
28	
29	
30	
31	
32	
33	
34	1

Names	Height in inches
Heidi	45
Liu	49
Chun	50
Maribel	51
Tony	51
Mitch	52
Mary	52
Agnes	53
Deion	53
John	53
Sefrona	54
Jametta	54
Ruth	55
Carolyn	55
Bill	55
Jamal	56
Juan	56
Curtis	56
Morton	56
Carlena	56
Kareem	57
Bob	57
Jenny	58
Anne	60
Emmy	62
Clark	64
Kim	64

(a)

```
stem leaf
   4 5, 9
   5 0, 1, 1, 2, 2, 3, 3, 3, 4, 4, 5, (5), 6, 6, 6, 6, 6, 6, 7, 7, 8
   6 0, 2, 4, 4
```

(b)

Figure 19.21 Computer-generated (a) table and (b) stem-and-leaf plot for heights of fifth-grade students

the other set is entered to the right of the stem. Notice how writing out the stem-and-leaf plot on grid paper ensures that the "leaves" on each stem are correctly spaced, much as a grid helped Autumn with her line plot (see Figure 19.5).

Box-and-Whisker Plots

Older children study one final means of representing data, the **box-and-whisker plot**. A box-and-whisker plot graphically represents the median, the first and third quartiles, and the extreme values of a data set. The data for a box-and-whisker plot are fairly easy to obtain, consisting of the high and low data points and three medians. The diagram below shows a box plot with each of the key five data points labeled.

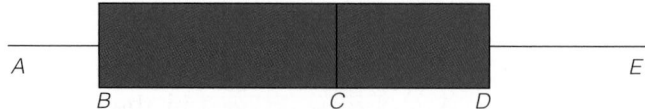

A: Low data point
B: Median of lower half of data, also called the *first quartile*
C: Median of the entire data set
D: Median of the upper half of data, also called the *third quartile*
E: High data point

The box-and-whisker plot shows each quarter of data. The whisker from A to B displays the first, or lower, quarter of data. The whisker from D to E displays the upper, or fourth, quarter of data. The box of the box-and-whisker plot shows the second and

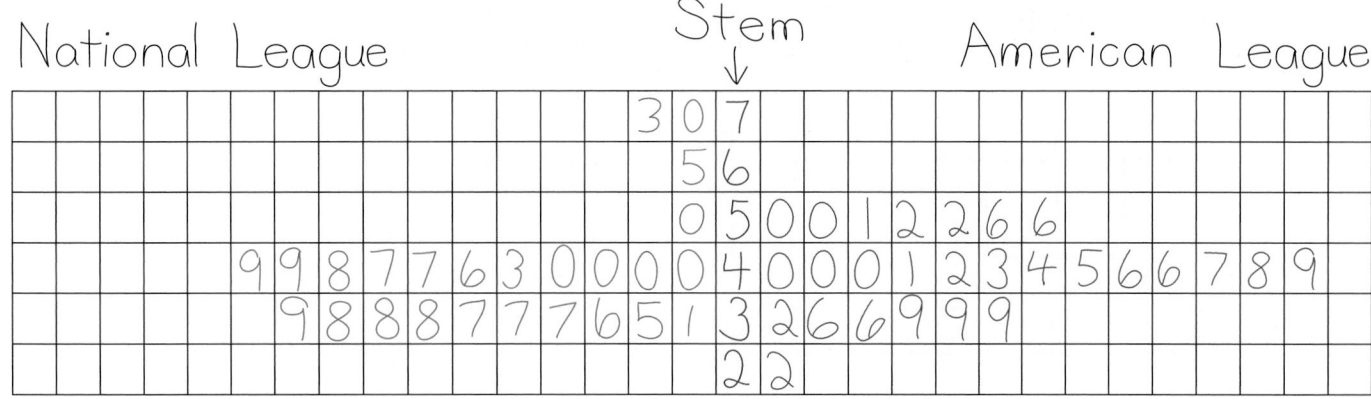

Figure 19.23 Student-drawn double stem-and-leaf plot of home run champions in major league baseball over the past 25 years

third quarters, separated by the median line at C. The entire box represents the middle 50% of data. The *interquartile range* is the difference between the first and third quartiles.

The relative length of each whisker and the two parts of the box represent how scattered the data are in each of the quarters. In this example the fourth quarter of data has a wider range than the data in the first quarter, because the whisker for the fourth quarter is longer than the whisker for the first quarter. Compare the second and third quarters. Can you tell which quarter has the wider range? The box-and-whisker plot shows that the box for the second quarter is longer than the box for the third quarter, so the second quarter has a wider range.

Although the box-and-whisker plot used here is displayed with no scale to evaluate any of the key data points, the comparison between the range of data in the various quarters is clearly represented. A completely developed box-and-whisker plot will have a scale across the bottom of the display so that the key data points can be evaluated. Consider Figure 19.24, which records the pulse rates of a sixth-grade class. The data are ordered so that determining

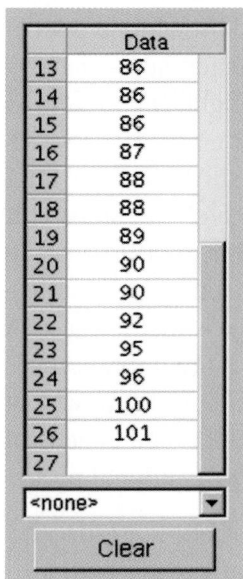

Figure 19.24 Pulse rates of a sixth-grade class

the respective medians to construct a box-and-whisker plot is relatively simple.

> 73, 75, 78, 79, 79, 80, 82, 82, 84, 84, 85, 85, 86,
> 86, 86, 87, 88, 88, 89, 90, 90, 92, 95, 96, 100, 101

The low and high pulse rates are 73 and 101, respectively. The median for the entire data set is the thirteenth pulse rate, 86. The median for the entire data set is 85.5. The median data value in a set with an even number of values, such as in the case of the entire set of values in this problem, is found by computing the mean of the two terms in the middle: $(85 + 86)/2 = 85.5$. Both the upper half and the lower half of the data have an odd number of data terms. In this case the median term for both sets is the middle term (82 and 90, respectively). We now have our key data points, and the resulting box-and-whisker plot is shown in Figure 19.25. The interquartile range is $81 - 90$.

Another use of box-and-whisker plots is for comparison of two different data sets. Figure 19.26 shows the box-and-whisker plots for the pulse rates of two classes. Although the second class had fewer students, the box-and-whisker plot allows for a comparison of the data. The mean average of both classes was the same, which makes the box-and-whisker plot even more valuable in comparing the pulse rates of the two classes. As a comparison of the two box-and-whisker plots shows, the pulse rates from Class B are higher, with a higher median and a smaller range for the middle 50% of data. Such a conclusion would be difficult to reach using only tables, means, and bar graphs.

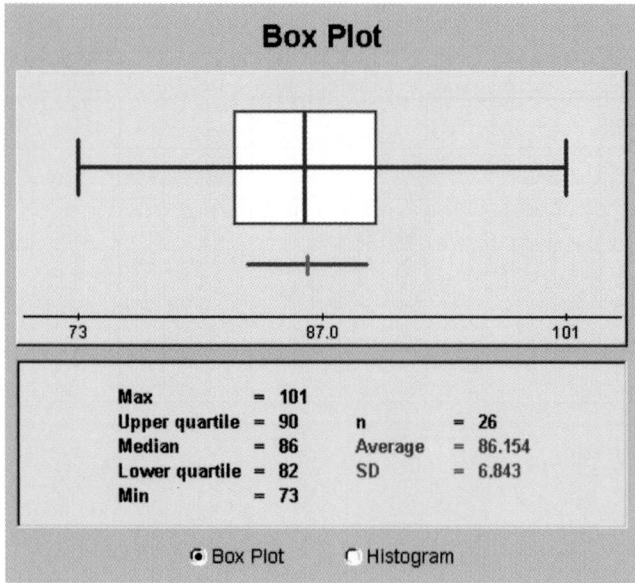

Box Plot

73   87.0   101

Max	= 101
Upper quartile	= 90
Median	= 86
Lower quartile	= 82
Min	= 73

n = 26
Average = 86.154
SD = 6.843

○ Box Plot   ○ Histogram

Figure 19.25 Box-and-whisker plot of a class's pulse rates. This box-and-whisker plot was drawn using the program Box Plot in Data Analysis and Probability 6–8, available at http://nlvm.usu.edu/en/nav/vlibrary.html. The box-and-whisker plot shows that the data for the highest quarter of data has a wider range than the data for the other three quarters.

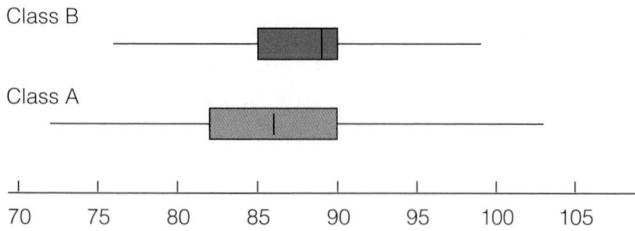

Class B

Class A

70   75   80   85   90   95   100   105

Figure 19.26 Box-and-whisker plot of class pulse rates

It is relatively easy to represent data on a box-and-whisker plot. Finding the five key data points requires little computation. Students can use computer software or graphing calculators to make box-and-whisker plots or draw their own. However, just because students can make box-and-whisker plots is not the reason to introduce them. It is important to consider box-and-whisker plots with students who have the mathematical maturity to understand what they represent: the variability of data around the middle.

A box-and-whisker plot might be considered an intermediate step between finding the mean and standard deviation. The mean can be misleading if the data contain a few outliers (see p. 514). A box-and-whisker plot displays data in such a way that the range of each quarter of data can be easily observed. Long whiskers and a long box indicate that the data have a wide range and are spread out. Short whiskers and a short box indicate that the data are close together in a short range. Students' understanding of this aspect of data is necessary before introducing box-and-whisker plots. Otherwise students will be performing rote procedures with little understanding of or appreciation for their results. See the companion website activity "Box-and-Whisker Plot Pulses," which challenges students to use box-and-whisker plots to compare two sets of data.

Ⓔ XERCISE

How familiar are you with the graphs described in this chapter? Which ones do you think you understand best? Have you seen or used stem-and-leaf plots before? What kinds of questions are answered by the stem-and-leaf plot for the 12 cities? for the home run champions? ●●●

Extending Children's Understanding of Statistics

For younger children the use of statistics is often limited to the mode of a data set. They will also notice the extremes in a data set, such as the tallest person and the shortest person. Older children learn to consider other statistical terms and concepts with the data they have gathered. In a set of data that records the height of students in a classroom, older students might observe several characteristics, such as outliers and the mean and median height. *High* refers to the highest number, or the tallest child, and *low* refers to the lowest number, or the shortest child. Subtracting the low from the high gives the statistical measure called the **range**. **Outlier** refers to a piece of data that is widely distanced from other data on either the high or the low end of a distribution. A student who is markedly shorter or taller than others in a class would be a statistical outlier. Discussion of the highs, the lows, and the range of data is natural in dealing with bar graphs and stem-and-leaf plots:

- What is the height of the shortest student? the tallest student? Is the height of any student an outlier?

- What is the largest number of brothers and sisters of anyone in the class? the smallest number?

- What is the range in the number of brothers and sisters?

- What is the highest score for the games? the lowest score? Is there an outlier among the scores?

- What is the difference between the high and low scores?

- Which city has the largest population? Which has the smallest population?

- Is any population an outlier? What is the difference between the largest and the smallest cities?

POINT OF VIEW

At [elementary] grade levels (3–5) students should pose questions about themselves and their environment, issues in their school or community, and content they are studying in different subject areas. . . . Once a question is posed, students can develop a plan to collect information to address the question. (National Council of Teachers of Mathematics, 2000, p. 177)

Data are analyzed in different ways depending on the questions being considered. The table, graph, stem-and-leaf plots, and box-and-whisker plots make it easy to answer the most commonly asked questions. The height measurement activity and its table, bar graph, and stem-and-leaf plot (see Figure 19.20) provide a source of data for working with statistical concepts. The question "How tall are the children in this class?" can be answered by all three representations. The table shows the data only in numerical form, whereas the bar graph and the stem-and-leaf plot show it in numerical and visual forms. All these forms of presentation can be used to analyze the data. The table and both graphs show the lows and highs and the range of heights in numerical terms.

MISCONCEPTION

Many students think that the median of a set must be a data entry for the set. As with the mean, the median need not be a value that is included in the set. Thus in the set 12, 14, 16, 18, the median 15 $\left(\frac{14 + 16}{2}\right)$ is not a data item in the set.

The statistical concept **median**, or middle number in a data set, analyzes the data in a different way. To introduce the concept, have students form a row by height from shortest to tallest. Beginning at each end, children count simultaneously toward the center. When only one child is left, that child is at the middle and has the median height (assuming an odd number of children to count off). Half the children are taller than that child and half are shorter. (Some children on one or both sides of the middle child may have the same height.) In a class with an odd number of children, the middle child's height is the median. In a class with an even number of children, there are two middle children. The median

Research for the Classroom

A recent research study (Meyer et al., 1999) compared data presented in two common formats: tables and graphs. The findings are not completely consistent with the widespread preference in the print media for displaying data in graphical form. The researchers found that for specific comparisons of data facts or points, students performed better when the data were presented in table form than when the data were presented in a graphical form. On the other hand, graphs were clearly superior for finding trends in the data. Any pattern or structure in data is transformed into a visual pattern by a graphical representation. The visual appearance of data in tables is unaffected by any pattern characteristic of the data. The investigators found that "graphic displays may indeed lead to the spontaneous detection of larger units of information and of patterns in the displayed data" (Meyer et al., 1999, p. 587). In sum, tables have a valid and important place in data display, especially when individual data points are being compared. Graphs are better suited for portraying data with a pattern or trend to them. Graphs enable the viewer to discern the larger picture that the data show, especially when there are many items in the data set.

Research on measures of central tendency has revealed much about how students think about mode, median, and mean. Watson and Moritz (2000) found that when students think of the average of a set of data, such as the price of a home, they first think of "middles" (median), then "mosts" (mode) with the mean a distant third. Konold and Pollatsek (2002), in subsequent research, observed that students view the mean in four different aspects: as a typical value, as a fair share, as a way to reduce data, and as a "signal amid noise". They suggested that focusing on the signal aspect of the mean can help students move beyond the mean as simply a fair share or typical value and to the more conceptually rich notion of the mean as a way to evaluate and compare sets of data.

is halfway between their heights, and the median height belongs to an "imaginary" child. Knowing the median, you can say, "Half the children are shorter than 55 inches, and half are taller than 55 inches; the low is 45 inches, the high is 64 inches, and the range is 19 inches." Both the bar graph and the stem-and-leaf plot can be used to determine the median. In the bar graph children can find the middle height for their class by simultaneously counting from the low bar and the high bar toward the center of the graph until the middle or middle pair of heights is reached. A similar procedure can be used to find the median of a stem-and-leaf plot.

Looking again at Figure 19.20, we see that by counting up and down from both ends of the data simultaneously, the middle value of 55 can be easily determined. Another method to find the median could be to count the total number of heights, in this case 27. The median is the 14th height and can be determined by counting off 14 heights from either the high end or the low end of the data displayed on the stem-and-leaf graph. Students should have many experiences in ordering data and then determining the median.

The **mean**, or arithmetic mean, is another way to answer questions about the children's heights. The mean, or **mean average**, is the most common measure of central tendency. It is computed by summing all the data in a set and then dividing that sum by the number of data items. If children add all the heights and divide by the number of students, they find the mean. Rather than telling students how to determine a mean (or mean average), use activities such as those in Activities 19.9 and 19.10 to help them discover its meaning and how to determine it. See the companion website activity "An Average

---

ACTIVITY 19.9   Finding Mean Averages

Level: Grades 3–5

Setting: Small groups

Objective: Students describe the meaning of mean average and compute mean averages from small collections of data.

Materials: Fifteen large wooden or plastic blocks; calculators, one for each group; lists of data, such as the heights of students in the class, number of pets owned by each class member, population of the 12 largest cities in North America, the number of brothers and sisters of each class member, area of each state west of the Rocky Mountains or in New England—a different list for each group

- In a place visible to all students, arrange five stacks of blocks, as illustrated here. Discuss with students the number of blocks in each stack.

- Demonstrate the meaning of mean average by having a student remove enough blocks from the tallest stack to put atop the shortest stack so that both stacks match the middle stack. Have another student do the same with the second and fourth stacks. Each stack has three blocks; 3 is the mean average for the set of blocks.

- Discuss the concept of mean average as being the idea that all the highs and lows are evened out until everything is the same.

- Have children meet in groups of four to discuss how to determine the mean average for the blocks without shifting blocks from one stack to another. Use the children's thinking as the basis for discussion to help them learn the addition-division process for determining a mean average, or mean. The mean average for the blocks is determined by adding 1 + 2 + 3 + 4 + 5 = 15; 15 ÷ 5 = 3. Emphasize that a mean average is determined by finding the sum of all the numbers in a set and then dividing the sum by the number of numbers.

- Give each group one set of data. Have them divide tasks to solve their problem. One student calls out the numbers one by one, a second enters them into a calculator, a third reads the calculator display to ensure accuracy of entries, and the fourth counts the number of entries and records the sum. Once the sum is determined, it is divided by the number of entries to find the mean average.

- Use the results to discuss the strengths and weaknesses of using mean averages with data. One use of a measure such as mean average is to make inferences. The mean average of the children's heights is probably a good indicator of the heights of similar groups of children, so they can be used to infer heights of other groups. The mean average size of North American cities cannot be used to infer the sizes of cities on other continents.

Activity," which helps students understand how the mean average progressively changes as more data in a set become available.

The differences between the three measures of central tendency—the mean, median, and mode—might be illustrated with the following problem:

- The ages of the workers at Hamburger Haven are 18, 20, 18, 19, 19, 18, 20, 21, 22, 45, and 54. Compute the mean, median, and mode for the workers' ages.

The mean is 25, the median is 20, and the mode is 18. Each of these values is a middle value, but they convey different information about the data set. The mode reveals the most common data value but does not indicate other values in the set, their frequency, or the range of values. The median is the value in the middle of the data set when the values are ar-

ranged in order of magnitude. The number of data values that are larger than the median is equal to the number of values that are smaller than the median. The mean is affected by extreme values in the data set because the mean is computed using all the data values. In this data set the two high values pull the value of the mean up so that it is higher than most of the values in the data set.

Suppose that the 54-year-old worker leaves Hamburger Haven and is replaced by a 21-year-old worker. How do the measures of central tendency change? In this case neither the mode nor the median change values. The mean is affected by the change in workers. It is now 22. This demonstrates the sensitivity of the mean to extreme values in a data set.

Mean, median, and mode are all ways of describing what is typical of a data set. They are all consid-

---

ACTIVITY 19.10 Over and Under the Mean (Reasoning and Proof)

Level: Grades 4 and 5

Setting: Student pairs

Objective: Students compute the mean and then compare it to the original data.

Materials: Centimeter cubes, centimeter grid paper

- Pass out 25 cubes to each pair of students.
- Have students form stacks of 3, 6, 5, 7, 1, and 2 cubes, and record the height of each stack on the grid paper by shading in the appropriate number of squares.
- Ask students to make all stacks the same height by moving the cubes from one stack to another. Once students have evened out the stacks, discuss how students moved the cubes. What plan did they use to make the stacks the same height?
- Now ask students to compare the height of the evened out stacks (4) to the heights of the original stacks. They can do this by drawing an average line at the height of the mean, 4 cubes high, on their sketch of the original stacks. Ask students to figure out how many cubes were originally higher than the 4-cube stack. Ask how many cubes were originally missing from the 4-cube stack.
- Students should find that the two values are the same.
- There are 6 cubes above the 4-cube line, and 6 cubes are missing below the 4-cube line. This is the result of evening off the stacks of cubes, and it is true for all means or mean averages. Repeat with stacks of 7, 3, 4, and 6, and 7, 5, 6, 3, and 4.
- As a culminating discussion, record the results of students' findings on the board.

$3 + 6 + 5 + 7 + 1 + 2 = 24 \rightarrow 4$

$7 + 3 + 4 + 6 = 20 \rightarrow 5$

$7 + 5 + 6 + 3 + 4 = 25 \rightarrow 5$

- Ask students to reflect on how they might determine the mean for several stacks of cubes without shifting cubes to even out the stacks. The recorded data will suggest to students that one way to divide up the cubes evenly is to divide the total number of cubes by the number of stacks.

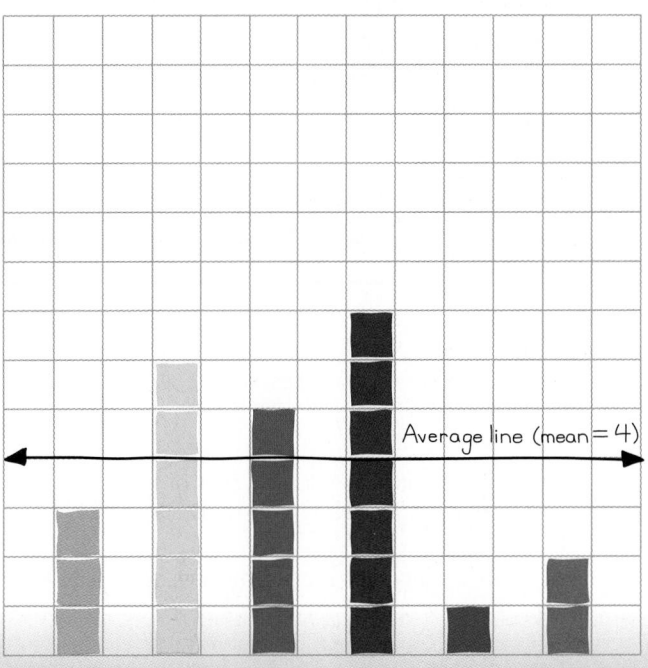

Average line (mean = 4)

ered measures of central tendency and are used to represent typical pieces of data from a whole set of data. Although each measure displays a central value for a data set, each one focuses on the center or average of a set of data in a different way. The measures might result in decidedly different central values for the same data set, and yet each one is sometimes referred to as an average. Each of these averages has strengths and weaknesses that are important for older students to begin to understand. Many middle school students can confidently determine the mean, median, and mode, but they are unable to discern when to use each of these measures of central tendency and what the implications of each one are. It is important to help students use these measures of central tendency as tools to solve problems, to view these central data as end solutions.

As mentioned earlier, the mode is used with categorical data, or with numerical data when the most frequent number is needed. The mode is useful to the manager of a convenience store who must decide what size bottles of soda to order. The median and mean both refer to numerical data. The mean is more sensitive to extreme outliers, whereas the median tends to be more immune to one or two extreme data values. Thus housing prices tend to list the median prices of homes and not the mean. Activity 19.11 presents one data set for students to analyze using these three measures of central tendency.

What, if any, inferences can be drawn from mean averages for the other sets of data used in this chapter? As previously suggested, a weakness of mean average is that one large or small outlier in a sample can distort the mean average for that sample. The mean average of the world's 12 largest cities is influenced very much by the population of Tokyo. With it, the mean average is 20,467,000; without it, the mean average is 19,270,000. This shows that one very large city increases the mean average by more than 1 million compared to the mean average without it. In the height situation it is possible that one or two children at one or the other end of the range can distort the mean average if they are unusually short or tall for their age group and the group is not large.

Investigations involving amounts of data so large that operations on them are time-consuming and cumbersome to perform with paper and pencil are easily done with computer programs. A typical program contains spreadsheet functions for sorting high to low, computing averages, and treating data in other ways. Activity 19.12 describes an interdisciplinary activity that uses a spreadsheet and graphing program for an investigation about rainfall.

ACTIVITY 19.11 Comparing Averages (Communication)

Level: Grades 5 and 6

Setting: Small groups

Objective: Students compute and then compare all three averages (mean, median, mode) for a set of data.

Materials: Calculators

- Present students with the following ages of workers at Henrietta's Hamburger Heaven: 17, 17, 17, 18, 19, 21, 22, 45, 58.

- Have students compute the mean, median, and mode for the ages of the workers.

- Present students with the following task: "Write three different radio advertisements, each using one of the 'averages' (mean, median, mode). Your advertisement will offer jobs by featuring the 'average' age of workers."

- Have groups read their advertisements to the class and explain who they hope to attract to work at Henrietta's Hamburger Heaven.

- In a concluding discussion, ask students which advertisement appealed to them, and have them write out their reasons.

ACTIVITY 19.12 Using and Interpreting Data (Representation)

Level: Grades 4–6

Setting: Whole class

Objective: Students apply knowledge of statistics, tables, and graphs to investigate rainfall patterns.

Materials: Local rainfall statistics for a recent 10-year period, computer graphing program

- Have students obtain month-by-month data on a community's rainfall for the last 10 years and enter the data into a software spreadsheet. Information can be obtained from the U.S. Weather Service, television weather reporters, or newspapers.

- This is a good activity to conduct with classes in other states by e-mail. Students in participating cities can share rainfall information. (see chart on p. 516)

- After students have entered the raw data into the database, have them generate questions about them. Which year had the most rain in the last 10 years? the least rain?

Which month had the most rain in the last 10 years? the least rain?

- Which months have the highest average rainfall? the lowest average?

- Make a copy of each spreadsheet in a new computer file so that students can experiment with the data without changing the original. Use the spreadsheet program to calculate monthly and yearly totals and averages. Use the Sort or Arrange function to compare the most and least rain for each month and year.

- Create graphs of the rainfall data, using the software graphing program. A bar graph is good for showing total rainfall by year. A line graph is useful for showing month-by-month rainfall averages or to compare monthly rainfall for different years. A circle graph can be used to compare rainfall by seasons.

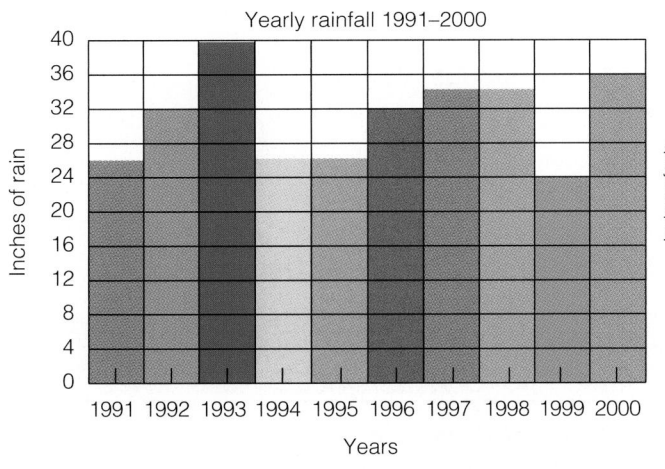

Yearly rainfall 1991–2000

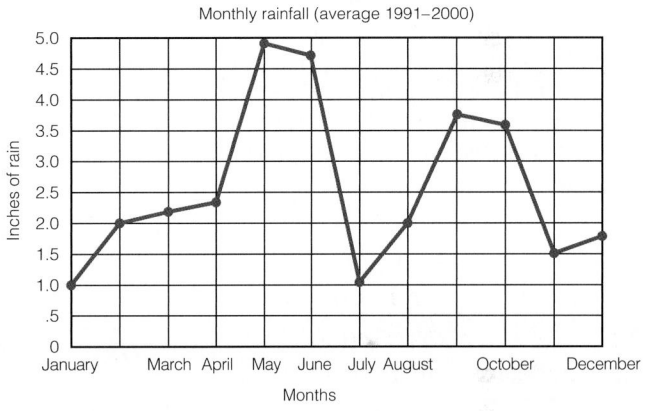

Monthly rainfall (average 1991–2000)

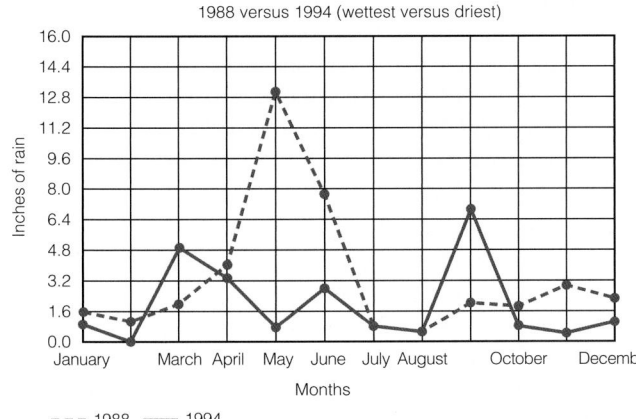

1988 versus 1994 (wettest versus driest)

- - - 1988   —— 1994

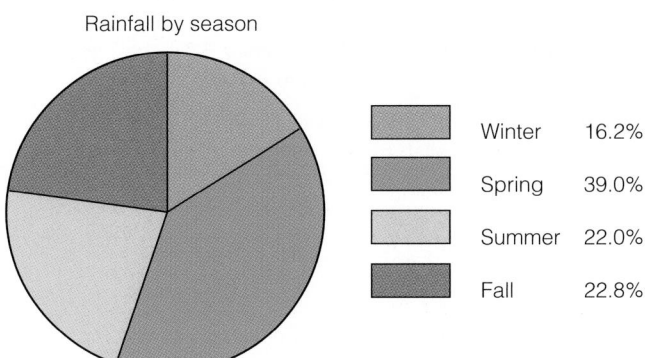

Rainfall by season

Winter	16.2%
Spring	39.0%
Summer	22.0%
Fall	22.8%

	MONTHLY RAINFALL (IN INCHES)										TOTAL EACH MONTH	AVERAGE EACH MONTH
	1991	1992	1993	1994	1995	1996	1997	1998	1999	2000		
January	1.57	0.14	1.66	1.87	0.17	1.08	0.00	1.78	1.17	1.04	10.48	1.05
February	0.63	3.30	1.03	0.90	0.79	2.61	1.10	4.06	0.00	3.50	17.92	1.79
March	0.76	1.86	2.04	2.06	1.48	3.77	0.84	1.99	5.15	1.54	21.49	2.15
April	0.35	3.95	3.38	2.19	0.62	6.15	3.24	0.32	2.83	0.32	23.35	2.33
May	6.67	3.54	13.22	3.21	1.44	1.69	3.87	10.17	0.71	4.54	49.06	4.91
June	0.26	4.59	7.41	5.05	1.78	7.07	7.61	2.43	2.80	8.60	47.60	4.76
July	0.03	1.33	0.92	0.19	0.92	0.21	0.77	2.78	0.84	3.19	11.18	1.12
August	0.26	2.29	0.71	0.19	3.07	1.75	2.10	2.40	0.58	6.17	19.52	1.95
September	10.23	1.49	2.06	0.00	0.80	1.46	6.77	2.23	7.04	5.01	37.09	3.71
October	1.65	7.83	1.99	7.79	6.24	3.69	4.37	0.11	0.76	2.25	36.68	3.67
November	1.57	0.86	2.73	0.91	3.32	1.11	3.03	1.66	0.51	0.03	15.73	1.57
December	1.94	0.30	2.22	0.89	5.03	0.11	0.91	4.84	1.11	0.28	17.63	1.76
TOTAL EACH YEAR	25.92	31.48	39.37	25.25	25.66	30.70	34.61	34.77	23.50	36.47	307.73	
AVG BY MONTH	2.16	2.62	3.28	2.10	2.14	2.56	2.88	2.90	1.96	3.04		30.773

ⒺXERCISE

Here are the heights (in centimeters) of 15 children: **126, 142, 139, 156, 148, 137, 135, 141, 145, 141, 151, 140, 135, 143, 134. Organize the data in a form suitable for determining the high, low, range, median, mean, and mode, and then determine the value(s) for each term. Is there an outlier? If so, what is it?** ●●●

Activity 19.13 is an assessment activity that summarizes the concepts of central tendency that we have explored in this chapter.

ACTIVITY 19.13 Assessment Activity

- -

Level: Grades 5 and 6

The Johnsonville Intermediate School girls basketball team has 10 players. The heights of the Johnsonville Jewels are 47 inches, 63 inches, 52 inches, 54 inches, 48 inches, 49 inches, 66 inches, 50 inches, 53 inches, and 48 inches. Complete the following exercises:

1. Find the mode for the team heights.
2. Find the median for the team heights.
3. Find the mean for the team heights.
4. Which of the three heights seems to you to be the best for the average height of the team? Explain your choice.
5. Write a news flash describing the Johnsonville team to the next team that the Johnsonville Jewels will play, the Tipps Tornadoes. Be sure to include one of the "average" heights in your news flash.

Take-Home Activity

The following letter may be completed as a family activity and returned to school. Possible in-school activities include finding total costs and the range, median, and mode of prices; comparing present prices with 1970 prices and figuring the percent difference; and preparing graphs to compare prices. Students can select data about which to write "surprising facts" in their journals. Older students can compare typical salaries in 1970 with those of today and determine whether costs of school supplies today are comparable to 1970 costs.

Dear Family,

Your child is working on a back-to-school project to begin the school year.

One objective of the project is to demonstrate the use of mathematics in the world around us. A common experience for students who return to school at the end of the summer is to purchase new school supplies. We will be talking in class about the costs of school supplies and comparing present-day costs with what these materials cost in the early 1970s, perhaps a time when your parents were purchasing back-to-school supplies for you.

Please assist your child as needed to find the present-day prices for these items. You might try news ads, catalogs, or a nearby store. Your child will record the price of each item on the list below and then find the total for all the items in each list, using mental math, pencil and paper, or a calculator.

Be sure to compare today's prices with the 1970s prices for each item with your child.

Please have your child return this activity sheet to class at the beginning of next week. We will use the sheet in class to explore several aspects of the data you collect. If you have any questions or concerns, please feel free to contact me at school.

Thank you,

Your Child's Teacher

(continued)

Name: _____

BACK-TO-SCHOOL SHOPPING

Back-to-School Data Sheet	Today's price	1970s price
1. Number 2 pencil	_____	$0.03
2. 12-inch ruler with inch and centimeter markings	_____	$0.10
3. Four-function calculator	_____	$79.99
4. Retractable pen (2)	_____	$0.10 each
5. Compass	_____	$0.25
6. One 4-ounce container of glue	_____	$0.25
7. 5 portfolio folders with pockets	_____	$0.15 each
8. 3 felt-tipped pens (red, blue, black)	_____	$0.20 each
9. 100-pack index cards	_____	$0.15
10. Spiral notebook	_____	$0.59
11. Roll of cellophane tape	_____	$0.25
12. Box of tissues	_____	$0.24
13. 24-crayon box	_____	$0.39
14. Note pad	_____	$0.10

Summary

Because much information is provided to the public by the mass media in tabular and graphic form, the ability to organize data and use tables and graphs effectively is a valuable problem-solving and reasoning skill. Children's early classification, sorting, and organizing activities develop a foundation for understanding tables and graphs.

Children create their own tables and graphs to build both understanding and skill in interpreting them. Children can provide much of the data they use for organizing and reporting in tables and graphs. Shoe preferences, pets, heights, and favorite pizzas, ice cream, and television shows are examples of information children can collect.

Data from surveys, almanacs and other secondary sources can be used by students. Primary-grade students construct and read tallies, line plots, and object, picture, and bar graphs. Older children use picture, bar, line, circle graphs, stem-and-leaf plots, and box-and-whisker plots. Calculators and computer graphing programs help students organize data and prepare graphs.

The development of statistical concepts should also be based on children's data. When children describe information, they learn statistical concepts and their names: most frequent, or mode; lowest to highest and range; middle, or median number; mean, or average; and outlier. Descriptive statistics help students summarize and communicate the main points about information they have collected.

Study Questions and Activities

1. Children should serve as the source of most of the data used in making tables and graphs. Think of 10 topics (in addition to the ones listed in this chapter) about which children could collect information. These could involve other children in the classroom or school, teachers, the school building, the parking lot and street, transportation to and from school, and things and people at home.

2. Tables are shown in Figures 19.1, 19.2, 19.6, and 19.8, and also in Activity 19.4. Graphs appropriate for each table are shown in the chapter. Select a different topic, and create a set of data about it. Write an activity plan for constructing a table and several graphs for that topic. Make a list of five questions children could ask and answer based on the table and graphs.

3. Collect data on the number of pairs of shoes owned by students in your class. Have them list the shoes in categories: dress, casual, athletic, and so on. Create a table and three graphs from the information. Compare your data, table, and graph with those of other students.

4. Examine a copy of *USA Today* with a classmate. What types of graphs are shown in the paper? Are they effective in displaying data? Are any of the graphs misleading?

5. Write three to five questions for students based on the graphs you found in *USA Today*.

6. Give two real-life situations for each of the measures of central tendency: the mean, the median, and the mode.

7. Old Faithful is a geyser in Yellowstone National Park with a reputation for erupting faithfully about every hour. Actually the time between eruptions can vary from 50 to 100 minutes. If you had eruption data for two weeks, which measure of central tendency would you use to report the average time between eruptions?

Praxis (http://www.ets.org/praxis/) The hand spans of ninth-grade students at Tyler High are approximately normally distributed, with a mean of 7 inches and a standard deviation of 1 inch. Of the following groups of measurements of hand span, which is expected to contain the largest number of ninth graders?

a. Less than 6 inches

b. Greater than 7 inches

c. Between 6 and 8 inches

d. Between 5 and 7 inches

NAEP (http://nces.ed.gov/nationsreportcard/) The pie chart shows the portion of time Pat spent on homework in each subject last week. If Pat spent 2 hours on mathematics, about how many hours did Pat spend on homework altogether?

A   4
B   8
C   12
D   16

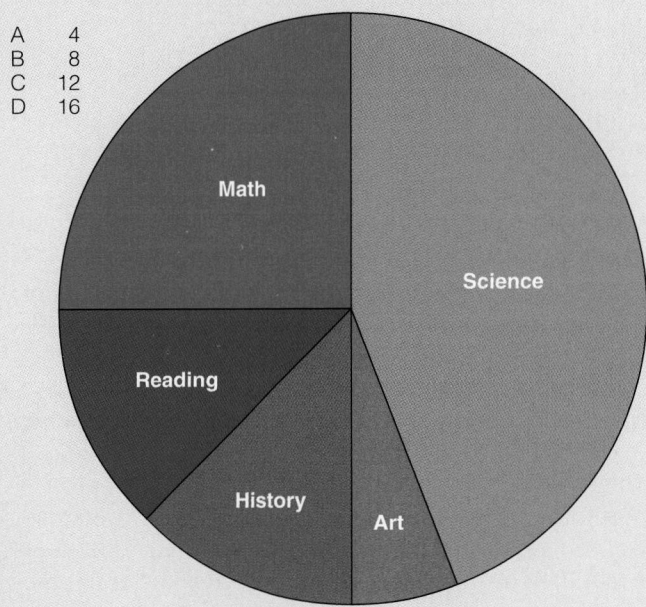

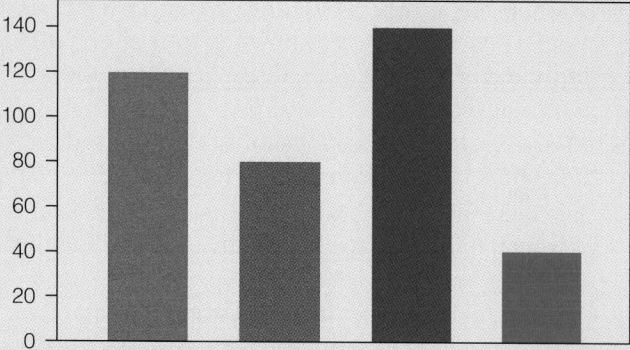

TIMSS (http://nces.ed.gov/timss/) The graph shows the number of pens, pencils, rulers, and erasers sold by a store in one week.

The names of the items are missing from the graph. Pens were the item most often sold, and fewer erasers than any other items were sold. More pencils than rulers were sold. How many pencils were sold?

Using Children's Literature

Jocelyn, Marthe. (2000). *Hannah's collection.* New York: Penguin Books for Young Readers. (Grades K–3)

Hannah is a collector with lots of different collections. She sorts her collections in different ways. One day she sorts her button collection by size, another day by color, another day by shape. So it goes with all her collections. Hannah has a problem, though. She can bring only one collection to school. What to bring? Hannah uses such mathematical concepts as number sense, patterns, geometry, and computation to make her surprise decision.

Tasks related to the reading could include:

- How many different collections does Hannah have?
- Which one is your favorite collection?
- How many different things does Hannah have in all her collections?
- What two different collections can you make using anything from Hannah's collections?
- Tell about a collection you have at home or one you would like to start.

Morgan, Rowland. (1997). *In the next three seconds.* New York: Penguin Books for Young Readers. (Grades 4–6)

In the Next Three Seconds is a book that contains many data items about what will happen in the next three seconds, minutes, hours, days, and so forth. For example, "In the next three seconds, Britons will eat 3,600 potatoes." Students could take one of the statistic items and extrapolate the data for a longer or shorter time period. They could also take the given data and apply it proportionally to another setting (e.g., How many potatoes will Americans eat in the next three seconds?). Students could then display the resulting data in a poster or present it to the class in an oral report.

Teacher's Resources

Bright, G., Brewer, W., McClain, K., & Mooney, E. (2003). *Navigating through data analysis in grades 6–8.* Reston, VA: National Council of Teachers of Mathematics.

Burrill, G., & Elliot, P. (Eds.). (2006). *Thinking and reasoning with data and chance: Sixty-eighth yearbook.* Reston, VA: National Council of Teachers of Mathematics.

Carter, Rick. (1996). *Chance, statistics, and graphs: Handling data.* Reston, VA: National Council of Teachers of Mathematics.

Chapin, S., Lozoil, A., MacPherson, J., & Rezba, C. (2002). *Navigating through data analysis and probability in grades 3–5.* Reston, VA: National Council of Teachers of Mathematics.

Cuomo, Celia. (1993). *In all probability: Investigations in probability and statistics—Teachers guide, grades 3–6.* Berkeley: University of California Press.

Curcio, Frances R. (1989). *Developing graph comprehension.* Reston, VA: National Council of Teachers of Mathematics.

Dilke, O. A. (1987). *Reading the past: Mathematics and measurement.* London: British Museum Press.

Lindquist, Mary M. (Ed.). (1995). *Curriculum and evaluation standards for school mathematics: Addenda series, grades K–6—Making sense of data.* Reston, VA: National Council of Teachers of Mathematics.

Sheffield, L., Cavanaugh, M., Dacey, L., Findell, C., Greenes, C., & Small, M. (2002). *Navigating through data analysis and probability in prekindergarten–grade 2.* Reston, VA: National Council of Teachers of Mathematics.

Steen, Lynn Arthur (Ed.). (1997). *Why numbers count: Quantitative literacy for tomorrow's America.* New York: College Entrance Examination Board.

Strauss, Stephen. (1995). *The sizeaurus.* New York: Kodansha International.

Children's Bookshelf

Arnold, Caroline. (1984). *Charts and graphs: Fun, facts, and activities.* New York: Franklin Watts. (Grades K–4)

Ash, Russell. (1996). *Incredible comparisons.* New York: Dorling Kindersley. (Grades 4–7)

Birch, David. (1993) *The king's chessboard.* New York: Puffin Books. (Grades 3–5)

Burns, Marilyn. (1975). *The I hate mathematics book.* Boston: Little, Brown. (Grades 5–8)

Guinness Book of World Records. (2006). Available at http://www.guinnessworldrecords.com

Lambert, David. (1998). *Dinosaur data book.* New York: Gramercy. (Grades 3–6)

Leedy, Loreen. (2000). *Measuring Penny*. New York: Henry Holt. (Grades 3–5)

Morgan, Rowland. (1997). *In the next three seconds*. New York: Lodestar. (Grades 3–8)

Nagala, Ann Whitehead, & Bickel, Cindy. (2002). *Tiger math: Learning to graph from a baby tiger*. New York: Henry Holt. (Grades 3–6)

Pittman, Helena Clare. (1994). *Counting Jennie*. Minneapolis: Carolrhoda. (Grades K–3)

Rex, Michael. (1997) *The fattest, tallest, biggest snowman ever*. New York: Cartwheel. (Grades 3–5)

Singh, S.(2002). *The code book: How to make it, break it, back it, crack it*. New York: Delacorte Press. (Grades 4–7)

Technology Resources

Computer Software

We used three computer software programs in this chapter. All three are available on the Internet:

http://nces.ed.gov/nceskids/Graphing/

http://math.about.com

http://nlvm.usu.edu/en/nav/vlibay.html

Students can use these free programs to organize data in spreadsheets and to report it using one or more of many different graph formats. There are many other programs on the Internet and a number of commercial software programs, such as Tabletop by Sunburst and SmartDraw.com, that allow older students to work with large data sets and produce sophisticated graphs.

Internet Sites

These websites contain interesting data to analyze and represent:

http://www.census.gov

http://nces.4ed.gov.nceskids

http://www.usatoday.com/edcae/home/html?Loc-vanity

Internet Game

The game Data Picking, available at **http://www.bbc.co.uk/education/mathsfile/**, involves several skills relative to understanding data collection and representation. In the game students "survey" people by clicking on their image and recording their responses on an electronic tally sheet. They record the information as they collect it and compile it at the end of the surveying. The next task is to select the graph that best represents the specific data they have collected. The sounds that accompany the game are amusing to most students but can distract some students who might better play the game with the mute button activated.

For Further Reading

Bombaugh, Ruth, & Jefferys, Lynn. (2006). Body math. *Mathematics Teaching in the Middle Grades* 11(8), 378–384.

The authors describe a project that combines mathematics and science in one exploration. Students gather data by surveying classmates in their school. They analyze the collected data to make conclusions about their school population.

Fiecht, Louis. (1999). Making charts: Do your students really understand the data? *Mathematics Teaching in the Middle Grades* 5(1), 16–18.

A discussion of common student misunderstandings of various graphs. Actual student comments are included in the article.

Goldsby, Dianne. (2004). "Lollipop" statistics. *Mathematics Teaching in the Middle Grades* 9(1), 12–16.

Goldsby describes how middle-grade students obtained data from an entire school and then represented it graphically.

Harper, Suzanne. (2004). Students' interpretations of misleading graphs. *Mathematics Teaching in the Middle Grades* 9(6), 340–343.

Students examine misleading graphs and make conclusions based on their perceptions of the graphs and their knowledge of data representation. The article highlights typical student misconceptions.

Methany, Dixie. (2001). Consumer investigations: What is the "best" chip? *Teaching Children Mathematics* 7(7), 418–420.

Students construct tables, charts, and graphs to display the data they gather about various popular snack chips. These representations are used in a presentation to convince classmates about their selection of the best snacking chips.

Martinie, Sherry. (2006). Families ask: Data analysis and statistics in the middle school. *Mathematics Teaching in the Middle* Grades 12(1), 48–53.

In this article the author describes the statistics curriculum that is appropriate for upper elementary school students.

Moore, Deborah. (1999). Some like it hot: Promoting measurement and graphical thinking using temperature. *Teaching Children Mathematics* 5(9), 538–543.

Moore describes a program in which students use various graphs to represent temperature and then use the graphs to make several analyses.

Olson, Melfried, Sakshaug, Lynae, & Olson, Judith (Eds.). (1998). Problem solvers: You gotta have heart—and blood! *Teaching Children Mathematics* 4(6), 352–353.

This feature presents a topic around which teachers can build a unit of study. Data about America's blood from the American Red Cross and other sources can be used in a statistics unit. Several websites offering additional information are noted in the article.

CHAPTER 20

Investigating Probability

An understanding of probability is essential for everyday living in our society. There is a 40% chance of rain. Should you cancel those picnic plans? Traffic to the beach resort has been terrible the past few weekends. What is the likelihood of heavy traffic this coming weekend? The medication your physician recommends causes side effects in about 10% of patients. Should you expect to suffer from side effects? The lottery jackpot is up to $15 million, does that improve your chances of winning? You were involved in a traffic accident with some minor damage. Will your automobile insurance premiums increase? An understanding of the principles of probability can help you to analyze these and similar situations and make decisions based on the mathematics of probability.

Probability is essentially a ratio that describes the likelihood that an event will or will not occur, although the study of probability involves proportional reasoning. Even young children explore probability situations. Thus the study of probability begins in the primary grades and continues through high school. Probability is a challenging topic for some children because at times it seems to be counterintuitive. That is, the probability involved in a particular situation can challenge children's beliefs and feelings. A favorite number, athlete, or even color will influence how a child views a specific situation. Past experiences also shade a child's outlook, and these factors can muddy and even contradict probability principles in the child's mind. A young child who needs to spin a 2 to win a board game may be convinced that she will spin a 2 because "2 is my favorite number." An older child is confident that his favorite baseball player will get a hit late in a game because he has been hitless up to now and is "due to get a hit." With appropriate experiences early in their schooling, children can put aside such erroneous thinking and see situations through a mathematical filter and make valid decisions based on their understanding of probability principles.

In this chapter you will read about:

1 Historical (empirical) and mathematical (theoretical) probability

2 How the law of large numbers and the gambler's fallacy affect teaching probability

3 Activities for younger children to develop their probability thinking

4 Exploration activities for older children to compute numerical probabilities

5 Sampling and simulations

6 A take-home probability experiment

Two Types of Probability

In elementary school two different types of probability are introduced: mathematical probability and historical probability. **Mathematical probability** is based on the mathematics of chance, or the arithmetic probability of an event occurring. For example:

- What is the chance a six will come up when this die stops rolling?

- What is the chance of drawing a yellow marble from the bag of colored marbles?

The answers to these and other questions can be computed using the mathematics principles of probability theory. Understanding probability enables older children to interpret information in newspapers and magazines and on the Internet. Many problem-solving activities involving data require children to construct tables and graphs, search for patterns, perform computations, make estimations, draw conclusions, and communicate results during a study of mathematical probability.

POINT OF VIEW
People use different, sometimes competing, intuitive, and personal theories when reasoning about probability tasks. (Shaughnessy, 2003, p. 223)

Historical probability is based on information accumulated over time about such things as weather and climate, driving experiences of teenagers and elders, or voting trends in electoral districts. For example:

- Is it likely to rain on our picnic if we plan it for the end of March?

- Who is more likely to be involved in an accident, a teenage driver or a person over 70?

- What type of candidate is most likely to be elected in that voting district?

Historical probability furnishes information for these questions and guides decision making about each topic. Health insurance premiums offer an example of how past information is used to affect the present. Health insurance premiums depend on many different factors, such as age, gender, occupation, family medical history, personal health, habits (such as smoking), residence, and marital status. Insurance companies have collected data on thousands of people on factors such as these. These empirical data are used to predict the likelihood that a person with a specific combination of factors will make a claim. Although an insurance company cannot predict whether a specific individual will make a claim, by analyzing the characteristics of thousands of previously insured persons, the company can predict the likelihood that the person will make a claim and can adjust the person's insurance premiums accordingly.

What Teachers Should Know About Teaching Probability

Probability, more than any other mathematics study, is the focus of superstitions, hunches, and erroneous beliefs. Students at every level can retain tightly held misconceptions about probability. To leave such misconceptions behind, students require many activities in which they generate and analyze data from probability situations. With enough experiences with probability situations, students will build a solid foundation for basic concepts of probability theory.

A well-developed unit on weather can introduce elementary-level students to historical probability and how it connects mathematics to everyday living. People who work outdoors (e.g., farmers) depend on weather records for planning their work. Others use daily weather reports and predictions to make daily decisions (e.g., road crews, construction workers, professional baseball players). Ask, "Historically, why is baseball played during summer and basketball during winter?" or "What time of year are outdoor concerts held in New England?" or "What time of year is a good time to plant a garden?"

Knowledge about both types of probability empowers students to make wise decisions in a wide variety of situations. For instance, many everyday decisions are influenced by a knowledge of past events. If you plan a picnic in July, what are the chances that the weather will be rainy? In West Texas or California's Sacramento Valley, rainfall records suggest that rain is unlikely. If you are in Hawaii or Florida, rainfall records indicate that rain is a likely occurrence. The negligible chance of winning a lottery may help dissuade a person from purchasing a ticket. When people buy an appliance, such as a television set or a refrigerator, they may study the reliability ratings of different models. Based on laboratory testing and the personal experiences of owners, appliances are rated for reliability. In other words, problems are less likely for some appliances than for others, based on past performance.

In dealing with probability, however, nothing is guaranteed. Rain has happened in July in West Texas and in the Sacramento Valley, and it can be dry in Hawaii or Florida; an appliance reported to be reliable can experience mechanical problems.

Both weather and appliance reliability offer opportunities to learn about historical probability in the classroom. Students can obtain historical data about local weather from the U.S. Weather Service (see **http://iwin.nws.noaa.gov**) or from a local meteorologist and estimate the chances of snow, rain, or sun during different seasons. Television weather reporters can be a source of weather data in your part of the country. *Consumer Reports* and other sources provide background information on the reliability of appliances.

The probability of any event happening ranges from 0 to 1. An event with a probability of 1 is certain to happen, such as the sun rising in the east, water freezing at 32°F, or rolling a number from 1 to 6 with a single number cube. An event with a probability of 0 will never happen, such as the sun rising in the west, pigs growing wings and flying, or rolling a 9 with a single number cube. Events having a probability of 0 or 1 encourage students to make lists of events with such extreme probabilities, drawing on their personal experiences or creating fantasy events, such as the probability that Donald Duck will hold his temper. Activity 20.1 provides students with the opportunity to develop their understanding of such extreme probability events.

When an event has a probability between 0 and 1, the event may or may not occur. An event that may or may not happen is fraught with uncertainty. Knowing the probability of the event happening removes some of the uncertainty and gives some indication of the likelihood of such an event. Still, there can be no guarantee that a specific event will or will not happen if the probability is between 0 and 1. Even events with probabilities that are close to either 0 or 1 are not certain. Snowfall in Wisconsin in January is a near certain event with a probability close to 1, perhaps $\frac{98}{100}$ or 0.98, but it cannot be absolutely guaranteed to happen. Similarly, getting nothing but 10 heads or 10 tails when 10 coins are tossed is an unlikely event, as is rainfall in an Arizona desert in August. Both of these events have probabilities close to 0, less than 1%. Because the probability is not 0, however, neither event is impossible.

The NCTM standard for probability at this level reflects the interest that younger children have in events with some uncertainty.

NCTM Standards Correlation

The probability standards are as follows:
Develop and evaluate inferences and predictions that are based on data

Pre-K–2 Expectations

In prekindergarten through grade 2 all students should:

- discuss events related to students' experiences as likely or unlikely.

POINT OF VIEW

At this level (Pre-K–2), probability experiences should be informal and often take the form of answering questions about the likelihood of events, using such vocabulary as more likely and less likely. (National Council of Teachers of Mathematics, 2000, p. 114)

POINT OF VIEW

In this informal study of probability, the notions of more likely and less likely should come from students' experiences rather than mathematical situations such as rolling dice or drawing names from a hat. . . . Probability is sometimes regarded as the least intuitive branch of mathematics because people have difficulties developing correct intuitions about fundamental ideas in probability. (Tarr, 2002, p. 482)

Accordingly, younger children who are studying probability may simply designate events as likely or unlikely rather than try to quantify their likelihood with a specific numerical probability. Such events should be drawn from their own experiences and from familiar settings. Activity 20.2 presents students with the task of locating the probability of common, familiar events along a probability number line, labeled *impossible*, *unlikely*, *likely*, and *certain* to happen. In Activity 20.3 children experiment with tossing a paper cup to gather information about the various probabilities. The companion website activity "Pick a Vowel" has students examine their name for the probability of picking a vowel from the letters that make up their name. In the companion website activity "Gathering Experimental Data" students flip tacks (or toothpaste caps) to determine the likely probabilities of each outcome.

ACTIVITY 20.1   Guaranteed to Happen (or Not to Happen)

Level: Grades K–2

Setting: Small groups

Objective: Students designate and list certain and impossible events.

Materials: Paper and pencils

- Tell students that they are going to decide whether the events in a list you will be giving to them are impossible (e.g., an elephant roller skating) or certain (e.g., the sun coming up every morning). Ask student volunteers to give one or two examples of each type of event.

- Distribute the following list to student groups, and give them the time to decide as a group whether each event is impossible or certain. Ask each group to select a recorder who will write out the group's decision about each event, and a reporter who will report the group's decisions to the class.

  1. It will snow in July at Disney World.
  2. A dog will knit a hat.
  3. A ball thrown into the air comes back down.
  4. A fish will breathe underwater.
  5. You will go a week without watching television.
  6. You pass GO in a game of Monopoly.
  7. You eat lunch at school this week.
  8. 7 + 6 = 13.
  9. Tomorrow night you will go to bed at midnight.
  10. You roll a 14 with a pair of number cubes.

- When groups are ready, have each reporter relate the group's decisions to the whole class. Discuss any event that a group cannot agree on or that does not seem to fit either category.

- During these discussions, have students explain the reasons for their decisions. For example, some students will state that it is not impossible to go a week without watching television, but others will insist that it is impossible to do so.

- Ask each group to write out two events that are certain to happen and two events that are impossible to happen.

- As each group shares its events with the entire class, have each student write down whether the event is certain or impossible. After each group reports its events, have students report their designations and discuss them as a class.

- You will likely find that students will view many situations from their own experience. Some students will suggest that it is impossible for them to stay up past 11 p.m., whereas others will have done so and so will not view that as an impossible event. The discussion that takes place after a group reveals its findings is thus a critical part of the activity. It is in such discussions that a teacher can discern the thinking of the students.

ACTIVITY 20.2 Maybe or Maybe Not (Reasoning and Proof)

Level: Grades 2–4

Setting: Small groups

Objective: Students designate events along a probability number line.

Materials: Sticky note paper, colored pencils, poster boards

- Pass out the materials to students.

- Draw on the board a probability number line like the one shown here, and discuss with the class what each word means. Ask student volunteers to give an example of an event that fits each of the four categories.

Impossible	Unlikely	Likely	Certain

- Ask each group to draw the probability line so that it fills their poster board.

- Distribute the following event list to each group. Ask students to make a sketch on the sticky note paper to represent each event.

Events for the Probability Number Line

1. It will snow here in December.
2. School will be closed on Thanksgiving Day.
3. A pig will fly.
4. When you drop a glass onto the floor, it will break.
5. When you shoot a basketball, you score a basket.
6. A cat will bark.
7. The school bus will not stop to pick up any students.
8. You will sit at your desk today at school.
9. $17 - 8 = 8$.
10. The sun will shine at midnight.

- Once the sketches are completed, have each group put its sticky notes on the probability line where members agree they should be placed.

- Post each group's poster, and discuss possible differences in the group results as a class.

- As you discuss the group posters, note any groups that put their sticky notes in between the categories. For example, a group may place a sticky note close to, but not on, *certain*. They might reason, for example, that "School is always closed on Thanksgiving Day, but there might be an emergency that makes the school stay open, so you can't be positive school will be closed."

ACTIVITY 20.3 Tossing Paper Cups

Level: Grades 1–3

Setting: Whole class

Objective: Students explain the concept of likely and unlikely events.

Materials: A paper cup for every student, paper and pencils

- Tell the students that they are going to investigate what happens when a paper cup is tossed in the air. Ask them to suggest what results could happen when this is done. They will probably answer, "Land on its side," "Land right side up," and "Land upside down." List these possibilities, but probe for others. They might add "Get hung in the light fixture" or "Fall in the trash can." List all the answers, and ask the children to classify them as likely or unlikely.

- Have the students work in pairs. Each pair lists the suggested outcomes on a paper, then tosses the paper cup 20 times and tallies how often it actually lands in each of the suggested ways. Set standards for acceptable tosses; children should not deliberately try to hang the cup on a light fixture or toss it into a trash can. One child tosses 10 times while the other records results; they exchange roles for the second 10 tosses.

- Tell the children to rate each event in terms of how often it occurred. Young children will simply note the frequency as being "often," "not often," or "never." Then have them decide whether an event is likely or unlikely to happen. Older children in this activity should calculate a common fraction with a denominator of 20 that expresses the probability for each suggested outcome. Using the fractions as a guide, they identify a number that indicates the likelihood of each event happening. The number is a decimal fraction on a scale of 0 (can't happen) to 1 (happens every time).

- Broaden the experience by having pairs toss different objects, such as toothpaste caps, half-pint milk cartons, thumbtacks, and plastic animals.

Extending Probability Understanding

MISCONCEPTION
Children without probability experiences will often reason that every possibility, no matter how unlikely, has an equal chance of happening. They develop understanding through recording the results of many probability activities.

Children in grade 3 and higher are able to reason more thoughtfully about probability situations. They are able to move beyond simply assigning events as likely or unlikely to using principles of probability to compute or predict the probability of an event. The NCTM standards for older children are as follows:

Develop and evaluate inferences and predictions that are based on data

Grades 3–5 Expectations
In grades 3–5 all students should:
- propose and justify conclusions and predictions that are based on data and design studies to further investigate the conclusions or predictions.

Grades 6–8 Expectations
In grades 6–8 all students should:
- use observations about differences between two or more samples to make conjectures about the populations from which the samples were taken;
- make conjectures about possible relationships between two characteristics of a sample on the basis of scatterplots of the data and approximate lines of fit;
- use conjectures to formulate new questions and plan new studies to answer them.

The standard suggests that computing numerical probability is appropriate for elementary school children in grades 3 and above, using various manipulatives and activities to generate data. Experimenting with dice is a common classroom probability activity. With one die, six outcomes are possible. If a die is fair, or unbiased, any of the six sides is equally likely to show after it is rolled. Therefore the chances of rolling any given number are one chance in six. When the probability of an event is quantified, it can be expressed in three different ways: as a common fraction, as an equivalent decimal fraction, and as an equivalent percent. When probability is expressed as a common fraction, it takes the general form:

$$P = \frac{\text{Number of times the specific event occurs}}{\text{Number of times all events occur}}$$

Thus the chances of getting a 5 on a die is expressed as $\frac{1}{6}$, because there is one chance of rolling a 5 out of a total of six possible outcomes. In a few rolls of a die one number may occur more frequently than the other five, but after many rolls the probability is that each number will occur equally, and each number will be rolled $\frac{1}{6}$ of the number of total rolls.

Probabilities from both historical and mathematical situations are expressed in the same ways. The probability of getting heads when a coin is tossed is 1 out of 2 and is expressed as $\frac{1}{2}$, 0.50, or 50%. If rain has occurred 980 times during the 31 days of July for the past 40 years, the historical probability is $\frac{980}{1,240}$ (1,240 = 31 × 40), or 0.79, or 79%, that it will rain in July this year. Because probability is expressed in common fraction, decimal fraction, or percent form, it is critical that students have a working knowledge of these different representations before they begin to compute theoretical probabilities. Students without knowledge of fractional representations may perform the proper calculations to compute a probability, but they will not be flexible in their interpretation of any fractions.

Students discover the probability of getting a certain number by rolling a die and keeping a tally of the results. Because a small number of rolls—say, 36—with one die may not produce experimental results that match the mathematical, or theoretical, probability of getting each number, students need to make a large number of rolls. If each child in a class rolls a die 36 times, combining all the tallies shows that the experimental, or *empirical*, probability of the die comes close to, or *approximates*, the theoretical probability. Figure 20.1 shows the results of rolling one die 36 times. The table in

Number	Times
1	ⅢⅢ
2	ⅢⅢ I
3	ⅢⅢ II
4	ⅢⅢ
5	ⅢⅢ II
6	ⅢⅢ I

Figure 20.1 Results of rolling a die 36 times

Figure 20.2 shows the results of using a computer program to roll one die 500 times. Notice that the results for 500 rolls more closely match the theoretical probabilities than do the results for only 36 rolls.

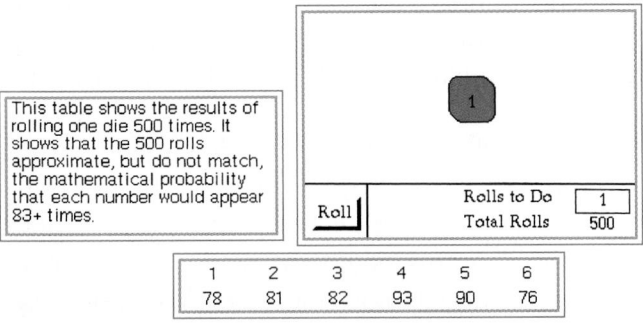

This table shows the results of rolling one die 500 times. It shows that the 500 rolls approximate, but do not match, the mathematical probability that each number would appear 83+ times.

Roll			Rolls to Do	1
			Total Rolls	500

1	2	3	4	5	6
78	81	82	93	90	76

Figure 20.2 Results of rolling one die using the program at http://www2.whidbey.net/ohmsmith/webwork/javascript/diceroll.htm

The results of the computer program in Figure 20.2 illustrate the Law of Large Numbers. The Law of Large Numbers stipulates that the greater the number of events or trials that occur for a particular situation, the closer to theoretical probability the results will be. When students collect experimental or empirical data from dice rolls, coin flips, and other events, unless they record a large number of events, it is unlikely that the empirical results will match theoretical results.

As the data of the computer program show, for many trials the results closely mirror theoretical results. Students need a large number of events before any conclusions can be drawn about probabilities. Students who are just beginning to gather data for probabilities tend to draw conclusions from the data of few events. For example, a child who picks three blue marbles in a row from a bag of marbles may declare that all the marbles in the bag are blue, when in fact six are blue and four are green.

Probability investigations and computations can be adapted to the interests and mathematical maturity of upper elementary grade students. In simple investigations with spinners, dice, and coin, students keep records and discuss the results of their experiments. When children use a five-colored spinner (see photo), they find that the likelihood of getting a certain color is 1 in 5, $\frac{1}{5}$. With the spinner numbered 1–6 shown in the photo, an event such as having the spinner stop on 4 is 1 in 6, $\frac{1}{6}$. Students will know that chances of winning many popular board games are equal for each player when they understand the mathematical probabilities associated with the dice or spinners that control moves on the board.

Probability Investigations

Coins provide many opportunities for probability investigations. Students can put a coin in a soft plastic cup and shake it before dumping it onto a mat. For each coin event, or *trial*, the result is either a head or a tail. Children keep a tally of the number of heads and tails for 40 trials, as shown in Figure 20.3. For each flip the chances of a head or a tail are equal. Over the long run the number of heads and tails will be about equal, or close to 50-50 (50%-50%). In the unlikely event that they are not, children should con-

Courtesy of NASCO

Probability devices

sider the reasons. They should consider the question of whether the coin is a *fair* one. A coin, or any other device, is fair when the observed chances approximate the mathematical chances. If, however, a head on a coin occurs many more times than tails, the coin might be bent or nicked or made unfair in some other fashion. If that is not the case, does the way the coin is tossed contribute to the disparity? All possible reasons should be considered. In the companion website activity "Dice Data" students predict the results of rolling a single die 60 times and then do the rolling.

Heads 卌 卌 卌 |||
Tails 卌 卌 卌 卌 ||

Figure 20.3 Tally of coin flips

Older students work with more complex probability experiments. The work with a pair of dice in Activity 20.4 introduces them to the idea that different probabilities exist for events occurring in the same activity. The table here shows the possible sums for rolling a pair of dice.

	1	2	3	4	5	6
1	2	3	4	5	6	7
2	3	4	5	6	7	8
3	4	5	6	7	8	9
4	5	6	7	8	9	10
5	6	7	8	9	10	11
6	7	8	9	10	11	12

After building such a table, the teacher asks why 6, 7, and 8 have more occurrences than 2 and 3, or 11 and 12. Many children will claim that there are only three ways to roll a 7 because, for example, they perceive 6 + 1 and 1 + 6 as a single possibility. One reason they do so is that the commutative law for addition postulates that 6 + 1 = 1 + 6. Using two different colored dice can help children understand why 6 (red die) + 1 (green die) is different from 1 (red die) + 6 (green die).

An extension of this activity can be made by using three or four regular dice or by investigating results with pairs of tetrahedral and icosahedral dice (see the six dice at the top center of the photo on p. 529). Children should record data in tables as they work. As a further extension, students could compute the theoretical probability of rolling each sum and compare that number with the classroom results (empirical probability). In Activity 20.5 students mark a blank number cube for a board game they design.

Probability experiments can be varied by using different objects and by varying the number of trials. A coin-tossing experiment using one, two, three, four, and five coins leads to an interesting pattern as the number of outcomes increases. When one coin is tossed, only two possible outcomes can happen: heads or tails. When two coins are tossed, the outcomes can be two heads (HH), two tails (TT), or one head and one tail. However, because each coin can land independently, there are two ways to get one head and one tail, so there are four possible outcomes: TT, TH, HT, and HH. Thus the chance of tossing two coins and getting two tails (or two heads) is $\frac{1}{4}$, or 25%. With three coins, eight outcomes are possible: HHH, HHT, HTH, HTT, THH, THT, TTH, and TTT. The combinations for one, two, and three coins are shown in a triangular arrangement in Figure 20.4. After children have worked out combinations for one, two, and three coins, ask them to look for a pattern to see if they can predict the combinations for four coins. If they cannot, list combinations for four coins, enter their numbers into the triangle in Figure 20.4, and look for a pattern again. Soon the students will see that each number in a lower line is the sum of adjacent numbers above it in the previous row. For example, the 3 in row 3 is the sum of the two numbers above it in row 2 (1 and 2). Extend the pattern to 10 coins and see what happens to the number of possibilities.

The arrangement of numbers in Figure 20.4 is called Pascal's triangle, named after the 17th-

			1				
1 coin			1		1		H, T
2 coins		1		2		1	HH, HT, TH, TT
3 coins	1		3		3		1	HHH, HHT, HTH, THH, HTT, THT, TTH, TTT
4 coins			———————			
5 coins			———————			

Figure 20.4 Pascal's triangle

ACTIVITY 20.4 Tossing Dice

Level: Grades 4–6

Setting: Whole class

Objective: Students determine the probability of an event.

Materials: Two dice for each pair of children, tally sheet for each pair of children, pencils, centimeter or half-inch squared paper, marking pens, calculator, large sheet of 1-inch squared paper

- Students work in pairs. Give each team of children a pair of dice. The first task is to determine what sums are possible when two dice are rolled and the numbers are totaled. Have the children guess which of the sums will be more frequent or less frequent when rolling two dice. (Students with experience rolling one die often guess that all the numbers will have the same frequency.)

- The children roll the dice 50 times and tally each sum as it occurs. One child rolls the dice 25 times while the other records; then they exchange roles.

Tally sheet										
2	3	4	5	6	7	8	9	10	11	12

- When all pairs are finished and have counted tallies for each sum, discuss their results. Ask why some numbers came up more frequently than others. Consider the ways the dice can make 2 and the ways they can make 7. Ask if any pairs had one number come up more often than any middle-range numbers, say, 3 or 10. This provides an opportunity to discuss how small samples, such as 50 rolls of the dice, do not always produce the expected outcome.

- Each pair of children uses an Internet program, if available, to make a bar graph showing the results of their tosses. Have students make their graph on squared paper if an Internet program is not available.

- As a follow-up to the activity, have two children calculate the totals for each column for all the tally sheets and prepare a bar graph showing the class totals. Compare this graph with the students' graphs. Does the classroom graph align with the mathematical probabilities more closely than the students' graphs?

- Some computer programs can be used for a similar activity.

- The following tables and graphs show results of 100 and 500 "rolls" of dice with the program found at http://nces.ed.gov/nceskids/probability/.

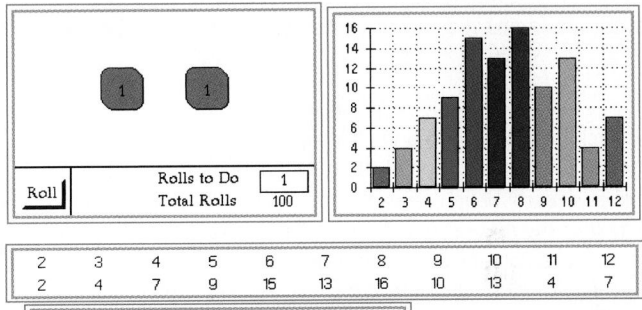

2	3	4	5	6	7	8	9	10	11	12
2	4	7	9	15	13	16	10	13	4	7

This table and graph show the number of times two dice stopped for each number during 100 rolls. Seven did not occur as often as I expected, because it was fewer than 6 and 8 and it tied 10. I expected it to be the most. Math Tools software was used for this activity.

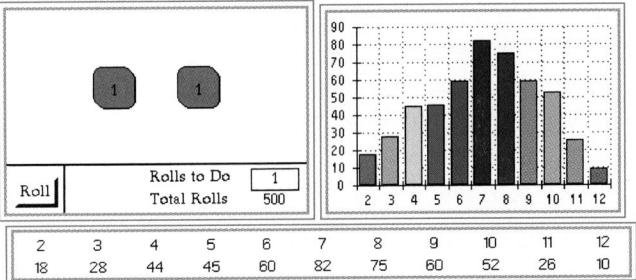

2	3	4	5	6	7	8	9	10	11	12
18	28	44	45	60	82	75	60	52	26	10

This table and graph show the results of rolling two dice 500 times. The graph shows that the number 7 came up more than any other number. It also shows that even with 500 rolls the numbers do not meet mathematical expectations because 8 came up 15 times more than 6 and mathematically they should be the same. Math Tools software was used for this activity.

century mathematician Blaise Pascal, who studied and wrote about it. You can create problem cards to guide students' investigation of many interesting questions based on Pascal's triangle. Here are some examples:

- What is the sum of each row of the triangle? Can you describe the sequence of numbers that includes each sum?

- When six coins are tossed, what is the probability of getting three heads and three tails? What percent of the possible outcomes is this?

- What is the probability of getting four heads and four tails when eight coins are tossed? What percent of the possible outcomes is this?

- Will the percent of possible outcomes for five heads and five tails when 10 coins are tossed be greater or less than the percent for four heads and four tails when 8 coins are tossed? Why do you think this is so?

- When you toss seven coins, what is the probability of getting three heads and four tails? What is the probability of getting four heads and three tails? Is each of these probabilities the same percent of the total outcomes? How do you explain this?

ⒺXERCISE

Complete Pascal's triangle to include tosses for 10 coins. Now answer the preceding questions. ●●●

French mathematician and philosopher Blaise Pascal (1623–1662) is considered one of the cofounders of probability theory. Pascal began his explorations into probability as the result of the request of a friend, Antoine Gombard. Gombard had a question about how to divide up the stakes of a dice game when the game was cut short. Pascal's exploration of his friend's query led him to write to another mathematician, Pierre de Fermat, and their correspondence established the principles of probability.

Pierre de Fermat (1601–1665), cofounder of probability theory with Pascal, was a solicitor for the French government by day and an amateur mathematician by night. But what a mathematician! He has been called Prince of the Amateurs because of his refusal to publish any of his mathematics discoveries; yet he had a hand in the development of probability, calculus, number theory, coordinate geometry, and plane geometry.

Combinations

Pascal's triangle is useful for determining all the possible combinations of feasible events in a probability situation. It is impossible to determine the probability of any event without determining all the conceivable combinations of possible events. Older students can find all possible combinations for an event by using a probability tree. The probability tree shown in Figure 20.5 was drawn by Sal, a fifth-grade student. The tree shows all the possible combinations of outfits that he can wear using the following articles of clothing: three pairs of pants (tan, gray, and black), three shirts (gray, tan, and white), and two pairs of shoes (black and tan). This probability tree shows 18 possible outfit combinations with these three articles of clothing. In his probability tree Sal has highlighted the single combination of clothing that will result in an outfit that is all tan. If Sal's little sister were to randomly select his clothing for a school day, there is a $\frac{1}{18}$ probability that he would be dressed in all tan. Students will also discover that the number of combinations can be expressed as a multiplicative relationship:

(number of pants choices) $\times$ (number of shoe choices) $\times$ (number of shirt choices) = number of different outfits

Students who are beginning their study of combinations in probability require much experience listing

---

ACTIVITY 20.5   Designer Number Cubes

Level: Grades 4–6

Setting: Small groups

Objective: Students design their own number cubes for a new board game.

Materials: Blank number cubes, colored markers, poster board

- Ask students what games they have played that use dice or number cubes. Discuss the chances of rolling a 3 with a single number cube. How does the chance of rolling a 3 compare to the chance of rolling a 6? a 1?

- Describe to students a board game that involves moving a game piece along a 25-square-long path. A few squares can contain commands such as "Move ahead," "Lose a turn," or "Move back." Each group will design a game board with a 25-square path from start to finish.

- The game will use a single designer number cube for moving the game piece. Each group will design a new number cube. Their designer cube will not show each number from 1 to 6 but will show some numbers more than once, and some numbers not at all. Each number cube must contain at least three numbers on the six faces, and no more than two numbers can have the same chance of coming up. Students might use different colors for each number.

- Students display their finished game boards to the class. They describe their number cube and show the chances of rolling each number represented on their number cube.

- Have groups exchange game boards and number cubes and play each other's games.

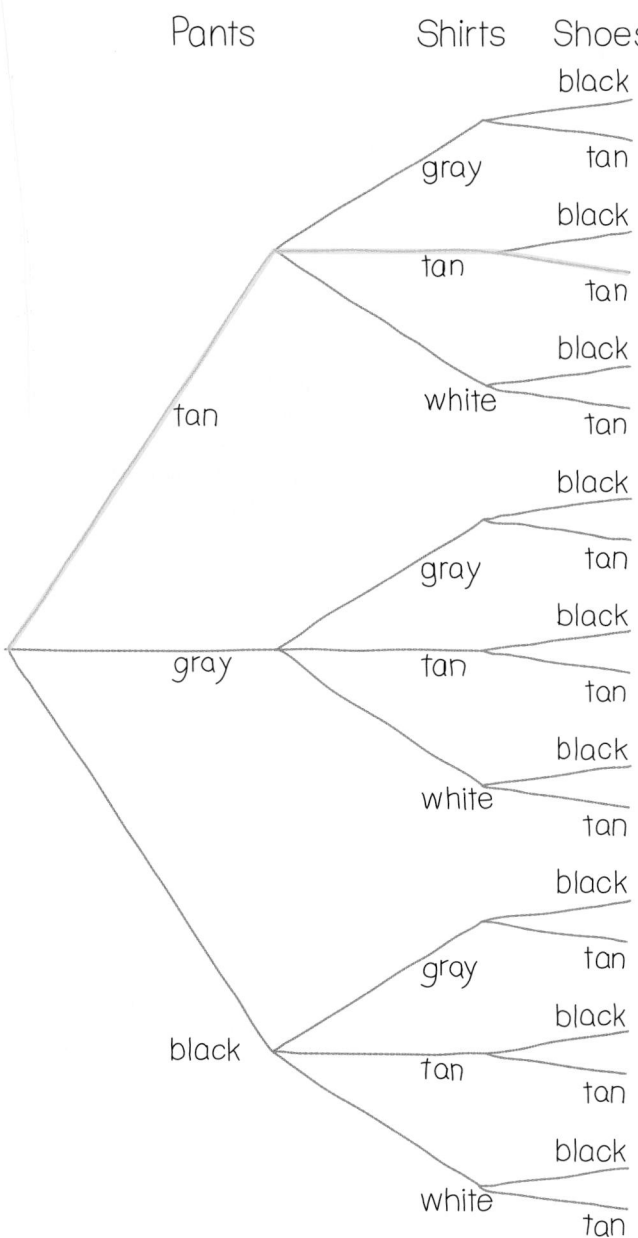

Pants   Shirts   Shoes

Figure 20.5 Student-drawn probability tree: Outfit combinations

combinations using a probability tree. Activity 20.6 asks students to use a probability tree to determine the total number of different breakfast meals that are possible from a fast-food restaurant.

MULTICULTURALCONNECTION

Although Pascal's triangle bears the name of Blaise Pascal, he was not the first to explore its properties. Chinese mathematician Chu Shih-Chieh wrote about the same triangle in 1303, more than 300 years before Pascal made his discovery of it. The triangle bears Pascal's name because he investigated its properties more deeply.

Eventually, middle school students learn how to compute combinations in various situations. They also study *permutations*, which are a type of combination in which the order of the individual items is important, such as the letters in a word. For example, consider the three letters C, A, and T. There is only a single combination with these three letters: C, A, and T (in any order). Six possible permutations can be formed with these same three letters. The probability tree in Figure 20.6 shows the six possibilities: CAT, CTA, ACT, ATC, TCA, and TAC.

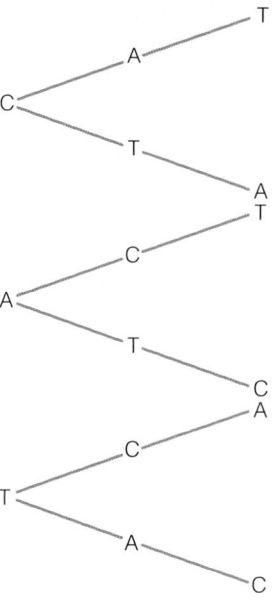

Figure 20.6 Probability tree: Permutations of CAT

Sampling

Sampling, another probability technique, involves choosing one or a few items from a larger group and drawing conclusions about the larger group based on the sample. Public opinion surveys, for example, are based on the opinions of sometimes fewer than 1,000 people. Because the survey is taken from a sample of people who are carefully selected to be representative of the entire country, such surveys are reasonably accurate representations of the opinions of the entire population. Children can use colored candies, marbles, beads, or blocks for sampling experiments.

Activity 20.7 describes a simple sampling process that can be used to estimate the colors of marbles in a bag or box. Activity 20.8 is a similar activity, in which students use a cumulative sampling strategy. They find that by combining the results of several independent samples, they can make a better estimate about the entire group. As with experimental probability results, the larger the sample, the better the resulting data are for making predictions.

Geometric Probability

In addition to dice, coins, and shoes, students can gather data from area relationships between geometric figures. Children have an intuitive understanding

ACTIVITY 20.6 Probability Tree (Representation)

Level: Grades 3–5

Setting: Groups of three students

Objective: Students build a probability tree to solve a real-life problem.

Materials: Pencil and paper, markers, poster board

- Relate to students that Henrietta's Hamburger Heaven has decided to offer breakfast meals. The plan is to have the following foods:
  - Three kinds of breakfast sandwiches: egg and cheese; ham, egg, and cheese; and bacon, egg, and cheese
  - Four types of breads: English muffin, bagel, croissant, and biscuit
  - Two drinks: coffee and orange juice

- Have groups select a reporter, a recorder, and a resident artist for the activity.

- Each group is to build a probability tree to display all these data and to answer the questions that follow.

- Once groups have designed a probability tree that they all agree is correct, have each group copy the tree onto a poster board.

- Groups are to use their probability tree to answer each of the questions and to explain how they used the tree to get their answers. Once all groups have completed the questions, have groups take turns with the questions and use their probability tree to explain their answers to the rest of the class.

1. You go to Henrietta's Hamburger Heaven every morning and eat a different breakfast combination. How many mornings would it be before you had the exact same breakfast again?

2. What is the chance that someone across the room eating breakfast has ordered the same combination that you ordered for breakfast?

3. Henrietta is thinking of adding tea as a beverage. If she does add tea to the breakfast menu, how many different breakfast combinations would there be?

4. The tea idea didn't work out. Instead of adding tea as a drink selection, Henrietta drops the tea and adds another bread: toast. Now how many breakfast combinations are there?

5. The toast idea didn't work either. Now Henrietta is going to add another sandwich: sausage, egg, and cheese. How many different breakfast combinations are there now?

6. Using the answers to the last four questions, explain how many different ice cream cones you could order from Iggy's Ice Cream Igloo. Iggy offers 12 flavors, plain or sugar cones, and nuts, sprinkles, or chocolate bits as a topping. You may make a new probability tree, or just part of one, to help you get the total number of different sundaes.

ACTIVITY 20.7 Sampling (Communication)

Level: Grades 4–6

Setting: Groups of four

Objective: Students conduct and explain a simple sampling investigation.

Materials: Bags of 100 plastic beads or chips of three or four different colors, one bag for each group of four students; record sheet for each group; pencils. Prepare two or three bags with the same number of beads or chips of each color and the rest with different numbers of beads or chips of each color.

- Use the roundtable cooperative plan. The children number off: 1, 2, 3, 4. Child 1 has the bag, and child 2 has the tally sheet and pencil. Child 1 draws an object from the bag, notes its color, and replaces it while child 2 makes a tally mark for its color on the record sheet.

- Drawing and tallying, the children rotate through the group after each draw until 50 draws have been made.

Tally sheet		
Color of marbles	Count	Total
Blue	ꜰꜰꜰ ꜰꜰꜰ IIII	14
Red	ꜰꜰꜰ ꜰꜰꜰ II	12
Yellow	ꜰꜰꜰ ꜰꜰꜰ ꜰꜰꜰ ꜰꜰꜰ IIII	24

- After 50 draws, have the students study the total for each color and guess how many of each color are in the bag. Remember, there are 100 objects in the bag!

- Use the totals to create percentages: 14 blue beads in 50 draws $= \frac{14}{50} = 28\%$, or 28 blue beads of 100; 12 red beads in 50 draws $= \frac{12}{50} = 24\%$, or 24 red beads in 100; 24 yellow beads in 50 draws $= \frac{24}{50} = 48\%$, or 48 yellow beads in 100.

- Share results of the draws. Do any of the groups believe that they may have the same number of beads or chips of each color in the bag? Do they believe that each bag has a different number of beads or chips of each color?

- Have children remove and count each color of bead or chip. How accurate were the results of the samplings? Did any bags contain the same number beads or chips of each color? If so, were they the same ones predicted during the earlier discussion? Are the children satisfied that drawing 50 objects enabled them to make accurate predictions?

To extend the activity, tell children to take a bag home to repeat the process by drawing more than 50 or fewer than 50 objects and tallying the results. Discuss whether the accuracy decreases when fewer objects are drawn. Does it increase when more are drawn? Does there appear to be a number beyond which accuracy does not increase?

ACTIVITY 20.8 Multiple Drawing Sampling

Level: Grades 5 and 6

Setting: Groups of four

Objective: Students use multiple drawings to estimate the contents of bags.

Materials: Bag with 100 plastic beads of four colors, two record sheets for each team, calculators

Mixed beads

- Tell the children that each bag contains 100 beads of four different colors. Their task is to estimate the number of each color. They will draw five beads at a time without looking and return the beads after each draw. Children

work in a roundtable format. Child 1 has a bag, child 2 has a record sheet, child 3 has a calculator, and child 4 has a record sheet. Child 1 draws five objects, and child 2 writes the number of each color on a record sheet. Child 3 uses the calculator to determine the percent that each color is of the total, and child 4 writes the percent on a record sheet.

- Functions rotate until each child has performed each role twice. After each draw, students calculate a running total for each color and use it to estimate the fraction for each color of bead.

	Red	Green	Black	Yellow
TRIAL 1	3	1	0	1
TRIAL 1 %	$3/5 = 60\%$	$1/5 = 20\%$	0%	$1/5 = 20\%$
TRIAL 2	2	2	1	0
CUMULATIVE %	$5/10 = 50\%$	$3/10 = 30\%$	$1/10 = 10\%$	$1/10 = 10\%$
TRIAL 3	3	0	1	1
CUMULATIVE %	$8/15 = 53\%$	$3/15 = 20\%$	$2/15 = 13\%$	$2/15 = 13\%$
TRIAL 4				

- After five beads have been drawn four times, each team estimates the number of beads and the percent of each color.

- Repeat the process to make a total of eight drawings, and again estimate the number and percent of each color.

- Count the actual objects to check the estimates. Follow up with a discussion similar to the one described in Activity 20.7.

of targets and bull's-eyes. The bull's-eye is the smallest part of the target and carries the highest number of points. The largest parts of a target (the easiest to hit) carry the fewest points.

Spinners that children use to play board games are an example of geometric probability. In the spinner pictured in Figure 20.7a, all the numbers have an equal chance of coming up because each number has a region that is equal in size to all the other individual regions. The spinners in Figures 20.7b and 20.7c show that 1 will come up twice as often as 2, a relationship that could be predicted by visual inspection or by gathering data from a number of spins. In Figure 20.7b the area of region 1 is $\frac{1}{4}$ of the area of the spinner template, and the area of region 2 is $\frac{1}{8}$ of the template. In Figure 20.7d the area marked 1 is $\frac{1}{4}$ the area of the template, and the area marked 2 is $\frac{1}{8}$

of the template. In both cases the area marked 1 is twice as large as the area marked 2. With a sufficient number of spins, this 2:1 ratio would be approached with experimental data. Activity 20.9 extends the concept of geometric probability on a spinner by having students design their own spinner templates. In Activity 20.10 students use an interactive activity on the Internet to explore probability on a spinner.

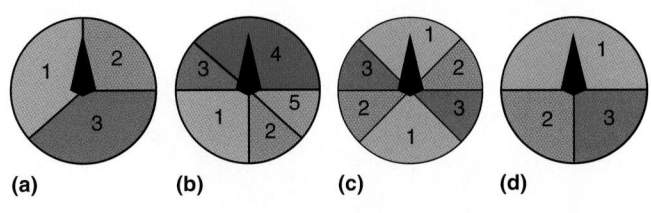

(a)   (b)   (c)   (d)

Figure 20.7 Probability spinners

ACTIVITY 20.9 Spinner Probability

Level: Grades 4–6

Setting: Small groups

Objective: Students design their own templates for spinners, predict probabilities, and test their predictions.

Materials: Spinners with blank templates, paper and colored pencils

- Show students a spinner from a board game (or from a game you have designed) with all numbers having an equal chance of coming up (see Figure 20.7a).

- Have students discuss why this is a fair spinner. Probe for students to recognize that equal areas on the spinner have an equal chance of coming up.

- Challenge students to design two different spinner templates on which the numbers (or colors) do not have an

equal chance of coming up. They should use three to six numbers or colors for the spinner template.

- Once a group draws a new spinner template, have them predict how often the spinner will land on each number or color in 100 spins. Each group should build identical templates of their spinner for each person in the group. Then the group should make 100 spins and collect data to verify their predictions for the template.

- Have groups take turns displaying their templates to the class. Each group can challenge classmates to predict about how often each number or color will come up in the 100 spins, based on visual inspection of the spinner.

Students can make their own spinner with a paper clip. Students can use a pencil to secure one end of the paper clip spinner and spin the paper clip to replicate a spinner. In Chapter 14 the black-line masters that show fraction circles can also be used as templates for spinners.

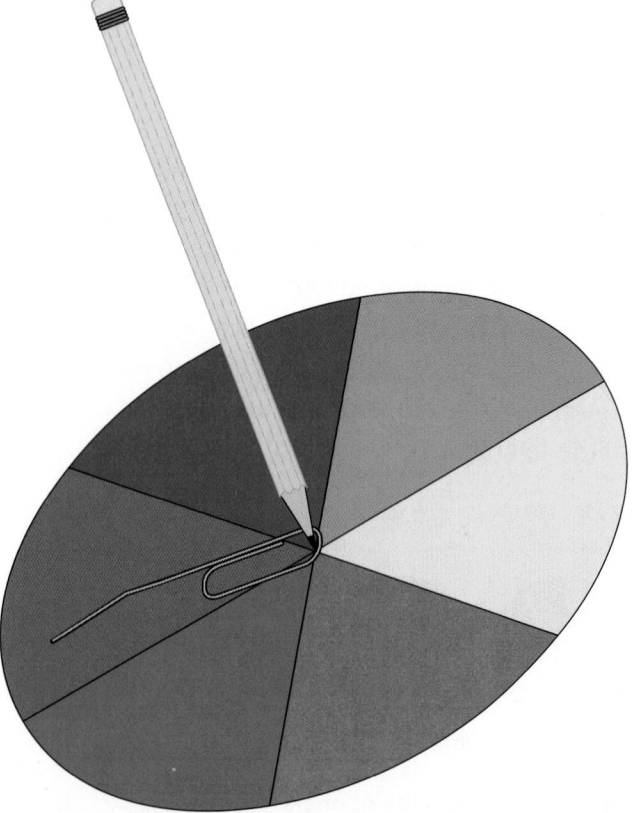

EXERCISE

Describe the probabilities shown in Figure 20.7. ●●●

Expected Value

Expected value is a topic that can have much appeal to older children. They may be familiar with the television show *Wheel of Fortune* or carnival games of chance that use a spinning wheel. Once students have ample experiences designing spinners for probability explorations, they are able to use the principles of probability to explore the expected value of specific spinners. Consider the spinner shown here.

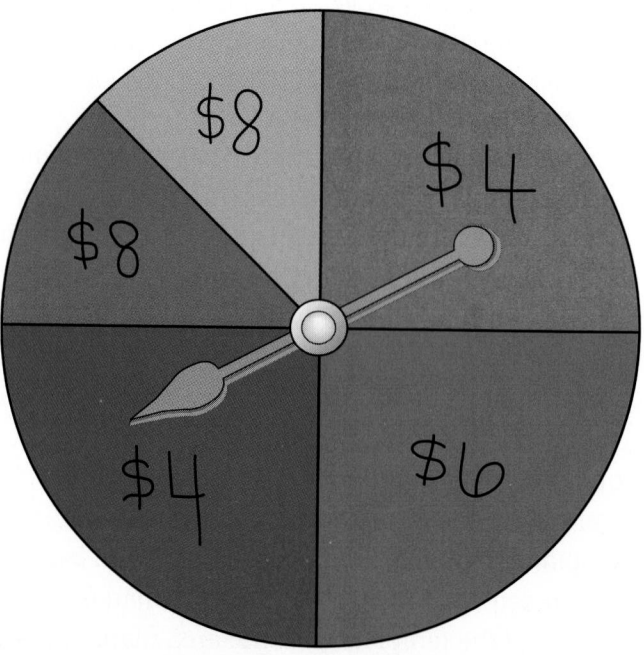

ACTIVITY 20.10 Design Your Own Spinner (Internet Activity)

Level: Grades 5 and 6

Setting: Groups of three students

Objective: Students design a spinner according to predetermined probabilities.

Materials: Internet access

- Go to http://nlvm.usu.edu/en/nav/vlibrary.html and follow the links to Spinners in 3–5 Data and Probability.
- Demonstrate how to change the spinner by increasing or decreasing the share of each color and by increasing and decreasing the number of colors in the spinner.
- Show how to "spin" the spinner and record the results.

- Ask students to design a spinner with three colors so that the spinner has an equal probability of landing on each color.
- Check on each group's design, and then have students check their spinner design by recording the data for 30 spins.
- Discuss the role of the Law of Large Numbers in the data that result. (These data will not always show a 10-10-10 result.) Combine the data from all groups to obtain an experimental result that is closer to the theoretical prediction of $\frac{1}{3}$ for each color.

This spinner will pay out to the player the amounts shown in each sector of the spinner. Expected value concepts enable students to determine the expected payout for the spinner. Naturally any prediction such as this assumes a large number of spins, so the Law of Large Numbers is a factor in making any prediction. It is impossible to predict the result of a single spin. Rather, the probabilities shown here specify the tendency of the spinner for many spins.

For this spinner the chance of landing on each sector is

$$\$4 = \frac{1}{2} \qquad \$6 = \frac{1}{4} \qquad \$8 = \frac{1}{8}$$

The probability of landing in each sector can be combined with the posted winnings for each sector to determine the expected value or expected winnings for playing a game of chance with this spinner:

$$(\frac{1}{2} \times \$4) + (\frac{1}{4} \times \$6) + (\frac{1}{8} \times \$8) + (\frac{1}{8} \times \$8)$$
$$= \$2 + \$1.50 + \$1.00 + \$1.00$$
$$= \$5.50$$

In the long run, with many spins, the expected value or winnings per spin is $5.50. Thus, if a charitable organization were to hold a fundraiser and include a game using this spinner to raise funds for their charity, the price of each spin would have to exceed $5.50. Any lower price to play would result in the charity paying out more money than the game earns. A charge of $5.50 to play would mean that the game would break even in the long run and not earn any funds. So, if the organization charges at least

$6.00 to play, they will likely raise some funds using this spinner.

Students can explore expected value using spinners that they have produced from earlier activities. They can also design original spinners with different payouts for each sector and determine the break-even price to use the spinner in a game of chance. Students might then test their findings by recording the results of spinning their spinner. Again, the Law of Large Numbers requires that students collect data from a large number of spins. In this case perhaps 50 spins will produce enough data to support the students' computations.

Both Activities 20.9 and 20.10 used spinners to develop probability concepts. In Activity 20.9 students built their own spinners, and in Activity 20.10 students used an Internet program to simulate using a spinner. Activity 20.11 is an assessment activity that probes students' understanding of probability in a geometric setting. Note that the dimensions of the figures in the game board are not given. We suggest making a game board that resembles the game board that is shown but does not duplicate it. One of the tasks of the activity is to assign an appropriate number of points according to the probability of landing a penny in each figure. With no specific dimensions given for any of the figures, students must use empirical probability to assign points to each figure. (In this case the chances of a penny landing anywhere on the target is totally random, in contrast to a game of darts or pitching pennies, in which players aim for one particular region of the target.) As in all the other probability activities, the chance

Research for the Classroom

Research has confirmed the persistence of characteristics similar to the gambler's fallacy in children who are learning probability principles (e.g., Watson & Moritz, 1999; Shaughnessy, 1992, pp. 470–472). Individuals who believe the gambler's fallacy predict that a probability event will be influenced by past events—that the coin or slot machine has a memory. For example, if a coin has come up heads 10 times in a row, a believer in the gambler's fallacy will reason that the next flip of the coin has to come up tails because "tails is due." This reasoning is similar to that of individuals who play a single slot machine for a large number of tries, believing that eventually the machine has to pay out. Research with students drawing colored balls out of a bag revealed that they expected a 50-50 distribution of the two colors. They persisted in their belief through many trials of drawing the balls out of the bag (and then replacing them), anticipating that the next draw and subsequent draws would equalize the colors they had already drawn, as if the marbles or the bag had a memory of the preceding events.

Related research has found that students will make predictions of the likelihood of an event based on how common the event is to them or how easily the event can be duplicated or simulated (Shaughnessy, 2003). For example, when asked whether there was a greater number of two-person groups or eight-person groups possible out of a total of ten people, students responded that more two-person groups were possible, although this is untrue by a large factor. The reason is that these students could easily compose many different two-person groups in a short time compared to the time needed to construct eight-person groups. Thus they persisted in their conclusion that more two-person groups would be possible. Children will predict that they will select their favorite color marble out of a bag, even if there are few of those marbles compared to the other colors.

These research results and many others underscore the effects of personal experiences and beliefs that result in misconceptions. Students will bring to school experiences with specific events, ranging from board games with dice and spinners to personal preferences regarding colors. These outside influences will prejudice their thinking about probability. Some students may even believe that God or their mental powers will influence a coin flip or a roll of the dice. The classroom teacher must be aware of these factors and work to help students leave their misconceptions behind.

ACTIVITY 20.11   Geometric Probability (Assessment Activity)

Level: Grades 3–5

The game board you see here is designed for tossing pennies. Here are the rules for playing the game.

- If the penny lands off the game board, it doesn't count, and the player gets another turn.
- If the penny lands on the board but misses the figures, the player still scores 1 point.

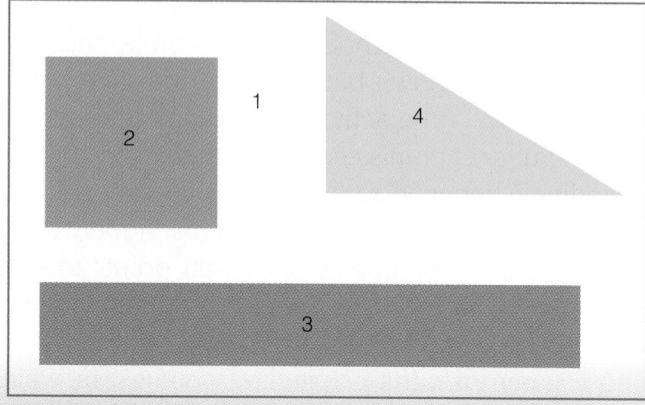

Just one thing: A player has to pick up the penny with his or her eyes closed and then drop it on the game board. Thus a player cannot really aim for any part of the board. Use what you know about areas and probability to give the chance of landing on each part of the game board.

1. What are the chances that the penny will land in the rectangle? in the square? in the triangle? on the game board but not in any figure?

2. Are the points on the game board OK? Do you think that the points should be different to make the game board fairer? How would you change the game board, and why?

3. Suppose that you designed a new game board with a circle, square, and triangle. What would be true about the size of these three figures if the chances of dropping a penny in each of them were equal?

of an individual event occurring is totally random. If events were not totally random, they could not be predicted over the long run by theoretical probability and the results would not be effective for predicting future results unless the same nonrandom factors, such as aiming at a particular part of the target, were reproduced exactly.

Simulations

Simulations are used to determine the probability of an event when there are no data from previous events, it is not possible to gather experimental data of the event, or the theoretical probability is impossible to compute. Simulations must be constructed carefully so that the data will properly represent the actual event. Activity 20.12 describes a simulation activity for students. In this simulation rolling a single number cube represents finding toy prizes in random boxes of cereal.

> Probability simulations with dice or similar manipulatives that are also used for games of chance are called the Monte Carlo method, after the famous Casino de Monte Carlo in Monaco. Simulations were first used by physicists working on the Manhattan Project during World War II. The simulations were used to develop shields and dampers for nuclear bombs and reactors, something that could not be done by direct experimentation.

ACTIVITY 20.12   A Probability Simulation (Connections)

Level: Grades 3–5

Setting: Small groups

Objective: Students conduct a simulation to explore the probability of a real-life situation.

Materials: One number cube per student

- Describe to students how and why simulations are used to determine the chance of an event happening. Stress that simulations are sometimes necessary because it is impossible to gather experimental data from the event to determine the probabilities involved.

- Ask students what prizes or toys they have collected from cereal boxes or fast food meal packs. Probe for students to tell how many different individual figures or toys there were in a particular collection they mention.

- Have students select a reporter and a recorder for their group.

- Describe to students a promotion for a new cereal, Breakfast Bash. The Breakfast Bash manufacturers have put one of six different action figures in each cereal box: Handy José, Sharp Simone, Mighty Miguel, Lucky Luisa, Super Sam, and Crafty Crissy. Ask students to estimate in their groups about how many boxes of cereal they would have to buy to be likely to collect all six action figures.

- Relate that one way to find out would be if they all bought many boxes of cereal and recorded the data. Have students discuss why that strategy is impractical.

- Because it is impractical to collect the experimental data, explain to students that using a number cube can replace actually buying boxes of cereal.

- Ask students what it is about a single number cube that relates to the problem of deciding how many boxes of cereal to buy in order to collect all six action figures. (Answer: There are six action figures and six numbers on the faces of the number cube.)

- As a class, assign one number from the number cube to each action figure. Be sure that each group's recorder writes out which figure each number represents for the group to use as a reference. Because each number represents an action figure, one roll of the number cube can represent opening a box of cereal. Whatever number comes up will represent the specific action figure in that box.

- Have each student roll a number cube until each number on the cube has come up. Be sure that each student records the results of each roll, using tally marks in a table like the one shown here. When all the numbers have come up, students should count the number of times they rolled the number cube.

1	2	3	4	5	6

- Have the group reporter tell the group's results, and write the results on the board. Ask students to think of the number of rolls that seems to best represent the overall results for the class. Is it the mean, median, or mode of the data? Ask students how to evaluate outliers such as 7 rolls or 32 rolls.

- Ask students about the role of the Law of Large Numbers in this simulation. One classroom set of data is not really sufficient to make a prediction about the number of boxes. More data are needed.

Take-Home Activities

This take-home project involves sampling data to predict how many minutes of commercials run in an hour of television time. Students will need a television and VCR to complete this project. If some students in the class do not have access to a VCR or digital video recorder at home, they might work with a student who has a VCR or complete the project in school using a tape you have made.

Dear Parents,

Your daughter/son will be using a television and VCR to conduct a probability experiment. They will record one hour of evening television and then analyze the taped material. Their data findings will be combined with data from other students in the class to predict the amount of commercial content in a typical hour of network television. This will help them to understand how sampling is used in mathematics to make predictions.

Analyze the recorded material with your child. Have them explain what they are doing and how the data they record will be used.

If I can answer any questions, please contact me at school.

1. Have your child record one hour of any network television station. Be sure your hour runs during the evening, between 5 and 11.

2. Have your child start the program from the beginning, and then press fast forward. After a short time, your child should stop the tape and note whether there is a commercial or a program playing.

3. Have your child press fast forward again and again stop the tape. What is playing now, a commercial or a show?

4. Your child should repeat this process 30 times. Help your child keep a careful record of commercials and programs that are playing at each stop. If the program runs out, your child can move back to the beginning and continue the process.

5. With your child, use the data results to predict how many minutes out of the 60 minutes are commercials.

6. Time how long the commercials actually last in the hour you taped.

7. Compare your prediction to the actual length of commercial time.

8. Have your child bring the data to class on Wednesday. We will combine data to determine what is a reasonable estimate of commercial time in an hour of typical network evening television.

9. Be sure your child reports back to you the results of the class data and analysis.

Summary

Younger children first learn about probability when they describe real-life events as impossible or certain, likely or unlikely. Older children conduct probability experiments to develop important problem-solving skills and an understanding of chance. They perform experiments, record and organize data, examine data for patterns, establish numerical odds, and make predictions from their observations.

Probabilities are derived from analysis of previous events and from mathematical sources. Historical probability is based on accumulated data that pertain to particular events, such as rainfall or appliance reliability. Mathematical probability deals with the mathematics of chance, such as flipping coins and rolling dice. Children's work with probability is largely exploratory; formal instruction may be limited to mature students in the upper elementary grades. However, a teacher models correct terminology so that children can develop a vocabulary about probability.

Study Questions and Activities

1. Have a roommate or family member make and give you a collection of objects in a bag or box similar to one of the collections in Activity 14.7. Use the method explained in Activity 14.7 to determine the characteristics of the set of objects. Compare your predictions with the actual objects in the bag or box.

2. Examine the local or state lottery. Find out the chances of winning the grand prize. How many tickets would you have to purchase to be assured of having a 50% chance of winning?

3. Explain why one mathematician has called lotteries "a tax on people who do not understand mathematics."

4. Monitor the time it takes you to brush your teeth for the next few days. Use the data to predict how long you will need to brush your teeth the next time you brush.

5. Some reports suggest that the chance of dying from a bee sting in the United States is greater than the chance of dying from a snakebite. Does this seem reasonable to you? How are such probabilities determined?

6. There is a 60% chance of rain tonight. Discuss with a classmate whether you would still plan on going to an outdoor concert.

   Praxis (http://www.ets.org/praxis/) A two-sided coin is unfairly weighted so that when it is tossed, the probability that heads will result is twice the probability that tails will result. If the coin is to be tossed three separate times, what is the probability that tails will result on exactly two of the tosses?

   a. $\frac{2}{9}$

   b. $\frac{3}{8}$

   c. $\frac{4}{9}$

   d. $\frac{2}{3}$

   NAEP (http://nces.ed.gov/nationsreportcard/) There are 15 girls and 11 boys in a mathematics class. If a student is selected at random to run an errand, what is the probability that a boy will be selected?

   a. $\frac{4}{26}$

   b. $\frac{11}{26}$

   c. $\frac{15}{26}$

   d. $\frac{11}{15}$

   e. $\frac{15}{11}$

   TIMSS (http://nces.ed.gov/timss/) In a school there were 1,200 students (boys and girls). A sample of 100 students was selected at random, and 45 boys were found in the sample. Which of these is most likely to be the number of boys in the school?

   a. 430

   b. 500

   c. 540

   d. 600

Using Children's Literature

Holtzman, Caren. (1997). *No fair!* New York: Scholastic. (Grades 2–4)

Probability as it relates to fairness is the theme of this book. Two central characters, David and Kristy, play games against each other. As they play, several issues arise. Who gets to choose the game? Do they each have a fair chance of winning? The story examines probability in the context of fair games.

Cushman, Jean. (1991). *Do you wanna bet? Your chance to find out about probability.* New York: Clarion. (Grades 4–6)

This book is a collection of problem situations that involve probability. Probability with coins, playing cards, the weather, and sampling are some of the ideas in the problem stories. A changing cast of characters is confronted with a problem to solve, the answer to which is found by the principles of probability (e.g., Given a 60% chance of rain tomorrow, should the friends still plan a hike for the next day?). The solution for each story problem immediately follows the story presentation in the text and is explained at the same level as the story itself. This book could almost serve as a self-tutorial in basic probability principles.

Teacher's Resources

Bright, G., Frierson, D., Tarr, J., & Thomas, C. (2003). *Navigating through probability in grades 6–8*. Reston, VA: National Council of Teachers of Mathematics.

Burrill, G., & Elliot, P. (Eds.). (2006). *Thinking and reasoning with data and chance: Sixty-eighth yearbook*. Reston, VA: National Council of Teachers of Mathematics.

Carter, Rick. (1996). *Chance, statistics, and graphs: Handling data*. Reston, VA: National Council of Teachers of Mathematics.

Chapin, Suzanne, Koizol, Alice, MacPherson, Jennifer, & Rezba, Carol. (2003). *Navigating through data analysis and probability in grades 3–5*. Reston, VA: National Council of Teachers of Mathematics.

Cuomo, Celia. (1993). *In all probability: Investigations in probability and statistics—Teachers guide, grades 3–6*. Berkeley: University of California Press.

Peterson, Ivars. (1998). *The jungles of randomness: A mathematical safari*. New York: Wiley.

Sheffield, Linda, Cavanaugh, Mary, Dacey, Linda, Findell, Carol, Greenes, Carole, & Small, Marian. (2002). *Navigating through data analysis and probability in prekindergarten–grade 2*. Reston, VA: National Council of Teachers of Mathematics.

Weaver, Jefferson Hale. (2001). *What are the odds? The chances of extraordinary events in everyday life*. Amherst, NY: Prometheus Books.

Children's Bookshelf

Barrett, Judi. (1978). *Cloudy with a chance of meatballs*. New York: Atheneum. (Grades 4–7)

Burns, Marilyn. (1975). *The I hate mathematics book*. Boston: Little, Brown. (Grades 5–8)

Cushman, Jean. (1991). *Do you wanna bet? Your chance to find out about probability*. New York: Clarion. (Grades 4–7)

Franco, Betsy, & Salermo, Steven. (2004). *Counting our way to the 100h day*. New York: Simon & Schuster. (Grades K–3)

Holtzman, Caren. (1997). *No fair*! New York: Scholastic. (Grades 2–4)

Morgan, Rowland. (1997). *In the next three seconds*. New York: Lodestar. (Grades 3–8)

Technology Resources

Computer Software

We have used two computer software programs from the Internet in this chapter:
http://www2.whidbey.net/ohmsmith/webwork/javascript/diceroll.htm and http://nces.ed.gov/nceskids/probability/.

There are other Internet sites for probability activities listed in this section. Some websites provide data tables along with the experiments, and some also build graphs to display the resulting data.

Internet Sites

For coin flipping simulations see:

http://www.shodor.org/interactivate/activities/chances/index.html

http://www2.whidbey.net/ohmsmath/webwork/javascript/cointoss.htm

For adjustable spinners and dice simulations see:

http://www.shodor.org/interactivate/activities/spinner/index.html

http://www2.whidbey.net/ohmsmath/webwork/javascript/spinner.htm

http://nlvm.usu.edu/en/nav/vlibrary.html

A virtual representation of the cereal prize simulation (Activity 20.12) can be found at
http://www.mste.uiuc.edu/users/reese/cereal/default.html.

Three Internet sites that enable students to use geometry contexts to solve probability problems are:

http://www.explorelearning.com/index.cfm?method=cResource.dspResourcesForCourse&CourseID=233

http://www.mste.uiuc.edu/activity/estpi/

http://www.mste.uiuc.edu/activity/rocket/

Internet Game

The game Fish Tank, available at **http://www.bbc.co.uk/education/mathsfile/**, challenges students to move red and yellow fish in and out of an aquarium to match the given probabilities of randomly capturing a red fish. The game has three levels of difficulty and sound effects to heighten children's interest. The sound can be turned off for children who become distracted.

For Further Reading

Abaugh, F., Scholten, C., & Essex, K. (2001). Data in the middle grades: A probability web quest. *Mathematics Teaching in the Middle School* 7(2), 90–95.

In this article Abaugh and colleagues describe how to use Internet-based materials and applets to introduce principles of probability.

Aspinwall, L., & Shaw, K. (2000). Enriching students' mathematical intuitions with probability games and tree diagrams. *Mathematics Teaching in the Middle School* 6(4), 214–220.

Aspinwall and Shaw present several games for students to explore using tree diagrams in order to build students' intuitions in probability.

Coffey, David, & Richardson, Mary. (2005). Rethinking fair games. *Mathematics Teaching in the Middle School* 10(6), 298–303.

Coffey and Richardson examine the fairness of a common matching game and use a probability tree to determine the game's fairness.

Ewbank, W., & Ginter, J. (2002). Probability on a budget. *Mathematics Teaching in the Middle School* 7(7), 280–283.

Ewbank and Ginter present several exploration lesson plans designed to help students understand probability. The experiments involve cheaply made manipulatives and are easily incorporated into a middle school classroom.

Frykholm, Jeffrey. (2001). Eenie, meenie, minie, moe . . . Building on intuitive notions of chance. *Teaching Children Mathematics* 8(2), 112–115.

Frykholm summarizes research on probability in the early grades, offers several activities in probability for younger children, and suggests some potential topics in probability for action research.

Nicholson, Cynthia. (2005). Is chance fair? One student's thoughts on probability. *Teaching Children Mathematics* 11, 83–89.

Nicholson describes students' typical misconceptions about probability as revealed in the thinking of one fifth-grade student.

Penner, Elizabeth, & Lehrer, Richard. (2000). The shape of fairness. *Teaching Children Mathematics* 7(4), 210–214.

Penner and Lehrer describe a project in which first- and second-graders design a model for a fair game of chance using experimentation and revisions to achieve a fair model.

Phillips-Bey, Carol. (2004). TI-73 calculator activities. *Mathematics Teaching in the Middle School* 9(9), 500–508.

Phillips-Bey describes how to use the technology of the TI-73 calculator to simulate rolling dice. The results of the simulation are then used to determine the fairness of various dice games.

Tarr, James. (2002). Providing opportunity to learn probability concepts. *Teaching Children Mathematics* 8(8), 482–487.

This article provides an overview of the NCTM standards for probability for grades K–2 and 3–5, including connections to other mathematics topics.

Weist, L., & Quinn, R. (1999). Exploring probability through an even-odds dice game. *Mathematics Teaching in the Middle School* 4(6), 358–362.

In this article Weist and Quinn describe probability explorations using several types of dice. Students develop game strategies based on probability principles and the data they generate.

Appendix A
NCTM Table of Standards and Expectations

Number and Operations

Standard

Instructional programs from prekindergarten through grade 12 should enable all students to—

Understand numbers, ways of representing numbers, relationships among numbers, and number systems

Understand meanings of operations and how they relate to one another

Compute fluently and make reasonable estimates

Pre-K–2

Expectations:

In prekindergarten through grade 2 all students should—

- count with understanding and recognize "how many" in sets of objects;
- use multiple models to develop initial understandings of place value and the base-ten number system;
- develop understanding of the relative position and magnitude of whole numbers and of ordinal and cardinal numbers and their connections;
- develop a sense of whole numbers and represent and use them in flexible ways, including relating, composing, and decomposing numbers;
- connect number words and numerals to the quantities they represent, using various physical models and representations;
- understand and represent commonly used fractions, such as $\frac{1}{4}$, $\frac{1}{3}$, and $\frac{1}{2}$.

- understand various meanings of addition and subtraction of whole numbers and the relationship between the two operations;
- understand the effects of adding and subtracting whole numbers;
- understand situations that entail multiplication and division, such as equal groupings of objects and sharing equally.

- develop and use strategies for whole-number computations, with a focus on addition and subtraction;
- develop fluency with basic number combinations for addition and subtraction;
- use a variety of methods and tools to compute, including objects, mental computation, estimation, paper and pencil, and calculators.

Grades 3–5

Expectations:

In grades 3–5 all students should—

- understand the place-value structure of the base-ten number system and be able to represent and compare whole numbers and decimals;
- recognize equivalent representations for the same number and generate them by decomposing and composing numbers;
- develop understanding of fractions as parts of unit wholes, as parts of a collection, as locations on number lines, and as divisions of whole numbers;
- use models, benchmarks, and equivalent forms to judge the size of fractions;
- recognize and generate equivalent forms of commonly used fractions, decimals, and percents;
- explore numbers less than 0 by extending the number line and through familiar applications;
- describe classes of numbers according to characteristics such as the nature of their factors.

- understand various meanings of multiplication and division;
- understand the effects of multiplying and dividing whole numbers;
- identify and use relationships between operations, such as division as the inverse of multiplication, to solve problems;
- understand and use properties of operations, such as the distributivity of multiplication over addition.

- develop fluency with basic number combinations for multiplication and division and use these combinations to mentally compute related problems, such as 30 × 50;
- develop fluency in adding, subtracting, multiplying, and dividing whole numbers;
- develop and use strategies to estimate the results of whole-number computations and to judge the reasonableness of such results;
- develop and use strategies to estimate computations involving fractions and decimals in situations relevant to students' experience;
- use visual models, benchmarks, and equivalent forms to add and subtract commonly used fractions and decimals;
- select appropriate methods and tools for computing with whole numbers from among mental computation, estimation, calculators, and paper and pencil according to the context and nature of the computation and use the selected method or tools.

Number and Operations

Standard

Grades 6–8

Grades 9–12

Instructional programs from prekindergarten through grade 12 should enable all students to—

Expectations:

In grades 6–8 all students should—

Expectations:

In grades 9–12 all students should—

Understand numbers, ways of representing numbers, relationships among numbers, and number systems

- work flexibly with fractions, decimals, and percents to solve problems;
- compare and order fractions, decimals, and percents efficiently and find their approximate locations on a number line;
- develop meaning for percents greater than 100 and less than 1;
- understand and use ratios and proportions to represent quantitative relationships;
- develop an understanding of large numbers and recognize and appropriately use exponential, scientific, and calculator notation;
- use factors, multiples, prime factorization, and relatively prime numbers to solve problems;
- develop meaning for integers and represent and compare quantities with them.

- develop a deeper understanding of very large and very small numbers and of various representations of them;
- compare and contrast the properties of numbers and number systems, including the rational and real numbers, and understand complex numbers as solutions to quadratic equations that do not have real solutions;
- understand vectors and matrices as systems that have some of the properties of the real-number system;
- use number-theory arguments to justify relationships involving whole numbers.

Understand meanings of operations and how they relate to one another

- understand the meaning and effects of arithmetic operations with fractions, decimals, and integers;
- use the associative and commutative properties of addition and multiplication and the distributive property of multiplication over addition to simplify computations with integers, fractions, and decimals;
- understand and use the inverse relationships of addition and subtraction, multiplication and division, and squaring and finding square roots to simplify computations and solve problems.

- judge the effects of such operations as multiplication, division, and computing powers and roots on the magnitudes of quantities;
- develop an understanding of properties of, and representations for, the addition and multiplication of vectors and matrices;
- develop an understanding of permutations and combinations as counting techniques.

Compute fluently and make reasonable estimates

- select appropriate methods and tools for computing with fractions and decimals from among mental computation, estimation, calculators or computers, and paper and pencil, depending on the situation, and apply the selected methods;
- develop and analyze algorithms for computing with fractions, decimals, and integers and develop fluency in their use;
- develop and use strategies to estimate the results of rational-number computations and judge the reasonableness of the results;
- develop, analyze, and explain methods for solving problems involving proportions, such as scaling and finding equivalent ratios.

- develop fluency in operations with real numbers, vectors, and matrices, using mental computation or paper-and-pencil calculations for simple cases and technology for more-complicated cases;
- judge the reasonableness of numerical computations and their result.

Algebra

Standard

Instructional programs from prekindergarten through grade 12 should enable all students to—	Pre-K–2	Grades 3–5
	Expectations: In prekindergarten through grade 2 all students should—	**Expectations:** In grades 3–5 all students should—
Understand patterns, relations, and functions	■ sort, classify, and order objects by size, number, and other properties; ■ recognize, describe, and extend patterns such as sequences of sounds and shapes or simple numeric patterns and translate from one representation to another; ■ analyze how both repeating and growing patterns are generated.	■ describe, extend, and make generalizations about geometric and numeric patterns; ■ represent and analyze patterns and functions, using words, tables, and graphs.
Represent and analyze mathematical situations and structures using algebraic symbols	■ illustrate general principles and properties of operations, such as commutativity, using specific numbers; ■ use concrete, pictorial, and verbal representations to develop an understanding of invented and conventional symbolic notations.	■ identify such properties as commutativity, associativity, and distributivity and use them to compute with whole numbers; ■ represent the idea of a variable as an unknown quantity using a letter or a symbol; ■ express mathematical relationships using equations.
Use mathematical models to represent and understand quantitative relationships	■ model situations that involve the addition and subtraction of whole numbers, using objects, pictures, and symbols.	■ model problem situations with objects and use representations such as graphs, tables, and equations to draw conclusions.
Analyze change in various contexts	■ describe qualitative change, such as a student's growing taller; ■ describe quantitative change, such as a student's growing two inches in one year.	■ investigate how a change in one variable relates to a change in a second variable; ■ identify and describe situations with constant or varying rates of change and compare them.

Algebra

Standard

	Grades 6–8	Grades 9–12
Instructional programs from prekindergarten through grade 12 should enable all students to—	**Expectations:** In grades 6–8 all students should—	**Expectations:** In grades 9–12 all students should—
Understand patterns, relations, and functions	■ represent, analyze, and generalize a variety of patterns with tables, graphs, words, and, when possible, symbolic rules; ■ relate and compare different forms of representation for a relationship; ■ identify functions as linear or nonlinear and contrast their properties from tables, graphs, or equations.	■ generalize patterns using explicitly defined and recursively defined functions; ■ understand relations and functions and select, convert flexibly among, and use various representations for them; ■ analyze functions of one variable by investigating rates of change, intercepts, zeros, asymptotes, and local and global behavior; ■ understand and perform transformations such as arithmetically combining, composing, and inverting commonly used functions, using technology to perform such operations on more-complicated symbolic expressions; ■ understand and compare the properties of classes of functions, including exponential, polynomial, rational, logarithmic, and periodic functions; ■ interpret representations of functions of two variables.
Represent and analyze mathematical situations and structures using algebraic symbols	■ develop an initial conceptual understanding of different uses of variables; ■ explore relationships between symbolic expressions and graphs of lines, paying particular attention to the meaning of intercept and slope; ■ use symbolic algebra to represent situations and to solve problems, especially those that involve linear relationships; ■ recognize and generate equivalent forms for simple algebraic expressions and solve linear equations.	■ understand the meaning of equivalent forms of expressions, equations, inequalities, and relations; ■ write equivalent forms of equations, inequalities, and systems of equations and solve them with fluency—mentally or with paper and pencil in simple cases and using technology in all cases; ■ use symbolic algebra to represent and explain mathematical relationships; ■ use a variety of symbolic representations, including recursive and parametric equations, for functions and relations; ■ judge the meaning, utility, and reasonableness of the results of symbol manipulations, including those carried out by technology.
Use mathematical models to represent and understand quantitative relationships	■ model and solve contextualized problems using various representations, such as graphs, tables, and equations.	■ identify essential quantitative relationships in a situation and determine the class or classes of functions that might model the relationships; ■ use symbolic expressions, including iterative and recursive forms, to represent relationships arising from various contexts; ■ draw reasonable conclusions about a situation being modeled.
Analyze change in various contexts	■ use graphs to analyze the nature of changes in quantities in linear relationships.	■ approximate and interpret rates of change from graphical and numerical data.

Geometry

Standard

Instructional programs from prekindergarten through grade 12 should enable all students to—

Standard	Pre-K–2	Grades 3–5
	Expectations: In prekindergarten through grade 2 all students should—	**Expectations:** In grades 3–5 all students should—
Analyze characteristics and properties of two- and three-dimensional geometric shapes and develop mathematical arguments about geometric relationships	■ recognize, name, build, draw, compare, and sort two- and three-dimensional shapes; ■ describe attributes and parts of two- and three-dimensional shapes; ■ investigate and predict the results of putting together and taking apart two- and three-dimensional shapes.	■ identify, compare, and analyze attributes of two- and three-dimensional shapes and develop vocabulary to describe the attributes; ■ classify two- and three-dimensional shapes according to their properties and develop definitions of classes of shapes such as triangles and pyramids; ■ investigate, describe, and reason about the results of subdividing, combining, and transforming shapes; ■ explore congruence and similarity; ■ make and test conjectures about geometric properties and relationships and develop logical arguments to justify conclusions.
Specify locations and describe spatial relationships using coordinate geometry and other representational systems	■ describe, name, and interpret relative positions in space and apply ideas about relative position; ■ describe, name, and interpret direction and distance in navigating space and apply ideas about direction and distance; ■ find and name locations with simple relationships such as "near to" and in coordinate systems such as maps.	■ describe location and movement using common language and geometric vocabulary; ■ make and use coordinate systems to specify locations and to describe paths; ■ find the distance between points along horizontal and vertical lines of a coordinate system.
Apply transformations and use symmetry to analyze mathematical situations	■ recognize and apply slides, flips, and turns; ■ recognize and create shapes that have symmetry.	■ predict and describe the results of sliding, flipping, and turning two-dimensional shapes; ■ describe a motion or a series of motions that will show that two shapes are congruent; ■ identify and describe line and rotational symmetry in two- and three-dimensional shapes and designs.
Use visualization, spatial reasoning, and geometric modeling to solve problems	■ create mental images of geometric shapes using spatial memory and spatial visualization; ■ recognize and represent shapes from different perspectives; ■ relate ideas in geometry to ideas in number and measurement; ■ recognize geometric shapes and structures in the environment and specify their location.	■ build and draw geometric objects; ■ create and describe mental images of objects, patterns, and paths; ■ identify and build a three-dimensional object from two-dimensional representations of that object; ■ identify and draw a two-dimensional representation of a three-dimensional object; ■ use geometric models to solve problems in other areas of mathematics, such as number and measurement; ■ recognize geometric ideas and relationships and apply them to other disciplines and to problems that arise in the classroom or in everyday life.

Geometry

Standard

	Grades 6–8	Grades 9–12
Instructional programs from prekindergarten through grade 12 should enable all students to—	**Expectations:** In grades 6–8 all students should—	**Expectations:** In grades 9–12 all students should—
Analyze characteristics and properties of two- and three-dimensional geometric shapes and develop mathematical arguments about geometric relationships	■ precisely describe, classify, and understand relationships among types of two- and three-dimensional objects using their defining properties; ■ understand relationships among the angles, side lengths, perimeters, areas, and volumes of similar objects; ■ create and critique inductive and deductive arguments concerning geometric ideas and relationships, such as congruence, similarity, and the Pythagorean relationship.	■ analyze properties and determine attributes of two- and three-dimensional objects; ■ explore relationships (including congruence and similarity) among classes of two- and three-dimensional geometric objects, make and test conjectures about them, and solve problems involving them; ■ establish the validity of geometric conjectures using deduction, prove theorems, and critique arguments made by others; use trigonometric relationships to determine lengths and angle measures.
Specify locations and describe spatial relationships using coordinate geometry and other representational systems	■ use coordinate geometry to represent and examine the properties of geometric shapes; ■ use coordinate geometry to examine special geometric shapes, such as regular polygons or those with pairs of parallel or perpendicular sides.	■ use Cartesian coordinates and other coordinate systems, such as navigational, polar, or spherical systems, to analyze geometric situations; ■ investigate conjectures and solve problems involving two- and three-dimensional objects represented with Cartesian coordinates.
Apply transformations and use symmetry to analyze mathematical situations	■ describe sizes, positions, and orientations of shapes under informal transformations such as flips, turns, slides, and scaling; ■ examine the congruence, similarity, and line or rotational symmetry of objects using transformations.	■ understand and represent translations, reflections, rotations, and dilations of objects in the plane by using sketches, coordinates, vectors, function notation, and matrices; ■ use various representations to help understand the effects of simple transformations and their compositions.
Use visualization, spatial reasoning, and geometric modeling to solve problems	■ draw geometric objects with specified properties, such as side lengths or angle measures; ■ use two-dimensional representations of three-dimensional objects to visualize and solve problems such as those involving surface area and volume; ■ use visual tools such as networks to represent and solve problems; ■ use geometric models to represent and explain numerical and algebraic relationships; ■ recognize and apply geometric ideas and relationships in areas outside the mathematics classroom, such as art, science, and everyday life.	■ draw and construct representations of two- and three-dimensional geometric objects using a variety of tools; ■ visualize three-dimensional objects and spaces from different perspectives and analyze their cross sections; ■ use vertex-edge graphs to model and solve problems; ■ use geometric models to gain insights into, and answer questions in, other areas of mathematics; ■ use geometric ideas to solve problems in, and gain insights into, other disciplines and other areas of interest such as art and architecture.

Measurement

Standard

Instructional programs from prekindergarten through grade 12 should enable all students to—

Understand measurable attributes of objects and the units, systems, and processes of measurement

Apply appropriate techniques, tools, and formulas to determine measurements

Pre-K–2

Expectations:

In prekindergarten through grade 2 all students should—

- recognize the attributes of length, volume, weight, area, and time;
- compare and order objects according to these attributes;
- understand how to measure using nonstandard and standard units;
- select an appropriate unit and tool for the attribute being measured.

- measure with multiple copies of units of the same size, such as paper clips laid end to end;
- use repetition of a single unit to measure something larger than the unit, for instance, measuring the length of a room with a single meterstick;
- use tools to measure;
- develop common referents for measures to make comparisons and estimates.

Grades 3–5

Expectations:

In grades 3–5 all students should—

- understand such attributes as length, area, weight, volume, and size of angle and select the appropriate type of unit for measuring each attribute;
- understand the need for measuring with standard units and become familiar with standard units in the customary and metric systems;
- carry out simple unit conversions, such as from centimeters to meters, within a system of measurement;
- understand that measurements are approximations and how differences in units affect precision;
- explore what happens to measurements of a two-dimensional shape such as its perimeter and area when the shape is changed in some way.

- develop strategies for estimating the perimeters, areas, and volumes of irregular shapes;
- select and apply appropriate standard units and tools to measure length, area, volume, weight, time, temperature, and the size of angles;
- select and use benchmarks to estimate measurements;
- develop, understand, and use formulas to find the area of rectangles and related triangles and parallelograms;
- develop strategies to determine the surface areas and volumes of rectangular solids.

Measurement

Standard

Instructional programs from prekindergarten through grade 12 should enable all students to—	Grades 6–8	Grades 9–12
	Expectations: In grades 6–8 all students should—	**Expectations:** In grades 9–12 all students should—
Understand measurable attributes of objects and the units, systems, and processes of measurement	■ understand both metric and customary systems of measurement; ■ understand relationships among units and convert from one unit to another within the same system; ■ understand, select, and use units of appropriate size and type to measure angles, perimeter, area, surface area, and volume.	■ make decisions about units and scales that are appropriate for problem situations involving measurement.
Apply appropriate techniques, tools, and formulas to determine measurements	■ use common benchmarks to select appropriate methods for estimating measurements; ■ select and apply techniques and tools to accurately find length, area, volume, and angle measures to appropriate levels of precision; ■ develop and use formulas to determine the circumference of circles and the area of triangles, parallelograms, trapezoids, and circles and develop strategies to find the area of more-complex shapes; ■ develop strategies to determine the surface area and volume of selected prisms, pyramids, and cylinders; ■ solve problems involving scale factors, using ratio and proportion; ■ solve simple problems involving rates and derived measurements for such attributes as velocity and density.	■ analyze precision, accuracy, and approximate error in measurement situations; ■ understand and use formulas for the area, surface area, and volume of geometric figures, including cones, spheres, and cylinders; ■ apply informal concepts of successive approximation, upper and lower bounds, and limit in measurement situations; ■ use unit analysis to check measurement computations.

Data Analysis and Probability

Standard

Instructional programs from prekindergarten through grade 12 should enable all students to—

	Pre-K–2	Grades 3–5
	Expectations: In prekindergarten through grade 2 all students should—	**Expectations:** In grades 3–5 all students should—
Formulate questions that can be addressed with data and collect, organize, and display relevant data to answer them	■ pose questions and gather data about themselves and their surroundings; ■ sort and classify objects according to their attributes and organize data about the objects; ■ represent data using concrete objects, pictures, and graphs.	■ design investigations to address a question and consider how data-collection methods affect the nature of the data set; ■ collect data using observations, surveys, and experiments; ■ represent data using tables and graphs such as line plots, bar graphs, and line graphs; ■ recognize the differences in representing categorical and numerical data.
Select and use appropriate statistical methods to analyze data	■ describe parts of the data and the set of data as a whole to determine what the data show.	■ describe the shape and important features of a set of data and compare related data sets, with an emphasis on how the data are distributed; ■ use measures of center, focusing on the median, and understand what each does and does not indicate about the data set; ■ compare different representations of the same data and evaluate how well each representation shows important aspects of the data.
Develop and evaluate inferences and predictions that are based on data	■ discuss events related to students' experiences as likely or unlikely.	■ propose and justify conclusions and predictions that are based on data and design studies to further investigate the conclusions or predictions.
Understand and apply basic concepts of probability		■ describe events as likely or unlikely and discuss the degree of likelihood using such words as certain, equally likely, and impossible; ■ predict the probability of outcomes of simple experiments and test the predictions; ■ understand that the measure of the likelihood of an event can be represented by a number from 0 to 1.

Data Analysis and Probability

Standard

	Grades 6–8	Grades 9–12
Instructional programs from prekindergarten through grade 12 should enable all students to—	**Expectations:** **In grades 6–8 all students should—**	**Expectations:** **In grades 9–12 all students should—**
Formulate questions that can be addressed with data and collect, organize, and display relevant data to answer them	■ formulate questions, design studies, and collect data about a characteristic shared by two populations or different characteristics within one population; ■ select, create, and use appropriate graphical representations of data, including histograms, box plots, and scatterplots.	■ understand the differences among various kinds of studies and which types of inferences can legitimately be drawn from each; ■ know the characteristics of well-designed studies, including the role of randomization in surveys and experiments; ■ understand the meaning of measurement data and categorical data, of univariate and bivariate data, and of the term variable; ■ understand histograms, parallel box plots, and scatterplots and use them to display data; ■ compute basic statistics and understand the distinction between a statistic and a parameter.
Select and use appropriate statistical methods to analyze data	■ find, use, and interpret measures of center and spread, including mean and interquartile range; ■ discuss and understand the correspondence between data sets and their graphical representations, especially histograms, stem-and-leaf plots, box plots, and scatterplots.	■ for univariate measurement data, be able to display the distribution, describe its shape, and select and calculate summary statistics; ■ for bivariate measurement data, be able to display a scatterplot, describe its shape, and determine regression coefficients, regression equations, and correlation coefficients using technological tools; ■ display and discuss bivariate data where at least one variable is categorical; ■ recognize how linear transformations of univariate data affect shape, center, and spread; ■ identify trends in bivariate data and find functions that model the data or transform the data so that they can be modeled.
Develop and evaluate inferences and predictions that are based on data	■ use observations about differences between two or more samples to make conjectures about the populations from which the samples were taken; ■ make conjectures about possible relationships between two characteristics of a sample on the basis of scatterplots of the data and approximate lines of fit; ■ use conjectures to formulate new questions and plan new studies to answer them.	■ use simulations to explore the variability of sample statistics from a known population and to construct sampling distributions; ■ understand how sample statistics reflect the values of population parameters and use sampling distributions as the basis for informal inference; ■ evaluate published reports that are based on data by examining the design of the study, the appropriateness of the data analysis, and the validity of conclusions; ■ understand how basic statistical techniques are used to monitor process characteristics in the workplace.

(Standard continues on page 554)

Data Analysis and Probability

Standard

	Grades 6–8	Grades 9–12
Instructional programs from prekindergarten through grade 12 should enable all students to—	**Expectations:** **In grades 6–8 all students should—**	**Expectations:** **In grades 9–12 all students should—**
Understand and apply basic concepts of probability	■ understand and use appropriate terminology to describe complementary and mutually exclusive events; ■ use proportionality and a basic understanding of probability to make and test conjectures about the results of experiments and simulations; ■ compute probabilities for simple compound events, using such methods as organized lists, tree diagrams, and area models.	■ understand the concepts of sample space and probability distribution and construct sample spaces and distributions in simple cases; ■ use simulations to construct empirical probability distributions; ■ compute and interpret the expected value of random variables in simple cases; ■ understand the concepts of conditional probability and independent events; ■ understand how to compute the probability of a compound event.

Appendix B

Black-Line Masters

Full-sized versions of the black-line masters shown in this appendix are available on the text's companion website—**www.thomsonedu.com/education/kennedy**.

1	2	3	4	5	6	7	8	9	10
11	12	13	14	15	16	17	18	19	20
21	22	23	24	25	26	27	28	29	30
31	32	33	34	35	36	37	38	39	40
41	42	43	44	45	46	47	48	49	50
51	52	53	54	55	56	57	58	59	60
61	62	63	64	65	66	67	68	69	70
71	72	73	74	75	76	77	78	79	80
81	82	83	84	85	86	87	88	89	90
91	92	93	94	95	96	97	98	99	100

BLM 10.1 Hundreds chart

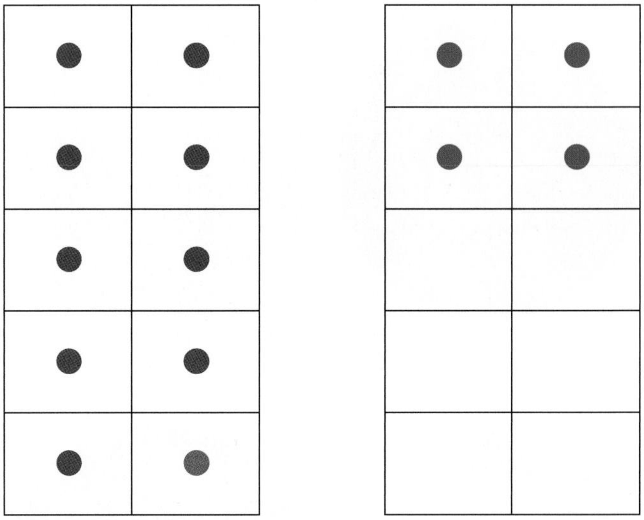

BLM 11.2 Tens frame

+	0	1	2	3	4	5	6	7	8	9
0										
1										
2										
3										
4										
5										
6										
7										
8										
9										

BLM 11.1 Blank addition chart

×	0	1	2	3	4	5	6	7	8	9
0										
1										
2										
3										
4										
5										
6										
7										
8										
9										

BLM 11.3 Blank multiplication chart

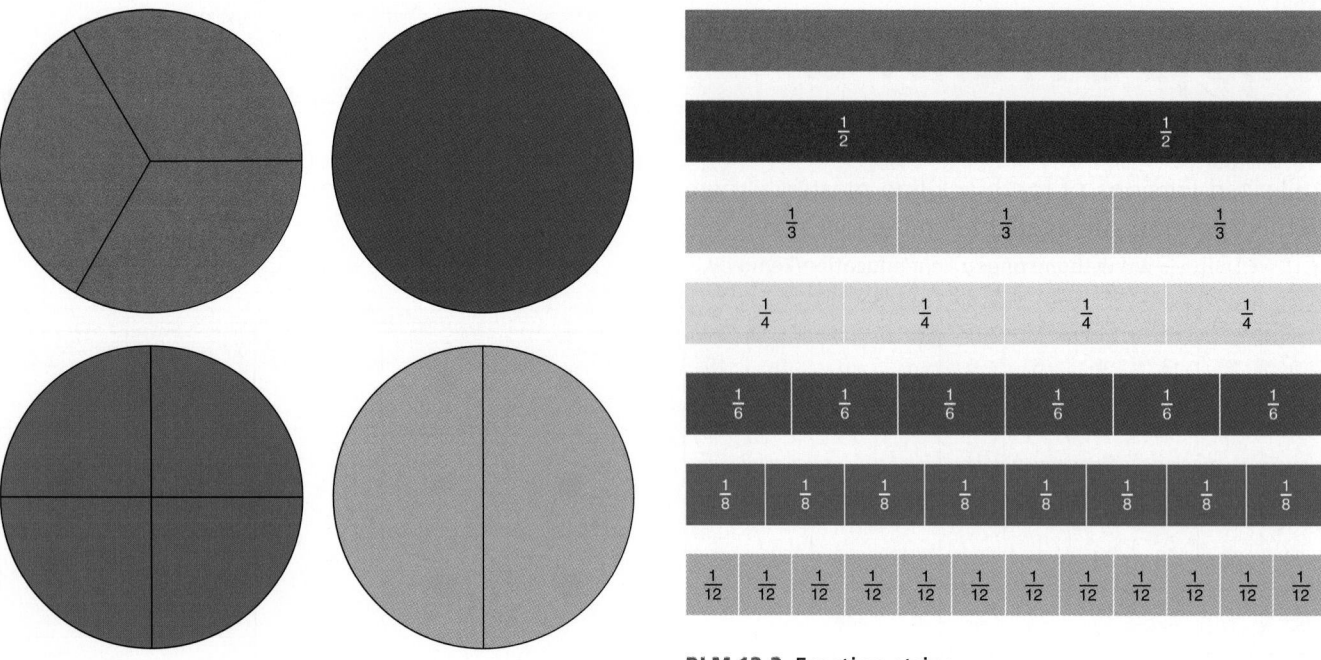

BLM 13.1 Fraction circle 1

BLM 13.3 Fraction strips

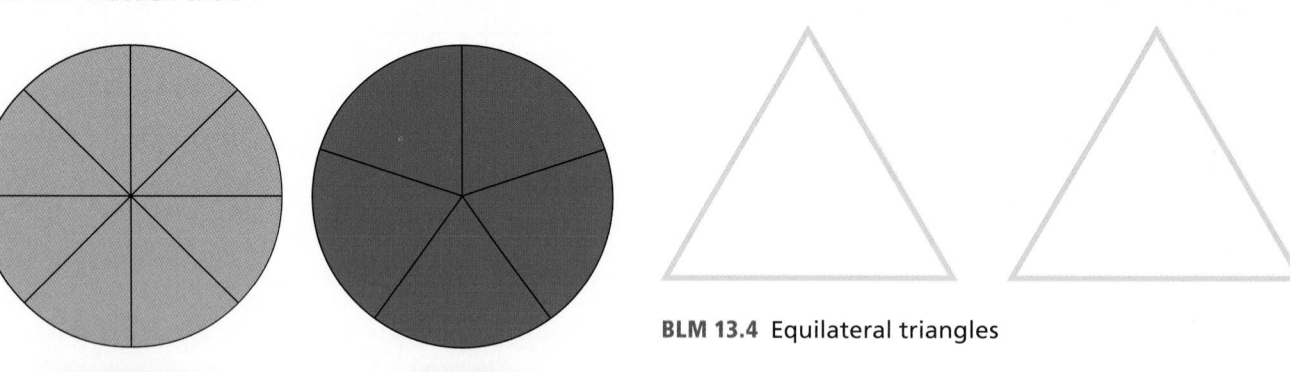

BLM 13.2 Fraction circle 2

BLM 13.4 Equilateral triangles

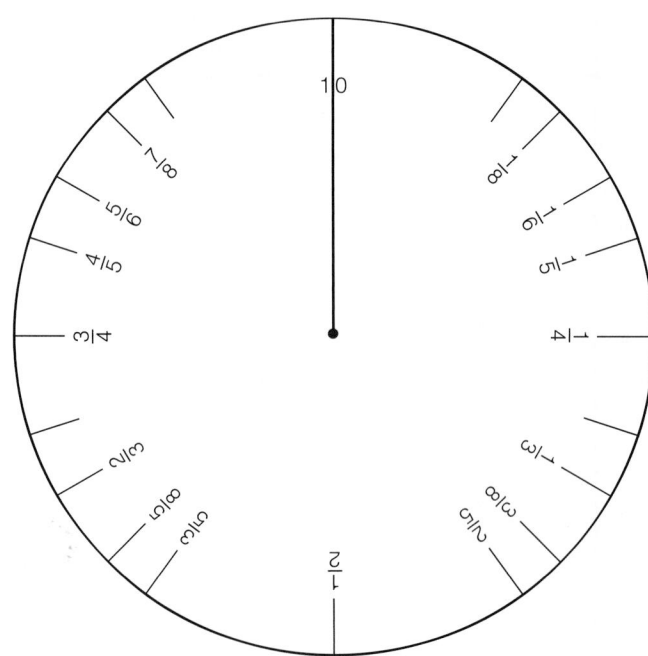

BLM 13.5 Fraction wheel 1

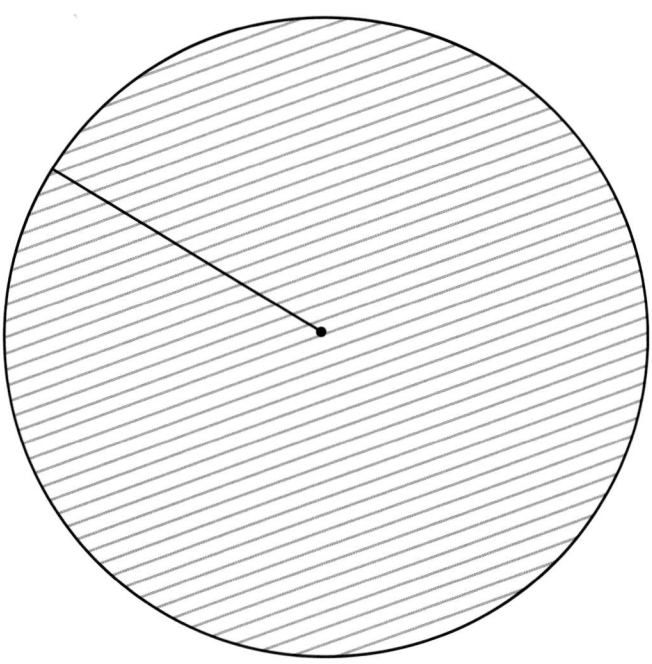

BLM 13.6 Fraction wheel 2

BLM 17.1 Isometric dot paper

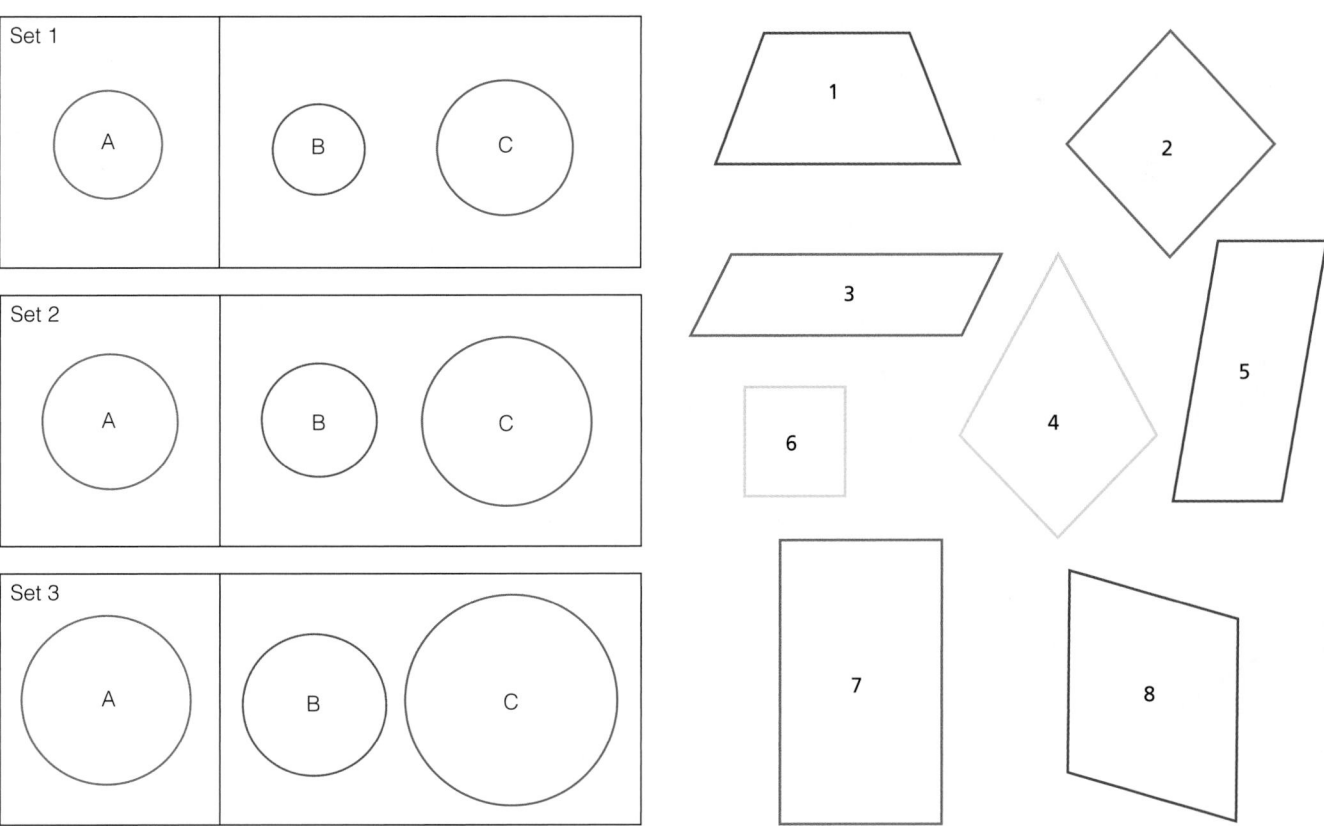

BLM 13.7 Decimal circles

BLM 17.2 Sorting shapes 1

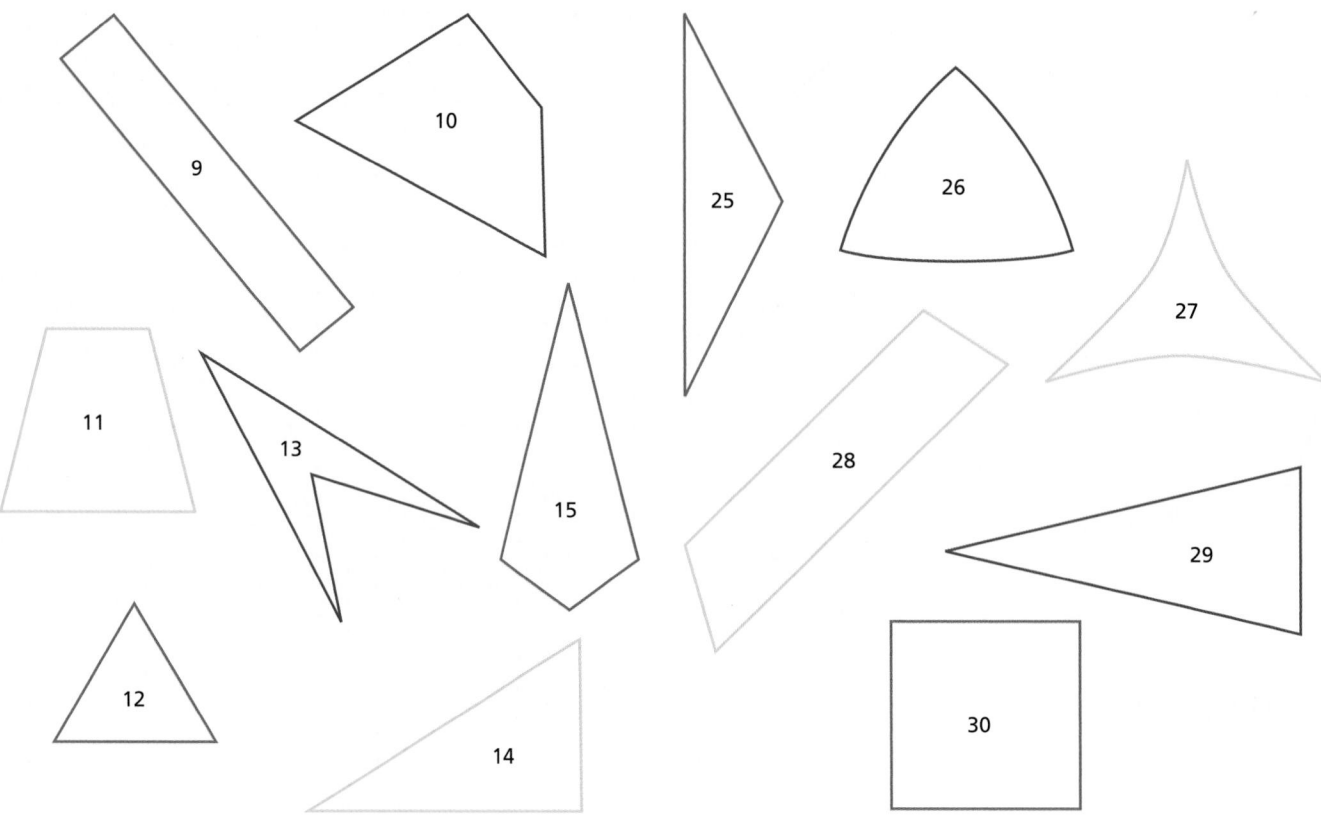

BLM 17.3 Sorting shapes 2

BLM 17.5 Sorting shapes 4

BLM 17.4 Sorting shapes 3

BLM 17.6 Sorting shapes 5

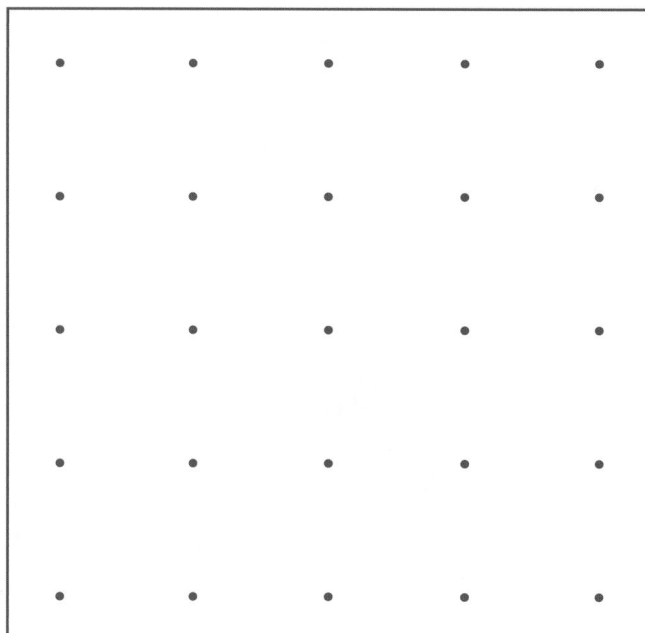

BLM 17.7 Geoboard pattern

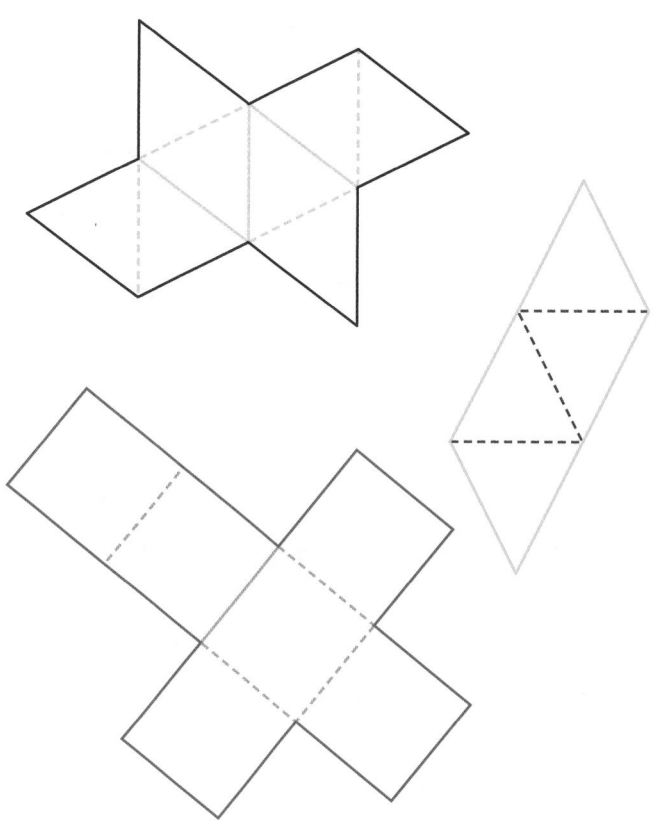

BLM 17.9 Nets for platonic solids: tetrahedron, cube, and octahedron. Fold along dotted lines and tape together to form each solid.

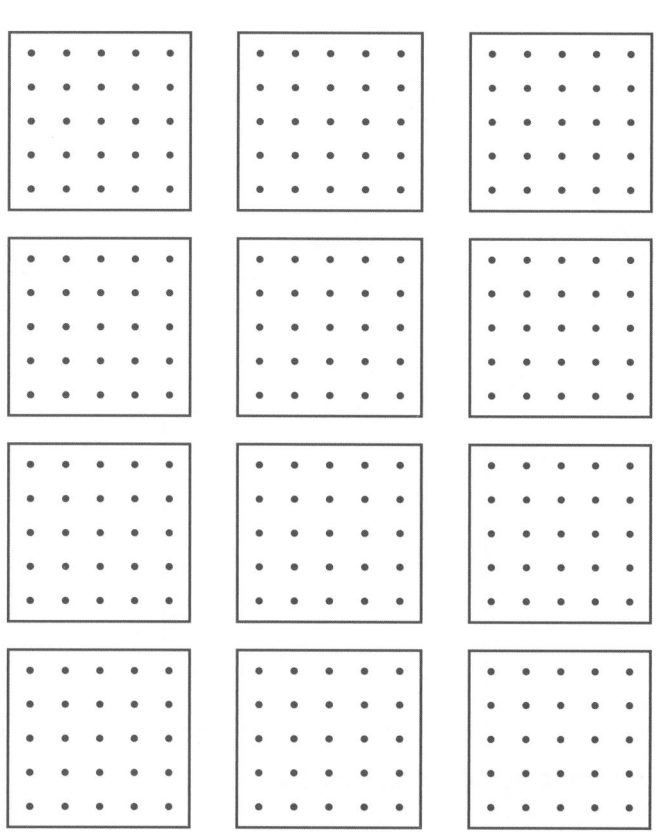

BLM 17.8 Geoboard record keeping

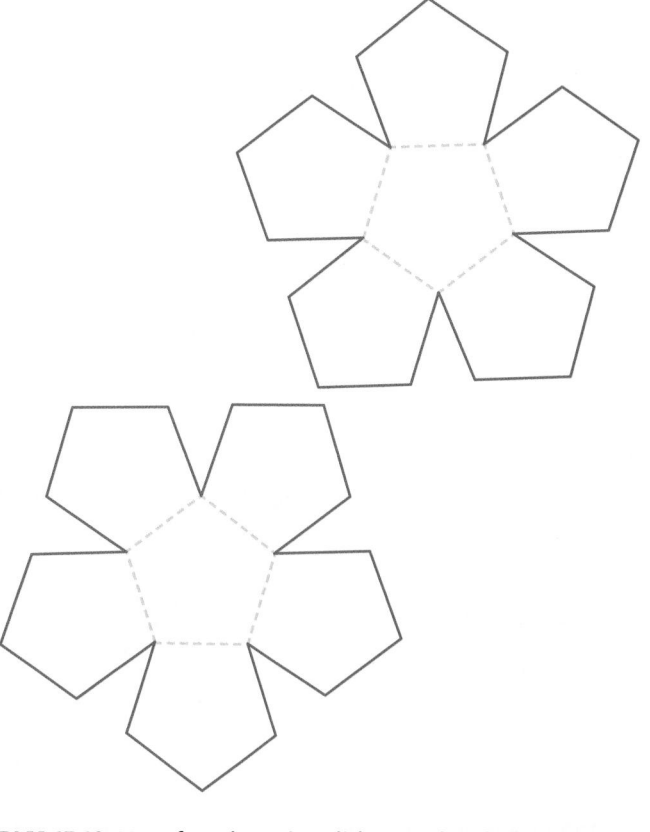

BLM 17.10 Nets for platonic solids: regular dodecahedron. Cut out both shapes and fold along dotted lines. The two shapes fit together to form a single regular dodecahedron.

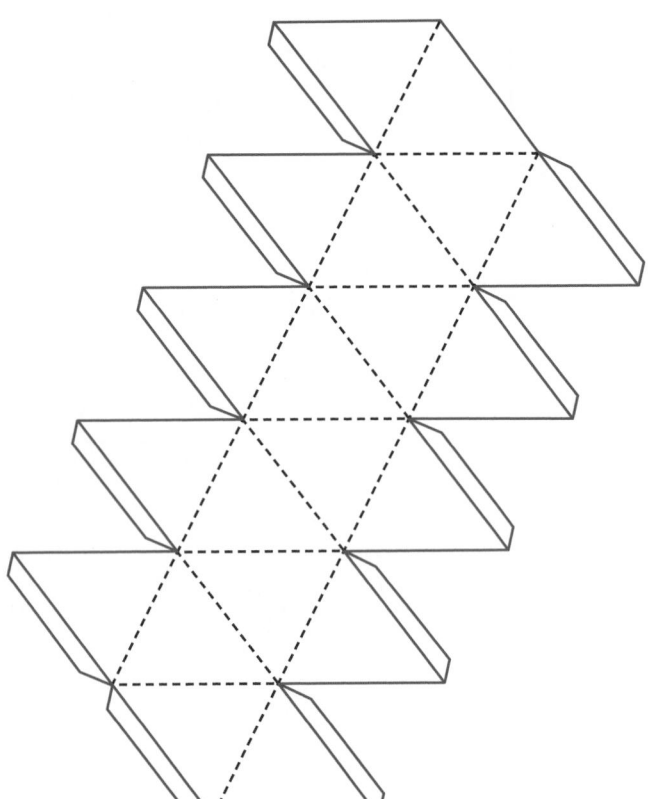

BLM 17.11 Nets for platonic solids: regular icosahedron. Fold on dotted lines and glue, using the tabs.

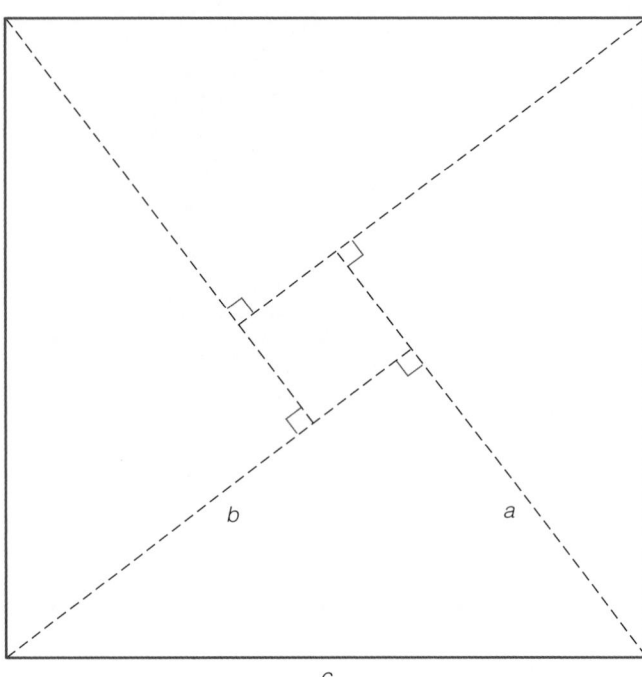

BLM 17.13 Pythagorean puzzle A

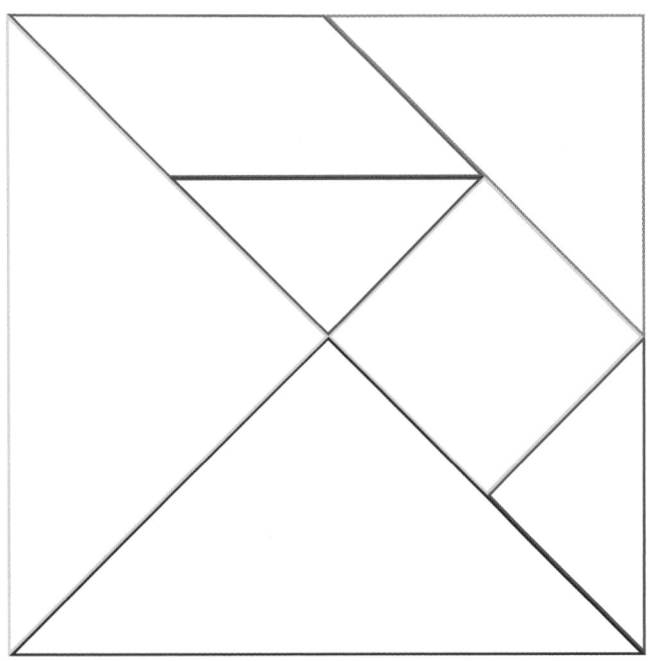

BLM 17.12 Tangram template. Copy onto card stock and laminate before cutting out.

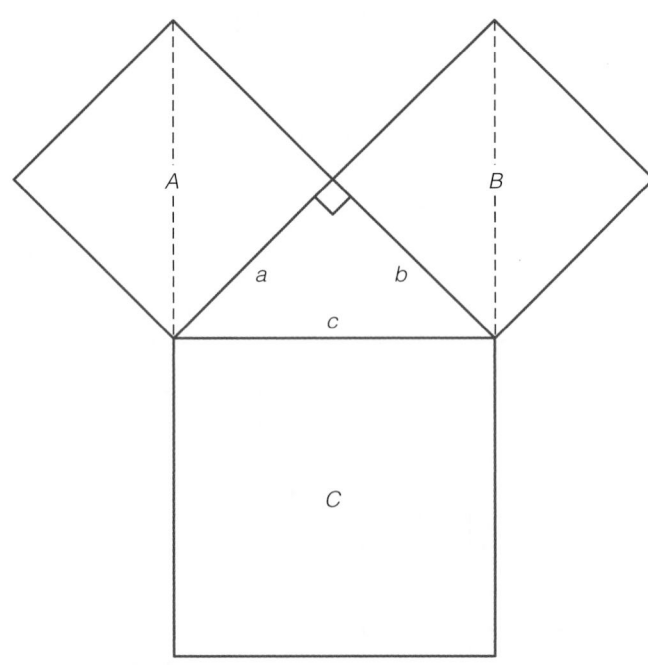

BLM 17.14 Pythagorean puzzle B

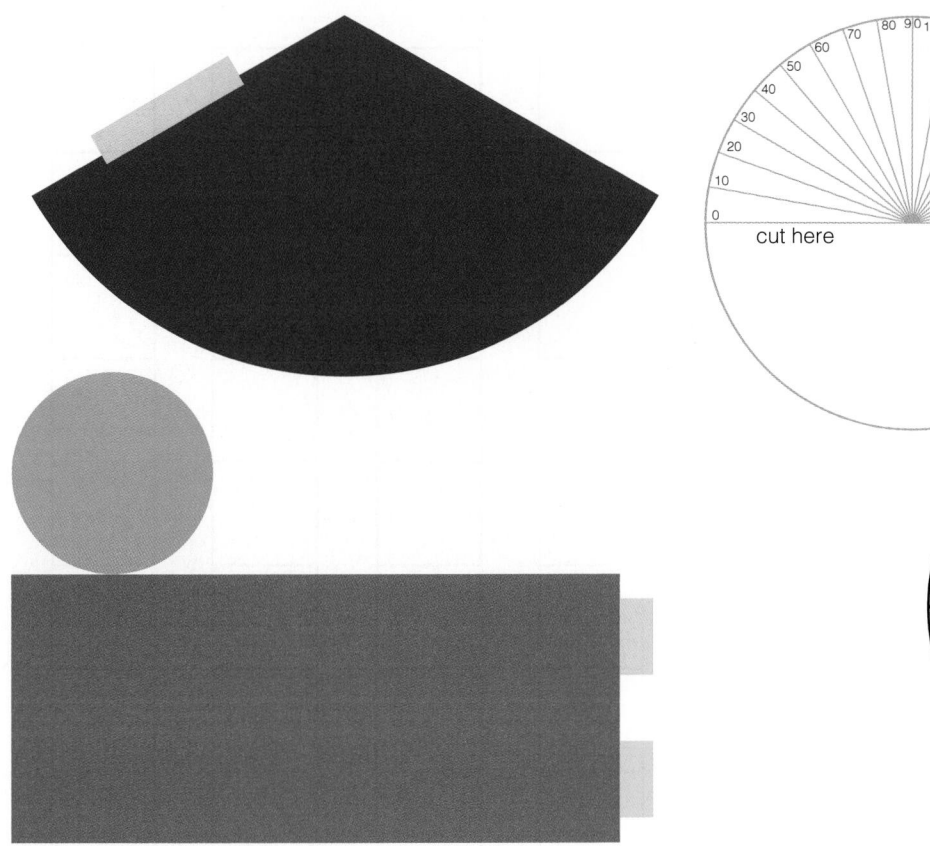

BLM 18.1 Cylinder and cone template for volume relationship. Print on card stock before cutting out.

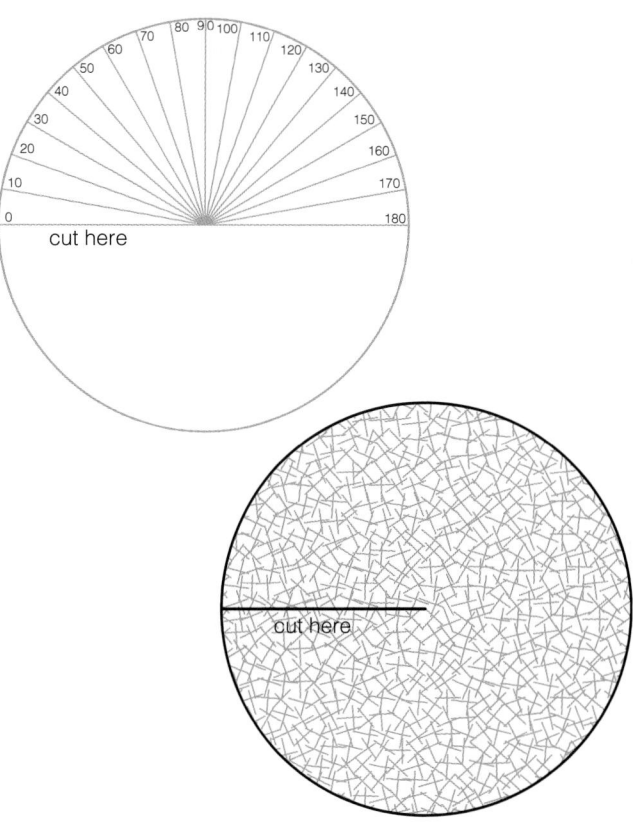

BLM 18.3 Angle wheel. Cut to the center of both circles along the indicated radius. Face the blank sides of both circles against each other. Fit the centers of the two circles together along the two cut radii.

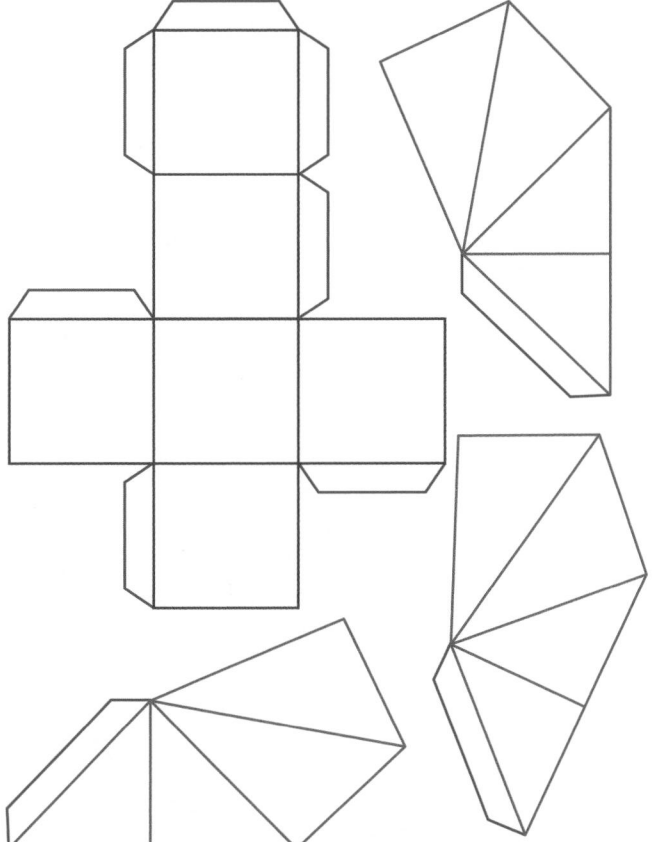

BLM 18.2 Cube and pyramid template for volume relationship. Print on card stock before cutting out.

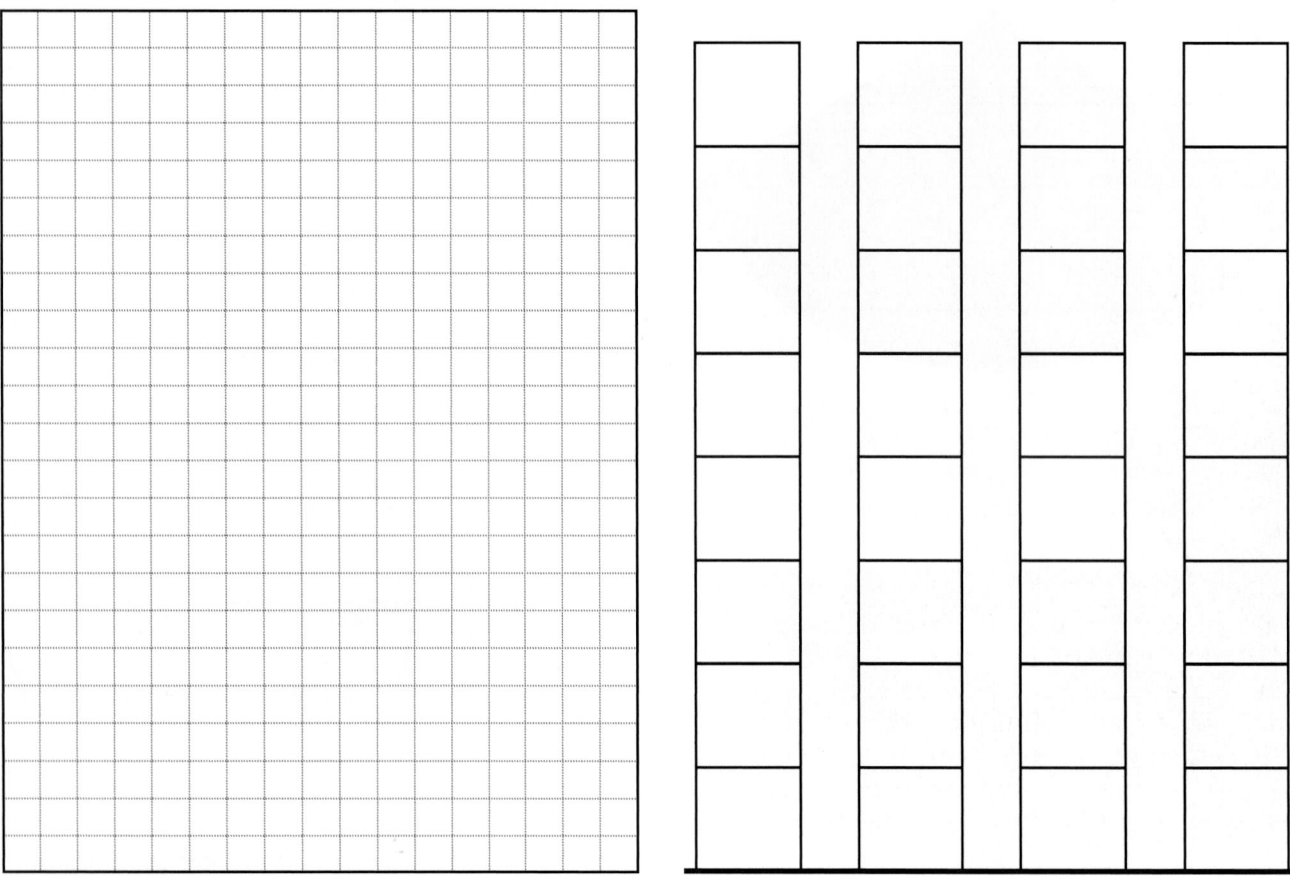

BLM 19.1 Centimeter grid

BLM 19.3 Bar graph template

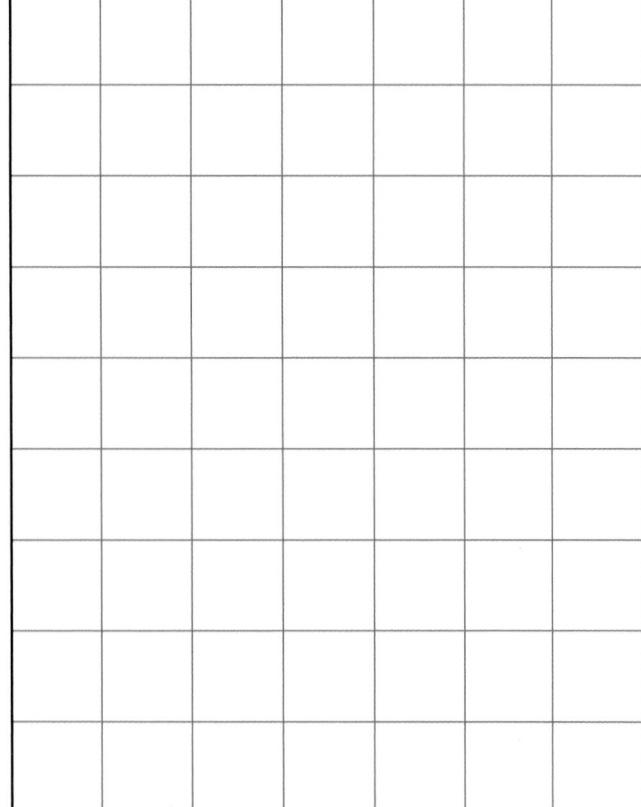

BLM 19.2 Inch grid

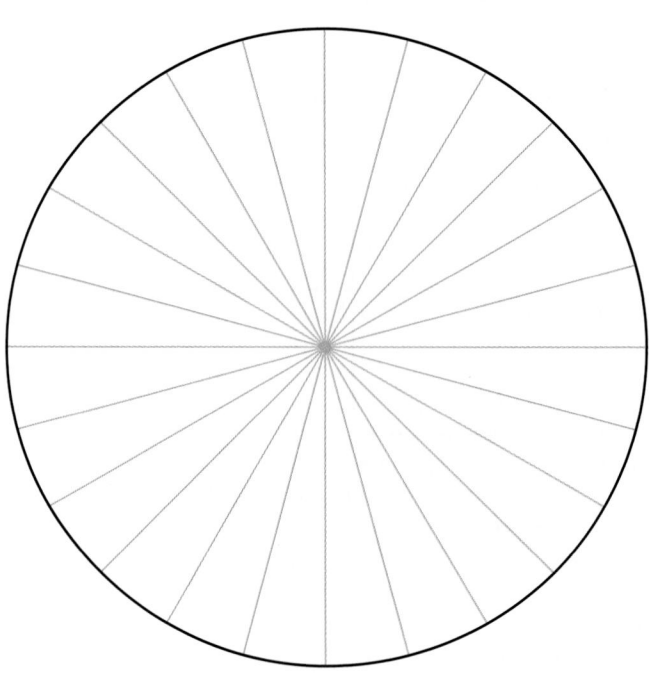

BLM 19.4 Circle graph

Glossary

A

acute triangle A triangle whose angles are all less than 90 degrees. Compare with *obtuse triangle* and *right triangle*.

addends In addition, the numbers being added to arrive at a sum.

algorithm A step-by-step procedure for calculation.

alternative algorithm An algorithm that is different from the traditional or conventional algorithm used most frequently in a culture.

analytic scoring rubric A detailed assessment of overall quality of an assignment or task. The analytical scoring rubric lists several performance objectives and gives a rubric for each performance indicator. Compare with *holistic scoring rubric*.

anecdotal record A written note about what a student did and said.

array In the geometric interpretation of multiplication, the graphic arrangement of objects in rows and columns.

associative property of addition The order in which addends are added does not change the sum. Applies to three or more addends. See also *commutative property of addition*.

associative property of multiplication When three or more factors are multiplied, the order in which they are paired for computation does not affect the product. See also *commutative property of multiplication*.

B

bar graph A graphical representation of numerical data that uses vertical or horizontal bars. Bar graphs are used to display categorical data.

base The number to which a percent is applied. Example: 50% of *60* (the base) is 30. See also *percent* and *percentage*.

behaviorism A theory of learning that focuses on observable behaviors and on ways to increase behaviors deemed positive and decrease behaviors deemed undesirable.

bell curve See *normal distribution*.

benchmark (1) Specific grade level learning target provided by state and local schools. (2) In estimation, a referent that gives students a comparison unit or amount to use for an estimate. Without a benchmark, students have a hard time making a reasonable estimate and refining it.

bimodal When there are two modes for a set of data.

box-and-whisker plot A graphical representation of the median, the first and third quartiles, and the extreme values of a data set. The data for a box-and-whisker plot are fairly easy to obtain, consisting of the high and low data points and three medians.

C

cardinal number A number that tells how many objects are in a set. Compare with *nominal number* and *ordinal number*.

Cartesian cross-product A multiplication strategy that involves the number of one-to-one combinations of objects in two or more sets. It shows the total number of possibilities made by choosing one option from each group of choices. Also called *combinations*. Compare with *geometric interpretation* and *repeated addition*.

Cartesian geometry See *coordinate geometry*.

classification Matching groups of objects sharing common characteristics, or attributes. Classification is an important skill in all subject areas. Also called *sorting* or *grouping* or *categorizing*.

classroom action research The process in which teachers conduct research in their classrooms by asking and answering questions about student learning and effective teaching. Teachers describe, explain, and try methods to improve their students' learning. They assess student learning by collecting data, drawing conclusions, and changing their techniques to increase learning.

closed questions Questions that call for short, specific answers.

cognitive-developmental theories Theories such as those of Jean Piaget, Richard Skemp, and Jerome Bruner that propose levels of successively more complex intellectual understanding or conceptualization.

combinations See *Cartesian cross-product*.

commutative The property in which the order of the numbers in a mathematical function does not matter. For example, addition is commutative; subtraction is not.

commutative law of addition See *commutative property of addition*.

commutative law of multiplication See *commutative property of multiplication*.

commutative property of addition The order of addends does not affect the sum. Also called *commutative law of addition*. See also *associative property of addition*.

commutative property of multiplication When the order of factors is switched, the product is the same. Also called *commutative law of multiplication*. See also *associative property of multiplication*.

comparison subtraction Compares the size of two sets or the measure of two objects. The quantity of both sets or measurement of both objects is known. The comparison question in subtraction asks "how much larger" or "how much smaller" one set is than the other. "What is the *difference*" is another way of expressing comparison between the two sets. Compare with *completion subtraction*, *takeaway subtraction*, and *whole-part-part subtraction*.

compatible numbers A mental computation strategy that looks for easy combinations of 10, 100, or 1,000.

compensation An alternative approach to calculation often used in addition and subtraction in which the original numbers are adjusted to make an easier calculation and then corrected, or compensated, in the final answer.

completion subtraction Comparison between an existing set and a desired set, or between an incomplete set and a completed set. The question for completion is "how many more are needed?" or "how much more is needed?" Compare with *comparison subtraction*, *takeaway subtraction*, and *whole-part-part subtraction*.

composite number A number that has several factors. Compare with *prime number*.

computational fluency The ability to compute with confidence and ease in a variety of situations using the appropriate operation and computational strategy and determining whether the result is reasonable and useful.

concrete operational stage Third stage of Piaget's developmental stages. Occurs around ages 7 to 12 when children master the underlying structure of number, geometry, and measurement. Work with concrete objects is the foundation for developing mathematical concepts represented by pictures, symbols, and mental images. Compare with *formal operational stage*, *preoperational stage*, and *sensorimotor stage*.

congruent The property in which one object fits exactly on the other. If all points on one line segment match exactly with all points on another segment, they are congruent. Any two plane or space figures are congruent when all their corresponding points match exactly. Compare with *similar*.

constructivism A learning theory that holds that learning is a result of building or constructing meaning from many experiences; individuals construct their understanding from physical and social interactions through the formation of schema—complex cognitive relationships.

continuous Qualitative in nature. Continuous properties can be subdivided into progressively smaller and smaller units that can take on an infinite number of values; to make *quantitative* comparisons about them, they must be measured. Compare with *discrete*.

cooperative group learning A grouping strategy that is designed to increase student participation by capitalizing on the social aspects of learning.

coordinate geometry Using a coordinate grid formed by two number lines—one extending horizontally and the other vertically—to locate objects on the grid. Also called *Cartesian geometry*.

counting A number concept in which a sequence of words is related to increasing number: 1, 2, 3, 4, 5, ...

counting-on A particularly effective learning strategy for addition. Following examples of the "plus 1" rule such as 5 + 1, 8 + 1, and 2 + 1, students will generalize "adding 1 is just counting to the next number." "Plus 2" and "plus 3" are extensions.

criterion-referenced test A standardized test that provides diagnostic information for teachers because it shows which concepts and skills each student has mastered instead of comparing students to each other as in a norm-referenced test. Mastery is determined by the number of items answered correctly for each performance objective and the number of objectives mastered. Compare with *norm-referenced test*.

D

decimal system A number system in which place value is based on powers of 10. The starting position is called the units

or ones place. From any place in the system, the next position to the left is 10 times greater, and the position to the right is one-tenth as large. This characteristic makes it possible to represent whole numbers of any size as well as decimal fractions with the system. The metric system for measurement and the United States monetary system are decimal systems.

decomposition The traditional subtraction algorithm, commonly called *borrowing*, which involves regrouping or trading down from a larger place value to a smaller place value before subtraction.

denominator In a common fraction, the number of equal-sized parts into which the whole, or unit, has been subdivided. For example, the "2" in $\frac{1}{2}$ is the denominator. Compare with *numerator*.

density A measure of the mass to volume ratio of a substance or object. The higher the mass to volume ratio, the greater the density will be.

density property of numbers There is always another number between any two numbers.

difference The degree or amount by which one set differs from another set.

directed teaching/thinking lesson Structured, but interactive, method of teaching mathematics in which manipulatives, discussion, and performance of tasks encourage student thinking, for small groups or the whole class.

discrete Quantitative in nature; countable. Compare with *continuous*.

distributive property of multiplication and division over addition The operations of multiplication and division may be carried on a sum or on addends of that sum.

dividend In division, the number being divided.

divisor In division, the number by which the dividend is divided; the known factor. Compare with *quotient*.

E

equal-addition algorithm An alternative algorithm for subtraction that is based on the fact that adding or subtracting the same amount to the sum and one addend will not change the difference between the two numbers.

equal participation One of the basic principles for implementing cooperative learning successfully, in which team members have equal opportunity to participate; an activity is not dominated by one member, nor can members choose not to participate. In traditional instruction, interchanges are often between the teacher and one student at a time. Compare with *individual accountability* and *positive interdependence*.

equilateral triangle A triangle with three equal, or congruent, sides. Compare with *isosceles triangle* and *scalene triangle*.

estimation A reasonable guess, hypothesis, or conjecture based on numerical information. Compare with *rounding*.

even numbers The set of numbers divisible by 2 with no remainder. Compare with *odd numbers*.

F

factors Numbers multiplied together.

flexible grouping The teacher uses different instructional groups appropriate to the task or situation.

formal operational stage Fourth stage of Piaget's developmental stages. Occurs around ages 11 to 13 when more sophisticated ways of thinking about mathematics, including proportional reasoning, propositional reasoning, and correlational reasoning, begin and continue to develop during the teenage years and into adulthood. Enables children and adults to form hypotheses, analyze situations to consider all factors that bear upon them, draw conclusions, and test them against reality. Compare with *concrete operational stage*, *preoperational stage*, and *sensorimotor stage*.

fundamental theorem of arithmetic Every composite number has only one set of prime factors.

G

geometric interpretation A multiplication strategy that shows the graphic arrangement of objects in rows and columns, called *rectangular arrays*. Compare with *Cartesian cross-product* and *repeated addition*.

greatest common factor The common factor with the largest value.

H

heuristic A general strategy or procedure that applies to all problem solving in mathematics and parallels the scientific method.

Hindu-Arabic numeration system A base-10 system that developed in Asia and the Middle East. It is the number system that we use today.

histogram A type of bar graph that represents the frequency of data that have been grouped into several intervals. Histograms are used to display numerical data, rather than categorical data, as with bar graphs.

historical probability One of two types of probability, historical probability is based on information accumulated over time about a wide range of topics. These empirical data can then be used to predict the likelihood of certain events. Compare with *mathematical probability*.

holistic scoring rubric A judgment of overall quality of an assignment or task. Compare with *analytical scoring rubric*.

I

identity element A number that does not change the value of another number during an arithmetic operation. The number 0 is an identity element for both addition and subtraction because adding or subtracting 0 does not change the value of a number. The number 1 is an identity element for both multiplication and division because multiplying or dividing by 1 does not change the value of a number.

idiocentric Self-centered. Refers to children's perspective on the world, including their understanding of space.

inclusion Rather than being placed in isolated special education settings, more and more students with disabilities are being included in the regular classroom, sometimes with instructional support from aides or special education teachers. Teachers work with students with a variety of cognitive abilities, learning styles, social problems, and physical challenges.

individual accountability One of the basic principles for implementing cooperative learning successfully, in which team members are held accountable for contributions and results of the team effort. Every student on the team is responsible for learning the content and skill, and the team is accountable for all the team members' being successful. Compare with *equal participation* and *positive interdependence*.

information processing A cognitive theory that uses a computer as a metaphor for learning. Instinctual behavior is similar to read only memory (ROM) in a computer; it is preprogrammed. Random access memory (RAM) is short-term memory the computer receives and stores temporarily, but does not retain when turned off. Learning becomes permanent when new ideas and experiences are transferred from short-term memory and stored in long-term memory for later retrieval and use. Information is stored in the computer's permanent memory based on the needs and choices of the computer user.

integer A positive or negative whole number, including 0.

inverse operation For addition; take-away subtraction "undoes" addition. Division is the inverse operation of multiplication.

isosceles triangle A triangle with two congruent sides. Compare with *equilateral triangle* and *scalene triangle*.

iteration In direct measurement, applying a unit of measure one or more times to an object being measured.

L

learning center An area in the classroom set up with materials that students may use in their learning.

learning modalities Learning styles. Do learners prefer to process information visually, auditorily, kinesthetically, or in some combination? Do learners prefer to learn individually or in groups, with quiet or background noise, in structured or open-ended assignments?

least common multiple The common multiple with the smallest value.

Likert-type scale A rating scale that indicates the levels of performance for a specific concept or skill on a number line.

line A set of points that extends infinitely. A line can be curved or straight.

line graph A graphical representation that shows patterns, trends, and relationships.

line plot A graphical representation of each item of data as an individual entry.

line symmetry Symmetry that produces mirror images that can be "folded" along the symmetry line onto one another. Each side of the symmetry is a mirror image of the other. Compare with *point symmetry*.

lowest common denominator The common denominator with the smallest value.

M

"make 10" A strategy used in addition based on finding number combinations for 10 such as $8 + 5 = 10 + 3$. See also *compatible numbers*.

manipulatives Sometimes called "objects to think with," include a variety of objects—for example, blocks, scales, coins, rulers, puzzles, and containers.

mastery assessment See *summary assessment*.

mathematical probability One of two types of probability, mathematical probability is based on the mathematics of chance, or the arithmetic probability of an event's occurring. "What is the chance a six will come up when this die stops rolling?" "What is the chance of drawing a yellow marble from the bag of colored marbles?" Compare with *historical probability*.

mean A measure of central tendency used to describe the middle value of a set of data. The mean is computed by summing all the data in a set and then dividing that sum by the number of data items. Also called *mean average*. Compare with *median* and *mode*.

mean average See *mean*.

meaning theory See *constructivism*.

measurement division When the known factor is the number belonging to each group and the unknown factor is the number of groups. Measurement division asks "How many groups of a known size can be made?" Also called *repeated subtraction* because the number in each group is repeatedly subtracted from the total. Compare with *partitive division*.

median A measure of central tendency used to describe the middle value of a set of data. The median is the middle number in a data set. Compare with *mean* and *mode*.

mode A measure of central tendency used to describe the middle value of a set of data. The mode is the number or response that appears most frequently. Compare with *mean* and *median*.

multiple intelligences A theory, first proposed by Howard Gardner in 1983, that asserts that people are capable, or even gifted, in different ways and that no single description of intelligence exists. Gardner initially identified seven intelligences: linguistic, logical/mathematical, spatial, body/kinesthetic, musical, interpersonal, and intrapersonal. An eighth intelligence has since been added: naturalist.

multiplicand The second factor in a multiplication sentence such as $3 \times 7 = 21$ that names the number of objects in a set.

multiplier The first factor in a multiplication sentence such as $3 \times 7 = 21$. It is called the multiplication operator or multiplier because it acts on the second factor.

N

near doubles An addition strategy that relates an unknown sum such as $7 + 8$ to a known sum that is a double such as $7 + 7$ or $8 + 8$.

near squares A multiplication strategy that relates an unknown product such as 4×5 to a known product that is a square such as 4×4 and 5×5.

net A two-dimensional shape that can be cut, folded, and taped to form a geometric solid.

nominal number A number that is used to identify or name, although it may code other information. Compare with *cardinal number* and *ordinal number*.

nonproportional materials Place-value materials that do not show value with their size. Money is the most familiar non-proportional material. For example, dimes are not 10 times as large as pennies, and dollar coins or bills are not 10 times as large as dimes. Compare with *proportional materials*.

normal distribution A graphic display of the number of students at each percentile rank. Also called a *bell curve*.

norm-referenced test A standardized test that compares the scores of students who have taken the test to each other. The norm-referenced standardized test is reported in percentile scores from the lowest score of 1 percentile to the highest of 99 percentile. Compare with *criterion-referenced test*.

numeral A written symbol that represents a number, for example, 0, 1, 2, 3, 4, 5, 6, 7, 8, and 9 in the Hindu-Arabic numeration system.

numerator In a common fraction, the number of parts being considered at a particular time. For example, the "1" in $\frac{1}{2}$ is the numerator. Compare with *denominator*.

O

object graph A graphical representation in which actual objects are part of the graph. Compare with *picture graph*.

object permanence The ability of children to learn to recognize persons and things and to hold mental images when the people or things can no longer be seen. Essential for recalling past experiences to connect with new experiences.

obtuse triangle A triangle having one angle larger than 90 degrees. Compare with *acute triangle* and *right triangle*.

odd numbers The set of numbers not divisible by 2 evenly, and which cannot be organized into pairs. Compare with *even numbers*.

open-ended questions Questions that ask students to explain their reasoning.

order A basic thinking/learning skill that involves the arrangement of objects, events, and ideas. Order has a beginning, middle, and end, but placement within the order may be arbitrary. Compare with *sequence* and *seriation*.

ordinal number A number that is used to designate location in a sequence. Compare with *cardinal number* and *nominal number*.

outlier A piece of data that is widely distanced from other data on either the high or the low end of a distribution.

overlearning Learning, practicing, and drilling the same math fact, procedure, or algorithm many times to achieve the ability to use it without prompting.

P

partitive division When the number of groups is known but the size of each group is not known. The action involves distributing, or sharing, the number as evenly as possible into the given number of groups. Partitive division asks "How many are in each group?" Also called *sharing division*. Compare with *measurement division*.

percent The rate applied to the base. Example: *50%* (the percent) of 60 is 30. See also *base* and *percentage*.

percentage The amount or quantity derived when a percent is applied to a base. Example: 50% of 60 is *30* (the percentage). See also *base* and *percent*.

performance indicator Specifies how the student demonstrates the performance objective. The objective in instruction becomes the performance indicator in assessment. The performance indicator describes what the teacher expects to see the student do, say, write, or demonstrate the objective. It may include situation and the criterion for success.

performance objective Describes the expected student learning so that teachers and students understand what they are working toward. Performance objectives guide what the teacher teaches, what students are to learn, and what is going to be assessed during and after instruction.

picture graph A graphical representation in which drawings or pictures are used to represent the actual objects in the data set. Compare with *object graph.*

place value In the Hindu-Arabic number system, a pattern of increasing/decreasing powers of 10 on which whole numbers are based.

plane figure A shape that has two dimensions, such as a square, triangle, rectangle, circle, and ellipse.

Platonic solid See *regular solid.*

point A location in space that has no dimension.

point symmetry Symmetry found as an object is rotated about its center, resulting in the same image being formed several times. Also called *rotational symmetry.* Compare with *line symmetry.*

polygon A closed figure with no curved lines. Polygons are named for the number of sides they have: triangle (3), quadrilateral (4), pentagon (5), hexagon (6), heptagon (7), octagon (8), enneagon (9), decagon (10), ...

polyhedron A space figure made up of plane faces. *Poly* and *hedron* are Greek terms meaning "many" and "seat" (formed by two flat surfaces), so *polyhedron* means "many flat surfaces."

positive interdependence One of the basic principles for implementing cooperative learning successfully, in which team success is achieved through the successes and contributions of each member. Compare with *equal participation* and *individual accountability.*

practice In a constructivist sense, providing many rich and stimulating experiences with a concept or skill rather than using repetition of the same experience.

preoperational stage Second stage of Piaget's developmental stages. Occurs around ages 2 or 3 to 6 or 7 when children gradually change from being egocentric and dominated by their idiosyncratic perceptions of the world. They begin to become aware of feelings and points of view of others in their world. Children develop symbol systems, including objects, pictures, actions, and language, to represent their experience. Compare with *concrete operational stage*, *formal operational stage*, and *sensorimotor stage.*

prime number A number that has only one set of factors—the number 1 and itself. Compare with *composite number.*

principle of compensation The smaller a measurement unit is, the more of these units will be required to measure an attribute.

problem-based learning Classroom investigations. Thorp and Sage describe problem-based learning as "focused, experiential learning (minds-on, hands-on) organized around the investigation and resolution of messy, real-world problems."

problem-based projects or investigations Students investigate a problem (initiated by teacher or student) by exploring, applying concepts and skills, expanding ideas, and drawing conclusions.

process-oriented problem Focuses on the process students employ to solve a problem. For example, a calculator frees students from computational boredom and allows them to concentrate on the *process* they use to find the answer. They can think about the problem itself rather than the computations the problem requires. Compare with *product-oriented problem.*

product The result of multiplication.

product-oriented problem Concentrates students' efforts on getting the answer by using familiar algorithms. The answer, or the product, is the focus. Such problems enable students to apply their algorithms in real-life situations, and appreciate how empowering such algorithms are, in contrast to sterile rote computations performed from a set of skill problems on a worksheet. Compare with *process-oriented problem.*

proportional materials Place-value materials that show value with their size. For example, when the manipulative piece representing one unit is determined, the tens piece is 10 times larger, and the hundreds piece is 10 times the tens unit. Compare with *nonproportional materials.*

Q

quotient In division, the result; the unknown factor. Compare with *divisor.*

R

range A statistical measure obtained by subtracting the low from the high.

rational counting Meaningful counting that begins when children connect number words to objects such as apples, blocks, toy cars, or fingers. Compare with *rote counting.*

reflection A mirror image created when an object is reversed across a reference line; commonly called *flip.* Compare with *rotation* and *translation.*

regrouping and renaming (1) Exchange between place values. (2) The traditional, or conventional, algorithm for addition, commonly referred to as "carrying."

regular polygon A polygon with congruent sides *and* congruent angles, such as a square, equilateral triangle, or regular hexagon.

regular solid A polyhedron with congruent faces, that is, with the same number of faces meeting at each vertex. There are five regular solids, also called Platonic solids: (1) hexahedron, or cube; (2) tetrahedron; (3) octahedron; (4) dodecahedron; and (5) icosahedron.

remainder (1) In take-away situations, the answer to the question or problem that asks "how much is left" or "how many are left" after part of a set is removed. (2) In division, the groups or objects that are not evenly divided.

repeated addition A multiplication strategy that involves the total number belonging to multiple groups having the same number; related to skip counting. Compare with *Cartesian cross-product* and *geometric interpretation.*

repeated subtraction division See *measurement division.*

right triangle A triangle having a 90-degree angle. Compare with *acute triangle* and *obtuse triangle.*

rotation A transformation resulting from an object being turned about a fixed point; commonly called *turn.* Compare with *reflection* and *translation.*

rotational symmetry See *point symmetry.*

rote counting A memorized list of number words, such as 1, 2, 3, 4, . . . , that provides prior knowledge for number concepts. Compare with *rational counting.*

rounding A way to express vital information about a number without being unnecessarily detailed. Compare with *estimation.*

running record A handy way to keep track of student progress. A running record is made by taping index cards on a clipboard and jotting down anecdotal notes or individual checklists about each student.

S

scaffold To frame student instruction that supports new skills and concepts based on student experiences. Teachers pre-assess or learn about the background knowledge of their students and plan their instruction accordingly.

scalene triangle A triangle with no congruent sides. Compare with *equilateral triangle* and *isosceles triangle*.

scope The range of topics, concepts, and skills to be taught.

scoring rubric Description added to each number in a rating scale to create a uniform understanding for levels of performance.

sensorimotor stage First stage of Piaget's developmental stages. Occurs between birth and age 2 or 3. Foundations for later mental growth and mathematical understanding are developed at this stage. Compare with *concrete operational stage, formal operational stage,* and *preoperational stage.*

sequence (1) The organization of knowledge and skills across grade levels. (2) A basic thinking/learning skill that involves the arrangement of objects, events, and ideas. In sequence, order has meaning. Compare with *order* and *seriation.*

seriation A basic thinking/learning skill that involves the arrangement of objects, events, and ideas. Arrangement is based on gradual changes of an attribute and is often used in measurement. Compare with *order* and *sequence.*

sharing division See *partitive division.*

similar The property in which two or more objects have the same shape, but differ in size; the corresponding sides are proportional. Compare with *congruent.*

simultaneous interaction A feature of cooperative learning that involves several students at the same time.

skip counting Counting in groups of 2, 3, 4, 5, ... Skip counting encourages fast and flexible counting and is connected to multiplication and division.

social constructivism Cognitive learning theory that emphasizes the importance of social interactions in developing concepts.

space figure A shape that has three dimensions, such as boxes and blocks, balls and world globes, cones, pyramids, and eggs.

spatial perception See *spatial sense.*

spatial sense The ability to perceive objects in relation to one another and to oneself; the ability to mentally change the orientation of an object in relation to other objects or to oneself. Also called *spatial perception.*

squared facts When a number is multiplied by itself, such as 4×4 or 7×7.

stem-and-leaf plot A graphical representation that displays numerical data by using the leftmost digit of the data as a stem, and the remaining digits as leaves on the graph. Stem-and-leaf plots are especially useful in comparing raw data.

stimulus-response (S-R) theory Drill and practice of facts and mathematical procedures is based on a belief that repetition establishes strong bonds.

sum In addition, the total found when adding numbers.

summative assessment Assessment following instruction to determine if students have mastered the concepts and skills and can apply them in problem-solving situations. Summative assessment provides accountability for students and for teachers. Also called *mastery assessment.*

symmetry The property of a shape in which there is an exact reflection of form on opposite sides of a dividing line or plane.

T

take-away subtraction Used when part of an original set is moved, lost, eaten, or spent. In take-away situations, the question or problem asks "how much is left" or "how many are left" after part of the set is removed. The answer is called the *remainder.* Compare with *comparison subtraction, completion subtraction,* and *whole-part-part subtraction.*

terminating decimal A fraction whose quotient eventually terminates when converted to a decimal with the division algorithm.

tessellation Tiling pattern made when a surface is completely covered with one geometric figure or a combination of figures in a repeating pattern.

test bias When items on a test provide an advantage or a disadvantage due to content or wording that is more familiar to one group than another. Minority students and those learning English may experience test bias, although students who speak English also interpret questions differently depending on geographic, cultural, and linguistic backgrounds.

tracking Grouping students by ability and keeping students together for long periods. Tracking frequently works to the detriment of lower-ability students with instruction that deemphasizes concepts and overemphasizes isolated skills. Tracking also isolates the lower-ability students from the modeling and support of more proficient students. The lower-track students often have the least qualified and least experienced teachers and the least opportunity for a full and balanced curriculum.

traditional algorithm The algorithm that is most commonly used and taught in a culture.

transitivity Transferring the measurement characteristic of an object to another object in order to make a comparison.

translation Transformation in which an object is relocated in a plane; commonly called *slide.* Compare with *reflection* and *rotation.*

U

unit fraction A fraction in which the numerator is 1.

W

whole number A number used for counting discrete quantities.

whole-part-part subtraction Identifies the size of a subgroup within a larger group. The whole group has a common characteristic, but parts or subgroups have distinct characteristics. Whole-part-part subtraction identifies membership in two subgroups that are included in the whole group. The number in one part of the whole is known, and the question posed is "how many belong" in the other part. Compare with *comparison subtraction, completion subtraction,* and *takeaway subtraction.*

Z

zone of proximal development The gap between current knowledge or skill and the desired knowledge or skill. Students are able to learn within their zone of proximal development. If students do not have the requisite background for learning, the teacher provides experiences that develop the foundation for successful learning.

References

Chapter 1

National Council of Teachers of Mathematics. (2000). *Principles and standards for school mathematics*. Reston, VA: Author.

Chapter 2

Hoppe, C. (1999, April 19). The big house: Nation's largest dorm buzzes like a small city. *Dallas Morning News*, p. 1A.

National Council of Teachers of Mathematics. (2000). *Principles and standards for school mathematics*. Reston, VA: Author.

Schroeder, T., & Lester, F., Jr. (1989). Developing understanding in mathematics via problem solving. In P. R. Trafton (Ed.), *New directions in elementary school mathematics* (pp. 31–42). Reston, VA: National Council of Teachers of Mathematics.

Silver, E. A., Kirkpatrick, J., & Schlesinger, B. (1990). *Thinking through mathematics*. New York: College Entrance Board.

Thorp, L., & Sage, S. (1999). *Problems as possibilities*. Alexandria, VA: Association for Supervision and Curriculum Development.

Chapter 3

Adler, I. (1966). Mental growth and the art of teaching. *Arithmetic Teacher* 13(7), 66–70.

Ambrose, R., & Falkner, K. (2001). Developing spatial understanding through building polyhedrons. *Teaching Children Mathematics* 8(8), 442–447.

Ambrose, R., Levi, L., & Fennema, E. (2002). The complexity of teaching for gender equity. In J. Trentacosta (Ed.), *Multicultural and gender equity in the mathematics classroom* (pp. 236–242). Reston, VA: National Council of Teachers of Mathematics.

Barnette, R., & Rivers, C. (2004, October 13). The persistence of gender myths in math. *Education Week*, p. 39.

Bilger, B. (2004, July 26). Annals of childhood: Nerd camp. *The New Yorker*, p. 71.

Bley, N. S., & Thornton, C. (2001). *Teaching mathematics to students with learning disabilities*. Austin, TX: Pro-Ed.

Bruner, J. (1960). *The process of education*. Cambridge, MA: Harvard University Press.

Burns, M. (1993). The 12 most important things you can do to be a better math teacher. *Instructor* 102(7), 28–31.

Campbell, P. B. (1995). Redefining the "girl problem" in mathematics. In W. G. Secada, E. Fennema, & L. B. Adajian (Eds.), *New directions for equity in mathematics education* (pp. 225–241). Cambridge, England: Cambridge University Press.

Carbo, M., Dunn, R., & Dunn, K. (1986). *Teaching students to read through their individual learning styles*. Englewood Cliffs, NJ: Prentice-Hall.

Chacon, P., & Soto-Johnson, H. (1994). Encouraging young women to stay in the mathematics pipeline: Mathematics camp for young women. *School Science and Mathematics* 103(16), 274–284.

D'Ambrosio, U. (1985). *Socio-cultural bases for mathematics education*. São Paulo: Universidade Estadual de Campinas (Unicamp).

D'Ambrosio, U. (1997). Diversity, equity, and peace: From dream to reality. In J. J. Trentacosta & M. J. Kenney (Eds.), *Multicultural and gender equity in the mathematics classroom: The gift of diversity* (pp. 243–248). Reston, VA: National Council of Teachers of Mathematics.

Davenport, L. R. (1994). *Promoting interest in mathematical careers among girls and women*. Columbus, OH: ERIC/CSMEE.

Delpit, L. (1999). *Ten factors to success in urban classrooms*. Presentation at Fall Conference of Coalition of Essential Schools, Atlanta, Georgia.

Dienes, Z. P. (1969). *Building up mathematics*. London: Hutchison Education.

Education Week, 2000. Available at http://edcounts.edweek.org/createtable/viewtable.php

Galda, L., & Cullinan, B. (2006). *Literature and the child* (6th ed.). Belmont, CA: Wadsworth.

Gallagher, A., & Kaufman, J. (2004). *Gender differences in mathematics: An integrational psychological approach*. Cambridge, England: Cambridge University Press.

Gardner, H. (1983). *Frames of the mind: The theory of multiple intelligences*. New York: Basic Books.

Gershaw, D. (2006). *Gender differences in math*. Available at http://www.jiska.com

Goldin, G. A. (1990). Epistemology, constructivism, and discovery learning in mathematics. In R. B. Davis, C. A. Maher, & N. Noddings (Eds.), *Constructivist views on the teaching and learning of mathematics*. Reston, VA: National Council of Teachers of Mathematics.

Goral, M., & Gnadinger, C. (2006). Using storytelling to teach mathematics. *Australian Primary Mathematics Classroom* 11(1), 4–8.

Greenes, C., & Tsankova, J. (Eds.). (2004). *Challenging young children mathematically*. Special Monograph on Early Childhood Mathematics. Golden, CO: National Council of Supervisors of Mathematics.

Grouws, D., & Cebulla, K. (2002). *Improving student achievement in mathematics: Recommendations for the classroom*. ERIC Clearinghouse for Science, Mathematics, and Environmental Education, ERIC Digest. Available at http://www.ericse.org/digests/dse00-10.html

Guild, P., & Garger, S. (1998). *Marching to different drummers* (2nd ed.). Alexandria, VA: Association for Supervision and Curriculum Development, and Reston, VA: National Council of Teachers of Mathematics.

Hart, L. (1983). *Human brain and human learning*. Oak Creek, AZ: Books for Educators.

Hiebert, J., & Lefevre, P. (1986). Conceptual and procedural knowledge in mathematics: An introductory analysis. In J. Hiebert (Ed.), *Conceptual and procedural knowledge: The case of mathematics* (pp. 1–16). Hillsdale, NJ: Erlbaum.

Huber, B., & Scanlon, R. (1995). Gender in the classroom. *Journal of Educational Computing Research* 13(3), 27–36.

Jensen, E. (1998). *Teaching with the brain in mind*. Alexandria, VA: Association for Supervision and Curriculum Development.

Johnson, A. (1991). *Classic math: Stories from the history of mathematics*. New York: Pearson.

Johnson, A. (1999). *Famous problems and their mathematicians*. Boulder, CO: Libraries Unlimited.

Johnson, A. (2007). *In a different voice: Teaching mathematics to limited English proficient students*. Boston: Allyn & Bacon.

Kagan, S., & Kagan, M. (1998). *Multiple intelligences: The complete MI book*. San Clemente, CA: Kagan Cooperative Learning.

Krutetskii, V. A. (1976). *The psychology of mathematical abilities in school children*. Chicago: University of Chicago Press.

Ladson-Billings, G. (1995). Making mathematics meaningful in multicultural contexts. In W. Secada, E. Fennema, & L. Byrd (Eds.), *New directions for equity in mathematics education* (pp. 35–47). Cambridge, England: Cambridge University Press.

Lefrancois, G. R. (2000). *Theories of human learning*. Belmont, CA: Wadsworth.

Levine, S. C., Huttenlocher, J., Taylor, A., & Lanrock, H. (1999). Early sex differences in spatial skills. *Developmental Psychology* 35, 940–949.

Linn, M. C., & Petersen, A. C. (1986). A meta-analysis of gender differences in spatial ability: Implications for mathematics and science. In J. S. Hyde & M. C. Linn (Eds.), *The psychology of gender: Advances through meta-analysis* (pp. 67–100). Baltimore: Johns Hopkins University Press.

McCook, A. (2005, April 1). Girls say they stink at math even when they don't. *Reuters*.

Mercer, M. D. (1992). *Students with learning difficulties*. New York: Macmillan.

National Assessment of Educational Progress. (2005). Available at http://www.nces.ed.gov/nationsreportcard

National Council of Teachers of Mathematics. (1989). *Curriculum and evaluation standards for school mathematics*. Reston, VA: Author.

National Council of Teachers of Mathematics. (1991). *Professional standards for teaching mathematics*. Reston, VA: Author.

National Council of Teachers of Mathematics. (2000). *Principles and standards for school mathematics*. Reston, VA: Author.

Piaget, J. (1952). *The child's conception of number*. New York: Humanities Press.

Renzulli, J., & Park, S. (2002). *Giftedness and high school dropouts: Personal, family, and school-related factors*. New York: National Research Center of the Gifted and Talented.

Ridge, H. L., & Renzulli, J. F. (1981). Teaching mathematics to the talented and gifted. In V. J. Glennon (Ed.), *The mathematics education of exceptional children and youth: An interdisciplinary approach* (pp. 196–201). Reston, VA: National Council of Teachers of Mathematics.

Ruf, D. (2006). *Losing our minds: Gifted children left behind*. Waco, TX: Prufrock Press.

Sadker, D., & Sadker, M. (1994). *Failing at fairness: How our schools cheat girls*. New York: Scribners.

Schneider, S. (1998). *Overcoming underachievement*. Philadelphia: Pennsylvania Association for Gifted Education.

Secada, W. G. (1991). Agenda setting: Enlightened self-interest and equity in mathematics education. *Peabody Journal of Education* 66(2), 22–56.

Sells, L. W. (1978). Mathematics: A critical filter. *Science Teacher* 45(2), 28–29.

Shermo, D. (2004, March 2). Schools facing tight budgets leave gifted programs behind. *New York Times*, p. 1.

Steeh, J. (2002, April 17). Gender difference in math interest and performance. *University of Michigan News Service*.

Sutton, J., & Krueger, A. (Eds.). (2002). *Ed thoughts: What we know about mathematics teaching and learning*. Aurora, CO: Midcontinent Research for Education and Learning.

Tapasak, R. C. (1990). Differences in expectancy: Attribution patterns of cognitive components in male and female math performance. *Contemporary Educational Psychology* 15(3), 284–298.

Virginia Department of Education. (2004). *Mathematics: Strategies for teaching limited English learning enhanced scope and sequence*. Richmond, VA: Department of Education.

Vygotsky, L. S. (1962). *Thought and language*. Cambridge, MA: MIT Press.

Wadsworth, B. J. (1984). *Piaget's theory of cognitive and affective development* (3rd ed.). New York: Longman.

Weinbrenner, S. (2001). *Teaching gifted kids in the regular classroom*. Minneapolis: Free Spirit Publications.

Zahorik, J. A. (1995). *Constructivist teaching*. Bloomington, IN: Phi Delta Kappa Educational Foundation.

Zanger, V. (1998). Math storybooks. *Teaching Children Mathematics* 5(2), 98–103.

Chapter 4

Ambrose, R., & Falkner, K. (2001). Developing spatial understanding through building polyhedron. *Teaching Children Mathematics* 8(8), 442–447.

Bransford, J. D., Brown, A. L., & Cocking, R. R. (1999). *How people learn: Brain, mind, experience, and school*. Washington, DC: National Academy Press.

Brownell, W. A. (1986). *Arithmetic Teacher* 34(2), 38–42. Reprint of original article published in 1951.

Bruner, J. (1960). *The process of education*. Cambridge, MA: Harvard University Press.

Burns, M. (1983). The 12 most important things you can do to be a better math teacher. *Instructor* 102(7), 28–31.

Dienes, Z. P. (1969). *Building up mathematics*. London: Hutchinson Education.

English, L. D. (Ed.). (2003). *Handbook of international research in mathematics education*. Mahway, NJ: Erlbaum.

Goldin, G. A. (1990). Epistemology, constructivism, and discovery learning in mathematics. In R. B. Davis, C. A. Maher, & N. Noddings (Eds.), *Constructivist views on the teaching and learning of mathematics*. Reston, VA: National Council of Teachers of Mathematics.

Grouws, D. (1992). *Handbook of research on mathematics teaching and learning*. New York: Macmillan Library Reference.

Grouws, D., & Cebulla, K. (2002). Improving student achievement in mathematics: Recommendations for the classroom. *ERIC Digest*. Available at http://www.ericse.org/digests/dse00-10.htm

Hart, L. (1983). *Human brain and human learning*. Oak Creek, AZ: Books for Educators.

Hiebert, J., & Lefevre, P. (1986). Conceptual and procedural knowledge in mathematics: An introductory analysis. In J. Hiebert (Ed.), *Conceptual and procedural knowledge: The case of mathematics* (pp. 1–16). Hillsdale, NJ: Erlbaum.

Jensen, E. (1998). *Teaching with the brain in mind*. Alexandria, VA: Association for Supervision and Curriculum Development.

Lefrancois, G. R. (2000). *Theories of human learning*. Belmont, CA: Wadsworth.

National Council of Teachers of Mathematics. (2000). *Principles and standards for school mathematics*. Reston, VA: Author.

Sowder, J., & Schappelle, B. (2002). *Lessons learned from research*. Reston, VA: National Council of Teachers of Mathematics.

Vygotsky, L. S. (1962). *Thought and language*. Cambridge, MA: MIT Press.

Zahorik, J. A. (1995). *Constructivist teaching*. Bloomington, IN: Phi Delta Kappa Educational Foundation.

Chapter 5

Burns, M. (1990). The math solution: Using groups of four. In N. Davidson (Ed.), *Cooperative learning in mathematics* (pp. 21–46). Menlo Park, CA: Addison-Wesley.

Gagne, R. (1985). *The conditions of learning and theory of instruction*. New York: Holt, Rinehart & Winston.

Kagan, S. (1994). *Cooperative learning*. San Clemente, CA: Kagan Learning Cooperative.

Little Soldier, L. (1989). Cooperative learning and the Native American student. *Phi Delta Kappan* 71(2), 161–167.

Malloy, C. (1997). Including African American students in the mathematics community. In J. J. Trentacosta & M. J. Kenney (Eds.), *Multicultural and gender equity in the mathematics classroom: The gift of diversity* (pp. 23–33). Reston, VA: National Council of Teachers of Mathematics.

Marzano, R. J. (2003). *What works in schools: Translating research into action*. Alexandria, VA: Association for Supervision and Curriculum Development.

Marzano, R., Pickering, D., & Pollock, J. (2004). *Classroom instruction that works*. Alexandria, VA: Association for Supervision and Curriculum Development.

National Supervisors of Mathematics. (1994). *Supporting leaders in mathematics education: A source book of essential information*. Available at http://www.utdanacenter.org/mathtoolkit/support/concept_manip.php

Slavin, R. (1987). Ability grouping and student achievement in elementary schools: A best-evidence synthesis. *Review of Educational Research* 57(3), 293–336.

Slavin, R. (Ed.). (1989). *School and classroom organization*. Hillsdale, NJ: Erlbaum.

Wong, H., & Wong, R. (1998). *The first days of school: How to be an effective teacher*. Sunnyvale, CA: Harry K. Wong Publications.

Chapter 6

Alejandre, S., & Moore, V. (2003). Technology as a tool in the primary classroom. *Teaching Children Mathematics* 10(1), 16–21.

Anderson, G. (2000). *An empirical comparison of the proportion of cooperative play of 4-year-old preschool children observed as they interact in four centers: Block, computer, housekeeping and manipulative*. Atlanta: National Association for the Education of Young Children.

Battista, M. (2001). Research-based perspective on teaching school geometry. In J. Brophy (Ed.), *Subject-specific instructional methods and activities* (pp. 73–101). New York: JAI Press and Elsevier Science.

Battista, M. (2002). Learning geometry in a dynamic computer environment. *Teaching Children Mathematics* 8(6), 333–338.

Beglau, M. (2005). Can technology narrow the Black-White achievement gap? The eMINTS instructional model of inquiry-based teaching, combined with multimedia tools in the classroom improves test scores for all students. *THE Journal* 32(12), 13–15.

Borja, R. (2006, May 10). Researchers weigh benefits of one computer per lap. *Education Week*.

Canavale, D. (2005, December 13). Michigan considers requiring high-school students to take at least one online course. *Chronicle of Higher Education*.

Cassidy, J. (2006, May 1). Me media. *The New Yorker*.

Clements, D., & McMillan, S. (1996). Rethinking "concrete" manipulatives. *Teaching Children Mathematics* 2, 11–13.

Clements, D., & Sarama, J. (2002). The role of technology in early childhood learning. *Teaching Children Mathematics* 8(6), 340–342.

Cordes, C., & Miller, E. (2000). Fool's gold: A critical look at computers in childhood. Available at http://www.alliancefor childhood.net/projects/computers_reports.htm

Dirr, P. (2004). *Measuring the impact of technology on classroom teaching and learning*. Alexandria, VA: U.S. Army Test and Evaluation Command.

Dunham, P. H., & Dick, T. P. (1994). Research on graphing calculators. *Mathematics Teacher* 87, 440–444.

Ellington, A. (2003). A meta-analysis of the effects of calculators in students' achievement and attitude levels in precollege mathematics classes. *Journal for Research in Mathematics Education* 5(34), 433–463.

Flores, A. (2002). Learning and teaching mathematics with technology. *Teaching Mathematics* 7(3), 153.

Grouws, D., & Cebula, K. (2004). *Improving student achievement in mathematics*. Brussels: International Academy of Education.

Groves, S. (1994). *Calculators: A learning environment to promote number sense*. Paper presented at the annual meeting of the American Educational Research Association, New Orleans, April.

Hillman, S., & Malotka, C. (2004). Changing views: Fearless families conquering technology together. *Mathematics Teaching in the Middle School* 4(10), 169–179.

Hoyt, R., Gonsalves, J., Braxton, P., Bevilacqua, B., Lipner, C., Badley, L., & Klofkorn, L. (1995). *Math around the world: Teacher's guide*. Berkeley, CA: GEMS.

Humbree, R., & Dassart, D. (1994). Effects of hand-held calculators in pre-college mathematics education: A meta-analysis. *Journal for Research in Mathematics Education* 17, 83–99.

Johnson, A., Bass, L., & Bellman, A. (2004). *TI-83/84 PLUS activities*. Needham, MA: Prentice Hall.

Keller, B., & Hart, E. (2002). *Improving students' spatial visualization skills and teachers' pedagogical content knowledge by using on-line curriculum-embedded applets*. Reston, VA: National Council of Teachers of Mathematics.

Learning in the Real World. (2006). *Computers' role in education*. Available at http://www.realworld.org

Marshall, J. (2002). *Learning with technology: Evidence that technology can, and does, support learning*. San Diego: Cable in the Classroom.

Martine, S. (2005). Games in the middle school. *Mathematics Teaching in the Middle School* 1(2), 94–100.

Moyer, P., Bolyard, J., & Spikell, M. (2002). What are virtual manipulatives? *Teaching Children Mathematics* 8(6), 372–377.

National Council of Teachers of Mathematics. (2000). *Principles and standards for school mathematics*. Reston, VA: Author.

National Council of Teachers of Mathematics. (2005). *Computation, calculators, and common sense*. Reston, VA: Author.

North Central Regional Education Laboratory. (2005). *Critical issue: Using technology to improve student achievement*. Naperville, IL: Author.

Oppenheimer, T. (1997). The computer delusion. *Atlantic Monthly*, 280(1), 45–62.

Prensky, M. (2000). *Digital game-based learning*. New York: McGraw-Hill.

Schacter, J. (1999). *The impact of education technology on student achievement: What the most current research has to say*. Santa Monica, CA: Miliken Exchange on Education Technology.

Sherry, L., & Jesse, D. (2000). *The impact of technology on student achievement*. Denver: RC Research Corp.

Sinclair, N., & Crespo, S. (2006). Learning mathematics in dynamic computer environments. *Teaching Children Mathematics* 12(9), 436–440.

Usiskin, Z. (1987). Paper presented at the Northwest Mathematics Teachers Annual Conference, Portland, Oregon.

Wenglinsky, H. (1998). *Does it compute? The relationship between educational technology and student achievement in mathematics*. Princeton, NJ: ETS Policy Information Center.

Chapter 7

Herman, J. L., Aschbacher, P. R., & Winters, L. (1992). *A practical guide to alternative assessment*. Alexandria, VA: Association for Supervision and Curriculum Development.

National Council of Teachers of Mathematics. (2000). *Principles and standards for school mathematics*. Reston, VA: Author.

Norwood, K. S., & Carter, G. (1994). Journal writing: An insight into students' understanding. *Teaching Children Mathematics* 1(3), 146–148.

Vygotsky, L. S. (1962). *Thought and language*. Cambridge, MA: MIT Press.

Chapter 8

Bruer, J. T. (1999). In search of brain-based education. *Phi Delta Kappan* 80(2), 648–657.

Burns, M. (1994). *What are you teaching my child?* Sausalito, CA: Math Solutions Inc. (video). Available at http://www.math solutions.com/mb/content/publications

Burns, M. (2000). *About teaching mathematics: A K–8 resource* (2nd ed.). Sausalito, CA: Math Solutions Publications.

Cuevas, G., & Yeatts, K. (2001). *Navigations through algebra, 3–5*. Reston, VA: National Council of Teachers of Mathematics.

Greenes, C., Cavanaugh, M., Dacey, L., Findell, C., & Small, M. (2001). *Navigations through algebra, PK–2*. Reston, VA: National Council of Teachers of Mathematics.

Hart, L. (1983). *Human brain and human learning*. Village of Oak Creek, AZ: Books for Educators.

Hutchins, P. (1986). *The doorbell rang*. New York: Greenwillow Books.

Lechner, G. (1983). *Creative problem solving in school mathematics*. Boston: Houghton Mifflin.

Leiva, M. A. (Ed.). (1991). *Curriculum and evaluation standards for school mathematics: Addenda series, grades K–6, kindergarten book*. Reston, VA: National Council of Teachers of Mathematics.

National Council of Teachers of Mathematics. (2000). *Principles and standards for school mathematics*. Reston, VA: Author.

Polya, G. (1957). *How to solve it*. Garden City, NY: Doubleday.

Schroeder, T., & Lester, F., Jr. (1989). Developing understanding in mathematics via problem solving. In P. R. Trafton (Ed.), *New directions in elementary school mathematics* (pp. 31–42). Reston, VA: National Council of Teachers of Mathematics.

Skolnick, J., Langbort, C., & Day, L. (1982). *How to encourage girls in math and science*. Palo Alto, CA: Dale Seymour.

Sutton, J., and Krueger, A. (2002). *EDThoughts: What we know about mathematics teaching and learning*. Aurora, CO: Midcontinent Research for Education and Learning.

Swensson, A., et al. (1997). *Changes in intelligence from 1960 to 1995 in relation to cohort, gender, and socioeconomic background*. Paper presented at the annual meeting of the American Education Research Association, Chicago, March.

Chapter 9

Caulfield, R. (2000). Numbers matter: Born to count. *Early Childhood Education Journal* 28(1), 63–65.

Copeland, R. (1984). *How children learn mathematics*. New York: Macmillan.

Gelman, R., & Gallistel, C. R. (1978). *The child's understanding of number*. Cambridge, MA: Harvard University Press.

Johnson, A. (1999). *Famous problems and their mathematicians*. Englewood, CO: Libraries Unlimited.

Jones, G., et al. (1992). *First-grade children's understanding of multidigit numbers*. Paper presented at the annual meeting of the American Educational Research Association, San Francisco, April.

Marzano, R. J. (2003). *What works in schools: Translating research into action*. Alexandria, VA: Association for Supervision and Curriculum Development.

National Council of Teachers of Mathematics. (1994). Editorial. *Teaching Children Mathematics* 1(3), 171.

National Council of Teachers of Mathematics. (2000). *Principles and standards for school mathematics*. Reston, VA: Author.

Piaget, J. (1952). *The child's conception of number*. New York: Humanities Press.

Suggate, J., Aubrey, C., & Pettitt, D. (1997). The number knowledge of four to five year olds at school entry and at the end of their first year. *European Early Childhood Research Journal* 5(2), 85–101.

Wright, R. J. (1994). A study of the numerical development of 5-year-olds and 6-year-olds. *Educational Studies in Mathematics* 24(1), 25–44.

Chapter 10

Ainsworth, S., Bibby, P., & Wood, D. (2002). Examining the effects of different multiple representation systems in learning primary mathematics. *Journal of the Learning Sciences* 11(1), 25–61.

Kamii, C. (1986). *Children reinvent arithmetic*. New York: Teachers College Press.

Montague, M., & van Garderen, D. (2003). A cross-sectional study of mathematics achievement, estimation skills, and academic self-perception in students of varying ability. *Journal of Learning Disabilities* 36(5), 437–448.

Murphy, C. (2004). How do children come to use a taught mental calculation strategy? *Educational Studies in Mathematics* 56, 3–18.

National Council of Teachers of Mathematics. (1989). *Curriculum and evaluation standards for school mathematics*. Reston, VA: Author.

National Council of Teachers of Mathematics. (2000). *Principles and standards for school mathematics*. Reston, VA: Author.

Chapter 11

Baroody, A. (2006). Why children have difficulties mastering the basic number combinations and how to help them. *Teaching Children Mathematics* 13(1), 22–31.

Baroody, A., Lai, M.-L., & Mix, K. (2005). The development of young children's number and operations sense and its implication for early childhood education. In B. Spodek & O. Saracho (Eds.), *Handbook of research on the education of young children* (pp. 223–247). Hillsdale, NJ: Erlbaum.

Fennell, S. (1992). Ideas. *Arithmetic Teacher* 39(4).

National Council of Teachers of Mathematics. (2000). *Principles and standards for school mathematics*. Reston, VA: Author.

Thompson, F. (1991). Two-digit addition and subtraction. *Arithmetic Teacher* 38(5), 10–13.

Chapter 12

Graham, A. O., & Tanenhaus, E. (1993). Multiplication and division: From whole numbers to rational numbers. In D. Grouws (Ed.), *Research ideas for the classroom: Middle grades mathematics* (pp. 113–119). Reston, VA: National Council of Teachers of Mathematics.

National Council of Teachers of Mathematics. (1989). *Curriculum and evaluation standards for school mathematics*. Reston, VA: Author.

National Council of Teachers of Mathematics. (2000). *Principles and standards for school mathematics*. Reston, VA: Author.

Thompson, F. (1991). Two-digit addition and subtraction. *Arithmetic Teacher* 38(5), 10–13.

Chapter 13

Ball, D. (1993). Halves, pieces, and truths: Constructing and using representational contexts in teaching fractions. In T. Carpenter, E. Kennedy, & T. Romberg (Eds.), *Rational numbers: An integration of research* (pp. 157–196). Hillsdale, NJ: Erlbaum.

Burns, M. (1989). The math solution: Using groups of four. In N. Davidson (Ed.), *Cooperative learning in mathematics* (pp. 21–46). Menlo Park, CA: Addison-Wesley.

Hunting, R. (1999). Rational-number learning in the early years: What is possible? In J. V. Copley (Ed.), *Mathematics in the Early Years* (pp. 151–183). Reston, VA: National Council of Teachers of Mathematics.

National Council of Teachers of Mathematics. (1989). *Curriculum and evaluation standards for school mathematics*. Reston, VA: Author.

National Council of Teachers of Mathematics. (2000). *Principles and standards for school mathematics*. Reston, VA: Author.

Smith, J. (2002). The development of students' knowledge of fractions and ratios. In B. Litwiller & G. Bright (Eds.), *Making sense of fractions, ratios, and proportions* (pp. 18–28). Reston, VA: National Council of Teachers of Mathematics.

Chapter 14

Aksu, M. (1997). Student performance in dealing with fractions. *Journal of Educational Research* 90(6), 375–383.

Beaton, A., Mills, I., Gonzalez, D., Kelly, D., & Smith, T. (1996). *Mathematics achievement in the middle school: IEA's third international mathematics and science study*. Boston: Center for the Study of Testing, Evaluation, and Educational Policy.

Casio. (1994). *Activities for Casio FX 55 fraction calculator*. Dover, NJ: Author.

Chancellor, D. (Ed.). (1991). Calendar mathematics. *Arithmetic Teacher* 39(1), 287–291.

Christ, G. (2000). *A world of mathematics: Activities for grades 4, 5, and 6 using the TI-15*. Dallas: Texas Instruments Inc.

Graeber, A., & Tanenhaus, E. (1993). Multiplication and division: From whole numbers to rational numbers. In D. T. Owens (Ed.), *Research ideas for the classroom: Middle grades mathematics* (pp. 99–117). Reston, VA: National Council of Teachers of Mathematics.

Johnson, A. (1999). The thinking of students: Krystal's method. *Mathematics Teaching in the Middle School* 5(3), 148–150.

Muschla, J., & Muschla, G. (1995). *Math teachers' book of lists*. Englewood Cliffs, NJ: Prentice Hall.

National Council of Teachers of Mathematics. (1989). *Curriculum and evaluation standards for school mathematics*. Reston, VA: Author.

National Council of Teachers of Mathematics. (2000). *Principles and standards for school mathematics*. Reston, VA: Author.

Olson, J., Olson, M., & Schielack, J. (2002). *Explorations: Integrating hand-held technology into the elementary mathematics classroom*. Dallas: Texas Instruments Inc.

Owens, D., & Super, D. (1993). Teaching and learning decimal fractions. In D. T. Owens (Ed.), *Research ideas for the classroom: Middle grades mathematics* (pp. 137–158). Reston, VA: National Council of Teachers of Mathematics.

Sutton, J., & Krueger, A. (Eds.). (2002). *Ed thoughts: What we know about mathematics teaching and learning*. Aurora, CO: Mid-Continent Research and Education.

Chapter 15

Kaput, J., & West, M. (1994). Missing value proportional reasoning problems: Factors affecting informal reasoning patterns. In G. Harel & J. Confrey (Eds.), *The development of multiplicative reasoning in the learning of mathematics* (pp. 237–292). Albany: State University of New York Press.

National Council of Teachers of Mathematics. (1989). *Curriculum and evaluation standards for school mathematics*. Reston, VA: Author.

National Council of Teachers of Mathematics. (2000). *Principles and standards for school mathematics*. Reston, VA: Author.

Chapter 16

Brown, E., & Jones, E. (2005). Using clock arithmetic to teach algebra concepts. *Teaching Mathematics in the Middle School* 2(11), 104–109.

Carraher, D., Schliemann, A., Brizuela, B., & Earnest, D. (2006). Arithmetic and algebra in early mathematics education. *Journal for Research in Mathematics Education* 37(2), 87–115.

Dobrynina, G. (2001). *Reasoning processes of grades 4–6 students solving two- and three-variable problems*. Ph.D. dissertation, Boston University.

Greenes, C. (2004). Algebra! It's elementary. *ENC Focus Review* 11(2), 8.

Greenes, C., Cavanaugh, M., Dacey, L., Findell, C., & Small, M. (2001). *Navigations through algebra, PK–2*. Reston, VA: National Council of Teachers of Mathematics.

Hart, L. (1983). *Human brain and human learning*. Village of Oak Creek, AZ: Books for Educators.

Leiva, M. A. (Ed.). (1991). *Curriculum and evaluation standards for school mathematics: Addenda series, grades K–6, kindergarten book*. Reston, VA: National Council of Teachers of Mathematics.

National Council of Teachers of Mathematics. (2000). *Principles and standards for school mathematics*. Reston VA: Author.

National Research Council, Mathematical Sciences Education Board. (1989). *Everybody counts: A report to the nation on the future of mathematics education*. Washington, DC: National Academy Press.

Tsankova, E. (2003). *Algebraic reasoning of first through third grade students solving systems of two linear equations with two variables*. Ph.D. dissertation, Boston University.

Williams, S., & Molina, D. (1997). *Algebra, what all students can learn: The nature and role of algebra in the K–1 curriculum—Proceedings of a national symposium*. Washington, DC: National Academy Press.

Chapter 17

Casey, B., Pezaris, E., Anderson, K., & Bassi, J. (2004). Research rationale and recommendations for spatially-based mathematics: Evening the odds for young girls and boys. In C. Greenes & J. Tsankova (Eds.), *Challenging young children mathematically* (pp. 28–39). Special Monograph on Early Childhood Mathematics. Golden, CO: National Council of Supervisors of Mathematics.

Casey, M., Nuttall, R., & Pezaris, E. (1997). Mediators of gender differences in mathematics college entrance test scores: A comparison of spatial skills with internalized abilities and anxieties. *Developmental Psychology* 33, 669–680.

Clements, D., & Battista, M. (1992). *Geometry and spatial reasoning*. In D. Grouws (Ed.), *Handbook of research on mathematics teaching and learning* (pp. 420–464). Reston, VA: National Council of Teachers of Mathematics.

Del Grande, J., & Morrow, L. (1989). *Addenda series, grades K–6, geometry and spatial sense*. Reston, VA: National Council of Teachers of Mathematics.

Fuys, D., & Tischler, R. (1988). *The van Hiele model of thinking in geometry among adolescents*. Reston, VA: National Council of Teachers of Mathematics.

Gardner, H. (1982). *Multiple intelligences: The theory in practice*. New York: Basic Books.

Keller, B., & Hart, E. (2002). Improving students' spatial visualization skills and teachers' pedagogical content knowledge by using on-line curriculum-embedded applets. Unpublished manuscript.

Levine, S. C., Huttenlocher, J., Taylor, A., & Lanrock, H. (1999). Early sex differences in spatial skills. *Developmental Psychology* 35, 940–949.

Linn, M., & Petersen, A. (1986). A meta-analysis of gender differences in spatial ability: Implications for mathematics and science achievement. In J. S. Hyde & M. C. Linn (Eds.), *The psychology of gender: Advances through meta-analysis* (pp. 67–101). Baltimore: Johns Hopkins University Press.

National Council of Teachers of Mathematics. (1989). *Curriculum and evaluation standards for school mathematics*. Reston, VA: Author.

National Council of Teachers of Mathematics. (2000). *Principles and standards for school mathematics*. Reston, VA: Author.

Piaget, J., Inhelder, B., & Szeminska, A. (1960). *The child's conception of geometry*. New York: Basic Books.

Taylor, L., Stevens, J., Peregoy, J., & Bath, B. (1991). American Indians, mathematical attitudes, and the standards. *Arithmetic Teacher* 38(6), 14–21.

Wheatley, G. H. (1992). Spatial sense and the construction of abstract units in tiling. *Arithmetic Teacher* 39(8), 10–11.

Chapter 18

Burns, M. (1989). The math solution: Using groups of four. In N. Davidson (Ed.), *Cooperative learning in mathematics*. Menlo Park, CA: Addison-Wesley.

Johnson, A., & Norris, K. (2007). The beginnings of the metric system. *Mathematics Teaching in the Middle School* 12(5), 28–32.

Kempe, C. H., et al. (Eds.). (1997). *Current periodic diagnosis and treatment 1997*. Norwalk, CT: Appleton & Lange.

Lubinski, C. A., & Thiessen, D. (1996). Exploring measurement through literature. *Teaching Children Mathematics* 2(5), 260–263.

National Council of Teachers of Mathematics. (1989). *Curriculum and evaluation standards for school mathematics*. Reston, VA: Author.

National Council of Teachers of Mathematics. (2000). *Principles and standards for school mathematics*. Reston, VA: Author.

Reece, C. S., & Kamii, C. (2000a). The concept of volume: Why do young children measure inaccurately? *School Science and Mathematics* 101(7), 356–361.

Reece, C. S., & Kamii, C. (2000b). The measurement of time: Children's construction of transitivity, iteration of unit, and conservation of speed. *School Science and Mathematics* 101(3), 125–130.

Chapter 19

Kilpatrick, J., Swafford, J., & Findell, B. (Eds.). (2001). *Adding it up: Helping children learn mathematics*. Washington, DC: National Academy Press.

Konold, C., & Pollatsek, A. (2002). Data analysis as the search for signals in noisy processes. *Journal for Research in Mathematics Education* 33, 259–289.

Meyer, J., Shomo, M. K., & Gopher, D. (1999). Information structure and the relative efficacy of tables and graphs. *Human Factors* 41(4), 570–589.

National Council of Teachers of Mathematics. (2000). *Principles and standards for school mathematics*. Reston, VA: Author.

Watson, J., & Moritz, J. (2000). Developing concepts of sampling. *Journal for Research in Mathematics Education* 31, 44–70.

Whitin, D. (2006). Learning to talk back to a statistic. In G. Burrill & P. Elliott (Eds.), *Thinking and reasoning with data and chance*. Reston, VA: National Council of Teachers of Mathematics.

Chapter 20

Bright, G., & Hoffner, K. (1993). Measurement, probability, statistics, and graphing. In *Research ideas for the classroom: Middle grades mathematics*. Reston, VA: National Council of Teachers of Mathematics.

National Council of Teachers of Mathematics. (2000). *Principles and standards for school mathematics*. Reston, VA: Author.

Orlando, L. (2006). *The multicultural game book*. La Jolla, CA: Muze.

Shaughnessy, M. (1992). Research in probability and statistics: Reflections and directions. In D. Grouws (Ed.), *Handbook of research on mathematics teaching and learning* (pp. 465–494). Reston, VA: National Council of Teachers of Mathematics.

Shaughnessy, M. (2003). Research of students' understandings of probability. In J. Kilpatrick, W. Martin, & D. Schifter (Eds.), *A research companion to principles and standards for school mathematics* (pp. 216–226). Reston, VA: National Council of Teachers of Mathematics.

Tarr, J. (2002). Providing opportunities to learn probability concepts. *Teaching Children Mathematics* 8(8), 482–487.

Watson, J. M., & Moritz, J. B. (1999). The beginning of statistical inference: Comparing two data sets. *Educational Studies in Mathematics* 37, 145–168.

Index